REGRESSION
AND
FORECASTING

C22.0103   Stern School of Business

Selected Chapters from
Business Statistics by Example, Fifth Edition

TERRY SINCICH

Sept. 2001

Pearson
Custom
Publishing

Prentice
Hall

Cover Art: "Excavations," by Brian Stevens.

Taken from:

Business Statistics by Example, Fifth Edition,
by Terry Sincich
Copyright © 1996 by Prentice-Hall, Inc.
A Pearson Education Company
Upper Saddle River, New Jersey 07458

This special edition published in cooperation with Pearson Custom Publishing

Printed in the United States of America

10 9 8 7 6 5 4 3 2 1

Please visit our web site at www.pearsoncustom.com

ISBN 0–536–62724–X

BA 992957

PEARSON CUSTOM PUBLISHING
75 Arlington Street, Suite 300, Boston, MA 02116
A Pearson Education Company

CONTENTS

10 COLLECTING EVIDENCE TO SUPPORT A THEORY: GENERAL CONCEPTS OF HYPOTHESIS TESTING 469

11 HYPOTHESIS TESTING: APPLICATIONS 510

12 SIMPLE LINEAR REGRESSION AND CORRELATION 580

13 MULTIPLE REGRESSION AND MODEL BUILDING   660

14 ANALYSIS OF VARIANCE   784

18 NONPARAMETRIC STATISTICS 1061

19 ELEMENTS OF DECISION ANALYSIS 1129

EXERCISE DATA SETS ON DISK

PREFACE

Approach

Business Statistics by Example, Fifth Edition is designed as an introductory text in statistics for business and economics majors whose mathematical background is limited to basic algebra. As suggested by the title, the approach taken by this text is to teach statistical concepts and methods through examples that are motivated by real data sets and reinforced through the use of statistical computing. Many of the examples arise as questions posed about the data sets. The text's practical orientation helps students relate statistics to real-life problems. In addition, it is hoped that this approach will encourage students to develop critical thinking skills that will allow them to realize greater success upon entering the working world. The pedagogical orientation of this text is not unique. In fact, it is consistent with the philosophy espoused by The American Statistical Association (ASA)-sponsored annual conference on "Making Statistics More Effective in Schools of Business." The following pages demonstrate how the "by example" approach is brought to life in the text.

"By Example" Introduction of Concepts

Each section includes numerous fully worked examples to demonstrate how to solve various types of statistical problems encountered in the real world.

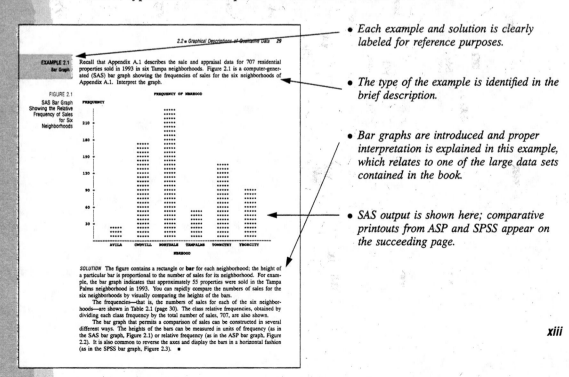

- *Each example and solution is clearly labeled for reference purposes.*

- *The type of the example is identified in the brief description.*

- *Bar graphs are introduced and proper interpretation is explained in this example, which relates to one of the large data sets contained in the book.*

- *SAS output is shown here; comparative printouts from ASP and SPSS appear on the succeeding page.*

Full Integration of Computer-Generated Output

A printout taken from one of four major statistical packages, SPSS, MINITAB, SAS, and ASP, accompanies every statistical technique presented, allowing instructors to emphasize interpretations of the statistical results rather than the calculations required to obtain the results.

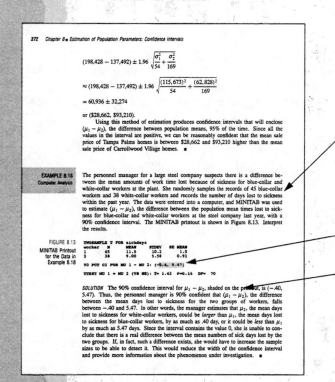

- *This example presents a realistic situation in which a personnel manager uses MINITAB output with a 90% confidence interval to assess the difference in average work time lost for different populations in a large steel company. The student is asked to interpret the results.*

- *Significant values are shaded in the printout to reinforce understanding.*

- *The solution walks the student through an analysis of the output.*

Real Data Sets

Appendix A describes the following large data sets, which are available to adopters on a $3\frac{1}{2}''$ diskette as ASCII files for use with any software package.

A.1 Sales and Appraisals of Residential Properties in Tampa, Florida

A.2 *Business Week*'s 1994 Executive Compensation Scoreboard

A.3 Characteristics of HMO Physicians in a Managed-Care System

A.4 Federal Trade Commission Rankings of Domestic Cigarette Brands

A.5 Diameters of Manufactured Steel Rods

A.6 Sealed-Bid Data for Fixed and Competitive Highway Construction Contracts

A.7 Commitment and Turnover of Employees at an Aerospace Firm

Through examples and exercises, these data sets are used, among other things, to: (i) develop the notion of a population and a sample, (ii) demonstrate the need for data description, (iii) develop the notion of a sampling distribution, and (iv) motivate various inferential methods.

Tested, Referenced Exercises

Because most students learn best by doing, the text contains more than 1,000 real data-based exercises. References are drawn from a wide variety of sources, as evidenced by the list contained in the front endpapers of this book. The exercise sets, which appear at the end of every section, are divided into **Learning the Mechanics** and **Applying the Concepts**. An additional set of exercises is found at the end of each chapter. These Supplementary Exercises pull together concepts from the entire chapter and test students' comprehension of the major ideas.

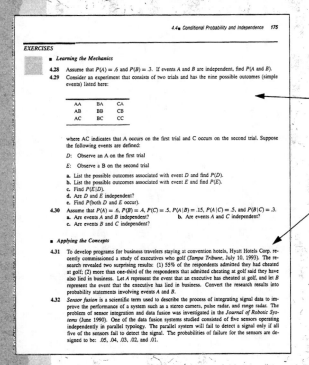

• *(Learning the Mechanics) Straightforward applications of new concepts presented in the section. These mechanical exercises provide practice and test comprehension of basic techniques and definitions.*

• *(Applying the Concepts) Realistic exercises that allow students to see applications of statistics to the solutions of real-world problems. Nearly all of these exercises contain data or information extracted from newspaper articles, magazines, and journals. Once the mechanics are mastered, these exercises develop students' skills in problem solving.*

Computer Software Tutorials: SAS, SPSS, MINITAB, ASP

A brief tutorial for each of the major statistical packages is included in a separate manual that accompanies the text. Easy-to-follow instructions on how to employ the statistical analysis commands for SAS, SPSS, MINITAB, and ASP allow students with access to a statistical package to produce statistical results for analysis. Most of the commands provided are appropriate for either the mainframe or PC version of the software.

Free ASP Software

A Statistical Package for Business, Economics, and the Social Sciences (DMC Software, Inc.), is packaged free with every copy of the text. This user-friendly, totally menu-driven program contains all of the major statistical applications covered in the text, plus many more.

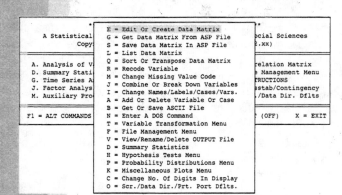

- *Students with no knowledge of computer programming are able to create and analyze data sets quickly.*

- *The ASP tutorial contains start-up procedures and instructions on the use of ASP.*

- *Minimal hardware requirements: IBM-compatible PC, 512K*

Case Studies to Pull It All Together

Two real-world case studies based on interesting business problems or current events conclude each chapter.

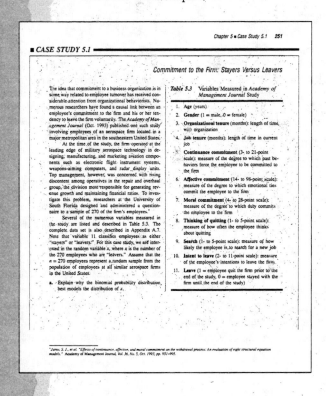

- *Questions posed about the case encourage students to apply the statistical techniques learned in the chapter to solve a practical problem.*

- *The complete data set is described in Appendix A.7 and is available on the data disk that accompanies the text.*

- *Computer output is provided, allowing students to focus on interpretation of results.*

Major Content Changes

The fifth edition contains several substantial modifications, additions, and enhancements including:

Chapter 1

Collecting data. The importance of collecting data with random (and representative) samples is emphasized by moving this material from its original location in Chapter 7 to Section 1.4. The section on types of data (originally in Chapter 2) has also been moved to this chapter (Section 1.3).

Chapter 9

Sample survey methods. For each sample survey method presented, advantages and disadvantages of the technique are discussed and highlighted (boxed).

Chapter 12

Early introduction to simple linear regression computer printouts. To avoid overemphasizing formulas and numerical calculations, a computer printout of a simple linear regression analysis is presented early (Section 12.3). This allows the student to concentrate on interpretation of the regression results.

Chapter 15

Total Quality Management (TQM). A new section on total quality management (Section 15.1) has been added to the chapter on statistical process and quality control.

Chapter 16

Consolidation of two time series chapters. The two time series chapters of the previous edition (Chapters 16 and 17) have been combined into a single, more concise chapter without omitting any of the topics. Again, emphasis on calculation formulas is reduced in favor of computer printouts. A new section on forecasting using lagged values of the dependent variable has also been added (Section 16.10).

Chapter 17

Odds-ratios in logistic regression. The material on logistic regression (Section 17.4) has been expanded to include a discussion of odds and interpretation of the β coefficients as odds-ratios.

Supplements for the Instructor

Instructor's Solutions Manual (by Mark Dummeldinger)

Solutions to all of the even-numbered exercises and Case Studies are given in this manual. Careful attention has been paid to ensure that all methods of solution and notation are consistent with those used in the core text. Solutions to the odd-numbered exercises are found in the Student's Solutions Manual.

Printed Test Bank (by Mark Dummeldinger)

This multiple-choice test item file follows the organization and approach of the text.

ESATEST III

ESATEST III incorporates three levels of test creation: (1) selection of questions from a test bank, (2) addition of new questions with the ability to import text and graphics files from WordPerfect, Microsoft Word, and Wordstar, and (3) algorithmic generation of multiple questions from a single question template. ESATEST III has a full-featured graphics editor supporting the complex formulas and graphics required by the statistics discipline. It is available in a Windows platform.

PowerPoint Lecture Tool

This versatile Windows-based tool may be used by professors in a number of different manners:

> Slide show in an electronic classroom
>
> Printed and used as transparency masters
>
> Printed copies may be distributed to students as a convenient note-taking device.

Included on the software disk are learning objectives, thinking challenges, concept presentation slides, and examples with worked solutions.

Data Disks

The data sets described in Appendix A and the data for all exercises containing approximately 20 or more observations are available on $3\frac{1}{2}''$ diskettes in ASCII format. A list of these exercises precedes the preface.

ASP Statistical Software

As described earlier in the Preface, this software comes packaged FREE with each copy of the text.

Computer Software Tutorials: SAS, SPSS, MINITAB, ASP

This self-contained manual provides the four software appendices. Keystroke commands and an extensive use of software output instructs the student in the use of the chosen statistical software package. This manual may be packaged free with each copy of the text.

Supplements Available for Purchase By Students

Student's Solutions Manual (by Nancy S. Boudreau)

Fully worked solutions to all of the odd-numbered exercises are provided in this manual. Careful attention has been paid to ensure that all methods of solution and notation are consistent with those used in the core text.

MINITAB Supplement (by David D. Krueger and Ruth K. Meyer)

The MINITAB computer supplement was developed to be used with the following releases of the software: DOS version 8.0, VAX version 9.0, and Windows or Mac version 10. The supplement, which was written especially for the student with no previous experience with computers, provides step-by-step descriptions of how to use MINITAB effectively as an aid in data analysis. Where appropriate, simulation examples are included. Exercises, many of which are drawn from the text, conclude each chapter.

Student Versions of SPSS

Student versions of SPSS's latest release of its award-winning and market-leading commercial data analysis package are available for student purchase. Designed specifically for hands-on classroom teaching and learning of data analysis, statistics, and research methods, Windows and PowerMac versions of the software allow the user to take full advantage of the easy-to-use graphical user interface combined with the traditional power of SPSS. Details on all current products are available from the publisher.

ConStatS (by Tufts University)

ConStatS is a set of Microsoft Windows-based programs designed to help college students understand concepts taught in a first-semester course on probability and statistics. Under development at Tufts University for over eight years, ConStatS helps improve students' conceptual understanding of statistics by engaging them in an active, experimental style of learning. ConStats is available for individual purchase or to schools on a site license basis. A companion ConStatS workbook is also available.

ACKNOWLEDGMENTS

I wish to acknowledge the many individuals who provided their invaluable assistance during the preparation of the original text and subsequent revisions. Their efforts are much appreciated. The reviewers are listed below:

William Applebaugh (University of Wisconsin-Eau Claire), Edwin F. Baumgartner (LeMoyne College), Randal Beek (Millikin University), Jim Bellis (IBM Corporation), Elaine Bohanon (Bemidji State University), John S. Bowdidge (Southwest Missouri State University), Barbara J. Bulmahn (Indiana University at Fort Wayne), John Cameron (Rockhurst College), P. L. Claypool (Oklahoma State University), Ronald L. Coccari (Cleveland State University), Robert Cochran (University of Wyoming), Murray Cohen (University of South Florida), Joyce Curry-Daly (California Polytechnic), Paul Dussue (SUNY–Oswego), Janice Marie Dykacz (Essex Community College), Joan Girard (Edison Community College), Damodar Golhar (Western Michigan University), Gavin Gregory (University of Texas at El Paso), Derek Hart (McGill University), Burt Holland (Temple University), Geoffrey B. Holmewood (Hudson Valley Community College), Gail Hoyt (University of Richmond), Rod Hurley (Hillsborough County Community College), Larry Jensen (Kutztown University), Thomas B. Laase (University of Southern Colorado), Carolyn Likins (Millikin University), James T. McClave (University of Florida), William Mendenhall (University of Florida), LaVern J. Meyer (Millikin University), Daniel Mihalko (Western Michigan University), Glenn W. Milligan (Ohio State University), S. Mishra (University of Southern Alabama), Amitava Mitra (Auburn University), Maurice Monahan (South Dakota State University), Carolyn Monroe (Baylor University), Kris K. Moore (Baylor University), Paul Nelson (Kansas State University), Patricia Odell (Bryant College), Bill Redmond (Bismarck State College), Larry J. Ringer (Texas A&M University), John B. Rushton (Metropolitan State College), Dale G. Sauers (York College), Susan Schott (University of Central Florida), Fay Sewell (Montgomery Community College), Brian E. Smith (McGill University), William L. Toth (Henry Ford Community College), Manel Wijesinha (Pennsylvania State University–York), Charles W. Zimmerman (Robert Morris College), Cathleen Zucco (LeMoyne College)

Finally, I owe very special thanks to my wife, Faith Sincich, who not only provided the necessary moral support one needs when undertaking a project like this, but also did an excellent job of typing, cutting, pasting, proofing, editing, and solving exercises. Without her, the fifth edition of this text could not have been completed.

Chapter 1

INTRODUCTION: STATISTICS AND DATA

Each year, *Business Week* conducts a salary survey of chief executive officers at the top 500 companies in the United States. The data collected from the survey are reported in the "Executive Compensation Scoreboard." Think of the task of collecting, summarizing, and analyzing these data. Then think of statistics! In this chapter and throughout this text, we discuss how you can use the science of statistics to solve such problems. The data from the "Executive Compensation Scoreboard" are discussed in greater detail in Case Study 1.1.

■ CONTENTS

1.1 What Is Statistics?

Consider the following recent items from the news media:

Time, June 13, 1994

According to a "Recent College Graduates Survey" conducted by the U.S. Department of Education, 81% of business graduates say their job is related to their major. In contrast, 95% of health professionals say their job is related to their major, whereas only 30% of history graduates are working in their area of expertise.

U.S. News & World Report, March 22, 1993

According to *U.S. News'* fourth annual survey of "America's Best Graduate Schools," an MBA degree candidate received an average of only one job offer prior to graduation, compared to 3.8 job offers a decade ago. On some campuses last year, one in five MBA candidates had not received a single job offer by graduation.

The Wall Street Journal, July 14, 1992

Video card games (e.g., video poker), once legal only in casinos, are now available for play in laundromats and grocery stores of states that have a lottery. These video card games are beginning to create adult addicts, many of them women, who gamble until they are broke or in debt. In a study of 52 women in Gamblers Anonymous, 90% were video poker players. After they became hooked on video poker, 75% exhausted their family savings, 33% embezzled from their employers, 25% declared bankruptcy, and 10% turned to prostitution to raise money.

Chance, Vol. 5, Summer/Fall 1992

Folk wisdom suggests that the final outcome of a professional basketball game is heavily dependent on what happens in the last quarter (final 12 minutes), if not the final 2 minutes, of playing time. Information for 189 National Basketball Association games was collected from the box scores reported in the *St. Louis Post-Dispatch*. In these games, the team leading after three quarters of play won 150 times and lost only 39 times—a "leader–win" percentage of almost 80%.

Tampa Tribune, December 7, 1994

Cigarette packages deceive smokers by listing very low tar and nicotine contents and should instead disclose the maximum amount smokers can inhale, according to a federal panel of tobacco experts. R. J. Reynolds tobacco company warned that if the ranges of nicotine in ultralight and light brands overlap, a smoker might move up to the higher-yield (and better-tasting) brand.

Every day we are inundated with bits of information—data—like those in the examples above, whether we are in the classroom, on the job, or at home. Many of you taking this course are studying to be (or may already be) managers of a business or firm. Some of you will be **data producers**, but most of you will be **data users**. As such, you will need to be able to make sense out of the mass of data that others produce for you. What specialized tools will enable you to become effective data users? The answer is **statistics**.

A common misconception is that a statistician is simply a "number cruncher," or a person who calculates and summarizes numbers, like baseball batting averages or unemployment rates. Statistics involves numbers, but there is much more to it than that.

According to *The Random House College Dictionary* (1994 ed.), statistics is "the science that deals with the collection, classification, analysis, and interpretation of numerical facts or data." In short, statistics is the **science of data**—a science that will enable you to be proficient data producers and efficient data users.

Definition 1.1

Statistics is the science of data. This involves collecting, classifying, summarizing, organizing, analyzing, and interpreting data.

In this chapter, we explore the different types of data that you will encounter in business, and we introduce you to some ideas on methods for collecting data. The various statistical methods for summarizing, analyzing, and interpreting that data are presented in the chapters that follow.

1.2 Types of Data

Data are obtained by measuring some characteristic or property of the objects (usually people or things) of interest to us. These objects upon which the measurements (or observations) are made are called **experimental units**, and the properties being measured are called **variables** (since, in virtually all studies of interest, the property varies from one observation to another).

Definition 1.2

An **experimental unit** is an object (person or thing) upon which we collect data.

Definition 1.3

A **variable** is a characteristic that differs, or varies, from one observation to the next.

EXAMPLE 1.1
Characteristics of Data

By law, the dollar value of each residential property in the United States must be assessed each year for tax purposes. Typically, these assessments are performed by a local government official (e.g., the city or county property appraiser). Appendix A.1 provides information on the location, appraised values, and sale prices for 707 residential properties sold in six Tampa, Florida, neighborhoods in 1993. Each row of the data set pertains to a single residential property and gives the following information:

1. Neighborhood in which the property is located (NBRHOOD)
2. Directional location of the property within the city (LOCATION)
3. Appraised value of the land (LANDVAL)
4. Appraised value of improvements (IMPROVAL)
5. Sale price of the property (SALEPRIC)
6. Ratio of sale price to total appraised value of land and improvements (SALTOAPR)

Data for 10 properties from Appendix A.1 are shown in Table 1.1.* For this data set, identify the following:

a. The experimental unit
b. The variables measured

SOLUTION

a. Since data have been collected on each residential property sold in Tampa in 1993, these residential properties are the experimental units.

b. The variables (characteristics) measured on each residential property are the six items previously listed—namely, neighborhood, location, appraised land value, appraised improvements value, sale

---

*The complete data set is available on a $3\frac{1}{2}$ " diskette from the publisher.

Table 1.1   Data for Ten Residential Properties from Appendix A.1

PROPERTY	NBRHOOD	LOCATION	LANDVAL	IMPROVAL	SALEPRIC	SALTOAPR
1	CWDVILL	NW	22824	92775	157500	1.36247
2	CWDVILL	NW	28936	108072	150000	1.09483
3	CWDVILL	NW	26695	74837	121300	1.19470
4	NORTDALE	NW	18770	71357	97000	1.07626
5	NORTDALE	NW	18900	86439	102800	0.97590
6	TAMPALMS	NE	43294	98074	152500	1.07874
7	TOWNCTRY	SW	12558	28166	57000	1.39967
8	TOWNCTRY	SW	14511	30183	68400	1.53041
9	TOWNCTRY	SW	21998	62076	85100	1.01220
10	YBORCITY	SE	5633	14696	14000	0.68867

Source: Hillsborough County (Florida) Property Appraisers Office.

price, and ratio of sale price to total appraised value. These are called *variables* since their values vary from one property to another (i.e., they are not constant). ■

All data (and, consequently, the variables we measure) are either **quantitative** or **qualitative** in nature.[*] Quantitative data are data that can be measured on a numerical scale. In general, qualitative data take values that are nonnumerical; they can only be classified. The statistical tools that we use to analyze data depend on whether the data are quantitative or qualitative. Thus, it is important to be able to distinguish between the two types of data.

Definition 1.4

Quantitative data are observations measured on a numerical scale.

Definition 1.5

Nonnumerical data that can only be classified into one of a group of categories are **qualitative data**.

---

[*]*A finer breakdown of data types into nominal, ordinal, interval, and ratio data is possible.* **Nominal** *data are qualitative data with categories that cannot be meaningfully ordered.* **Ordinal** *data are also qualitative data, but a distinct ranking of the groups from high to low exists.* **Interval** *and* **ratio** *data are two different types of quantitative data. For most statistical applications (and all the methods presented in this introductory text), it is sufficient to classify data as either quantitative or qualitative.*

> **EXAMPLE 1.2**
> Identifying Data Types

Refer to the data set of Appendix A.1 described in Example 1.1. Determine the data type (quantitative or qualitative) of each of the six variables measured.

SOLUTION The first two variables listed are qualitative since the data they produce are values that are nonnumerical; they can only be classified into categories or groups. For example, values of LOCATION are northwest (NW), northeast (NE), southwest (SW), and southeast (SE). Similarly, values for NBRHOOD are Tampa Palms, Carrollwood Village, Town & Country, etc. We can classify a residential property according to NBRHOOD and LOCATION, but we cannot express these two variables as meaningful numerical quantities.

[*Caution:* The values of a qualitative variable may be coded or recorded numerically. For example, location could have been coded 1, 2, 3, and 4 for NW, NE, SW, and SE, respectively. Nevertheless, the data are qualitative since each observation can only be classified into one of a group of categories.]

The last four variables are all quantitative. LANDVAL, IMPROVAL, and SALEPRIC are measured in dollars, whereas SALTOAPR is a ratio of two quantitative variables. ■

> **EXAMPLE 1.3**
> Identifying Data Types

Marketers are keenly interested in the factors that motivate coupon usage by consumers. A study reported in the *Journal of Consumer Marketing* (Spring 1988) asked a sample of 290 shoppers to respond to the following questions:

1. Do you collect and redeem coupons?
2. Are you price-conscious while shopping?
3. On average, how much time per week do you spend clipping and collecting coupons?

Classify the responses to the questions as quantitative or qualitative data.

SOLUTION Possible responses to questions 1 and 2 are "Always," "Occasionally," and "Never." These responses cannot be quantified; they can only be classified into categories. Consequently, data for the first two questions will be qualitative. In contrast, responses to the third question, "How much time per week do you spend collecting coupons," will be numerical in nature. Possible responses are "30 minutes, "2 hours," etc. Thus, data for the third variable are quantitative. ■

As noted in Example 1.2, qualitative data can be converted into quantitative data by assigning numbers to each category of the qualitative variable. To illustrate, consider question 1 in Example 1.3, "Do you collect and redeem coupons?" Suppose we assign the number 1 to all consumers who respond "Always" or "Occasionally," and a number 0 to all who respond "Never." Then the sum of all the 0's and 1's in the data set will equal the total number of the 290 consumers surveyed who redeem coupons. Qualitative variables cannot always be converted into meaningful quantitative variables, but it can be done (as shown here) when the observations are classified into two categories. Consequently, when a value of "0" is assigned to one of the categories and a value of "1" to the other category, the sum of the observations will equal the number of experimental units falling in the "1" category.

To summarize, knowing the type (quantitative or qualitative) of data that you want to analyze is one of the keys to selecting the appropriate statistical method to use. A second key involves the concept of population and samples, as discussed in the next section.

EXERCISES

■ *Applying the Concepts*

1.1 *Business Horizons* (Jan.–Feb. 1993) conducted a comprehensive study of 800 chief executive officers who run the country's largest global corporations. The purpose of the study was to build a profile of the CEOs based on their aggregate social background characteristics. Several of the variables measured for each CEO are listed here. Classify each variable as quantitative or qualitative.
  a. State of birth   **b.** Age   **c.** Educational level
  d. Tenure with firm   **e.** Total compensation   **f.** Area of expertise

1.2 In Hawaii, condemnation proceedings have been under way since 1980 to enable private citizens to own the property that their homes are built on. (Prior to 1980, only estates were permitted to own land, and homeowners leased the land from the estate.) The new law requires estates to sell land to homeowners at a fair market price. As part of a study to estimate the fair market value of its land (called the "leased fee" value), a large Hawaiian estate collected the data shown in the accompanying table for five properties.
  a. Identify the experimental units.
  b. State whether each of the variables measured is quantitative or qualitative.

Property	Leased Fee Value $ thousands	Lot Size 1,000 sq. ft.	Neighborhood	Location of Lot
1	70.7	13.5	Cove	Cul-de-sac
2	52.6	9.6	Highlands	Interior
3	87.1	17.6	Cove	Corner
4	43.2	7.9	Highlands	Interior
5	144.3	13.8	Golf Course	Cul-de-sac

1.3 A study was conducted to examine the differences in job performance of white-collar workers with type A and type B behavior (*Journal of Human Stress*, Summer 1985). Type A workers exhibit on-the-job traits such as explosiveness, accelerated speech, ambitiousness, impatience, hostility, a tendency to challenge others, and the general appearance of tension; type B behavior is generally characterized by opposite attributes and qualities. The data for several workers at a large Canadian manufacturing firm who took part in the study are given in the table. [*Note:* Job performance of each worker was measured on a 5-point scale (a higher score indicates better performance) based on ratings of immediate supervisors.]

Worker	Behavior Type	Age	Managerial Level	Number of Employees Supervised	Performance Rating
1	A	47	Upper	22	3
2	B	28	Middle	10	5
3	B	52	Upper	105	2
4	A	30	Lower	3	1

Source: Jamal, M. "Type A behavior and job performance: Some suggestive findings." *Journal of Human Stress* (now *Behavioral Medicine*), Summer 1985, pp. 60–67. Reprinted with permission of the Helen Dwight Reid Educational Foundation. Published by Heldref Publications, 4000 Albermarle St., N.W., Washington, D.C. 20016. Copyright © 1985.

a. Identify the experimental units.

b. State whether each of the variables measured is quantitative or qualitative.

1.4 The data in the accompanying table were obtained from the Environmental Protection Agency (EPA) *1993 Gas Mileage Guide* for new automobiles.

a. Identify the experimental units.

b. State whether each of the variables measured is quantitative or qualitative.

Model Name	Manufacturer	Transmission	Engine Size (liters)	Number of Cylinders	Estimated City Miles/Gallon	Estimated Highway Miles/Gallon
NSX	Acura	Automatic	3.0	6	18	23
Colt	Dodge	Manual	1.5	4	32	40
318i	BMW	Automatic	1.8	4	22	30
Aerostar	Ford	Automatic	4.0	6	16	22
Camry	Toyota	Manual	2.2	4	22	30

Source: 1993 Gas Mileage Guide, EPA Fuel Economy Estimates, Oct. 1992.

1.5 *U.S. News & World Report*'s "1994 Home Guide" provides information on prices of existing homes in 100 U.S. cities. Several of the variables recorded for each home in the *U.S. News* survey include:

a. City

b. Region of county

c. Home type (starter, trade-up, or deluxe)

d. Number of days on market

e. Sale price

Identify the type of data (quantitative or qualitative) produced by each variable.

1.3 Fundamental Elements of a Statistical Analysis

When you examine a data set, you will be doing so because the data characterize some phenomenon of interest to you. In statistics, the data set that is the target of your interest is called a **population**. Notice that a statistical population does not refer to a group of people; it refers to a set of measurements. This data set, which is typically large, exists in fact or is part of an ongoing operation and hence is conceptual. Some examples of business phenomena and their corresponding populations are shown in Table 1.2.

Definition 1.6

A **population** is a collection (or set) of data that decribe some phenomenon of interest to you.

Table 1.2   Some Typical Populations

Phenomenon	Experimental Units	Population	Type
a. Current year, new residential construction prices	Residential properties sold this year	Set of prices of all new residential properties	Existing
b. Starting salary of a graduating MBA this year	MBAs graduating this year	Set of starting salaries of all MBAs who graduated this year	Existing
c. Profit per job in a construction company	Jobs	Set of profits for all jobs performed recently or to be performed in the near future	Part existing, part conceptual
d. Quality of items produced on an assembly line	Manufactured items	Set of quality measurements for all items manufactured over the recent past and in the future	Part existing, part conceptual

If you have the population in hand—that is, if you have every measurement in the population—then statistical methodology can help you describe the set of data. In this text, we present graphical and numerical ways to make sense out of a large mass of data. The branch of statistics devoted to this application is called **descriptive statistics**.

Definition 1.7

The branch of statistics devoted to the organization, summarization, and description of data sets is called **descriptive statistics**.

Many populations are too large to measure each observation; others cannot be measured because they are conceptual. For example, population **a** in Table 1.2 cannot be measured since it would be impossible to identify all new residential properties sold this year in the United States. Even if we could identify them, it would be too costly and time-consuming to research and record their sale prices. Population **d** in Table 1.2 cannot be measured because it is partly conceptual. Even though we may be able to record the quality measurements of all items manufactured over the recent past, we cannot measure quality in the future. Because of this problem, we are required to select a subset of values, called a **sample**, from a population.

Definition 1.8
A **sample** is a subset of data selected from a population.

EXAMPLE 1.4
Population and Sample

Refer to the sale price–appraisal data of Appendix A.1 described in Example 1.1. Recall that the data set includes the sale prices of all residential properties sold in 1993 in six specific Tampa neighborhoods: Tampa Palms, Carrollwood Village, Town & Country, Ybor City, Avila, and Northdale.

a. Suppose the target of your interest is the sale price data of Appendix A.1. Describe the target population.

b. Suppose the target of your interest is the sale prices of all residential properties sold in Tampa in 1993. Are the data of Appendix A.1 a population or a sample?

SOLUTION

a. Appendix A.1 contains information on the sale prices of all residential properties sold in 1993 in the six specific neighborhoods. Consequently, the target population is the set of sale prices for all residential properties sold in 1993 in the six Tampa neighborhoods.

b. Since we are interested in examining sale prices for all residential properties sold in Tampa in 1993, the target population will contain all these sale prices. Appendix A.1, however, contains only sale prices for properties in six neighborhoods; consequently, the data represent a sample from the target population. ■

EXAMPLE 1.5
Identifying Population and Sample

A University of Minnesota survey of brand names (e.g., Levi's, Lee, and Calvin Klein) and private labels manufactured for retail chains found a high percentage of jeans with incorrect waist and/or inseam sizes on the label. The researchers found that only 18 of 240 pairs, or 7.5%, of men's five-pocket, prewashed jeans sold in

Minneapolis stores were correctly labeled—that is, came within a half inch of their label sizes (*Tampa Tribune*, May 20, 1991). In this study, identify the following:

a. The population   **b.** The sample
c. A parameter of interest   **d.** The inference made about the population

SOLUTION

a. The researchers are interested in men's five-pocket, prewashed jeans manufactured for retail outlets in Minnesota. Consequently, the experimental units in the population are *all* pairs of men's five-pocket, prewashed jeans manufactured for retail outlets in Minnesota. The measurement (or variable) of interest is the label status of each pair of jeans: inseam and/or waist sizes labeled correctly or incorrectly. Note that this is a qualitative variable. In this example, the measurements could have been recorded as 1's and 0's, where a 1 would represent a correctly labeled inseam/waist size and a 0 would represent an incorrectly labeled inseam/waist size.

b. The sample consists of the collection of label status measurements (1's and 0's) for the 240 pairs of jeans examined in the study.

c. A parameter of interest to the researchers is the true percentage of jeans with correct inseam/waist sizes on the label.

d. Since 7.5% of the jeans in the sample had correct labels, the inference is that 7.5% of all jeans in the population have correct labels (i.e., an estimate of the parameter of interest is 7.5%). This leads to the conclusion reached by the University of Minnesota researchers: A high percentage (over 90%) of the men's five-pocket, prewashed jeans manufactured for retail outlets in the state have incorrect inseam/waist size labels. Note that the researchers do not provide a measure of reliability for this inference. Enough information is available, however, to calculate such a measure. We will show in Chapter 8 that, with a high degree of "confidence," the estimate of 7.5% is within 3.4% of the true percentage. That is, we are confident that the true percentage is no lower than 4.1% and no higher than 10.9%. ■

Statistical studies of the type described in Example 1.5 are also called **enumerative studies**. An enumerative study involves using samples to make inferences about some aspect of a population. The population is well defined in this type of study; that is, it is possible to list (or count) all the experimental units in the population—hence, the name "enumerative."

Definition 1.9

An **enumerative study** involves making inferences about a well-defined population based on sample data.

A second type of study, called an **analytic study**, involves analyzing and making inferences about **processes**. The main goal of an analytic study is to predict or improve process performance in the future.

Definition 1.10

A **process** is a series of actions or operations that produces or generates data over time.

Definition 1.11

An **analytic study** involves collecting and analyzing process data for the purpose of predicting or improving the future performance of the process.

EXAMPLE 1.6
Process Data

Record orange juice production in Florida was expected to lower the average price of orange juice in 1993. As a result, sales of grapefruit juice declined. Table 1.3 lists annual sales of grapefruit juice (in millions of gallons) from 1987 to 1992. Suppose the Florida Citrus Department wants to use these data to predict grapefruit sales in 1995.

a. Describe the process of interest.
b. Identify the type of statistical study to be employed.
c. Is the data set, Table 1.3, a population or a sample?

Table 1.3 Annual Sales of Grapefruit Juice

Year	Gallons millions
1987	58.2
1988	54.1
1989	53.4
1990	48.0
1991	50.2
1992	45.6

Source: Florida Citrus Department.

SOLUTION

a. The process of interest is the series of operations that grapefruit juice producers use to grow, produce, market, and sell their product. It is a process because it generates sales data (in gallons) over time—one observation per year.

b. According to Definition 1.11, this study is clearly analytic in nature since the Florida Citrus Department is interested in forecasting grapefruit juice sales in 1995.

c. In analytic studies, the data produced by a process are considered to be a sample. Since the Florida Citrus Department is ultimately interested in future grapefruit juice sales, the data of Table 1.3 represent a sample from a conceptual population consisting of grapefruit juice sales for all years, past and future. ■

The tools used to conduct a statistical study will depend on whether the study is enumerative or analytic; thus, it is important to be able to distinguish between the two types of studies.

Definition 1.12

The branch of statistics concerned with using sample data to make an inference about a population is called **inferential statistics**. When proper sampling techniques are used, this methodology also provides a **measure of reliability** for the inference.

Numbers that summarize some particular characteristic of a population are called **parameters**; similarly, summary measures used to describe a sample are called **statistics**.

Definition 1.13

A **parameter** is a numerical summary measure used to describe a characteristic of a population.

Definition 1.14

A **statistic** is a numerical summary measure used to describe a characteristic of a sample.

In future chapters, we will discover statistical methods that enable us to infer the nature of the population (for example, estimate the value of some unknown parameter) from the information in the sample. The branch of statistics devoted to this application is called **inferential statistics**. In addition, the methodology provides **measures of reliability** for each inference obtained from a sample. This last point is one of the major contributions of inferential statistics. Anyone can examine a sample and make a "guess" about the nature of the population. For example, we might estimate that the average price of new residential properties sold last year was $88,000. But statistical methodology enables us to go one step further. When the sample is selected in a specified way from the population, we can also say how accurate our estimate will be, that is, how close the estimate of $88,000 will be to the true average.

   The key facts to remember in this section are summarized in the accompanying boxes.

The Objective of Statistics

1. To describe data sets
2. To use sample data to make inferences about a population

The Major Contribution of Inferential Statistics

Statistical methodology allows us to provide a measure of reliability for every statistical inference based on a properly selected sample.

EXERCISES

■ *Applying the Concepts*

1.6   A panel of tobacco experts convened by the National Cancer Institute recommends that cigarette manufacturers put more descriptive labels on their cigarette packages, including a disclaimer that "light" brands are not really more healthful than "regular" (nonlight) brands (*Tampa Tribune*, Dec. 7, 1994). The panel's recommendations are based, in part, on data collected by the Federal Trade Commission (FTC). Each year, the FTC tests all domestic cigarette brands for carcinogens such as tar and nicotine. (See Case Study 2.1.) Suppose our goal is to compare the average nicotine content of all domestic light cigarette brands to the average nicotine content of all domestic regular cigarette brands. To do this, we record the nicotine contents (in milligrams) of 25 light cigarette brands and 25 regular cigarettes brands.
   a. Describe the target populations. (Give the precise statistical definitions.)
   b. Describe the samples.
   c. What are the parameters of interest?

1.7   An assembly line that mass produces automobile gear shifts is monitored for quality. Each hour, quality control inspectors select 50 gear shifts from the production line and test for defects. The hourly proportion of defectives among the 50 tested serves as a measure of the quality of the process. If the percentage of defectives for any 1 hour exceeds a specified upper limit, adjustments will be made to the assembly line to improve future quality.

a. Describe the process of interest to the manufacturer of the automobile gear shifts.

b. Describe the sample.

1.8 Potential advertisers value television's well-known Nielsen ratings as a barometer of a TV show's popularity among viewers. The Nielsen rating of a certain TV program (e.g., NBC's popular hit comedy series, "Seinfeld") is an estimate of the proportion of viewers, expressed as a percentage, who tune their sets to the program on a given night at a given time. A typical Nielsen survey consists of 165 families selected nationwide who regularly watch television. Suppose we are interested in the Nielsen ratings for the latest episode of "Seinfeld."

a. Is the study enumerative or analytic?

b. Identify the target population.

c. Identify the sample.

1.9 The prime interest rates for the past 7 years are listed in the table. Suppose you are interested in using this information to forecast the prime interest rate in 1994.

Year	Prime Rate, %
1987	8.22
1988	9.32
1989	10.87
1990	10.01
1991	8.46
1992	6.25
1993	6.15

Source: U.S. Department of Labor, Federal Reserve Board.

a. What type of statistical study is to be employed?

b. Identify the sample.

c. Describe the conceptual population of interest.

1.10 Pesticides applied to an extensively grown crop can result in inadvertent ambient air contamination. *Environmental Science & Technology* (Oct. 1993) reported on thion residues of the insecticide chlorpyrifos used on dormant orchards in the San Joaquin Valley, California. Ambient air specimens were collected daily at an orchard site during an intensive period of spraying—a total of 13 days—and the thion level (ng/m^3) was measured each day.

a. Identify the population of interest to the researchers.

b. Identify the sample.

1.11 A study of merit raises at 16 U.S. corporations was conducted to determine the extent to which merit pay policies for employees are actually tied to performance (*Personnel Journal*, Mar. 1986). One phase of the study focused on the 3,990 merit raises (measured as percentage increases in salary) awarded during a year to one of the largest of the 16 firms. The analysis revealed that over half of the merit increases were between 7% and 10%.

a. Identify the variable of interest. Is it quantitative or qualitative?

b. Do the 3,990 merit raises represent a population or a sample? Explain.

1.4 Collecting Data

Enumerative Studies

Enumerative studies, you will recall, involve sampling and using information in the sample to make inferences about a well-defined population. For these applications, it is essential that we obtain a **representative sample**.

Definition 1.15

A **representative sample** exhibits characteristics similar to those possessed by the target population.

For example, consider the problem of estimating the average price of residential properties sold last year in the United States. It would be unwise to base our estimate on data collected for a sample of properties sold in Orange County, California, since this area has one of the highest-priced housing markets in the United States. Our estimate would certainly be *biased* high and, consequently, would not be very reliable.

The most common way to satisfy the requirement of "representative sample" in enumerative studies is to select a (simple) **random sample**.

Definition 1.16

A **random sample** of n experimental units is one selected from the population in such a way that every different sample of size n has an equal probability (or chance) of selection.*

How can a random sample be generated? If the population is not too large, each observation may be recorded on a piece of paper and placed in a suitable container. After the collection of papers is thoroughly mixed, the researcher can remove n pieces of paper from the container; the elements named on these n pieces of paper are the ones to be included in the sample. Lottery officials utilize such a technique in generating the winning numbers for Florida's weekly 6/49 Lotto game. Forty-nine white Ping-Pong balls (the population), each identified from 1 to 49 in black numerals, are placed into a clear plastic drum and mixed by blowing air into the container. The Ping-Pong balls bounce at random until a total of six balls pop into a tube attached to the drum. The numbers on the six balls (the random sample) are the winning Lotto numbers.

---

*A more formal definition of probability will be provided in Chapter 4.

This method of random sampling is fairly easy to implement if the population is relatively small. It is not feasible, however, when the population consists of a large number of observations. Since it is also very difficult to achieve a thorough mixing, the procedure provides only an approximation to random sampling. Most scientific studies, however, rely on **random number generators** to automatically generate the random sample. Random number generators can be found in a table of random numbers (such as Table 1 of Appendix B) and in computers. In fact, almost all of the statistical software packages available today (e.g., SAS, SPSS, MINITAB) have procedures for generating random samples. We illustrate the use of these random number generators in the following examples.

EXAMPLE 1.7
Random Numbers

Consider the set of 707 sale prices described in Appendix A.1 and stored on a $3\frac{1}{2}''$ diskette. Suppose we designate this data set as our target population. Use a table of random numbers to generate a random sample of five sale prices from the population.

SOLUTION A portion of the random number table in Appendix B (Table 1) is reproduced in Table 1.4. The steps for obtaining a random sample using this table are outlined in the box on page 18. The five random numbers and the associated observations on sale price are shown in Table 1.5.

Table 1.4   Reproduction of a Portion of Table 1 in Appendix B

		Column					
		1	2	3	4	5	6
Row	1	10480	15011	01536	02011	81647	91646
	2	22368	46573	25595	85393	30995	89198
	3	24130	48360	22527	97265	76393	64809
	4	42167	93093	06243	61680	07856	16376
	5	37570	39975	81837	16656	06121	91782
	6	77921	06907	11008	42751	27756	53498
	7	99562	72905	56420	69994	98872	31016
	8	96301	91977	05463	07972	18876	20922
	9	89579	14342	63661	10281	17453	18103
	10	85475	36857	53342	53988	53060	59533
	11	28918	69578	88231	33276	70997	79936
	12	63553	40961	48235	03427	49626	69445
	13	09429	93969	52636	92737	88974	33488
	14	10365	61129	87529	85689	48237	52267
	15	07119	97336	71048	08178	77233	13916

■

Using a Table of Random Numbers to Generate a Random Sample of Size n from a Population of N Elements

STEP 1 The elements (sale prices) in the population are numbered from 001 to 707 on the data disk. This labeling implies that we will obtain random numbers of three digits from the table, selecting only those numbers with values less than or equal to 707. Note that Table 1.4 gives 5-digit random numbers in each column. Consequently, we will use only the first three digits of each random number.

STEP 2 Arbitrarily, let's begin in row 1, column 1 of the table. The random number entry given there is 10480. From the first three digits, the random number generated is 104 (shaded in Table 1.4). Thus, we will choose the sale price numbered 104 in the population as our first element of the random sample.

STEP 3 Proceeding horizontally to the right across the columns (this choice of direction is arbitrary), we find the next entry in the table to be 150. Therefore, the sale price numbered 150 represents the second element in the sample. Continuing in this manner, we see that the remaining elements to be included in the sample are those numbered 015, 020, 816 (skip), 916 (skip), and (proceeding to row 2) 223.

Table 1.5   Random Sample of Five Sale Prices Selected from the Population Described in Appendix A.1

Random Number	Sale Price
104	$100,000
150	59,000
15	315,000
20	57,000
223	109,000

EXAMPLE 1.8
Selecting a Random Sample

Assume, again, that our target population is the data set consisting of the 707 sale prices on the data disk. Use the computer to select a random sample of size $n = 25$ from the population.

SOLUTION   We used the random number generator of the SAS statistical software package to obtain the sample of 25 sale prices.* The SAS printout listing these 25 random

---

*The SAS commands used to generate the sample are given in the Computer Tutorial, Appendix C. SPSS, MINITAB, and ASP commands are given in Appendices D, E, and F, respectively.

FIGURE 1.1	PROPERTY	SALEPRIC
SAS-Generated Random Sample of 25 Sale Prices from Appendix A.1	14	300000
	36	113500
	39	127000
	58	120700
	119	69900
	130	68500
	151	230000
	152	167000
	162	256000
	222	150500
	237	130000
	249	99500
	262	106000
	283	90000
	299	85000
	344	82000
	356	102900
	360	100300
	393	92000
	410	100700
	452	310000
	483	85000
	501	52200
	574	76000
	588	47500

numbers and associated sale prices is shown in Figure 1.1. Consequently, the 25 sale prices shown in Figure 1.1 represent the sample. ■

Although random sampling represents one of the simplest of the multitude of sampling techniques available for research, most of the statistical techniques presented in this introductory text assume that such a sample (or sample that closely approximates a random sample) has been collected. We consider a few of the other, more sophisticated, sampling methods in Chapter 9.

Analytic Studies

Recall that analytic studies involve analyzing process data—that is, data collected sequentially over time. Sampling plans for process data are fairly easy to implement. For example, if we are interested in forecasting the annual price of gold, we might simply collect gold prices (in dollars per ounce) for each of the past 10 years. Then, our sample would consist of annual gold prices for the past 10 years. Or, if we are monitoring a manufacturing process (say, electronic components) to improve future quality, we might inspect one randomly selected item each hour for a period of 48 consecutive hours. The 48 quality measurements, recorded sequentially in time, represent our sample.

More information on sampling plans for process data is provided in Chapters 15 and 16.

EXERCISES

▪ *Learning the Mechanics*

1.12 Use a random number table to generate a random sample of size $n = 5$ from a population with 1,000 observations.

1.13 Use a computer to generate a random sample of $n = 20$ observations from a population that contains 10,000 elements.

1.14 Appendix A.4 contains information on the tar contents (in milligrams) of 500 cigarette brands tested by the Federal Trade Commission. Use a random number generator to produce a random sample of $n = 20$ tar measurements from the data described in Appendix A.4. (The data are available on a $3\frac{1}{2}''$ diskette from the publisher.)

▪ *Applying the Concepts*

1.15 Many opinion surveys are conducted by mail. In such a sampling procedure, a random sample of persons is selected from among a list of people who are supposed to constitute a target population (e.g., purchasers of a product). Each is sent a questionnaire and is requested to complete and return the questionnaire to the pollster. Why might this type of survey yield a sample that would produce biased inferences?

1.16 Test marketing is used by companies to gauge consumer preferences for a new product. Conventional marketing tests usually involve sampling 3% of the target population over a 1-year period, a slow and expensive process to carry out. *Fortune* (Oct. 29, 1984) reports that many companies are turning to alternative methods that use a much smaller sample over a much shorter time span. One such method, called *simulated test marketing*, is described as follows. "A consumer recruited at a shopping center reads an ad for a new product and gets a free sample to take home. Later, she rates it in a telephone interview." The telephone responses are used by the test-marketing firm to predict potential sales volume. Simulated marketing tests appear to identify potential failures reasonably well, but "they don't do such a good job predicting the upside potential of products." Why might the sampling procedure yield a sample of consumer preferences that underestimates sales volume of a successful new product?

1.17 Researchers who publish in professional business journals are typically university professors. Consequently, the data upon which the research is based are sometimes obtained by using students in an experimental setting. For example, the *Academy of Management Journal* (Oct. 1993) published a study on the relationship between employee commitment and employee turnover at an aerospace firm. A major part of the study involved measuring and analyzing the commitment of employees (and former employees) of the firm. A secondary portion of the study, however, utilized commitment data measured on a sample of students in an undergraduate management class. In general, comment on the use of students as experimental units in business studies.

1.18 A file clerk is assigned the task of selecting a random sample of 26 company accounts (from a total of 5,000) to be audited. The clerk is considering two sampling methods:

METHOD A. Organize the 5,000 company accounts in alphabetical order (according to the first letter of the client's last name); then randomly select one account card for each of the 26 letters of the alphabet.

METHOD B. Assign each company account a four-digit number from 0001 to 5000. From a table of random numbers, choose 26 four-digit numbers (in the range of 0001–5000) and match the numbers with the corresponding company account.

Which of the two methods would you recommend to the file clerk? Which sampling method could possibly yield a nonrepresentative sample?

SUMMARY

In this chapter, we identify the types of problems for which statistical procedures are useful—namely, describing data sets and using *sample* data to make *inferences* about a sampled *population*. Basic to the application of these techniques is the identification of a population of data that truly characterizes the phenomenon of interest.

Most statistical problems involve sampling and using a sample to make inferences about the sampled population. For example, the ratios of sale price to total appraised value for the six neighborhoods (described in Appendix A.1) could be viewed as samples of the ratios of property value to appraised value for their respective neighborhoods. Do these sample values suggest a difference in the distributions of the ratios of property value to appraised value among the six neighborhoods? Statistical methods to be covered later will help us answer this question and will provide us with a *measure of reliability* for our decision.

The remainder of this course will examine some basic statistical procedures for describing and analyzing data sets. We will learn how to use sample data to infer the nature of the sampled population and to do so with a known degree of reliability. The proper statistical technique will depend on several factors, including the type of data (quantitative or qualitative) collected. (Consult the flow chart on the inside front cover of this text for a guide to selecting the proper method.)

KEY TERMS

Analytic study	Population	Reliability
Data	Qualitative data	Representative sample
Enumerative study	Quantitative data	Sample
Experimental unit	Random number generator	Variable
Inference	Random sample	

SUPPLEMENTARY EXERCISES

■ *Learning the Mechanics*

1.19 Use a random number table or a computer to generate a random sample of 10 observations from a population with 40,000 elements.

1.20 Appendix A.5 describes data on the diameters (in inches) of 500 steel rods manufactured on a production line. Use a random number generator to produce a random sample of $n = 15$ diameters from the data set. (The data are available on a $3\frac{1}{2}''$ diskette from the publisher.)

■ *Applying the Concepts*

1.21 State whether each of the following variables is quantitative or qualitative.
  a. Number of acres in a plot of land
  b. Mode of transportation (to and from work) for a city employee
  c. Type of residential water-heating system
  d. Time required for a product to be shipped from one city to another

1.22 Want to avoid an Internal Revenue Service audit of your personal income tax return? If so, then try living in Newark, New Jersey, or in Boston. Research Institute of America (RIA) found that only .55% of returns in those two cities were audited in 1987, in contrast to 1.45% in Anchorage, Alaska, 1.44% in San Francisco, and 1.36% in Manhattan (*Wall Street Journal*, Mar. 22, 1989). For this RIA study, identify or describe the following:
  a. Population   **b.** Sample
  c. Experimental unit   **d.** Inference

1.23 When Nissan introduced its new Infiniti luxury cars in 1989, its television ad campaign was renowned for a novel gimmick: The automobiles were nowhere in sight. The Infiniti ads, which depicted lushly photographed trees, boulders, lightning bolts, and ocean waves (but no cars), were found by a nationwide Gallup poll of 1,000 consumers to be the best-recalled commercial on television (*Time*, Jan. 22, 1990).
  a. Is the study enumerative or analytic?
  b. Describe the population of interest to the pollsters.
  c. Identify the sample.
  d. Are the data collected quantitative or qualitative?
  e. What is the inference made by the Gallup poll?

1.24 Do most state lottery winners who win big payoffs quit their jobs within 1 year of winning? No, according to a study conducted by sociologist and professor, H. Roy Kaplan (*Journal of the Institute for Socioeconomic Studies*, Sept. 1985). Kaplan mailed questionnaires to over 2,000 lottery winners who won at least $50,000 in the past 10 years. Of the 576 who responded, only 11% had quit their jobs during the first year after striking it rich. In this study, identify the following:
  a. The population
  b. The sample
  c. The inference made about the population

1.25 A study conducted to examine the differences in job performance of white-collar workers with type A and type B behavior (*Journal of Human Stress*, Summer 1985). Type A workers exhibit on-the-job traits such as explosiveness, accelerated speech, high-achievement ambitions, impatience with slowness, free-floating hostility, a tendency to challenge others, and the general appearance of tension; type B behavior is generally characterized by opposite attributes and qualities. Samples of 103 type A workers and 104 type B workers at a large Canadian manufacturing firm took part in the study. Job performance of each worker was measured on a 5-point scale (a higher score indicates better performance) based on the ratings of immediate supervisors.

    a. Describe the two populations of interest in the study.

    b. Identify the variable being measured, and state whether it is quantitative or qualitative.

    c. Would you expect the samples of type A and type B workers to adequately represent the corresponding populations described in part **a**?

    d. Explain how the researchers could use the sample information to estimate the difference in "average" performance ratings of the two populations described in part **a**.

    e. Would you expect the observed sample difference to equal the population difference? Explain.

1.26 An enumerative study was conducted to explore the relation of self-esteem and positive inequity to on-the-job productivity (*Journal of Personality*, Dec. 1985). Eighty students enrolled in an industrial psychology course at a private New England university served as participants. All students were asked to complete a proofreading task and were compensated for their work on an hourly basis. However, some students were overpaid for each hour they worked (positive inequity condition), whereas the others were given fair compensation (equity condition). The results of the study revealed that individuals of high self-esteem were more productive (i.e., completed more of the task) in the positive inequity condition than in the equity condition. However, the reverse was true for students of low self-esteem.

    a. The variable of interest in this study is productivity, measured as amount of the task completed. Is this variable quantitative or qualitative in nature?

    b. In this study, we can envision four experimental conditions: (1) high self-esteem/positive inequity, (2) high self-esteem/equity, (3) low self-esteem/positive inequity, and (4) low self-esteem/equity. Describe the populations corresponding to the four conditions.

    c. Identify the samples. Assume that 20 students were assigned to each of the four experimental conditions.

    d. Do you think the samples adequately represent the populations described in part **a**?

    e. Do you think the results of the study were obtained by analyzing the data in the populations, or were they derived from sample information?

1.27 A successful discount clothing store, in business for 30 years, must order a particular brand of blue jeans from the manufacturer 1 month in advance. To avoid large losses, the store must be able to predict the monthly demand for blue jeans for each month of the year. Suppose the store has ready access to the monthly sales records (i.e., the number of blue jeans sold by the store during each month) for the past 10 years. This information will be used to project monthly demand.

    a. What type of statistical study is to be employed?

    b. If the discount store views the monthly blue jeans sales data over the past 10 years as a sample selected from a population, describe the conceptual population.

    c. Suggest a way in which the discount clothing store could use the monthly sales records over the past 10 years to project monthly blue jeans demand.

1.28 Automated customer checkout systems, more formally known as Universal Product Code (UPC) symbol-scanning systems, are used by virtually all retail food marketers. With automated checkers, the cashier brushes the item across a scanning window located on the counter. A laser beam is then activated to read the price code several times, verify its accuracy, and transmit the price to the checkstand to be printed on the receipt tape. Customers who shop at supermarkets with automated checkers can expect faster checkout times and a more accurate and detailed receipt tape. Consider the customer checkout times for a sample of 500 grocery shoppers at a supermarket that uses automated checkers. (Customer checkout time is defined here as the total length of time required for service personnel to check the prices of the customer's food items, total the prices, accept payment, and return change.)

    a. Identify the variable measured and its type.

    b. Describe the population from which the sample is selected.

    c. Suppose you were to use the average of the 500 customer checkout times to estimate the average checkout time of all customers who shop at the supermarket. Would you expect the sample average to equal the average for the population? Explain.

■ CASE STUDY 1.1

The Executive Compensation Scoreboard

How much are the top corporate executives being paid, and are they worth it? To answer these questions, *Business Week* magazine compiles its Executive Compensation Scoreboard each year based on a survey of executives at the highest-ranking companies listed in the *Business Week 1000*. Among the 360 companies surveyed in 1994, nearly 70% of the chief executives earned more than $1 million in 1993.[*]

The top spot in the survey was claimed by Michael D. Eisner, chairman of Walt Disney Corporation. According to *Business Week*, Eisner earned $203,010,590 in salary, bonuses, and stock options, "more than any other chief executive of a public or private corporation has made in a single year—or probably in the history of American business." Eisner's staggering salary computes to $78,081 per hour!

To determine which executives are worth their pay, *Business Week* calculates several useful benchmarks as part of the Executive Compensation Scoreboard. One of these, the focus of this case study, is the ratio of total shareholder return (measured by the dollar value of a $100 investment in the company made 3 years earlier) to total executive pay (in $ thousands). For example, a $100 investment in Walt Disney Corporation in 1991 was worth $170 at the end of 1993. When this shareholder return ($170) is divided by CEO Michael Eisner's total 1993 compensation in thousands, the result is a shareholder return-to-pay ratio of only .00084—one of the lowest among all other executives in the survey.

The total 1993 compensations and shareholder return-to-pay ratios for the 361 CEOs in the *Business Week* survey are described in Appendix A.2. In addition, the industry group (e.g., high tech, transportation, consumer products, etc.) of each CEO is listed. This information will permit us to make pay-for-performance comparisons of executives in the industry groups later

in this text. Suppose you are interested in determining which CEOs in *Business Week*'s Executive Compensation Scoreboard are "worth" their 1993 pay. To accomplish this, you will rank the 360 CEOs in the survey based on the ratio of shareholder return to executive pay.

a. Describe the target population for this problem. Does the population adequately characterize the pay-for-performance of CEOs in the *Business Week* survey? Explain.

b. Suppose you were interested in characterizing the pay-for-performance of CEOs at *all* U.S. companies in 1993. Would the data in Appendix A.2 represent a population or a sample? Explain.

c. Refer to part **b**. Do you think the sample is representative of the target population? Explain.

d. The variables recorded in Appendix A.2 are listed here. Identify the type (quantitative or qualitative) of each.
- (1) Industry type
- (2) Chief executive officer (CEO)
- (3) Company/corporation
- (4) 1993 salary ($ thousands)
- (5) Change in salary from 1992 ($ thousands)
- (6) Long-term compensation ($ thousands)
- (7) Total compensation ($ thousands)
- (8) Return on $100 investment ($)
- (9) Return-to-total pay ratio
- (10) Rating[†] (1 = excellent, 2 = above average, 3 = average, 4 = below average, 5 = poor)

e. Use the computer or a random number table to select a random sample of 10 CEO return-to-pay ratios from the data described in Appendix A.2. (The data are available on a $3\frac{1}{2}$" diskette from the publisher.)

---

[*] *Source:* "Executive Compensation Scoreboard." Business Week, *Apr. 25, 1994.*

[†] *To obtain the performance rating,* Business Week *compared an executive's return-to-pay ratio with those of others within the same industry group and assigned a rating of 1 to those executives with the highest ratios (relative to the others in the group), a rating of 2 to those with the next highest ratios, etc.*

■ CASE STUDY 1.2

HMO Physicians: Cost-effective?

During the past 20 years, health-care costs have escalated at a rapid rate. To make health care more affordable, health maintenance organizations (HMOs) designed insurance packages that allow patients to obtain as much service as possible at low or minimal personal expense. An HMO is usually made up of an independent group of physicians who provide primary and special health care to patients in a geographical area. Since most HMOs are "unmanaged," the system provides only marginally beneficial services and is usually not cost-effective.

In contrast, the object of a "managed" health-care system is to provide the patients with care that is genuinely needed, not what the patients think they want or what the physicians want to provide. A "case manager" authorizes any out-of-ordinary testing, referral to physicians other than the primary-care physician, and referral to a hospital for admission. Most experts view primary-care physicians (e.g., general practitioners, family physicians, general internists, pediatricians) as the best case managers by virtue of their generalized professional training. However, one question that remains to be answered is whether some case managers are more cost-effective than others.

To investigate this phenomenon, a study was conducted by a network of private practicing physicians in Florida, called the Tampa Bay Area Doctors (TBAD). Appendix A.3 describes the total costs accrued per patient per month by 186 TBAD physicians in 1989.* In addition to total cost, Appendix A.3 includes the following information on the physicians:

- Primary specialty (general practice, internal medicine, pediatrics, family practice, or other)
- Secondary specialty (yes or no)
- Years of experience
- Country of medical residency (U.S. or foreign)
- Country of medical school (U.S. or foreign)
- Gender (male or female)
- Total patient-months
- Certification level (0, 1, or 2)

By examining total costs of the TBAD physicians, we can determine whether there exists an identifiable subgroup of physicians who consistently have lower total health-care costs for the patients they manage. (For example, one theory is that experienced primary-care physicians without a secondary specialty who obtained their degree at a U.S. medical school will be most cost-effective.) Such an analysis will be the subject of a later case study.

a. Give a scenario where the data in Appendix A.3 would represent the target population.

b. Give a scenario where the data in Appendix A.3 would represent a sample. For this sample, what is the target population? Is the sample representative of the population? Explain.

c. Identify the type (quantitative or qualitative) of each variable included in Appendix A.3.

d. Use the computer or a random number table to select a random sample of 20 HMO physicians from Appendix A.3. List the characteristics (variables) for each of these 20 physicians. (The data are available on a $3\frac{1}{2}''$ diskette from the publisher.)

---

*Source: Lane, W., and Sincich, T. "Selection of Cost-Effective Primary-Care Physician Case Managers." Medical Interface, Oct. 1992.

Chapter 2

GRAPHICAL METHODS FOR DESCRIBING DATA SETS

The U.S. surgeon general lists tar, nicotine, and carbon monoxide as hazardous substances that are found in cigarette smoke. Consequently, each year the Federal Trade Commission (FTC) tests and ranks each domestic cigarette brand according to these substances. The most recent data collected by the FTC include 500 cigarette brands. A graphical method for summarizing and making sense of this data set is the topic of Case Study 2.1. Graphical methods that rapidly convey the information contained in a data set are discussed in this chapter.

■ CONTENTS

2.1 The Objective of Data Description

The objective of data description is to summarize the characteristics of a data set. Ultimately, we want to make the data more comprehensible and meaningful. In this chapter, we show you how to construct charts and graphs that convey the nature of a data set. The procedure that we use to accomplish this objective in a particular situation depends on the type of data, quantitative or qualitative, that we want to describe.

2.2 Graphical Descriptions of Qualitative Data

Bar graphs and **pie charts** are two of the most widely used graphical methods for describing qualitative data sets. Essentially, they show how many observations fall in each qualitative category.

The observations for foreman in charge, a qualitative variable, could fall into one of a number of categories or **classes.** If three foremen were used in the manufacturing operation, then the number of classes would be three. If the variable Foreman in charge was observed on a number of shifts, we would find that foreman 1 was in charge, say, n_1 times; foreman 2, n_2 times; and foreman 3, n_3 times.

The summary information that we seek on qualitative variables is either the number of observations falling in each class or the proportion of the total number of observations falling in each class. Bar graphs can be constructed to show either type of information. Pie charts usually show the proportions or percentages of the total number of measurements falling in the classes. Although bar graphs and pie charts can be easily constructed by hand, you will probably rely on a statistical computer software package to produce the graphs for presentation purposes.

Definition 2.1

A **class** is one of the categories into which qualitative data can be classified.

Definition 2.2

The **frequency** for a particular class is the number of observations falling in that class.

Definition 2.3

The **relative frequency** for a particular class is equal to the class frequency divided by the total number of observations.

Recall that Appendix A.1 describes the sale and appraisal data for 707 residential properties sold in 1993 in six Tampa neighborhoods. Figure 2.1 is a computer-generated (SAS) bar graph showing the frequencies of sales for the six neighborhoods of Appendix A.1. Interpret the graph.

FIGURE 2.1

SAS Bar Graph
Showing the Relative
Frequency of Sales
for Six
Neighborhoods

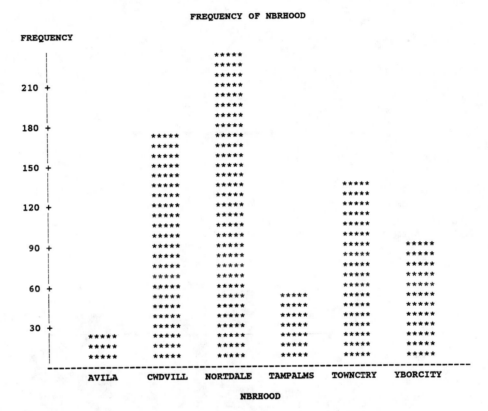

SOLUTION The figure contains a rectangle or **bar** for each neighborhood; the height of a particular bar is proportional to the number of sales for its neighborhood. For example, the bar graph indicates that approximately 55 properties were sold in the Tampa Palms neighborhood in 1993. You can rapidly compare the numbers of sales for the six neighborhoods by visually comparing the heights of the bars.

The frequencies—that is, the numbers of sales for each of the six neighborhoods—are shown in Table 2.1 (page 30). The class relative frequencies, obtained by dividing each class frequency by the total number of sales, 707, are also shown.

The bar graph that permits a comparison of sales can be constructed in several different ways. The heights of the bars can be measured in units of frequency (as in the SAS bar graph, Figure 2.1) or relative frequency (as in the ASP bar graph, Figure 2.2). It is also common to reverse the axes and display the bars in a horizontal fashion (as in the SPSS bar graph, Figure 2.3). ■

Table 2.1 Frequencies and Relative Frequencies of Sales for the Six Neighborhoods of Appendix A.1

Neighborhood	Class Frequency	Relative Frequency
1. Avila	24	.034
2. Carrollwood Village	169	.239
3. Northdale	235	.333
4. Tampa Palms	54	.076
5. Town & Country	138	.195
6. Ybor City	87	.123
TOTAL	707	1.000

FIGURE 2.2

ASP Bar Graph Showing Relative Frequency of Sales for Six Neighborhoods

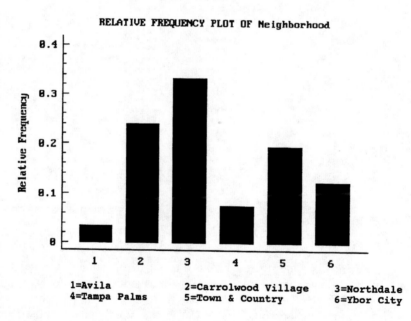

RELATIVE FREQUENCY PLOT OF Neighborhood

1=Avila
4=Tampa Palms
2=Carrolwood Village
5=Town & Country
3=Northdale
6=Ybor City

FIGURE 2.3

SPSS Horizontal Bar Graph Showing Frequency of Sales for Six Neighborhoods

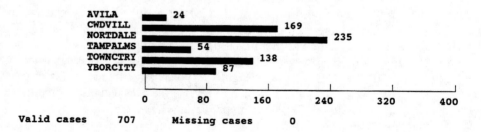

Valid cases   707   Missing cases   0

EXAMPLE 2.2
Pie Chart

An ASP pie chart for the neighborhood sales data is shown in Figure 2.4. Show that the pie chart conveys the same information as the bar chart in Figure 2.2.

SOLUTION The total number of sales for the six neighborhoods (the pie) is split into six pieces. The size (angle) of the slice assigned to a neighborhood is proportional to the relative frequency for that neighborhood. For example, since a complete circle spans 360°, the slice assigned to the Tampa Palms neighborhood is 7.6% of 360°, or

$$(.076)(360) = 27.4°$$

It is common to show the proportion of measurements in each class on the pie chart as indicated. ■

FIGURE 2.4

ASP Pie Chart
Showing Relative
Frequency of Sales
for Six
Neighborhoods

NBRHOODS: (1=AVILA 2=CARWOOD 3=NORTDLE 4=TAMPLMS 5=TWNCTY 6=YBOR)

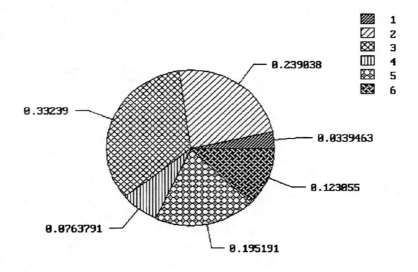

EXAMPLE 2.3
Relative Frequency Bar
Graph

Refer to the data on HMO physicians described in Appendix A.3. One of the several variables measured is the primary specialty of each physician (see Case Study 1.2). Figure 2.5 (page 32) is a SAS relative frequency bar graph giving the percentage breakdown according to primary specialty for the 186 physicians. Interpret the figure.

SOLUTION Each of the 186 physicians in the HMO has been classified according to primary specialty, a qualitative variable; six primary specialty groups are shown in the figure. The height of each bar is proportional to the percentage of the 186 physicians with that particular primary specialty. For example, approximately 10% of the 186 physicians (about 18 physicians) consider family practice as their primary specialty, whereas the highest percentage of these physicians (30%, or about 54) are pediatricians. ■

FIGURE 2.5

SAS Bar Chart Showing Percentages of Physicians in Primary Specialty Groups

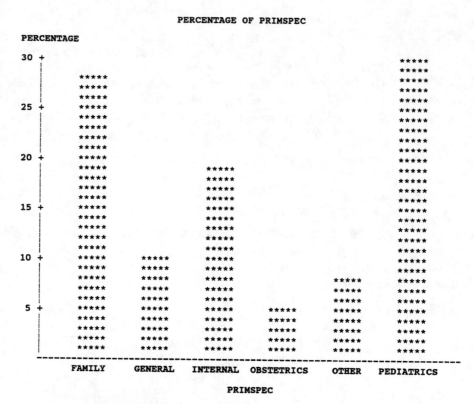

EXAMPLE 2.4
Horizontal Bar Graph

Refer to Example 2.3. Another qualitative variable measured on each physician is certification level. A certified doctor has completed training and passed the American Medical Association (AMA) Board of Physicians' examination. An uncertified physician can be one of two types: a young physician who has completed training but has not yet taken or passed the AMA board exam, or an older physician who is ineligible for certification but was granted a license to practice by the AMA. The levels of certification recorded in Appendix A.3 are 0, 1, and 2, where 0 = uncertified, board-ineligible; 1 = board-certified; and 2 = uncertified, board-eligible. Figure 2.6 is an ASP horizontal bar graph showing the frequencies of certification level. Interpret the graph.

FIGURE 2.6

ASP Frequency Bar Graph of Physician Certification Levels

FREQUENCY PLOT

VARIABLE: Certification

	FRQ.	CUM.	%	CUM.	FREQUENCY PLOT
x < 0	0	0	0	0	
x = 0	27	27	14.5	14.5	*****
x = 1	122	149	65.6	80.1	************************
x = 2	37	186	19.9	100	*******
x > 2	0	186	0	100	
TOTAL	**186**		**100**		

SOLUTION Each of the 186 HMO physicians has been classified according to certification level. The length of the horizontal bar adjacent to each category label is proportional to the number of physicians with that particular certification level. The row of the graph labeled x = 1 reveals that the majority of physicians (122 of 186, or 65.6%) are board-certified. Of the remaining (uncertified) physicians, 27 are board-ineligible (x = 0 row) and 37 are board-eligible (x = 2 row). ■

Constructing a Bar Graph

STEP 1   Summarize the data in a frequency table. The table should contain the frequency and relative frequency for each class (or category) of the qualitative variable.

STEP 2   Draw horizontal and vertical axes on graph paper. The vertical axis can represent either class frequency or class relative frequency. The classes (or categories) of the qualitative variable will be marked under the horizontal axis.

STEP 3   Draw in the bars for each class (or category). The height of the bar should be proportional to either the class frequency or class relative frequency.

EXERCISES

■ *Learning the Mechanics*

2.1   The *Journal of Performance of Constructed Facilities* (Feb. 1990) reported on the performance dimensions of water distribution networks in the Philadelphia area. For one part of the study, the following data were collected for a sample of water pipe sections:

1. Pipe diameter (inches)
2. Pipe material
3. Age (year of installation)
4. Location
5. Pipe length (feet)
6. Stability of surrounding soil (unstable, moderately stable, or stable)
7. Corrosiveness of surrounding soil (corrosive or noncorrosive)
8. Internal pressure (pounds per square inch)
9. Percentage of pipe covered with land cover
10. Breakage rate (number of times pipe had to be repaired as a result of breakage)

a. Identify the qualitative variables measured.

b. Refer to part **a.** List the statistical methods available for summarizing the data produced by the qualitative variables.

2.2 Complete the following table:

Grade on Business Statistics Exam	Frequency	Relative Frequency
A: 90–100	16	.08
B: 80–89	36	18 / 45
C: 65–79	90	
D: 50–64	30	15
F: Below 50	28	14
TOTAL	200	1.00

2.3 Many U.S. corporations have experimented with alternatives to the traditional 5-day, 40-hour work week. Suppose a company surveyed its employees concerning the type of work week they would prefer: a 6-day, 48-hour work week; a 5-day, 40-hour work week; a 4-day, 40-hour work week; or a 3-day, 40-hour work week. Twenty-five employees responded as shown in the table.

Employee	Work Week	Employee	Work Week
1	5-day, 40-hour	14	4-day, 40-hour
2	5-day, 40-hour	15	6-day, 48-hour
3	3-day, 40-hour	16	4-day, 40-hour
4	6-day, 48-hour	17	5-day, 40-hour
5	4-day, 40-hour	18	5-day, 40-hour
6	4-day, 40-hour	19	5-day, 40-hour
7	5-day, 40-hour	20	4-day, 40-hour
8	3-day, 40-hour	21	3-day, 40-hour
9	6-day, 48-hour	22	5-day, 40-hour
10	5-day, 40-hour	23	3-day, 40-hour
11	4-day, 40-hour	24	4-day, 40-hour
12	5-day, 40-hour	25	5-day, 40-hour
13	4-day, 40-hour		

a. Identify the type of variable measured.

b. Identify the classes.

c. Compute the frequency of each class.

d. Compute the relative frequency of each class.

e. Construct a relative frequency bar graph for the data on work-week preferences.

■ *Applying the Concepts*

2.4 The *Journal of Consumer Marketing* (Summer 1992) reported on a study of company response to letters of consumer complaints. Marketing students at a large midwest public university "were asked to write letters of complaint to companies whose products legitimately caused them to be dissatisfied." Of the 750 students in the class, 286 wrote letters of complaint. The table shows the type of response received from the companies and number of each type.

Type of Response	Number
Letter and product replacement	42
Letter and good coupon	36
Letter and cents-off coupon	29
Letter and refund check	23
Letter, refund check, and coupon	13
Letter only	76
No response	67
Total	286

Source: Clark, G. L., Kaminski, P. F., and Rink, D. R. "Consumer complaints: Advice on how companies should respond based on an empirical study." *Journal of Consumer Marketing,* Vol. 9, No. 3, Summer 1992, p. 8 (Table 1).

a. Display the study results in a relative frequency bar graph.

b. What percentage of consumers received a response to their letter of complaint?

2.5 The accompanying table lists 17 men's cologne (fragrance) brands rated by *Consumer Reports* (Dec. 1993). The balance and intensity of each brand are rated.

a. The balance ratings are summarized in the accompanying SPSS printout. Interpret the results.

BALANCE

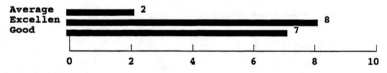

b. Summarize the intensity ratings with an appropriate graphical method.

Fragrance Brand	Balance Rating	Intensity Rating
Aramis	Good	Strong
Brut	Average	Very strong
Drakkar Noir	Excellent	Very strong
Egoïste	Good	Strong

(continued)

Fragrance Brand	Balance Rating	Intensity Rating
English Leather	Good	Medium
Escape for Men	Excellent	Strong
Eternity for Men	Excellent	Very strong
Gravity	Excellent	Strong
Lancer	Excellent	Strong
Obsession for Men	Excellent	Strong
Old Spice	Good	Strong
Polo	Average	Very strong
Preferred Stock	Excellent	Strong
Realm for Men	Excellent	Strong
Safari for Men	Good	Very strong
Stetson	Good	Medium
Tribute	Good	Strong

Source: *Consumer Reports*, Dec. 1993, p. 773.

2.6 An investigation of the waiting time experienced by customers at a large Boston bank was conducted (*Sloan Management Review*, Winter 1991). With the aid of video cameras, the researchers recorded the actual time each of 277 customers waited in line for a bank teller. As customers finished their transactions, they were interviewed by the researchers and asked about perceived waiting time. In addition to perceived and actual waiting time, the researchers asked customers to describe their wait in line. Customers generally fell into three categories: "watchers" who enjoy observing people and events at the bank, "impatients" who could think of nothing more boring than waiting in line, and "neutrals" who fell somewhere in the middle. The accompanying table gives the breakdown, in percentages, of the 277 customers falling in the three categories of watchers, impatients, and neutrals.

Summary of Customer Interest Level

Category	Percentage
Watchers	21
Impatients	45
Neutrals	34

Source: Katz, K. L., Larson, B. M., and Larson, R. C. "Prescription for the waiting-in-line blues: Entertain, enlighten, and engage." *Sloan Management Review*, Winter 1991, p. 49 (Fig. 5).

a. Are the data quantitative or qualitative?

b. Describe the data summarized in the table graphically. Interpret the graph.

2.7   Every year during the July 4th holiday, police and fire chiefs alert us to the dangers of fireworks. Although the danger is real (about 12,000 Americans are injured by fireworks each year), more than twice as many Americans are injured using skateboards as by fireworks. The accompanying table, reported in *Consumers' Research* (June 1995), provides a breakdown of the 849,500 injuries that occurred in 1993 related to the seven most dangerous products. Construct and interpret a frequency bar graph for the data.

Product	Number of Injuries (thousands)
Bicycles	600
In-line skates	76
Sleds	55
Trampolines	46
Aquariums/pet supplies	32
Skateboards	28
Fireworks	12.5
Total	849.5

Source: Consumer Product Safety Commission.

2.8   Investors in the 1990s are faced with a plethora of stocks, mutual funds, and bonds in which to invest. The bond market alone held $440 billion in net assets in 1993. The accompanying table describes the different types of bonds available in 1993. Summarize the data with a graphical method. Interpret the results.

Bond Type	Number
U.S. Government	310
Investment Grade Corp.	186
Medium Grade Corp.	50
"Junk" Corporation	90
Investment Grade Muni.	631
High Yield Muni.	26
Global	94
Total	1,387

Source: Bogle, J. C. "A crystal ball look at the U.S. markets in the 1990's." *Journal of Financial Planning*, Jan. 1993, p. 17 (Exhibit 12).

2.9   Real estate investment trusts (REITs) are corporations or trusts that sell stock and combine capital from investors to buy properties or make real estate loans. Since REITs must meet federal guidelines and are regulated by the Internal Revenue Service, only a limited number exist. Currently, there are 219 REITs operating nationwide. The major type of properties owned by these 219 REITs are summarized in the table.

Type of Property	Percent of REITs
Health care	17
Hotels	2
Industrial	11
Office	20
Residential	15
Retail	21
Other	14
Total	100

Source: Chicago Tribune, Sept. 1992.

a. Display the data with a pie chart.
b. Interpret the pie chart.
c. Does the pie chart describe population or sample data? Explain.

2.10 Refer to the *Business Horizons* study of 800 CEOs, Exercise 1.1. A summary of the birth regions of the CEOs is displayed in the table. Illustrate the data with a bar graph.

Region of Birth	Percent of CEOs
Northeast	37
South	18
Midwest	32
West	7
Outside U.S.A.	6
	100

Source: Bassiry, G. R., and Dekmejian, R. H. "America's global companies: A leadership profile." Business Horizons, Jan.–Feb. 1993, p. 48. Reprinted from Business Horizons, Jan.–Feb. 1993. Copyright 1993 by the Foundation for the School of Business at Indiana University. Used with permission.

2.11 The University of Miami conducted a study for the U.S. Department of Labor concerning barriers to women's upward mobility in the workplace. General characteristics of the 176 female executives throughout the country who participated in the survey are illustrated in the pie charts. Use this information to describe the typical female executive.

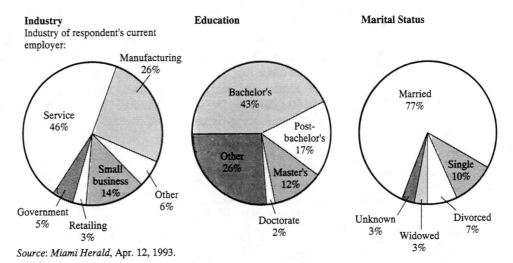

Industry
Industry of respondent's current
employer:

Manufacturing 26%
Service 46%
Small business 14%
Other 6%
Government 5%
Retailing 3%

Education

Bachelor's 43%
Post-bachelor's 17%
Other 26%
Master's 12%
Doctorate 2%

Marital Status

Married 77%
Single 10%
Unknown 3%
Widowed 3%
Divorced 7%

Source: Miami Herald, Apr. 12, 1993.

2.12 Most emergency-care patients in Florida use some type of insurance coverage, public or private, to pay for treatment. Surprisingly, over 20% of these patients have no insurance coverage of any kind to help pay emergency-care costs (*Annals of Emergency Medicine,* Oct. 1992). Data collected on 1,645 emergency-care patients treated at Florida hospitals were classified according to primary party responsible for payment. The data are summarized in the accompanying table. Construct and interpret a pie chart for the data.

Primary Insurance	Number of Patients
Self-responsible	339
Medicare	288
Medicaid	120
Commercial	526
HMO/PPO	238
Workers Compensation	134
Total	1,645

Source: Mitchell, T. A., and Remmel, R. J. "Level of uncompensated care delivered by emergency physicians in Florida." *Annals of Emergency Medicine,* Vol. 21, No. 10, Oct. 1992, p. 55 (Table 2).

2.3 Graphical Descriptions of Quantitative Data: Stem-and-Leaf Displays

Stem-and-leaf displays and **histograms** are two of the most popular graphical methods for describing quantitative data sets. Like the bar graphs and pie charts of Section 2.2, they show either the number of observations that fall in each class (class frequency) or the proportion of the total number of observations falling in each class (class relative frequency). The difference is that the classes do not represent categories of a qualitative variable; instead, they are formed by grouping the numerical values of the quantitative variable that you want to describe.

For small data sets (say, 30 or fewer observations) with measurements with only a few digits, stem-and-leaf displays can be constructed easily and quickly by hand. Histograms, on the other hand, are better suited to the description of large data sets, and they permit greater flexibility in the choice of the classes. In this section, we present stem-and-leaf displays for small data sets. We will illustrate the procedure using a sample of 25 sale prices selected from the data of Appendix A.1. The data are shown in Table 2.2.

Table 2.2   Sale Prices for a Sample of Properties from Appendix A.1

	Sale Price, Hundreds of Dollars			
660	595	1,060	500	630
899	1,295	749	820	843
710	950	720	575	760
1,090	770	682	1,016	650
425	367	1,480	945	1,120

EXAMPLE 2.5
Stem-and-Leaf Display

Construct a stem-and-leaf display for the sale price data shown in Table 2.2.

SOLUTION   Since all the sale prices in Appendix A.1 are given to the nearest hundred dollars, we have simplified the numbers in the data set by dropping the last two zeros. Thus, the first number in the table is 660, representing a sale price of $66,000. We will designate the last two digits (60) of this number as its **leaf**; we will call the remaining digit (6) its **stem,** as illustrated here.

Stem	Leaf
6	60

The stem and leaf of the number 899 are 8 and 99, respectively. Similarly, the stem and leaf of the number 1,090 are 10 and 90, respectively.

The first step in forming a stem-and-leaf display for this data set is to list all stem possibilities in a column starting with the smallest stem (3, corresponding to the number 367) and ending with the largest (14, corresponding to the number 1,480), as shown in Figure 2.7a. The next step is to place the leaf of each number in the data set in the row of the display corresponding to the number's stem. For example, for the number 660, the leaf 60 is placed in stem row 6. Similarly, for the number 899, the leaf 99 is placed in stem row 8. The usual convention is to list the leaves of each stem in increasing order. After the leaves of the 25 numbers are placed in the appropriate stem rows, the completed stem-and-leaf display will appear as shown in Figure 2.7a.   ■

FIGURE 2.7

Stem-and-Leaf
Display of 25 Sale
Prices in Table 2.2

a. Stem-and-leaf display

Stems	Leaves
3	67
4	25
5	00, 75, 95
6	30, 50, 60, 82
7	10, 20, 49, 60, 70
8	20, 43, 99
9	45, 50
10	16, 60, 90
11	20
12	95
13	
14	80

b. Frequency and relative frequency
tabulation for the stem-and-leaf display

Frequency	Relative Frequency
1	$\frac{1}{25}$
1	$\frac{1}{25}$
3	$\frac{3}{25}$
4	$\frac{4}{25}$
5	$\frac{5}{25}$
3	$\frac{3}{25}$
2	$\frac{2}{25}$
3	$\frac{3}{25}$
1	$\frac{1}{25}$
1	$\frac{1}{25}$
0	0
1	$\frac{1}{25}$
Totals 25	1

You can see that the stem-and-leaf display in Figure 2.7 partitions the data set into 12 categories (called **classes**) corresponding to the 12 stems. The class corresponding to 3 would contain all numbers from 300 to 399; the class corresponding to the stem 4 would contain all numbers from 400 to 499. The number of leaves in each class gives the class frequency. Thus, a stem-and-leaf display provides the frequencies needed to construct frequency and relative frequency distributions for a data set. A **frequency distribution** is a bar graph for a quantitative data set. A **relative frequency distribution** conveys the same information, but the heights of the bars are proportional to the class relative frequencies.

EXAMPLE 2.6
Frequency Distribution

Construct a frequency distribution for the data contained in the stem-and-leaf display in Figure 2.7a.

SOLUTION The frequencies and relative frequencies for 12 classes (corresponding to the 12 stems) are given in Figure 2.7b. Figure 2.8 (page 42) shows the frequency distribution for the data.[*] Bars are constructed over each class, with the height of each bar proportional to the class frequency.

---

[*]*Detailed instructions for constructing a frequency distribution will be given in the next section. At this point, our goal is simply to convert the information contained in the stem-and-leaf display into graphical form.*

FIGURE 2.8

A Frequency
Distribution for the
Sale Price Data of
Figure 2.7

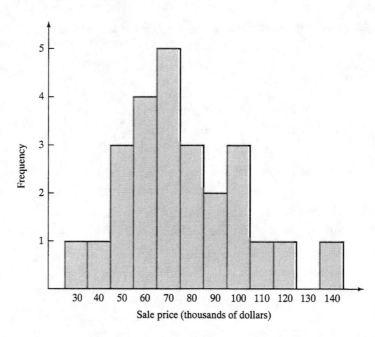

Notice that if you tip the stem-and-leaf display (Figure 2.7a) on its side, you obtain the same type of bar graph as provided by the frequency distribution. Both figures show that the 25 sale prices are scattered over the interval from $30,000 to less than $150,000, with most falling between $50,000 and $100,000. Both methods provide a good visual description of the data.

One advantage of a stem-and-leaf display over a frequency distribution is that the original data are preserved. That is, you can look at the display and resurrect the exact values of the data. A stem-and-leaf display also arranges the data in an orderly fashion and makes it easy to determine certain numerical characteristics to be discussed in Chapter 3. The third advantage is that the classes and the numbers falling in them are quickly determined once we have selected the digits that we want to use for the stems and leaves. A disadvantage of the stem-and-leaf display is that there is sometimes not much flexibility in choosing the stems.

For the data in Table 2.2, two stem and leaf options are possible. We could define the stems and leaves as shown in Figure 2.7a. Or, we could let only the last digit represent the leaf, in which case the number 660 would have the stem 66 and the leaf 0:

Stem	Leaf
66	0

The associated stem-and-leaf display for the data of Table 2.2 would contain 113 stems, 36, 37, ..., 148, and each of the stems would contain either a single leaf or none at all. Clearly, this choice of stems and leaves would not provide as much information about the data as does the display of Figure 2.7a. Consequently, we are left with the option of using a stem-and-leaf display that produces 12 stems (and thus, 12 classes) or one that produces 113 stems.*

Most statistical computer software packages have routines to produce stem-and-leaf displays. A MINITAB stem-and-leaf display for the data of Table 2.2 is shown in Figure 2.9. The stems, 3, 4, 5, ..., 14, are given in the second column and the leaves are given in the third column of the printout. You can see that MINITAB has chosen to use 12 stems, as in Figure 2.7a. MINITAB uses only a single digit—the number in the tens place—to represent a leaf.† Thus, the leaf 6 in stem row 3 of the MINITAB printout (Figure 2.9) represents the value 367 in Table 2.2; the leaf 2 in stem row 4 represents the value 425; and so forth.‡

FIGURE 2.9

MINITAB Stem-and-Leaf Display for Sale Prices in Table 2.2

```
Stem-and-leaf of salepric   N  = 25
Leaf Unit = 10

     1       3  6
     2       4  2
     5       5  079
     9       6  3568
    (5)      7  12467
    11       8  249
     8       9  45
     6      10  169
     3      11  2
     2      12  9
     1      13
     1      14  8
```

Constructing a Stem-and-Leaf Display

1. Decide how the stems and leaves will be defined.
2. List the stems in order in a column, starting with the smallest stem and ending with the largest.
3. Proceed through the data set, placing the leaf for each observation in the appropriate stem row. (You may want to place the leaves of each stem in increasing order.)

---

*By sacrificing some of the simplicity of our procedure, we could define the stems and leaves so that the number of stems falls between 12 and 113. We omit discussion of this topic.

†In MINITAB, the leaf will always be the digit immediately to the right of the stem.

‡The numbers in the first column of the MINITAB printout give the cumulative number of observations from the stem row to the nearest "end" of the distribution.

EXERCISES

■ *Learning the Mechanics*

2.13 Consider the following sample data:

213	228	241	268	234	303	274	316
319	320	227	226	224	267	303	266
265	237	288	291	285	270	254	215

a. Using the first two digits of each number as a stem, list the stem possibilities in order.
b. Place the leaf for each observation in the appropriate stem row to form a stem-and-leaf display.

2.14 A sample of 20 measurements is shown here:

26	34	21	32	42	36	28	38	17	39
22	12	56	39	25	41	30	23	27	19

a. Using the first digit as a stem, list the stem possibilities in order.
b. Place the leaf for each observation in the appropriate stem row to form a stem-and-leaf display.

2.15 Consider the following sample data:

5.9	5.3	1.6	7.4	8.6	1.2	2.1
4.0	7.3	8.4	8.9	6.7	4.5	6.3
7.6	9.7	3.5	1.1	4.3	3.3	8.4
1.6	8.2	6.5	1.1	5.0	9.4	6.4

a. Using the first digit as a stem, construct a stem-and-leaf display.
b. Use the stem-and-leaf display from part **a** to construct a frequency distribution for the data.

■ *Applying the Concepts*

2.16 Multinational corporations are firms with both domestic and foreign assets/investments. The foreign revenue (as a percentage of total revenue) generated by each of the top 20 U.S.-based multinationals is listed in the accompanying table.
a. Construct a stem-and-leaf display for the data.
b. Turn the stem-and-leaf display constructed in part **a** on its side to form a frequency distribution for the data.

c. Interpret the graph obtained in part **b.**

d. What proportion of the 20 multinational firms generated at least 50% of their revenue from foreign investments/sales?

Exxon	73.2	Procter & Gamble	39.9
IBM	58.9	Philip Morris	19.6
GM	26.6	Eastman Kodak	40.9
Mobil	64.7	Digital	54.1
Ford	33.2	GE	12.4
Citicorp	52.3	United Technologies	32.9
EI duPont	39.8	Amoco	26.1
Texaco	42.3	Hewlett-Packard	53.3
ITT	43.3	Xerox	34.6
Dow Chemical	54.1	Chevron	20.5

Source: Forbes, July 23, 1990, pp. 362–363.

2.17   If you are an undergraduate student in business, are you thinking about going to graduate school and obtaining your MBA? If so, you will want answers to several questions before you make your decision. To provide prospective students with "as much comparative educational information as possible beyond the adjective burdened generalizations offered by college marketing brochures," *U.S. News & World Report* each year conducts its Survey of America's Best Graduate and Professional Schools. The accompanying table lists the top 25 business schools according to the survey. The data include a school's overall score (based on a weighted average of rankings in five areas), out-of-state tuition costs, average GMAT scores of entering MBAs, acceptance rate, and average starting salary of MBAs who obtained employment. MINITAB stem-and-leaf displays for the five quantitative variables listed in the table are also shown. Interpret the results.

School	Overall Score	Tuition	GMAT	Acceptance Rate	Starting Salary
Harvard University	100.0	$18,550	640	16.3%	$65,500
Stanford University	99.8	19,239	680	12.0	65,000
University of Pennsylvania (Wharton)	95.5	18,800	644	25.1	60,095
Northwestern University (Kellogg)	94.0	18,780	635	20.3	55,500
University of Michigan	92.2	18,200	621	31.9	56,220
Mass. Institute of Tech. (Sloan)	92.0	19,500	650	20.7	60,000
Duke University (Fuqua)	90.8	18,500	631	30.1	54,000
Dartmouth College (Tuck), (N.H.)	90.0	18,750	651	19.5	57,500
University of Chicago	89.8	19,250	637	36.2	55,000
Columbia University	88.2	19,000	630	46.9	55,000
University of Virginia (Darden)	84.9	14,227	610	25.8	54,000
Cornell University (Johnson)	81.4	18,500	635	36.7	53,000
Carnegie Mellon University (Pa.)	80.7	18,500	638	33.8	54,000

(continued)

School	Overall Score	Tuition	GMAT	Acceptance Rate	Starting Salary
Univ. of California at Berkeley (Haas)	80.5	10,617	636	24.2	54,000
Univ. of California at L.A. (Anderson)	79.2	11,246	633	21.5	54,000
New York University (Stern)	78.0	17,200	616	35.1	55,000
Yale University	77.9	19,275	651	37.6	55,000
University of Texas at Austin	76.8	6,452	634	23.9	45,000
U.N.C., Chapel Hill (Kenan/Flagler)	76.5	8,680	620	17.0	54,100
Indiana University at Bloomington	76.4	12,000	605	38.4	47,000
University of Southern California	73.4	15,730	622	31.2	54,000
Georgetown University	72.4	17,460	608	43.8	50,000
Purdue University (Krannert), (Ind.)	72.0	8,192	608	28.9	45,500
University of Rochester (Simon), (N.Y.)	71.8	16,980	616	31.4	48,000
Vanderbilt University (Owen), (Tenn.)	71.6	17,500	607	48.9	43,100

Source: "The best graduate schools." *U.S. News & World Report*, Mar. 22, 1993, p. 58.

```
Stem-and-leaf of Score      N = 25
Leaf Unit = 1.0

    5      7  11223
   11      7  666789
   (4)     8  0014
   10      8  89
    8      9  00224
    3      9  59
    1     10  0
```

```
Stem-and-leaf of Tuition    N = 25
Leaf Unit = 100

    1      6  4
    1      7
    3      8  16
    3      9
    4     10  6
    5     11  2
    6     12  0
    6     13
    7     14  2
    8     15  7
    9     16  9
   12     17  245
   (8)    18  25555778
    5     19  02225
```

```
Stem-and-leaf of GMAT       N = 25
Leaf Unit = 1.0

    4     60  5788
    7     61  066
   10     62  012
   (9)    63  013455678
    6     64  04
    4     65  011
    1     66
    1     67
    1     68  0
```

```
Stem-and-leaf of AccRate    N = 25
Leaf Unit = 1.0

    1      1  2
    4      1  679
    9      2  00134
   12      2  558
   (5)     3  01113
    8      3  56678
    3      4  3
    2      4  68
```

```
Stem-and-leaf of Salary     N = 25
Leaf Unit = 1000

    1      4  3
    3      4  55
    4      4  7
    5      4  8
    6      5  0
    7      5  3
  (12)     5  444444455555
    6      5  67
    4      5
    4      6  00
    2      6
    2      6  55
```

2.18 Researchers at Miami University (Ohio) studied the incidence of humor in advertisements placed in American, British, and German trade magazines (*Industrial Marketing Management*, 1993). A total of 665 ads were evaluated. The accompanying table gives the breakdown of the number of ads evaluated by the various industries.

Industry	Number of Ads	Industry	Number of Ads
Accountancy	21	Hotels	13
Aeronautics	20	Insurance	29
Agriculture	31	Laundry	13
Baking	35	Marketing/advertising	37
Business	26	Medical	33
Chemistry	25	Mining	27
Computers	25	Music	19
Dairy	17	Packaging	31
Dental	29	Paper/pulp	25
Electronics	16	Plastics	31
Environment	17	Safety	26
Fishing	20	Security	20
Fur	7	Toys	15
Graphics	16	Travel	19
Grocery	22		

Source: McCullough, L. S., and Taylor, R. K. "Humor in American, British, and German ads." *Industrial Marketing Management*, Vol. 22, 1993, p. 21 (Table 1).

a. Construct a stem-and-leaf display for the data, using a single-digit stem.
b. Repeat part **a**, using a two-digit stem.
c. Which of the two figures constructed in parts **a** and **b** provides more information about the ad data? Explain.

2.19 Under a voluntary cooperative inspection program, all passenger cruise ships arriving at U.S. ports are subject to unannounced inspection. The purpose of these inspections is to achieve levels of sanitation that will minimize the potential for gastrointestinal disease outbreaks on these ships. Ships are rated on a scale of 0 to 100 points, depending on how well they meet the Centers for Disease Control sanitation standards. In general, the lower the score, the lower the level of sanitation. The table on page 48 lists the sanitation inspection scores for 91 international cruise ships during 1992.
a. A MINITAB stem-and-leaf display of the data is shown on page 48. Identify the stems and leaves of the graph.
b. A score of 86 or higher at the time of inspection indicates the ship is providing an accepted standard of sanitation. Use the MINITAB graph to estimate the proportion of ships that have an accepted sanitation standard.
c. Locate the inspection score of 70 (Pacific Star) on the stem-and-leaf display.

Ship	Score	Ship	Score	Ship	Score
Americana	89	Hanseatic Renaissance	82	Seabourn Pride	99
Amerikanis	97	Holiday	91	Seabourn Spirit	92
Azure Seas	83	Horizon	94	Seabreeze 1	96
Britanis	93	Island Princess	87	Seaward	89
Caribbean Prince	84	Jubilee	89	Sky Princess	97
Caribe 1	90	Mardi Gras	92	Society Explorer	66
Carla C	90	Meridian	95	Song of America	95
Carnivale	92	Nantucket Clipper	89	Song of Flower	99
Celebration	95	New Shoreham II	95	Song of Norway	92
Club Med 1	94	Nieuw Amsterdam	97	Southward	89
Costa Classica	91	Noordam	92	Sovereign of the Seas	93
Costa Marina	91	Nordic Empress	93	Star Princess	94
Costa Riviera	91	Nordic Prince	92	Starship Atlantic	87
Crown Monarch	94	Norway	84	Starship Majestic	94
Crown Odyssey	88	Pacific Princess	88	Starship Oceanic	97
Crown Princess	88	Pacific Star	70	Starward	96
Crystal Harmony	99	Queen Elizabeth 2	98	Stella Solaris	94
Cunard Countess	96	Regent Sea	87	Sun Viking	90
Cunard Princess	89	Regent Star	74	Sunward	95
Daphne	86	Regent Sun	95	Triton	86
Dawn Princess	86	Rotterdam	92	Tropicale	93
Discovery 1	93	Royal Princess	93	Universe	92
Dolphin IV	96	Royal Viking Sun	86	Victoria	96
Ecstasy	94	Sagafjord	89	Viking Princess	90
Emerald Seas	95	Scandinavian Dawn	87	Viking Serenade	96
Enchanted Isle	86	Scandinavian Song	90	Vistafjord	94
Enchanted Seas	96	Scandinavian Sun	89	Westerdam	91
Fair Princess	87	Sea Bird	86	Wind Spirit	96
Fantasy	97	Sea Goddess I	97	Yorktown Clipper	92
Festivale	94	Sea Lion	91		
Golden Odyssey	89	Sea Princess	88		

Source: Center of Environmental Health and Injury Control, Miami. Fla. (reported in *Tampa Tribune,* May 17, 1992).

```
Stem-and-leaf of SanLevel   N = 91
Leaf Unit = 1.0


     1     6 6
     1     6
     2     7 0
     2     7
     3     7 4
     3     7
     3     7
     3     8
     5     8 23
     7     8 44
    18     8 66666677777
    31     8 8888999999999
    42     9 00000111111
   (15)    9 222222222333333
    34     9 4444444445555555
    18     9 66666666777777
     4     9 8999
```

2.20 The Customer Satisfaction Index, compiled monthly by J. D. Powers & Associates, is designed to measure customer satisfaction with new automobiles in the areas of repair, reliability, and experience at the dealership. The index is based on questionnaires completed by drivers 1 year after they bought their cars. In 1992, an index of 129 was considered average, with ratings above 129 considered "above average" and ratings below 129 considered "below average" in terms of overall customer satisfaction. The table lists the 1992 Customer Satisfaction Index for the top 10 rated automobiles.

Auto (Manufacturer)	Foreign (F) or Domestic (D)	Customer Satisfaction Index
Lexus (Toyota)	F	179
Infiniti (Nissan)	F	167
Saturn (GM)	D	160
Acura (Honda)	F	148
Mercedes-Benz	F	145
Toyota	F	144
Audi (VW)	F	139
Cadillac (GM)	D	138
Honda	F	138
Jaguar (Ford)	D	137

Source: J. D. Powers & Associates, 1992. Customer Satisfaction StudySM.

a. Construct a stem-and-leaf display of the Customer Satisfaction Index for the 10 top-rated automakers.

b. Circle the Customer Satisfaction Index values for all foreign automakers on the graph, part **a.** Do customers tend to be more satisfied with foreign automakers?

2.21 How strong an effect do characteristics such as brand name or store name have on a buyer's perception of the quality of a product? Numerous studies have been conducted to investigate this phenomenon, but the results seem to vary depending on the method used to analyze the data, type of product, price, etc. An article in the *Journal of Marketing Research* (Aug. 1989) summarized the results of 15 studies that investigated the effect of brand name on product quality and 17 studies that examined the effect of store name on quality. In all studies (the experimental units), an effect size index was computed. The index ranges from 0 to 1.00; values closer to 0 indicate small effects and values near 1 indicate the presence of large effects. Stem-and-leaf displays of effect size index for the two groups of studies are illustrated on page 50. Compare and contrast the two figures. Which variable, brand name or store name, seems to have the stronger effect on perceived quality? Explain.

Brand Name (15 studies)			Store Name (17 studies)	
Stem	**Leaf**		**Stem**	**Leaf**
.6	0		.6	
.5	7		.5	
.4			.4	3 4
.3	4		.3	
.2	5 5		.2	
.1	0 1 1 2 4		.1	2
.0	3 3 5 5 7		.0	0 0 0 1 1 2 2 3 3 6 7 8 8

Source: Rao, A. R., and Monroe, K. B. "The effect of price, brand name, and store name on buyers' perceptions of product quality: An integrative review." *Journal of Marketing Research,* Vol. 26, Aug. 1989, p. 354 (Table 2).

2.4 Graphical Descriptions of Quantitative Data: Histograms

Frequency (or **relative frequency**) **histograms** are similar to the bar graphs of Section 2.2 except that the classes represent intervals of values of the quantitative data. In contrast to stem-and-leaf displays, histograms are more suited for describing larger data sets and measurements with more than a few digits.

EXAMPLE 2.7
Constructing a Histogram

Table 2.3 gives the sales prices for 50 properties selected from the 707 sale prices of Appendix A.1. Construct a relative frequency histogram for the data.

Table 2.3 Sale Prices for a Sample of Properties Selected from Appendix A.1

		Sale Prices		
99,000	45,000	61,500	78,400	48,500
123,000	60,000	155,000	77,000	56,400
65,700	50,000	140,000	49,600	59,500
115,000	45,500	112,000	58,500	25,000
63,000	70,000	62,000	46,000	110,000
76,000	77,100	61,900	36,500	25,000
58,000	45,500	55,000	38,000	89,500
87,000	63,500	31,700	44,900	90,000
68,000	51,600	75,300	40,000	32,000
50,500	79,000	47,000	48,000	103,000

SOLUTION

STEP 1   The first step in constructing the relative frequency histogram for this sample is to define the **class intervals** (categories) into which the data will fall. To do this, we need to know the smallest and largest sale prices in the data set. These prices are $25,000 and $155,000, respectively. Since we want the smallest price to fall in the lowest class interval and the largest price to fall in the highest class interval, the class intervals must span sale prices ranging from $25,000 to $155,000.

STEP 2   The second step is to choose the **class interval width;** this will depend on how many intervals we want to use to span the sale price range and whether we want to use equal or unequal interval widths. For this example, we will use equal class interval widths (the most popular choice) and 11 class intervals. (See the note in the box on page 54 about choosing the number of class intervals.)

Note that the price range is equal to

Range = Largest measurement − Smallest measurement

$$= \$155,000 - \$25,000 = \$130,000$$

Since we chose to use 11 class intervals, the class interval width should approximately equal

$$\text{Class interval width} \approx \frac{\text{Range}}{\text{Number of class intervals}}$$

$$\approx \frac{130,000}{11} = 11,818.2$$

$$\approx \$12,000$$

We shall start the first class slightly below the smallest observation ($25,000) and choose the starting point so that no observation can fall on a class boundary. Since sale prices are recorded to the nearest hundred dollars, we can do this by choosing the lower class boundary of the first class interval to be $24,050. [*Note:* We could just as easily have chosen $24,025, $24,075, $24,090, or any one of many other points below and near $25,000.] Then the class intervals will be $24,050 to $36,050, $36,050 to $48,050, and so on. The class intervals are shown in the second column of Table 2.4 (page 52).

STEP 3   The third step in constructing a histogram is to obtain each class frequency, i.e., the number of observations falling within each class. This is done by examining each sale price in Table 2.3 and recording by tally (as shown in the third column of Table 2.4) the class in which it falls. The tally for each class gives the class frequencies shown in column 4 of Table 2.4. Finally, we calculate the class relative frequency as

$$\text{Class relative frequency} = \frac{\text{Class frequency}}{\text{Total number of observations}}$$

$$= \frac{\text{Class frequency}}{50}$$

These values are shown in the fifth column of Table 2.4 at the top of page 52.

Table 2.4   Tabulation of Data for the Sale Prices of Table 2.3

Class	Class Interval	Tally	Class Frequency	Class Relative Frequency
1	24,050–36,050	////	4	.08
2	36,050–48,050	̶H̶H̶ ̶H̶H̶	10	.20
3	48,050–60,050	̶H̶H̶ ̶H̶H̶ /	11	.22
4	60,050–72,050	̶H̶H̶ ///	8	.16
5	72,050–84,050	̶H̶H̶ /	6	.12
6	84,050–96,050	///	3	.06
7	96,050–108,050	//	2	.04
8	108,050–120,050	///	3	.06
9	120,050–132,050	/	1	.02
10	132,050–144,050	/	1	.02
11	144,050–156,050	/	1	.02
		TOTALS	50	1.00

STEP 4   The final step is to draw the graph. Mark off the class intervals along a horizontal line, as shown in Figure 2.10. Then construct over each class interval a bar with the

FIGURE 2.10

Class Intervals for the
Data of Table 2.4

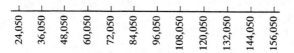

FIGURE 2.11

Relative Frequency
Histogram for the
Data of Table 2.4

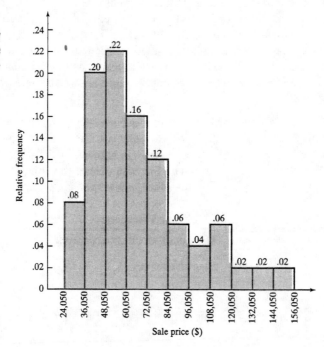

height proportional to the class frequency (**frequency histogram**) or the class relative frequency (**relative frequency histogram**). Since we desire a relative frequency histogram, the bar heights will be proportional to the class relative frequencies. The resulting histogram is shown in Figure 2.11. ■

EXAMPLE 2.8
Interpreting a Histogram

Interpret the histogram for the 50 sale prices, Figure 2.11.

SOLUTION Remember that a histogram, like a bar graph or stem-and-leaf display, conveys a visual picture of the data. In particular, a histogram will identify a range of values where most of the data fall. You can see that most of the 50 residential properties in the sample had sale prices between $36,050 and $84,050. The four classes (bars) associated with this interval have relative frequencies of .20, .22, .16, and .12, respectively. The sum of these relative frequencies is .70. Thus, 70% of the residential properties in the sample had sale prices between $36,050 and $84,050.

Note also that none of the sale prices was less than $24,050, but several large sales caused the distribution to be spread unusually far to the right. We say that such a distribution is **rightward skewed** (or **positively skewed**). Similarly a **leftward** (or **negatively**) **skewed** distribution has a histogram that tails out to the left because of several unusually small values. Illustrations of rightward and leftward skewed distributions, as well as a **nonskewed** (or **symmetric**) distribution, are shown in Figure 2.12.

FIGURE 2.12
Skewed and
Nonskewed
Distributions

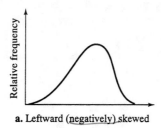 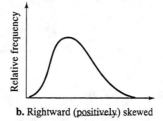 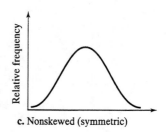

a. Leftward (negatively) skewed   **b.** Rightward (positively) skewed   **c.** Nonskewed (symmetric) ■

In Examples 2.7 and 2.8, suppose we had spanned the range with three classes instead of 11. Then almost all the sale prices would have fallen in a single class and the resulting histogram would not have been nearly as informative as Figure 2.11. Or, suppose that we had chosen to span the interval from $25,000 to $155,000 with 50 classes. Then many classes would have contained only a few sale prices and others would have been empty. Again, such a figure would not have been as informative as Figure 2.11. You can see that the choice of number of classes is crucial when constructing a histogram.

A good rule of thumb in deciding on the number of class intervals is to use a small number when you want to describe a small amount of data—say, five or six classes for up to 25 observations. You can increase the number of classes (as we did) for 50 observations, and you may want to use 15 or 20 classes for large amounts of data. Remember that the objective is to obtain a graph that rapidly conveys a visual picture of the data. If your first choice of class interval width is not satisfactory, we recommend that you choose a different interval width and try again.

The steps employed in constructing a relative frequency distribution are summarized in the accompanying box.

Constructing a Histogram

1. Examine the data to determine the smallest and the largest measurements.
2. Divide the interval between the smallest and the largest measurements into between 5 and 20 equal subintervals called **classes** (see next box). These classes should satisfy the following requirement:

   Each measurement falls into one and only one subinterval.

   Note that this requirement implies that no measurement falls on a boundary of a subinterval.
3. Compute the frequency or relative frequency of measurements falling within each subinterval.
4. Using a vertical axis of about three-fourths the length of the horizontal axis, plot each frequency or relative frequency as a rectangle over the corresponding subinterval.

Rule of Thumb for Determining the Number of Classes in a Histogram

Number of Observations in a Data Set	Number of Classes
Less than 25	5 or 6
25–50	7–14
More than 50	15–20

The important concept to use in visually interpreting a histogram is as follows:

Interpreting a Histogram

The percentage of the total number of measurements falling within a particular interval is proportional to the area of the bar that is constructed above the interval. For example, if 30% of the area under the distribution lies over a particular interval, then 30% of the observations fell in that interval.

EXAMPLE 2.9

Interpreting a Histogram

Figure 2.13 is a computer-generated (SAS) relative frequency histogram that describes all 707 sale prices (recorded in $ thousands) of Appendix A.1.[*]

a. Interpret the graph.

b. Visually estimate the proportion of sale prices between $70,000 and $110,000.

FIGURE 2.13

SAS Relative Frequency Distribution for the 707 Residential Sale Prices of Appendix A.1

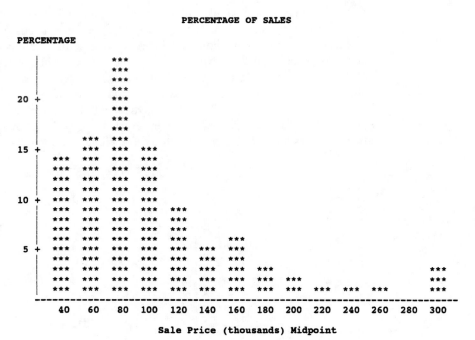

SOLUTION

a. Note that the classes are marked in intervals of $20,000 along the horizontal axis of the SAS histogram, Figure 2.13, with the midpoint

---

[*]*Note that the computer-generated relative frequency distribution leaves "gaps" between the bars. However, the resulting figure should not be confused with a bar graph for qualitative data. When drawn by hand, the bars of a relative frequency distribution are adjacent, with no gaps. (See Figure 2.11.)*

(rather than the class boundaries) of each interval shown.* You can see that the sale prices tend to pile up near $80,000—the class from $70,000 to $90,000 has the greatest relative frequency (or percentage). Since this histogram "tails" out to the right, the data are rightward skewed.

b. The interval $70,000 to $110,000 spans two sale price classes: 70,000—90,000 and 90,000—110,000. The proportion of sale prices between $70,000 and $110,000 is equal to the sum of the relative frequencies associated with these two classes. These two class relative frequencies are (approximately) .24 and .15, respectively. Therefore, the approximate proportion of sale prices between $70,000 and $110,000 is

$$.24 + .15 = .39 = 39\% \quad ■$$

The preceding examples illustrate histograms with equal class interval widths. Histograms with unequal class widths can also be constructed. For example, the relative frequency histogram shown in Figure 2.14 describes the quantitative variable, age at which people start their own business. The data were obtained from a recent survey of National Federation of Independent Businesses (NFIB) members. Note that the eight middle class intervals all have the same width (5 years), but the first and last class intervals do not. The first class includes all NFIB members 20 years or younger, and the last class includes all members over age 60. By allowing the classes at the two extremes to have different widths, we obtain a more informative graphical display of the data.

FIGURE 2.14

Relative Frequency Histogram for Age at Which People Start Businesses

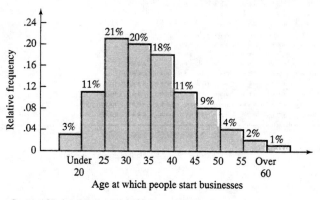

Source: National Federation of Independent Businesses.

The last class interval (identified by midpoint at $300,000) actually includes all sale prices that exceed the lower class boundary, $290,000.

EXERCISES

■ *Learning the Mechanics*

2.22   A sample of 20 measurements is shown here:

26	34	21	32	32	36	28	38	17	39
22	12	26	39	25	31	30	23	27	19

   a. Using a class interval width of 5, give the upper and lower boundaries for six class intervals, where the lower boundary of the first class is 10.5.
   b. Determine the relative frequency for each of the six classes specified in part **a.**
   c. Construct a relative frequency histogram using the results of part **b.**

2.23   Consider the sample data shown here:

5.9	5.3	1.6	7.4	8.6	1.2	2.1
4.0	7.3	8.4	8.9	6.7	4.5	6.3
7.6	9.7	3.5	1.1	4.3	3.3	8.4
1.6	8.2	6.5	1.1	5.0	9.4	6.4

   a. Find the difference between the largest and the smallest measurements.
   b. Divide the difference obtained in part **a** by 5 to determine the approximate class interval width for five class intervals.
   c. Specify upper and lower boundaries for each of the five class intervals.
   d. Construct a frequency histogram for the data.

■ *Applying the Concepts*

2.24   Century 21 Real Estate compiled data on more than 600,000 sales of single-family homes in the United States in 1990. Based on the average price, the realty company found that Hawaii had the most expensive homes (average price of $281,042) and North Dakota had the least expensive (average price of $51,334). The average prices of single-family homes for all 50 states are listed in the table on page 58.
   a. Construct a histogram for the data.
   b. Are the data on average prices skewed right, skewed left, or symmetric?

State	1990 Average Price	State	1990 Average Price	State	1990 Average Price
Ala.	$ 64,734	La.	$ 56,991	Ohio	$ 68,569
Alaska	86,215	Maine	90,972	Okla.	49,828
Ariz.	82,514	Md.	114,074	Ore.	69,133
Ark.	53,750	Mass.	168,840	Pa.	88,510
Calif.	166,423	Mich.	71,246	R.I.	127,628
Colo.	70,879	Minn.	67,357	S.C.	72,614
Conn.	152,157	Miss.	59,413	S.D.	54,346
Del.	95,504	Mo.	60,992	Tenn.	63,953
Fla.	77,785	Mont.	60,607	Texas	65,638
Ga.	78,655	Neb.	61,157	Utah	60,122
Hawaii	281,042	Nev.	101,784	Vt.	96,538
Idaho	59,328	N.H.	115,288	Va.	98,708
Ill.	94,707	N.J.	141,701	Wash.	86,667
Ind.	73,593	N.M.	73,449	W. Va.	58,667
Iowa	51,478	N.Y.	124,245	Wis.	64,666
Kan.	58,075	N.C.	77,077	Wyo.	62,728
Ky.	64,205	N.D.	51,334		

Source: *USA Today,* Mar. 22, 1991. Copyright 1991, USA Today. Reprinted with permission.

2.25 "Deep hole" drilling is a family of drilling processes used when the ratio of hole depth to hole diameter exceeds 10. Successful deep hole drilling depends on the satisfactory discharge of the drill chip. An experiment was conducted to investigate the performance of deep hole drilling when chip congestion exists (*Journal of Engineering for Industry,* May 1993). An analysis of drill chip congestion was performed using data generated via computer simulation. The simulated distribution of the length (in millimeters) of 50 drill chips is displayed here in a frequency histogram.

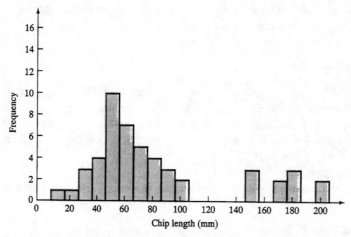

Source: Chin, Jih-Hua, et al. "The computer simulation and experimental analysis of chip monitoring for deep hole drilling." *Journal of Engineering for Industry, Transactions of the ASME,* Vol. 115, May 1993, p. 187 (Figure 12).

    a. Convert the frequency histogram into a relative frequency histogram.

    b. Based on the graph, part **a**, would you expect to observe a drill chip with a length of at least 190 mm? Explain.

2.26 Beginning in 1991, the nation's Department of Education began taking corrective and punitive actions against colleges and universities with high student-loan default rates. Those schools with default rates above 60% face suspension from the government's massive student-loan program, whereas schools with default rates between 40% and 60% are mandated to reduce their default rates by 5% a year or face a similar penalty (*Tampa Tribune*, June 21, 1989). A list of 66 colleges and universities in Florida with their student-loan default rate is provided in the table.

College/University	Default Rate	College/University	Default Rate
Florida College of Business	76.2	Brevard CC	9.4
Ft. Lauderdale College	48.5	College of Boca Raton	9.1
Florida Career College	48.3	Florida International Univ.	8.7
United College	46.8	Santa Fe CC	8.6
Florida Memorial College	46.2	Edison CC	8.5
Bethune Cookman College	43.0	Palm Beach Junior College	8.0
Edward Waters College	38.3	Eckerd College	7.9
Florida College of Medical and Dental Careers	32.6	University of Tampa	7.6
International Fine Arts College	26.5	Lakeland College of Business	7.2
Tampa College	23.9	Pensacola Junior College	6.8
Miami Technical College	23.3	University of Miami	6.7
Tallahassee CC	20.6	Florida Institute of Tech.	6.7
Charron Williams College	20.2	University of West Florida	6.3
Florida CC	19.1	Palm Beach Atlantic College	6.0
Miami-Dade CC	19.0	University of Central Florida	5.7
Broward CC	18.4	Seminole CC	5.6
Daytona Beach CC	16.9	Polk CC	5.6
Lake Sumter CC	16.7	Phillips Junior College	5.6
Florida Technical College	16.6	Nova University	5.5
Florida A&M University	15.8	Rollins College	5.5
Prospect Hall College	15.1	St. Leo College	5.5
Hillsborough CC	14.4	Gulf Coast CC	5.4
Pasco-Hernando CC	13.5	Southern College	5.3
Orlando College	13.5	Flagler College	4.7
Jones College	13.1	Florida Atlantic University	4.4
Webber College	11.8	University of South Florida	4.2
Warner Southern College	11.8	Manatee Junior College	4.1
Central Florida CC	11.8	Florida State University	4.0
Indian River CC	11.8	University of North Florida	3.9
St. Petersburg CC	11.3	Barry University	3.1
Valencia CC	10.8	University of Florida	3.1
Florida Southern College	10.3	Stetson University	2.9
Lake City CC	9.8	Jacksonville University	1.5

a. Construct a relative frequency histogram for the data using 12 classes to span the range.

b. Repeat part **a**, but use only three classes to span the range. Compare this with the relative frequency distribution you constructed in part **a**. Which is more informative? Why does an inadequate number of classes limit the information conveyed by the relative frequency distribution?

c. Repeat part **a**, but use 25 classes. Comment on the information provided by this graph as compared with that of part **a**.

d. Refer to the histogram, part **a**. Estimate the proportion of Florida colleges and universities with a default rate of 40% or higher. Shade the bars in the histogram corresponding to this area.

e. Note that Florida College of Business has a default rate nearly 30% higher than the next highest rate. Omit the value for Florida College of Business from the data set, and reconstruct the histogram.

f. Compare the histograms constructed in parts **a** and **e**. Which graph is more informative? Explain.

2.27 Refer to the *Sloan Management Review* (Winter 1991) study of customer waiting time at a Boston bank, Exercise 2.6.

a. Consider the data set consisting of the differences between the perceived and actual waiting times of the 277 customers. Are the data qualitative or quantitative?

b. A graph describing the data of part **b** is shown here. What type of graph is displayed? Interpret the graph. In particular, obtain the approximate percentage of customers who overestimated their waiting time in line at the Bank of Boston.

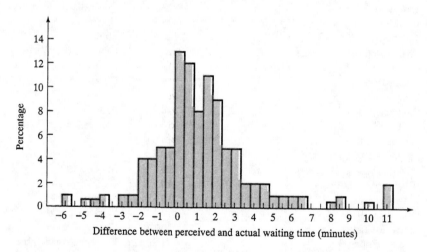

Difference between perceived and actual waiting time (minutes)

Source: Katz, K. L., Larson, B. M., and Larson, R. C. "Prescription for the waiting-in-line blues: Entertain, enlighten, and engage." *Sloan Management Review,* Winter 1991, p. 48 (Fig. 3).

2.28 According to the 1990 U.S. Census, nearly half of the counties in the country exhibited a declining population trend between 1980 and 1990. In particular, the population of several major metropolitan counties also declined. For example, Wayne County (Detroit), Michigan, lost nearly 10% of its residents between 1980 and 1990. Many demographers feel this reflects "urban flight," a reversal of the 1970s trend of people migrating from rural to metropolitan counties (*USA Today*, Mar. 19, 1991). The accompanying table lists the 49 largest counties in the United States (based on 1990 population) and their percentage change in population from 1980 to 1990. A MINITAB frequency histogram (with interval midpoints marked on the vertical axis) for the data is shown here. Interpret the graph.

County (Nearest Big City)	Percentage Change	County (Nearest Big City)	Percentage Change
Los Angeles (Los Angeles)	18.5	Tarrant (Fort Worth, Tex.)	35.9
Cook (Chicago)	−2.8	Oakland (Pontiac, Mich.)	7.1
Harris (Houston)	17.0	Sacramento (Sacramento)	32.9
Orange (Los Angeles)	24.7	Hennepin (Minneapolis)	9.7
Kings (New York City)	3.1	St. Louis (St. Louis)	2.0
Maricopa (Phoenix)	40.6	Erie (Buffalo)	−4.6
Wayne (Detroit)	−9.7	Franklin (Columbus, Ohio)	10.6
Queens (New York City)	3.2	Milwaukee (Milwaukee)	−.6
Dade (Miami)	19.2	Westchester (White Plains, N.Y.)	1.0
Dallas (Dallas)	19.0	Hamilton (Cincinnati)	−.8
Philadelphia (Philadelphia)	−6.1	Palm Beach (Palm Beach, Fla.)	49.7
King (Seattle)	18.7	Hartford (Hartford, Conn.)	5.4
Santa Clara (San Jose, Calif.)	15.6	Pinellas (St. Petersburg, Fla.)	16.9
New York (New York City)	4.1	Honolulu (Honolulu)	9.7
San Bernardino (Los Angeles)	58.5	Hillsborough (Tampa)	28.9
Cuyahoga (Cleveland)	−5.8	Fairfield (Bridgeport, Conn.)	2.5
Middlesex (Boston)	2.3	Shelby (Memphis)	6.3
Allegheny (Pittsburgh)	−7.8	Bergen (Hackensack, N.J.)	−2.4
Suffolk (New York City)	2.9	Fairfax (Va./Washington)	37.4
Nassau (New York City)	−2.6	New Haven (New Haven, Conn.)	5.6
Alameda (Oakland)	15.7	Contra Costa (San Francisco)	22.5
Broward (Ft. Lauderdale, Fla.)	23.3	Marion (Indianapolis)	4.25
Bronx (New York City)	3.0	DuPage (Chicago)	18.6
Bexar (San Antonio)	19.9	Essex (Newark, N.J.)	−8.6
Riverside (Los Angeles)	76.5		

Source: U.S. Census Bureau, 1990 Census.

```
Histogram of PctChnge    N = 49

Midpoint    Count
     -10        5    *****
       0       16    ****************
      10        7    *******
      20       13    *************
      30        2    **
      40        3    ***
      50        1    *
      60        1    *
      70        0
      80        1    *
```

2.29 Electrical engineers recognize that high neutral current in computer power systems is a potential problem. To determine the extent of the problem, a survey of the computer power system load currents at 146 U.S. sites was taken (*IEEE Transactions on Industry Applications*, July/ Aug. 1990). A relative frequency histogram for the load capacities (measured as a percentage) of the 146 sites in the sample is shown here.

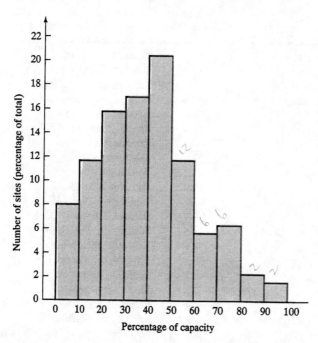

Source: Gruzs, T. M. "A survey of neutral currents in three-phase computer power systems." *IEEE Transactions on Industry Applications*, Vol. 26, No. 4, July/Aug. 1990, p. 722 (Figure 6).

a. Approximately what proportion of the 146 computer sites had a load capacity between 20% and 30%?

b. Approximately what proportion of the 146 computer sites had a load capacity of 50% or more?

2.30 Are major colleges and universities lax in hiring minorities to fill top positions in their athletic programs? A *USA Today* survey of 62 Division I schools found that only 12.5% of the jobs in the athletic department are held by minorities (blacks, Hispanics, native Americans, and Asians). In contrast, the 1990 Census shows minorities represent 19.7% of the U.S. population (*USA Today*, Mar. 19, 1991). The results of the survey are reproduced in the table. The 62 schools were selected based on the Top 25 polls for men's and women's basketball during the 1989–1990 season and the final 1990 Top 25 football poll. (Northwestern declined to respond, and Seton Hall did not supply figures.)

School	Total Positions	Positions Held by Minority	Percentage Minority
Georgetown	30	8	26.7
Houston	43	11	25.6
Miami	55	14	25.5
Arizona	67	15	22.4
Long Beach State	53	11	20.8
USC	65	13	20.0
Pittsburgh	54	10	18.5
Oklahoma State	34	6	17.6
Oklahoma	63	11	17.5
Washington	63	11	17.5
Southern Mississippi	35	6	17.1
Stanford	71	12	16.9
Iowa	72	12	16.7
Georgia Tech	52	8	15.4
Michigan State	60	9	15.0
Illinois	54	8	14.8
Kentucky	54	8	14.8
Ohio State	64	9	14.1
Colorado	43	6	14.0
LSU	59	8	13.6
Purdue	53	7	13.2
New Mexico State	38	5	13.2
UCLA	84	11	13.1
Clemson	48	6	12.5
North Carolina	57	7	12.3
Kansas	49	6	12.2
Utah	33	4	12.1
Louisville	34	4	11.8
Georgia	60	7	11.7
Florida	61	7	11.5
Louisiana Tech	26	3	11.5
Syracuse	52	6	11.5
Arkansas	44	5	11.4
Northern Illinois	53	6	11.3
Alabama	54	6	11.1
Western Kentucky	18	2	11.1
UNLV	55	6	10.9
Connecticut	37	4	10.8
South Carolina	49	5	10.2

(continued)

(continued)

School	Total Positions	Positions Held by Minority	Percentage Minority
East Tennessee State	30	3	10.0
Texas-El Paso	30	3	10.0
Rutgers	42	4	9.5
North Carolina State	44	4	9.1
Texas[a]	67	6	9.0
Michigan	58	5	8.6
Penn State	82	7	8.5
St. John's	60	5	8.3
Nebraska	64	5	7.8
Mississippi State	52	4	7.7
Providence	13	1	7.7
Mississippi	40	3	7.5
Florida State	53	4	7.5
Indiana	57	4	7.0
Tennessee[a]	73	5	6.8
Duke	45	3	6.7
Virginia	60	4	6.7
BYU	51	3	5.9
Princeton	44	2	4.5
Notre Dame	47	2	4.3
Stephen F. Austin	27	1	3.7

[a] Numbers combined from separate men's/women's athletic programs.
Source: USA Today, Mar. 19, 1991.

a. Do the data represent a sample or a population? Explain.
b. Describe the data on percentage of minority positions in the athletic department of the 60 colleges and universities with a graphical technique. Interpret the graph.

SUMMARY

In this chapter, we presented methods for describing data sets of *qualitative* or *quantitative* variables. We first define data categories and then record the number of observations falling in each category. *Bar graphs* or *pie charts* can then be constructed for qualitative data, and *stem-and-leaf displays* or *histograms* can be constructed for quantitative data.

If the data are quantitative and the number of observations is small, the categorization and the determination of class frequencies can be done automatically by constructing a stem-and-leaf display. Once the stem of a number is defined, the data classes are determined. The number of leaves associated with each stem in the stem-and-leaf display can easily be counted to determine the class frequency. The stem-and-leaf display provides a graphical picture of the data set, showing how the observations are spread from the smallest to the largest. It also enables us to reconstruct the exact values of the observations. This feature of the stem-and-leaf display will be useful in determining the values of certain numerical descriptive measures of the data set to be discussed in Chapter 3.

Large sets of data are best described using *frequency* or *relative frequency histograms*. Usually, class intervals of equal width are defined. Bars are then constructed over each interval with the bar height proportional to the interval relative frequency. Since the bars are of equal width, the area of a particular bar, as a proportion of the total area of all bars, is equal to the class relative frequency of that bar. This property enables us to examine a relative frequency histogram and visually estimate the proportion of the total number of observations in the data set that fall in specific intervals. Thus, the histogram provides a good graphical description of the location and distribution of the observations in a data set.

Note the differences and similarities between the bar graph used to describe qualitative data and the histogram used to describe quantitative data. Whereas the classes in a bar graph are unrelated, the classes that categorize quantitative data are connected intervals on a real line—the upper class boundary of one interval is the lower class boundary of the next. The interpretations of bar graphs and histograms are similar: The height of a bar is proportional to a class frequency (or relative frequency). Thus, both convey at a glance a graphical picture of the proportions of observations falling in the data classes.

KEY TERMS

Bar graph	Class interval	Relative frequency histogram
Class	Class relative frequency	Rightward skewed
Class boundaries (lower and upper)	Frequency histogram	Skewed distribution
Class frequency	Leftward skewed	Stem-and-leaf display
	Pie chart	Symmetric distribution

SUPPLEMENTARY EXERCISES

2.31 Casual restaurants—eateries featuring basic entrees, relaxed decors, and moderate prices—will be the major trend for restaurants in the 1990s, according to a Gallup survey for the National Restaurant Association (*Tampa Tribune*, Mar. 10, 1990). Gallup surveyed 1,000 adults about their attitudes toward casual and fine dining. One question asked how often the respondents eat out. The results are provided in the accompanying table. Use the appropriate graphical technique to describe the data.

Frequency of Eating Out	Type of Restaurant	
	Casual	Fine
Once a week	29%	4%
2–3 times a month	24	9
Once a month	17	12
Once every few months	12	16
Once every 6 months	6	13
Once a year	4	15
Less than once a year	8	31
Totals	100%	100%

Source: 1990 National Restaurant Association Gallup Survey.

2.32 A Purdue University study was conducted to examine the reasons why individual investors select certain investment portfolios (*Quarterly Review of Economics & Business,* Autumn 1989). A list of 3,000 accounts was obtained, at random, from the computerized customer records of a large, nationwide financial brokerage house. Each individual investor on the list was mailed a lengthy questionnaire. A total of 972 completed questionnaires were returned with information on the (1) gender, (2) marital status, (3) age, (4) annual income, (5) education, and (6) occupation of the individual investors. The data were tabulated to form an "investor profile." The number of investors in each category of the six variables is shown in the accompanying table.

(1) Gender		*(2) Marital Status*		*(3) Age*	
Male	782	Married	784	21–25	1
Female	190	Unmarried	188	26–34	29
				35–44	117
				45–54	274
				55–64	252
				65 & over	299

(4) Annual Income		*(5) Education*	
Under $5,000	1	High school diploma	225
5,000–9,999	80	Bachelor's degree	526
10,000–14,999	148	Master's degree	90
15,000–19,999	129	Law degree	63
20,000–24,999	173	Ph.D.	28
25,000–49,999	251	Medical degree	40
50,000–99,999	132		
100,000–149,999	27		
150,000 & over	15		

(6) Occupation

Professional & technical	265	Farm owner	15
Managerial	157	Service worker	5
Proprietor	124	Clerical	23
Sales	53	Craftsman	18
Housewife	69	Retired	217
Operative & laborer	8	Unemployed	18

Source: Krehbiel, T. L., and McCarthy, P. "An analysis of the determinants of portfolio selection."
Quarterly Review of Economics & Business, Vol. 29, No. 3, 1989, p. 46.

a. Identify the type (quantitative or qualitative) of each variable measured.
b. Identify the population of interest to the researchers.
c. Identify the sample of interest to the researchers.
d. Describe each variable with the appropriate graphical technique.

2.33 Researchers have been creating thin films of tiny diamonds since the early 1950s, but industry has only recently utilized diamond thin films in the manufacture of such products as cutting tools, stereo loudspeaker tweeters, heat sinks, sunglasses, and components for scientific instruments. According to the Philadelphia Institute for Scientific Information (ISI), the United States and Japan are preeminent in current research on diamond thin films (*The Scientist*, June 11, 1990). Each of 251 published papers was categorized according to the author's country of residence. The results are shown in the accompanying table. Use an appropriate graphical technique to summarize the data. Do you agree with ISI's assessment of the United States and Japan with regard to diamond thin-film research?

Country	Number of Papers on Diamond Thin-Film Research
U.S.	105
Japan	63
United Kingdom	20
Germany	17
Italy	7
Others	39
Total	251

Source: Grissom, A. "U.S. and Japan sparkle in diamond thin film research." *The Scientist*, June 11, 1990, p. 17 (Table 1).

2.34 The Global Auto Scoreboard, compiled by *Business Week*, is a comprehensive analysis of the world's 25 largest automobile manufacturers (based on world market share). The total number of units (autos and trucks) produced by each manufacturer in 1989 is provided in the table at the top of page 68.

Rank	Manufacturer	Country	Worldwide Production thousands of units
1	General Motors	U.S.A.	7,946
2	Ford	U.S.A.	6,336
3	Toyota	Japan	4,115
4	Volkswagen	Germany	2,948
5	Nissan	Japan	2,930
6	Chrysler	U.S.A.	2,382
7	Fiat	Italy	2,436
8	Peugeot	France	2,216
9	Renault	France	2,053
10	Honda	Japan	1,960
11	Mazda	Japan	1,460
12	Mitsubishi Motors	Japan	1,335
13	Hyundai	South Korea	819
14	Suzuki	Japan	875
15	Daimler	Germany	803
16	Daihatsu	Japan	600
17	Fuji Heavy	Japan	530
18	BMW	Germany	523
19	Rover	Britain	535
20	Volvo	Sweden	465
21	Isuzu	Japan	590
22	KIA Motors	South Korea	412
23	Daewoo Motors	South Korea	200[a]
24	Lada	Soviet Union	140[a]
25	Saab-Scania	Sweden	138

[a] Estimated

Source: Business Week, May 7, 1990, pp. 54–55.

a. Construct a relative frequency bar graph to describe the worldwide production of the 25 largest auto manufacturers. Interpret the graph.

b. Nine countries are represented by the 25 largest auto manufacturers. Construct a relative frequency bar graph to describe the worldwide production of the nine countries. Interpret the graph.

c. Construct a relative frequency bar graph to describe the worldwide production of the nine Japanese firms represented in the table. Interpret the graph.

2.35 Over the past decade, federal and state governments have proposed and implemented several new programs designed to improve automobile and highway safety standards. These include stricter drunken driving laws and mandatory-use seat belt laws in many states and federal guidelines related to airbags in new automobiles. Three Northeastern University professors conducted a survey of U.S. residents "in an attempt to gauge their opinions concerning existing and proposed automobile safety standards" (*Transportation Journal*, Summer 1986). It was hoped that the results of the survey would aid federal and state government officials in the planning and design of automobile safety programs. The survey elicited usable responses from a sample of 380 residents. The responses to two of the questions in the survey are summarized in the accompanying tables. Use a graphical method to describe the two data sets and interpret the results.

Question: How Often Do You Use Your Safety Seat Belts?

Response	*Percentage*
Always	40%
Frequently	23%
Infrequently	20%
Never	17%

Question: Would You Purchase an Optional Automobile Safety Air Bag at a Price of $500 or $1,000?

	Percentage	
Response	*$500*	*$1,000*
Definitely would	16%	5%
Probably would	17%	12%
Not sure	18%	17%
Probably would not	21%	22%
Definitely would not	28%	44%

Source: Lieb, R. C., Wiseman, F., and Moore, T. E. "Automobile safety programs: The public viewpoint." *Transportation Journal*, Vol. 25, No. 4, Summer 1986, pp. 22–30.

2.36 Low employment rates are often associated with a healthy economy. The 1989 unemployment rates for Florida's 67 counties are listed in the table.

County	Unemployment Rate, %	County	Unemployment Rate, %	County	Unemployment Rate, %
Alachua	3.1	DeSoto	5.2	Hernando	6.4
Baker	6.4	Dixie	6.5	Highlands	6.7
Bay	9.6	Duval	5.8	Hillsborough	4.9
Bradford	3.5	Escambia	6.3	Holmes	6.8
Brevard	5.2	Flagler	5.0	Indian River	6.4
Broward	5.1	Franklin	6.3	Jackson	6.1
Calhoun	8.8	Gadsden	5.8	Jefferson	5.1
Charlotte	4.7	Gilchrist	5.7	Lafayette	6.4
Citrus	6.3	Glades	7.8	Lake	6.2
Clay	5.1	Gulf	8.3	Lee	3.9
Collier	4.6	Hamilton	8.0	Leon	4.0
Columbia	8.2	Hardee	8.6	Levy	5.8
Dade	6.4	Hendry	12.2	Liberty	3.9

(continued)

County	Unemployment Rate, %	County	Unemployment Rate, %	County	Unemployment Rate, %
Madison	7.1	Palm Beach	6.0	St. Lucie	10.0
Manatee	4.6	Pasco	6.4	Sumter	7.0
Marion	6.1	Pinellas	4.6	Suwannee	7.4
Martin	6.4	Polk	8.5	Taylor	9.1
Monroe	3.0	Putnam	7.5	Union	4.1
Nassau	5.7	Santa Rosa	7.1	Volusia	5.4
Okaloosa	6.2	Sarasota	3.7	Wakulla	5.3
Okeechobee	8.9	Seminole	5.1	Walton	6.8
Orange	5.0	St. Johns	5.7	Washington	8.1
Osceola	5.2				

Source: *Florida Statistical Abstract*, 1990 (Table 6.10).

a. Construct a stem-and-leaf display for the data.

b. Construct a relative frequency distribution using the class intervals 0–1.01, 1.01–2.02, 2.02–3.03, etc.

c. Compare the figures constructed in parts **a** and **b**. On which graph is it easier to locate the unemployment rate of 6.2% for Lake County? Which graph is easier to use to find the percentage of Florida counties with unemployment rates greater than 6.06%?

2.37 How educated are casino gamblers? Do college-educated gamblers play different casino games than those with no college background? These were the questions of interest in a recent survey of the U.S. gaming industry conducted by Harrah's Casino. The answers are provided in the following table.

	Percent Attended College	Percent with No College Education
Table Games (Blackjack, Craps, Roulette)	65	35
Slot/Video Machines	50	50

a. Construct a pie chart to describe the college attendance of casino gamblers who play table games such as blackjack, craps, and roulette.

b. Construct a pie chart to describe the college attendance of casino gamblers who play slot and/or video machines.

c. Compare the two pie charts, parts **a** and **b**. What inference can you make?

2.38 A study of merit raises at 16 U.S. corporations was conducted to discover the extent to which merit pay policies for employees are actually tied to performance (*Personnel Journal*, Mar. 1986). One phase of the study focused on the distribution of merit raises (measured as percentage increase in salary) awarded at the companies. The frequency distribution of the 3,990 merit increases awarded at one of the largest firms in the study is reproduced in the figure.

a. Approximately how many of the firm's employees were awarded merit increases between 6% and 10%?

b. Is the distribution skewed? If so, is it skewed to the right or skewed to the left?

c. Approximately what proportion of the 3,990 merit increases were less than 5%?

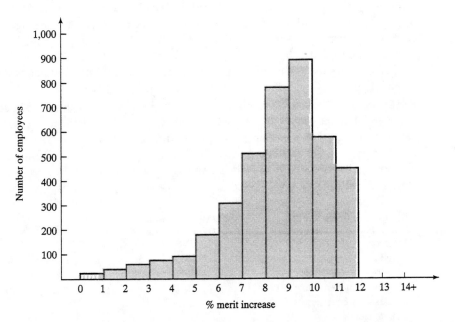

2.39 The *Wall Street Journal* (Feb. 27, 1987) reported the results of a survey on employee life insurance policies offered by U.S. companies. One question focused on the lowest group-life benefit offered to employees. The percentages in each of the response categories are illustrated in the accompanying figure.

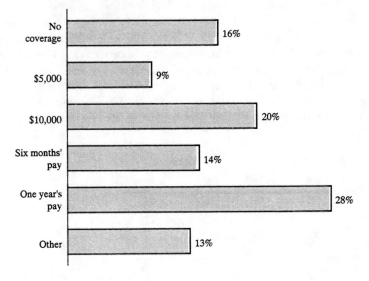

Source: Hewitt Associates.

a. What type of graphical method is used to describe the survey results?

b. What percentage of the companies surveyed offer no group-life coverage?

c. If 1,000 companies participated in the survey, how many offer $10,000 as the lowest group-life benefit?

d. Do you think the results of the survey are based on the data in the population or on a sample? Explain.

2.40 Each year, the Business Economics Division of the U.S. Department of Labor classifies each business failure into one of the following eight categories, based on the reason for failure: (1) neglect, (2) fraud, (3) lack of experience in the line, (4) lack of managerial experience, (5) unbalanced experience, (6) incompetence, (7) disaster, or (8) unknown reasons. These classifications are based on the opinions of informed creditors and information in Business Economics Division reports. A summary of 1,463 recent failures of construction enterprises is given in the table.

Underlying Cause	Relative Frequency
Neglect	.008
Fraud	.002
Lack of line experience	.076
Lack of managerial experience	.161
Unbalanced experience	.215
Incompetence	.477
Disaster	.004
Reason unknown	.057

a. Use an appropriate graphical method to describe the 1,463 construction business failures.

b. Visually estimate the percentage of construction businesses that failed because of inadequate experience or incompetence.

2.41 Reporting in the *New England Journal of Medicine* (Mar. 18, 1991), the Center for Disease Control (CDC) confirmed what many former cigarette smokers have learned from experience: People who quit smoking tend to gain weight. The CDC's research team reviewed data on 1,885 smokers and 768 former smokers who were studied over a 13-year period. Weight gain over the study period was classified as slight (3 kilograms or less), moderate (between 3 and 8 kilograms), significant (between 8 and 13 kilograms), and major (more than 13 kilograms). The smokers/quitters were also classified according to gender to compare male versus female weight gain. The percentages of men and women in the four weight-gain categories are provided in the table.

Gain	Quitters Men	Quitters Women	Smokers Men	Smokers Women
Slight	55	50	66	63
Moderate	22	26	24	23
Significant	14	10	8	9
Major	9	14	2	5
Total	100	100	100	100

Source: *Time,* Mar. 25, 1991, p. 55.

a. Describe the data with the appropriate graphical technique. Construct one graph for each column of the table.

b. Compare the four graphs, part **a.** Do quitters tend to gain more weight than smokers? Do female quitters tend to gain more weight than male quitters?

2.42 In Florida, civil engineers are designing roads with the latest safety-oriented construction methods in response to the fact that in 1988 more people in Florida were killed by accidents as a result of bad roads than by guns. A total of 135 traffic accidents that occurred during the year have been attributed to poorly constructed roads (*Tampa Tribune*, Nov. 14, 1989). A breakdown of the poor road conditions that caused the accidents is shown in the accompanying table. Construct and interpret a frequency bar graph for the data.

Poor Road Condition	*Number of Fatalities*
Obstructions without warning	7
Road repairs/under construction	39
Loose surface material	13
Soft or low shoulders	20
Holes, ruts, etc.	8
Standing water	25
Worn road surface	6
Other	17
Total	135

Source: Florida Department of Highway Safety and Motor Vehicles, 1989.

2.43 The palatability of a new food product can often be determined by preliminary market taste tests. Experience has shown that a test in which as few as 50 people taste and evaluate a new product under controlled conditions can reveal a major problem in consumer acceptability, if one exists. Suppose 50 individuals agreed to participate in a taste test for a new product—chocolate peanut butter. After tasting the product, each person was asked to mark a ballot rating overall acceptability on a scale from -3 to $+3$ ($-3 =$ terrible, $-2 =$ very poor, $-1 =$ poor, $0 =$ average, $+1 =$ good, $+2 =$ very good, and $+3 =$ excellent). The results are displayed in the accompanying graph.

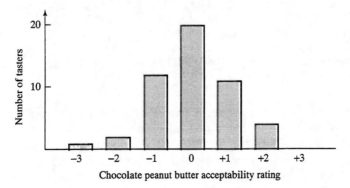

a. What type of graphical tool is used to describe the results of the taste test?

b. What information is conveyed by the graph?

c. What proportion of the 50 tasters rated the new chocolate peanut butter as "terrible"?

2.44 A study was conducted to evaluate the advertisement awareness and sales effectiveness of advertising campaigns for 18 confectionery brands (*Journal of the Market Research Society*, Jan. 1986). For each brand, an ad awareness index (maximum = 100) was determined from a consumer survey, and a sales effectiveness index (maximum = 100) was estimated from market shares. The accompanying frequency distributions were used to summarize the data.

Distribution of 18 Campaigns by Ad Awareness Effectiveness (maximum = 100)

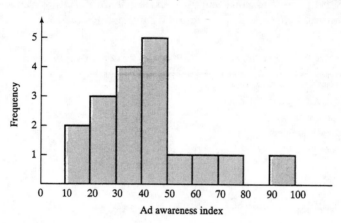

Distribution of 18 Campaigns by Sales Effectiveness (maximum = 100)

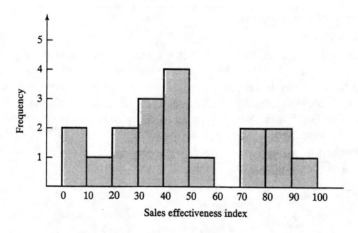

Source: Broadbent, S., and Colman, S. "Advertising effectiveness: across brands." *Journal of the Market Research Society*, Vol. 28, No. 1, 1986, pp. 15–23.

a. How many of the 18 brands had an ad awareness index of 40 or less?

b. How many of the 18 brands had a sales effectiveness index of 70 or more?

c. Use the information provided by the frequency distribution to construct a relative frequency distribution for the 18 ad awareness indexes. Interpret the graph.

d. Use the information provided by the frequency distribution to construct a relative frequency distribution for the 18 sales effectiveness indexes.

2.45 Many industries worldwide currently use newly designed robots to perform certain assembly tasks that often require as many as 10 people to complete. Approximately 33,600 industrial robots were employed in the United States in 1990. The pie chart shows how the robots were used at U.S. industrial plants. Interpret the pie chart.

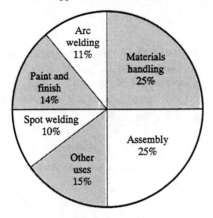

U.S. Robot Applications in 1990 (33,600 units)

Source: Info Graphics, News America Syndicate.

2.46 Personal computers (PCs) are crucial to the success of any large corporation competing in the 1990s. Ten years ago, however, companies were just beginning to incorporate PCs into their corporate strategy (*Wall Street Journal*, Sept. 16, 1985). The table lists the companies that had installed the most PCs for the work place in 1985.

Company	Installed PCs	Company	Installed PCs	Company	Installed PCs
General Motors	31,000	Sperry	4,700	Time	1,700
General Electric	18,000	General Dynamics	4,700	J. P. Morgan & Co.	1,600
Westinghouse	12,000	Travelers	4,500	American Can	1,500
Citicorp	10,000	Merrill Lynch	4,400	Wells Fargo	1,400
Du Pont	10,000	Dun & Bradstreet	4,300	Upjohn	1,400
Ford Motor Co.	9,000	Touche Ross & Co.	4,100	Northwestern Mutual	1,400
Pacific Bell	7,000	3M	4,000	LTV Steel	1,200
Chase Manhattan Bank	6,700	Intel	4,000	Pillsbury	1,000
Exxon	6,000	Security Pacific	3,000	General Mills	1,000
Peat, Marwick, Mitchell	5,600	Lockheed	3,000	Nabisco	1,000
United Technologies	5,000	Allied Products	2,500	Federal Express	1,000
McDonnell Douglas	5,000	Chevron	2,400	R. J. Reynolds	1,000
Hughes Aircraft	5,000	Union Carbide	2,200	Bechtel	1,000
Aetna Life & Casualty	5,000	Mobil	2,000	Teledyne	1,000
TRW	5,000	PG&F	2,000		
Boeing	5,000	Chemical Bank	1,700		

Source: Infoworld, 1985.

a. Construct a relative frequency distribution for the data.

b. What proportion of the companies had installed 6,000 or more PCs in 1985? Shade the bars in the relative frequency distribution corresponding to this area.

c. Note that General Motors had installed nearly twice as many PCs as the next highest company. Omit the value for General Motors from the data set and reconstruct the relative frequency distribution.

d. Compare the relative frequency distributions obtained in parts **a** and **c**. Which graph is more informative? Explain.

2.47 According to a survey of job placement offices at 161 colleges and universities nationwide, 26% fewer job offers were made to graduating students in 1986 than in the previous year (*The College Edition of National Business Employment Weekly*, Fall 1986). Of the 32,965 job offers made to graduating seniors in 1986, 10,951 were to business students. A breakdown of these 10,951 offers by business major is shown in the table.

Business Major	Number of Job Offers
Accounting	6,575
Business Administration & Management	1,934
Management Information Systems	607
Marketing & Distribution	1,835
Total	10,951

Source: College Placement Council 1986 Salary Survey.

a. Are the data quantitative or qualitative?

b. Use an appropriate graphical method to describe the data.

c. What generalizations can you make based on the data?

2.48 One of the major problems encountered in starting a small business is cash flow. Where is the financing necessary to start a small business obtained? The following information on financing sources for small business starts was reported in the *Wall Street Journal* (May 20, 1985).

Source	Relative Frequency
One major capital source:	
Personal savings (PS)	.23
Friends; relatives (FR)	.02
Institutional lenders (IL)	.07
Individual investors (II)	.03
Government (G)	.01
Other major source	.04
Two major capital sources (primary source listed first):	
PS/IL	.23
PS/FR	.11

(continued)

Source	Relative Frequency
PS/II	.02
FR/PS	.03
FR/IL	.02
IL/PS	.11
IL/FR	.03
Other	.05
Total	1.00

Source: Simison, R. L. "In search of the cash-cow." *Wall Street Journal*, May 20, 1985, p. 15c.

a. Summarize the information in the table with an appropriate graph.
b. What percentage of small business starts require only one major source of financing?
c. What percentage of small business starts use personal savings as a source of financing?

2.49 Many hospitals have developed their own computer system software for processing outpatient billings and other accounting services. The *1982 National Survey on Hospital Data Processing* gave the accompanying information on the vendors who supply the computer hardware for 341 hospitals that developed their own financial system software.

Hardware Vendor	Number of Hospitals
Burroughs	45
Data General	6
Digital Equipment	8
Honeywell	8
IBM	188
NCR	50
Others	36

Source: *Modern Health Care*, May 1983, p. 188. Reprinted with permission. Copyright Crain Communications, Inc., 740 N. Rush, Chicago, Ill. 60611. All rights reserved.

a. Classify the variable of interest, hardware vendor, as quantitative or qualitative.
b. What type of graphical method is appropriate for summarizing the data in the table?
c. Construct an appropriate graph to summarize the data.
d. What percentage of hospitals surveyed purchased their computer hardware equipment from Burroughs?
e. What percentage of hospitals surveyed did not purchase their computer hardware equipment from IBM?

■ CASE STUDY 2.1

Warning: Cigarette Smoke Is Hazardous to Your Health

An ongoing campaign of heavy advertising and warnings in the media by the U.S. surgeon general has made both cigarette smokers and nonsmokers well aware of the dangers of inhaling the excess tar and nicotine from a burning cigarette. In addition to tar and nicotine, the surgeon general lists another hazardous substance that affects cigarette smokers: carbon monoxide. According to the surgeon general, "Breathing carbon monoxide, a product of incomplete combustion, reduces the ability of blood to carry oxygen. For smokers, this occurs at the same time that inhaled nicotine is increasing the heart's oxygen needs. Research [conducted by the surgeon general] has indicated carbon monoxide can be particularly hazardous to pregnant women smokers and heart disease patients."

As a result of these findings, the Federal Trade Commission (FTC) annually ranks American cigarette brands in terms of the amount of carbon monoxide, tar, and nicotine in their smoke. The test results are obtained as follows: A 20-part sequential smoking machine is used to "smoke" cigarettes to a 23-millimeter butt length. Based on tests of 100 cigarettes per brand, the carbon monoxide, tar, and nicotine concentrations (rounded to the nearest milligram) in the residual "dry" particulate matter are determined.

Appendix A.4 describes the results of the FTC's 1993 tests of 500 cigarette brands.* In addition to carbon monoxide, tar, and nicotine content (all recorded in milligrams), the following characteristics are listed for each brand:

Light type: Regular (R), Light (L), Extra light (E), or Super Light (X)
Filter type: Filter (F) or Nonfilter (NF)
Menthol type: Menthol (M) or Nonmenthol (NM)
Pack hardness: Hard pack (HP) or Soft pack (SP)
Length (in millimeters): 70, 85, 100, or 120

a. Classify each of the variables in Appendix A.4 as either quantitative or qualitative.

b. Describe each of the variables in Appendix A.4 with a graphical technique. Interpret each graph.

c. Use a graphical method to compare the tar contents of filter and nonfilter cigarettes.

d. Use a graphical method to compare the nicotine contents of hard pack and soft pack cigarettes.

[*Note*: The data of Appendix A.4 are available on a $3\frac{1}{2}$" diskette from the publisher.]

*Source: "Tar, nicotine, and carbon monoxide of the smoke of 568 varieties of domestic cigarettes." Federal Trade Commission report, 1994.

■ *CASE STUDY 2.2*

Statistical Quality Control: Fudging the Data

Statistics plays a key role in monitoring the quality of a manufactured product and in controlling the quality of products shipped to consumers.

In his essay "Making Things Right," W. Edwards Deming gave several illustrations of statistical control of quality drawn from the production line. In one example, Deming examined the quality control process for a manufacturer of steel rods. Rods produced with diameters smaller than the **lower specification limit (LSL)** of 1 centimeter fit too loosely in their bearings and ultimately must be rejected (thrown out). To determine whether the diameter setting of the machine that produces the rods is correct, 500 rods are selected from the day's production and their diameters are recorded. The 500 diameters for one day's production are provided in Appendix A.5. [Note: The data were simulated based on information provided in the essay.]

a. Use one or more of the methods discussed in this chapter to describe and summarize the data. [*Note:* The data of Appendix A.5 are available on a $3\frac{1}{2}''$ diskette from the publisher.]

b. The manufacturing process is out of control if more

than 10% of the rods produced have diameters below the LSL. Use your results from part **a** to determine whether the process is out of control.

c. There has been speculation that some of the inspectors are unaware of the trouble that an undersized rod diameter would cause later in the manufacturing process. Consequently, these inspectors may be passing rods with diameters that are barely below the LSL and recording them as 1.000 centimeter. Is there any evidence to support the claim that the inspectors "fudged" the data? Explain.

d. The inspectors admitted that they were, in fact, passing rods barely below the LSL and fudging the diameters. When the inspection process was corrected for the next day's sample of 500 rods, 105 were found to be defective. Based on this new and more accurate information, is the process out of control? [*Note:* This new information led to a finding of an incorrect machine setting on the production line. When the setting was corrected, the process was back in control.]

*From Tanur, J., et al. (eds.). Statistics: A Guide to the Unknown. Pacific Grove, Calif.: Brooks/Cole Publishing, 1978, pp. 279–281.

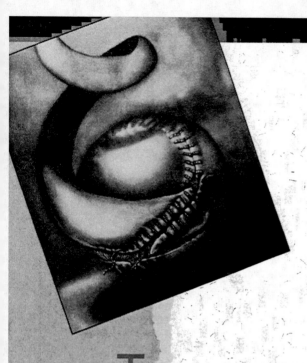

Chapter 3

NUMERICAL METHODS FOR DESCRIBING QUANTITATIVE DATA

To prevent bid-rigging in the highway construction industry, the Florida Department of Transportation (DOT) has developed a system to monitor and analyze sealed bid data. A key variable is the ratio of low bid price to DOT estimated price. How could you describe the ratios for a sample of highway contracts with a single number? We will show you in this chapter how **numerical descriptive measures** can be used to describe the characteristics of a set of measurements, and we will apply this to the Florida highway construction industry in Case Study 3.2.

3.1 Why We Need Numerical Descriptive Measures

It is probably true that a picture is worth a thousand words, and it is certainly true when the goal is to describe a quantitative data set. But sometimes you will want to discuss the major features of a data set and it may not be convenient to produce a stem-and-leaf display or histogram for the data. When this situation occurs, we seek a few summarizing numbers, called **numerical descriptive measures,** that create in our minds a picture of the relative frequency distribution.

3.2 Types of Numerical Descriptive Measures

Examine Figure 3.1, a reproduction of the computer-generated (SAS) histogram for the 707 residential sale prices described in Appendix A.1. If you were allowed to choose two numbers that would help you to construct a mental image of the distribution, which two would you choose? We think you would probably choose

1. A number that is located near the "center" of the distribution (see Figure 3.2a on page 82)
2. A number that measures the "spread" of the distribution (see Figure 3.2b)

For distributions of data shaped like Figure 3.2, a number that would describe the "center" of the distribution would be visually located near the spot where most of the data seem to be concentrated. Consequently, numbers that fulfill this role are

FIGURE 3.1

SAS Histogram for the Sale Prices (in Thousands of Dollars) of Appendix A.1

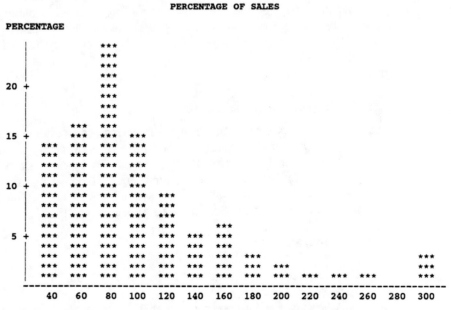

FIGURE 3.2

Numerical
Descriptive Measures

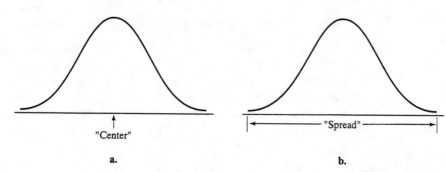

a.

b.

called **measures of central tendency.** We will define and describe several measures of central tendency for data sets in Section 3.4.

The amount of "spread" in a data set is a measure of the variation in the data. Consequently, numerical descriptive measures that perform this function are called **measures of variation** or **measures of dispersion.** As you will subsequently see (Section 3.5), there are several ways to measure the variation in a data set.

Measures of central tendency and data variation are not the only types of numerical measures for describing data sets. Some are constructed to measure the **skewness** of a distribution. Recall from Section 2.4 that skewness describes the tendency of the distribution to tail out to the right (or left). For example, the histogram in Figure 3.1 is **skewed to the right** (or **positively skewed**).

We will concentrate in this chapter on measures of central tendency and measures of variation. Although numerical descriptive measures of skewness are beyond the scope of this text, knowing whether a distribution of data is skewed or symmetric is important when describing the data with measures of central tendency and variation (Section 3.6). As you read this material, keep in mind our goal of using a pair of numbers to create a mental image of a relative frequency distribution. Relate each numerical descriptive measure to this objective, and verify that it fulfills the role it is intended to play.

3.3 Summation Notation

Suppose a data set was obtained by observing a quantitative variable x. For example, x may represent the quantitative sale price of a residential property. By observing x (sale price) for the 707 properties of Appendix A.1, we obtained the data set consisting of 707 sale prices. If we want to represent a particular observation in a data set, say, the 50th one, we represent it by the symbol x with a subscript 50. For example, the sale price for the 50th observation in Appendix A.1 is \$86,000. Therefore,

$$x_{50} = \$86,000$$

The complete sale price data of Appendix A.1 would be represented by the symbols $x_1, x_2, x_3, \ldots, x_{707}.$

Most of the formulas that we shall use require the summation of numbers. For example, we may want to sum the observations in a data set, or we may want to square each observation and then sum the squares of all the observations. The sum of the observations in a data set will be represented by the symbol

Σx

This symbol is read "summation x." The symbol Σ (sigma) is giving you an instruction: It is telling you to sum a set of numbers. The variable to be summed, x, is shown to the right of the Σ symbol.

EXAMPLE 3.1
Finding Sums

Suppose the variable x is used to represent the number of bathrooms in a given residence. Five residential properties are examined, and the value of x is recorded for each. The observations are 2, 1, 3, 2, 3.

a. Find Σx.   b. Find Σx^2.

SOLUTION

a. The symbol Σx tells you to sum the x values in the data set. Therefore,

$$\Sigma x = 2 + 1 + 3 + 2 + 3 = 11$$

b. The symbol Σx^2 tells you to sum the squares of the x values in the data set. Therefore,

$$\Sigma x^2 = (2)^2 + (1)^2 + (3)^2 + (2)^2 + (3)^2$$
$$= 4 + 1 + 9 + 4 + 9 = 27 \quad \blacksquare$$

EXAMPLE 3.2
Finding Sums

Refer to Example 3.1.

a. Find $\Sigma(x - 3)$.   b. Find $\Sigma(x - 3)^2$.   c. Find $\Sigma x^2 - 3$.

SOLUTION

a. The symbol $\Sigma(x - 3)$ tells you to subtract 3 from each x value and then sum. Therefore,

$$\Sigma(x - 3) = (2 - 3) + (1 - 3) + (3 - 3) + (2 - 3) + (3 - 3)$$
$$= (-1) + (-2) + 0 + (-1) + 0 = -4$$

b. The symbol $\Sigma(x - 3)^2$ tells you to subtract 3 from each x value in the data set, square these differences, and then sum them as follows:

$$\Sigma(x-3)^2 = (2-3)^2 + (1-3)^2 + (3-3)^2 + (2-3)^2 + (3-3)^2$$
$$= (-1)^2 + (-2)^2 + (0)^2 + (-1)^2 + (0)^2$$
$$= 1 + 4 + 0 + 1 + 0 = 6$$

c.   The symbol $\Sigma x^2 - 3$ tells you first to sum the squares of the x values, and then subtract 3 from this sum:

$$\Sigma x^2 - 3 = (2)^2 + (1)^2 + (3)^2 + (2)^2 + (3)^2 - 3$$
$$= 4 + 1 + 9 + 4 + 9 - 3 = 24 \quad ▪$$

Meaning of Summation Notation Σx

Sum observations on the variable that appears to the right of the summation symbol.

EXERCISES

▪ *Learning the Mechanics*

3.1   A data set contains the observations 5, 1, 3, 2, 1. Find:
   a. Σx
   b. Σx^2 40
   c. $\Sigma(x-1)$
   d. $\Sigma(x-1)^2$
   e. $(\Sigma x)^2$ 144

3.2   Suppose a data set contains the observations 3, 8, 4, 5, 3, 4, 6. Find:
   a. Σx 33
   b. Σx^2
   c. $\Sigma(x-5)^2$
   d. $\Sigma(x-2)^2$
   e. $(\Sigma x)^2$ 1089

3.3   Refer to Exercise 3.1. Find:

   a. $\Sigma x^2 - \dfrac{(\Sigma x)^2}{5}$
   b. $\Sigma(x-2)^2$
   c. $\Sigma x^2 - 10$

3.4   Refer to Exercise 3.2. Find:

   a. $\Sigma x^2 - \dfrac{(\Sigma x)^2}{7}$
   b. $\Sigma(x-4)^2$
   c. $\Sigma x^2 - 15$ 25

3.5   A data set contains the observations 6, 0, −2, −1, 3. Find:

   a. Σx
   b. Σx^2
   c. $\Sigma x^2 - \dfrac{(\Sigma x)^2}{5}$

3.4 Measures of Central Tendency

The word *center*, as applied to a relative frequency distribution, is not a well-defined term. In our minds, we know vaguely what we mean: a number somewhere near the "middle" of the distribution, a single number that tends to typify the data set. The measures of central tendency that we define often generate different numbers for the same data set but all will satisfy our general objective. If we visually imagine a hump-shaped distribution, all measures of central tendency will fall near the middle of the hump.

The most common measure of the central tendency of a data set is familiar to you and is called the **arithmetic mean** of the data. The arithmetic mean, or **average,** is defined in the box.

Definition 3.1

The **arithmetic mean** of sample of n observations, x_1, x_2, ..., x_n, is denoted by the symbol $\bar{x}$ (read "x-bar") and is computed as

$$\bar{x} = \frac{\text{Sum of the } x \text{ values}}{\text{Number of observations}} = \frac{\Sigma x}{n}$$

Note: From now on, we will refer to an arithmetic mean simply as a **mean.**

EXAMPLE 3.3

Computing a Mean

Find the mean for the data set consisting of the observations 5, 1, 6, 2, 4.

SOLUTION The data set contains $n = 5$ observations. Therefore,

$$\bar{x} = \frac{\Sigma x}{n} = \frac{5 + 1 + 6 + 2 + 4}{5}$$
$$= \frac{18}{5} = 3.6 \quad \blacksquare$$

EXAMPLE 3.4

Interpreting a Mean

Find the mean for the 707 sale prices of Appendix A.1. Locate it on the histogram shown in Figure 3.1. Does the mean fall near the center of the distribution?

SOLUTION With such a large data set, it is impractical to calculate numerical descriptive measures by hand or calculator. We will rely on one of the numerous statistical software packages available for calculating the mean. Figure 3.3 (page 86) is a SAS printout giving descriptive statistics for the sale price data. The mean of the 707 sale prices, shaded on the printout, is $\bar{x} = \$106,405$.

This mean, or average, sale price should be located near the center of the histo-

FIGURE 3.3

SAS Descriptive Statistics for 707 Sale Prices of Appendix A.1

UNIVARIATE PROCEDURE

Variable=SALEPRIC

Moments

N	707	Sum Wgts	707
Mean	106405.3	Sum	75228578
Std Dev	85414.25	Variance	7.2956E9
Skewness	5.033051	Kurtosis	44.46102
USS	1.316E13	CSS	5.151E12
CV	80.27252	Std Mean	3212.334
T:Mean=0	33.124	Prob>|T|	0.0001
Sgn Rank	125139	Prob>|S|	0.0001
Num ^= 0	707		

Quantiles(Def=5)

100% Max	1146000	99%	425000
75% Q3	126000	95%	230000
50% Med	87000	90%	179000
25% Q1	68000	10%	36000
0% Min	8500	5%	20000
		1%	10000
Range	1137500		
Q3-Q1	58000		
Mode	70000		

Extremes

Lowest	Obs	Highest	Obs
8500(	702)	475000(	456)
8500(	645)	605000(	18)
9000(	698)	775000(	20)
9000(	696)	805000(	472)
9000(	652)	1146000(	21)

gram for the 707 sale prices. If you examine Figure 3.1, you will see that the mean $\bar{x}$ does indeed fall near the center of the mound-shaped portion of the distribution. If we did not have Figure 3.1 available, we could reconstruct the distribution in our minds as a mound-shaped figure centered in the vicinity of $\bar{x} = \$106,405$. ▪

A second measure of central tendency for a data set is the **median.** For large data sets, the median M for a data set is a number chosen so that half the observations are less than the median and half are larger. Since the areas of the bars used to construct the histogram are proportional to the numbers of observations falling within the classes, it follows that the median is a value of x that divides the area of the histogram into two equal portions. Half the area will lie to the left of the median (see Figure 3.4) and half will lie to the right. For example, the median for the 707 sale prices of Appendix A.1 (shaded in Figure 3.3) is $87,000. You can see from Figure 3.1 that this sale price divides the data into two sets of equal size. Half the 707 sale prices are less than $87,000; half are larger.

EXAMPLE 3.5

Computing a Median: *n* Odd

Find the median for the data set consisting of the observations 7, 4, 3, 5, 3.

SOLUTION We first arrange the data in increasing (or decreasing) order:

FIGURE 3.4

The Median Divides
the Area of a Relative
Frequency
Distribution into Two
Equal Portions

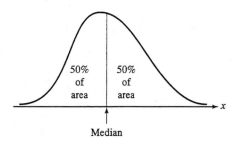

50%
of
area

50%
of
area

x

Median

3   3   4   5   7

Since we have an *odd number of measurements,* the choice for the median is easy: We will choose 4. Half the remaining measurements are less than 4 and half are greater than 4. ■

EXAMPLE 3.6
Computing a Median:
n Even

Suppose you have an *even number of measurements* in the data set—say, 5, 7, 3, 1, 4, 6. Find the median.

SOLUTION If we arrange the data in increasing order, we obtain

1   3   4   5   6   7

You can see that there are now many choices for the median. Any number between 4 and 5 will divide the data set into two groups of three each. There are many ways to choose this number, but the simplest is to choose the median as the point halfway between the two middle numbers when the data are arranged in order. Thus, the median is

$$M = \frac{4 + 5}{2} = 4.5 \quad ■$$

Definition 3.2

The **median** M of a sample of n observations, $x_1, x_2, \ldots, x_n$, is defined as follows:

If n is odd: The middle observation when the data are arranged in order. [The number in the $(n + 1)/2$ position is the median.]

If n is even: The number halfway between the two middle observations—that is, the mean of the two middle observations—when the data are arranged in order. [The two middle observations are those in the $n/2$ and $(n/2 + 1)$ positions.]

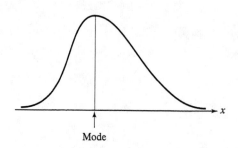

Mode

A third measure of central tendency for a data set is the **mode**. The mode is the value of *x* that occurs with greatest frequency (see Figure 3.5). If the data have been grouped into classes, we will define the mode as the center of the class with the largest class frequency (or relative frequency). For example, you can see that the sale price mode is $70,000 (shaded in Figure 3.3) and that the modal class is $70,000–$90,000 (Figure 3.1).

Definition 3.3

The **mode** of a data set is the value of *x* that occurs with greatest frequency.
The **modal class** is the class with the largest class frequency.

The mean, median, and mode are shown (Figure 3.6) on the graph of the relative frequency distribution for the 707 sale prices of Appendix A.1. Which is the best measure of central tendency for this data set? The answer depends on the type of descriptive information you want. If you want the "average" sale price, or "center of gravity," for the sale price distribution, then the mean is the desired measure. If your notion of a typical or "central" sale price is one that is larger than half the sale prices and less than the remainder, then you will prefer the median. The mode is rarely the preferred measure of central tendency because the measurement that occurs most often does not necessarily lie in the "center" of the distribution. There are situations, however, where the mode is preferred. For example, if the relative frequency of occurrence of residential property sale prices can be viewed as a measure of homeowner preference (e.g., the greatest frequency of sales occurred in the class with the midpoint at $80,000), then the mode might be the preferred measure of central tendency. More realistically, a retailer of women's shoes would be interested in the modal shoe size of potential customers.

In making your decision, you should know that *the mean is sensitive to very large or very small measurements*. Consequently, the mean will shift toward the direction of skewness and may be a misleading measure of central tendency in some situations. You can see from Figure 3.6 that the mean falls to the right of the median and that the sale prices are skewed to the right. The high sale prices of a relatively few properties influence the mean much more than the median. For this reason, the median is sometimes called a **resistant** measure of central tendency since it, unlike the mean, is resistant to the influence of extreme measurements. For data sets that are ex-

FIGURE 3.6

Location of the Mean, Median, and Mode for the Sale Price Data of Appendix A.1

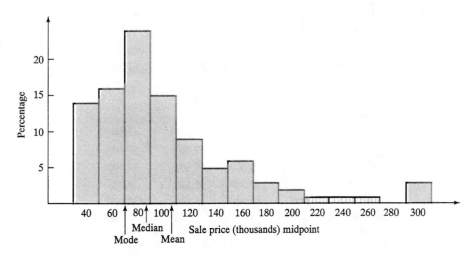

tremely skewed, the median would better represent the "center" of the distribution. (This explains why the median price of new homes, rather than the mean, is reported each month by the federal government.)

Warning

For data sets that are extremely skewed, be wary of using the mean as a measure of the "center" of the distribution. In this situation, a more meaningful measure of central tendency may be the median, which is more resistant to the influence of extreme measurements.

Most of the inferential statistical methods discussed in this text are based, theoretically, on mound-shaped distributions of data with little or no skewness. For these situations, the mean and the median will be, for all practical purposes, the same. Since the mean has nicer mathematical properties than the median, it is the preferred measure of central tendency for these inferential techniques.

EXERCISES

■ *Learning the Mechanics*

3.6   Calculate the mean for samples with the following characteristics:
   a. $n = 10$ and $\Sigma x = 500$ **b.** $n = 20$ and $\Sigma x = 400$ **c.** $n = 500$ and $\Sigma x = 100$

3.7   Find the mean and median for the data set consisting of the five measurements 3, 9, 0, 7, 4.

3.8   Find the mean and median for the following sample of $n = 6$ measurements: 7, 3, 4, 1, 5, 6.

3.9 Calculate the mean, median, and mode for each of the following samples:
    a. 3, 4, 4, 5, 5, 5, 6, 6, 7   **b.** 3, 4, 4, 5, 5, 5, 6, 6, 70
    c. −50, −49, 0, 0, 49, 50   **d.** −50, −49, 0, 9, 9, 81

3.10 The sample of $n = 50$ sale prices of residential properties listed in Table 2.3 is reproduced here.

Sale Prices

99,000	45,000	61,500	78,400	48,500
123,000	60,000	155,000	77,000	56,400
65,700	50,000	140,000	49,600	59,500
115,000	45,500	112,000	58,500	25,000
63,000	70,000	62,000	46,000	110,000
76,000	77,100	61,900	36,500	25,000
58,000	45,500	55,000	38,000	89,500
87,000	63,500	31,700	44,900	90,000
68,000	51,600	75,300	40,000	32,000
50,500	79,000	47,000	48,000	103,000

  a. Compute the mean and median, and locate these values on the relative frequency distribution for the data set (see Figure 2.11 on page 52). Notice that they fall near the center of the distribution.
  b. Find the **modal class** (the class with the greatest relative frequency) or the relative frequency distribution shown in Figure 2.11. Compare your answer with the mean and median obtained in part **a**.
  c. Suppose that a distribution of data is skewed to the right. Would you expect the mean of this data set to be larger or smaller than the median? Does your answer agree with the results of part **a**?

■ *Applying the Concepts*

3.11 The *U.S. News & World Report* data on the top 25 graduate business schools, Exercise 2.17, are reproduced here.

School	Overall Score	Tuition	GMA	Acceptance Rate	Starting Salary
Harvard University	100.0	$18,550	640	16.3%	$65,500
Stanford University	99.8	19,239	680	12.0	65,000
University of Pennsylvania (Wharton)	95.5	18,800	644	25.1	60,095
Northwestern University (Kellogg)	94.0	18,780	635	20.3	55,500
University of Michigan	92.2	18,200	621	31.9	56,220
Mass. Institute of Tech. (Sloan)	92.0	19,500	650	20.7	60,000
Duke University (Fuqua)	90.8	18,500	631	30.1	54,000
Dartmouth College (Tuck), (N.H.)	90.0	18,750	651	19.5	57,500

(continued)

School	*Overall Score*	*Tuition*	*GMA*	*Acceptance Rate*	*Starting Salary*
University of Chicago	89.8	19,250	637	36.2	55,000
Columbia University	88.2	19,000	630	46.9	55,000
University of Virginia (Darden)	84.9	14,227	610	25.8	54,000
Cornell University (Johnson)	81.4	18,500	635	36.7	53,000
Carnegie Mellon University (Pa.)	80.7	18,500	638	33.8	54,000
Univ. of California at Berkeley (Haas)	80.5	10,617	636	24.2	54,000
Univ. of California at L.A. (Anderson)	79.2	11,246	633	21.5	54,000
New York University (Stern)	78.0	17,200	616	35.1	55,000
Yale University	77.9	19,275	651	37.6	55,000
University of Texas at Austin	76.8	6,452	634	23.9	45,000
U.N.C., Chapel Hill (Kenan/Flagler)	76.5	8,680	620	17.0	54,100
Indiana University at Bloomington	76.4	12,000	605	38.4	47,000
University of Southern California	73.4	15,730	622	31.2	54,000
Georgetown University	72.4	17,460	608	43.8	50,000
Purdue University (Krannert), (Ind.)	72.0	8,192	608	28.9	45,500
University of Rochester (Simon), (N.Y.)	71.8	16,980	616	31.4	48,000
Vanderbilt University (Owen), (Tenn.)	71.6	17,500	607	48.9	43,100

Source: "The best graduate schools." *U.S. News & World Report*, Mar. 22, 1993, p. 58.

```
                    UNIVARIATE PROCEDURE

                    Variable=ACCRATE

                         Moments

N                25    Sum Wgts             25
Mean         29.488    Sum               737.2
Std Dev    9.668045    Variance        93.4711
Skewness    0.23658    Kurtosis       -0.53464
USS        23981.86    CSS            2243.306
CV         32.78637    Std Mean       1.933609
T:Mean=0   15.25024    Prob>|T|        0.0001
Sgn Rank      162.5    Prob>|S|        0.0001
Num  ^= 0        25

                   Quantiles(Def=5)

    100% Max      48.9        99%       48.9
     75% Q3       36.2        95%       46.9
     50% Med      30.1        90%       43.8
     25% Q1       21.5        10%         17
      0% Min        12         5%       16.3
                               1%         12
    Range        36.9
    Q3-Q1        14.7
    Mode           12

                       Extremes

    Lowest     Obs     Highest     Obs
       12(       2)      37.6(      17)
     16.3(       1)      38.4(      20)
       17(      19)      43.8(      22)
     19.5(       8)      46.9(      10)
     20.3(       4)      48.9(      25)
```

a. Calculate the mean, median, and mode for the GMAT scores of the 25 business schools.

b. Interpret the results, part **a**.

c. Descriptive statistics for the acceptance rates of the 25 business schools is shown in the accompanying SAS printout. Locate and interpret the measures of central tendency displayed on the printout.

3.12 Refer to the *Industrial Marketing Management* (1993) study of advertisements placed in trade magazines, Exercise 2.18. For convenience, the data on number of ads by industry are reproduced here.

Industry	Number of Ads	Industry	Number of Ads
Accountancy	21	Hotels	13
Aeronautics	20	Insurance	29
Agriculture	31	Laundry	13
Baking	35	Marketing/advertising	37
Business	26	Medical	33
Chemistry	25	Mining	27
Computers	25	Music	19
Dairy	17	Packaging	31
Dental	29	Paper/pulp	25
Electronics	16	Plastics	31
Environment	17	Safety	26
Fishing	20	Security	20
Fur	7	Toys	15
Graphics	16	Travel	19
Grocery	22	29	668

Source: McCullough, L. S., and Taylor, R. K. "Humor in American, British, and German ads." *Industrial Marketing Management*, Vol. 22, 1993, p. 21 (Table 1).

a. Compute and interpret the mean number of ads for this study. *22.93*

b. Compute and interpret the median number of ads for this study.

c. Compute and interpret the mode of the number of ads for this study.

d. Refer to the stem-and-leaf display you constructed in Exercise 2.18. Which measure of central tendency best describes the data?

3.13 Refer to the Centers for Disease Control study of sanitation levels for 91 international cruise ships, Exercise 2.19. A MINITAB printout of the descriptive statistics for the data is shown here. (Recall that sanitation scores range from 0 to 100.) Interpret the numerical descriptive measures of central tendency displayed on the printout.

	N	MEAN	MEDIAN	TRMEAN	STDEV	SEMEAN
sanlevel	91	91.044	92.000	91.580	5.566	0.583

	MIN	MAX	Q1	Q3		
sanlevel	66.000	99.000	89.000	95.000		

3.14 Recall that Appendix A.1 describes the sale prices for properties sold in six specific residential neighborhoods. The mean and median sale prices (to the nearest dollar) for the six data sets are shown in the accompanying table. Use these measures of central tendency to comment on the skewness of the relative frequency distributions for the six data sets.

Neighborhood	Mean Sale Price	Median Sale Price
Avila	$297,004	$192,000
Carrollwood Village	137,492	125,000
Northdale	94,391	91,000
Tampa Palms	198,428	170,000
Town & Country	70,477	69,000
Ybor City	25,764	23,400

3.15 Organizational behaviorists and social psychologists are keenly interested in the process by which decision makers escalate their commitment to an ineffective course of action. This phenomenon has been labeled many things, including the "sunk cost" effect, the "knee-deep-in-the-big-muddy" effect, and the "too-much-invested-to-quit" effect, but is most commonly known as "entrapment." Fifty-two introductory psychology students took part in a laboratory experiment designed to explore whether individuals' tendencies to view prior outcomes as revealing of their self-identity would heighten entrapment (*Administrative Science Quarterly,* Mar. 1986). The experiment consisted of 30 trials in which points were "awarded" based on the accuracy of students' judgments of geometric patterns of various shapes. The total points awarded on each trial are listed in the table.

5	5	4	7	24	6
10	12	11	15	11	10
3	23	4	20	5	4
7	5	6	6	15	5
15	10	13	9	4	6

Source: Brockner, J., et al. "Escalation of commitment to an ineffective course of action: The effect of feedback having negative implications for self-identity." *Administrative Science Quarterly,* Vol. 31, No. 1, Mar. 1986, p. 115. Reprinted by permission of *Administrative Science Quarterly.* Copyright 1986.

a. Construct a relative frequency distribution for data.
b. Compute the mean, median, and mode (modal class) for the data set and locate them on the relative frequency distribution. Do these measures of central tendency appear to locate the center of the distribution of data?

3.16 What are the top corporate executives being paid? To answer this question, *Business Week* magazine conducts a survey of corporate executives each year. (See Case Studies 1.1 and 3.1.)

Business Week's 1994 survey of executives at 360 companies revealed a 15% increase in salaries and bonuses from 1992 to 1993, reversing two consecutive years of declining salaries. The top 20 corporate executives and their 1993 total pay (salary plus bonus long-term compensation) are shown in the table. Assume that these represent a sample of the highest-paid corporate executives in the United States.

Corporate Executive (Company)	1993 Total Pay (in thousands)
1. Michael D. Eisner (Walt Disney)	$203,011
2. Sanford I. Weill (Travelers)	52,810
3. Joseph R. Hyde (Autozone)	32,220
4. Charles N. Mathewson (Intl. Game Tech.)	22,231
5. Alan C. Greenberg (Bear Stearns)	15,915
6. H. Wayne Huizenga (Blockbuster)	15,557
7. Norman E. Brinker (Brinker Intl.)	14,925
8. Roberto C. Goizueta (Coca-Cola)	14,513
9. C. Robert Kidder (Duracell)	14,172
10. Thomas M. Hahn (Georgia-Pacific)	13,680
11. H. Brewster Atwater (General Mills)	13,177
12. James C. Morgan (Applied Materials)	12,833
13. Richard H. Jenrette (Equitable Cos.)	12,380
14. Harry A. Merlo (Louisiana-Pacific)	12,051
15. John H. Bryan (Sara Lee)	11,889
16. David R. Whitwam (Whirlpool)	11,837
17. Charles S. Sanford (Bankers Trust)	11,811
18. Frank V. Cahouet (Mellon Bank)	11,516
19. Walter J. Sanders (Adv. Micro Devices)	11,488
20. Stanley C. Gault (Goodyear)	11,278

Source: "That eye-popping executive pay." *Business Week*, Apr. 25, 1994, p. 53.

a. Find the mean total pay for the 20 CEOs.
b. Find the median.
c. Which of the two measures of central tendency, the mean or the median, better describes the total pay distribution of the top corporate executives in 1993? Explain.

3.17   Refer to the *Journal of Marketing Research* article on the effect of brand name and store name on product quality, Exercise 2.21. The stem-and-leaf displays showing the distribution of effect size (an index ranging from 0 to 1) for the 15 brand-name studies and the 17 store-name studies are reproduced here.

a. Calculate the mean, median, and mode of effect size for the 15 brand-name studies. Which measure of central tendency best describes the data set?
b. Calculate the mean, median, and mode of effect size for the 17 store-name studies. Which measure of central tendency best describes the data set?
c. Combine the data for the two studies, and compute the mean, median, and mode of effect size. Which measure of central tendency best describes the combined data set?

Brand Name (15 studies)

Stem	Leaf
.6	0
.5	7
.4	
.3	4
.2	5 5
.1	0 1 1 2 4
.0	3 3 5 5 7

Store Name (17 studies)

Stem	Leaf
.6	
.5	
.4	3 4
.3	
.2	
.1	2
.0	0 0 0 1 1 2 2 3 3 4 6 7 8 8

Source: Rao, A. R., and Monroe, K. B. "The effect of price, brand name, and store name on buyers' perceptions of product quality: An integrative review." *Journal of Marketing Research*, Vol. 26, Aug. 1989, p. 354 (Table 2).

3.5   Measures of Data Variation

Just as measures of central tendency locate the "center" of a relative frequency distribution, **measures of variability** measure its "spread." Examine the histogram for the 707 sale prices (Figure 3.6) and think how you might describe its spread. The first thought that probably comes to mind is the **range.**

Definition 3.4

The **range** of a quantitative data set is equal to the difference between the largest and the smallest measurements in the set.

EXAMPLE 3.7
Computing a Range

Find the range for the data set consisting of the observations 3, 7, 2, 1, 8.

SOLUTION   The smallest and largest members of the data set are 1 and 8, respectively. Therefore,

Range = Largest measurement − Smallest measurement

$$= 8 - 1 = 7   ■$$

The range of a data set is easy to acquire, but it is an insensitive measure of variation and is not very informative. For an example of its insensitivity, consider Figure 3.7 (page 96). Both relative frequency distributions have the *same range,* but it is clear that the relative frequency distribution in Figure 3.7b indicates much less data variation than the distribution in Figure 3.7a. Most of the observations in Figure 3.7b lie close to the mean. In contrast, most of the observations in Figure 3.7a deviate substantially from the center of the distribution. Since the ranges for the two distributions

FIGURE 3.7

Two Relative
Frequency
Distributions That
Have Equal Ranges,
but Show Differing
Amounts of Data
Variation

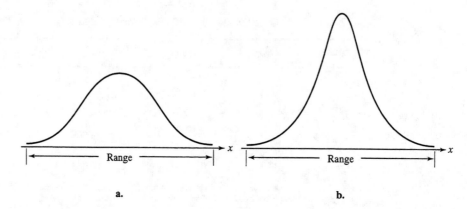

a.

b.

are equal, it is clear that the range is a fairly insensitive measure of data variation. The range was unable to detect the differences in data variation for the data sets represented in Figure 3.7.

To demonstrate the fact that the range is not very informative, examine the relative frequency distribution in Figure 3.6 and note that most of the data fall between $30,000 and $310,000—i.e., visually, we see the range as approximately $280,000. But if you examine the set of all 707 sale prices in Appendix A.1, you will find that the smallest observation is $8,500, the largest is $1,146,000, and the range is really $1,137,500 (see the SAS printout, Figure 3.3 on page 86). In other words, the range for the data set quantifies the spread of the extreme largest and smallest members of the data set, and thus is insensitive to the variability of the remaining measurements in the set.

A more useful measure of spread is the **variance**. The variance of a data set is based on how much the observations "deviate" from their mean. The **deviation** between an observation x and the mean $\bar{x}$ of a sample is the difference

$$x - \bar{x}$$

If a sample data set contains n observations, the **sample variance** is equal to the "average" of the squared deviations of all n observations. That is, the sample variance, denoted by the symbol s^2, is*

$$s^2 = \frac{\Sigma(x - \bar{x})^2}{n - 1}$$

The larger the value of s^2, the more spread out (i.e., the more variable) the sample data.

---

*We use $(n - 1)$ rather than n in the denominator of s^2 to obtain a mathematically good estimator of the true population variance. When n is used in the denominator, the value of s^2 tends to underestimate the population variance. Dividing by $(n - 1)$ adjusts for the underestimation problem.

Definition 3.5

The **variance**, s^2, of a set of n sample measurements is equal to the sum of squares of deviations of the measurements about their mean, divided by $(n - 1)$:

$$s^2 = \frac{\Sigma(x - \bar{x})^2}{n - 1}$$

Note: A shortcut formula for calculating s^2 is

$$s^2 = \frac{\Sigma x^2 - (\Sigma x)^2/n}{n - 1} = \frac{\Sigma x^2 - n(\bar{x})^2}{n - 1}$$

The greater the value of s^2, the more variation in the sample data.

EXAMPLE 3.8
Computing a Variance

Find the variance for the sample measurements 3, 7, 2, 1, 8.

SOLUTION The five observations are listed in the first column of Table 3.1. You can see that $\Sigma x = 21$ and, therefore,

$$\bar{x} = \frac{\Sigma x}{n} = \frac{21}{5} = 4.2$$

This value of $\bar{x}$, 4.2, is subtracted from each observation to determine how much each observation deviates from the mean. These deviations are shown in the second column of Table 3.1. A *negative deviation* means that the observation fell *below* the mean; a *positive deviation* indicates that the observation fell *above* the mean. **Notice that the sum of the deviations equals 0. This will be true for all data sets.**

Table 3.1 Data and Computation Table

Observation x	$x - \bar{x}$	$(x - \bar{x})^2$
3	−1.2	1.44
7	2.8	7.84
2	−2.2	4.84
1	−3.2	10.24
8	3.8	14.44
Totals 21	0	38.80

The squares of the deviations are shown in the third column of Table 3.1. The total at the bottom of the column gives the sum of squares of deviations,

$$\Sigma(x - \bar{x})^2 = 38.8$$

Then the **sample variance** is

$$s^2 = \frac{\Sigma(x - \bar{x})^2}{n - 1} = \frac{38.8}{4} = 9.7 \quad \blacksquare$$

The procedure illustrated in Example 3.8 for calculating a variance is tedious and often leads to rounding errors in finding the sum of squares of deviations, $\Sigma(x - \bar{x})^2$. A shortcut formula for calculating the sum of squares of deviations and the variance (shown in the box) is illustrated in the following example.

EXAMPLE 3.9
Computing a Variance

Use the shortcut procedure to calculate the sample variance, s^2, for the data set of Example 3.8.

SOLUTION The shortcut procedure provides an easy way to compute $\Sigma(x - \bar{x})^2$, the numerator of the sample variance calculation. Instead of calculating the deviation of each measurement from the mean, we calculate the squares of the observations, as shown in Table 3.2.

Table 3.2 Table for Calculating a Standard Deviation: Shortcut Procedure

Observation	
x	x^2
3	9
7	49
2	4
1	1
8	64
Totals 21	127

Then it can be shown (proof omitted) that

$$\Sigma(x - \bar{x})^2 = \boxed{\Sigma x^2 - \frac{(\Sigma x)^2}{n}}$$

Substituting the sum of squares Σx^2 and the sum Σx of the observations into this formula, we obtain

$$\Sigma(x - \bar{x})^2 = \Sigma x^2 - \frac{(\Sigma x)^2}{n} = 127 - \frac{(21)^2}{5}$$

$$= 127 - 88.2 = 38.8$$

This is exactly the same total that we obtained for the sum of squares of deviations in Table 3.1. Finally, we have

$$s^2 = \frac{\Sigma(x - \bar{x})^2}{n - 1} = \frac{38.8}{4} = 9.7$$

as we obtained in Example 3.8. ■

How can we interpret the value of the sample variance calculated in Example 3.8? We know that data sets with large variances are more variable (i.e., more spread out) than data sets with smaller variances. But what information can we obtain from the number $s^2 = 9.7$? One interpretation is that the average squared deviation of the sample measurements from their mean is 9.7. However, a more practical interpretation can be obtained by calculating the square root of this number.

A third measure of data variation, the **standard deviation**, is obtained by taking the square root of the variance. This results in a number with units of measurement equal to the units of the original data. That is, if the units of measurement for the sample observations are feet, dollars, or hours, the standard deviation of the sample is measured in feet, dollars, or hours (instead of feet^2, dollars^2, or hours^2). Like the variance, the standard deviation measures the amount of spread in a quantitative data set.

Definition 3.6

The **standard deviation** of a set of n sample measurements is equal to the square root of the variance:

$$s = \sqrt{s^2}$$

$$= \sqrt{\frac{\Sigma(x - \bar{x})^2}{n - 1}}$$

The standard deviation of the five sample measurements in Examples 3.8 and 3.9 is

$$s = \sqrt{s^2} = \sqrt{9.7} = 3.1$$

Now that you know how to calculate a standard deviation, we will demonstrate how it can be used to measure the spread or variation of a relative frequency distribution in the next section.

3.6 Interpreting the Standard Deviation

In this section, we give two rules for interpreting the standard deviation. Both rules use the mean and standard deviation of a data set to determine an interval of values within which most of the measurements fall. For samples, the intervals take the form

$$\bar{x} \pm (k)s$$

where k is any positive constant (usually 1, 2, or 3). The particular rule you apply will depend on the shape of the relative frequency distribution for the data set, as the following examples illustrate.

EXAMPLE 3.10
Interpreting s

Recall that each year, the Federal Trade Commission ranks domestic cigarette brands according to the amount of carbon monoxide (CO), in milligrams, emitted in smoke (Case Study 2.1). The 1994 CO rankings of a sample of 500 brands are described in Appendix A.4. Suppose we want to describe the distribution of CO measurements for this sample. To do so, we require the mean and standard deviation of the measurements.

    a. Calculate $\bar{x}$ and s for the data set.

    b. Form an interval by measuring 1 standard deviation on each side of the mean, i.e., $\bar{x} \pm s$. Also, form the intervals $\bar{x} \pm 2s$ and $\bar{x} \pm 3s$.

    c. Find the proportions of the total number (500) of CO measurements falling within these intervals.

SOLUTION

    a. Rather than compute $\bar{x}$ and s by hand, we utilize the computer. A MINITAB printout giving numerical descriptive measures for the data set is shown in Figure 3.8. The mean and standard deviation, shaded on the printout, are

$$\bar{x} = 11.02 \quad \text{and} \quad s = 4.01$$

FIGURE 3.8

MINITAB Printout: Descriptive Statistics for 500 CO Measurements in Appendix A.4

	N	MEAN	MEDIAN	TRMEAN	STDEV	SEMEAN
CO	500	11.015	12.000	11.127	4.011	0.179

	MIN	MAX	Q1	Q3		
CO	0.500	19.000	8.000	14.000		

    b. The intervals $\bar{x} \pm s$, $\bar{x} \pm 2s$, and $\bar{x} \pm 3s$ are formed as follows:

$$\bar{x} \pm s = 11.02 \pm 4.01$$
$$= (11.02 - 4.01,\ 11.02 + 4.01)$$
$$= (7.01,\ 15.03)$$
$$\bar{x} \pm 2s = 11.02 \pm 2(4.01)$$
$$= 11.02 \pm 8.02$$
$$= (11.02 - 8.02,\ 11.02 + 8.02)$$
$$= (3.00,\ 19.04)$$
$$\bar{x} \pm 3s = 11.02 \pm 3(4.01)$$
$$= 11.02 \pm 12.03$$
$$= (11.02 - 12.03,\ 11.02 + 12.03)$$
$$= (-1.01,\ 23.05)$$

c. It is too tedious to check by hand each of the CO measurements of Appendix A.4 to determine whether it falls within the three intervals, so we did it by computer. The proportions of the total number of CO measurements falling within the three intervals are shown in Table 3.3. The three intervals, $\bar{x} \pm s$, $\bar{x} \pm 2s$, and $\bar{x} \pm 3s$, are also shown on a SAS relative frequency histogram for the CO data displayed in Figure 3.9 (page 102). If you visually estimate the proportions of the total area under the histogram that lie over the three intervals, you will obtain proportions approximately equal to those given in Table 3.3.

Table 3.3 Proportions of the Total Number of CO Measurements in Intervals $\bar{x} \pm s$, $\bar{x} \pm 2s$, $\bar{x} \pm 3s$

Interval	Number of Observations in Interval	Proportion in Interval
$\bar{x} \pm s$ or (7.01, 15.03)	324	.648
$\bar{x} \pm 2s$ or (3.00, 19.04)	485	.970
$\bar{x} \pm 3s$ or (−1.01, 23.05)	500	1.000

Will the proportions of the total number of observations falling within the intervals $\bar{x} \pm s$, $\bar{x} \pm 2s$, and $\bar{x} \pm 3s$ remain fairly stable for most distributions of data? To examine this possibility, consider the next example.

FIGURE 3.9

SAS Histogram for
CO Measurements of
Appendix A.4

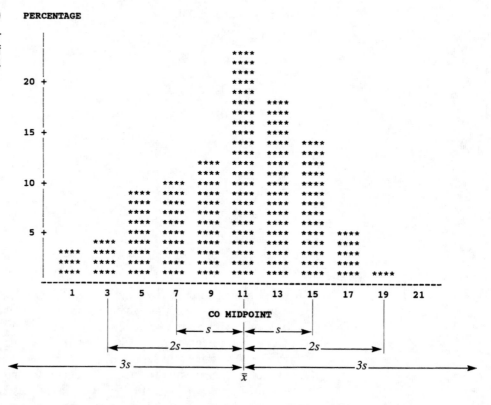

EXAMPLE 3.11
Descriptive Statistics

Calculate the mean and standard deviation of each of the following data sets:

a. The 707 sales-to-appraisal ratios of residential properties described in Appendix A.1

b. The 360 returns on investments described in Appendix A.2

c. The 186 per-member per-month costs of physicians described in Appendix A.3

d. The 500 tar contents of cigarettes described in Appendix A.4

SOLUTION Because of the large amounts of data involved, we computed the means and standard deviations on a computer. They are shown in Table 3.4. The SPSS relative frequency histograms for the four data sets are shown in Figures 3.10–3.13 (pages 103–104). ■

Table 3.4   Means and Standard Deviations for Four Data Sets

	Data Set	Appendix	Mean	Standard Deviation
a.	Sales-to-appraisal ratios	A.1	1.21	.27
b.	Returns on investments	A.2	$211.80	$152.10
c.	Physician costs	A.3	$102.96	$366.31
d.	Tar content of cigarettes, mg	A.4	11.06	4.93

FIGURE 3.10

SPSS Relative
Frequency
Distribution for the
707 Sales-to-
Appraisal Ratios of
Residential
Properties in
Appendix A.1

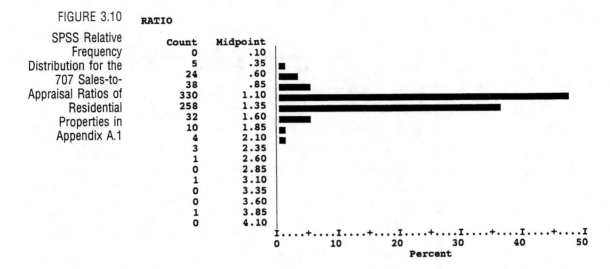

FIGURE 3.11

SPSS Relative
Frequency
Distribution for the
360 Returns on
Investments in
Appendix A.2

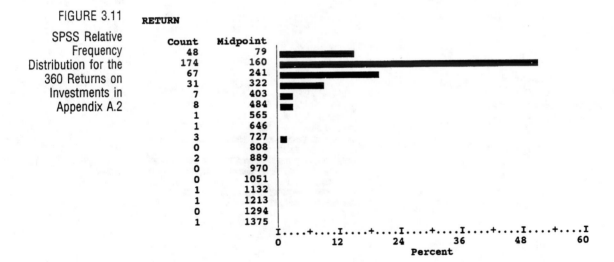

The means and standard deviations of Table 3.4 were used to calculate the intervals $\bar{x} \pm s$, $\bar{x} \pm 2s$, and $\bar{x} \pm 3s$ for each data set. We obtained a computer count of the number and proportion of the total number of observations falling within each interval. These proportions are presented in Table 3.5a–d (page 105).

Tables 3.3 and 3.5a–d demonstrate a property that is common to many data sets. The percentage of observations that lie within 1 standard deviation of the mean $\bar{x}$, i.e., in the interval $\bar{x} \pm s$, is fairly large and variable, usually from 60% to 80% of the total number, but the percentage can reach 90% or more for highly skewed distributions of data. The percentage within 2 standard deviations of $\bar{x}$, i.e., in the interval $\bar{x} \pm 2s$, is

FIGURE 3.12

SPSS Relative
Frequency
Distribution for the
186 Per-Member Per-
Month Costs of
Physicians in
Appendix A.3

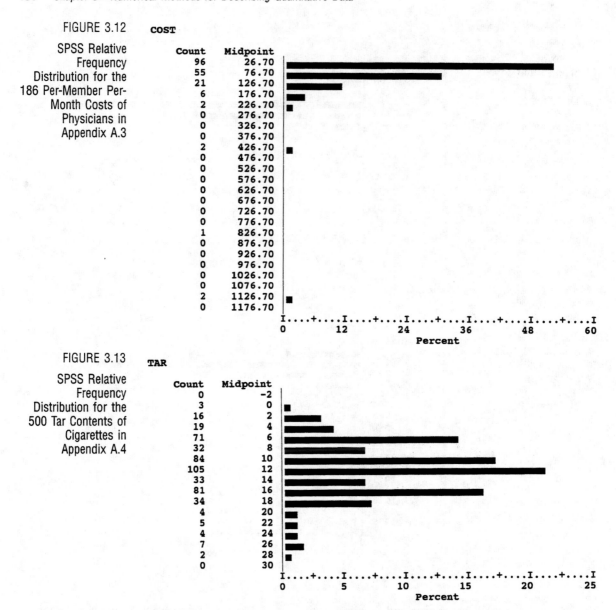

FIGURE 3.13

SPSS Relative
Frequency
Distribution for the
500 Tar Contents of
Cigarettes in
Appendix A.4

close to 95% but, again, the percentage will be larger for highly skewed sets of data. Finally, the percentage of observations within 3 standard deviations of $\bar{x}$, i.e., in the interval $\bar{x} \pm 3s$, is almost 100%, meaning that almost all of the observations in a data set will fall within this interval. This property, which seems to hold for most data sets that contain at least 20 observations and are *mound-shaped*, is called the **Empirical Rule.** The Empirical Rule provides a very good rule of thumb for forming a mental image of a distribution of sample data when you know the mean and standard deviation of the data set. Calculate the intervals $\bar{x} \pm s$, $\bar{x} \pm 2s$, and $\bar{x} \pm 3s$, and then picture the observations grouped as described in the box and shown in Figure 3.14 (page 106).

Table 3.5 Proportions of the Total Number of Observations
Falling Within $\bar{x} \pm s$, $\bar{x} \pm 2s$, and $\bar{x} \pm 3s$

a. Sales-to-Appraisal Ratios

Interval		*Proportion in Interval*
$\bar{x} \pm s$ or	(.94, 1.48)	.850
$\bar{x} \pm 2s$ or	(.67, 1.76)	.943
$\bar{x} \pm 3s$ or	(.40, 2.03)	.986

b. Returns on Investments

Interval		*Proportion in Interval*
$\bar{x} \pm s$ or	($59.7, $363.9)	.881
$\bar{x} \pm 2s$ or	($-92.4, $516.1)	.928
$\bar{x} \pm 3s$ or	($-244.6, $668.2)	.936

c. Physician Costs

Interval		*Proportion in Interval*
$\bar{x} \pm s$ or	($-263.35, $469.27)	.978
$\bar{x} \pm 2s$ or	($-629.66, $835.58)	.984
$\bar{x} \pm 3s$ or	($-995.97, $1,201.89)	.995

d. Tar Contents of Cigarettes

Interval		*Proportion in Interval*
$\bar{x} \pm s$ or	(6.13, 15.99)	.582
$\bar{x} \pm 2s$ or	(1.20, 20.92)	.940
$\bar{x} \pm 3s$ or	(-3.73, 25.85)	.999

The Empirical Rule

If a distribution of sample data is mound-shaped with mean $\bar{x}$ and standard deviation s, then the proportions of the total number of observations falling within the intervals $\bar{x} \pm s$, $\bar{x} \pm 2s$, and $\bar{x} \pm 3s$ are as follows:

$\bar{x} \pm s$: Usually between 60% and 80%. The percentage will be approximately 70% for distributions that are nearly symmetric, but larger (near 90%) for highly skewed distributions.

$\bar{x} \pm 2s$: Close to 95% for symmetric distributions. The percentage will be larger (near 100%) for highly skewed distributions.

$\bar{x} \pm 3s$: Near 100%

FIGURE 3.14

Illustration of the
Empirical Rule

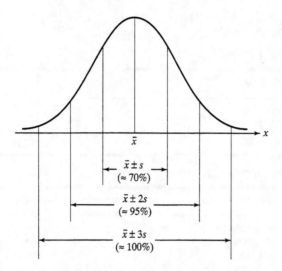

Note that the relative frequency histograms of sales-to-appraisal ratios (Figure 3.10) and physician costs (Figure 3.12) are highly skewed. Consequently, actual percentages of observations falling within the intervals $\bar{x} \pm s$, $\bar{x} \pm 2s$, $\bar{x} \pm 3s$ for these data sets will tend to be on the high side of the range of values given by the Empirical Rule. On the other hand, the mound-shaped distribution of tar contents of cigarettes (Figure 3.13) is nearly symmetric; consequently, the percentages falling within the three intervals are very close to the values given by the Empirical Rule.

Can the Empirical Rule be applied to data sets with non–mound-shaped relative frequency distributions or relative frequency distributions of unknown shape? The answer, unfortunately, is no. However, in these situations we can apply a more conservative rule, called **Tchebysheff's theorem.**

The theorem states (proof omitted) that at least $1 - 1/k^2$ of the total number of observations in a sample data set will fall within the interval $\bar{x} \pm ks$, where k is a constant. We present the theorem in the following box for two useful values of k, $k = 2$ and $k = 3$. [*]

Tchebysheff's Theorem

For any set of sample measurements with mean $\bar{x}$ and standard deviation s, the proportions of the total number of observations in the sample falling within the intervals $\bar{x} \pm 2s$ and $\bar{x} \pm 3s$ are as follows:

$\bar{x} \pm 2s$:   At least <u>75%</u>
$\bar{x} \pm 3s$:   At least 89%

---

[*]*For $k = 1$, $1 - 1/k^2 = 1 - 1/(1)^2 = 0$. Thus, Tchebysheff's theorem states that at least 0% of the observations fall within $\bar{x} \pm s$. Consequently, no useful information is provided about the interval.*

Note that Tchebysheff's theorem applies to any set of sample measurements, regardless of the shape of the relative frequency distribution. The rule is conservative in the sense that the specified percentage for any interval is a lower bound on the actual percentage of measurements falling in that interval. For example, Tchebysheff's theorem states that at least 75% of the 500 CO measurements in Appendix A.4 will fall in the interval $x \pm 2s$. We know (from Table 3.3) that the actual percentage (97%) is closer to the Empirical Rule's value of 95%. Consequently, whenever you know that a relative frequency distribution for a data set is mound-shaped, the Empirical Rule will give more precise estimates of the true percentages falling within the intervals $\bar{x} \pm s$, $\bar{x} \pm 2s$, and $\bar{x} \pm 3s$.

The last example in this section demonstrates the use of these rules in statistical inference.

EXAMPLE 3.12
Application of Empirical Rule

Travelers who have no intention of showing up often fail to cancel their hotel reservations in a timely manner. These travelers are known, in the parlance of the hospitality trade, as "no-shows." To protect against no-shows and late cancellations, hotels invariably overbook rooms. A recent study reported in the *Journal of Travel Research* examined the problems of overbooking rooms in the hotel industry. The data in Table 3.6, extracted from the study, represent daily numbers of late cancellations and no-shows for a random sample of 30 days at a large (500-room) hotel. Based on this sample, what is the minimum number of rooms the hotel should overbook each day?

Table 3.6   Hotel No-Shows for a Sample of 30 Days

18	16	16	16	14	18	16	18	14	19
15	19	9	20	10	10	12	14	18	12
14	14	17	12	18	13	15	13	15	19

Source: Toh, R. S. "An inventory depletion overbooking model for the hotel industry." *Journal of Travel Research*, Vol. 23, No. 4, Spring 1985, p. 27. The *Journal of Travel Research* is published by the Travel and Tourism Research Association (TTRA) and the Business Research Division, University of Colorado at Boulder.

SOLUTION   To answer this question, we need to know a range of values where most of the daily numbers of no-shows fall. This requires that we compute $\bar{x}$ and s, and examine the shape of the relative frequency distribution for the data.

Figure 3.15 (page 108) is a MINITAB printout that shows a stem-and-leaf display and descriptive statistics of the sample data. Notice from the stem-and-leaf display that the distribution of daily no-shows is mound-shaped and only slightly skewed on the low (top) side of Figure 3.15. Thus, the Empirical Rule should give a good estimate of the percentage of days that fall within 1, 2, and 3 standard deviations of the mean.

The mean and standard deviation of the sample data, shaded on the MINITAB printout, are $\bar{x} = 15.133$ and $s = 2.945$, respectively. From the Empirical Rule, we know that about 95% of the daily number of no-shows fall within 2 standard deviations of the mean, i.e., within the interval

FIGURE 3.15

MINITAB Printout
Describing the No-
Show Data,
Example 3.12

```
Stem-and-leaf of noshows   N  = 30
Leaf Unit = 0.10

    1     9 0
    3    10 00
    3    11
    6    12 000
    8    13 00
   13    14 00000
   (3)   15 000
   14    16 0000
   10    17 0
    9    18 00000
    4    19 000
    1    20 0
```

	N	MEAN	MEDIAN	TRMEAN	STDEV	SEMEAN
noshows	30	15.133	15.000	15.231	2.945	0.538

	MIN	MAX	Q1	Q3
noshows	9.000	20.000	13.000	18.000

$$\bar{x} \pm 2s = 15.133 \pm 2(2.945)$$

$$= 15.133 \pm 5.890$$

or between 9.243 no-shows and 21.023 no-shows. (If we count the number of measurements in this data set, we find that actually 29 out of 30, or 96.7%, fall in this interval.) From this result, the large hotel can infer that there will be at least 9.243 (or, rounding up, 10) no-shows per day. Consequently, the hotel can overbook at least 10 rooms per day and still be highly confident that all reservations can be honored.   ■

EXERCISES

■ *Learning the Mechanics*

3.18   Calculate the range, variance, and standard deviation of each of the following samples:
   a. 0, 2, 4, 6, 8, 10   **b.** 0, 4, 5, 5, 6, 10   **c.** 4, 4, 4, 4, 4, 4

3.19   Calculate the variance and standard deviation of samples for which:
   a. $n = 10$, $\Sigma x^2 = 331$, $\Sigma x = 50$ **b.** $n = 25$, $\Sigma x^2 = 163{,}456$, $\Sigma x = 2{,}000$
   c. $n = 5$, $\Sigma x^2 = 26.46$, $\Sigma x = 11.5$

3.20   Find the range, variance, and standard deviation for the following data set:

3	9	0	7	4

Use the shortcut procedure to calculate s^2.

3.21 Find the range, variance, and standard deviation for the following $n = 25$ measurements:

2	1	7	6	5	3	8	5	2
4	5	6	3	4	4	6	9	4
3	4	5	5	7	3	5		

$\bar{x} = 4.64$
range $= 8$

3.22 Refer to the data given in Exercise 3.21. Construct the intervals $\bar{x} \pm s$, $\bar{x} \pm 2s$, and $\bar{x} \pm 3s$. Determine the number of observations falling within each interval, and find the corresponding proportions. Compare your results with the Empirical Rule and Tchebysheff's theorem.

3.23 Suppose a data set has a nearly symmetric, mound-shaped distribution. Make a statement about the percentage of measurements contained in each of the following intervals:
a. $\bar{x} \pm s$ **b.** $\bar{x} \pm 2s$ **c.** $\bar{x} \pm 3s$

3.24 Suppose a data set has a non-mound-shaped distribution. Make a statement about the percentage of measurements contained in each of the following intervals:
a. $\bar{x} \pm s$ **b.** $\bar{x} \pm 2s$ **c.** $\bar{x} \pm 3s$

■ *Applying the Concepts*

3.25 Based on an analysis of automobile insurance claims, the Highway Loss Data Institute (HLDI) compiles injury and collision-loss data for popular cars, station wagons, and vans. The data in the table, reported in *Consumer's Research* (Nov. 1993), are the HLDI collision-damage ratings of large station wagons and minivans. The collision-damage rating reflects how much, compared to other cars, is paid out by insurance companies to the model's owners for collision damage repairs. The higher the rating, the greater the amounts paid for collision-damage repairs.

Vehicle Model	Collision-Damage Rating
Chevrolet Astro 4-wheel drive	50
Plymouth Voyager	59
Chevrolet Caprice	77
Oldsmobile Silhouette	72
Dodge Caravan	60
GMC Safari	60
Mazda MPV 4-wheel drive	121
Toyota Previa	77
Chevrolet Lumina APV	71
Ford Aerostar	74
Chevrolet Astro	59
Mazda MPV	114
Pontiac Trans Sport	72

    a. Compute the mean collision-damage rating of the cars listed in the table.

    b. Compute the standard deviation of the collision-damage ratings.

    c. Suppose you have recently purchased a new minivan. Give an interval that is highly likely to contain the collision-damage rating of your new car.

3.26 Refer to the *Journal of Performance of Constructed Facilities* (Feb. 1990) study of water distribution networks, Exercise 2.1. The internal pressure readings (measured in pounds per square inch, psi) for a sample of pipe sections had a mean of 7.99 psi and a standard deviation of 2.02 psi.

    a. Use this information to construct an interval that captures about 95% of the pressure readings sampled.

    b. Would you expect to observe an internal pressure reading of 20 psi? Explain.

3.27 The *Tampa Bay Business Journal* recently surveyed the 25 largest certified public accountant (CPA) firms in the Tampa, Florida, area. The accompanying data give the number of CPAs employed by each firm.

110	60	102	86	106
63	24	29	16	16
20	28	25	25	20
18	14	8	6	16
12	11	10	11	6

Source: *Tampa Bay Business Journal*, Mar. 8–14, 1991.

    a. Compute $\bar{x}$, s^2, and s for the data set.

    b. What percentage of the measurements would you expect to find in the interval $\bar{x} \pm 2s$?

    c. Count the number of measurements that actually fall within the interval of part **b** and express the interval count as a percentage of the total number of measurements. Compare this result with the answer to part **b**.

3.28 Refer to the data on student-loan default rates for 66 Florida colleges, Exercise 2.26. An SPSS printout giving descriptive statistics for the data set is displayed here.

```
Number of Valid Observations (Listwise) =        66.00

Variable   DEFRATE

Mean            14.682            S.E. Mean        1.741
Std Dev         14.141            Variance       199.974
Kurtosis         5.427            S.E. Kurt         .582
Skewness         2.204            S.E. Skew         .295
Range           74.700            Minimum          1.50
Maximum         76.20             Sum            969.000

Valid Observations -       66     Missing Observations -          0
```

    a. Locate the mean default rate on the printout.

    b. Locate the variance and standard deviation of the default rates on the printout.

    c. What proportion of measurements would you expect to find within 2 standard deviations of the mean?

d. Determine the proportion of measurements (default rates) that actually fall within the interval of part **c**. Compare this result with your answer to part **c**.

e. Suppose the college with the highest default rate (Florida College of Business, 76.2%) was omitted from the analysis. Would you expect the mean to increase or decrease? Would you expect the standard deviation to increase or decrease?

f. Calculate the mean and standard deviation for the data set with Florida College of Business excluded. Compare these results with your answer to part **e**.

g. Answer parts **c** and **d** using the recalculated mean and standard deviation. This problem illustrates the dramatic effect a single observation can have on the analysis.

3.29 Refer to the Federal Trade Commission's rankings of 500 cigarette brands, Appendix A.4 (see Case Study 2.1). The accompanying SAS printout provides numerical descriptive measures for the nicotine content (in milligrams) of the cigarettes.

```
                       UNIVARIATE PROCEDURE

                        Variable=NICOTINE

                             Moments

            N                500   Sum Wgts         500
            Mean          0.8425   Sum           421.25
            Std Dev     0.345525   Variance    0.119388
            Skewness    -0.17036   Kurtosis    0.162504
            USS         414.4775   CSS         59.57437
            CV          41.01187   Std Mean    0.015452
            T:Mean=0    54.52246   Prob>|T|      0.0001
            Sgn Rank       62625   Prob>|S|      0.0001
            Num ^= 0         500

                        Quantiles(Def=5)

            100% Max       1.9       99%         1.7
             75% Q3        1.1       95%         1.4
             50% Med       0.9       90%         1.2
             25% Q1        0.7       10%         0.4
              0% Min      0.05        5%         0.1
                                      1%         0.1

            Range         1.85
            Q3-Q1          0.4
            Mode           0.8

                            Extremes

           Lowest    Obs      Highest    Obs
           0.05(    336)      1.7(     344)
           0.05(    335)      1.8(     330)
           0.05(     93)      1.8(     333)
            0.1(    327)      1.8(     349)
            0.1(    325)      1.9(     152)


                  Histogram              #        Boxplot
      1.95+*                             1          0
         .**                             3          0
         .**                             3          |
         .**                             3          |
         .**                             4          |
         .*******                       13          |
         .*********                     17          |
         .************************      49          |
         .*********************         42       +-----+
         .***************************   56       |     |
         .******************************** 64    *-----*
         .******************************** 70    | + |
         .**************************      54       +-----+
         .*********                      18          |
         .*********************          41          |
         .***********                    22          |
         .**                             3           |
         .****                           8           |
         .*************                  26          |
      0.05+**                            3           0
          ----+----+----+----+----+----+
          * may represent up to 2 counts
```

a. Use the information in the printout to describe the relative frequency histogram for nicotine content.

b. Is the data set better described by the Empirical Rule or Tchebysheff's theorem?

3.30 Refer to the data on population change of the 49 largest U.S. counties, Exercise 2.28. For convenience, the data are reproduced in the accompanying table.

County (Nearest Big City)	Percentage Change	County (Nearest Big City)	Percentage Change
Los Angeles (Los Angeles)	18.5	Tarrant (Fort Worth, Tex.)	35.9
Cook (Chicago)	−2.8	Oakland (Pontiac, Mich.)	7.1
Harris (Houston)	17.0	Sacramento (Sacramento)	32.9
Orange (Los Angeles)	24.7	Hennepin (Minneapolis)	9.7
Kings (New York City)	3.1	St. Louis (St. Louis)	2.0
Maricopa (Phoenix)	40.6	Erie (Buffalo)	−4.6
Wayne (Detroit)	−9.7	Franklin (Columbus, Ohio)	10.6
Queens (New York City)	3.2	Milwaukee (Milwaukee)	−.6
Dade (Miami)	19.2	Westchester (White Plains, N.Y.)	1.0
Dallas (Dallas)	19.0	Hamilton (Cincinnati)	−.8
Philadelphia (Philadelphia)	−6.1	Palm Beach (Palm Beach, Fla.)	49.7
King (Seattle)	18.7	Hartford (Hartford, Conn.)	5.4
Santa Clara (San Jose, Calif.)	15.6	Pinellas (St. Petersburg, Fla.)	16.9
New York (New York City)	4.1	Honolulu (Honolulu)	9.7
San Bernardino (Los Angeles)	58.5	Hillsborough (Tampa)	28.9
Cuyahoga (Cleveland)	−5.8	Fairfield (Bridgeport, Conn.)	2.5
Middlesex (Boston)	2.3	Shelby (Memphis)	6.3
Allegheny (Pittsburgh)	−7.8	Bergen (Hackensack, N.J.)	−2.4
Suffolk (New York City)	2.9	Fairfax (Va./Washington)	37.4
Nassau (New York City)	−2.6	New Haven (New Haven, Conn.)	5.6
Alameda (Oakland)	15.7	Contra Costa (San Francisco)	22.5
Broward (Ft. Lauderdale, Fla.)	23.3	Marion (Indianapolis)	4.25
Bronx (New York City)	3.0	DuPage (Chicago)	18.6
Bexar (San Antonio)	19.9	Essex (Newark, N.J.)	−8.6
Riverside (Los Angeles)	76.5		

Source: U.S. Census Bureau, 1990 Census.

a. Compute $\bar{x}$ and s.

b. Calculate the intervals $\bar{x} \pm s$, $\bar{x} \pm 2s$, and $\bar{x} \pm 3s$.

c. Calculate the percentage of observations falling in the interval $\bar{x} \pm 2s$.

d. Does the Empirical Rule adequately describe the distribution of percentage change in population for the U.S. counties?

3.31 Nevada continues to be the leading gold producer in the United States. According to the U.S. Bureau of Mines, it ranks among the top four regional producers worldwide (trailing South Africa, Russia, and Australia). The data in the table represent the production (in thousands of ounces) for the top 30 gold mines in the state.

1,467.8	228.0	111.3	76.0	55.1	40.0
318.0	222.6	89.1	72.5	54.1	32.4
296.9	214.6	82.0	66.0	50.0	30.9
256.0	207.3	81.5	60.4	50.0	30.3
254.5	120.7	78.8	60.0	44.5	30.0

Source: *Engineering & Mining Journal,* June 1990, p. 38

a. Summarize the data using a graphical technique.
b. Calculate the mean, median, and standard deviation of the data.
c. What proportion of Nevada mines have production values that lie within 2 standard deviations of the mean?
d. Note the extremely large production value, 1,467.8, for the first mine listed in the table. Recalculate the mean, median, and standard deviation with the production measurement for this mine deleted.
e. Explain how the three numerical descriptive measures (mean, median, and standard deviation) are affected by the deletion of the measurement, 1,467.8.

3.32 A Harris Corporation/University of Florida study was undertaken to determine whether a manufacturing process performed at a remote location can be established locally. Test devices (pilots) were set up at both the old and new locations, and voltage readings on the process were obtained. A "good process" was considered to be one with voltage readings of at least 9.2 volts (with larger readings being better than smaller readings). The table contains voltage readings for 30 production runs at each location. Descriptive statistics for both sample data sets are provided in the SAS printout on page 114. Use the Empirical Rule to compare the voltage reading distributions for the two locations.

Old Location			*New Location*		
9.98	10.12	9.84	9.19	10.01	8.82
10.26	10.05	10.15	9.63	8.82	8.65
10.05	9.80	10.02	10.10	9.43	8.51
10.29	10.15	9.80	9.70	10.03	9.14
10.03	10.00	9.73	10.09	9.85	9.75
8.05	9.87	10.01	9.60	9.27	8.78
10.55	9.55	9.98	10.05	8.83	9.35
10.26	9.95	8.72	10.12	9.39	9.54
9.97	9.70	8.80	9.49	9.48	9.36
9.87	8.72	9.84	9.37	9.64	8.68

Source: Harris Corporation, Melbourne, Fla.

Analysis Variable : VOLTAGE

```
------------------------------ LOCATION=NEW ------------------------------
```

N Obs	N	Minimum	Maximum	Mean	Std Dev
30	30	8.5100000	10.1200000	9.4223333	0.4788757

```
------------------------------ LOCATION=OLD ------------------------------
```

N Obs	N	Minimum	Maximum	Mean	Std Dev
30	30	8.0500000	10.5500000	9.8036667	0.5409155

3.7 Measures of Relative Standing

In some situations, you may want to describe the relative position of a particular measurement in a data set. For example, suppose a property in the data set of Appendix A.1 sold for $107,500. You might want to know whether this is a relatively small or large sale price, etc. What percentage of the sale prices were less than $107,500? What percentage were larger? Descriptive measures that locate the relative position of a measurement—in relation to the other measurements—are called **measures of relative standing**. One measure that expresses this position in terms of a percentage is called a **percentile** for the data set.

Definition 3.7

Let $x_1, x_2, \ldots, x_n$ be a set of n measurements arranged in increasing (or decreasing) order. The **pth percentile** is a number x such that $p\%$ of the measurements fall below the pth percentile and $(100 - p)\%$ fall above it.

A sale price of $179,000 falls at the 90th percentile of the sale price data in Appendix A.1. This tells you that 90% of the sale prices were less than $179,000 and $(100 - 90)\% = 10\%$ were greater.

The median, by definition, is the 50th percentile. The 25th percentile, the median, and the 75th percentile are often used to describe a data set because they divide the data set into four groups, each containing one-fourth (25%) of the observations. They would also divide the relative frequency distribution for a data set into four parts, each containing the same area (.25), as shown in Figure 3.16. Consequently, the 25th percentile, the median, and the 75th percentile are called the **lower quartile**, the **mid-quartile**, and the **upper quartile**, respectively, for a data set.

FIGURE 3.16

Locations of the
Lower and Upper
Quartiles

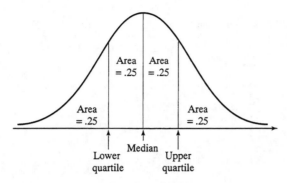

Definition 3.8

The **lower quartile**, Q_L, for a data set is the 25th percentile.

Definition 3.9

The **mid-quartile** (median), *M*, for a data set is the 50th percentile.

Definition 3.10

The **upper quartile**, Q_U, for a data set is the 75th percentile.

For large data sets, percentiles can be found by locating the corresponding areas under the relative frequency distribution; however, they are usually found via the computer. Figure 3.17 (page 116) is a SAS printout describing the sale price data set in Appendix A.1. The values of Q_L, *M*, Q_U, and the 90th percentile are shaded on the printout. From these values, we know that 25% of the 707 sale prices fall below the lower quartile, $68,000; 50% fall below the median, $87,000; 75% fall below the upper quartile, $126,000; and 90% fall below the 90th percentile, $179,000.

When the sample data set is small, it may be impossible to find a measurement in the data set that exceeds, say, *exactly* 25% of the remaining measurements. Consequently, percentiles for small data sets are not well defined. The box on page 116 describes a procedure for finding quartiles and other percentiles with small data sets.

FIGURE 3.17

SAS Descriptive
Statistics for Sale
Price Data of
Appendix A.1

UNIVARIATE PROCEDURE

Variable=SALEPRIC

Moments

N	707	Sum Wgts	707
Mean	106405.3	Sum	75228578
Std Dev	85414.25	Variance	7.2956E9
Skewness	5.033051	Kurtosis	44.46102
USS	1.316E13	CSS	5.151E12
CV	80.27252	Std Mean	3212.334
T:Mean=0	33.124	Prob>$|T|$	0.0001
Sgn Rank	125139	Prob>$|S|$	0.0001
Num ^= 0	707		

Quantiles(Def=5)

100% Max	1146000		99%	425000
75% Q3	126000		95%	230000
50% Med	87000		90%	179000
25% Q1	68000		10%	36000
0% Min	8500		5%	20000
			1%	10000
Range	1137500			
Q3-Q1	58000			
Mode	70000			

Extremes

Lowest	Obs	Highest	Obs
8500(	702)	475000(	456)
8500(	645)	605000(	18)
9000(	698)	775000(	20)
9000(	696)	805000(	472)
9000(	652)	1146000(	21)

Finding Quartiles (and Percentiles) with Small Data Sets

1. Rank the n measurements in the data set in increasing order of magnitude.

2. Calculate the quantity $\frac{1}{4}(n+1)$ and round to the nearest integer. The measurement with this rank represents the lower quartile or 25th percentile. *Note:* If $\frac{1}{4}(n+1)$ falls halfway between two integers, round up.

3. Calculate the quantity $\frac{3}{4}(n+1)$ and round to the nearest integer. The measurement with this rank represents the upper quartile or 75th percentile. *Note:* If $\frac{3}{4}(n+1)$ falls halfway between two integers, round down.

GENERAL.   To find the pth percentile, calculate the quantity $p(n+1)/100$ and round to the nearest integer. The measurement with this rank is the pth percentile.

One advantage of a stem-and-leaf display is that the display makes it easy to locate the median and the upper and lower quartiles for a data set. We will illustrate with an example.

<table>
<tr><td>EXAMPLE 3.13</td></tr>
<tr><td>Finding Percentiles</td></tr>
</table>

Find the lower quartile, the median, the upper quartile, and the 90th percentile for the 25 sale prices in Table 2.2.

SOLUTION The stem-and-leaf display for the data of Table 2.2 is reproduced for convenience in Figure 3.18.

FIGURE 3.18

Stem-and-Leaf
Display for the Data
of Table 2.2

Stem	Leaf
3	67
4	25
5	00, 75, 95
6	30, 50, 60, 82
7	10, 20, 49, 60, 70
8	20, 43, 99
9	45, 50
10	16, 60, 90
11	20
12	95
13	
14	80

Since there are 25 observations in the data set, $\frac{1}{4}(n+1) = \frac{1}{4}(26) = 6.5$. Since this value is halfway between 6 and 7, we round *up* to 7. Thus, the lower quartile Q_L will be the seventh observation when the data are arranged in order from smallest to largest. We can locate Q_L by proceeding down the stem-and-leaf display until we reach the stem (6) that contains the seventh leaf. Of the leaves in this stem, 50 represents the seventh leaf; therefore, $Q_L = 650$ (corresponding to $65,000).

The median of the data set is the 13th observation when the data are arranged in order. Counting leaves from the top of the display, you can see that the 13th leaf is the next-to-largest leaf in stem 7, namely, 60. Therefore, the median is $M = 760$ (corresponding to $76,000).

To find the upper quartile Q_U, we calculate $\frac{3}{4}(n+1) = \frac{3}{4}(26) = 19.5$. Since this value is halfway between 19 and 20, we round *down* to 19. Thus, the upper quartile is the 19th leaf from the top (or the seventh leaf from the bottom) of the diagram. It is the largest leaf (50) in stem 9. Therefore, $Q_U = 950$ (corresponding to $95,000).

Finally, we find the 90th percentile: $90(n+1)/100 = 90(26)/100 = 23.4$, or 23 (after rounding). Thus, the 90th percentile is the 23rd leaf from the top (or third leaf from the bottom) of the stem-and-leaf display. This value is 1,120 (corresponding to $112,000). ■

When a data set is large, the locations of the quartiles relative to the median help us detect possible skewness in the frequency distribution for a data set. For example, if Q_L is farther away from the median than Q_U, then the distribution is likely to be skewed to the left, as shown in Figure 3.19a (page 118). If Q_U is farther away from

FIGURE 3.19

Locations of the
Quartiles and Median
for Various Types of
Skewness

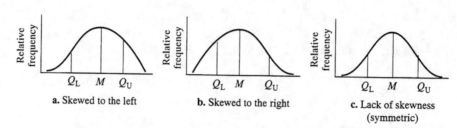

a. Skewed to the left   **b.** Skewed to the right   **c.** Lack of skewness (symmetric)

the median than Q_L, then the distribution is likely to be skewed to the right, as in Figure 3.19b. Lack of skewness is suggested when Q_L and Q_U are approximately equidistant from the median, as depicted in Figure 3.19c.

Another measure of relative standing is the **z score** for a measurement. For example, suppose you were told that $200,000 lies 1.10 standard deviations above the mean of the 707 sale prices of Appendix A.1 (i.e., the sale price has a z score of 1.10). The distance that a measurement x lies above or below the mean $\bar{x}$ of a data set, measured in units of the standard deviation s, is called the **z score** for the measurement. Knowing that most of the sale prices will be less than 2 standard deviations from the mean (i.e., will have z scores less than 2 in absolute value) and almost all will be within 3 standard deviations (i.e., will have z scores less than 3 in absolute value), you would have a good idea of the relative standing of the $200,000 sale price.

Definition 3.11

The sample **z score** for the measurement x is

$$z = \frac{x - \bar{x}}{s}$$

A negative z score indicates that the observation lies to the left of the mean; a positive z score indicates that the observation lies to the right of the mean.

EXAMPLE 3.14

Computing z Scores

As can be seen in Figure 3.17, the mean and standard deviation for the 707 sale prices of Appendix A.1 are $\bar{x} = \$106,405$ and $s = \$85,414$, respectively. Use these values to find the z score for a sale price of $200,000.

SOLUTION Substituting the values of x, $\bar{x}$, and s into the formula for z, we obtain

$$z = \frac{x - \bar{x}}{s} = \frac{200,000 - 106,405}{85,414} = 1.10$$

Since the z score is positive, we conclude that the $200,000 sale price lies a distance of 1.10 standard deviations above (to the right of) the mean of $106,405. ▪

In the next section we discuss how percentiles and z scores can be used to detect unusual observations in a data set.

EXERCISES

■ *Learning the Mechanics*

3.33 State the percentage of measurements that are above and below each of the following percentiles:

a. 20th percentile **b.** Median **c.** 76th percentile
d. Lower quartile **e.** Upper quartile

3.34 The 24 sample measurements of Exercise 2.13 are reproduced here:

213	228	241	268	234	303	274	316
319	320	227	226	224	267	203	266
265	237	288	291	285	270	254	215

a. Use the stem-and-leaf display you constructed in Exercise 2.13 to find Q_L, M, and Q_U.
b. Find the 90th percentile of the data set.

3.35 Compute the z score corresponding to each x value, assuming $\bar{x} = 20$ and $s = 5$.
a. $x = 12$ **b.** $x = 23$ **c.** $x = 28$

3.36 Compute z scores for each of the following situations. Then determine which x value lies the greatest distance above the mean; the greatest distance below the mean.
a. $x = 77$, $\bar{x} = 58$, $s = 8$ **b.** $x = 8.8$, $\bar{x} = 11$, $s = 2$
c. $x = 0$, $\bar{x} = -5$, $s = 1.5$ **d.** $x = 2.9$, $\bar{x} = 3$, $s = .1$

3.37 The 28 sample measurements of Exercise 2.15 are reproduced here:

5.9	5.3	1.6	7.4	8.6	1.2	2.1
4.0	7.3	8.4	8.9	6.7	4.5	6.3
7.6	9.7	3.5	1.1	4.3	3.3	8.4
1.6	8.2	6.5	1.1	5.0	9.4	6.4

a. Use the stem-and-leaf display you constructed in Exercise 2.15 to find Q_L, M, and Q_U.
b. Find the 10th percentile of the data set.

■ *Applying the Concepts*

3.38 Refer to the *U.S. News & World Report* study of the top 25 graduate business schools, Exercise 3.11. Descriptive statistics for the starting salary variable are shown in the ASP printout at the top of page 120.

```
                                  SUMMARY STATISTICS

                                  StartingSalary
                                  ----------------
                        Mean =    53980.6
                     Maximum =    65500
                     Minimum =    43100
                       Range =    22400
           Valid Observations =      25
              Missing Values =       0
          Sample Standard Dev. =   5491.99
             Sample Variance =      3.0162E7
         Sample Coef. Of Var. =      0.10174
        Standard Error Of Mean =   1098.4
                      Median =    54000
              First Quartile =    53000
              Third Quartile =    55500
          Interquartile Range =    2500
         Lower Adjacent Value =    50000
         Upper Adjacent Value =    57500
               Minor Outliers =       5
               Major Outliers =       4
           Standard Deviation =    5381.03
                    Variance =      2.89555E7
        Coefficient Of Var. =      0.0996846
                         Sum =      1.34952E6
              Sum Of Squares =      7.35715E10
          Sum Of Squared Dev. =     7.23888E8
               Second Moment =      2.89555E7
                Third Moment =      5.41867E9
               Fourth Moment =      2.59401E15
       Coefficient Of Skewness =    6.95546E-3
       Coefficient Of Kurtosis =    3.09392
```

a. Locate the measures of relative standing on the printout and interpret their values.

b. Calculate a measure of relative standing for the starting salary of Stanford graduates. Interpret this result.

3.39 Descriptive statistics for the 707 ratios of residential sale prices to appraised values (Appendix A.1) are displayed in the accompanying MINITAB printout. Locate and interpret the measures of relative standing on the printout.

	N	MEAN	MEDIAN	TRMEAN	STDEV	SEMEAN
Ratio	707	1.2131	1.2013	1.2068	0.2710	0.0102

	MIN	MAX	Q1	Q3
Ratio	0.2919	3.9519	1.1136	1.3095

3.40 Refer to Exercise 3.39. Find and interpret the z score for a residential property with a sales-to-appraisal ratio of .92.

3.41 Refer to the data on trade magazine advertisements given in Exercise 3.12.
a. Compute Q_L and Q_U for the data set. Interpret these values.
b. Compute the 40th percentile for the data set. Interpret the result.
c. Find the z score for the medical industry. Interpret the result.

3.42 Refer to the Harris Corporation study on voltage readings at two locations, Exercise 3.32.
a. Calculate the z score for a voltage reading of 10.50 at the old location.
b. Calculate the z score for a voltage reading of 10.50 at the new location.
c. Based on the results of parts **a** and **b**, at which location is a voltage reading of 10.50 more likely to occur? Explain.

3.43 The hotel no-show data presented in Example 3.12 are reproduced here.

18	16	16	16	14	18	16	18	14	19
15	19	9	20	10	10	12	14	18	12
14	14	17	12	18	13	15	13	15	19

Source: Toh, R. S. "An inventory depletion overbooking model for the hotel industry." *Journal of Travel Research*, Vol. 23, No. 4, Spring 1985, p. 27. The *Journal of Travel Research* is published by the Travel and Tourism Research Association (TTRA) and the Business Research Division, University of Colorado at Boulder.

a. Construct a stem-and-leaf display for the data.
b. Compute and interpret the values of Q_L, M, and Q_U.
c. Compute and interpret the 90th percentile for the data.

3.44 Refer to the *Administrative Science Quarterly* entrapment experiment, Exercise 3.15. The data (i.e., total points awarded) for the 30 trials are reproduced here:

5	5	4	7	24	6
10	12	11	15	11	10
3	23	4	20	5	4
7	5	6	6	15	5
15	10	13	9	4	6

Source: Brockner, J., et al. "Escalation of commitment to an ineffective course of action: The effect of feedback having negative implications for self-identity." *Administrative Science Quarterly*, Vol. 31, No. 1, Mar. 1986, p. 115. Reprinted by permission of *Administrative Science Quarterly*, Copyright 1986.

a. Calculate and interpret a measure of relative standing for a trial in which five points were awarded.
b. Calculate and interpret a measure of relative standing for a trial in which 20 points were awarded.

3.45 Refer to the data on percentage change in population for U.S. counties given in Exercise 3.30.
a. Compute and interpret the values of Q_L, M, and Q_U.
b. Compute and interpret a measure of relative standing for Riverside County (Los Angeles).

3.8 Methods for Detecting Outliers

Sometimes inconsistent observations are included in a data set. For example, when we discuss sale prices for residential properties, we generally think of properties with typical residential dwellings located within the city limits. But suppose one of the properties is a tract of farmland located in the unincorporated part of the city. Clearly, the sale price for this property could be much larger than the other sale prices because of the additional acreage, and we probably would not want to include it in the data set.

An unusual observation that lies outside the range of the data values we want to describe is called an **outlier**.

Outliers are often attributable to one of several causes. First, the measurement associated with the outlier may be invalid. For example, the experimental procedure used to generate the measurement may have malfunctioned, the experimenter may have misrecorded the measurement, or the data might have been coded incorrectly in the computer. Second, the outlier may be the result of a misclassified measurement. That is, the measurement belongs to a population different from that from which the rest of the sample was drawn, as in the case of the sale price for the tract of farmland described in the preceding paragraph. Finally, the measurement associated with the outlier may be recorded correctly and from the same population as the rest of the sample, but represents a rare (chance) event. Such outliers occur most often when the relative frequency distribution of the sample data is extremely skewed, because such a distribution has a tendency to include extremely large or small observations relative to the others in the data set.

Definition 3.12

An observation (or measurement) that is unusually large or small relative to the other values in a data set is called an **outlier**. Outliers typically are attributable to one of the following causes:

1. The measurement is observed, recorded, or entered into the computer incorrectly.
2. The measurement comes from a different population.
3. The measurement is correct, but represents a rare (chance) event.

The most obvious method for determining whether an observation is an outlier is to calculate its z score (Section 3.7), as the following example illustrates.

EXAMPLE 3.15
Outliers: z Score Method

One of the residential properties in Appendix A.1 has a sale price of $1,146,000. Is this observation an outlier?

SOLUTION Recall from Example 3.14 that $\bar{x} = \$106,405$ and $s = \$85,414$ for the 707 sale prices of Appendix A.1. Therefore, the z score for the sale price of $1,146,000 is

$$z = \frac{x - \bar{x}}{s} = \frac{1,146,000 - 106,405}{85,414} = 12.17$$

Both the Empirical Rule and Tchebysheff's theorem (Section 3.6) tell us that almost all the observations in a data set will have z scores less than 3 in absolute value. Since a z score as large as 12.17 is highly improbable, the sale price of $1,146,000 is called an outlier. Some research by the county property appraiser's office revealed that the sale price for this property was correctly recorded, but that the property was one of the few sold in 1993 in a subdivision (Avila) inhabited by the city's most wealthy residents.   ■

Another procedure for detecting outliers is to construct a **box plot** of the data. With this method, we construct intervals similar to the $\bar{x} \pm 2s$ and $\bar{x} \pm 3s$ intervals of the Empirical Rule; however, the intervals are based on a quantity called the **interquartile range** instead of the standard deviation s.

Definition 3.13

The **interquartile range**, **IQR**, is the distance between the upper and lower quartiles:

$$IQR = Q_U - Q_L$$

You can see from Figure 3.20 that the interquartile range is also a measure of data variation: The larger the interquartile range, the more variable the data tend to be.

FIGURE 3.20
The Interquartile
Range

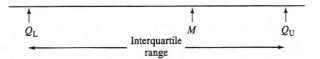

The box plot procedure is especially easy to use for small data sets because the quartiles and interquartile range can be quickly determined. We will illustrate the procedure in Example 3.16.

EXAMPLE 3.16
Outliers: Box Plot Method

Refer to the sale price data of Table 2.2. Construct a box plot for the data and check for outliers.

SOLUTION

STEP 1   Find Q_L, Q_U, and IQR. From Example 3.13, $Q_L = 650$ and $Q_U = 950$; therefore, the interquartile range for the data set is

$$IQR = Q_U - Q_L = 950 - 650 = 300$$

STEP 2   Construct a box with Q_L and Q_U located at the lower corners (see Figure 3.21, page 124). The base width will then be equal to the interquartile range.

STEP 3   Locate the **inner fences**, which lie a distance of $1.5(IQR) = 1.5(300) = 450$ below Q_L

FIGURE 3.21

A Box Plot for the
Data of Table 2.2

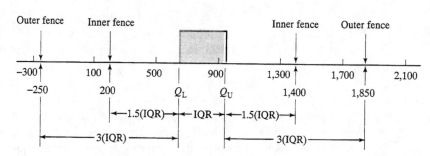

and above Q_U. These values, $Q_L - 1.5(IQR) = 650 - 450 = 200$ and $Q_U + 1.5(IQR)$
$= 950 + 450 = 1,400$, are located on the box plot shown in Figure 3.21.

STEP 4   Locate the **outer fences**, which lie a distance of $1.5(IQR) = 450$ below the lower inner
fence and above the upper inner fence. Thus, the outer fences for this data set are located at -250 and $1,850$, as indicated in Figure 3.21.

STEP 5   Observations that fall between the inner and outer fences (usually indicated by asterisks) are deemed to be **suspect outliers**. Observations falling outside the outer fences
(usually indicated by small circles) are judged **highly suspect outliers**. Checking the
data set in Table 2.2, you can see that only the observation 1,480 (representing a sale
price of $148,000) falls outside the inner fences. Since it lies between the outer
fences, it would be judged a suspect outlier and is located on the box plot with an asterisk (*).   ■

Constructing a Box Plot

1. Calculate the median, M, lower and upper quartiles, Q_L and Q_U,
   and the interquartile range, IQR, for the measurements in a data
   set.

2. Construct a box with Q_L and Q_U located at the lower corners (see
   Figure 3.21). The base width will then be equal to IQR. Draw a
   vertical line inside the box to locate the median, M.

3. Construct two sets of limits on the box plot. **Inner fences** are located a distance of $1.5(IQR)$ below Q_L and above Q_U; **outer fences**
   are located a distance of $3(IQR)$ below Q_L and Q_U (see Figure
   3.21).

4. Observations that fall between the inner and outer fences are called
   suspect outliers. Locate the suspect outliers on the box plot using
   asterisks (*). Observations that fall outside the outer fences are
   called **highly suspect outliers**. Use small circles (o) to locate
   highly suspect outliers.

For large data sets, box plots can be constructed using an available statistical computer software package. A MINITAB box plot for the data in Table 2.2 is shown in Figure 3.22. Note that Q_L and Q_U are indicated on the box plot with the symbol I (called a **hinge**). The plus (+) symbol locates the median on the box plot and the asterisk (*) identifies the suspect outlier at 1,480. To further highlight extreme values, MINITAB adds dashed lines—called **whiskers**—to the box plot of Figure 3.22. The left whisker extends to the smallest sale price in the region between Q_L and the lower inner fence, whereas the right whisker extends to the largest price in the region between Q_U and the upper inner fence.

FIGURE 3.22

MINITAB Box Plot for
the Data of Table 2.2

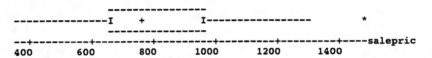

The z score and box plot methods both establish rule-of-thumb limits outside of which a measurement is deemed to be an outlier (see the accompanying box). Usually, the two methods produce similar results. However, the presence of one or more outliers in a data set can inflate the computed value of *s*. Consequently, it will be less likely that an errant observation would have a z score larger than 3 in absolute value. In contrast, the values of the quartiles used to calculate the intervals for a box plot are not affected by the presence of outliers.

Rules of Thumb for Detecting Outliers

z scores: Observations with z scores greater than 3 in absolute value are considered outliers. (For some highly skewed data sets, observations with z scores greater than 1 in absolute value may be outliers.)

Box plots: Observations falling between the inner and outer fences are deemed **suspect outliers**. Observations falling beyond the outer fence are deemed **highly suspect outliers**.

EXAMPLE 3.17
Identifying Outliers

Each county in the state of Florida negotiates an annual contract for bread to supply the county's public schools. Sealed bids are submitted by vendors, and the lowest bid (price per pound of bread) is selected as the bid winner. This process works extremely well in competitive markets, but it has the potential to increase the cost of purchasing if the markets are noncompetitive or if collusive practices are present. The latter occurred in the early 1980s in the Florida bread market. In several markets the suppliers of white bread were found guilty of "price-fixing," i.e., setting the price of bread several cents above the fair, or competitive, price.

For this example, we have obtained the winning (or low) bid prices for a random sample of 303 white-bread contracts awarded in eight geographic markets over a 6-year period in Florida. (For confidentiality, the specific years and markets are not identified.) Descriptive statistics and a histogram for the data are shown in the SAS printouts, Figures 3.23a and 3.23b.

a. Use the z score method to identify any outliers in the bid-price data.

b. Use the box plot method to identify any outliers in the bid-price data.

SOLUTION

a. The mean and standard deviation of the sample bid prices are shaded on the SAS printout, Figure 3.23a. To check for outliers we would use these values, $\bar{x} = .243$ and $s = .052$, to calculate z scores for all $n = 303$ bid prices in the data set. For the purposes of this example, we will focus only on the largest bid prices in the sample. Notice that the five highest prices are given at the bottom of the printout, Figure 3.23a, in the section titled Extremes. The z scores for these prices (corresponding to contracts #17, #303, #233, #224, and #295) are computed as follows:

$$x_{17} = .364: \quad z = \frac{.364 - .243}{.052} = 2.33$$

$$x_{303} = .375: \quad z = \frac{.375 - .243}{.052} = 2.54$$

$$x_{233} = .405: \quad z = \frac{.405 - .243}{.052} = 3.12$$

$$x_{224} = .410: \quad z = \frac{.410 - .243}{.052} = 3.21$$

$$x_{295} = .440: \quad z = \frac{.440 - .243}{.052} = 3.79$$

All five prices have z scores that exceed 2; the prices for contracts #233, #224, and #295 have z scores that exceed 3.

Which of these cutoffs, 2 or 3, should be used with this data set? Since the shape of the (horizontal) histogram shown in Figure 3.23b is mound-shaped and only slightly skewed to the high (top) side, the Empirical Rule best describes the distribution of bid prices. Thus, we expect nearly all the bid prices to fall within 3 standard deviations of the sample mean. Those falling beyond this range are considered outliers and should be investigated for cause. In this example, the bid prices corresponding to contracts #233, #224, and #295 are outliers. Further investigation of these bread contracts may reveal that they were not from the population of competitively bid prices, but were "fixed" during collusion.

FIGURE 3.23

SAS Printouts for
Example 3.17

a. Descriptive statistics for bid price data

UNIVARIATE PROCEDURE

Variable=PRICE

Moments

N	303	Sum Wgts	303
Mean	0.242777	Sum	73.56131
Std Dev	0.051701	Variance	0.002673
Skewness	0.674997	Kurtosis	0.243131
USS	18.66622	CSS	0.807249
CV	21.29577	Std Mean	0.00297
T:Mean=0	81.73874	Prob>$\|T\|$	0.0001
Sgn Rank	23028	Prob>$\|S\|$	0.0001
Num ^= 0	303		
W:Normal	0.948543	Prob<W	0.0001

Quantiles(Def=5)

100% Max	0.44	99%	0.375
75% Q3	0.2793	95%	0.328889
50% Med	0.23	90%	0.312
25% Q1	0.2052	10%	0.186667
0% Min	0.145	5%	0.173333
		1%	0.153333
Range	0.295		
Q3-Q1	0.0741		
Mode	0.2		

Extremes

Lowest	Obs	Highest	Obs
0.145(	145)	0.364(	17)
0.150267(	1)	0.375(	303)
0.153333(	288)	0.405333(	233)
0.153333(	282)	0.41(	224)
0.153333(	193)	0.44(	295)

b. Histogram and box plot for bid price data

UNIVARIATE PROCEDURE

Variable=PRICE

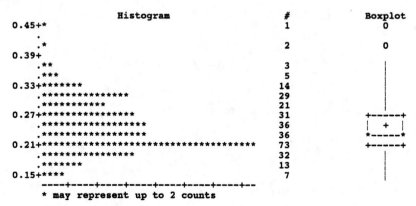

```
                    Histogram              #        Boxplot
   0.45+*                                  1           0
       .
       .*                                  2           0
   0.39+
       .**                                 3           |
       .***                                5           |
   0.33+*******                           14           |
       .**************                    29           |
       .**********                        21           |
   0.27+****************                  31        +-----+
       .*****************                 36        |  +  |
       .*****************                 36        *-----*
   0.21+*****************************************  73  +-----+
       .****************                  32           |
       .*******                           13           |
   0.15+****                               7           |
       ----+----+----+----+----+----+----+--
       * may represent up to 2 counts
```

b. A SAS box plot for the bid price data set is shown in Figure 3.23b. Like the MINITAB box plot, the plus (+) symbol locates the median bid price. However, SAS uses zeros (0) to locate suspect outliers. You can see from the box plot in Figure 3.23b that the two highest bid prices are identified as suspect outliers. ■

EXERCISES

■ *Learning the Mechanics*

3.46 Consider a sample data set with $n = 50$ observations and the following numerical descriptive measures: $Q_L = 98$, $M = 110$, and $Q_U = 122$.
 a. Find IQR.
 b. Find the inner fences of a box plot.
 c. Find the outer fences of a box plot.

3.47 Construct a box plot for the 24 sample measurements reproduced in Exercise 3.34.

3.48 Construct a box plot for the 28 sample measurements reproduced in Exercise 3.37.

■ *Applying the Concepts*

3.49 Recall that Appendix A.3 describes the per-member per-month costs of a sample of 186 physicians in a managed-care HMO. The mean and standard deviation of the costs are (from Table 3.4) $\bar{x} = \$102.96$ and $s = \$366.31$. One of the physicians in the data set had a per-member per-month cost of $4,725.10.
 a. Calculate and interpret the z score for this physician's cost. Is the observation an outlier?
 b. A careful examination of this physician's data (observation #166) reveals a total member-months value of 1. In other words, the physician treated only a single patient during a single month of the year at a cost of $4,725.10. Based on this information, how would you classify this outlier?

3.50 SPSS was used to generate descriptive statistics for the executive salary data of Exercise 3.16. The printouts are displayed here.

```
        TOTALPAY

Valid cases:      20.0   Missing cases:      .0   Percent missing:      .0


Mean      25964.70  Std Err    9572.113  Min    11278.00  Skewness    4.1251
Median    13428.50  Variance   1.83E+09  Max    203011.0  S E Skew     .5121
5% Trim   16944.72  Std Dev    42807.79  Range  191733.0  Kurtosis   17.6186
                                         IQR    3975.500  S E Kurt     .9924

Percentiles         25.0000   75.0000
HAVERAGE          11850.00   15825.50
TUKEY'S HINGES    11863.00   15736.00
```

 a. Use the information on the SPSS printout to construct a box plot for the data.
 b. Do you detect any outliers in the sample of 20 corporate executive salaries?

c. The four highest paid CEOs were removed from the data set. An SPSS box plot for the remaining 16 CEO salaries follows. Interpret the results.

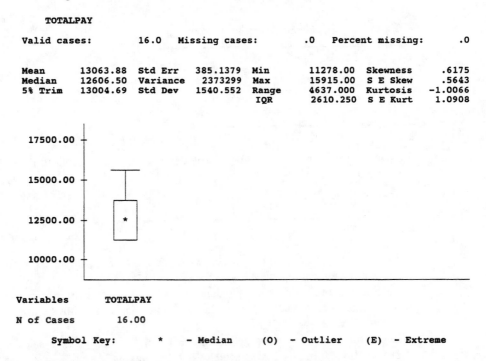

```
TOTALPAY

Valid cases:         16.0   Missing cases:      .0   Percent missing:      .0


Mean      13063.88  Std Err   385.1379  Min    11278.00  Skewness     .6175
Median    12606.50  Variance  2373299   Max    15915.00  S E Skew     .5643
5% Trim   13004.69  Std Dev   1540.552  Range  4637.000  Kurtosis   -1.0066
                                        IQR    2610.250  S E Kurt    1.0908
```

```
17500.00 -


15000.00 -


12500.00 -       *


10000.00 -
```

```
Variables      TOTALPAY

N of Cases        16.00

        Symbol Key:       *    - Median    (O)  - Outlier    (E)  - Extreme
```

3.51 Refer to the voltage reading data supplied in Exercise 3.32.
 a. Construct a box plot for the data at the old location. Do you detect any outliers?
 b. Use the method of z scores to detect outliers at the old location.
 c. Construct a box plot for the data at the new location. Do you detect any outliers?
 d. Use the method of z scores to detect outliers at the new location.
 e. Compare the distributions of voltage readings at the two locations by placing the box plots, parts **a** and **c**, side by side vertically.

3.52 Refer to the hotel no-show data of Example 3.12 and Exercise 3.43.
 a. Use the stem-and-leaf display and the results of Exercise 3.43 to form a box plot for the data.
 b. How would you classify the observations that lie between the inner and outer fences of the box plot?
 c. How would you classify the observations that lie outside the outer fences of the box plot?
 d. Use z scores to detect suspect outliers in the data. Do your results agree with the box plot? Explain.

3.53 Refer to the data on percentage change in population of U.S. counties given in Exercises 2.28 and 3.45.
 a. Use the results of Exercise 3.30 to construct a box plot for the data.
 b. Use the box plot to detect any suspect or highly suspect outliers.
 c. Are the outliers the same as those identified by using z scores?

3.54 The data in the accompanying table represent sales, in thousands of dollars per week, for a random sample of 24 fast-food outlets located in four cities.

City	Weekly Sales ($ thousands)
A	6.3, 6.6, 7.6, 3.0, 9.5, 5.9, 6.1, 5.0, 3.6
B	2.8, 6.7, 5.2
C	82.0, 5.0, 3.9, 5.4, 4.1, 3.1, 5.4
D	8.4, 9.5, 8.7, 10.6, 3.3

A computer-generated (MINITAB) box plot for the data is reproduced here.

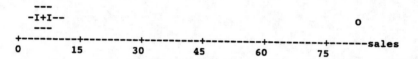

a. Examine the box plot. Do you detect any outliers? If so, identify the city and the weekly sales measurement associated with the outlier.

b. Calculate $\bar{x}$ and s for the sample data. Then use this information to compute the z score for the outlier(s) identified in part **a**. Is the result consistent with the box plot constructed in part **a**? Explain.

c. A careful check of the sales records revealed that the weekly sales value for the first fast-food outlet in city C was actually 8.2, but was incorrectly recorded as 82.0. When this recording error is corrected, the MINITAB box plot appears as shown here. Repeat parts **a** and **b** for the corrected sales data set.

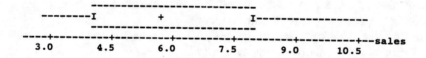

3.9 Numerical Descriptive Measures for Populations

When you analyze a sample, you are doing so for a reason. Presumably, you want to use the information in the sample to infer the nature of some larger set of data—the population. For example, we might want to know something about the complete set of 1993 property values for all properties in Tampa, Florida. If we take the value for each property to be the sale price that the owner *would have received* in 1993 (if the property had been sold), then the conceptual set of sale prices for *all* residential properties in the city would be the population of interest to us. However, most of the properties in the city *were not sold* in 1993 and, consequently, we can never obtain all the sale prices that constitute the population. We do know that the entire population of sale prices has a relative frequency distribution (the exact form of which is unknown to us), and we will want to infer the nature of this distribution based on the sample of 707 sale prices contained in Appendix A.1. It is natural that we would want to use the descriptive measures of this sample to infer the nature of the population relative frequency distribution.

Numerical descriptive measures that characterize the relative frequency distribution for a population are called **parameters**. Since we will often use numerical descriptive measures of a sample to estimate the corresponding unknown numerical descriptive measures of the population, we need to make a distinction between the numerical descriptive measure symbols for the population and for the sample.

Definition 3.14

Numerical descriptive measures (e.g., mean, median, standard deviation) of the relative frequency distribution for a population are called **parameters**.

In our previous discussion, we used the symbols $\bar{x}$ and s to denote the mean and standard deviation, respectively, of a sample of n observations. Similarly, we will use the symbol μ (mu) to denote the mean of a population and the symbol σ (sigma) to denote the standard deviation of a population. As you will subsequently see, we will use the sample mean $\bar{x}$ to estimate the population mean μ, and the sample standard deviation s to estimate the population standard deviation σ. In doing so, we will be using the sample to help us infer the nature of the population relative frequency distribution.

Sample and Population Numerical Descriptive Measures

Sample mean: $\bar{x}$	*Population mean:* μ
Sample standard deviation: s	*Population standard deviation:* σ
Sample z score: $z = \dfrac{x - \bar{x}}{s}$	*Population z score:* $z = \dfrac{x - \mu}{\sigma}$

SUMMARY

Numerical descriptive measures enable us to construct a mental image of the relative frequency distribution for a data set. The two most important types of numerical descriptive measures are those that measure *central tendency* and *data variation*.

Three numerical descriptive measures are used to locate the "center" of a relative frequency distribution: the *mean*, the *median*, and the *mode*. Each conveys a special piece of information. In a sense, the mean is the balancing point for the data. The median, which is insensitive to *out-*

liers, divides the data; half of the observations will be less than the median, and half will be larger. The mode is the value of x that occurs with greatest frequency. The mode locates the point where the relative frequency distribution achieves its maximum relative frequency.

The range and the standard deviation measure the spread of a relative frequency distribution. In particular, we can obtain a very good notion of the way data are distributed by constructing the intervals $\bar{x} \pm s$, $\bar{x} \pm 2s$, and $\bar{x} \pm 3s$ and referring to the *Empirical Rule* or *Tchebysheff's theorem*. The percentages of the total number of observations falling within these intervals will be approximately as shown in the table.

Interval	Empirical Rule (mound-shaped)	Tchebysheff's Theorem
$\bar{x} \pm s$	60% to 80%	At least 0%
$\bar{x} \pm 2s$	95%	At least 75%
$\bar{x} \pm 3s$	Almost 100%	At least 89%

Percentiles, *quartiles*, and *z scores* measure the relative position of a measurement within a data set. The *lower* and *upper quartiles* and the distance between them can also help us visualize a data set. *Box plots*, constructed from intervals based on the *interquartile range*, and *z* scores provide an easy way to detect possible outliers in the data.

KEY TERMS

Box plots
Empirical Rule
Inner and outer fences
Interquartile range
Mean
Measures of central tendency
Measures of data variation or spread

Measures of relative standing
Median
Numerical descriptive measures
Outlier
Parameter
Percentile
Quartile

Range
Resistant measure
Skewness
Standard deviation
Tchebysheff's theorem
z score

KEY SYMBOLS

For a Sample	For a Population
Mean: $\bar{x}$	Mean: μ
Variance: s^2	Variance: σ^2
Standard deviation: s	Standard deviation: σ

KEY FORMULAS

Sample mean: $\bar{x} = \dfrac{\Sigma x}{n}$

Sample variance: $s^2 = \dfrac{\Sigma(x - \bar{x})^2}{n - 1} = \dfrac{\Sigma x^2 - \dfrac{(\Sigma x)^2}{n}}{n - 1} = \dfrac{\Sigma x^2 - n(\bar{x})^2}{n - 1}$

Sample standard deviation: $s = \sqrt{s^2}$

Interquartile range: $\text{IQR} = Q_U - Q_L$

Sample z score: $z = \dfrac{x - \bar{x}}{s}$

Population z score: $z = \dfrac{x - \mu}{\sigma}$

SUPPLEMENTARY EXERCISES

3.55 Refer to the *Forbes* study of multinational corporations, Exercise 2.16. The foreign revenue (expressed as a percentage of total revenue) of the 20 U.S.-based multinational firms in the sample is listed here.

Exxon	73.2	Procter & Gamble	39.9
IBM	58.9	Philip Morris	19.6
GM	26.6	Eastman Kodak	40.9
Mobil	64.7	Digital	54.1
Ford	33.2	GE	12.4
Citicorp	52.3	United Technologies	32.9
EI duPont	39.8	Amoco	26.1
Texaco	42.3	Hewlett-Packard	53.3
ITT	43.3	Xerox	34.6
Dow Chemical	54.1	Chevron	20.5

Source: Forbes, July 23, 1990, pp. 362–363.

a. Calculate the mean of the data set. Interpret this value.
b. Calculate the median of the data set. Interpret this value.

c. Which measure of central tendency best describes the data?

d. Calculate the standard deviation of the data set. Interpret this value.

e. Comment on the relative standing of the foreign revenue of Amoco.

3.56 Laws to protect infants and children as occupants of motor vehicles, i.e., child-restraint laws, have been in effect in all 50 states since 1985. However, there is little uniformity among the laws, and in each state some children are excluded from coverage due to age, vehicle type, seating position, unregistered vehicles, etc. As part of a study to show the limiting effects of exemptions to the coverage of child-restraint laws, the number of children (0–5 years) killed in motor vehicles in each state from 1976 to 1980 was recorded and the percentage of deaths not covered due to exemptions was calculated. The state percentages are given in the table, followed by a MINITAB analysis of the data.

State	Percentage	State	Percentage	State	Percentage
AK	14	LA	37	OH	26
AL	41	MA	8	OK	17
AR	44	MD	42	OR	20
AZ	49	ME	55	PA	36
CA	27	MI	32	RI	0
CO	47	MN	36	SC	37
CT	29	MO	50	SD	37
DE	29	MS	68	TN	41
FL	15	MT	57	TX	30
GA	50	NC	76	UT	50
HI	8	ND	53	VA	47
IA	10	NE	45	VT	50
ID	46	NH	9	WA	18
IL	17	NJ	5	WI	46
IN	27	NM	40	WV	26
KS	70	NV	11	WY	60
KY	38	NY	27		

Source: Teret, S. P., Jones, A. S., Williams, A. F., and Wells, J. K. "Child restraint laws: An analysis of gaps in coverage." *American Journal of Public Health*, Vol. 76, No. 1, Jan. 1986, p. 33 (Table 3).

	N	MEAN	MEDIAN	TRMEAN	STDEV	SEMEAN
PctKill	50	35.06	37.00	34.68	17.92	2.53

	MIN	MAX	Q1	Q3
PctKill	0.00	76.00	19.50	47.50

a. Locate and interpret the measures of central tendency shown on the printout.

b. Locate and interpret the measures of variation shown on the printout.

c. Calculate the proportion of states with percentages falling within 1 standard deviation of the mean.

d. Calculate the proportion of states with percentages falling within 2 standard deviations of the mean.

e. Calculate the proportion of states with percentages falling within 3 standard deviations of the mean.

f. Which rule, Tchebysheff's theorem or the Empirical Rule, best describes the distribution of state percentages of child motor vehicle deaths?

3.57 According to one study, "The majority of people who die from fire and smoke in compartmentalized fire-resistive buildings—the type used for hotels, motels, apartments, and other health-care facilities—die in the attempt to evacuate" (*Risk Management*, Feb. 1986). The accompanying data represent the numbers of victims who attempted to evacuate for a sample of 14 recent fires at compartmentalized fire-resistive buildings reported in the study.

Fire	Number of Victims
Las Vegas Hilton (Las Vegas)	5
Inn on the Park (Toronto)	5
Westchase Hilton (Houston)	8
Holiday Inn (Cambridge, Ohio)	10
Conrad Hilton (Chicago)	4
Providence College (Providence)	8
Baptist Towers (Atlanta)	7
Howard Johnson (New Orleans)	5
Cornell University (Ithaca, New York)	9
Wesport Central Apartments (Kansas City, Missouri)	4
Orrington Hotel (Evanston, Illinois)	0
Hartford Hospital (Hartford, Connecticut)	16
Milford Plaza (New York)	0
MGM Grand (Las Vegas)	36

Source: Macdonald, J. N. "Is evacuation a fatal flaw in fire fighting philosophy?" *Risk Management*, Vol. 33, No. 2, Feb. 1986, p. 37.

a. Construct a stem-and-leaf display for the data.
b. Compute the mean, median, and mode for the data set. Which measure of central tendency appears to best describe the center of the distribution of data?
c. Compute the range, variance, and standard deviation for the data set. Which measure of variation is most useful for describing the data?
d. The MGM Grand fire in Las Vegas was treated separately in the *Risk Management* analysis because of the size of the high-rise hotel and other unique factors. Do the data support treating the MGM Grand fire deaths differently from the other measurements in the sample? Explain.

3.58 Refer to the *Quarterly Review of Economics & Business* (Autumn 1989) study of $n = 972$ individual investors and their investment portfolios, Exercise 2.32. Two quantitative variables of interest to the researchers were $x_1 =$ dollar value of portfolio and $x_2 =$ number of securities held by each of the 972 investors. Descriptive statistics for the two variables follow.

	Mean	Standard Deviation	Minimum	Maximum
Dollar value of portfolio, x_1	$35,007	$64,699	$21.25	$1,801,000
Number of securities held, x_2	7,715	7,046	1.00	60

Source: Krehbiel, T. L., and McCarthy, P. "An analysis of the determinants of portfolio selection." *Quarterly Review of Economics & Business,* Vol. 29, No. 3, 1989, p. 46.

a. Give an interval of x_1 values within which most of the investors fall.
b. Give an interval of x_2 values within which most of the investors fall.

3.59 It is well known that worker absenteeism is costly and leads to decreased production efficiency at most firms. A study was conducted to investigate employee absenteeism at a medium-size assembly and packaging plant in Great Britain (*Journal of Occupational Psychology*, 1985). Workers in each of three departments—packaging, assembly, and maintenance—were monitored over a 2-year period and the number of days of unanticipated absences due to sickness was recorded each week. The accompanying table gives the mean and standard deviation of number of days absent per 1,000 employees for each department.

	Packaging Department	Assembly Department	Maintenance Department
Mean number of days per 1,000 employees	39.24	17.38	14.56
Standard deviation	9.88	5.16	6.88

Source: Moch, M. K., and Fitzgibbons, D. E. "The relationship between absenteeism and production efficiency: An empirical assessment." *Journal of Occupational Psychology,* Vol. 58, 1985, pp. 39–47.

a. Use the information in the table to sketch your mental images of the three relative frequency distributions. Construct them on the same graph so that you can see how they appear relative to each other.
b. Estimate the proportion of weeks in which between 19.48 and 59.00 days of unanticipated absences per 1,000 workers occur in the packaging department.
c. In a typical week, how many days of unanticipated absences per 1,000 workers would you expect to occur in the assembly department?
d. Repeat part **c** for the maintenance department.

3.60 One way in which stock market analysts measure the price volatility of an individual stock relative to the market is to compute the stock's *beta value*. Beta values greater than 1 indicate that the stock's price has changed faster than the average market price, whereas beta values less than 1 indicate that the stock's price has changed slower than the average market price. The accompanying table lists the ticker abbreviations and beta values for a recent sample of 25 Standard & Poor's 500 stocks.

Ticker	Beta	Ticker	Beta	Ticker	Beta
AL	1.489	JCP	.561	TL	1.137
BX	.987	KO	.548	UPJ	.951
CMK	.746	LIT	1.502	VO	1.317
DOC	1.220	MAT	1.662	WEN	1.731
ECH	.907	NSM	2.014	WIN	.196
FNC	.859	PRD	1.358	XON	.980
GS	.722	REV	.879	ZE	1.304
HIA	1.736	S	.688		
ID	1.187	T	.132		

a. Calculate $\bar{x}$, s^2, and s for the 25 beta values. How many beta values lie within the interval $\bar{x} \pm 2s$? Does this result agree with the Empirical Rule?

b. Calculate the median. Interpret this value.

c. Find the 80th percentile of the 25 beta values.

d. The ticker abbreviation S represents Sears & Roebuck stock. Find the z score of the beta value for Sears & Roebuck. Interpret this value.

3.61 *Scram* is the term used by nuclear engineers to describe a rapid emergency shutdown of a nuclear reactor. The nuclear industry has made a concerted effort to significantly reduce the number of unplanned scrams. The accompanying table gives the number of scrams at each of 56 U.S. nuclear reactor units in a recent year. A MINITAB printout showing both a graphical and numerical description of the data is also provided on page 138.

Number of Scrams

1	0	3	1	4	2	10	6	5	2	0	3	1	5
4	2	7	12	0	3	8	2	0	9	3	3	4	7
2	4	5	3	2	7	13	4	2	3	3	7	0	9
4	3	5	2	7	8	5	2	4	3	4	0	1	7

a. Fully interpret the results.

b. Would you expect to observe a nuclear reactor in the future with 11 unplanned scrams? Explain.

c. Suppose the data for nuclear reactors with 12 and 13 scrams were omitted from the analysis. Would you expect $\bar{x}$ to increase or decrease? Would you expect s to increase or decrease?

d. Recalculate $\bar{x}$ and s, excluding the observations 12 and 13. Compare these results with your answer to part **c**.

```
Stem-and-leaf of SCRAMS    N  = 56
Leaf Unit = 0.10

    6      0  000000
   10      1  0000
   19      2  000000000
  (10)     3  0000000000
   27      4  00000000
   19      5  00000
   14      6  0
   13      7  000000
    7      8  00
    5      9  00
    3     10  0
    2     11
    2     12  0
    1     13  0
```

```
                    ----------------
          --------I    +       I--------------------      *    *
                    ----------------
          +----------+----------+----------+----------+----------+------SCRAMS
        0.0        2.5        5.0        7.5       10.0       12.5
```

	N	MEAN	MEDIAN	TRMEAN	STDEV	SEMEAN
SCRAMS	56	4.036	3.000	3.820	3.027	0.404

	MIN	MAX	Q1	Q3
SCRAMS	0.000	13.000	2.000	5.750

3.62 To qualify for college, high school graduates must take and pass either one of two approved college entrance examinations: the Scholastic Aptitude Test (SAT) or the American College Test (ACT). Five high school graduates have applied to your university or college. Three completed the SAT and two completed the ACT. Scores on the SAT have a mean of 850 and a standard deviation of 100, whereas scores on the ACT have a mean of 18 and a standard deviation of 2. The applicants' scores are listed in the table.

Applicant	Exam Taken	Score
1	SAT	915
2	SAT	815
3	SAT	780
4	ACT	20
5	ACT	17

a. Find the respective z scores for each of the applicants.

b. If the five applicants are ranked from highest to lowest entirely on the basis of entrance exam score *in relation to the type of exam taken* (highest score receiving rank 1, and so forth), which applicant would have the highest rank? The lowest? [*Hint:* Use your results from part **a**.]

3.63 The variation of the rates of return on a bond is often used to measure the level of risk associated with buying the bond—the greater the variation, the higher the level of risk. The accompanying table presents a portion of the results of a simulation study to compare the performance of zero-coupon bonds (those for which the interest coupons have been removed and therefore pay no interest) to bonds with coupon payments attached. The rates of return on zero-coupon bonds are determined solely by the changes in bond prices, whereas the return on coupon bonds depends also on the market interest rate. The simulation study yielded means and standard deviations of the rates of return for both zero-coupon and coupon bonds at a fixed interest rate. The results for a market interest rate of 14% are shown in the table.

	Zero-Coupon Bonds	*Coupon-Attached Bonds*
Mean	12.48%	12.48%
Standard deviation	20.80%	14.56%

Source: Potter, T. "Your finances." *American Bar Association Journal*, Aug. 1984.
Reprinted with permission from the ABA Journal, The Lawyer's Magazine.

a. Use the Empirical Rule to sketch the relative frequency distributions for the rates of return of both zero-coupon bonds and coupon-attached bonds.

b. Compute the z score for a zero-coupon bond with a rate of return of −20%. Interpret this value.

c. Compute the z score for a coupon-attached bond with a rate of return of −20%. Interpret this value.

3.64   Refer to the Customer Satisfaction Index, Exercise 2.20. Recall that the index is designed to measure customer satisfaction with new automobiles and automakers. (An index of 100 is considered average, with ratings above 100 considered above average, and ratings below 100 considered below average in terms of overall customer satisfaction.) The data are reproduced in the table.

Auto (Manufacturer)	Foreign (F) or Domestic (D)	Customer Satisfaction Index
Lexus (Toyota)	F	179
Infiniti (Nissan)	F	167
Saturn (GM)	D	160
Acura (Honda)	F	148
Mercedes-Benz	F	145
Toyota	F	144
Audi (VW)	F	139
Cadillac (GM)	D	138
Honda	F	138
Jaguar (Ford)	D	137

Source: J. D. Powers and Associates, 1992. Customer Satisfaction Study.

a. Calculate the mean satisfaction rating for the 10 automakers listed in the table.
b. Calculate the median satisfaction rating for the 10 automakers listed in the table.
c. Calculate the standard deviation of the satisfaction ratings.
d. Find the 90th percentile of the satisfaction ratings.
e. Find the z score for Cadillac. Interpret this value.
f. Calculate the mean satisfaction rating of the seven foreign automakers in the sample. Compare this value to the mean for the three domestic automakers. Does it appear that customers are more satisfied with foreign than with domestic automakers? [*Note:* We discuss a more formal statistical technique for comparing the two means in Chapter 11.]

3.65 Industrial engineers periodically conduct "work measurement" analyses to determine the time used to produce a single unit of output. At a large processing plant, the total number of man-hours required per day to perform a certain task was recorded for 50 days. This information will be used in a work measurement analysis. The total number of man-hours required for each of the 50 days is listed here, accompanied by a SAS printout (page 141) summarizing and describing the data.

128	119	95	97	124	113	109	124	132	97
146	128	103	135	114	124	131	133	131	88
100	112	111	150	117	128	142	98	108	120
138	133	136	120	112	109	100	111	131	113
118	116	98	112	138	122	97	116	92	122

a. Locate the mean, median, and mode of the data set on the printout and interpret their values.
b. Locate the range, variance, and standard deviation of the data set on the printout, and interpret their values.
c. Construct the intervals $\bar{x} \pm s$, $\bar{x} \pm 2s$, and $\bar{x} \pm 3s$. Count the number of observations that fall within each interval and find the corresponding proportions. Compare the results to the Empirical Rule. Do you detect any outliers?
d. Examine the box plot for the data shown on the printout. Do you detect any outliers?
e. Locate the 90th percentile for the data on the printout, and interpret its value.

3.66 The notion of using the Empirical Rule and the interval $\bar{x} \pm 2s$ to detect outliers is well documented in business and industry. In the 1960s, a beverage company was one of the first to apply the procedure to determine whether to conduct a search for specific causes of consumer complaints. (Consumer complaints primarily concerned chipped bottles that looked dangerous.) For one of the firm's brands, the complaint rate was known to have a mound-shaped distribution with a mean of 26.01 per 10,000 bottles sold and a standard deviation of 11.28 when the bottling process was operating properly (*Journal of Marketing Research*, Aug. 1964). The complaint rate observed during a later 2-week period was 93.12 complaints per 10,000 bottles sold.

a. Compute the z score for the observed rate of 93.12.
b. Give a general interpretation of the z value computed in part **a**.
c. Use the Empirical Rule to determine whether the observed rate is due to chance or whether

SAS Printout for Exercise 3.65

UNIVARIATE PROCEDURE

Variable=MANHOURS

Moments

N	50	Sum Wgts	50
Mean	117.82	Sum	5891
Std Dev	15.01114	Variance	225.3343
Skewness	0.00906	Kurtosis	-0.69123
USS	705119	CSS	11041.38
CV	12.74074	Std Mean	2.122896
T:Mean=0	55.49967	Prob>$\|T\|$	0.0001
Sgn Rank	637.5	Prob>$\|S\|$	0.0001
Num ^= 0	50		

Quantiles(Def=5)

100% Max	150	99%	150
75% Q3	131	95%	142
50% Med	117.5	90%	137
25% Q1	109	10%	97
0% Min	88	5%	95
		1%	88
Range	62		
Q3-Q1	22		
Mode	97		

Extremes

Lowest	Obs	Highest	Obs
88(	44)	138(	7)
92(	40)	138(	49)
95(	21)	142(	16)
97(	42)	146(	3)
97(	31)	150(	35)

```
Stem Leaf                        #        Boxplot
  15 0                           1           |
  14 26                          2           |
  13 1112335688                 10        +-----+
  12 0022444888                 10        |     |
  11 1122233466789              13        *--+--*
  10 003899                      6        +-----+
   9 2577788                     7           |
   8 8                           1           |
     ----+----+----+----+
Multiply Stem.Leaf by 10**+1
```

it is due to some specific cause. (In actuality, a search for a possible problem in the bottling process led to a discovery of rough handling of the bottled beverage in the warehouse by newly hired workers. As a result, a training program for new workers was instituted.)

3.67 A unique approach to determining the cost of a firm's common equity capital was investigated (*Journal of Business Research*, Mar. 1980). The methodology of this approach depends on the shareholders' perceptions of growth rates for (1) the firm's common stock price, (2) cash dividends per share, and (3) earnings per share. (The growth rate, defined over a 10–15-year period, is the average percentage at which the firm's common stock price, cash dividends, and earnings per share *increase* each year.) The data in the table at the top of page 142 summarize the growth rate estimates (percentages) of the 229 shareholders of Apex Industries, Inc. (a pseudonym) for each of the three categories defined.

Item	Mean	Standard Deviation
Common stock price	16.82	13.64
Cash dividends per share	16.17	20.76
Earnings per share	28.29	23.46

Source: Scott, D. F., Jr., Petty, J. W., and Shepherd, C. W. "Determining the cost of common equity capital: The direct method." *Journal of Business Research*, Mar. 1980, 8, pp. 89–103.

a. Construct the interval $\bar{x} \pm 2s$ for each of the three Apex stock items. (A negative growth rate implies an annual decrease in the stock item.)

b. Assume that the estimated growth rate for each item has a relative frequency distribution that is nearly mound-shaped. Approximate the proportion of the measurements that fall within the interval $\bar{x} \pm 2s$ for each of the three data sets.

c. Considering the wide range of the intervals you computed in part **a**, would you feel comfortable using the mean projected growth rate of the sample to estimate the true growth rate for each of the respective stock items? Is it possible that the sample mean projected growth rates could lead to poor cost of capital estimates? [*Note:* We give a detailed discussion on the reliability of the sample mean as an estimate of the population mean in Chapters 8 and 9.]

3.68 Refer to the *U.S. News & World Report* survey of the top 25 graduate business schools, Exercises 3.11 and 3.38. An ASP analysis of the out-of-state tuition costs for the data set is shown in the accompanying printout. Completely interpret the results.

```
                       SUMMARY STATISTICS

                               Tuition
                         ----------------
                 Mean =  16045.1
              Maximum =  19500
              Minimum =   6452
                Range =  13048
    Valid Observations =     25
       Missing Values =      0
   Sample Standard Dev. =  4028.49
       Sample Variance =     1.62287E7
   Sample Coef. Of Var. =     0.251072
  Standard Error Of Mean =    805.697
               Median =  18200
        First Quartile =  14227
        Third Quartile =  18780
    Interquartile Range =   4553
   Lower Adjacent Value =   8192
   Upper Adjacent Value =  19500
        Minor Outliers =      1
        Major Outliers =      0
    Standard Deviation =   3947.09
             Variance =     1.55796E7
    Coefficient Of Var. =     0.246
                  Sum = 401128
         Sum Of Squares =     6.82564E9
     Sum Of Squared Dev. =     3.89489E8
         Second Moment =     1.55796E7
          Third Moment =    -7.21444E10
         Fourth Moment =     7.11096E14
  Coefficient Of Skewness =   0.234639
  Coefficient Of Kurtosis =   2.92967
```

(continued)

STEM AND LEAF PLOT

VARIABLE: Tuition

STEM AND LEAF PLOT   OF (ROUNDED) Tuition (*10^-2):
```
 6|5
 7|
 8|27
 9|
10|6
11|2
12|0
13|
14|2
15|7
16|
17|0255
18|25556888
19|02335
    TOTAL = 25
```

BOX AND WHISKER PLOT

VARIABLE: Tuition

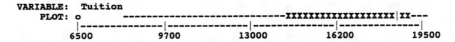

```
    PLOT: o        ---------------------------XXXXXXXXXXXXXXXXXX|XX---
          |---------------|---------------|---------------|---------------|
          6500            9700            13000           16200           19500
```

■ CASE STUDY 3.1

Are CEOs Really Worth Their Pay?

In Case Study 1.1, we described the data in *Business Week*'s 1994 Executive Compensation Scoreboard (Appendix A.2). Recall that the scoreboard attempts to determine which of the 360 chief executive officers (CEOs) in the survey are worth their pay by computing the ratio of total shareholder return (measured by the dollar value of a $100 investment in the company made 3 years earlier) to total executive pay (in thousands of dollars) over the same 3-year period. The lower the return-to-pay ratio, the less likely the CEO is worth his pay to prospective investors in the firm.

The CEOs in the 1990 scoreboard are categorized by nine industry groups as follows: industrial high-tech, industrial low-tech, consumer products, financial, transportation, telecommunications, services, utilities, and resources. The objective of this case study is to make pay-for-performance comparisons of executives within industry groups.

An ASP printout describing the return-to-pay ratios of CEOs in the industrial high-tech (IHT) industry group is displayed in Figure 3.24. Parts **a–f** refer to this printout.

a. Find and interpret the measures of central tendency given on the printout.

b. Find and interpret the measures of variation given on the printout.

c. Find and interpret the measures of relative standing given on the printout.

d. Is the distribution of return-to-pay ratios for industrial high-tech CEOs better described by the Empirical Rule or Tchebysheff's theorem? Explain.

e. Do you detect any outliers in the data set? If so, identify them.

f. Identify the CEOs that fall below the 10th percentile of return-to-pay ratios for the industrial high-tech group.

Now select one of the other eight industry groups in Appendix A.2 and answer the following questions: [*Note:* The data of Appendix A.2 are available on a $3\frac{1}{2}''$ diskette from the publisher.]

g. Construct a stem-and-leaf display of the shareholder return-to-pay ratios. Is the distribution best described by the Empirical Rule or Tchebysheff's theorem?

h. Calculate the mean, median, and mode of the shareholder return-to-pay ratios. Which measure of central tendency best describes the center of the distribution?

i. Calculate the range, variance, and standard deviation of the shareholder return-to-pay ratios.

j. Use your answers to parts **g–i** to estimate the percentage of return-to-pay ratios that fall within 2 standard deviations of the mean.

k. Calculate the actual percentage of return-to-pay ratios that fall within 2 standard deviations of the mean. Compare the results with your answer to part **j**.

l. Identify any outliers in the return-to-pay ratio distribution using z scores.

m. Repeat part **l** using box plots. Compare the results of the two approaches.

n. Delete any outliers identified in parts **l–m** from the data set. Then repeat parts **g–i**. Which measure of central tendency is most affected by the deletion of outliers? Which measure of variation?

FIGURE 3.24

Return-to-Pay Ratio
Descriptive Statistics
for Industrial High-
Tech CEOs

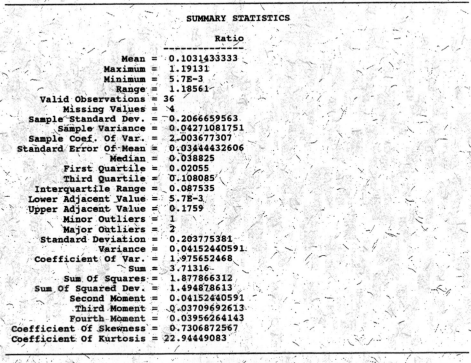

```
                            SUMMARY STATISTICS

                                Ratio
                            ------------
                 Mean =   0.1031433333
              Maximum =   1.19131
              Minimum =   5.7E-3
                Range =   1.18561
    Valid Observations =   36
        Missing Values =   4
   Sample Standard Dev. =   0.2066659563
        Sample Variance =   0.04271081751
    Sample Coef. Of Var. =   2.003677307
  Standard Error Of Mean =   0.03444432606
                 Median =   0.038825
          First Quartile =   0.02055
          Third Quartile =   0.108085
     Interquartile Range =   0.087535
    Lower Adjacent Value =   5.7E-3
    Upper Adjacent Value =   0.1759
          Minor Outliers =   1
          Major Outliers =   2
      Standard Deviation =   0.203775381
               Variance =   0.04152440591
       Coefficient Of Var. =   1.975652468
                   Sum =   3.71316
           Sum Of Squares =   1.877866312
       Sum Of Squared Dev. =   1.494878613
           Second Moment =   0.04152440591
            Third Moment =   0.03709692613
           Fourth Moment =   0.03956264143
    Coefficient Of Skewness =   0.7306872567
    Coefficient Of Kurtosis =   22.94449083
```

```
                            STEM AND LEAF PLOT

VARIABLE:  Ratio
MAJOR OUTLIERS ARE EXCLUDED FROM PLOT

STEM AND LEAF PLOT OF (ROUNDED) Ratio (*10^2):
0 111111
0 2222223333
0 44455
0 667
0 99
1 111
1 23
1 5
1
1 8
2
2
2 5
2
2

    TOTAL = 34
```

```
                            BOX AND WHISKER PLOT

VARIABLE:  Ratio
    PLOT:  -X|XX----    o           o                                 o
        |----------|----------|----------|----------|
        0.01       0.3        0.6        0.89       1.19
```

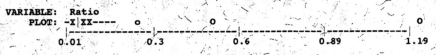

■ CASE STUDY 3.2

Bid Collusion in the Highway Contracting Industry

Many products and services are purchased by governments, cities, states, and businesses on the basis of competitive bids, and frequently contracts are awarded to the lowest bidders. As we learned in Example 3.17, such a process is prone to price-fixing or bid collusion by the bidders. Recall that price-fixing involves setting the bid price above the fair, or competitive, price to increase profit margin.

Numerous methods exist for detecting the possibility of collusive practices among bidders. According to Rothrock and McClave (1979), these procedures involve the detection of significant departures from normal market conditions, such as (1) systematic rotation of the winning bid, (2) stable market shares over time, (3) geographic market divisions, (4) lack of relationship between delivery costs and bid levels, (5) high degree of uniformity and stability in bid levels over time, and (6) presence of a baseline point pricing scheme.[*]

In this case study, we examine a data set collected during the late 1970s and early 1980s involving road construction contracts in the state of Florida. During this time period, the Office of the Florida Attorney General (FLAG) suspected numerous contractors of practicing bid collusion. The investigations led to an admission of guilt by several of the contractors. Although these contractors were heavily fined, they avoided harsher punishment by identifying which road construction contracts were competitively bid and which involved fixed bids. By comparing the bid prices (and other important bid variables) of the fixed contracts to the competitive contracts, the Florida attorney general was able to establish invaluable benchmarks for detecting bid-rigging in the future. (In fact, the benchmarks led to a virtual elimination of bid-rigging in road construction in the state.)

Appendix A.6 describes FLAG's data for 279 road construction contracts. For each contract, the following variables were measured:

1. Price of contract ($) bid by lowest bidder
2. Department of Transportation (DOT) engineer's estimate of fair contract price ($)
3. Ratio of low (winning) bid price to DOT engineer's estimate of fair price
4. Status (fixed or competitive) of contract
5. District in which construction project is located
6. Number of bidders on contract
7. Estimated number of days to complete work
8. Length of road project (miles)
9. Percentage of costs allocated to liquid asphalt
10. Percentage of costs allocated to base material
11. Percentage of costs allocated to excavation
12. Percentage of costs allocated to mobilization
13. Percentage of costs allocated to structures
14. Percentage of costs allocated to traffic control
15. Subcontractor utilization (yes or no)

For this case study, we focus on the quantitative variable LBERATIO (ratio of low-bid price to DOT estimate of fair price). Theoretically, the ratio will be near 1 for competitive bids. The larger the ratio, the more evidence that an unusually high bid (and possibly price-fixing) has occurred.

a. Of the 279 contracts, 194 were competitively bid and 85 were fixed (i.e., involved some type of bid collusion). Descriptive statistics for both sets of contracts are provided in the SAS printouts in Figure 3.25 (competitive) and Figure 3.26 (fixed) (page 148). In addition, side-by-side box plots for the two sets of contracts are shown in Figure 3.27 (page 149). Use the methods of this chapter to an-

---

[*] Rothrock, T. P., and McClave, J. T. "An analysis of bidding competition in the Florida school bidding competition using a statistical model." Paper presented at the TIMS/ORSA Joint National Meeting, Chicago, 1979.

alyze the road construction contract data. In particular, comment on the belief that fixed bids result in higher ratios of low-bid price to DOT estimate than competitively bid contracts.

b. The DOT divides the state of Florida into five different districts based on geographic location. Suppose you are hired by the DOT to compare the ratios of low-bid price to DOT estimate for the five districts. Perform an analysis of LBERATIO (similar to that of part a) by district. [*Note:* The data of Appendix A.6 are available on $3\frac{1}{2}''$ diskette from the publisher.]

FIGURE 3.25

Descriptive Statistics for Competitive Contracts

```
------------------------------ STATUS = COMPET ------------------------------
                         UNIVARIATE PROCEDURE
        Variable=LBERATIO       LOW BID/ESTIMATE(DOT) RATIO
                              Moments

                   N            194  Sum Wgts          194
                   Mean     0.907248  Sum          176.0062
                   Std Dev  0.136927  Variance     0.018749
                   Skewness 0.034461  Kurtosis    -0.918657
                   USS      163.2998  CSS           3.61855
                   CV       15.09254  Std Mean     0.009831
                   T:Mean=0 92.28655  Prob>|T|       0.0001
                   Sgn Rank   9457.5  Prob>|S|       0.0001
                   Num ^= 0      194
                   W:Normal 0.978221  Prob<W         0.2297

                           Quantiles(Def=5)

           100% Max   1.350088         99%   1.302152
            75% Q3     0.99483         95%   1.120844
            50% Med   0.913298         90%   1.054544
            25% Q1    0.820453         10%   0.754458
             0% Min   0.532556          5%   0.669066
                                        1%   0.559258
           Range      0.817532
           Q3-Q1      0.174377
           Mode       0.532556

                             Extremes

           Lowest     Obs       Highest      Obs
           0.532556(   24)      1.209417(    16)
           0.559258(   20)      1.239872(   100)
           0.561543(   35)      1.285623(   115)
           0.564582(   15)      1.302152(   164)
           0.569583(   54)      1.350088(   157)


       Stem Leaf                              #       Boxplot
         13 5                                 1          0
         13 0                                 1          0
         12 9                                 1          0
         12 14                                2          |
         11 677                               3          |
         11 01123                             5          |
         10 5555666889                       10          |
         10 0000000112222233334444444        25          |
          9 555566667777778888888899999      27      +-----+
          9 00111111112222222233333334444    29      *--+--*
          8 5555556666666677777777788888999  31      +-----+
          8 00000011111112222222333344       26      +-----+
          7 5556677788999999                 16          |
          7 013444                            6          |
          6 677                               3          |
          6 24                                2          |
          5 66679                             5          |
          5 3                                 1          0
         ----+----+----+----+----+----+----+-
       Multiply Stem.Leaf by 10**-1
```

FIGURE 3.26

Descriptive Statistics
for Fixed Contracts

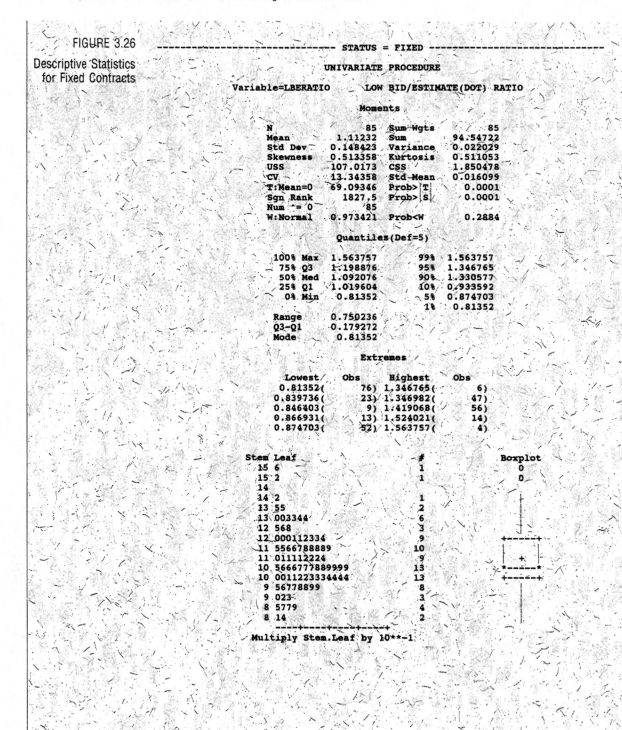

```
------------------------------ STATUS = FIXED ------------------------------
                            UNIVARIATE PROCEDURE

      Variable=LBERATIO       LOW BID/ESTIMATE(DOT) RATIO

                                Moments

              N            85   Sum Wgts           85
              Mean      1.11232  Sum          94.54722
              Std Dev  0.148423  Variance     0.022029
              Skewness 0.513358  Kurtosis     0.511053
              USS      107.0173  CSS          1.850478
              CV       13.34358  Std Mean     0.016099
              T:Mean=0 69.09346  Prob>|T|       0.0001
              Sgn Rank   1827.5  Prob>|S|       0.0001
              Num ^= 0       85
              W:Normal 0.973421  Prob<W         0.2884

                            Quantiles(Def=5)

              100% Max  1.563757    99%    1.563757
               75% Q3   1.198876    95%    1.346765
               50% Med  1.092076    90%    1.330577
               25% Q1   1.019604    10%    0.933592
                0% Min   0.81352     5%    0.874703
                                     1%     0.81352

              Range    0.750236
              Q3-Q1    0.179272
              Mode      0.81352

                                Extremes

              Lowest     Obs       Highest     Obs
              0.81352(    76)   1.346765(      6)
              0.839736(   23)   1.346982(     47)
              0.846403(    9)   1.419068(     56)
              0.866931(   13)   1.524021(     14)
              0.874703(   52)   1.563757(      4)


     Stem Leaf                        #     Boxplot
      15 6                            1        0
      15 2                            1        0
      14
      14 2                            1
      13 55                           2        |
      13 003344                       6        |
      12 568                          3        |
      12 000112334                    9     +-----+
      11 5566788889                  10     |     |
      11 011112224                    9     |     |
      10 5666777889999               13     *--+--*
      10 0011223334444               13     +-----+
       9 56778899                     8        |
       9 023                          3        |
       8 5779                         4        |
       8 14                           2        |
         ----+----+----+----+
     Multiply Stem.Leaf by 10**-1
```

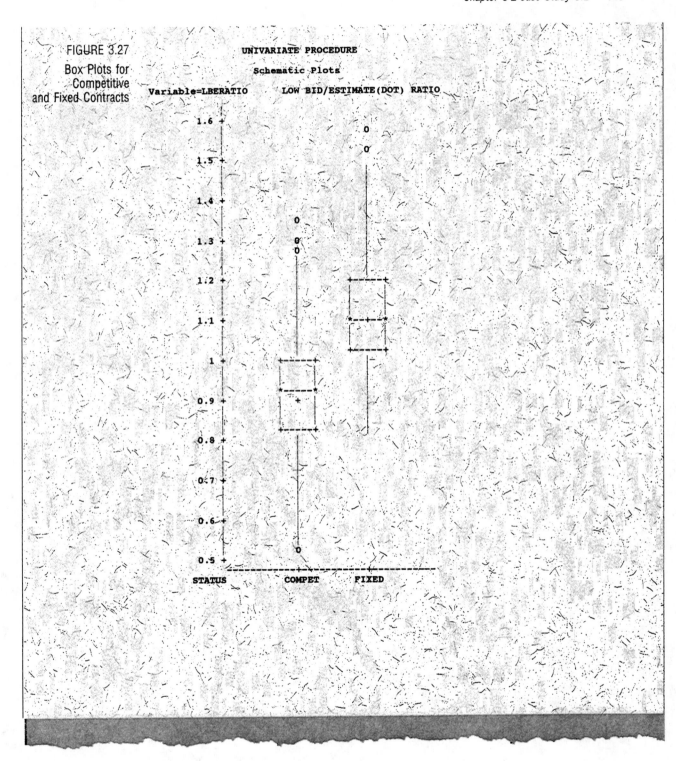

FIGURE 3.27

Box Plots for Competitive and Fixed Contracts

UNIVARIATE PROCEDURE

Schematic Plots

Variable=LBERATIO   LOW BID/ESTIMATE(DOT) RATIO

Chapter 4

PROBABILITY: BASIC CONCEPTS

How would you like to win a state lottery (Case Study 4.1) or choose the grand prize on "Let's Make a Deal" (Case Study 4.2)? What does each of these ventures have to do with statistics? The answer is **uncertainty**. The return in real dollars on most investments cannot be predicted with certainty. Neither can we be certain that an inference about a population, based on the partial information contained in a sample, will be correct. In this chapter, we learn how probability can be used to measure uncertainty, and we take a brief glimpse at its role in assessing the reliability of statistical inferences.

■ CONTENTS

4.1 The Role of Probability in Statistics

If you play blackjack, a popular gambling game, you know that whether you win in any one game is an outcome that is very uncertain. Similarly, investing in bonds, stock, or a new business is a venture whose success is subject to uncertainty.

Much like playing blackjack and investing, making inferences based on sample data is also subject to uncertainty. A sample rarely tells a perfectly accurate story about the population from which it was selected. There is always a margin of error (as the pollsters tell us) when sample data are used to estimate the proportion of people in favor of a particular political candidate, some consumer product, or some political or social issue. There is always uncertainty about how far the sample estimate will depart from the true population proportion of affirmative answers that you are attempting to estimate. Consequently, a <u>measure of the amount of uncertainty</u> associated with an estimate (which we called the **reliability of an inference** in Chapter 1) plays a major role in statistical inference.

How do we measure the uncertainty associated with events? Anyone who has observed a daily newscast can answer that question. The answer is **probability**. For example, it may be reported that the probability of rain on a given day is 20%. Such a statement acknowledges that it is uncertain whether it will rain on the given day and indicates that the forecaster measures the likelihood of its occurrence as 20%. (We give a formal definition of probability in the next section.)

Probability also plays an important role in decision making. To illustrate, suppose you have an opportunity to invest in an oil exploration company. Past records show that for 10 out of 10 previous oil drillings (a sample of the company's experiences), all 10 resulted in dry wells. What do you conclude? Do you think the chances are better than 50–50 that the company will hit a producing well? Should you invest in this company? We think your answer to these questions will be an emphatic "no." If the company's exploratory prowess is sufficient to hit a producing well 50% of the time, a record of 10 dry wells out of 10 drilled is an event that is just too improbable. Do you agree?

In this chapter, we examine the meaning of probability and develop some basic properties of probability that will be useful in our study of statistics.

4.2 Experiments, Events, and the Probability of an Event

In the language employed in a study of probability, the word *experiment* has a very broad meaning. In this language, an **experiment** is the process of making an observation or taking a measurement on the experimental unit. For example, suppose you are dealt a single card from a standard 52-card bridge deck. Observing the outcome (i.e., the number and suit of the card) could be viewed as an experiment. Counting the number of defective light bulbs produced per hour in a manufacturing process is an experiment. Similarly, recording the annual sales of a corporation is an experiment. Observing the annual average inflation rate is an experiment. Note that most experiments result in outcomes (or measurements) that cannot be predicted with certainty in advance.

Definition 4.1

The process of making an observation or taking a measurement on one or more experimental units is called an **experiment**.

EXAMPLE 4.1
Listing Outcomes

Consider the following experiment. You are dealt one card from a standard 52-card bridge deck. List some possible outcomes of this experiment that cannot be predicted with certainty in advance.

SOLUTION Some possible outcomes of this experiment that cannot be predicted with certainty in advance are as follows (see Figure 4.1):

a. You draw an ace of hearts.   **b.** You draw an 8 of diamonds.
c. You draw a spade.   **d.** You do not draw a spade.

FIGURE 4.1

Possible Outcomes of
Card-Drawing
Experiment,
Example 4.1

a.　　　　　　　b.　　　　　　　c.　　　　　　　d.　　　■

EXAMPLE 4.2
Listing Outcomes

Consider the following experiment. A sample of 500 is selected from among a large number of homeowners to determine the proportion who own a personal computer (PC) for their home use. The response of each of the homeowners is recorded. List some possible outcomes of this experiment that cannot be predicted with certainty in advance.

SOLUTION Since we are observing the responses of 500 homeowners (where homeowners are the experimental units), this experiment can result in a very large number of outcomes. Three of the many possible outcomes are listed here:

a. Exactly 287 of the 500 homeowners own a PC.
b. Exactly 100 own a PC.
c. A particular homeowner, the Jones family, owns a PC.

Clearly, we could define many other outcomes of this experiment that cannot be predicted in advance. ■

In the language of probability theory, outcomes of experiments are called **events**.

Definition 4.2

Outcomes of experiments are called **events**. [*Note*: To simplify our discussion, we will use italic capital letters, *A, B, C,* ..., to denote specific events.]

The outcomes for each of the experiments described in Examples 4.1 and 4.2 are shrouded in uncertainty; that is, prior to conducting the experiment, we cannot be certain whether a particular event will occur. The uncertainty is measured by the **probability** of the event.

EXAMPLE 4.3
Interpreting a Probability

Suppose we perform the following experiment: Toss a coin and observe whether the upside of the coin is a head or a tail. Define the event *H* by

H: Observe a head

What do we mean when we say that the probability of *H*, denoted by *P(H)*, is equal to $\frac{1}{2}$?

SOLUTION   Stating that the probability of observing a head is $P(H) = \frac{1}{2}$ does *not* mean that exactly half of a number of tosses will result in heads. (For example, we do not expect to observe exactly 1 head in 2 tosses of a coin or exactly 5 heads in 10 tosses of a coin.) Rather, it means that, in a very long series of tosses, we believe that approximately half would result in a head. Therefore, the number $\frac{1}{2}$ measures the likelihood of observing a head on a single toss of the coin.   ■

The relative frequency concept of probability discussed in Example 4.3 is illustrated in Figure 4.2 (page 154). The graph shows the proportion of heads observed after *n* = 25, 50, 75, 100, 125, ..., 1,450, 1,475, and 1,500 computer-simulated repetitions of a coin-tossing experiment. The number of tosses is marked along the horizontal axis of the graph, and the corresponding proportions of heads are plotted on the vertical axis above the values of *n*. We have connected the points by line segments to emphasize the fact that the proportion of heads moves closer and closer to .5 as *n* gets larger (as you move to the right on the graph).

Although most people think of the probability of an event as the proportion of times the event occurs in a very long series of trials, some experiments can never be repeated. For example, if you invest $50,000 in starting a new business, the probability that your business will survive 5 years has some unknown value that you will never be able to evaluate by repetitive experiments. The probability of this event occurring is a number that has some value, but it is unknown to us. The best that we could do, in estimating its value, would be to attempt to determine the proportion of

FIGURE 4.2

The Proportion of Heads in *n* Tosses of a Coin

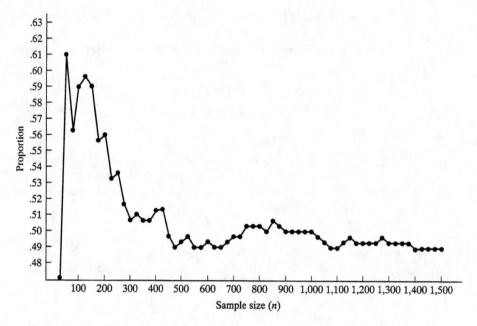

similar businesses that survived 5 years and take this as an approximation to the desired probability. In spite of the fact that we may not be able to conduct repetitive experiments, the relative frequency definition for probability appeals to our intuition.

Definition 4.3

The **probability of an event** A, denoted by $P(A)$, is a number between 0 and 1 that measures the likelihood that A will occur when the experiment is performed. $P(A)$ can be approximated by the proportion of times that A is observed when the experiment is repeated a very large number of times.

In the next section, we give some rules for finding the probability of an important type of event.

■ *Applying the Concepts*

4.1 Consider the following experiment: Toss a single die and observe the number showing on the upper face.
  a. If this experiment were to be repeated over and over again in a very long series of trials, what proportion of the experimental outcomes do you think would result in a 5?

    b. What does it mean to say, "The probability that the outcome is a 5 is $\frac{1}{6}$"?

    c. Perform the experiment a large number of times and calculate the proportion of outcomes that result in a 5. Note that as the number of repetitions becomes larger and larger, this proportion moves closer and closer to $\frac{1}{6}$.

4.2   Consider the following experiment. Thirteen cards are dealt face up from a standard, well-mixed, 52-card bridge deck, and their suits (hearts, spades, clubs, and diamonds) are observed. Define the event A as follows:

A: 4 hearts, 4 spades, 3 clubs, and 2 diamonds are observed

It can be shown that the probability of A is .01796, i.e., $P(A) = .01796$. What do we mean by the statement, "$P(A) = .01796$"?

4.3   A power plant that discharges its waste into a nearby gulf performed the following experiment each day for a period of 1 year (365 days): A water sample is selected from an area near the plant's discharge, analyzed for the presence of polychlorinated biphenyl, known as PCB (a dangerous chemical), and the amount of PCB (in parts per million) in the sample is recorded. Suppose the power plant observed that the amount of PCB in the water samples exceeded government pollution standards on two of the days. Find the approximate probability of A, where A is the event that, on any randomly selected day, the amount of PCB in the water sample will exceed the standard.

4.4   In New York City, the leading cause of death on the job is not construction accidents, machinery malfunctions, or car crashes—it is homicide! A Federal Bureau of Labor Statistics study revealed that of the 177 New York City workers who died of injuries sustained on the job in 1991, 122 were homicide victims (*New York Times*, Feb. 25, 1993). Use this information to estimate the probability that an on-the-job death of a New York City worker is the result of a homicide.

4.5   U.S. Department of Labor estimates showed that unemployment in the labor force was 7.6% in August 1994. That is, of all those who were considered eligible workers in August 1994, 7.6% were unemployed. Suppose we selected one eligible worker from the labor force in August 1994 and determined that person's employment status. Based on the Department of Labor estimate, what is the probability that this person was unemployed?

4.6   A Current Population Survey found only one of every 10 full-time wage and salary workers is on an evening or night shift (*Monthly Labor Review*, Nov. 1986). Find the probability that a full-time worker is on an evening or night shift. Interpret your result.

4.7   During the 1989 U.S. Open golf tournament, four professional golfers (Doug Weaver, Jerry Pate, Nick Price, and Mark Wiebe) made holes in one (aces) on the sixth hole at Oak Hill Country Club—all on the same day! How unlikely is such a feat? According to *Golf Digest* (Mar. 1990), the probability of a Professional Golf Association (PGA) tour pro making an ace on a given hole is approximately $\frac{1}{3,000}$. The estimate is based on the ratio of the number of aces made on the PGA tour to the total number of rounds played.

    a. Interpret the probability of $\frac{1}{3,000}$.

    b. *Golf Digest* also estimates the probability of any four players getting aces on the same hole on the same day during the next U.S. Open as $\frac{1}{150,000}$. Interpret this probability.

4.8   The *San Francisco Examiner* (Oct. 15, 1992) reported on a large-scale Kaiser Permanente study of expectant parents to assess the risk of their children being born with cystic fibrosis. The Kaiser study used genetic DNA analysis of the parents to determine whether the unborn child is likely to have the disease. Based on the study, the following risk assessment table was compiled.

		Father		
		Untested	*Test Positive*	*Test Negative*
	Untested	Unknown	1 in 100	1 in 16,500
Mother	*Test Positive*	1 in 100	1 in 4	1 in 660
	Test Negative	1 in 16,500	1 in 660	1 in 106,000

a. If both parents test positive, what is the probability of the child developing cystic fibrosis?
b. If both parents test negative, what is the probability of the child developing cystic fibrosis?

4.3 Mutually Exclusive Events

One special property of events can be seen in the examples of the preceding section. Two events are said to be **mutually exclusive** if, when one occurs, the other cannot occur. To illustrate, the events listed in parts **c** and **d** of Example 4.1 are mutually exclusive. You cannot conduct an experiment and "draw a spade" (the event listed in part **c**) yet at the same time "not draw a spade" (the event listed in part **d**). If one of these two events occurs when an experiment is conducted, the other event cannot occur. Therefore, we say that they are mutually exclusive events.

Definition 4.4

Two events are said to be **mutually exclusive** if, when one of the two events occurs in an experiment, the other cannot occur.

EXAMPLE 4.4
Mutually Exclusive Events

Refer to Example 4.2 and redefine the following events:

A: Exactly 287 of the 500 homeowners own a PC

B: Exactly 100 own a PC

C: A particular homeowner, the Jones family, owns a PC

State whether the following pairs of events are mutually exclusive.

    a. *A* and *B*   **b.** *A* and *C*   **c.** *B* and *C*

SOLUTION   **a.**   Events *A* and *B* are mutually exclusive because if you have observed exactly 287 homeowners who own a PC, then you could not, at the same time, have observed exactly 100.

b. Events *A* and *C* are *not* mutually exclusive because the Jones family may be one of the homeowners among the 287 in event *A* who own a PC. Therefore, it is possible for both events *A* and *C* to occur simultaneously.

c. Events *B* and *C* are not mutually exclusive for the same reason given in part **b.** ▪

EXAMPLE 4.5
Mutually Exclusive Events

Suppose an experiment consists of selecting two electric light switches from an assembly line for inspection. Define the following events:

A: The first switch is defective

B: The second switch is defective

Are *A* and *B* mutually exclusive events?

SOLUTION Events *A* and *B* are not mutually exclusive because both could occur when the inspection is made. That is, both the first and the second switch could be defective. ▪

If two events *A* and *B* are mutually exclusive, then the probability that *either A or B* occurs is equal to the sum of their probabilities. We will illustrate with an example.

EXAMPLE 4.6
Summing Probabilities

Consider the following experiment: You toss two coins and observe the upper faces of the two coins. What is the probability that you toss exactly one head?

SOLUTION The experiment can result in one of four mutually exclusive events. One possibility is that you will observe a head on coin 1, call it H_1, and a head on coin 2, H_2. We could denote this event as $H_1 H_2$. Similarly, we could observe a head on coin 1 and a tail on coin 2; call this $H_1 T_2$. The other two possible outcomes are a tail on coin 1 and a head on coin 2, $T_1 H_2$; and tails on both coins, $T_1 T_2$. These four events represent the most basic outcomes of the experiment and are called **simple events**. The collection of all possible simple events in an experiment is called the **sample space**. The sample space for this coin-tossing experiment is shown diagrammatically in Figure 4.3 (page 158).* ▪

---

*The graphical representation that shows all possible simple events in an experiment is called a **Venn diagram**.*

FIGURE 4.3

Four Mutually
Exclusive Outcomes
(Simple Events) and
Associated
Probabilities When
Tossing a Pair of
Coins

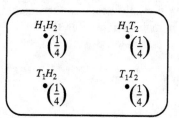

Definition 4.5

Simple events are mutually exclusive events that represent the most basic outcomes of an experiment.

Definition 4.6

The **sample space** of an experiment is the collection of all its simple events.

Since the chance of tossing either a head or a tail on each coin is $\frac{1}{2}$ (recall Example 4.3), we would expect each of the four simple events of Figure 4.3 to occur with approximately equal relative frequency $(\frac{1}{4})$ if the coin-tossing experiment were repeated over and over again a large number of times. Since you will observe exactly one head only if T_1H_2 occurs or if H_1T_2 occurs, and these simple events are mutually exclusive, either one or the other of these events will occur $(\frac{1}{4} + \frac{1}{4}) = \frac{1}{2}$ of the time. Therefore, the probability of observing exactly one head in the toss of two coins is equal to the probability of observing *either T_1H_2 or H_1T_2*, which is $\frac{1}{2}$. You can verify this result experimentally, using the simulation procedure employed in Section 4.2.

Probability Rule #1

The Additive Rule for Mutually Exclusive Events

If two events A and B are mutually exclusive, then **the probability that either A or B occurs** is equal to the sum of their respective probabilities:

$$P(A \text{ or } B) = P(A) + P(B)$$

Although Example 4.6 utilized the concept of simple events, the additive probability rule shown in the box applies to any two mutually exclusive events. You can now see why the concept of mutually exclusive events is important. We will illustrate with several more examples.

EXAMPLE 4.7
Applying Probability
Rule #1

In August 1994, PepsiCo stock was selling for $31 per share on the New York Stock Exchange. A survey of a large number of stock analysts at Smith Barney, Inc., yielded the following probability estimates for three events related to the price of PepsiCo 1 year later:

Event	Probability
A: Less than $31 per share (sell)	.05
B: Between $32 and $50 per share (buy)	.75
C: Greater than $50 per share (attractive buy)	.20

Find the probability that PepsiCo will sell for more than $31 per share next year.

SOLUTION The three conditions of the economy listed in events A, B, and C represent three mutually exclusive events with the probabilities shown. The event of interest, that the price of PepsiCo will exceed $31 per share next year, will occur if either event B or event C occurs. Therefore, using probability rule #1, we have

$$P(B \text{ or } C) = P(B) + P(C)$$
$$= .75 + .20 = .95 \quad ■$$

EXAMPLE 4.8
Applying Probability
Rule #1

Consider the following experiment: Two dice are tossed, and the numbers of dots on the upper faces of the dice are observed. Find the probability that the sum of the two numbers is equal to 7 (a winning number in the game of craps).

SOLUTION Mark the dice so that they are identified as die #1 and die #2. Then there are $6 \times 6 = 36$ distinctly different ways that the dice could fall. You could observe a 1 on die #1 and a 1 on die #2; a 1 on die #1 and a 2 on die #2; a 1 on die #1 and a 3 on die #2, etc. In other words, you can pair the six values (shown on the six sides) of die #1 with the six values of die #2 in $6 \times 6 = 36$ mutually exclusive ways. These 36 combinations represent the simple events (and, hence, the sample space) for the experiment. The sums associated with the simple events are shown in Figure 4.4 (page 160).

Since there are 36 possible ways the dice could fall and since these ways should occur with equal frequency, the probability of observing any one of the 36 events shown in the figure is $\frac{1}{36}$. Then to find the probability of tossing a 7, we need only to add the probabilities of those events corresponding to a sum on the dice equal to 7.

If we denote the event that you observe a 6 on die #1 and a 1 on die #2 as (6, 1), etc., then, as shown in Figure 4.4, you will toss a 7 if you observe a (6, 1), (5, 2), (4,3), (3,4), (2,5), or (1,6). Therefore, the probability of tossing a 7 is

FIGURE 4.4

The Sum of the Dots for the 36 Mutually Exclusive Outcomes in the Tossing of a Pair of Dice

Die #1

Die #2	⚀	⚁	⚂	⚃	⚄	⚅
⚀	2	3	4	5	6	7
⚁	3	4	5	6	7	8
⚂	4	5	6	7	8	9
⚃	5	6	7	8	9	10
⚄	6	7	8	9	10	11
⚅	7	8	9	10	11	12

$$P(7) = P[(6, 1) \text{ or } (5, 2) \text{ or } (4, 3) \text{ or } (3, 4) \text{ or } (2, 5) \text{ or } (1, 6)]$$

$$= P(6, 1) + P(5, 2) + P(4, 3) + P(3, 4) + P(2, 5) + P(1, 6)$$

$$= \frac{1}{36} + \frac{1}{36} + \frac{1}{36} + \frac{1}{36} + \frac{1}{36} + \frac{1}{36} = \frac{6}{36} = \frac{1}{6} \quad ▪$$

Example 4.8 suggests a modification of probability rule #1 when an experiment can result in one and only one of a number of equally likely (equiprobable) mutually exclusive events.

Probability Rule #2

The Probability Rule for an Experiment That Results in One of a Number of Equally Likely Mutually Exclusive Events

Suppose an experiment can result in one and only one of M equally likely mutually exclusive events and that m of these events result in event A. Then the probability of event A is

$$P(A) = \frac{m}{M}$$

EXAMPLE 4.9

Applying Probability Rule #2

As a contestant on "Let's Make a Deal," you have selected, by chance, two doors from among four doors offered. Unknown to you, there are prizes behind only two of the four doors. What is the probability that you win at least one of the two prizes?

SOLUTION Identify the four doors as D_1, D_2, D_3, and D_4, and let D_3 and D_4 be the two doors that hide the two prizes. Then the six distinctly different and mutually exclusive ways that the two doors may be selected from the four are

$$(D_1D_2),\ (D_1D_3),\ (D_1D_4),\ (D_2D_3),\ (D_2D_4),\ (D_3D_4)$$

STEP 1   Since the doors were selected by chance, we would expect the likelihood that any one pair would be chosen to be the same as for any other pair. Also, since the experiment can result in only one of these pairs, $M = 6$.

STEP 2   You can see from the listed outcomes that the number of pairs that result in a choice of D_3 or D_4 is $m = 5$. (These are the last five pairs listed.)

STEP 3   Using probability rule #2, the probability of selecting at least one of the two doors with prizes is

$$P(\text{At least one of } D_3 \text{ or } D_4) = \frac{m}{M} = \frac{5}{6} \quad ▪$$

Examples 4.6–4.9 identify the properties of the probabilities of all events, as summarized in the box.

Properties of Probabilities

1. The probability of an event always assumes a value between 0 and 1.
2. If two events A and B are mutually exclusive, then the probability that either A or B occurs is equal to $P(A) + P(B)$.
3. If we list all possible simple events associated with an experiment, then the sum of their probabilities will always equal 1.

Before concluding this section, we will comment on two important mutually exclusive events and their probabilities. Consider the dice-tossing experiment (Example 4.8) and define the following two events:

A: The sum of the two numbers on the dice is 7

$\overline{A}$:   The sum of the two numbers on the dice is not 7

Thus, $\overline{A}$ is the event that A *does not occur*. You can see that A and $\overline{A}$ are mutually exclusive events and, further, since A occurs $\frac{1}{6}$ of the time in a long series of trials (see Example 4.8), then $\overline{A}$ will occur $\frac{5}{6}$ of the time. In other words,

$$P(A) + P(\overline{A}) = 1$$

Definition 4.7

The Rule of Complements

The **complement** of an event A, denoted by the symbol $\overline{A}$, is the event that A does not occur. (See Figure 4.5.)

FIGURE 4.5
Complementary
Events A and $\overline{A}$ in a
Sample Space

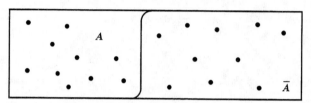

Complementary events are important because sometimes it is difficult to find the probability of an event A, but easy to find the probability of its complement $\overline{A}$. In this case, we can find $P(A)$ using the relationship stated in the box.

Probability Rule #3

Probability Relationship for Complementary Events

$$P(A) = 1 - P(\overline{A})$$

EXERCISES

■ *Learning the Mechanics*

4.9 In the toss of a single fair (balanced) die, the following outcomes (simple events) are equally likely:

Simple Event	Probability
1	1/6
2	1/6
3	1/6
4	1/6
5	1/6
6	1/6

Define the following events:

A: Observe a number less than 4

B: Observe an odd number

C: Observe an even number

a. Find the probabilities of events *A*, *B*, and *C*.

b. List the outcomes (simple events) in the complements of events *A*, *B*, and *C*.

c. Find the probabilities of $\overline{A}$, $\overline{B}$, and $\overline{C}$.

d. Are any of the pairs of events, *A* and *B*, *A* and *C*, or *B* and *C*, complementary? Explain.

4.10 An experiment has five possible outcomes (simple events) with the following probabilities:

Simple Event	Probability
S_1	.15
S_2	.20
S_3	.20
S_4	.25
S_5	.20

a. Find the probability of each of the following events:

A: Outcome S_1, S_2, or S_4 occurs.

B: Outcome S_2, S_3, or S_5 occurs.

C: Outcome S_4 does not occur.

b. List the simple events in the complements of events *A*, *B*, and *C*.

c. Find the probabilities of $\overline{A}$, $\overline{B}$, and $\overline{C}$.

4.11 Suppose an experiment involves tossing two coins and observing the upper faces of the coins. Find the probabilities of

a. *A:*   Observing exactly two heads

b. *B:*   Observing exactly two tails

c. *C:*   Observing at least one head

d. Describe the complement of event *A* and find its probability.

4.12 Two dice are tossed and the upper faces of the dice are observed. Use Figure 4.4 to find the probability that the sum shown on the dice is equal to

a. 12   **b.** 5   **c.** 11

4.13 Refer to the dice-tossing experiment in Exercise 4.12. Find the approximate probability of tossing a total of 7 by conducting an experiment similar to the experiments illustrated in Figure 4.2: Toss a pair of dice a large number of times and record the proportion of times a 7 is observed. Compare your value with the exact probability, $\frac{1}{6}$.

4.14 Refer to Examples 4.6 and 4.7. Verify that property 3 (shown in the box titled Properties of Probabilities, page 161) holds for each of these examples.

▪ Applying the Concepts

4.15 Environmental engineers classify U.S. consumers into five mutually exclusive groups based on consumers' feeling about environmentalism as follows:

1. *Basic browns* claim they do not have the knowledge to understand environmental problems.
2. *True-blue greens* use biodegradable products.
3. *Greenback greens* support requiring new cars to run on alternative fuel.
4. *Sprouts* recycle newspapers regularly.
5. *Grousers* believe industries, not individuals, should solve environmental problems.

The proportion of consumers in each group is shown in the table. Suppose a U.S. consumer is selected at random and his or her feeling about environmentalism determined.

Basic browns	.28
True-blue greens	.11
Greenback greens	.11
Sprouts	.26
Grousers	.24

Source: The Orange County (Calif.) Register, Aug. 7, 1990.

a. List the simple events for the experiment.
b. Assign reasonable probabilities to the simple events.
c. Find the probability that the consumer is either a basic brown or a grouser.
d. Find the probability that the consumer supports environmentalism in some fashion (i.e., is either a true-blue green, greenback green, or sprout).

4.16 The National Highway Safety Traffic Administration maintains the Fatal Accident Report System (FARS) file. The FARS file documents every motor vehicle crash (since Jan. 1, 1975) on a U.S. public road in which a fatality occurred. Based on over 800,000 deaths recorded in the FARS file, the types of crashes that account for all car occupant fatalities is distributed as follows:

Type of Crash	*Proportion*
Single-car crash	.45
Two-car crash	.22
Car crashing with another noncar vehicle (e.g., a truck)	.25
Crash involving 3 or more vehicles	.08
TOTAL	1.00

Source: Evans, L. "Small cars, big cars: What is the safety difference?" Chance, Vol. 7, No. 3, Summer 1994, p. 9.

Consider a recent car crash that resulted in a fatality.

a. What is the probability that a single-car crash occurred?   45%

b. What is the probability that a two-car crash occurred?   41%

c. What is the probability that two or more vehicles were involved in the crash?   55%

4.17   "Employee Burnout: America's Newest Epidemic" is the name of a survey of American workers commissioned by Northwestern National Life Insurance Company. The main topic of the study was job-related stress. The origins of job stress, according to the responses of 600 workers, are summarized in the accompanying pie chart.

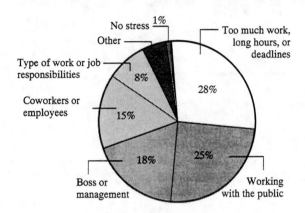

Source: *Tampa Tribune*, May 8, 1991.

Suppose one of the 600 workers in the survey is selected at random.

a. What is the probability that the worker attributes on-the-job stress to his to her "boss or management"?

b. What is the probability that the worker attributes on-the-job stress to "too much work, long hours, or deadlines"?

c. What is the probability that the worker has on-the-job stress?

d. What is the probability that the worker attributes on-the-job stress to people (e.g., coworkers, employees, boss, management, or the public)?

4.18   Local area merchants often use "scratch off" tickets with promises of grand prize giveaways to entice customers to visit their stores. One such game, called Jackpot, was recently used in Tampa, Florida. Residents were mailed game tickets with 10 " play squares" and the instructions: "Scratch off your choice of ONLY ONE Jackpot Play Square. If you reveal any 3-OF-A-KIND combination, you WIN. Call NOW to make an appointement to claim your prize." All 10 play squares, of course, have winning 3-of-a-kind combinations. On one such ticket, three cherries (worth up to $1,000 in cash or prizes) appeared in play squares numbered 1, 2, 3, 4, 5, 6, 7, and 9; three lemons (worth a 10-piece microwave cookware set) appeared in play square number 8; and three sevens (worth a whirlpool spa) appeared in play square 10.

a. If you play Jackpot, what is the probability that you win a whirlpool spa?

b. If you play Jackpot, what is the probability that you win $1,000 in cash or prizes?

4.19   An improved method for measuring the electrical resistivity of concrete has been developed that eliminates difficulties due to polarization effects and capacitive resistance (*Magazine of Concrete Research*, Dec. 1985). The method was tested on concrete specimens with different water–cement mixes. Three different water weight ratios (40%, 45%, and 50%) and three different amounts of cement (300, 350, and 400 kilograms per cubic meter) were examined.

a. List all possible water–cement mixes for this experiment.

b. Suppose we determine the water–cement mix that yields the highest electrical resistivity. Before the experiment is performed, should equal probabilities be assigned to the simple events? Why or why not?

4.20 An *Industry Week* (Nov. 15, 1993) survey of 500 chief executive officers posed the question: "If you could live your life over again, what would you do differently?" The responses are summarized in the table.

What would you do differently?	Number of CEOs
Nothing	153
More or better education	102
Change professions	45
Spend more time with family	37
Start own company	34
Enjoy life	25
Make better decisions	25
Be myself	24
Marry differently	16
Other responses	39
TOTAL	500

a. Find the probability that a randomly selected CEO would do nothing differently if given the chance to live life over again.

b. Find the probability that a randomly selected CEO would get a better education or change professions if given the chance to live life over again.

4.21 In high-volume machining centers, cutting tools are replaced at regular heuristically chosen intervals. These intervals are generally untimely, i.e., either the tool is replaced too early or too late. The *Journal of Engineering for Industry* (Aug. 1993) reported on an automated real-time diagnostic system designed to replace the cutting tool of a drilling machine at optimum times. To test the system, data were collected over a broad range of machining conditions. A total of eight machining conditions (of a possible 168) were used in the study. These are described below:

Experiment	Workpiece Material	Drill Size in.	Drill Speed rpm	Feed Rate ipr
1	Cast iron	.25	1,250	.011
2	Cast iron	.25	1,800	.005
3	Steel	.25	3,750	.003

(continued)

Experiment	Workpiece Material	Drill Size in.	Drill Speed rpm	Feed Rate ipr
4	Steel	.25	2,500	.003
5	Steel	.25	2,500	.008
6	Steel	.125	4,000	.0065
7	Steel	.125	4,000	.009
8	Steel	.125	3,000	.010

a. Suppose one (and only one) of the 168 possible machining conditions will detect a flaw in the system. What is the probability that the experiment conducted in the study will detect the system flaw?

b. Suppose the system flaw occurs when drilling steel material with a .25-inch drill size at a speed of 2,500 rpm. Of the 168 possible machining conditions, only 7 of these have such a configuration. Find the probability that the experiment conducted in the actual study will detect the system flaw.

4.22 International commercial banks that loan money to developing countries always run the risk of the country's rescheduling its debt. Consequently, it is important that the bank be able to distinguish between countries that have a tendency to reschedule their debts and countries that do not. A study was conducted to investigate the incidence of debt rescheduling of developing countries (*Journal of International Business Statistics*, Summer 1986). During the 1960s and early 1970s, there were only 21 incidents of debt rescheduling out of a sample of 238 observations. (Here, an observation consists of a year–country combination. That is, for a particular country in a particular year, it was determined whether the country rescheduled its debt.) In contrast, a study of 30 developing countries over the 8-year period 1975–1982 (i.e., $30 \times 8 = 240$ observations) found 40 incidents of debt rescheduling.

a. Suppose you select one of the sample of 238 country–year observations during the 1960s and early 1970s. What is the probability that the developing country rescheduled its debt during the year?

b. Answer part **a** assuming that you select one of the sample of 240 year–country observations during 1975–1982.

c. Compare the probabilities obtained in parts **a** and **b**. In which of the two periods is it more likely to find a rescheduled debt?

4.23 In 1987, Congress enacted the Surface Transportation and Uniform Act, which allowed states to increase the speed limit to 65 miles per hour (mph) on interstate highways located outside of an urban area of 50,000 or more persons. In a study of traffic fatalities on interstate highways, the Fatal Accident Reporting System discovered that 96% of the interstate highway miles eligible to be posted at 65 mph are rural interstates, and 97% of these eligible miles were actually posted at 65 mph (*American Journal of Public Health*, Oct. 1989).

a. For a particular 1-mile stretch of interstate highway eligible to be posted at 65 mph, estimate the probability that the 1-mile stretch is posted at 65 mph.

b. For a particular 1-mile stretch of interstate highway eligible to be posted at 65 mph, estimate the probability that the 1-mile stretch is not rural.

c. Are the events in parts **a** and **b** mutually exclusive? Explain.

4.24 Enhanced protection against corrosion of steel sheet is a top priority of automakers. At Mazda Motor Corporation (Japan), there is a strong preference for thin, plated alloy coatings to improve protection against rust and adhesion. The accompanying table gives the breakdown of steel sheet usage in Mazda's 626s exported to the United States. Suppose a single steel sheet is randomly selected from among those sheets used in the production of a Mazda 626, and we are interested in the type of steel sheet that is selected.

Type of Steel Sheet	Percentage Used
Cold rolled	27
Cold rolled, high strength	12
Cold rolled, plated	30
Cold rolled, high strength, plated	15
Hot rolled	8
Hot rolled, high strength	5
Hot rolled, plated	3
	100

Source: Chandler, H. E. "Materials trends at Mazda Motor Corporation." *Metal Progress*, Vol. 129, No. 6, May 1986, p. 57 (Figure 3).

a. What is the probability that the steel sheet will be of the hot-rolled, high-strength type?
b. What is the probability that the steel sheet will be of the cold-rolled type?
c. What is the probability that the steel sheet will not be plated?

4.25 In business, how often do corporate managers commit a "courageous" act, i.e., voice an unpopular position, speaking out despite the possibility that the action might hurt their careers? A *Psychology Today* (Sept. 1986) study of the actions of American managers from 1969 to 1983 revealed that managers were six times more likely to act courageously during the years 1981–1983 than during the recessionary period of 1972–1974. The table gives the probability of a courageous act for each of the periods studied. [*Note:* These probabilities were obtained by dividing the number of courageous acts reported in a given period by the total number reported over the years 1969–1983.]

Period	Probability of a Courageous Act
1969–1971	.21
1972–1974	.07
1975–1977	.13
1978–1980	.15
1981–1983	44

Source: Hornstein, H. A. "When corporate courage counts." *Psychology Today,* Sept. 1986, p. 58. Copyright © 1986 (APA). Reprinted with permission.

a. Verify that the probabilities in the table sum to 1.

b. What is the probability that a courageous act committed by an American manager in the study period occurred prior to 1975?

c. What is the probability that a courageous act committed by an American manager in the study period did not occur during 1981–1983?

4.26 Market researchers are keenly interested in consumer preferences for the various benefits offered by a product. Researchers at the University of Pennsylvania conducted a study of consumer preferences for shampoo benefits *(Journal of the Market Research Society,* Jan. 1984). Part of the study involved a survey of 186 undergraduate business students. Each respondent was shown a list of 13 benefits and asked to select up to four benefits that he or she most strongly desires in a shampoo brand. The group of benefits selected by a respondent is termed a *benefit bundle.* The 13 benefits are as follows:

Body	Thickness	Contains protein
Bounciness	Softness	Natural ingredients
Control	Manageability	Repairs split ends
Luster	Gentle action	Conditions hair
Protection against dandruff		

a. Suppose a respondent is permitted to select two benefits from those listed in the first column. List the outcomes for this experiment.

b. Assuming that the benefit bundles from part **a** are equally likely, what is the probability that a respondent will select the {Body, Luster} bundle as most desirable?

c. Assuming the benefit bundles from part **a** are equally likely, what is the probability that a respondent will select Control as one of the two benefits?

4.27 After Evelyn Marie Adams won the New Jersey weekly lottery twice within a 4-month period in 1986, the event was widely reported as an amazing feat that beat the odds of 1 in 17 trillion. Although the probability of the event, 1/17,000,000,000,000, is technically correct, it does not take into account a fundamental law of statistics called "the law of very large numbers." In the words of Harvard statisticians Perci Diaconis and Frederick Mosteller *(Journal of the American Statistical Association,* Dec. 1989), the law states that "with a large enough sample, any outrageous thing is apt to happen." Diaconis and Mosteller go on to explain that "one in 17 trillion is the odds that a given person (e.g., Ms. Adams) who buys a single ticket for exactly two New Jersey lotteries will win both times." The true question, they say, is, "What is the chance that some person, out of all the millions and millions who buy lottery tickets in the United States, hits a lottery twice in a lifetime?" Based on a 7-year study of state lottery winners, Purdue statisticians Stephen Samuels and George McCabe estimated the "odds are better than even that there will be a double lottery winner somewhere in the United States" *(Wall Street Journal,* Feb. 27, 1990).* Let A be the event that you buy a New Jersey lottery ticket for exactly two different weeks and win both times. Let B be the event that any person wins a state lottery twice.

Reprinted by permission of the Wall Street Journal. © 1990 Dow Jones & Company, Inc. All rights reserved worldwide.

a. Are the events A and B mutually exclusive?

b. What is the probability of A?

c. What is the probability of B?

d. Explain why the probabilities, parts **b** and **c**, are so drastically different.

4.4 Conditional Probability and Independence

The event probabilities we have discussed thus far give the relative frequencies of occurrence of the events when an experiment is repeated a very large number of times. They are called **unconditional probabilities** because no special conditions are assumed other than those that define the experiment.

Sometimes we may want to revise the probability of an event when we have additional knowledge that might affect its outcome. To give a simple example, we found that the probability of observing a 7 when two dice are tossed is $\frac{1}{6}$ (see Example 4.8). But suppose you are given the information that the sum of the two numbers showing on the dice is even. Would you still believe that the probability of observing a 7 on that particular toss is $\frac{1}{6}$? Intuitively, you will realize that the probability of observing a 7 is now 0. Since you know that an even number occurred, the outcome 7 cannot have occurred (because 7 is an odd number). The probability of observing a 7, *given that you know some other event has already occurred*, is called the **conditional probability** of the event.

> **Definition 4.8**
>
> The probability of an event A, given that an event B has occurred, is called the **conditional probability of A given B** and is denoted by the symbol
>
> $P(A|B)$
>
> *Note:* The vertical bar between A and B is read "given."

EXAMPLE 4.10
Conditional Probability

A box contains three fuses, one good and two defective. Two fuses are drawn in sequence, first one and then the other.

a. What is the probability that the second fuse drawn is defective?

b. What is the probability that the second fuse drawn is defective if you know, for certain, that the first fuse drawn is defective?

SOLUTION

a. We will denote the good fuse by G and the two defective fuses as D_1 and D_2. If the fuses are drawn at random from the box, the six possible orders of selection are:

$$(G, D_1), (G, D_2), (D_1, G), (D_1, D_2), (D_2, G), (D_2, D_1)$$

STEP 1   Since these six mutually exclusive events are equally likely and comprise all possible outcomes of the draw, we have $M = 6$.

STEP 2   Next, we must find the number of selections in which a defective fuse is selected in the second draw. You can see from the listed draws that $m = 4$.

STEP 3   Using probability rule #2, we conclude that the unconditional probability of obtaining a defective fuse on the second draw is

$$P(\text{Defective fuse on the second draw}) = \frac{m}{M} = \frac{4}{6} = \frac{2}{3}$$

b.   The probability of observing a defective fuse on the second draw, given that you have observed a defective fuse on the first draw, is the conditional probability $P(A|B)$, where:

A: Observe a defective fuse on the second draw

B: Observe a defective fuse on the first draw

If the first fuse drawn from the box is defective, then the box now contains only two fuses, one defective and one nondefective. This means that there is a 50% chance of drawing a defective fuse on the second draw, given that a defective fuse has already been drawn. That is,

$$P(A|B) = \frac{1}{2}$$

The probability obtained in part **a**, the unconditional probability of event A, was equal to $\frac{2}{3}$. Clearly, the probability has changed when we know that event B has occurred.   ■

EXAMPLE 4.11
Conditional Probability

A balanced coin is tossed 10 times, resulting in 10 tails. If the coin is tossed one more time, what is the probability of observing a head?

SOLUTION   We are asked to find the conditional probability of event A, given that event B has occurred, where

A: The 11th toss results in a head

B: The first 10 tosses resulted in 10 heads

Intuitively, it may seem reasonable to expect the probability of observing a head on the 11th toss (given that the 10 previous tosses resulted in heads) to be greater than $\frac{1}{2}$, but such is not the case. If the coin is truly balanced and is tossed in an unbiased manner, then the probability of observing a head on the 11th toss is still $\frac{1}{2}$. (This has been verified both theoretically and experimentally). Therefore, this is a case where the conditional probability of an event A is equal to the unconditional probability of A.   ■

Example 4.11 illustrates an important relationship that exists between some pairs of events. If the probability of one event does not depend on whether a second event has occurred, then the events are said to be **independent.**

Definition 4.9

Two events A and B are said to be **independent** if

$P(A|B) = P(A)$ or if $P(B|A) = P(B)$

Note: If one of these equalities is true, then the other will also be true.

The notion of independence is particularly important when we want to find the probability that *both* of two events will occur. When the events are independent, the probability that both events will occur is equal to the product of their unconditional probabilities.

Probability Rule #4

The Probability That Both of Two Independent Events A and B Occur

If two events A and B are independent, then the **probability that both A and B occur** is equal to the product of their respective unconditional probabilities:

$P(A \text{ and } B) = P(A)P(B)$

Probability rule #4 can be extended to apply to any number of independent events. For example, if A, B, and C are independent events, then

$$P(\text{All of the events, } A, B, \text{ and } C, \text{ occur}) = P(\text{both } A \text{ and } B \text{ occur})P(C)$$

$$= P(A)P(B)P(C)$$

EXAMPLE 4.12
Applying Probability
Rule #4

Find the probability of observing two heads in two tosses of a balanced coin.

SOLUTION   Define the following events:

A: Observe a head on the first toss

B: Observe a head on the second toss

Since we know that events *A* and *B* are independent and that $P(A) = P(B) = \frac{1}{2}$, the probability that we observe two heads, i.e., both events *A* and *B*, is

$$P(\text{Observe two heads}) = P(A)P(B)$$

$$= \left(\frac{1}{2}\right)\left(\frac{1}{2}\right) = \frac{1}{4}$$

You can see that this answer agrees with our reasoning in Example 4.6.   ■

We now consider a problem in statistical inference.

EXAMPLE 4.13
Making an Inference Based
on a Probability

Experience has shown that a manufacturing operation produces, on the average, only one defective unit in 10. These are removed from the production line, repaired, and returned to the warehouse. Suppose that during a given period of time you observe five defective units emerging in sequence from the production line.

    a.   If prior history has shown that defective units usually emerge randomly from the production line, what is the probability of observing a sequence of five consecutive defective units?

    b.   If the event in part **a** really occurred, what would you conclude about the process?

SOLUTION

    a.   If the defectives really occur randomly, then whether any one unit is defective should be independent of whether the others are defective. The unconditional probability that any one unit is defective is known to be $\frac{1}{10}$. We will define the following events:

    D_1: The first unit is defective

    D_2: The second unit is defective

    ⋮   ⋮

    D_5: The fifth unit is defective

    Then

$$P(D_1) = P(D_2) = P(D_3) = P(D_4) = P(D_5) = \frac{1}{10}$$

and the probability that all five are defective is

$$P(\text{All five are defective}) = P(D_1)P(D_2) \cdots P(D_5)$$

$$= \left(\frac{1}{10}\right)\left(\frac{1}{10}\right)\left(\frac{1}{10}\right)\left(\frac{1}{10}\right)\left(\frac{1}{10}\right)$$

$$= \frac{1}{100,000}$$

b. We do not need an understanding of probability to know that something must be wrong with the production line. Intuition would tell us that observing five defectives in sequence is highly improbable (given past history), and we would immediately infer that past history no longer describes the condition of the process. In fact, we would infer that something is disturbing the stability of the process. ■

Example 4.13 illustrates how you can use your knowledge of probability and the probability of a sample event to make an inference about some population. The technique, called the **rare event approach**, is summarized in the box.

Rare Event Approach to Making Statistical Inferences

Suppose we calculate the probability of an event A *based on certain assumptions about the sampled populations.* If $P(A) = p$ is small (say, p less than .05) and we observe that A occurs, then we can reach one of two conclusions:

1. Our original assumption about the sampled population is correct, and we have observed a rare event, i.e., an event that is highly improbable. (For example, we would conclude that the production line of Example 4.13, in fact, produces only 10% defectives. The fact that we observed five defectives in a sample of five was an unlucky and rare event.)

2. Our original assumption about the sampled population is incorrect. (In Example 4.13, we would conclude that the line is producing more than 10% defectives, a situation that makes the observed sample—five defectives in a sample of five—more probable.)

Using the rare event approach, we prefer conclusion 2. The fact that event A did occur in Example 4.13 leads us to believe that $P(A)$ is much higher than p, and that our original assumption about the population is incorrect.

EXERCISES

∎ **Learning the Mechanics**

4.28 Assume that $P(A) = .6$ and $P(B) = .3$. If events A and B are independent, find $P(A$ and $B)$.

4.29 Consider an experiment that consists of two trials and has the nine possible outcomes (simple events) listed here:

AA	BA	CA
AB	BB	CB
AC	BC	CC

where AC indicates that A occurs on the first trial and C occurs on the second trial. Suppose the following events are defined:

D: Observe an A on the first trial

E: Observe a B on the second trial

a. List the possible outcomes associated with event D and find $P(D)$.
b. List the possible outcomes associated with event E and find $P(E)$.
c. Find $P(E|D)$.
d. Are D and E independent?
e. Find $P($both D and E occur).

4.30 Assume that $P(A) = .6$, $P(B) = .4$, $P(C) = .5$, $P(A|B) = .15$, $P(A|C) = .5$, and $P(B|C) = .3$.
a. Are events A and B independent?   *no*   **b.** Are events A and C independent?   *no*
c. Are events B and C independent?   *no*

∎ **Applying the Concepts**

4.31 To develop programs for business travelers staying at convention hotels, Hyatt Hotels Corp. recently commissioned a study of executives who golf (*Tampa Tribune*, July 10, 1993). The research revealed two surprising results: (1) 55% of the respondents admitted they had cheated at golf; (2) more than one-third of the respondents that admitted cheating at golf said they have also lied in business. Let A represent the event that an executive has cheated at golf, and let B represent the event that the executive has lied in business. Convert the research results into probability statements involving events A and B.

4.32 *Sensor fusion* is a scientific term used to describe the process of integrating signal data to improve the performance of a system such as a stereo camera, pulse radar, and range radar. The problem of sensor integration and data fusion was investigated in the *Journal of Robotic Systems* (June 1990). One of the data fusion systems studied consisted of five sensors operating independently in parallel typology. The parallel system will fail to detect a signal only if all five of the sensors fail to detect the signal. The probabilities of failure for the sensors are designed to be: .05, .04, .03, .02, and .01.

a. Find the probability that the parallel system fails.

b. If the parallel system fails, make an inference about the probabilities of failure for the five sensors.

4.33 Nightmares about college exams appear to be common among college graduates. In a recent survey of 30- to 45-year-old graduates from Transylvania University, 50 of 188 respondents admitted they had recurring dreams about college exams (*Tampa Tribune*, Dec. 12, 1988). Of these 50, 47 felt distress, anguish, fear, or terror in their dreams. (For example, some dreamers "couldn't find the building or they walked in and all the students were different." Other dreamers either overslept or did not realize they were enrolled in the class.)

a. Calculate the approximate probability that a 30- to 45-year-old graduate of Transylvania University has recurring dreams about college exams. Why is this probability approximate?

b. Refer to part **a**. Given that the graduate has recurring dreams, what is the approximate probability that the dreams are unpleasant (i.e., that the graduate feels distress, anguish, fear, or terror in the dreams)?

c. Are the events {Graduate has recurring dreams} and {Dreams are unpleasant} independent?

4.34 According to a report from the Newspaper Advertising Bureau, 40% of all primary car maintainers are women (*American Demographics*, June 1985). Consequently, advertisements for car care products, traditionally geared toward men, are now being aimed at women also. Consider the population consisting of all primary car maintainers.

a. What is the probability that a primary car maintainer, selected from the population, is a woman? A man?   *40%*   *60%*

b. What is the probability that both primary car maintainers in a sample of two selected from the population are women?   *16%*

4.35 An article in *IEEE Computer Applications in Power* (Apr. 1990) describes "an unmanned watching system to detect intruders in real time without spurious detections, both indoors and outdoors, using video cameras and microprocessors." The system was tested outdoors under various weather conditions in Tokyo, Japan. The numbers of intruders detected and missed under each condition are provided in the table.

a. Under cloudy conditions, what is the probability that the unmanned system detects an intruder?   *0.9744*

b. Given that the unmanned system missed detecting an intruder, what is the probability that the weather condition was snowy?   *0.12*

	Weather Condition				
	Clear	*Cloudy*	*Rainy*	*Snowy*	*Windy*
Intruders detected	21	228	226	7	185
Intruders missed	0	6	6	3	10
TOTALS	21	234	232	10	195

Source: Kaneda, K., et al. "An unmanned watching system using video cameras." *IEEE Computer Applications in Power*, Apr. 1990, p. 24.

4.36 Since 1961, parcels of land that may contain oil have been placed in a lottery with the winner receiving leasing rights (at $1 per acre per year) for a period of 10 years. United States citizens 21 years or older are eligible and are entitled to one entry per lottery by paying a $10 filing fee to the Bureau of Land Management (see *The Federal Oil & Gas Leasing System*, Federal Resource Registry, 1993). For several months in 1980, however, the lottery was suspended to investigate a player who won three parcels of land in 1 month. The number of entries for the three lotteries were 1,836, 1,365, and 495, respectively. An Interior Department audit stated that "federal workers did a poor job of shaking the drum before the drawing."

  a. Find the probability that a player would win on three parcels involving 1,836 entries, 1,365 entries, and 495 entries.

  b. Is this probability consistent with the Interior Department's explanation of this particular event?

  c. Based on your knowledge of probability and rare events, would you make the same inference as that made by the auditor? Explain.

4.37 A manufacturer guarantees that the failure rate of its new solar-powered battery is only 1 in 20. A new system to be used in a space vehicle operates on one of these batteries. To increase the reliability of the system, three batteries are installed, each designed to operate if the preceding batteries in the chain fail. If the system is operated in a practical situation, what is the probability that all three batteries would fail?

4.38 Periodically, magazine publishers promote their products by mailing "sweepstakes" packets to consumers. These packets offer the chance to win a grand prize of $1 million or more, with no obligation to purchase any of the advertised products. Despite the low odds of winning, marketing experts have found that the sweepstakes contests dramatically increase consumer interest and orders. The U.S. government investigated the legitimacy of popular sweepstakes conducted by Publishers Clearing House, American Family Publishers, and Reader's Digest. On a nationwide basis, the odds of winning the grand prize are 1 in 181,795,000 for the current Publishers Clearing House sweepstakes, 1 in 200,000,000 for the American Family Publishers sweepstakes, and 1 in 84,000,000 for the Reader's Digest sweepstakes (*Gainesville Sun*, Jan. 24, 1985).

  a. Calculate the probability of winning the grand prize in the Publishers Clearing House sweepstakes.

  b. Repeat part **a** for the American Family Publishers sweepstakes.

  c. Repeat part **a** for the Reader's Digest sweepstakes.

4.39 Refer to Exercise 4.38. Suppose you enter the sweepstakes contests of all three companies.

  a. What is the probability that you win the grand prize in all three contests?

  b. What is the probability that you do not win any of the three grand prizes?

  c. Use the probability computed in part **b** to calculate the probability of winning at least one of the three grand prizes. [*Hint*: The complement of "at least one" is "none."]

4.40 According to NASA, each space shuttle in the U.S. fleet has 1,500 "critical items" that could lead to catastrophic failure if rendered inoperable during flight. NASA estimates that the chance of at least one critical-item failure within the shuttle's main engines is about 1 in 63 for each mission (*Tampa Tribune*, Dec. 3, 1993). To build the space station *Freedom*, NASA plans to fly eight shuttle missions a year during the remainder of the 1990s.

  a. Find the probability that at least one of the eight shuttle flights scheduled next year results in a critical-item failure.

  b. Find the probability that at least one of the 40 shuttle missions scheduled over the next 5 years results in a critical-item failure.

4.41 A large-volume retailer of high-fidelity stereo needles boasts that only 1% of the needles he sells need to be replaced after 5 years of continuous use (i.e., on the average, 1 in every 100 needles sold needs to be replaced after 5 years of use). Four customers are randomly chosen from among those customers who have recently purchased stereo needles from the retailer.

   a. If the retailer's claim is true, what is the probability that all four customers will need to replace their stereo needles after 5 years of continuous use?

   b. Suppose that the event described in part **a** actually occurs. What would you infer about the retailer's claim?

4.42 According to the National Highway Traffic Safety Administration, "as many as 9 out of 10 heavily used cars, such as those from the leasing companies, may have had their mileage rolled back when resold" (reported in the *Orlando Sentinel*, Apr. 13, 1984). Officials estimate that an altered odometer adds $750 to the price of a used car. Suppose you are considering buying a used car from an auto leasing company that has three cars available. Assume also that 90% of all used cars sold by the company have falsified odometer readings and that the three available cars represent a random sample of used cars sold by the company.

   a. What is the probability that all three cars have falsified odometer readings?

   b. What is the probability that none of the three cars has a falsified odometer reading?

   c. Suppose a salesman claims that none of the three cars has a falsified odometer reading. What would you infer about the claim?

4.43 The game of craps is played with two dice. A player throws both dice, winning unconditionally if he produces either of the outcomes 7 or 11 (the sum of the numbers showing on the two dice), which are designated as *naturals*. If the player casts the outcome 2, 3, or 12—referred to as *craps*—he loses unconditionally.

   a. Find the probability of a player throwing a natural.

   b. Find the probability of a player throwing craps.

   c. Suppose a "hot" player has thrown five naturals in a row. What is the probability that the player throws a natural on the next toss?

   d. Suppose a "cold" player has thrown five craps in a row. What is the probability that the player throws craps on the next toss?

4.5 The Additive and Multiplicative Laws of Probability (Optional)

In this optional section, we define some standard probability notation and give two laws for finding probabilities. Although these laws are not required for a study of the remaining material in the text, they are needed to complete an introductory coverage of probability.

When both of two events A and B occur, as discussed in Section 4.4, this is called the **intersection of A and B** and is denoted $A \cap B$. When either A or B occurs, as discussed in Section 4.3, this is called the **union of A and B** and is denoted by $A \cup B$.

Definition 4.10

The **intersection** of A and B, denoted by $A \cap B$, is the event that both A and B occur. (See Figure 4.6.)

Definition 4.11

The **union** of A and B, denoted by $A \cup B$, is the event that either A or B occurs. (See Figure 4.7.)

FIGURE 4.6

Illustration of the Intersection of Two Events, $A \cap B$

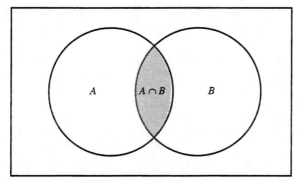

FIGURE 4.7

Illustration of the Union of Two Events, $A \cup B$

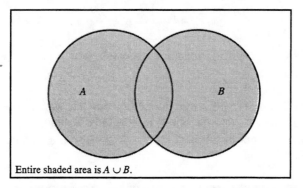

Entire shaded area is $A \cup B$.

Probability rule #4 (Section 4.4) gave a formula for finding the probability that both events A and B occur (i.e., $A \cap B$) for the special case where A and B are independent events. We now give a formula, called the **Multiplicative Law of Probability,** that applies in general, that is, regardless of whether A and B are independent events.

Probability Rule #5

The Multiplicative Law of Probability

The probability that **both** of two events A and B occur is

$$P(A \text{ and } B) = \boxed{P(A \cap B) = P(A)P(B|A)} = P(B)P(A|B)$$

EXAMPLE 4.14

Applying Probability Rule #5

Refer to Example 4.10, where we selected two fuses from a box that contained three, two of which were defective. Use the Multiplicative Law of Probability to find the probability that you first draw defective fuse D_1 and then draw D_2.

SOLUTION Define the following events:

A: The second draw results in D_2

B: The first draw results in D_1

The probability of event B is $P(B) = \frac{1}{3}$. Also, from Example 4.10, the conditional probability of A given B is $P(A|B) = \frac{1}{2}$. Then, the probability that both events A *and* B occur is

$$P(A \text{ and } B) = P(B)P(A|B) = \left(\frac{1}{3}\right)\left(\frac{1}{2}\right) = \frac{1}{6}$$

You can verify this result by rereading Example 4.10.   ■

An additive probability rule, probability rule #1, was given for the event that either A or B occurs (i.e., $A \cup B$), but it applies only to the case where A and B are mutually exclusive events. A rule that applies in general is given by the **Additive Law of Probability.**

Probability Rule #6

The Additive Law of Probability

The probability that **either** an event A **or** an event B **or both** occur is

$$P(A \text{ or } B \text{ or both}) = \boxed{P(A \cup B) = P(A) + P(B) - P(A \cap B)}$$

EXAMPLE 4.15
Applying Probability
Rule #6

Suppose an experiment consists of tossing a pair of coins and observing the upper faces. Define the following events:

A: Observe at least one head

B: Observe at least one tail

Use the Additive Law of Probability to find the probability of observing either *A or B or* both.

SOLUTION   We want to find $P(A \cup B)$; however, we know the answer to this question before we start because the probability of observing at least one head or at least one tail is 1—i.e., the event is a certainty. To obtain this answer using the Additive Law of Probability, we could use the method of Example 4.6 to find

$$P(A) = P(\text{At least one head}) = \frac{3}{4}$$

$$P(B) = P(\text{At least one tail}) = \frac{3}{4}$$

The event that both A and B occur—observing at least one head and at least one tail—is the event that you observe exactly one head and exactly one tail. We found this probability in Example 4.6 to be $P(A \cap B) = \frac{1}{2}$. Therefore,

$$P(A \text{ or } B \text{ or both}) = P(A \cup B) = P(A) + P(B) - P(A \cap B)$$

$$= \frac{3}{4} + \frac{3}{4} - \frac{1}{2} = 1$$

This answer confirms what we already knew, that the probability of the event is equal to 1.   ■

Important: In Examples 4.14 and 4.15, two key words helped us identify which probability law to employ. In Example 4.14, the key word was "and," as in "find the probability that both *A and B* occur." The word *and* implies intersection; therefore, we use the Multiplicative Law of Probability. Alternatively, the key word was "or" in Example 4.15, as in "find the probability that either *A or B or* both occur." The word *or* implies union; therefore, we use the Additive Law of Probability.

EXAMPLE 4.16
Applying All Probability
Rules

A survey of 1,000 small business ventures classified each according to the profitability of the business (profitable or unprofitable), and according to whether the business had been in operation less than 2 years, 2 to 5 years, or more than 5 years. The percentages of businesses falling in the six categories are shown in Table 4.1. Suppose we use the percentages contained in the table to give the approximate probabilities that a single business would fall in the respective categories. We define the following events:

A: The business is profitable

B: The business has been in existence for more than 5 years

Table 4.1 Results of Profitability Survey of 1,000 Small Businesses

| | Length of Time in Business, Years | | | |
	Less than 2	2–5	More than 5	TOTALS
Profitable	2	8	14	24
Unprofitable	16	35	25	76
TOTALS	18	43	39	100

a. Find the probability that both A and B occur.
b. Find the conditional probability that A will occur given that B has occurred.
c. Find the probability that A will not occur.
d. Find the probability that either A or B or both occur.

SOLUTION

a. We can see from the table that 14% of the businesses were both profitable (A) and had survived more than 5 years (B). Therefore,

$$P(A \text{ and } B) = P(A \cap B) = .14$$

b. Again, examining Table 4.1, we find that 24% of all the businesses were profitable and 39% had survived more than 5 years. Therefore,

$$P(A) = .24 \quad \text{and} \quad P(B) = .39$$

To find $P(A|B)$, we substitute the answer to part **a** and the value of $P(B)$ into the formula for the Multiplicative Law of Probability. Thus,

$$P(A \text{ and } B) = P(A \cap B) = P(B)P(A|B)$$

or

$$.14 = (.39)P(A|B)$$

Solving for $P(A|B)$ yields

$$P(A|B) = \frac{.14}{.39} = .359$$

c. The event that A does not occur is the complement of A, denoted by the symbol $\overline{A}$. Since A is the event that a business is profitable, $\overline{A}$ is the event that a business is unprofitable. Recall that $P(A)$ and $P(\overline{A})$ bear a special relationship to each other:

$$P(A) + P(\overline{A}) = 1$$

From part **b**, we have $P(A) = .24$. Therefore,

$$P(\overline{A}) = 1 - .24 = .76$$

which can be verified by examining Table 4.1.

d. The probability that either A or B or both occur is given by the Additive Law of Probability. From parts **a** and **b** we know that

$$P(A) = .24$$
$$P(B) = .39$$
$$P(A \cap B) = .14$$

Then,

$$P(A \text{ or } B \text{ or both}) = P(A \cup B) = P(A) + P(B) - P(A \cap B)$$
$$= .24 + .39 - .14 = .49 \quad ■$$

EXERCISES

■ *Learning the Mechanics*

P (A∩B)= 0.4

4.44 For two events A and B, $P(A) = .5$, $P(B) = .6$, and P(both A and B occur) $= .4$. Find the probability that either A or B or both occur. 0 5+ 0.6- 0.4= 0.⁊

4.45 For two events A and B, $P(A) = .3$, $P(B) = .5$, and P(both A and B occur) $= .2$. Find the probability that either A or B or both occur.

4.46 Consider the experiment of tossing a pair of dice. Define events A and B as follows:

A: Observe a sum of 7

B: Observe a 4 on at least one die

a. List the possible outcomes in event A and find $P(A)$.
b. List the possible outcomes in event B and find $P(B)$.
c. Find $P(A \cap B)$ using the Multiplicative Law of Probability. Then list the possible outcomes associated with this event and find $P(A \cap B)$ by summing the probabilities of these outcomes.
d. Find $P(A \cup B)$ using the Additive Law of Probability. Then list the possible outcomes associated with this event and find $P(A \cup B)$ by summing the probabilities of these outcomes.

▪ Applying the Concepts

4.47 Refer to the *Transportation Journal* study of automobile safety, Exercise 2.35. The researchers also investigated the frequency of safety seat-belt usage among automobile owners. Each in a sample of 387 drivers was classified according to frequency of use (always, frequently, infrequently, and never) and state of residence (states with mandatory safety seat-belt laws, states with pending mandatory laws, and states without mandatory laws). The result are shown in the table.

| | Seat-belt Usage | | | | |
State of Residence	Always	Frequently	Infrequently	Never	Totals
Mandatory Seat-Belt Law	67	24	18	19	128
Pending Mandatory Seat-Belt Law	27	20	23	8	78
No Mandatory Seat-Belt Law	63	42	38	38	181
TOTALS	157	86	79	65	387

Source: Lieb, R. C., Wiseman, F., and Moore, T. E. "Automobile safety programs: The public viewpoint." *Transportation Journal*, Vol. 25, No. 4, Summer 1986, p. 25.

Suppose we select one of the 387 drivers in the study.
a. Find the probability that the driver resides in a state with no mandatory seat-belt law.
b. Find the probability that the driver uses safety seat belts infrequently.
c. Find the probability that the driver resides in a state with a pending mandatory seat-belt law and never uses seat belts.
d. Find the probability that the driver either resides in a state with a mandatory seat-belt law or always uses seat belts.
e. Given that the driver never uses seat belts, what is the probability that the driver resides in a state with no mandatory seat-belt law?
f. Given that the driver resides in a state with a pending mandatory seat-belt law, what is the probability that the driver frequently uses seat belts?

4.48 Refer to the Jackpot scratch-off game described in Exercise 4.18. Recall that eight of the 10 play squares reveal three cherries, "worth up to $1,000 in cash or prizes." Given that you scratch off three cherries, you will receive one of the following prizes (with associated probabilities):

$1,000 cash (.0000125)	Grandfather clock (.0000625)
$500 cash (.0000125)	Designer watch (.0000625)
VCR (.0000125)	Assorted prizes (.9998375)

a. Given that you scratch off three cherries, find the probability that you win cash.

b. What is the unconditional probability that you win cash in Jackpot?

4.49 According to the National Association of State Boards of Accountancy (NASBA), the probability is .20 that a first-time candidate passes all subjects in the Uniform CPA Examination (*New Accountant*, Sept. 1993). Given that a first-time candidate fails, the probability that such a candidate passes all subjects increases to .30 on repeat examinations. Use this information to find the probability that a candidate passes the Uniform CPA Examination on his or her second attempt.   *0.24*

4.50 In the summer of 1941, two incredible and well-publicized events occurred during the major league baseball season: (1) Ted Williams of the Boston Red Sox became the last player to record a batting average over .400, and (2) Joe DiMaggio of the New York Yankees had at least one hit in 56 consecutive games—the longest hitting streak in major league baseball history. Baseball fans and experts alike continually argue about which accomplishment is more likely to be duplicated first. *Chance* (Fall 1991) assessed the probabilities of the events occurring within the next 50 years as $P(\text{Bat over }.400) = .035$ and $P(\text{56-game hitting streak}) = .016$ under specific conditions (i.e., a league batting average of .270).

   a. Suppose a current major league baseball star has just completed a 56-game hitting streak. What is the probability that he will end the season with a batting average of over .400? Assume the two events, {Bat over .400} and {56-game hitting streak}, are dependent.

   b. Explain why it is not possible to calculate the conditional probability of part **a.**

   c. Calculate the conditional probability of part **a,** assuming the two events are independent.

   d. Based on your knowledge of baseball, batting averages, and hitting streaks, assess the likelihood of the two events being independent.

4.51 A recent survey of the American public showed that a majority believe that when they retire, their retirement income (from Social Security, company retirement plans, etc.) will be inadequate. A breakdown of the percentages in each category is shown in the table on page 186. Assume that the percentage of the total number of people who fall in a given cell of the table gives the approximate probability that a person selected at random will fall in that cell category. Define the following events:

A: A person believes that his or her retirement income will be inadequate

B: The major source of retirement income will be a Social Security pension

C: The major source of retirement income will be a job pension

Find:

a. $P(A)$ **b.** $P(B)$ **c.** $P(C)$ **d.** $P(A \cap B)$

e. $P(B \cap C)$ **f.** $P(A \cup B)$ **g.** $P(B|A)$

		Primary Type of Retirement Support				
		Social Security	Job Pensions	Personal Savings	Other	TOTALS
Believe Support	*Adequate*	16	9	11	1	37
Will Be	*Inadequate*	41	12	4	6	63
	TOTALS	57	21	15	7	100

4.52 The National Acid Precipitation Assessment Program (NAPAP) has recently concluded a 10-year study of acid rain. In its report, NAPAP estimates the probability of an Adirondack lake being acidic at .14. Given that the Adirondack lake is acidic, the probability that it comes by its acidity naturally is .25 (*Science News*, Sept. 15, 1990). Use this information to find the probability that an Adirondack lake is naturally acidic.   3.5%

4.53 A national study of 1,006 female adults showed that 58% have a sewing machine in their homes (*Journal of Advertising Research*, Feb./Mar. 1984). Of those who have sewing machines, 36% have sewn a garment that required use of a sewing pattern in the past 12 months. Based on these figures, what is the probability that a female adult selected from those surveyed has a machine and has sewn a garment that required use of a sewing pattern in the past 12 months?

4.54 The merging process from an acceleration lane to the through lane of a freeway constitutes an important aspect of traffic operation at interchanges. From a study of parallel and tapered interchange ramps in Israel, the table provides information on traffic lags (where a lag is defined as an interval of time between arrivals of major streams of vehicles) accepted and rejected by drivers in the merging lane.

Type of Interchange Lane	Traffic Condition on Freeway	Number of Merging Drivers Accepting the First Available Lag	Number of Merging Drivers Rejecting the First Available Lag
Tapered	Heavy traffic	16	115
	Little traffic	67	121
Parallel	Heavy traffic	40	139
	Little traffic	144	331

Source: Polus, A., and Livneh, M. "Vehicle flow characteristics on acceleration lanes." *Journal of Transportation Engineering*, Vol. III, No. 6, Nov. 1985, pp. 600–601 (Table 4).

a. What is the probability that a driver in a tapered merging lane with heavy traffic will accept the first available lag?

b. What is the probability that a driver in a parallel merging lane will reject the first available lag in traffic?

c. Given that a driver accepts the first available lag in little traffic, what is the probability that the driver is in a parallel merging lane?

SUMMARY

In this chapter, we introduced the notion of *experiments* whose outcomes could not be predicted with certainty in advance. The uncertainty associated with these outcomes (events) was measured by their *probabilities*—the relative frequencies of their occurrence in a very large number of repetitions of the experiment.

We presented several rules for finding the probabilities of events. The first two rules enable us to find the probability that either one or the other of two events will occur when the events are *mutually exclusive* (probability rule #1), and when all possible outcomes of the experiment are both mutually exclusive and equiprobable (probability rule #2). Probability rule #3 provides a formula for finding the probability that both of two events will occur when the two events are *independent*. Probability rule #4 gives the probability of the *complement* of an event. In the optional section of this chapter, we gave two probability rules that apply in general: the Multiplicative Law of Probability for the intersection of two events and the Additive Law of Probability for the union of two events. These probability rules are summarized here for convenience.

Probability Rules

1. *Additive Rule:* If two events A and B are mutually exclusive, then

$$P(A \text{ or } B) = P(A \cup B) = P(A) + P(B)$$

In general,*

$$P(A \text{ or } B \text{ or both}) = P(A \cup B) = P(A) + P(B) - P(A \text{ and } B)$$

2. *Modified Additive Rule for Equally Likely Mutually Exclusive Events:* If an experiment results in one and only one of M equally likely mutually exclusive events, of which m of these result in an event A, then

$$P(A) = \frac{m}{M}$$

3. *Multiplicative Rule:* If two events A and B are independent, then

$$P(A \text{ and } B) = P(A \cap B) = P(A)P(B)$$

In general,*

$$P(A \text{ and } B) = P(A \cap B) = P(A)P(B|A) = P(B)P(A|B)$$

4. *Rule of Complements:* $P(A) = 1 - P(\overline{A})$

Finally, we used the *rare event approach* to illustrate how probability plays a role in statis-

---

*From the optional section in this chapter.

tical inference. We drew a sample from a population and then, based on the probability of observing the sample under various assumptions about the population, we made a decision concerning the nature of the sampled population.

We will not be using the probability rules to solve probability problems in the succeeding chapters because the sample probabilities that we need are too difficult to obtain (that is, their calculation is beyond the scope of this text). Nevertheless, the basic concepts of probability covered in this chapter will be of considerable benefit in understanding how probability plays a role in the inferential methods that follow.

KEY TERMS

Complementary events	Intersection*	Simple events
Conditional probability	Mutually exclusive events	Uncertainty
Event	Probability	Union*
Experiment	Rare event approach	
Independent events	Sample space	

SUPPLEMENTARY EXERCISES

[Note: Starred (*) exercises refer to the optional section in this chapter.]

4.55   Video card games (e.g., video poker), once only legal in casinos, are now available for play in laundromats and grocery stores in states that employ a lottery. Because these video games are less intimidating than the traditional casino table games (e.g., blackjack, roulette, and craps), experts speculate that more women are becoming addicted to them. The *Wall Street Journal* (July 14, 1992) reported on the gambling habits of 52 women in Gamblers Anonymous.

a. Of the 52 women, 47 were video poker players. Use this information to assess the likelihood that a female member of Gamblers Anonymous (GA) is or was addicted to video poker.

b. Refer to part **a**. Of the 47 video poker players, 35 gambled until they exhausted their family savings. Express this information in a probability statement.

* **c.** Use the probabilities, parts **a** and **b**, to find the probability that a female member of GA was addicted to video poker and gambled until she exhausted her family savings.

4.56   The loan officer of a bank performs the following experiment: Observe the size of a loan request and the financial characteristics (as they relate to credit risk) of the applicant. If the experiment is conducted once (that is, the loan officer observes the characteristics described above for a single loan application), some of the events he or she might observe are as follows:

From the optional section in this chapter.

A: The loan request exceeds $100,000

B: The loan request exceeds $60,000

C: The applicant's net worth is $185,000

Explain whether the pairs of events, *A* and *B*, *A* and C, *B* and C, are mutually exclusive.

4.57 A study on shoplifting for the National Mass Retailing Institute (reported in the *Orlando Sentinel*, Dec. 11, 1983) revealed that retailers blame shoplifting for only 30% of their shrinkage (disappearance of inventory). Fifty percent of the shrinkage is attributed to employee theft and 20% to poor paperwork control.
a. Find the probability that a missing sales item was stolen.
b. Find the probability that a missing sales item was not stolen.

4.58 The accompanying table summarizes the results of a report on the survival rates of U.S. corporations. The first column lists various ages (in years) of the firms, and the second column gives the percentage of all U.S. corporations that survive to the specified age. Of those firms that survive to the specified age, the third column gives the percentages surviving at least 5 years beyond that age.

Age	Percentage Surviving to Specified Age	Percentage Surviving at Least 5 Years Beyond Specified Age
5	38%	55%
10	21	65
15	14	70
20	10	73
25	7	76
50	2	83
75	1	86
100	.5	88

Source: Nystrom, P. C., and Starbuck, W. H. "To avoid organizational crises, unlearn."
Organizational Dynamics, Spring 1984, Vol. 12, No. 4, p. 54.

a. Find the probability that a new corporation survives to age 15 years. (Assume that the survival rates remain unchanged.)
b. Find the probability that a new corporation survives to at least age 15 years, given that it has survived to age 10 years.
c. Find the probability that a new corporation does not survive to age 5 years (i.e., fails before 5 years).

4.59 According to the *Wall Street Journal* (Sept. 23, 1985) "the rise in recent years of high-powered betting syndicates has become one of the hot controversies in sports betting." A syndicate is a group of high-stakes bettors who pool their resources and cover every combination of a pari-mutuel bet. Suppose your betting syndicate wants to cover all possible outcomes of a quinella bet in jai-alai. To win a quinella, a bettor must pick players (of the eight) who finish in the top two positions ("win" and "place") in a single game without regard to their order of finish. List the different quinella bets that must be made, i.e., list the different ways in which two players can be selected from the eight.

4.60 Managers of oil exploration portfolios make decisions on which prospects to pursue based, in part, on the level of risk associated with each venture. The problem of risk analysis in oil exploration was recently examined using the outcomes and associated probabilities for a single prospect shown in the table.

Outcome, Barrels	Probability
0 (dry hole)	.60
50,000	.10
100,000	.15
500,000	.10
1,000,000	.05
	1.00

Source: Kinchen, A. L. "Projected outcomes of exploration programs based on current program status and the impact of prospects under consideration." *Journal of Petroleum Technology*, Vol. 38, No. 4, Apr. 1986, p. 462. Copyright 1986 Society of Petroleum Engineers of AIME.

a. What is the probability that a single oil well prospect will result in no more than 100,000 barrels of oil?

b. What is the probability that a single oil well prospect will strike oil?

c. Two identical oil well prospects were also considered. List the possible outcomes if the two wells are drilled. Assume that the outcomes listed in the table are the only possible outcomes for any one well. [*Hint:* One possible outcome is two dry holes.]

d. Use the information in the table to calculate the probabilities of the outcomes listed in part **c.** (Assume that the individual outcomes of the two wells are independent of each other.)

e. Refer to part **d.** Find the probability that at least one of the two oil prospects strikes oil.

4.61 As part of an advertising campaign to attract new listeners, an AM radio station conducts a cash jackpot drawing each weekday morning. Every morning a name is chosen at random from the local phone directory (residential phones only) and that person is called for a chance to win money. A listener whose last name begins with a "Y" calls the radio station and inquires about her chance of being selected. She is informed that since there are 26 letters in the alphabet, the probability of choosing a last name beginning with "Y" is $\frac{1}{26}$. Is this probability correct? Explain.

4.62 Pennsylvania's twice-weekly Big 4 lottery game allows players to bet an amount between 50¢ and $5.00 on a four-digit number of their choice. For a winning ticket, payoffs have been as high as $25,000. On June 8, 1983, lottery officials suspended play on the number 3526 (which corresponds to the record strike-out total recorded by Philadelphia Phillies pitcher and Hall-of-Famer Steve Carlton earlier that week) because of heavy betting that left the state with a potential liability—if the number were to be selected—of $5 million. A similar situation occurred when play was suspended on the number 4077 during the week of March 2, 1983, when the last installment of the old television series "M ∗ A ∗ S ∗ H" was broadcast.

a. If lottery officials select the winning number at random, what is the probability that it would be 3526? Use the fact that there are 10,000 different four-digit numbers that could be selected.

b. Lottery officials also reported heavy betting on other groupings of the numbers 3, 5, 2, and 6. How many different rearrangements of these four digits are possible?

c. What is the probability that the winning number would be some rearrangement of the digits 3, 5, 2, and 6?

4.63   The most common data-collection method in consumer and market research is the telephone survey. However, a major problem with consumer telephone surveys is nonresponse. How likely are consumers to be at home to take the call and, if at home, how likely are they to take part in the survey? To answer these and other questions, Kerin and Peterson (1983) directed a study of over 250,000 random-digit dialings of both listed and unlisted telephone numbers across the United States. The study enabled the researchers to assess the probabilities of various outcomes on the first dialing attempt, as shown in the accompanying table.

Result of Dialing Attempt	*Probability*
No answer	.347
Busy signal	.020
Out-of-service	.203
No eligible person at home	.291
Business number	.041
Eligible person at home—refusal	.014
Eligible person at home—completed interview	.084

Source: Kerin, R. A., and Peterson, R. A. *Journal of Advertising Research,* Apr./May. 1983.

a. What is the probability that a single call will result in no answer, a busy signal, or an out-of-service number?

b. What is the probability that an eligible person will be at home to take the call?

c. Given that an eligible person is at home to take the call, what is the probability that he or she will refuse to participate in the interview? (This probability is known as the *refusal rate.*)

4.64   To assist the Occupational Safety and Health Administration in the development of federal safety standards, the Bureau of Labor Statistics conducted a survey of workers who suffer serious hand injuries on the job *(Engineering News-Record,* Mar. 3, 1983). The Bureau reported that, despite their relatively small numbers, carpenters account for 4% of all job-related hand injuries. The survey also indicated that 29% of the injured workers attributed their injuries to the pace at which they were working, and 13% of those injured workers wearing hand protection claimed their gloves actually caused the accident. Suppose a worker sustains a hand injury. Assume that the events previously described are independent.

a. Find the probability that the injured worker is a carpenter whose injury was caused by the pace at which he was working.

b. Find the probability that the injured worker attributes the cause of the accident to his protective hand gloves (given that the worker was wearing hand protection).

4.65   The Department of Housing collects data on loan size, loan value, default status, and various other characteristics of all FHA home mortgages. Housing planners and credit institutions use this information to assess the risk of default in home mortgages. The accompanying table gives the probability of default for several different types of home loans at 95%–100% of value.

Loan	Race of Homeowner	Home Location	Probability of Default
Above $20,750	White	City	.0344
Below $20,750	White	City	.0389
Above $20,750	Black	City	.1250
Above $20,750	Black	Suburb	.1695

Source: FHA Cross Reference File, 1978. Data also reported in Evans, R. D., Mans, B. A., and Weinstein, R. I. "Expected loss and mortgage default risk." *Quarterly Journal of Business and Economics*, Winter 1985, Vol. 24, No. 1, p. 77.

a. What is the probability that a white homeowner, located in the city, will default on a loan of greater than $20,750?

b. What is the probability that a black homeowner, located in the city, will default on a loan of greater than $20,750?

c. Suppose that 70% of the blacks who own homes are city dwellers and 30% reside in the suburbs. What is the probability that a black homeowner will default on a loan of greater than $20,750?

4.66   A weekly business periodical operates with two high-speed printing presses (presses #1 and #2). The manufacturer of these high-speed presses claims that, when operating properly, the machines shut down for repairs on only 1% of the operating days. Suppose the presses operate independently—that is, the chance of one press breaking down is in no way influenced by the current operating condition of the other. One operating day is randomly selected and the performance of the presses is observed.

a. What is the probability that press #1 will be shut down for repairs?

b. What is the probability that press #2 will not need to be shut down for repairs?

c. What is the probability that both presses will be shut down for repairs?

d. Suppose both presses actually do need to be shut down for repairs during the operating day. Based on this observation, what would you infer about the press manufacturer's claim?

4.67   Under "Operation Greenback," U.S. customs officials are using computers to help trace large sums of money from the illegal narcotics trade to the kingpins—those people who do not actually handle the drugs but who realize profits from drug sales. The computer monitors cash transactions at state and federal banks and flags all unusual transactions. Because some transactions are completely legitimate, investigators cross-reference the list of possible offenders with a list of suspected or convicted criminals. When a "hit" or match is made, the name is investigated by federal law enforcement agencies.

Suppose the computer detects four unusual cash transactions at a Miami bank. These four names are then cross-referenced with a list of suspected Miami drug dealers. Assume that the outcomes ("hit" or "miss") of the four transactions are equally likely.

a. What is the probability of exactly two matches?
b. What is the probability of at least one match?
c. Do you think that the assumption of equally likely outcomes is reasonable? Explain.

*4.68 A small company conducted a survey of its employees to determine their attitudes toward a buyout of the company's stock. The company's 1,040 employees were asked whether they favored the buyout and whether they planned to retire within the next 15 years. The numbers of employees falling in the four buyout–retirement categories are shown in the table. Suppose a single employee is to be randomly selected from among the 1,040.

| | | *Favor Buyout* | | |
		No	*Yes*	*Totals*
Retirement	*No*	464	182	646
Within 15 Years	*Yes*	179	215	394
Totals		643	397	1,040

a. What is the probability that the employee favors a buyout?   38.17%   37.88
b. What is the probability that the employee will retire within the next 15 years?
c. What is the probability that the employee favors the buyout given that he or she plans to retire within the next 15 years?   20.67%
d. Is an employee's attitude toward the buyout independent of his or her retirement plans? no

*4.69 A brewery utilizes two bottling machines, but they do not operate simultaneously. The second machine acts as a back-up system to the first machine, and operates only when the first breaks down during operating hours. The probability that the first machine breaks down during operating hours is .20. If in fact the first breaks down, then the second machine is turned on and has a probability of .30 of breaking down.

a. What is the probability that the brewery's bottling system is not working during operating hours? [*Hint:* The system is not working when both bottling machines break down during operating hours. Use the Multiplicative Law of Probability.]   0.06
b. The *reliability* of the bottling process is the probability that the system is working during operating hours. Find the reliability of the bottling process at the brewery. [*Hint:* Use your answer to part **a** and the notion of complementary events.]   0.94

4.70 Recent survey research reveals a tremendous variability in consumer purchasing experience and behavior in less developed countries (LDCs). For example, one large multinational corporation failed in its attempt to sell baby food in Africa using a package designed for its home country—Africans interpreted the labels to mean the jars contained ground-up babies! How do multinational corporations market and adapt consumer products from developed countries in LDCs? To answer this question, Hill and Still (1984) surveyed subsidiaries of consumer goods manufacturers with operations in LDCs. The survey results were used to assess the likelihood that a specific factor (e.g., consumer preference or social custom) caused the change in a product characteristic (e.g., brand name). The probabilities for three product characteristics are shown in the table on page 194.

	Product Characteristic		
Factor	Brand Name	Labeling	Package Aesthetics
Consumer preferences	.363	.314	.530
Competition	.018	.205	.269
Literacy and education	.200	.051	.000
Legal considerations	.309	.340	.000
Sociocultural customs and taboos	.072	.051	.037
Other	.038	.039	.164

Source: Adapted from Hill, J. S., and Still, R. R. "Adapting products to LDC tastes." *Harvard Business Review,* Mar.-Apr. 1984, Vol. 62, No. 2, p. 96.

a. Show that the factor probabilities sum to 1 for each product characteristic.
b. Given that the brand name of a product is changed, what is the probability that the change is caused by a marketing factor (i.e., either consumer preference or competition)?
c. Repeat part **b** for the product characteristic labeling.
d. Repeat part **b** for the product characteristic package aesthetics.
e. For each of the three product characteristics, find the probability that the factor causing the change is not an LDC's customs and taboos.

4.71 Most national advertisers use mixed-media advertising campaigns that include both television and magazines. The key to a successful campaign is the correct apportionment of the advertising budget to be spent in each medium. The *Journal of Marketing Research* (Feb. 1984) reported on a model for evaluating mixed-media advertising schedules, based on the probabilities of the following events:

A: A consumer views a typical television show in the schedule   0.2

B: A consumer reads a typical magazine issue in the schedule   0.08

C: A consumer views a typical television show and reads a typical magazine issue in the schedule   0.03

D: A consumer is *not* exposed to either a typical television show or a typical magazine issue in the schedule

Assume that an individual is selected from the population of potential buyers of a product. The advertisers of the product have developed a mixed-media campaign, with the following probabilities:

$P(A) = .20$ $P(B) = .08$ $P(C) = .03$

a. Find P(Either A or B or both occur).   0.25
b. Describe, in words, the probability of part **a.**
c. Describe the event $\overline{D}$.
d. Use your answers to parts **a–c** and the probability relationship for complementary events to find $P(D)$.   0.75

4.72 Food labeled as "low calorie" is required by law to contain no more than 40 calories per serving. The Food and Drug Administration (FDA) suspects a company is marketing illegally labeled cans of "low calorie" chocolate pudding—i.e., the cans contain more than 40 calories per serving, even though they are labeled as "low calorie." From a supermarket shelf containing 10 cans of "low calorie" chocolate pudding, the FDA randomly selects three for inspection. Unknown to the FDA, exactly seven of the 10 cans contain more than 40 calories per serving.

a. What is the probability that the FDA observes all three cans to be legally labeled—that is, the cans contain no more than 40 calories per serving? Use the fact that the number of different ways the FDA can select three of the 10 cans for inspection is 120.

b. What is the probability that the FDA observes at least one of the three cans to be illegally labeled?

c. If the event of part **b** actually occurred, would you consider it to be a rare event if in fact seven of the 10 cans are illegally labeled?

4.73 Refer to Exercise 4.43. In the two-dice game of craps, a player wins if he throws a *natural* (a 7 or 11) and loses if he throws *craps* (a 2, 3, or 12). However, if the sum of the two dice is 4, 5, 6, 8, 9, or 10 (each of these is known as a *point*), the player continues throwing the dice until the same outcome (point) is repeated (in which case the player wins), or the outcome 7 occurs (in which case the player loses). For example, if a player's first toss results in a 6, the player continues to toss the dice until a 6 or 7 occurs. If a 6 occurs first, the player wins. If a 7 occurs first, the player loses.

a. What is the probability that a player throws a point on the first toss? [*Hint:* Find P(Either 4 or 5 or 6 or 8 or 9 or 10).]

b. If a player throws a point of 6 on the first toss, what is the probability that the player wins the game on the next toss?

c. If a player throws a point of 6 on the first toss, what is the probability that the player loses the game on the next toss?

4.74 Refer to Exercises 4.43 and 4.73. From the information provided by these exercises, it can be seen that there are basically three events that result in a win for the craps player:

A: The player throws a 7 on the first toss

B: The player throws an 11 on the first toss

C: The player throws a point on the first toss, and throws the same point on a subsequent toss before throwing a 7

Since the events *A*, *B*, and *C* form pairs of mutually exclusive events, the probability that the player wins the game—i.e., the probability of *making a pass*—is simply $P(A) + P(B) + P(C)$. It can be shown (proof omitted) that the probability of a player making a pass is .493.

a. Interpret this win probability.

b. In most casinos, betting that a player makes a pass pays off at *even odds*—i.e., for every $1 bet, you win $1 if the player makes a pass. Considering the .493 probability of winning, do you think that the even payoff odds are "fair"? That is, if you repeatedly bet on a player to make a pass, would you expect to win as much money as you lose? [*Hint:* When the payoff odds for a winning bet are even, the game is deemed *fair* if the probability of winning the bet is .50.]

4.75 *Science Digest* magazine features an interesting and informative columnist, known only by the eerie name of Dr. Crypton. Each month Dr. Crypton presents mind-twisters, riddles, puzzles, and enigmas that very often can be solved using the laws of probability. In the January 1982 issue, Dr. Crypton offered this view of what is commonly called the "birthday problem": [*]

> Surely you have been in a situation in which a small group of people compared birthdays and found, to their surprise, that at least two of them were born on the same day of the same month. Suppose there are 10 people in the group. Intuition may suggest that the odds of two sharing a birthday are quite poor. Probability theory, however, shows the odds are better than one in nine.
>
> If you like to win bets, you should keep in mind that for a group of 23 people the odds are in favor of at least two of them sharing a birthday. (For 22 people, the odds are slightly against this.)

a. Find the probability that no two of a group of 23 people share the same birthday. [*Hint:* Since there are 365 days in a year, any of which may be the birthday of one of the 23 people, the probability that none of the people in the group share a birthday is

$$\left(\frac{365}{365}\right) \cdot \left(\frac{364}{365}\right) \cdot \left(\frac{363}{365}\right) \cdots \left(\frac{343}{365}\right)$$

Person   Person   Person   Person
#1   #2   #3   #23

Compute this probability.]

b. Using the rule of complements, find the probability that at least two of 23 people will share the same birthday.

c. Use the steps outlined in parts **a** and **b** to find the probability that at least two of 22 people will share the same birthday.

■ CASE STUDY 4.1

Lottery Buster!

"Welcome to the Wonderful World of Lottery Bu$ters." So begins the premier issue of *Lottery Buster*, a monthly publication for players of the state lottery games. *Lottery Buster* provides interesting facts and figures on the nearly 40 state lotteries currently operating in the United States and, more importantly, tips on how to increase a player's odds of winning the lottery.

New Hampshire, in 1963, was the first state in modern times to authorize a state lottery as an alternative to increasing taxes. (Prior to this time, beginning in 1895, lotteries were banned in America because of corruption.) Since then, lotteries have become immensely popular for two reasons. First, they lure you with the opportunity to win millions of dollars with a $1 investment, and second, when you lose, at least you know your money is going to a good cause.

The popularity of the state lottery has brought with it an avalanche of "experts" and "mathematical wizards" (such as the editors of *Lottery Buster*) who provide advice on how to win the lottery—for a fee, of course! These experts—the legitimate ones, anyway—base their "systems" of winning on their knowledge of probability and statistics.

For example, more experts would agree that the "golden rule" or "first rule" in winning lotteries is *game selection*. State lotteries generally offer three types of games: Instant (scratch-off) tickets, Daily Numbers (Pick-3 and Pick-4), and the weekly Pick-6 Lotto game.

The Instant game involves scratching off the thin opaque covering on a ticket with the edge of a coin to determine whether you have won or lost. The cost of a ticket is 50¢ and the amount won ranges from $1 to $100,000 in most states, and to as much as $1 million in others. *Lottery Buster* advises against playing the Instant game because it is "a pure chance play, and you can win only by dumb luck. No skill can be applied to this game."

The Daily Numbers game permits you to choose either a three-digit (Pick-3) or four-digit (Pick-4) number at a cost of $1 per ticket. Each night, the winning number is drawn. If your number matches the winning number, you win a large sum of money, usually

$100,000. You do have some control over the Daily Numbers game (since you pick the numbers that you play) and, consequently, there are strategies available to increase your chances of winning. However, the Daily Numbers game, like the Instant game, is not available for out-of-state play. For this reason, and the fact that payoffs are relatively small, lottery experts prefer the weekly Pick-6 Lotto game.

To play Pick-6 Lotto, you select six numbers of your choice from a field of numbers ranging from 1 to N, where N depends on which state's game you are playing. For example, Florida's Lotto game involves picking six numbers ranging from 1 to 49 (denoted 6/49) as shown on the Florida Lotto ticket, Figure 4.8 (page 198). Delaware's Lotto is a 6/30 game, and Pennsylvania's is a 6/40 game. The cost of a ticket is $1, and the payoff, if your six numbers match the winning numbers drawn at the end of each week, is $6 million or more, depending on the number of tickets purchased. (To date, Pennsylvania has had the largest weekly payoff of $106 million.) In addition to the grand prize, you can win second-, third-, and fourth-prize payoffs by matching five, four, and three of the six numbers drawn, respectively. You do not have to be a resident of the state to play the state's Lotto game. Anyone can play by calling a toll-free "hotline" number.

a. Consider Florida's 6/49 Lotto game. Use the formula given in the next box to calculate the number of samples of $n = 6$ numbers that can be selected from a total of $N = 49$ numbers. (This number represents the total number of simple events in the sample space, i.e., the number of possible ways in which you can choose the six numbers from the 49 available.) If you purchase a single $1 ticket, what is the probability that you win the grand prize (i.e., match all six numbers)?

b. Repeat part a for Delaware's 6/30 game.

c. Repeat part a for Pennsylvania's 6/40 game.

d. Since you can play any state's Lotto game,

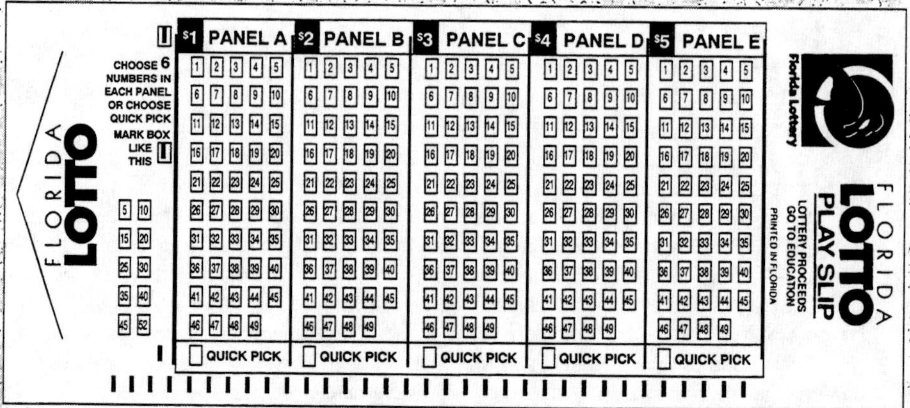

FIGURE 4.8

Reproduction of Florida 6/49 Lotto Ticket

Combinatorial Rule for Determining the Number of Different Samples That Can Be Selected from a Population

The number of different samples of n objects that can be selected from among a total of N is denoted $\binom{N}{n}$ and is equal to

$$\binom{N}{n} = \frac{N!}{n!\,(N-n)!}$$

where

$N! = N(N-1)(N-2)(N-3)\cdots(3)(2)(1)$ and is read N factorial

$n! = n(n-1)(n-2)(n-3)\cdots(3)(2)(1)$

$0! = 1$

---

which of the three, Florida, Delaware, or Pennsylvania, would you choose to play? Why?

e. One strategy used to increase your odds of winning a Lotto is to employ a *wheeling system*. In a complete wheeling system, you select more than six numbers, say seven, and play every combination of six of those seven numbers. Suppose you choose to "wheel" the following seven numbers in a

6/40 game: 2, 7, 18, 23, 30, 32, 39. How many tickets would you need to purchase to have every possible combination of the seven numbers? List the six numbers on each of these tickets.

f. Refer to part **e**. What is the probability of winning the 6/40 Lotto when you wheel seven numbers? Does the strategy, in fact, increase your odds of winning?

g. Another strategy is to play neighboring

pairs. Neighboring pairs are two consecutive numbers that come up together on the winning ticket. In one state lottery, for example, 79% of the winning tickets had at least one neighboring pair. Thus, some "experts" feel that you have a better chance of winning if you include at least one neighboring pair in your number selection. Calculate the probability of winning the 6/40 Lotto with the six numbers: 2, 15, 19, 20, 27, 37. [*Note*: 19, 20 is a neighboring pair.] Compare this probability to the one in part c. Comment on the neighboring pairs strategy.

a b c d e f g

a b c d e f   a b c d g f
a g c d e f   a b c d e g
a b g d e f   g b c d e f
a b e g e f

■ CASE STUDY 4.2

To Switch or Not to Switch?

Marilyn vos Savant, who is listed in *Guinness Book of World Records Hall of Fame* for "Highest IQ," writes a monthly column in the Sunday newspaper supplement *Parade Magazine*. Her column, "Ask Marilyn," is devoted to games of skill, puzzles, and mind-bending riddles. In a recent issue, vos Savant posed the following question:

Suppose you're on a game show, and you're given a choice of three doors. Behind one door is a car; behind the others, goats. You pick a door—say, #1—and the host, who knows what's behind the doors, opens another door—say, #3—which has a goat. He then says to you, 'Do you want to pick door #2?' Is it to your advantage to switch your choice?

Marilyn's answer was, "Yes, you should switch. The first door has a $\frac{1}{3}$ chance of winning [the car], but the second door has a $\frac{2}{3}$ chance [of winning the car]." Needless to say, vos Savant's surprising answer led to thousands of critical letters disagreeing with her. Many of the letters were from Ph.D. mathematicians; some of the more interesting and critical letters (that were printed in her next column) are condensed below:

- "May I suggest you obtain and refer to a standard textbook on probability before you try to answer a question of this type again?" (University of Florida)

- "Your logic is in error, and I am sure you will receive many letters on this topic from high school and college students. Perhaps you should keep a few addresses for help with future columns." (Georgia State University)

- "You are utterly incorrect about the game-show question, and I hope this controversy will call some public attention to the serious national crisis in mathematical education. If you can admit your error you will have contributed constructively toward

the solution of a deplorable situation. How many irate mathematicians are needed to get you to change your mind?" (Georgetown University)

- "I am in shock that after being corrected by at least three mathematicians, you still do not see your mistake." (Dickinson State University)

- "You are the goat!" (Western State University)

- "You're wrong, but look on the positive side. If all the Ph.D.'s were wrong, the country would be in serious trouble." (U.S. Army Research Institute)

The logic employed by those who disagree with vos Savant is as follows: Once the host shows you door #3 (a goat), only two doors remain. The probability of the car being behind door #1 (your door) is $\frac{1}{2}$; similarly, the probability is $\frac{1}{2}$ for door #2. Therefore, in the long run (i.e., over a long series of trials), it doesn't matter whether you switch to door #2 or keep door #1. Approximately 50% of the time you will win a car, and 50% of the time you will "win" a goat.

Who is correct, the Ph.D. mathematicians or Marilyn? By answering the following series of questions, you will arrive at the correct solution.

a. Prior to the taping of the game show, the host randomly decides behind which of the three doors to put the car; the goats will go behind the remaining two doors. List the simple events for this experiment. [*Hint:* One simple event is $C_1 G_2 G_3$, i.e., car behind door #1 and goats behind door #2 and door #3.]

b. Randomly choose one of the three doors, as the contestant does in the game show. Now, for each simple event in part **a**, circle the selected door and put an × through one of the remaining two doors that hides a goat. (This is the door that the host shows the contestant—always with a goat behind it.)

Source: Parade Magazine, Feb. 17, 1991.

c. Refer to the altered simple events in part **b.** Assume your strategy is to keep the door originally selected. Count the number of simple events for which this is a "winning" strategy (i.e., you win the car). Assuming equally likely simple events, what is the probability that you win the car?

d. Repeat part **c,** but assume your strategy is to always switch doors.

e. Based on the probabilities of parts **c** and **d,** is it to your advantage to switch your choice?

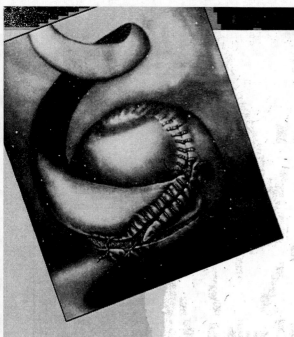

Chapter 5

DISCRETE PROBABILITY DISTRIBUTIONS

Organizational behavior researchers have found a causal link between employees' commitment to a firm and employee turnover. Consider the number x of employees who leave the firm for a job at another company. What values of x signal a general lack of employee commitment to the firm? To answer this question, we must know something about the probability distribution of x. In this chapter, we learn about several different types of discrete probability distributions that provide good models for many business data. We apply one of these probability distributions to answer questions concerning stayers and leavers at an organization in Case Study 5.1.

■ CONTENTS

5.1 Random Variables

In a practical business setting, an experiment (as defined in Chapter 4) involves selecting a sample of data consisting of one or more observations on some variable. For example, we might survey 1,000 consumers concerning their preferences for toothpaste and record x, the number who prefer a particular brand. Or, we might randomly select a single property from Appendix A.1 and record its total appraised value, x. Since we can never know with certainty in advance the exact value that we will observe when we record x for a single performance of the experiment, we call x a **random variable**.

Definition 5.1

A **random variable** is a variable that assumes numerical values associated with events of an experiment.

The random variables described above are examples of two different types of random variables—**discrete** and **continuous**. The number x of consumers in a sample of 1,000 who prefer a particular brand of toothpaste is said to be a discrete random variable because it can assume only a countable number of values—namely, 0, 1, 2, 3, ..., 999, 1,000. In contrast, the appraised value of a property is a continuous random variable because it could theoretically assume any one of an infinite number of values—namely, any value from \$0 upward. Of course, in practice, we record appraised value to the nearest dollar but, *in theory*, the appraised value of a property could assume any value, say, \$51,144.13471.

A good way to distinguish between discrete and continuous random variables is to imagine the values that they may assume as points on a line. Discrete random variables may assume any one of a countable number (say, 10, 21, or 100) of values corresponding to points on a line. In contrast, a continuous random variable can theoretically assume *any* value corresponding to the points in one or more intervals on a line. For example, the appraised value of a property could be represented by any of the infinitely large number of points on some portion of the positive half of a line.

Definition 5.2

A **discrete random variable** is one that can assume only a countable number of values.

Definition 5.3

A **continuous random variable** can assume any value in one or more intervals on a line.

EXAMPLE 5.1
Types of Random Variables

Suppose you randomly select a single work day at the IBM Corporation. Classify each of the following random variables as discrete or continuous:

    a. Number of nonsalaried employees who report for work that day

    b. Total value of sales orders (in dollars) for personal computers made that day

SOLUTION

    a. The number of nonsalaried employees reporting for work on a given day is a discrete random variable because it can assume only a countable number of values (for example, 1, 2, 3, ..., 48,855, 48,856, and so on). It is not continuous because the number reporting for work *must be an integer*; the variable can never assume values such as .5 or 47,504.2116.

    b. The total value of sales orders taken on a given day is a continuous random variable that could assume any value (for example, $20,417.31), corresponding to the points on the line interval from 0 to some maximum amount. ■

The focus of this chapter is discrete random variables. Continuous random variables are the topic of Chapter 6.

5.2 Probability Models for Discrete Random Variables

We learned in Chapter 4 that we make inferences based on the probability of observing a particular sample outcome. Since we never know the *exact* probability of some event, we must construct probability models for the values assumed by random variables.

For example, if we toss a die, we assume that the values 1, 2, 3, 4, 5, and 6 represent equiprobable events, i.e., $P(1) = P(2) = \cdots = P(6) = \frac{1}{6}$. In doing so, we have constructed a probabilistic model for a theoretical population of x values, where x is the number of dots showing on the upper face of the die. This population is "theoretical" in the sense that we would observe x for an infinite number of die tosses. A bar graph for the theoretical population would appear as shown in Figure 5.1.

FIGURE 5.1

The Probability Distribution for x, the Number of Dots Observed on a Balanced Die

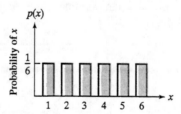

Figure 5.1, which gives the relative frequency for each value of x in an infinite number of tosses of a die, is called the **probability distribution for the discrete random variable** x.

Definition 5.4

The **probability distribution for the discrete random variable** x is a table, graph, or formula that gives the probability of observing each value of x. If we denote the probability of x by the symbol $p(x)$, the probability distribution has the following properties:

1. $0 \le p(x) \le 1$ for all values of x
2. $\displaystyle\sum_{\text{all } x} p(x) = 1$

EXAMPLE 5.2
Properties of a Probability Distribution

Consider the following consumer-sampling situation. Draw a random sample of $n = 5$ consumers from a very large number—say, 10,000—and record the number x of consumers who favor toothpaste brand A. Suppose 2,000 of the consumers actually prefer brand A. Replace the five consumers in the population and randomly draw a new sample of $n = 5$ consumers. Record the value of x again. Repeat this process over and over again 100,000 times.

a. Construct a relative frequencies distribution for the 100,000 values of x shown in Table 5.1.

b. Assuming that the relative frequencies of Table 5.1 are good approximations to the probabilities of x, show that the properties of a probability distribution are satisfied.

Table 5.1   Relative Frequencies for 100,000 Observations on x, the Number of People in a Sample of $n = 5$ Who Prefer Brand A

x	*Frequency*	*Relative Frequency*	$p(x)$
0	32,891	.32891	.32768
1	40,929	.40929	.40960
2	20,473	.20473	.20480
3	5,104	.05104	.05120
4	599	.00599	.00640
5	4	.00004	.00032
			1.00000

SOLUTION **a.** The relative frequency histogram for the values of x is shown in Figure 5.2. This figure provides a very good approximation to the probability distribution for x, the number of consumers in a sample of $n = 5$ who prefer brand A (assuming that 20% of the consumers in the population prefer brand A).

FIGURE 5.2

Relative Frequency Histogram for Example 5.2

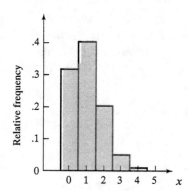

b. We use the relative frequencies of Table 5.1 as approximations to the probabilities of $x = 0$, $x = 1$, ..., $x = 5$. Note that each probability (relative frequency) is between 0 and 1. Summing these probabilities, we obtain

$$.32891 + .40929 + .20473 + .05104 + .00599 + .00004 = 1$$

Thus, the properties of a discrete probability distribution are satisfied. ■

In the next section, we show you how to find the mean and variance for this probability distribution. Then, in the following section, we discuss a good theoretical model for this distribution. As you will subsequently learn, this model will give the exact probabilities, $p(x)$, for the values of x shown in Table 5.1.

EXERCISES

■ *Learning the Mechanics*

5.1 Consider the probability distribution shown in the table.

x	−5	0	2	5
$p(x)$	.2	.3	.4	.1

a. List the values that x may assume.
b. What value of x is most probable?
c. Find the probability that x is greater than 0.
d. What is the probability that $x = -5$?
e. Verify that the sum of the probabilities equals 1.

5.2   A discrete random variable can assume five possible values, as listed in the accompanying probability distribution.

x	1	2	4	5	8
$p(x)$	.20	.25	—	.30	.10

a. Find the missing value for $p(4)$.
b. Find the probability that $x = 2$ or $x = 4$.
c. Find the probability that x is less than or equal to 4.

5.3   The probability distribution for a discrete random variable x is given by the formula,

$$p(x) = (.8)(.2)^{x-1}, \quad x = 1, 2, 3, \ldots$$

a. Calculate $p(x)$ for $x = 1$, $x = 2$, $x = 3$, $x = 4$, and $x = 5$.
b. Sum the probabilities of part **a**. Is it likely to observe a value of x greater than 5?
c. Find $P(x = 1$ or $x = 2)$.

■ *Applying the Concepts*

5.4   Refer to Exercise 4.17. The pie chart describing the origins of job stress for American workers is reproduced here. Let x be the number of workers that must be sampled until the first worker with no stress is found.

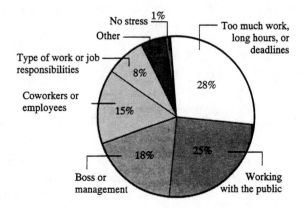

Source: *Tampa Tribune*, May 8, 1991.

a. List the possible values of x.
b. Refer to part **a**. If you sum the probabilities for these x values, what result will you obtain?
c. Find $p(1)$.
d. Find $p(2)$. [*Hint:* Use probability rule #4 for two independent events (Chapter 4).]
e. We show, in optional Section 5.7, that the probability distribution of x is given by the formula $p(x) = \pi(1 - \pi)^{x-1}$, where π is the probability that a single worker has no on-the-job stress. Use this formula to find $p(12)$.

5.5 The director of marketing for a small computer manufacturer believes the discrete probability distribution shown in the figure characterizes the number, x, of new computers the firm will lease next year.

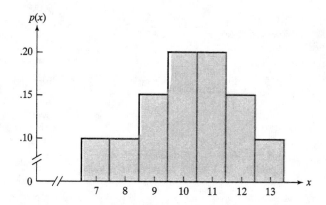

a. Is this a valid probability distribution? Explain.
b. Display the probability distribution in tabular form.
c. What is the probability that exactly nine computers will be leased?
d. What is the probability that fewer than 12 computers will be leased?

5.6 According to a *Wall Street Journal* survey of businesses that use personal computers (PCs) in the office, 70% use IBM PCs. If two surveyed businesses are selected, find the probability distribution of x, the number of businesses that use IBM PCs in the office. [*Hint:* The possible outcomes of the experiment are (I, I—both companies use IBM PCs), (I, N—the first company uses IBM PCs and the second does not), (N, I), and (N, N). For each outcome, determine the value of x and then calculate its probability using probability rule #4 (Chapter 4).]

5.3 The Expected Value and Variance of a Discrete Random Variable

Often, the sample collected in an experiment (such as the consumer sample survey of Example 5.2) is quite large. For example, the Gallup and Harris survey results reported in the news media are usually based on sample sizes from $n = 1,000$ to $n = 2,000$ people. Since we would not want to calculate $p(x)$ for values of n this large, we need an easy way to describe the probability distribution for x. To do this, we must know the mean and standard deviation for the distribution. That is, we must know the mean μ and standard deviation σ for the theoretical population of x values modeled by the probability distribution. Then we can describe it using either the Empirical Rule or Tchebysheff's theorem of Chapter 3.

Definition 5.5

The **mean** μ (or **expected value**) of a discrete random variable x is equal to the sum of the products of each value of x and the corresponding value of $p(x)$:

$$\mu = \Sigma x p(x)$$

Definition 5.6

The **variance** σ^2 of a discrete random variable x is equal to the sum of the products of $(x - \mu)^2$ and the corresponding value of $p(x)$:

$$\sigma^2 = \Sigma(x - \mu)^2 p(x) = \Sigma x^2 p(x) - \mu^2$$

Definition 5.7

The **standard deviation** σ of a random variable x is equal to the positive square root of the variance.

EXAMPLE 5.3
Computing μ and σ

Consider the sample survey of $n = 5$ consumers, described in Example 5.2. The graph of the probability distribution for x, the number of consumers in the sample who favor toothpaste brand A, is reproduced in Figure 5.3 (page 210).

    a. Find the mean μ for this distribution. That is, find the expected value of x.

    b. Interpret the value of μ.

    c. Find the standard deviation of x.

SOLUTION   **a.** By Definition 5.5, the mean μ is given by

$$\mu = \Sigma x p(x)$$

where $p(x)$ is given in Table 5.1. Since x can take values $x = 0, 1, 2, ..., 5$, we have

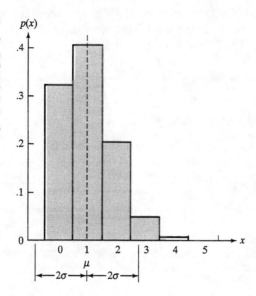

FIGURE 5.3

Probability
Distribution for *x*, the
Number of
Consumers in a
Sample of *n* = 5 Who
Prefer Toothpaste
Brand A

$$\mu = 0p(0) + 1p(1) + 2p(2) + \cdots + 5p(5)$$
$$= 0(.32768) + 1(.40960) + 2(.20480) + 3(.05120)$$
$$+ 4(.00640) + 5(.00032)$$
$$= 1.0$$

b.   The value of μ can also be obtained by adding the 100,000 values of *x* shown in Table 5.1 and dividing the sum by $n = 100,000$:

$$\mu = \frac{\Sigma x}{n}$$

$$= \frac{32{,}891(0) + 40{,}929(1) + 20{,}473(2) + 5{,}104(3) + 599(4) + 4(5)}{100{,}000}$$

$$= 1.0$$

Consequently, the value $\mu = 1.0$ implies that, *over a long series of surveys* similar to the one described in Example 5.2, the average number of consumers in the sample of 5 who favor toothpaste brand A will equal 1. The key to the interpretation of μ is to think in terms of repeating the experiment over a long series of trials (i.e., in the long run). Then μ represents the average *x* value of this large number of trials.

c.   By Definition 5.6, we obtain

$$\sigma^2 = \Sigma x^2 p(x) - \mu^2 = (0)^2 p(0) + (1)^2 p(1) + \cdots + (5)^2 p(5) - (1)^2$$

$$= (0)\,(.32768) + (1)\,(.40960) + (4)\,(.20480) + (9)\,(.05120)$$

$$+ (16)\,(.00640) + (25)\,(.00032) - (1)$$

$$= .80$$

Then by Definition 5.7, the standard deviation σ is given by

$$\sigma = \sqrt{\sigma^2} = \sqrt{.80} = .894 \quad ■$$

EXAMPLE 5.4
Empirical Rule Application

Refer to Example 5.3. Locate the interval $\mu \pm 2\sigma$ on the graph of the probability distribution for x. Confirm that most of the (theoretical) population falls within this interval.

SOLUTION Recall that $\mu = 1.0$ and $\sigma = .894$ for this distribution. Then

$$\mu - 2\sigma = 1.0 - 2(.894) = -.788$$

$$\mu + 2\sigma = 1.0 + 2(.894) = 2.788$$

The interval from $-.788$ to 2.788, shown in Figure 5.3, includes the values of $x = 0$, $x = 1$, and $x = 2$. Thus, the probability (relative frequency) that a population value falls within this interval is

$$p(0) + p(1) + p(2) = .32768 + .40960 + .20480 = .94208$$

This certainly agrees with the Empirical Rule, which states that approximately 95% of the data will lie within 2σ of the mean μ. ■

In the remainder of this chapter, we present several discrete probability distributions that provide useful models for many types of data encountered in business.

EXERCISES

■ *Learning the Mechanics*

5.7   Find μ and σ for the probability distribution given in Exercise 5.1.

5.8   Find μ and σ for the probability distribution given in Exercise 5.2.

▪ *Applying the Concepts*

5.9   In Exercise 4.36, we introduced you to the oil-lease lottery conducted by the Bureau of Land Management. Given various probabilities of winning, it is interesting to compute the expected gain associated with a single $10 entry. For example, it is estimated that the probability of winning on a parcel worth $25,000 to $150,000 is approximately $\frac{1}{5,000}$.

    a. Use the values stated above to calculate the expected gain associated with a single $10 entry. Interpret this result.

    b. Suppose you enter the lottery for three parcels of land. If the probability that you will win $25,000 on a single entry is $\frac{1}{5,000}$, what is the expected gain for the $30 investment in the three parcels? [*Hint:* The gain can assume one of four values, depending on whether the number x of wins is 0, 1, 2, or 3.]

5.10   Refer to Exercise 5.5, which shows the probability distribution of x, the number of new computers the firm will lease next year.

    a. Calculate μ and σ.

    b. Interpret the value of μ.

    c. Locate the interval $(\mu - 2\sigma, \mu + 2\sigma)$ on the graph constructed in Exercise 5.5.

    d. Find the probability that x falls within the interval of part **c**. Compare your result to the Empirical Rule.

5.11   Refer to the probability distribution of x, the number of businesses that use IBM PCs in the office, provided in Exercise 5.6.

    a. Calculate μ and σ.

    b. Interpret the value of μ.

    c. Find an interval that captures approximately 95% of the values of x in the theoretical population.

5.4 The Binomial Probability Distribution

Consumer preference and opinion polls (i.e., sample surveys) are conducted frequently in business. Some recent examples include polls to determine: (1) the number of voters in favor of legalizing casino gambling in a particular state, (2) the number of Americans in favor of government-controlled health care, and (3) the number of baseball fans who support a strike by the Major League Baseball Players Association. Consequently, it is useful for us to know the probability distribution of the number x in a random sample of n experimental units (people) who exhibit some characteristic or prefer some specific proposition. This probability distribution, known as a **binomial probability distribution**, is applicable when the sample size n is small relative to the number N of experimental units in the population.

Strictly speaking, the binomial probability distribution applies only to sampling that satisfies the conditions of a **binomial experiment**, as listed in the box.

In real life, there are probably few experiments that satisfy exactly the conditions for a binomial experiment. However, there are many that satisfy approximately—at least for all practical purposes—these conditions. Consider, for example, a sample survey. As suggested above, when the number N of elements in the population is large and the sample size n is small relative to N, the sampling satisfies, approximately, the conditions of a binomial experiment. The next two examples illustrate the point.

Conditions Required for a Binomial Experiment

1. A sample of n experimental units is selected from a population.

2. Each experimental unit possesses one of two characteristics. We conventionally call the characteristic of interest a "success" and the other a "failure."

3. The probability that a single experimental unit possesses the "success" characteristic is equal to π. This probability is the same for all experimental units.

4. The outcome for any one experimental unit is independent of the outcome for any other experimental unit (i.e., the draws are independent).

5. The random variable x counts the number of "successes" in n trials.

EXAMPLE 5.5
Checking Binomial
Conditions

Suppose a sample of $n = 2$ elements is randomly selected from a population containing $N = 10$ elements, three of which are designated as successes and seven as failures. Explain why this sampling procedure violates the conditions of a binomial experiment.

SOLUTION The probability of selecting a success on the first draw is equal to $\frac{3}{10}$—that is, the number of successes in the population (3) divided by the total number of elements in the population (10). In contrast, the probability of a success on the second draw is either $\frac{2}{9}$ or $\frac{3}{9}$, depending on whether a success was selected on the first draw. In other words, selecting a success on the second draw is dependent on the outcome of the first draw, and this is a violation of condition 4 required for a binomial experiment. ■

EXAMPLE 5.6
Checking Binomial
Conditions

Suppose a sample of size $n = 2$ is randomly selected from a population containing $N = 1,000$ elements, 300 of which are successes and 700 of which are failures. Explain why this sampling procedure satisfies, approximately, the conditions required for a binomial experiment.

SOLUTION The probability of a success on the first draw is the same as in Example 5.5—namely, $\frac{300}{1,000} = \frac{3}{10}$. The probability of a success on the second draw is either $\frac{299}{999} = .2993$ or $\frac{300}{999} = .3003$, depending on whether the first draw resulted in a success or a failure. But since these conditional probabilities are approximately equal to the unconditional probability $\left(\frac{3}{10}\right)$ of drawing a success on the second draw, we can say that, *for all practical purposes*, the sampling satisfies the conditions of a binomial experiment. Thus, when N is large and n is small relative to N (say, n/N less than .05), we can use the binomial probability distribution to calculate the probability of observing x successes in a survey sample. ■

The binomial probability distributions for a sample of $n = 10$ and $\pi = .1$, $\pi = .3$, $\pi = .5$, $\pi = .7$, and $\pi = .9$ are shown in Figure 5.4. Note that the probability distribution is skewed to the right for small values of π, skewed to the left for large values of π, and symmetric for $\pi = .5$.

The formula used for calculating probabilities of the binomial probability distribution is shown in the following box.

FIGURE 5.4

Binomial Probability
Distribution for
$n = 10$, $\pi = .1, .3, .5,$
$.7, .9$

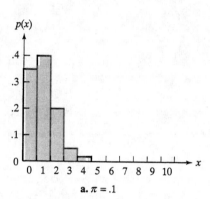

a. $\pi = .1$

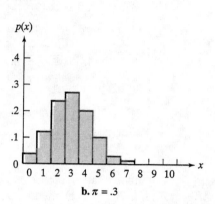

b. $\pi = .3$

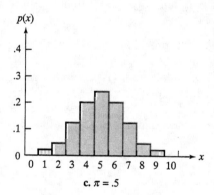

c. $\pi = .5$

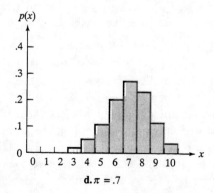

d. $\pi = .7$

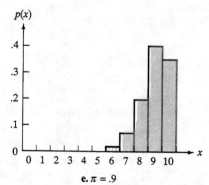

e. $\pi = .9$

The Binomial Probability Distribution

$$p(x) = \binom{n}{x}\pi^x(1-\pi)^{n-x}, \quad x = 0, 1, 2, \ldots, n$$

where

n = Sample size (number of trials)

x = Number of successes in n trials

π = Probability of success on a single trial

$$\binom{n}{x} = \frac{n!}{x!\,(n-x)!}$$

Assumption: The sample size n is small relative to the number N of elements in the population (say, n/N smaller than $\frac{1}{20}$).
[*Note:* $x! = x(x-1)(x-2)(x-3)\cdots(3)(2)(1)$ and $0! = 1$.]

EXAMPLE 5.7
Computing Binomial Probabilities

Verify that the consumer survey experiment described in Example 5.2 is a binomial experiment. Then use the binomial probability distribution to calculate the exact probabilities of $x = 0, x = 1, \ldots, x = 5$.

SOLUTION The sample survey satisfies the five requirements for a binomial experiment given in the box:

1. A sample of $n = 5$ consumers (experimental units) is selected from a population.
2. Each consumer surveyed possesses one of two characteristics: favor toothpaste brand A (a "success") or do not favor toothpaste brand A (a "failure").
3. The proportion of people in the population who prefer toothpaste brand A is .2; thus, the probability of a "success" is $\pi = .2$. Since the sample size $n = 5$ is small relative to the population size $N = 10,000$, this probability remains the same for all trials.
4. The response for any one consumer is independent of the response for any other consumer.
5. We are counting x = the number of consumers in the sample who favor toothpaste brand A.

To calculate the binomial probabilities, we substitute the values of $n = 5$ and $\pi = .2$ and each value of x into the formula for $p(x)$:

$$p(x) = \binom{n}{x} \pi^x (1 - \pi)^{n-x} = \frac{n!}{x!\,(n-x)!} \pi^x (1 - \pi)^{n-x}$$

Thus, remembering that $0! = 1$, we have

$$P(x = 0) = p(0) = \binom{5}{0} (.2)^0 (.8)^5$$

$$= \frac{5!}{0!5!} (.2)^0 (.8)^5 = (1)(1)(.32768)$$

$$= .32768$$

Similarly,

$$P(x = 1) = p(1) = \binom{5}{1} (.2)^1 (.8)^4 = \frac{5!}{1!4!} (.2)^1 (.8)^4 = .40960$$

$$P(x = 2) = p(2) = \binom{5}{2} (.2)^2 (.8)^3 = \frac{5!}{2!3!} (.2)^2 (.8)^3 = .20480$$

$$P(x = 3) = p(3) = \binom{5}{3} (.2)^3 (.8)^2 = \frac{5!}{3!2!} (.2)^3 (.8)^2 = .05120$$

$$P(x = 4) = p(4) = \binom{5}{4} (.2)^4 (.8)^1 = \frac{5!}{4!1!} (.2)^4 (.8)^1 = .00640$$

$$P(x = 5) = p(5) = \binom{5}{5} (.2)^5 (.8)^0 = \frac{5!}{5!0!} (.2)^5 (.8)^0 = .00032$$

Note that these probabilities are approximately equal to the relative frequencies reported in Table 5.1. ■

EXAMPLE 5.8
Summing Binomial Probabilities

Refer to Example 5.7. Find the probability that three or more persons in the sample prefer brand A.

SOLUTION The values that a random variable x can assume are always mutually exclusive events—i.e., you could not observe $x = 2$ and, at the same time, observe $x = 3$. Therefore, the event "x is 3 or more" (the event that $x = 3$ or $x = 4$ or $x = 5$) can be found using probability rule #2 (Chapter 4). Thus,

$$P(x = 3 \text{ or } x = 4 \text{ or } x = 5) = P(x = 3) + P(x = 4) + P(x = 5)$$

$$= p(3) + p(4) + p(5)$$

Substituting the probabilities found in Example 5.7, we obtain

$$P(x = 3 \text{ or } x = 4 \text{ or } x = 5) = .05120 + .00640 + .00032 = .05792 \quad ■$$

In some situations, we will want to compare an observed value of x obtained from an opinion poll (or other binomial experiment) with some theory or claim associated with the sampled population. In particular, we will want to see whether the observed value of x represents a *rare event*, assuming that the claim is true.

EXAMPLE 5.9
Statistical Inference

A manufacturer of O-ring seals used to prevent hot gases from leaking through the joints of rocket boosters claims that 95% of all seals that it produces will function properly. Suppose you randomly select 10 of these O-ring seals, test them, and find that only six prevent gas from leaking. Is this sample outcome highly improbable (that is, does it represent a *rare event*) if the manufacturer's claim is true?

SOLUTION If π is in fact equal to .95 (or some larger value), then observing a small number, x, of O-ring seals that function properly would represent a rare event. Since we observed $x = 6$, we want to know the probability of observing a value of $x = 6$ or some other value of x even more contradictory to the manufacturer's claim, i.e., we want to find the probability that $x = 0$ or $x = 1$ or $x = 2$ or ... or $x = 6$. Using the additive rule for values of $p(x)$, we obtain

$$P(x = 0 \text{ or } x = 1 \text{ or } x = 2 \text{ or } ... \text{ or } x = 6)$$
$$= p(0) + p(1) + p(2) + p(3) + p(4) + p(5) + p(6)$$

As you saw in Example 5.7, the calculation of the binomial probabilities in the sum can be very tedious. In practice, we refer to one of the many tables that give partial sums of the values of $p(x)$, called **cumulative probabilities**, for a wide range of values of n and π. Table 2 of Appendix B includes cumulative binomial tables for $n = 5, 6, 7, 8, 9, 10, 15, 20,$ and 25. A reproduction of the cumulative binomial probability table for $n = 10$ is shown in Table 5.2 (page 218).

In general, to find the sum of the binomial probabilities $p(x)$ for $x = 0, 1, 2, ...,$ k using Table 2 in Appendix B, locate the tabled entry corresponding to the row $x = k$ under the appropriate column for π. The cumulative sum of probabilities for this example is given in the column corresponding to $\pi = .95$ and the row corresponding to $x = 6$. Therefore,

$$P(x \le 6) = p(0) + p(1) + p(2) + p(3) + p(4) + p(5) + p(6) = .0010$$

This small probability (shaded in Table 5.2) tells us that observing as few as six good O-ring seals out of 10 is indeed a rare event, if in fact the manufacturer's claim is true. Such a sample result suggests either that the manufacturer's claim is false or that the 10 O-ring seals tested do not represent a random sample from the manufacturer's total production. Perhaps they came from a particular production line that was temporarily malfunctioning.   ■

Table 5.2 Reproduction of a Portion of Table 2 in Appendix B: Cumulative Binomial Probability Distribution, $n = 10$

k	.01	.05	.1	.2	.3	.4	.5	.6	.7	.8	.9	.95	.99
0	.9044	.5987	.3487	.1074	.0282	.0060	.0010	.0001	.0000	.0000	.0000	.0000	.0000
1	.9957	.9139	.7361	.3758	.1493	.0464	.0107	.0017	.0001	.0000	.0000	.0000	.0000
2	.9999	.9885	.9298	.6778	.3828	.1673	.0547	.0123	.0016	.0001	.0000	.0000	.0000
3	1.0000	.9990	.9872	.8791	.6496	.3823	.1719	.0548	.0106	.0009	.0000	.0000	.0000
4	1.0000	.9999	.9984	.9672	.8497	.6331	.3770	.1662	.0473	.0064	.0001	.0000	.0000
5	1.0000	1.0000	.9999	.9936	.9527	.8338	.6230	.3669	.1503	.0328	.0016	.0001	.0000
6	1.0000	1.0000	1.0000	.9991	.9894	.9452	.8281	.6177	.3504	.1209	.0128	.0010	.0000
7	1.0000	1.0000	1.0000	.9999	.9984	.9877	.9453	.8327	.6172	.3222	.0702	.0115	.0001
8	1.0000	1.0000	1.0000	1.0000	.9999	.9983	.9893	.9536	.8507	.6242	.2639	.0861	.0043
9	1.0000	1.0000	1.0000	1.0000	1.0000	.9999	.9990	.9940	.9718	.8926	.6513	.4013	.0956

Using the formulas in Definitions 5.5, 5.6, and 5.7, you can show (proof omitted) that the mean, variance, and standard deviation for a binomial probability distribution are as listed in the following box.

> ### Mean, Variance, and Standard Deviation for a Binomial Probability Distribution
>
> $$\mu = n\pi$$
>
> $$\sigma^2 = n\pi(1 - \pi)$$
>
> $$\sigma = \sqrt{n\pi(1 - \pi)}$$
>
> where
>
> $n = $ Sample size
>
> $\pi = $ Probability of success on a single trial
>
> $= $ Proportion of experimental units in a large population that are "successes"

For *large samples*, the mean and the variance of the binomial probability distribution (in conjunction with the Empirical Rule or Tchebysheff's theorem) can be used to make inferences about the sampled population, as illustrated in the next example.

EXAMPLE 5.10
Computing Binomial
μ and σ

People who work at high-stress jobs frequently develop stress-related physical problems (e.g., high blood pressure, ulcers, and irritability). In a recent study it was found that 40% of the large number of business executives surveyed have symptoms of stress-induced problems. Consider a group of 1,500 randomly selected business executives and assume that the probability of an executive with stress-induced problems is $\pi = .40$. Let x be the number of business executives in the sample of 1,500 who develop stress-related problems.

    a.   What are the mean and standard deviation of x?

    b.   Based on the Empirical Rule, within what limits would you expect x to fall?

    c.   Suppose you observe $x = 800$ executives with symptoms of stress-induced problems. What can you infer about the value of π?

SOLUTION   **a.**   Since $n = 1,500$ executives in the sample is small relative to the large number of business executives in the population, the number x of executives with stress-induced problems is a binomial random variable with $\pi = .4$. We use the formulas for μ and σ given in the box to obtain the mean and standard deviation of this binomial distribution:

$$\mu = n\pi = (1,500)(.4) = 600$$

$$\sigma = \sqrt{n\pi(1 - \pi)} = \sqrt{(1,500)(.4)(.6)} = \sqrt{360} = 18.97$$

    b.   According to the Empirical Rule, most (about 95%) of the x values will fall within 2 standard deviations of the mean. Thus, we would expect the number of sampled executives with stress-induced problems to fall in the interval from

$$\mu - 2\sigma = 600 - 2(18.97) = 562.06$$

to

$$\mu + 2\sigma = 600 + 2(18.97) = 637.94$$

    c.   Using the rare event approach of Chapter 4, we want to determine whether observing $x = 800$ executives with stress-induced problems is unusual, assuming $\pi = .40$. You can see that this value of x is highly improbable when $\pi = .40$ since it lies a long way outside the interval $\mu \pm 2\sigma$. The z score for this value of x is

$$z = \frac{x - \mu}{\sigma} = \frac{800 - 600}{18.97} = 10.54$$

Clearly, if $\pi = .40$, the probability that the number, x, of executives with stress-induced problems in the sample is 800 or larger is almost 0. Therefore, we are inclined to believe (based on the sample value of $x = 800$) that the proportion of executives with stress-induced problems is much higher than $\pi = .40$. ■

EXERCISES

▪ *Learning the Mechanics*

5.12 A coin is tossed 10 times and the number of heads is recorded. To a reasonable degree of approximation, is this a binomial experiment? Check to determine whether each of the five conditions required for a binomial experiment is satisfied.

5.13 Compute each of the following:

  a. $4!$ **b.** $\dfrac{4!}{1!3!}$ **c.** $\binom{5}{3}$ **d.** $(.4)^3$ **e.** $\binom{5}{3}(.4)^3(.6)^2$

5.14 Four coins are selected from a group of five pennies and five dimes. (Once selected, a coin cannot be selected again; this is called **sampling without replacement**.) Let x equal the number of pennies in the sample of four coins. To a reasonable degree of approximation, is this a binomial experiment? Determine whether each of the five conditions required for a binomial experiment is satisfied.

5.15 Consider a binomial experiment with $n = 4$ trials and probability of success $\pi = .5$.
  a. Use the formula for the binomial probability distribution to find the probabilities for $x = 0$, 1, 2, 3, and 4. Construct a graph, similar to Figure 5.4, of the probability distribution.
  b. Find the probability that x is less than 2.
  c. Find the probability that x is less than or equal to 2.
  d. Locate the probabilities computed in parts **b** and **c** on the graph that you constructed in part **a**.
  e. Verify that (except for rounding) the sum of the probabilities for $x = 0$, 1, 2, 3, and 4 equals 1.

5.16 Let x be a binomial random variable with parameters $n = 4$ and $\pi = .2$.
  a. Find the probability that x is less than 2.
  b. Find the probability that x is equal to 2 or more.
  c. How are the events in parts **a** and **b** related?
  d. What relationship must the probabilities of the events in parts **a** and **b** satisfy?

5.17 Refer to the cumulative binomial probability table for $n = 5$, given in Table 2 of Appendix B.

  a. Find $\displaystyle\sum_{x=0}^{2} p(x) = p(0) + p(1) + p(2)$ when $\pi = .3$.

  b. Find $\displaystyle\sum_{x=0}^{4} p(x)$ when $\pi = .3$.

  c. Find $\displaystyle\sum_{x=4}^{5} p(x)$ when $\pi = .3$. $\left[\textit{Hint:}\ \displaystyle\sum_{x=4}^{5} p(x) = 1 - \sum_{x=0}^{3} p(x).\right]$

  d. Find $p(2)$ when $\pi = .3$. $\left[\textit{Hint:}\ p(2) = \displaystyle\sum_{x=0}^{2} p(x) - \sum_{x=0}^{1} p(x).\right]$

5.18 Refer to the cumulative binomial probability table for $n = 10$ and $\pi = .4$, given in Table 2 of Appendix B.
   a. Find the probability that x is less than or equal to 8.
   b. Find the probability that x is less than 8.
   c. Find the probability that x is larger than 8.

5.19 Calculate μ and σ for a binomial probability distribution with
   a. $n = 10$ and $\pi = .1$ **b.** $n = 15$ and $\pi = .1$
   c. $n = 20$ and $\pi = .1$ **d.** $n = 25$ and $\pi = .1$

5.20 Find the mean and standard deviation for each of the following binomial probability distributions:
   a. $n = 100$ and $\pi = .99$ **b.** $n = 100$ and $\pi = .8$
   c. $n = 100$ and $\pi = .5$ **d.** $n = 100$ and $\pi = .2$
   e. $n = 100$ and $\pi = .01$
   Use the values of μ and σ to construct rough sketches of the five binomial probability distributions.

■ *Applying the Concepts*

5.21 A study of 5-year trends in the logistics information systems of industries found that the greatest computerization advances were in transportation (*Industrial Engineering*, July 1990). Currently, 90% of all industries contain shipping open-order files in their computerized data base. In a random sample of 10 industries, let x equal the number that include shipping open-order files in their computerized data base.
   a. Verify that the probability distribution of x can be modeled using the binomial distribution.
   b. Find $P(x = 7)$.
   c. Find $P(x > 5)$.
   d. Find the mean and variance of x. Interpret the results.

5.22 In a study, *Consumer Reports* (Feb. 1992) found widespread contamination and mislabeling of seafood in supermarkets in New York City and Chicago. The study revealed one alarming statistic: 40% of the swordfish pieces available for sale had a level of mercury above the Food and Drug Administration (FDA) maximum amount. In a random sample of three swordfish pieces, find the probability that:
   a. All three swordfish pieces have mercury levels above the FDA maximum.
   b. Exactly one swordfish piece has a mercury level above the FDA maximum.
   c. At most one swordfish piece has a mercury level above the FDA maximum.

5.23 *Chance* (Summer 1993) reported on a study of the success rate of National Football League (NFL) field goal kickers. Data collected over three NFL seasons (1989–1991) revealed that NFL kickers, in aggregate, made 75% of all field goals attempted. However, when the kicks were segmented by distance (yards), the rate of successful kicks varied widely. For example, 95% of all short field goals (under 30 yards) were made, whereas only 58% of all long field goals (over 40 yards) were successful. Consider x, the number of field goals made in a random sample of 20 kicks attempted last year in an NFL game. Is x (approximately) a binomial random variable? Explain.

5.24 The *Wall Street Journal* (Nov. 2, 1983) reported on a survey conducted to evaluate the public's opinion concerning the honest and ethical behavior of business executives. The survey included a representative sample of 1,558 adults selected from among all adults in the United States. Each person in the sample was asked to respond "yes" or "no" to each of a series of questions. If this sample were randomly selected from among all adults in the United States, would the number x responding "yes" to a particular question possess (approximately) a binomial probability distribution? Explain.

5.25 Electrical engineers recognize that high neutral current in computer power systems is a potential problem. A recent survey of computer power system load currents at U.S. sites found that 10% of the sites had high neutral to full-load current ratios (*IEEE Transactions on Industry Applications*, July/Aug. 1990). In a sample of 20 computer power systems selected from the large number of sites in the country, let x be the number with high neutral to full-load current ratios.

a. Find and interpret the mean of x.
b. Find and interpret the standard deviation of x.

5.26 *Occupational Outlook Quarterly* (Spring 1993) reported that 1% of all the drywall installers employed in the construction industry are women. In a random sample of 10 drywall installers, find the probability that at most one is a woman.

5.27 Refer to the *IEEE Computer Applications in Power* (Apr. 1990) study of an outdoor unmanned watching system to detect trespassers, Exercise 4.35. In snowy weather conditions, the system detected 7 out of 10 intruders; thus, the researchers estimated the system's probability of intruder detection in snowy conditions at .70.

a. Assuming the probability of intruder detection in snowy conditions is only .50, find the probability that the unmanned system detects at least 7 of the 10 intruders.
b. Based on the result, part **a**, comment on the reliability of the researcher's estimate of the system's detection probability in snowy conditions.

5.28 According to the American Hotel and Motel Association, women are expected to account for half of all business travelers by the year 2000. To attract these women business travelers, hotels are providing more amenities that women particularly like, such as shampoo, conditioner, and body lotion. A survey of American hotels found that 86% offer shampoo in their guest rooms (*Wall Street Journal*, Oct. 14, 1988). Consider a random sample of five hotels, and let x be the number that provide shampoo as a guest room amenity.

a. To a reasonable degree of approximation, is this a binomial experiment?
b. What is a "success" in the context of this experiment?
c. What is the value of π?
d. Find the probability that $x = 4$.
e. Find the probability that $x \geq 4$.

5.29 *Organic Gardening* magazine conducted a poll to determine whether consumers would prefer organically grown fruits and vegetables over those grown with fertilizers and pesticides (*New York Times*, Mar. 21, 1989). If the costs of the two food types were the same, 85% said they would prefer the organic food. Surprisingly, 50% said they would prefer the organic food even if they had to pay more for it. Consider the preferences of a random sample of $n = 25$ consumers.

a. Assuming the percentages in the poll are reflective of the population, find the probability that at least 20 of the 25 consumers would prefer the organically grown food, if the costs were the same.

b. Assuming the percentages in the poll are reflective of the population, find the probability that at least 20 of the 25 consumers would prefer the organically grown food, if the costs were higher than food grown with fertilizers and pesticides.

5.30   Do you have the basic skills necessary to succeed in college? Most likely, your college professor does not think so. According to a survey conducted by the Carnegie Foundation for the Advancement of Teaching, over 70% of college professors consider their students "seriously unprepared in basic skills" that should have been learned in high school (*Tampa Tribune*, Nov. 6, 1989). In a sample of 25 college faculty at your institution, let x represent the number who agree that students lack basic skills. Assume that $\pi = .70$ at your institution.
a. What is the probability that x is less than 20?
b. What is the probability that x is less than nine?
c. What is the probability that x is more than nine?
d. If, in fact, x is less than nine, make an inference about the value of π at your institution.

5.31   A study of vehicle flow characteristics on acceleration lanes (i.e., merging ramps) at a major freeway in Israel found that one out of every six vehicles uses less than one-third of the acceleration lane before merging into traffic (*Journal of Transportation Engineering*, Nov. 1985). Suppose we monitor the location of the merge for the next five vehicles that enter the acceleration lane.
a. What is the probability that none of the vehicles will use less than one-third of the acceleration lane?
b. What is the probability that exactly two of the vehicles will use less than one-third of the acceleration lane?

5.32   When you graduate, will you find a job of your own choosing? A Gallup survey for the National Occupational Information Coordinating Committee revealed that only 40% of American workers hold the types of job they had planned to have (*Tampa Tribune*, Jan. 12, 1990). The majority of those employed attribute their job to simple chance or lack of choice. Let x be the number of American workers in a sample of $n = 250$ who consciously chose their job or career.
a. Is this a binomial experiment? Explain.
b. What is π, the probability of success?
c. What is the mean of x?
d. Within what limits would you expect x to fall?
e. Give a value of x that would contradict the finding that 40% of American workers hold jobs they had planned for. Explain.

5.5 The Poisson Probability Distribution

The **Poisson probability distribution,** named for the French mathematician Siméon D. Poisson (1781–1840), provides a good model for the probability distribution of the number of "rare events" that occur randomly in time, distance, or space. Some random variables that may possess (approximately) a Poisson probability distribution are the following:

1. The number of accidents that occur per month (or week, day, etc.) in a manufacturing plant
2. The number of arrivals per minute (or hour, etc.) at a medical clinic or other servicing facility
3. The number of defects detected by quality control inspectors in a new Honda Accord
4. The number of days in a given year in which a 30-point change occurs in the Dow Jones Industrial Stock Index
5. The number of breakdowns per month in a large mainframe computer

The characteristics of a Poisson random variable are listed in the box, followed by a formula for its probability distribution.

Characteristics of a Poisson Random Variable

1. The experiment consists of counting the number, x, of times a particular event occurs during a given unit of time, or a given area or volume (or weight, or distance, or any other unit of measurement).
2. The probability that an event occurs in a given unit of time, area, or volume is the same for all the units.
3. The number of events that occur in one unit of time, area, or volume is independent of the number that occur in other units.

The Poisson Probability Distribution

$$p(x) = \frac{\mu^x e^{-\mu}}{x!}, \quad x = 0, 1, 2, ..., \infty$$

where

$x =$ Number of rare events per unit of time, distance, or space

$\mu =$ Mean value of x

$e = 2.71828...$

Figure 5.5 shows how the shape of the Poisson distribution changes as its mean μ changes. The figure gives graphs of $p(x)$ for $\mu = 1, 2, 3,$ and 4.

Calculating Poisson probabilities requires a calculator or a table of values of $e^{-\mu}$ for various values of μ (e is the base of natural logarithms and is equal to 2.718...). We give an abbreviated set of values of $e^{-\mu}$ in Table 3 of Appendix B. More com-

FIGURE 5.5

Histograms of the
Poisson Distribution
for $\mu = 1, 2, 3,$ and 4

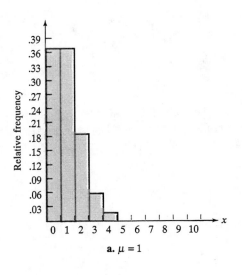

a. $\mu = 1$

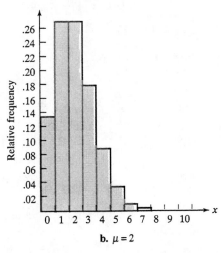

b. $\mu = 2$

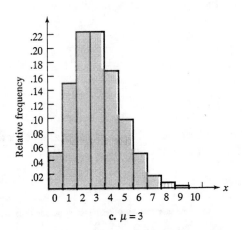

c. $\mu = 3$

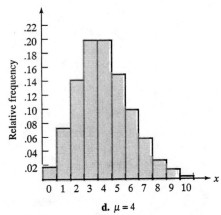

d. $\mu = 4$

plete tables of values of $e^{-\mu}$ can be found in numerous books of mathematical tables. In addition, we give cumulative Poisson probabilities in Table 4 of Appendix B. This table will save you some computational labor if your value of μ is listed in the table.

EXAMPLE 5.11
Cumulative Poisson
Probability

The quality control inspector in a diamond-cutting operation has found that the mean number of defects per diamond (defects discernible to the eye of a jeweler) is $\mu = 1.5$. What is the probability that a randomly selected diamond contains more than one such defect?

SOLUTION The probability distribution of x, the number of discernible defects per diamond, can be approximated by a Poisson probability distribution with $\mu = 1.5$. The probability that a diamond contains more than one defect is

$$P(x > 1) = p(2) + p(3) + p(4) + \cdots$$

$$= 1 - [p(0) + p(1)]$$

$$= 1 - P(x \le 1)$$

To find $p(0)$ and $p(1)$, we can substitute into the formula for $p(x)$. Or, we can find the probability using the table of cumulative Poisson probabilities given in Table 4 of Appendix B. Table 4 gives values of $P(x \le k)$ for selected values of μ and k. In this case,

$$k = 1 \quad \text{and} \quad \mu = 1.5$$

Locating these values in Table 4 of Appendix B, we find

$$P(x \le 1) = .5578$$

Therefore, the probability that the number x of defects per diamond is more than one is

$$P(x > 1) = 1 - P(x \le 1)$$

$$= 1 - .5578 = .4422 \quad ■$$

The mean μ of the Poisson probability distribution appears in the formula for $p(x)$. It is given, with the variance and standard deviation of x, in the accompanying box.

Mean, Variance, and Standard Deviation of a Poisson Probability Distribution

$$\text{Mean} = \mu \qquad \sigma^2 = \mu \qquad \sigma = \sqrt{\mu}$$

EXAMPLE 5.12
Computing Poisson
μ **and** σ

Suppose the mean number of employee accidents per month at a particular manufacturing plant is 3.4. Find the mean, variance, and standard deviation of x, the number of accidents in a randomly selected month. Is it likely that x will be as large as 12?

SOLUTION We are given the fact that $\mu = 3.4$. Therefore,

$\sigma^2 = 3.4$

and

$\sigma = \sqrt{3.4} = 1.84$

Then the z score corresponding to $x = 12$ is

$$z = \frac{x - \mu}{\sigma} = \frac{12 - 3.4}{1.84} = 4.67$$

Since $x = 12$ lies 4.67 standard deviations away from its mean, we know (from the Empirical Rule) that this is a highly improbable event. ■

In addition to the applications of the Poisson distribution that we have described, it can also be used to approximate a binomial probability distribution when the number n of trials in the binomial experiment is large, π is small, and $n\pi$ is not too large—say, $n\pi < 7$. The Poisson distribution used to make the approximation is one with a mean equal to $n\pi$, the same as the mean of the approximated binomial distribution.

> **The Poisson Approximation
> to the Binomial Probability Distribution**
>
> Use a Poisson distribution with $\mu = n\pi$. To obtain an adequate approximation, n must be large, π small, and $n\pi < 7$.

EXAMPLE 5.13
Poisson Approximation to Binomial

Use the Poisson probability distribution to approximate $p(1)$ and $p(2)$ for a binomial probability distribution with $n = 20$ and $\pi = .1$. Compare your results with the exact values of those binomial probabilities derived from Table 2 of Appendix B.

SOLUTION The value $n = 20$ was chosen for this example, not because it is large, but because we can calculate the exact values of $p(x)$ for $n = 20$ and $\pi = .1$ from Table 2 of Appendix B. This will enable us to compare the Poisson approximations with the exact values. Note that $n\pi = (20)(.1) = 2 < 7$. To find the Poisson probability corresponding to $p(1)$, we substitute $\mu = n\pi = 2$ and $x = 1$ into the formula for the Poisson probability distribution. Thus,

$$p(x) = \frac{\mu^x e^{-\mu}}{x!}$$

and

$$p(1) = \frac{(2)^1 e^{-2}}{1!}$$

where e^{-2}, given in Table 3 of Appendix B (or obtained from a pocket calculator), is .135335. Then

$$p(1) = \frac{(2)(.135335)}{1} = .2707$$

Similarly,

$$p(2) = \frac{(2)^2 e^{-2}}{2!} = \frac{(4)(.135335)}{2} = .2707$$

The Poisson and binomial probabilities for $x = 1$ and $x = 2$ are compared in the table. You can see that the Poisson probabilities provide reasonably good approximations to their binomial equivalents. In general, the approximations improve as the value of n increases.

x	Poisson $p(x)$	Binomial $p(x)$
1	.2707	.2701
2	.2707	.2852

EXAMPLE 5.14
Poisson Approximation to
Binomial Application

A manufacturer of transistors claims that the company's transistors are 99.9% reliable or, equivalently, that the probability a transistor is defective is .001. If the transistors are sold in batches of 800 and you buy a batch, what is the probability that none in the batch is defective?

SOLUTION Assume that the 800 transistors in the batch represent a random selection of transistors from among the large number produced by the manufacturer and, therefore, that the sampling represents a binomial experiment with $n = 800$ and probability $\pi = .001$ that a single transistor is defective. Then, since n is large, π is small, and $n\pi = (800)(.001) = .8 < 7$, we can approximate the binomial probability, $p(0) = \binom{800}{0}(.001)^0 (.999)^{800}$, using the Poisson probability distribution with $\mu = n\pi = .8$.

Substituting $x = 0$ and $\mu = .8$ into the formula for the Poisson probability distribution, we obtain

$$p(0) \approx \frac{(.8)^0 e^{-.8}}{0!} = \frac{(1)(.449329)}{1} = .449$$

Thus, the probability that you will receive a defect-free batch is approximately .45. ■

EXERCISES

■ **Learning the Mechanics**

5.33 Use Table 3 of Appendix B to find each of the following:
   a. $e^{-4.5}$ **b.** $e^{-2.0}$ **c.** $e^{-6.0}$ **d.** $e^{-1.3}$
   e. $\dfrac{(8.2)^3 e^{-8.2}}{3!}$ **f.** $\dfrac{(1.5)^4 e^{-1.5}}{4!}$ **g.** $\dfrac{(3.0)^2 e^{-3.0}}{2!}$

5.34 Assume that x has a Poisson probability distribution. Use Table 4 of Appendix B to find each of the following probabilities:
   a. $P(x = 5)$ when $\mu = 3.0$ **b.** $P(x \geq 4)$ when $\mu = 7.5$
   c. $P(x \leq 2)$ when $\mu = 5.5$ **d.** $P(x = 8)$ when $\mu = 4.0$

5.35 Suppose x has a Poisson probability distribution with $\mu = 2.5$.
   a. Graph $p(x)$ for $x = 0, 1, 2, ..., 10$.
   b. Find μ and σ.
   c. Locate $\mu \pm 2\sigma$ on the graph of part **a**. What is the probability that x falls within $\mu \pm 2\sigma$?

5.36 Suppose x has a Poisson probability distribution with $\mu = 6.0$.
   a. Graph $p(x)$ for $x = 0, 1, 2, ..., 12$.
   b. Find μ and σ.
   c. Locate $\mu \pm 2\sigma$ on the graph of part **a**. What is the probability that x falls within $\mu \pm 2\sigma$?

5.37 Suppose x has a binomial probability distribution with $n = 100$ and $\pi = .02$. Use the Poisson approximation to the binomial distribution to find:
   a. $P(x \geq 3)$ **b.** $P(x = 5)$ **c.** $P(x = 0)$ **d.** $P(x < 2)$

5.38 Suppose x has a binomial probability distribution with $n = 500$ and $\pi = .01$. Use the Poisson approximation to the binomial distribution to find:
   a. $P(x = 4)$ **b.** $P(x \leq 2)$ **c.** $P(x > 6)$ **d.** $P(x = 9)$

■ **Applying the Concepts**

5.39 Refer to the *Journal of Transportation Engineering* study described in Exercise 5.31. Suppose the number of vehicles using the acceleration lane per minute has a mean equal to 1.1.
   a. What is the probability that more than two vehicles will use the acceleration lane in the next minute?
   b. What is the probability that exactly three vehicles will use the acceleration lane in the next minute?

5.40 The Environmental Protection Agency (EPA) has established national ambient air quality standards in an effort to control air pollution. Currently, the EPA limit on ozone levels in air is set at 12 parts per hundred million (pphm). A 1990 study examined the long-term trend in daily ozone levels in Houston, Texas.* One of the variables of interest is x, the number of days in a year on which the ozone level exceeds the EPA threshold of 12 pphm. The mean number of exceedences in a year is estimated to be 18. Assume that the probability distribution for x can be modeled with the Poisson distribution.

a. Compute $P(x \geq 20)$.

b. Compute $P(5 \leq x \leq 10)$.

c. Estimate the standard deviation of x. Within what range would you expect x to fall in a given year?

d. The study revealed a decreasing trend in the number of exceedences of the EPA threshold over the past several years. The observed values of x for the past six years were 24, 22, 20, 15, 14, and 16. Explain why this trend casts doubt on the validity of the Poisson distribution as a model for x. [*Hint:* Consider characteristic #3 of the Poisson random variable.]

5.41 A can company reports that the number of breakdowns per 8-hour shift on its machine-operated assembly line follows a Poisson distribution, with a mean of 1.5.

a. What is the probability of exactly two breakdowns during the midnight shift?

b. What is the probability of fewer than two breakdowns during the afternoon shift?

c. What is the probability of no breakdowns during three consecutive 8-hour shifts? (Assume the machine operates independently across shifts.)

5.42 The number x of computer input errors per minute made by a particular computer programmer has a Poisson distribution with an average of .75 error per minute.

a. Find the mean and variance of x.

b. What is the probability that the programmer will make at least one error in a particular minute?

c. What is the probability that the programmer will make no errors in a particular minute?

5.43 Refer to the *American Journal of Public Health* (AJPH) report on traffic fatalities on rural interstate highways, Exercise 4.23. One year prior to the AJPH report, the American Automobile Association (AAA) sponsored an analysis of the effect of the 65-mile-per-hour speed limit in the state of Indiana. The AAA study found that Indiana averaged 90 fatalities per year on rural interstates. For a given year, within what range would you expect the number of traffic fatalities on rural interstates in Indiana to fall?

5.44 The random variable x, the number of people who arrive at a cashier's counter in a bank during a specified period of time, often possesses (approximately) a Poisson probability distribution. If the mean arrival rate, μ, is known, the Poisson probability distribution can be used to aid in the design of the customer service facility. Suppose you estimate that the mean number of arrivals per minute for cashier service at a bank is one person per minute.

a. What is the probability that in a given minute, the number of arrivals will be two or more?

b. Can you tell the bank manager that the number of arrivals will rarely exceed two per minute?

5.45 A random sample of 230 people is selected and all are asked whether they would prefer to own a personal computer (PC) or a videocassette recorder (VCR). Assuming that 3% of the public would prefer a PC, approximate the probability that 10 people in the sample would prefer a PC to a VCR.

---

*Shively, Thomas S. "An analysis of the trend in ozone using nonhomogeneous Poisson processes." Paper presented at the annual meeting of the American Statistical Association, Anaheim, Calif., Aug. 1990.

5.46 *Lead time* is a term used by retailers to describe the time period during which a stock item is replenished. In one study, the Poisson probability distribution was used to describe x, the number of customers in a 7-day lead time period in a large U.S. Air Force base supply account (*Management Science*, Apr. 1983). Two types of items were analyzed separately: items that cost $5 or less and items that cost more than $5. For items that cost $5 or less, the mean number of customers during lead time was estimated to be .09; for items that cost over $5, the mean was estimated to be .15.

a. Find the mean and variance for the number x of customers who demand items that cost $5 or less. Within what limits would you expect x to fall?

b. Find the mean and variance for the number x of customers who demand items that cost over $5. Within what limits would you expect x to fall?

c. What is the probability that no customers will demand an item that costs $5 or less during lead time?

d. What is the probability that no customers will demand an item that costs more than $5 during lead time?

e. What is the probability that at least one customer will demand an item that costs $5 or less during lead time?

f. What is the probability that at least one customer will demand an item that costs more than $5 during lead time?

5.6 The Hypergeometric Probability Distribution (Optional)

We noted in Section 5.4 that one of the applications of the binomial probability distribution is its use as the probability distribution for the number x of favorable (or unfavorable) responses in a public opinion or market survey. Ideally, it is applicable when sampling is **with replacement**—that is, each item drawn from the population is observed and returned to the population before the next item is drawn. Practically speaking, the sampling in surveys is rarely conducted with replacement. Nevertheless, the binomial probability distribution is still appropriate if the number N of elements in the population is large and the sample size n is small relative to N.

When sampling is **without replacement,** and the number of elements N in the population is small (or when the sample size n is large relative to N), the number of "successes" in a random sample of n items has a **hypergeometric probability distribution.** The defining characteristics and probability for a hypergeometric random variable are stated in the boxes.

Characteristics That Define a Hypergeometric Random Variable

1. The experiment consists of randomly drawing n elements without replacement from a set of N elements, S of which are "successes" and $N - s$ of which are "failures."

2. The hypergeometric random variable x is the number of S's in the draw of n elements.

The Hypergeometric Probability Distribution

$$p(x) = \frac{\binom{S}{x}\binom{N-S}{n-x}}{\binom{N}{n}}$$

where

N = Number of elements in the population

S = Number of "successes" in the population

n = Sample size

x = Number of "successes" in the sample

$$\binom{S}{x} = \frac{S!}{x!\,(S-x)!}$$

$$\binom{N-S}{n-x} = \frac{(N-S)!}{(n-x)!\,(N-S-n+x)!}$$

$$\binom{N}{n} = \frac{N!}{n!\,(N-n)!}$$

Assumptions:

1. The sample of n elements is randomly selected from the N elements of the population.
2. The value of x is restricted so that all factorials are nonnegative.

EXAMPLE 5.15
Computing Hypergeometric
Probabilities

Suppose you plan to select four of 10 new stock issues (stock issued by new companies) and that, unknown to you, three of the 10 will result in substantial profits and seven will result in losses.

    a. What is the probability that all three of the profitable issues will appear in your selection?

    b. What is the probability that at least two of the three profitable issues will appear in your selection?

    c. Graph the probability distribution for x, the number of profitable issues in the sample of $n = 4$.

SOLUTION   For this problem, the number of elements in the population is $N = 10$, the number of successes is $S = 3$, and the sample size is $n = 4$.

a. We use the formula for the hypergeometric probability distribution to compute the probability of observing exactly $x = 3$ successes in the sample of $n = 4$:

$$p(x) = \frac{\binom{S}{x}\binom{N-S}{n-x}}{\binom{N}{n}}$$

or

$$p(3) = \frac{\binom{3}{3}\binom{7}{1}}{\binom{10}{4}} = \frac{\left(\frac{3!}{3!0!}\right)\left(\frac{7!}{1!6!}\right)}{\left(\frac{10!}{4!6!}\right)}$$

$$= \frac{(1)(7)}{210} = \frac{1}{30}$$

b. The probability of observing at least two successes in the sample of $n = 4$ is

$$P(x \geq 2) = p(2) + p(3)$$

Since we have calculated $p(3)$ in part **a**, we need to find

$$p(2) = \frac{\binom{3}{2}\binom{7}{2}}{\binom{10}{4}} = \frac{\left(\frac{3!}{2!1!}\right)\left(\frac{7!}{2!5!}\right)}{\left(\frac{10!}{4!6!}\right)}$$

$$= \frac{(3)(21)}{210} = \frac{3}{10}$$

Then

$$P(x \geq 2) = p(2) + p(3) = \frac{1}{30} + \frac{3}{10} = \frac{1}{30} + \frac{9}{30} = \frac{1}{3}$$

c. Since x can assume only the values 0, 1, 2, 3, and $p(2)$ and $p(3)$ were calculated in parts **a** and **b**, we need to calculate $p(0)$ and $p(1)$:

$$p(0) = \frac{\binom{3}{0}\binom{7}{4}}{\binom{10}{4}} = \frac{\left(\frac{3!}{0!3!}\right)\left(\frac{7!}{4!3!}\right)}{210} = \frac{35}{210} = \frac{1}{6}$$

FIGURE 5.6

Probability Histogram for the Hypergeometric Probability Distribution of Example 5.15

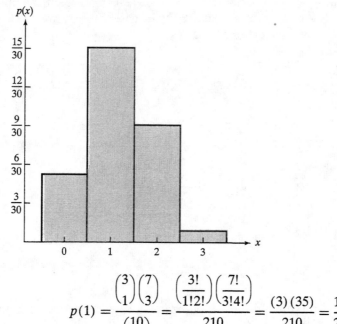

$$p(1) = \frac{\binom{3}{1}\binom{7}{3}}{\binom{10}{4}} = \frac{\left(\frac{3!}{1!2!}\right)\left(\frac{7!}{3!4!}\right)}{210} = \frac{(3)(35)}{210} = \frac{1}{2}$$

Using a probability histogram to display these values of $p(x)$, we obtain the graph shown in Figure 5.6. ■

The mean, variance, and standard deviation for a hypergeometric probability distribution are shown in the box.

Mean, Variance, and Standard Deviation for a Hypergeometric Probability Distribution

$$\mu = \frac{nS}{N}$$

$$\sigma^2 = n\left(\frac{S}{N}\right)\left(\frac{N-S}{N}\right)\left(\frac{N-n}{N-1}\right)$$

$$\sigma = \sqrt{n\left(\frac{S}{N}\right)\left(\frac{N-S}{N}\right)\left(\frac{N-n}{N-1}\right)}$$

EXAMPLE 5.16
Empirical Rule Application

An experiment is conducted to select a suitable catalyst for the commercial production of ethylenediamine, a product used in soaps. Suppose a chemical engineer randomly selects $n = 30$ catalysts for testing from among a group of $N = 60$ catalysts. Unknown to the engineer, $S = 14$ of the 60 catalysts are highly acidic. What is the probability that the number x of highly acidic catalysts selected for testing is less than 3?

SOLUTION The probability that fewer than $x = 3$ catalysts in the sample of $n = 30$ will be highly acidic is

$$P(x \le 2) = p(0) + p(1) + p(2)$$

where $p(x)$ is given by the hypergeometric probability distribution. When n, S, and x are relatively large, the calculation of $p(x)$ can be tedious. Therefore, we can save a lot of effort by calculating μ and σ and using the Empirical Rule to obtain some notion of the magnitude of $P(x \le 2)$. In this example, we have

$$\mu = \frac{nS}{N} = \frac{(30)(14)}{60} = 7$$

$$\sigma = \sqrt{n\left(\frac{S}{N}\right)\left(\frac{N-S}{N}\right)\left(\frac{N-n}{N-1}\right)} = \sqrt{30\left(\frac{14}{60}\right)\left(\frac{46}{60}\right)\left(\frac{30}{59}\right)}$$
$$= 1.65$$

and the z score (see Definition 3.11) corresponding to $x = 2$ is

$$z = \frac{x - \mu}{\sigma} = \frac{2 - 7}{1.65} = -3.03$$

Therefore, $x = 2$ lies more than 3σ away from its mean μ. Since our knowledge of the Empirical Rule tells us that it is highly improbable that an observation will lie more than 3σ away from its mean, we would conclude that the probability that x is less than or equal to 2 is very small.

The graph of $p(x)$ shown in Figure 5.7 (page 236) provides a visual confirmation of our conclusion. We have located the mean μ and the interval $\mu \pm 2\sigma$ on the graph. You can see that most of the probability distribution falls within the interval $\mu \pm 2\sigma$ and that the probability that $x \le 2$ is very small. ■

FIGURE 5.7

Graph of $p(x)$ for
Example 5.16

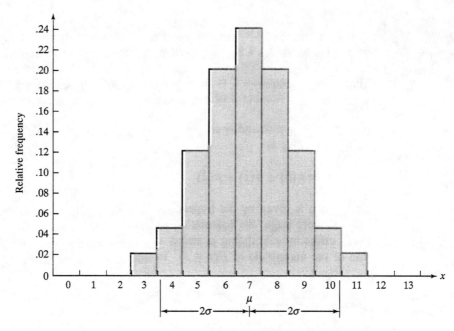

EXERCISES

■ *Learning the Mechanics*

5.47   Suppose x has a hypergeometric probability distribution with $N = 6$, $n = 4$, and $S = 2$.
   a. Compute $p(x)$ for $x = 0, 1, 2$.
   b. Graph the probability distribution $p(x)$.
   c. Compute μ and σ.
   d. Locate the interval $\mu \pm 2\sigma$ on the graph of part **b**. What is the probability that x will fall within $\mu \pm 2\sigma$?

5.48   Suppose x has a hypergeometric probability distribution with $N = 10$, $n = 5$, and $S = 4$.
   a. Compute $p(x)$ for $x = 0, 1, 2, 3, 4$.
   b. Graph the probability distribution $p(x)$.
   c. Compute μ and σ.
   d. Locate the interval $\mu \pm 2\sigma$ on the graph of part **b**. What is the probability that x will fall within $\mu \pm 2\sigma$?

5.49   Suppose x has a hypergeometric probability distribution with $N = 12$, $n = 7$, and $S = 5$. Compute each of the following:
   a. $P(x = 3)$ **b.** $P(x \le 2)$ **c.** $P(x = 5)$
   d. $P(x > 3)$ **e.** μ **f.** σ
   g. The probability that x will fall within the interval $\mu \pm 2\sigma$

5.50   Suppose x has a hypergeometric probability distribution with $N = 8$, $n = 5$, and $S = 3$. Compute each of the following:

a. $P(x = 1)$ **b.** $P(x \le 1)$ **c.** $P(x \ge 2)$
d. $P(x = 4)$ **e.** μ **f.** σ
g. The probability that x will fall within the interval $\mu \pm 2\sigma$

■ *Applying the Concepts*

5.51 Suppose you are purchasing small lots of cathode ray tubes (CRTs) for computer terminals. Since it is very costly to test a single CRT, it may be desirable to test a sample of CRTs from the lot rather than every CRT in the lot. Such a sampling plan would be based on a hypergeometric probability distribution. For example, assume that each lot contains seven CRTs. You decide to sample three CRTs per lot and to reject the lot if you observe one or more defectives in the sample.
a. If the lot contains one defective CRT, what is the probability that you will accept the lot?
b. What is the probability that you will accept the lot if it contains three defective CRTs?

5.52 A College Placement Council survey found that 90% of college students would be willing to work long hours on the job (*Personnel Journal*, July 1984). Suppose 15 recent college graduates have applied for three entry-level management positions at a high-tech firm. Of these applicants, only two would not be willing to work long, hard hours on the job. Since the applicants are judged from their resumes to have equal ability and talent, the firm will randomly select three applicants for the three openings.
a. What is the probability that both applicants who would be unwilling to work long, hard hours on the job are selected?
b. What is the probability that at least one of the applicants who would be unwilling to work long, hard hours on the job is selected?

5.53 Based on data provided by the U.S. Department of Health and Human Resources, *U.S. News & World Report* (Sept. 28, 1992) estimates that 1 out of every 5 kidney transplants fails within a year. Suppose that exactly 3 of the next 15 kidney transplants fail within a year. Consider a random sample of 3 of the 15 patients.
a. Find the probability that all 3 of the sampled kidney transplant operations result in failure within a year.
b. Find the probability that at least 1 of the 3 sampled kidney transplants fails within a year.

5.54 A commercial for Trident sugarless chewing gum claims that "three out of four dentists who recommend sugarless gum to their patients recommend Trident." Suppose this claim was established following a survey of four dentists randomly selected from a group of 20 dentists who were known to recommend sugarless gum to their patients. What is the probability that at least three of the four dentists surveyed would recommend Trident if in fact only half of the original group of 20 dentists favor that brand? Does your probability calculation strengthen or weaken the gum manufacturer's claim? Explain.

5.55 Refer to Exercise 4.35. As reported in *IEEE Computer Applications in Power* (Apr. 1990), an outdoor, unmanned computerized video monitoring system detected seven out of 10 intruders in snowy conditions. Suppose that two of the intruders had criminal intentions. What is the probability that both of these intruders were detected by the system?

5.56 An article in *The American Statistician* (May 1991) described the use of probability in a reverse cocaine sting. Police in a mid-size Florida city seized 496 foil packets in a cocaine bust. To convict the drug traffickers, police had to prove that the packets contained genuine cocaine.

Consequently, the police lab randomly selected and chemically tested four of the packets; all four tested positive for cocaine. This result led to a conviction of the traffickers.

a. Of the 496 foil packets confiscated, suppose 331 contain genuine cocaine and 165 contain an inert (legal) powder. Find the probability that four randomly selected packets will test positive for cocaine.

b. Police used the 492 remaining foil packets (i.e., those not tested) in a reverse sting operation. Two of the 492 packets were randomly selected and sold by undercover officers to a buyer. Between the sale and the arrest, however, the buyer disposed of the evidence. Given that four of the original 496 packets tested positive for cocaine, what is the probability that the two packets sold in the reverse sting did not contain cocaine? Assume the information provided in part **a** is correct.

c. *The American Statistician* article demonstrates that the conditional probability, part **b**, is maximized when the original 496 packets consist of 331 packets containing genuine cocaine and 165 containing inert powder. Recalculate the probability, part **b**, assuming that 400 of the original 496 packets contain cocaine.

5.57 A task force established by the Environmental Protection Agency was scheduled to investigate 20 industrial firms to check for violations of pollution control regulations. However, budget cutbacks have drastically reduced the size of the task force, and they will be able to investigate only three of the 20 firms. If five of the firms are actually operating in violation of regulations, find the probability that:

a. None of the three sampled firms will be found in violation of regulations.

b. All three firms investigated will be found in violation of regulations.

c. At least one of the three firms will be operating in violation of pollution control regulations.

5.7 The Geometric Probability Distribution (Optional)

Suppose you were to flip a coin over and over again. What is the probability that more than five coin flips would occur before you observe the first head? Or, suppose you were to invest in a series of identical and independent business ventures. What is the probability that you would have to make more than four investments before you observe the first success? Or, suppose that the length of time between the sales of a large computer is measured in days and that the probability of making a sale on any one day is the same as on any other. If the event (sale or no sale) that occurs on any one day is independent of the occurrence on any other day, what is the probability that as many as 30 days would elapse between sales?

The probability distribution that provides answers to these questions is called the **geometric probability distribution.** It is based on a series of independent identical trials of the type encountered in a binomial experiment (discussed in Section 5.4). The difference between this experiment and the binomial experiment is that the number of trials is not fixed. Instead, the trials continue until the first "success" is observed. The probability distribution for x, the number of trials until the first success, is given in the box.

The Geometric Probability Distribution

$$p(x) = \pi(1 - \pi)^{x-1} \text{ for } x = 1, 2, 3, \ldots$$

where

π = Probability of "success" on a single trial

x = Number of trials until the first "success" is observed

EXAMPLE 5.17
Computing Geometric Probabilities

An insurance company expects its salespersons to achieve minimum monthly sales of $50,000. Suppose the probability that a particular salesperson sells $50,000 of insurance in any given month is .8. If the sales of insurance in any one month are independent of the sales in any other, what is the probability that exactly 3 months will elapse before the salesperson reaches the acceptable minimum monthly sales? Graph $p(x)$.

SOLUTION Let π be the probability that the salesperson will achieve the minimum $50,000 sales in a given month, and let x be the number of months until the first acceptable sales month occurs. Then x has a geometric probability distribution with $\pi = .8$, and the probability that $x = 3$ is

$$p(x) = \pi(1 - \pi)^{x-1}$$
$$= (.8)(.2)^{3-1} = (.8)(.04) = .032$$

A probability histogram for $p(x)$ is shown in Figure 5.8 (page 240). ■

The mean, variance, and standard deviation for a geometric probability distribution are shown in the next box.

Mean, Variance, and Standard Deviation for a Geometric Probability Distribution

$$\mu = \frac{1}{\pi}$$

$$\sigma^2 = \frac{1 - \pi}{\pi^2} \qquad \sigma = \sqrt{\frac{1 - \pi}{\pi^2}}$$

when π = Probability of a "success" on a single trial

FIGURE 5.8

Probability
Histogram for the
Geometric
Probability
Distribution of
Example 5.17

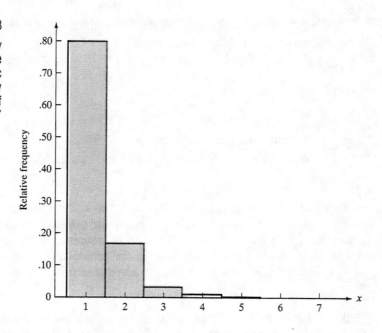

EXAMPLE 5.18

μ, σ, and Statistical
Inference

The drilling records for an oil company suggest that the probability it will hit oil in productive quantities at a certain offshore location is .2. Suppose the company plans to drill a series of wells.

a. Find the mean and standard deviation of the number x of wells that must be drilled before the company hits its first productive well.

b. Is it likely that x could be as large as 15?

SOLUTION For this example, x has a geometric probability distribution and the probability of success (i.e., hit oil in productive quantities) is $\pi = .2$.

a. Using the formulas given in the box, we have

$$\mu = \frac{1}{\pi} = \frac{1}{.2} = 5$$

and

$$\sigma = \sqrt{\frac{1 - \pi}{\pi^2}} = \sqrt{\frac{.8}{(.2)^2}} = 4.47$$

b. The z score corresponding to $x = 15$ is

$$z = \frac{x - \mu}{\sigma} = \frac{15 - 5}{4.47} = 2.24$$

This means that $x = 15$ lies 2.24 standard deviations above its mean, $\mu = 5$. Since the Empirical Rule tells us that approximately 95% of a large number of observations will lie within 2 standard deviations of their mean, it seems that the likelihood of observing a value of x as large as 15 is relatively small.

As in Example 5.16, we will provide a visual confirmation of our conclusions. A histogram of the geometric probability distribution is shown in Figure 5.9. The mean and the interval $\mu \pm 2\sigma$ are indicated on the graph. You can see that most of the probability distribution falls in the interval $\mu \pm 2\sigma$, and the probability that x is as large as 15 is small.

FIGURE 5.9

Graph of $p(x)$ for Example 5.18

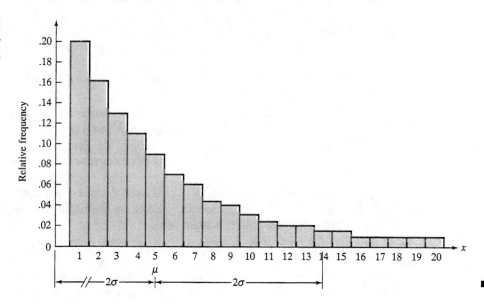

EXERCISES

■ *Learning the Mechanics*

5.58 Suppose x has a geometric probability distribution with $\pi = .7$.
  a. Graph $p(x)$ for $x = 1, 2, 3, 4$.
  b. Compute μ and σ.
  c. Locate the interval $\mu \pm 2\sigma$ on the graph of part **a**. What is the probability that x will fall within the interval $\mu \pm 2\sigma$?

5.59 Suppose x has a geometric probability distribution with $\pi = .3$.
  a. Graph $p(x)$ for $x = 1, 2, 3, \ldots, 8$.
  b. Compute μ and σ.
  c. Locate the interval $\mu \pm 2\sigma$ on the graph of part **a**. What is the probability that x will fall within the interval $\mu \pm 2\sigma$?

5.60 Suppose x has a geometric probability distribution with $\pi = .1$. Find:

  a. $P(x = 7)$ **b.** $P(x = 10)$ **c.** $P(x \le 3)$ **d.** $P(x > 5)$

  e. $P(7 \le x \le 10)$ **f.** μ **g.** σ

5.61   Suppose x has a geometric probability distribution with $\pi = .4$. Find:

  a. $P(x = 2)$ **b.** $P(x \ge 4)$ **c.** $P(x < 3)$ **d.** $P(x = 5)$

  e. $P(x > 1)$ **f.** μ **g.** σ

■ *Applying the Concepts*

5.62   The National Aeronautics and Space Administration (NASA) estimates that the chance of a "critical item" failure within a space shuttle's main engine is approximately 1 in 63 (*Tampa Tribune*, Dec. 3, 1993). The failure of a critical item during flight will lead directly to a shuttle catastrophe.

  a. On average, how many shuttle missions will fly before a critical item failure occurs?

  b. What is the standard deviation of the number of missions before a critical item failure occurs?

  c. Give an interval that will capture the number of missions before a critical item failure occurs with probability of approximately .95.

5.63   The manufacturer of a price-reading optical scanner claims that the probability it will misread the price of any product by misreading the "bar code" on a product's label is .001. At the time one of the scanners was installed in a supermarket, the store manager tested its performance. Let x be the number of trials (i.e., the number of prices read by the scanner) until the first misread price is observed.

  a. Find the probability distribution for x. (Assume the trials represent independent events.)

  b. If the manufacturer's claim is correct, what is the probability that the scanner will not misread a price until after the fifth price is read?

  c. If in fact the third price is misread, what inference would you make about the manufacturer's claim? Explain.

5.64   The most common data-collection method in consumer and market research is the telephone survey. A major problem with consumer telephone surveys, however, is nonresponse. How likely are consumers to be at home to take the call and, if at home, how likely are they to take part in the survey? To answer these and other questions, a study of over 250,000 random-digit dialings of both listed and unlisted telephone numbers was directed across the United States (*Journal of Advertising Research*, Apr./May 1983). The probability of a completed interview on the first dialing attempt was assessed to be .084.

  a. What is the probability that five calls must be made before the first completed interview is obtained?

  b. What is the probability that at least five calls must be made before the first completed interview is obtained?

  c. Find the mean number of calls that must be made before the first completed interview is obtained. Find the standard deviation.

5.65   According to *Engineering News-Record* (Dec. 1, 1983), the District of Columbia mandates that at least one-half of all jobs created by city contracts be filled by local residents. Suppose you want to survey jobs created by city contracts after the mandate was issued to determine the level of compliance with the new law. If in fact only 40% of all jobs created by city contracts are filled by local residents,

a. What is the expected number of jobs you would have to survey before you find one that has been filled by a local resident?

b. What is the probability that you will not find a job filled by a local resident until after the fourth job surveyed?

5.66 Environmental engineers classify consumers into one of five categories (see Exercise 4.15 for a description of each group). The probabilities associated with the groups are given here.

Basic browns	.28
True-blue greens	.11
Greenback greens	.11
Sprouts	.26
Grousers	.24

Source: The *Orange County (Calif.) Register*, Aug. 7, 1990.

Let x equal the number of consumers that must be sampled until the first environmentalist is found. [*Note*: From Exercise 4.15, an environmentalist is a true-blue green, greenback green, or sprout.]

a. Find μ and σ, the mean and standard deviation of x.

b. Use the information, part **a**, to form an interval that will include x with a high probability.

5.67 A manufacturer uses electrical fuses in an electronic system. The fuses are purchased in large lots and tested sequentially until the first defective fuse is observed. Assume that the lot contains 5% defective fuses.

a. What is the probability that the first defective fuse will be one of the first five fuses tested?

b. Find the mean, variance, and standard deviation for x, the number of fuses tested until the first defective fuse is observed.

c. Within what limits would you expect x to fall?

5.68 Refer to Exercise 5.46. Recall that researchers developed a model for the demand during lead time for items stocked in a large U.S. Air Force base supply account (*Management Science*, Apr. 1983). Let x represent the number of units of a particular item (e.g., electronic items) demanded per customer during lead time. The researchers approximated the probability distribution of x using a geometric distribution with $\pi = .875$.

a. Interpret the value of π. [*Hint*: Substitute $x = 1$ into the formula for $p(x)$.]

b. Find the mean and variance of x.

c. Find the probability that customers will demand $x = 2$ units during lead time.

d. Find the probability that customers will demand three or more units during lead time.

5.69 "The sufficiently prolonged continuation of a low probability makes a given outcome inevitable," writes A. J. Coale in *Population and Development Review* (Sept. 1985). The "inevitable" event Coale is specifically referring to is a nuclear war. Experts agree that the probability of a nuclear war occurring in a given year is small, but not zero. According to Coale, then, "over hundreds of years this makes nuclear war virtually certain." Suppose the probability of a nuclear war occurring in any given year is only .01. What is the probability of a nuclear war occurring in the next 5 years? 10 years? 15 years? 20 years?

SUMMARY

This chapter introduces the notion of *random variables* and then focuses on *discrete* random variables, those that can assume a countable number of values. A complete list (or graph or formula) that gives the probabilities associated with each value of a discrete random variable x is called its probability distribution.

The *binomial random variable* is one of many discrete random variables encountered in business and economics. The binomial probability distribution provides a good model for the probability distribution of the number x of favorable (or unfavorable) responses when the number N of events in the population is large relative to the sample size n—a situation that generally occurs with public opinion polls and sample surveys.

A second discrete probability distribution covered in this chapter was the *Poisson probability distribution*. It provides a good model for the distribution of the number x of some rare event per unit of time, space, or distance. It also provides a good approximation to the binomial probability distribution when n is large, π is small, and $n\pi < 7$.

Two other discrete probability distributions, both related to the binomial, were discussed in optional sections of this chapter. When the number N in the population is small relative to the sample size n, the number x of successes in n trials follows a *hypergeometric probability distribution*. The *geometric probability distribution* provides a good model for x, the number of trials until the first success is observed in a sequence of identical trials of the type conducted in a binomial experiment.

KEY TERMS

Binomial experiment	Cumulative binomial probabilities	Poisson probability distribution
Binomial probability distribution	Discrete random variable	Random variable
Binomial random variable	*Geometric probability distribution	*Sampling with replacement
Continuous random variable	*Hypergeometric probability distribution	*Sampling without replacement

KEY FORMULAS

Discrete probability distribution:

$$\mu = \Sigma x p(x) \qquad \sigma^2 = \Sigma (x - \mu)^2 p(x) = \Sigma x^2 p(x) - \mu^2$$

---

*From the optional sections in this chapter.

Binomial probability distribution:

$$p(x) = \binom{n}{x} \pi^x (1 - \pi)^{n-x}, \quad x = 0, 1, 2, \ldots, n$$

$$\mu = n\pi \qquad \sigma^2 = n\pi(1 - \pi) \qquad \sigma = \sqrt{n\pi(1 - \pi)}$$

Poisson probability distribution:

$$p(x) = \frac{\mu^x e^{-\mu}}{x!}, \quad x = 0, 1, 2, \ldots, \infty$$

$$\text{Mean} = \mu \qquad \sigma^2 = \mu \qquad \sigma = \sqrt{\mu}$$

*Hypergeometric probability distribution:

$$p(x) = \frac{\binom{S}{x}\binom{N-S}{n-x}}{\binom{N}{n}}, \quad x = 0, 1, 2, \ldots, n$$

$$\mu = \frac{nS}{N} \qquad \sigma^2 = n\left(\frac{S}{N}\right)\left(\frac{N-S}{N}\right)\left(\frac{N-n}{N-1}\right)$$

$$\sigma = \sqrt{n\left(\frac{S}{N}\right)\left(\frac{N-S}{N}\right)\left(\frac{N-n}{N-1}\right)}$$

*Geometric probability distribution:

$$p(x) = \pi(1 - \pi)^{x-1}, \quad x = 0, 1, 2, \ldots, \infty$$

$$\mu = \frac{1}{\pi} \qquad \sigma^2 = \frac{1 - \pi}{\pi^2} \qquad \sigma = \sqrt{\frac{1 - \pi}{\pi^2}}$$

SUPPLEMENTARY EXERCISES

[*Note: Starred (*) exercises refer to the optional sections in this chapter.*]

5.70 The *Tampa Tribune* (Aug. 14, 1988) reported on death rates at major hospitals in the country. Department of Health and Human Services studies revealed that many hospitals had significantly more or fewer deaths than were "expected." However, the author cautions that "large

---

*From the optional sections in this chapter.

numbers (of patients) are necessary for meaningful [death] results," especially when rates are extremely small. To illustrate, the following hypothetical situation was considered. A small hospital has 100 patients, each of whom has received a certain operation. Suppose the expected death rate for this operation is 1 per 100 (i.e., .01). Let x be the number of the 100 patients who die from the operation.

a. What probability distribution best models the distribution of x? Why?

b. What is the expected value of x?

c. Suppose that the last of the 100 patients is the only one to die from the operation (i.e., $x = 1$). Does the observed death rate match the expected death rate?

d. Now, suppose the second death occurs in the 101st patient. Does the observed death rate match the expected? [*Hint*: Use $n = 101$ and $x = 2$.]

5.71 According to the *Training and Development Journal* (Aug. 1984), statistics show that between 10% and 20% of the labor force are considered "troubled employees" who suffer from mental health problems such as alcohol, drug abuse, and psychological stress disorders. Suppose that 20% of a firm's 10,000 employees are "troubled employees." Let x be the number of "troubled employees" in a sample of 15 randomly selected employees. What is the probability that:

a. x is greater than 10?

b. x is 2 or less?

c. x is 0?

d. If none of the 15 employees admits to being a "troubled employee," what would you infer? [*Hint*: Refer to your answer to part **c.**]

*5.72 One recent survey found that almost half of all business executives report symptoms of stress-induced problems (see Example 5.10). Suppose a project team consisting of four business executives is to be selected at random from a group of 10 executives at an international trade organization. Unknown to the firm, three of the 10 executives are currently experiencing stress-related physical problems.

a. What is the probability that the project team will include at least one executive with stress-related physical problems?

b. What is the probability that the project team will include exactly one executive with stress-related physical problems?

c. What is the probability that the project team will include all three executives with stress-related physical problems?

d. Within what limits would you expect the number of executives with stress-related physical problems on the project team to fall?

5.73 E. M. Matsumura and K. W. Tsui applied the Poisson approximation to the binomial distribution in audit sampling (*Journal of Accounting Research*, Spring 1982). They counted the number of errors in a sample of 100 transactions from each account. For one particular account, they estimated that the probability a transaction would be in error is .06.

a. Use the Poisson approximation to the binomial to find the probability that at least one of the 100 audited transactions for this account will be in error.

b. For a different account, Matsumura and Tsui estimated that the probability a transaction would be in error is .03. Repeat part **a** for this account.

c. Use your answers to parts **a** and **b** to find the probability that both accounts will show at least one of the 100 audited transactions in error. (Assume that the two events of parts **a** and **b** are independent.)

5.74 In a recent national study, it was discovered that four out of every 10 full-time employees claim they participate in their companies' purchasing decisions on a regular basis (*Journal of Advertising Research*, Aug./Sept. 1984). Let x be the number of full-time employees in a sample of $n = 500$ who regularly participate in their companies' purchasing decisions.

   a. Is this a binomial experiment? Explain.

   b. What is π, the probability of success?

   c. What is the expected value of x?

   d. Within what interval would you expect x to fall?

   e. Would the value $x = 185$ contradict the statement that "four out of every 10 employees regularly participate in their firms' buying decisions"? Explain.

5.75 Lesser developed countries experiencing rapid population growth often face severe traffic control problems in their large cities. Traffic engineers have determined that elevated rail systems may provide a feasible solution to these traffic woes. Studies indicate that the number of maintenance-related shutdowns of the elevated rail system in a particular country has a distribution with a mean equal to 6.5 per month.

   a. Find the probability that at least five shutdowns of the elevated rail system will occur next month in the country.

   b. Find the probability that exactly four shutdowns will occur next month.

5.76 Associated Merchandising Corporation conducted a survey of shoppers at malls in eight major U.S. cities in 1983. The survey revealed that 82% of the shoppers feel there is more credibility in buying a similar or identical piece of merchandise at regular discount stores than on sale at department stores (*The Discount Merchandiser*, Aug. 1983). Suppose the survey consisted of a sample of 1,000 shoppers and assume that, in fact, $\pi = .82$.

   a. Compute μ, the mean number of shoppers in a sample of 1,000 who feel there is more credibility in buying merchandise at regular discount stores.

   b. Compute σ.

   c. Construct the interval $\mu \pm 2\sigma$.

   d. Would you expect to see as few as 600 shoppers in 1,000 who feel there is more credibility in buying at regular discount stores? Explain.

*5.77 Of the next 20 electronic switches manufactured on a production line, two will be defective. A quality control inspector will randomly select five of the next 20 switches and check for defects.

   a. What is the probability that the quality control inspector will select the two defective switches?

   b. What is the probability that the quality control inspector will select at least one of the defective switches?

   c. The quality control inspector will use the proportion of defectives in the sample of five to estimate the rate at which defective switches are produced for the entire production line. How many defectives can the inspector expect to select in the sample of five?

5.78 James S. Trefil wrote about the role of probabilities and expected values in our everyday lives (*Smithsonian*, Sept. 1984). Trefil illustrates expected value theory by applying it to junk-mail contests, ploys used by advertisers to interest readers in their products. He writes:

> If you are on a junk-mail list, you probably get regular notices announcing that "You may have already won the $10,000 jackpot!" Is it really worth answering the ad? Well, suppose the mailing went to 100,000 people. Your

chances of winning are then 1 in 100,000. Over many contests, therefore, you would expect to win an average of $10,000 × ($\frac{1}{100,000}$), or ten cents per game ... . You will note that the expected [winnings] in this case is less than the price of the postage stamp you need to enter the contest. In fact, you can expect to lose ... cents every time you play, so the reaction "It's not worth answering this" is correct.

Suppose you randomly select $n = 10$ junk-mail contests to enter, each offering a $10,000 jackpot if you win. Assume that the probability of your winning any one contest is 1 in 100,000 or .00001. Let x be the number of contests that you win.

a. Find the expected value of x.

b. Now let y be the amount of money you win on any one contest. In Trefil's illustration, either $y = $10,000$ (i.e., you win the contest) or $y = 0$ (i.e., you lose the contest). In this particular case, it can be shown that $E(y) = $10,000 E(x)$. Find your expected winnings, $E(y)$.

c. Find $E(y)$ if you enter only a single contest (i.e., $n = 1$). Does this value agree with Trefil's "ten cents" per game?

d. Now suppose you decide to enter a series of junk-mail contests until you win one contest. What is the probability that you will not win a junk-mail contest until after the fifth contest you enter?

e. Refer to part d. Find the mean and standard deviation of the number of junk-mail contests you must enter before you can expect to win. Within what range do you expect the number of contests you must enter to fall?

5.79 The safety supervisor at a large manufacturing plant believes the expected number of industrial accidents per month is 4.1.

a. What is the probability that exactly two accidents will occur next month?

b. What is the probability that at least four accidents will occur next month?

5.80 Computer technology has developed to the point where most industrial "robots" are programmed to operate through microprocessors. The probability that one such computerized robot breaks down during any one 8-hour shift is .2. Find the probability that the robot will operate for at most five shifts before breaking down.

5.81 According to *Organizational Dynamics* (Spring 1984), 38% of all new U.S. corporations survive to age 5 years.

a. What is the probability that the first new corporation to survive to age 5 years will be one of the first three new corporations formed this year?

b. Find the mean, variance, and standard deviation of x, the number of new corporations formed until the first corporation to survive to age 5 years is observed.

5.82 According to the National Highway Traffic Safety Administration, "as many as 9 out of 10 heavily used cars, such as those from leasing companies, may have had their mileage rolled back when resold" (reported in *Orlando Sentinel*, Apr. 13, 1984). Suppose you will purchase for your firm two used cars from an auto leasing company that has 10 cars available. Unknown to you, 9 of the 10 cars have falsified odometer readings.

a. What is the probability that both of the cars you purchase have falsified odometer readings?

b. What is the probability that at least one of the two cars you purchase has a falsified odometer reading?

5.83 Pharmacists periodically conduct polls to determine the health status of their customers. One such survey of 2,000 Americans was conducted for the Proprietary Association, a trade group of the over-the-counter drug industry (reported in the *Orlando Sentinel*, Mar. 19, 1984). The respondents were asked to report the number x of minor physical ailments they might expect to experience in a typical 2-week period. The average value of x for the survey was found to be 4.5.

a. Find the probability that an individual will experience $x = 2$ minor ailments in a typical 2-week period.

b. Find the probability that a person will experience $x \geq 5$ minor ailments in a typical 2-week period.

c. Find the probability that a person will experience no minor ailments in a typical 2-week period.

5.84 Benzene, a solvent commonly used to synthesize plastics and found in consumer products such as paint strippers and high-octane unleaded gasoline, has been classified by scientists as a leukemia-causing agent. Let x be the level (in parts per million) of benzene in the air at a petrochemical plant. Then x can take on the values 0, 1, 2, 3, ..., 1,000,000, and can be approximated by a Poisson probability distribution. In 1978, the federal government lowered the maximum allowable level of benzene in the air at a workplace from 10 parts per million (ppm) to 1 ppm. Any industry in violation of these government standards is subject to severe penalties, including implementation of expensive measures to lower the benzene level.

a. Suppose the mean level of benzene in the air at petrochemical plants is $\mu = 5$ ppm. Find the probability that a petrochemical plant exceeds the government standard of 1 ppm.

b. Repeat part **a**, assuming that $\mu = 2.5$.

c. The *Florida Times-Union* (Apr. 2, 1984) reported on a study by Gulf Oil that revealed that 88% of benzene-using industries expose their workers to 1 ppm or less of the solvent. Suppose you randomly sampled 55 of the benzene-using industries in the country and determined y, the number in violation of government standards. Use the Poisson approximation to the binomial to find the probability that none of the sampled industries violates government standards. Compare this probability to the exact probability computed using the binomial probability distribution. (You can compute the binomial probability using a hand calculator.)

d. Refer to part **c**. Use the fact that 88% of benzene-using industries expose their workers to 1 ppm or less of benzene to approximate μ, the mean level of benzene in the air at these industries. [*Hint:* Search Table 4 of Appendix B for the value of μ that yields $P(x \leq 1)$ closest to .88.]

5.85 As a college student, are you frequently depressed and overwhelmed by the pressure to succeed? According to the American Council on Education (ACE), the level of stress among college freshmen is rising rapidly. In a 1988 survey of 308,007 full-time college freshmen conducted for the ACE by UCLA's Higher Education Research Institute, more than 10% reported frequently "feeling depressed," compared with 8.2% in 1985 (*Tampa Tribune*, Jan. 9, 1989). Assume that 10% of all college freshmen frequently feel depressed.

a. On average, how many of the 308,007 college freshmen surveyed would you expect to report frequent feelings of depression if the true percentage in the population is 8.2% (the 1985 figure)?

b. Find the standard deviation of the number of the 308,007 freshmen surveyed who frequently feel depressed if the true percentage is 8.2%.

c. Suppose that 30,800 of the college freshmen surveyed reported frequent feelings of depression. (This number, 30,800, is approximately the number observed in the actual study.) Calculate the z score for 30,800.

d. Based on the result, part **c**, what would you infer about the true percentage of college freshmen in 1988 who frequently feel depressed? Explain.

*5.86 Many analysts on Wall Street subscribe to the adage "As January goes, so goes the year." The so-called "January Indicator" has been used to forecast the performance of the market for the rest of the year. To investigate the performance of the January Indicator, *Barron's* (Mar. 12, 1984) tracked the monthly Dow Jones Industrial Average (DJA) from 1969 to 1982, a period of 14 years (168 months). For each year, the net change in the DJA during the month of January was compared to the year-end net change in order to determine whether the January index made the "correct call." A similar analysis was performed for the months February through December on the hunch that there might be other, less obvious months with predictive power as good as or better than January's. Each month's 14-year performance record is summarized in the table. Suppose you were to randomly sample 5 of the 14 years from 1969 to 1982. Let x be the number of years in which the January Indicator correctly predicts market performance.

a. Explain why the binomial probability distribution is *not* a good model. Specify the correct probability distribution for x.

b. Find $P(x = 5)$.

c. Find $P(x \leq 2)$.

d. Repeat parts **b** and **c** for the November indicator.

e. Repeat parts **b** and **c** for the September indicator.

Month	*Number of Correct Calls Out of 14*	*Percent Accuracy*
January	10	71%
February	8	57
March	9	64
April	11	79
May	10	71
June	9	64
July	9	64
August	10	71
September	3	21
October	6	43
November	10	71
December	7	50
Total (168 months)	102	61%

Source: Arms, R. W. "Indicators for all seasons? A closer look at January's signal record." *Barron's,* Mar. 12, 1984, pp. 66, 86.

■ CASE STUDY 5.1

Commitment to the Firm: Stayers Versus Leavers

The idea that commitment to a business organization is in some way related to employee turnover has received considerable attention from organizational behaviorists. Numerous researchers have found a causal link between an employee's commitment to the firm and his or her tendency to leave the firm voluntarily. The *Academy of Management Journal* (Oct. 1993) published one such study involving employees of an aerospace firm located in a major metropolitan area in the southeastern United States.

At the time of the study, the firm operated at the leading edge of military aerospace technology in designing, manufacturing, and marketing aviation components such as electronic flight instrument systems, weapons-aiming computers, and radar display units. Top management, however, was concerned with rising discontent among operatives in the repair and overhaul group, the division most responsible for generating revenue growth and maintaining financial ratios. To investigate this problem, researchers at the University of South Florida designed and administered a questionnaire to a sample of 270 of the firm's employees.

Several of the numerous variables measured in the study are listed and described in Table 5.3. The complete data set is also described in Appendix A.7. Note that variable 11 classifies employees as either "stayers" or "leavers." For this case study, we are interested in the random variable x, where x is the number of the 270 employees who are "leavers." Assume that the $n = 270$ employees represent a random sample from the population of employees at all similar aerospace firms in the United States.

a. Explain why the binomial probability distribution best models the distribution of x.

Table 5.3 Variables Measured in *Academy of Management Journal* Study

1. **Age** (years)

2. **Gender** (1 = male, 0 = female)

3. **Organizational tenure** (months): length of time with organization

4. **Job tenure** (months): length of time in current job

5. **Continuance commitment** (3- to 21-point scale): measure of the degree to which past behaviors force the employee to be committed to the firm

6. **Affective commitment** (14- to 98-point scale): measure of the degree to which emotional ties commit the employee to the firm

7. **Moral commitment** (4- to 28-point scale): measure of the degree to which duty commits the employee to the firm

8. **Thinking of quitting** (1- to 5-point scale): measure of how often the employee thinks about quitting

9. **Search** (1- to 5-point scale): measure of how likely the employee is to search for a new job

10. **Intent to leave** (2- to 11-point scale): measure of the employee's intentions to leave the firm

11. **Leave** (1 = employee quit the firm prior to the end of the study, 0 = employee stayed with the firm until the end of the study)

*Jaros, S. J., et al. "Effects of continuance, affective, and moral commitment on the withdrawal process: An evaluation of eight structural equation models." Academy of Management Journal, Vol. 36, No. 5, Oct. 1993, pp. 951–995.

b. A claim is made that the true proportion of "leavers" at all U.S. aerospace firms is $\pi = .10$. Find the expected value and variance of x. Interpret these values.

c. A SAS printout giving the frequency and relative frequency of "stayers" and "leavers" in the data set of Appendix A.7 is displayed in Figure 5.10. Use this information to make an inference about the claim in part **b.**

FIGURE 5.10

SAS Frequency Distribution of Stayers and Leavers

LEAVE	Frequency	Percent	Cumulative Frequency	Cumulative Percent
0 (STAYER)	222	82.2	222	82.2
1 (LEAVER)	48	17.8	270	100.0

■ CASE STUDY 5.2

The Chevalier's Dilemma (Optional)

After reading our discussion of probability theory (Chapter 4) and probability distributions (Chapter 5), you may wonder where and when the notion of probability began. Since probability theory is really the study of chance events, it is not surprising that the idea of probability first occurred to gamblers in their effort to improve the "odds" of winning games of chance.

According to James S. Trefil, "Most historians date the study of the theory of chance occurrences from a day in 1654 when Antoine Gombaud, Chevalier de Méré, Sieur de Baussey, walked into a gaming room in Paris."* Trefil relates the following story about de Méré that is known to students of probability as "The Chevalier's Dilemma":

In progress was a popular gambling diversion of the time, a game in which the player bet the house that he could roll a die four times in a row without getting a 6. If he did so, he collected his winnings; if a 6 came up, he lost. De Méré and every other gambler in the room knew that this game was stacked in favor of the house. But de Méré got to thinking about a slightly more complicated game: one involving two dice. What sort of game could you set up by betting that you could roll two dice a certain number of times without getting a double 6? The conventional gambling wisdom of the time said the break-even point was 24 throws: fewer than this would put the odds too heavily in favor of the gambler, greater than this would favor the house. De Méré thought the conventional wisdom wrong, and his calculations eventually involved such giants of French mathematics as Blaise Pascal and Pierre de Fermat. One of the first products of modern probability theory was the realization that the real break-even point for the double die game was 25 throws, not 24.

The Chevalier's Dilemma can be solved by considering the discrete random variable x, where x is the number of throws of two dice until the first "double 6" occurs.

a. What probability distribution best models the distribution of x? Why?

b. Define a "success" for this distribution.

c. What are the values of π and $(1 - \pi)$?

d. Find $P(x = 25)$.

e. Find $P(x > 24)$, the probability that double 6's will not occur until after the 24th throw. [*Hint:* It can be shown (proof omitted) that for the geometric probability distribution, $P(x > k) = (1 - \pi)^k$.]

f. Find $P(x < 24)$, the probability that double 6's will occur before the 24th throw. [*Hint:* Since $P(x < k) = 1 - P(x > k - 1)$, the hint given in part d implies that $P(x < k) = 1 - (1 - \pi)^{k-1}$.]

g. Refer to the probabilities computed in parts e and f. Check to verify that more than 24 throws puts the "odds" in favor of the gambler, and fewer than 24 throws puts the "odds" in favor of the house. (This reasoning was used to support the original belief that the break-even point for the double-die game was 24 throws.)

A version of the dice game of interest to de Méré can be formally described as follows:

Outcome	Winnings ($)
Gambler wins: $X > B$	1
Gambler loses: $X < B$	-1[a]
Tie: $X = B$	0

[a]*The gambler forfeits $1.*

"The Chevalier's Dilemma" is to find the break-even point B. In the language of probability, the break-even point is the value of B such that a gambler's expected winnings in a long series of dice throws is \$0. This expected value can be written as

$$E(\text{Winnings}) = (1)P(X > B) + (-1)P(X < B)$$
$$+ (0)P(X = B)$$
$$= P(X > B) - P(X < B)$$

Using the hints given in parts **d** and **e**, we have

$$E(\text{Winnings}) = (1 - \pi)^B - [1 - (1 - \pi)^{B-1}]$$
$$= (1 - \pi)^B + (1 - \pi)^{B-1} - 1$$

We must find an integer B such that

$$E(\text{Winnings}) = 0 \text{ or } (1 - \pi)^B + (1 - \pi)^{B-1} - 1 = 0$$

h. Find $E(\text{Winnings})$ for $B = 24$.

i. Find $E(\text{Winnings})$ for $B = 25$.

j. Do the results of parts **h** and **i** support the Chevalier de Méré's findings that the break-even point is 25 throws, not 24? [*Hint:* Check to see that $E(\text{Winnings})$ is closer to 0 for $B = 25$ than for $B = 24$.]

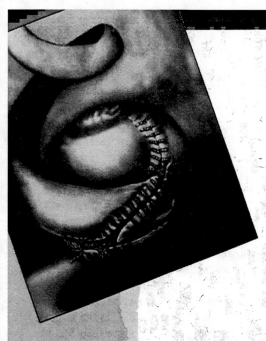

Chapter 6

CONTINUOUS PROBABILITY DISTRIBUTIONS

According to one theory of stock price behavior, publicized and popularized by B. G. Malkiel's book, *A Random Walk Down Wall Street*, stock prices actually change (walk) upward and downward in a random manner and produce a relative frequency distribution of changes in price that has a familiar bell-shaped curve known as a **normal distribution**. Does the real world of stock price changes agree with this theory? In this chapter, we study the characteristics of normal distributions (and other continuous distributions) and learn how to identify improbable or rare events. We use these tools to test the random-walk stock price theory in Case Study 6.1.

■ CONTENTS

6.1 Probability Models for Continuous Random Variables

Suppose you want to predict your company's annual sales, its profit, the sale price of a home, the annual return on an investment, or an evening's winnings at blackjack. If you do, you will need to know something about continuous random variables.

Recall that continuous random variables are those that can assume (at least theoretically) any of the infinitely large number of values contained in an interval. Thus, we might envision a population of the sale prices of houses, the annual returns on a large number of similar investments, or the gains (or losses) of many evenings of blackjack. Since our ultimate goal is to make inferences about a population based on the measurements contained in a sample, we shall need to know the probability that the sample observations (or sample statistics) assume specific values.

For example, suppose we are interested in the daily change in price for a particular stock sold on the New York Stock Exchange (NYSE). Then the set of daily price changes for all past and all future days that the stock is sold on the NYSE is the target population. What is the probability that stock's price will increase by more than $1.00 in a single trading day? This probability can be obtained only if we know the relative frequency distribution of the population of daily changes. For example, let Figure 6.1 represent the *hypothetical* relative frequency distribution for the population. Then the probability that a daily change in the stock's price will exceed $1.00 is approximately .2, the area shaded under the curve in Figure 6.1.

FIGURE 6.1

Hypothetical Relative Frequency Distribution of Daily Changes in Stock's Price

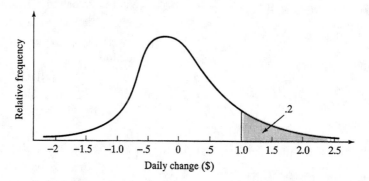

The problem, of course, is that future daily changes in the stock's price are unknown. Hence, we do not know the *exact* shape of the population relative frequency distribution sketched in Figure 6.1. Then, as in the case of a coin-tossing experiment, we postulate a model, i.e., we select a smooth curve (similar to the one shown in Figure 6.1) as a **model** for the population relative frequency distribution. To find the probability that a particular observation (say, a daily price change) will fall in a particular interval, we use the model and find the area under the curve that falls over that interval. Of course, for this approximate probability to be realistic, we must be fairly certain that the model and the population relative frequency distribution are very similar. In Chapter 7, we show why we believe that the models we use are good approximations to reality. In the next section, we introduce one of the most important and useful models for population relative frequency distributions and show how it can be used to find probabilities associated with specific sample observations.

6.2 The Normal Probability Distribution

One of the most useful models for the population relative frequency distribution is known as the **normal distribution**. A graph of the normal distribution (often called the **normal curve**) is shown in Figure 6.2.* The normal distribution was proposed by C. F. Gauss (1777–1855) as a model for the relative frequency distribution of *errors*, such as errors of measurement. Amazingly, this curve provides an adequate model for the relative frequency of data collected from many different disciplines.

FIGURE 6.2

The Normal Curve, with Mean μ and Standard Deviation σ

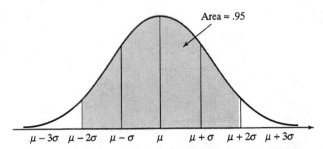

You can see from the figure that the normal curve is mound-shaped and symmetric about its mean μ. Furthermore, approximately 68% of the area under a normal curve lies within the interval $\mu \pm \sigma$. Approximately 95% of the area lies within the interval $\mu \pm 2\sigma$ (shaded in Figure 6.2), and almost all (99.7%) lies within the interval $\mu \pm 3\sigma$. Note that these percentages agree with the Empirical Rule of Section 3.6. (This is because the Empirical Rule is based on data that can be modeled by a normal distribution.)

Remember that areas under the normal curve have a probabilistic interpretation. Thus, if a population of measurements has approximately a normal distribution, then the probability that a randomly selected observation falls within the interval $\mu \pm 2\sigma$ is approximately .95.

Properties of the Normal Curve

1. Mound-shaped (or bell-shaped)
2. Symmetric about μ
3. $P(\mu - \sigma < x < \mu + \sigma) \approx .68$
4. $P(\mu - 2\sigma < x < \mu + 2\sigma) \approx .95$
5. $P(\mu - 3\sigma < x < \mu + 3\sigma) \approx .997$

---

*The formula for the normal curve, denoted f(x) and called the **normal probability density function**, is

$$f(x) = \frac{1}{\sigma\sqrt{2\pi}} \, e^{-(1/2)\,[(x-\mu)/\sigma]^2}$$

Although always mound-shaped and symmetric, the exact shape of the normal curve will depend on the specific values of μ and σ. Three different normal curves are shown in Figure 6.3. You can see from Figure 6.3 that the mean μ measures the location of the distribution and the standard deviation σ measures its spread.

The areas under the normal curve have been computed and are given in Table 5 of Appendix B. Since the normal curve is symmetric, we need give areas on only one side of the mean. Consequently, the entries in Table 5 are areas between the mean and a point x to the right of the mean.

FIGURE 6.3

Three Normal Distributions with Different Means and Standard Deviations

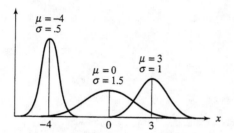

Since the values of μ and σ vary from one normal distribution to another, the easiest way to express a distance from the mean is in terms of a z score. Recall (Section 3.8) that a z **score measures the number of standard deviations that a point** x **lies from the mean** μ. Thus,

$$z = \frac{x - \mu}{\sigma}$$

is the distance between x and μ, expressed in units of σ.

EXAMPLE 6.1
Computing a z Value

Suppose a population relative frequency distribution has mean $\mu = 500$ and standard deviation $\sigma = 100$. Give the z score corresponding to $x = 650$.

SOLUTION The value $x = 650$ lies 150 units above $\mu = 500$. This distance, expressed in units of σ ($\sigma = 100$), is 1.5. We can get this answer directly by substituting x, μ, and σ into the formula for z:

$$z = \frac{x - \mu}{\sigma} = \frac{650 - 500}{100}$$

$$= \frac{150}{100} = 1.5 \quad \blacksquare$$

A partial reproduction of Table 5 of Appendix B is shown in Table 6.1. The entries in the complete table give the areas to the right of the mean for distances from $z = .00$ to $z = 3.09$.

Table 6.1   Reproduction of Part of Table 5 of Appendix B

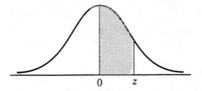

z	.00	.01	.02	.03	.04	.05	.06	.07	.08	.09
.0	.0000	.0040	.0080	.0120	.0160	.0199	.0239	.0279	.0319	.0359
.1	.0398	.0438	.0478	.0517	.0557	.0596	.0636	.0675	.0714	.0753
.2	.0793	.0832	.0871	.0910	.0948	.0987	.1026	.1064	.1103	.1141
.3	.1179	.1217	.1255	.1293	.1331	.1368	.1406	.1443	.1480	.1517
.4	.1554	.1591	.1628	.1664	.1700	.1736	.1772	.1808	.1844	.1879
.5	.1915	.1950	.1985	.2019	.2054	.2088	.2123	.2157	.2190	.2224
.6	.2257	.2291	.2324	.2357	.2389	.2422	.2454	.2486	.2517	.2549
.7	.2580	.2611	.2642	.2673	.2704	.2734	.2764	.2794	.2823	.2852
.8	.2881	.2910	.2939	.2967	.2995	.3023	.3051	.3078	.3106	.3133
.9	.3159	.3186	.3212	.3238	.3264	.3289	.3315	.3340	.3365	.3389
1.0	.3413	.3438	.3461	.3485	.3508	.3531	.3554	.3577	.3599	.3621
1.1	.3643	.3665	.3686	.3708	.3729	.3749	.3770	.3790	.3810	.3830
1.2	.3849	.3869	.3888	.3907	.3925	.3944	.3962	.3980	.3997	.4015
1.3	.4032	.4049	.4066	.4082	.4099	.4115	.4131	.4147	.4162	.4177
1.4	.4192	.4207	.4222	.4236	.4251	.4265	.4279	.4292	.4306	.4319
1.5	.4332	.4345	.4357	.4370	.4382	.4394	.4406	.4418	.4429	.4441

EXAMPLE 6.2
Using the Standard
Normal Table

Find the area under a normal curve between the mean and a point $z = 1.26$ standard deviations to the right of the mean.

SOLUTION   To locate the proper entry, proceed down the left (z) column of the table to the row corresponding to $z = 1.2$. Then move across the top of the table to the column headed .06. The intersection of the .06 column and the 1.2 row contains the desired area, .3962 (shaded in Table 6.1), as shown in Figure 6.4.

FIGURE 6.4

The Tabulated Area
Given in Table 5 of
Appendix B
Corresponding to
$z = 1.26$

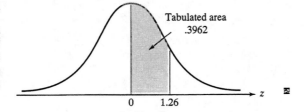

The normal distribution of the z statistic (as shown in Figure 6.4) is called the **standard normal distribution**. The mean of a standard normal distribution is always equal to 0 (since $z = 0$ when $x = \mu$); the standard deviation is always equal to 1 (proof omitted). Since the mean is 0, z values to the right of the mean are positive; those to the left are negative.

EXAMPLE 6.3
Area Between 0 and Negative z

Find the area beneath a standard normal curve between the mean $z = 0$ and the point $z = -1.26$.

SOLUTION The best way to solve a problem of this type is to draw a sketch of the distribution (see Figure 6.5). Since $z = -1.26$ is negative, we know that it lies to the left of the mean, and the area that we seek is the shaded area shown.

FIGURE 6.5

Standard Normal Distribution for Example 6.3

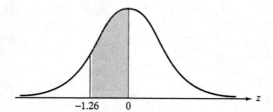

Since the normal curve is symmetric, the area between the mean 0 and $z = -1.26$ is exactly the same as the area between the mean 0 and $z = +1.26$. We found this area in Example 6.2 to be .3962. Therefore, the area between $z = -1.26$ and $z = 0$ is .3962. ■

EXAMPLE 6.4
Area Between $-z$ and z

Find the probability that a normally distributed random variable will lie within $z = 2$ standard deviations of its mean.

SOLUTION The probability that we seek is the shaded area shown in Figure 6.6. Since the area between the mean and $z = 2.0$ is exactly the same as the area between the mean and $z = -2.0$, we need find only the area between the mean and $z = 2$ standard deviations to the right of the mean and multiply by 2. This area is given in Table 5 of

FIGURE 6.6

Standard Normal Distribution for Example 6.4

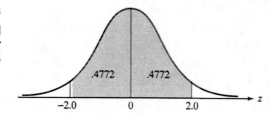

Appendix B as .4772. Therefore, the probability P that a normally distributed random variable will lie within 2 standard deviations of its mean is

$$P = 2(.4772) = .9544 \quad ■$$

| EXAMPLE 6.5 |
| Area Above z |

Find the probability that a normally distributed random variable x will lie more than $z = 2$ standard deviations above its mean.

SOLUTION The probability we seek is the darkly shaded area shown in Figure 6.7. The total area under a standard normal curve is 1; half this area lies to the left of the mean, half to the right. Consequently, the probability P that x will lie more than 2 standard deviations above the mean is equal to .5 less the area A:

$$P = .5 - A$$

FIGURE 6.7

Standard Normal
Distribution for
Example 6.5

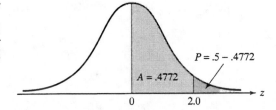

The area A corresponding to $z = 2.0$ is .4772. Therefore,

$$P = .5 - .4772 = .0228 \quad ■$$

| EXAMPLE 6.6 |
| Area Between Two Positive |
| z Values |

Find the area under the normal curve between $z = 1.2$ and $z = 1.6$.

SOLUTION The area A that we seek lies to the right of the mean because both z values are positive. It will appear as the shaded area shown in Figure 6.8. Let A_1 represent the area between $z = 0$ and $z = 1.2$, and A_2 represent the area between $z = 0$ and $z = 1.6$. Then the area A that we desire is

$$A = A_2 - A_1$$

FIGURE 6.8

Standard Normal
Distribution for
Example 6.6

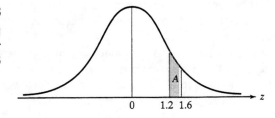

From Table 5 of Appendix B, we obtain

$$A_1 = .3849 \quad \text{and} \quad A_2 = .4452$$

Then

$$A = A_2 - A_1 = .4452 - .3849 = .0603 \quad \blacksquare$$

EXAMPLE 6.7
Finding z_α

Let $z_{.10}$ denote the value of z such that the area to the right of $z_{.10}$ is .10. Find $z_{.10}$.

SOLUTION The z value that we seek appears as shown in Figure 6.9. Note that we show an area to the right of z equal to .10. Since the total area to the right of the mean $z = 0$ is equal to .5, the area between the mean 0 and the unknown z value is $.5 - .1 = .4$ (as shown in the figure). Consequently, to find $z_{.10}$, we must look in Table 5 of Appendix B for the z value that corresponds to an area equal to .4.

FIGURE 6.9

Standard Normal
Distribution for
Example 6.7

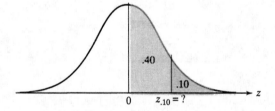

The area .4000 does not appear in Table 5. The closest values are .3997, corresponding to $z = 1.28$, and .4015, corresponding to $z = 1.29$. Since the area .3997 is closer to .4000 than to .4015, we will choose $z = 1.28$ as our answer. That is, $z_{.10} = 1.28$. $\blacksquare$

Examples 6.2–6.7 demonstrate how to solve the following two types of normal probability problems:

1. Examples 6.2–6.6 use Table 5 of Appendix B to **find areas under the standard normal curve**. These problems may be further classified into one of three types:
   a. Finding the area between the mean, $\mu_z = 0$, and some value of z—say, z_0—that is located above or below $\mu_z = 0$ (Examples 6.2 and 6.3)
   b. Finding the area between the values z_1 and z_2, where z_1 or z_2 is not equal to 0 (Examples 6.4 and 6.6)
   c. Finding the area in either the upper or the lower tail of the standard normal z distribution (Example 6.5)

2. Example 6.7 uses Table 5 of Appendix B to **find the z value, denoted z_α, corresponding to an area** α in the upper tail of the standard normal z distribution. A similar procedure may be used to find a z value corresponding to a lower-tail area under the curve.

Many distributions of data that occur in the real world are approximately normal, but few are *standard* normal. However, Examples 6.8–6.11 use what you have learned about the standard normal curve to solve the same two types of problems involving *any* normal distribution:

1. Finding the probability that a normal random variable x falls between the values x_1 and x_2, or the probability that it falls in either the upper or the lower tail of the normal distribution   (Examples 6.8–6.10)
2. Finding the value of x—say, x_0—that places a probability P in the upper (or lower) tail of a normal distribution   (Example 6.11)

EXAMPLE 6.8
Application: Finding a
Normal Probability

Medical research has linked excessive consumption of salt to hypertension (high blood pressure). Yet, salt is America's second leading food additive (after sugar), both in factory-processed foods and home cooking. The average amount of salt consumed per day by an American is 15 grams (15,000 milligrams), although the actual physiological minimum daily requirement for salt is only 220 milligrams. Suppose that the amount of salt intake per day is approximately normally distributed with a standard deviation of 5 grams. What proportion of all Americans consume between 14 and 22 grams of salt per day?

SOLUTION The proportion P of Americans who consume between $x = 14$ grams and $x = 22$ grams of salt is the total shaded area in Figure 6.10a (page 264). Before we can compute this area, we need to determine the z values that correspond to $x = 14$ and $x = 22$. Substituting $\mu = 15$ and $\sigma = 5$ into the formula for z, we compute the z value for $x = 14$ as

$$z_1 = \frac{x - \mu}{\sigma} = \frac{14 - 15}{5} = \frac{-1}{5} = -.20$$

The corresponding z value for $x = 22$ is

$$z_2 = \frac{x - \mu}{\sigma} = \frac{22 - 15}{5} = \frac{7}{5} = 1.40$$

Figure 6.10b[*] shows these z values along with P. From this figure, we see that

---

[*]*Actually, the shape of the standard normal distribution shown in Figure 6.10b differs from the shape of the normal distribution in Figure 6.10a because the distributions have different variances. In fact, the normal curve associated with Figure 6.10b ($\sigma = 1$) will be more peaked and narrower than that for Figure 6.10a ($\sigma = 5$) since the variance is smaller. Nevertheless, the tail area P shaded on the two distributions is identical. For pedagogical reasons, we show the distributions with similar shapes.*

FIGURE 6.10

Normal Curve
Sketches for
Example 6.8

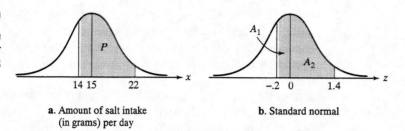

a. Amount of salt intake
(in grams) per day

b. Standard normal

$P = A_1 + A_2$, where A_1 is the area corresponding to $z_1 = -.20$, and A_2 is the area corresponding to $z_2 = 1.4$. These values, given in Table 5 of Appendix B, are $A_1 = .0793$ and $A_2 = .4192$. Thus,

$$P = A_1 + A_2 = .0793 + .4192 = .4985$$

So 49.85% of Americans consume between 14 and 22 grams of salt per day. ■

The technique for finding the probability that a normal random variable falls between two values is summarized in the next box.

Finding the Probability That a Normal Random Variable Falls
Between Two Values, x_1 and x_2

1. Make two sketches of the normal curve, one representing the normal distribution of x and the other, the standard normal z distribution.

2. Show the approximate locations of x_1 and x_2 on the sketch of the x distribution. Be sure to locate x_1 and x_2 correctly relative to the mean μ. For example, if x_1 is larger than μ, then it should be located to the right of μ; if x_1 is less than μ, then it should be located to the left of μ.

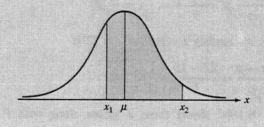

3. Find the values of z corresponding to x_1 and x_2:

$$z_1 = \frac{x_1 - \mu}{\sigma} \quad \text{and} \quad z_2 = \frac{x_2 - \mu}{\sigma}$$

4. Locate the values of z_1 and z_2 on your sketch of the z distribution.

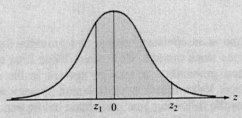

5. Use the table of areas under the standard normal curve, given in Table 5 of Appendix B, to find the area between z_1 and z_2. This will be the probability that x falls between x_1 and x_2.

EXAMPLE 6.9

Application: Finding a Normal Probability

Refer to Example 6.8. Physicians recommend that those Americans who want to reach a level of salt intake at which hypertension is less likely to occur should consume less than 1 gram of salt per day. What is the probability that a randomly selected American consumes less than 1 gram of salt per day?

SOLUTION The probability P that a randomly selected American consumes less than 1 gram of salt per day is represented by the shaded area in Figure 6.11a. The z value corresponding to $x = 1$ (shown in Figure 6.11b) is

$$z = \frac{x - \mu}{\sigma} = \frac{1 - 15}{5} = \frac{-14}{5} = -2.80$$

Since the area to the left of $z = 0$ is equal to .5, the probability that x is less than or equal to 1 is $P = .5 - A$, where A is the tabulated area corresponding to $z = -2.80$.

FIGURE 6.11

Normal Curve Sketches for Example 6.9

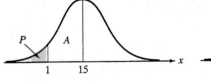

a. Amount of salt intake (in grams) per day

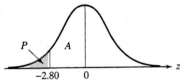

b. Standard normal

This value, given in Table 5 of Appendix B, is $A = .4974$. Then, the probability that a randomly selected American consumes no more than 1 gram of salt per day is

$$P = .5 - A$$
$$= .5 - .4974$$
$$= .0026 \quad ■$$

EXAMPLE 6.10

Application: Finding a Normal Probability

Value Line is an advisory service that provides investors with forecasts of the movement of the stock market. Each week Value Line selects one stock that it believes has the highest probability of moving upward in the coming months. Over a certain 3-year period, Value Line's stock selection strategy was highly successful. However, its selections the following year performed below par, according to Value Line's *Selection & Opinion*, which listed the performance of the stock selections to date. Performance was measured as the percentage change in stock price since the date of recommendation. The mean percentage change of the stocks was −19.9, and the standard deviation was 18.6. Assume that the percentage change in stock price over the period of interest can be modeled by a normal probability distribution.

What is the probability that the percentage change of a stock recommended by Value Line over the period is greater than 0? (This is the probability that the stock will "gain" or move upward.)

SOLUTION The percentage change, x, of Value Line's stocks is assumed to be approximately normal with $\mu = -19.9$ and standard deviation $\sigma = 18.6$. We want to find the probability that x exceeds 0, i.e., $P(x > 0)$. This is the area P under the normal curve shaded in Figure 6.12a. To use the standard normal tables, we must find this probability on the standard normal curve (Figure 6.12b). This amounts to finding the z value corresponding to 0%. Substituting $x = 0$, $\mu = -19.9$, and $\sigma = 18.6$ into the formula for z, we obtain

$$z = \frac{x - \mu}{\sigma} = \frac{0 - (-19.9)}{18.6} = \frac{19.9}{18.6} = 1.07$$

Thus, we have $P(x > 0) = P(z > 1.07)$. Therefore, $P(z > 1.07) = (.5 - A)$, where A is the area between $\mu = 0$ and $z = 1.07$. This area, given in Table 5 of Appendix B, is .3577. It follows that

$$P(x > 0) = P(z > 1.07) = .5 - A = .5 - .3577 = .1423$$

FIGURE 6.12

Normal Curve Sketches for Example 6.10

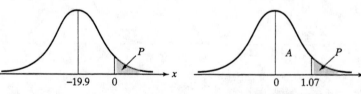

a. Percentage change, x b. Standard normal, z ■

EXAMPLE 6.11
Application: Finding a Value
of the Normal
Random Variable

Refer to Example 6.10. For this 3-year period, 10% of the stocks recommended by Value Line had percentage changes below what value of x?

SOLUTION We want to find a value of x_0 of the normal random variable x, percentage change, such that $P(x < x_0) = .10$. Unlike Example 6.10, where we were given a value of x and asked to find a corresponding probability, here we are given a probability $P = .10$ and asked to locate the corresponding value of x. We call P the **tail probability associated with x_0**. The value x_0, along with its tail probability, is shown in Figure 6.13a.

FIGURE 6.13
Normal Curve Areas
for Example 6.11

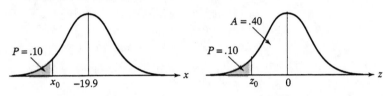

a. Percentage change, x b. Standard normal, z

Notice that x_0 must be located to the left of (i.e., below) the mean for $P(x < x_0)$ to be so small. The location of x_0 is not arbitrary, but depends on the value of P. To see this more clearly, try placing x_0 above (to the right of) the mean of -19.9. Now (mentally) shade in the corresponding tail probability P, i.e., the area to the left of x_0. You can see that this area cannot possibly equal $.10$—it is too large ($.50$ or greater). Thus, x_0 must lie to the left of -19.9.

The first step, then, in solving problems of this type is to determine the location of x_0 relative to the mean μ. The second step is to find the corresponding z value for x_0, call it z_0, where

$$z_0 = \frac{x_0 - \mu}{\sigma} = \frac{x_0 - (-19.9)}{18.6}$$

Thus, z_0 represents the number of standard deviations that x_0 lies from the mean μ. Once we locate z_0, we can use the equivalent relation

$$x_0 = \mu + z_0(\sigma) = -19.9 + z_0(18.6)$$

to find x_0.

You can see from Figure 6.13b that z_0 is the z value that corresponds to the area $A = .40$ in Table 5 of Appendix B. In the body of the table, we see the value closest to $.40$ is $.3997$. The z value corresponding to this area is $z_0 = -1.28$. (Note that z_0 is negative because it lies to the left of 0.) Substituting into the formula above, we have

$$x_0 = -19.9 + z_0(18.6) = -19.9 + (-1.28)(18.6) = -43.71$$

Thus, 10% of the stocks recommended by Value Line had percentage changes below -43.71. ∎

To help in solving problems of this type throughout the remainder of the chapter, we outline in the box the steps leading to the solutions.

The Determination of a Particular Value of the Normal Random Variable Given an Associated Tail Probability

1. Make a sketch of the relative frequency distribution of the normal random variable x. Shade the tail probability P, and locate the corresponding value x_0 on the sketch. Remember that x_0 will be to the right or the left of the mean μ depending on the value of P.

2. Make a sketch of corresponding relative frequency distribution of the standard normal random variable z. Locate z_0, the z value corresponding to x_0, and shade the area coresponding to P.

3. Compute the area A associated with z_0 as follows:

$$A = .5 - P$$

4. Use the area A, i.e., the area between 0 and z_0 in Table 5 of Appendix B. (If you cannot find the exact value of A in the table, use the closest value.) Note that z_0 will be negative if you place x_0 to the left of the mean in step 1.

5. Compute x_0 as follows:

$$x_0 = \mu + z_0(\sigma)$$

The preceding examples should help you to understand the use of the table of areas under the normal curve. The practical applications of this information to inference making will become apparent in the following chapters.

EXERCISES

■ *Learning the Mechanics*

6.1 Find the area under the standard normal curve:
  a. Between $z = 0$ and $z = 1.2$
  b. Between $z = 0$ and $z = 1.49$
  c. Between $z = -.48$ and $z = 0$
  d. Between $z = -1.37$ and $z = 0$
  e. For values of z larger than 1.33
  Show the z values and the corresponding area of interest on a sketch of the normal curve for each part of the exercise.

6.2 Find the area under the standard normal curve:
  a. Between $z = 0$ and $z = 1.96$
  b. Between $z = -1.96$ and $z = 0$
  c. Between $z = -1.96$ and $z = 1.96$
  d. For values of z larger than .55
  e. For values of z less than -1.24
  Show the values of z and corresponding area of interest on a sketeh of the normal curve for each part of the exercise.

6.3   Find the z value (to two decimal places) that corresponds to a tabulated area (Table 5 of Appendix B) equal to:

a. .1000   **b.** .3200   **c.** .4000   **d.** .4500   **e.** .4750

Show the area and corresponding value of z on a sketch of the normal curve for each part of the exercise.

6.4   Find the value of z (to two decimal places) that cuts off an area in the upper tail of the standard normal curve equal to:

a. .025   **b.** .05   **c.** .005   **d.** .01   **e.** .10

Show the area and corresponding value of z on a sketch of the normal curve for each part of the exercise.

6.5   Suppose a normal random variable x has mean $\mu = 20.0$ and standard deviation $\sigma = 4.0$. Find the z score corresponding to:

a. $x = 23.0$ **b.** $x = 16.0$ **c.** $x = 13.5$ **d.** $x = 28.0$ **e.** $x = 12.0$

For each part of the exercise, locate x and μ on a sketch of the normal curve. Check to make sure that the sign and magnitude of your z score agree with your sketch.

6.6   Find the approximate value for z_0 such that the probability that z is larger than z_0 is:

a. $P = .10$ **b.** $P = .15$ **c.** $P = .20$ **d.** $P = .25$

Locate z_0 and the corresponding probability P on a sketch of the normal curve for each part of the exercise.

6.7   Find the approximate value of z_0 such that the probability that z is less than z_0 is:

a. $P = .10$ **b.** $P = .15$ **c.** $P = .30$ **d.** $P = .50$

Locate z_0 and the corresponding probability P on a sketch of the normal curve for each part of the exercise.

■ *Applying the Concepts*

6.8   Researchers have developed sophisticated intrusion-detection algorithms to protect the security of computer-based systems. These algorithms use principles of statistics to identify unusual or expected data, i.e., "intruders." One popular intrusion-detection system assumes the data being monitored are normally distributed (*Journal of Information Systems*, Spring 1992). As an example, the researcher considered system data with a mean of .27, a standard deviation of 1.473, and an intrusion-detection algorithm that assumes normal data.

a. Find the probability that a data value observed by the system will fall between −.5 and .5.

b. Find the probability that a data value observed by the system exceeds 3.5.

c. Comment on whether a data value of 4 observed by the system should be considered an "intruder."

6.9   "Cents off" coupons have been traditionally viewed by economists as price discriminators between two segments of the product's customers: loyal consumers with a high value of time who choose not to use the coupon (and pay full price), and customers with a low value of time who redeem the coupon to realize a lower price. In contrast, marketers view "cents off" coupons simply as a form of advertisement or promotion of a product; very few customers are expected to take advantage of the reduced price. A study was conducted to investigate these two competing interpretations of "cents off" coupons (*Quarterly Journal of Business and Economics*,

Autumn 1986). Price comparisons of a particular brand of paper towels purchased with and without coupons resulted in a mean difference of 2.75¢ and a standard deviation of 3.45¢. Assume that the price difference x (in cents) is normally distributed.

a. Find $P(x > 9)$.
b. Find $P(x > 5)$.
c. Find $P(x < 0)$.

6.10 Researchers at the University of Rochester studied the friction that occurs in the paper-feeding process of a photocopier (*Journal of Engineering for Industry*, May 1993). The coefficient of friction is a proportion that measures the degree of friction between two adjacent sheets of paper in the feeder stack. Assume the friction coefficient for a certain copier system is normally distributed, with $\mu = .55$ and $\sigma = .013$. (Higher coefficients correspond to a higher degree of friction.) During system operation, the friction coefficient is measured at a randomly selected time.

a. Find the probability that the friction coefficient falls between .53 and .56.
b. Is it likely to observe a friction coefficient below .50? Explain.

6.11 Pacemakers are used to control the heartbeat of cardiac patients, with over 120,000 of the devices implanted each year. A single pacemaker is made up of several biomedical components that must be of a high quality for the pacemaker to work. It is vitally important for manufacturers of pacemakers to use parts that meet specifications. One particular plastic part, called a connector module, mounts on the top of the pacemaker. Connector modules are required to have a length between .304 inch and .322 inch to work properly. Any module with length outside these limits is "out-of-spec." *Quality* (Aug. 1989) reported on one supplier of connector modules that had been shipping out-of-spec parts to the manufacturer for 12 months.

a. The lengths of the connector modules produced by the supplier were found to follow an approximate normal distribution with mean $\mu = .3015$ inch and standard deviation $\sigma = .0016$ inch. Use this information to find the probability that the supplier produces an out-of-spec part.
b. Once the problem was detected, the supplier's inspection crew began to employ an automated data-collection system designed to improve product quality. After 2 months, the process was producing connector modules with mean $\mu = .3146$ inch and standard deviation $\sigma = .0030$ inch. Find the probability that an out-of-spec part will be produced. Compare your answer to part **a**.

6.12 The U.S. Department of Agriculture (USDA) has recently patented a process that uses a bacterium for removing bitterness from citrus juices (*Chemical Engineering*, Feb. 3, 1986). In theory, almost all the bitterness could be removed by the process, but for practical purposes the USDA aims at 50% overall removal. Suppose a USDA spokesman claims that the percentage of bitterness removed from an 8-ounce glass of freshly squeezed citrus juice is normally distributed with mean 50.1 and standard deviation 10.4. To test this claim, the bitterness removal process is applied to a randomly selected 8-ounce glass of citrus juice.

a. Find the probability that the process removes less than 33.7% of the bitterness.
b. Refer to your answer to part **a**. If the test on the single glass of citrus juice yielded a bitterness removal percentage of 33.7%, would you tend to doubt the USDA spokesman's claim?

6.13   Behaviorists have developed an instrument designed to measure the maturity of small groups. The 10-item questionnaire is based on the assumptions that a mature group is able to function independently of its leader, is active, is organized, and has an established working history, whereas an immature group has the opposite attributes. Krayer (1988) divided a class of undergraduate college students into two groups, mature and immature, based on their answers to the 10-item questionnaire. A final project was then assigned and, at the end of the semester, student performances were evaluated. A summary of the grades on the project for the two groups is provided in the table. Assume these represent population means and standard deviations.

Group	Mean Grade	Standard Deviation
Mature	91.50	8.48
Immature	84.20	6.98

Source: Krayer, K. L. "Exploring group maturity in the classroom." *Small Group Behavior,* Vol. 19, No. 2, May 1988.

   a. Assuming the population of project grades for the mature group is approximately normal, find the probability that a mature student will score below 80 on the final project.
   b. Repeat part **a** for the immature group.
   c. Why might the assumption of normality in parts **a** and **b** be suspect? [*Hint*:   Consider the fact that the highest grade that can be assigned to a project is 100.]

6.14   Foresters "cruising" British Columbia's boreal forest have determined that the diameter at breast height of white spruce trees in a particular community is approximately normal, with mean 17 meters and standard deviation 6 meters. *
   a. Find the probability that the breast height diameter of a randomly selected white spruce in the forest community is less than 12 meters.
   b. Suppose you observe a white spruce with a breast height diameter of 12 meters. Is this an unusual event? Explain.
   c. Find the probability that the breast height diameter of a randomly selected white spruce in the forest community will exceed 37 meters.
   d. Suppose you observe a tree in the forest community with a breast height diameter of 38 meters. Is this tree likely to be a white spruce? Explain.

6.15   How does the stock market react when a firm announces its stock earnings in the *Wall Street Journal*? To examine this issue, a comprehensive study of 240 stocks was conducted over a 10-year period (*The Accounting Review*, Jan. 1991). One of the variables used to measure market reaction was excess trading volume. Excess trading volume is defined as the difference between the percentage of shares traded on the day of the earnings announcement and the average percentage of shares traded for a 3-day period prior to the announcement. The researcher assumes that excess trading volume, when standardized, has an approximate standard normal distribution. Let x equal the standardized excess trading volume for a particular stock.

Scholz, H. "Fish Creek Community Forest: Exploratory statistical analysis of selected data," working paper, Northern Lights College, British Columbia, Canada.

       a. What is the mean of x?

       b. What is the standard deviation of x?

       c. Find the median (50th percentile) of x.

       d. Find the lower quartile (25th percentile) of x.

       e. Find the upper quartile (75th percentile) of x.

6.16   Refer to Exercise 6.15. Using simulation, the researcher found that standardized excess trading volume x is approximately normal, but with mean $\mu = -1.767$ and standard deviation $\sigma = .956$.

       a. Find $P(x < 0)$.

       b. Find $P(x < Q_L)$, where Q_L is the lower quartile of a standard normal (z) distribution.

       c. Find $P(x < Q_U)$, where Q_U is the upper quartile of a standard normal (z) distribution.

       d. Based on the results, parts **a–c**, how well does the standard normal (z) distribution approximate the true distribution of x?

6.17   An empirical study of auditory nerve response rates was reported in the *Journal of the Acoustical Society of America* (Feb. 1986). Cats (selected because of their keen sense of hearing) were exposed to bursts of noise in a laboratory setting and the number of spikes per 200 milliseconds of noise burst received by the auditory nerve fibers of each, called the response rate, was recorded. A key question addressed by the researcher is whether the tone can be detected reliably when background noise is present. Let x represent the auditory nerve response rate under two conditions: when the stimulus is background noise only (N) and when the stimulus is a tone plus background noise (T). Empirical research has found that the probability distribution of x under either condition N or T can be approximated by a normal distribution. Based on the results of the study, the two normal distributions have means $\mu_N = 10.1$ spikes per burst and $\mu_T = 13.6$ spikes per burst, respectively, and equal variances $\sigma_N^2 = \sigma_T^2 = 2$. Given these conditions, an observer sets a threshold C and decides that a tone is present if $x \geq C$ and decides that no tone is present if $x < C$.

       a. For a threshold of $C = 11$ spikes per burst, find the probability of detecting the tone given that the tone is present. That is, find $P(x \geq 11)$ under condition T. (This is known as the **detection probability**.)

       b. For a threshold of $C = 11$ spikes per burst, find the probability of detecting the tone given that only background noise is present. That is, find $P(x \geq 11)$ under condition N. (This is known as the **probability of false alarm**.)

       c. Usually, it is desirable to maximize detection probability while minimizing false alarm probability. Can you find a value of C that will both increase the detection probability (part **a**) and decrease the probability of false alarm (part **b**)? [*Hint:* Sketch the two probability distributions for conditions N and T, side by side, allowing some overlap between them. For any value C, shade the two probabilities in parts **a** and **b**. As you move C right or left, what happens to the probabilities?]

6.18   A television cable company receives numerous phone calls throughout the day from customers reporting service troubles and from would-be subscribers to the cable network. Most of these callers are put "on hold" until a company operator is free to help them. The company has determined that the length of time a caller is on hold is normally distributed with a mean of 3.1 minutes and a standard deviation of .9 minute. Company experts have decided that if as many as 5% of the callers are put on hold for 4.8 minutes or longer, more operators should be hired.

a. What proportion of the company's callers are put on hold for at least 4.8 minutes? Should the company hire more operators? Show the pertinent quantities on a sketch of the normal curve.

b. At this company, 5% of the callers are put on hold for longer than x minutes. Find the value of x, and show the pertinent quantities on a sketch of the normal curve.

6.3 Descriptive Methods for Assessing Normality

In the chapters that follow, we learn how to make inferences about the population based on information in the sample. Several of these techniques are based on the assumption that the population is approximately normally distributed. Consequently, it will be important to determine whether the sample data come from a normal population before we can properly apply these techniques.

Several descriptive methods can be used to check for normality. In this section, we consider the three methods summarized in the next box.

Determining Whether the Data Are
from an Approximately Normal Distribution

1. Construct either a **relative frequency histogram** or a **stem-and-leaf display** for the data. If the data are approximately normal, the shape of the graph will be similar to the normal curve, Figure 6.2 (i.e., mound-shaped and symmetric about the mean).

2. Find the **interquartile range**, IQR, and **standard deviation**, s, for the sample; then calculate the ratio IQR/s. If the data are approximately normal, then IQR/$s \approx 1.3$.

3. Construct a **normal probability plot** for the data. (See the box on page 276.) If the data are approximately normal, the points will fall (approximately) on a straight line.

EXAMPLE 6.12
Detecting Normality

Consider the data set consisting of the tar contents of 500 cigarette brands, Appendix A.4. Numerical and graphical descriptive measures for the data are shown on the SAS printouts, Figures 6.14a–c (pages 274–275). Determine whether the tar contents have an approximate normal distribution.

SOLUTION　As a first check, we examine the horizontal frequency histogram of the data shown in Figure 6.14b. Clearly, the tar contents fall in an approximately mound-shaped, symmetric distribution centered around the mean of 11.06 milligrams. Thus, from check 1 in the box, the data appear to be approximately normal.

FIGURE 6.14

SAS Printout for Example 6.12 (Tar Contents of Appendix A.4)

a. Descriptive statistics

UNIVARIATE PROCEDURE

Variable=TAR

Moments

N	500	Sum Wgts	500
Mean	11.059	Sum	5529.5
Std Dev	4.931192	Variance	24.31665
Skewness	0.360265	Kurtosis	0.37881
USS	73284.75	CSS	12134.01
CV	44.58985	Std Mean	0.22053
T:Mean=0	50.14746	Prob>$\vert$T$\vert$	0.0001
Sgn Rank	62625	Prob>$\vert$S$\vert$	0.0001
Num ^= 0	500		
W:Normal	0.959723	Prob<W	0.0001

Quantiles(Def=5)

100% Max	27	99%	25.5
75% Q3	15	95%	18
50% Med	11	90%	17
25% Q1	8	10%	5
0% Min	0.5	5%	4
		1%	1
Range	26.5		
Q3-Q1	7		
Mode	11		

Extremes

Lowest	Obs	Highest	Obs
0.5(	336)	26(	179)
0.5(	335)	26(	330)
0.5(	93)	26(	333)
1(	327)	27(	51)
1(	325)	27(	344)

b. Histogram and box plot

UNIVARIATE PROCEDURE

Variable=TAR

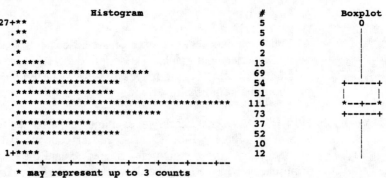

```
                    Histogram                         #        Boxplot
     27+**                                             5          0
       .**                                             5          |
       .**                                             6          |
       .*                                              2          |
       .*****                                          13         |
       .***********************                        69         |
       .******************                             54      +-----+
       .****************                               51      |     |
       .******************************************     111     *--+--*
       .************************                       73      +-----+
       .*************                                  37         |
       .*****************                              52         |
       .****                                           10         |
      1+****                                           12         |
        ----+----+----+----+----+----+----+--
        * may represent up to 3 counts
```

FIGURE 6.14 *(cont.)*

SAS Printout for
Example 6.12 (Tar
Contents of
Appendix A.4)

c. Normal probability plot

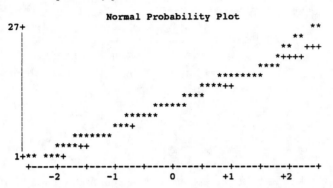

Check 2 in the box requires that we find the interquartile range (i.e., the difference between the 75th and 25th percentiles) and the standard deviation of the data set, and compute the ratio of these two numbers. The ratio IQR/s for a sample from a normal distribution will approximately equal 1.3.* The values of IQR and s, shaded in Figure 6.14a, are IQR = $Q_U - Q_L = 7$ and $s = 4.93$. Then the ratio is

$$\frac{IQR}{s} = \frac{7}{4.93} = 1.42$$

Since this value is approximately equal to 1.3, we have further confirmation that the data are approximately normal.

A third descriptive technique for checking normality is a **normal probability plot**. In a normal probability plot, the observations in the data set are ordered and then plotted against the standardized expected values of the observations under the assumption that the data are normally distributed. When the data are, in fact, normally distributed, an observation will approximately equal its expected value. Thus, a linear (straight–line) trend on the normal probability plot suggests that the data are from an approximate normal distribution, whereas a nonlinear trend indicates that the data are nonnormal.

Normal probability plots can be constructed by hand, as shown in the box (page 276). However, it is easier to generate these plots by computer. A SAS normal probability plot for the 500 tar measurements is shown in Figure 6.14c. Notice that the ordered measurements (represented by the plotting symbol "*") fall reasonably close to a straight line (plotting symbol "+"). Thus, check 3 also suggests that the data are likely to be approximately normally distributed. ■

You can see that this property holds for normal distributions by noting that the z values, obtained from Table 5 in Appendix B, corresponding to the 75th and 25th percentiles are .67 and −.67, respectively. Since σ =1 for a standard normal (z) distribution, IQR/σ = [.67 − (−.67)]/1 = 1.34.

Constructing a Normal Probability Plot for a Data Set

1. List the observations in the sample data set in ascending order, where x_i represents the ith ordered value.

2. For each observation, calculate the corresponding tail area of the standard normal (z) distribution,

$$A = \frac{i - .375}{n + .25}$$

where n is the sample size.

3. Calculate the estimated expected value of x_i under normality using the following formula:

$$E(x_i) = (s)[Z(A)]$$

where s is the sample standard deviation and $Z(A)$ is the z value that cuts off an area A in the lower tail of the standard normal distribution. [*Note*: $Z(A)$ will be negative when $A < .5$, and $Z(A)$ will be positive when $A > .5$.]

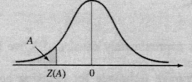 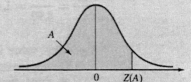

4. Plot the ordered observations, x_i, on the vertical axis and the corresponding estimated expected values, $E(x_i)$, on the horizontal axis.

The checks for normality given in the box are simple, yet powerful, techniques to apply, but they are only descriptive in nature. It is possible (although unlikely) that the data are nonnormal even when the checks are reasonably satisfied. Thus, we should be careful not to claim that the 500 tar measurements in Appendix A.4 are, in fact, normally distributed. We can only state that it is reasonable to believe that the data are from a normal distribution.[*]

---

[*]*Statistical tests of normality that provide a measure of reliability for the inference are available. However, these tests tend to be very sensitive to slight departures from normality, i.e., they tend to reject the hypothesis of normality for any distribution that is not perfectly symmetrical and mound-shaped.*

EXERCISES

■ *Applying the Concepts*

6.19 Refer to the *Journal of Information Systems* study of intrusion-detection systems, Exercise 6.8. According to the study, many intrusion-detection systems assume that the data being monitored are normally distributed when such data are clearly nonnormal. Consequently, the intrusion-detection system may lead to inappropriate conclusions. The researcher considered the following data on input–output (I/O) units utilized by a sample of 44 users of a system.

15	5	2	17	4	3	1	1	0	0	0	0
0	0	0	20	9	0	0	0	1	6	1	3
1	0	6	0	0	0	0	1	14	0	7	0
2	9	4	0	0	0	9	10				

Source: O'Leary, D. E. "Intrusion-detection systems." *Journal of Information Systems*, Spring 1992, p. 68 (Table 2).

Based on the accompanying MINITAB printouts, assess whether the data are normally distributed.

```
Stem-and-leaf of I/O      N  = 44
Leaf Unit = 1.0


   (26)    0  00000000000000000000111111
    18     0  2233
    14     0  445
    11     0  667
     8     0  999
     5     1  0
     4     1
     4     1  45
     2     1  7
     1     1
     1     2  0
```

	N	MEAN	MEDIAN	TRMEAN	STDEV	SEMEAN
I/O	44	3.432	1.000	2.850	5.160	0.778

	MIN	MAX	Q1	Q3
I/O	0.000	20.000	0.000	5.750

6.20 Refer to the *Small Group Behavior* study of mature and immature groups, Exercise 6.13. A stem-and-leaf display and normal probability plot for each of the two groups are shown in the SAS printouts on page 278. Based on these graphs, assess whether the grade distributions are approximately normal.

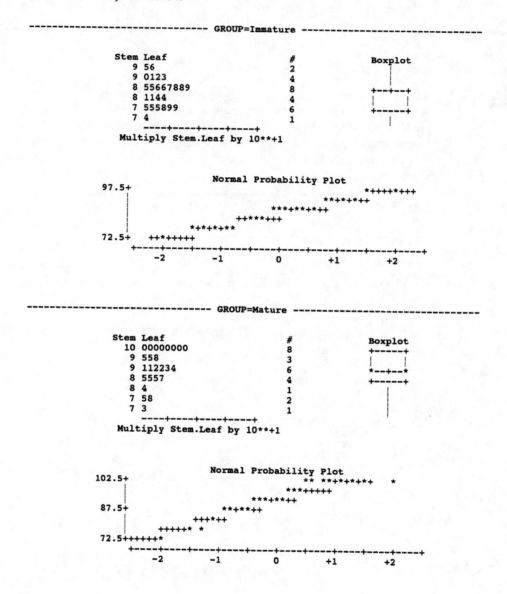

```
------------------------------ GROUP=Immature ------------------------------

        Stem Leaf                        #            Boxplot
         9 56                            2                 |
         9 0123                          4                 |
         8 55667889                      8            +--+--+
         8 1144                          4            |     |
         7 555899                        6            +-----+
         7 4                             1                 |
           ----+----+----+----+
        Multiply Stem.Leaf by 10**+1
```

```
                        Normal Probability Plot
        97.5+                                       *++++*+++
            |                                 **+*+*++
            |                            ***+**+*++
            |                        ++****+++
            |                   *+*+*+**
        72.5+    ++*+++++
            +----+----+----+----+----+----+----+----+----+----+
               -2        -1        0        +1        +2
```

```
------------------------------ GROUP=Mature ------------------------------

        Stem Leaf                        #            Boxplot
        10 00000000                      8            +-----+
         9 558                           3            |     |
         9 112234                        6            *--+--*
         8 5557                          4            +-----+
         8 4                             1                 |
         7 58                            2                 |
         7 3                             1                 |
           ----+----+----+----+
        Multiply Stem.Leaf by 10**+1
```

```
                        Normal Probability Plot
       102.5+                            **  **+*+*+*+   *
            |                         ***+++++
            |                     ***+**++
        87.5+                 **+**++
            |             +++*++
            |         +++++* *
        72.5++++++*
            +----+----+----+----+----+----+----+----+----+----+
               -2        -1        0        +1        +2
```

6.21 At the end of each academic semester, the Career Resource Center at the University of Florida mails out questionnaires pertaining to employment status and starting salary of all students who graduated that particular semester. From fall 1989 through spring 1991, 1,795 graduates returned the questionnaire and indicated they had secured a job as of the date of graduation. The accompanying SAS printouts describe the 1,795 starting salaries. Use this information to assess whether the data are approximately normal.

UNIVARIATE PROCEDURE

Variable=SALARY

Moments

N	1795	Sum Wgts	1795
Mean	28474.83	Sum	51112325
Std Dev	9369.484	Variance	87787229
Skewness	1.093351	Kurtosis	2.301454
USS	1.613E12	CSS	1.575E11
CV	32.90444	Std Mean	221.1482
T:Mean=0	128.759	Prob>|T|	0.0
Sgn Rank	805955	Prob>|S|	0.0
Num ^= 0	1795		
W:Normal	0.934422	Prob<W	0.0

Quantiles(Def=5)

100% Max	80000		99%	60000
75% Q3	33000		95%	46000
50% Med	27000		90%	40000
25% Q1	22000		10%	19000
0% Min	7100		5%	16000
			1%	10000
Range	72900			
Q3-Q1	11000			
Mode	20000			

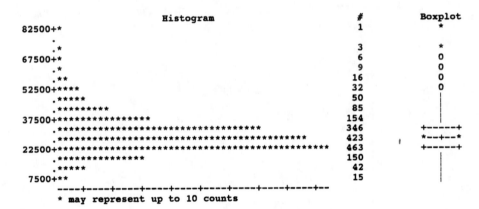

```
              Histogram                              #       Boxplot
  82500+*                                            1          *
       .
       .*                                            3          *
  67500+*                                            6          0
       .*                                            9          0
       .**                                          16          0
  52500+****                                         32          0
       .*****                                        50          |
       .********                                      85          |
  37500+****************                             154         |
       .***********************************         346      +-----+
       .**************************************      423      *--+--*
  22500+****************************************    463      +-----+
       .***************                             150         |
       .*****                                        42         |
   7500+***                                          15         |
       ----+----+----+----+----+----+----+----+--
       * may represent up to 10 counts
```

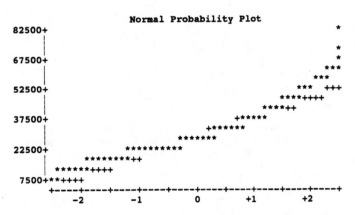

```
                   Normal Probability Plot
  82500+                                              *
       |
  67500+                                             *
       |                                            *
       |                                          ***
  52500+                                       ***
       |                                    *** +++
       |                                 ****++++
  37500+                              ****++
       |                          +*****
       |                       +******
  22500+               *********
       |        ********++
   7500+**++++
       +----+----+----+----+----+----+----+----+----+----+
           -2        -1         0        +1        +2
```

6.22 Refer to the study of British Columbia's boreal forest, Exercise 6.14. The diameters at breast height (in meters) for a sample of 28 trembling aspen trees are listed here. Determine whether the sample data are from an approximately normal distribution.

12.4	17.3	27.3	19.1	16.9	16.2	20.0
16.6	16.3	16.3	21.4	25.7	15.0	19.3
12.9	18.6	12.4	15.9	18.8	14.9	12.8
24.8	26.9	13.5	17.9	13.2	23.2	12.7

Source: Sholtz, H. "Fish Creek Community Forest: Exploratory statistical analysis of selected data," working paper, Northern Lights College, British Columbia, Canada.

6.23 Recall that Appendix A.1 describes the sale prices of residential properties in six neighborhoods in Tampa, Florida. For each neighborhood, use the computer to determine whether the sale price data are approximately normal (The data are available on a $3\frac{1}{2}$"diskette from the publisher.)

6.24 A histogram describing the length (in millimeters) of 50 drill chips, Exercise 2.25, is reproduced here. Does it appear that the 50 drill chip lengths come from an approximately normal population?

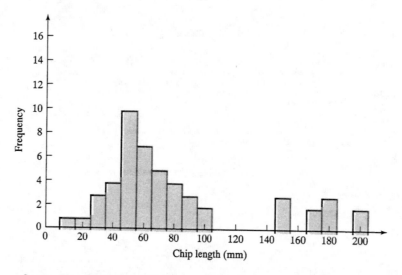

Source: Chin, Jih-Hua et al. "The computer simulation and experimental analysis of chip monitoring for deep hole drilling." *Journal of Engineering for Industry, Transactions of the ASME*, Vol. 115, May 1993, p. 187 (Figure 12).

6.25 The Harris Corporation data on voltage readings at two locations, Exercise 3.32, are reproduced here. Determine whether the voltage readings at each location are approximately normal.

	Old Location			New Location	
9.98	10.12	9.84	9.19	10.01	8.82
10.26	10.05	10.15	9.63	8.82	8.65
10.05	9.80	10.02	10.10	9.43	8.51
10.29	10.15	9.80	9.70	10.03	9.14
10.03	10.00	9.73	10.09	9.85	9.75
8.05	9.87	10.01	9.60	9.27	8.78
10.55	9.55	9.98	10.05	8.83	9.35
10.26	9.95	8.72	10.12	9.39	9.54
9.97	9.70	8.80	9.49	9.48	9.36
9.87	8.72	9.84	9.37	9.64	8.68

Source: Harris Corporation, Melbourne, Fla.

6.4 The Normal Approximation to the Binomial Distribution

It can be shown (proof omitted) that the binomial probability distribution of Chapter 5 becomes more nearly normal as the sample size n becomes larger. That is, the histogram for a binomial random variable is shaped nearly like a normal distribution when n is large. Consequently, we can use the normal probability tables to approximate binomial probabilities using the technique of Section 6.2.

The normal approximation to a binomial probability distribution is reasonably good even for small samples—say, n as small as 10—when $\pi = .5$, and the distribution of x is therefore symmetric about its mean $\mu = n\pi$. When π is near 0 (or 1), the binomial probability distribution will tend to be skewed to the right (or left), but this skewness will disappear as n becomes large. In general, the approximation will be good when n is large enough so that both $n\pi$ and $n(1 - \pi)$ are greater than or equal to 5.

> ### Condition Required to Apply a Normal Approximation to a Binomial Probability Distribution
> The approximation will be good if both $n\pi \geq 5$ and $n(1 - \pi) \geq 5$.

EXAMPLE 6.13
Normal Approximation to Binomial

Suppose x has a binomial probability distribution with $n = 10$ and $\pi = .5$.

a. Graph $p(x)$ and superimpose on the graph a normal distribution with $\mu = n\pi$ and $\sigma = \sqrt{n\pi(1 - \pi)}$.

b. Use Table 2 of Appendix B to find $P(x \leq 4)$.

c. Use the normal approximation to the binomial probability distribution to find an approximation to $P(x \leq 4)$.

SOLUTION   **a.**   The graphs of $p(x)$ and a normal distribution with

$$\mu = n\pi(10)(.5) = 5$$

and

$$\sigma = \sqrt{n\pi(1 - \pi)} = \sqrt{10(.5)(.5)} = 1.58$$

are shown in Figure 6.15. Note that $n\pi = n(1-\pi) = 5$; thus, the normal distribution with $\mu = 5$ and $\sigma = 1.58$ provides a good approximation to $p(x)$.

FIGURE 6.15

A Binomial Probability Distribution ($n = 10$, $\pi = .5$) and the Approximating Normal Distribution ($\mu = n\pi = 5$ and $\sigma = \sqrt{n\pi(1 - \pi)}$ $= 1.58$)

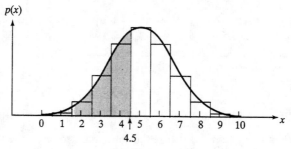

b.   From Table 2 of Appendix B we obtain

$$\sum_{x=0}^{4} p(x) = .3770$$

c.   By examining Figure 6.15, you can see that $P(x \le 4)$ is the area under the normal curve to the left of $x = 4.5$. Note that the area to the left of $x = 4$ would *not* be appropriate because it would omit half the probability rectangle corresponding to $x = 4$. We need to add .5 to 4 before calculating the probability to correct for the fact that we are using a continuous probability distribution to approximate a discrete probability distribution. The value .5 is called the **continuity correction factor** for the normal approximation to the binomial probability (see the next box). The z value corresponding to the corrected value $x = 4.5$ is

$$z = \frac{x - \mu}{\sigma} = \frac{4.5 - 5}{1.58} = \frac{-.5}{1.58} = -.32$$

The area between $z = 0$ and $z = .32$, given in Table 5 of Appendix B, is $A = .1255$. Therefore,

$$P(x \le 4) \approx .5 - A = .5 - .1255 = .3745$$

Thus, the normal approximation to $P(x \le 4) = .3770$ is quite good, although n is as small as 10. The sample size would have to be larger in order to apply the approximation if π were not equal to .5. ▪

Continuity Correction for the Normal Approximation to a Binomial Probability

Let x be a binomial random variable with parameters n and π, and let z be a standard normal random variable. Then

$$P(x \le a) = P\left[z < \frac{(a + .5) - \mu}{\sigma}\right] \quad \text{(see Fig. 6.16a)}$$

$$P(x \ge a) = P\left[z > \frac{(a - .5) - \mu}{\sigma}\right] \quad \text{(see Fig. 6.16b)}$$

$$P(a \le x \le b) = P\left[\frac{(a - .5) - \mu}{\sigma} < z < \frac{(b + .5) - \mu}{\sigma}\right] \quad \text{(see Fig. 6.16c)}$$

where $\mu = n\pi$ and $\sigma = \sqrt{n\pi(1 - \pi)}$.

Note: $P(x < a) = P(x \le a - 1)$ and $P(x > a) = P(x \ge a + 1)$

FIGURE 6.16

Illustration of Continuity Correction for the Normal Approximation to the Binomial Distribution

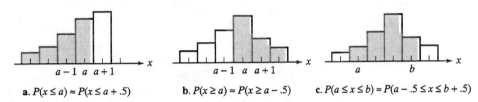

a. $P(x \le a) \approx P(x \le a + .5)$ **b.** $P(x \ge a) \approx P(x \ge a - .5)$ **c.** $P(a \le x \le b) \approx P(a - .5 \le x \le b + .5)$

In sample surveys and opinion polls conducted by professional pollsters, such as Harris, Gallup, and CNN, the sample size n is typically large (usually, $n \ge 500$). When such a large n is used, the continuity correction can be conveniently omitted from normal approximation calculations without jeopardizing the validity of the results. This point is illustrated in the next example.

EXAMPLE 6.14

Continuity Correction with Large n

Suppose x is a binomial random variable with $n = 2,000$ and $\pi = .5$.

a. Use the normal approximation to find $P(x \ge 1,049)$.
b. Repeat part **a**, but do not use the continuity correction factor.

SOLUTION

a. First, we find the mean and standard deviation of x:

$$\mu = n\pi = 2,000(.5) = 1,000$$

$$\sigma = \sqrt{n\pi(1 - \pi)} = \sqrt{2,000(.5)(.5)} = 22.36$$

Using the continuity correction factor, $P(x \ge 1,049)$ corresponds to $P(x \ge 1,048.5)$. The normal approximation proceeds as follows:

$$P(x \geq 1,048.5) = P\left(z \geq \frac{1,048.5 - \mu}{\sigma}\right)$$

$$= P\left(z \geq \frac{1,048.5 - 1,000}{22.36}\right)$$

$$= P(z \geq 2.17)$$

$$= .5 - .4850 \quad \text{(from Table 5, Appendix B)}$$

$$= .0150$$

b.   Ignoring the continuity correction factor, we obtain:

$$P(x \geq 1,049) = P\left(z \geq \frac{1,049 - \mu}{\sigma}\right)$$

$$= P\left(z \geq \frac{1,049 - 1,000}{22.36}\right)$$

$$= P(z \geq 2.19)$$

$$= .5 - .4857 \quad \text{(from Table 5, Appendix B)}$$

$$= .0143$$

You can see that the two probabilities, parts **a** and **b**, are nearly identical. For practical reasons, then, the continuity correction can be ignored when using the normal approximation to a binomial distribution with a large n. ▪

EXERCISES

▪ *Learning the Mechanics*

6.26   Let x a binomial random variable with $n = 15$ and $\pi = 3$. (0.3)
  a. Use Table 2 of Appendix B to find $P(x \leq 8)$.
  b. Use the normal approximation to the binomial probability distribution to find an approximation to $P(x \leq 8)$. Compare to your answer in part **a**.

6.27   Suppose x is a binomial random variable with n and π as specified in the cases below. For each case, decide whether the normal distribution provides a good approximation to the binomial distribution.
  a. $n = 23$, $\pi = .30$ **b.** $n = 3$, $\pi = .01$ **c.** $n = 100$, $\pi = .97$ **d.** $n = 15$, $\pi = .45$

6.28   Suppose x has a binomial distribution with $n = 1,000$ and $\pi = .40$. Find approximations to each of the following probabilities:
  a. $P(x \leq 440)$ **b.** $P(x > 420)$ **c.** $P(410 \leq x \leq 415)$ **d.** $P(x \leq 410)$

6.29 Let x be a binomial random variable with $n = 20$ and $\pi = .6$.
  a. Use Table 2 of Appendix B to find $P(x > 13)$.
  b. Use the normal approximation to the binomial probability distribution to find an approximation to $P(x > 13)$. Compare to your answer in part **a**.

■ *Applying the Concepts*

6.30 One of the keys to developing successful information systems is to implement structured design and programming techniques. Computer-aided software engineering (CASE) technology provides several automated tools (e.g., data flow diagrams) that can facilitate structured techniques. The *Journal of System Management* (July 1989) reported that 60% of information systems (IS) professionals make extensive use of data flow diagrams in their work. In a sample of 150 IS professionals, what is the approximate probability that at least half make extensive use of data flow diagrams?

6.31 According to the U.S. Department of Labor, women are vastly underrepresented in high-technology jobs related to computers. In the category of computer systems analyst—the fastest growing and highest paid computer-related job—women constitute only 30% of the work force (*Wall Street Journal*, Sept. 16, 1985).
  a. Use the normal approximation to the binomial to calculate the probability that more than half of a random sample of 20 computer systems analysts are women.
  b. Use the normal approximation to the binomial to calculate the probability that five or fewer of a random sample of 20 computer systems analysts are women.
  c. Use the binomial tables to calculate the exact probabilities in parts **a** and **b**. Does the normal distribution provide a good approximation to the binomial distribution?

6.32 The merging process from an acceleration lane to the through lane of a freeway constitutes an important aspect of traffic operation at interchanges. A study of parallel interchange ramps in Israel revealed that many drivers do not use the entire length of parallel lanes for acceleration, but for seeking, as soon as possible, an appropriate gap in the major stream of traffic for merging (*Transportation Engineering Journal*, Nov. 1985). At one site (Yavneh), 54% of the drivers use less than half the lane length available before merging. Suppose we plan to monitor the merging patterns of a random sample of 330 drivers at the Yavneh site.
  a. What is the approximate probability that fewer than 100 of the drivers will use less than half the acceleration lane length before merging?
  b. What is the approximate probability that 200 or more of the drivers will use less than half the acceleration lane length before merging?

6.33 Quality control is a problem with items that are mass produced. The production process must be monitored to ensure that the rate of defective items is kept at an acceptably low level. One method of dealing with this problem is lot acceptance sampling, in which a random sample of items produced is selected and each item in the sample is carefully tested. The entire lot of items is then accepted or rejected, based on the number of defectives observed in the sample. Suppose a manufacturer of pocket calculators randomly chooses 200 stamped circuits from a day's production and determines x, the number of defective circuits in the sample. If a sample defective rate of 6% or less is considered acceptable and, unknown to the manufacturer, 8% of the entire day's production of circuits is defective, find the approximate probability that the lot of stamped circuits will be rejected.

6.34 How well does a college engineering degree prepare you for the work place? A 2-year nation-wide survey of engineers and engineering managers in "specific high-demand" industries revealed that only 34% believe that their companies make good use of their learned skills (*Chemical Engineering*, Feb. 3, 1986). In a random sample of 50 engineers and engineering managers, consider the number x who believe that their employer makes good use of their college engineering background. Find the approximate probability that:

a. $x \leq 10$ **b.** $x \geq 25$ **c.** $20 \leq x \leq 30$

6.5 The Uniform Probability Distribution (Optional)

Suppose you were to randomly select a number x represented by a point in the interval $a \leq x \leq b$. Then x is called a **uniform random variable**, and its probability distribution is called a **uniform distribution**. The uniform probability distribution has a rectangular shape, as shown in Figure 6.17. Note that the height of the rectangle is constant and equal to $1/(b-a)$. This guarantees that the total area under the rectangle will be 1.*

FIGURE 6.17

The Uniform Probability Distribution

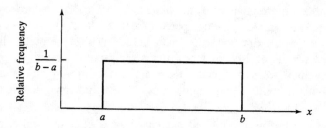

The uniform probability distribution provides a good model for continuous random variables that are randomly (or evenly) distributed over a certain interval. Any one value of a uniform random variable is as likely to occur as any other value; consequently, the distribution is evenly spread over the entire region of possible values.

The formulas for calculating probabilities, the mean, and standard deviation of the uniform distribution are given in the box. We illustrate the use of these formulas with an example.

---

*Recall that the area of a rectangle is equal to (Base) × (Height). For the uniform distribution, Base = $(b-a)$, Height = $1/(b-a)$; thus,

$$(Base) \times (Height) = (b-a)\left(\frac{1}{b-a}\right) = 1$$

The Probability Distribution, Mean, and Standard Deviation
for a Uniform Random Variable

Let x be a **uniform random variable** in the interval $a \leq x \leq b$. Then the probability distribution for x is a rectangle with height $1/(b-a)$ over the interval $a \leq x \leq b$. Probabilities of x (i.e., areas under the uniform curve) are given by

$$P(x < c) = \frac{c-a}{b-a} \quad \text{for } a \leq c \leq b$$

$$P(x > c) = \frac{b-c}{b-a} \quad \text{for } a \leq c \leq b$$

$$P(c < x \leq d) = \frac{d-c}{b-a} \quad \text{for } a \leq c < d \leq b$$

The mean and standard deviation of x are given by

$$\mu = \frac{a+b}{2} \qquad \sigma = \frac{b-a}{\sqrt{12}}$$

EXAMPLE 6.15
Computing Uniform μ
and σ

A quality control inspector for a company that manufactures field rifles for the Department of Defense believes that one of the production lines is producing firing pins of varying lengths. Suppose the pins turned out by this production line have lengths that can be modeled by a uniform probability distribution over the interval .95 to 1.05 inches.

    a. Calculate the mean and standard deviation of x, the length of the firing pins produced by this line.

    b. Graph the probability distribution and locate μ, $\mu \pm \sigma$, and $\mu \pm 2\sigma$ on the graph.

SOLUTION
    a. To calculate the mean and standard deviation of x, we substitute $a = .95$ inch and $b = 1.05$ inches in the formulas given in the box. Thus,

$$\mu = \frac{a+b}{2} = \frac{.95 + 1.05}{2} = 1.00 \text{ inch}$$

and

$$\sigma = \frac{b-a}{\sqrt{12}} = \frac{1.05 - .95}{\sqrt{12}} = \frac{.10}{3.464} = .029 \text{ inch}$$

FIGURE 6.18

Probabillity
Distribution for *x,*
Example 6.15

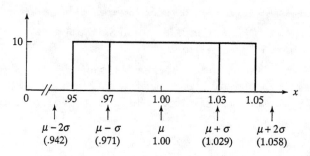

b.   The graph of this distribution is shown in Figure 6.18. Note that the height of the rectangle is

$$\frac{1}{b-a} = \frac{1}{1.05 - .95} = \frac{1}{.10} = 10$$

The mean and 1- and 2-standard-deviation intervals around the mean are shown on the horizontal axis. You can see that all (100%) of the firing pin lengths fall within $\mu \pm 2\sigma$. ■

EXAMPLE 6.16

Finding a Uniform
Probability

Refer to Example 6.15. Suppose that firing pins with lengths less than .97 inch or greater than 1.03 inches do not meet specifications and must be discarded. Find the fraction of pins produced by the line that must be scrapped.

SOLUTION   To find the fraction of firing pins that do not meet specifications, we must find the probability that *x* is either less than .97 inch or greater than 1.03 inches. According to the rule of complements (see Chapter 4), this probability is equal to 1 minus the probability that *x* falls between $c = .97$ and $d = 1.03$ inches (see Figure 6.19), i.e.,

$$P(\text{Do not meet specifications}) = P(x < .97 \text{ or } x > 1.03)$$

$$= 1 - P(.97 < x < 1.03)$$

From the previous box, the probability of the complement is computed as

$$P(c < x < d) = \frac{d-c}{b-a} = \frac{1.03 - .97}{1.05 - .95} = \frac{.06}{.10} = .60$$

FIGURE 6.19

The Probability That
the Pin Length, *x,* Is
Less Than .97 or
Greater Than 1.03
Inches

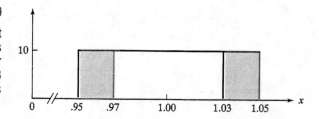

Thus,

$$P(\text{Do not meet specifications}) = 1 - .60 = .40$$

That is, 40% of the firing pins manufactured by this production line must be discarded unless the problem is identified and corrected. ■

EXERCISES

■ *Learning the Mechanics*

6.35 Find μ and σ for a uniform random variable x distributed over the interval $a \le x \le b$ for each of the following values of a and b:
a. $a = 2$, $b = 10$ **b.** $a = -5$, $b = 5$ **c.** $a = 0$, $b = 1$ **d.** $a = 60$, $b = 75$
Locate μ and σ on a graph of the probability distribution for each interval.

6.36 Suppose x is a uniform random variable over the interval $1 \le x \le 3$. Find the following probabilities:
a. $P(x < 2.5)$ **b.** $P(x > 1.7)$ **c.** $P(1.5 < x < 2)$
d. $P(x < 2)$ **e.** $P(1.1 \le x \le 1.6)$ **f.** $P(x \le 1.3)$

6.37 Suppose x has a uniform distribution with $a = 100$ and $b = 200$.
a. Find μ and σ.
b. Locate the interval $\mu \pm 2\sigma$ on a graph of the probability distribution.
c. Calculate $P(\mu - 2\sigma \le x \le \mu + 2\sigma)$. How does this value compare to the Empirical Rule or Tchebysheff's theorem?

■ *Applying the Concepts*

6.38 Researchers at the University of California–Berkeley have designed, built, and tested a switched-capacitor circuit for generating random signals (*International Journal of Circuit Theory and Applications,* May–June 1990). The circuit's trajectory was shown to be uniformly distributed on the interval (0,1).
a. Give the mean and variance of the circuit's trajectory.
b. Compute the probability that the trajectory falls between .2 and .4.
c. Would you expect to observe a trajectory that exceeds .995? Explain.

6.39 A manufacturing company has developed a fuel-efficient machine that combines pressure washing with steam cleaning. It is designed to deliver 7 gallons of cleaner per minute at 1,000 pounds per square inch for pressure washing. In fact, it delivers an amount at random anywhere between 6.5 and 7.5 gallons per minute. Assume that x, the amount of cleaner delivered, is a uniform random variable with $a = 6.5$ and $b = 7.5$.
a. Find the mean and standard deviation of x. Graph the probability distribution for x, showing the locations of the mean and 1- and 2-standard-deviation intervals around the mean.
b. Find the probability that more than 7.2 gallons of cleaner are dispensed per minute.

6.40 The Department of Transportation (DOT) has determined that the winning (low) bid x (in dollars) on a road construction contract has a uniform distribution with $a = \frac{2}{5}d$ and $b = 2d$, where d is the DOT estimate of the cost of the job.

a. Find the mean and standard deviation of x. Graph the probability distribution for x, showing the locations of the mean and 1- and 2-standard-deviation intervals around the mean.

b. What fraction of the winning bids on road construction contracts are less than the DOT estimate?

6.41 The amount of time x between pauses on a full-screen-edit terminal (i.e., the time required for the terminal to process an edit command and make the corrections on the screen) is uniformly distributed between .5 and 2.25 seconds.

a. Find the mean and variance of x.

b. Locate the interval $\mu \pm 2\sigma$ on a graph of the probability distribution and compute $P(\mu - 2\sigma < x < \mu + 2\sigma)$. Compare your result with Tchebysheff's theorem.

c. What is the probability the terminal will process an edit command and make the appropriate corrections on the screen in less than 1 second?

6.6 The Exponential Probability Distribution (Optional)

Many continuous random variables can assume only nonnegative values. The probability distribution for data of this type can often be modeled by an **exponential probability distribution**.

In business, the exponential probability distribution is used to approximate the relative frequency distribution of the length of time between arrivals at a service counter (computer center, supermarket checkout counter, hospital clinic, etc.) when the probability of a customer arrival in any one unit of time is equal to the probability of arrival during any other. It is also used as a model for the length of life of industrial equipment or products when the probability that an "old" component will operate at least t additional time units, given that it is now functioning, is the same as the probability that a "new" component will operate at least t time units. Equipment subject to periodic maintenance and parts replacement often exhibits this property of "never growing old."

A special property of the exponential probability distribution is that its mean equals its standard deviation. Thus, the exponential distribution depends on only a single parameter value, μ, since $\mu = \sigma$. Graphs of the exponential distribution for several values of μ are shown in Figure 6.20.

The formulas for calculating probabilities of the exponential random variable, its mean, and its standard deviation are shown in the box.

The Probability Distribution for an Exponential Random Variable

Let x have an **exponential distribution** with mean μ and standard deviation μ, where $x > 0$. Probabilities of x are given by

$$P(x \geq c) = e^{-c/\mu}$$

$$P(x \leq c) = 1 - e^{-c/\mu}$$

$$P(c \leq x \leq d) = e^{-c/\mu} - e^{-d/\mu}$$

[*Note:* Values $e^{-c/\mu}$ can be found in Table 3 of Appendix B.]

FIGURE 6.20

Exponential
Distributions

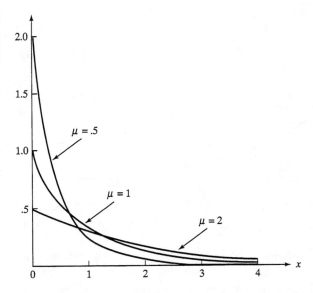

EXAMPLE 6.17
Computing Exponential
Probabilities

The exponential distribution is related to the Poisson probability distribution of Section 5.5. In fact, it can be shown (proof omitted) that if the number of arrivals at a service counter follows a Poisson probability distribution with mean number of arrivals per unit time equal to $1/\mu$, then the length of time x between any pair of successive arrivals (i.e., the *interarrival time)* will have an exponential distribution with mean μ. Consider a supermarket checkout counter with mean number of customers per minute equal to $\frac{1}{2} = .5$ (i.e., $\mu = 2$).

a. Find the probability that the length of time between a pair of successive arrivals of customers at the counter exceeds 3 minutes.

b. Within what range do you expect most of the interarrival times to fall?

SOLUTION

a. Assuming that the number of arrivals (per minute) at the supermarket checkout counter follows a Poisson distribution, we know that x, the length of time between a pair of successive arrivals, is an exponential random variable with mean $\mu = 2$ minutes. The probability we want to find, $P(x \geq 3)$, is the area A shaded in the graph of the exponential distribution shown in Figure 6.21 (page 292). The desired probability can be found by substituting

$$c = 3 \quad \text{and} \quad \mu = 2$$

into the formula given in the box:

$$A = P(x \geq c)$$
$$= e^{-c/\mu}$$
$$= e^{-3/2}$$
$$= e^{-1.5}$$

FIGURE 6.21

Exponential
Distribution ($\mu = 2$)
for Example 6.17

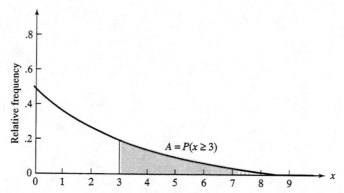

Referring to Table 3 of Appendix B (or a hand calculator), we find

$$A = e^{-1.5} = .2231$$

Thus, the probability that the time between arriving customers at the checkout counter exceeds 3 minutes is approximately .22.

b. The mean and standard deviation of x, the interarrival times, are

$$\mu = 2 \text{ minutes}$$

and

$$\sigma = 2 \text{ minutes}$$

Using either the Empirical Rule or Tchebysheff's theorem (Chapter 3), we expect most of the x's to fall in the interval

$$\mu \pm 2s = 2 \pm 2(2) = 2 \pm 4$$

or $(-2,6)$. Since the interarrival time x cannot be negative, we expect x to range anywhere from 0 to 6 minutes. In fact, the probability that x falls in this interval is

$$
\begin{aligned}
P(0 \leq x \leq 6) &= 1 - P(x > 6) \\
&= 1 - e^{-6/2} \\
&= 1 - e^{-3} \\
&= 1 - .0498 \\
&= .9502 \quad ■
\end{aligned}
$$

EXERCISES

■ *Learning the Mechanics*

6.42 Suppose x has an exponential probability distribution with $\mu = 7$. Find the following probabilities:

      a. $P(x > 3)$ **b.** $P(x \le 10)$ **c.** $P(4 < x < 12)$
      d. $P(x \ge 5.5)$ **e.** $P(x < 7)$

6.43   Suppose x has an exponential distribution with $\mu = .5$.
      a. Find $P(x > 2)$.
      b. Find $P(x \le .75)$.
      c. Find the standard deviation of x.

6.44   Suppose x has an exponential distribution with $\mu = 2$.
      a. Calculate σ.
      b. Locate the interval $\mu \pm 2\sigma$ on a graph of the exponential distribution. What percentage of the x values do you expect to fall in this interval?
      c. Calculate the probability that x falls in the interval $\mu \pm 2\sigma$. Compare this value to your answer to part **b**.

■ *Applying the Concepts*

6.45   The lifetime x (in hours) of the central processing unit of a certain type of microcomputer is an exponential random variable with mean $\mu = 1,000$.
      a. Find the variance of the lifetime of the central processing unit.
      b. What is the probability that a central processing unit will have a lifetime of at least 2,000 hours?
      c. What is the probability that a central processing unit will have a lifetime of at most 1,500 hours?

6.46   In finding and correcting errors in a computer program (*debugging*) and determining the program's reliability, computer software experts have noted the importance of the distribution of the time until the next program error is found. Suppose this random variable has an exponential distribution. One computer programmer believes that the mean time between finding program errors is $\mu = 24$ days. Suppose a programming error is found today.
      a. Assuming that $\mu = 24$, find the probability that it will take at least 60 days to discover the next programming error.
      b. If the next programming error takes at least 60 days to find, what would you infer about the programmer's claim that the mean time between the detection of programming errors is $\mu = 24$ days? Why?

6.47   From past experience, a manufacturer knows that the relative frequency distribution of the length of time x (in months) between major customer product complaints can be modeled by an exponential distribution with $\mu = 4$. Fifteen months after the manufacturer tightened its quality control requirements, the first complaint arrived. Does this suggest that the mean time between major customer complaints may have increased? [*Hint:* Find $P(x \ge 15)$.]

6.48   The number of industrial accidents can often be modeled by an exponential distribution (*Technometrics*, May 1985). Suppose the number of accidents per hour at an industrial plant is exponentially distributed with mean $\mu = .5$.
      a. What is the probability that at least one accident will occur in a randomly selected hour at the industrial plant?
      b. What is the probability that fewer than two accidents will occur in a randomly selected hour at the industrial plant?
      c. Within what range do you expect the number of accidents per hour to fall?

6.49 A part processed in a flexible manufacturing system (FMS) is routed through a set of operations, some of which are sequential and some of which are parallel. In addition, an FMS operation can be processed by alternative machines. An article in *IEEE Transactions* (Mar. 1990) gave an example of an FMS with four machines operating independently. The repair rates for the machines (i.e., the time, in hours, it takes to repair a failed machine) are exponentially distributed with means $\mu_1 = 1$, $\mu_2 = 2$, $\mu_3 = .5$, and $\mu_4 = .5$, respectively.

a. Find the probability that the repair time for machine 1 exceeds 1 hour.

b. Repeat part **a** for machine 2.

c. Repeat part **a** for machines 3 and 4.

d. If all four machines fail simultaneously, find the probability that the repair time for the entire system exceeds 1 hour.

SUMMARY

This chapter introduced an important probability model for continuous random variables—the *normal distribution.* Since the normal distribution is a model for a population relative frequency distribution, it follows that the total area under the curve is equal to 1, and areas under the curve correspond to the probabilities of drawing observations that fall within particular intervals.

When the sample size *n* is large, the normal distribution provides a good approximation to the binomial probability distribution. You will learn in Chapter 7 why we expect many other population relative frequency distributions to be approximately normally distributed. You will also begin to develop an understanding of how areas under the normal curve can be used to assess the uncertainty associated with sample inferences.

Two other continuous probability distributions with business applications were discussed in optional sections. The *uniform distribution* provides a good model for random variables that are randomly, or evenly, distributed. The *exponential distribution* is used to approximate the distribution of the length of time between certain events, such as arrivals at a service counter, customer complaints, failures of an electronic component, etc.

KEY TERMS

*Exponential distribution

Normal approximation to the
   binomial

Normal curve

Normal distribution

Normal probability plot

Probabilistic model

Standard normal distribution

*Uniform distribution

From the optional sections.

KEY FORMULAS

Normal distribution:

$$z \text{ score} = \frac{x - \mu}{\sigma} \qquad x_0 = \mu + z_0 \sigma$$

Normal approximation to binomial:

$$P(x \leq a) \approx P\left[z < \frac{(a + .5) - \mu}{\sigma}\right]$$

$$P(x \geq a) \approx P\left[z > \frac{(a - .5) - \mu}{\sigma}\right]$$

$$P(a \leq x \leq b) \approx P\left[\frac{(a - .5) - \mu}{\sigma} < z < \frac{(b + .5) - \mu}{\sigma}\right]$$

Uniform distribution ($a \leq x \leq b$):

$$P(x \leq c) = \frac{c - a}{b - a}, \quad \text{for } a \leq c \leq b$$

$$P(x \geq c) = \frac{b - c}{b - a}, \quad \text{for } a \leq c \leq b$$

$$P(c \leq x \leq d) = \frac{d - c}{b - a}, \quad \text{for } a \leq c < d \leq b$$

$$\mu = \frac{a + b}{2} \qquad \sigma = \frac{b - a}{\sqrt{12}}$$

Exponential distribution:

(Mean $= \mu$)

$$P(x \geq c) = e^{-c/\mu}$$

$$P(x \leq c) = 1 - e^{-c/\mu}$$

$$P(c \leq x \leq d) = e^{-c/\mu} - e^{-d/\mu}$$

$$\mu = \mu \qquad \sigma = \mu$$

*From the optional sections.

SUPPLEMENTARY EXERCISES

[Note: Starred (*) exercises are from the optional sections in this chapter.]

6.50 How reliable are security analysts' forecasts of corporate earnings growth? According to David Dreman of *Forbes* magazine, "Astrology might be better" (*Forbes*, Mar. 26, 1984). Dreman reported on a study of annual earnings estimates made by institutional brokerage analysts covering the more widely followed companies between 1977 and 1981. The study revealed that "the average annual error by the analysts was a staggering 31.3% over the 5-year period." Suppose the annual forecast error by security analysts is normally distributed with a mean of 31.3% and a standard deviation of 10%. Suppose you obtain a security analyst's forecast of annual earnings for a particular corporation.

a. What is the probability that the forecast error will be between 20% and 25%?

b. What is the probability that the forecast error will be greater than 50%?

6.51 State governments are beginning to tighten up their antitrust laws and stiffen penalties against highway construction bid riggers. Suppose it is known that the bids received on a 110-mile highway construction project are normally distributed with a mean of $290 million and a standard deviation of $40 million.

a. Find the probability that a contractor selected at random would have a bid of $200 million or less.

b. Twenty percent of the bids received on similar projects fall below what value?

6.52 A food processor packages instant orange juice in small jars. The weights of the filled jars are approximately normally distributed with a mean of 10.82 ounces and a standard deviation of .30 ounce.

a. Find the probability that the weight of a randomly selected jar of instant orange juice will exceed 10.2 ounces.

b. Suppose the Food and Drug Administration sets the minimum weight of the jars at 10 ounces. Jars with weights below the allowable minimum must be removed from the supermarket shelf. What proportion of the jars should we expect to be removed from the supermarket shelf?

c. Two percent of the packaged jars are below what weight?

For parts **a–c**, show the pertinent quantities on a sketch of the normal curve.

6.53 *Meta-analysis* is a procedure used to compare the findings of independent studies on the same subject matter. Stock et al. (1985) conducted a meta-analysis of the relation between race and subjective well-being among noninstitutionalized adults based on results obtained from 54 sources. For each source, a measure of the relationship between race and well-being, called "effect size," was calculated. (Effect sizes ranged from −1 to 1, with positive values implying that whites had a higher subjective well-being than blacks and negative values implying the reverse.) A stem-and-leaf display (see Chapter 2) of the 54 effect sizes is reproduced here. The mean and standard deviation of the data were .10 and .09, respectively.

a. Examine the stem-and-leaf display. Is the distribution of effect sizes approximately normal?

b. Assuming normality, calculate the probability that a randomly selected study on the relationship between race and subjective well-being will have a negative effect size. (Assume $\mu = .10$ and $\sigma = .09$.)

c. Use the stem-and-leaf display to calculate the actual percentage of the 54 effect sizes that were negative. Compare the result to your answer to part **b**.

Stem	Leaf
.3	01
.2	567
.2	00024
.1	556999
.1	000112223444
.0	56666778889
.0	2
−.0	1000
−.0	998
−.1	22111
−.1	6
−.2	4

Source: Stock, W. A., Okun, M. A., Haring, M. J., and Witter, R. A. "Race and subjective well-being in adulthood: A black–white research synthesis." *Human Development*, Vol. 28, 1985, p. 195. By permission of S. Karger AG, Basel.

6.54 Refer to the *Wall Street Journal* study on the ethical behavior of business executives, described in Exercise 5.24. Let x be the number in a sample of 1,558 executives who condone unethical behavior in business. Suppose x has a binomial distribution with $\pi = .15$.
    a. Calculate the approximate probability that x exceeds 232.
    b. Calculate the approximate probability that x is less than or equal to 300.

6.55 The length of time between breakdowns of an essential piece of equipment is an important factor in deciding on the amount of auxiliary equipment needed to assure continuous service. A machine room foreman believes the time between breakdowns of a particular electrical generator is best approximated by an exponential distribution with mean equal to 10 days.
    a. What is the standard deviation of this exponential distribution?
    b. Assuming that the foreman has correctly characterized the distribution for the time between breakdowns and that the generator broke down today, what is the probability that the generator will break down again within the next 14 days?
    c. What is the probability that the generator will operate for more than 20 days without a breakdown?

6.56 Refer to the data on physician costs, Appendix A.3. Using a computer, determine whether the data are approximately normal.

*6.57 The problem of passenger congestion prompted a large international airport to install a monorail connecting its main terminal to the three concourses, A, B, and C. The engineers designed the monorail so that the amount of time a passenger at concourse B must wait for a monorail car has a uniform distribution ranging from 0 to 10 minutes.
    a. Find the mean and variance of x, the time a passenger at concourse B must wait for the monorail. (Assume that the monorail travels sequentially from concourse A, to concourse

B, to concourse C, back to concourse B, and then returns to concourse A. The route is then repeated.)

b. If it takes the monorail 1 minute to go from concourse to concourse, find the probability that a hurried passenger can reach concourse A less than 4 minutes after arriving at the monorail station at concourse B.

*6.58 Many products are mass-produced on automated assembly lines. The probability distribution of the length of time between the arrivals of successive manufactured components off the assembly line is often (approximately) exponential. Suppose the mean time between arrivals of magnetron tubes manufactured on an assembly line is 20 seconds.

a. What is the probability that a particular interarrival time (the time between the arrivals of two magnetron tubes) is less than 10 seconds?

b. What is the probability that the next four interarrival times are all less than 10 seconds?

c. What is the probability that an interarrival time will exceed 1 minute?

6.59 The average life of a certain steel-belted radial tire is advertised as 60,000 miles. Assume that the life of the tires is normally distributed with a standard deviation of 2,500 miles. (The life of a tire is defined as the number of miles the tire is driven before blowing out.)

a. Find the probability that a randomly selected steel-belted radial tire will have a life of 61,800 miles or less.

b. Find the probability that a randomly selected steel-belted radial tire will have a life between 62,000 miles and 66,000 miles.

c. To avoid a tire blowout, the company manufacturing the tires will warn purchasers to replace each tire after it has been used for a given number of miles. What should the replacement time (in miles) be so that only 1% of the tires will blow out?

For parts **a–c**, show the pertinent quantities on a sketch of the normal curve.

*6.60 Suppose we are counting events that occur according to a Poisson distribution, such as the number of data-processing jobs submitted to a computer center. If it is known that exactly one such event has occurred in a given interval of time, say $(0, t)$, then the actual time of occurrence is uniformly distributed over this interval. Suppose that during a given 30-minute period, one data-processing job was submitted. Find the probability that the job was submitted during the last 5 minutes of the 30-minute period.

6.61 *USA Today* (Aug. 8, 1985) reported on a survey on the perceived fairness of the federal income tax. Let x be the number of the 2,052 adults surveyed who believe the current version of the tax law is unfair.

a. Assuming that 60% of all adults believe the tax is unfair, find the approximate probability that x is greater than 1,300.

b. If you actually find that more than 1,300 adults in the survey believe the tax is unfair, what could you infer about the 60% figure of part **a**? Explain.

*6.62 The shelf life of a product is a random variable that is related to consumer acceptance and, ultimately, to sales and profit. Suppose the shelf life of bread is best approximated by an exponential distribution with mean equal to 2 days. What fraction of the loaves stocked today would you expect to be saleable (i.e., not stale) 3 days from now?

6.63 One common ploy of advertisements for new automobiles is to list the Environmental Protection Agency (EPA) estimated miles per gallon (mpg) for the make of car being advertised. A recent advertisement in a national magazine boasts that the Dodge Aries-K station wagon has the highest mileage of all six-passenger cars. Its EPA estimated miles per gallon is listed as 28 mpg. The EPA tests cars under conditions (weather, brand of gasoline, speed, terrain, etc.) ideally suited for maximum mileage performance. Nevertheless, even under identical conditions, it is unreasonable and impractical to assume that all Dodge Aries-K station wagons tested will obtain the same gas mileage. It is most likely, then, that the 28 mpg figure is the average miles per gallon obtained by the sample of station wagons tested. Let us assume that the EPA estimated mpg for this type of car is accurate, i.e., the true mean mpg obtained under "ideal" conditions for all Dodge Aries-K station wagons is, in fact, 28. Also, suppose the distribution of miles per gallon is approximately normal with a standard deviation of 2.

a. What proportion of all Dodge Aries-K station wagons tested under "ideal" conditions will obtain at least 32 mpg?

b. What is the probability that a Dodge Aries-K station wagon tested under "ideal" conditions will obtain less than 20 mpg?

c. Fifteen percent of all Dodge Aries-K station wagons tested will obtain an mpg rating above a particular value. Find this value.

d. Suppose you test your new Dodge Aries-K station wagon under "ideal" conditions and find that your car obtains 20 mpg. Does this result imply that you have bought a "lemon," or is it more likely that the EPA estimated mpg figure of 28 is too high? [*Hint:* Use your answer to part **b.**]

■ CASE STUDY 6.1

A Random Walk Down Wall Street

In his lively and insightful book *A Random Walk Down Wall Street*,* Burton G. Malkiel devotes Chapter 6 to "Technical Analysis and the Random-Walk Theory." In brief, this chapter discusses the theory used by some stock market technical analysts to forecast the upward or downward movement of specific stocks or the market as a whole.

Technical analysts called **chartists** believe that "knowledge of a stock's past behavior can help predict its probable future behavior." According to Malkiel, chartists strongly favor stocks that have made an upward move, and they advocate selling stocks that have moved downward in price. Similarly, when the stock market averages have shown strength and moved upward, they forecast further upward movement in the market averages. Malkiel clearly has little faith in the forecasts of chartists. He states, "On close examination, technicians are often seen with holes in their shoes and frayed shirt collars. I, personally, have never known a successful technician, but I have seen wrecks of several unsuccessful ones. (This is, of course, in terms of following their own technical advice. Commissions from urging customers to act on their recommendations are very lucrative.)" In brief, Malkiel does not agree that knowledge of a stock's past performance can be used to predict its future behavior.

The antithesis of the theory held by chartists is known as the **random-walk theory**. According to this theory, the price movement of a stock (or the stock market) today is completely independent of its movement in the past; the price will rise or fall today by a random amount. A sequence of these random increases and decreases is known as a **random walk**. Note that this theory does not rule out the possibility of long-term trends—say, a long-term upward trend in stock prices fueled by increased earnings or dividends. It simply states that the *daily* change in price is independent of the changes that have occurred in the past.

To support the random-walk theory, Malkiel generated the stock price chart for several fictitious stocks by tossing a coin to decide whether a stock would move up (a head) or down (a tail) by a fixed amount, say, $.50, on a given day. This procedure was repeated for a large number of days. The movement of the fictitious stock was plotted, thus revealing its random walk. We performed an equivalent coin-tossing experiment for this case, and our fictitious stock chart for 50 days is shown in Figure 6.22. You can see how the price seems to surge upward and downward in this chart (suggesting short-term trends), although the coin tossings were independent.

One way that we can refine the random-walk theory is to postulate the probability distribution of the daily price change in a stock (or the daily change in a market average). Although stock prices change by discrete amounts, the most common assumption is that the change has a distribution that is approximately normal. To examine this theory, we recorded the daily change in the Standard & Poor's (S&P) Stock Index for each market day during a recent 5-year period. The relative frequency distribution for these changes, shown in Figure 6.23 (page 302), has a mean equal to $.095 and a standard deviation equal to $1.527. Does this distribution differ markedly from a normal distribution with $\mu = .095$ and $\sigma = 1.527$?

Statistical tests are available to detect distributional departures from normality, but they are beyond the scope of this text. Nevertheless, we can get an indication of the answer by applying the descriptive methods of Section 6.3. A SAS printout showing descriptive statistics for the 1,264 daily changes in the S&P Index is displayed in Figure 6.24 (pages 303–304). Does it appear that the daily change has a distribution that is approximately normal?

---

*Malkiel, B. G. A Random Walk Down Wall Street. New York: Norton, 1975.

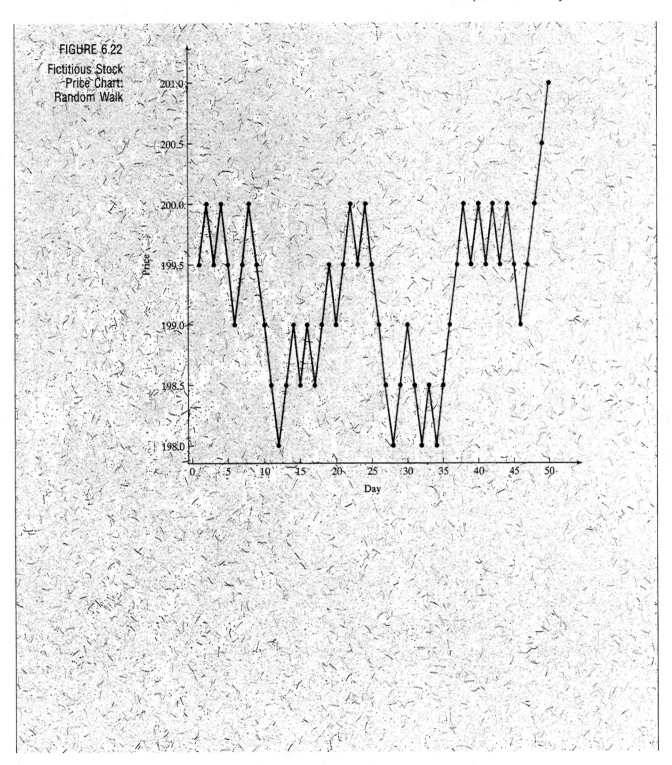

FIGURE 6.22

Fictitious Stock
Price Chart:
Random Walk

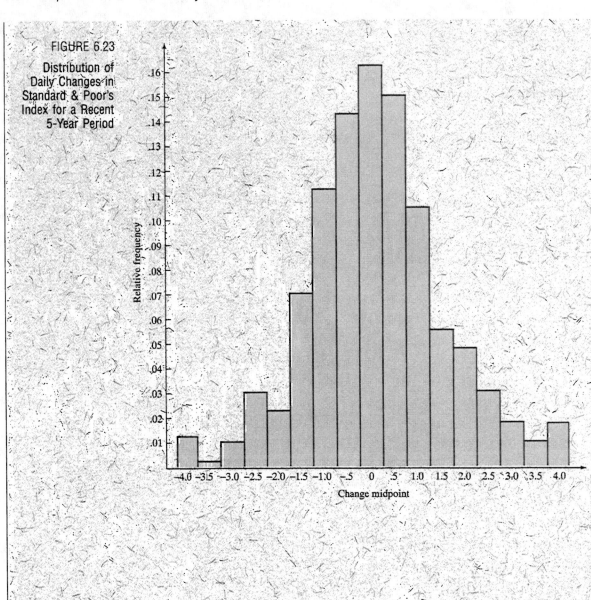

FIGURE 6.23

Distribution of Daily Changes in Standard & Poor's Index for a Recent 5-Year Period

FIGURE 6.24   **a.** SAS descriptive statistics for daily changes in S&P Index for 5-year period

UNIVARIATE PROCEDURE

Variable=CHANGE

Moments

N	1264	Sum Wgts	1264
Mean	0.094636	Sum	119.62
Std Dev	1.526847	Variance	2.331263
Skewness	-0.37318	Kurtosis	4.487836
USS	2955.705	CSS	2944.385
CV	1613.388	Std Mean	0.042946
T:Mean=0	2.20361	Prob>|T|	0.0277
Sgn Rank	25400	Prob>|S|	0.0495
Num ^= 0	1261		

Quantiles(Def=5)

100% Max	5.38	99%	4.34
75% Q3	0.895	95%	2.69
50% Med	0.035	90%	1.92
25% Q1	-0.79	10%	-1.53
0% Min	-11.88	5%	-2.31
		1%	-4.11
Range	17.26		
Q3-Q1	1.685		
Mode	0.79		

Extremes

Lowest	Obs	Highest	Obs
-11.88(	1187)	4.95(	158)
-7.74(	1140)	4.95(	1244)
-6.43(	1235)	5.03(	1176)
-5.83(	1016)	5.11(	1059)
-5.71(	1121)	5.38(	213)

FIGURE 6.24 (cont.)   **b.** SAS plots describing daily changes in S&P Index for 5-year period

```
                              UNIVARIATE PROCEDURE

        Variable=CHANGE

                                  Histogram                    #        Boxplot
            5.5+*                                               3           0
              .**                                              11           0
              .****                                            31           0
              .**********                                      74
              .*********************                          169
              .***********************************************357        +--+--+
              .*************************************************377      +-----+
              .**********************                         166
              .*******                                         55
              .*                                                8           0
              .*                                                7           0
              .*                                                3           0
              .*                                                1           *
              .*                                                1           *
              .
           -11.5+*                                               1          *
              ----+----+----+----+----+----+----+----+----+----+----+---
              * may represent up to 8 counts


                              Normal Probability Plot
            5.5+                                                    *
               .                                              ***
               .                                       ******++
               .                                 +*******
               .                            *******
               .                    **********
               .            *******+
               .      ******++
               .  +++***
               .  ***
               .  *
               .  *
               .  *
           -11.5+*
               +----+----+----+----+----+----+----+----+----+----+
                   -2        -1         0        +1        +2
```

■ CASE STUDY 6.2

Break–Even Analysis—When to Market a New Product

The inherent risk involved with marketing a new product is a key consideration for market researchers. How much will it cost to produce? Should the product be marketed? And if marketed, what should be the price of the new product? Will it be profitable? Various statistical models have been developed to aid speculators and businesses in making such decisions. Typically, these decision models are based on the assumption that production costs and selling price are known, and that the quantity produced is determined without knowledge of the demand for the product.

One area of marketing research that uses decision models is called **break-even analysis**. The underlying assumption of break-even analysis is that the demand for a product is normally distributed, with known mean μ and standard deviation σ. Of interest is the relationship between actual demand D and the break-even point BE, where the break-even point is defined as the number of units of the product the company must sell to "break even" on the investment.

Shih (1981) developed two practical decision criteria using break-even analysis.[*] Both decision rules require knowledge of probability and the normal distribution.

Under the assumption that demand is normally distributed, decision rule A is equivalent to marketing the product when $\mu \geq BE$. Thus, no knowledge of σ is needed to arrive at a decision.

The probability $P(D \geq BE)$ is often called the **level of risk**. Shih's second decision criterion "allows top management to vary the level of risk it could tolerate [for each new product] in light of its outlook on the uncertainty."

Under the normality assumption, decision rule B can be implemented in either of two ways:

1. Given the values of μ and σ, calculate $P(D \geq BE)$ using the standard normal probability table. Then compare this probability to the specified level of risk p. If $P(D \geq BE) > p$, market the new product.

Decision Rule A

Market the new product if the chance is better than 50% that demand D will exceed the break-even point BE—that is, market the product if

$$P(D \geq BE) > .5$$

Decision Rule B

For a specified level of risk $p\,(0 \leq p \leq 1)$, market the new product if

$$P(D \geq BE) > p$$

---

[*] *Shih, W. "A general decision model for cost-volume-profit analysis under uncertainty: A reply."* The Accounting Review, *Vol. 56, No. 2, 1981, pp. 404–408.*

2. Calculate the **break-even average demand** M, such that the probability of break-even or better is equal to the specified level of risk p. That is, compute

$$M = BE - z_p \sigma$$

where $P(z > z_p) = p$. Market the new product if $\mu \geq M$.

Suppose a company wants to decide whether to market a new type of ceiling fan. From past experience, the company knows that the number of ceiling fans of this type sold per year follows a normal distribution with a mean of 4,000 and a standard deviation of 500.

Marketing researchers have also determined that the company needs to sell 3,500 units to break even for the year.

a. According to decision rule A, should the company market the new ceiling fans?

b. Use a sketch of the normal distribution to show that if $P(D \geq BE) > .5$, then it must be true that $\mu \geq BE$.

c. Suppose that the minimum level of risk the company is willing to tolerate is $p = .8$. Use decision rule B to arrive at a decision. Show that the two ways of implementing the rule lead to the same decision.

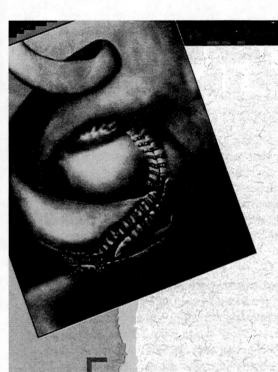

Chapter 7

SAMPLING AND SAMPLING DISTRIBUTIONS

F inancial managers use statistics to aid them in determining when to investigate a high cost or poor performance. The rule utilizes the sample mean and sample standard deviation of some measure of performance (e.g., time to perform a laboratory test). Knowing the mean and standard deviation of a sample, how can we estimate the true mean? And, what is the reliability of this estimate? The behavior of sample statistics, described by their probability distributions, is the topic of Chapter 7. We apply this knowledge to the financial management problem in Case Study 7.2.

■ CONTENTS

7.1 Why the Method of Sampling Is Important

We now return to the objective of statistics—namely, the use of sample information to infer the nature of a population. Predicting your company's annual sales from its sales records of the last 10 years, the annual return on an investment from the results of a number of similar investments, and an evening's winnings at blackjack based on your previous (successful and unsuccessful) treks to the casino are examples of statistical inferences, and each involves an element of uncertainty. In this chapter, we discuss a technique for measuring the uncertainty associated with making inferences.

EXAMPLE 7.1
Representative Samples

Researchers have determined that the time patients spend waiting in physicians' offices plays an important role in an efficiently run practice (*Journal of Business*, Oct. 1977). Suppose an orthodontist is interested in examining the waiting times of his patients over the past year as part of an annual evaluation of his practice. Now, unknown to the orthodontist, suppose the population relative frequency distribution for the waiting time for each of the orthodontist's 2,000 patients last year appears as in Figure 7.1. (We emphasize that this example is for illustration only. In actual practice, the entire population of 2,000 waiting times may not be easily accessible.) Now, assume that a member of his staff provides the orthodontist with the relative frequency distributions of waiting times for each of two samples of 50 patients (Figures 7.2a and 7.2b) selected from the 2,000 patients last year.

Compare the distributions of patient waiting times for the two samples. Which appears to better characterize patient waiting time for the population?

SOLUTION It is clear that the two samples lead to quite different conclusions about the same population from which they were both selected. From Figure 7.2b, we see that 20% of the sampled patients waited in the orthodontist's office at least 50 minutes be-

FIGURE 7.1

Relative Frequency
Distribution of
Waiting Times for
2,000 Patients

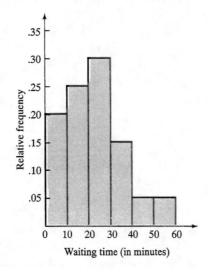

FIGURE 7.2

Relative Frequency
Distribution of
Waiting Times for
Each of Two Samples
of 50 Patients
Selected from 2,000
Patients

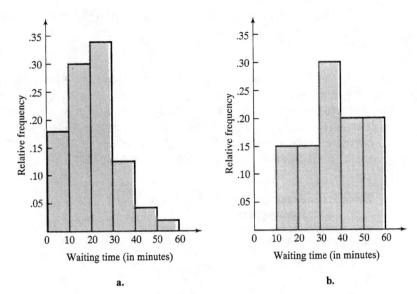

a.

b.

fore being served, whereas from Figure 7.2a, we see that only 2% of the sampled patients had such a long wait. This may be compared to the relative frequency
distribution for the population (shown in Figure 7.1), in which we observe that 5% of
all the patients last year waited at least 50 minutes. In addition, note that none of the
patients in the second sample (Figure 7.2b) had waits of less than 10 minutes, whereas
18% of the patients in the first sample (Figure 7.2a) had waits of less than 10
minutes. This value from the first sample compares favorably with the 20% of the
waiting times for the entire population (Figure 7.1) that were less than 10 minutes.

To rephrase the question posed in the example, we could ask: Which of the two
samples is more representative of, or characteristic of, patient waiting time for all
2,000 of the orthodontist's patients last year? Clearly, the information provided by the
first sample (Figure 7.2a) gives a better picture of the actual population of waiting
times. Its relative frequency distribution is more similar to that for the entire population (Figure 7.1) than is the one provided by the second sample (Figure 7.2b). Thus,
if the orthodontist were to rely on information from the second sample only, he may
have a distorted, or *biased*, impression of the true situation with respect to patient
waiting time last year. ■

How is it possible that two samples from the same population can provide (apparently) contradictory information about the population? The key issue is the method
by which the samples are obtained. Example 7.1 demonstrates that great care must be
taken to select a sample that will give an unbiased picture of the population about
which inferences are to be made. We learned (Chapter 1) that one way to cope with
this problem is to use **random sampling**. You will recall (Definition 1.16) that random sampling is a process that guarantees that every sample of size n has an equal
chance of selection. Thus, with random sampling, the possibility of sample bias is

greatly reduced. In addition, random sampling provides a probabilistic basis for evaluating the reliability of an inference.

EXAMPLE 7.2
Comparing μ to $\bar{x}$

Refer to the 707 sale prices of residential properties described in Appendix A.1, and assume that this data set is our target population. In Example 1.8, we used the computer (SAS) to generate a random sample of $n = 25$ sale prices from Appendix A.1. These 25 sale prices are listed in Table 7.1. Compute the mean of the sample, and compare it to the mean μ of the target population. (Recall, from Chapter 3, that the mean of all 707 residential sale prices is $\mu = \$106,405$.)

Table 7.1 Random Sample of 25 Sale Prices from Appendix A.1

Observation	Property #	Sale Price
1	14	$300,000
2	36	113,500
3	39	127,000
4	58	120,700
5	119	69,900
6	130	68,500
7	151	230,000
8	152	167,000
9	162	256,000
10	222	150,500
11	237	130,000
12	249	99,500
13	262	106,000
14	283	90,000
15	299	85,000
16	344	82,000
17	356	102,900
18	360	100,300
19	393	92,000
20	410	100,700
21	452	310,000
22	483	85,000
23	501	52,200
24	574	76,000
25	588	47,500

SOLUTION A MINITAB printout giving descriptive statistics for the sample of 25 sale prices is displayed in Figure 7.3. The mean of the sample, $\bar{x} = \$126,488$, is shaded on the printout. Note that the sample mean deviates from the true mean, $\mu = \$106,405$, by about $20,000. We can never know for certain how much $\bar{x}$ will deviate from μ. However, because we used random sampling to generate the sample,

FIGURE 7.3

MINITAB Printout for Example 7.2

	N	MEAN	MEDIAN	TRMEAN	STDEV	SEMEAN
SalePric	25	126488	100700	121943	72334	14467

	MIN	MAX	Q1	Q3
SalePric	47500	310000	83500	140250

we can compute the probability of obtaining a sample mean "close" to the population mean. This information allows us to attach a measure of reliability to any inferences made about μ. ■

In the next two sections, we demonstrate how to judge the performance of a sample mean computed from a random sample.

7.2 Sampling Distributions

With inferential statistics, the ultimate goal is to use information from the sample to make an inference about the nature of the population. In many situations, the objective will be to estimate a numerical characteristic of the population, called a **parameter**, using information in the sample. To illustrate, in Example 7.2, we computed $\bar{x} = \$126,488$, the mean sale price for a random sample of $n = 25$ residential properties from Appendix A.1. In other words, we used the sample information to compute a **statistic**—namely, the sample mean $\bar{x}$.

Definition 7.1

A numerical descriptive measure of a population is called a **parameter**.

Definition 7.2

A quantity computed from the observations in a sample is called a **statistic**.

You may have observed that the value of a population parameter (e.g., the mean μ) is constant (although it is usually unknown to us); its value does not vary from sample to sample. However, the value of a sample statistic (e.g., the sample mean, $\bar{x}$) is highly dependent on the particular sample selected. If, in Example 7.2, we had used a different random number generator (e.g., MINITAB or a random number table), we would have obtained a different random sample of 25 observations, and thus a different value of $\bar{x}$.

Since statistics vary from sample to sample, any inferences based on them will necessarily be subject to some uncertainty. How, then, do we judge the reliability of a sample statistic as a tool in making an inference about the corresponding population parameter? Fortunately, the uncertainty of a statistic generally has characteristic properties that are known to us, and that are reflected in its **sampling distribution**. Knowledge of the sampling distribution of a particular statistic provides us with information about its performance over the long run.

Definition 7.3

The **sampling distribution** of a sample statistic (based on n observations) is the relative frequency distribution of the values of the statistic theoretically generated by taking repeated random samples of size n and computing the value of the statistic for each sample.

The notion of a sampling distribution can be illustrated with the data of Appendix A.1. Assume that our interest focuses *only* on the sale prices of the 707 residential properties sold in 1993 in one of the six Tampa (Fla.) neighborhoods. In particular, we wish to estimate the mean sale price of all such properties. Then the target population consists of the 707 observations on sale price described in Appendix A.1. (Although the true value of μ, the mean of these 707 observations, is already known to us, this example will serve to illustrate the concepts.)

EXAMPLE 7.3
Concept of a Sampling Distribution

How could we physically generate the sampling distribution of $\bar{x}$, the mean of a random sample of $n = 5$ observations, from the population of 707 sale price values in Appendix A.1?

SOLUTION The sampling distribution for the statistic $\bar{x}$, based on a random sample of $n = 5$ measurements, would be generated in this manner: Select a random sample of five measurements from the population of 707 observations on sale price in Appendix A.1; compute and record the value of $\bar{x}$ for this sample. Now return these five measurements to the population and repeat the procedure; i.e., draw another random sample of $n = 5$ measurements and record the value of $\bar{x}$ for this sample. Return these measurements and repeat the process. If this sampling procedure could be repeated an infinite number of times, as shown in Figure 7.4 (page 313), the infinite number of values of $\bar{x}$ obtained could be summarized in a relative frequency distribution, called the **sampling distribution of $\bar{x}$**. ■

The task described in Example 7.3, which may seem impractical if not impossible, is not performed in actual practice. Instead, the sampling distribution of a statistic is obtained by applying mathematical theory or computer simulation, as illustrated in the next example.

FIGURE 7.4

Generating the
Theoretical Sampling
Distribution of the
Sample Mean, $\bar{X}$

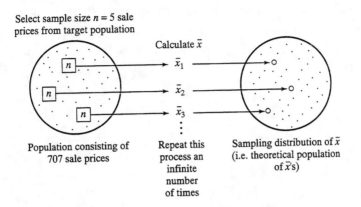

EXAMPLE 7.4	Use computer simulation to find the approximate sampling distribution of $\bar{x}$, the mean
Approximating a Sampling	of a random sample of $n = 5$ observations from the population of 707 sale prices in
Distribution by Computer	Appendix A.1.

SOLUTION We obtained a large number—namely, 100—computer-generated random samples of size $n = 5$ from the target population. The first 10 samples are presented in Table 7.2.

Table 7.2   First 10 Samples of $n = 5$ Sale Prices from Appendix A.1

Sample	Sale Prices (dollars)				
1	157,500	135,900	129,000	83,400	60,000
2	84,700	127,000	61,000	105,000	65,900
3	91,500	84,000	68,000	26,900	24,900
4	74,500	83,000	83,000	49,000	11,500
5	255,000	170,000	63,900	54,000	36,000
6	135,000	130,000	129,000	79,500	84,900
7	159,000	71,500	57,900	82,000	36,900
8	111,900	62,700	68,000	21,500	9,000
9	127,000	42,500	86,200	33,678	12,000
10	163,000	79,000	86,000	89,000	36,000

For example, the first computer-generated sample contained the measurements 157,500, 135,900, 129,000, 83,400, and 60,000. The corresponding value of the sample mean is

$$\bar{x} = \frac{\sum x}{n} = \frac{157,000 + 135,900 + 129,000 + 83,400 + 60,000}{5} = \$113,160$$

For each sample of five observations, the sample mean $\bar{x}$ was computed. The 100 values of $\bar{x}$ are summarized in the SAS relative frequency distribution shown in Figure

7.5. This distribution approximates the sampling distribution of $\bar{x}$ for a sample of size $n = 5$.

FIGURE 7.5

SAS Relative
Frequency
Distribution:
Sampling
Distribution of $\bar{x}$; 100
Random Samples of
$n = 5$ Sale Prices
from Appendix A.1

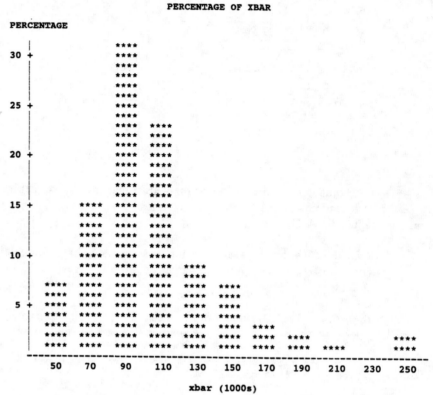

Let us compare the relative frequency distribution for $\bar{x}$ (Figure 7.5) with the relative frequency distribution for the population, shown in Figure 7.6 (page 315). Note that the values of $\bar{x}$ in Figure 7.5 tend to cluster around the population mean, $\mu = \$106,405$. Also, the values of the sample mean are less spread out (i.e., they have less variation) than the population values shown in Figure 7.6. These two observations are borne out by comparing the means and standard deviations of the two sets of observations, Table 7.3.

Table 7.3 Comparison of the Population Distribution and the Approximate Sampling Distribution of $\bar{x}$, Based on 100 Samples of Size $n = 5$

	Mean	*Standard Deviation*
Population of 707 sale prices *(Figure 7.6)*	$\mu = \$106,405$	$\sigma = \$85,414$
100 values of $\bar{x}$ ***based on samples of size*** $n = 5$ *(Figure 7.5)*	$\$106,755$	$\$45,483$

FIGURE 7.6

SAS Relative
Frequency
Distribution of
Population of 707
Sale Prices in
Appendix A.1

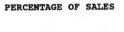

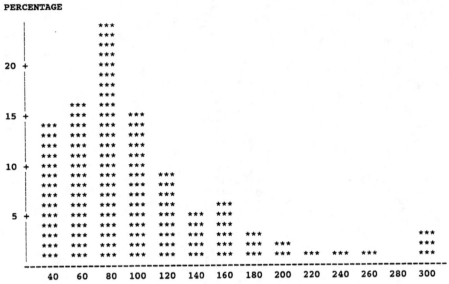

PERCENTAGE OF SALES

PERCENTAGE

Sale Price (thousands) Midpoint

EXAMPLE 7.5
Impact of *n* on Sampling
Distribution of *x̄*

Refer to Example 7.4. Simulate the sampling distribution of $\bar{x}$ for samples of size $n = 25$ from the population of 707 sale-price observations. Compare the result with the sampling distribution of $\bar{x}$ based on samples of size $n = 5$, obtained in Example 7.4.

SOLUTION We obtained 100 computer-generated random samples of size $n = 25$ from the target population. A SAS relative frequency distribution for the 100 corresponding values of $\bar{x}$ is shown in Figure 7.7 (page 316).

It can be seen that, as with the sampling distribution based on samples of size $n = 5$, the values of $\bar{x}$ tend to center about the population mean. However, a visual inspection shows that the variation of the $\bar{x}$ values about their mean in Figure 7.7 is less than the variation in the values of $\bar{x}$ based on samples of size $n = 5$ (Figure 7.5). The mean and standard deviation for these 100 values of $\bar{x}$ based on samples of size $n = 25$ are shown in Table 7.4 (page 316) for comparison with previous results.

From Table 7.4 we observe that, as the sample size increases, there is less variation in the sampling distribution of $\bar{x}$; that is, the values of $\bar{x}$ tend to cluster more closely about the population mean as n gets larger. This intuitively appealing result will be stated formally in the next section.

FIGURE 7.7

SAS Relative Frequency Distribution: Sampling Distribution of $\bar{x}$; 100 Random Samples of Size $n = 25$ Sale Prices from Appendix A.1

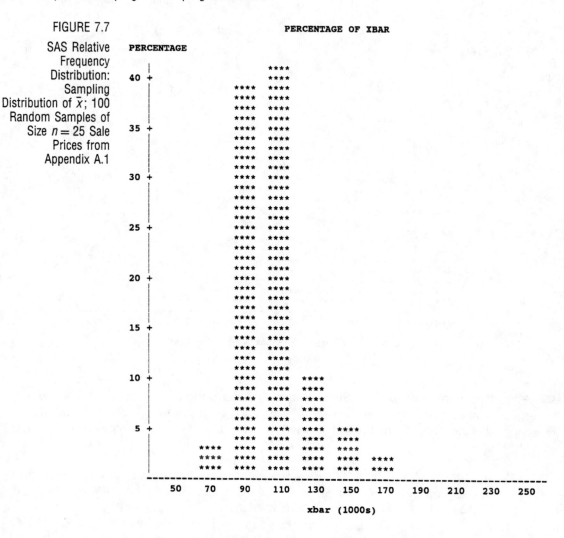

Table 7.4 Comparison of the Population Distribution and the Approximate Sampling Distribution of $\bar{x}$, Based on 100 Samples of Size $n = 25$

	Mean	Standard Deviation
Population of 707 sale prices (Figure 7.6)	$\mu = \$106,405$	$\sigma = \$85,414$
100 values of $\bar{x}$ based on samples of size $n = 5$ (Figure 7.5)	$\$106,755$	$\$45,483$
100 values of $\bar{x}$ based on samples of size $n = 25$ (Figure 7.7)	$\$105,743$	$\$18,812$

EXERCISES

■ Learning the Mechanics

7.1   The table contains 50 random samples of $n = 5$ measurements selected from a population with $\mu = 4.5$ and $\sigma^2 = 8.25$.

Sample	Sample	Sample	Sample
1, 8, 0, 6, 6	6, 7, 0, 4, 3	4, 5, 2, 6, 6	8, 4, 7, 6, 9
2, 1, 7, 2, 9	0, 5, 9, 9, 6	9, 3, 7, 1, 3	6, 9, 4, 4, 2
4, 5, 7, 7, 1	4, 4, 7, 5, 6	1, 9, 6, 9, 2	2, 3, 7, 6, 3
3, 6, 1, 8, 1	6, 6, 5, 5, 6	5, 1, 2, 3, 4	2, 0, 6, 3, 3
9, 8, 6, 2, 9	5, 0, 6, 6, 5	4, 5, 3, 4, 8	1, 9, 0, 3, 2
6, 8, 8, 3, 5	3, 0, 4, 9, 6	5, 6, 7, 8, 2	8, 9, 2, 7, 0
9, 5, 7, 7, 9	3, 0, 7, 4, 1	3, 8, 6, 0, 1	1, 5, 0, 5, 1
7, 6, 4, 4, 7	3, 6, 4, 2, 0	1, 4, 4, 9, 0	7, 8, 7, 7, 6
6, 5, 6, 4, 2	1, 5, 0, 5, 8	7, 7, 9, 8, 1	9, 3, 7, 3, 9
8, 6, 8, 6, 0	4, 6, 2, 6, 2	9, 2, 9, 8, 7	5, 1, 1, 4, 0
1, 6, 0, 0, 9	1, 8, 8, 2, 1	6, 8, 9, 6, 0	2, 5, 7, 7, 9
6, 8, 5, 2, 8	9, 0, 6, 1, 7	3, 4, 6, 7, 0	3, 0, 6, 9, 7
2, 4, 9, 4, 6	3, 7, 3, 4, 3		

a. Calculate $\bar{x}$ for each of the 50 samples.

b. Construct a relative frequency distribution for the 50 sample means. This figure represents an approximation to the sampling distribution of $\bar{x}$ based on samples of size $n = 5$.

c. Compute the mean and standard deviation for the 50 sample means. Locate these values of the relative frequency distribution of part **b**. Note how the sample means cluster about $\mu = 4.5$.

7.2   Refer to Exercise 7.1. Combine pairs of samples (moving down the columns of the table) to obtain 25 samples of $n = 10$ measurements.

a. Calculate $\bar{x}$ for each of the 25 samples.

b. Construct a relative frequency distribution for the 25 sample means. This figure represents an approximation to the sampling distribution of $\bar{x}$ based on samples of size $n = 10$. Compare with the figure constructed in Exercise 7.1.

c. Compute the mean and standard deviation for the 25 sample means and locate them on the relative frequency distribution. Note how the sample means cluster about $\mu = 4.5$.

d. Compare the standard deviations of the two sampling distributions in Exercises 7.1 and 7.2. Which sampling distribution has less variation?

■ Applying the Concepts

7.3   Suppose we want to assess the talents of residential property appraisers in Tampa, Florida, in 1993. One method would be to consider the population of ratios of sale price to total appraised value for all residential properties sold in six neighborhoods during 1993. The data are described in Appendix A.1.

a. Which parameter of the target population may be of particular interest? What value would you expect this parameter to assume? [*Hint:* Consider the cases where the sale price for a piece of property (i) is equal to the total appraised value, (ii) exceeds the total appraised value, and (iii) is less than the total appraised value.]

b. Use Table 1 of Appendix B or a computer to generate 50 random samples of size $n = 10$ from the target population. (Alternatively, each class member could generate several random samples, and the results for the entire class could be pooled.) Construct the approximate sampling distribution of the sample mean, $\bar{x}$. Compare with the population relative frequency distribution shown in Figure 7.6. [*Note:* The data of Appendix A.1 are available on a $3\frac{1}{2}''$ diskette from the publisher.]

7.4 Refer to Exercise 7.3. We have reason to expect that the population relative frequency distribution for ratio of sale price to total appraised value would be markedly skewed to the right because no such value can be less than 0, most values would presumably be near 1, and, occasionally, very large values would be observed. Now, recalling from Section 3.4 that the mean is sensitive to very large observations, one could argue that the population median ratio would provide more information than would the mean about the abilities of property appraisers.

Suppose an investigator has proposed two different statistics (call them *A* and *B*) for estimating the population median. In an attempt to judge which of the statistics is more suitable, you simulated the approximate sampling distributions for each of the statistics, based on random samples of size $n = 10$, with the results shown in the figures. Comment on the two sampling distributions. Which of the statistics, *A* or *B*, would you recommend for use? (In the next section, we discuss desirable properties of a sampling distribution.)

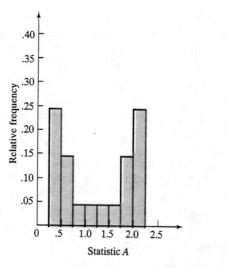
Statistic *A*

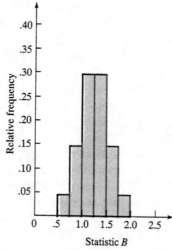
Statistic *B*

7.5 Use computer simulation or Table 1 in Appendix B to obtain 30 random samples of size $n = 5$ from the population of 186 per-member, per-month cost of HMO physicians described in Appendix A.3. [*Note:* The data are available on a $3\frac{1}{2}''$ diskette from the publisher.] Again, each class member could generate several random samples and the results could be pooled.

    a. Calculate $\bar{x}$ for each of the 30 samples. Construct a relative frequency distribution for the 30 sample means.

    b. Compute the average of the 30 sample means.

    c. Compute the standard deviation of the 30 sample means.

    d. Locate the average of the 30 sample means, computed in part **b**, on the relative frequency distribution. This value could be used as an estimate for μ, the mean of the entire population of 186 physician costs.

7.6   Repeat parts **a**, **b**, **c**, and **d** of Exercise 7.5, but use random samples of size $n = 10$. Compare the relative frequency distribution with that of Exercise 7.5a. Do the values of $\bar{x}$ generated from samples of size $n = 10$ tend to cluster more closely about μ?

7.7   Generate the sampling distribution of $\bar{x}$, the mean of a random sample of $n = 20$ observations from the population of tar contents in cigarettes described in Appendix A.4. [*Note:* The data are available on a $3\frac{1}{2}''$ diskette from the publisher.]

7.3 The Sampling Distribution of $\bar{X}$; the Central Limit Theorem

Estimating the mean sale price for all residential properties sold in a certain city, or the average increase in value over the previous year for parcels of land in a certain development, or the mean value per acre of property zoned for industrial use in a particular area are all examples of practical problems in which the goal is to make an inference about the mean, μ, of some target population. In previous sections, we have indicated that the sample mean $\bar{x}$ is often used as a tool for making an inference about the corresponding population parameter μ, and we have shown how to approximate its sampling distribution. The following theorem, of fundamental importance in statistics, provides information about the actual sampling distribution of $\bar{x}$.

> *The Central Limit Theorem*
>
> If the sample size is sufficiently large, then the mean $\bar{x}$ of a random sample from a population has a sampling distribution that is approximately normal, *regardless of the shape of the relative frequency distribution of the target population*. As the sample size increases, the better will be the normal approximation to the sampling distribution.

The sampling distribution of $\bar{x}$, in addition to being approximately normal for large n, has other known characteristics that are summarized in the next box.

> *Properties of the Sampling Distribution of* $\bar{x}$
>
> If $\bar{x}$ is the mean of a random sample of size n from a population with mean μ and standard deviation σ, then:
>
>   *(continued)*

1. The sampling distribution of $\bar{x}$ has a mean equal to the mean of the population from which the sample was selected. That is, if we let $\mu_{\bar{x}}$ denote the mean of the sampling distribution of $\bar{x}$, then

$$\mu_{\bar{x}} = \mu$$

2. The sampling distribution of $\bar{x}$ has a standard deviation equal to the standard deviation of the population from which the sample was selected, divided by the square root of the sample size. That is, if we let $\sigma_{\bar{x}}$ denote the standard deviation of the sampling distribution of $\bar{x}$ (also called the **standard error of $\bar{x}$**), then

$$\sigma_{\bar{x}} = \frac{\sigma}{\sqrt{n}}$$

EXAMPLE 7.6
Properties of the Sampling Distribution of $\bar{x}$

Show that the empirical evidence obtained in Examples 7.4 and 7.5 supports the central limit theorem and the two properties of the sampling distribution of $\bar{x}$. Recall that, in Examples 7.4 and 7.5, we obtained repeated random samples of sizes $n = 5$ and $n = 25$ from the population of sale prices described in Appendix A.1. For this target population, we know the values of the parameters μ and σ:

Population mean: $\mu = \$106,405$

Population standard deviation: $\sigma = \$85,414$

SOLUTION   In Figures 7.5 and 7.7, we noted that the values of $\bar{x}$ tend to cluster about the population mean, $\mu = \$106,405$. This is guaranteed by property 1, which implies that, in the long run, the average of *all* values of $\bar{x}$ that would be generated in infinite repeated sampling would be equal to μ.

We also observed, from Table 7.4, that the standard deviation of the sampling distribution of $\bar{x}$, called the **standard error of $\bar{x}$**, decreases as the sample size increases from $n = 5$ to $n = 25$. Property 2 quantifies the decrease and relates it to the sample size. As an example, note that for our approximate (simulated) sampling distribution based on samples of size $n = 5$, we obtained a standard deviation of \$45,483, whereas property 2 tells us that, for the actual sampling distribution of $\bar{x}$, the standard deviation is equal to

$$\sigma_{\bar{x}} = \frac{\sigma}{\sqrt{n}} = \frac{\$85,414}{\sqrt{5}} = \$38,198$$

Similarly, for samples of size $n = 25$, the sampling distribution of $\bar{x}$ actually has a standard deviation of

$$\sigma_{\bar{x}} = \frac{\sigma}{\sqrt{n}} = \frac{\$85,414}{\sqrt{25}} = \$17,083$$

The value we obtained by simulation was $18,812.

Finally, for sufficiently large samples, the central limit theorem guarantees an approximately normal distribution for $\bar{x}$, regardless of the shape of the original population. In our examples, the population from which the samples were selected is seen in Figure 7.6 to be highly skewed to the right. Note from Figures 7.5 and 7.7 that, although the sampling distribution of $\bar{x}$ tends to be mound-shaped in each case, the normal approximation improves when the sample size is increased from $n = 5$ (Figure 7.5) to $n = 25$ (Figure 7.7). ■

EXAMPLE 7.7
Illustration of Central Limit Theorem

Three population relative frequency distributions that provide reasonably accurate probability models for certain types of business phenomena are the **normal distribution** (which we discussed in Section 6.2), the **uniform distribution** (optional Section 6.5), and the **exponential distribution** (optional Section 6.6). Their vastly different shapes are shown in Figure 7.8.* Simulate the sampling distributions of $\bar{x}$ by drawing 1,000 samples of $n = 5$ observations from populations that have the relative frequency distributions shown in Figure 7.8. Repeat the procedure for $n = 15$, 25, 50, and 100. Does the central limit theorem appear to provide adequate information about the shapes of the sampling distribution of $\bar{x}$?

SOLUTION For each population and each sample size n, we obtained 1,000 computer-generated random samples. The SPSS relative frequency distributions for the 1,000 values of $\bar{x}$ obtained for samples of size $n = 5$, 15, 25, 50, and 100 from the uniform distribution are displayed in Figure 7.9 (pages 322–323). Similarly, the simulated (SPSS) sampling distributions of $\bar{x}$ for samples from the normal and exponential distributions are shown in Figures 7.10 and 7.11 (pages 323–326), respectively.

FIGURE 7.8

Three Population Relative Frequency Distributions

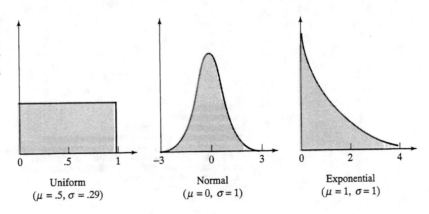

Uniform
($\mu = .5$, $\sigma = .29$)

Normal
($\mu = 0$, $\sigma = 1$)

Exponential
($\mu = 1$, $\sigma = 1$)

---

*For those who have not covered optional Sections 6.5 and 6.6, it is not necessary to go back and read this material. Simply note the shape of the distributions in Figure 7.8.

FIGURE 7.9

Sampling
Distributions of $\overline{x}$:
Uniform Population

a. $n = 5$

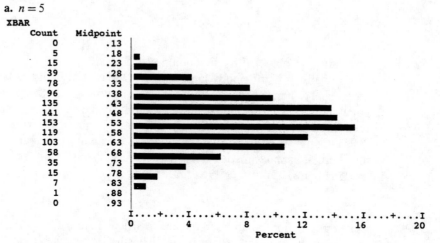

b. $n = 15$

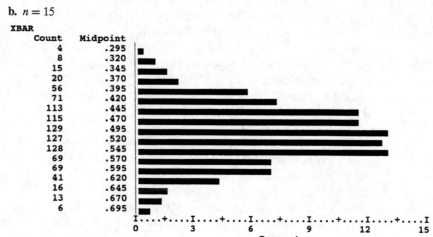

c. $n = 25$

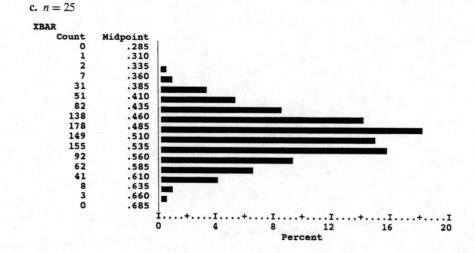

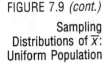

FIGURE 7.9 *(cont.)*

Sampling
Distributions of x̄:
Uniform Population

d. $n = 50$

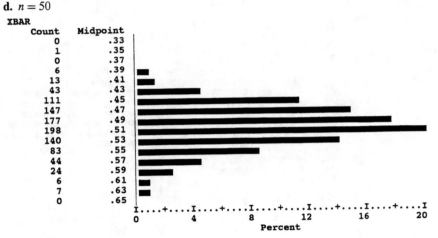

XBAR Count	Midpoint
0	.33
1	.35
0	.37
6	.39
13	.41
43	.43
111	.45
147	.47
177	.49
198	.51
140	.53
83	.55
44	.57
24	.59
6	.61
7	.63
0	.65

Percent (0, 4, 8, 12, 16, 20)

e. $n = 100$

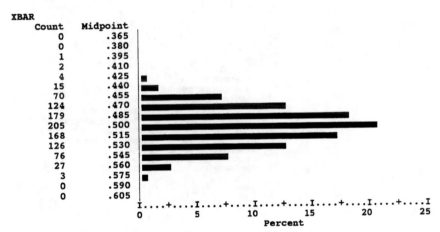

XBAR Count	Midpoint
0	.365
0	.380
1	.395
2	.410
4	.425
15	.440
70	.455
124	.470
179	.485
205	.500
168	.515
126	.530
76	.545
27	.560
3	.575
0	.590
0	.605

Percent (0, 5, 10, 15, 20, 25)

FIGURE 7.10

Sampling
Distributions of x̄:
Normal Population

a. $n = 5$

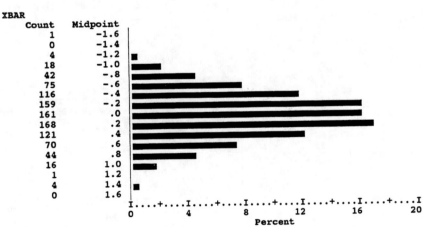

XBAR Count	Midpoint
1	-1.6
0	-1.4
4	-1.2
18	-1.0
42	-.8
75	-.6
116	-.4
159	-.2
161	.0
168	.2
121	.4
70	.6
44	.8
16	1.0
1	1.2
4	1.4
0	1.6

Percent (0, 4, 8, 12, 16, 20)

FIGURE 7.10 *(cont.)*

Sampling
Distributions of $\overline{x}$:
Normal Population

b. $n = 15$

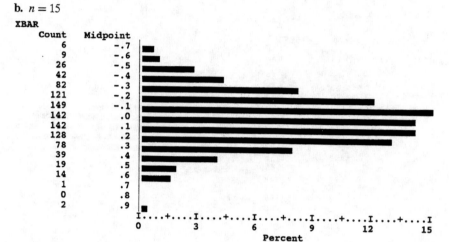

c. $n = 25$

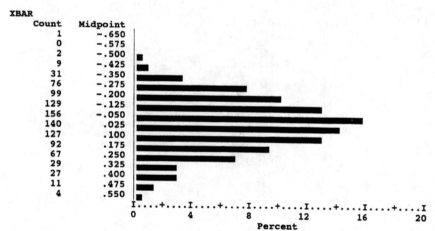

d. $n = 50$

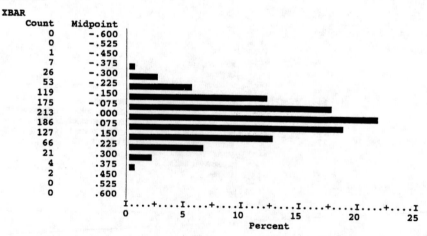

FIGURE 7.10 *(cont.)*   **e.** $n = 100$

Sampling
Distributions of $\overline{x}$:
Normal Population

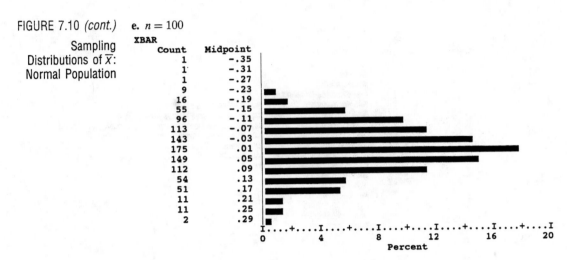

FIGURE 7.11   **a.** $n = 5$

Sampling
Distributions of $\overline{x}$:
Exponential
Population

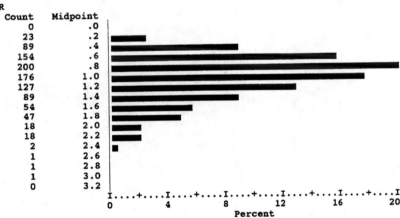

b. $n = 15$

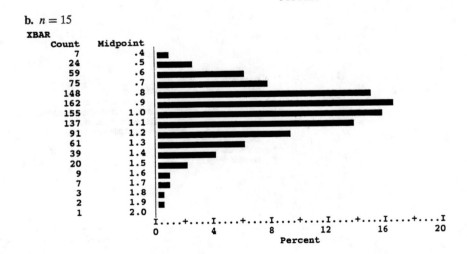

FIGURE 7.11 *(cont.)*

Sampling
Distributions of $\overline{x}$:
Exponential
Population

c. $n = 25$

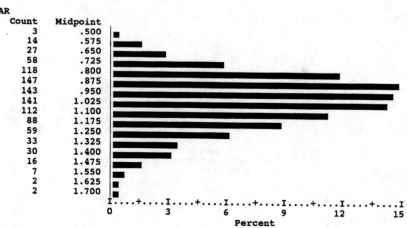

d. $n = 50$

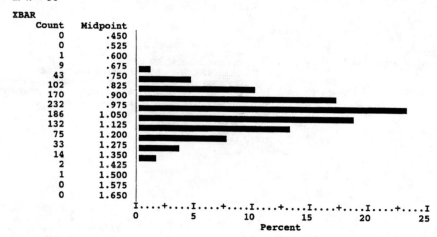

e. $n = 100$

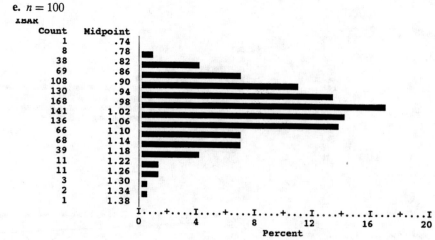

Examine each of the figures and three patterns emerge. First, you can see that the values of $\bar{x}$ tend to cluster about the mean of the probability distribution from which the samples were taken. Second, as n increases, there is less variation in the sampling distribution. Third, as the sample size n increases, the shape of the sampling distribution of $\bar{x}$ tends toward the shape of the normal distribution (symmetric and mound-shaped), regardless of the shape of the relative frequency distribution of the sampled population shown in Figure 7.8.

The results of our computer simulations thus offer visual verification of the central limit theorem and the other properties of the sampling distribution of $\bar{x}$ given in the box. (It is interesting to note that when sampling from a normal population, the sampling distribution of $\bar{x}$ is approximately normal for all values of n simulated in this example. In fact, it can be shown theoretically that when the relative frequency distribution of the target population is normal, the sample mean will have a normal sampling distribution, regardless of the sample size.)   ■

EXAMPLE 7.8
Application of Concepts

Engineers responsible for the design and maintenance of aircraft pavements traditionally use pavement-quality concrete. A study was conducted at Luton Airport (United Kingdom) to assess the suitability of concrete blocks as a surface for aircraft pavements (*Proceedings of the Institute of Civil Engineers*, Apr. 1986). The original pavement-quality concrete of the western end of the runway was overlaid with 80-mm-thick concrete blocks and a series of plate-bearing tests was carried out to determine the load classification number (LCN)—a measure of breaking strength—of the surface. Let $\bar{x}$ represent the mean LCN of a sample of 25 concrete block sections on the western end of the runway.

a. Prior to resurfacing, the mean LCN of the original pavement-quality concrete of the western end of the runway was known to be $\mu = 60$ and the standard deviation was $\sigma = 10$. If the mean strength of the new concrete block surface is no different from that of the original surface, describe the sampling distribution of $\bar{x}$.

b. If the mean strength of the new concrete block surface is no different from that of the original surface, find the probability that $\bar{x}$, the sample mean LCN of the 25 concrete block sections, exceeds 65.

c. The plate-bearing tests on the new concrete block surface resulted in $\bar{x} = 73$. Based on this result, what can you infer about the true mean LCN of the new surface?

SOLUTION

a. Although we have no information about the shape of the relative frequency distribution of the breaking strengths (LCNs) for sections of the new surface, we can apply the central limit theorem to conclude that the sampling distribution of $\bar{x}$, the mean LCN of the sample, is approximately normally distributed. In addition, if $\mu = 60$ and $\sigma = 10$, the mean $\mu_{\bar{x}}$, and the standard deviation, $\sigma_{\bar{x}}$, of the sampling distribution are given by

$$\mu_{\bar{x}} = \mu = 60$$

and

$$\sigma_{\bar{x}} = \frac{\sigma}{\sqrt{n}} = \frac{10}{\sqrt{25}} = 2$$

b. If the two surfaces are of equal strength, then $P(\bar{x} \geq 65)$, the probability of observing a mean LCN of 65 or more in the sample of 25 concrete block sections, is equal to the shaded area shown in Figure 7.12.

Since the sampling distribution is approximately normal, with mean and standard deviation as obtained in part **a**, we can compute the desired area by obtaining the z score for $\bar{x} = 65$:

$$z = \frac{\bar{x} - \mu_{\bar{x}}}{\sigma_{\bar{x}}} = \frac{65 - 60}{2} = 2.50$$

Thus, $P(\bar{x} \geq 65) = P(z \geq 2.50)$, and this probability (area) may be found using Table 5 of Appendix B and the methods of Chapter 6:

$$P(\bar{x} \geq 65) = P(z \geq 2.50)$$

$$= .5 - A \quad \text{(see Figure 7.12)}$$

$$= .5 - .4938 = .0062$$

c. If there is no difference between the true mean strengths of the new and original surfaces (i.e., $\mu = 60$ for both surfaces), the probability that we would obtain a sample mean LCN for concrete block of 65 or greater is only .0062. Observing $\bar{x} = 73$ provides strong evidence that the true mean breaking strength of the new surface exceeds $\mu = 60$. Our reasoning stems from the rare event philosophy

FIGURE 7.12

Sampling
Distributions of $\overline{x}$ in
Example 7.8

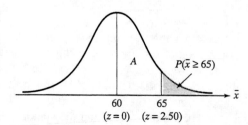

of Chapter 4, which states that such a large sample mean ($\bar{x} = 73$) is very unlikely to occur if $\mu = 60$. ■

In practical terms, the central limit theorem and the two properties of the sampling distribution of $\bar{x}$ assure us that the sample mean $\bar{x}$ is a reasonable statistic to use in making inferences about the population mean μ, and they allow us to compute a measure of the reliability of inferences made about μ. (This topic will be treated more thoroughly in Chapter 8.)

As was noted earlier, we will not be required to obtain sampling distributions by simulation or by mathematical arguments. Rather, for all the statistics to be used in this course, the sampling distribution and its properties (which are a matter of record) will be presented as the need arises.

In addition to simple random sampling, other, more sophisticated sampling procedures have been developed. An introduction to this particular area of statistics, known as **survey sampling,** is the topic of optional Chapter 9.

EXERCISES

■ *Learning the Mechanics*

7.8   Suppose a random sample of n measurements is selected from a population with mean $\mu = 60$ and variance $\sigma^2 = 100$. For each of the following values of n, give the mean and standard deviation of the sampling distribution of the sample mean, $\bar{x}$:
   a. $n = 10$ **b.** $n = 25$ **c.** $n = 50$ **d.** $n = 75$
   e. $n = 100$ **f.** $n = 500$ **g.** $n = 1,000$

7.9   Suppose a random sample of $n = 100$ measurements is selected from a population with mean μ and standard deviation σ. For each of the following values of μ and σ, give the values of $\mu_{\bar{x}}$ and $\sigma_{\bar{x}}$:
   a. $\mu = 10$, $\sigma = 20$ **b.** $\mu = 20$, $\sigma = 10$
   c. $\mu = 50$, $\sigma = 300$ **d.** $\mu = 100$, $\sigma = 200$

7.10   A random sample of $n = 225$ observations is selected from a population with $\mu = 70$ and $\sigma = 30$. Calculate each of the following probabilities:
   a. $P(\bar{x} > 72.5)$ **b.** $P(\bar{x} < 73.6)$ **c.** $P(69.1 < \bar{x} < 74.0)$ **d.** $P(\bar{x} < 65.5)$

7.11   A random sample of $n = 50$ observations is selected from a population with $\mu = 21$ and $\sigma = 6$. Compute each of the following probabilities:
   a. $P(\bar{x} < 23.1)$ **b.** $P(\bar{x} > 21.7)$ **c.** $P(22.8 < \bar{x} < 23.6)$

■ *Applying the Concepts*

7.12   The National Institute for Occupational Safety and Health (NIOSH) recently completed a study to evaluate the level of exposure of workers to the chemical dioxin, 2,3,7,8-TCDD. The distribution of TCDD levels in parts per trillion (ppt) in production workers at a Newark, New Jersey, chemical plant had a mean of 293 ppt and a standard deviation of 847 ppt (*Chemosphere*, Vol. 20, 1990). A graph of the distribution is shown here.

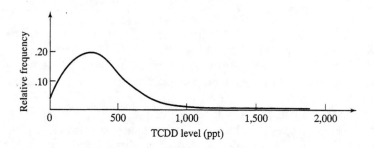

In a random sample of $n = 50$ workers selected at the New Jersey plant, let $\bar{x}$ represent the sample mean TCDD level.
a. Find the mean and standard deviation of the sampling distribution of $\bar{x}$.
b. Draw a sketch of the sampling distribution of $\bar{x}$. Locate the mean on the graph.
c. Find the probability that $\bar{x}$ exceeds 550 ppt.

7.13 Many firms are using research and development limited partnerships (R&D LPs) as innovative fundraising vehicles. According to the Securities and Exchange Commission (SEC), funds raised through an R&D LP should be reported as debt on the firm's balance sheet; many firms, however, violate this policy. To gain more insight into this problem, the *Accounting Review* (Jan. 1991) investigated the financial statements of firms with R&D LPs. The mean and standard deviation of the population, consisting of present values of all R&D LPs, were estimated to be $\mu = \$28.5$ million and $\sigma = \$51.8$ million. Consider a random sample of $n = 75$ R&D LPs selected from the population.
a. Describe the sampling distribution of $\bar{x}$, the mean present value of the sample of 75 R&D LPs.
b. What is the probability that $\bar{x}$ falls between $25.2 and $36.6 million?
c. What is the probability that $\bar{x}$ is less than $30 million?

7.14 "Cost estimation" is the term used to describe the process by which engineers estimate the cost of work contracts (e.g., road construction, building construction) that are to be awarded to the lowest bidder. The engineers' estimate is the baseline against which the low (winning) bid is compared. A study investigated the factors that affect the accuracy of engineers' estimates (*Cost Engineering*, Oct. 1988), where accuracy is measured as the percentage difference between the low bid and the engineers' estimate. One of the most important factors is number of bidders—the more bidders on the contract, the more likely the engineers are to overestimate the cost. For building contracts with five bidders, the mean percentage error was −7.02 and the standard deviation was 24.66. Consider a sample of 50 building contracts, each with 5 bidders.
a. Describe the sampling distribution of $\bar{x}$, the mean percentage difference between the low bid and the engineers' estimate, for the 50 contracts.
b. Find $P(\bar{x} < 0)$. (This is the probability of an overestimate.)
c. Suppose you observe $\bar{x} = -17.83$ for a sample of 50 building contracts. Based on the information above, are all these contracts likely to have five bidders? Explain.

7.15 The rash of recent incidents of unethical business tactics has organizations searching for ways to discourage unethical behavior. But how much will a company's stated concern for ethical conduct influence the behavior of its decision makers? To answer this question, researchers at Marquette University presented MBA students (believed to be representative of entry-level managers) with decision-making situations that were clearly unethical in nature (*Journal of Business Ethics*, Vol. 6, 1987). The subjects' decisions were then rated on a scale of 1 ("definitely unethical") to 5 ("definitely ethical"). When no references to ethical concern by the "company" were explicitly stated, the ratings had a mean of 3.00 and a standard deviation of 1.03. Assume that these values represent the population mean and standard deviation, respectively, under the condition "no reference to ethical concern."

  a. Suppose we present a random sample of 30 entry-level managers with a similar situation and record the ratings of each. Find the probability that $\bar{x}$, the sample mean rating, is greater than 3.40.

  b. Refer to part **a**. Prior to making their decisions, the 30 entry-level managers were all read a statement from the president of the "company" concerning the company's code of business ethics. The code advocates socially responsible behavior by all employees. The researchers theorize that the population mean rating of the managers under this condition will be larger than for the "no reference to ethical concern" condition. (A higher mean indicates a more ethical response.) If the sample mean, $\bar{x}$, is 3.55, what can you infer about the population mean under the "stated concern" condition? [*Hint:* Use your answer to part **a**.]

7.16 Studies by neuroscientists at the Massachusetts Institute of Technology (MIT) reveal that melatonin, which is secreted by the pineal gland in the brain, functions naturally as a sleep-inducing hormone (*Tampa Tribune*, Mar. 1, 1994). After male volunteers were given various doses of melatonin or placebos, they were placed in a dark room at midday and told to close their eyes and fall asleep on demand. Of interest to the MIT researchers is the time x (in minutes) required for each volunteer to fall asleep. With the placebo (i.e., no hormone), the researchers found that the mean time to fall asleep was 15 minutes. Assume that with the placebo treatment $\mu = 15$ and $\sigma = 5$.

  a. Consider a random sample of $n = 20$ men who are given the sleep-inducing hormone, melatonin. Let $\bar{x}$ represent the mean time to fall asleep for this sample. If the hormone is *not* effective in inducing sleep, describe the sampling distribution of $\bar{x}$.

  b. Refer to part **a**. Find $P(\bar{x} \leq 6)$.

  c. In the actual study, the mean time to fall asleep for the 20 volunteers was $\bar{x} = 5$. Use this result to make an inference about the true value of μ for those taking the melatonin.

7.17 Research conducted by a tobacco company indicates that the relative frequency distribution of the tar content of low-tar cigarettes has a mean, μ, equal to 3.9 milligrams of tar per cigarette and a standard deviation, σ, equal to 1.0 milligram. Suppose a sample of 20 low-tar cigarettes is randomly selected from the population and the tar content is measured in each.

  a. Assuming that the tobacco company's claim is true, find the probability that the mean tar content of the sample is greater than 4.15 milligrams—that is, compute $P(\bar{x} > 4.15)$.

  b. Use the first sample of 20 measurements generated in Exercise 7.7 to compute the sample mean tar content, $\bar{x}$.

  c. Based on the probability computed in part **a** and the result of part **b**, make an inference about the true value of μ stated by the tobacco company.

7.18 By definition, an entrepreneur is "one who undertakes to start and conduct an enterprise or business, assuming full control and risks" (Funk and Wagnall's *Standard Dictionary*). Thus, a distinguishing characteristic of entrepreneurs is their propensity for taking risks. R. H. Brockhaus used a choice dilemma questionnaire (CDQ) to measure the risk-taking propensities of successful entrepreneurs (*Academy of Management Journal*, Sept. 1980). He found that the CDQ scores of entrepreneurs had a mean of 71 and a standard deviation of 12. (Lower scores are associated with a greater propensity for taking risks.) Let $\bar{x}$ be the mean CDQ score for a random sample of $n = 50$ entrepreneurs.

a. Describe the sampling distribution of $\bar{x}$.

b. Find $P(69 \leq \bar{x} \leq 72)$.

c. Find $P(\bar{x} \leq 67)$.

d. Would you expect to observe a sample mean CDQ score of 67 or lower? Explain.

SUMMARY

The objective of most statistical investigations is to make an inference about a *population parameter*. Since we often base inferences upon information contained in a *sample* from the target population, it is essential that the sample be properly selected. We described a procedure for obtaining a *random sample* using a table of random numbers or a computer.

After the sample has been selected, we compute a *statistic* that contains information about the target parameter. The *sampling distribution* of the statistic characterizes the relative frequency distribution of values of the statistic over an infinitely large number of samples.

The *central limit theorem* provides information about the sampling distribution of the sample mean, $\bar{x}$. In particular, if you have used random sampling, the sampling distribution of $\bar{x}$ will be approximately normal if the sample size is sufficiently large.

KEY TERMS

Biased	Parameter	Sample
Central limit theorem	Population	Sampling distribution
Computer simulation	Random sample	Statistic

KEY FORMULAS

Sampling distribution of $\bar{x}$:

Mean: $\mu_{\bar{x}} = \mu$

Standard deviation: $\sigma_{\bar{x}} = \dfrac{\sigma}{\sqrt{n}}$

SUPPLEMENTARY EXERCISES

7.19 Let $\bar{x}_{25}$ represent the mean of a random sample of size 25 obtained from a population with mean $\mu = 17$ and standard deviation $\sigma = 10$. Similarly, let $\bar{x}_{100}$ represent the mean of a random sample of size 100 selected from the same population.

a. Describe the sampling distribution of $\bar{x}_{25}$.

b. Describe the sampling distribution of $\bar{x}_{100}$.

c. Which of the probabilities, $P(15 < \bar{x}_{25} < 19)$ or $P(15 < \bar{x}_{100} < 19)$, would you expect to be the larger?

d. Calculate the two probabilities in part **c**. Was your answer to part **c** correct?

7.20 The manufacturer of a new instant-picture camera claims that its product has "the world's fastest-developing color film by far." Extensive laboratory testing has shown that the relative frequency distribution for the time it takes the new instant camera to begin to reveal the image after shooting has a mean of 9.8 seconds and a standard deviation of .55 second. Suppose 50 of these cameras are randomly selected from the production line and tested. The time until the image is first revealed, x, is recorded for each.

a. Describe the sampling distribution of $\bar{x}$, the mean time it takes the sample of 50 cameras to begin to reveal the image.

b. Find the probability that the mean time until the image is first revealed for the 50 sampled cameras is greater than 9.70 seconds.

c. If the mean and standard deviation of the population relative frequency distribution for the times until the cameras begin to reveal the image are correct, would you expect to observe a value of $\bar{x}$ less than 9.55 seconds? Explain.

d. Refer to part **a**. Describe the changes in the sampling distribution of $\bar{x}$ if the sample size were decreased from $n = 50$ to $n = 20$.

e. Repeat part **d** if the sample size were increased from $n = 50$ to $n = 100$.

7.21 *Flextime* is a term used to describe formalized flexible working hours on the job. Many managers believe that flextime reduces worker tardiness, absenteeism, and turnover, and increases job satisfaction and performance. In one study conducted by B. F. Harvey and F. Luthans, it was found that a sample of $n = 27$ flextime workers at a state human service agency had a mean job satisfaction rating of $\bar{x} = 35.33$ (*Michigan State University Business Topics*, Summer 1979). Assume that the distribution of job satisfaction ratings of all flextime workers has a population mean of $\mu = 35$ and a standard deviation of $\sigma = 10$.

a. Find $P(\bar{x} \geq 35.33)$.

b. Find $P(\bar{x} \leq 28.71)$.

c. Does a sample mean of $\bar{x} = 35.33$ represent a rare event? Explain.

d. Does a sample mean of $\bar{x} = 28.71$ represent a rare event? Explain.

e. The value $\bar{x} = 28.71$ actually represents the sample mean job satisfaction rating of workers on a fixed schedule. Use your answer to part **d** to make an inference about the true population mean satisfaction rating of workers on a fixed schedule.

7.22 The U.S. Army Engineering and Housing Support Center recently sponsored a study of the reliability, availability, and maintainability (RAM) characteristics of small diesel and gas-powered systems at commercial and military facilities (*IEEE Transactions on Industry Applications*, July/August, 1990). The study revealed that the time, x, to perform corrective maintenance on continuous diesel auxiliary systems has an approximate exponential distribution with an estimated mean of 1,700 hours.

    a. Assuming $\mu = 1,700$, find the probability that the mean time to perform corrective maintenance for a sample of 70 continuous diesel auxiliary systems exceeds 2,500 hours.

    b. If you observe $\bar{x} > 2,500$, what inference would you make about the value of μ?

7.23 As part of industrial quality control programs, it is common practice to monitor the quality characteristics of a product. For example, the amount of alkali in soap might be monitored by randomly selecting from the production process and analyzing $n = 30$ test quantities twice each day. If the sample mean $\bar{x}$ falls within specified control limits, the process is deemed to be in control. If $\bar{x}$ is outside the limits, the monitor flashes a warning signal and suggests that something is wrong with the process. Suppose the lower and upper control limits are located, respectively, $3\sigma_{\bar{x}}$ below and above μ, the true mean amount of alkali in the soap.

    a. For the soap process, experience has shown that $\mu = 2\%$ and $\sigma = 1\%$. Specify the lower and upper control limits for the process. [*Hint:* Calculate $\mu - 3\sigma_{\bar{x}}$ and $\mu + 3\sigma_{\bar{x}}$.]

    b. If the process is in control, what is the probability that $\bar{x}$ falls outside the control limits? Use the fact that the probability that $\bar{x}$ falls outside the control limits is given by

$$1 - P(\text{Process is in control}) = 1 - P(\mu - 3\sigma_{\bar{x}} < \bar{x} < \mu + 3\sigma_{\bar{x}})$$

7.24 A telephone company has determined that during nonholidays the number of phone calls that pass through the main branch office each hour has a relative frequency distribution with a mean μ of 80,000 and a standard deviation σ of 35,000.

    a. Describe the shape of the sampling distribution of $\bar{x}$, the mean number of incoming phone calls per hour for a random sample of 60 nonholiday hours.

    b. What is the mean of the sampling distribution in part **a**?

    c. What is the standard deviation of the sampling distribution in part **a**?

    d. Find the probability that $\bar{x}$, the mean number of incoming phone calls per hour for a random sample of 60 nonholiday hours, will be larger than 91,970.

    e. Suppose the telephone company wishes to determine whether the true mean number of incoming calls per hour during holidays is the same as for nonholidays. To accomplish this, the company randomly selects 60 hours during a holiday period, monitors the incoming phone calls each hour, and computes $\bar{x}$, the sample mean number of incoming phone calls. If the sample mean is computed to be $\bar{x} = 91,970$ calls per hour, do you believe that the true mean for holidays is $\mu = 80,000$ (the same as for nonholidays)? Assume that the standard deviation of the number of incoming calls per hour for holidays is 35,000.

7.25 A manufacturer of photocopy machines buys back many of its photocopiers from businesses that are clearing their old inventory. Thus, the depreciation time of the photocopiers—i.e., the time until the resale value of the photocopiers diminishes—is of importance to the company. Suppose that, unknown to the company, the depreciation time of its copy machines has a relative frequency distribution with a true mean of 45 months and a standard deviation of 10 months.

    a. What is the probability that a sample of 25 photocopiers sold to various businesses will have a mean depreciation time between 40 and 44 months?

    b. What is the probability that the sample mean will be less than 42 months?

    c. Suppose the sample represents the depreciation times of 25 photocopiers sold to businesses during a period when the U.S. economy was in a deep recession. Why might the sample information be biased?

7.26 One of the monitoring methods used by the Environmental Protection Agency (EPA) to determine whether sewage treatment plants are conforming to standards is to take 36 1-liter specimens from the plant's discharge during the period of investigation. Chemical methods are applied to determine the percentage of sewage in each specimen. If the sample data provide evidence to indicate that the true mean percentage of sewage exceeds a limit set by the EPA, the treatment plant must undergo mandatory repair and retooling. One particular plant, at which the mean sewage discharge limit has been set at 15%, is suspected of being in violation of the EPA standard.

a. Unknown to the EPA, the relative frequency distribution of sewage percentages in 1-liter specimens at the plant in question has a mean, μ, of 15.7% and a standard deviation, σ, of 2.0%. Thus, the plant is in violation of the EPA standard. What is the probability that the EPA will obtain a sample of 36 1-liter specimens with a mean sewage percentage less than 15%, even though the plant is violating the sewage discharge limit?

b. Suppose the EPA computes $\bar{x} = 14.95\%$. Does this result lead you to believe that the sample of 36 1-liter specimens obtained by the EPA was not random, but biased in favor of the sewage treatment plant? Explain. [*Hint:* Use your answer to part **a.**]

7.27 This year a large insurance firm began a program of compensating its salespeople for sick days not used. The firm decided to pay each salesperson a bonus for every unused sick day. In previous years, the number of sick days used per salesperson per year had a relative frequency distribution with a mean of 9.2 and a standard deviation of 1.8. To determine whether the compensation program has effectively reduced the mean number of sick days used, the firm randomly sampled 81 salespeople and recorded the number of sick days used by each at year's end.

a. Assuming that the compensation program was not effective in reducing the average number of sick days used, find the probability that the 81 randomly selected salespeople produce a sample mean less than 8.76 days. [*Hint:* If the compensation program was not effective, then the mean and standard deviation of the relative frequency distribution of number of sick days used per salesperson this year is the same as in previous years, i.e., $\mu = 9.2$ and $\sigma = 1.8$.]

b. If the sample mean number of sick days used is computed to be $\bar{x} = 8.76$ days, is there sufficient evidence to conclude that the compensation program was effective, i.e., that the true mean number of sick days used per salesperson this year is less than 9.2, the mean for previous years?

7.28 A large freight elevator can transport a maximum of 9,800 pounds (4.9 tons). Suppose a load of cargo containing 49 boxes must be transported via the elevator. Experience has shown that the weights of boxes for this type of cargo have a relative frequency distribution with $\mu = 205$ pounds and $\sigma = 14$ pounds. Based on this information, what is the probability that all 49 boxes can be safely loaded onto the freight elevator and transported? [*Hint:* For all 49 boxes to be safely loaded onto the freight elevator, their total weight must not exceed the maximum of 9,800 pounds. This implies that $\bar{x}$, the average weight of the 49 boxes, must not exceed $9,800/49 = 200$ pounds. Thus the desired probability can be found by computing $P(\bar{x} < 200)$.]

7.29 Suppose we select a random sample of 40 recently issued building permits for improvements to existing residential structures and record the value, x, of each permit. Prior experience has shown that, in a particular county, the relative frequency distribution for the value of such building permits has a mean of $\mu = \$8,000$ and a standard deviation of $\sigma = \$1,500$.

a. Describe the sampling distribution of $\bar{x}$, the mean value of a sample of 40 building permits.

b. What is the probability that the mean value of the permits in the sample will be less than $7,500?

c. What is the probability that the mean value of the permits in the sample will be between $7,500 and $8,500?

7.30 Suppose you are in charge of student ticket sales for a major college football team. From past experience, you know that the number of tickets purchased by a student standing in line at the ticket window has a relative frequency distribution with a mean of 2.4 and a standard deviation of 2.0. For today's game, there are 100 eager students standing in line to purchase tickets. If only 250 tickets remain, what is the probability that all 100 students will be able to purchase the tickets they desire?

7.31 As part of a study to determine the relationship between the length of time patients wait in the physician's office and certain demand and cost factors, researchers obtained data on the typical patient waiting times for 4,500 physicians in the five largest specialties: general practice, general surgery, internal medicine, obstetrics/gynecology, and pediatrics (*Journal of Business*, Oct. 1977). They reported a mean waiting time of $\mu = 24.7$ minutes and a standard deviation of $\sigma = 19.3$ minutes. Assume that the 4,500 observations in that data set represent the *actual* waiting times of all patients who visited a particular pediatrician last year and that the values of μ and σ are unavailable to the pediatrician. To determine whether the "optimal" mean waiting time for his practice has been attained, the pediatrician has one of his staff monitor the waiting times for 100 randomly selected patients during the year and compute the sample average waiting time, $\bar{x}$.

a. Find the probability that $\bar{x}$ falls between 20 minutes and 27 minutes.

b. From experience, the pediatrician has learned that the maximum operational efficiency for his practice is attained when the sample mean waiting time, $\bar{x}$, is less than 25 minutes. Find $P(\bar{x} < 25)$.

■ CASE STUDY 7.1

TV Telephone Polls—Dial 900 to Register Your Opinion

Recently, it has become popular for television networks to conduct surveys of its viewers by telephone. Unlike the traditional "scientific" telephone survey in which the opinions of a random sample of people are elicited, the TV network provides two or more "900" telephone numbers (each corresponding to a different opinion), which the viewer can call at a cost of 50¢ per call. Because the calls are electronically monitored, the results can be shown "live" almost immediately after the polling period ends.

One of the first polls of this type was conducted by ABC-TV following the 1980 Carter-Reagan presidential debate. ABC provided viewers with two numbers—one for Carter, the other for Reagan—to automatically register their opinion on who gained the most in the debate.

Several other more recent TV telephone polls are described briefly as follows:

- Each week during the National Football League (NFL) season, a CBS affiliate in Jacksonville, Florida, allowed callers to choose which of two teams to watch on Sunday afternoon, the Atlanta Falcons or Tampa Bay Buccaneers. The phone numbers were provided each Wednesday and Thursday night before the game during the station's 11 P.M. newscast.

- The cable TV sports network, ESPN, conducted a poll of its viewers to gauge sportsfans' opinions on whether Pete Rose, the famous (now retired) baseball player, should be ineligible for the Hall of Fame because of his gambling activities and tax-evasion conviction.

- The cable news network CNN provided phone numbers for viewers of its popular "Larry King Live" talk show to voice their opinion on the guilt or innocence of O. J. Simpson, the former NFL star accused of murdering his ex-wife and another man.

Explain why the sample of opinions collected by each of the TV surveys described above could have produced biased results.

■ **CASE STUDY 7.2**

A Decision Problem for Financial Managers: When to Investigate Cost Variances

Financial managers are faced daily with the job of controlling costs, and several useful management techniques for implementing that control are available. In this case study, we focus on a method that has been received favorably in the health-care field—**cost variance analysis**.

In variance analysis, actual performance (usually measured as either cost or level of activity) is compared against some standard of expected performance. The difference between the two measures of performance is called a *variance*.* These differences, or variances, can direct managers to potential problem areas or situations where costs are out of control. The question is, which variances should the manager investigate? That is, when is the deviation between expected and actual results large enough to warrant an expensive investigation?

W. A. Robbins and F. A. Jacobs[†] discuss the relevant issues surrounding the cost variance investigation decision problem. They illustrate the problem as follows:

Suppose a laboratory technician is able to perform a given test in 45 minutes, "on average," and management observes the test performed during the previous week took 60 minutes, on average, to perform. An investigation of this 15-minute unfavorable variance might reveal the technicians are being poorly supervised, resulting in an inefficient use of their time. On the other hand, management might find newly installed laboratory testing equipment is more sophisticated and requires a longer set-up time than originally anticipated, perhaps an additional 15 minutes on average. The investigation in this latter situation may result in management changing their expectation (standard) of efficient performance to 60 minutes or to some other new time dictated by the new technology.

In either instance, the variance has directed attention to a problem that can be corrected upon investigation.

Robbins and Jacobs developed a statistical model for the cost variance investigation decision problem. "The model," they write, "is based on the concept that a standard [usually the mean or average of an activity distribution] is best described by a band or area of acceptability, rather than a single point. The UCL and LCL [upper and lower control limits] form the bounds on the area of acceptability. Any variations falling within this area are considered to be due to random causes and do not require investigation. If a variance falls outside these limits, it is deemed to have a controllable source (nonrandom) and should be considered for possible investigation." The decision model is illustrated in Figure 7.13.

The control limits of the decision model can be either arbitrarily selected by management or mathematically calculated. For the purposes of this case study, consider the following three decision rules, each with a different method of calculating LCL and UCL:

RULE 1. $LCL = \mu - p\mu$ and $UCL = \mu + p\mu$

where

μ = Mean (or expected) level of activity

p = Percentage of mean $(0 < p < 1)$

$\bar{x}$ = Actual mean activity level of a sample of n observations

Acceptable area: $(\mu - p\mu) < \bar{x} < (\mu + p\mu)$
(Do not investigate)

RULE 2. $LCL = \mu - 2\sigma$ and $UCL = \mu + 2\sigma$

---

*The word variance is used loosely here. Students should not confuse its meaning with the statistical definition of variance given in Chapter 3.

[†]Robbins, W. A., and Jacobs, F. A. "A decision problem for financial managers: When to investigate cost variances." Healthcare Financial Management, Sept. 1985, pp. 36–41.

FIGURE 7.13

Decision Model for Case Study 7.2

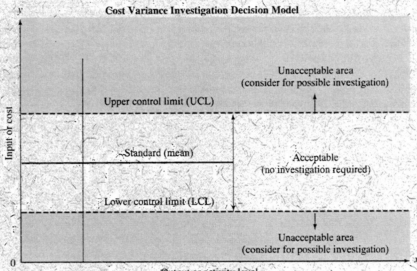

Cost Variance Investigation Decision Model

where

μ = Mean (or expected) level of activity

σ = Standard deviation of distribution of expected activity levels

$\bar{x}$ = Actual mean activity level of a sample of n observations

Acceptable area: $(\mu - 2\sigma) < \bar{x} < (\mu + 2\sigma)$
(Do not investigate)

RULE 3. $LCL = \mu - \dfrac{2\sigma}{\sqrt{n}}$ and $UCL = \mu + \dfrac{2\sigma}{\sqrt{n}}$

where

μ = Mean (or expected) level of activity

σ = Standard deviation of expected activity

$\bar{x}$ = Actual mean activity level of a sample of n observations

Acceptable area: $\left(\mu - \dfrac{2\sigma}{\sqrt{n}} \right) < \bar{x} < \left(\mu + \dfrac{2\sigma}{\sqrt{n}} \right)$

(Do not investigate)

To illustrate the differences among the three rules, we use a variation of a problem proposed by Robbins and Jacobs. Suppose the time required to fill a certain type of prescription in a hospital pharmacy is expected to have a probability distribution with $\mu = 24$ minutes and $\sigma = 2.7$ minutes. As a check on the prescription-filling process, the manager of the pharmacy sampled $n = 30$ prescriptions of this type and recorded the time it took to fill each prescription. If the sample mean, $\bar{x}$, falls outside the control limits, the manager will conduct a costly investigation of the prescription-filling process.

a. Suppose the process is out of control, i.e., the mean time required to fill the prescription is greater than the expected mean of $\mu = 24$. Assuming the actual mean is $\mu = 26$, describe the sampling distribution of the sample mean, $\bar{x}$.

b. Using the expected mean ($\mu = 24$), calculate LCL and UCL for rule 1 when $p = .10$. (This is a situation in which management believes a time variance of 10%, greater than or less than the mean, is significant enough to warrant an investigation.) Assuming the process is out of control (i.e., $\mu = 26$), what is the probability that $\bar{x}$ falls outside the control limits? This can be viewed as the probability that the manager will proceed with an investigation when, in fact, the process is out of control. [*Hint:* Use the sampling distribution from part **a** to calculate the probability.]

c. Using the expected mean ($\mu = 24$), calculate LCL and UCL for rule 2. Assuming the process is out of control (i.e., $\mu = 26$), what is the probability that $\bar{x}$ falls outside the control limits?

d. Using the expected mean ($\mu = 24$), calculate LCL and UCL for rule 3. Assuming the process is out of control (i.e., $\mu = 26$), what is the probability that $\bar{x}$ falls outside the control limits?

e. Based on the three probabilities computed in parts **b–d**, which decision rule would you recommend? Explain.

Chapter 8

ESTIMATION OF POPULATION PARAMETERS: CONFIDENCE INTERVALS

P ublic opinion surveys (e.g., the Gallup poll) are popular tools for estimating the proportion of the general public who believe in some cause, favor some product, prefer a presidential candidate, etc. How should we use the information provided by these sample surveys to calculate the estimate, and how accurate will it be? How does the sample size affect the accuracy of the estimate? These questions about estimating population parameters will be answered in this chapter.

You will learn how sample size and other factors affect the behavior of sample statistics. In Case Study 8.2, we examine public opinion surveys.

■ CONTENTS

8.1 Introduction

In preceding chapters, we learned that populations are characterized by numerical descriptive measures (parameters), and that inferences about parameter values are based on statistics computed from the information in a sample selected from the population of interest. In this chapter, we demonstrate how to estimate population parameters and assess the reliability of our estimates, based on knowledge of the sampling distributions of the statistics being used.

EXAMPLE 8.1
Selecting a Point Estimate

Suppose we are interested in estimating the average sale price of all residential properties sold in six Tampa (Fla.) neighborhoods in 1993. Recall that the target population consists of the 707 observations on sale price described in Appendix A.1. (Although we already know the value of the population mean, we use this example to illustrate the concepts involved in estimation.) How could one estimate the parameter of interest in this situation?

SOLUTION An intuitively appealing estimate of a population mean, μ, is the sample mean, $\bar{x}$, computed from a random sample of n observations from the target population. Assume, for example, that we obtain a random sample of size $n = 100$ from the sale price measurements of Appendix A.1 and then compute the value of the sample mean to be $\bar{x} = \$104,560$. This value of $\bar{x}$ provides a **point estimate** of the population mean. ■

Definition 8.1

A **point estimate** of a parameter is a statistic, a single value computed from the observations in a sample, that is used to estimate the value of the target parameter.

How reliable is a point estimate for a parameter? To be truly practical and meaningful, an inference concerning a parameter (in this case, estimation of the value of μ) not only must consist of a point estimate, but also must be accompanied by a measure of the realiability of the estimate; that is, we must be able to state how close our estimate is likely to be to the true value of the population parameter. This can be done by using the characteristics of the sampling distribution of the statistic that was used to obtain the point estimate; the procedure is illustrated in the next section.

8.2 Estimation of a Population Mean: Normal (z) Statistic

Recall from Section 7.3 that, for sufficiently large sample sizes, the sampling distribution of the sample mean, $\bar{x}$, is approximately normal, as indicated in Figure 8.1.

FIGURE 8.1

Sampling
Distribution of $\bar{x}$

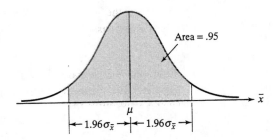

EXAMPLE 8.2
Reliability of Interval
Estimate

Refer to Example 8.1. Recall that our target population is the data set of Appendix A.1, and we are interested in estimating μ, the mean sale price of residential properties in the six neighborhoods. Suppose we plan to take a sample of $n = 100$ measurements from the population of sale prices in Appendix A.1 and construct the interval

$$\bar{x} \pm 1.96\,\sigma_{\bar{x}} = \bar{x} \pm 1.96(\sigma/\sqrt{n})$$

where σ is the population standard deviation of the 707 sale price values and $\sigma_{\bar{x}} = \sigma/\sqrt{n}$ is the standard error of $\bar{x}$. In other words, we will construct an interval 1.96 standard deviations around the sample mean, $\bar{x}$. What can we say about how likely it is that this interval will contain the true value of the population mean, μ?

SOLUTION We arrive at a solution by the following three-step process:

STEP 1 First note that the area beneath the sampling distribution of $\bar{x}$ between $\mu - 1.96\,\sigma_{\bar{x}}$ and $\mu + 1.96\,\sigma_{\bar{x}}$ is approximately .95. (This area, shaded in Figure 8.1, is obtained from Table 5 of Appendix B.) This implies that before the sample of measurements is drawn, the probability that $\bar{x}$ will fall within the interval $\mu \pm 1.96\,\sigma_{\bar{x}}$ is .95.

STEP 2 If in fact the sample yields a value of $\bar{x}$ that falls within the interval $\mu \pm 1.96\,\sigma_{\bar{x}}$, then it is also true that the interval $\bar{x} \pm 1.96\,\sigma_{\bar{x}}$ will contain μ, as demonstrated in Figure 8.2. For a particular value of $\bar{x}$ (shown with a vertical arrow) that falls within the interval $\mu \pm 1.96\,\sigma_{\bar{x}}$, a distance of $1.96\,\sigma_{\bar{x}}$ is marked off both to the left and to the right of $\bar{x}$. You can see that the value of μ must fall within $\bar{x} \pm 1.96\,\sigma_{\bar{x}}$.

FIGURE 8.2

Sampling
Distribution of $\bar{x}$ in
Example 8.2

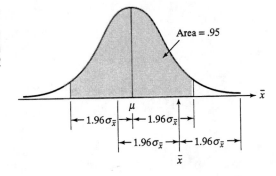

STEP 3   Steps 1 and 2 combined imply that, before the sample is drawn, the probability that the interval $\bar{x} \pm 1.96\,\sigma_{\bar{x}}$ will enclose μ is approximately .95. ■

The interval $\bar{x} \pm 1.96\,\sigma_{\bar{x}}$ in Example 8.2 is called a large-sample 95% **confidence interval** for the population mean μ. The term *large-sample* refers to the sample being of a sufficiently large size that we can apply the central limit theorem to determine the form of the sampling distribution of $\bar{x}$. Empirical research has found that a sample size n exceeding a value between 20 and 30 will usually yield a sampling distribution of $\bar{x}$ that is approximately normal. This result led many practitioners to adopt the rule of thumb that a sample size of $n \ge 30$ is required to use large-sample confidence interval procedures. Keep in mind, though, that 30 is not a magical number and, in fact, is quite arbitrary.

Definition 8.2

A **confidence interval** for a parameter is an interval of numbers within which we expect the true value of the population parameter to be contained. The endpoints of the interval are computed based on sample information.

EXAMPLE 8.3
95% Confidence Interval

Refer to Example 8.2. Suppose a random sample of 100 observations from the population of sale prices yielded a sample mean of $\bar{x} = \$104{,}560$. Construct a 95% confidence interval for μ, the population mean sale price, based on this sample information. Recall that the standard deviation of the population of sale prices is $\sigma = \$85{,}414$.

SOLUTION A 95% confidence interval for μ, based on a sample of size $n = 100$, is given by

$$\bar{x} \pm 1.96\,\sigma_{\bar{x}} = \bar{x} \pm 1.96\left(\frac{\sigma}{\sqrt{n}}\right)$$

$$= 104{,}560 \pm 1.96\left(\frac{85{,}414}{\sqrt{100}}\right)$$

$$= 104{,}560 \pm 16{,}741$$

or (87,819, 121,301). Hence, we estimate that the population mean sale price falls within the interval from \$87,819 to \$121,301. ■

How much confidence do we have that μ, the true population mean sale price, lies within the interval (\$87,819, \$121,301)? Although we cannot be certain whether the sample interval contains μ (unless we calculate the true value of μ for all 707 observations), we can be reasonably sure that it does. This confidence is based on the interpretation of the confidence interval procedure: If we were to select repeated random samples of size $n = 100$ sale prices and form an interval of 1.96 standard deviations around $\bar{x}$ for each sample, then approximately 95% of the intervals constructed in this manner would contain μ. Thus, we are 95% confident that the particular interval ($87,819, $121,301) contains μ; this is our measure of the reliability of the point estimate $\bar{x}$.

EXAMPLE 8.4
Theoretical Interpretation of a Confidence Interval

To illustrate the classical interpretation of a confidence interval, we generated 40 random samples, each of size $n = 100$, from the population of sale prices described in Appendix A.1. For each sample, the sample mean was calculated and used to construct a 95% confidence interval for μ as in Example 8.3. Interpret the results, which are shown in Table 8.1.

Table 8.1 95% Confidence Intervals for μ for 40 Random Samples of 100 Sale Prices from Appendix A.1

Sample	$\bar{x}$	Lower Limit	Upper Limit	Sample	$\bar{x}$	Lower Limit	Upper Limit
1	$104,044	$87,303	$120,785	21	$109,943	$93,202	$126,684
2	121,859	105,118	138,600	22	113,225	96,484	129,966
3	116,747	100,006	133,488	*23	124,067	107,326	140,808
*4	141,645	124,904	158,386	24	112,826	96,085	129,567
5	112,226	95,485	128,967	25	109,831	93,090	126,572
6	103,052	86,311	119,793	26	97,857	81,116	114,598
7	96,266	79,525	113,007	27	90,853	74,112	107,594
8	96,454	79,713	113,195	28	104,390	87,649	121,131
9	104,701	87,960	121,442	29	102,840	86,099	119,581
10	94,714	77,973	111,455	30	97,488	80,747	114,229
11	102,741	86,000	119,482	31	96,527	79,786	113,268
12	98,636	81,895	115,377	32	100,503	83,762	117,244
13	100,254	83,513	116,995	33	107,079	90,338	123,820
14	107,001	90,260	123,742	34	105,728	88,987	122,469
15	109,453	92,712	126,194	35	102,936	86,195	119,677
16	105,970	89,229	122,711	36	118,646	101,905	135,387
17	107,441	90,700	124,182	37	109,725	92,984	126,466
18	102,927	86,186	119,668	38	94,719	77,978	111,460
19	119,725	102,984	136,466	39	112,671	95,930	129,412
20	114,238	97,497	130,979	40	113,897	97,156	130,638

Note: Asterisks (*) identify the intervals that do not contain $\mu = 106,405$.

SOLUTION For the target population of 707 sale prices, we have previously obtained the population mean value, $\mu = \$106,405$ (Section 3.4). In the 40 repetitions of the confidence interval procedure described above, only two of the intervals (those based on samples 4 and 23, indicated by asterisks in Table 8.1) do not contain the value of μ, whereas the remaining 38 of the 40 intervals (or 95% of the 40 intervals) do contain the true value of μ.

Keep in mind that, in actual practice, you would not know the true value of μ, and you would not perform this repeated sampling; rather you would select a single random sample and construct the associated 95% confidence interval. The one confidence interval you form may or may not contain μ, but you can be fairly sure it does because of your *confidence in the statistical procedure*, the basis for which was illustrated in this example. ■

Suppose you want to construct an interval that you believe will contain μ with some degree of confidence other than 95%; in other words, you want to choose a **confidence coefficient** other than .95.

Definition 8.3

The **confidence coefficient** is the proportion of times that a confidence interval encloses the true value of the population parameter if the confidence interval procedure is used repeatedly a very large number of times.

The first step in constructing a confidence interval with any desired confidence coefficient is to notice from Figure 8.1 that, for a 95% confidence interval, the confidence coefficient of .95 is equal to the total area under the sampling distribution (1.00), less .05 of the area, which is divided equally between the two tails of the normal distribution. Thus, each tail has an area of .025. Second, consider that the tabulated value of z (from Table 5 of Appendix B) that cuts off an area of .025 in the right tail of the standard normal distribution is 1.96 (see Figure 8.3). The value $z = 1.96$ is also the distance, in terms of standard deviations, that $\bar{x}$ is from each endpoint of the 95% confidence interval. By assigning a confidence coefficient other than .95 to a confidence interval, we change the area under the sampling distribution between the endpoints of the interval, which in turn changes the tail area associated with z. Thus, this z value provides the key to constructing a confidence interval with any desired confidence coefficient. In our subsequent discussion, we will use the notation defined in the next box.

FIGURE 8.3

Tabulated z Value Corresponding to a Tail Area of .025

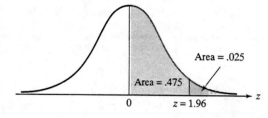

Area = .475

Area = .025

0      $z = 1.96$ z

> **Definition 8.4**
>
> We define $z_{\alpha/2}$ to be the z value such that an area of $\alpha/2$ lies to its right (see Figure 8.4).

Now, if an area of $\alpha/2$ lies beyond $z_{\alpha/2}$ in the right tail of the standard normal (z) distribution, then an area of $\alpha/2$ lies to the left of $-z_{\alpha/2}$ in the left tail (Figure 8.4) because of the symmetry of the distribution. The remaining area, $(1 - \alpha)$, is equal to the confidence coefficient—that is, the probability that $\bar{x}$ falls within $z_{\alpha/2}$ standard deviations of μ is $(1 - \alpha)$. Thus, a large-sample confidence interval for μ, with confidence coefficient equal to $(1 - \alpha)$, is given by

$$\bar{x} \pm z_{\alpha/2}\, \sigma_{\bar{x}}$$

FIGURE 8.4

Locating $z_{\alpha/2}$ on the Standard Normal Curve

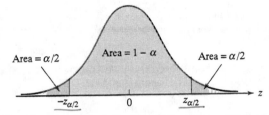

EXAMPLE 8.5

Finding z for a 90% Confidence Interval

In statistical problems using confidence interval techniques, .90 is a very common confidence coefficient. Determine the value of $z_{\alpha/2}$ that would be used in constructing a 90% confidence interval for a population mean based on a large sample.

SOLUTION   For a confidence coefficient of .90, we have

$$1 - \alpha = .90$$
$$\alpha = .10$$
$$\alpha/2 = .05$$

and we must obtain the value $z_{\alpha/2} = z_{.05}$ that locates an area of .05 in the upper tail of the standard normal distribution. Since the total area to the right of 0 is .50, $z_{.05}$ is the value such that the area between 0 and $z_{.05}$ is $.50 - .05 = .45$. From the body of Table 5 in Appendix B we find $z_{.05} = 1.645$ (see Figure 8.5, page 348). We conclude that a large-sample 90% confidence interval for a population mean is given by

$$\bar{x} \pm 1.645\, \sigma_{\bar{x}} \quad ■$$

In Table 8.2 (page 348), we present the values of $z_{\alpha/2}$ for the most commonly used confidence coeffcients.

FIGURE 8.5

Location of $z_{\alpha/2}$ for Example 8.5

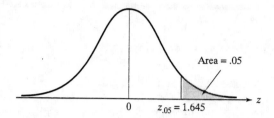

Area = .05

$0 \quad z_{.05} = 1.645$

Table 8.2 Commonly Used Confidence Coefficients and Their Corresponding z Values

Confidence Coefficient $1 - \alpha$	$\alpha/2$	$z_{\alpha/2}$
.90	.05	1.645
.95	.025	1.96
.98	.01	2.33
.99	.005	2.58

A summary of the large-sample confidence interval procedure for estimating a population mean appears in the accompanying box.

Large-Sample $(1 - \alpha)100\%$ Confidence Interval for a Population Mean, μ

$$\bar{x} \pm z_{\alpha/2}\sigma_{\bar{x}} = \bar{x} \pm z_{\alpha/2}\left(\frac{\sigma}{\sqrt{n}}\right)$$

where $z_{\alpha/2}$ is the z value that locates an area of $\alpha/2$ to its right, σ is the standard deviation of the population from which the sample was selected, n is the sample size, and $\bar{x}$ is the value of the sample mean.

Assumption: The sample size n is large (usually $n \geq 30$).

[*Note*: When the value of σ is unknown (as will usually be the case), the sample standard deviation s may be used to approximate σ in the formula for the confidence interval. The approximation is generally quite satisfactory for large samples.]

EXAMPLE 8.6

99% Confidence Interval

Based on the set of all residential properties that were sold in the six Tampa (Fla.) neighborhoods during 1993, we want to assess the collective ability of the city's real estate appraisers. A random sample of $n = 50$ observations from the population of values of the ratio of sale price to total appraised value is listed in Table 8.3. Estimate

Table 8.3 Random Sample of $n = 50$ Ratios
of Sale Price to Total Appraised Value

1.36	1.29	1.41	1.07	1.91
1.23	1.06	1.16	1.10	1.04
1.08	1.20	1.22	1.13	1.26
1.22	1.22	1.05	1.12	1.23
1.33	.84	1.60	.60	.69
1.09	1.55	1.34	1.11	2.13
2.08	2.07	1.01	1.32	1.16
1.21	1.64	1.18	1.20	1.74
1.80	2.47	1.48	1.70	1.36
1.27	1.22	1.33	.92	.96

μ, the mean ratio of sale price to total appraised value for all properties sold in 1993, using a 99% confidence interval. Interpret the interval in terms of the problem.

SOLUTION The general form of a large-sample 99% confidence interval for μ is

$$\bar{x} \pm 2.58 \, \frac{\sigma}{\sqrt{n}}$$

To compute the interval, we require the sample mean $\bar{x}$ and the population standard deviation σ. In most practical business applications, however, the value of σ will be unknown. For large samples, the fact that σ is unknown poses only a minor problem since the sample standard deviation s provides a good approximation to σ. Consequently, we may substitute s for σ in the confidence interval formula given in the box.[*]

A SAS printout showing descriptive statistics for the sample of $n = 50$ ratios is displayed in Figure 8.6 (page 350). The values of $\bar{x}$ and s, shaded on the printout, are $\bar{x} = 1.315$ and $s = .366$. Substituting these values into the formula, we obtain the approximate 99% confidence interval

$$1.315 \pm 2.58 \left(\frac{.366}{\sqrt{50}} \right)$$

or (1.181, 1.449). We can be 99% confident that the interval (1.181, 1.449) encloses the true mean ratio of sale price to total appraised value for all residential properties sold in the six Tampa neighborhoods in 1993. Since all the values in the interval exceed 1, we conclude that there was a general tendency for the sale price of a property in these neighborhoods to exceed its total appraised value. Further investigation

---

[*] *We discuss an alternative form of the confidence interval when σ is unknown in Section 8.3.*

FIGURE 8.6

SAS Descriptive
Statistics for $n = 50$
Sample Ratios

```
Analysis Variable : SALTOAPR

N Obs   N      Minimum        Maximum          Mean         Std Dev
------------------------------------------------------------------------
  50   50    0.6000000      2.4700000      1.3152000      0.3657491
------------------------------------------------------------------------
```

would be required to relate this phenomenon to the skills of the appraisers in this city. ■

EXAMPLE 8.7

Effect of $(1 - \alpha)$ on the
Width of the Confidence
Interval

Refer to Example 8.6.

a. Using the sample information provided in Example 8.6, construct a 95% confidence interval for the mean ratio of sale price to total appraised value for properties sold in the six neighborhoods.

b. For a fixed sample size, how is the width of the confidence interval related to the confidence coefficient?

SOLUTION

a. The form of a large-sample 95% confidence interval for a population mean μ is

$$\bar{x} \pm 1.96 \, \frac{\sigma}{\sqrt{n}} \approx \bar{x} \pm 1.96 \, \frac{s}{\sqrt{n}}$$

$$= 1.315 \pm 1.96 \left(\frac{.366}{\sqrt{50}} \right)$$

$$= 1.315 \pm .101$$

or (1.214, 1.416).

b. The 99% confidence interval for μ was determined in Example 8.6 to be (1.181, 1.449). The 95% confidence interval, obtained in part **a** and based on the same sample information, is narrower than the 99% confidence interval. This relationship holds in general, as noted in the accompanying box. ■

Relationship Between Width of Confidence Interval and Confidence Coefficient

For a given sample size, the width of the confidence interval for a parameter increases as the confidence coefficient increases. Intuitively, the interval must become wider for us to have greater confidence that it contains the true parameter value.

EXAMPLE 8.8

Effect of *n* on the Width of the Confidence Interval

Refer to Example 8.6.

a.   Assume that the given values of the statistics $\bar{x}$ and s were based on a sample of size $n = 100$ instead of a sample of size $n = 50$. Construct a 99% confidence interval for μ, the population mean ratio of sale price to total appraised value.

b.   For a fixed confidence coefficient, how is the width of the confidence interval related to the sample size?

SOLUTION

a.   Substituting the values of the sample statistics into the general formula for a 99% confidence interval for μ yields

$$\bar{x} \pm 2.58\ \frac{\sigma}{\sqrt{n}} \approx 1.315 \pm 2.58 \left(\frac{.366}{\sqrt{100}} \right)$$

$$= 1.315 \pm .094$$

or (1.221, 1.409).

b.   The 99% confidence interval based on a sample of size $n = 100$, constructed in part **a**, is narrower than the 99% confidence interval based on a sample of size $n = 50$, constructed in Example 8.6. This will also hold true in general, as noted in the box.   ▪

Relationship Between Width of Confidence Interval and Sample Size

For a fixed confidence coefficient, the width of the confidence interval decreases as the sample size increases. In other words, larger samples generally provide more information about the target population than do smaller samples.

In this section, we have introduced the concepts of point and interval estimation of the population mean μ, based on the large-sample z statistic. The general theory appropriate for the estimation of μ also carries over to the estimation of other population parameters. Hence, in subsequent sections, we present only the point estimate, its sampling distribution, the general form of a confidence interval for the parameter of interest, and any assumptions required for the validity of the procedure.

EXERCISES

■ *Learning the Mechanics*

8.1   In a large-sample confidence interval for a population mean, what does the confidence coefficient represent?

8.2   Use Table 5 of Appendix B to determine the value of $z_{\alpha/2}$ that would be used to construct a large-sample confidence interval for μ for each of the following confidence coefficients:
a. .85   **b.** .95   **c.** .975

8.3   Suppose a random sample of size $n = 100$ produces a mean of $\bar{x} = 81$ and a standard deviation of $s = 12$.
a. Construct a 90% confidence interval for μ.   **b.** Construct a 95% confidence interval for μ.
c. Construct a 99% confidence interval for μ.

8.4   A random sample of size n is selected from a population with unknown mean μ and standard deviation σ. Calculate a 95% confidence interval for μ for each of the following situations:
a. $n = 35$, $\bar{x} = 26$, $s^2 = 228.2$ **b.** $n = 70$, $\bar{x} = 24.1$, $s^2 = 198.4$
c. $n = 105$, $\bar{x} = 24.2$, $s^2 = 216.9$

8.5   A random sample of size 400 is taken from an unknown population with mean μ and standard deviation σ. The following values are computed:

$$\Sigma x = 2,280 \qquad \Sigma x^2 = 38,532$$

a. Find a 90% confidence interval for μ.
b. Find a 99% confidence interval for μ.

8.6   The mean and standard deviation of a random sample of n measurements are equal to 22 and 16, respectively.
a. Construct a 95% confidence interval for μ if $n = 100$.
b. Construct a 95% confidence interval for μ if $n = 500$.

■ *Applying the Concepts*

8.7   Give a precise interpretation of the statement, "We are 95% confident that the interval estimate contains μ."

8.8   When a university professor attempts to publish a research article in a professional journal, the manuscript goes through a rigorous review process. Usually, anywhere from three to five reviewers read and critique the article, then pass judgment on whether the article should be published. Recently, a study was undertaken to seek information on how reviewers for research journals pursue their activities (*Academy of Management Journal*, Mar. 1989). A sample of 73 reviewers for the Academy of Management's *Journal* (*AMJ*) and *Review* (*AMR*) were asked how many hours they spent per paper for a typical complete review process. The sample mean and standard deviation were computed to be $\bar{x} = 5.4$ hours and $s = 3.6$ hours.
a. Find the point estimate for μ, the true mean number of hours spent by a reviewer in conducting a complete review of a paper submitted to *AMJ* or *AMR*.
b. Compute a 99% confidence interval for μ.
c. Interpret the interval, part **b**.

8.9   Adult students are enrolling in colleges and universities in ever-increasing numbers, and many are majoring in marketing. A study was conducted to determine the attitudes of marketing faculty toward the adult students in their classes (*Journal of Marketing Education*, Summer 1987). A sample of 290 faculty, drawn at random from the American Marketing Association's membership directory, responded to a series of attitudinal statements, the first of which was, "Adult students (i.e., undergraduates 24 years or older) participate more actively in classroom discussions than do younger students." Attitudes were measured using a 5-point Likert scale (1 = strongly agree, 2 = agree, 3 = no opinion, 4 = disagree, and 5 = strongly disagree). For the participation statement, the mean attitudinal score for the sample was 1.94 and the standard deviation was .92.

    a. Estimate the true mean attitudinal score of marketing faculty with regard to classroom participation of adult students using a 98% confidence interval. Interpret the result.

    b. How could you reduce the width of the confidence interval in part **a**?

8.10   According to a study reported in *Administrative Science Quarterly* (June 1988), the salary gap between a chief executive officer (CEO) of a firm and a vice president (VP) is often very large, and the gap appears to increase the more VPs a firm employs. Based on data collected for a sample of 105 U.S. firms drawn from *Business Week*'s Executive Compensation Scoreboard, the mean and standard deviation of the number of VPs employed by a firm are $\bar{x} = 19.4$ and $s = 10.1$. Use this information to estimate the true mean number of VPs at U.S. firms with a 90% confidence interval. Interpret the result.

8.11   Chemical engineers at the University of Murcia (Spain) conducted a series of experiments to determine the most effective membrane to use in a passive sampler (*Environmental Science & Technology*, Vol. 27, 1993). The effectiveness of a passive sampler was measured by the sampling rate, recorded in cubic centimeters per minute. In one experiment, six passive samplers were positioned with their faces parallel to the air flow and with an air velocity of 90 centimeters per second. After 6 hours, the sampling rate of each was determined. Based on the results, a 95% confidence interval for the mean sampling rate was calculated to be (49.66, 51.48).

    a. What is the confidence coefficient for the interval?

    b. Give a theoretical interpretation of the confidence coefficient, part **a**.

    c. Give a practical interpretation of the confidence interval.

    d. What assumptions, if any, are required for the interval to yield valid inferences?

8.12   Refer to the data on ratio of shareholder return to executive salary for CEOs described in Appendix A.2. A random sample of 50 return-to-pay ratios selected from the data set are shown here. A MINITAB printout showing descriptive statistics for the sample and a 95% confidence interval for the mean return-to-pay ratio of all CEOs is also shown at the top of page 354.

.03	.051	.047	.091	.026
.049	.029	.01	.037	.031
.086	.02	.005	.019	.206
.029	.018	.081	.005	.206
.017	.049	.062	.005	.112
.023	.033	.036	.021	.122
.031	.033	.02	.048	.072
.051	.14	.086	.041	.032
.025	.042	.02	.032	.02
.025	.047	.091	.026	.122

	N	MEAN	STDEV	SE MEAN	95.0 PERCENT C.I.
ratio	50	0.05120	0.04530	0.00641	(0.03832, 0.06408)

a. Use the data in the table to verify the 95% confidence interval shown on the MINITAB printout.

b. Interpret the interval.

c. How could you reduce the width of the confidence interval? Are there any drawbacks to reducing the interval width? Explain.

8.13 Refer to the data on physician costs described in Appendix A.3. The president of the health maintenance organization (HMO) wants to estimate the average per-member per-month cost of the physicians in the HMO.

a. Use one of the methods of Chapter 7 to select a random sample of 30 physician costs. [*Note:* The data are available on a $3\frac{1}{2}''$ diskette from the publisher.]

b. Use the data from part **a** to construct a 97% confidence interval for the true average physician cost of this HMO.

c. What is the confidence coefficient for the interval of part **b**? Interpret this value.

d. Based on your interval obtained in part **b**, would you expect the true mean physician cost to exceed $200 per member per month?

8.14 Refer to the data on student-loan default rates for 66 Florida colleges, Exercise 2.26. A MINITAB printout showing descriptive statistics for the sample data and a 95% confidence interval for the mean student-loan default rate is displayed here.

	N	MEAN	STDEV	SE MEAN	95.0 PERCENT C.I.
defrate	66	14.68	14.14	1.74	(11.20, 18.16)

a. Use the descriptive statistics in the MINITAB printout to verify the 95% confidence interval shown on the printout.

b. Interpret the interval.

c. How could you reduce the width of the confidence interval? Are there any drawbacks to reducing the interval width? Explain.

d. Would you feel comfortable using the 95% confidence interval to make an inference about the true mean student-loan default rate of all U.S. colleges? Explain.

8.3 Estimation of a Population Mean: Student's *t* Statistic

In the previous section, we discussed the estimation of a population mean based on large samples and known population standard deviation σ. However, time or cost limitations may often restrict the number of sample observations that may be obtained, so that the estimation procedures of Section 8.2 would not be applicable.

With small samples, the following two problems arise:

PROBLEM 1 Since the central limit theorem applies only to large samples, we are not able to assume that the sampling distribution of $\bar{x}$ is approximately normal. For small samples, the sampling distribution of $\bar{x}$ depends on the particular form of the relative frequency distribution of the population being sampled.

PROBLEM 2   The sample standard deviation s may not be a satisfactory approximation to the population standard deviation σ if the sample size is small. Thus, replacing σ with s in the large-sample formula given in Section 8.2 is not appropriate.

Fortunately, we may proceed with estimation techniques based on small samples if we can make the following assumption:

Assumption Required for Estimating μ Based on Small Samples

The population from which the sample is selected has an approximate normal distribution.

If this assumption is valid, then we may again use $\bar{x}$ as a point estimate for μ, and the general form of a small-sample confidence interval for μ is as shown in the next box.*

Small-Sample Confidence Interval for μ

$$\bar{x} \pm t_{\alpha/2}\left(\frac{s}{\sqrt{n}}\right)$$

where the distribution of t is based on $(n-1)$ degrees of freedom.

When you compare this to the large-sample confidence interval for μ, you will see that the sample standard deviation s replaces the population standard deviation σ. Also, the sampling distribution upon which the confidence interval is based is known as a **Student's t distribution**.[†] Consequently, we must replace the value of $z_{\alpha/2}$ used in a large-sample confidence interval by a value obtained from the t distribution.

The t distribution is very much like the z distribution. In particular, both are symmetric and mound-shaped, and have a mean of 0. However, the t distribution is flatter, i.e., more variable (see Figure 8.7, page 356). Also, the distribution of t depends on a quantity called its **degrees of freedom (df)**, which is equal to $(n-1)$ when estimating a population mean based on a small sample of size n. Intuitively, we can think of the number of degrees of freedom as the amount of information available for estimating, in addition to μ, the unknown quantity σ^2. Table 6 of Appendix B, a portion of which is reproduced in Table 8.4, gives the value of t_α that locates an area of α in the upper tail of the t distribution for various values of α and for degrees of freedom ranging from 1 to 120.

---

*When sampling is from a normal population with σ known, the appropriate confidence interval is $\bar{x} \pm z_{\alpha/2}\,(\sigma/\sqrt{n})$ regardless of the size of the sample. This results from the fact that the sampling distribution of $\bar{x}$ is normal whenever the population is normally distributed. (See Section 7.3.)

[†] The result was first published in 1908 by W. S. Gosset, who wrote under the pen name of Student. Thereafter, the distribution became known as Student's t.

FIGURE 8.7

Comparison of the *z* Distribution to the *t* Distribution

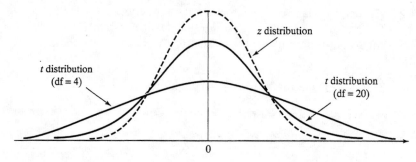

Table 8.4   Reproduction of a Portion of Table 6 of Appendix B

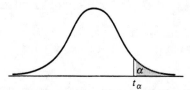

Degrees of Freedom	$t_{.100}$	$t_{.050}$	$t_{.025}$	$t_{.010}$	$t_{.005}$	$t_{.001}$	$t_{.0005}$
1	3.078	6.314	12.706	31.821	63.657	318.31	636.62
2	1.886	2.920	4.303	6.965	9.925	22.326	31.598
3	1.638	2.353	3.182	4.541	5.841	10.213	12.924
4	1.533	2.132	2.776	3.747	4.604	7.173	8.610
5	1.476	2.015	2.571	3.365	4.032	5.893	6.869
6	1.440	1.943	2.447	3.143	3.707	5.208	5.959
7	1.415	1.895	2.365	2.998	3.499	4.785	5.408
8	1.397	1.860	2.306	2.896	3.355	4.501	5.041
9	1.383	1.833	2.262	2.821	3.250	4.297	4.781
10	1.372	1.812	2.228	2.764	3.169	4.144	4.587
11	1.363	1.796	2.201	2.718	3.106	4.025	4.437
12	1.356	1.782	2.179	2.681	3.055	3.930	4.318
13	1.350	1.771	2.160	2.650	3.012	3.852	4.221
14	1.345	1.761	2.145	2.624	2.977	3.787	4.140
15	1.341	1.753	2.131	2.602	2.947	3.733	4.073

Characteristics of Student's t Distribution

1. Symmetric distribution
2. Mean of 0
3. More variable (flatter) than the standard normal (*z*) distribution
4. Depends on a quantity called **degrees of freedom (df)**
5. For large samples (i.e., large df values), the *t* and *z* distributions are nearly equivalent.

EXAMPLE 8.9
Finding *t* Values

Use Table 6 of Appendix B to determine the *t* value that would be used to construct a 95% confidence interval for μ based on a sample of size $n = 14$.

SOLUTION   For a confidence coefficient of .95, we have

$$1 - \alpha = .95$$

$$\alpha = .05$$

$$\frac{\alpha}{2} = .025$$

We thus require the value of $t_{.025}$ for a *t* distribution based on $(n - 1) = (14 - 1) = 13$ degrees of freedom. In Table 8.4 at the intersection of the column labeled $t_{.025}$ and the row corresponding to df = 13, we find the entry 2.160 (see Figure 8.8). Hence, a 95% confidence interval for μ, based on a sample of $n = 14$ observations, would be given by

$$\bar{x} \pm 2.160 \left(\frac{s}{\sqrt{14}} \right)$$

FIGURE 8.8

Location of $t_{.025}$ for
Example 8.9

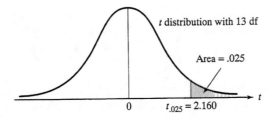

t distribution with 13 df

Area = .025

0      $t_{.025} = 2.160$ *t*

EXAMPLE 8.10
"Large" Sample

Recall that when estimating μ in Section 8.2, we used the arbitrary cutoff point of $n = 30$ for distinguishing between large and small samples. Explain why $n \geq 30$ is selected as the arbitrary cutoff.

SOLUTION   In Appendix B, the values in the last row of Table 6 (corresponding to df = ∞) are the values from the standard normal *z* distribution. This phenomenon occurs because, as the sample size increases, the *t* distribution becomes more and more like the *z* distribution (recall Figure 8.7). By the time *n* reaches 30, i.e., df = 29, there is very little difference between tabulated values of *t* and *z*. Of course, the values $n = 40$, $n = 60$, and even $n = 120$ could also have been selected as the cutoff for defining a "large" sample. However, $n = 30$ seems to be the smallest value of *n* for which the *t* values reasonably approximate the corresponding *z* values.   ■

EXAMPLE 8.11
Small-Sample Confidence
Interval for μ

The Geothermal Loop Experimental Facility, located in the Salton Sea in southern California, is a U.S. Department of Energy operation for studying the feasibility of generating electricity from the hot, highly saline water of the Salton Sea. Operating experience has shown that these brines leave silica scale deposits on metallic plant piping, causing excessive plant outages. Jacobsen et al. (*Journal of Testing and Evaluation*, Vol. 9, No. 2, Mar. 1981, pp. 82–92) have found that scaling can be reduced somewhat by adding chemical solutions to the brine. In one screening experiment, each of five antiscalants was added to an aliquot of brine, and the solutions were filtered. A silica determination (parts per million of silicon dioxide) was made on each filtered sample after a holding time of 24 hours, with the following results:

229	255	280	203	229

Estimate the mean amount of silicon dioxide present in the five antiscalant solutions. Use a 99% confidence interval.

SOLUTION The first step in constructing the confidence interval is to compute the mean, $\bar{x}$, and standard deviation, s, of the sample of five silicon dioxide amounts. These values, $\bar{x} = 239.2$ and $s = 29.3$, are provided in the MINITAB printout, Figure 8.9.

FIGURE 8.9

MINITAB Descriptive
Statistics for
Example 8.1

	N	MEAN	MEDIAN	TRMEAN	STDEV	SEMEAN
ppm	5	239.2	229.0	239.2	29.3	13.1

	MIN	MAX	Q1	Q3
ppm	203.0	280.0	216.0	267.5

For a confidence coefficient of $1 - \alpha = .99$, we have $\alpha = .01$ and $\alpha/2 = .005$. Since the sample size is small ($n = 5$), our estimation technique requires the assumption that the amount of silicon dioxide present in an antiscalant solution has an approximately normal distribution (i.e., the sample of five silicon amounts is selected from a normal population).

Substituting the values for $\bar{x}$, s, and n into the formula for a small-sample confidence interval for μ, we obtain

$$\bar{x} \pm t_{\alpha/2}\left(\frac{s}{\sqrt{n}}\right) = \bar{x} \pm t_{.005}\left(\frac{s}{\sqrt{n}}\right)$$

$$= 239.2 \pm t_{.005}\left(\frac{29.3}{\sqrt{5}}\right)$$

where $t_{.005}$ is the value corresponding to an upper-tail area of .005 in the Student's t distribution based on $(n - 1) = 4$ degrees of freedom. From Table 6 of Appendix B, the required t value is $t_{.005} = 4.604$. Substitution of this value yields

$$239.2 \pm t_{.005}\left(\frac{29.3}{\sqrt{5}}\right) = 239.2 \pm (4.604)\left(\frac{29.3}{\sqrt{5}}\right)$$

$$= 239.2 \pm 60.3$$

or 178.9 to 299.5 ppm. Thus, if the distribution of silicon dioxide amounts is approximately normal, then we can be 99% confident that the interval (178.9, 299.5) encloses μ, the true mean amount of silicon dioxide present in an antiscalant solution. ■

EXAMPLE 8.12
Computer Analysis

Refer to Example 8.6 and the problem of estimating μ, the mean ratio of sale price to total appraised value, based on a large sample ($n = 50$) of properties. A MINITAB printout showing a 99% confidence interval for μ is displayed in Figure 8.10. Compare the results to the interval calculated in Example 8.6.

FIGURE 8.10
MINITAB Printout for Example 8.12

	N	MEAN	STDEV	SE MEAN	99.0 PERCENT C.I.
saltoapr	50	1.3152	0.3657	0.0517	(1.1766, 1.4538)

SOLUTION The 99% confidence interval, shaded on the MINITAB printout, is (1.1766, 1.4538). The interval calculated in Example 8.6 is (1.181, 1.449). The differences in the endpoints of the interval, although relatively minor, are due to the fact that σ is unknown for the target population. As do most statistical software packages, MINITAB computes the confidence interval using the t statistic, i.e.,

$$\bar{x} \pm t_{.005}\left(\frac{s}{\sqrt{n}}\right)$$

where $t_{.005} \approx 2.68$ (based on $n - 1 = 49$ df). The confidence interval in Example 8.6, you will recall, was calculated using the z statistic, i.e.,

$$\bar{x} \pm z_{.005}\left(\frac{s}{\sqrt{n}}\right)$$

where $z_{.005} = 2.58$. Theoretically, the MINITAB confidence interval is the correct one, since $\bar{x}$ has a t distribution when σ is unknown. The confidence interval in Example 8.6 is approximate. But you can see that the approximation is good when the sample size n is large. ■

Before concluding this section, we will comment on the assumption that the sampled population is normally distributed. In the real world, we rarely know whether a sampled population has an exact normal distribution. However, empirical studies indicate that moderate departures from this assumption do not seriously affect the confidence coefficients for small-sample confidence intervals. For example, if the population of silicon dioxide amounts for the antiscalant solutions of Example 8.11 has a distribution that is mound-shaped but nonnormal, it is likely that the actual confidence coefficient for the 99% confidence interval will be close to .99—at least close enough to be of practical use. As a consequence, the small-sample confidence interval given in the box is frequently used by experimenters when estimating the population mean of a nonnormal distribution as long as the distribution is mound-shaped and only moderately skewed.

For populations that depart greatly from normality, other estimation techniques (such as robust estimation) or methods that are distribution-free (called **nonparametric** methods) are recommended. Nonparametric statistics are the topic of Chapter 18.

EXERCISES

■ *Learning the Mechanics*

8.15 Use Table 6 of Appendix B to determine the value of $t_{\alpha/2}$ that would be used in the construction of a confidence interval for a population mean from each of the following combinations of confidence coefficient and sample size:
a. Confidence coefficient .99, $n = 18$ **b.** Confidence coefficient .95, $n = 10$
c. Confidence coefficient .90, $n = 15$

8.16 Give two reasons why the interval estimation procedure of Section 8.2 may not be applicable when the sample size is small.

8.17 The mean and standard deviation of n measurements randomly sampled from a normally distributed population are 33 and 4, respectively. Construct a 95% confidence interval for μ when:
a. $n = 5$ **b.** $n = 15$ **c.** $n = 25$

8.18 The following data represent a random sample of five measurements from a normally distributed population:

7	4	2	5	7

a. Find a 90% confidence interval for μ. **b.** Find a 99% confidence interval for μ.

8.19 How are the t distribution and the z distribution similar? How are they different?

8.20 A random sample of $n = 10$ measurements from a normally distributed population yielded $\bar{x} = 9.4$ and $s = 1.8$.
a. Calculate a 90% confidence interval for μ. **b.** Calculate a 95% confidence interval for μ.
c. Calculate a 99% confidence interval for μ.

■ *Applying the Concepts*

8.21 In Exercise 3.16, we listed the total 1993 compensations (salaries, fees, bonuses, etc.) for the top 20 corporate executives, as determined by a *Business Week* survey. For convenience, the data are repeated in the accompanying table.

	Corporate Executive (Company)	1993 Total Pay (in thousands)
1.	Michael D. Eisner (Walt Disney)	$203,011
2.	Sanford I. Weill (Travelers)	52,810
3.	Joseph R. Hyde (Autozone)	32,220
4.	Charles N. Mathewson (Intl. Game Tech.)	22,231
5.	Alan C. Greenberg (Bear Stearns)	15,915
6.	H. Wayne Huizenga (Blockbuster)	15,557
7.	Norman E. Brinker (Brinker Intl.)	14,925
8.	Roberto C. Goizueta (Coca-Cola)	14,513
9.	C. Robert Kidder (Duracell)	14,172
10.	Thomas M. Hahn (Georgia-Pacific)	13,680
11.	H. Brewster Atwater (General Mills)	13,177
12.	James C. Morgan (Applied Materials)	12,833
13.	Richard H. Jenrette (Equitable Cos.)	12,380
14.	Harry A. Merlo (Louisiana-Pacific)	12,051
15.	John H. Bryan (Sara Lee)	11,889
16.	David R. Whitwam (Whirlpool)	11,837
17.	Charles S. Sanford (Bankers Trust)	11,811
18.	Frank V. Cahouet (Mellon Bank)	11,516
19.	Walter J. Sanders (Adv. Micro Devices)	11,488
20.	Stanley C. Gault (Goodyear)	11,278

Source: "That Eye-Popping Executive Pay." *Business Week*, Apr. 25, 1994, p. 53.

a. Compute $\bar{x}$ and s.
b. Calculate a 95% confidence interval for the mean total compensation of the highest-paid corporate executives in 1993.
c. What assumption is required for the confidence interval procedure of part **b** to be valid?
d. Why might the interval, part **b**, be biased upward?

8.22 Each year, thousands of manufacturers' sales promotions are conducted by North American packaged goods companies, but promotion managers are frequently dissatisfied with their results. An exploratory study was conducted to examine the objectives and impact of such sales promotions. A sample of Canadian packaged goods companies provided information on examples of past sales promotions, including trade promotions. For the 21 "successful" trade promotions (where "success" is determined by the company managers) identified in the sample, the mean incremental profit was $53,000 and the standard deviation was $95,000 (*Journal of Marketing*, July 1986).

    a. Find a 90% confidence interval for the true mean incremental profit of "successful" trade promotions.

    b. State the assumptions required for this confidence interval to be valid.

    c. Give two ways in which you could reduce the width of the interval obtained in part **a**. Which would you recommend?

8.23 Many North American cities have built or are considering building light rail transit (LRT) systems as an alternative to the heavy rail transit systems that employ large passenger trains and subways. LRT systems are similar to the early 1900s streetcar, but are typically longer, quieter, faster, and more comfortable. In one study, the characteristics of LRT operations were examined in 10 cities that have built or are planning to build LRT systems (*Journal of the American Planning Association*, Spring 1984). One characteristic of importance to urban planners is the farebox recovery rate, computed by dividing passenger revenues by operating costs. The sample of 10 cities had a mean farebox recovery rate of .604 and a standard deviation of .163.

    a. Construct a 95% confidence interval for the true mean farebox recovery rate for LRT systems in North American cities.

    b. How would the width of the confidence interval change if the sample size were increased from $n = 10$ to $n = 20$?

    c. What assumption is required for the confidence interval procedure of part **a** to be valid?

8.24 Refer to the *Journal of Marketing Research* study of the effect of brand name and store name on product quality, Exercises 2.21 and 3.17. The stem-and-leaf displays showing the distribution of effect size (an index ranging from 0 to 1) for the 15 brand-name studies and the 17 store-name studies are reproduced here.

Brand Name (15 studies)		*Store Name (17 studies)*	
Stem	**Leaf**	**Stem**	**Leaf**
.6	0	.6	
.5	7	.5	
.4		.4	3 4
.3	4	.3	
.2	5 5	.2	
.1	0 1 1 2 4	.1	2
.0	3 3 5 5 7	.0	0 0 0 1 1 2 2 3 3 4 6 7 8 8

Source: Rao, A. R., and Monroe, K. B. "The effect of price, brand name, and store name on buyers' perceptions of product quality: An integrative review." *Journal of Marketing Research*, Vol. 26, Aug. 1989, p. 354 (Table 2).

    a. Use the method of this section to find a 95% confidence interval for the mean effect size for all brand-name studies. Interpret the result.

    b. Repeat part **a** for store-name studies.

    c. Why might the validity of the confidence intervals, parts **a** and **b**, be suspect?

8.25 The *Consumer's Research* (Nov. 1993) data on the collision-damage ratings of station wagons and minivans, Exercise 3.25, are reproduced here. Recall that a higher rating implies a greater amount paid for collision-damage repairs.

Vehicle Model	Collision-damage Rating
Chevrolet Astro 4-wheel drive	50
Plymouth Voyager	59
Chevrolet Caprice	77
Oldsmobile Silhouette	72
Dodge Caravan	60
GMC Safari	60
Mazda MPV 4-wheel drive	121
Toyota Previa	77
Chevrolet Lumina APV	71
Ford Aerostar	74
Chevrolet Astro	59
Mazda MPV	114
Pontiac Trans Sport	72

a. In Exercise 3.25, you computed $\bar{x} = 74.31$ and $s = 20.94$ for the sample data. Use this information to construct a 98% confidence interval for μ, the true average collision-damage rating of all station wagons and minivans.

b. Is there evidence to indicate that μ is less than 100? Explain.

8.26 Refer to the *Forbes* study of multinational firms, Exercises 2.16 and 3.55. The foreign revenue (expressed as a percentage of total revenue) of the 20 U.S.-based multinational firms in the sample is reproduced here. A MINITAB analysis of the data follows.

Exxon	73.2	Procter & Gamble	39.9
IBM	58.9	Philip Morris	19.6
GM	26.6	Eastman Kodak	40.9
Mobil	64.7	Digital	54.1
Ford	33.2	GE	12.4
Citicorp	52.3	United Technologies	32.9
EI duPont	39.8	Amoco	26.1
Texaco	42.3	Hewlett-Packard	53.3
ITT	43.3	Xerox	34.6
Dow Chemical	54.1	Chevron	20.5

Source: Forbes, July 23, 1990, pp. 362–363.

	N	MEAN	STDEV	SE MEAN	95.0 PERCENT C.I.
Revenue%	20	41.13	15.97	3.57	(33.66, 48.61)

a. Locate a 95% confidence interval for the mean foreign revenue percentage of all U.S.-based multinational firms on the MINITAB printout.

b. Interpret the interval, part **a**.

c. What assumption is required for the interval estimation procedure to be valid?

d. Use one of the methods of Section 6.3 to determine whether the assumption, part **c**, is approximately satisfied.

8.4 Estimation of a Population Proportion

We now consider the method for estimating the binomial proportion of successes—that is, the proportion of elements in a population that have a certain characteristic. For example, a television marketing executive would be interested in the percentage of viewers who are tuned to a particular TV program on a given night; a mortgage lending institution would be interested in estimating the proportion of its customers who will default on their loans; or a supplier of heating oil might be interested in the proportion of homes in its service area heated by natural gas. How would you estimate a binomial proportion π (e.g., the proportion of viewers who are tuned to a particular TV program), based on information contained in a sample from the population? The following examples illustrate the procedure.

EXAMPLE 8.13
Selecting a Point Estimate

Do most state lottery winners who win big payoffs quit their jobs? Not according to a study conducted by sociologist and professor H. Roy Kaplan (*Journal of the Institute for Socioeconomic Studies*, Sept. 1985). Kaplan mailed questionnaires to lottery winners who won at least $50,000 in the past 10 years. Of the 576 who responded, only 63 had quit their jobs during the first year after striking it rich. Estimate π, the true proportion of all state lottery winners (at least $50,000) who quit their jobs during the first year after striking it rich.

SOLUTION A logical candidate for a point estimate of the population proportion π is the proportion of observations in the sample that have the characteristic of interest (called a "success"); we will call this sample proportion p. If we let x represent the number of state lottery winners in the sample who quit their jobs (i.e., the number of "successes" in the sample), then the sample proportion is given by

$$p = \frac{x}{n} = \frac{\text{Number of lottery winners in sample who quit job}}{\text{Total number of lottery winners in sample}}$$

$$= \frac{63}{576} = .11$$

That is, 11% of the lottery winners in the sample quit their job during the first year after striking it rich; the value $p = .11$ serves as our point estimate of the population proportion π. ▪

To assess the reliability of the point estimate p, we must know its sampling distribution. This information may be derived by an application of the central limit theorem (details are omitted here). Properties of the sampling distribution of p (illustrated in Figure 8.11) are given in the box.

FIGURE 8.11

Sampling
Distribution of p

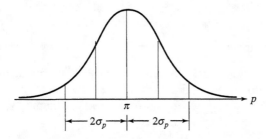

Sampling Distribution of the Sample Proportion, p

For sufficiently large samples, the sampling distribution of $p = x/n$ is approximately normal with

Mean: $\mu_p = \pi$

Standard deviation: $\sigma_p = \sqrt{\dfrac{\pi(1 - \pi)}{n}}$

where

$\pi =$ True population proportion of "successes"

$x =$ Number of successes in the samples

$n =$ Sample size

A large-sample confidence interval for π may be constructed by using a procedure analogous to that used for estimating a population mean. We begin with the point estimator p, then add and subtract a certain number of standard deviations of p to obtain the desired level of confidence. The details are given in the next box.

Large-Sample $(1 - \alpha)100\%$ Confidence Interval for a Population Proportion, π

$$p \pm z_{\alpha/2}\sigma_p \approx p \pm z_{\alpha/2}\sqrt{\frac{pq}{n}}$$

where $p = x/n$ is the sample proportion of observations with the characteristic of interest, and $q = 1 - p$.

(continued)

[*Note:* The interval is approximate since we have substituted the sample values p and q for the corresponding population values required for σ_p.]

Assumption: The sample size n is sufficiently large so that the approximation is valid. As a rule of thumb, the condition of a "sufficiently large" sample size will be satisfied if the interval $p \pm 2\sigma_p$ does not contain 0 or 1.

Note that we must substitute p and q into the formula for $\sigma_p = \sqrt{\pi(1 - \pi)/n}$ to construct the interval. This approximation will be valid as long as the sample size n is sufficiently large. Many researchers adopt the rule of thumb that n is "sufficiently large" if the interval $p \pm 2\sqrt{pq/n}$ does not contain 0 or 1.

EXAMPLE 8.14

95% Confidence Interval for π

Refer to Example 8.13. Construct a 95% confidence interval for π, the population proportion of state lottery winners who quit their job within 1 year of striking it rich.

SOLUTION For a confidence coefficient of .95, we have $1 - \alpha = .95$, $\alpha = .05$, and $\alpha/2 = .025$; the required z value is $z_{.025} = 1.96$. In Example 8.13, we obtained $p = x/n = \frac{63}{576} = .11$. Thus, $q = 1 - .11 = .89$. Substituting these values into the general formula for a confidence interval for π yields

$$p \pm z_{\alpha/2}\sqrt{\frac{pq}{n}} = .11 \pm 1.96\sqrt{\frac{(.11)(.89)}{576}} = .11 \pm .03$$

or (.08, .14). ■

EXAMPLE 8.15

90% Confidence Interval for π

Potential advertisers value television's well-known Nielsen ratings as a barometer of a TV show's popularity among viewers. The Nielsen rating of a certain TV program is an estimate of the proportion of viewers, expressed as a percentage, who tune their sets to the program on a given night. In a random sample of 165 families who regularly watch television, a Nielsen survey indicated that 101 of the families were tuned to NBC's "Seinfeld" on the night of its premiere. Estimate π, the true proportion of all TV-viewing families who watched the premiere of "Seinfeld," using a 90% confidence interval. Interpret the interval.

SOLUTION In this problem, the variable of interest is the response (yes or no) to the question, Did you watch "Seinfeld" on the night of its premiere? The sample proportion of families that watched the premiere of "Seinfeld" is

$$p = \frac{x}{n} = \frac{\text{Number of families in sample that watched the premiere}}{\text{Number of families in sample}}$$

$$= \frac{101}{165} = .612$$

Thus $q = 1 - .612 = .388$. From the formula in the box, the approximate 90% confidence interval is

$$p \pm z_{.05}\sqrt{\frac{pq}{n}} = .612 \pm 1.645 \sqrt{\frac{(.612)(.388)}{165}}$$

$$= .612 \pm .062$$

or (.550, 674).

We are 90% confident that the interval from .550 to .674 encloses the true proportion of TV-viewing families that watched the premiere of "Seinfeld." If we repeatedly selected random samples of $n = 165$ families and constructed a 90% confidence interval based on each sample, then we would expect 90% of the confidence intervals constructed to contain π. ■

Although small-sample procedures are available for the estimation of a population proportion π, they are beyond the scope of this introductory text. However, most surveys of binomial populations (e.g., opinion polls) performed in the business world use samples that are large enough to employ the procedure presented in this section.

EXERCISES

■ *Learning the Mechanics*

8.27 Random samples of n measurements are selected from a population with unknown proportion of successes π. Compute an estimate of σ_p for each of the following combinations of sample size n and sample proportion of successes p.
a. $n = 250$, $p = .4$ **b.** $n = 500$, $p = .85$ **c.** $n = 100$, $p = .25$

8.28 Random samples of n measurements are selected from a population with unknown proportion of successes π. Calculate a 95% confidence interval for π for each of the following combinations of sample size n and sample proportion of successes p.
a. $n = 500$, $p = .38$ **b.** $n = 100$, $p = .45$ **c.** $n = 1,000$, $p = .43$

8.29 The proportion of successes in a random sample of size n is $p = .20$.
a. Find a 95% confidence interval for π if $n = 100$.
b. Find a 95% confidence interval for π if $n = 500$.

8.30   A random sample of size 150 is selected from a population and the number of successes is 60.
   a. Find p, the sample proportion of successes.
   b. Construct a 90% confidence interval for π.
   c. Construct a 95% confidence interval for π.
   d. Construct a 99% confidence interval for π.

▪ *Applying the Concepts*

8.31   A University of Minnesota survey of brand names (e.g., Levi's, Lee, and Calvin Klein) as well as private labels manufactured for retail chains found a high percentage of jeans with incorrect waist and/or inseam measurements on the label. The study found that only 18 of 240 pairs of men's five-pocket, prewashed jeans sold in Minneapolis stores came within a half-inch of all their label measurements (*Tampa Tribune*, May 20, 1991). Let π represent the true proportion of men's five-pocket, prewashed jeans sold in Minneapolis that have inseam and waist measurements that fall within .5 inch of the labeled measurements.
   a. Find a point estimate of π.
   b. Find an interval estimate of π. Use a confidence coefficient of .90.
   c. Interpret the interval, part **b**.

8.32   Colleges and universities nationwide are facing an onslaught of budget reductions mandated by state governments. The reduced budget is forcing college administrators to reduce costs and/or raise revenue by raising student tuition and fees, freezing faculty salaries, increasing faculty teaching loads, and increasing class sizes. According to *U.S. News & World Report* (Sept. 28, 1992), a national sample of 2,527 college presidents and deans found that 1,769 plan on increasing class sizes to ease the financial strain. Estimate the true fraction of colleges nationwide that are planning to increase class sizes with a 95% confidence interval.

8.33   When choosing a product to purchase, what do you consider most: price or quality? In a poll of 2,000 American adults conducted by Roper Starch Worldwide, 64% claim they mainly base their buying decisions on price (*Tampa Tribune*, Oct. 31, 1993).
   a. Construct a 99% confidence interval for the true percentage of American adults who base their buying decisions more on price than on quality.
   b. Interpret the interval.
   c. How would the width of the confidence interval, part **a**, change if the confidence coefficient was decreased from .99 to .95?

8.34   The "Black Hole" survey, sponsored by the Professional Employment Research Council, reports on the toughest jobs to fill on recruiters' lists. In the most recent survey, 95 of 285 recruiters listed engineering positions as the "toughest to fill" (*Industrial Engineering*, Aug. 1990). Estimate the true percentage of recruiters who find it toughest to fill engineering positions. Use a 99% confidence interval.

8.35   As part of a cooperative research agreement between Japan and the United States, a full-scale reinforced concrete building was designed and tested under simulated earthquake loading conditions in Japan (*Journal of Structural Engineering*, Jan. 1986). For one part of the study, several U.S. design engineers were asked to evaluate the new design. Of the 48 engineers surveyed, 36 believed the shear wall of the structure to be too lightly reinforced.
   a. Find a 95% confidence interval for the true proportion of U.S. design engineers who consider the shear wall of the building too lightly reinforced.
   b. Is the sample large enough for the interval estimation procedure to be valid?

8.36 An American Housing Survey (AHS) conducted by the U.S. Department of Commerce revealed that 705 of 1,500 sampled homeowners are "do-it-yourselfers"—they did most of the work themselves on at least one of their home improvements or repairs (Bureau of the Census, *Statistical Brief*, May 1992). Using a 95% confidence interval, estimate the true proportion of American homeowners who do most of the home improvement/repair work themselves. Interpret the result.

8.37 According to an Internal Revenue Service (IRS) study, most IRS officials believe that taxpayers are unethical when filing their taxes. Of a sample of 800 IRS executives and managers from across the country, only 144 rated the ethics of the average taxpayer as good or excellent (*Arizona Republic*, Mar. 23, 1991). Estimate the true proportion of IRS officials who rate the ethics of the average taxpayer as good or excellent with a 99% confidence interval. Interpret the result.

8.38 "Are today's undergraduates more willing to cheat in order to get good grades?" This was the question posed to a national sample of 5,000 college professors by the Carnegie Foundation for the Advancement of Teaching. Given the "make it at all costs" mentality of the past decade, it is not surprising that 43% of the professors responded yes (*Tampa Tribune*, March 7, 1990). Based on this survey, estimate the proportion of all college professors who believe their undergraduate students are more willing to cheat to get good grades. Use a confidence coefficient of .90.

■ 8.5 Estimation of the Difference Between Two Population Means: Independent Samples

In Sections 8.2 and 8.3, we learned how to estimate the mean μ of a single population. We now proceed to a technique for using the information in two samples to estimate the difference between two population means. For example, we may want to compare the mean sale prices for residential properties in two neighborhoods, or the mean gasoline consumptions that may be expected this year for drivers in two areas of the country, or the mean output of union and nonunion workers at a steel company. The technique to be presented is a straightforward extension of that used for estimation of a single population mean.

Large-Sample Estimation

EXAMPLE 8.16
Selecting a Point Estimate

Use the data of Appendix A.1 to estimate the difference between the mean sale prices for all residential properties sold in the Tampa, Florida, neighborhoods Carrollwood Village and Tampa Palms.

SOLUTION Let the subscript 1 refer to Tampa Palms and the subscript 2 to Carrollwood Village. Define the following notation:

μ_1 = Population mean sale price of all Tampa Palms residential properties

μ_2 = Population mean sale price of all Carrollwood Village residential properties

Similarly, let $\bar{x}_1$ and $\bar{x}_2$ denote the respective sample means; s_1 and s_2, the respective sample standard deviations; and n_1 and n_2, the respective sample sizes. An analysis of the data of Appendix A.1 is summarized in Table 8.5.

Table 8.5 Summary of Information for Example 8.16

	Tampa Palms	Carrollwood Village
Sample size	$n_1 = 54$	$n_2 = 169$
Sample mean	$\bar{x}_1 = \$198{,}428$	$\bar{x}_2 = \$137{,}492$
Sample standard deviation	$s_1 = \$115{,}673$	$s_2 = \$62{,}828$

Now, to estimate $(\mu_1 - \mu_2)$, it seems logical to use the difference between the sample means

$$\bar{x}_1 - \bar{x}_2 = \$198{,}428 - \$137{,}492 = \$60{,}936$$

as our point estimate of the difference between the population means. The properties of the point estimate $(\bar{x}_1 - \bar{x}_2)$ are summarized by its sampling distribution, shown in the accompanying box (see also Figure 8.12). ■

FIGURE 8.12

Sampling Distribution of $(\bar{x}_1 - \bar{x}_2)$

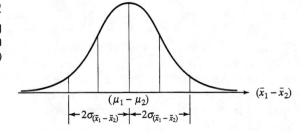

Sampling Distribution of $(\bar{x}_1 - \bar{x}_2)$

For sufficiently large sample sizes (say, $n_1 \geq 30$ and $n_2 \geq 30$), the sampling distribution of $(\bar{x}_1 - \bar{x}_2)$, based on independent random samples from two populations, is approximately normal with

Mean: $\mu_{(\bar{x}_1 - \bar{x}_2)} = (\mu_1 - \mu_2)$

Standard deviation: $\sigma_{(\bar{x}_1 - \bar{x}_2)} = \sqrt{\dfrac{\sigma_1^2}{n_1} + \dfrac{\sigma_2^2}{n_2}}$

where σ_1^2 and σ_2^2 are the variances of the two populations from which the samples were selected.

As was the case with large-sample estimation of a single population mean, the requirement of "large" sample sizes enables us to apply the central limit theorem to obtain the sampling distribution of $(\bar{x}_1 - \bar{x}_2)$; it also justifies the use of s_1^2 and s_2^2 as approximations to the respective population variances, σ_1^2 and σ_2^2.

The procedure for forming a large-sample confidence interval for $(\mu_1 - \mu_2)$ appears in the accompanying box.

Large-Sample $(1 - \alpha)100\%$ Confidence Interval for $(\mu_1 - \mu_2)$

$$(\bar{x}_1 - \bar{x}_2) \pm z_{\alpha/2}\, \sigma_{(\bar{x}_1 - \bar{x}_2)} = (\bar{x}_1 - \bar{x}_2) \pm z_{\alpha/2} \sqrt{\frac{\sigma_1^2}{n_1} + \frac{\sigma_2^2}{n_2}}$$

$$\approx (\bar{x}_1 - \bar{x}_2) \pm z_{\alpha/2} \sqrt{\frac{s_1^2}{n_1} + \frac{s_2^2}{n_2}}$$

[*Note:* We have used the sample variances s_1^2 and s_2^2 as approximations to the corresponding population parameters.]

Assumptions:

1. The two random samples are selected in an independent manner from the target populations. That is, the choice of elements in one sample does not affect, and is not affected by, the choice of elements in the other sample.
2. The sample sizes n_1 and n_2 are sufficiently large. (We recommend $n_1 \geq 30$ and $n_2 \geq 30$.)

EXAMPLE 8.17
Large-Sample 95%
Confidence Interval for
$\mu_1 - \mu_2$

Refer to Example 8.16. Assume the data described in Appendix A.1 represent independent random samples of properties sold in the Tampa neighborhoods. Construct a 95% confidence interval for $(\mu_1 - \mu_2)$, the difference between the mean sale prices for all residential properties in Tampa Palms and Carrollwood Village. Interpret the interval.

SOLUTION The general form of a 95% confidence interval for $(\mu_1 - \mu_2)$, based on large samples from the target populations, is given by

$$(\bar{x}_1 - \bar{x}_2) \pm z_{.025} \sqrt{\frac{\sigma_1^2}{n_1} + \frac{\sigma_2^2}{n_2}}$$

Recall that $z_{.025} = 1.96$, and use the information in Table 8.5 to make the following substitutions to obtain the desired confidence interval:

$$(198,428 - 137,492) \pm 1.96 \sqrt{\frac{\sigma_1^2}{54} + \frac{\sigma_2^2}{169}}$$

$$\approx (198,428 - 137,492) \pm 1.96 \sqrt{\frac{(115,673)^2}{54} + \frac{(62,828)^2}{169}}$$

$$= 60,936 \pm 32,274$$

or ($28,662, $93,210).

Using this method of estimation produces confidence intervals that will enclose $(\mu_1 - \mu_2)$, the difference between population means, 95% of the time. Since all the values in the interval are positive, we can be reasonably confident that the mean sale price of Tampa Palms homes is between $28,662 and $93,210 higher than the mean sale price of Carrollwood Village homes. ■

EXAMPLE 8.18
Computer Analysis

The personnel manager for a large steel company suspects there is a difference between the mean amounts of work time lost because of sickness for blue-collar and white-collar workers at the plant. She randomly samples the records of 45 blue-collar workers and 38 white-collar workers and records the number of days lost to sickness within the past year. The data were entered into a computer, and MINITAB was used to estimate $(\mu_1 - \mu_2)$, the difference between the population mean times lost to sickness for blue-collar and white-collar workers at the steel company last year, with a 90% confidence interval. The MINITAB printout is shown in Figure 8.13. Interpret the results.

FIGURE 8.13
MINITAB Printout
for the Data in
Example 8.18

```
TWOSAMPLE T FOR sickdays
worker    N       MEAN     STDEV    SE MEAN
1        45       11.5     10.2       1.5
2        38       9.00     5.58       0.91

90 PCT CI FOR MU 1 - MU 2:  (-0.4, 5.47)

TTEST MU 1 = MU 2 (VS NE):  T= 1.42   P=0.16   DF=  70
```

SOLUTION The 90% confidence interval for $\mu_1 - \mu_2$, shaded on the printout, is $(-.40, 5.47)$. Thus, the personnel manager is 90% confident that $(\mu_1 - \mu_2)$, the difference between the mean days lost to sickness for the two groups of workers, falls between $-.40$ and 5.47. In other words, the manager estimates that μ_2, the mean days lost to sickness for white-collar workers, could be *larger* than μ_1, the mean days lost to sickness for blue-collar workers, by as much as .40 day, or it could be *less* than μ_1 by as much as 5.47 days. Since the interval contains the value 0, she is unable to conclude that there is a real difference between the mean numbers of sick days lost by the two groups. If, in fact, such a difference exists, she would have to increase the sample sizes to be able to detect it. This would reduce the width of the confidence interval and provide more information about the phenomenon under investigation. ■

Small-Sample Estimation

When estimating the difference between two population means based on small samples from each population, we must make specific assumptions about the relative frequency distributions of the two populations, as indicated in the box.

> **Assumptions Required for Small-Sample Estimation of $(\mu_1 - \mu_2)$**
>
> 1. Both of the populations from which the samples are selected have relative frequency distributions that are approximately normal.
> 2. The variances σ_1^2 and σ_2^2 of the two populations are equal.
> 3. The random samples are selected in an independent manner from the two populations.

Figure 8.14 illustrates the form of the population distributions implied by assumptions 1 and 2. Observe that both populations have relative frequency distributions that are approximately normal. Although the means of the two populations may differ, we require the variances σ_1^2 and σ_2^2, which measure the spreads of the two distributions, to be equal. When these assumptions are satisfied, we may use the Student's t distribution (specified in the next box) to construct a confidence interval for $(\mu_1 - \mu_2)$, based on small samples (say, $n_1 < 30$ or $n_2 < 30$) from the respective populations. Since we assume that the two populations have equal variances (i.e., $\sigma_1^2 = \sigma_2^2 = \sigma^2$), we construct an estimate of σ^2 based on the information contained in *both* samples. This **pooled estimate** is denoted s_p^2 and is computed as shown in the box.

FIGURE 8.14

Assumptions Required for Small-Sample Estimation of $(\mu_1 - \mu_2)$: Normal Distributions with Equal Variances

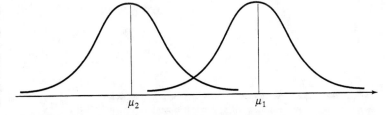

> **Small-Sample $(1 - \alpha)100\%$ Confidence Interval for $(\mu_1 - \mu_2)$**
>
> $$(\bar{x}_1 - \bar{x}_2) \pm t_{\alpha/2}\sqrt{s_p^2\left(\frac{1}{n_1} + \frac{1}{n_2}\right)}$$
>
> where
>
> $$s_p^2 = \frac{(n_1 - 1)s_1^2 + (n_2 - 1)s_2^2}{n_1 + n_2 - 2}$$
>
> and the value of $t_{\alpha/2}$ is based on $(n_1 + n_2 - 2)$ degrees of freedom.

EXAMPLE 8.19
Small-Sample 95%
Confidence Interval
for $\mu_1 - \mu_2$

A key aspect of organizational buying is negotiation. S. W. Clopton investigated several issues pertaining to buyer–seller negotiations (*Journal of Marketing Research*, Feb. 1984). One aspect of the analysis involved a comparison of two types of bargaining strategies—competitive bargaining and coordinative bargaining. A *competitive strategy* is characterized by inflexible behavior aimed at forcing concessions, whereas a *coordinative strategy* involves a problem-solving orientation to negotiations with a high degree of trust and cooperation. A sample of organizational buyers were recruited to participate in a particular negotiation experiment. In one negotiation setting where the maximum profit was fixed, eight buyers used the competitive bargaining strategy and eight buyers used the coordinative bargaining strategy.

Data on the individual savings for the two groups of buyers are provided in Table 8.6.

a. Construct a 95% confidence interval for the difference between the mean buyer savings of the two strategies.

b. In theory, the mean buyer savings for the competitive strategy will be less than the corresponding mean for the coordinative strategy. Use the result, part **a**, to make an inference about this theory.

Table 8.6   Data for Example 8.19

Competitive Bargaining	Coordinative Bargaining
$1,857	$1,544
1,700	2,640
1,829	1,645
2,644	2,275
1,566	2,137
663	2,327
1,712	2,152
1,679	2,130

Source: Clopton, S.W. "Seller and buying firm factors affecting industrial buyers' negotiation behavior and outcomes." *Journal of Marketing*, Feb. 1984, pp. 39–53, published by the American Marketing Association.

SOLUTION

a. Let μ_1 and μ_2 represent the true mean savings of buyers using the competitive and coordinative bargaining strategies, respectively. Since the samples selected for the study are small ($n_1 = n_2 = 8$), the following assumptions are required:

1. The populations of buyer savings under the competitive and coordinative strategies both have approximately normal distributions.

2. The variances of the populations of buyer savings for the two bargaining strategies are equal.

FIGURE 8.15

MINITAB Printout for
Example 8.19

```
TWOSAMPLE T FOR Compete VS Coordin

            N      MEAN    STDEV   SE MEAN
Compete   8      1706     538      190
Coordin   8      2106     357      126

95 PCT CI FOR MU Compete - MU Coordin: (-890, 90)

TTEST MU Compete = MU Coordin (VS NE): T= -1.75  P=0.10  DF=  14

POOLED STDEV =        457
```

3. The samples were independently and randomly selected.

To compute the confidence interval, we must find $\bar{x}_1$, $\bar{x}_2$, s_1, and s_2. These summary statistics are given in the MINITAB printout, Figure 8.15, as $\bar{x}_1 = 1,706$, $\bar{x}_2 = 2,106$, $s_1 = 538$, and $s_2 = 357$. Since we have assumed that the two populations have equal variances (i.e., $\sigma_1^2 = \sigma_2^2 = \sigma^2$), the next step is to compute an estimate of this common variance. Our pooled estimate is given by

$$s_p^2 = \frac{(n_1 - 1)s_1^2 + (n_2 - 1)s_2^2}{n_1 + n_2 - 2} = \frac{(8-1)(538)^2 + (8-1)(357)^2}{8+8-2}$$

$$= 208,446$$

The 95% confidence interval for $(\mu_1 - \mu_2)$ will be based on the value of $t_{.025}$, where t has $(n_1 + n_2 - 2) = (8+8-2) = 14$ degrees of freedom. From Table 6 of Appendix B, we obtain $t_{.025} = 2.145$. We now substitute the appropriate quantities into the general formula:

$$(\bar{x}_1 \pm \bar{x}_2) \pm t_{.025} \sqrt{s_p^2 \left(\frac{1}{n_1} + \frac{1}{n_2} \right)}$$

$$= (1,706 - 2,106) \pm 2.145 \sqrt{208.446 \left(\frac{1}{8} + \frac{1}{8} \right)}$$

$$= -400 \pm 490$$

or $(-890, 90)$.

We estimate with 95% confidence that the difference $(\mu_1 - \mu_2)$ falls in the interval from -890 to 90. Note that this interval is also given (shaded) on the MINITAB printout, Figure 8.15.

b. From the 95% confidence interval, part **a**, we can infer that μ_1, the mean buyer savings for the competitive bargaining strategy, is anywhere from \$890 less to \$90 more than μ_2, the corresponding mean for coordinative bargaining. Since 0 is included in the interval, there is no evidence to support the theory that μ_1 is less than μ_2. ■

As with the one-sample case, the assumptions required for estimating $(\mu_1 - \mu_2)$ with small samples do not have to be satisfied exactly for the interval estimate to be useful in practice. Slight departures from these assumptions do not seriously affect the level of confidence in the procedure. For example, when the variances σ_1^2 and σ_2^2 of the sampled populations are unequal, researchers have found that the small-sample confidence interval for $(\mu_1 - \mu_2)$ given in the box will still yield valid results in practice as long as the two populations are normal and the sample sizes are equal, i.e., $n_1 = n_2$. In the case where $\sigma_1^2 \neq \sigma_2^2$ and $n_1 \neq n_2$, an approximate confidence interval for $(\mu_1 - \mu_2)$ can be constructed by modifying the degrees of freedom associated with the t distribution.

In the box, we give the approximate small-sample confidence intervals for $(\mu_1 - \mu_2)$ for two situations when the assumption of equal variances is violated: $n_1 = n_2$ and $n_1 \neq n_2$.

Approximate Small-Sample $(1 - \alpha)100\%$ Confidence Interval for $(\mu_1 - \mu_2)$ When $\sigma_1^2 \neq \sigma_2^2$

$$n_1 = n_2 = n: \quad (\bar{x}_1 \pm \bar{x}_2) \pm t_{\alpha/2} \sqrt{\frac{s_1^2}{n} + \frac{s_2^2}{n}}$$

where the distribution of t depends on $v = n_1 + n_2 - 2 = 2(n - 1)$ degrees of freedom.

$$n_1 \neq n_2: \quad (\bar{x}_1 - \bar{x}_2) \pm t_{\alpha/2} \sqrt{\frac{s_1^2}{n} + \frac{s_2^2}{n}}$$

where the distribution of t has degrees of freedom equal to

$$v = \frac{(s_1^2/n_1 + s_2^2/n_2)^2}{\dfrac{(s_1^2/n_1)^2}{n_1 - 1} + \dfrac{(s_2^2/n_2)^2}{n_2 - 1}}$$

[*Note:* In the case of $n_1 \neq n_2$, the value of v will not generally be an integer. Round v down to the nearest integer to use the t table (Table 6 of Appendix B).]

Assumptions:

1. Both of the populations from which the samples are selected have relative frequency distributions that are approximately normal.
2. The random samples are selected in an independent manner from the two populations.

EXERCISES

■ **Learning the Mechanics**

8.39 Independent random samples are selected from two populations with means μ_1 and μ_2, respectively. Calculate estimates of $\mu_{(\bar{x}_1 - \bar{x}_2)}$ and $\sigma_{(\bar{x}_1 - \bar{x}_2)}$ for each of the following situations:

a. $\bar{x}_1 = 150$, $s_1^2 = 36$; $\bar{x}_2 = 140$, $s_2^2 = 24$; $n_1 = n_2 = 35$

b. $\bar{x}_1 = 125$, $s_1^2 = 225$, $n_1 = 90$; $\bar{x}_2 = 112$, $s_2^2 = 90$, $n_2 = 60$

8.40 Consider two independent random samples, 30 observations selected from population 1 and 40 selected from population 2. The resulting sample means and variances are shown in the table.

Sample from Population 1	Sample from Population 2
$\bar{x}_1 = 15$	$\bar{x}_2 = 23$
$s_1^2 = 16$	$s_2^2 = 100$
$n_1 = 30$	$n_2 = 40$

a. Construct a 90% confidence interval for $(\mu_1 - \mu_2)$.
b. Construct a 95% confidence interval for $(\mu_1 - \mu_2)$.
c. Construct a 99% confidence interval for $(\mu_1 - \mu_2)$.

8.41 To use the t statistic in a small-sample confidence interval for the difference between the means of two populations, what assumptions must be made about the two populations? About the two samples?

8.42 The accompanying tables show summary statistics for random samples selected from two normal populations that are assumed to have the same variance. In each case, find s_p^2, the pooled estimate of the common variance.

a.	Sample from Population 1	Sample from Population 2	**b.**	Sample from Population 1	Sample from Population 2
	$\bar{x}_1 = 552$	$\bar{x}_2 = 369$		$\bar{x}_1 = 10.8$	$\bar{x}_2 = 8.4$
	$s_1^2 = 4{,}400$	$s_2^2 = 7{,}481$		$s_1^2 = .313$	$s_2^2 = .499$
	$n_1 = 6$	$n_2 = 7$		$n_1 = 8$	$n_2 = 8$

8.43 Independent random samples from two normal populations produced the sample means and variances listed in the next table.

Sample from Population 1	Sample from Population 2
$n_1 = 14$	$n_2 = 7$
$\bar{x}_1 = 53.2$	$\bar{x}_2 = 43.4$
$s_1^2 = 96.8$	$s_2^2 = 102.0$

a. Find a 90% confidence interval for $(\mu_1 - \mu_2)$.
b. Find a 95% confidence interval for $(\mu_1 - \mu_2)$.
c. Find a 99% confidence interval for $(\mu_1 - \mu_2)$.

8.44 Two independent random samples selected from normal populations produced the summary statistics shown in the table.

Sample 1	Sample 2
$\bar{x}_1 = 25$	$\bar{x}_2 = 23$
$s_1^2 = 16$	$s_2^2 = 20$

a. Find a 95% confidence interval for $(\mu_1 - \mu_2)$ if $n_1 = n_2 = 100$.
b. Find a 95% confidence interval for $(\mu_1 - \mu_2)$ if $n_1 = n_2 = 10$ and $\sigma_1^2 = \sigma_2^2$.
c. Find a 95% confidence interval for $(\mu_1 - \mu_2)$ if $n_1 = n_2 = 10$ and $\sigma_1^2 \neq \sigma_2^2$.
d. Find a 95% confidence interval for $(\mu_1 - \mu_2)$ if $n_1 = 10$, $n_2 = 20$, and $\sigma_1^2 = \sigma_2^2$.
e. Find a 95% confidence interval for $(\mu_1 - \mu_2)$ if $n_1 = 10$, $n_2 = 20$, and $\sigma_1^2 \neq \sigma_2^2$.

▪ *Applying the Concepts*

8.45 The label "Machiavellian" was derived from the 16th-century Florentine writer Niccolo Machiavelli, who wrote on ways of manipulating others to accomplish one's objective. Critics often accuse marketers of being manipulative and unethical, or Machiavellian in nature. S. D. Hunt and L. B. Chanko explored the question of whether "marketers are more Machiavellian than others" (*Journal of Marketing*, Summer 1984). The Machiavellian scores (measured by the Mach IV scale) for a sample of marketing professionals were recorded and compared to the Machiavellian scores for other groups of people, including a sample of college students in an earlier study. The results are summarized in the accompanying table. (Higher scores are associated with Machiavellian attitudes.)

	Marketing Professionals	College Students
Sample size	1,076	1,782
Mean score	85.7	90.7
Standard deviation	13.2	14.3

a. Construct a 99% confidence interval for the mean difference in Machiavellian scores between marketing professionals and college students.

b. Interpret the interval constructed in part **a.**

8.46 Refer to the Harris Corporation/University of Florida study to determine whether a manufacturing process performed at a remote location can be established locally, Exercise 3.32. Test devices (pilots) were set up at both the old and new locations and voltage readings on 30 production runs at each location were obtained. The data are reproduced in the table. Descriptive statistics are displayed in the accompanying SAS printout. [*Note*: Larger voltage readings are better than smaller voltage readings.]

Old Location			New Location		
9.98	10.12	9.84	9.19	10.01	8.82
10.26	10.05	10.15	9.63	8.82	8.65
10.05	9.80	10.02	10.10	9.43	8.51
10.29	10.15	9.80	9.70	10.03	9.14
10.03	10.00	9.73	10.09	9.85	9.75
8.05	9.87	10.01	9.60	9.27	8.78
10.55	9.55	9.98	10.05	8.83	9.35
10.26	9.95	8.72	10.12	9.39	9.54
9.97	9.70	8.80	9.49	9.48	9.36
9.87	8.72	9.84	9.37	9.64	8.68

Source: Harris Corporation, Melbourne, Fla.

```
              Analysis Variable : VOLTAGE


------------------------------ LOCATION=OLD ------------------------------

  N Obs   N     Minimum      Maximum        Mean         Std Dev
  ----------------------------------------------------------------
    30    30    8.0500000   10.5500000    9.8036667     0.5409155
  ----------------------------------------------------------------


------------------------------ LOCATION=NEW ------------------------------

  N Obs   N     Minimum      Maximum        Mean         Std Dev
  ----------------------------------------------------------------
    30    30    8.5100000   10.1200000    9.4223333     0.4788757
  ----------------------------------------------------------------
```

a. Compare the mean voltage readings at the two locations using a 90% confidence interval.

b. Based on the interval, part **a,** does it appear that the manufacturing process can be established locally?

8.47 The *American Journal of Small Businesses* (Winter 1988) reported on a survey designed to compare female managers at large firms with those at small firms (less than 100 employees). Previous studies indicate that female managers in large and small companies are quite similar.

In this study, independent random samples of 86 female managers at small firms and 91 female managers at large firms were compared on several job-related variables. The following question was asked: "How many times have you been promoted in the last three years?" The responses for the two groups of female managers are summarized in the table.

Small Firms	Large Firms
$n_1 = 86$	$n_2 = 91$
$\bar{x}_1 = 1.0$	$\bar{x}_2 = .9$
$s_1 = 1.1$	$s_2 = 1.1$

Source: Anderson, R. L., and Anderson, K. P. "A comparison of women in small and large companies." *American Journal of Small Businesses,* Vol. 12, No. 3, Winter 1988, p. 28 (Table 2).

a. Compute a point estimate for the difference between the mean number of promotions awarded to female managers at small firms and at large firms.
b. Compare the mean number of promotions awarded to the two groups of female managers with a 90% confidence interval.
c. Interpret the interval, part **b**.
d. How could the researchers reduce the width of the interval, part **b**?

8.48 An experiment was conducted to determine whether individuals could be taught how to make decisions rationally and whether such training would improve the quality of their career decisions (*Journal of Vocational Behavior*, Aug. 1986). A sample of 69 California community college students, all classified as rational decision makers, were randomly divided into two groups. The experimental group (34 students) received instruction in rational decision making, whereas the control group (35 students) did not. At the end of the instruction period, all subjects completed a multiple-choice test designed to assess the extent to which an individual knows how to apply rational principles in job-decision situations. The results are summarized in the table. (Higher scores indicate greater adherence to the rational style of decision making.) Construct a 90% confidence interval for the difference between the mean test scores of the two groups of students. Interpret the interval.

	Experimental (Training) Group	Control (No Training) Group
Sample size	34	35
Mean	50.26	47.34
Standard deviation	6.67	11.52

Source: Krumboltz, J. D., et al. "Teaching a rational approach to career decision making: Who benefits most?" *Journal of Vocational Behavior,* Vol. 29, No. 8, Aug. 1986, pp. 1–6 (Table 1).

8.49 Consider the total appraised values of residential properties described in Appendix A.1. Suppose you want to compare the mean appraisals of properties in two Tampa neighborhoods, Northdale and Ybor City.

a. Use one of the methods of Chapter 7 to generate random samples of size $n_1 = n_2 = 5$ from the total appraised values for the two neighborhoods. Compute the mean and standard deviation for each sample. [*Note:* The data are available on a $3\frac{1}{2}''$ diskette from the publisher.]

b. Use the information from part **a** to construct a 90% confidence interval for the difference between the mean appraised values of properties in the two neighborhoods. Does the interval provide evidence that the mean appraised value in Ybor City is less than the mean appraised value in Northdale?

c. State the assumptions necessary for the estimation procedure you used in part **b** to be valid.

d. Repeat part **a**, but select independent random samples of size $n_1 = n_2 = 30$. Compute $\bar{x}$ and s for the two samples.

e. Use the sample information from part **d** to construct a 90% confidence interval for the difference between the mean appraised values of properties in the two neighborhoods. Compare this interval to the interval you found in part **b**. How have the increased sample sizes affected the width of the 90% confidence interval?

f. Does the interval from part **e** provide evidence that the mean appraisal in Ybor City is less than the mean appraisal in Northdale? Which interval, the interval of part **b** or the interval of part **e**, would you recommend for making inferences concerning the difference between the means? Why?

8.50 Many business decisions are made because of offered incentives that are intended to make the decision maker "feel good." How does such a positive affect influence the risk preference of decision makers? This question was the subject of a study conducted at Ohio State University. Before the experiment began, subjects were divided randomly into two groups: the "positive affect" group and the control group. Each subject in the positive affect group was given a bag of candies as a token of appreciation for participating in the study, whereas the control group subjects were not given the gift. All subjects were then given 10 gambling chips (worth $10) as a reward for participating in the study, and presented with a choice of (1) betting five chips on any one of the bets available in roulette, or (2) not betting. After a short explanation of the probabilities associated with the different roulette bets, the subjects were instructed to indicate on a scale of .00 to 1.00, marked at intervals of .10, the riskiest bet they were willing to make (i.e., what the probability of winning would have to be for them to bet). A summary of the results (winning probabilities) is given in the table.

	Positive Affect Group	Control Group
Number of subjects	11	13
Mean probability of winning	.65	.52
Standard deviation	.18	.15

Source: Isen, A. M., and Geva, N. "The influence of positive affect on acceptable level of risk: The person with the large canoe has a large worry." *Organizational Behavior and Human Decision Processes,* Vol. 39, 1987, p. 149.

a. Construct a 95% confidence interval for the difference between the mean probabilities of winning indicated by the two groups of subjects.

b. Interpret the interval obtained in part **a**. Is there evidence of a difference between the mean probabilities selected by subjects in the two groups?

c. What assumptions are required for the inference made in part **b** to be valid?

8.51 Refer to Exercise 8.24. Use the information in the stem-and-leaf displays to find a 95% confidence interval for the difference between the mean effect sizes of brand-name studies and store-name studies. Comment on any assumptions required for the interval estimate to be valid and whether they are reasonably satisfied.

8.6 Estimation of the Difference Between Two Population Means: Matched Pairs

The procedures for estimating the difference between two population means presented in Section 8.5 were based on the assumption that the samples were randomly and independently selected from the target populations. Sometimes we can obtain more information about the difference between population means, $(\mu_1 - \mu_2)$, by selecting **paired observations**.

EXAMPLE 8.20
Drawback to Using Independent Samples

Suppose you want to compare two methods for training managers of a large corporation to be more assertive. One way to design the experiment is to randomly select 20 managers from among all available managers and then randomly assign 10 to method 1 and 10 to method 2 (see Figure 8.16). The assertiveness test scores obtained after completion of the experiment would represent independent random samples of scores attained by managers trained by two different methods. The difference between the mean assertiveness scores, $(\mu_1 - \mu_2)$, could be estimated using the small-sample confidence interval procedure described in Section 8.5.

a. Comment on the potential drawbacks of using independent random samples to estimate $(\mu_1 - \mu_2)$.

b. Propose a better method of sampling, one that will yield more information on the parameter of interest.

FIGURE 8.16

Independent Random Samples of Managers, Example 8.20

	Method 1	Method 2
	1	2
	5	3
	6	4
	8	7
Manager	11	9
Identification	14	10
Number	15	12
	17	13
	19	16
	20	18

SOLUTION

a. Assume that method 1 is truly more effective than method 2 in teaching assertiveness skills to managers. A potential drawback to the independent sampling plan shown in Figure 8.16 is that the differences in the assertiveness scores of managers due to experience, education, personality, and other factors are not taken into account. For example, by chance, the sampling plan may assign the 10 "worst" managers to method 1 and the 10 "best" managers to method 2. This unbalanced assignment may mask the fact that method 1 is more effective than method 2, i.e., the resulting confidence interval on $(\mu_1 - \mu_2)$ may fail to show that μ_1 exceeds μ_2.

b. A better method of sampling is one that attempts to remove the variation in assertiveness scores due to extraneous factors such as experience and education. One way to do this is to match the managers in pairs, where the managers in each pair have similar experience, education, etc. From each pair, one member would be randomly selected to be taught by method 1; the other member would be assigned to the class taught by method 2 (see Figure 8.17). The differences between the **matched pairs** of assertiveness scores should provide a clearer picture of the true difference in assertiveness for the two training methods because the matching would tend to cancel the effects of the extraneous factors that formed the basis of the matching.

FIGURE 8.17

Matched Pairs
Experiment, Example
8.20 (Pair members
identified as manager
A and manager B)

Manager Pair	Assignment	
	Method 1	Method 2
1	A	B
2	B	A
⋮	⋮	⋮
10	A	B

The sampling plan shown in Figure 8.17 is commonly known as a **matched-pairs experiment**. In the box on page 384, we give the procedure for estimating the difference between two population means based on matched-pairs data. You can see that once the differences in the paired observations are obtained, the analysis proceeds as a one-sample problem. That is, a confidence interval on a single mean (the mean of the difference, μ_d) is computed.

$(1 - \alpha)100\%$ Confidence Interval for $\mu_d = (\mu_1 - \mu_2)$: Matched Pairs

Let $d_1, d_2, ..., d_n$ represent the differences between the pairwise observations in a random sample of n matched pairs, $\bar{d}$ = mean of the n sample differences, and s_d = standard deviation of the n sample differences.

Large Sample	Small Sample
$$\bar{d} \pm z_{\alpha/2}\left(\frac{\sigma_d}{\sqrt{n}}\right)$$	$$\bar{d} \pm t_{\alpha/2}\left(\frac{s_d}{\sqrt{n}}\right)$$
where σ_d is the population standard deviation of differences Assumption: $n \geq 30$ [Note: When σ_d is unknown (as is usually the case), use s_d to approximate σ_d.]	where $t_{\alpha/2}$ is based on $(n - 1)$ degrees of freedom Assumption: The population of paired differences is normally distributed.

EXAMPLE 8.21
95% Confidence Interval for μ_d

Refer to the comparison of two methods for training managers to be more assertive, Example 8.20. Suppose that the $n = 10$ pairs of managerial assertiveness test scores were as shown in Table 8.7. (Higher scores indicate higher levels of assertiveness.) Find a 95% confidence interval for the difference in mean levels of assertiveness, $\mu_d = (\mu_1 - \mu_2)$.

Table 8.7 Managerial Assertiveness Test Scores for Example 8.21

					Manager Pair					
	1	2	3	4	5	6	7	8	9	10
Method 1 score	78	63	72	89	91	49	68	76	85	55
Method 2 score	71	44	61	84	74	51	55	60	77	39
Pair difference	7	19	11	5	17	−2	13	16	8	16

SOLUTION The differences between the $n = 10$ matched pairs of assertiveness test scores are computed as

$$d = (\text{Method 1 score}) - (\text{Method 2 score})$$

and are shown in the third row of Table 8.7.

To proceed with this small-sample estimation, we must assume that these differences are from an approximately normal population. The mean and standard deviation of these sample differences are shown (shaded) on the SPSS printout, Figure 8.18. From the printout, $\overline{d} = 11.0$ and $s_d = 6.53$.

FIGURE 8.18

SPSS Printout for
Example 8.21

```
----------------------------------------------------------------------------

Number of Valid Observations (Listwise) =          10.00

Variable        Mean    Std Dev   Minimum   Maximum    N  Label

SCORDIFF       11.00      6.53     -2.00     19.00     10
----------------------------------------------------------------------------
```

The value of $t_{.025}$, based on $(n - 1) = (10 - 1) = 9$ degrees of freedom, is given in Table 6 of Appendix B as $t_{.025} = 2.262$. Substituting these values into the formula for the confidence interval, we obtain

$$\overline{d} \pm t_{.025} \left(\frac{s_d}{\sqrt{n}} \right) = 11.0 \pm 2.262 \left(\frac{6.53}{\sqrt{10}} \right)$$

$$= 11.0 \pm 4.7$$

or (6.3, 15.17).

We estimate with 95% confidence that the difference between mean managerial assertiveness test scores for methods 1 and 2 falls within the interval from 6.3 to 15.7. Since all the values within the interval are positive, method 1 seems to produce a mean assertiveness score that is statistically larger than the mean score for method 2. ■

Often, the pairs of observations in a matched-pairs experiment arise naturally by recording two measurements on the same experimental unit at two different points in time. For example, a recent study investigated the effectiveness of a prescription drug in improving the SAT scores of nervous test takers. The experimental units (the objects upon which the measurements are taken) were 22 high school juniors who took the SAT twice, once without and once with the drug. Thus, two measurements were taken on each junior: (1) SAT score with no drug and (2) SAT score with the drug. These two observations, taken for all students in the study, formed the "matched pairs" of the experiment.

In an analysis of matched-pairs observations, it is important to stress that the pairing of the experimental units must be performed before the data are collected. Recall that the objective is to compare two methods of "treating" the experimental units. By using matched pairs of units that have similar characteristics, we are able to cancel the effects of the variables used to match the pairs.

EXERCISES

■ **Learning the Mechanics**

8.52   A random sample of 10 paired observations yielded the following summary information:

$$\bar{d} = 2.3 \qquad s_d = 2.67$$

a. Find a 90% confidence interval for μ_d.   b. Find a 95% confidence interval for μ_d.
c. Find a 99% confidence interval for μ_d.

8.53   The data for a random sample of four paired observations are shown in the table.

Pair	Observation from Population A	Observation from Population B
1	2	0
2	5	7
3	10	6
4	8	5

a. Calculate the difference within each pair, subtracting observation B from observation A. Use the differences to calculate $\bar{d}$ and s_d.
b. If μ_1 and μ_2 are the means of populations A and B, respectively, express μ_d in terms of μ_1 and μ_2.
c. Construct a 95% confidence interval for μ_d.

8.54   The data for a random sample of seven paired observations are shown in the accompanying table. Find a 90% confidence interval for $\mu_d = (\mu_A - \mu_B)$.

Pair	Observation from Population A	Observation from Population B
1	48	54
2	50	56
3	47	50
4	50	55
5	63	64
6	65	65
7	55	61

8.55   A random sample of $n = 50$ paired observations yielded the following summary statistics:

$$\bar{d} = 19.3 \qquad s_d = 5.2$$

Construct a 95% confidence interval for μ_d.

8.56 List the assumptions required to construct a valid small-sample confidence interval for μ_d based on matched-pairs data.

■ *Applying the Concepts*

8.57 Traditionally, real estate appraisers use a cost and/or income approach to valuate tenanted real estate. A new method, called discounted cash flow (DCF) analysis, is now available. If it is applied properly, researchers believe DCF analysis to be the premier valuation tool of appraisers. *The Appraisal Journal* (Jan. 1993) compared the results of a DCF analysis to that of a feasibility study (which involves both the cost and income approach) for estimating annual rental rates of properties. The projected rental rates are listed in the accompanying table.

	Projected Annual Rental Rates	
Year	*DCF Analysis*	*Feasibility Study*
1	$12.00	$17.00
2	12.00	17.68
3	12.36	18.39
4	12.98	19.12
5	14.02	19.89
6	15.42	20.68
7	16.96	21.51
8	18.66	22.37
9	19.59	23.27
10	20.57	24.20
11	21.60	25.16

Source: Bottum, M. S. "Discounted cash flow analyses: Tests of reasonableness." *The Appraisal Journal*, Jan. 1993, p. 139 (Table 1).

a. Construct a 99% confidence interval for the mean difference between annual rental rates projected by the DCF and feasibility methods.

b. According to the study, the DCF analysis is reasonable if the mean DCF rental rate does not exceed the mean feasibility rental rate. Use the interval, part **a**, to make an inference about the two means in question.

8.58 A new weight-reducing technique, consisting of a liquid protein diet, is currently undergoing tests by the Food and Drug Administration (FDA) before its introduction into the market. The following is a typical test performed by the FDA. The weights of a random sample of five people are recorded before they are introduced to the liquid protein diet. The five individuals are then instructed to follow the liquid protein diet for 3 weeks. At the end of this period, their weights (in pounds) are again recorded. The results of one such test are listed in the next table.

Person	Weight Before Diet	Weight After Diet
1	150	143
2	195	190
3	188	185
4	197	191
5	204	200

a. Construct a 95% confidence interval for the difference between the true mean weights before and after the diet is used.

b. What assumptions are necessary to ensure the validity of the procedure you used?

8.59 One desirable characteristic of water pipes is that the quality of the water they deliver is equal to or near the quality of the water entering the system at the water treatment plant. A type of ductile iron pipe has provided an excellent water delivery system for the St. Louis County Water Company. The chlorine level of water emerging from the South water treatment plant and at the Fire Station (Fenton Zone 13) was measured over a 12-month period, with the results shown in the accompanying table. Estimate the mean difference in monthly chlorine content between the two locations using a 90% confidence interval.

		Month										
		Jan.	Feb.	Mar.	Apr.	May	June	July	Aug.	Sept.	Oct.	Nov.	Dec.
Location	South Plant	2.0	2.0	2.1	1.9	1.7	1.8	1.7	1.9	2.0	2.0	2.1	2.2
	Fire Station	2.2	2.2	2.1	2.0	1.9	1.9	1.8	1.7	1.9	1.9	1.8	2.0

Source: "St. Louis County standardizes pipes and procedures for reliability." Staff Report, Water and Sewage Works, Dec. 1980.

8.60 Pesticides applied to an extensively grown crop can result in inadvertent area-wide air contamination. *Environmental Science & Technology* (Oct. 1993) reported on air deposition residues of the insecticide diazinon used on dormant orchards in the San Joaquin Valley, California. Ambient air samples were collected and analyzed at an orchard site for each of 11 days during the most intensive period of spraying. The levels of diazinon residue (in ng/m^3) during the day and at night are recorded in the table. The researchers want to know whether the mean diazinon residue levels differ from day to night.

Date	Diazinon Residue Day	Diazinon Residue Night	Date	Diazinon Residue Day	Diazinon Residue Night
Jan. 11	5.4	24.3	Jan. 17	6.1	104.3
12	2.7	16.5	18	7.7	96.9
13	34.2	47.2	19	18.4	105.3
14	19.9	12.4	20	27.1	78.7
15	2.4	24.0	21	16.9	44.6
16	7.0	21.6			

Source: Selber, J. N., et al. "Air and fog deposition residues for organophosphate insecticides used on dormant orchards in the San Joaquin Valley, California." *Environmental Science & Technology,* Vol. 27, No. 10, Oct. 1993, p. 2240 (Table IV).

a. Analyze the data using a 90% confidence interval.
b. What assumptions are necessary for the validity of the interval estimation procedure of part **a**?
c. Use the interval, part **a**, to answer the researchers' question.

8.61 A recent supermarket advertisement states: "Winn-Dixie offers you the lowest total food bill! Here's the proof!" The "proof" (shown below) is a side-by-side listing of the prices of 60 grocery items purchased at Winn-Dixie and at Publix on the same day.

Item	Winn-Dixie	Publix	Item	Winn-Dixie	Publix
Big Thirst Towel	1.21	1.49	Post Golden Crisp	2.78	2.99
Camp Crm/Broccoli	.55	.67	Surf Detergent	2.29	1.89
Royal Oak Charcoal	2.99	3.59	Sacramento T/Juice	.79	.89
Combo Chdr/Chz Snk	1.29	1.29	SS PruneJuice	1.36	1.61
Sure Sak Trash Bag	1.29	1.79	V8 Cocktail	1.18	1.29
Dow Handi Wrap	1.59	2.39	Rodd KosherDill	1.39	1.79
White Rain Shampoo	.96	.97	Bisquick	2.09	2.19
Kraft Italian Drs	.99	1.19	Soup Start Bf Veg	1.39	2.03
BC Hamburger Helper	1.46	1.75	Camp Pork & Beans	.44	.49
Comstock Chrry Pie	1.29	1.69	Sunsweet Pit Prune	.98	1.33
Dawn Liquid King	2.59	2.29	DM Vgcls Grdn Duet	1.07	1.13
DelMonte Ketchup	1.05	1.25	Argo Corn Starch	.69	.89
Silver Floss Kraut	.77	.81	Sno Drop Bowl Clnr	.53	1.15
Trop Twist Beverag	1.74	2.15	Cadbury Milk Choc	.79	1.29
Purina Kitten Chow	1.09	1.05	Andes Crm/De Ment	1.09	1.30
Niag Spray Starch	.89	.99	Combat Ant & Roach	2.33	2.39
Soft Soap Country	.97	1.19	Joan/Arc Kid Bean	.45	.56
Northwood Syrup	1.13	1.37	La Vic Salsa Pican	1.22	1.75
Bumble Bee Tuna	.58	.65	Moist N Beef/Chz	2.39	3.19
Mueller Elbow/Mac	2.09	2.69	Ortega Taco Shells	1.08	1.33
Kell Nut Honey Crn	2.95	3.25	Fresh Step Cat Lit	3.58	3.79
Cutter Spray	3.09	3.95	Field Trial Dg/Fd	3.49	3.79
Lawry Season Salt	2.28	2.97	Tylenol Tablets	5.98	5.29
Keb Graham Crust	.79	1.29	Rolaids Tablets	1.88	2.20
Spiffits Glass	1.98	2.19	Plax Rinse	2.88	3.14
Prog Lentil Soup	.79	1.13	Correctol Laxative	3.44	3.98
Lipton Tea Bags	2.07	2.17	Tch Scnt Potpourri	1.50	1.89
Carnation Hot Coco	1.59	1.89	Child Enema 2.250	.98	1.15
Crystal Hot Sauce	.70	.87	Gillette Atra Plus	5.00	5.24
C/F/N/ Coffee Bag	1.17	1.15	Colgate Shave	.94	1.10

Source: Advertisement in *Tampa Tribune*, June 2, 1991.

a. Explain why the data should be analyzed as matched pairs.

b. A MINITAB printout showing a 95% confidence interval for $(\mu_{\text{Winn}} - \mu_{\text{Publix}})$, the difference between the mean prices of grocery items purchased at the two supermarkets, is shown here. Interpret the result.

```
              N    MEAN    STDEV   SE MEAN   95.0 PERCENT C.I.
Diff          60  -0.2540  0.2741   0.0354   ( -0.3248, -0.1832)
```

8.62 A corporation's name is sometimes changed in the belief that a new name, as a sign of positive change for investors, will lead to a jump in company stock prices. Corporate identity consultants, who provide companies with names and marketing strategies, cannot seem to agree on how name changes affect stock prices. To shed more light on the question, the *Wall Street Journal* studied a sample of 10 corporate stocks, shown in the table, each of which underwent a recent name change. For each stock, the rate of return from the date of the name change through February 23, 1987, is recorded and compared to the rate of return on the Standard & Poor's 500 Index (S&P 500) over the same period.

New Name	Date Changed	Old Name	Stock[a]	S&P 500[a]	Diff.[b]
Unisys	11/25/86	Burroughs	32.8%	14.7%	+18.1
Trinova	8/1/86	Libbey–Owens–Ford	46.5	22.6	+23.9
USX	7/9/86	U.S. Steel	47.2	18.8	+28.4
Varity	6/17/86	Massey–Ferguson	−13.0	18.2	−31.2
Enron	4/10/86	HNG/Internorth	26.3	23.1	+3.2
Navistar Int'l	2/20/86	Int'l Harvester	−10.3	31.5	−41.8
Fidata	2/20/85	Bradford National	−41.9	68.4	−110.3
Figgie Int'l	6/1/81	A-T-O	326.9	113.0	+213.9
Citicorp	3/26/74	First National City Corp.	26.7	189.2	−162.5
Exxon	11/1/72	Standard Oil (N.J.)	283.2	153.1	+130.1

[a]*Total return, assuming reinvestment of dividends, for company's stock and Standard & Poor's 500 Index from date of name change through close of trading Monday.*

[b]*Number of percentage points the total return led or trailed the S&P 500.*

Source: Smith, R. "Motives vary as firms play name games at record pace." *Wall Street Journal,* Feb. 27, 1987.

a. Construct a 95% confidence interval for the true mean difference between the rates of return for stocks with name changes and the S&P 500.

b. Interpret the interval obtained in part **a.** Does it appear that a name change has an effect on stock performance? Explain.

8.7 Estimation of the Difference Between Two Population Proportions

This section extends the method of Section 8.4 to the case in which we want to estimate the difference between two population proportions. For example, one may be interested in comparing the proportions of defective items produced by two machines, or the proportions of homes in two states that are heated by natural gas, or the proportions of U.S. and Japanese firms that employ industrial robots.

EXAMPLE 8.22
Point Estimate for $\pi_1 - \pi_2$

Over the years, one of the issues studied in depth by organizational behavior theorists involves the area of ethical management decision making. Prior to 1980, these studies focused on the male manager because the management field was male-dominated. Today, with women entering management careers in record numbers, researchers are studying the differences in ethical perceptions between male and female managers. In one study, 48 of 50 female managers responded that concealing one's on-the-job errors was very unethical, whereas only 30 of 50 male managers responded in like manner (*Journal of Business Ethics*, Aug. 1987). Construct a point estimate for the difference between the proportions of female and male managers who believe that concealing one's errors is very unethical.

SOLUTION   For this example, define

π_1 = Population proportion of female managers who believe that concealing on-the-job errors is unethical

π_2 = Population proportion of male managers who believe that concealing on-the-job errors is unethical

x_1 = Number of females in the sample who believe that concealing on-the-job errors is unethical

x_2 = Number of males in the sample who believe that concealing on-the-job errors is unethical

As a point estimate of $(\pi_1 - \pi_2)$, we will use the difference between the corresponding sample proportions $(p_1 - p_2)$, where

$$p_1 = \frac{x_1}{n_1} = \frac{48}{50} = .96$$

and

$$p_2 = \frac{x_2}{n_2} = \frac{30}{50} = .60$$

Thus, the point estimate of $(\pi_1 - \pi_2)$ is

$$(p_1 - p_2) = .96 - .60 = .36 \quad \blacksquare$$

To judge the reliability of the point estimate $(p_1 - p_2)$, we must know the characteristics of its performance in repeated independent sampling from two binomial populations. This information is provided by the sampling distribution of $(p_1 - p_2)$, illustrated in Figure 8.19 and described in the accompanying box.

FIGURE 8.19

Sampling Distribution of $(p_1 - p_2)$

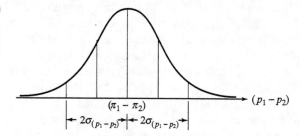

Sampling Distribution of $(p_1 - p_2)$

For sufficiently large sample sizes, n_1 and n_2, the sampling distribution of $(p_1 - p_2)$, based on independent random samples from two binomial populations, is approximately normal with

Mean: $\mu_{(p_1 - p_2)} = (\pi_1 - \pi_2)$

and

Standard deviation: $\sigma_{(p_1 - p_2)} = \sqrt{\dfrac{\pi_1(1 - \pi_1)}{n_1} + \dfrac{\pi_2(1 - \pi_2)}{n_2}}$

It follows that a large-sample confidence interval for $(\pi_1 - \pi_2)$ may be obtained as shown in the next box.

Large-Sample $(1 - \alpha)100\%$ Confidence Interval for $(\pi_1 - \pi_2)$

$$(p_1 - p_2) \pm z_{\alpha/2}\, \sigma_{(p_1 - p_2)} \approx (p_1 - p_2) \pm z_{\alpha/2} \sqrt{\dfrac{p_1 q_1}{n_1} + \dfrac{p_2 q_2}{n_2}}$$

where p_1 and p_2 are the sample proportions of observations with the characteristic of interest, $q_1 = 1 - p_1$, and $q_2 = 1 - p_2$.

[*Note:* We have followed the usual procedure of substituting the sample values $p_1, q_1, p_2,$ and q_2 for the corresponding population values required for $\sigma_{(p_1 - p_2)}$.]

(continued)

Assumption: The samples are sufficiently large so that the approximation is valid. As a general rule of thumb, we will require that the intervals

$$p_1 \pm 2 \sqrt{\frac{p_1 q_1}{n_1}} \quad \text{and} \quad p_2 \pm 2 \sqrt{\frac{p_2 q_2}{n_2}}$$

do not contain 0 or 1.

EXAMPLE 8.23
95% Confidence Interval
for $\pi_1 - \pi_2$

Refer to Example 8.22. Estimate the difference between the proportions of female and male managers who believe that concealing one's errors is very unethical, using a 95% confidence interval. Interpret your results.

SOLUTION For a confidence coefficient of .95, we will use $z_{.025} = 1.96$ in constructing the confidence interval. From Example 8.22, we have $n_1 = 50$, $n_2 = 50$, $p_1 = .96$, and $p_2 = .60$. Thus, $q_1 = 1 - .96 = .04$, $q_2 = 1 - .60 = .40$, and the 95% confidence interval for $(\pi_1 - \pi_2)$ is given by

$$(p_1 - p_2) \pm z_{.025} \sqrt{\frac{p_1 q_1}{n_1} + \frac{p_2 q_2}{n_2}} = (.96 - .60) \pm 1.96 \sqrt{\frac{(.96)(.04)}{50} + \frac{(.60)(.40)}{50}}$$

$$= .36 \pm .146$$

or (.214, .506). Thus, we estimate that the interval (.214, .506) encloses the difference $(\pi_1 - \pi_2)$ with 95% confidence. It appears that there are between 21% and 51% more female managers than male managers who believe that concealing on-thejob errors is very unethical. ∎

Small-sample estimation procedures for $(\pi_1 - \pi_2)$ will not be discussed here for the reasons outlined at the end of Section 8.4.

EXERCISES

∎ *Learning the Mechanics*

8.63 Suppose you want to estimate $\pi_1 - \pi_2$, the difference between the proportions of two populations. Based on independent random samples, you can compute the sample proportions of successes, p_1 and p_2, respectively. Estimate $\mu_{(p_1 - p_2)}$ and $\sigma_{(p_1 - p_2)}$ for each of the following results:

a. $n_1 = 150$, $p_1 = .3$; $n_2 = 130$, $p_2 = .4$ **b.** $n_1 = 100$, $p_1 = .10$; $n_2 = 100$, $p_2 = .05$
c. $n_1 = 200$, $p_1 = .76$; $n_2 = 200$, $p_2 = .96$

8.64   Independent random samples are taken from two populations. The accompanying table shows the sample sizes and the sample proportions of observations with the characteristic of interest.

Sample from Population 1	Sample from Population 2
$n_1 = 400$	$n_2 = 350$
$p_1 = .50$	$p_2 = .60$

   a. Find a 90% confidence interval for $(\pi_1 - \pi_2)$.
   b. Find a 95% confidence interval for $(\pi_1 - \pi_2)$.
   c. Find a 99% confidence interval for $(\pi_1 - \pi_2)$.

8.65   Independent random samples of 250 observations each are selected from two populations. The samples from populations 1 and 2 produced, respectively, 100 and 75 observations possessing the characteristic of interest.
   a. Construct a 90% confidence interval for $(\pi_1 - \pi_2)$.
   b. Construct a 99% confidence interval for $(\pi_1 - \pi_2)$.

8.66   Independent random samples from populations 1 and 2 produced sample proportions $p_1 = .44$ and $p_2 = .52$.
   a. Find a 95% confidence interval for $(\pi_1 - \pi_2)$ if $n_1 = n_2 = 500$.
   b. Find a 99% confidence interval for $(\pi_1 - \pi_2)$ if $n_1 = n_2 = 500$.

■ *Applying the Concepts*

8.67   Over the last decade, the University of California at Los Angeles (UCLA) has conducted an annual survey of Collegiate Schools of Business computer usage. The *Journal of Computer Information Systems* (Spring 1993) reported on the level of microcomputer use of instructional software (e.g., word processing, spreadsheets, simulation, statistics) at the business schools. In the 1991 survey of 163 schools, 142 reported that WordPerfect was the choice word processing package. In contrast, the 1987 survey found that 52 of 113 schools used WordPerfect.
   a. Construct a 95% confidence interval for the difference between the proportions of business schools in 1991 and 1987 that prefer WordPerfect as a word-processing package.
   b. Interpret the interval, part **a**.

8.68   According to an American Heart Association (AHA) researcher, "people who are hostile and mistrustful are more likely to die young or develop life-threatening heart disease than those with more trusting hearts," (*Tampa Tribune*, Jan. 17, 1989). A sample of 118 male doctors, lawyers, and workers in a large industrial firm in Chicago were divided into two groups based on a standard psychological test designed to measure hostility. Of the 35 men who scored high in hostility, 7 died at a relatively early age (i.e., between the ages of 25 and 50). In contrast, only 4 of the 83 men whose hostility rating was low died at an early age.
   a. Estimate the true difference between the proportion of men with high hostility scores who die at an early age and the corresponding proportion of men with low hostility scores. Use a 95% confidence interval.
   b. Are the sample sizes large enough for the interval in part **a** to be valid?

c. Interpret the interval in part **a.** Do you agree with the AHA researcher?

8.69 Refer to the *American Journal of Small Businesses* study of female managers, Exercise 8.47. The two groups of managers surveyed were also asked whether they would change jobs if given the opportunity. Of the 86 small-firm managers, 65 responded negatively, whereas 51 of the 91 large-firm managers answered no.

a. Construct a 95% confidence interval for the difference between the percentages who would not change jobs if given the opportunity for the two groups of female managers.

b. Interpret the interval, part **a.**

8.70 *Social Science Quarterly* (Sept. 1993) reported on a study of gender differences among workers in the computer software industry. Questionnaires were administered to a sample of 298 females and 264 males who were employed full-time in software-related jobs. In the female sample, 89 had professional occupations (e.g., programmers, analysts, computer scientists) and 209 had nonprofessional jobs (computer and peripheral equipment operators). In contrast, the male sample included 150 professionals and 114 nonprofessionals. Use a 90% confidence interval to compare the proportions of male and female software workers who hold professional positions.

8.71 The Egyptian National Scientific and Technical Information Network (ENSTINET) operates an on-line data base search service of existing U.S. data bases. A data base "search" occurs when a specific request is executed by ENSTINET during a single session. In situations when the search produces irrelevant or no output, the search is "rerun." According to *Information Processing & Management* (Vol. 22, No. 3, 1986), ENSTINET performed 342 data base searches in 1982, of which 40 were rerun. In 1985, 83 of 2,117 searches required reruns. Assuming the two samples of data base searches are independent and random, construct a 95% confidence interval for the difference between the proportions of data base search reruns performed by ENSTINET in 1982 and 1985. Interpret the interval.

8.72 The city of Niagara Falls, New York, and the surrounding county are known to contain a large number of toxic-waste disposal sites (dump sites). Following the negative publicity of the "Love Canal" (located in Niagara Falls), the New York State Department of Health funded a death-certificate study to determine whether lung cancer in Niagara County might be associated with exposure to pollution from the dump sites (*Environmental Research*, Feb. 1989). The study involved a comparison of two samples. The first sample (called cases) comprised the $n_1 = 327$ residents of Niagara County who died of cancer of the trachea, bronchus, or lung. The second sample (called controls) consisted of $n_2 = 667$ residents of Niagara County who died from causes other than respiratory cancers. Of the 327 cases, 50 resided near dump sites containing lung carcinogens; of the 667 controls, 102 resided near dump sites containing lung carcinogens.

a. Compare the percentages of cases and controls with residences near dump sites with a 90% confidence interval.

b. If the confidence coefficient were decreased to .80, would you expect the width of the interval to increase, decrease, or stay the same? Would you recommend decreasing the confidence coefficient to .80? Explain.

8.8 Choosing the Sample Size

In the preceding sections, we have overlooked a problem that usually must be faced in the initial stages of an experiment. Before constructing a confidence interval for a parameter of interest, we will have to decide on the number n of observations to be included in a sample. Should we sample $n = 10$ observations, $n = 20$, or $n = 100$? To answer this question we need to decide how wide a confidence interval we are willing to tolerate and the measure of confidence—that is, the confidence coefficient—that we wish to place in it. The following example will illustrate the method for determining the appropriate sample size for estimating a population mean.

EXAMPLE 8.24

Sample Size for Estimating μ

A mail-order house wants to estimate the mean length of time between shipment of an order and receipt by the customer. The management plans to randomly sample n orders and determine, by telephone, the number of days between shipment and receipt for each order. If the management wants to estimate the mean shipping time correct to within .5 day with confidence coefficient equal to .95, how many orders should be sampled?

SOLUTION We will use $\bar{x}$, the sample mean of the n measurements, to estimate μ, the mean shipping time. Its sampling distribution will be approximately normal, and the probability that $\bar{x}$ will lie within

$$1.96\,\sigma_{\bar{x}} = 1.96\left(\frac{\sigma}{\sqrt{n}}\right)$$

of the mean shipping time, μ, is approximately .95 (see Figure 8.20). Therefore, we want to choose the sample size n so that $1.96\,\sigma/\sqrt{n}$ equals .5 day:

$$1.96\left(\frac{\sigma}{\sqrt{n}}\right) = .5$$

FIGURE 8.20

Sampling
Distribution of the
Sample Mean, $\bar{x}$

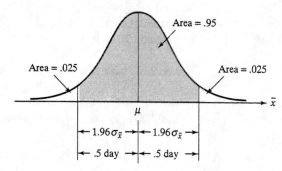

FIGURE 8.21

Hypothetical Relative
Frequency
Distribution of
Population of
Shipping Times for
Example 8.24

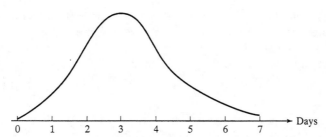

To solve the equation $1.96\sigma/\sqrt{n} = .5$, we need to know the value of σ, a measure of variation of the population of all shipping times. Since σ is unknown (as will usually be the case in practical applications), we must approximate its value using the standard deviation of some previous sample data or deduce an approximate value from other knowledge about the population. Suppose, for example, that we know almost all shipments will be delivered within 7 days. Then the population of shipping times might appear as shown in Figure 8.21.

Figure 8.21 provides the information we need to find an approximation for σ. Since the Empirical Rule tells us that almost all the observations in a data set will fall within the interval $\mu \pm 3\sigma$, it follows that the range of a population is approximately 6σ. If the range of the population of shipping times is 7 days, then

$$6\sigma = 7 \text{ days}$$

and σ is approximately equal to $\frac{7}{6}$ or 1.17 days.

The final step in determining the sample size is to substitute this approximate value of σ into the equation obtained previously and solve for n. Thus, we have

$$1.96\left(\frac{1.17}{\sqrt{n}}\right) = .5$$

or

$$\sqrt{n} = \frac{1.96(1.17)}{.5} = 4.59$$

Squaring both sides of this equation yields

$$n = 21.07$$

We will follow the usual convention of rounding the calculated sample size upward. Therefore, the mail-order house must sample approximately $n = 22$ shipping times to estimate the mean shipping time correct to within .5 day with confidence coefficient equal to .95.   ■

In Example 8.24, we wanted our sample estimate to lie within .5 day of the true mean shipping time, μ, with probability .95, where .95 represents the confidence coefficient. We could calculate the sample size for a confidence coefficient other than .95 by changing the z value in the equation. In general, if we want $\bar{x}$ to lie within a distance d of μ with probability $(1 - \alpha)$, we would solve for n in the equation

$$z_{\alpha/2}\left(\frac{\sigma}{\sqrt{n}}\right) = d$$

where the value of $z_{\alpha/2}$ is obtained from Table 5 of Appendix B. The solution is given by

$$n = \left(\frac{z_{\alpha/2}\sigma}{d}\right)^2$$

For example, for a confidence coefficient of .90, we would require a sample size of

$$n = \left(\frac{1.645\sigma}{d}\right)^2$$

Choosing the Sample Size for Estimating a <u>Population Mean μ</u> to Within d Units with Confidence Coefficient $(1 - \alpha)$

$$n = \left(\frac{z_{\alpha/2}\sigma}{d}\right)^2$$

[*Note:* The population standard deviation σ will usually have to be approximated.]

The procedures for determining the sample sizes needed to estimate a population proportion, the difference between two population means, or the difference between two population proportions are analogous to the procedure for determining the sample size for estimating a population mean. In the remainder of this section, we will present the appropriate formulas and illustrate their use with examples. We first consider the estimation of a population proportion.

> **Choosing the Sample Size for Estimating a __Population Proportion__ π to Within d Units with Confidence Coefficient $(1 - \alpha)$**
>
> $$n = \left(\frac{z_{\alpha/2}}{d}\right)^2 \pi(1 - \pi)$$
>
> where π is the value of the population proportion that you are attempting to estimate.
>
> [*Note:* This technique requires a previous estimate of π. If none is available, use $\pi = .5$ for a conservative choice of *n*.]

EXAMPLE 8.25
Sample Size for Estimating π

In Example 8.13, a study was conducted to estimate the proportion of state lottery winners who quit their job within 1 year of striking it rich. Suppose the researcher wants to acquire an estimate of π that is correct to within .01 with 90% confidence. How many lottery winners would have to be included in the researcher's sample?

SOLUTION For a confidence coefficient of $(1 - \alpha) = .90$, we have $\alpha = .10$. Thus, to calculate *n* using the equation given in the box, we must find the value of $z_{\alpha/2} = z_{.05}$ and find an approximation for the unknown population proportion π.

From Table 5 of Appendix B, the *z* value corresponding to an area of $\alpha/2 = .05$ in the upper tail of the standard normal distribution is $z_{.05} = 1.645$. As an approximation to π, we will use the sample estimate, $p = .11$, obtained for the sample of 576 lottery winners in Example 8.13.

Substituting the value of .11 for π and $z_{.05} = 1.645$ into the equation for *n*, we have

$$n = \left(\frac{z_{\alpha/2}}{d}\right)^2 \pi(1 - \pi) = \left(\frac{1.645}{.01}\right)^2 (.11)(.89) = 2,649.2$$

Therefore, to estimate π to within .01 with 90% confidence, the researcher will have to sample approximately $n = 2,650$ lottery winners. ■

In Example 8.25, we used a prior estimate of π in computing the required sample size. If such prior information were not available, we could approximate π in the sample size equation using $\pi = .5$. The nearer the substituted value of π is to .5, the larger will be the sample size obtained from the formula. Hence, if you take $\pi = .5$ as the approximation to π, you will always obtain a sample size that is at least as large as required.

The procedure for determining the sample sizes for estimating the difference between a pair of population means is summarized in the next box.

> *Choosing the Sample Sizes for Estimating the Difference* $(\mu_1 - \mu_2)$
> *Between a Pair of Population Means Correct to Within d Units with*
> *Confidence Coefficient* $(1 - \alpha)$
>
> $$n_1 = n_2 = \left(\frac{z_{\alpha/2}}{d}\right)^2 (\sigma_1^2 + \sigma_2^2)$$
>
> where n_1 and n_2 are the numbers of observations sampled from each of the two populations, and σ_1^2 and σ_2^2 are the variances of the two populations.

EXAMPLE 8.26
Sample Size for
Estimating $\mu_1 - \mu_2$

Refer to Example 8.24. Suppose the mail-order house wanted to estimate the difference in mean shipping times for two different express services. If the company specifies that the estimated difference in means is to be correct to within $d = .5$ day with 99% confidence, how many shipping times would have to be included in each sample?

SOLUTION We will assume that the population standard deviations are approximately equal and will estimate them using the value $\sigma \approx 1.17$ obtained in Example 8.24. Consulting Table 5 of Appendix B, we find that for $\alpha = .01$, $z_{\alpha/2} = z_{.005} \approx 2.58$. Substituting these values into the equation for the required sample sizes, we obtain

$$n_1 = n_2 = \left(\frac{z_{\alpha/2}}{d}\right)^2 (\sigma_1^2 + \sigma_2^2) = \left(\frac{2.58}{.5}\right)^2 [2(1.17)^2] = 72.9$$

Therefore, to estimate the difference in mean shipping times correct to within .5 day with 99% confidence, the mail-order house will have to sample approximately 73 shipments for each express service. ■

In the next box, we give the equation for determining the sample sizes required to estimate the difference between two population proportions.

> *Choosing the Sample Sizes for Estimating the Difference* $(\pi_1 - \pi_2)$
> *Between Two Population Proportions to Within d Units with*
> *Confidence Coefficient* $(1 - \alpha)$
>
> $$n_1 = n_2 = \left(\frac{z_{\alpha/2}}{d}\right)^2 [\pi_1(1 - \pi_1) + \pi_2(1 - \pi_2)]$$
>
> where π_1 and π_2 are the proportions for populations 1 and 2, respectively, and n_1 and n_2 are the numbers of observations to be sampled from each population.

EXAMPLE 8.27
Sample Size for
Estimating $\pi_1 - \pi_2$

A soft-drink bottler wants to assess the effect of an advertising campaign designed to increase customer recognition of a new cola drink. Random samples of consumers are to be selected from the marketing area both before and after the advertising campaign and asked whether they have heard of the new cola drink. Suppose the bottler wants to estimate the difference in the proportions of consumers who recognize the brand name of the cola drink correct to within .05 with confidence coefficient equal to .95. How many people should be included in each sample? (Assume that samples of equal size are to be selected before and after the campaign.)

SOLUTION We have no prior information on the values of π_1 and π_2. Therefore, to be certain that the sample sizes are large enough to estimate $(\pi_1 - \pi_2)$ to within .05 with confidence coefficient .95, we will approximate both π_1 and π_2 with the value .5. The z value corresponding to $(1 - \alpha) = .95$ is $z_{\alpha/2} = z_{.025} = 1.96$. Substituting these values into the formula for n_1 and n_2, we obtain

$$n_1 = n_2 = \left(\frac{z_{\alpha/2}}{d}\right)^2 [\pi_1(1 - \pi_1) + \pi_2(1 - \pi_2)]$$

$$= \left(\frac{1.96}{.05}\right)^2 [(.5)(.5) + (.5)(.5)]$$

$$= 768.3$$

Therefore, the bottler should include approximately 769 consumers in each of the two samples. ■

The formulas given in this section are appropriate when the sample size n is small relative to the population size N. For situations in which n may be large relative to N, adjustments to these formulas must be made. Sample size determination for this special case is one of the topics discussed in optional Chapter 9.

EXERCISES

■ *Learning the Mechanics*

8.73 Determine the sample size needed to estimate μ for each of the following situations:
    a. $d = 3$, $\sigma = 40$, $(1 - \alpha) = .95$
    b. $d = 5$, $\sigma = 40$, $(1 - \alpha) = .95$
    c. $d = 5$, $\sigma = 40$, $(1 - \alpha) = .99$

8.74 Find the sample size needed to estimate π for each of the following situations:
    a. $d = .04$, $\pi \approx .9$, $(1 - \alpha) = .90$

b. $d = .04$, $\pi \approx .5$, $(1 - \alpha) = .90$

c. $d = .01$, $\pi \approx .5$, $(1 - \alpha) = .90$

8.75 Find the appropriate value of $n_1 = n_2$ needed to estimate $(\mu_1 - \mu_2)$ to within:

a. 5 units with probability .95 (Assume $\sigma_1 \approx 12$ and $\sigma_2 \approx 15$.)

b. 5 units with probability .99 (Assume $\sigma_1 \approx 12$ and $\sigma_2 \approx 15$.)

c. 1 unit with probability .90 (Asssume $\sigma_1^2 \approx 100$ and $\sigma_2^2 \approx 120$.)

8.76 Assuming that $n_1 = n_2$, find the appropriate sample sizes needed to estimate $(\pi_1 - \pi_2)$ for each of the following situations:

a. $d = .01$, $(1 - \alpha) = .99$, $\pi_1 \approx .3$, $\pi_2 \approx .6$

b. $d = .05$, $(1 - \alpha) = .95$, $\pi_1 \approx .2$, $\pi_2 \approx .08$

c. $d = .05$, $(1 - \alpha) = .90$, $\pi_1 \approx .5$, $\pi_2 \approx .5$

■ Applying the Concepts

8.77 Refer to the *Journal of Marketing* study on the incremental profit of trade promotions of Canadian packaged goods companies, introduced in Exercise 8.22. How many successful trade promotions must be sampled to estimate the true mean incremental profit to within $10,000 with 90% confidence? Use the sample standard deviation from Exercise 8.22, $s = \$95,000$, as an estimate of σ.

8.78 Some power plants are located near rivers or oceans so that the available water can be used for cooling the condensers. As part of an environmental impact study, suppose a power company wants to estimate the difference in mean water temperature between the discharge of its plant and the offshore waters. How many sample measurements must be taken at each site to estimate the true difference between means to within .2°C with 95% confidence? Assume the range in readings will be about 4°C at each site and the same number of readings will be taken at each site.

8.79 Rat damage creates a large financial loss in the production of sugar cane. One aspect of the problem that has been investigated by the United States Department of Agriculture concerns the optimal place to locate rat poison. To be more effective in reducing rat damage, should the poison be located in the middle of the field or on the outer perimeter? One way to answer this question is to determine where the greater amount of damage occurs. If damage is measured by the proportion of cane stalks that have been damaged by rats, how many stalks from each section of the field should be sampled to estimate the true difference between the proportions of stalks damaged in the two sections to within .02 with probability .95? (Assume that samples of equal size are to be selected from each section.)

8.80 *Cost Engineering* (Oct. 1988) reports on a study of the percentage difference between the low bid and the engineer's estimate of the cost for building contracts (see Exercise 7.14). For contracts with four bidders, the mean percentage error is $\mu = -7.02$ and the standard deviation is $\sigma = 24.66$. Suppose you want to estimate the mean percentage error for building contracts with five bidders. How many five-bidder contracts must be sampled to estimate with 90% confidence the mean to within 5 percentage points of its true value? Assume that the standard deviation for five-bidder contracts is approximately equal to the standard deviation for four-bidder contracts.

8.81 Many people believe that a national lobby's successful fight against gun-control legislation is reflecting the will of a minority of Americans. Suppose you are interested in estimating the true proportion of Americans who favor gun-control legislation. How many people should you include in your sample to estimate this proportion to within .03 of its true value with probability .90? Assume that no prior information exists concerning the value of the population proportion.

8.82 Do colleges provide good value for the dollar? A majority of Americans do not think so, according to a Media General–Associated Press telephone poll. Of the 1,348 adult Americans who participated in the nationwide poll, 805 believe tuition at most private colleges and universities is too high for the quality of education provided (*Gainesville Sun*, Sept. 1, 1987). How many adult Americans must be surveyed to estimate the true proportion who believe college tuition is too high to within .02 of its true value, with 95% confidence? Use the information provided in the telephone poll to compute an estimate of π.

8.9 Estimation of a Population Variance (Optional)

In the previous sections, we considered interval estimates for population means or proportions. In this optional section, we discuss a confidence interval for a population variance, σ^2.

EXAMPLE 8.28
Estimating σ^2

Refer to the Federal Trade Commission (FTC) rankings of domestic cigarette brands (see Case Study 2.1). It is important for the FTC to know how stable the tar contents of the cigarettes are. That is, how large is the variation σ^2 in the population of cigarette tar measurements?

a. Identify the paramenter of interest to the FTC.

b. Explain how to build a confidence interval for the parameter, part **a.**

SOLUTION

a. The FTC is interested in the *variation* of the tar contents. Consequently, the target population parameter is σ^2, the variance of tar measurements for all cigarettes in the population.

b. Intuitively, it seems reasonable to use the sample variance s^2 to estimate σ^2 and to construct our confidence interval around this value. However, unlike sample means and sample proportions, the sampling distribution of the sample variance s^2 does not possess a normal (z) distribution or a t distribution.

Rather, when certain assumptions are satisfied (we discuss these later), the sampling distribution of s^2 possesses approximately a **chi-square** (χ^2) distribution.[*] The chi-square probability distribution, like the t distribution, is characterized by a quantity called the *degrees of freedom* associated with the distribution. Several chi-square probability distributions with different degrees of freedom are shown in Figure 8.22 (page 404). Unlike z and t distributions, the chi-square distribution is not symmetric about 0.

---

[*] *In this section and throughout this text we will use the words chi-square and the Greek symbol χ^2 interchangeably.*

FIGURE 8.22

Several Chi-Square
Probability
Distributions

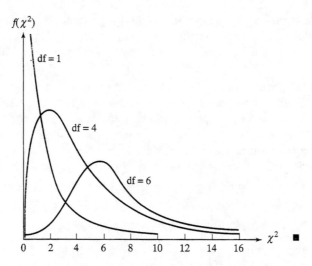

EXAMPLE 8.29

Finding Values of χ^2

Tabulated values of the χ^2 distribution are given in Table 7 of Appendix B; a partial reproduction of this table is shown in Table 8.8. Entries in the table give an upper-tail value of χ^2, call it χ^2_α, such that $P(\chi^2 > \chi^2_\alpha) = \alpha$. Find the tabulated value of χ^2 corresponding to 9 degrees of freedom that cuts off an upper-tail area of .05.

SOLUTION The value of χ^2 that we seek appears (shaded) in the partial reproduction of Table 7 of Appendix B given in Table 8.8. The columns of the table identify the value of α associated with the tabulated value of χ^2_α and the rows correspond to the degrees of freedom. For this example, we have df $= 9$ and $\alpha = .05$. Thus, the tabulated value of χ^2 corresponding to 9 degrees of freedom is

$$\chi^2_{.05} = 16.9190 \quad ■$$

We use the tabulated values of χ^2 to construct a confidence interval for σ^2, as the next example illustrates.

EXAMPLE 8.30

95% Confidence
Interval for σ^2

Refer to Example 8.28. Recall that the FTC determined the tar contents for a sample of 500 cigarette brands. The following summary statistics (see Table 3.4) were obtained: $\bar{x} = 11.06$ milligrams and $s = 4.93$ milligrams. Use this information to construct a 95% confidence interval for the true variation in tar contents of domestic cigarette brands.

SOLUTION A $(1 - \alpha)100\%$ confidence interval for σ^2 depends on the quantities s^2, $(n - 1)$, and critical values of χ^2 as shown in the box on page 406. Note that $(n - 1)$ represents the degrees of freedom associated with the χ^2 distribution. To construct the interval, we first locate the critical values $\chi^2_{(1 - \alpha/2)}$ and χ^2_α. These are the values

Table 8.8   Reproduction of Part of Table 7 of Appendix B

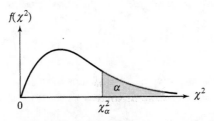

Degrees of Freedom	$\chi^2_{.100}$	$\chi^2_{.050}$	$\chi^2_{.025}$	$\chi^2_{.010}$	$\chi^2_{.005}$
1	2.70554	3.84146	5.02389	6.63490	7.87944
2	4.60517	5.99147	7.37776	9.21034	10.5966
3	6.25139	7.81473	9.34840	11.3449	12.8381
4	7.77944	9.48773	11.1433	13.2767	14.8602
5	9.23635	11.0705	12.8325	15.0863	16.7496
6	10.6446	12.5916	14.4494	16.8119	18.5476
7	12.0170	14.0671	16.0128	18.4753	20.2777
8	13.3616	15.5073	17.5346	20.0902	21.9550
9	14.6837	16.9190	19.0228	21.6660	23.5893
10	15.9871	18.3070	20.4831	23.2093	25.1882
11	17.2750	19.6751	21.9200	24.7250	26.7569
12	18.5494	21.0261	23.3367	26.2170	28.2995
13	19.8119	22.3621	24.7356	27.6883	29.8194
14	21.0642	23.6848	26.1190	29.1413	31.3193
15	22.3072	24.9958	27.4884	30.5779	32.8013
16	23.5418	26.2962	28.8454	31.9999	34.2672
17	24.7690	27.5871	30.1910	33.4087	35.7185
18	25.9894	28.8693	31.5264	34.8053	37.1564
19	27.2036	30.1435	32.8523	36.1908	38.5822

of χ^2 that cut off an area of $\alpha/2$ in the lower and upper tails, respectively, of the chi-square distribution (see Figure 8.23).

FIGURE 8.23
The Location of
$\chi^2_{(1-\alpha/2)}$ and
$\chi^2_{\alpha/2}$ for a Chi-Square Distribution

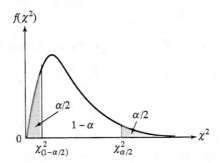

A $(1-\alpha)100\%$ Confidence Interval for a Population Variance, σ^2

$$\frac{(n-1)s^2}{\chi^2_{\alpha/2}} \le \sigma^2 \le \frac{(n-1)s^2}{\chi^2_{(1-\alpha/2)}}$$

where $\chi^2_{\alpha/2}$ and $\chi^2_{(1-\alpha/2)}$ are values of χ^2 that locate an area of $\alpha/2$ to the right and $\alpha/2$ to the left, respectively, of a chi-square distribution based on $(n-1)$ degrees of freedom.

Assumption: The population from which the sample is selected has an approximate normal distribution.

For a 95% confidence interval, $(1-\alpha) = .95$ and $\alpha/2 = .05/2 = .025$. Therefore, we need the tabulated values $\chi^2_{.025}$ and $\chi^2_{.975}$ for $(n-1) = 499$ df. Looking in the df = 500 row of Table 7 of Appendix B (the row with the df values closest to 499), we find

$$\chi^2_{.025} = 563.852 \quad \text{and} \quad \chi^2_{.975} = 439.936$$

Substituting into the formula given in the box, we obtain

$$\frac{(500-1)(4.93)^2}{563.852} \le \sigma^2 \le \frac{(500-1)(4.93)^2}{439.936}$$

$$21.51 \le \sigma^2 \le 27.57$$

We are 95% confident that the true variance in tar contents of domestic cigarette brands falls between 21.51 and 27.57. ■

EXAMPLE 8.31
Estimating σ

Refer to Example 8.30. Find a 95% confidence interval for σ, the true standard deviation of tar measurements.

SOLUTION   A confidence interval for σ is obtained by taking the square roots of the lower and upper endpoints of a confidence interval for σ^2. Thus, the 95% confidence interval is

$$\sqrt{21.51} \le \sigma \le \sqrt{27.57}$$

$$4.64 \le \sigma \le 5.25$$

Thus, we are 95% confident that the true standard deviation of tar measurements falls between 4.64 milligrams and 5.25 milligrams. ■

Note that the procedure for calculating a confidence interval for σ^2 in Example 8.30 (and the confidence interval for σ in Example 8.31) requires an assumption regardless of whether the sample size n is large or small (see box). We must assume that the population from which the sample is selected has an approximate normal distribution. It is reasonable to expect this assumption to be satisfied in Examples 8.30 and 8.31 since the histogram of the 500 tar measurements in the sample, shown previously in Figure 3.13, is approximately normal.

EXERCISES

■ **Learning the Mechanics**

8.83 For each of the following combinations of α and degrees of freedom (df), use Table 7 of Appendix B to find the values of $\chi^2_{\alpha/2}$ and $\chi^2_{1-\alpha/2}$ that would be used to form a confidence interval for σ^2.
   a. $\alpha = .05$, df $= 7$ **b.** $\alpha = .10$, df $= 16$
   c. $\alpha = .01$, df $= 10$ **d.** $\alpha = .05$, df $= 20$

8.84 Given the following values of $\bar{x}$, s, and n, calculate a 90% confidence interval for σ^2.
   a. $\bar{x} = 21$, $s = 2.5$, $n = 50$ **b.** $\bar{x} = 1.3$, $s = .02$, $n = 15$
   c. $\bar{x} = 167$, $s = 31.6$, $n = 22$ **d.** $\bar{x} = 9.4$, $s = 1.5$, $n = 5$
   What assumption about the population must be satisfied for the confidence interval to be valid?

8.85 Refer to Exercise 8.84. For each part **a–d**, calculate a 90% confidence interval for σ.

8.86 A random sample of $n = 6$ observations from a normal distribution resulted in the following measurements: 8, 2, 3, 7, 11, 6. Find a 95% confidence interval for σ^2.

■ **Applying the Concepts**

8.87 A machine used to fill beer cans must operate so that the amount of beer actually dispensed varies very little. If too much beer is released, the cans will overflow, causing waste. If too little beer is released, the cans will not contain enough beer, causing complaints from customers. A random sample of the fills for 20 cans yielded a standard deviation of .07 ounce. Estimate the true variance of the fills using a 95% confidence interval.

8.88 Refer to Exercise 8.12 and the MINITAB printout showing descriptive statistics for the sample of 50 return-to-pay ratios of CEOs selected from Appendix A.2. Use the information on the printout to construct a 90% confidence interval for σ, the true standard deviation of the return-to-pay ratios of CEOs. Interpret the interval.

8.89 *Jitter* is a term used to describe the variation in conduction time of a modular pulsed water power system. Low throughput jitter is critical to successful waterline technology. An investigation of throughput jitter in the plasma opening switch of a prototype system (*Journal of Applied Physics*, Sept. 1993) yielded the following descriptive statistics on conduction time for $n = 18$ trials:

$\bar{x} = 334.8$ nanoseconds $s = 6.3$ nanoseconds

(Conduction time is defined as the length of time required for the downstream current to equal 10% of the upstream current.)

a. Construct a 95% confidence interval for the true standard deviation of conduction times of the prototype system.

b. A system is considered to have low throughput jitter if the true conduction time standard deviation is less than 7 nanoseconds. Does the prototype system satisfy this requirement? Explain.

8.90 Polychlorinated biphenyls (PCBs), used in the manufacture of large electrical transformers and capacitors, are extremely hazardous contaminants when released into the environment. The Environmental Protection Agency (EPA) is experimenting with a new device for measuring PCB concentration in fish. To check the precision of the new instrument, seven PCB readings were taken on the same fish specimen. The data are recorded here (in parts per million):

6.2	5.8	5.7	6.3	5.9	5.8	6.0

a. Construct a 90% confidence interval for the variance in the instrument readings.

b. Suppose the EPA requires an instrument to yield PCB readings with a variance of less than .1. Does the new instrument meet the EPA's specifications?

8.91 Refer to Exercise 8.26 and the data on foreign revenue (expressed as a percentage) of U.S.-based multinational firms. The MINITAB printout summarizing the data is reproduced here.

	N	MEAN	MEDIAN	TRMEAN	STDEV	SEMEAN
Revenue%	20	41.13	40.40	40.95	15.97	3.57

	MIN	MAX	Q1	Q3
Revenue%	12.40	73.20	28.18	53.90

a. Form a 95% confidence interval for the variation in foreign revenue percentages of all U.S.-based multinational firms. Interpret the interval.

b. What assumption is required for the interval, part **a**, to be valid? Is the assumption reasonably satisfied? (Refer to your answer to part **d** of Exercise 8.26.)

SUMMARY

This chapter presented the technique of *estimation*—that is, using sample information to make an inference about the value of a population parameter, or the difference between two population parameters. In each instance, we presented the *point estimate* of the parameter of interest, its sampling distribution, the general form of a *confidence interval*, and any assumptions required for the validity of the procedure. These results are collected in Tables 8.9a and 8.9b. In addition, we provided techniques for determining the sample size necessary to estimate each of these parameters.

Table 8.9a Summary of Estimation Procedures: One-Population Cases

Parameter	Point Estimate	Standard Error	$(1-\alpha)100\%$ Confidence Interval	Assumptions/Conditions
μ Population mean	$\bar{x}$ Sample mean	$\sigma/\sqrt{n}$ where σ is standard deviation of sample population	$\bar{x} \pm z_{\alpha/2}(\sigma/\sqrt{n})$ $\approx \bar{x} \pm z_{\alpha/2}(s/\sqrt{n})$	$n \geq 30$ (large sample) Random sample
μ Population mean	$\bar{x}$ Sample mean	(see above)	$\bar{x} \pm t_{\alpha/2}(s/\sqrt{n})$ where $t_{\alpha/2}$ is based on $(n-1)$ degrees of freedom	$n < 30$ (small sample) Random sample Relative frequency distribution of population is approximately normal.
μ_d Population mean difference, matched pairs	$\bar{d}$ Sample mean difference	$\sigma_d/\sqrt{n}$ where σ_d is standard deviation of population of differences	$\bar{d} \pm t_{\alpha/2}(s_d/\sqrt{n})$ where $t_{\alpha/2}$ is based on $(n-1)$ degrees of freedom	$n < 30$ (small sample) Random sample Relative frequency distribution of population of differences is approximately normal.
π Proportion of population with specified charateristic(s)	Sample proportion with specified characteristics(s): $$p = \frac{\text{Number in sample with characteristic}}{n}$$ where n is number of observations sampled	$\sqrt{\frac{\pi(1-\pi)}{n}}$	$p \pm z_{\alpha/2}\sqrt{\frac{\pi(1-\pi)}{n}}$ $\approx p \pm z_{\alpha/2}\sqrt{\frac{pq}{n}}$ where $q = 1-p$	The interval $p \pm 2\sqrt{\frac{pq}{n}}$ does not contain 0 or 1 (large sample). Random sample
σ^2 Population variance (optional)	s^2 Sample variance	(not required)	$\dfrac{(n-1)s^2}{\chi^2_{\alpha/2}} \leq \sigma^2 \leq \dfrac{(n-1)s^2}{\chi^2_{(1-\alpha/2)}}$ where the values $\chi^2_{\alpha/2}$ and $\chi^2_{(1-\alpha/2)}$ are based on $(n-1)$ degrees of freedom	Relative frequency distribution of population is approximately normal. Random sample

Table 8.9b Summary of Estimation Procedures: Two-Population Cases

Parameter	Point Estimate	Standard Error	$(1-\alpha)100\%$ Confidence Interval	Assumptions/ Conditions
$(\mu_1 - \mu_2)$ Difference between population means, independent samples	$(\bar{x}_1 - \bar{x}_2)$ Difference between sample means	$\sqrt{\dfrac{\sigma_1^2}{n_1} + \dfrac{\sigma_2^2}{n_2}}$ where σ_1^2 and σ_2^2 are the variances of the sampled populations	$(\bar{x}_1 - \bar{x}_2) \pm z_{\alpha/2}\sqrt{\dfrac{\sigma_1^2}{n_1} + \dfrac{\sigma_2^2}{n_2}}$ $\approx (\bar{x}_1 - \bar{x}_2) \pm z_{\alpha/2}\sqrt{\dfrac{s_1^2}{n_1} + \dfrac{s_2^2}{n_2}}$	$n_1 \geq 30$ and $n_2 \geq 30$ (large samples) Samples are randomly and independently selected from the two populations.
$(\mu_1 - \mu_2)$ Difference between population means, independent samples	$(\bar{x}_1 - \bar{x}_2)$ Difference between sample means	(see above)	$(\bar{x}_1 - \bar{x}_2) \pm t_{\alpha/2}\sqrt{s_p^2\left(\dfrac{1}{n_1} + \dfrac{1}{n_2}\right)}$ where $s_p^2 = \dfrac{(n_1-1)s_1^2 + (n_2-1)s_2^2}{n_1 + n_2 - 2}$ and $t_{\alpha/2}$ is based on $(n_1 + n_2 - 2)$ degrees of freedom	$n_1 < 30$ or $n_2 < 30$ (small samples) 1. Relative frequency distributions of both populations are approximately normal. 2. Variances of both populations are equal. 3. Samples are randomly and independently selected from the two populations.
$\mu_d = (\mu_1 - \mu_2)$ Difference between population means, matched pairs			(see Table 8.9a)	
$(\pi_1 - \pi_2)$ Difference between population proportions	$(p_1 - p_2)$ Difference between sample proportions	$\sqrt{\dfrac{\pi_1(1-\pi_1)}{n_1} + \dfrac{\pi_2(1-\pi_2)}{n_2}}$	$(p_1 - p_2) \pm z_{\alpha/2}$ $\times \sqrt{\dfrac{\pi_1(1-\pi_1)}{n_1} + \dfrac{\pi_2(1-\pi_2)}{n_2}}$ $\approx (p_1 - p_2) \pm z_{\alpha/2}$ $\times \sqrt{\dfrac{p_1 q_1}{n_1} + \dfrac{p_2 q_2}{n_2}}$ where $q_1 = 1 - p_1$ and $q_2 = 1 - p_2$	The intervals $p_1 \pm 2\sqrt{\dfrac{p_1 q_1}{n_1}}$ and $p_2 \pm 2\sqrt{\dfrac{p_2 q_2}{n_2}}$ do not contain 0 or 1 (large samples). Samples are randomly and independently selected from the two populations.

KEY TERMS

*Chi-square (χ^2) distribution	Independent samples	Proportion
Confidence coefficient	Matched pairs	Standard error
Confidence interval	Point estimate	*t* statistic
Degrees of freedom	Pooled estimate of variance	

KEY FORMULAS

Large-sample confidence interval for means or proportions:

Point estimator $\pm (z_{\alpha/2})$ (Standard error)

Small-sample confidence interval for means:

Point estimator $\pm (t_{\alpha/2})$ (Standard error)

[*Note:*   The respective point estimator and standard error for each parameter discussed in this chapter are provided in Table 8.9.]

*Confidence interval for variances:

$$\frac{(n-1)s^2}{\chi^2_{\alpha/2}} \le \sigma^2 \le \frac{(n-1)s^2}{\chi^2_{(1-\alpha/2)}}$$

SUPPLEMENTARY EXERCISES

[Note: List the assumptions necessary to ensure the validity of the interval estimation procedures you use to solve these exercises. Exercises marked with an asterisk (*) are from the optional section in this chapter.]

8.92 What do college recruiters think are the most important topics to be covered in a job interview? To answer this and other questions, researchers elicited the opinions of recruiters interviewing at a small midwestern college and a large midwestern university (*Journal of Occupational Psychology*, 1984). Recruiters were asked to rate on a 105-point scale the importance of each in a list of 25 interview topics [where 0 = least important (can often be omitted without hurting the interview), 52.5 = average importance (can sometimes be omitted without hurting the interview), and 105 = most important (can never be omitted without hurting the

---

*From the optional section in this chapter.

interview)]. The topic concerning "applicant's skill in communicating ideas to others" received the highest ratings of the $n = 58$ college recruiters who returned the questionnaire. The sample mean rating and sample standard deviation for this topic were $\bar{x} = 84.84$ and $s = 15.67$, respectively.

a. Give a point estimate for the true mean rating of "applicant's skill in communicating ideas to others" by all college recruiters.

b. Use the sample information to construct a 95% confidence interval for the true mean rating.

c. What is the confidence coefficient for the interval of part **b**? Interpret this value.

8.93 R. Brodie and C. A. de Kluyver recently performed a comparison of market shares for frequently purchased brands of consumer goods in New Zealand (*Journal of Marketing Research*, May 1984). A portion of their analysis focused on two brands of chocolate biscuits (brand A and brand B). For each brand, 28 bimonthly observations on market share were obtained spanning the years 1975–1980. The data are summarized in the table. Construct a 99% confidence interval for the difference between the mean market shares of the two brands of chocolate biscuits. Interpret the result.

	Brand A	Brand B
Sample size	28	28
Mean	.540	.330
Standard deviation	.038	.030

8.94 What do managers stress most on the job? In a survey prepared for Towers, Perrin, Forster and Crosby (an international management consultant firm), 462 senior human resource and compensation executives in private industry, government, and nonprofit organizations were asked this question (*Personnel Journal*, Oct. 1984). The most frequent response, given by 226 of 462 managers, was "pay employees for performance." Construct a 95% confidence interval for the true proportion of managers who stress pay for performance on the job.

8.95 Americans shop for food, clothing, housewares, furniture, and other necessities and luxuries week after week. But is shopping considered a pleasant or unpleasant experience? According to R. H. Bruskin's "Update on America" study, about one in three individuals feels shopping is an unpleasant experience (*Journal of Marketing Research*, Feb./Mar. 1984). A national sample of 2,025 male and female adults was surveyed to determine each respondent's opinion on the pleasantness of shopping. The survey produced the results shown in the table.

	Males	Females
Sample size	1,012	1,013
Number who think shopping is an unpleasant experience	425	283

a. Compute the proportion of males in the sample who think shopping is an unpleasant experience.

b. Compute the proportion of females in the sample who think shopping is an unpleasant experience.

c. Construct a 98% confidence interval for the difference between the true proportions of males and females who think shopping is an unpleasant experience.

d. Which group, males or females, appears to dislike shopping more?

8.96 Gerald Appel, president of Signalert Corporation, an investment advisory firm, has found what he believes to be an indicator of upturns in the stock market. As he explains in *Barron's* (Feb. 27, 1984), "only rarely does the market fall with such velocity that the spread between the weekly [New York Stock Exchange] index and the [10-week] moving average [of that index] stretches to −4.0 or more. Such a dramatic plunge nearly always has indicated a market that is deeply oversold and ready for either recovery or at least a respite from selling pressure." Appel dubs this market signal "the major bottom indicator." Between 1970 and 1984, the major bottom indicator signaled a buy eight times. The performance of these major bottom indicators (measured as percentage gain in NYSE index) for two points in time, 4 weeks and 13 weeks after buy, is shown in the accompanying table.

Percentage Gain in NYSE Index

Buy Signal	4 Weeks After Buy	13 Weeks After Buy
1	.0	11.1
2	3.0	4.7
3	18.4	13.5
4	1.5	5.4
5	5.5	11.9
6	7.0	22.1
7	2.5	−2.5
8	−4.6	19.9

Source: Appel, G. "Have we hit bottom? A trusty indicator signals a possible turn in the market." *Barron's*, Feb. 27, 1984, p. 24.

a. Construct a 95% confidence interval for the mean difference in percentage gains in the NYSE index for the two time periods.

b. On average, is it more profitable to hold the stock 4 weeks or 13 weeks after the buy signal? Explain.

8.97 Refer to the problem of estimating total compensation of all corporate executives, Exercise 8.21. Recall that the sample data used to form the interval may be biased. Suppose you want to collect an unbiased sample of CEOs to estimate the true mean total compensation of all corporate executives in 1993 to within $500,000 with 95% confidence. How many executives should be sampled? [*Hint:* Use the value of s calculated in Exercise 8.21 as an estimate of σ.]

8.98 A study was conducted to investigate the perceived unit effectiveness of purchasing companies (*Journal of Applied Behavioral Science*, Vol. 22, 1986). The researchers define unit effectiveness as "the relative ability of the members of a unit [e.g., office] to mobilize their centers of power to produce, adapt, and handle temporarily unpredicted overloads of work." A sample of 115 purchasing agents participated in the study by responding to questionnaires on the organizational effectiveness of his or her office. Each agent rated each of eight "effectiveness" items on a scale of 1 to 5 (where 1 = not effective and 5 = very effective). The sum of the eight values was used as a measure of perceived unit effectiveness. A summary of the results follows:

$$\bar{x} = 29.07 \qquad s = 4.68$$

a. Construct a 95% confidence interval for the true mean "perceived unit effectiveness" rating of all purchasing agents.
b. Interpret the interval obtained in part **a**.
c. How could the researcher reduce the width of the confidence interval in part **a**? Are there any drawbacks to reducing the interval width? Explain.

8.99 A study was conducted to investigate job satisfaction of industrial workers in Bangladesh (*Human Relations*, Vol. 40, 1987). A random sample of 1,558 workers was divided into two groups based on years of experience. Of the 206 workers with less than 5 years of experience, 165 indicated that they were satisfied with their job, whereas 1,179 of the 1,352 workers with 5 or more years of experience were satisfied overall with their job.

a. Calculate a 90% confidence interval for the difference between the proportions who expressed overall satisfaction with their job for the two groups of Bangladesh workers, those with less than 5 years of experience and those with 5 or more years of experience.
b. Interpret the interval obtained in part **a**.

8.100 The pesticide Temik is used for controlling insects that feed on potatoes, oranges, and other crops. According to federal standards, drinking water wells with levels of Temik above 1 part per billion are considered contaminated. The accompanying table lists the results of tests for Temik contamination conducted in five states over the past 5 years.

State	Number of Wells Tested	Number of Contaminated Wells
New York	10,500	2,750
Wisconsin	700	105
Maine	124	82
Florida	825	4
Virginia	76	17

Source: Orlando Sentinel Star, July 4, 1983.

a. For each state, construct a 95% confidence interval for the true proportion of wells contaminated with Temik.
b. Find a 90% confidence interval for the difference between the proportions of wells in Wisconsin and Maine that are contaminated with Temik.

8.101 Are Japanese managers and their workers more motivated than their American counterparts? To investigate one aspect of this question, A. Howard, K. Shudo, and M. Umeshima surveyed middle-age Japanese and American business managers (*Personnel Psychology*, Winter 1983). The Japanese sample consisted of 100 managers selected at a 2-day management seminar in

Tokyo and Osaka, whereas the American sample was made up of 211 managers employed in the Bell System. Each manager was administered the Sarnoff Survey of Attitudes Toward Life (SSATL), which measures motivation for upward mobility. The SSATL scores are summarized in the table. (Higher scores indicate a greater motivation for upward mobility.)

	American Managers	*Japanese Managers*
Sample size	211	100
Mean SSATL score	65.75	79.83
Standard deviation	11.07	6.41

a. Find a 95% confidence interval for the difference in mean SSATL scores for American and Japanese managers.

b. Interpret the interval obtained in part **a**. Does it appear that Japanese managers, on average, are more motivated for upward mobility than American managers?

c. Suppose you would like to reduce the width of the interval obtained in part **a**. How many managers of each group should you sample to estimate the difference in mean SSATL scores to within one point with 95% confidence? (Assume equal sample sizes will be selected from each group.)

8.102 More than 12 million tin-coated steel cans are removed from the municipal waste streams of our cities and recycled each day, according to a study conducted by the American Iron and Steel Institute. Suppose it is desired to estimate the mean number of tin cans recovered from mixed refuse per year in American cities. A random sample of eight American cities yielded the following summary statistics on number of tin cans (in millions) recovered per city last year:

$$\bar{x} = 105.7 \qquad s = 9.3$$

a. Construct a 95% confidence interval for the true mean number of tin cans removed annually from mixed refuse for recycling in American cities.

b. Interpret the interval obtained in part **a**.

c. What assumption is required for the interval estimate of part **a** to be valid?

*8.103 Refer to Exercise 8.102. Find a 95% confidence interval for the variance of the number of tin cans removed from mixed refuse for recycling. Interpret the interval.

8.104 The growth of "off-price" retail stores has been phenomenal. Off-price stores are specialty stores that claim to sell brand-name and designer women's career clothes, casual wear, and active wear for less than traditional retail stores. A study was conducted to investigate apparel price variation in off-price and department stores. The average prices of 20 fall women's apparel items at both off-price stores and department stores in Montgomery County, Maryland, were recorded for each of 13 weeks. The data are shown in the following table.

Week	Off-Price Store Average Price	Department Store Average Price	Week	Off-Price Store Average Price	Department Store Average Price
1	$55.63	$81.18	8	$55.16	$74.98
2	55.63	81.80	9	54.11	71.66
3	55.32	79.36	10	54.65	68.64
4	54.11	79.18	11	53.01	68.56
5	54.79	79.55	12	42.61	67.39
6	54.36	78.21	13	50.66	67.01
7	55.33	77.70			

Source: Kirby, G. M., and Dardis, R. "Resarch note: A pricing study of women's apparel in off-price and department stores." *Journal of Retailing,* Vol. 62, No. 3, Fall 1986, p. 325.

a. Estimate the mean difference between the average retail prices of the items at the two types of stores. Use a 99% confidence interval.

b. Why is the design used for this experiment preferable to independent random sampling?

8.105 According to an advertisement, the twin-blade Daisy shaver from Gillette shaves legs smoother, closer, and safer than any single-blade shaver. Gillette based this claim on the results of an uncontrolled consumer survey where the consumers used the product in their own homes and shaved according to their own routine. An independent survey was conducted with 13 women ranging in age from 19 to 50. Each woman shaved one leg with a Daisy and the other leg with a Lady Bic (a competing single-blade disposable razor for women) according to her own routine, then gave her opinion as to which of the two shavers gave a "smoother, closer, and safer" shave. The results are as follows: "Nine of the women chose the Daisy as being superior in all three categories; two said they could tell no difference; one chose the Lady Bic as being superior in all three categories; and one said the Bic gave a closer shave while the Daisy gave a smoother shave."[*]

a. Give a point estimate of the true proportion of women (tested under conditions similar to those of the independent survey) who prefer the Daisy shave to the Lady Bic shave in all three categories.

b. Using your answer to part **a**, construct a 98% confidence interval for the true proportion of women who prefer the Daisy shaver to the Lady Bic shaver.

c. Why might the interval estimate of part **b** lead to unreliable inferences about the true population proportion? Explain.

d. Give two ways in which you could reduce the width of the interval in part **b**. Which of the two do you recommend?

e. How many women should be sampled to estimate the true proportion who prefer the Daisy shaver to within .05 with 99% confidence?

8.106 During the budget preparation process at a hospital, forecasts of in-patient utilization (measured in patient-days) for the coming fiscal year play a pivotal role. Planners at Sisters of St. Joseph of Peace Health and Hospital Services, Bellevue, Washington, have developed a budget early warning technique (BEWT) for forecasting future fiscal year utilizations. The method involves

---

[*]Hill, J. *"Watch this space—Gillette Daisy shave does a job on the legs."* Gainesville Sun, *Apr. 26, 1981.*

collecting past data on monthly utilization and calculating, for each month, the ratio of monthly utilization to utilization for the entire fiscal year preceding the month. Confidence intervals established on this utilization ratio enable planners to establish budget forecasts. At one of the smaller (50 beds) Sisters of St. Joseph's hospitals, the April utilization ratios for each of the past 10 years were calculated and found to have a sample mean of .0817 and a sample standard deviation of .0069 (*Hospital & Health Services Administration*, Jan./Feb. 1986). Establish a 99% confidence interval for μ, the true mean April utilization ratio. Interpret the interval.

*8.107 Refer to the *Journal of the American Planning Association* study of light rail transit (LRT) systems, Exercise 8.23. Recall that a sample of 10 cities with LRT systems had a mean farebox recovery rate of .604 and a standard deviation of .163. Use this information to find a 99% confidence interval for the true standard deviation of the population of farebox recovery ratios. Interpret the interval.

■ CASE STUDY 8.1

An Aspirin a Day Keeps the Heart Doctor Away

According to the National Center for Health Statistics, heart disease is the leading cause of death in the United States; heart attacks and strokes account for about 40% of all deaths. With this statistic in mind, it is no surprise that the following headline appeared across the front page of nearly every U.S. daily newspaper in late January 1988: "Aspirin cuts the risk of heart attack."

The exciting news was based on a nationwide study of 22,071 U.S. physicians, the results of which were reported in the *New England Journal of Medicine* (Jan. 27, 1988). The U.S. Physicians' Health Study, as it is known, involved a randomized clinical trial in which about half (11,037) of the physicians were assigned at random to receive one Bufferin brand aspirin tablet every other day. The other half (11,034) received a placebo, a harmless and ineffective substitute. The study was "double-blind" so that neither the participants (i.e., the physicians) nor the medical scientists who were conducting the research knew which tablet, the Bufferin or the placebo, was being administered. After 5 years, the researchers found that the incidence of fatal heart attacks among the "placebo" group was over 3 times greater than that for the "aspirin" group. (See Table 8.10.) Based on these findings, the study was halted so that those physicians who were taking the placebo could immediately switch to aspirin and receive its "extreme beneficial effects on fatal heart attacks."

The good news of the U.S. Physicians' Health Study was followed by an avalanche of television commercials for aspirin, promoting its new-found status as the "heart attack prevention drug." Unfortunately, the excitement over the "cure" for heart disease was short-lived "and turned to confusion, when," according to *Chance* (Fall 1988), "three days later a headline in the *New York Times* read, 'Value of Daily Aspirin Disputed in British Study of Heart Attacks.' It seemed that a similar study conducted in England did not show that aspirin had any beneficial effect in reducing the risk of heart attack."

The 6-year British study involved 5,139 doctors in which two-thirds (3,429) were randomly chosen to take daily aspirin. The remaining physicians (1,710) were not given a placebo, but instead were instructed "to avoid aspirin and products containing aspirin unless some specific indication for aspirin was thought to have developed." The results, reported in the *British Medical Journal* (Jan. 1988), showed that the fatal heart attack rate was essentially the same in both groups. (See Table 8.10b.)

a. Consider the results of the U.S. Physicians' Health Study. Construct a 95% confidence interval for the true difference between the fatal heart attack rates of the aspirin group and the placebo group. Interpret the interval.

b. Now consider the results of the British study. Construct a 95% confidence interval for the true difference between the heart attack rates of the aspirin group and the control group. Interpret the interval.

c. Refer to parts a and b. Does your inference about the beneficial effect of aspirin in the prevention of heart attacks depend on which study you consider?

d. Why might the two studies yield contrasting results? [*Hint:* Consider one or more of the following issues: sample size; the fact that the U.S. study used physicians who had extraordinarily low cardiovascular mortality rates; double-blind study versus unblinded study; placebo versus "no aspirin."]

* Greenhouse, J. B., and Greenhouse, S. W. "An aspirin a day...?" Change: New Directions for Statistics and Computing, *Vol. 1, No. 4, Fall 1988, pp. 24–31, New York, Springer-Verlag.*

Table 8.10   Results of Two Studies on the Use of Aspirin
in the Prevention of Heart Attacks

a. U.S. Physicians' Health Study	Aspirin Group	Placebo Group
Sample size	11,037	11,034
Number of fatal heart attacks	5	18

b. British Study	Aspirin Group	Control Group
Sample size	3,429	1,710
Number of fatal heart attacks	89	47

■ CASE STUDY 8.2 ■

Public Opinion Polls: How Accurate Are They?

[In the 1984 presidential election, then incumbent] Ronald Reagan captured 59% of the nation's popular votes, and all of the electoral votes save those in challenger Walter Mondale's home state. Published preelection polls generally picked Reagan as the likely winner. Yet, even late in the campaign, quite discrepant estimates of the victory margin were appearing. At the extremes, a Gordon Black survey conducted for *USA Today* gave Reagan a lead over Mondale by 60% to 35%, with 5% undecided, while a Roper Poll for the Public Broadcasting Station (PBS) showed Reagan ahead 52.5% to 42.5%, also with 5% undecided. Earlier polls, even when simultaneous, had diverged more widely.

The above is the opening paragraph of an article published in a 1986 issue of *Science* magazine.* The authors, P. E. Converse and M. W. Traugott, both directors at the Institute for Social Research, University of Michigan, are writing on the accuracy of public opinion polls. "Discrepancies as glaring as [the two polls referenced in the above paragraph] are not common for reputable sample surveys of the same population at the same time," they state, "but they do occur. And while polls reported in the national media tend to state error margins, usually plus or minus three percentage points, a reader diligent enough to compare competing polls ... is likely to conclude that error margins must somehow exceed this three percentage point value by an appreciable amount."

The "three percentage point" error margin the authors are referring to arises from the sampling error associated with estimating a population proportion π. From Section 8.4, we know that this sampling error is proportional to the standard error of the sample proportion, σ_p, where

$$\sigma_p = \sqrt{\frac{\pi(1-\pi)}{n}}$$

Since most conventional opinion polls utilize a sample size of $n = 1,500$, a conservative estimate of σ_p is

$$\sigma_p \approx \sqrt{\frac{(.5)(.5)}{1,500}}$$

$$= .0129$$

(Note that we substituted $\pi = .5$ into the equation to obtain this value. Recall from Section 8.8 that $\pi = .5$ is a conservative estimate of π because it is the value that maximizes σ_p.) For a 95% confidence interval for π, the bound on the error of estimation is approximately

$$2\sigma_p \approx 2(.0129)$$

$$= .0258$$

Rounding up, we obtain $2\sigma_p \approx .03$, or 3%. In other words, the estimate of π will be within about 3% of the true value at confidence level .95 when a sample of size $n = 1,500$ is employed.

a. Assuming that the *USA Today* poll referenced previously included a sample of 1,500 voters, find a 95% confidence interval for π, the true proportion of voters who favored Reagan just prior to the 1984 presidential election.

b. Repeat part a for the PBS poll.

c. Compare the two intervals obtained in parts a and b. If the two samples were selected from the same population (i.e., the population of eligible voters) at

*Source: Converse, P. E., and Traugott, M.W. "Assessing the accuracy of polls and surveys." Science, Vol. 234, 1986, pp. 1094–1098. Copyright 1986 by the AAAS.

the same time, would you expect to see such disparate results? Explain.

Converse and Traugott note that the plus or minus three percent "refers only to the most obvious source of variability, the error arising because the population at issue has not been fully enumerated, but merely sampled." In addition to sampling error, they identify several other reasons why such discrepancies in public opinion polls exist:

1. The target populations for the polls are often not the same. For example, one poll may sample the population of eligible voters, whereas another may sample the population consisting of those citizens who actually do vote.

2. Most national surveys, although they claim to cover the entire adult population of the United States, miss a small margin of the population. "Few surveys include Alaska or Hawaii, or institutionalized members of the population in hospitals, barracks, dormitories, and jails." Also, telephone surveys miss about "8% of the household population [that] remains inaccessible by residential phone."

3. Every survey is faced with the problem of nonresponse by eligible sample members, either by a refusal of the polled person to answer questions or by failure of the polling service to contact the selected member. This leads to biased survey results, even when repeated attempts to contact the person are made. For example, during the 1984 campaign, the authors found that "Democratic partisans were more accessible at early calls than Republican ones. A trial heat gave Reagan a mere three percentage point margin over Mondale among those interviewed at one call; ... after up to 30 callbacks for the most difficult to locate respondents, the lead had advanced to 13 percentage points."

4. The way the written questionnaire or verbal questions are constructed and asked has a significant impact on the survey results. For example, researchers have found that "both black and white respondents report positions on race-related issues that are less supportive of blacks when talking to white interviewers than when talking to black ones."

In optional Chapter 9, we discuss several alternative sample survey techniques designed to reduce the sampling error introduced by some of these problems.

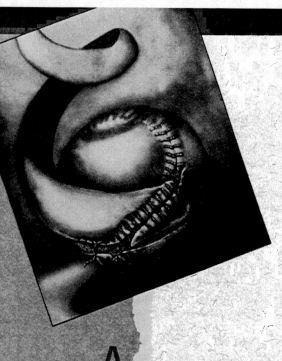

Chapter 9

INTRODUCTION TO SAMPLE SURVEY METHODS (OPTIONAL)

According to a survey of nearly 200 *Fortune* 500 companies, more than 86% rely on university-based education programs to aid in the development of their top-level executives. Suppose we want to construct a confidence interval for the true percentage of *Fortune* 500 firms that utilize university-based executive education programs. The estimation procedures discussed in Chapter 8 are based on the assumption that the number N of elements in the population is large relative to the sample size n. Since the sample size ($n = 200$) represents a significant proportion of the total number of firms ($N = 500$) in the target population, the formula for the confidence interval must be adjusted. In this optional chapter, we present methods for estimating population parameters when the sample size is large relative to the population size. The *Fortune* 500 survey problem is addressed in Exercise 9.4.

■ CONTENTS

9.1 Why Sample Survey Methods Are Useful

In the preceding chapter, we presented methods for estimating population parameters based on simple random sampling. We assumed that the sampling was achieved using a random number generator or that the sampling procedure approximated (to a reasonable degree) random sampling. **All of the estimation procedures were based on the assumption that the number N of elements in the population was large relative to the sample size n.**

Sampling in the real world, particularly conducting surveys of consumer preferences or opinions and surveys of business conditions, is not so simple. It is often difficult to identify and list the people in the population that is to be sampled, and the costs of contacting the people in the sample depend on the type of survey conducted. In some cases, the number n of people in the sample may represent a significant proportion of the number N of people in the population.

The branch of statistics devoted to designing and conducting business surveys, consumer preference polls, and so forth, and dealing with problems such as the one identified above, is known as **survey sampling**. In this chapter, we introduce several methods for choosing the sample size and estimating population parameters for sample surveys in which n is large relative to N.

9.2 Terminology

Our discussion of survey sampling begins with definitions of several important terms. The relationships among these terms are shown graphically in Figure 9.1.

FIGURE 9.1

Illustration of Survey
Sampling Terms

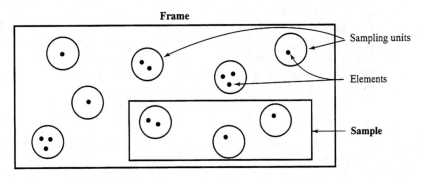

Definition 9.1

An **element** is the object upon which an observation (measurement) is made.

Definition 9.2

A **sampling unit** is a single element or a set of elements. The elements in two or more sampling units are nonoverlapping. That is, an element can be in one and only one sampling unit.

Definition 9.3

A **frame** is a list of all sampling units in the population.

Definition 9.4

A **sample** is a subset of sampling units selected from the frame.

The key to survey sampling is to properly identify the frame from which the sample is to be selected. The following two examples illustrate the point.

EXAMPLE 9.1
Identifying a Frame

A marketing research firm wants to sample the opinions of adults in a city concerning some new product. The firm decides to randomly select a sample of $n = 2,000$ adults from the city and elicit the opinion of each. Identify the frame for this survey.

SOLUTION Each adult who might appear in the sample is a **sampling unit**, and the list of all possible sampling units (adults) in the city is the **frame.** For this particular example, an adult in the city is both a sampling unit and an element of the sample; that is, each sampling unit contains only a single element. ■

EXAMPLE 9.2
ntifying the Elements of
a Sample Survey

Refer to Example 9.1. A less-expensive way to sample approximately the same number of adults would be to randomly select $n = 1,000$ households from among all households in the city and then record the opinions of all adults in each sampled household. Identify the elements, sampling units, and frame for this survey.

SOLUTION Since households are actually sampled from the city, a sampling unit would be a household, and the list of all households in the city would be the frame. Since opinions are recorded for each adult in a household, each of the adults is an element of the sample. This type of sampling, which involves sampling **clusters** of elements (in this example, a cluster is the set of elements in a single household), is called **cluster sampling.** ■

For most sampling situations (e.g., those discussed in the preceding chapters of this text, and that of Example 9.1) sampling units contain a single element, or **experimental unit**. The need to make a distinction between a sampling unit and an element of the sample occurs in survey sampling because cluster sampling (Example 9.2) is frequently employed.

9.3 A Finite Population Correction Factor

Which sample contains the greater amount of information about a population mean μ, a sample of $n = 10$ from a population of $N = 1,000$ or a sample of $n = 10$ from a population of $N = 1,000,000$? Although we might think that a sample of $n = 10$ out of 1,000 contains more information than $n = 10$ out of 1,000,000, they contain approximately the same amount of information about μ. This is because, for both sampling situations, the sample size n is small relative to N. Thus, when the sample size n is small relative to N (and N is large), the number N of elements in the population has no effect on the amount of information in the sample available for estimating μ.

Suppose we were to sample $n = 100$ from a population containing $N = 200$ elements. Intuitively, we would feel that this sample, which represents 50% of the elements in the population, contains more information about μ than a sample of $n = 10$ from $N = 1,000$ or $n = 20$ from $N = 1,000,000$. This time our intuition is correct. When the ratio n/N is large—say, larger than .05—we must adjust the width of the confidence interval for a population parameter. As you will subsequently see, the procedure for constructing a confidence interval for estimating a population mean μ or a population proportion π is the same as that given in Chapter 8, except that the width is now multiplied by the finite population correction factor shown in the next box.

Finite Population Correction Factor[*]

$$\sqrt{\frac{N-n}{N}} = \sqrt{1 - \frac{n}{N}}$$

The finite population correction factors for some ratios of sample size to population size are given in Table 9.1 (page 426). The table shows, for example, that if the sample represents only 1% of the population, the finite population correction factor is .995. This means that the confidence interval for μ or π, based on a 1% sample, will be almost the same width (99.5% as wide) as the confidence interval for μ or π presented in Chapter 8. In other words, if the sample size is 1% or less of the number of elements in the population, there is little need to make a finite population correction. However, if the sample size represents 50% of the number of elements in the popula-

---

[*]*Alternatively, we could define the finite population correction factor as* $\sqrt{(N-n)/(N-1)}$. *In practice, the two formulas will yield nearly identical results.*

tion, the confidence interval for μ or π will be only 70.7% as wide as the interval computed using the formulas in Chapter 8. Therefore, when the ratio of sample size n to population size N is larger than some small value—say, .05—the finite population correction factor should be used to compute confidence intervals for population parameters. If the ratio is smaller than .05, there is no harm in making the finite population correction but it will have little effect on the width of the computed confidence interval.

Table 9.1   Some Finite Population
Correction Factor Values

Ratio of Sample Size n to Population Size N (n/N)	*Value of Finite Population Correction Factor*
.01	.995
.05	.975
.10	.949
.20	.894
.30	.837
.50	.707
.80	.447

The following sections present point estimates and approximate confidence intervals for population parameters using several different sample survey methods. First, in Sections 9.4 and 9.5, we discuss the familiar simple random sampling technique. Then, we introduce two other types of samples and present their estimation methods in the remaining sections. As you read these sections, note the finite population correction factor in the formulas for the confidence intervals.

9.4 Estimation: Simple Random Sampling

In this section, we assume that each sampling unit contains a single element and that the sample is randomly selected from a frame consisting of all sampling units in the population. This type of sample is called a **simple random sample**.

Definition 9.5

A **simple random sample** of n sampling units from a population of N sampling units is one selected in such a way that every different sample of n sampling units has an equal probability of selection. *Note:* Each sampling unit in a simple random sample contains a single element.

In addition to giving the formulas for point estimators and confidence intervals for a population proportion π and a population mean μ, we also give corresponding formulas for a population total τ. For example, if μ is the mean value of some variable x taken over all N sampling units in a population, then τ is the sum (or total) of these N values of x. Since the formulas for estimating a mean μ or proportion π are identical to those given in Chapter 8 (except for the finite population correction factor), we will omit examples of these estimation problems and refer you to the appropriate sections in Chapter 8. Example 9.1 illustrates estimation of a population total τ.

The formulas for the confidence intervals for μ, τ, and π are approximate because the sampling distributions of the statistics used to form the intervals deviate somewhat from the normal distribution. These formulas are given in the boxes.

Estimation of a Population Mean μ: Simple Random Sampling

Point estimator: $\hat{\mu} = \bar{x} = \dfrac{\Sigma x}{n}$

Approximate 95% confidence interval: $\bar{x} \pm 1.96 \dfrac{s}{\sqrt{n}} \sqrt{\dfrac{N - n}{N}}$

where

$$s = \sqrt{\dfrac{\Sigma (x_i - \bar{x})^2}{n - 1}}$$

n = Number of sampling units in the sample

N = Number of sampling units in the population

Estimation of a Population Total τ: Simple Random Sampling

Point estimator: $\hat{\tau} = N\bar{x}$

Approximate 95% confidence interval: $\hat{\tau} \pm 1.96 \dfrac{Ns}{\sqrt{n}} \sqrt{\dfrac{N - n}{N}}$

where

$\bar{x}$ = Sample mean s = Sample standard deviation

n = Number of sampling units in the sample

N = Number of sampling units in the population

Estimation of a Population Proportion π: Simple Random Sampling

Point estimator: $\hat{\pi} = p = \dfrac{x}{n}$

Approximate 95% confidence interval: $p \pm 1.96 \sqrt{\dfrac{p(1-p)}{n}} \sqrt{\dfrac{N-n}{N}}$

where

x = Number of sampling units possessing a specific attribute

n = Number of sampling units in the sample

N = Number of sampling units in the population

EXAMPLE 9.3
Estimating τ with a Simple Random Sample

The term *shrinkage*, as it relates to a department store, is the loss in inventory resulting from theft or other unexplained reasons. A particular department store merchandises 2,409 items. To estimate the total shrinkage (in dollars) in its inventory, the store decided to randomly sample $n = 200$ items and to calculate the shrinkage for each item. The mean shrinkage per item for the sample was found to be \$31.07 and the sample standard deviation was \$112.94. Find an approximate 95% confidence interval for the total shrinkage for the store.

SOLUTION For this example we are given that $n = 200$, $N = 2,409$, $\bar{x} = 31.07$, and $s = 112.94$. Then

$$\hat{\tau} = N\bar{x} = 2,409(31.07) = \$74,847.63$$

and a 95% confidence interval for τ is

$$\hat{\tau} \pm 1.96 \frac{Ns}{\sqrt{n}} \sqrt{\frac{N-n}{N}}$$

$$74,847.63 \pm (1.96) \frac{(2,409)(112.94)}{\sqrt{200}} \sqrt{\frac{2,409 - 200}{2,409}}$$

or \$74,847.63 ± \$36,108.13. Therefore, we estimate that the interval from \$38,739.50 to \$110,955.76 contains the actual total shrinkage τ for the store. The confidence coefficient for the interval is approximately .95. ■

EXERCISES

■ *Learning the Mechanics*

9.1   Suppose you want to estimate a population mean μ with $N = 300$, $n = 30$, $\bar{x} = 680$, and $s = 22$. Find an approximate 95% confidence interval for μ.

9.2   Suppose you want to estimate a population total τ with $N = 3,500$, $n = 100$, $\bar{x} = 50.2$, and $s = 3.7$. Find an approximate 95% confidence interval for τ.

9.3   Suppose you want to estimate a population proportion π with $N = 5,000$, $n = 800$, and sample proportion $p = .81$. Find an approximate 95% confidence interval for π.

■ *Applying the Concepts*

9.4   The *Training and Development Journal* (June 1984) reported on a survey of 183 *Fortune* 500 companies regarding executive development in university-based education programs. One of the main questions posed by the survey asked, "What techniques are used most frequently by *Fortune* 500 companies for management development?" Thirty-eight of the 183 companies indicated that they use campus-based executive education programs as one of their techniques for management development.
  a. Calculate the finite population correction factor for a simple random sample of 183 companies selected from the *Fortune* 500.
  b. Find an approximate 95% confidence interval for the proportion of *Fortune* 500 companies that use university-based education programs as one of their techniques for management development.

9.5   Because external audits can be quite expensive, many companies are creating or augmenting internal audit departments to lower auditing costs. W. A. Wallace conducted a survey of the audit departments of 32 diverse companies (*Harvard Business Review*, Mar.–Apr. 1984). The main goal of the study was to determine the effect of internal audit departments on external audit fees. The mean external audit fee paid by the 32 companies during the year was $779,030 and the standard deviation was $1,083,162. Assuming that the 32 sampled companies were selected from a total of 95 similar companies in the Southwest, calculate an approximate 95% confidence interval for the mean external audit fee paid by all Southwest companies during the year.

9.6   A sample survey is undertaken to determine the proportion of voters in a certain county who favor a proposal to create urban "enterprise job zones" that would seek to attract new business and job opportunities in declining areas of the county's cities. A random sample of 1,000 voters is selected from the 50,840 eligible voters in the county. Of the 1,000 voters, 620 said they would favor the proposal. Use the techniques outlined in this section to find an approximate 95% confidence interval for the true proportion of the county's voters who favor the creation of urban enterprise job zones.

9.7   A large credit corporation is conducting an investigation of its delinquent creditors, i.e., creditors who are more than 1 month behind in payment. The company randomly samples 40 of its 272 delinquent accounts and records the dollar amount overdue for each. These accounts produce the following sample statistics:

$$\bar{x} = \$371 \qquad s = \$66$$

   a. Find an approximate 95% confidence interval for the mean delinquency per account for all creditors who are more than 1 month behind in payment.

   b. Find an approximate 95% confidence interval for the total amount overdue for all creditors who are more than 1 month behind in payment.

9.8 One piece of information of great interest to an individual who wants to contract for the services of a home builder is the proportion of the builder's construction projects that are completed on or before the target date. A large-volume builder in Phoenix, Arizona, has begun 200 home construction projects over the past year. The records for a random sample of 60 of these projects indicated that 27 of the projects were completed on time and 33 extended beyond the estimated completion date. Estimate π, the proportion of this builder's projects that are completed by the target date, using an approximate 95% confidence interval.

9.9 A specialty manufacturer wants to purchase remnants of sheet aluminum foil. The foil, all of which is the same thickness, is stored on 7,462 rolls, each containing a varying amount of foil. To obtain an estimate of the total number of square feet of foil on all the rolls, the manufacturer randomly sampled 100 rolls and measured the number of square feet of foil on each roll. The sample mean was 47.4 and the sample variance was 153.1. Find an approximate 95% confidence interval for the total amount of foil on the 7,462 rolls.

9.5 Choosing the Sample Size: Simple Random Sampling

The method for choosing the sample size for estimating μ, τ, or π is similar to the procedure described in Section 8.8. We equate the formula for the half-width of the confidence interval to the desired half-width, d, and solve for n. The formulas for finding n, based on sampling from a population containing N sampling units (with known variance σ^2), are shown in the boxes.

Approximate Sample Size to Obtain a 95% Confidence Interval for a Population Mean μ or Total τ: Simple Random Sampling

$$n = \frac{N\sigma^2}{(N-1)D + \sigma^2}$$

where

N = Number of sampling units in the population

σ^2 = Population variance

$$D = \begin{cases} \dfrac{d^2}{4} & \text{when estimating } \mu \\[2ex] \dfrac{d^2}{4N^2} & \text{when estimating } \tau \end{cases}$$

d = Desired half-width of the confidence interval

Approximate Sample Size to Obtain a 95% Confidence Interval for Population Proportion π: Simple Random Sampling

$$n = \frac{N\pi(1-\pi)}{(N-1)D + \pi(1-\pi)}$$

where

$\pi = $ Population proportion

$$D = \frac{d^2}{4}$$

$d = $ Desired half-width of the confidence interval

EXAMPLE 9.4

Selecting *n* for a Simple Random Sample

The confidence interval for the total shrinkage for the department store in Example 9.3 was quite wide. Suppose the store manager wants to increase the size of the sample so that the interval half-width is approximately $10,000. Approximately how many items would have to be included in the survey to obtain this 95% confidence interval for τ?

SOLUTION The formula for *n* is

$$n = \frac{N\sigma^2}{(N-1)D + \sigma^2}$$

where

$N = 2,409$

$d = \$10,000$

$$D = \frac{d^2}{4N^2} = \frac{(10,000)^2}{4(2,409)^2} = 4.3079$$

To solve for *n*, we need an approximate value for the population variance, σ^2. We could guess the value σ (and consequently, σ^2) if we had no prior information but, in this case, we have an estimate of σ—namely, $s = 112.94$, from Example 9.3. Using this value as an approximation to σ and substituting it along with the values of N and D into the formula, we find

$$n = \frac{N\sigma^2}{(N-1)D + \sigma^2} \approx \frac{(2,409)(112.94)^2}{(2,409 - 1)(4.3079) + (112.94)^2} = 1,328.6$$

Rounding this value upward, we have $n = 1,329$. Therefore, to estimate the total shrinkage τ to within $10,000 with 95% confidence, the store manager would require a simple random sample of $n = 1,329$ items. ■

Unlike in Example 9.4, survey samplers interested in estimating μ or τ will rarely have an estimate of σ readily available to use in the formula for determining n. Rather than guess its value, many *presample* the population and use the value of s from the presample (or **pilot sample**) to estimate σ. Typically, the presample is a relatively small sample (say, $n = 10$ or $n = 20$) that can be conveniently obtained. In the case of estimating a population proportion π, if no prior estimate of π is available, it is advisable to use $\pi = .5$ as an estimate. As we learned in Chapter 8, using $\hat{\pi} = .5$ leads to a conservative sample size (i.e., a value of n that is larger than the actual sample size necessary).

EXERCISES

■ *Learning the Mechanics*

9.10 Find the sample size needed to estimate a population mean μ with 95% confidence if $N = 2,000$, $d = 6$, and $\sigma^2 \approx 225$.

9.11 Find the sample size needed to estimate a population total τ with 95% confidence if $N = 510$, $d = 4,000$, and $\sigma^2 \approx 720$.

9.12 Find the sample size needed to estimate a population proportion π with 95% confidence if $N = 800$, $d = .10$, and $\pi \approx .33$.

■ *Applying the Concepts*

9.13 Suppose you want to reduce the width of the confidence interval constructed in Exercise 9.6. How many voters should be selected to estimate the true proportion of the county's voters who favor the creation of urban enterprise zones to within .02, with 95% confidence?

9.14 Suppose you want to reduce the width of the confidence interval obtained in Exercise 9.7, part **a**. How many of the credit corporation's 272 delinquent accounts must be sampled to estimate the mean amount overdue per account to within $10 of the true value, with 95% confidence?

9.15 Suppose you want to reduce the width of the confidence interval constructed in Exercise 9.9. How many rolls of sheet aluminum foil should be sampled to estimate the total amount of foil on the 7,462 rolls to within 10,000 square feet of its true value, with 95% confidence?

9.6 Other Types of Samples: Stratified, Cluster, and Systematic Samples

Selecting a random sample can be difficult and costly. For example, suppose we want to sample the opinion of all working women in a certain community on the issue of gender bias in the workplace. The first obstacle to the sample selection is acquiring a frame, a complete listing of all the women working in the population. The second obstacle is contacting the women who appear in the sample to obtain their opinions.

To reduce the difficulty and costs associated with acquiring a frame and selecting the sample, and to increase the precision of the sample information, people trained in selecting samples have devised some modifications to the simple random sampling procedure described in Sections 9.4 and 9.5. In this section, we introduce three alternative methods of sampling, the first of which is **stratified random sampling**.

EXAMPLE 9.5 Selecting a Stratified Random Sample	Suppose we wish to sample the opinions of all heads of household in a state on some issue (e.g., legalized casino gambling), and further suppose that the state contains 10 counties (see Figure 9.2). It might be difficult to obtain a frame listing all households within the state, but suppose we know that each county possesses a frame—namely, the households listed on its tax roll. Suppose, also, that the demographics and socio-economic status of households vary widely among counties. How could we proceed with the sampling?

FIGURE 9.2

Map of a Fictitious
State with 10
Counties

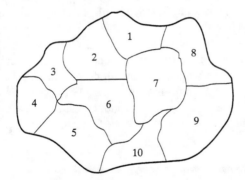

SOLUTION Instead of combining the 10 frames and selecting a random sample from the whole state, it would be easier and less costly to select a random sample of heads of household from each county. This would enable us to obtain sample opinions not only for each county (so that particular counties could be compared) but also for the entire state. This method of sampling is called **stratified random sampling** because the population is partitioned into a number of **strata** and random samples are then selected from among the elements in each **stratum**. Stratification is advantageous because it allows you to acquire sample information on the individual strata as well as on the entire population. It is often less costly to select the sample and, because the variability of observations within a stratum (county) is usually less than the variability in observations between strata, stratification may provide more accurate estimates of strata and population parameters. ■

Definition 9.6

A **stratified random sample** is obtained by partitioning the sampling units in the population into nonoverlapping subpopulations called **strata**. Random samples are then selected from each stratum.

A second alternative sampling method, called **cluster sampling**, is based on the random selection of clusters of elements from a population.

EXAMPLE 9.6
Selecting a Cluster Sample

Suppose we want to sample the opinions of the heads of household in a city, but we know that many households, for one reason or another, are not listed on the tax roll. How could we proceed?

SOLUTION   Since the tax roll cannot be used as a frame, we could construct a frame by numbering on a map each of the city blocks. The list of all blocks in the city would then provide a frame for selecting a random sample of *city blocks*, each representing a **cluster** of households. After the random sample of clusters is selected, interviewers are sent out to contact and interview all heads of household within each cluster (block) that appears in the sample. The information contained in the clusters is ultimately combined to make inferences about the population of heads of household within the city. The advantages of cluster sampling are clear: It is often easy to form a frame consisting of clusters, and it is less costly to conduct interviews within clusters than to interview individual elements selected at random from the population.   ■

Definition 9.7

A **cluster sample** is a random sample in which the sampling units consist of clusters of elements.

The third alternative type of sampling to be discussed here is **systematic sampling.** This method is also used to reduce the difficulty and cost of selecting a sample.

EXAMPLE 9.7
Selecting a Systematic Sample

Suppose our objective is to sample the opinions of all persons who use the downtown area of a city concerning a prospective increase in bus fares. Since it would be difficult, if not impossible, to construct a frame consisting of all people who use the downtown area, how should we proceed?

SOLUTION   The sample could be collected by *systematically* questioning every fifth person (or every 10th person or, in general, every kth person) encountered at a particular street location. Although this type of sampling is easy and inexpensive, the disadvantage is that it is difficult to obtain the sampling distribution of a statistic computed from the sample data. This makes it difficult to assess the accuracy of estimates based on a systematic sample.[*] ■

Definition 9.8

A **systematic sample** is obtained by systematically selecting every kth element in the population when the elements are ordered from 1 to N.

Stratified, cluster, and systematic samples are just a few of the many sampling plans available for conducting sample surveys. We discuss stratified and cluster sampling in more detail in the remainder of this chapter.

9.7 Estimation: Stratified Random Sampling

EXAMPLE 9.8
Devising a Sampling Plan

A television station wants to estimate the proportion of households in a three-county area that receive the station's evening news telecast. One of the counties is essentially urban and consists primarily of a small city. The other two counties are rural. It is expected that the proportion of viewers will vary substantially between the urban and rural areas. Devise a sampling plan for the TV station.

SOLUTION Since we expect substantial differences between the proportion of households in the urban and rural areas that receive the evening news telecast, it is advisable to treat the three counties as subpopulations of the complete three-county population and to use the county tax rolls to construct the frames for sampling. Using this procedure, the station would be able to estimate the proportion of viewing households in each of the three counties. It could then combine this information and obtain a single estimate of the proportion of viewers for the three-county area. ■

The sampling method used by the television station in Example 9.8 is **stratified random sampling**. Recall from Definition 9.6 that, in stratified random sampling, the sampling units are partitioned into nonoverlapping sets called **strata.** When groups of people are being sampled, the strata might be determined by geographical boundaries,

---

[*] *One alternative is to treat the systematic sample the same as a simple random sample. This approach is dangerous, however, if a periodic or cyclical pattern exists in the data. (For example, if prices are sampled every 30th day at a retail outlet, the prices will tend to be too low due to end-of-the-month clearance sales.) Another alternative is to select multiple systematic samples (e.g., one sample for each street location in Example 9.7) and treat them as clusters in a cluster sample. Whatever method is employed, the standard errors of the estimate will be only approximate.*

as was the case for the television viewers survey. Or, the strata might be determined organizationally. For example, in sampling the opinions of the employees of a corporation, you might partition the corporation's employees into three nonoverlapping sets—salaried employees, union hourly employees, and nonunion hourly employees.

Stratified random sampling has certain advantages over simple random sampling, as enumerated in the box.

Advantages of Stratified Random Sampling

1. You are able to obtain estimates of strata parameters as well as estimates of the parameters of the complete population.

2. Parameter estimates are usually more accurate than those obtained by simple random sampling. This is because strata are usually selected so that the variability of observations taken *within* strata is less than the variability *between* strata. This enables you to make more accurate estimates of the individual strata parameters and, consequently, to obtain more accurate estimates of the overall population parameters.

3. Sampling administrative costs are often less than for simple random sampling. For example, it may be easier to obtain frames for the strata, and the costs of collecting the sample (e.g., travel costs) may be less than for simple random sampling.

The accompanying boxes give the notation used in stratified random sampling, as well as the formulas for the point and interval estimators of μ, τ, and π. We give examples illustrating the estimation of a population proportion π and a mean μ. Estimation of a population total τ is performed in a similar manner; we leave this problem as an exercise for you.

Notation: Stratified Random Sampling

k = Number of strata

N_i = Number of sampling units in the ith stratum

N = Number of sampling units in the population

$= N_1 + N_2 + \cdots + N_k$

n_i = Number of sampling units randomly selected from the ith stratum

n = Total number of sampling units selected from the population

$= n_1 + n_2 + \cdots + n_k$

(continued)

$\bar{x}_i$ = Sample mean of the n_i observations selected from the ith stratum

s_i^2 = Sample variance computed from the n_i observations selected from the ith stratum

p_i = Sample proportion computed from the n_i observations selected from the ith stratum

---

Estimation of the Population Mean μ: Stratified Random Sampling

Point estimator: $\hat{\mu} = \bar{\bar{x}} = \dfrac{1}{N}\,(N_1\bar{x}_1 + N_2\bar{x}_2 + \cdots + N_k\bar{x}_k)$

Approximate 95% confidence interval: $\bar{\bar{x}} \pm 1.96 \sqrt{\dfrac{1}{N^2}\Sigma N_i^2\,\dfrac{s_i^2}{n_i}\!\left(\dfrac{N_i - n_i}{N_i}\right)}$

Estimation of the Population Total τ: Stratified Random Sampling

Point estimator: $\hat{\tau} = N\bar{\bar{x}} = N_1\bar{x}_1 + N_2\bar{x}_2 + \cdots + N_k\bar{x}_k$

Approximate 95% confidence interval: $\hat{\tau} \pm 1.96 \sqrt{\Sigma N_i^2\,\dfrac{s_i^2}{n_i}\!\left(\dfrac{N_i - n_i}{N_i}\right)}$

Estimation of a Population Proportion π: Stratified Random Sampling

Point estimator: $\hat{\pi} = \bar{p} = \dfrac{1}{N}\,(N_1 p_1 + N_2 p_2 + \cdots + N_k p_k)$

Approximate 95% confidence interval: $\bar{p} \pm 1.96 \sqrt{\dfrac{1}{N^2}\Sigma N_i^2\,\dfrac{p_i(1 - p_i)}{n_i - 1}\!\left(\dfrac{N_i - n_i}{N_i}\right)}$

EXAMPLE 9.9

Estimating π with a
Stratified Sample

Refer to the survey of households in Example 9.8. Suppose the television station selected $n_1 = n_2 = n_3 = 500$ households from each of the three counties. The number of households in each county along with the sample proportions that view the station's news telecast are shown in Table 9.2.

Table 9.2 Strata Sizes, Sample Sizes, and Proportions for Example 9.9

County	Number N_i of Households per County	Number n_i of Households Sampled per County	Sample Proportion per County
1 (Urban)	48,107	500	.27
2 (Rural)	12,419	500	.18
3 (Rural)	6,875	500	.17

a. Find an approximate 95% confidence interval for the proportion π of households that view the newscast for the three-county population.

b. Find an approximate 95% confidence interval for the proportion π_1 of urban households that view the telecast.

SOLUTION

a. The point estimator of the proportion π of households that view the station's news telecast is

$$\bar{p} = \frac{1}{N}(N_1 p_1 + N_2 p_2 + N_3 p_3)$$

where, from Table 9.2,

$$N = N_1 + N_2 + N_3 = 48,107 + 12,419 + 6,875 = 67,401$$

and

$$p_1 = .27, \, p_2 = .18, \text{ and } p_3 = .17$$

Then

$$\bar{p} = \frac{1}{67,401}[48,107(.27) + 12,419(.18) + 6,875(.17)]$$

$$= \frac{16,393.06}{67,401} = .24$$

The approximate 95% confidence interval for π is

$$\bar{p} \pm 1.96 \sqrt{\frac{1}{N^2} \Sigma N_i^2 \frac{p_i(1-p_i)}{n_i - 1} \left(\frac{N_i - n_i}{N_i} \right)}$$

Substituting into the formula, we have $.24 \pm 1.96 \sigma_{\bar{p}}$, where

$$\sigma_{\bar{p}} = \sqrt{\frac{1}{(67,401)^2} \left\{ (48.107)^2 \frac{(.27)(.73)}{500} \left(\frac{48,107 - 500}{48,107} \right) + (12,419)^2 \frac{(.18)(.82)}{500} \left(\frac{12,419 - 500}{12,419} \right) + (6,875)^2 \frac{(.17)(.83)}{500} \left(\frac{6,875 - 500}{6,875} \right) \right\}}$$

$$= .24 \pm 1.96(.0145)$$

$$= .24 \pm .028$$

or (.212, .268). Thus, the proportion of households that view the newscast for the three-county population falls between .212 and .268, with 95% confidence.

b. The urban county sample was a simple random sample of 500 households selected from among the 48,107 households in stratum 1. Therefore, we use the formula from Section 9.4 to find the confidence interval for π_1:

$$p_1 \pm 1.96 \sqrt{\frac{p_1(1-p_1)}{n_1}} \sqrt{\frac{N_1 - n_1}{N_1}}$$

Note that the finite population correction factor

$$\frac{N_1 - n_1}{N_1} = \frac{48,107 - 500}{48,107} = .990$$

is very close to 1.0 and can be ignored. (In fact, the correction factors for all three counties are very close to 1 and could have been ignored in the calculation of the confidence interval of part **a**.) Therefore, the approximate 95% confidence interval for the proportion π_1 of households in the urban county that view the news telecast is

$$.27 \pm 1.96 \sqrt{\frac{(.27)(.73)}{500}}$$

$$.27 \pm .039$$

or .231 to .309. ■

EXAMPLE 9.10

Estimating μ with a Stratified Sample

The television survey of Example 9.9 also asked each household to give the approximate number of hours per week that the household views television. The means and standard deviations for the strata samples are shown in Table 9.3.

Table 9.3 Sample Means and Standard Deviations for Hours per Week of Television Viewing

County	Number N_i of Households per County	Number n_i of Households Sampled per County	$\bar{x}_i$	s_i^2
1 (Urban)	48,107	500	14.35	237.24
2 (Rural)	12,419	500	18.74	168.47
3 (Rural)	6,875	500	19.98	131.01

a. Find an approximate 95% confidence interval for the mean viewing time per week of households in the three-county viewing area.

b. Find an approximate 95% confidence interval for the mean viewing time per week for households in the urban county.

SOLUTION

a. In Example 9.9, we found the population size to be $N = 67,401$. Substituting into the formula for $\bar{\bar{x}}$, we find the point estimator of μ to be

$$\bar{\bar{x}} = \frac{1}{N} \ (N_1 \bar{x}_1 + N_2 \bar{x}_2 + N_3 \bar{x}_3)$$

$$= \frac{1}{67,401} \ [48,107(14.35) + 12,419(18.74) + 6,875(19.98)]$$

$$= 15.73 \text{ hours per week}$$

The approximate 95% confidence interval for μ is

$$\bar{\bar{x}} \pm 1.96 \sqrt{\frac{1}{N^2} \Sigma N_i^2 \ \frac{s_i^2}{n_i} \left(\frac{N_i - n_i}{N_i} \right)}$$

Since the finite population correction factors

$$\frac{N_1 - n_1}{N_1} = .99 \qquad \frac{N_2 - n_2}{N_2} = .96 \qquad \frac{N_3 - n_3}{N_3} = .93$$

are close to 1, they may be ignored in the confidence interval formula. Then we have

$$\bar{\bar{x}} \pm 1.96 \sqrt{\frac{1}{N^2} \Sigma N_i^2 \frac{s_i^2}{n_i}}$$

$$= 15.73 \pm 1.96 \sqrt{\frac{1}{(67,401)^2} \left[\frac{(48,107)^2(237.24)}{500} + \frac{(12,419)^2(168.47)}{500} + \frac{(6,875)^2(131.01)}{500} \right]}$$

$$= 15.73 \pm 1.96(.506) = 15.73 \pm .99$$

or (14.74, 16.72). We estimate the mean viewing time per week of households in the three-county area to fall between 14.74 and 16.72 hours, with (approximate) 95% confidence.

b. As noted in Example 9.9, the sample selected from the urban county, stratum 1, was a simple random sample. Then, according to the formula in Section 9.4, an approximate 95% confidence interval for the mean weekly television viewing time for the urban households of stratum 1 is

$$\bar{x}_1 \pm 1.96 \frac{s_1}{\sqrt{n}} \sqrt{\frac{N-n}{N}}$$

$$= 14.35 \pm 1.96 \sqrt{\frac{237.24}{500}} \sqrt{\frac{48,107-500}{48,107}} = 14.35 \pm 1.34$$

or from 13.01 to 15.69 hours per week. ■

Note of caution: Stratified random sampling will produce a more accurate parameter estimate (i.e., an estimate with a smaller variance) than that obtained by simple random sampling whenever *the variance of observations within strata is less than the overall population variance.* However, if the variances within strata are large, stratified random sampling may actually yield an estimate that is less accurate than the estimate produced by a simple random sample. Consequently, for stratified random sampling to succeed, the strata must be carefully selected so that the data within each stratum are homogeneous.

EXERCISES

■ **Learning the Mechanics**

9.16 A survey based on a stratified random sample produced the data shown in the accompanying table. Find an approximate 95% confidence interval for the population mean μ.

	Stratum			
	1	*2*	*3*	*4*
N_i	4,000	3,000	5,000	10,000
n_i	80	60	100	200
$\bar{x}_i$	23.4	29.5	18.6	20.2
s_i	3.3	4.8	9.1	2.7
p_i	.6	.5	.7	.3

9.17 Refer to Exercise 9.16. Find an approximate 95% confidence interval for the population total τ.

9.18 Refer to Exercise 9.16. Find an approximate 95% confidence interval for the population proportion π.

■ **Applying the Concepts**

9.19 A wholesale food distributor who services four store chains in a large metropolitan area is considering adding a new product to his stock. To determine whether demand is great enough for the new product, he will test market the product in each of the four chains to estimate average monthly sales. For administrative convenience, stratified random sampling is used with each chain as a stratum. (No information on stratum variances is available.) The number of stores in the four chains (or strata) are: $N_1 = 24$, $N_2 = 36$, $N_3 = 30$, and $N_4 = 30$. The distributor has enough funds to obtain data on monthly sales in $n = 20$ stores. Using a proportional allocation scheme, the distributor randomly samples $n_1 = 4$, $n_2 = 6$, $n_3 = 5$, and $n_4 = 5$ stores from the four strata. After 1 month, the sales (in $ thousands) of the new product at the sampled stores showed the following results:

	Chain		
1	*2*	*3*	*4*
9.4	9.1	10.8	9.2
9.0	9.9	9.6	11.0
10.2	9.3	10.0	9.4
11.0	10.5	9.3	9.1
	11.1	9.3	11.3
	10.1		

a. Summary statistics (e.g., $\bar{x}$ and s) on monthly sales at each of the four store chains are displayed in the accompanying MINITAB printout. Use this information to construct a 95% confidence interval for the true mean monthly sales of the new product.

	N	MEAN	MEDIAN	TRMEAN	STDEV	SEMEAN
Chain1	4	9.900	9.800	9.900	0.887	0.443
Chain2	6	10.000	10.000	10.000	0.746	0.304
Chain3	5	9.800	9.600	9.800	0.628	0.281
Chain4	5	10.000	9.400	10.000	1.061	0.474
Total	20	9.930	9.750	9.906	0.773	0.173

b. Suppose the distributor had decided to take a simple random sample of $n = 20$ stores from the total of $N = 120$ stores in the four chains. Treat the 20 observations on monthly sales shown in the table as the simple random sample and construct a 95% confidence interval for the true mean monthly sales of the new product.

c. Compare the 95% confidence intervals, parts **a** and **b**. Which sampling scheme resulted in a more precise estimate of the true mean monthly sales of the new product?

d. Give a reason why the result, part **c**, occurred. [*Hint:* Compare the individual stratum sample variances to the overall sample variance, s_2.]

e. Can you think of a way to stratify the $n = 20$ monthly sales observations that will yield an estimate of the mean with a smaller variance?

9.20 Suppose you want to estimate the total amount of money spent on textbooks each quarter by students at your university. To reduce the variability in the data, you decide to consider student classes (freshman, sophomore, junior, senior) as strata. You randomly sample 50 students in each class and obtain an estimate of the total amount spent on textbooks during the quarter for each student. From the information given in the table, construct an approximate 95% confidence interval for the population total amount spent on textbooks per quarter by students at your university.

Class	N_i, Total Number of Students	$\bar{x}_i$, Average Amount Spent on Textbooks	s_i^2, Variance
Freshman	4,085	$75.20	62.50
Sophomore	3,520	62.00	86.50
Junior	5,525	45.15	31.40
Senior	5,070	42.85	39.70

9.21 Temik is a pesticide used for controlling insects that feed on potatoes, oranges, and other crops. Recently, drinking-water wells in several states have been found to be contaminated with Temik. According to federal standards, wells with levels of Temik above 1 part per billion are considered contaminated. To estimate the proportion of wells in Florida that are contaminated, a stratified sampling scheme is devised based on geographical area. A random sample of wells is selected from each of three regions and Temik tests are conducted to determine the number of contaminated wells. The accompanying table shows the total number of wells, the number sampled, and the proportion contaminated for each of the three strata. Estimate the true proportion of wells in Florida that are contaminated, with an approximate 95% confidence interval.

Region	N_i, Total Number of Drinking Wells	n_i, Number of Sampled Wells	p_i, Sample Proportion Contaminated
Panhandle	320	150	.013
Central Florida	716	300	.020
South Florida	1,025	400	.025

9.22 A tobacco company will use an estimate of the average number of cigarettes smoked per day by its employees in its next advertising campaign. The company expects a difference in amounts smoked by men and women, so it has decided to stratify by gender. From the company's 535 male employees, 50 are selected, and of the 366 female employees, 40 are sampled. An estimate of the number of cigarettes smoked per day by each is recorded. The table gives the respective means and variances of the samples.

Gender	N_i	n_i	$\bar{x}_i$	s_i^2
Men	535	50	8.5	16.8
Women	366	40	5.2	21.2

a. Estimate the average number of cigarettes smoked per day by the company employees with an approximate 95% confidence interval.
b. Estimate the average number of cigarettes smoked per day by male employees of the company with a 95% confidence interval.
c. Estimate the average number of cigarettes smoked per day by female employees of the company with a 95% confidence interval.

9.8 Choosing the Sample Size: Stratified Random Sampling

Before choosing the sample size n for a stratified random sampling design, we must decide on how we plan to allocate the n sampling units to the strata. For example, we could use equal sample sizes. Then, if there were $k = 4$ strata, we would allocate one-fourth of the n sampling units to each stratum. Or, we might want to make the strata sample sizes proportional to the numbers of sampling units in the strata. Using this procedure, we would select large samples from strata containing a large number of sampling units and small samples from strata containing a small number of sampling units.

Regardless of how the sample is to be allocated to the strata, we will assume that the proportion allocated to stratum 1 is w_1, the proportion allocated to stratum 2 is w_2, and, in general, the proportion allocated to stratum i is w_i, $i = 1, 2, \ldots, k$. Then the formulas giving the approximate numbers n of observations needed to construct 95% confidence intervals for μ, τ, and π are shown in the next two boxes.

Approximate Sample Size n to Obtain a 95% Confidence Interval for a Population Mean μ and Total τ: Stratified Random Sampling

$$n = \frac{\Sigma\left(\dfrac{N_i^2\sigma_i^2}{w_i}\right)}{N^2D + \Sigma(N_i\sigma_i^2)}$$

where

w_i = Proportion of sampling units allocated to stratum i

σ_i^2 = Variance of the sampling units in stratum i

$$D = \begin{cases} \dfrac{d^2}{4} & \text{when estimating } \mu \\[2mm] \dfrac{d^2}{4N^2} & \text{when estimating } \tau \end{cases}$$

d = Desired half-width of the confidence interval

Approximate Sample Size n to Obtain a 95% Confidence Interval for a Population Proportion π: Stratified Random Sampling

$$n = \frac{\Sigma\left(\dfrac{N_i^2\pi_i(1-\pi_i)}{w_i}\right)}{N^2D + \Sigma N_i\pi_i(1-\pi_i)}$$

where

π_i = Subpopulation proportion for stratum i

w_i = Proportion of sampling units allocated to stratum i

$$D = \frac{d^2}{4}$$

d = Desired half-width of the confidence interval

EXAMPLE 9.11
Selecting n for a
Stratified Sample

Refer to Example 9.9. Suppose the television station planned to conduct another survey of the three counties to estimate the proportion π of households that regularly tune in to a particular program. The station wants to use sample sizes approximately proportional to the numbers of sampling units in the strata—say, $w_1 = .7$, $w_2 = .2$, and $w_3 = .1$. Find the approximate sample size n and the strata sample sizes, n_1, n_2, and n_3, needed to find a 95% confidence interval for π with half-width equal to $d = .015$.

SOLUTION For this example, we have

$$d = .015$$

$$w_1 = .7 \qquad\qquad w_2 = .2 \qquad\qquad w_3 = .1$$

$$N_1 = 48,107 \qquad N_2 = 12,419 \qquad N_3 = 6,875$$

$$D = \frac{d^2}{4} = \frac{(.015)^2}{4} = .0000563$$

Suppose we have no prior information on the strata proportions. Then we would use the conservative values, $\pi_1 = \pi_2 = \pi_3 = .5$. This procedure would yield a solution for n that would, in most cases, be larger than required. Thus,

$$n = \frac{\Sigma \left[\dfrac{N_i^2 \pi_i (1 - \pi_i)}{w_i} \right]}{N^2 D + \Sigma N_i \pi_i (1 - \pi_i)}$$

$$= \frac{\left[\dfrac{(48,107)^2(.5)^2}{.7} + \dfrac{(12,419)^2(.5)^2}{.2} + \dfrac{(6,875)^2(.5)^2}{.1} \right]}{(67,401)^2(.0000563) + (48,107)(.5)^2 + (12,419)(.5)^2 + (6,875)(.5)^2}$$

$$= 4,172.5$$

or $n = 4,173$. Applying the strata weights, we should sample

$$n_1 = w_1 n = .7(4,173) = 2,921$$

$$n_2 = w_2 n = .2(4,173) = 835$$

$$n_3 = w_3 n = .1(4,173) = 417$$

households from stratum 1, stratum 2, and stratum 3, respectively. ▪

The choice of the strata sample sizes for stratified random sampling can also be based on the costs of contacting and observing the sampling units within the strata.

For example, it may be less costly to make an observation within one stratum than within another. This method for allocating the sample to the strata is beyond the scope of this text.

EXERCISES

■ *Learning the Mechanics*

9.23 Consider the stratified sampling plan with three strata shown in the table. Find the sample sizes n_1, n_2, and n_3 needed to estimate the population mean μ to within $d = 2$ with 95% confidence.

	Stratum		
	1	*2*	*3*
N_i	2,000	1,000	5,000
w_i	.25	.10	.65
σ_i^2 *(estimate)*	225	300	170
π_i *(estimate)*	.30	.50	.45

9.24 Refer to Exercise 9.23. Find the sample sizes n_1, n_2, and n_3 needed to estimate the population total τ to within $d = 10,000$ with 95% confidence.

9.25 Refer to Exercise 9.23. Find the sample sizes n_1, n_2, and n_3 needed to estimate the population proportion π to within .05 with 95% confidence.

■ *Applying the Concepts*

9.26 Suppose you want to reduce the width of the confidence interval obtained in Exercise 9.20. How many students should be sampled from each class to estimate the total amount spent on textbooks per quarter to within $8,000 of the true value, with 95% confidence?

9.27 Suppose you want to reduce the width of the confidence interval constructed in Exercise 9.21. How many wells need to be tested in each geographical region to estimate the true proportion of Florida wells contaminated with Temik to within .005, with 95% confidence? Assume that 10% of the wells sampled will be in the Panhandle, 30% in central Florida, and 60% in south Florida.

9.28 Suppose you want to reduce the width of the confidence interval constructed in Exercise 9.22. How many of the company's male and female employees must be sampled to estimate the average number of cigarettes smoked per day by company employees to within .5 of the true value, with 95% confidence? Assume that equal numbers of males and females are to be selected.

9.29 *Scanner-based test marketing* is a sophisticated method of product testing used by major U.S. manufacturers. In a scanner-based test, .1% of the U.S. population is sampled from selected market areas. According to *Fortune* (Oct. 29, 1984): "Consumers in a selected market get identification cards, which they present at supermarket checkout counters. Scanners record what they buy, how much, and how often. Consumers do not know which products are being tested and competitors can't get the scanner information. The results go to a central computer for analysis." A typical scanner-based test lasts 1 year and costs approximately $225,000 (a conventional, 3-year market test costs $600,000). Assume that some sort of stratified sampling plan is implemented in scanner-based test marketing, with the different test markets (i.e., geographical regions) representing the strata.

a. What are the sampling units in the stratified sample? What is the frame?

b. Why is it more advantageous to use a stratified sampling plan rather than a simple random sample of .1% of all U.S. consumers?

c. Suppose a scanner-based test is used to test a new product in three major U.S. markets: Los Angeles, Chicago, and New York. How many consumers must be sampled in each market to estimate the true proportion who would be willing to try the new product to within .10? Use the sample size weights $w_1 = .4$, $w_2 = .2$, and $w_3 = .4$ for Los Angeles ($N_1 = 3,000,000$), Chicago ($N_2 = 1,000,000$), and New York ($N_3 = 5,000,000$), respectively.

9.9 Estimation: Cluster Sampling

Recall from Section 9.6 that a **cluster sample** is a random sample of sampling units in which each sampling unit is a cluster of one or more elements of the sample. (See Definition 9.7.) Suppose, for example, that you want to sample the opinions of adults in a community. It would be easier and less costly to obtain the opinions of one or more adults by randomly sampling households than by sampling individual adults. Thus, a household would be a sampling unit and the group of adults within a household would represent a cluster. Note that the number of elements within the clusters can vary from cluster to cluster. Two advantages of cluster sampling are given in the box.

Advantages of Cluster Sampling

1. With cluster sampling, it is sometimes easier to construct a frame for the population.

2. Cluster sampling reduces the cost of sampling when costs of obtaining observations on the elements increase as the distance between elements increases.

The notation and the formulas for the estimation of μ, τ, and π are given in the boxes. We illustrate their application with two examples.

Notation: Cluster Sampling

N = Number of clusters in the population

n = Number of clusters in a simple random sample

m_i = Number of elements in cluster i, $i = 1, 2, ..., n$

$\overline{m}$ = Average size of the clusters in the sample

M = Number of elements in the population

$$= \sum_{i=1}^{N} m_i$$

$\overline{M} = \dfrac{M}{N}$ = Average size of the clusters in the population

x_i = Total of all observations in cluster i

Estimation of the Population μ: Cluster Sampling

Point estimator: $\overline{x} = \dfrac{\Sigma x_i}{\Sigma m_i}$

where

Σx_i = Sum of the sample cluster totals

Σm_i = Sum of the sample cluster sizes

Approximate 95% confidence interval:

$$\overline{x} \pm 1.96 \sqrt{\left(\frac{N-n}{Nn\overline{M}^2}\right) \Sigma \frac{(x_i - \overline{x}m_i)^2}{n-1}}$$

Estimation of the Population Total τ: Cluster Sampling

Point estimator: $M\overline{x} = M \dfrac{\Sigma x_i}{\Sigma m_i}$

where $\overline{x}$ is the point estimator of μ.

(continued)

Approximate 95% confidence interval:

$$M\bar{x} \pm 1.96 \sqrt{N^2 \left(\frac{N-n}{Nn}\right) \Sigma \frac{(\bar{x}_i - \bar{x}m_i)^2}{n-1}}$$

Estimation of the Population Proportion π: Cluster Sampling

Point estimator: $p = \dfrac{\Sigma a_i}{\Sigma m_i}$

where

a_i = Number of elements in cluster i possessing the attribute of interest

Σm_i = Sum of the sample cluster sizes

Approximate 95% confidence interval:

$$p \pm 1.96 \sqrt{\left(\frac{N-n}{Nn\overline{M}^2}\right) \Sigma \frac{(a_i - pm_i)^2}{n-1}}$$

EXAMPLE 9.12
Estimating μ with
Cluster Sampling

A newspaper publishing company wanted to estimate the mean number of newspaper subscriptions per household in a town containing 3,416 households. To reduce the cost of sampling, the company divided the town into 214 nonoverlapping geographic areas (mostly town blocks), and 10 blocks were randomly selected from among the 214. The number of newspapers received by each household in a sampled block was recorded. The number of households and the number of subscriptions per household are shown in Table 9.4. Find an approximate 95% confidence interval for the mean number of newspaper subscriptions per household in the town.

SOLUTION   For this example, $N = 214$, $n = 10$, $\Sigma m_i = 136$, $\Sigma x_i = 196$, and $M = 3,416$. Then the mean number of households per cluster for the sample is

$$\overline{m} = \frac{\Sigma m_i}{n} = \frac{136}{10} = 13.6$$

and the average cluster size for the population is

Table 9.4   Number of Newspaper Subscriptions per Household
for a Sample of $n = 10$ Clusters

Cluster	Cluster Size m_i	Subscriptions Per Household	Cluster Total x_i
1	16	0, 1, 1, 0, 1, 0, 1, 1, 1, 1, 1, 0, 1, 1, 0, 1	11
2	10	2, 1, 1, 3, 2, 2, 1, 2, 2, 3	19
3	14	1, 1, 2, 1, 1, 1, 2, 1, 1, 0, 1, 1, 1, 1	15
4	12	2, 1, 2, 1, 1, 1, 2, 2, 1, 1, 1, 2	17
5	13	1, 1, 1, 0, 1, 2, 0, 1, 1, 1, 1, 1, 2	13
6	12	3, 1, 2, 2, 3, 2, 3, 3, 4, 2, 3, 3	31
7	18	1, 0, 1, 1, 0, 1, 1, 1, 1, 1, 1, 2, 1, 1, 1, 1, 0, 1	16
8	10	2, 3, 3, 2, 3, 4, 2, 3, 2, 2	26
9	14	1, 1, 2, 1, 1, 2, 1, 2, 2, 2, 1, 2, 1, 1	20
10	17	2, 1, 3, 2, 2, 1, 2, 2, 1, 1, 2, 2, 2, 1, 2, 1, 1	28
	$\Sigma m_i = 136$		$\Sigma x_i = 196$

$$\overline{M} = \frac{M}{N} = \frac{3,416}{214} = 15.96$$

The point estimate of μ, the mean number of subscriptions per household for the sample, is

$$\bar{x} = \frac{\Sigma x_i}{\Sigma m_i} = \frac{196}{136} = 1.44$$

To find an approximate 95% confidence interval, we first need to obtain the sample estimate of the variance of the cluster totals:

$$\frac{\Sigma(x_i - \bar{x}m_i)^2}{n-1} = \frac{1}{(10-1)} \{[11 - (1.44)(16)]^2 + [19 - (1.44)(10)]^2 + \cdots + [28 - (1.44)(17)]^2\}$$

$$= \frac{659.16}{9} = 73.24$$

Substituting this quantity along with the values of N, n, and $\overline{M}$ into the formula for the 95% confidence interval, we obtain

$$\bar{x} \pm 1.96 \sqrt{\frac{N-n}{Nn\overline{M}^2} \Sigma \frac{(x_i - \bar{x}m_i)^2}{n-1}} = 1.44 \pm 1.96 \sqrt{\left[\frac{214 - 10}{(214)(10)(15.96)^2}\right](73.24)}$$

$$= 1.44 \pm .17$$

or 1.27 to 1.61. Our estimate of the mean number of subscriptions per household falls between 1.27 and 1.61, with 95% confidence. ■

EXAMPLE 9.13
Estimating π with Cluster Sampling

A wholesaler of electric lightbulbs received complaints that some of its bulbs failed to light. The complaints pertained to a shipment of 6,000 packages of bulbs, with four bulbs to each package. A random sample of 400 packages was selected from among the 6,000 in the shipment, and each of the 1,600 bulbs was tested to determine whether it was defective. The testing showed 53 failures among the 1,600 tested (i.e., $p = \frac{53}{1,600} = .033$), with

$$\frac{\Sigma(a_i - pm_i)^2}{n - 1} = \frac{\Sigma[a_i - (.033)(4)]^2}{400 - 1} = .1402$$

Find an approximate 95% confidence interval for the proportion π of lightbulbs in the shipment that are defective.

SOLUTION For this example, we have $N = 6,000$, $n = 400$, and $\overline{M} = M/N = 4$. Then the approximate 95% confidence interval for π is given by

$$p \pm 1.96 \sqrt{\left(\frac{N - n}{Nn\overline{M}^2}\right)\frac{\Sigma(a_i - pm_i)^2}{n - 1}} = .033 \pm 1.96 \sqrt{\left[\frac{6,000 - 400}{(6,000)(400)(4)^2}\right](.1402)}$$

$$= .033 \pm .009$$

or .024 to .042. ■

Note of caution: Cluster sampling is intended to provide maximum information on the parameter of interest at minimum cost when a frame listing all population elements is not available, or when the cost of obtaining observations increases as the distance between elements increases. *For samples of the same size, however, simple random sampling will generally lead to a parameter estimate with a smaller variance than with cluster sampling.* Consequently, if a frame is available and the cost of sampling is not prohibitive, simple random sampling (or stratified random sampling) is preferred. In applications where cost is a major concern, cluster sampling allows selection of a larger sample than would be practical if simple random sampling were employed, and this larger sample compensates for the loss of precision in estimating the parameter.

EXERCISES

■ *Learning the Mechanics*

9.30 The table shows the results of a sample survey based on cluster sampling with $N = 300$, $n = 8$, and $M = 1,280$. Find an approximate 95% confidence interval for the population mean μ.

					Cluster			
	1	2	3	4	5	6	7	8
m_i	2	4	2	2	5	3	4	3
x_i	6.0	5.2	8.1	16.7	28.0	3.4	15.5	12.6

9.31 Refer to Exercise 9.30. Find an approximate 95% confidence interval for the population total τ.

9.32 Find an approximate 95% confidence interval for the population proportion π using the information shown in the table. A survey based on cluster sampling with $N = 100$, $n = 10$, and $M = 2,500$ was used to collect the data.

					Cluster					
	1	2	3	4	5	6	7	8	9	10
m_i	20	30	31	22	25	16	44	27	22	25
a_i	6	10	12	7	4	1	15	10	11	9

■ *Applying the Concepts*

9.33 To emphasize safety, a taxicab company wants to estimate the proportion of unsafe tires on their fleet of 250 cabs.
  a. Describe how the estimate could be obtained using simple random sampling.
  b. Describe how the estimate could be obtained using cluster sampling.
  c. Explain why cluster sampling may be more practical than simple random sampling in this problem.

9.34 A heavy equipment manufacturer wanted to estimate the mean cost of maintenance and repair for a new model of bulldozer sold last year. Although the manufacturer can locate the construction companies that have purchased the bulldozers, it is unlikely that individual maintenance records are kept for each and every machine. Consequently, it is easier to construct a frame of construction companies and to treat the collection of bulldozers within each company as a cluster. The total number of bulldozers sold last year was 1,804. Twenty construction companies were randomly selected from a set of 279 that purchased the new bulldozer last year. A listing of the number of bulldozers purchased by each construction company along with the total cost (in dollars) of annual repair and maintenance (R&M) for the purchased bulldozers is shown in the next table. Estimate the mean cost for the year per bulldozer for repair and maintenance with an approximate 95% confidence interval.

Company	Number of Bulldozers	R&M Cost	Company	Number of Bulldozers	R&M Cost
1	3	1,270	11	2	494
2	10	5,860	12	6	1,980
3	6	4,310	13	10	7,740
4	10	7,940	14	3	1,144
5	2	500	15	15	12,130
6	3	968	16	3	1,770
7	4	1,490	17	4	1,052
8	3	2,710	18	4	2,617
9	2	390	19	12	3,985
10	5	1,785	20	6	2,463

9.35 One of the problems encountered by fresh fruit growers is spoilage of the fruit during transport to market. Each day during the harvest, a Florida citrus grower, using a fleet of 75 trucks, transports fresh fruit to 15 markets to be sold. (The trucks are routed to their nearest markets.) To estimate the total amount of spoilage for the day, five markets are randomly selected and the number of bushels of spoiled fruit transported by each truck to the sampled market is recorded. Given the data in the table, construct an approximate 95% confidence interval for the total number of bushels of spoiled fruit transported to the 15 markets at the end of the day.

Market	Number of Trucks	Total Number of Bushels of Spoiled Fruit
1	6	16.2
2	2	3.4
3	8	5.0
4	3	10.7
5	2	12.8

9.36 A large manufacturing company is considering a new health insurance plan for its employees. Before putting the plan into effect, the company wants to estimate the proportion of its employees who favor the new health insurance proposal. The company's sampling scheme is to randomly select nine of its 45 manufacturing plants scattered throughout the country and to use each plant as a cluster. The employees at each of the nine plants are interviewed and their opinions regarding the new health insurance plan are recorded. Use the data in the table to obtain an estimate of the true proportion of this company's employees who favor the new health insurance plan. Use an approximate 95% confidence interval. [*Hint:* Use the average size of the clusters in the sample to estimate the population average cluster size.]

Plant	Number of Employees	Number Favoring the New Plan
1	112	98
2	75	65
3	83	71
4	154	123
5	108	97
6	68	61
7	102	92
8	95	90
9	83	65

9.10 Choosing the Sample Size: Cluster Sampling

The formulas for selecting the approximate sample size to construct a 95% confidence interval for μ, τ, and π are shown in the boxes.

Approximate Sample Size n to Obtain 95% Confidence Interval for a Population Mean μ: Cluster Sampling

$$n = \frac{N\sigma_c^2}{ND + \sigma_c^2}$$

where

σ_c^2 = Variance of the cluster total x

$$D = \frac{d^2\overline{M}^2}{4}$$

d = Desired half-width of the confidence interval

In a practical situation, σ_c^2 is unknown and must be approximated by an estimate obtained from an earlier sample. Or, a small sample can be taken to obtain an estimate,

$$s_c^2 = \frac{\Sigma(x_i - \bar{x}m_i)^2}{n-1}$$

Approximate Sample Size n to Obtain 95% Confidence Interval
for a Population Total τ: Cluster Sampling

$$n = \frac{N\sigma_c^2}{ND + \sigma_c^2}$$

where

$\sigma_c^2 = $ Variance of the cluster total x

$$D = \frac{d^2}{4N^2}$$

$d = $ Desired half-width of the confidence interval

In a practical situation, σ_c^2 is unknown and must be approximated by an estimate obtained from an earlier sample. Or, a small sample can be taken to obtain an estimate,

$$s_c^2 = \frac{\Sigma(x_i - \bar{x}m_i)^2}{n-1}$$

Approximate Sample Size n to Obtain 95% Confidence Interval
for a Population Proportion π: Cluster Sampling

$$n = \frac{N\sigma_c^2}{ND + \sigma_c^2}$$

where

$\sigma_c^2 = $ Variance of the number a of successes in a cluster

$$D = \frac{d^2\bar{M}^2}{4}$$

$d = $ Desired half-width of the confidence interval

In a practical situation, σ_c^2 is unknown and must be approximated by an estimate obtained from an earlier sample. Or, a small sample can be taken to obtain an estimate,

$$s_c^2 = \frac{\Sigma(a_i - pm_i)^2}{n-1}$$

<table>
<tr><td>

EXAMPLE 9.14
Selecting *n* for a
Cluster Sample

</td><td>

An automobile dealership wants to survey car owners in a city to estimate the mean age of privately owned automobiles. The surveying organization has decided to use households as sampling units and to record the age for each automobile owned by the household. The frame consists of 12,140 households. If the dealership wants to estimate the mean age of the automobiles to within 3 months (.25 year), how many households should be included in the sample?

</td></tr>
</table>

SOLUTION The formula for calculating the number *n* of households to be included in the sample is

$$n = \frac{N\sigma_c^2}{ND + \sigma_c^2} \quad \text{where} \quad D = \frac{d^2\overline{M}^2}{4}$$

We know that $N = 12{,}140$ households and $d = .25$ year, but we will have to approximate $\overline{M}$ and σ_c^2 because the values of these quantities are unknown.

Recall that $\overline{M}$ is the average number of elements per cluster for all clusters in the population. If the city required city licenses for automobiles, we could determine M, the number of automobiles in the city, and we could calculate $\overline{M} = M/N = M/12{,}140$. If the value of M were unavailable, we would have to guess the mean number of automobiles per household. We will assume that $\overline{M} = 1.8$ is a reasonable value for this example.

The quantity σ_c^2 is the variance of the total age x of the automobiles within a household. The total age x of all automobiles per household could be as small as 0 (if the household owned no automobiles) and might be as large as 20 (if members of the household owned four automobiles averaging 5 years in age). If we set the range of values from 0 to 20 years equal to $4\sigma_c$, we find $\sigma_c \approx \frac{20}{4} = 5$ and $\sigma_c^2 \approx 25$.

Substituting the values of N and d and our approximations to $\overline{M}$ and σ_c^2 into the formula for n, we have

$$D = \frac{d^2\overline{M}^2}{4} = \frac{(.25)^2(1.8)^2}{4} = .050625$$

$$n = \frac{N\sigma_c^2}{ND + \sigma_c^2} = \frac{(12{,}140)(25)}{(12{,}140)(.050625) + 25} = 474.5$$

Therefore, to find a 95% confidence interval for the mean length of life of all automobiles in the city correct to within 3 months, the survey should include approximately 475 households. ■

EXERCISES

■ *Learning the Mechanics*

9.37 Consider a cluster sampling plan with $N = 200$, $M = 1,500$, and $\sigma_c^2 \approx 96$. Find the sample size (i.e., number of clusters) needed to estimate the population mean μ to within $d = 1$ of the true value, with 95% confidence.

9.38 Refer to Exercise 9.37. Find the sample size (i.e., number of clusters) needed to estimate the population total τ to within $d = 800$ of the true value, with 95% confidence.

9.39 Consider a cluster sampling plan with $N = 100$, $M = 2,500$, and $\sigma_c^2 \approx 6$. Find the sample size (i.e., number of clusters) needed to estimate the population proportion π to within .06 of the true value, with 95% confidence.

■ *Applying the Concepts*

9.40 Suppose you want to reduce the width of the interval constructed in Exercise 9.34. How many construction companies should be included in the sample to estimate the true mean annual expenditure per bulldozer to within $50? (Use the information given in Exercise 9.34 to compute an estimate of σ_c^2.)

9.41 Suppose you want to reduce the width of the interval obtained in Exercise 9.35. How many markets must be sampled to estimate the total number of bushels of spoiled fruit to within 60 bushels of the true value? (Use the information provided in Exercise 9.35 to compute an estimate of σ_c^2.)

9.42 Suppose you want to reduce the width of the interval constructed in Exercise 9.36. How many manufacturing plants must be sampled to estimate the true proportion of company employees who favor the new health insurance plan to within .03? (Use the information provided in Exercise 9.36 to obtain an estimate of σ_c^2.)

9.11 Problems of Nonresponse and Invalid Responses

Before concluding this introduction to sample surveys, we will mention two important problems associated with conducting a survey. The first is the problem of **nonresponse**, i.e., the inability of an interviewer to contact one or more of the persons (or elements) listed in the sample or the refusal of a sampled person to respond. Nonresponse is an important problem because the exclusion of the nonrespondents may produce a serious bias in the resulting sample. For example, it is quite common for television stations to request viewers to call in their opinions regarding some political candidate or issue. (See Case Study 7.1.) This type of "sampling" is likely to include people who want to produce a strong showing for one side or the other and exclude people who are less ardent in expressing their political opinions. Nonresponse often occurs in mailed surveys because busy people, a particular and unique social class, are too busy to complete the survey's questionnaire. Methods for coping with nonresponse (based primarily on resampling the nonresponders) are available and are discussed in the literature.

Another problem encountered in some business surveys is the difficulty in eliciting valid responses from persons included in the sample. For example, suppose that one question in a survey of employees asks whether the employee wrongly took sick leave during the year and used it for vacation. An employee who was habitual in misusing sick leave might want to hide the fact by falsifying his or her response to the question. Sampling techniques using a **randomized response model** are available for coping with this problem. With this method, each person is presented two questions, one sensitive and one of a trivial nature. One of the questions is randomly selected by some mechanism and the person interviewed responds "yes" or "no." The interviewer does not know which question has been answered, but the technique enables us to obtain an estimate of the proportion of employees who misuse sick leave.

SUMMARY

This chapter presented sampling and estimation procedures useful in designing and evaluating data collected in business surveys. The object of the designs is to facilitate and reduce the cost of sampling. Two of the most commonly used sampling designs, *stratified random sampling* and *cluster sampling*, were described in this chapter. Stratified random sampling partitions the population into nonoverlapping subpopulations called *strata*. A random sample is then selected from each stratum. Cluster sampling involves the random selection of sampling units, each of which is a cluster of elements.

Methods for constructing approximate 95% confidence intervals for three population parameters, μ, τ, and π, were presented for simple random sampling, stratified random sampling, and cluster sampling designs. In addition, we presented the formula used to select the sample size for each estimation procedure.

One unique feature of the estimation procedures presented in this chapter is that they take into account the relative sizes of the sample and the population. This is important in some surveys when the number N of sampling units in the population is small and/or the number n of elements in the sample is large relative to N.

The material presented in this chapter represents only an introduction to the large body of methodology dealing with *survey sampling*.

KEY TERMS

Cluster	Randomized response model	Stratified random sample
Cluster sample	Sample	Survey sampling
Element	Sampling unit	Systematic sample
Frame	Simple random sample	
Nonresponse	Strata	

KEY FORMULAS

	95% Confidence Interval	*Sample Size* *(d = desired half-width)*

Simple Random Sampling

Population mean μ

$$\bar{x} \pm 1.96 \, \frac{s}{\sqrt{n}} \sqrt{\frac{N-n}{n}}$$

$$n = \frac{N\sigma^2}{(N-1)(d^2/4) + \sigma^2}$$

Population total τ

$$N\bar{x} \pm 1.96 \, \frac{Ns}{\sqrt{n}} \sqrt{\frac{N-n}{n}}$$

$$n = \frac{N\sigma^2}{(N-1)(d^2/4N^2) + \sigma^2}$$

Population proportion π

$$p \pm 1.96 \sqrt{\frac{p(1-p)}{n}} \sqrt{\frac{N-n}{n}}$$

$$n = \frac{N\pi(1-\pi)}{(N-1)(d^2/4) + \pi(1-\pi)}$$

Stratified Random Sampling

Population mean μ

$$\frac{\Sigma N_i \bar{x}_i}{N} \pm 1.96 \sqrt{\frac{1}{N^2} \Sigma N_i^2 \frac{s_i^2}{n_i} \left(\frac{N_i - n_i}{N_i} \right)}$$

$$n = \frac{\Sigma \left(\dfrac{N_i^2 \sigma_i^2}{w_i} \right)}{N^2(d^2/4) + \Sigma N_i \sigma_i^2}$$

Population total τ

$$\Sigma N_i \bar{x}_i \pm 1.96 \sqrt{\Sigma N_i^2 \frac{s_i^2}{n_i} \left(\frac{N_i - n_i}{N_i} \right)}$$

$$n = \frac{\Sigma \left(\dfrac{N_i^2 \sigma_i^2}{w_i} \right)}{N^2(d^2/4N^2) + \Sigma N_i \sigma_i^2}$$

Population proportion π

$$\frac{\Sigma N_i p_i}{N} \pm 1.96 \sqrt{\frac{1}{N^2} \Sigma N_i^2 \frac{p_i(1-p_i)}{n_i - 1} \left(\frac{N_i - n_i}{N_i} \right)}$$

$$n = \frac{\Sigma \left[\dfrac{N_i^2 \pi_i(1-\pi_i)}{w_i} \right]}{N^2(d^2/4) + \Sigma N_i \pi_i(1-\pi_i)}$$

Cluster Sampling

Population mean μ

$$\bar{x} \pm 1.96 \sqrt{\left(\frac{N-n}{Nn\overline{M}^2} \right) \frac{\Sigma(x_i - \bar{x}m_i)^2}{n-1}}$$

$$n = \frac{N\sigma_c^2}{N(d^2\overline{M}^2/4) + \sigma_c^2}$$

where $\bar{x} = \Sigma x_i / \Sigma m_i$

Population total τ

$$M\bar{x} \pm 1.96 \sqrt{N^2 \left(\frac{N-n}{Nn} \right) \frac{\Sigma(x_i - \bar{x}m_i)^2}{n-1}}$$

$$n = \frac{N\sigma_c^2}{N(d^2/4N^2) + \sigma_c^2}$$

Population proportion π $\qquad p \pm 1.96 \sqrt{\left(\dfrac{N-n}{Nn\overline{M}^2}\right)\dfrac{\Sigma(a_i - pm_i)^2}{n-1}}$ $\qquad\qquad n = \dfrac{N\sigma_c^2}{N(d^2\overline{M}^2/4) + \sigma_c^2}$

where $p = \Sigma a_i / \Sigma m_i$

SUPPLEMENTARY EXERCISES

9.43 A simple random sample of size $n = 50$ was selected from a population with $N = 4{,}000$ and produced the following results:

$$\bar{x} = 461.7 \qquad s = 98.8 \qquad p = .44$$

a. Find an approximate 95% confidence interval for the population mean μ.
b. Find an approximate 95% confidence interval for the population total τ.
c. Find an approximate 95% confidence interval for the population proportion π.
d. How large a sample must be selected to reduce the half-width of the interval of part **a** to $d = 15$?

9.44 A survey based on a stratified random sample produced the information shown in the table.

	Stratum		
	1	2	3
N_i	500	600	450
n_i	20	20	20
$\bar{x}_i$	7.2	11.0	9.8
s_i^2	3.1	3.0	4.2
p_i	.82	.75	.71

a. Find an approximate 95% confidence interval for the population mean μ.
b. Find an approximate 95% confidence interval for the population total τ.
c. Find an approximate 95% confidence interval for the population proportion π.
d. How large a sample must be selected from each stratum to reduce the half-width of the interval of part **b** to $d = 200$? Assume samples of equal size are to be selected from the three strata.

9.45 The information given in the next table was obtained from a survey based on cluster sampling with $N = 900$, $n = 5$, and $M = 5{,}400$.

	Cluster				
	1	*2*	*3*	*4*	*5*
Number of elements (m$_i$)	4	10	3	6	5
Total of all observations	181	363	107	310	294
Number of elements possessing the attribute of interest	1	4	1	2	2

a. Find an approximate 95% confidence interval for the population mean μ.
b. Find an approximate 95% confidence interval for the population total τ.
c. Find an approximate 95% confidence interval for the population proportion π.
d. How many clusters must be selected to reduce the half-width of the interval in part **c** to $d = .03$?

9.46 A wholesale seafood business serves a city with three distinctly different market areas. To decide how to allocate sales effort and where to locate retail markets, the wholesaler wants to obtain an estimate of the mean monthly seafood consumption per household in the city. Random samples of 400 households are selected from within each of the three markets, and an estimate of the dollar amount spent per month on seafood is obtained from each household. The number of households in each market along with sample means and variances are shown in the table.

	Market		
	1	*2*	*3*
N_i	20,800	6,400	12,600
n_i	400	400	400
$\bar{x}_i$	$5.31	$9.49	$6.75
s_i^2	16.83	15.10	23.78

a. Identify the sampling plan for this experiment.
b. Give a reason why the sampling plan was used.
c. Find an approximate 95% confidence interval for the mean monthly seafood consumption per household in the city.
d. Find an approximate 95% confidence interval for the total amount spent per month on seafood in the city.

9.47 Refer to Exercise 9.46. As part of the survey, the number of sampled households that purchase seafood directly from the wholesaler was counted. Use the information given in the accompanying table to find an approximate 95% confidence interval for the proportion of households in the city that purchase seafood directly from the wholesaler.

	Market		
	1	*2*	*3*
Number of sampled households that purchase seafood directly from wholesaler	28	17	45

9.48 As part of an appraisal of the retail value of homes in a particular section of a city, a real estate appraiser wants to estimate the proportion of adult males who own their homes. The area is divided into 200 clusters, each containing five city blocks. The plan is to select clusters at random and collect information on all adult males who live in the area and who own their homes.

a. Give one or more reasons why cluster sampling is selected over simple random sampling in this application.

b. How many clusters should be sampled to estimate the true proportion of adult males who own their homes to within .02? Assume that σ_c^2, the variance of the number of adults in a cluster who own their homes, is approximately .22 and that the average cluster size is approximately 100.

9.49 Refer to Exercises 3.16 and 8.21. The total 1993 compensations (salaries, fees, bonuses, etc.) for the top 20 corporate executives, as determined by a *Business Week* survey, are reproduced in the table. Assume that these 20 values represent a random sample of total 1993 compensations for the 100 highest-paid corporate executives in the United States. Calculate an approximate 95% confidence interval for the mean compensation of the highest-paid corporate executives in 1993.

	Corporate Executive (Company)	*1993 Total Pay (in Thousands)*
1.	Michael D. Eisner (Walt Disney)	$203,011
2.	Sanford I. Weill (Travelers)	52,810
3.	Joseph R. Hyde (Autozone)	32,220
4.	Charles N. Mathewson (Intl. Game Tech.)	22,231
5.	Alan C. Greenberg (Bear Stearns)	15,915
6.	H. Wayne Huizenga (Blockbuster)	15,557
7.	Norman E. Brinker (Brinker Intl.)	14,925
8.	Roberto C. Goizueta (Coca-Cola)	14,513
9.	C. Robert Kidder (Duracell)	14,172
10.	Thomas M. Hahn (Georgia-Pacific)	13,680
11.	H. Brewster Atwater (General Mills)	13,177
12.	James C. Morgan (Applied Materials)	12,833
13.	Richard H. Jenrette (Equitable Cos.)	12,380
14.	Harry A. Merlo (Louisiana-Pacific)	12,051
15.	John H. Bryan (Sara Lee)	11,889
16.	David R. Whitwam (Whirlpool)	11,837
17.	Charles S. Sanford (Bankers Trust)	11,811
18.	Frank V. Cahouet (Mellon Bank)	11,516
19.	Walter J. Sanders (Adv. Micro Devices)	11,488
20.	Stanley C. Gault (Goodyear)	11,278

Source: "That Eye-Popping Executive Pay." *Business Week*, Apr. 25, 1994, p. 53.

9.50 Refer to Exercise 9.49. How many of the highest-paid executives must be sampled to estimate the true mean 1993 compensation to within $500,000 with 95% confidence?

9.51 Before implementing a plan designed to reduce flight time, and hence conserve fuel and energy, the Air Force needs an estimate of the total number of miles flown by a certain type of aircraft during a given month. Air Force records show that a total of 1,500 planes of this type in the fleet are harbored at 96 different airfields across the country. The Air Force randomly selects six of the airfields and monitors the flight mileage of each plane at each airfield for 1 month. The data (thousands of miles flown) are shown in the accompanying table. Treat the collection of all aircraft of this type at each airfield as a cluster, and find an approximate 95% confidence interval for the total number of miles flown per month.

Airfield	Number of Airplanes	Miles Flown
1	20	36
2	10	25
3	18	16
4	18	24
5	10	15
6	16	20

9.52 An economist wants to use a stratified sampling plan to estimate the mean annual income of families in a mainly industrial community. The city is divided into three relatively homogeneous areas. One section houses primarily factory workers (360 households); one, mostly company executives (74 households); and the remaining area, mostly farmers (95 households).

a. Why is stratified random sampling selected over simple random sampling in this application?

b. How many households must be randomly sampled from each city section to estimate the true mean annual income to within $750? (Assume that samples of equal size are to be selected and that the estimated variances of the annual incomes for the three sections are 9,100,000 for factory workers, 25,000,000 for company executives, and 17,000,000 for farmers.)

■ CASE STUDY 9.1

The New Hite Report—Controversy over the Numbers

In 1968, researcher Shere Hite shocked conservative America with her now-famous "Hite Report" on the permissive sexual attitudes of American men and women. Twenty years later, Hite was surrounded by controversy again with her book, *Women and Love: A Cultural Revolution in Progress* (Knopf Press, 1988). In this new Hite report, she reveals some starting statistics describing how women feel about contemporary relationships:

- 84% of women are not emotionally satisfied with their relationship
- 95% of women report "emotional and psychological harassment" from their men
- 70% of women married 5 years or more are having extramarital affairs
- Only 13% of women married more than 2 years are "in love"

Hite conducted the survey by mailing out 100,000 questionnaires to women across the country over a 7-year period. Each questionnaire consisted of 127 open-ended questions, many with numerous subquestions and follows-ups. Hite's instructions read: "It is not necessary to answer every question! Feel free to skip around and answer those questions you choose." Approximately 4,500 completed questionnaires were returned for a response rate of 4.5%, and they form the data set from which these percentages were determined. Hite claims that these 4,500 women are a representative sample of all women in the United States, and therefore, the survey results imply that vast numbers of women are "suffering a lot of pain in their love relationships with men." Many people disagree, however, saying that only unhappy women are likely to take the time to answer Hite's 127 essay questions, and thus her sample is representative only of the discontented.

The views of several statisticians and expert survey researchers on the validity of Hite's "numbers" were presented in an article in *Chance* magazine (Summer 1988). A few of the more critical comments follow.*

- Hite used a combination of haphazard sampling and volunteer respondents to collect her [data]. First, Hite sent questionnaires to a wide variety of organizations and asked them to circulate the questionnaires to their members. She mentions that they included church groups, women's voting and political groups, women's rights organizations and counseling and walk-in centers for women. These groups would not seem to be representative of women in general; there is an over-representation of feminist groups and of women in troubled circumstances. In addition, the use of groups to distribute the questionnaires meant that gatekeepers had the power of assuring a zero response rate by not distributing the questionnaire, or conversely of greatly stimulating returns by endorsing the study in some fashion. Second, Hite also relied on volunteer respondents who wrote in for copies of the questionnaire. These volunteers seem to have been recruited from readers of her past books and those who saw interviews on television and in the press. This type of volunteer respondent is the exact opposite of the randomly selected respondent utilized in standard survey research and even more potentially unrepresentative than the group samples cited above. **(Tom Smith, National Opinion Research Center)**

- So few people responded, it's not representative of any group, except the odd group who agreed to respond. Hite has no assurance that even her claimed 4.5% response rate is correct. How do we know how many people passed their hands over these questionnaires? You don't want to fill it out, you give it to your sister, she gives it to a friend. You'll get one response, but that questionnaire may have been turned down by five people. **(Donald**

---

* Streitfeld, D. *"Shere Hite and the trouble with numbers."* Chance: New Directions for Statistics and Computing, *Vol. 1, No. 3, Summer 1988, pp. 26–31. Springer-Verlag, © 1988, the* Washinton Post. *Reprinted with permission.*

Rubin, Professor and Chairman, Department of Statistics, Harvard University)

- When you get instructions to answer only those questions you wish to, you're likely to skip some. Isn't it more likely that, for example, a woman who feels strongly about affairs would be more likely answer questions on that subject than a woman who does not feel as strongly? Thus, her finding that 70% of all women married over five years are having affairs is meaningless because she does not report how many people answered each question. I cannot tell whether this means 70% of 1,000 women or 70% of 10 women. **(Judith Tanur, Professor of Sociology and Statistical Specialist in Survey Methodology, State University of New York, Stony Brook)**

- Even in good samples, where you have a 50% or 70% response rate, you usually have some skews—say, with income, race, or region. If she can do a sample like this, she's got the Rosetta Stone, and I'll come study from her. **(Martin Frankel, Professor of Statistics & CIS, Baruch College, commenting on Hite's claim that her sample matches that of the U.S. female population in terms of demographic balance.)**

- According to Hite, whether you're 18 or 71, you're going to answer the questions the same way.

Whether white, black, Hispanic, Middle Eastern, or Asian American, you're going to answer the same way. Whether you make $5,000 a year or over $75,000, you'll answer the questions the same way. I've never seen anything like this in my career—and the Kinsey Institute collects data from everybody. **(June Reinisch, Director of Kinsey Institute, Indiana University, commenting on Hite's numbers showing that no matter what the demographic breakdown of the women married 5 years or more, about 70% are having extramarital affairs.)**

a. Identify the population of interest to Shere Hite. What are the experimental units?

b. Identify the variables of interest to Hite. Are they quantitative or qualitative variables?

c. Describe how Hite obtained her sample.

d. What inferences did Hite make about the population? Comment on the reliability of these inferences.

e. Discuss the difficulty in obtaining a simple random sample of women across the United States to take part in a survey similar to the one conducted by Shere Hite.

f. Describe a sampling plan that will lead to more reliable inferences than the one employed by Hite.

■ CASE STUDY 9.2 ■

Increasing Survey Response Rates: The Foot and the Face Techniques

As discussed in Section 9.11, sample surveys often suffer from a lack of a suitable number of respondents; any inferences derived from surveys with low response rates could very well be biased. Many strategies have been devised for the purpose of increasing survey response rates. Although these compliance-gaining tactics originated in the nonbusiness behavioral sciences (social psychology, personality, etc.), much attention has recently been given to them in business and marketing literature.

Mowen and Cialdini[*] give brief descriptions of various manipulative strategies. The most popular of these among business and marketing researchers is the "foot-in-the door" or, more simply, the "foot" principle. Mowen and Cialdini write: "In using this compliance-gaining tactic, a requester first makes a request so small that nearly anyone would comply, in effect getting a 'foot in the-door.' After compliance with the first request occurs, a second, larger request is made—actually the one desired from the outset." For example, Hansen and Robinson[†] conducted an experiment in which a random group of subjects were contacted by phone and initially asked whether they had purchased a new car within the last 3 years. If they had, they were asked some basic questions on general perceptions toward automobile dealers, such as, "All car dealers overcharge on their repair work; do you agree or disagree?" After the brief (no longer than 5 minutes) "foot-in-the-door" interview, the subject was asked if he or she would be willing to participate in the mail portion of the survey (the desired, larger request). This "foot" technique has been shown to increase response rates in a number of business settings, typical of the one described above. The key to the success of the "foot" principle, say Hansen and Robinson, is that it allows the respondent to become involved in the subject area, which eventually leads to a greater degree of participation in the subsequent larger request.

A second strategy discussed by Mowen and Cialdini is labeled the "door-in-the-face" principle. In the "face" approach, the person administering the survey "begins with an initial request so large that nearly everyone refuses it (i.e., the door is slammed in his face). [After the first refusal,] the requester then retreats to a smaller favor—actually the one desired from the outset." The "face" principle is based on the social rule of reciprocation that states, "One should make concessions to those who make concessions to oneself." Mowen and Cialdini explain: "The requester's movement from the initial, extreme favor to the second, more moderate one is seen by the [potential respondent] as a concession. To reciprocate this concession, the [respondent] must move from his or her initial position of noncompliance with the large request to a position of compliance with the smaller request." The key to the successful "face" approach is that the respondent perceive the original request as being legitimate, and that a concession be clearly made in the movement from the large to the small request.

An example of the "door-in-the-face" technique is given by Mowen and Cialdini. Subjects were approached by experimenters representing a fictitious corporation, the California Mutual Insurance Company. The experimenters' initial request went as follows:

> Hello. I'm doing a survey for the California Mutual Insurance Company. For each of the last twelve years, we have been on campus to gather survey information on safety in the home or dorm. The survey takes about one hour to administer. Would you be willing to take an hour, right now, to answer the questions?

---

[*] Mowen, J. C., and Cialdini, R. B. *"On implementing the door-in-the-face compliance technique in a business context."* Journal of Marketing Research, *Vol. 17, May 1980, pp. 253–258.*

[†] Hansen, R. A., and Robinson, L. M. *"Testing the effectiveness of alternative foot-in-the-door manipulations."* Journal of Marketing Research, *Vol. 17, Aug. 1980, pp. 359–363.*

After the subject declined to participate, the experimenter would make the second, smaller request:

> Oh, ... well, look, one part of the survey is particularly important and is fairly short. It will take only fifteen minutes to administer. If you take fifteen minutes right now to complete this short survey, it would really help us out.

The "foot-in-the-door" and "door-in-the-face" strategies present an interesting contrast in sample survey designs. The "foot" approach uses an initial, small request to enhance the likelihood of compliance with a second, larger (desired) request; the "face" approach uses an initial, large request to increase the response rate on a second, smaller (desired) request.

a. Think of a business survey that might be best implemented by using the "foot" approach.

b. Repeat part a for the "face" approach.

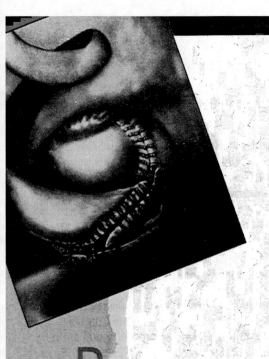

Chapter 10

COLLECTING EVIDENCE TO SUPPORT A THEORY: GENERAL CONCEPTS OF HYPOTHESIS TESTING

P harmaceutical companies use a technique called *drug screening* to test thousands of compounds for the few that may be effective. The decision on any one particular drug is made by using sample information to infer the value of the drug's "mean effectiveness," e.g., whether the mean exceeds some numerical value. In this chapter, we learn how sample data can be used to make decisions about population parameters. We will examine drug screening in greater detail in Case Study 10.1.

10.1 The Relationship Between Statistical Tests of Hypotheses and Confidence Intervals

As stated in Chapter 8, there are two general methods for making inferences about population parameters: We can estimate their values using confidence intervals (the subject of Chapter 8) or we can make decisions about them. Making decisions about specific values of the population parameters—**testing hypotheses** about these values—is the topic of this chapter.

It is important to point out that confidence intervals and hypothesis tests are related and that either can be used to make decisions about parameters. For example, suppose an investigator for the Environmental Protection Agency (EPA) wants to determine whether the mean level μ of a certain type of pollutant released into the atmosphere by a chemical company meets the EPA guidelines. If 3 parts per million is the upper limit allowed by the EPA, the investigator would want to use sample data (daily pollution measurements) to decide whether the company is violating the law, i.e., to decide whether $\mu > 3$. If, say, a 99% confidence interval for μ contained only numbers greater than 3, then the EPA would be confident that the mean exceeds the established limit.

As a second example, consider a manufacturer who purchases terminal fuses in lots of 10,000 and suppose that the supplier of the fuses guarantees that no more than 1% of the fuses in any given lot are defective. Since the manufacturer cannot test each of the 10,000 fuses in a lot, he must decide whether to accept or reject a lot based on an examination of a sample of fuses selected from the lot. If the number x of defective fuses in a sample of, say, $n = 100$ is large, he will reject the lot and send it back to the supplier. Thus, he wants to decide whether the proportion π of defectives in the lot exceeds .01, based on information contained in a sample. If a confidence interval for π falls below .01, then the manufacturer will accept the lot and be confident that the proportion of defectives is less than 1%; otherwise, he will reject it.

The examples in the preceding paragraphs illustrate how a confidence interval can be used to make a decision about a parameter. Note that both applications are one-directional: The EPA wants to determine whether $\mu > 3$, and the manufacturer wants to know whether $\pi > .01$. (In contrast, if the manufacturer is interested in determining whether $\pi > .01$ or $\pi < .01$, the inference would be two-directional.)

Recall from Chapter 8 that to find the value of z (or t) used in a $(1 - \alpha)100\%$ confidence interval, the value of α is divided in half and $\alpha/2$ is placed in both the upper and lower tails of the z (or t) distribution. Consequently, confidence intervals are designed to be two-directional. Use of a two-directional technique in a situation where a one-directional method is desired will lead the researcher (e.g., the EPA or the manufacturer) to understate the level of confidence associated with the method. As we explain in this chapter, hypothesis tests are appropriate for either one- or two-directional decisions about a population parameter.

This chapter will treat the general concepts involved in hypothesis testing; specific applications will be demonstrated in Chapter 11.

10.2 Formulation of Hypotheses

When a researcher in any field sets out to test a new theory, he or she first formulates a **hypothesis**, or claim, which he or she believes to be true. For example, a real estate appraiser may claim that the mean appraised value of improvements for properties in neighborhood A differs from the mean appraised value of improvements for properties in neighborhood B. In statistical terms, the hypothesis that the researcher tries to establish is called the **alternative hypothesis**, or **research hypothesis**. To be paired with the alternative hypothesis is the **null hypothesis**, which is the "opposite" of the alternative hypothesis. In this way, the null and alternative hypotheses, both stated in terms of the appropriate population parameters, describe two possible states of nature that cannot simultaneously be true. When the researcher begins to collect information about the phenomenon of interest, he or she generally tries to present evidence that lends support to the alternative hypothesis. As you will subsequently learn, we take an indirect approach to obtaining support for the alternative hypothesis: Instead of trying to show that the alternative hypothesis is true, we attempt to produce evidence to show that the null hypothesis (which may often be interpreted as "no change from the status quo") is false.

Definition 10.1

A statistical **hypothesis** is a statement about the numerical value of a population parameter.

Definition 10.2

The **alternative** (or **research**) **hypothesis**, denoted by H_a, is usually the hypothesis for which the researcher wants to gather supporting evidence.

Definition 10.3

The **null hypothesis**, denoted by H_0, is usually the hypothesis that the researcher wants to gather evidence against (i.e., the hypothesis to be "tested").

EXAMPLE 10.1
Choosing H_0 and H_a

A metal lathe is checked periodically by quality control inspectors to determine whether it is producing machine bearings with a mean diameter of .5 inch. If the mean diameter of the bearings is larger or smaller than .5 inch, then the process is out of control and must be adjusted. Formulate the null and alternative hypotheses that could be used to test whether the bearing production process is out of control.

SOLUTION The hypotheses must be stated in terms of a population parameter. Thus, we define

μ = True mean diameter (in inches) of all bearings produced by the lathe

If either $\mu > .5$ or $\mu < .5$, then the metal lathe's production process is out of control. Since we wish to be able to detect either possibility, the null and alternative hypotheses would be

H_0: $\mu = .5$ (i.e., the process is in control)

H_a: $\mu \neq .5$ (i.e., the process is out of control) ■

EXAMPLE 10.2
Choosing H_0 and H_a

Since 1970, cigarette advertisements have been required by law to carry the following statement: "Warning: The surgeon general has determined that cigarette smoking is dangerous to your health." However, this warning is often located in inconspicuous corners of the advertisements and printed in small type. Consequently, a spokesperson for the Federal Trade Commission (FTC) believes that over 80% of those who read cigarette advertisements fail to see the warning. Specify the null and alternative hypotheses that would be used in testing the spokesperson's theory.

SOLUTION The FTC spokesperson wants to make an inference about π, the true proportion of all readers of cigarette advertisements who fail to see the surgeon general's warning. In particular, the FTC spokesperson wishes to collect evidence to support the claim that π is greater than .80; thus, the null and alternative hypotheses are

H_0: $\pi \leq .80$

H_a: $\pi > .80$

The sign in H_0 is "$\leq$" because we want to cover all situations for which H_a *does not* occur. In other words, the event that H_0 occurs is the complement of the event that H_a occurs. ■

An accepted convention in hypothesis testing is to write H_0 with an equality sign (=). Consequently, in Example 10.2 we may also write the null hypothesis as H_0: $\pi = .80$. The reasoning is as follows: Since the alternative of interest is that $\pi > .80$, then any evidence that would cause you to reject the null hypothesis H_0: $\pi = .80$ in favor of H_a: $\pi > .80$ would also cause you to reject H_0: $\pi = \pi'$, for any value of π' that is *less than* .80. In other words, H_0: $\pi = .80$ represents the worst possible case, from the researcher's point of view, if in fact the alternative hypothesis is *not* correct. Thus, for mathematical ease, we combine all possible situations for describing the opposite of H_a into one statement involving an equality.

An alternative hypothesis may hypothesize a change from H_0 in a particular direction, or it may merely hypothesize a change without specifying a direction. In Example 10.2, the researcher is interested in detecting departure from H_0 in a particular direction; interest focuses on whether the proportion of cigarette advertisement readers who fail to see the surgeon general's warning is greater than .80. This test is called a **one-tailed** (or **one-sided**) **test**. In contrast, Example 10.1 illustrates a **two-tailed** (or **two-sided**) **test** in which we are interested in whether the mean diameter of the machine bearings differ in either direction from .5 inch, i.e., whether the process is out of control.

Definition 10.4

A **one-tailed test** of hypothesis is one in which the alternative hypothesis is directional, and includes either the symbol "<" or ">."

Definition 10.5

A **two-tailed test** of hypothesis is one in which the alternative hypothesis does not specify departure from H_0 in a particular direction; such an alternative is written with the symbol "$\neq$."

EXAMPLE 10.3
Hypotheses for Formulating a One-Tailed Test

Prior to the institution of a new safety program, the average number of on-the-job accidents per day at a factory was 4.5. To determine whether the safety program has been effective, the factory will test

$$H_0: \quad \mu = 4.5$$

where μ is the true mean number of on-the-job accidents per day at the factory. Formulate the appropriate alternative hypothesis for the factory.

SOLUTION The factory is interested in detecting whether the true mean number of on-the-job accidents per day is less than 4.5, for if it is the case that $\mu < 4.5$, then the new safety program has been effective in reducing the average number of on-the-job accidents. Thus, the alternative hypothesis of interest to the factory is

$$H_a: \quad \mu < 4.5$$

Note that the null hypothesis

$$H_0: \quad \mu = 4.5$$

actually represents all possible situations for which the safety program has not reduced the true mean number of on-the-job accidents, i.e., $\mu \geq 4.5$. Since the alternative is directional—that is, since the factory is interested in detecting a departure from H_0 in the direction of values of μ smaller than 4.5—a one-tailed test is to be performed. ▪

EXAMPLE 10.4
Formulating Hypotheses
for a Two-Tailed Test

A study was conducted to determine the impact of a multifunction workstation (MFWS) on the way managers work (*Datamation*, Feb. 15, 1986). Two groups of managers at a St. Louis-based defense agency took part in the study: a group of managers who currently use MFWS software and a control group of non-MFWS users. To determine whether the proportion of MFWS users who rely on the computer as their major information source differs from the corresponding proportion of non-MFWS users, the researcher tested the null hypothesis

$$H_0: (\pi_1 - \pi_2) = 0$$

where π_1 and π_2 represent the true proportion of MFWS users and non-MFWS users, respectively, who rely on the computer as their major information source. Specify the appropriate alternative hypothesis for this test.

SOLUTION The researcher is interested only in detecting whether there is a difference between the proportions of MFWS and non-MFWS users who rely on the computer as their major information source. If there is a difference, then $\pi_1 \neq \pi_2$, or, equivalently, the difference between proportions $(\pi_1 - \pi_2)$ differs from 0. Thus, the alternative hypothesis of interest to the researcher is the two-tailed alternative

$$H_a: (\pi_1 - \pi_2) \neq 0 \quad ▪$$

EXERCISES

▪ *Applying the Concepts*

10.1 Explain the difference between an alternative hypothesis and a null hypothesis.

10.2 A *Harvard Business Review* (Sept.– Oct. 1985) survey was conducted to determine whether a difference exists between the proportions of male executives and female executives who agree with the statement "A woman executive is invariably paid less than her male counterpart." Formulate the appropriate null and alternative hypotheses for the study.

10.3 Kimberly Clark Corporation, the makers of Kleenex, periodically conducts market surveys to determine the average number of tissues used by people when they have a cold. Currently, the company puts 60 tissues in a box. Suppose marketing experts at the company want to test whether the mean number of tissues used by people with colds exceeds 60. Formulate the appropriate null and alternative hypotheses for the study.

10.4 A study reported in the *Academy of Management* (Mar. 1982) investigated whether the mean performance appraisal of "leavers" at a large national oil company is less than the mean performance appraisal of "stayers." Formulate the appropriate null and alternative hypotheses for the study.

10.5 Cannibalism among chickens is common when the birds are confined in small areas. A breeder and seller of live chickens wants to test whether the mortality rate due to cannibalism is less than .04 for a certain breed of chickens. Formulate the appropriate null and alternative hypotheses for the study.

10.6 A management consultant who has worked for both Japanese and American organizations wants to compare the average motivational levels of Japanese and American managers. Formulate the appropriate null and alternative hypotheses for the study.

10.7 State whether each of the tests in Exercises 10.2–10.6 is one-tailed or two-tailed.

10.3 Decisions and Consequences for a Hypothesis Test

The goal of any hypothesis-testing situation is to make a decision; in particular, we will decide whether to reject the null hypothesis, H_0, in favor of the alternative hypothesis, H_a. Although we would like to be able to make a correct decision always, we must remember that the decision will be based on sample information, and thus we are subject to make one of two types of error, as the following examples illustrate.

EXAMPLE 10.5
Errors in Hypothesis Tests

Identify the two types of errors that can be made in a hypothesis test.

SOLUTION The null hypothesis can be either true or false; further, we will make a decision either to reject or accept the null hypothesis. Thus, four possible situations may arise in testing a hypothesis, as summarized in Table 10.1. Note that an error occurs in two of the four situations. We can reject H_0 when H_0 is true (a **Type I error**), or we can accept H_0 when H_0 is false (a **Type II error**).

Table 10.1   Conclusions and Consequences for Testing a Hypothesis

		True State of Nature	
		H_0 true (H_a false)	H_0 false (H_a true)
Decision	Accept H_0	Correct decision	Type II error
	Reject H_0	Type I error	Correct decision

Note that we risk a Type I error only if the null hypothesis is rejected, and we risk a Type II error only if the null hypothesis is accepted. Thus, we may make no error, or we may make either a Type I error or a Type II error, but not both. Notationally, let α represent the probability of a Type I error and let β represent the probability of a Type II error. There is an intuitively appealing relationship between the probabilities for the two types of error: *As α increases, β decreases; similarly, as β increases, α decreases. The only way to reduce α and β simultaneously is to increase the amount of information available in the sample, i.e., to increase the sample size.*

Definition 10.6

A **Type I error** occurs if we reject a null hypothesis when it is true. The probability of committing a Type I error is usually denoted by α.

Definition 10.7

A **Type II error** occurs if we accept a null hypothesis when it is false. The probability of making a Type II error is usually denoted by β.

EXAMPLE 10.6
Specifying Type I and
Type II Errors

Refer to Example 10.3. Specify what Type I and Type II errors would represent, in terms of the problem.

SOLUTION A Type I error is that of incorrectly rejecting the null hypothesis. In our example, this would occur if we conclude that the new safety program is effective in reducing μ, the mean number of on-the-job accidents, when, in fact, it is ineffective. The consequence of making such an error would be that unnecessary time, effort, and money would be invested in an ineffectual safety program.

A Type II error, that of incorrectly accepting the null hypothesis, would occur if we conclude that μ is equal to 4.5 accidents per day when in fact μ is less than 4.5 accidents per day. The practical significance of making a Type II error is that the new safety program (thought to be ineffective) will be discontinued, when in fact it was effective in reducing the mean number of on-the-job accidents. ■

Subsequently, we will see that the probability of making a Type I error is controlled by the researcher (see Section 10.4); thus, it is often used as a measure of the reliability of the conclusion and is called the **significance level** of the test.

Definition 10.8

The probability, α, of making a Type I error is called the **level of significance** (or **significance level**) for a hypothesis test.

In actual practice, we will carefully avoid stating a decision in terms of "accept the null hypothesis H_0." Instead, if the sample does not provide enough evidence to support the alternative hypothesis, H_a, we prefer a decision "fail to reject H_0," or "insufficient evidence to reject H_0." This is because, if we were to "accept H_0," the reliability of the conclusion would be measured by β, the probability of a Type II error (i.e., the probability of accepting H_0 when H_0 is false). Unfortunately, the value of β is not constant, but depends on the specific alternative value of the parameter and is difficult to compute in most testing situations. (Guidelines on how to calculate an estimate of β are given in optional Section 10.6.)

In summary, we recommend the following procedure for formulating hypotheses and stating conclusions.

Formulating Hypotheses and Stating Conclusions

1. State the hypothesis you want to support as the alternative hypothesis, H_a.

2. The null hypothesis, H_0, will be the opposite of H_a and will contain an equality sign.

3. If the sample evidence supports the alternative hypothesis, you will reject the null hypothesis and will know that the probability of having made an incorrect decision (when in fact H_0 is true) is α, a quantity that you can manipulate to be as small as you wish.

4. If the sample does not provide sufficient evidence to support the alternative hypothesis, then conclude that the null hypothesis cannot be rejected on the basis of your sample. In this situation, you may wish to obtain a larger sample to collect more information about the phenomenon under study.

EXAMPLE 10.7
Logic of Hypothesis Testing

The logic used in hypothesis testing has often been likened to that used in the courtroom in which a defendant is on trial for committing a crime. Assume that the judge has issued the standard instruction to the jury: The defendant should be acquitted unless evidence of guilt is beyond a "reasonable doubt."

a. Formulate appropriate null and alternative hypotheses for judging the guilt or innocence of the defendant.

b. Interpret the Type I and Type II errors in this context.

c. If you were the defendant, would you want α to be small or large? Explain.

SOLUTION

a. Under our judicial system, a defendant is "innocent until proven guilty." That is, the burden of proof is *not* on the defendant to prove his or her innocence; rather, the court must collect sufficient evidence to support the claim that the defendant is guilty. Thus, the null and alternative hypotheses would be

H_0:   Defendant is innocent

H_a: Defendant is guilty

b.   The four possible outcomes are shown in Table 10.2. A Type I error would be to conclude that the defendant is guilty, when in fact he or she is innocent; a Type II error would be to conclude that the defendant is innocent, when in fact he or she is guilty.

Table 10.2   Conclusions and Consequences, Example 10.7

		True State of Nature	
		Defendant is innocent	Defendant is guilty
Decision of Court	Defendant is innocent	Correct decision	Type II error
	Defendant is guilty	Type I error	Correct decision

c.   Most would probably agree that the Type I error in this situation is by far the more serious. Thus, we would want α, the probability of committing a Type I error, to be very small indeed.   ■

A convention that is generally observed when formulating the null and alternative hypotheses of any statistical test is to *state H_0 so that the possible error of incorrectly rejecting H_0 (Type I error) is considered more serious than the possible error of incorrectly accepting H_0 (Type II error)*. In many cases, the decision as to which type of error is more serious is admittedly not as clear-cut as that of Example 10.7; a little experience will help to minimize this potential difficulty.

EXERCISES

■ *Applying the Concepts*

10.8   Refer to Exercise 10.2. Interpret the Type I and Type II errors in the context of the problem.

10.9   Refer to Exercise 10.3. Interpret the Type I and Type II errors in the context of the problem.

10.10   Refer to Exercise 10.4. Interpret the Type I and Type II errors in the context of the problem.

10.11   Refer to Exercise 10.5. Interpret the Type I and Type II errors in the context of the problem.

10.12   Refer to Exercise 10.6. Interpret the Type I and Type II errors in the context of the problem.

10.13   Explain why each of the following statements is incorrect:

  a. The probability that the null hypothesis is correct is equal to α.
  b. If the null hypothesis is rejected, then the test proves that the alternative hypothesis is correct.
  c. In all statistical tests of hypothesis, $\alpha + \beta = 1$.

10.14 Last month, a large supermarket chain received many consumer complaints about the quantity of chips in 16-ounce bags of a particular brand of potato chips. Suspecting that the complaints were merely the result of the potato chips settling to the bottom of the bags during shipping, but wanting to be able to assure its customers they were getting their money's worth, the chain decided to test the following hypotheses concerning μ, the mean weight (in ounces) of a bag of potato chips in the next shipment of chips received from their largest supplier:

H_0: $\mu = 16$

H_a: $\mu < 16$

If there is evidence that $\mu < 16$, then the shipment would be refused and a complaint registered with the supplier.
  a. What is a Type I error, in terms of the problem?
  b. What is a Type II error, in terms of the problem?
  c. Which type of error would the chain's customers view as more serious? Which type of error would the chain's supplier view as more serious?

10.15 Why do we avoid stating a decision in terms of "accept the null hypothesis H_0"?

10.4 Test Statistics and Rejection Regions

In this section we describe how to arrive at a decision in a hypothesis-testing situation. Recall that when making any type of statistical inference (of which hypothesis testing is a special case), we collect information by obtaining a random sample from the population(s) of interest. In all our applications, we will assume that the appropriate sampling process has already been carried out.

EXAMPLE 10.8
Format of a Test

Suppose we want to test the hypotheses

H_0: $\mu = 72$

H_a: $\mu > 72$

What is the general format for carrying out a statistical test of hypothesis?

SOLUTION Once we have specified H_0 and H_a (step 1), the second step is to obtain a random sample from the population of interest. The information provided by this sample, in the form of a sample statistic, will help us decide whether to reject the null hypothesis. The sample statistic upon which we base our decision is called the **test statistic**.

The third step, then, is to determine a test statistic that is reasonable in the context of a given hypothesis test. For this example, we are hypothesizing about the value of the population mean μ. Since our best guess about the value of μ is the sample mean $\bar{x}$ (see Section 8.2), it seems reasonable to use $\bar{x}$ as a test statistic. We will learn how to choose the test statistic for other hypothesis-testing situations in the examples that follow.

The fourth step is to specify the range of possible computed values of the test statistic for which the null hypothesis will be rejected. That is, what specific values of the test statistic will lead us to reject the null hypothesis in favor of the alternative hypothesis? These specific values are known collectively as the **rejection region** for the test. For this example, we would need to specify the values of $\bar{x}$ that would lead us to believe that H_a is true, i.e., that μ is greater than 72. Again, we will learn how to find an appropriate rejection region in later examples.

Definition 10.9

The **test statistic** is a sample statistic, computed from the information provided by the sample, upon which the decision concerning the null and alternative hypotheses is based.

Definition 10.10

The **rejection region** is the set of possible computed values of the test statistic for which the null hypothesis will be rejected.

Finally, in the fifth step, we make our decision by observing whether the computed value of the test statistic lies within the rejection region. If the computed value falls within the rejection region, we reject the null hypothesis; otherwise, we do not (or "fail" to) reject the null hypothesis. ■

An outline of the hypothesis-testing procedure developed in Example 10.8 is given in the box. Each step in this approach will be explained in greater detail as we proceed.

Recall that the null and alternative hypotheses (step 1) will be stated in terms of specific population parameters. Thus, in step 3 we decide on a test statistic that will provide information about the target parameter.

Outline for Testing a Hypothesis

1. Specify the **null** and **alternative hypotheses**, H_0 and H_a, and the **significance level**, α.
2. Obtain a **random sample** from the population(s) of interest.

(continued)

3. Determine an appropriate **test statistic** and compute its value using the sample data.
4. Specify the **rejection region**. (This will depend on the value of α selected.)
5. Make the appropriate **conclusion** by observing whether the computed value of the test statistic lies within the rejection region. If so, reject the null hypothesis; otherwise, do not reject the null hypothesis.

Recall that the null and alternative hypotheses (step 1) will be stated in terms of specific population parameters. Thus, in step 3 we decide on a test statistic that will provide information about the target parameter.

EXAMPLE 10.9
Selecting a Test Statistic

Refer to Example 10.2. The spokesperson for the FTC wants to test

H_0: $\pi = .80$

H_a: $\pi > .80$

where π is the proportion of all readers of cigarette advertisements who fail to notice the surgeon general's warning. Suggest a test statistic that may be useful in deciding whether to reject H_0.

SOLUTION Since the target parameter is a population proportion π, it would be logical to use the sample proportion p as a tool in the decision-making process. Recall from Section 8.4 that p is the point estimate of π used in the interval estimation procedure. ■

EXAMPLE 10.10
Selecting a Test Statistic

A college recruiter believes that the mean starting salary of graduates with economic degrees is less than the mean starting salary of graduates with marketing degrees. Consequently, the recruiter wants to test:

H_0: $(\mu_1 - \mu_2) = 0$

H_a: $(\mu_1 - \mu_2) < 0$

where μ_1 and μ_2 are the population mean starting salaries of all economic graduates and marketing graduates, respectively. Suggest an appropriate test statistic in the context of this problem.

SOLUTION The parameter of interest is $(\mu_1 - \mu_2)$, the difference between two population means. Therefore, we will use $(\bar{x}_1 - \bar{x}_2)$, the difference between the corresponding sample means, as a basis for deciding whether to reject H_0. If the difference between the sample means $(\bar{x}_1 - \bar{x}_2)$ falls greatly below the hypothesized value of $(\mu_1 - \mu_2) = 0$, then we have evidence that disagrees with the null hypothesis. In fact, it would support the alternative hypothesis that $(\mu_1 - \mu_2) < 0$. Again, we are using the point estimate of the target parameter to form the test statistic in the hypothesis-testing approach. ■

Guideline for Step 3 of Hypothesis Testing

The test statistic to be used in a hypothesis test of a population parameter is based on the conventional point estimate of that parameter. Recall that the point estimate is a sample statistic, i.e., it is calculated from the sample data.

In step 4, we divide all possible values of the test statistic (or a standardized version of it) into two sets: the **rejection region** and its complement. If the computed value of the test statistic falls within the rejection region, we reject the null hypothesis. If the computed value of the test statistic does not fall within the rejection region, we do not reject the null hypothesis.

EXAMPLE 10.11
Decisions Based on the Test Statistic

Refer to Example 10.8. For the hypothesis test

H_0: $\mu = 72$

H_a: $\mu > 72$

indicate which decision you may make for each of the following values of the test statistic:

    a. $\bar{x} = 110$ **b.** $\bar{x} = 59$ **c.** $\bar{x} = 73$

SOLUTION

a. If $\bar{x} = 110$, then much doubt is cast upon the null hypothesis. In other words, *if the null hypothesis were true* (i.e., μ is in fact equal to 72), then it is very unlikely that we would observe a sample mean $\bar{x}$ as large as 110. We would thus tend to reject the null hypothesis on the basis of information contained in this sample.

b. Since the alternative of interest is $\mu > 72$, this value of the sample mean, $\bar{x} = 59$, provides no support for H_a. Thus, we would *not* reject H_0 in favor of H_a: $\mu > 72$ based on this sample.

c. Does a sample value of $\bar{x} = 73$ cast sufficient doubt on the null hypothesis to warrant its rejection? Although the sample mean $\bar{x} = 73$ is larger than the null hypothesized value of $\mu = 72$, is this due to chance variation, or does it provide strong enough evidence to conclude in favor of H_a? We think you will agree that the decision is not as clear-cut as in parts **a** and **b**, and that we need a more formal mechanism for deciding what to do in this situation.   ▪

We now illustrate how to determine a rejection region that takes into account such factors as the sample size and the maximum probability of a Type I error that you are willing to tolerate.

EXAMPLE 10.12
Rejection Region for Upper-Tailed Test

Refer to Example 10.11. Specify completely the form of the rejection region for a test of

H_0: $\mu = 72$

H_a: $\mu > 72$

at a significance level of $\alpha = .05$.

SOLUTION   We are interested in detecting a directional departure from H_0; in particular, we are interested in the alternative that μ is *greater than* 72. Now, what values of the sample mean $\bar{x}$ would cause us to reject H_0 in favor of H_a? Clearly, values of $\bar{x}$ that are "sufficiently greater" than 72 would cast doubt on the null hypothesis. But how do we decide whether a value—say, $\bar{x} = 73$—is "sufficiently greater" than 72 to reject H_0? A convenient measure of the distance between $\bar{x}$ and 72 is the z score, which "standardizes" the value of the test statistic $\bar{x}$:

$$z = \frac{\bar{x} - \mu_{\bar{x}}}{\sigma_{\bar{x}}} = \frac{\bar{x} - 72}{\sigma/\sqrt{n}} \approx \frac{\bar{x} - 72}{s/\sqrt{n}}$$

(The z score is obtained by using the values of $\mu_{\bar{x}}$ and $\sigma_{\bar{x}}$ that would be valid if the null hypothesis were true, i.e., if $\mu = 72$.) *The z score then gives us a measure of how many standard deviations the observed $\bar{x}$ is from what we would expect to observe if H_0 were true.*

Now examine Figure 10.1a (page 484) and observe that the chance of obtaining a value of $\bar{x}$ more than 1.645 standard deviations above 72 is only .05, *when the true value of μ is 72*. (We are assuming that the sample size is large enough to ensure that the sampling distribution of $\bar{x}$ is approximately normal.) Thus, if we observe a sample mean located more than 1.645 standard deviations above 72, then either H_0 is true and a relatively rare (with probability .05 or less) event has occurred, *or H_a is true and the population mean exceeds 72*. We would tend to favor the latter explanation for obtaining such a large value of $\bar{x}$, and would then reject the null hypothesis.

In summary, our rejection region for this example consists of all values of z that are greater than 1.645 (i.e., all values of $\bar{x}$ that are more than 1.645 standard deviations above 72). The **critical value** 1.645 is shown in Figure 10.1b. In this situation,

FIGURE 10.1

Location of Rejection
Region for Example
10.12

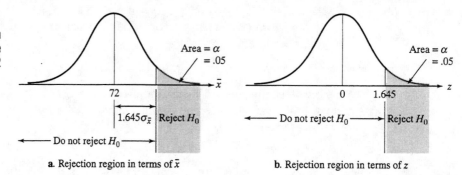

a. Rejection region in terms of $\bar{x}$ **b.** Rejection region in terms of z

the probability of a Type I error—that is, deciding in favor of H_a if in fact H_0 is true—is equal to $\alpha = .05$. ■

Definition 10.11

In specifying the rejection region for a particular test of hypothesis, the value at the boundary of the rejection region is called the **critical value**.

EXAMPLE 10.13
Rejection Region for Lower-Tailed Test

Specify the form of the rejection region for a test of

H_0: $\mu = 72$

H_a: $\mu < 72$

at a significance level of $\alpha = .01$.

SOLUTION Here, we want to be able to detect the directional alternative that μ is *less than* 72; in this case, it is "sufficiently small" values of the test statistic $\bar{x}$ that would cast doubt on the null hypothesis. As in Example 10.12, we will standardize the value of the test statistic to obtain a measure of the distance between $\bar{x}$ and the null hypothesized value of 72:

$$z = \frac{\bar{x} - \mu_{\bar{x}}}{\sigma_{\bar{x}}} = \frac{\bar{x} - 72}{\sigma/\sqrt{n}} \approx \frac{\bar{x} - 72}{s/\sqrt{n}}$$

This z value tells us how many standard deviations the observed $\bar{x}$ is from what would be expected *if H_0 were true*. (Again, we have assumed that the sample size n is large so that the sampling distribution of $\bar{x}$ will be approximately normal. The appropriate modifications for small samples will be discussed in Chapter 11.)

Figure 10.2a shows us that, *when the true value of μ is* 72, the chance of observ-

FIGURE 10.2

Location of Rejection
Region for Example
10.13

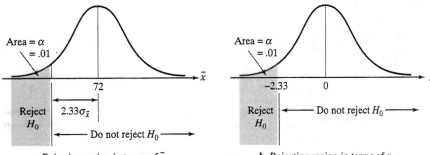

a. Rejection region in terms of $\bar{x}$ **b.** Rejection region in terms of z

ing a value of $\bar{x}$ more than 2.33 standard deviations below 72 is only .01. Thus, at significance level (probability of Type I error) equal to .01, we would reject the null hypothesis for all values of z that are less than -2.33 (see Figure 10.2b), i.e., for all values of $\bar{x}$ that lie more than 2.33 standard deviations below 72. ■

EXAMPLE 10.14

Rejection Region for Two-
Tailed Test

Specify the form of the rejection region for a test of

H_0: $\mu = 72$

H_a: $\mu \neq 72$

where we are willing to tolerate a .05 chance of making a Type I error.

SOLUTION For this two-sided (nondirectional) alternative, we would reject the null hypothesis for "sufficiently small" *or* "sufficiently large" values of the standardized test statistic

$$z = \frac{\bar{x} - \mu_{\bar{x}}}{\sigma_{\bar{x}}} = \frac{\bar{x} - 72}{\sigma/\sqrt{n}} \approx \frac{\bar{x} - 72}{s/\sqrt{n}}$$

Now, from Figure 10.3a (page 486), we note that the chance of observing a sample mean $\bar{x}$ more than 1.96 standard deviations below 72 *or* more than 1.96 standard deviations above 72, *when H_0 is true*, is only $\alpha = .05$. Thus, the rejection region consists of two sets of values: We will reject H_0 if z is either less than -1.96 or greater than 1.96 (see Figure 10.3b). For this rejection rule, the probability of a Type I error is .05. ■

The three previous examples all exhibit certain common characteristics regarding the rejection region, as indicated in the next box.

FIGURE 10.3

Location of Rejection
Region for
Example 10.14

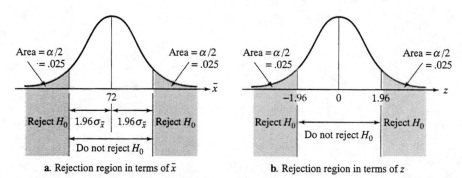

a. Rejection region in terms of $\bar{x}$ **b.** Rejection region in terms of z

---

Guidelines for Step 4 of Hypothesis Testing: Specifying the Rejection Region

1. The value of α, the probability of a Type I error, is specified in advance by the researcher. It can be made as small or as large as desired; typical values are $\alpha = .01$, $.02$, $.05$, and $.10$. For a fixed sample size, the size of the rejection region decreases as the value of α decreases (see Figure 10.4). That is, for smaller values of α, more extreme departures of the test statistic from the null hypothesized parameter value are required to permit rejection of H_0.

2. The test statistic (i.e., the point estimate of the target parameter) is standardized to provide a measure of how great its departure is from the null hypothesized value of the parameter. The standardization is based on the sampling distribution of the point estimate, assuming H_0 is true. (It is through the standardization that the rejection rule takes into account the sample sizes.) For means and proportions, the general formula is:

$$\text{Standardized test statistic} = \frac{\text{Point estimate} - \text{Hypothesized value}}{\text{Standard error of point estimate}}$$

3. The location of the rejection region depends on whether the test is one-tailed or two-tailed, and on the prespecified significance level, α.

   a. For a one-tailed test in which the symbol ">" occurs in H_a, the rejection region consists of values in the upper tail of the sampling distribution of the standardized test statistic. The critical value is selected so that the area to its right is equal to α. (See Figure 10.1b.)

   b. For a one-tailed test in which the symbol "<" occurs in H_a, the rejection region consists of values in the lower tail of the sampling distribution of the standardized test statistic. The critical value is selected so that the area to its left is equal to α. (See Figure 10.2b.)

   (continued)

> **c.** For a two-tailed test in which the symbol "$\neq$" occurs in H_a, the rejection region consists of two sets of values. The critical values are selected so that the area in each tail of the sampling distribution of the standardized test statistic is equal to $\alpha/2$. (See Figure 10.3b.)

FIGURE 10.4

Size of the Upper-Tail Rejection Region for Different Values of α

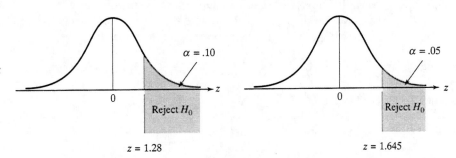

Once we have chosen the test statistic from the sample information and computed its value (step 3), we determine whether its standardized value lies within the rejection region so we can decide whether to reject the null hypothesis (step 5).

EXAMPLE 10.15

A Complete Hypothesis Test

Refer to Example 10.12. Suppose the following statistics were calculated based on a random sample of $n = 30$ measurements: $\bar{x} = 73$, $s = 13$. Perform a test of

H_0: $\mu = 72$

H_a: $\mu > 72$

at a significance level of $\alpha = .05$.

SOLUTION In Example 10.12, we determined the following rejection rule for the given value of α and the alternative hypothesis of interest:

Reject H_0 if $z > 1.645$.

The standardized test statistic, computed assuming H_0 is true, is given by

$$z = \frac{\bar{x} - \mu_{\bar{x}}}{\sigma_{\bar{x}}}$$

$$= \frac{\bar{x} - 72}{\sigma/\sqrt{n}}$$

$$\approx \frac{\bar{x} - 72}{s/\sqrt{n}}$$

$$= \frac{73 - 72}{13/\sqrt{30}} = .42$$

Since this value does not lie within the rejection region (shown in Figure 10.5), we fail to reject H_0 and conclude there is insufficient evidence to support the alternative hypothesis, H_a: $\mu > 72$. (Note that we do *not* conclude that H_0 is true; rather, we state that we have insufficient evidence to reject H_0.) ■

FIGURE 10.5

Location of Rejection Region and Test Statistic for Example 10.15

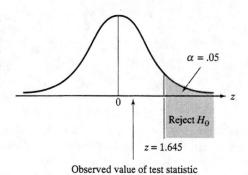

EXAMPLE 10.16
Hypothesis-Testing Application

Recall from Example 10.1 that a metal lathe that produces machine bearings is out of control if the mean diameter of the bearings differs from .5 inch. Suppose a random sample of $n = 50$ bearings produced a mean diameter of $\bar{x} = .46$ inch and a standard deviation of $s = .075$ inch. Perform a test, at significance level .05, of

H_0: $\mu = .5$

H_a: $\mu \neq .5$

where μ is the true mean diameter of all machine bearings being produced by the lathe.

SOLUTION   The standardized test statistic is computed as follows:

$$z = \frac{\bar{x} - \mu_{\bar{x}}}{\sigma_{\bar{x}}} = \frac{\bar{x} - .5}{\sigma/\sqrt{50}} \approx \frac{\bar{x} - .5}{s/\sqrt{50}}$$

$$= \frac{.46 - .5}{.075/\sqrt{50}} = -3.77$$

FIGURE 10.6

Location of Rejection Region and Test Statistic for Example 10.16

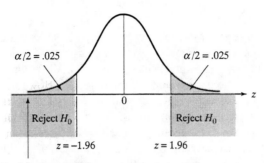

α/2 = .025   α/2 = .025

Reject H_0 Reject H_0

$z = -1.96$ $z = 1.96$

Observed value of test statistic
$z = -3.77$

This value lies within the rejection region shown in Figure 10.6; we therefore conclude that the mean diameter of the bearings is not equal to .5 inch. It appears that the machine needs adjustment. We acknowledge that we may be making a Type I error, with probability $\alpha = .05$. ■

In the subsequent discussions on hypothesis testing, we will not differentiate between the test statistic (point estimate) and its standardized value. We will employ the common usage, in which *test statistic* refers to the standardized value of the point estimate for the target parmeter. Thus, in Example 10.16, the value of the *test statistic* was computed to be $z = -3.77$.

EXERCISES

■ *Learning the Mechanics*

10.16 Suppose it is desired to test H_0: $\mu = 65$. Specify the form of the rejection region for each of the following (assume that the sample size will be sufficient to guarantee the approximate normality of the sampling distribution of $\bar{x}$):

   a. H_a: $\mu \neq 65$, $\alpha = .02$ **b.** H_a: $\mu > 65$, $\alpha = .05$

   c. H_a: $\mu < 65$, $\alpha = .01$ **d.** H_a: $\mu < 65$, $\alpha = .10$

10.17 Refer to Exercise 10.16. Calculate the test statistic for each of the following sample results:

   a. $n = 100$, $\bar{x} = 60$, $s = 15$ **b.** $n = 50$, $\bar{x} = 60$, $s = 15$

   c. $n = 50$, $\bar{x} = 70$, $s = 15$ **d.** $n = 50$, $\bar{x} = 70$, $s = 30$

10.18 Refer to Exercises 10.16 and 10.17. Give the appropriate conclusions for each of the tests, parts **a–d**.

10.19 For each of the following rejection regions, determine the value of α, the probability of a Type I error:

   a. $z < -1.96$ **b.** $z > 1.645$ **c.** $z < -2.58$ or $z > 2.58$

■ *Applying the Concepts*

10.20 Each year, hundreds of thousands of investors hope to strike it rich by playing in a controversial U.S. government lottery. For $75, one can compete for a federal oil and gas lease that the Interior Department assumes is practically worthless. All the land in the lottery is supposed to have been checked by the government for oil and gas. However, the *Wall Street Journal* (Mar. 29, 1984) reports on evidence suggesting that the Interior Department is including valuable oil leases in the lottery, some worth millions of dollars. Of 328 winners in a July 1980 lottery of Wyoming lands, 184 (or 56%) were able to sell their leases to an oil company for a substantial profit. Yet the Interior Department claims that at most 10% of the leases in the lottery are salable to an oil company. Let π represent the true proportion of lottery leases that are salable to an oil company. Then we want to test

H_0: $\pi = .10$

H_a: $\pi > .10$

a. Give the form of the rejection region for $\alpha = .05$. Locate the rejection region, α, and the critical value on a sketch of the normal curve.
b. Calculate the value of the test statistic. [*Hint*: The standard deviation of the point estimate p is (from Section 8.4) $\sqrt{\pi(1 - \pi)/n}$, where π is the hypothesized value in H_0.]
c. In terms of the problem, what is the proper conclusion?

10.21 Refer to Exercise 10.14. The supermarket chain randomly samples $n = 50$ bags of potato chips from the shipment and measures the weight of the chips in each. The mean weight of the sample was determined to be $\bar{x} = 15.7$ ounces, and the sample standard deviation was $s = .8$ ounce.
a. Calculate the appropriate (standardized) test statistic for this test.
b. Specify the form of the rejection region if the level of significance is $\alpha = .01$. Locate the rejection region, α, and the critical value on a sketch of the standard normal curve.
c. Use the results of parts **a** and **b** to make the proper conclusion in terms of the problem.

10.22 The Consumer Product Safety Commission strictly enforces guidelines that require specific safety warnings to be placed on all potentially dangerous products. *Human Factors* (Dec. 1984) reported on a University of Florida study to determine the impact of safety warnings on consumers. Each of 91 business undergraduates was presented with display boards containing information on price, smell, ease of application, and safety for two hypothetical brands of bug killers. One of the two brands was randomly assigned a safety warning (such as "Danger: Do Not Inhale"), whereas the other had no safety message. The students were then instructed to rate each brand regarding its safety on a scale of 1 to 25 (where 1 = very poor and 25 = very good). An analysis of the data led the researcher to conclude that "The brand of bug killer … with the safety warnings was perceived as significantly safer than the brand without the safety warnings."
a. The inference was based on the results of a statistical test of hypothesis for the parameter $\mu_1 - \mu_2$, where μ_1 is the mean safety rating of brand A (no safety warning) and μ_2 is the mean safety rating of brand B (safety warning). Write the appropriate null and alternative hypotheses.
b. Since each student rated each of the two brands, the data were analyzed as matched pairs. In Section 11.5, we will learn that when the data are collected as matched pairs and the

sample size is large ($n = 91$ students in this experiment), the test statistic is a z statistic. Give the rejection region for the test described in part **a**, for $\alpha = .01$.

c. The exact value of the test statistic was not reported in the article. However, from the information given, we know the value falls below $z = -2.33$. In terms of the problem, what is the appropriate conclusion?

10.5 Reporting Test Results: p-Values

The statistical hypothesis-testing technique that we have developed in Section 10.4 requires us to choose the significance level α (i.e., the maximum probability of a Type I error that we are willing to tolerate) before obtaining the data and computing the test statistic. By choosing α a priori, we in effect fix the rejection region for the test. Thus, no matter how large or how small the observed value of the test statistic, our decision regarding H_0 is clear-cut: Reject H_0 (i.e., conclude that the test results are statistically significant) if the observed value of the test statistic falls into the rejection region, and do not reject H_0 (i.e., conclude that the test results are insignificant) otherwise. This *"fixed" significance level*, α, then serves as a measure of the reliability of our inference. However, there is one drawback to a test conducted in this manner—namely, a measure of the *degree* of significance of the test results is not readily available. That is, if the value of the test statistic falls into the rejection region, we have no measure of the extent to which the data disagree with the null hypothesis.

EXAMPLE 10.17
The Degree of Disagreement Between Sample Data and H_0

A large-sample test of H_0: $\mu = 72$ versus H_a: $\mu > 72$ is to be conducted at a fixed significance level of $\alpha = .05$. Consider the following possible values of the computed test statistic:

$$z = 1.82 \quad \text{and} \quad z = 5.66$$

a. Which of the above values of the test statistic provides stronger evidence for the rejection of H_0?

b. How can we measure the extent of disagreement between the sample data and H_0 for each of the computed values?

SOLUTION

a. From Example 10.15, the appropriate rejection region for this test, at $\alpha = .05$, is given by

$$z > z_{.05} = 1.645$$

Clearly, for either of the test statistic values given above, $z = 1.82$ or $z = 5.66$, we will reject H_0; hence, the result in each case is statistically significant. Recall, however, that the appropriate test statistic for a large-sample test concerning μ is simply the z score for the observed sample mean $\bar{x}$, calculated by using the hypothesized value of μ in H_0 (in this case, $\mu = 72$). The larger the z score, the greater the distance (in units of standard deviations) that $\bar{x}$ is from the hypothesized value of $\mu = 72$. Thus, a z score of 5.66 would present stronger evidence that the true mean is larger than 72 than would a z score of 1.82. This reasoning stems from our knowledge of the sampling distribution of $\bar{x}$; if in fact $\mu = 72$, we would certainly not expect to observe an $\bar{x}$ with a z score as large as 5.66.

b. One way of measuring the amount of disagreement between the observed data and the value of μ in the null hypothesis is to calculate the probability of observing a value of the test statistic equal to or greater than the actual computed value, if in fact H_0 were true. That is, if z_c is the computed value of the test statistic, calculate

$$P(z \geq z_c)$$

assuming the null hypothesis is true. This "disagreement" probability, or *p-value*, is calculated here for each of the computed test statistics, $z = 1.82$ and $z = 5.66$, using Table 5 of Appendix B:

$$P(z \geq 1.82) = .5 - .4656 = .0344$$

$$P(z \geq 5.66) \approx .5 - .5 = 0$$

From the discussion in part **a**, you can see that the smaller the *p*-value the greater the extent of disagreement between the data and the null hypothesis—that is, the more significant the result. ■

In general, *p*-values for tests based on large samples are computed as shown in the accompanying box. (*p*-values for small-sample tests are discussed in Chapter 11.)

Measuring the Disagreement Between the Data and H_0: p-Values

Upper-tailed test: *p*-value $= P(z \geq z_c)$

Lower-tailed test: *p*-value $= P(z \leq z_c)$

Two-tailed test: *p*-value $= 2P(z \geq |z_c|)$

where z_c is the computed value of the test statistic and $|z_c|$ denotes the absolute value of z_c (which will always be positive).

Notice that the *p*-value for a two-tailed test is twice the probability for the one-tailed test. This is because the disagreement between the data and H_0 can be in two directions.

When publishing the results of a statistical test of hypothesis in journals, case studies, reports, etc., many researchers make use of *p*-values. Instead of selecting α a priori and then conducting a test as outlined in Section 10.4, the researcher will compute and report the value of the appropriate test statistic and its associated *p*-value. It is left to the reader of the report to judge the significance of the result—that is, the reader must determine whether to reject the null hypothesis in favor of the alternative, based on the reported *p*-value. This *p*-value is often referred to as the **observed significance level** of the test. The null hypothesis will be rejected if the observed significance level is *less* than the fixed significance level, α, chosen by the reader (see Figure 10.7). There are two inherent advantages of reporting test results in this manner: (1) Readers are permitted to select the maximum value of α that they would be willing to tolerate in carrying out a standard test of hypothesis in the manner outlined in this chapter; and (2) It is an easy way to present the results of test calculations performed by a computer. Most statistical software packages perform the calculations for a test, give the value of the test statistic, and report the observed significance level (*p*-value) of the test; this makes it easy for the user to decide whether to reject H_0.

FIGURE 10.7

Using *p*-Values to Make Conclusions

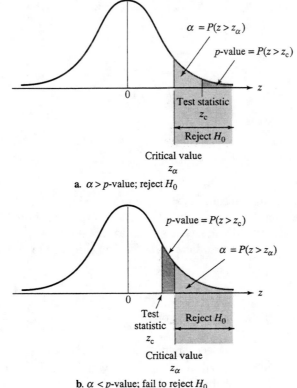

$\alpha = P(z > z_\alpha)$

p-value $= P(z > z_c)$

Test statistic z_c

Reject H_0

Critical value z_α

a. $\alpha > p$-value; reject H_0

p-value $= P(z > z_c)$

$\alpha = P(z > z_\alpha)$

Test statistic z_c

Reject H_0

Critical value z_α

b. $\alpha < p$-value; fail to reject H_0

> **Reporting Test Results As p-values: How to Decide Whether to Reject H_0**
>
> 1. Choose the maximum value of α that you are willing to tolerate.
> 2. If the observed significance level (*p*-value) of the test is less than the maximum value of α, then reject the null hypothesis (see Figure 10.7).

EXAMPLE 10.18

Calculating the *p*-Value for a One-Tailed Test

Refer to Example 10.15 and the test of H_0: $\mu = 72$ versus H_a: $\mu < 72$. Compute the observed significance level of the test and interpret its value.

SOLUTION In this large-sample test concerning a population mean μ, the computed value of the test statistic was $z_c = .42$. Since the test is upper-tailed, the associated *p*-value is given by

$$P(z \geq z_c) = P(z \geq .42) = .5 - .1628 = .3372 \quad \text{(see Figure 10.8)}$$

FIGURE 10.8

p-Value for Example 10.18

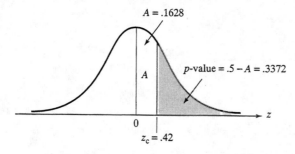

Thus, the observed significance level of the test is .3372. To reject the null hypothesis H_0: $\mu = 72$, we would have to be willing to risk a Type I error probability, α, of at least .3372. Most researchers would not be willing to take this risk and would deem the result insignificant (i.e., conclude that there is insufficient evidence to reject H_0). ▪

EXAMPLE 10.19

Calculating the *p*-Value for a Two-Tailed Test

Refer to Example 10.16 and the test of H_0: $\mu = .5$ versus H_a: $\mu \neq .5$.

    a. Compute the observed significance level of the test.
    b. Make the appropriate conclusion if you are willing to tolerate a Type I error probability of $\alpha = .01$.

SOLUTION

    a. The computed test statistic for this large-sample test about μ was given as $z_c = -3.77$. Since the test is two-tailed, the associated *p*-

value is

$$2P(z \geq |z_c|) = 2P(z \geq |-3.77|) = 2P(z \geq 3.77) \quad \text{(see Figure 10.9)}$$

Since $P(z \geq 3.77)$ is very near 0, the observed significance level of the test is approximately 0.

FIGURE 10.9
p-Value for Example
10.19

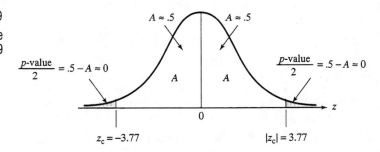

b. Since the approximate *p*-value of 0 is less than the maximum tolerable Type I error probability of $\alpha = .01$, we will reject H_0 and conclude that the mean diameter of the bearings is significantly different from .5 inch. In fact, we could choose an even smaller Type I error probability (e.g., $\alpha = .001$) and still have sufficient evidence to reject H_0. Thus, the result is highly significant. ■

Whether we conduct a test using *p*-values or the rejection region approach, our choice of a maximum tolerable Type I error probability becomes critical to the decision concerning H_0 and should not be hastily made. In either case, care should be taken to weigh the seriousness of committing a Type I error in the context of the problem.

EXERCISES

■ *Learning the Mechanics*

10.23 For a large-sample test of

$$H_0: \quad (\mu_1 - \mu_2) = 0$$

$$H_a: \quad (\mu_1 - \mu_2) > 0$$

compute the *p*-value associated with each of the following computed test statistic values:
a. $z_c = 1.96$ **b.** $z_c = 1.645$ **c.** $z_c = 2.67$ **d.** $z_c = 1.25$

10.24 For a large-sample test of

$$H_0: \quad (\pi_1 - \pi_2) = 0$$

$$H_a: \quad (\pi_1 - \pi_2) \neq 0$$

compute the p-value associated with each of the following computed test statistic values:

a. $z_c = -1.01$ b. $z_c = -2.37$ c. $z_c = 4.66$ d. $z_c = -1.45$

10.25 Give the approximate observed significance level of the test $H_0: \mu = 16$ for each of the following combinations of test statistic value and H_a:

a. $z_c = 3.05, \quad H_a: \mu \neq 16$ b. $z_c = -1.58, \quad H_a: \mu < 16$

c. $z_c = 2.20, \quad H_a: \mu > 16$ d. $z_c = -2.97 \quad H_a: \mu \neq 16$

■ *Applying the Concepts*

10.26 Refer to Exercise 10.2. Assume the following: p-value $= .217$, $\alpha = .10$. State the conclusion in the words of the problem.

10.27 Refer to Exercise 10.3. Assume the following: p-value $= .033$, $\alpha = .05$. State the conclusion in the words of the problem.

10.28 Refer to Exercise 10.4. Assume the following: p-value $= .001$, $\alpha = .05$. State the conclusion in the words of the problem.

10.29 Refer to Exercise 10.5. Assume the following: p-value $= .866$, $\alpha = .01$. State the conclusion in the words of the problem.

10.30 Refer to Exercise 10.6. Assume the following: p-value $= .025$, $\alpha = .01$. State the conclusion in the words of the problem.

10.31 Refer to Exercises 10.14 and 10.21. Compute the observed significance level (p-value) of the test. Interpret the result.

10.32 Refer to Exercise 10.20. Compute the approximate observed significance level (p-value) of the test. What is your decision regarding H_0 if you are willing to risk a maximum Type I error probability of only $\alpha = .01$?

10.6 Calculating the Probability of a Type II Error and the Power of a Test (Optional)

In Section 10.3, we discussed the problem with making the decision "accept H_0." The chance that we incorrectly accept H_0, i.e., accept H_0 when H_0 is in fact false, is β, the probability of a Type II error. Therefore, β serves as a measure of reliability for the decision "accept H_0." Unlike α, the value of β is typically not controlled by the researcher and, in most testing situations, is very difficult to calculate. Consequently, when the test statistic does not fall in the rejection region, we state our conclusion as "do not reject H_0" rather than risk making a Type II error with unknown probability of occurrence.

In certain situations, however, *it is possible to calculate β for a specified value of the parameter in H_a*, as the following example illustrates.

EXAMPLE 10.20
Calculating β

Suppose we want to conduct the test of hypothesis of Example 10.15,

$$H_0: \mu = 72$$

$$H_a: \mu > 72$$

at significance level $\alpha = .05$. Recall that the test was based on a random sample of $n = 30$ measurements, with $\bar{x} = 73$ and $s = 13$. Calculate the value of β if the value of μ in H_a is $\mu_a = 75$.

SOLUTION

STEP 1   The first step is to find the value of $\bar{x}$ on the border between the rejection region and the acceptance region. From Example 10.15, the rejection region is $z > 1.645$. Since the test statistic is calculated as

$$z = \frac{\bar{x} - 72}{\sigma / \sqrt{n}}$$

we can write the rejection region in terms of $\bar{x}$:

$$\frac{\bar{x} - 72}{\sigma / \sqrt{n}} > 1.645$$

or

$$\bar{x} > 72 + 1.645 \left(\frac{\sigma}{\sqrt{n}} \right)$$

Substituting $n = 30$ and $s = 13$ (as an approximation for σ) into the expression for the rejection region, we obtain

$$\bar{x} > 72 + 1.645 \left(\frac{13}{\sqrt{30}} \right) = 75.90$$

Thus, at $\alpha = .05$, we will reject H_0 if the sample mean $\bar{x}$ exceeds 75.90. Or equivalently, we will accept H_0 if $\bar{x} < 75.90$. These rejection and acceptance regions are illustrated in Figure 10.10 (page 498).

STEP 2   The next step is to write β as a probability statement involving $\bar{x}$:

$$\beta = P(\text{Type II error})$$

$$= P(\text{Accept } H_0 \text{ when } H_0 \text{ is false})$$

$$= P(\bar{x} < 75.90 \text{ when } \mu_a = 75)$$

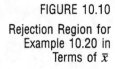

FIGURE 10.10

Rejection Region for Example 10.20 in Terms of $\bar{x}$

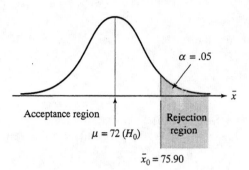

$\alpha = .05$

Acceptance region

Rejection region

$\mu = 72\ (H_0)$

$\bar{x}_0 = 75.90$

FIGURE 10.11

Value of β When $\mu_a = 75$

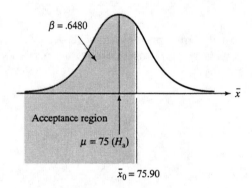

$\beta = .6480$

Acceptance region

$\mu = 75\ (H_a)$

$\bar{x}_0 = 75.90$

[Note that we have substituted $\mu_a = 75$ for "H_0 is false" because this is the value of μ specified in H_a.] This probability is shown in Figure 10.11.

STEP 3.   The final step is to calculate β using the standard normal (z) table (Table 5 of Appendix B):

$$\beta = P(\bar{x} < 75.90 \text{ when } \mu = 75)$$

$$= P\left(\frac{\bar{x} - \mu}{\sigma/\sqrt{n}} < \frac{75.90 - 75}{\sigma/\sqrt{n}}\right)$$

$$\approx P\left(z < \frac{75.90 - 75}{13/\sqrt{30}}\right)$$

$$= P(z < .38) = 5 + .1480 = .6480$$

Thus, the probability that the test procedure will lead us to incorrectly accept $H_0: \mu = 72$ when, in fact $\mu = 75$ is approximately .65. The fact that this probability is so large implies that it will be difficult to detect departures from H_0 for values of μ close, but not equal, to 72.   ■

Guidelines for Calculating β for a Large-Sample Test About μ

Consider a large-sample test of H_0: $\mu = \mu_0$ at significance level α. The value of β for a specific value of the alternative, $\mu = \mu_a$, is calculated as follows:

STEP 1   For one-tailed tests, find the value of $\bar{x}$ corresponding to the border of the rejection region. The calculation of this value, $\bar{x}_0$, depends on whether the test is upper-tailed or lower-tailed:

Upper-tailed test: $\bar{x}_0 = \mu_0 + z_\alpha\left(\dfrac{\sigma}{\sqrt{n}}\right) \approx \mu_0 + z_\alpha\left(\dfrac{s}{\sqrt{n}}\right)$

Lower-tailed test: $\bar{x}_0 = \mu_0 - z_\alpha\left(\dfrac{\sigma}{\sqrt{n}}\right) \approx \mu_0 - z_\alpha\left(\dfrac{s}{\sqrt{n}}\right)$

For two-tailed tests, two border values exist—one in the upper tail of the distribution $(\bar{x}_{0,\,U})$ and one in the lower tail $(\bar{x}_{0,\,L})$:

Two-tailed test: $\bar{x}_{0,\,U} \approx \mu_0 + z_{\alpha/2}\left(\dfrac{s}{\sqrt{n}}\right)$

$$\bar{x}_{0,\,L} \approx \mu_0 - z_{\alpha/2}\left(\dfrac{s}{\sqrt{n}}\right)$$

STEP 2   Write β as a probability involving the border value(s) of $\bar{x}$ and the alternative value of μ:

Upper-tailed test: $\beta = P(\bar{x} < \bar{x}_0 \text{ when } \mu = \mu_a)$

Lower-tailed test: $\beta = P(\bar{x} > \bar{x}_0 \text{ when } \mu = \mu_a)$

Two-tailed test: $\beta = P(\bar{x}_{0,\,L} < \bar{x} < \bar{x}_{0,\,U} \text{ when } \mu = \mu_a)$

STEP 3   Convert the border value(s) of $\bar{x}$ to z values in the probability statement of step 2. Then find the probability using Table 5 of Appendix B.

Upper-tailed test: $\beta \approx P\left(z < \dfrac{\bar{x}_0 - \mu_a}{s/\sqrt{n}}\right)$

Lower-tailed test: $\beta \approx P\left(z > \dfrac{\bar{x}_0 - \mu_a}{s/\sqrt{n}}\right)$

Two-tailed test: $\beta \approx P\left(\dfrac{\bar{x}_{0,\,L} - \mu_a}{s/\sqrt{n}} < z < \dfrac{\bar{x}_{0,\,U} - \mu_a}{s/\sqrt{n}}\right)$

EXAMPLE 10.21

Calculating β

Refer to Example 10.20. Calculate the value of β when the value of μ in H_a is $H_a = 80$.

SOLUTION From step 1 of Example 10.20, we know that the acceptance region for the test with $\alpha = .05$ is $\bar{x} < 75.90$. Thus, the value of $\bar{x}$ on the border of the rejection region is $\bar{x}_0 = 90$. Then for $\mu_a = 80$, we have

$$\beta = P(\text{Accept } H_0 \text{ when } H_0 \text{ is false})$$

$$= P(\bar{x} < \bar{x}_0 \text{ when } \mu = \mu_a)$$

$$= P(\bar{x} < 75.90 \text{ when } \mu_a = 80)$$

$$\approx P\left(\frac{\bar{x}_0 - \mu_a}{s/\sqrt{n}} < \frac{75.90 - 80}{13/\sqrt{30}}\right)$$

$$= P(z < -1.73)$$

From Table 5 of Appendix B, this probability is

$$\beta = .5 - .4582 = .0418 \quad (\text{see Figure 10.12}) \quad \blacksquare$$

FIGURE 10.12

Value of β When $\mu_a = 80$

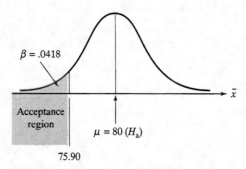

$\beta = .0418$

Acceptance region

$\mu = 80 (H_a)$

75.90

Examples 10.20 and 10.21 illustrate an important property of the statistical test of hypothesis: The value of β *decreases* as the true value of μ departs from the value hypothesized in H_0. In other words, the farther away the true value of μ lies from μ_0, the less likely you will be to incorrectly accept H_0 or, equivalently, the more likely you will be to correctly reject H_0. Also, it can be easily shown that β decreases as α increases for fixed n, or as n increases for fixed α. These properties of β are summarized in the box.

> **Properties of β for a Test of Hypothesis About μ**
>
> 1. β decreases as the distance between μ_0 and μ_a increases.
> 2. For fixed sample size n, β decreases as α increases.
> 3. For fixed significance level α, β decreases as n increases.

In practice, it is useful to interpret the value of $(1 - \beta)$, which is known as the **power of the test**. Since β and $(1 - \beta)$ are complementary probabilities, the power represents the probability that you will reject H_0 when H_0 is false, i.e., **the power of the test is the probability that you detect a departure from H_0 for a specific value of μ in H_a**. For example, the power of the test for $\mu_a = 80$ in Example 10.21 is

$$\text{Power} = 1 - \beta = 1 - .0418 = .9582$$

Thus, the test is very likely (probability of about .96) to lead to a rejection of H_0: $\mu = 72$ in favor of the alternative $H_a: \mu > 72$ when the true value of μ is $\mu_a = 80$. The greater the value of $(1 - \beta)$, the more powerful the test is for the particular alternative value of μ.

Definition 10.12

The **power** of a test is the probability that the test will lead to a rejection of the null hypothesis H_0 when, in fact, the alternative hypothesis H_a is true. For a particular alternative, the power is equal to $(1 - \beta)$.

EXAMPLE 10.22
Calculating Power

Refer to Example 10.21. Calculate the power of the test for the following values of μ_a: 73, 74, 75, ..., 85. Plot these values on a graph. What pattern do you observe?

SOLUTION For this upper-tailed $\alpha = .05$ test, the value of β for some alternative μ_a is given by

$$\beta \approx P\left(z < \frac{\bar{x}_0 - \mu_a}{s/\sqrt{n}}\right) = P\left(z < \frac{75.90 - \mu_a}{13/\sqrt{30}}\right)$$

Therefore, the power of the test is

$$\text{Power} = 1 - \beta \approx 1 - P\left(z < \frac{75.90 - \mu_a}{13/\sqrt{30}}\right)$$

Substituting $\mu_a = 73, 74, 75, \ldots, 85$ into the equation above and finding the respective probabilities from Table 5, Appendix B, we obtain the powers shown in Table 10.3.

Table 10.3   Power of the Test $H_0: \mu = 72$ vs. $H_a: \mu > 72$ for Several Different Values of μ_a

μ_a	Power	μ_a	Power
73	.1112	80	.9582
74	.2119	81	.9842
75	.3520	82	.9949
76	.5160	83	.9986
77	.6772	84	.9997
78	.8106	85	≈ 1.0000
79	.9049		

FIGURE 10.13

Power Curve for Example 10.22

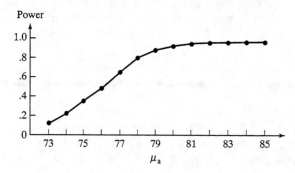

A plot of powers in Table 10.3 against μ_a is displayed in Figure 10.13. This graph is known as a **power curve** for the large-sample test.

Notice that the power of the test increases the farther μ_a deviates from the hypothesized value, $\mu_0 = 72$. That is, the greater the true value of μ deviates from the value hypothesized in H_0, the higher the probability of correctly rejecting H_0. Also, you can see that for alternative values of μ exceeding 83, the power of the test is approximately 1. ■

Since the power equals $(1 - \beta)$, the properties of the power are similar to those of β. These properties are summarized in the box.

Properties of Power $= (1 - \beta)$ ***for a Test of Hypothesis About*** μ

1. The power increases as the distance between μ_0 and μ_a increases.
2. For fixed sample size n, the power increases as α increases.
3. For fixed significance level α, the power increases as n increases.

When testing a hypothesis about a population parameter, we want to use the procedure with the highest power. In Chapter 11, we present testing procedures that have been shown to be most powerful for a general set of alternatives.

EXERCISES

■ Learning the Mechanics

10.33 How are β and the power of a test for a fixed alternative related?

10.34 Explain how you can increase the power of a test.

10.35 Suppose you want to test H_0: $\mu = \mu_0$ against H_a: $\mu > \mu_0$. Assuming $\sigma = 42$, find the value of $\bar{x}$ on the border of the rejection region if:
  a. $\mu_0 = 1{,}000$, $n = 36$, $\alpha = .01$
  b. $\mu_0 = 68$, $n = 100$, $\alpha = .05$
  c. $\mu_0 = 7.8$, $n = 85$, $\alpha = .10$

10.36 Suppose you want to test H_0: $\mu = 400$ against H_a: $\mu < 400$ at significance level $\alpha = .05$. Find the value of β for the following sets of values:
  a. $n = 100$, $s = 20$, $\mu_a = 395$ **b.** $n = 50$, $s = 20$, $\mu_a = 395$
  c. $n = 50$, $s = 20$, $\mu_a = 390$

10.37 Suppose you want to test H_0: $\mu = 25$ against H_a: $\mu \neq 25$. A sample size of $n = 100$ yielded a value of $s = 12$. Find the power of the test for the alternative $\mu_a = 23$ for each of the following values of α:
  a. .10   **b.** .05   **c.** .01

■ Applying the Concepts

10.38 Refer to Exercises 10.14 and 10.21. Calculate the power of the test if the true mean weight of the chips is 15 ounces. Interpret your result.

10.39 Refer to Examples 10.1 and 10.16. Calculate the power of the test if the true mean diameter of the bearings is .495 inch. Interpret your results.

SUMMARY

In this chapter, we have introduced the logic and general concepts involved in the statistical procedure of *hypothesis testing*. The techniques will be illustrated more fully with practical applications in Chapter 11.

KEY TERMS

Alternative hypothesis   Observed significance level   Rejection region
Critical value   One-tailed test   Test statistic
Fixed significance level   *p*-value   Two-tailed test
Hypothesis testing   *Power curve   Type I error
Null hypothesis   *Power of the test   Type II error

KEY SYMBOLS

H_0:   Null hypothesis

H_a: Alternative hypothesis

$\alpha = P(\text{Type I error}) = P(\text{Reject } H_0 \text{ when } H_0 \text{ is true})$

$\beta = P(\text{Type II error}) = P(\text{Accept } H_0 \text{ when } H_0 \text{ is false})$

*Power $= 1 - \beta$

SUPPLEMENTARY EXERCISES

[Note: Exercises marked with an asterisk (*) are from the optional section in this chapter.]

10.40 Explain the difference between the null hypothesis and the alternative hypothesis in a statistical test.

10.41 What are the two possible conclusions in a statistical test of hypothesis?

10.42 Define each of the following:
    a. Type I error   **b.** Type II error
    c. α **d.** β
    e. Critical value   **f.** Fixed level of significance
    g. One-tailed test   **h.** Two-tailed test
    ***i.** Power   **j.** Observed significance level
    k. *p*-value

10.43 When do you risk making a Type I error? A Type II error?

10.44 In a test of hypothesis, is the size of the rejection region increased or decreased when the significance level α is reduced?

---

*From the optional section.

*10.45 What happens to the power of the test as α is decreased?

10.46 If the calculated value of the test statistic falls in the rejection region, we reject H_0 in favor of H_a. Does this prove that H_a is correct? Explain.

10.47 Specify the form of the rejection region for a two-tailed test of hypothesis conducted at each of the following significance levels:

a. $\alpha = .01$ **b.** $\alpha = .02$ **c.** $\alpha = .04$

Locate the rejection region, α, and the critical values on a sketch of the standard normal curve for each part of the exercise. (Assume that the sampling distribution of the test statistic is approximately normal.)

10.48 For each of the following rejection regions, determine the value of α, the probability of a Type I error:

a. $z > 2.58$ **b.** $z < -1.29$ **c.** $z < -1.645$ or $z > 1.645$

Locate the rejection region, α, and the critical value(s) on a sketch of the standard normal curve.

10.49 Formulate the appropriate null and alternative hypotheses for each problem. Define all notation used.

a. A manufacturer of fishing line wants to show that the mean breaking strength of a competitor's 22-pound line is really less than 22 pounds.

b. An auto insurance investigator wants to determine whether there is a difference between the proportions of claims made against insurance company A and insurance company B that are in excess of $200.

c. A college placement center will conduct an investigation to determine whether the average starting salary for male graduates who seek jobs through the center is greater than the average starting salary for female graduates who seek jobs through the center.

d. Each year, *Computerworld* magazine reports on the Datapro ratings of all computer software vendors. Vendors are rated on a scale of 1 to 4 (1 = poor, 4 = excellent) in such areas as reliability, efficiency, ease of installation, and ease of use by a random sample of software users. A software vendor wants to determine whether its product has a higher mean Datapro rating than a rival vendor's product.

e. A craps player who has experienced a long run of bad luck at the craps table wants to test whether the casino dice are "loaded," i.e., whether the proportion of "sevens" occurring in many tosses of the two dice is different from $\frac{1}{6}$. (If the dice are fair, the probability of tossing a "seven" is $\frac{1}{6}$.)

10.50 Refer to Exercise 10.49e. Suppose that in the next 100 tosses of the two dice at the craps table, 5 resulted in the outcome of "seven."

a. Compute the test statistic appropriate for testing the hypothesis of Exercise 10.49e. (Use the hint given in Exercise 10.20.)

b. Set up the rejection region for the test if the craps player is willing to tolerate a Type I error probability of $\alpha = .10$. Locate the pertinent quantities on a sketch of the standard normal curve.

c. Give a full conclusion in terms of the problem.

d. What are the consequences of a Type I error for the craps player?

e. Find the *p*-value of the test and interpret its value.

10.51 Fiat Motors of North America, Inc., has been advertising its 2-year, 24,000-mile warranty. The warranty covers the engine, transmission, and drive train of all new Fiat-made cars for up to 2 years or 24,000 miles, whichever comes first. However, one Fiat dealer believes the 2-year part of the warranty is unnecessary since μ, the true mean number of miles driven by Fiat owners in 2 years, is greater than 24,000 miles. Suppose the dealer wishes to test

H_0: $\mu = 24,000$

H_a: $\mu > 24,000$

at a significance level of $\alpha = .01$.

a. Give the form of the rejection region for this test. Locate the rejection region, α, and the critical value on a sketch of the standard normal curve. (Assume the sample size will be sufficient to guarantee normality of the test statistic.)

b. A random sample of 32 new Fiat owners produced the following statistics on number of miles driven after 2 years: $\bar{x} = 24,517$ and $s = 1,866$. Calculate the appropriate test statistic.

c. Make the appropriate conclusion in terms of the problem.

d. Describe a Type I error in terms of the problem.

e. Describe a Type II error in terms of the problem.

f. Calculate the p-value of the test and interpret its value.

*g. Calculate β for $\mu_a = 25,000$.

*h. Calculate the power of the test for $\mu_a = 26,000$.

10.52 Suppose the observed significance level (p-value) of a test is .07.

a. For what values of α would you reject H_0?

b. For what values of α would you fail to reject H_0?

10.53 Refer to the data of Appendix A.2. Suppose we wish to test the null hypothesis that μ_1, the average return-to-pay ratio of CEOs in the automotive industry, is identical to μ_2, the average return-to-pay ratio of CEOs in the banking industry:

H_0: $(\mu_1 - \mu_2) = 0$

The alternative of interest is that the automotive industry mean is greater than the banking industry mean:

H_a: $(\mu_1 - \mu_2) > 0$

a. Interpret Type I and Type II errors in the context of the problem.

b. Which error has the more serious consequences for an automotive industry CEO? A banking industry CEO?

■ *CASE STUDY 10.1*

Drug Screening: A Statistical Decision Problem

Pharmaceutical companies are continually searching for new drugs. Charles W. Dunnett, in his essay* "Drug Screening: The Never-Ending Search for New and Better Drugs," writes that

> ... research chemists often know what types of chemical structures to look for to treat a particular disease, and the chemists can set about synthesizing compounds of the desired type. Sometimes, however, their knowledge may be vague; resulting in such a wide range of possibilities that many, many compounds have to be made and tested. In such a case, the search is very lengthy and requires years of effort by many people to develop a useful new drug.

Testing these thousands of compounds for the few that might be effective is known in the pharmaceutical industry as *drug screening*. Because of the obvious impact on human health, drug screening requires highly organized, efficient testing methods, and "anything that improves the efficiency of the testing procedure," writes Dunnett, "increases the chance of discovering a new cure."

Drug-screening techniques have improved tremendously over the years, and one of the major contributors to this continual improvement is the discipline of statistics. In fact, Dunnett views the drug-screening procedure in its preliminary stage in terms of a statistical decision problem: "In drug screening, two actions are possible: (1) to 'reject' the drug, meaning to conclude that the tested drug has little or no effect, in which case it will be set aside and a new drug selected for screening; and (2) to 'accept' the drug provisionally, in which case it will be subjected to further, more refined experimentation." Since it is the goal of the researcher to find a drug that effects a cure, the null and alternative hypotheses in a statistical test would take the following form:

H_0:   Drug is ineffective in treating a particular disease

H_a: Drug is effective in treating a particular disease

Dunnett comments on the possible errors associated with the drug-screening procedure: "To abandon a drug when in fact it is a useful one (a *false negative*) is clearly undesirable, yet there is always some risk in that. On the other hand, to go ahead with further, more expensive testing of a drug that is in fact useless (a *false positive*) wastes time and money that could have been spent on testing other compounds." Thus, to a statistician, a false positive result corresponds to a Type I error (i.e., to reject H_0 when in fact H_0 is true), and a false negative result corresponds to a Type II error (i.e., to fail to reject H_0 when in fact H_0 is false).

For this case study, we will consider the following hypothetical drug-screening experiment. A drug developed by a pharmaceutical company for possible treatment of cancerous tumors is to be screened. An investigator implants cancer cells in 100 laboratory mice. From this group, 50 mice are randomly selected and treated with the drug. The remaining 50 are left untreated, and comprise what is known as the *control group*. After a fixed length of time, the actual tumor weights of all the mice in the experiment are measured. If μ_1, the population mean tumor weight of all mice that could be treated with the drug, is significantly less than μ_2, the population mean tumor weight of all untreated mice, then the drug will be provisionally accepted and subjected to further testing; otherwise, the drug will be rejected.

a. Give the appropriate null and alternative hypotheses for the drug-screening test.

b. What are the Type I and Type II errors for this test? (Explain in terms of false positive and false negative results.)

c. Using a significance level of $\alpha = .01$, set up the rejection region for the test.

---

* From Tanur, J. M., et al., eds. Statistics: A Guide to the Unknown. *San Francisco: Holden-Day, 1978.*

d. The experimental results are summarized in Table 10.4. Compute the difference between sample means, $(\bar{x}_1 - \bar{x}_2)$. Explain why we should not base our decision on this value alone.

Table 10.4 Results of Drug-Screening Experiment

Treated Group	Control Group
$\bar{x}_1 = 1.23$ grams	$\bar{x}_2 = 1.37$ grams
$s_1 = .55$ gram	$s_2 = .21$ gram

e. Use the results given in the table to calculate the required test statistic. [*Hint:* The standard error of the point estimate is

$$\sqrt{\frac{\sigma_1^2}{n_1} + \frac{\sigma_2^2}{n_2}} \approx \sqrt{\frac{s_1^2}{n_1} + \frac{s_2^2}{n_2}}$$

from Section 8.5.]

f. Should the pharmaceutical company provisionally accept the drug and subject it to further testing?

■ CASE STUDY 10.2 ■

Schlitz Versus Budweiser—Mug to Mug

In 1980, the Schlitz Brewing Company reported that its beer sales had decreased 50% over a 5-year period. In an effort to revive depressed sales, then-CEO Frank Sellinger announced that Schlitz would broadcast a taste test featuring 100 beer drinkers on live television during half time of the December 28, 1980, National Football League AFC wildcard playoff game between the Houston Oilers and the Oakland Raiders.

During the live broadcast, Schlitz claimed that the 100 beer drinkers selected for the taste test were "loyal" drinkers of Budweiser, the industry's best-selling beer. Each of the participants was served two beers, one Schlitz and one Budweiser, in unlabeled ceramic mugs. Tasters were then told to make a choice by pulling an electronic switch left or right in the direction of the beer they preferred. (Prior to the test, the tasters were informed that one of the mugs contained their regular beer, Budweiser, and the other contained Schlitz, but the ordering was not revealed.) The percentage of the 100 "loyal" Budweiser drinkers who preferred Schlitz was then tabulated live, in front of millions of football fans.

One beer industry observer was quoted as calling the test "a giant roll of the dice." However, CEO Sellinger disagreed that the move was a gamble: "Some people thought it was risky to do live TV taste tests. But it didn't take nerve, it just took confidence."

The results of the live TV taste test showed that 46 of the 100 "loyal" Budweiser beer drinkers preferred Schlitz. Schlitz, of course, labeled the outcome "an impressive showing" in a magazine advertisement following the test. For the purposes of this case study, let us suppose that market experts hired by Schlitz informed the company that the taste test would be successful in boosting sales if more than 40 of the 100 Budweiser drinkers selected Schlitz as their favorite. Since 46 tasters pulled the switch in the direction of Schlitz, the brewer called the outcome "impressive," and anxiously awaited sales of Schlitz beer to increase. However, do these sample results indicate that the true proportion of "loyal" Budweiser drinkers who prefer Schlitz is larger than 40%? We can obtain an answer to this question by applying the general concepts of hypothesis testing outlined in this chapter.

a. Set up the null and alternative hypotheses of a test to determine whether the true proportion π of all "loyal" Budweiser drinkers who would prefer Schlitz over Budweiser in a similar taste test is larger than .40.

b. For a significance level of $\alpha = .05$, specify the form of the rejection region. Locate the rejection region, α, and the critical value on a sketch of the standard normal curve.

c. Recall from Section 8.4 that the sampling distribution of p, the sample proportion of Budweiser drinkers who prefer Schlitz, has a standard deviation given by $\sqrt{\pi(1 - \pi)}$. In Chapter 11, we will show that the appropriate test statistic for testing a hypothesis about a population proportion π is

$$z = \frac{p - \pi_0}{\sqrt{\pi_0(1 - \pi_0)}}$$

where π_0 is the hypothesized value of π specified in H_0. Use this formula and the results of the live taste test to compute the value of the test statistic.

d. What is the proper conclusion, in terms of the problem?

e. A valid test of hypothesis, of course, requires that the 100 tasters actually represent a random sample from the segment of the beer-drinking population who are truly "loyal" Budweiser drinkers. Discuss the problems with obtaining a truly random sample from the target population of "loyal" Budweiser drinkers. Do you think it is possible to select such a sample? In what way(s) could Schlitz have selected the sample (either intentionally or unintentionally) to bias the results in their favor?

---

*Reported in *Orlando* Sentinel Star, *Dec. 11, 1980.*

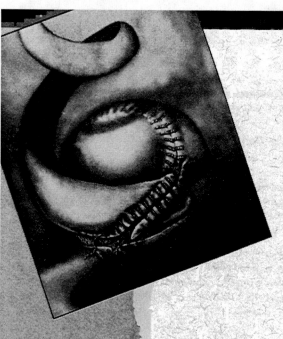

Chapter 11

HYPOTHESIS TESTING: APPLICATIONS

Recall that Appendix A.7 describes data collected on the commitment levels of two types of employees: those who stay with their firm for a relatively long period of time and those who leave for employment elsewhere. Do "stayers" tend to have a higher mean level of commitment to their firm than "leavers"? In this chapter, we learn how to apply the methodology of hypothesis testing to answer questions of this type. The commitment data are analyzed in Case Study 11.2.

■ CONTENTS

11.1 Diagnosing a Hypothesis Test: Determining the Target Parameter

In this chapter, we present applications of the hypothesis-testing logic developed in Chapter 10. Among the population parameters to be considered are those for which we developed estimation procedures in Chapter 8: μ, $(\mu_1 - \mu_2)$, π, and $(\pi_1 - \pi_2)$.

The concepts of a hypothesis test are the same for all these parameters; the null and alternative hypotheses, test statistic, and rejection region all have the same general form (see Chapter 10).[*] However, the manner in which the test statistic is actually computed depends on the parameter of interest. For example, in Chapter 10, we saw that the large-sample test statistic for testing a hypothesis about a population mean μ is given by

$$z = \frac{\bar{x} - \mu_0}{\sigma/\sqrt{n}} \qquad \text{(see Example 10.12)}$$

whereas the test statistic for testing a hypothesis about the parameter π is

$$z = \frac{p - \pi_0}{\sqrt{\dfrac{\pi_0(1 - \pi_0)}{n}}} \qquad \text{(see Case Study 10.2)}$$

The key, then, to correctly diagnosing a hypothesis test is to determine first the parameter of interest—a task that can sometimes present difficulties for the introductory statistics student, especially when the parameter is stated in words rather than symbols.

Those who are routinely successful in diagnosing a hypothesis test generally follow a three-step process. First, identify the experimental unit (i.e., the objects upon which the measurements are taken). Second, identify the type of variable, quantitative or qualitative, measured on each experimental unit. Third, determine the target parameter based on the phenomenon of interest and the variable measured. For quantitative data, the target parameter will be either a population mean or variance; for qualitative data, the parameter will be a population proportion.

Often, there are one or more key words in the statement of the problem that indicate the appropriate population parameter. In this section, we present several examples illustrating how to determine the parameter of interest. First, we state in the box at the top of page 512 the key words to look for when conducting a hypothesis test about a population parameter.

---

[*] *In optional Sections 11.7 and 11.8, we consider the population parameters σ^2 and σ_1^2 / σ_2^2. For these cases, the form of the test statistic and rejection region will be different.*

> ### *Diagnosing a Hypothesis Test: Determining the Target Parameter*
>
> | Parameter | Key Words or Phrases |
> |---|---|
> | μ | Mean; average |
> | $(\mu_1 - \mu_2)$ | Difference in means or averages; mean difference; comparison of means or averages |
> | π | Proportion; percentage; fraction; rate |
> | $(\pi_1 - \pi_2)$ | Difference in proportions, percentages, fractions, or rates; comparison of proportions, percentages, fractions, or rates |
> | σ^2 (optional) | Variance; variation; spread; precision |
> | σ_1^2 / σ_2^2 (optional) | Ratio of variances; difference in variation; comparison of variances |

EXAMPLE 11.1
Choosing the Target
Parameter

The "Pepsi Challenge" was a marketing strategy recently used by Pepsi-Cola. A consumer is presented with two cups of cola and asked to select the one that tastes best. Unknown to the consumer, one cup is filled with Pepsi, the other with Coke. Marketers of Pepsi claim that the true fraction of consumers who select their product will exceed .50. What is the parameter of interest to the Pepsi marketers?

SOLUTION In this problem, the experimental units are the consumers and the variable measured is *qualitative*—the consumer chooses either Pepsi or Coke. The key word in the statement of the problem is "fraction." Thus, the parameter of interest is π, where

$\pi = $ True fraction of consumers who favor Pepsi over Coke in the taste test

To test the hypothesis, the marketers will need to present a sample of consumers with the Pepsi Challenge and determine the number in the sample who select Pepsi over Coke. ■

EXAMPLE 11.2
Choosing the Target
Parameter

A broker wants to determine which of two over-the-counter stocks is, on average, more profitable. He will monitor the stocks' daily prices for 1 month and determine whether the mean prices are significantly different. What is the parameter of interest to the broker?

SOLUTION In this problem, the experimental units are days, and the variables measured are stock 1 daily price and stock 2 daily price—both *quantitative* in nature. The key words in the statement of this problem are "on average," "mean," and "different." Thus, there are two means to be compared,

$\mu_1 =$ Mean daily price of stock 1

and

$\mu_2 =$ Mean daily price of stock 2

and the parameter of interest is $(\mu_1 - \mu_2)$. Further, the sample data that the broker will collect will be paired since two measurements, stock 1 price and stock 2 price, will be recorded on the same day for each day in the 1-month study period. Therefore, a hypothesis test for matched pairs is appropriate. ▪

EXAMPLE 11.3
Choosing the Target Parameter

A quality control engineer wants to determine whether a difference exists in the proportions of bolts produced by two different assembly lines that are defective. What is the parameter of interest?

SOLUTION For the quality control engineer, the experimental units are the bolts produced by the assembly lines, and the variable measured is *qualitative*—either the bolt is defective or it is not. The two key words in the statement of the problem are "difference" and "proportions." Therefore, the parameter of interest is $(\pi_1 - \pi_2)$, where

$\pi_1 =$ Proportion of bolts produced by assembly line 1 that are defective

and

$\pi_2 =$ Proportion of bolts produced by assembly line 2 that are defective ▪

In the following sections, we present a summary of the hypothesis-testing procedures for each of the parameters listed in the previous box. In the exercises that follow each section, the target parameter can easily be identified by simply noting the title of the section. However, to properly diagnose a hypothesis test, it is essential to search for the key words in the statement of the problem. For practice, we strongly recommend that you read through all the Supplementary Exercises at the end of the chapter (where the specific parameter is not known a priori) and determine the parameter of interest before attempting to analyze the data.

11.2 Testing a Population Mean

When testing a hypothesis about a population mean, μ, the procedure that we use will depend on whether the sample size n is large (say, $n \geq 30$) or small. The accompanying box contains the elements of a large-sample hypothesis test for μ based on the z statistic. Note that for this case, the only assumption required for the validity of the procedure is that the sample size is in fact large so that the sampling distribution of $\bar{x}$ is normal. Technically, we must know the true population standard deviation σ to use the z statistic, and this is rarely, if ever, the case. However, we established in Chapter 8 that when n is large, the sample standard deviation s provides a good approximation to σ, and the z statistic can be approximated as shown in the box.

Large Samples

Large-Sample Test of Hypothesis About a Population Mean

One-Tailed Test

$H_0: \quad \mu = \mu_0$
$H_a: \quad \mu > \mu_0 \quad$ (or $H_a: \quad \mu < \mu_0$)

Two-Tailed Test

$H_0: \quad \mu = \mu_0$
$H_a: \quad \mu \neq \mu_0$

Test statistic: $\quad z = \dfrac{\bar{x} - \mu_0}{\sigma_{\bar{x}}} \approx \dfrac{\bar{x} - \mu_0}{s/\sqrt{n}}$

Rejection region:
$z > z_\alpha \quad$ (or $z < -z_\alpha$)

Rejection region:
$|z| > z_{\alpha/2}$

where z_α is the z value such that $P(z > z_\alpha) = \alpha$; and $z_{\alpha/2}$ is the z value such that $P(z > z_{\alpha/2}) = \alpha/2$. [*Note:* μ_0 is our symbol for the particular numerical value specified for μ in the null hypothesis.]

Assumption: The sample size must be sufficiently large (say, $n \geq 30$) so that the sampling distribution of $\bar{x}$ is approximately normal and that s provides a good approximation to σ.

EXAMPLE 11.4
Application: One-Tailed Test

Prior to the institution of a new safety program, the average number of on-the-job accidents per day at a factory was 4.5 (recall Example 10.3). To determine whether the safety program has been effective in reducing the average number of accidents per day, a random sample of 120 days is taken after the institution of the new safety program, and the number of accidents per day is recorded. The sample mean and standard deviation were computed as follows:

$$\bar{x} = 3.7 \qquad s = 2.6$$

a. Is there sufficient evidence to conclude (at significance level .01) that the average number of on-the-job accidents per day at the factory has decreased since the institution of the safety program?

b. What is the practical interpretation of the test statistic computed in part **a**?

SOLUTION   **a.**   To determine whether the safety program was effective, we will conduct a test of

$$H_0: \quad \mu = 4.5 \quad \text{(i.e., no change in average number of on-the-job accidents per day)}$$

$$H_a: \quad \mu < 4.5 \quad \text{(i.e., average number of on-the-job accidents per day has decreased)}$$

where μ represents the mean number of on-the-job accidents per day at the factory after institution of the new safety program. Note that the sample size $n = 120$ is sufficiently large so that the sampling distribution of $\bar{x}$ is approximately normal and that s provides a good approximation to σ. Since the required assumption is satisfied, we may proceed with a large-sample test about μ.

Using a significance level of $\alpha = .01$, we will reject the null hypothesis for this one-tailed test if

$$z < -z_{.01} = -2.33$$

This rejection region is shown in Figure 11.1.

FIGURE 11.1

Rejection Region for
Example 11.4

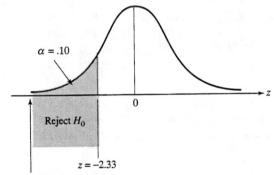

The computed value of the test statistic is

$$z \approx \frac{\bar{x} - \mu_0}{s/\sqrt{n}} = \frac{3.7 - 4.5}{2.6/\sqrt{120}} = -3.37$$

Since this value falls within the rejection region, there is sufficient evidence (at $\alpha = .01$) to conclude that the average number of on-the-job accidents per day at the factory has decreased since the institution of the safety program. It appears that the safety program was effective in reducing the average number of accidents per day.

b. If the null hypothesis is true, $\mu = 4.5$. Recall that for large samples, the sampling distribution of $\bar{x}$ is approximately normal, with mean $\mu_{\bar{x}} = \mu$ and standard deviation $\sigma_{\bar{x}} = \sigma/\sqrt{n}$. Then the z score for $\bar{x}$, under the assumption that H_0 is true, is given by

$$z = \frac{\bar{x} - 4.5}{\sigma/\sqrt{n}}$$

You can see that the test statistic computed in part **a** is simply the (approximate) z score for the sample mean $\bar{x}$, if in fact $\mu = 4.5$. A calculated z score of -3.37 indicates that the value of $\bar{x}$ computed from the sample falls a distance of 3.37 standard deviations below the hypothesized mean of $\mu = 4.5$. Of course, we would not expect to observe a z score this extreme if in fact $\mu = 4.5$. ■

EXAMPLE 11.5
Application: Two-Tailed Test

Refer to Example 8.6. In an attempt to assess the collective ability of Tampa, Florida, property appraisers, we collected a random sample of $n = 50$ observations from the population of values of ratio of sale price to total appraised value in Appendix A.1. (The data are reproduced in Table 11.1.) If the sale price for a piece of property were approximately equal to its total appraised value, then μ, the mean value of the ratio of sale price to total appraised value for all such properties, would equal 1.0. Consequently, we want to test the hypothesis that μ, the population mean ratio, is equal to 1.0 against the alternative that it is different from 1.0.

Table 11.1 Random Sample of $n = 50$ Ratios of Sale
Price to Total Appraised Value

1.36	1.29	1.41	1.07	1.91
1.23	1.06	1.16	1.10	1.04
1.08	1.20	1.22	1.13	1.26
1.22	1.22	1.05	1.12	1.23
1.33	.84	1.60	.60	.69
1.09	1.55	1.34	1.11	2.13
2.08	2.07	1.01	1.32	1.16
1.21	1.64	1.18	1.20	1.74
1.80	2.47	1.48	1.70	1.36
1.27	1.22	1.33	.92	.96

a. Suppose we want a very small chance of rejecting H_0, if in fact μ is equal to 0. That is, it is important that we avoid making a Type I error. Select an appropriate value of the significance level, α.

b. Test whether μ, the population mean ratio, is different from 1.0, using the significance level selected in part **a.** Use the p-value of the test to make your decision.

SOLUTION   **a.** The hypothesis-testing procedure that we have developed gives us the advantage of being able to choose any significance level that we desire. Since the significance level, α, is also the probability of a Type I error, we will choose α to be very small. In general, researchers who consider a Type I error to have very serious practical consequences should perform the test at a very low α value—say, $\alpha = .01$. Other researchers may be willing to tolerate an α value as high as .10 if a Type I error is not deemed a serious error to make in practice. For this example, we will test at $\alpha = .01$.

b. We formulate the following hypotheses:

$$H_0: \quad \mu = 1.0$$

$$H_a: \quad \mu \neq 1.0$$

The sample size is large ($n = 50$); thus, we may proceed with the large-sample (z) test about μ. The data (Table 11.1) were entered into a computer, and SAS was used to conduct the analysis. The SAS printout is displayed in Figure 11.2. The test statistic,

$$z \approx \frac{\bar{x} - 1}{s/\sqrt{n}} = 6.09$$

is shaded on the SAS printout under **T**. (Remember that for large n and σ unknown, the t distribution and z distribution are approximately equal.) The p-value of this test, shaded under **PROB > |T|**, is .0001.

From Section 10.5, we will reject H_0 if our chosen significance level α exceeds this p-value. Since $\alpha = .01$ is larger than p-value $= .0001$, we reject H_0 and conclude that the mean ratio of sale price to total appraised value is significantly different from 1.0 for the residential properties sold in Tampa during 1990. If the null hypothesis is true (i.e., if $\mu = 1.0$), then the probability that we have incorrectly rejected it is equal to $\alpha = .01$.   ■

FIGURE 11.2

SAS Printout for
Example 11.5

Analysis Variable : RATIO_1 (Ratio minus 1)

N Obs	Mean	Std Dev	Std Error	T	Prob>|T|
50	0.3152000	0.3657491	0.0517247	6.0937964	0.0001

The *practical* implications of the result obtained in Example 11.5 remain to be studied further. Perhaps there is a general tendency for Tampa's real estate appraisers to overappraise or underappraise a property's value. Alternatively, a tight housing market may tend to inflate the sale price for residential properties in the city. **It is not always the case that a statistically significant result implies a practically significant result.** The researcher must retain his or her objectivity and judge the practical significance using, among other criteria, his or her knowledge of the subject matter and the phenomenon under investigation.

EXAMPLE 11.6 Confidence Interval Versus Hypothesis Test	Recall from Example 8.6 that a 99% confidence interval for the mean ratio of sale price to total appraised value is (1.18, 1.45). Does the inference derived from this confidence interval agree with the two-tailed test, Example 11.5? Which gives more information, the test of Example 11.5 or the confidence interval of Example 8.6?

SOLUTION In Example 8.6, we concluded that μ exceeds 1 since all the numbers in the 99% confidence interval for μ are greater than 1. This, of course, agrees with our test in Example 11.5. The confidence interval, however, is more informative. Not only can we conclude that μ exceeds 1, but the interval estimate provides additional information on the magnitude of μ that the test cannot provide—namely, that the true mean ratio of sale price to total appraised value falls between 1.18 and 1.45. This implies that, on average, the property appraisers are appraising residential properties in Tampa anywhere from 18% to 45% *below* the sale price. Consequently, in *two-tailed* situations, it is more informative to construct a confidence interval for the target parameter than to conduct a test of hypothesis. ■

Small Samples

Time and cost considerations sometimes limit the sample size to a small number. In this case, the assumption required for a large-sample test of hypothesis about μ will be violated, and s will not provide a reliable estimate of σ. We need a procedure that is appropriate for use with small samples.

A hypothesis test about a population mean, μ, for small samples $(n < 30)$, is based on a t statistic. The elements of the test are listed in the box on page 519.

As we noticed in the development of estimation procedures, when we are making inferences based on small samples, more restrictive assumptions are required than when making inferences from large samples. In particular, the hypothesis test procedure requires the assumption that the population from which the sample is selected is approximately normal.

Notice that the test statistic given in the box is a t statistic and is calculated exactly as our approximation to the large-sample test statistic, z, given earlier in this section. Therefore, just like z, the computed value of t indicates the direction and approximate distance (in units of standard deviations) that the sample mean, $\bar{x}$, is from the hypothesized population mean, μ_0.

Small-Sample of Hypothesis About a Population Mean

One-Tailed Test   *Two-Tailed Test*

H_0: $\mu = \mu_0$ H_0: $\mu = \mu_0$
H_a: $\mu > \mu_0$ (or H_a: $\mu < \mu_0$) H_a: $\mu \neq \mu_0$

$$\text{Test statistic:}\quad t = \frac{\bar{x} - \mu_0}{s/\sqrt{n}}$$

Rejection region: *Rejection region:*
$t > t_\alpha$ (or $t < -t_\alpha$) $|t| > t_{\alpha/2}$

where the distribution of t is based on $(n-1)$ degrees of freedom; t_α is the t value such that $P(t > t_\alpha) = \alpha$; and $t_{\alpha/2}$ is the t value such that $P(t > t_{\alpha/2}) = \alpha/2$.

Assumption: The relative frequency distribution of the population from which the sample was selected is approximately normal.

EXAMPLE 11.7
Application: *p*-Values

The building specifications in a certain city require that the sewer pipe used in residential areas have a mean breaking strength of more than 2,500 pounds per lineal foot. A manufacturer who would like to supply the city with sewer pipe has submitted a bid and provided the following additional information: An independent contractor randomly selected seven sections of the manufacturer's pipe and tested each for breaking strength. The results (pounds per lineal foot) are shown here:

2,610	2,750	2,420	2,510	2,540	2,490	2,680

a. Compute $\bar{x}$ and s for the sample.

b. Is there sufficient evidence to conclude that the manufacturer's sewer pipe meets the required specifications? Use a significance level of $\alpha = .10$.

c. Compute the *p*-value of the test, part **b**. Interpret the result.

SOLUTION

a. The data were entered into a computer, and descriptive statistics were generated using SPSS. The SPSS printout is shown in Figure 11.3 on page 520. The values of the sample mean breaking strength and standard deviation of breaking strengths (shaded) are $\bar{x} = 2,571.4$ and $s = 115.1$.

b. The relevant hypothesis test has the following elements:

FIGURE 11.3

SPSS Printout for
Example 11.7

```
Paired samples t-test:   STRENGTH
                          MU

Variable     Number                 Standard   Standard
             of Cases    Mean       Deviation   Error

STRENGTH        7      2571.4286     115.098    43.503
MU              7      2500.0000       .000      .000
```

(Difference) Mean	Standard Deviation	Standard Error	2-Tail Corr. Prob.	t Value	Degrees of Freedom	2-Tail Prob.
71.4286	115.098	43.503	. .	1.64	6	.152

H_0: $\mu = 2{,}500$ (i.e., the manufacturer's pipe does not meet the city's specifications)

H_a: $\mu > 2{,}500$ (i.e., the pipe meets the specifications)

where μ represents the true mean breaking strength (in pounds per lineal foot) for all sewer pipe produced by this manufacturer. This small-sample $(n = 7)$ test requires the assumption that the relative frequency distribution of the population values of breaking strength for the manufacturer's pipe is approximately normal. Then the test will be based on a t distribution with $(n - 1) = 6$ degrees of freedom. We will thus reject H_0 if

$$t > t_{.10} = 1.440 \qquad \text{(see Figure 11.4)}$$

Substituting the values $\bar{x} = 2{,}571.4$ and $s = 115.1$ yields the test statistic

$$t = \frac{\bar{x} - \mu_0}{s/\sqrt{n}} = \frac{2{,}571.4 - 2{,}500}{115.1/\sqrt{7}} = 1.64$$

This value is also shaded on the SPSS printout of the test results, Figure 11.3. Since this value of t is larger than the critical value of 1.440, we reject H_0. There is sufficient evidence (at significance level $\alpha = .10$) that the manufacturer's pipe meets the city's building specifications.

c. p-values for small-sample tests are computed in the same way as those for large-sample tests, except that we use the t distribution rather than the z distribution. For this upper-tailed test, the computed value of the test statistic is $t_c = 1.64$, and the associated p-value is

$$P(t \geq t_c) = P(t \geq 1.64)$$

FIGURE 11.4

Rejection Region for
Example 11.7

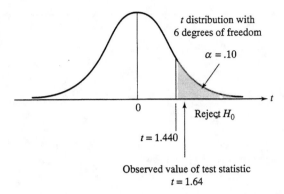

where the distribution of t is based on $(n-1)=6$ degrees of freedom. To find the p-value from the table of critical t values provided in Table 6 of Appendix B, search for the value 1.64 in the row corresponding to 6 df. You can see that 1.64 does not appear in this row but falls between the values 1.943 (in the $t_{.05}$ column) and 1.440 (in the $t_{.10}$ column). The p-value associated with 1.943 is .05, and the p-value associated with 1.440 is .10. Thus, the p-value associated with $t_c = 1.64$ is somewhere between .05 and .10. Since the exact p-value is unknown, we take the conservative approach and report the approximate p-value as the larger of the two endpoints—namely, .10. This (approximate) p-value indicates that the null hypothesis $H_0: \mu = 2,500$ will be rejected in favor of $H_a: \mu > 2,500$ for any fixed significance level α larger than or equal to .10.

Although we can approximate the p-value using Table 6 of Appendix B, usually we will rely on the computer to calculate its exact value. The two-tailed p-value for the test of part **b** is shaded on the SPSS printout, Figure 11.3. Recall (Section 10.5) that the p-value for a one-tailed test is half that for a two-tailed test; consequently, the exact p-value $= .152/2 = .076$. ■

Remember that the small-sample test of Example 11.7 requires the assumption that the sampled population has a relative frequency distribution that is approximately normal. If you know that the population is highly skewed (based on, for example, a stem-and-leaf plot of the sample data), then any inferences derived from the t test are suspect. In this case, we do not perform the t test; instead, we use one of the nonparametric statistical methods discussed in Chapter 18.

Warning

When the sampled population is decidedly nonnormal (e.g., highly skewed), any inferences derived from the small-sample t test for μ are suspect. In this case, one alternative is to use nonparametric sign test discussed in Section 18.2.

EXERCISES

■ *Learning the Mechanics*

11.1   Compute the approximate value of the test statistic z for each of the following situations:
  a. $H_0: \mu = 9.8$, $H_a: \mu > 9.8$; $\bar{x} = 10.0$, $s = 4.3$, $n = 50$
  b. $H_0: \mu = 80$, $H_a: \mu < 80$; $\bar{x} = 75$, $s^2 = 19$, $n = 86$
  c. $H_0: \mu = 8.3$, $H_a: \mu \neq 8.3$; $\bar{x} = 8.2$, $s = .79$, $n = 175$

11.2   A random sample of n observations is selected from a population with unknown mean μ and variance σ^2. For each of the following situations, specify the test statistic and rejection region.
  a. $H_0: \mu = 50$, $H_a: \mu > 50$; $n = 36$, $\bar{x} = 60$, $s^2 = 64$; $\alpha = .05$
  b. $H_0: \mu = 140$, $H_a: \mu \neq 140$; $n = 40$, $\bar{x} = 143.2$, $s = 9.4$; $\alpha = .01$
  c. $H_0: \mu = 10$, $H_a: \mu < 10$; $n = 50$, $\bar{x} = 9.5$, $s = .35$; $\alpha = .10$

11.3   To test the null hypothesis $H_0: \mu = 10$, a random sample of n observations is selected from a normal population. Specify the rejection region for each of the following combinations of H_a, n, and α:
  a. $H_a: \mu \neq 10$, $n = 15$, $\alpha = .05$ **b.** $H_a: \mu \neq 10$, $n = 15$, $\alpha = .01$
  c. $H_a: \mu < 10$, $n = 15$, $\alpha = .05$ **d.** $H_a: \mu > 10$, $n = 5$, $\alpha = .10$
  e. $H_a: \mu > 10$, $n = 25$, $\alpha = .10$

11.4   A random sample of n observations is selected from a normal population. For each of the following situations, specify the rejection region, test statistic, and conclusion.
  a. $H_0: \mu = 3,000$, $H_a: \mu \neq 3,000$; $\bar{x} = 2,958$, $s = 39$, $n = 8$; $\alpha = .05$
  b. $H_0: \mu = 6$, $H_a: \mu > 6$; $\bar{x} = 6.3$, $s = .3$, $n = 7$; $\alpha = .01$
  c. $H_0: \mu = 22$, $H_a: \mu < 22$; $\bar{x} = 13.0$, $s = 6$, $n = 17$; $\alpha = .05$

11.5   A random sample of 49 measurements produced the following sums:

$$\Sigma x = 50.3 \qquad \Sigma x^2 = 68$$

  a. Test the null hypothesis that $\mu = 1.18$ against the alternative that $\mu < 1.18$. Use $\alpha = .01$.
  b. Test the null hypothesis that $\mu = 1.18$ against the alternative that $\mu < 1.18$. Use $\alpha = .10$.
  c. Find the p-value of the test, part **a**.
  d. Find the p-value of the test, part **b**.

11.6   A random sample of five measurements from a normally distributed population yielded the following data:

12   4   3   5   5

  a. Test the null hypothesis that $\mu = 4$, against the alternative hypothesis that $\mu \neq 4$. Use $\alpha = .01$.
  b. Test the null hypothesis that $\mu = 4$, against the alternative hypothesis that $\mu > 4$. Use $\alpha = .01$.
  c. Find the p-value of the test, part **a**.
  d. Find the p-value of the test, part **b**.

■ *Applying the Concepts*

> [*Note:* In all the Applying the Concepts exercises for this chapter, you should carefully define any notation used, perform all steps of the relevant hypothesis test, state a conclusion in terms of the problem, and specify any assumptions required for the validity of the procedure.]

11.7 According to *Chance* (Fall 1994), the average number of faxes transmitted in the United States each minute is 88,000.
a. Set up the null and alternative hypotheses for testing this claim.
b. Describe how to collect the data necessary to carry out the test, part **a**.

11.8 Stocks on the National Association of Security Dealers (NASD) system were analyzed in *Financial Analysts Journal* (Jan./Feb. 1993). The annualized monthly returns for a sample of 13 large-firm NASD stocks were computed and are summarized as follows: $\bar{x} = 13.50\%$, $s = 23.84\%$. Conduct a test of hypothesis to determine whether the mean annualized monthly return for large-firm NASD stocks exceeds 10%. Use $\alpha = .05$.

11.9 "Deep hole" drilling is a family of drilling processes used when the ratio of hole depth to hole diameter exceeds 10. Successful deep hole drilling depends on the satisfactory discharge of the drill chip. An experiment was conducted to investigate the performance of deep hole drilling when chip congestion exists (*Journal of Engineering for Industry*, May 1993). The length (in millimeters) of 50 drill chips resulted in the following summary statistics: $\bar{x} = 81.2$ mm, $s = 50.2$ mm. Conduct a test to determine whether the true mean drill chip length, μ, differs from 75 mm. Use a significance level of $\alpha = .01$.

11.10 Radium-226 is a naturally occurring radioactive gas. Elevated levels of radium-226 in metropolitan Dade County (Florida) were recently investigated (*Florida Scientist*, Summer/Autumn 1991). The data in the accompanying table are radium-226 levels (measured in pCi/L) for 26 soil specimens collected in southern Dade County. The Environmental Protection Agency (EPA) has set maximum exposure levels of radium-226 at 4.0 pCi/L. Use the information in the accompanying MINITAB printout to determine whether the mean radium-226 level of soil specimens collected in southern Dade County is less than the EPA limit of 4.0 pCi/L. Use $\alpha = .10$.

1.46	.58	4.31	1.02	.17	2.92	.91	.43	.91
1.30	8.24	3.51	6.87	1.43	1.44	4.49	4.21	1.84
5.92	1.86	1.41	1.70	2.02	1.65	1.40	.75	

Source: Moore, H. E. and Gussow, D. G. "Radium and radon in Dade County ground water and soil samples." *Florida Scientist*, Vol. 54, No. 3/4, Summer/Autumn, 1991, p. 155 (portion of Table 3).

	N	MEAN	MEDIAN	TRMEAN	STDEV	SEMEAN
RadLevel	26	2.413	1.555	2.264	2.081	0.408

	MIN	MAX	Q1	Q3
RadLevel	0.170	8.240	0.993	3.685

11.11 Every so often, one of the major U.S. car manufacturers announces a recall of some of its automobiles that have been found to be defective. A study was conducted to investigate the impact of automobile recall announcements on the equity holders of the manufacturer's competitors (*Quarterly Journal of Business & Economics*, Autumn 1986). For each of a sample of 112 recalls that were severe in nature (e.g., problems that possibly could result in engine compartment and fuel tank fires, loss of steering or brake control, and repeated engine stalling), the researchers measured the abnormal rate of return for competitors' stocks 2 days after the recall was announced. (The abnormal return rate is the difference between the actual rate of return and the expected return that would have transpired in the absence of a recall.) A summary of the results follows:

$$\bar{x} = .0050 \qquad s = .0233$$

a. Is there sufficient evidence to conclude (at significance level $\alpha = .05$) that the average abnormal rate of return 2 days after the recall announcement exceeds 0? (If the average abnormal return rate is greater than 0, the researchers will conclude that the recall announcement had a positive impact on competitors' car sales.)

b. Conduct the test of part **a** assuming that the number of recall announcements in the sample is 25. Interpret the result.

c. Compute the *p*-values of the tests, parts **a** and **b**. Interpret the results.

11.12 Farm and power equipment dealers are typically dependent on a primary supplier organization for many of their business needs. These suppliers often demand control over many of the dealers' decisions. To determine the degree to which dealers are dependent on suppliers, a national survey of 226 farm and power equipment dealers was conducted. The study revealed the following summary statistics on the total number of suppliers engaged by the dealers:

$$\bar{x} = 3.12 \qquad s = 1.91$$

(*Academy of Management Journal*, Mar. 1989). Use this information to test the hypothesis that the true mean number of suppliers engaged by farm and power equipment dealers exceeds 2. Compute the *p*-value of the test and interpret the result.

11.13 The effect of machine breakdowns on the performance of a manufacturing system was investigated using computer simulation (*Industrial Engineering*, Aug. 1990). The simulation study focused on a single machine tool system with several characteristics, including a mean interarrival time of 1.25 minutes, a constant processing time of 1 minute, and a machine that breaks down 10% of the time. After $n = 5$ independent simulation runs of length 160 hours, the mean throughput per 40-hour week was $\bar{x} = 1,908.8$ parts. For a system with no breakdowns, the mean throughput for a 40-hour week will be equal to 1,920 parts. Assuming the standard deviation of the five sample runs was $s = 18$ parts per 40-hour week, test the hypothesis that the true mean throughput per 40-hour week for the system is less than 1,920 parts. Test using $\alpha = .05$.

11.14 How do the makers of Kleenex know how many tissues to put in a box? According to the *Wall Street Journal* (Sept. 21, 1984), the marketing experts at Kimberly Clark Corporation have "little doubt that the company should put 60 tissues in each pack." The researchers determined that 60 is "the average number of times people blow their nose during a cold" by asking hundreds of customers to keep count of their Kleenex use in diaries. Suppose a random sample of 250 Kleenex users yielded the following summary statistics on the number of times they blew their nose when they had a cold:

$$\bar{x} = 57 \qquad s = 26$$

Is this sufficient evidence to dispute the researchers' claim? Test at $\alpha = .05$.

11.15 Refer to Exercise 8.12 and the random sample of 50 return-to-pay ratios of CEOs selected from the data described in Appendix A.2. A SAS printout for testing the null hypothesis that the true mean return-to-pay ratio of CEOs is equal to .10 is displayed here. Interpret the results of the test.

```
Analysis Variable : RATIO_01 (Ratio minus .1)
```

N Obs	Mean	Std Dev	Std Error	T	Prob>|T|
50	-0.0488000	0.0452977	0.0064061	-7.6177919	0.0001

11.3 Testing a Population Proportion

The procedure described in the box is used to test a hypothesis about a population proportion π, based on a large sample from the target population. (Recall that π represents the probability of success in a binomial experiment.)

Large-Sample Test of Hypothesis About a Population Proportion

One-Tailed Test

$H_0: \quad \pi = \pi_0$

$H_a: \quad \pi > \pi_0 \quad$ (or $H_a: \quad \pi < \pi_0$)

Two-Tailed Test

$H_0: \quad \pi = \pi_0$

$H_a: \quad \pi \neq \pi_0$

Test statistic: $\quad z = \dfrac{p - \pi_0}{\sqrt{\pi_0(1 - \pi_0)/n}}$

Rejection region:

$z > z_\alpha \quad$ (or $z < -z_\alpha$)

Rejection region:

$|z| > z_{\alpha/2}$

where $p = x/n =$ sample proportion of "successes"

Assumption: The sample size n is large; this will usually be satisfied if the interval $p \pm 2\sqrt{p(1 - p)/n}$ does not contain 0 or 1.

For the procedure to be valid, the sample size must be sufficiently large to guarantee approximate normality of the sampling distribution of the sample proportion, p. A general rule of thumb for determining whether n is "sufficiently large" is that the interval $p \pm 2\sqrt{p(1 - p)/n}$ does not include 0 or 1.

EXAMPLE 11.8

Application: Rejection
Region Approach

An *American Demographics* study conducted in 1980 found that 40% of new car buyers were women. Suppose that in a random sample of $n = 120$ new car buyers in 1995, 57 were women. Does this evidence indicate that the true proportion of new car buyers in 1995 who were women is significantly larger than .40, the 1980 proportion? Use the rejection region approach, testing at significance level $\alpha = .05$.

SOLUTION   We wish to perform a large-sample test about a population proportion, π:

H_0: $\pi = .40$ (i.e., no change from 1980 to 1995)

H_a: $\pi > .40$ (i.e., proportion of new car buyers who were women was greater in 1995)

where π represents the true proportion of all new car buyers in 1995 who were women.

At significance level $\alpha = .05$, the rejection region for this one-tailed test consists of all values of z for which

$z > z_{.05} = 1.645$ (see Figure 11.5)

FIGURE 11.5

Rejection Region for
Example 11.8

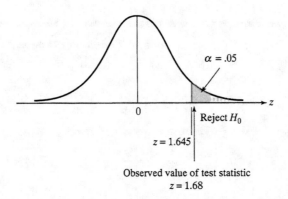

The test statistic requires the calculation of the sample proportion, p, of new car buyers who were women:

$$p = \frac{\text{Number of sampled new car buyers who were women}}{\text{Number of new car buyers sampled}}$$

$$= \frac{57}{120} = .475$$

Substituting, we obtain the following value of the test statistic:

$$z = \frac{p - \pi_0}{\sqrt{\pi_0(1 - \pi_0)/n}} = \frac{.475 - .40}{\sqrt{(.40)(.60)/120}} = 1.68$$

This value of z lies within the rejection region; we thus conclude that the proportion of new car buyers in 1995 who were women increased significantly from .40. The probability of our having made a Type I error (rejecting H_0 when, in fact, it is true) is $\alpha = .05$.

Note that the interval

$$p \pm 2\sqrt{p(1 - p)/n} = .475 \pm 2\sqrt{(.475)(.525)/120}$$

$$= .475 \pm .091$$

does not contain 0 or 1. Thus, the sample size is large enough to guarantee the validity of the hypothesis test. ■

EXAMPLE 11.9
Application: *p*-Values

Refer to Example 11.8. Calculate the observed significance level (p-value) of the test and interpret its value.

SOLUTION For this large-sample, upper-tailed test, the computed value of the test statistic is $z_c = 1.68$ Thus, the p-value is

$$P(z > z_c) = P(z > 1.68)$$

From Table 5, Appendix B, this probability is $.5 - .4535 = .0465$.

Remember, p-value $= .0465$ is the minimum α value that leads to a rejection of the null hypothesis. Consequently, we will reject H_0 for any α value exceeding .0465 (as in Example 11.8) but will fail to reject H_0 for α values below .0465. Therefore, a researcher who desires a Type I error rate of only $\alpha = .01$ or $\alpha = .02$ will have insufficient evidence to say that the proportion of new car buyers who were women in 1995 exceeds .40. ■

Although small-sample procedures are available for testing hypotheses about a population proportion, the details are omitted from our discussion. It is our experience that they are of limited utility, since most surveys of binomial populations (for example, opinion polls) performed in the real would use samples that are large enough to use the techniques of this section.

EXERCISES

■ *Learning the Mechanics*

11.16 A random sample of n observations is selected from a binomial population to test the null hypothesis that $\pi = .40$. Specify the rejection region for each of the following combinations of H_a and α:
  a. $H_a: \pi \neq .40, \quad \alpha = .05$ **b.** $H_a: \pi < .40, \quad \alpha = .05$ **c.** $H_a: \pi > .40, \quad \alpha = .10$
  d. $H_a: \pi < .40, \quad \alpha = .01$ **e.** $H_a: \pi \neq .40, \quad \alpha = .01$

11.17 A random sample of n observations is selected from a binomial population. For each of the following situations, specify the rejection region, test statistic value, and conclusion:
  a. $H_0: \pi = .10, \quad H_a: \pi > .10; \quad p = .13, \quad n = 200; \quad \alpha = .10$
  b. $H_0: \pi = .05, \quad H_a: \pi < .05; \quad p = .04, \quad n = 1,124; \quad \alpha = .05$
  c. $H_0: \pi = .90, \quad H_a: \pi \neq 90; \quad p = .73, \quad n = 125; \quad \alpha = .01$

11.18 A random sample of 100 observations from a binomial population resulted in 45 successes.
  a. Test the null hypothesis that the true proportion of successes in the population is .5 against the alternative hypothesis that $\pi < .5$. Use $\alpha = .05$.
  b. Test $H_0: \pi = .35$ against $H_a: \pi \neq .35$ at $\alpha = .05$.
  c. Test $H_0: \pi = .4$ against $H_a: \pi > .4$ at $\alpha = .05$.

■ *Applying the Concepts*

11.19 According to *Harpers* (Apr.–Aug. 1994), 52% of all Americans would rather spend a week in jail than be president of the United States.
  a. Set up the null and alternative hypotheses for testing this assertion.
  b. Describe how to collect the data necessary to carry out the test, part **a**.

11.20 Hospital patients over the age of 65 apparently face a high risk of serious treatment errors, according to a study in the *Journal of the American Geriatric Society* (Dec. 1990). The records of 122 randomly selected elderly patients were checked for errors in their prescribed medications. Of these, 73 patients were found to have at least one erroneously prescribed medication (i.e., they received an unneeded drug that might cause harmful side effects, or they failed to receive a necessary drug). Prior to the study, the researcher did not expect such a high error rate. Suppose the researcher wants to test whether the true percentage of elderly (over age 65) patients who have at least one erroneously prescribed drug exceeds .20.
  a. Set up the null and alternative hypothesis of interest to the researchers.
  b. Conduct the test, part **a**. Use $\alpha = .05$.
  c. Compute the p-value of the test. Interpret the result.

11.21 Researchers at the University of Rochester studied the friction that occurs in the paper-feeding process of a photocopier (*Journal of Engineering for Industry*, May 1993). The experiment involved monitoring the displacement of individual sheets of paper in a stack fed through the copier. If no sheet except the top one moved more than 25% of the total stroke distance, the feed was considered successful. In a stack of 100 sheets of paper, the feeding process was successful 94 times. The success rate of the feeder is designed to be .90. Test to determine whether the true success rate of the feeder exceeds .90. Use $\alpha = .10$.

11.22 To significantly reduce soil erosion in our country, the Conservation Title of the 1985 farm bill requires that conservation compliance be implemented by 1995. Despite controversy over the bill, the U.S. Soil Conservation Service (SCS) claims that 80% of farmers who already have a soil conservation plan think their plan is reasonable and practical (*Prairie Farmer*, Mar. 20, 1990). An independent survey conducted by *Prairie Farmer* magazine found that of 144 Indiana farmers who have a conservation plan, only 78 believe their plan is realistic.

a. Does this survey refute or support the SCS claim? Test using $\alpha = .01$.

b. Compute the *p*-value of the test. Interpret the result.

11.23 *Jeopardy!* is a television game show in which three contestants answer general-knowledge questions on a wide variety of topics and earn money for each correct answer. In the Final Jeopardy round, contestants bet an amount between $0 and their total accumulated earnings that they will answer the final question correctly. If the player answers correctly, the bet amount is added to the player's total; if the player answers incorrectly, the bet amount is subtracted from his or her total. The contestant with the highest total amount wins, thereby earning the right to defend his or her championship the next day. *Chance* (Spring 1994) collected data for a sample of 218 *Jeopardy!* games. In these 218 games, the defending champion won 126 times. Conduct a test of hypothesis to determine whether the defending *Jeopardy!* champion has a better than 50–50 chance of winning the next day. Use $\alpha = .01$.

11.24 Concerned about airport and airline security, the Federal Aviation Administration (FAA) has begun imposing sanctions against airlines that fail security tests. One series of tests conducted at Los Angeles International Airport (LAX) showed that security guards detected only 72 of the 100 mock weapons carried on by FAA inspectors or included in their carry-on luggage (*Gainesville Sun*, Dec. 11, 1987). According to the FAA, this "detection rate was well below the national rate of .80." Is there sufficient evidence to conclude that the mock weapon detection rate at LAX is less than the national rate of .80? Test using $\alpha = .10$.

11.25 Researchers at the University of South Florida College of Medicine conducted a study of the drug usage of U.S. physicians (*Journal of the American Medical Association*, May 6, 1992). The anonymous survey of 5,426 randomly selected physicians revealed that 7.9% (or 429) experienced substance abuse or drug dependency in their lifetime. Test the hypothesis that more than 5% of U.S. physicians have abused or depended on drugs in their lifetime. Use $\alpha = .10$.

11.26 Refer to the University of Minnesota study of label measurements on brand-name jeans, Exercise 8.31. Recall that 18 of 240 pairs of jeans sold in Minneapolis had waist or inseam measurements that fell within .5 inch of the value stated on the label. Use this information to test the hypothesis that the true percentage of jeans sold in Minneapolis with inseam and waist measurements that fall within .5 inch of the labels is less than 10%. Use the *p*-value approach to test the hypothesis.

11.4 Testing the Difference Between Two Population Means: Independent Samples

Suppose we want to compare the means of two populations based on independent random samples collected from the populations. In many practical applications, we want to determine whether the two means differ.

Large Samples

The procedure described in the accompanying box is applicable for testing a hypothesis about $(\mu_1 - \mu_2)$, the difference between two population means, when the sample sizes are sufficiently large.

Large-Sample Procedure for Testing H_0: $(\mu_1 - \mu_2) = 0$ [*]

One-Tailed Test

H_a: $(\mu_1 - \mu_2) > 0$
[or H_a: $(\mu_1 - \mu_2) < 0$]

Two-Tailed Test

H_a: $(\mu_1 - \mu_2) \neq 0$

Test statistic: $z = \dfrac{\bar{x}_1 - \bar{x}_2}{\sigma_{\bar{x}_1 - \bar{x}_2}} \approx \dfrac{\bar{x}_1 - \bar{x}_2}{\sqrt{\dfrac{s_1^2}{n_1} + \dfrac{s_2^2}{n_2}}}$

Rejection region:
$z > z_\alpha$ [or $z < -z_\alpha$]

Rejection region:
$|z| > z_{\alpha/2}$

Assumptions: **1.** The sample sizes n_1 and n_2 are sufficiently large—say, $n_1 \geq 30$ and $n_2 \geq 30$.
  2. The samples are selected randomly and independently from the target populations.

EXAMPLE 11.10
Application: Large Samples

Studies have shown that in a nonbusiness (e.g., academic) setting, those who tend to have job mobility are predominantly better performers. To examine the performance turnover relationship in a business setting, a researcher examined the personnel records of a large national oil company (*Academy of Management Journal*, Mar. 1982). The sample consisted of 174 employees who were classified as "stayers" (those who stayed with the company from 1964 through 1979) and 355 former employees who were classified as "leavers" (those who left the company at varying points during the 15-year period). The company's annual performance appraisals corresponding to the initial years of service were used to form an initial performance rating for each employee. Summary statistics on initial performance for the two groups of employees are provided in Table 11.2. (The ratings were assigned using a 5-point scale, where 1 = low performance and 5 = high performance.)

---

[*] *To test whether $(\mu_1 - \mu_2)$ is equal to some hypothesized nonzero value D_0 (i.e., H_0: $\mu_1 - \mu_2 = D_0$), use the test statistic*

$$z = \frac{(\bar{x}_1 - \bar{x}_2) - D_0}{\sigma_{(\bar{x}_1 - \bar{x}_2)}}$$

Table 11.2 Summary of Performance
Ratings, Example 11.10

Performance Ratings	
Stayers	Leavers
$n_1 = 174$	$n_2 = 355$
$\bar{x}_1 = 3.51$	$\bar{x}_2 = 3.24$
$s_1 = 51$	$s_2 = .52$

a. Is there evidence of a difference between the mean initial performance ratings of stayers and leavers? Test using $\alpha = .01$.

b. If the means do, in fact, differ, how large is the difference?

SOLUTION **a.** For this problem, let μ_1 represent the mean initial performance rating of stayers and μ_2 represent the mean initial performance rating
of leavers. Then the researcher wants to test the hypotheses

H_0: $(\mu_1 - \mu_2) = 0$ (i.e., no difference between mean initial performance
ratings of stayers and leavers)

H_a: $(\mu_1 - \mu_2) \neq 0$ (i.e., mean initial performance ratings of stayers and
leavers differ)

This two-tailed, large-sample (since both n_1 and n_2 exceed 30) test is
based on a z statistic. Thus, we will reject H_0 if $|z| > z_{\alpha/2} = z_{.005}$.
Since $z_{.005} = 2.58$, the rejection region is given by

$z > 2.58$ or $z < -2.58$ (see Figure 11.6 on page 532)

We compute the test statistic as follows:

$$z \approx \frac{\bar{x}_1 - \bar{x}_2}{\sqrt{\dfrac{s_1^2}{n_1} + \dfrac{s_2^2}{n_2}}} = \frac{3.51 - 3.24}{\sqrt{\dfrac{(.51)^2}{174} + \dfrac{(.52)^2}{355}}} = 5.68$$

Since this computed value of $z = 5.68$ lies in the rejection region,
there is sufficient evidence (at $\alpha = .01$) to conclude that the mean
initial performance rating of stayers is significantly different from
the mean initial performance rating of leavers. The probability of
our having committed a Type I error is $\alpha = .01$.

b. As we discovered in Section 11.2, the information provided by a
two-tailed test of hypothesis is limited. In part **a**, we determined

FIGURE 11.6

Rejection Region for
Example 11.10

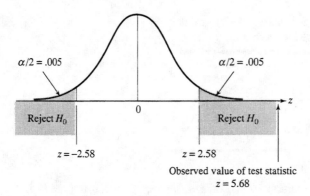

$\alpha/2 = .005$ $\alpha/2 = .005$

Reject H_0 Reject H_0

$z = -2.58$ $z = 2.58$

Observed value of test statistic
$z = 5.68$

that the mean initial performance ratings of the two groups of em-ployees differ; but we have only a point estimate of the magnitude of the difference, namely, $(\bar{x}_1 - \bar{x}_2) = (3.51 - 3.24) = .27$. To find an interval estimate of the difference, we construct a 99% con-fidence interval for $(\mu_1 - \mu_2)$:

$$(\bar{x}_1 - \bar{x}_2) \pm z_{.005} \sqrt{\frac{\sigma_1^2}{n_1} + \frac{\sigma_2^2}{n_2}} \approx (3.51 - 3.24) \pm 2.58 \sqrt{\frac{(.51)^2}{174} + \frac{(.52)^2}{355}}$$

$$= .27 \pm .12$$

or, (.15, .39). Note that the interval includes only positive numbers. This implies that the difference $(\mu_1 - \mu_2)$ is positive. That is, the mean initial performance rating of stayers (μ_1) exceeds the mean initial performance rating of leavers (μ_2). This differ-ence, although statistically significant, may be too small for the re-searcher to attach any practical significance to the result. ■

Small Samples

When the sample sizes n_1 and n_2 are inadequate to permit use of the large-sample pro-cedure of Example 11.10, modifications may be made to perform a small-sample test of hypothesis about the difference between two population means. The test procedure is based on assumptions that are, again, more restrictive than in the large-sample case. The elements of the hypothesis test and required assumptions are listed in the next box.

Small-Sample Procedure for Testing H_0: $(\mu_1 - \mu_2) = 0$ *

One-Tailed Test

H_a: $(\mu_1 - \mu_2) > 0$
[or H_a: $(\mu_1 - \mu_2) < 0$]

Two-Tailed Test

H_a: $(\mu_1 - \mu_2) \neq 0$

Test statistic: $t = \dfrac{\bar{x}_1 - \bar{x}_2}{\sqrt{s_p^2(1/n_1 + 1/n_2)}}$

Rejection region:
$t > t_\alpha$ [or $t < -t_\alpha$]

Rejection region:
$|t| > t_{\alpha/2}$

where $s_p^2 = \dfrac{(n_1 - 1)s_1^2 + (n_2 - 1)s_2^2}{n_1 + n_2 - 2}$

and the distribution of t is based on $(n_1 + n_2 - 2)$ degrees of freedom.

Assumptions: **1.** The populations from which the samples are selected both have approximately normal relative frequency distributions.
  2. The variances of the two populations are equal.
  3. The random samples are selected in an independent manner from the two populations.

EXAMPLE 11.11
Application: Small Samples

Refer to Example 8.19 and the *Journal of Marketing* study of competitive and coordinative bargaining strategies. A sample of 16 buyers was divided into two equal groups; one group of buyers used the competitive strategy whereas the other used the coordinative strategy. The individual buyer savings for the two groups are reproduced in Table 11.3. In theory, the mean buyer savings for the competitive strategy will be less than the corresponding mean for the coordinative strategy. Test the theory using $\alpha = .025$.

SOLUTION   We want to test the following hypothesis:

H_0: $(\mu_1 - \mu_2) = 0$ (i.e., no difference in mean buyer savings)

H_a: $(\mu_1 - \mu_2) < 0$ (i.e., the mean buyer savings for competitive strategy is less than the mean for coordinative strategy)

---

*To test whether $(\mu_1 - \mu_2)$ is equal to some hypothesized nonzero value D_0 (i.e., H_0: $\mu_1 - \mu_2 = D_0$), use the test statistic

$$t = \frac{(\bar{x}_1 - \bar{x}_2) - D_0}{\sqrt{s_p^2(1/n_1 + 1/n_2)}}$$

Table 11.3 Data for Example 11.11

Competitive Bargaining	Coordinative Bargaining
$1,857	$1,544
1,700	2,640
1,829	1,645
2,644	2,275
1,566	2,137
663	2,327
1,712	2,152
1,679	2,130

Source: Clopton, S. W. "Seller and buying firm factors affecting industrial buyers' negotiation behavior and outcomes." *Journal of Marketing*, Feb. 1984, pp. 39–53, published by the American Marketing Association.

where μ_1 and μ_2 are the true mean savings of buyers using the competitive and coordinative bargaining strategies, respectively. Since the samples selected for the study are small ($n_1 = n_2 = 8$), the following assumptions are required:

1. The populations of buyer savings under the competitive and coordinative strategies both have approximately normal distributions.
2. The variances of the populations of buyer savings for the two bargaining strategies are equal.
3. The samples were independently and randomly selected.

If these three assumptions are valid, the test statistic will have a t distribution with $(n_1 + n_2 - 2) = (8 + 8 - 2) = 14$ degrees of freedom. With a significance level of $\alpha = .025$, the rejection region is given by

$$t < -t_{.025} = -2.145 \qquad \text{(see Figure 11.7)}$$

FIGURE 11.7

Rejection Region for
Example 11.11

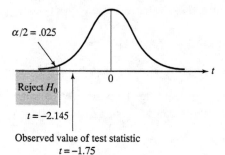

$\alpha/2 = .025$

Reject H_0

$t = -2.145$

Observed value of test statistic
$t = -1.75$

To compute the test statistic, we must find $\bar{x}_1$, $\bar{x}_2$, s_1, and s_2. These summary statistics are given in the MINITAB printout, Figure 11.8, as $\bar{x}_1 = 1,706$, $\bar{x}_2 = 2,106$, $s_1 = 538$, and $s_2 = 357$.

FIGURE 11.8

MINITAB Printout for
Example 11.11

```
TWOSAMPLE T FOR Compete VS Coordin
            N       MEAN     STDEV    SE MEAN
Compete  8         1706       538        190
Coordin  8         2106       357        126

95 PCT CI FOR MU Compete - MU Coordin: (-890, 90)

TTEST MU Compete = MU Coordin (VS NE): T= -1.75   P=0.10   DF=  14

POOLED STDEV =        457
```

Since we have assumed that the two populations have equal variances (i.e., that $\sigma_1^2 = \sigma_2^2 = \sigma_2$, we first compute an estimate of this common variance. Our pooled estimate is given by

$$s_p^2 = \frac{(n_1 - 1)s_1^2 + (n_2 - 1)s_2^2}{n_1 + n_2 - 2} = \frac{(8 - 1)(538)^2 + (8 - 1)(357)^2}{8 + 8 - 2}$$

$$= 208,446.5$$

Using this pooled sample variance to compute the test statistic, we obtain

$$t = \frac{\bar{x}_1 - \bar{x}_2 - D_0}{\sqrt{s_p^2 \left(\frac{1}{n_1} + \frac{1}{n_2}\right)}} = \frac{(1,706 - 2,106) - 0}{\sqrt{208,446.5 \left(\frac{1}{8} + \frac{1}{8}\right)}}$$

$$= -1.75$$

Since the computed value of t does not fall within the rejection region, we fail to reject the null hypothesis (at $\alpha = .025$). There is insufficient evidence that the mean savings of bargainers using the competitive strategy is less than the corresponding mean for bargainers using the coordinative strategy.

The analysis of the data in Table 11.3 could be performed using the t test procedure available in a statistical software package. The MINITAB analysis is shown at the bottom of Figure 11.8. The p-value of the two-tailed test, shaded on the printout, is .10; hence, the p-value of the one-tailed test is

$$p = \frac{.10}{2} = .05$$

Since this one-tailed p-value exceeds $\alpha = .025$, we cannot reject H_0. ■

As with the one-sample case, the assumptions required for testing $(\mu_1 - \mu_2)$ with small samples do not have to be satisfied exactly for the inferences to be useful in practice. Slight departures from these assumptions do not seriously affect the level of confidence in the procedure. Recall (Section 8.5) that when the variances σ_1^2 and σ_2^2 of the sampled populations are unequal, researchers have found that the formulas for small-sample inferences for $(\mu_1 - \mu_2)$ will still yield valid results in practice as long as the two populations are normal and the sample sizes are equal, i.e., $n_1 = n_2$.

This situation occurs in Example 11.11. The sample standard deviations given in Figure 11.8 are 538 and 357. Thus, it is very likely that the population standard deviations (and variances) are unequal.* However, since $n_1 = n_2 = 8$, the inference derived from the test is still valid if we use s_1^2 and s_2^2 as estimates for the population variances (rather than using the pooled sample variance s_p^2). In the case where $\sigma_1^2 \neq \sigma_2^2$ and $n_1 \neq n_2$, approximate tests for $(\mu_1 - \mu_2)$ can be performed by modifying the degrees of freedom associated with the t distribution and again substituting s_1^2 for σ_1^2 and s_2^2 for σ_2^2. These modifications are shown in the box.

Modifications to Small-Sample Tests of H_0: $(\mu_1 - \mu_2) = 0$ when $(\sigma_1^2 \neq \sigma_2^2)$

$$n_1 = n_2 = n$$

Test statistic: $\quad t = \dfrac{\bar{x}_1 - \bar{x}_2}{\sqrt{\dfrac{s_1^2}{n_1} + \dfrac{s_2^2}{n_2}}} = \dfrac{\bar{x}_1 - \bar{x}_2}{\sqrt{\dfrac{1}{n}(s_1^2 + s_2^2)}}$

Degrees of freedom: $\quad v = n_1 + n_2 - 2 = 2(n - 1)$

$$n_1 \neq n_2$$

Test statistic: $\quad t = \dfrac{\bar{x}_1 - \bar{x}_2}{\sqrt{\dfrac{s_1^2}{n_1} + \dfrac{s_2^2}{n_2}}}$

Degrees of freedom: $\quad v = \dfrac{(s_1^2/n_1 + s_2^2/n_2)^2}{\dfrac{(s_1^2/n_1)^2}{n_1 - 1} + \dfrac{(s_2^2/n_2)^2}{n_2 - 1}}$

[*Note:* The value of v will generally not be an integer. Round down to the nearest integer to use the t table (Table 6 of Appendix B).]

---

*A test of hypothesis for comparing two variances is discussed in optional Section 11.8.

Small-sample inferences about $(\mu_1 - \mu_2)$ are also valid if the populations deviate slightly from normality. On the other hand, when the sampled populations depart greatly from normality, the t test is invalid and any inferences derived from the procedure are suspect. For the nonnormal case, it is advisable to use one of the nonparametric statistical methods discussed in Chapter 18.

> ### Warning
>
> When the sampled populations are decidedly nonnormal (e.g., highly skewed), any inferences derived from the small-sample t test for $(\mu_1 - \mu_2)$ are suspect. In this case, one alternative is to use the nonparametric Wilcoxon rank sum test of Section 18.3.

EXERCISES

■ **Learning the Mechanics**

11.27 Two independent random samples, both large ($n > 30$), are selected from populations with unknown means μ_1 and μ_2. Specify the rejection region for each of the following combinations of H_0, H_a, and α:

a. $H_0: (\mu_1 - \mu_2) = 0$, $\quad H_a: (\mu_1 - \mu_2) \neq 0$; $\quad \alpha = .01$
b. $H_0: (\mu_1 - \mu_2) = 0$, $\quad H_a: (\mu_1 - \mu_2) \neq 0$; $\quad \alpha = .10$
c. $H_0: (\mu_1 - \mu_2) = 0$, $\quad H_a: (\mu_1 - \mu_2) > 0$; $\quad \alpha = .05$
d. $H_0: (\mu_1 - \mu_2) = 0$, $\quad H_a: (\mu_1 - \mu_2) < 0$; $\quad \alpha = .05$

11.28 Two independent random samples are selected from normal populations with unknown means μ_1 and μ_2 and variances $\sigma_1^2 = \sigma_2^2$. Specify the rejection region for each of the following combinations of H_a, n_1, n_2, and α when testing the null hypothesis $H_0: (\mu_1 - \mu_2) = 0$.

a. $H_a: (\mu_1 - \mu_2) \neq 0$; $\quad n_1 = 10$, $\quad n_2 = 10$, $\quad \alpha = .05$
b. $H_a: (\mu_1 - \mu_2) > 0$; $\quad n_1 = 8$, $\quad n_2 = 4$, $\quad \alpha = .10$
c. $H_a: (\mu_1 - \mu_2) < 0$; $\quad n_1 = 6$, $\quad n_2 = 5$, $\quad \alpha = .01$

11.29 Two independent random samples are selected from populations with means μ_1 and μ_2, respectively. The sample sizes, means, and standard deviations are shown in the table.

Sample 1	Sample 2
$\bar{x} = 7.0$	$\bar{x} = 6.0$
$s = 3.0$	$s = 1.0$
$n = 40$	$n = 60$

a. Test the null hypothesis $H_0: (\mu_1 - \mu_2) = 0$ against the alternative hypothesis $H_a: (\mu_1 - \mu_2) \neq 0$ at $\alpha = .05$.

b. Test $H_0: (\mu_1 - \mu_2) = .5$ against $H_a: (\mu_1 - \mu_2) \neq .5$. Use $\alpha = .05$

11.30 Independent random samples selected from two normal populations with equal variances produced the sample means and variances shown in the table.

Sample 1	Sample 2
$\bar{x}_1 = 64$	$\bar{x}_2 = 69$
$s_1^2 = 52$	$s_2^2 = 71$
$n_1 = 11$	$n_2 = 14$

a. Test $H_0: (\mu_1 - \mu_2) = 0$ against $H_a: (\mu_1 - \mu_2) \neq 0$. Use $\alpha = .01$.
b. Test $H_0: (\mu_1 - \mu_2) = 0$ against $H_a: (\mu_1 - \mu_2) < 0$. Use $\alpha = .10$.

11.31 Independent random samples from normal populations with equal variances produced these results:

Sample 1	Sample 2
4.8	5.0
5.2	4.7
5.0	4.9
4.9	4.8
5.1	

Test the null hypothesis $H_0: (\mu_1 - \mu_2) = 0$ against the alternative hypothesis $H_a: (\mu_1 - \mu_2) > 0$. Use $\alpha = .05$.

■ *Applying the Concepts*

11.32 Many computer software packages utilize menu-driven user-interfaces to increase "user-friend-liness." One feature that can be incorporated into the interface is a stacked menu display. Each time a menu item is selected, a submenu is displayed partially over the parent menu, thus creating a series of "stacked" menus. The *Special Interest Group on Computer Human Interaction Bulletin* (July 1993) reported on a study to determine the effects of the presence/absence of a stacked menu structure on search time. Twenty-two subjects were randomly placed in one of two groups; each was asked to search a menu-driven software package for a particular item. In the experimental group ($n_1 = 11$), the stacked menu format was used; in the control group ($n_2 = 11$), only the current menu was displayed.

a. The researcher's initial hypothesis is that the mean time required to find a target item does not differ for stacked and nonstacked menu displays. Describe the statistical method appropriate for testing this hypothesis.
b. What assumptions are required for inferences derived from the analysis to be valid?
c. The mean search times for the two groups were 11.02 seconds and 11.07 seconds, respectively. Is this enough information to conduct the test? Explain.
d. The observed significance level for the test, part **a**, exceeds .10. Interpret this result.

11.33 Does competition between separate research and development (R&D) teams in the U.S. Department of Defense, working independently on the same project, improve performance? To answer this question, performance ratings were assigned to each of 58 multisource (competitive) and 63 sole-source R&D contracts (*IEEE Transactions on Engineering Management*, Feb. 1990). With respect to quality of reports and products, the competitive contracts had a mean performance rating of 7.62, whereas the sole-source contracts had a mean of 6.95.

   a. Set up the null and alternative hypotheses for determining whether the mean quality performance rating of competitive R&D contracts exceeds the mean for sole-source contracts.

   b. Find the rejection region for the test using $\alpha = .05$.

   c. The *p*-value for the test was reported to be between .02 and .03. What is the appropriate conclusion?

11.34 An industrial plant wants to determine which of two types of fuel—gas or electric—will produce more useful energy at a lower cost. One measure of economical energy production, called the *plant investment per delivered quad*, is calculated by taking the amount of money (in dollars) invested in the particular utility by the plant, and dividing by the delivered amount of energy (in quadrillion British thermal units). The smaller this ratio, the less an industrial plant pays for its delivered energy. Random samples of 11 plants using electrical utilities and 16 plants using gas utilities were taken, and the plant investment/quad was calculated for each. The data are listed in the table, followed by a MINITAB printout of the analysis of the data. Do these data provide sufficient evidence at the $\alpha = .05$ level of significance to indicate a difference in the average investment/quad between the plants using gas and those using electrical utilities? What assumptions are required for the procedure you used to be valid?

Electric				Gas			
204.15	.57	62.76	89.72	.78	16.66	74.94	.01
.35	85.46	.78	.65	.54	23.59	88.79	.64
44.38	9.28	78.60		.82	91.84	7.20	66.64
				.74	64.67	165.60	.36

```
TWOSAMPLE T FOR electric VS gas
             N      MEAN    STDEV    SE MEAN
electric    11      52.4    62.4       19
gas         16      37.7    49.0       12

95 PCT CI FOR MU electric - MU gas: (-30, 59)

TTEST MU electric = MU gas (VS NE): T= 0.68  P=0.50  DF=  25

POOLED STDEV =       54.8
```

11.35 In the fall of 1989, the U.S. government mandated that every bottle or can of alcoholic beverage include a warning label listing the six risks of alcohol consumption. A study was conducted to determine the awareness of these risks by adolescents both before and after the labeling law was enacted (*American Journal of Public Health*, Apr. 1993). Awareness was measured in a sample of 1,211 12th-grade students immediately before the label was required to appear (1989) and in a sample of 2,006 12th-graders 1 year after the enactment of the law (1990). (*Awareness* was measured as the number of the six risks that were correctly identified by the adolescent.) According to the researchers, "in 1990 the average awareness score was 4.3 (standard deviation = 1.24), which was a statistically significant (p-value < .01) increase over the average of 3.6 (standard deviation = 1.26) in 1989." Comment on the validity of the researchers' statement.

11.36 As a result of recent advances in educational telecommunications, many colleges and universities are utilizing instruction by interactive television for "distance" education. For example, each semester, Ball State University televises six graduate business courses to students at remote off-campus sites (*Journal of Education for Business*, Jan./Feb. 1991). To compare the performance of the off-campus MBA students at Ball State (who take the televised classes) to the on-campus MBA students (who have a "live" professor), a test devised by the Assembly of Collegiate Schools of Business (AACSB) was administered to a sample of both groups of students. (The test included seven exams covering accounting, business strategy, finance, human resources, marketing, management information systems, and production and operations management.) The AACSB test scores (50 points maximum) are summarized in the table. Based on these results, the researchers report that "there was no significant difference between the two groups of students."

	Mean	Standard Deviation
On-Campus Students	41.93	2.86
Off-Campus TV Students	44.56	1.42

Source: Arndt, T. L. and LaFollette, W. R. "Interactive television and the nontraditional student." *Journal of Education for Business*, Jan./Feb. 1991, p. 184.

a. Note that the sample sizes were not given in the journal article. Assuming 50 students are sampled from each group, perform the desired analysis. Do you agree with the researchers' findings?

b. Repeat part **a**, but assume 15 students are sampled from each group.

11.37 According to a popular model of managerial behavior, the current state of automation in a manufacturing firm influences managers' perceptions of problems of automation. To investigate this proposition, researchers at Concordia University (Montreal) surveyed managers at firms with a high level of automation and at firms with a low level of automation (*IEEE Transactions on Engineering Management*, Aug. 1990). Each manager was asked to give his or her perception of the problems of automation at the firm. Responses were measured on a 5-point scale (1-no problem, 5-major problem). Summary statistics for the two groups of managers, provided in the table, were used to test the hypothesis of no difference in the mean perceptions of automation problems between managers of highly automated and less automated manufacturing firms.

	Sample Size	Mean	Standard Deviation
Low-Level Firms	17	3.274	.762
High-Level Firms	8	3.280	.721

Source: Farhoomand, A. F., Kira, D., and Williams, J. "Managers' perceptions towards automation in manufacturing." *IEEE Transactions on Engineering Management*, Vol. 37, No. 3, Aug. 1990, p. 230.

a. Conduct the test for the researchers, assuming that the perception variances for the two groups of managers are equal. Use $\alpha = .01$.

b. Conduct the test for the researchers if it is known that the perception variances differ for managers at low-level and high-level firms.

11.38 The *Journal of Organizational Behavior* (Vol. 13, 1992) reported on a study of workload and psychological strain in professionals. Independent random samples of 318 self-employed dentists and 84 dentists who were not self-employed took part in the survey. Psychological strain was measured two ways: self-esteem (40-point scale) and job satisfaction (20-point scale). Higher scores indicate a lower level of strain.

a. A test of the hypothesis that the mean self-esteem score for self-employed dentists is greater than the mean self-esteem score for dentists not self-employed was conducted. The test statistic was reported as $t = 1.92$ with a one-tailed observed significance level of $p = .03$. Interpret the results.

b. According to the researchers, "self-employed dentists enjoyed a significantly higher degree of job satisfaction ($\bar{x}_1 = 14.2$) than did the non–self-employed dentists ($\bar{x}_2 = 13.1$)." This inference was based on a test statistic of $t = 2.2$ and a one-tailed observed significance level of $p = .02$. Do you agree with the researchers' conclusions?

11.39 How does the employment status of wives affect their husbands' well-being? To answer this question, a random sample of 413 male accountants who were employed full-time and married took part in a survey reported in the *Academy of Management Journal* (Mar. 1989). In this sample, 214 wives were employed and 199 were unemployed. The job satisfaction levels of husbands in the two groups are summarized in the table.

	n	$\bar{x}$	s
Wives Employed	214	3.29	.65
Wives Unemployed	199	3.45	.58

Source: Parasuraman, S. et al. "Work and family variables as mediators of the relationship between wives' employment and husbands' well-being." *Academy of Management Journal*, Vol. 32, No. 1, Mar. 1989, p. 191.

a. Give the null and alternative hypotheses for testing whether the mean job satisfaction level of male accountants married to employed wives is less than the mean job satisfaction level of male accountants married to unemployed wives.

b. The test statistic and p-value, reported in the study, were $z \approx 2.6$ and p-value $< .01$. Verify these results.

c. Interpret the results, part **b**.

11.40 End-user computing (EUC) describes the use of computer resources by managers, professionals, and operators usually not formally educated in the computer field. Researchers at the University of Arkansas–Little Rock conducted a study of EUC systems at two types of firms: those with a formal policy controlling the EUC environment and those with no formal policy (*Journal of Computer Information Systems*, Spring 1993). Independent random samples of 36 data processing/information system (DP/IS) managers at firms with a formal EUC policy in-place and 46 DP/IS managers at firms without a formal policy participated in the study. Each manager was asked to rate (on a 5-point scale) each of 18 specific EUC policies at their firm (where 1 = no value and 5 = necessity). The mean ratings for the two groups of managers in each category are given in the table. Those that means are "significantly different" at $\alpha = .05$ are indicated by an asterisk. Interpret the results.

	Policy	*Mean Ratings of EUC Policies*	
		With Formal Policy (n = 36)	No Formal Policy (n = 46)
1.	Firm value	2.72	2.22
2.	Goals	3.06	2.70
*3.	Relationship with MIS	3.61	3.04
4.	Justifiable applications	3.28	2.96
5.	Hardware standards	4.39	4.22
*6.	Software standards: purchases	4.50	4.17
7.	Software standards: in-house	3.89	3.83
8.	Compatibility	4.11	3.91
9.	Role of networking	4.17	3.96
10.	Justifiable types of data	3.72	3.43
11.	Data security/integrity	4.06	4.35
12.	Data confidentiality	4.06	4.09
13.	Documentation of files	3.89	4.09
14.	Ownership of files	3.67	3.83
15.	Copyright infringements	3.94	3.83
*16.	Movement of hardware	3.00	3.65
17.	Training	2.61	2.74
*18.	Accountability	3.72	3.13

Source: Mitchell, R. B. and Neal, R. "Status of planning and control systems in the end-user computing environment." *Journal of Computer Information Systems*, Vol. 33, No. 3, Spring 1993, p. 28 (Table 2).

11.5 Testing the Difference Between Two Population Means: Matched Pairs

We explained in Section 8.6 that it may be possible to acquire more information on the difference between two population means by using data collected in matched pairs instead of independent samples. Consider, for example, an experiment to compare consumer evaluation of the durability of two types of jogging shoes, A and B. Ten daily joggers are to be randomly selected for the experiment, and each will be given one pair of each type of shoe. The joggers will be instructed to use one of the shoe types until, according to his or her evaluation, the shoe is no longer usable. The jogger will then shift to the other shoe type and repeat the experiment, with the order of use of shoe type randomly assigned for each jogger. The number of weeks of service for each type of shoe will be recorded for each jogger. The resulting data, matched on joggers, can be used to test a hypothesis about the difference between the mean usable lifetimes of the two types of shoes. The appropriate procedure for testing the equality of means is summarized in the box.

Matched Pairs Test of H_0: $(\mu_1 - \mu_2) = 0$ [*]

One-Tailed Test   *Two-Tailed Test*

H_a: $(\mu_1 - \mu_2) > 0$ H_a: $(\mu_1 - \mu_2) \neq 0$
[or H_a: $(\mu_1 - \mu_2) < 0$]

Large Samples

$$\text{Test statistic:} \quad t = \frac{\bar{d}}{\sigma_d / \sqrt{n}} \approx \frac{\bar{d}}{s_d / \sqrt{n}}$$

Rejection region: *Rejection region:*
$z > z_\alpha$ [or $z < -z_\alpha$] $|z| > z_{\alpha/2}$

Assumption: The sample size is sufficiently large (e.g., $n \geq 30$).

Small Samples

$$\text{Test statistic:} \quad t = \frac{\bar{d}}{s_d / \sqrt{n}}$$

Rejection region: *Rejection region:*
$t > t_\alpha$ [or $t < -t_\alpha$] $|t| > t_{\alpha/2}$

Assumptions: **1.** The relative frequency distribution of the population of differences is approximately normal.
                 2. The paired differences are randomly selected from the population of differences.

EXAMPLE 11.12
Application: Small Sample

Consider the experiment to compare consumer evaluation of the durability of two types of jogging shoes. Do the data given in Table 11.4 on page 544 provide sufficient information to indicate that, according to the ratings of habitual joggers, the

---

[*] *To test whether $(\mu_1 - \mu_2)$ is equal to some hypothesized nonzero value D_0 (i.e., H_0: $\mu_1 - \mu_2 = D_0$), use the test statistic*

$$t = \frac{\bar{d} - D_0}{s_d / \sqrt{n}}$$

Table 11.4 Weeks of Jogging for Example 11.12

							Jogger				
		1	2	3	4	5	6	7	8	9	10
Shoe Type	A	27	35	19	39	34	32	15	26	18	17
	B	23	28	16	31	38	30	17	22	15	16
d		4	7	3	8	−4	2	−2	4	3	1

mean length of usable service for shoe type A exceeds the corresponding mean for shoe type B? Test using $\alpha = .05$.

SOLUTION Let μ_1 and μ_2 represent the mean number of weeks of durable wear for shoe types A and B, respectively. To determine whether μ_1 exceeds μ_2, we want to test the hypotheses

H_0: $\mu_1 - \mu_2 = 0$ (i.e., $\mu_1 = \mu_2$)

H_a: $\mu_1 - \mu_2 > 0$ (i.e., $\mu_1 > \mu_2$)

Since the number of joggers (matched pairs) used in the study is small ($n = 10$), the test statistic will have a t distribution based on $(n - 1) = (10 - 1) = 9$ degrees of freedom. We will reject the null hypothesis if

$t > t_{.05} = 1.833$ (see Figure 11.9)

FIGURE 11.9

Rejection Region for
Example 11.12

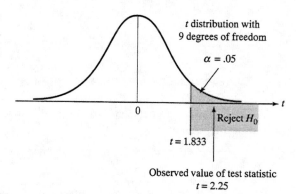

t distribution with
9 degrees of freedom

$\alpha = .05$

$t = 1.833$

Reject H_0

Observed value of test statistic
$t = 2.25$

To conduct the test, we must first calculate the difference d in length of use of the two shoe types for each jogger. These differences (where the observation for shoe type B is subtracted from the observation for shoe type A within each pair) are shown in the last row of Table 11.4. Next, we would calculate the mean $\bar{d}$ and standard deviation s_d for this sample of $n = 10$ differences to obtain the test statistic.

Rather than perform these calculations, we will rely on the output of a computer. An ASP printout for the analysis is shown in Figure 11.10.

FIGURE 11.10

ASP Printout for
Example 11.12

```
                HYPOTHESIS:  MEAN DIFFERENCE = 0

                        X = Difference(A-B)

        SAMPLE MEAN OF X  =    2.6
    SAMPLE VARIANCE OF X  =   13.3778
        SAMPLE SIZE OF X  =   10
                    x  =    0

            MEAN X - x  =    2.6
                     t  =    2.24792
                 D. F.  =    9
               P-VALUE  =    0.0511767
             P-VALUE/2  =    0.0255883
             SD. ERROR  =    1.15662


                    STEM AND LEAF PLOT

VARIABLE:   Difference(A-B)

STEM AND LEAF PLOT  OF Difference(A-B) (*10^2):
 -4| 00
 -3|
 -2| 00
 -1|
 -0|
  0|
  1| 00
  2| 00
  3| 00 00
  4| 00 00
  5|
  6|
  7| 00
  8| 00
```

From the printout we obtain the values of $\bar{d} = 2.6$ and $s_d^2 = 13.3778$; thus $s_d = \sqrt{13.3778} = 3.66$. Substituting into the formula for the test statistic, we have

$$t = \frac{\bar{d} - D_0}{s_d / \sqrt{n}} = \frac{2.6 - 0}{3.66 / \sqrt{10}} = 2.25$$

Since this value of the test statistic (shaded on the printout) exceeds the critical value, $t_{.05} = 1.833$, there is sufficient evidence to indicate that the mean number of weeks of durable service for shoe type A exceeds the mean for shoe type B.

Note that we can derive the same inference by examining the *p*-value of the test. The *p*-value for our one-tailed test, shaded in Figure 11.10, is .0256. Since this value is less than our preselected value of $\alpha = .05$, we have sufficient evidence to reject H_0.

The inference for this small-sample test is valid as long as the sample differences come from an approximately normal distribution. An ASP stem-and-leaf display for the data is shown at the bottom of Figure 11.10. The lack of strong skewness in the plot supports the assumption of normality required for this test. ■

EXAMPLE 11.13

Matched Pairs Versus Independent Samples

Refer to the matched pairs experiment of Example 11.12. Why did we collect the data in matched pairs rather than use independent random samples of joggers, with some assigned to use only shoe type A and others to use only shoe type B?

SOLUTION   Clearly, we expect some joggers to wear their shoes out more rapidly than others. To cancel out this variation from jogger to jogger, the experiment was designed so that each jogger would rate both shoe types. Then each shoe type within a given pair (i.e., for a given jogger) would be subjected to the same pattern of wear. By comparing usable service time *within* each jogger, we were able to obtain more information on the difference in mean usable service time than we could have obtained by independent random sampling. ▪

As in the previous section, we close this section with a warning.

> **Warning**
>
> It is inappropriate to apply the small-sample, matched-pairs t test when the population of differences is decidedly nonnormal (e.g., highly skewed). In this case, an alternative procedure is the nonparametric Wilcoxon signed ranks test of Section 18.4.

EXERCISES

▪ *Learning the Mechanics*

11.41   A matched-pairs experiment is used to test the null hypothesis $H_0: (\mu_1 - \mu_2) = 0$. For each of the following situations, specify the rejection region, test statistic value, and conclusion.
  a. $H_a: (\mu_1 - \mu_2) \neq 0$; $\bar{d} = 400$, $s_d = 435$, $n = 100$, $\alpha = .01$
  b. $H_a: (\mu_1 - \mu_2) > 0$; $\bar{d} = .48$, $s_d = .08$, $n = 5$, $\alpha = .05$
  c. $H_a: (\mu_1 - \mu_2) < 0$; $\bar{d} = -1.3$, $s_d^2 = .95$, $n = 6$, $\alpha = .10$

11.42   Consider the following summary statistics for a matched-pairs experiment:

$$\bar{d} = 10.5 \qquad s_d = 10$$

  a. Suppose $n = 10$. Test $H_0: (\mu_1 - \mu_2) = 0$ against $H_a: (\mu_1 - \mu_2) > 0$ at $\alpha = .05$.
  b. Suppose $n = 4$. Test $H_0: (\mu_1 - \mu_2) = 0$ against $H_a: (\mu_1 - \mu_2) > 0$ at $\alpha = .05$.

11.43   The data for a random sample of six paired observations are shown in the table.

Pair	Sample 1	Sample 2
1	6	4
2	2	1
3	5	8
4	10	7
5	8	6
6	4	2

a. Test the null hypothesis $H_0: (\mu_1 - \mu_2) = 0$ against the alternative hypothesis $H_a:$ $(\mu_1 - \mu_2) \neq 0$. Use $\alpha = .05$.

b. What assumptions must be made when performing a test of hypothesis based on matched-pairs data?

■ *Applying the Concepts*

11.44 The *Journal of Education for Business* (Apr. 1993) reported on a study of the effectiveness of a tailored library instruction program for students in a business strategy class. The goal of the study was to determine whether the mean level of student satisfaction with the college library after a student received the specialized instruction exceeded the mean satisfaction level prior to a student receiving the instruction.

a. Set up the null and alternative hypotheses for this test.

b. Describe how to collect the data using matched pairs.

11.45 Researchers at Purdue University compared human real-time scheduling in a processing environment to an automated approach that utilizes computerized robots and sensing devices (*IEEE Transactions*, Mar. 1993). The experiment consisted of eight simulated scheduling problems. Each task was performed by a human scheduler and by the automated system. Performance was measured by the *throughput rate*, defined as the number of good jobs produced weighted by product quality. The resulting throughput rates are shown in the accompanying table. Analyze the data using a test of hypothesis.

Task	Human Scheduler	Automated Method	Task	Human Scheduler	Automated Method
1	185.4	180.4	5	240.0	269.3
2	146.3	248.5	6	253.8	249.6
3	174.4	185.5	7	238.8	282.0
4	184.9	216.4	8	263.5	315.9

Source: Yih, Y., Liang, T., and Moskowitz, H. "Robot scheduling in a circuit board production line: A hybrid OR/ANN approach." *IEEE Transactions*, Vol. 25, No.2, Mar. 1993, p. 31 (Table 1).

11.46 When long-term resource allocation decisions (e.g., building a domed stadium or constructing a major highway system) meet with unexpected major setbacks, the decision maker must decide whether to abandon the project before irretrievable costs are incurred or to continue in the face of probable losses. Surprisingly, researchers have found that decision makers all too often persist, or even escalate resources, in these situations. In a study of resource allocation behavior reported in *Organizational Behavior and Human Decision Processes* (June 1986), 20 undergraduate business school students were asked to make resource allocation decisions for fictional Sunburst Investments, which had undertaken construction of an office park and tennis club. For one portion of the study, each student was asked to rate the options of finishing and not finishing the project on a 7-point scale (1 = very negative, 7 = very positive). The differences between the ratings of the two options (rating for finishing option minus rating for not finishing option) were calculated and the mean and standard deviation of the 20 sample differences obtained:

$$\bar{x} = -2.05 \qquad s = 1.85$$

a. Conduct a test to determine whether subjects rate the option of finishing more negative, on average, than the option of not finishing the project (i.e., test the hypothesis that the mean difference in ratings is less than 0). Use $\alpha = .10$.

b. What assumptions are required for the test of part **a** to be valid?

11.47 *USA Today* recently published the results of the *NCAA Graduation-Rates Report*. The report makes public, for the first time, the graduation rates of student athletes at individual universities. The data in the table represent a random sample of schools selected from the NCAA report. The percentage of students and the percentage of men's basketball players from the 1983–1984 and 1984–1985 freshmen classes who graduated within 6 years are presented in the table. Use a test of hypothesis to compare the mean graduation rates of students and male basketball players. Is there evidence (at $\alpha = .05$) of a difference between the two groups?

School	Graduation Rates, %	
	Students	Men's Basketball
Duquesne	70	86
Florida State	52	40
Seton Hall	58	60
Oklahoma	42	13
Michigan	81	50
UNLV	26	25
Virginia Tech	71	33
Drexel	68	70
Arizona	45	36
Georgia	60	13
San Diego State	36	0
Vanderbilt	77	83

Source: USA Today, Aug. 13, 1992.

11.48 Medical researchers believe that exposure to dust from cotton bract induces respiratory disease in susceptible cotton textile manufacturers. An experiment was conducted to determine the effect of air-dried green cotton bract extract (GBE) on the cells of mill workers not exposed to dust (*Environmental Research*, Feb. 1986). Blood samples taken on six non–cotton dust exposed laboratory volunteers were incubated with varying concentrations of GBE. After a short period of time, the cyclic AMP level (a measure of cell activity expressed in picomoles per million cells) of each blood sample was measured. The data for two GBE concentrations, 0 mg/ml (salt buffer, control solution) and .2 mg/ml, are reproduced in the table. [Note that one blood sample was taken from each worker, with one aliquot exposed to the salt buffer solution and the other to the GBE.] Analyze the data for the researchers.

Worker	*GBE Concentration, mg/ml* 0	.2
A	8.8	4.4
B	13.0	5.7
C	9.2	4.4
D	6.5	4.1
F	9.1	4.4
H	17.0	7.9

Source: Butcher, B. T., Reed, M. A., and O'Neil, C. E. "Biochemical and immunologic characterization of cotton bract extract and its effect on *in vitro* cyclic AMP production." *Environmental Research*, Vol. 39, No. 1, Feb. 1986, p. 119.

11.49 The traditional retail store audit is one of the most widely used marketing research tools among consumer packaged goods companies. The retail store audit involves periodic audits of a sample of retail audits to monitor inventory and purchases of a particular product. V. K. Prasad, W. R. Casper, and R. J. Schieffer conducted a study to compare market data yielded by retail store audits with an alternative, less costly auditing procedure—weekend selldown audits (*Journal of Marketing*, Winter 1984). The market shares of six major brands of beer distributed in eastern cities were estimated using each of the two store audit methods, with the results shown in the accompanying table. Is there sufficient evidence to indicate a difference in the mean estimates of beer brand market shares produced by the two auditing methods? Test using $\alpha = .05$.

Brand	*Traditional Store Audit*	*Weekend Selldown Audit*
1	18.0	19.0
2	15.3	17.3
3	8.9	8.5
4	6.5	4.9
5	5.3	6.1
6	3.4	3.0

11.50 Refer to the paired comparison of grocery items at Winn-Dixie and Publix supermarkets, Exercise 8.61. A SAS printout for testing the hypothesis of no difference between the mean prices of grocery items purchased at the two supermarkets is displayed at the top of page 550.

```
Analysis Variable : DIFF (Winn minus Publix)

N Obs         Mean        Std Dev       Std Error            T   Prob>|T|
-------------------------------------------------------------------------
   60   -0.2540000      0.2741223      0.0353890   -7.1773633     0.0001
-------------------------------------------------------------------------
```

a. Locate the test statistic on the SAS printout. Interpret its value.

b. Locate the *p*-value of the test statistic on the SAS printout. Interpret its value.

11.51 *Newsweek* (Nov. 16, 1987) reported on an experiment in which the drug propranolol was used to reduce anxiety in students taking the Scholastic Aptitude Test (SAT). (The drug, which interferes with adrenaline, has been used for heart conditions and minor stress for over 25 years.) Twenty-two high school juniors who had not performed as well as expected on the SAT were administered the "SAT pill" (i.e., propranolol) 1 hour prior to retaking the test in their senior year. The sample mean increase in SAT scores for these 22 students was $\bar{x}_d = 120$ points, compared to the national average increase of $\mu_d = 38$ points.

a. Assuming that the standard deviation of the difference in SAT scores for the sample of 22 students was $s_d = 125$, test the hypothesis that the true mean increase in SAT scores for those students who take an "SAT pill" prior to the exam exceeds the national average increase of 38. Use $\alpha = .05$.

b. Repeat part **a** assuming that the standard deviation of the differences in SAT scores for the sample was $s_d = 250$.

c. The *Newsweek* article did not provide the value of the sample standard deviation, s_d, of the matched pairs experiment. Given this omission, why should one interpret the results of the experiment with caution?

11.6 Testing the Difference Between Two Population Proportions

Suppose we are interested in comparing two population proportions. Then the target parameter about which we will test a hypothesis is $(\pi_1 - \pi_2)$. Recall that π_1 and π_2 also represent the probabilities of success for two independent binomial experiments. The method for performing a large-sample test of hypothesis about whether $(\pi_1 - \pi_2)$, the difference between two binomial proportions is 0 (i.e., whether $\pi_1 = \pi_2$), is outlined in the following box.

Large-Sample Procedure for Testing H_0: $(\pi_1 - \pi_2) = 0$ *

One-Tailed Test

H_a: $(\pi_1 - \pi_2) > 0$
[or H_a: $(\pi_1 - \pi_2) < 0$]

Two-Tailed Test

H_a: $(\pi_1 - \pi_2) \neq 0$

(continued)

$$\text{Test statistic:}^* \quad z = \frac{p_1 - p_2}{\sigma_{(p_1 - p_2)}} \approx \frac{p_1 - p_2}{\sqrt{pq(1/n_1 + 1/n_2)}}$$

Rejection region:
$$z > z_\alpha \quad [\text{or } z < -z_\alpha]$$
where

Rejection region:
$$|z| > z_{\alpha/2}$$

$$p_1 = \frac{x_1}{n_1} = \frac{\text{Number of successes in sample 1}}{n_1}$$

$$p_2 = \frac{x_2}{n_2} = \frac{\text{Number of successes in sample 2}}{n_2}$$

$$p = \frac{x_1 + x_2}{n_1 + n_2} = \frac{\text{Total number of successes in the combined samples}}{\text{Total sample size}}$$

$$q = 1 - p$$

Assumptions: The samples sizes n_1 and n_2 are large; that will usually be satisfied if the intervals

$$p_1 \pm 2 \sqrt{\frac{p_1 q_1}{n_1}} \quad \text{and} \quad p_2 \pm 2 \sqrt{\frac{p_2 q_2}{n_2}}$$

do not contain 0 or 1.   *Note:* $q_1 = 1 - p_1$ and $q_2 = 1 - p_2$.

Since we are testing $H_0: (\pi_1 - \pi_2) = 0$ or, equivalently, $H_0: \pi_1 = \pi_2$, the best estimate of $\pi_1 = \pi_2 = \pi$ is found by dividing the total number of successes in the combined samples by the total number of observations in the two samples. That is, if x_1 is the number of successes in sample 1 and x_2 is the number of successes in sample 2, then

$$p = \frac{x_1 + x_2}{n_1 + n_2}$$

In this case, the best estimate of the standard deviation of the sampling distribution of

---

**To test $H_0: (\pi_1 - \pi_2) = D_0$, where $D_0 \neq 0$, use the test statistic* $z = \dfrac{(p_1 - p_2) - D_0}{\sqrt{\dfrac{p_1 q_1}{n_1} + \dfrac{p_2 q_2}{n_2}}}$

$(p_1 - p_2)$ is found by substituting p for both π_1 and π_2:

$$\sigma_{(p_1 - p_2)} = \sqrt{\frac{\pi_1(1 - \pi_1)}{n_1} + \frac{\pi_2(1 - \pi_2)}{n_2}}$$

$$\approx \sqrt{\frac{pq}{n_1} + \frac{pq}{n_2}} = \sqrt{pq\left(\frac{1}{n_1} + \frac{1}{n_2}\right)}$$

The sample sizes n_1 and n_2 must be sufficiently large to ensure that the sampling distributions of p_1 and p_2, and hence of the difference $(p_1 - p_2)$, are approximately normal. The rule of thumb given in the box may be used to determine whether the sample sizes are "sufficiently large."

EXAMPLE 11.14
Application: One-Tailed Test

In recent years, there has been a trend toward both parents working outside the home. Do working mothers experience the same burdens and family pressures as their spouses? A popular belief is that the proportion of working mothers who feel they have enough spare time for themselves is significantly less than the corresponding proportion of working fathers. To test this claim, independent random samples of 100 working mothers and 100 working fathers were selected, and their views on spare time for themselves were recorded. A summary of the data is given in Table 11.5. (Assume that the spouses of all individuals sampled were also working outside the home.) Does the sample information support the belief that the proportion of working mothers who feel they have enough spare time for themselves is less than the corresponding proportion of working fathers? Test as significance level $\alpha = .01$.

Table 11.5   Data on Working Parents for Example 11.14

	Working Mothers	*Working Fathers*
Number Sampled	100	100
Number in Sample Who Feel They Have Enough Spare Time for Themselves	27	56

SOLUTION   We wish to perform a test of

H_0: $(\pi_1 - \pi_2) = 0$ (i.e., $\pi_1 = \pi_2$)

H_a: $(\pi_1 - \pi_2) < 0$ (i.e., $\pi_1 < \pi_2$)

where

π_1 = Proportion of all working mothers who feel they have enough spare time for themselves

π_2 = Proportion of all working fathers who feel they have enough spare time for themselves

For this large-sample, one-tailed test, the null hypothesis will be rejected if

$$z < -z_{.01} = -2.33 \quad \text{(see Figure 11.11)}$$

FIGURE 11.11

Rejection Region for
Example 11.14

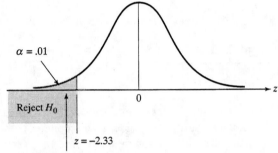

$\alpha = .01$

Reject H_0

$z = -2.33$

Observed value of test statistic
$z = -2.69$

The sample proportions p_1 and p_2 are computed for substitution into the formula for the test statistic:

p_1 = Sample proportion of working mothers who feel they have enough spare time for themselves

$$= \frac{27}{100} = .27$$

p_2 = Sample proportion of working fathers who feel they have enough spare time for themselves

$$= \frac{56}{100} = .56$$

The test statistic is given by

$$z = \frac{(p_1 - p_2) - D_0}{\sqrt{pq\left(\dfrac{1}{n_1} + \dfrac{1}{n_2}\right)}}$$

where

$$p = \frac{\left(\begin{array}{c}\text{Total number of sampled mothers and fathers who} \\ \text{feel they have enough spare time for themselves}\end{array}\right)}{\text{Total number of mothers and fathers sampled}}$$

$$= \frac{27 + 56}{100 + 100} = .415$$

and $q = 1 - p = .585$. Then we have

$$z = \frac{(.27 - .56) - 0}{\sqrt{(.415)(.585)(1/100 + 1/100)}} = -4.16$$

This value falls below the critical value of -2.33. Thus, at $\alpha = .01$, we reject the null hypothesis; there is sufficient evidence to conclude that the proportion of working mothers who feel they have enough spare time for themselves is significantly less than the corresponding proportion of working fathers; i.e., $\pi_1 < \pi_2$. ■

The inference derived from the test in Example 11.14 is valid only if the sample sizes, n_1 and n_2, are sufficiently large to guarantee that the intervals

$$p_1 \pm 2\sqrt{\frac{p_1 q_1}{n_1}} \quad \text{and} \quad p_2 \pm 2\sqrt{\frac{p_2 q_2}{n_2}}$$

do not contain 0 or 1. This requirement is satisfied for Example 11.14, as the following calculations show:

$$p_1 \pm 2\sqrt{\frac{p_1 q_1}{n_1}} = .27 \pm \sqrt{\frac{(.27)(.73)}{100}}$$

$$= .27 \pm .089 \quad \text{or} \quad (.181, .359)$$

$$p_2 \pm 2\sqrt{\frac{p_2 q_2}{n_2}} = .56 \pm 2\sqrt{\frac{(.56)(.44)}{100}}$$

$$= .56 \pm .099 \quad \text{or} \quad (.461, .659)$$

When the samples are not "sufficiently large," we must resort to another statistical technique.

> **Warning**
>
> The z test for comparing π_1 and π_2 is inappropriate when the sample sizes are not "sufficiently large" (see the rule of thumb given in the previous box). In this case, π_1 and π_2 can be compared using a statistical technique to be discussed in Section 18.4.

EXERCISES

■ Learning the Mechanics

11.52 Independent random samples of sizes n_1 and n_2 are selected from two binomial populations to test the null hypothesis $H_0: (\pi_1 - \pi_2) = 0$. For each of the following situations, specify the rejection region, test statistic value, and conclusion.

    a. $H_a: (\pi_1 - \pi_2) \neq 0$, $p_1 = .4$, $p_2 = .3$, $p = .343$, $n_1 = 1{,}500$, $n_2 = 2{,}000$, $\alpha = .01$

    b. $H_a: (\pi_1 - \pi_2) > 0$, $p_1 = .05$, $p_2 = .02$, $p = .035$, $n_1 = n_2 = 1{,}000$, $\alpha = .05$

    c. $H_a: (\pi_1 - \pi_2) < 0$, $p_1 = .60$, $p_2 = .65$, $p = .625$, $n_1 = n_2 = 120$, $\alpha = .01$

11.53 Independent random samples selected from two binomial populations produced the results given in the accompanying table.

	Sample 1	Sample 2
Number of Successes	82	76
Sample Size	100	100

    a. Test $H_0: (\pi_1 - \pi_2) = 0$ against $H_a: (\pi_1 - \pi_2) > 0$ at $\alpha = .05$.

    b. Suppose $n_1 = n_2 = 1{,}000$, but the sample estimates p_1, p_2, and p remain the same as in part **a**. Test $H_0: (\pi_1 - \pi_2) = 0$ against $H_a: (\pi_1 - \pi_2) > 0$ at $\alpha = .05$.

11.54 Independent random samples were selected from two binomial populations, 100 observations from population 1 and 150 from population 2. The numbers of successes were 78 and 87, respectively.

    a. At $\alpha = .05$, test $H_0: (\pi_1 - \pi_2) = 0$ against $H_a: (\pi_1 - \pi_2) > 0$.

    b. What assumptions must be made to conduct a large-sample test of hypothesis about $(\pi_1 - \pi_2)$?

■ Applying the Concepts

11.55 As a professional courtesy, physicians have traditionally provided health care free of charge or at a reduced rate to other physicians and their families. In 1966, 94% of a sample of 1,000 physicians offered this professional courtesy. To assess the extent to which this practice has changed over the years, the *New England Journal of Medicine* (Nov. 25, 1993) conducted a national survey of 2,224 physicians listed as current members of the American Medical Association (AMA). Of these physicians, 1,957 currently offer free or reduced-rate health care to fellow physicians. Is this sufficient evidence to conclude that the true proportion of physicians who offer the professional courtesy has decreased since 1966? Test using $\alpha = .10$.

11.56   Sports fans often argue that the outcomes of professional basketball games are not decided until the fourth (and last) quarter. In contrast, the conventional "wisdom" in Major League Baseball (MLB) suggests that most nine-inning games are "over" by the seventh inning. Can the outcome of a baseball game really be predicted based on the team leading after seven innings? And, is it really true that the team leading after three quarters of a National Basketball Association (NBA) game is no more likely to win than the trailing team? To answer these and other questions, University of Missouri researchers collected and analyzed data for 200 NBA games and 100 MLB games played during the 1990 regular season (*Chance*, Vol. 5, 1992). The accompanying table reports the number and percentage of games in which the team leading after three quarters or seven innings won. [*Note:* Tied games after three quarters or seven innings were removed from the data set.] Use a test of hypothesis to compare the win percentage of NBA teams leading after three quarters to the win percentage of MLB teams leading after seven innings. Test using $\alpha = .05$.

Sports	Games	Leader Wins	Leader Loses	% Reversals
NBA	189	150	39	20.6
MLB	92	86	6	6.5

Source: Cooper, H., DeNeve, K. M., and Mosteller, F. "Predicting professional sports game outcomes from intermediate game scores." *Chance: New Directions for Statistics and Computing,* Vol. 5, Nos. 3–4, 1992, pp. 18–22 (Table 1).

11.57   In 1982, 371 manufacturing and retailing companies were surveyed to determine the extent to which logistics information systems were implemented. A follow-up survey of 459 firms was conducted in 1987 to measure the 5-year trend in computerization of logistics information (*Industrial Engineering*, July 1990). One of the survey items focused on the percentage of firms that had computerized external market data. From 1982 to 1987, this percentage increased from 25% to 33%. Use this information to test for a significant increase in the percentage of firms with computerized external market data over the 5-year period. Test using $\alpha = .05$.

11.58   According to *Harvard Business Review* (July–Aug. 1986), approximately two-thirds of the 500 largest U.S. corporations have, in varying degrees, committed some form of unethical behavior. The lack of ethics in business has led many to question higher education's role in the ethics process. A more recent study found that the presence of ethics in the business school curriculum is sorely lacking. In a sample of 94 MBA programs, only 7 required a course on ethics, whereas 18 of 86 sampled undergraduate business programs required an ethics course (*Journal of Education for Business*, Nov.–Dec. 1990).

    a. Conduct a test to determine whether the percentage of business school programs that require an ethics course differs at the undergraduate and MBA level. Use $\alpha = .10$.

    b. Find the *p*-value of the test, part **a**. Interpret the result.

11.59   Calcium blockers are among several classes of medicines commonly prescribed to relieve high blood pressure. A study in Denmark has found that calcium blockers may also be effective in reducing the risk of heart attacks (*Tampa Tribune*, Mar. 23, 1990). A total of 897 Danish patients, each recovering from a heart attack, were given a daily dose of the drug Verapamil, a calcium blocker. After 18 months of follow-up, 146 of these patients had recurring heart attacks. In a control group of 878 people—each of whom took placebos—180 had a heart attack. Do the data provide sufficient evidence to infer that calcium blockers are effective in reducing the risk of heart attacks? Test using $\alpha = .01$.

11.60 Are black teachers in Florida's public universities earning tenure at the same rate as their white colleagues? A Florida university system study found that of the 20 black professors hired in 1983, only one had received tenure by their seventh year. Comparatively, 60 of the 150 white professors hired in 1983 earned tenure by their seventh year (*Tampa Tribune*, Sept. 16, 1990).

a. Is there sufficient evidence to indicate that black professors in Florida have a lower tenure rate than white professors? Test using $\alpha = .05$.

b. Find the *p*-value of the test, part **a**. Interpret the result.

11.61 In the travel industry, destination-specific travel literature (DSTL) refers to booklets, brochures, and pamphlets that describe a destination in detail (e.g., information on activities, facilities, and prices). DSTL is made available to travelers free of charge upon request. A study was undertaken to investigate the differences between information seekers (i.e., those who request DSTL) and nonseekers on a variety of consumer travel dimensions. Independent random samples of 288 seekers and 367 nonseekers were asked several questions about their "most recent pleasure trip or vacation of two or more days away from home." One interesting question asked whether the vacation was "active" (i.e., involved mainly challenging events or educational activities) or "passive" (i.e., involved mainly rest and relaxation). The number of passive vacations in each group is given in the table. Do the data provide sufficient evidence to indicate that information seekers are less likely to have a passive vacation than nonseekers? Test using $\alpha = .10$.

	Seekers	Nonseekers
Number Surveyed	288	367
Number Who Experienced a "Passive" Vacation	197	301

Source: Etzel, M. J. and Wahlers, R. G. "The use of requested promotional material by pleasure travelers." *Journal of Travel Research*, Vol. 23, No. 4, Spring 1985, pp. 2–6.

11.62 Are left-handed people more accident-prone than right-handers? This question was investigated at the Navy Personnel Research and Development Center in San Diego (*Tampa Tribune*, Aug. 23, 1993). In a sample of 231 male Navy enlisted personnel who are left-handed, 90 reported that they had been hospitalized for injuries. In contrast, 623 in a sample of 2,148 male Navy enlisted personnel who are right-handed admitted they had been hospitalized for injuries. Use this information to determine whether left-handers are more accident-prone than right-handers. Test using $\alpha = .01$.

11.7 Testing a Population Variance (Optional)

Hypothesis tests about a population variance σ^2 are conducted using the chi-square (χ^2) distribution introduced in Section 8.9. The test is outlined in the box. Note that the assumption of a normal population is required regardless of whether the sample size *n* is large or small.

Test of Hypothesis About a Population Variance σ^2

One-Tailed Test

H_0: $\sigma^2 = \sigma_0^2$
H_a: $\sigma^2 > \sigma_0^2$ (or H_a: $\sigma^2 < \sigma_0^2$)

Two-Tailed Test

H_0: $\sigma^2 = \sigma_0^2$
H_a: $\sigma^2 \neq \sigma_0^2$

Test statistic: $\chi^2 = \dfrac{(n-1)s^2}{\sigma_0^2}$

Rejection region:
$\chi^2 > \chi_\alpha^2$ (or $\chi^2 < \chi_{1-\alpha}^2$)

Rejection region:
$\chi^2 < \chi_{1-\alpha/2}^2$ or $\chi^2 > \chi_{\alpha/2}^2$

where χ_α^2 and $\chi_{1-\alpha}^2$ are values of χ^2 that locate an area of α to the right and α to the left, respectively, of a chi-square distribution based on $(n-1)$ degrees of freedom.

[*Note:* σ_0^2 is our symbol for the particular numerical value specified for σ^2 in the null hypothesis.]

Assumption: The population from which the random sample is selected has an approximate normal distribution.

EXAMPLE 11.15
Application: One-Tailed Test

A quality control supervisor in a cannery knows that the exact amount each can contains will vary, since there are certain uncontrollable factors that affect the amount of fill. The mean fill per can is important, but equally important is the variation σ^2 of the amount of fill. If σ^2 is large, some cans will contain too little and others too much. Suppose regulatory agencies specify that the standard deviation of the amount of fill for 8-ounce cans should be less than .1 ounce. The quality control supervisor sampled $n = 10$ 8-ounce cans and measured the amount of fill in each. The data (in ounces) are shown here. Is there sufficient evidence to indicate that the standard deviation, σ, of the fill measurements is less than .1 ounce?

7.96	7.90	7.98	8.01	7.97	7.96	8.03	8.02	8.04	8.02

SOLUTION Since the null and alternative hypotheses must be stated in terms of σ^2 (rather than σ), we will want to test the null hypothesis that $\sigma^2 = .01$ against the alternative that $\sigma^2 < .01$. Therefore, the elements of the test are

- H_0: $\sigma^2 = .01$ (i.e., $\sigma = .1$)
- H_a: $\sigma^2 < .01$ (i.e., $\sigma^2 < .1$)
- *Assumption:* The population of amounts of fill of the cans is approximately normal.

- *Test statistic*: $\quad \chi^2 = \dfrac{(n-1)s^2}{\sigma_0^2}$

- *Rejection region*: The smaller the value of s^2 we observe, the stronger the evidence in favor of H_a. Thus, we reject H_0 for "small values" of the test statistic. With $\alpha = .05$ and $(n-1) = 9$ df, the critical χ^2 value is found in Table 7 of Appendix B and illustrated in Figure 11.12. We will reject H_0 if $\chi^2 < 3.32511$. (Remember that the area given in Table 7 is the area to the *right* of the numerical value in the table. Thus, to determine the lower-tail value that has $\alpha = .05$ to its *left*, we use the $\chi^2_{.95}$ column in Table 7.)

FIGURE 11.12

Rejection Region for Example 11.15

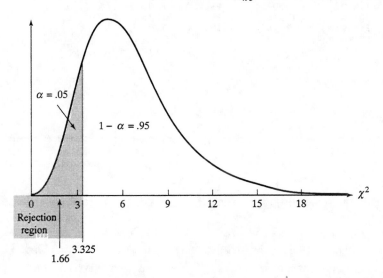

To compute the test statistic, we must find the sample standard deviation, s. Numerical descriptive statistics for the sample data are provided in the SAS printout, Figure 11.13 on page 560. The value of s, shaded in Figure 11.13, is $s = .043$. Substituting $s = .043$, $n = 10$, and $\sigma_0^2 = .01$ into the formula for the test statistic, we obtain

$$\chi^2 = \frac{(10-1)(.043)^2}{.01} = 1.66$$

- *Conclusion*: Since the test statistic, $\chi^2 = 1.66$, is less than 3.32511, the supervisor can conclude that the variance of the population of all amounts of fill is less than $.01(\sigma < .1)$ with 95% confidence. As usual, the confidence is in the procedure used—the χ^2 test. If this procedure is repeatedly used, it will incorrectly reject H_0 only 5% of the time. Thus, the quality control supervisor is confident in the decision that the cannery is operating within the desired limits of variability.

FIGURE 11.13

SAS Printout:
Descriptive Statistics
for Example 11.15

```
Variable=FILL
                Moments
N                     10  Sum Wgts             10
Mean               7.989  Sum               79.89
Std Dev         0.043063  Variance       0.001854
Skewness         -0.8538  Kurtosis       0.479371
USS            638.2579   CSS             0.01669
CV             0.539032   Std Mean       0.013618
T:Mean=0       586.6587   Prob>|T|         0.0001
Sgn Rank          27.5    Prob>|S|         0.0020
Num ^= 0          10

            Quantiles(Def=5)

    100% Max     8.04      99%      8.04
    75%  Q3      8.02      95%      8.04
    50%  Med     7.995     90%      8.035
    25%  Q1      7.96      10%      7.93
    0%   Min     7.9        5%      7.9
                           1%      7.9

    Range        0.14
    Q3-Q1        0.06
    Mode         7.96
```
■

EXERCISES

■ *Learning the Mechanics*

11.63 Calculate the test statistic for testing $H_0: \sigma^2 = \sigma_0^2$ in a normal population for each of the following:

a. $n = 25$, $\bar{x} = 17$, $s^2 = 8$, $\sigma_0^2 = 10$ **b.** $n = 12$, $\bar{x} = 6.2$, $s^2 = 1.7$, $\sigma_0^2 = 1$

c. $n = 50$, $\bar{x} = 106$, $s^2 = 31$, $\sigma_0^2 = 50$ **d.** $n = 100$, $\bar{x} = .35$, $s^2 = .04$, $\sigma_0^2 = .01$

11.64 A random sample of n observations, selected from a normal population, is used to test the null hypothesis $H_0: \sigma^2 = 9$. Specify the appropriate rejection region for each of the following:

a. $H_a: \sigma^2 > 9$, $n = 20$, $\alpha = .01$ **b.** $H_a: \sigma^2 \neq 9$, $n = 20$, $\alpha = .01$

c. $H_a: \sigma^2 < 9$, $n = 12$, $\alpha = .05$ **d.** $H_a: \sigma^2 < 9$, $n = 12$, $\alpha = .10$

11.65 A random sample of $n = 10$ observations yielded $\bar{x} = 231.7$ and $s^2 = 15.5$. Test the null hypothesis $H_0: \sigma^2 = 20$ against the alternative hypothesis $H_a: \sigma^2 < 20$. Use $\alpha = .05$. What assumptions are necessary for the test to be valid?

11.66 The following measurements represent a random sample of $n = 5$ observations from a normal population: 11, 7, 2, 9, 13. Is this sufficient evidence to conclude that $\sigma^2 \neq 2$? Test using $\alpha = .10$.

■ *Applying the Concepts*

11.67 Refer to the *Journal for Engineering for Industry* (May 1993) study of deep hole drilling under drill chip congestion, Exercise 11.9. Test to determine whether the true standard deviation of drill chip lengths differs from 75 mm. Recall that for $n = 50$ drill chips, $s = 50.2$.

11.68 Refer to the *Financial Analysts Journal* (Jan./Feb. 1993) study of NASD stocks, Exercise 11.8. Recall that the mean and standard deviation of the annualized monthly returns for 13 large-firm

NASD stocks was $\bar{x} = 13.50\%$ and $s = 23.84\%$. Conduct a test to determine whether the true standard deviation of the annualized monthly returns for all large-firm NASD stocks is less than 25%. Test using $\alpha = .05$.

11.69 The most common method of disinfecting water for potable use is free residual chlorination. Recently, preammoniation (i.e., the addition of ammonia to the water prior to applying free chlorine) has received considerable attention as an alternative treatment. In one study, 44 water specimens treated with preammoniation were found to have a mean effluent turbidity of 1.8 and a standard deviation of .16 (*American Water Works Journal*, Jan. 1986). Is there sufficient evidence to indicate that the variance of the effluent turbidity in water specimens disinfected by the preammoniation method exceeds .0016? (The value .0016 represents the known effluent turbidity variance of water specimens treated with free chlorine.) Test using $\alpha = .01$.

11.70 Refer to Exercise 11.15 and the sample of 50 return-to-pay ratios for CEOs selected from Appendix A.2. The data are reproduced here. Conduct a test to determine whether the true variance in the ratios differs from .0025. Test using $\alpha = .10$.

.03	.051	.047	.091	.026
.049	.029	.01	.037	.031
.086	.02	.005	.019	.206
.029	.018	.081	.005	.206
.017	.049	.062	.005	.112
.023	.033	.036	.021	.122
.031	.033	.02	.048	.072
.051	.14	.086	.041	.032
.025	.042	.02	.032	.02
.025	.047	.091	.026	.122

11.71 Refer to the EPA study on the precision of a new instrument designed for measuring PCB concentration in fish, Exercise 8.90. The seven PCB readings (in parts per million) taken on the same fish specimen are reproduced here:

6.2	5.8	5.7	6.3	5.9	5.8	6.0

Recall that the EPA requires the new instrument to yield PCB readings with a variance less than .1.

a. Test to determine whether the true variance in the instrument readings is less than .1. Use $\alpha = .10$.

b. In Exercise 8.90, part **b**, you used a 90% confidence interval for the true variance to determine whether the new instrument meets the EPA specifications. Why is the test, part **a**, preferable to the confidence interval?

11.72 Refer to the *Forbes* study of multinational firms, Exercises 8.26 and 8.91. The foreign revenue (expressed as a percentage of total revenue) of the 20 U.S.-based multinational firms in the sample is reproduced on page 562. A MINITAB analysis of the data follows.

Exxon	73.2	Procter & Gamble	39.9
IBM	58.9	Philip Morris	19.6
GM	26.6	Eastman Kodak	40.9
Mobil	64.7	Digital	54.1
Ford	33.2	GE	12.4
Citicorp	52.3	United Technologies	32.9
EI duPont	39.8	Amoco	26.1
Texaco	42.3	Hewlett-Packard	53.3
ITT	43.3	Xerox	34.6
Dow Chemical	54.1	Chevron	20.5

Source: Forbes, July 23, 1990, pp. 362–363.

	N	MEAN	MEDIAN	TRMEAN	STDEV	SEMEAN
Revenue%	20	41.13	40.40	40.95	15.97	3.57

	MIN	MAX	Q1	Q3
Revenue%	12.40	73.20	28.18	53.90

a. Test the hypothesis that the variation in foreign revenue percentages of all U.S.-based multinational firms differs from 100. Use $\alpha = .05$.

b. In Exercise 8.91, you computed a 95% confidence interval for the variance in foreign revenue percentages. Show that the inference derived from the confidence interval agrees with the test, part **a**. Why is the confidence interval preferred?

11.8 Testing the Ratio of Two Population Variances (Optional)

In this optional section, we present a test of hypothesis for comparing two population variances, σ_1^2 and σ_2^2. Variance comparison tests have broad applications in business. For example, a production manager may be interested in comparing the variation in the length of eye-screws produced on each of two assembly lines. A line with a large variation produces too many individual eyescrews that do not meet specifications (either too long or too short), even though the mean length may be satisfactory. Similarly, an investor might want to compare the variation in the monthly rates of return for two different stocks that have the same mean rate of return. In this case, the stock with the smaller variance may be preferred because it is less risky—that is, it is less likely to have many very low and very high monthly return rates.

Variance comparison tests can also be applied prior to conducting a small-sample t test for $(\mu_1 - \mu_2)$, discussed in Section 11.4. Recall that the t test requires the assumption that the variances of the two sampled populations are equal. If the two population variances are greatly different, any inferences derived from the t test are suspect. Consequently, it is important that we detect a significant difference between the two variances, if it exists, before applying the small-sample t test.

EXAMPLE 11.16

Setting up the Hypothesis Test

Suppose you want to conduct a test of hypothesis to compare two population variances. Let σ_1^2 represent the variance of population 1 and σ_2^2 represent the variance of population 2. Assume that independent random samples of size $n_1 = 13$ and $n_2 = 18$ are selected and that the two populations are both normal.

a. Set up the null and alternative hypotheses for testing whether σ_1^2 exceeds σ_2^2

b. Give the form of the test statistic.

c. Specify the rejection region for $\alpha = .05$.

SOLUTION

a. To select whether σ_1^2 exceeds σ_2^2, we test

$$H_0: \quad \sigma_1^2 = \sigma_2^2$$

$$H_a: \quad \sigma_1^2 > \sigma_2^2$$

However, the common statistical procedure for comparing the two variances makes an inference about the ratio, σ_1^2/σ_2^2. This is because the sampling distribution of the estimator of σ_1^2/σ_2^2 is well known when the *samples are randomly and independently selected from two normal populations.* Consequently, we typically write the null and alternative hypotheses as follows:

$$H_0: \quad \frac{\sigma_1^2}{\sigma_2^2} = 1$$

$$H_0: \quad \frac{\sigma_1^2}{\sigma_2^2} > 1$$

b. When the sample sizes are large, s_1^2 and s_2^2 are good estimates of σ_1^2 and σ_2^2, respectively. Therefore, the best estimate of σ_1^2/σ_2^2 is s_1^2/s_2^2. Consequently, the test statistic, called an F statistic, is

$$F = \frac{s_1^2}{s_2^2}$$

c. Under the assumption that both samples come from normal populations, the F statistic, $F = s_1^2/s_2^2$, possesses an F **distribution** with $v_1 = (n_1 - 1)$ numerator degrees of freedom and $v_2 = (n_2 - 1)$ denominator degrees of freedom.

Unlike the z and t distributions of the preceding sections, an F distribution can be symmetric about its mean, skewed to the left, or skewed to the right; its exact shape depends on the degrees of freedom—in this example, $v_1 = (n_1 - 1) = 12$ and $v_2 = (n_2 - 1) = 17$, respectively. An F distribution with $v_1 = 12$ numerator df and $v_2 = 17$ denominator df is shown in Figure 11.14. You can see that this particular F distribution is skewed to the right.

FIGURE 11.14

Rejection Region for
Example 11.16

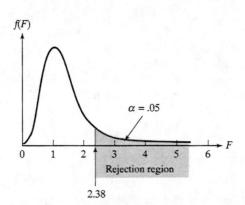

Upper-tail critical values of F are found in Tables 8, 9, 10, and 11 of Appendix B. Table 9 of Appendix B, partially reproduced in Table 11.6, gives F values that correspond to $\alpha = .05$ upper-tail areas for different pairs of degrees of freedom. The columns of the table correspond to various numerator degrees of freedom, whereas the rows correspond to various denominator degrees of freedom.

Thus, if the number of numerator degrees of freedom is 12 and the number of denominator degrees of freedom is 17, we find the F value,

$$F_{.05} = 2.38$$

As shown in Figure 11.14, $\alpha = .05$ is the tail area to the right of 2.38 in the F distribution with 12 numerator df and 17 denominator df. Thus, the probability that the F statistic will exceed 2.38 is $\alpha = .05$.

Given this information on the F distribution, we are now able to find the rejection region for this test. Logically, large values of $F = s_1^2/s_2^2$ will lead us to reject H_0 in favor of H_a. (If H_a is true, then $\sigma_1^2 > \sigma_2^2$. Consequently, s_1^2 will very likely exceed s_2^2 and F will be large.) How large? The critical F value depends on our choice of α. The general form of the rejection region is $F > F_\alpha$. For $\alpha = .05$, we have $F_{.05} = 2.38$ (based on $v_1 = 12$ and $v_2 = 17$ df). Thus, the rejection region is

Reject H_0 if $F > 2.38$.   ■

The elements of a hypothesis test for the ratio of two population variances, σ_1^2/σ_2^2, are given in the next box.

Table 11.6 Reproduction of Part of Table 9 of Appendix B; $\alpha = .05$

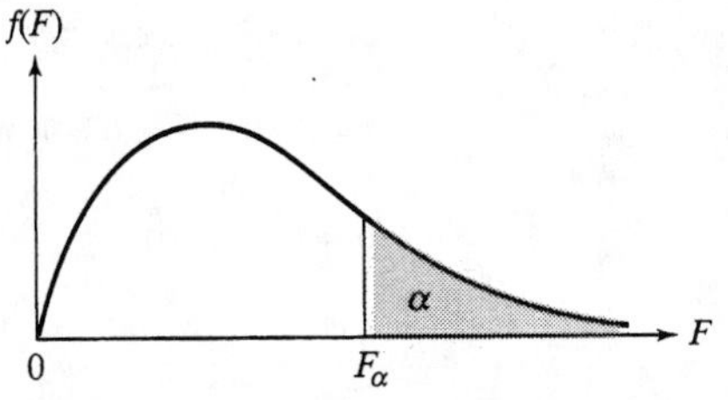

v_2 \ v_1	Numerator Degrees of Freedom 1	2	3	4	5	6	7	8	9
Denominator Degrees of Freedom 1	161.4	199.5	215.7	224.6	230.2	234.0	236.8	238.9	240.5
2	18.51	19.00	19.16	19.25	19.30	19.33	19.35	19.37	19.38
3	10.13	9.55	9.28	9.12	9.01	8.94	8.89	8.85	8.81
4	7.71	6.94	6.59	6.39	6.26	6.16	6.09	6.04	6.00
5	6.61	5.79	5.41	5.19	5.05	4.95	4.88	4.82	4.77
6	5.99	5.14	4.76	4.53	4.39	4.28	4.21	4.15	4.10
7	5.59	4.74	4.35	4.12	3.97	3.87	3.79	3.73	3.68
8	5.32	4.46	4.07	3.84	3.69	3.58	3.50	3.44	3.39
9	5.12	4.26	3.86	3.63	3.48	3.37	3.29	3.23	3.18
10	4.96	4.10	3.71	3.48	3.33	3.22	3.14	3.07	3.02
11	4.84	3.98	3.59	3.36	3.20	3.09	3.01	2.95	2.90
12	4.75	3.89	3.49	3.25	3.11	3.00	2.91	2.85	2.80
13	4.67	3.81	3.41	3.18	3.03	2.92	2.83	2.77	2.71
14	4.60	3.74	3.34	3.11	2.96	2.85	2.76	2.70	2.65

Test of Hypothesis for the Ratio of Two Population Variances, σ_1^2/σ_2^2

One-Tailed Test

$$H_0: \frac{\sigma_1^2}{\sigma_2^2} = 1$$

$$H_a: \frac{\sigma_1^2}{\sigma_2^2} > 1$$

$$\left[\text{or, } H_a: \frac{\sigma_1^2}{\sigma_2^2} < 1\right]$$

Two-Tailed Test

$$H_0: \frac{\sigma_1^2}{\sigma_2^2} = 1$$

$$H_a: \frac{\sigma_1^2}{\sigma_2^2} \neq 1$$

(continued)

Test statistic:

$$F = \frac{s_1^2}{s_2^2}$$

$$\left[\text{or, } F = \frac{s_2^2}{s_1^2} \right]$$

Test statistic:

$$F = \frac{\text{Larger sample variance}}{\text{Smaller sample variance}}$$

i.e.,

$$F = \begin{cases} \dfrac{s_1^2}{s_2^2} & \text{when} \quad s_1^2 > s_2^2 \\[2ex] \dfrac{s_2^2}{s_1^2} & \text{when} \quad s_2^2 > s_1^2 \end{cases}$$

Rejection region:
$$F > F_\alpha$$

Rejection region:
$$F > F_{\alpha/2}$$

where F_α and $F_{\alpha/2}$ are values that locate an area α and $\alpha/2$, respectively, in the upper tail of the F distribution with $v_1 =$ numerator degrees of freedom (i.e., the df for the sample variance in the numerator) and $v_2 =$ denominator degrees of freedom (i.e., the df for the sample variance in the denominator). [*Note:* $v_i = n_i - 1$, n_i is the sample size for the ith sample.]

Assumptions: **1.** Both of the populations from which the samples are selected have relative frequency distributions that are approximately normal.
2. The random samples are selected in an independent manner from the two populations.

EXAMPLE 11.17
Application: Comparing
Population Variances

Refer to the *Journal of Marketing* study described in Example 11.11. The researcher's objective is to compare the mean buyer savings for two bargaining strategies, competitive and coordinative. Since both samples of buyers are small ($n_1 = 8$ and $n_2 = 8$), the t test for $(\mu_1 - \mu_2)$ requires that both sampled populations of buyer savings be normal with equal variances. To check the latter assumption, the researcher wants to determine whether the variation in the savings of buyers using the competitive strategy differs from the variation in the savings of buyers using the coordinative strategy. Test using $\alpha = .10$.

SOLUTION Let

$\sigma_1^2 =$ Population variance of savings for buyers using the competitive bargaining strategy

$\sigma_2^2 =$ Population variance of savings for buyers using the coordinative strategy

For this test to yield valid results, we must assume that both samples of buyer savings come from normal populations and that the samples are independent.

Now, following the guidelines in the box, we list the elements of this two-tailed hypothesis test:

- H_0: $\dfrac{\sigma_1^2}{\sigma_2^2} = 1$ (i.e., $\sigma_1^2 = \sigma_2^2$)

- H_a: $\dfrac{\sigma_1^2}{\sigma_2^2} \neq 1$ (i.e., $\sigma_1^2 \neq \sigma_2^2$)

- *Test statistic:* $F = \dfrac{\text{Larger } s^2}{\text{Smaller } s^2} = \dfrac{s_1^2}{s_2^2} = \dfrac{(538)^2}{(357)^2} = 2.27$

(based on summary statistics shaded in the MINITAB printout, Figure 11.15).

FIGURE 11.15

MINITAB Printout for
Example 11.17

	N	MEAN	MEDIAN	TRMEAN	STDEV	SEMEAN
Compete	8	1706	1706	1706	538	190
Coordin	8	2106	2145	2106	357	126

	MIN	MAX	Q1	Q3
Compete	663	2644	1594	1850
Coordin	1544	2640	1766	2314

- *Rejection region:* For this two-tailed test, $\alpha = .10$ and $\alpha/2 = .05$. Thus, the rejection region is

  Reject H_0 if $F > 3.79$ (from Table 11.6)

- *Conclusion:* Since the test statistic, $F = 2.27$, does not fall in the rejection region, we fail to reject H_0. Therefore, at $\alpha = .10$, the data do not provide sufficient evidence to indicate a difference between the variances in savings of buyers using the two types of bargaining strategies. Although it appears that the assumption of equal variances required for the small-sample t test is satisfied, we must be careful not to flatly accept H_0: $\sigma_1^2 = \sigma_2^2$ without knowing the true value of β, the probability of a Type II error. ■

Example 11.17 illustrates the technique for calculating the test statistic and rejection region for a two-tailed F test. The reason we place the larger sample variance in the numerator of the test statistic is that only upper-tail values of F are shown in the F tables of Appendix B—no lower-tail values are given. By placing the larger sample variance in the numerator, we make certain that only the upper tail of the rejection region is used. The fact that the upper-tail area is $\alpha/2$ reminds us that the test is two-tailed.

The problem of not being able to locate an F value in the lower tail of the F distribution is easily avoided in a one-tailed test because we can control how we specify the ratio of the population variances in H_0 and H_a. That is, we can always make a one-tailed test an *upper-tailed* test. For example, if we want to test whether σ_1^2 is greater than σ_2^2, then we write the alternative hypothesis as

$$H_a: \quad \frac{\sigma_1^2}{\sigma_2^2} > 1 \quad (\text{i.e., } \sigma_1^2 > \sigma_2^2)$$

and the appropriate test statistic is $F = s_1^2 / s_2^2$. Conversely, if we want to test whether σ_1^2 is less than σ_2^2 (i.e., whether σ_2^2 is greater than σ_1^2), we write

$$H_a: \quad \frac{\sigma_2^2}{\sigma_1^2} > 1 \quad (\text{i.e., } \sigma_2^2 > \sigma_1^2)$$

and the corresponding test statistic is $F = s_2^2 / s_1^2$.

EXERCISES

■ **Learning the Mechanics**

11.73 Find $F_{.05}$ for an F distribution with:
  a. Numerator df = 7, denominator df = 25   **b.** Numerator df = 10, denominator df = 8
  c. Numerator df = 30, denominator df = 60   **d.** Numerator df = 15, denominator df = 4

11.74 Find F_α for an F distribution with 15 numerator df and 12 denominator df for the following values of α:
  a. $\alpha = .025$ **b.** $\alpha = .05$ **c.** $\alpha = .10$

11.75 Calculate the value of the test statistic for testing $H_0: \sigma_1^2/\sigma_2^2 = 1$ in each of the following cases:
  a. $H_a: \sigma_1^2/\sigma_2^2 > 1$; $s_1^2 = 1.75$, $s_2^2 = 1.23$ **b.** $H_a: \sigma_1^2/\sigma_2^2 < 1$; $s_1^2 = 1.52$, $s_2^2 = 5.90$
  c. $H_a: \sigma_1^2/\sigma_2^2 \neq 1$; $s_1^2 = 2,264$, $s_2^2 = 4,009$

11.76 Under what conditions does the sampling distribution of s_1^2 / s_2^2 have an F distribution?

■ **Applying the Concepts**

11.77 Wet samplers are standard devices used to measure the chemical composition of precipitation. The accuracy of the wet deposition readings, however, may depend on the number of samplers stationed in the field. Experimenters in The Netherlands collected wet deposition measurements using anywhere from one to eight identical wet samplers (*Atmospheric Environment*, Vol. 24A, 1990). For each sampler (or sampler combination), data were collected every 24 hours for an entire year; thus, 365 readings were collected per sampler (or sampler combination). When one wet sampler was used, the standard deviation of the hydrogen readings (measured as percentage relative to the average reading from all eight samplers) was

6.3%. When three wet samplers were used, the standard deviation of the hydrogen readings (measured as percentage relative to the average reading from all eight samplers) was 2.6%. Conduct a test to compare the variation in hydrogen readings for the two sampling schemes (i.e., one wet sampler versus three wet samplers). Test using $\alpha = .05$.

11.78 A study was conducted to compare the variation in the price of wholesale residual petroleum sold in rural (low-density) and urban (high-density) counties. In particular, the variable of interest was the natural logarithm of the ratio of county price to state price, i.e., log(county price/ state price). Based on independent random samples of 10 rural counties and 23 urban counties, the descriptive statistics shown in the table were obtained. Is there evidence of a difference between the variance in the log-price ratios of rural and urban counties?

	n	$\bar{x}$	s
Rural	10	.239	.310
Urban	23	.117	.199

Source: Saavedra, P. et al. "Geographical stratification of petroleum retailers and resellers." Paper presented at Joint Statistical Meetings, Anaheim, Calif., Aug. 1990.

11.79 An *Environmental Science & Technology* (Oct. 1993) study was conducted to compare the mean oxon/thion ratios at a California orchard under two weather conditions: foggy and clear/ cloudy. Test the assumption of equal variances required for the comparison of means to be valid. Use $\alpha = .02$.

Date		Condition	Thion	Oxon	Oxon/Thion Ratio
Jan.	15	Fog	38.2	10.3	.270
	17	Fog	28.6	6.9	.241
	18	Fog	30.2	6.2	.205
	19	Fog	23.7	12.4	.523
	20	Fog	62.3	(Air sample lost)	—
	20	Clear	74.1	45.8	.618
	21	Fog	88.2	9.9	.112
	21	Clear	46.4	27.4	.591
	22	Fog	135.9	44.8	.330
	23	Fog	102.9	27.8	.270
	23	Cloudy	28.9	6.5	.225
	25	Fog	46.9	11.2	.239
	25	Clear	44.3	16.6	.375

Source: Selber, J. N. et al. "Air and fog deposition residues of four organophosphate insecticides used on dormant orchards in the San Joaquin Valley, California." *Environmental Science & Technology*, Vol. 27, No. 10, Oct. 1993, p. 2,240 (Table V).

11.80 An experiment was conducted to study the effect of reinforced flanges on the torsional capacity of reinforced concrete T-beams (*Journal of the American Concrete Institute*, Jan.–Feb. 1983). Several different types of T-beams were used in the experiment, each type having a different flange width. The beams were tested under combined torsion and bending until failure (i.e., cracking). One variable of interest is the cracking torsion moment at the top of the flange of the T-beam. Cracking torsion moments for eight beams with 70-cm slab widths and eight beams with 100-cm slab widths are recorded here:

70-cm Slab Width	100-cm Slab Width
6.00	6.80
7.20	9.20
10.20	8.80
13.20	13.20
11.40	11.20
13.60	14.90
9.20	10.20
11.20	11.80

a. Is there evidence of a difference in the variation in the cracking torsion moments of the two types of T-beams? Use $\alpha = .10$.

b. What assumptions are required for the test to be valid?

11.81 An experiment was conducted in England to examine the diet metabolizable energy (ME) content of commercial cat foods. The researchers monitored the diets of 57 adult domestic short-haired cats; 28 cats were fed a diet of commercial canned cat food and 29 cats were fed a diet of dry cat food over a 3-week period. At the end of the trial, the ME content was determined for each cat, with the results shown in the table. Conduct a test to determine whether the variation in ME content of cats fed canned food differs from the variation in ME content of cats fed dry food. Use $\alpha = .10$.

	Canned Food	Dry Food
Sample Size	28	29
Mean ME Content	.96	3.70
Standard Deviation	.26	.48

Source: Kendall, P. T., Burger, I. N., and Smith, P. M. "Methods of estimation of the metabolizable energy content of cat foods." *Feline Practice*, Vol. 15, No. 2, Feb. 1986, pp. 38–44.

11.82 Heavy doses of ethylene oxide (ETO) in rabbits have been shown to alter significantly the DNA structure of cells. Although it is a known mutagen and suspected carcinogen, ETO is used quite frequently in sterilizing hospital supplies. A study was conducted to investigate the effect of ETO on hospital personnel involved with the sterilization process. Thirty-one subjects were randomly selected and assigned to one of two tasks: 18 subjects were assigned the task of opening the sterilization package that contains ETO (task 1); the remaining 13 subjects were assigned the task of opening and unloading the sterilizer gun filled with ETO (task 2). After the tasks were performed, researchers measured the amount of ETO (in milligrams) present in the bloodstream of each subject. A summary of the results appears in the table. Do the data provide sufficient evidence to indicate a difference in the variability of the ETO levels in subjects assigned to the two tasks? Test using $\alpha = .10$.

	Task 1	Task 2
Sample Size	18	13
Mean	5.90	5.60
Standard Deviation	1.93	3.10

SUMMARY

In this chapter, we have summarized the procedures for testing hypotheses about various population parameters. As we noted with the estimation techniques of Chapter 8, fewer assumptions about the sampled populations are required when the sample sizes are large. We also wish to emphasize that *statistical* significance differs from *practical* significance, and the two must not be confused. A reasonable approach to hypothesis testing blends a valid application of the formal statistical procedures with the researcher's knowledge of the subject matter.

KEY TERMS

Practical significance   Statistical significance

KEY FORMULAS

Large-sample test statistic:

$$z = \frac{\text{Estimator} - \text{Hypothesized}(H_0)\text{ value}}{\text{Standard error}}$$

Small-sample test statistic:

$$t = \frac{\text{Estimator} - \text{Hypothesized}(H_0)\text{ value}}{\text{Estimated standard error}}$$

Note: The respective estimators and standard errors for the population parameters μ, $(\mu_1 - \mu_2)$, π, and $(\pi_1 - \pi_2)$ are provided in Table 8.9 of Chapter 8. [The test statistics for the parameters σ^2 and σ_1^2/σ_2^2 from the optional sections are given below.]

Test statistic for σ^2: $\chi^2 = \dfrac{(n-1)s^2}{\sigma_0^2}$

Test statistic for σ_1^2/σ_2^2: $F = \dfrac{s_1^2}{s_2^2}$

SUPPLEMENTARY EXERCISES

[Note: Starred (*) exercises are from the optional sections of this chapter.]

11.83   When trees grown in greenhouses are replanted in their natural habitat, there is usually only a 50% survival rate. However, a recent General Telephone and Electronics (GTE) advertisement claimed that trees grown in a particular environment ideal for plant growth have a 95% survival rate when replanted. These trees are grown inside a mountain in Idaho where the air temperature, carbon dioxide content, and humidity are all constant, and there are no major disease or insect problems. A key growth ingredient—light—is supplied by specially made GTE Sylvania Super-Metalarc lamps. These lights help the young trees develop more fibrous root systems that aid in the transplantation. Suppose we wish to challenge GTE's claim, i.e., we want to test whether the true proportion of all trees grown inside the Idaho mountain that survive when replanted in their natural habitat is less than .95. We randomly sample 150 of the trees grown in the controlled environment, replant the trees in their natural habitat, and observe that 138 of the trees survive. Perform the test at a level of significance of $\alpha = .01$.

11.84   C. S. Patterson conducted an investigation of the financing policies and practices of large regulated public utilities (*Financial Management*, Summer 1984). One goal of Patterson's research was to determine whether public utilities operate at a debt level that maximizes shareholder wealth. A sample of 47 publicly held electric utilities identified in *Moody's Manual* as having revenues of $300 million or more took part in the study. The actual debt ratios (defined as long-term debt divided by total capital) of the companies were recorded, with the following results:

$\bar{x} = .485$ $\qquad$ $s = .029$

Prior to giving their actual debt ratios, the companies estimated that the mean debt ratio at which they should operate to maximize shareholder wealth is .459. Is there sufficient evidence to indicate that the actual mean debt ratio of public utilities differed from the optimum value .459? Test using $\alpha = .10$.

**From the optional sections of this chapter.*

11.85 Refer to the study on the differences in the ethical perceptions of male and female managers, described in Example 8.22. Another objective of the research was to determine how each gender perceived their counterparts would respond to the same set of ethical decision situations (*Journal of Business Ethics*, Aug. 1987). For example, the 50 male executives in the survey had an average self-rating of 2.44 on the question of whether using company materials and supplies for personal use is unethical (1 = very unethical, 5 = not at all unethical). When the 50 female executives were asked to estimate how the men would respond to such a question, the average rating was 3.06. Assuming that the variances in the ratings of the two samples are both equal to 2.2, conduct a test for a difference between the mean ethics ratings of the two groups using $\alpha = .05$. Interpret the result in the context of the problem.

11.86 Marketers spend billions of dollars annually to develop humorous advertising. But is humor in advertising an effective means of marketing a product? To determine the views of successful advertising practitioners concerning humor in advertising, T. J. Madden and M. G. Weinberger surveyed two groups of advertising personnel: (1) vice presidents/directors of research and (2) vice presidents/directors of creative services (*Journal of Advertising Research*, Aug./Sept. 1984). The two groups of executives, research and creative, were selected because historically they have conflicting views on advertising techniques and objectives. One hundred thirty-seven research directors and 145 creative directors took part in the study. The table shows the numbers of directors in each group who agreed with the stated communication objectives of humorous advertising. (Numbers are based on percentages given in the original article.) For each of the three communication objectives, conduct a test to determine whether the percentage who agree with the objective differs for the two groups of directors. Use $\alpha = .01$.

	Communication Objective	Research Sample $n_1 = 137$	Creative Sample $n_2 = 145$
1.	Humor helps gain awareness of new products	81	120
2.	Humor harms comprehension more than nonhumor	88	57
3.	Humor increases persuasion more than nonhumor	34	39

Source: Adapted from the *Journal of Advertising Research.* © Copyright 1984 by the Advertisting Research Foundation.

11.87 Are learning preferences of college students affected by program instruction, or do they remain stable over time? To answer this question, researchers administered the Learning Preference Inventory (LPI) exam to 37 junior students at the University of Illinois during the first week the students were on campus (*American Journal of Occupational Therapy*, Oct. 1984). The LPI measures preference for learning in a well-organized, teacher-directed class, with expectations, assignments, and goals clearly defined. The higher the LPI score, the greater the preference. Following four quarters of academic course work, which included independent study methods and small group tutorials as well as the traditional classroom lectures, the students were again administered the LPI. The differences between the LPI scores (score before minus score after) for the sample of 37 students had a mean of 4.11 and a standard deviation of 15.82.

a. Give the null and alternative hypotheses appropriate for testing whether the mean score on the LPI exam given at the beginning of the term differs from the mean score on the LPI exam given after four quarters of academic course work.

b. Note that the data were collected as matched pairs. For this application, what is the advantage of using a matched-pairs experiment rather than independent samples?

c. Conduct the test of part **a**, using $\alpha = .05$. Can you infer that students' preferences for learning in a teacher-structured atmosphere (as measured by the LPI) changed after four quarters of academic course work? Explain.

*11.88 The quality control department of a paper company measures the brightness (a measure of reflectance) of finished paper periodically throughout the day. Two instruments used to measure the paper specimens are subject to error, but they can be adjusted so that the mean readings for a control paper specimen are the same for both instruments. Suppose you are concerned about the precision of the two instruments—namely, that the variation in readings from instrument 2 exceeds that for instrument 1. To check this theory, five measurements of a single paper sample are made on both instruments. The data are shown in the table. Determine whether instrument 2 readings are less precise (i.e., more variable) than instrument 1. Test using $\alpha = .05$.

Instrument 1	Instrument 2
29	26
28	34
30	30
28	32
30	28

*11.89 A new gun-like apparatus has been devised to replace the needle in administering vaccines. The apparatus, which is connected to a large supply of the vaccine, can be set to inject different amounts of the serum, but the variance in the amount of serum injected in a given person must not be greater than .06 to ensure proper inoculation. A random sample of 25 injections resulted in a variance of .135. Do the data provide sufficient evidence to indicate the gun is not working properly? Use $\alpha = .10$.

*11.90 The testing department of a tire and rubber company schedules truck and passenger tires for durability tests. Currently, tires are scheduled twice weekly on flexible processors (machines that can handle either truck or passenger tires) using the shortest processing time (SPT) approach. Under SPT, the tire with the shortest processing time is scheduled first. Company researchers have developed a new scheduling rule that they believe will reduce the variation in flow time (i.e., the variation in the completion time of a test) and lead to a reduction in the variation in tardiness of a scheduled test. To compare the two scheduling rules, 64 tires were randomly selected and divided into two groups of equal size. One set of tires was scheduled using SPT, the other using the proposed rule. A summary of the flow times and tardiness (in hours) of the tire tests is provided in the table.

	Flow Time		Tardiness	
	Mean	*Variance*	*Mean*	*Variance*
SPT	158.28	8,532.80	5.26	452.09
Proposed Rule	117.07	5,208.53	4.52	319.41

a. Is there sufficient evidence at $\alpha = .05$ to conclude that the variation in flow time is less under the proposed scheduling rule than under the SPT approach?

b. Is there sufficient evidence at $\alpha = .05$ to conclude that the proposed scheduling rule will lead to a reduction in the variation in tardiness of tire tests?

11.91 According to a Gallup study for the American Society of Quality Control, "men focus on product performance and durability when assessing quality [of American-made goods] while women also consider the availability of service, whether a product can be repaired, and type of warranty" (*American Demographics*, June 1986). Overall, 58% of the women surveyed rated American products "high" in quality, compared to 43% of the men. Assuming that the sample survey included 500 men and 500 women, conduct a test to determine whether the true percentage of women who rate American products high in quality exceeds the true percentage of men. Use $\alpha = .01$.

11.92 A new insecticide is advertised to kill more than 95% of roaches upon contact. In a laboratory test, the insecticide was applied to 400 roaches and, although all 400 eventually died, only 384 died immediately after contact. Is this sufficient evidence to support the advertised claim? Base your decision on the computed *p*-value.

*11.93 It is essential in the manufacture of machinery to utilize parts that conform to specifications. In the past, diameters of the ball bearings produced by a certain manufacturer had a variance of .00156. To cut costs, the manufacturer instituted a less expensive production method. The variance of the diameters of 100 randomly sampled bearings produced by the new process was .00211. Do the data provide sufficient evidence to indicate that diameters of ball bearings produced by the new process are more variable than those produced by the old process? Test using $\alpha = .05$.

11.94 To examine potential gender differences in the industrial sales force, a sample of 244 males and a sample of 153 females were administered a questionnaire (*Journal of Personal Selling & Sales Management*, Summer 1990). All respondents were either sales managers or salespeople at one of 16 industrial firms located in the southeastern United States. One of the variables measured in the study was months of experience in sales. Summary statistics for this variable are given in the table.

	Males	*Females*
Sample Size	244	155
Mean Number of Months Experience	64.99	27.69
Standard Deviation	79.59	68.88

Source: Schul, P. L., Remington, S., and Berl, R. L. "Assessing gender differences in relationships between supervisory behaviors and job-related outcomes in the industrial sales force." *Journal of Personal Selling & Sales Management*, Summer 1990, Vol. X, p. 7 (Table 2).

a. Is there evidence of a difference between the mean number of months experience in sales of males and females? Test using $\alpha = .01$.

b. The *p*-value of the test, part **a**, was reported as $p < .001$. Interpret this result.

c. The researchers also compared the male and female samples with respect to the following variables: job satisfaction, pay satisfaction, motivation, and organizational commitment. Why might the results of these tests be misleading indicators of gender differences? [*Hint:* Consider the possibility that differences in experience may explain why the two groups differ with respect to job satisfaction, pay satisfaction, etc.]

11.95 To what extent, if any, can we influence local weather conditions? Some Texas farmers have hired a meteorologist to investigate the effectiveness of cloud seeding in the artificial production of rainfall. Two farming areas in Texas with similar past meteorological records were selected for the experiment. One is seeded regularly throughout the year, whereas the other is left unseeded. Data on the monthly precipitation (in inches) at the farms for the first 6 months of the year are recorded in the table. Using a significance level of $\alpha = .05$, test whether the true mean difference between the monthly precipitation in the seeded and unseeded farm areas is greater than 0.

Month	Seeded Farm Area	Unseeded Farm Area
1	1.75	1.62
2	2.12	1.83
3	1.53	1.40
4	1.10	0.75
5	1.70	1.71
6	2.42	2.33

11.96 "M*A*S*H"—a former CBS television comedy series about a mobile military hospital unit in the Korean War—was highly acclaimed for using a blend of comedy and drama to depict the realities of war and organizational life in general. Because the series had a devoted following of college students, Dyer and Dyer were interested in determining whether "M*A*S*H" shaped college students' views on organizational values and the type of people they would like as superiors, peers, and subordinates in the real work world (*Organizational Dynamics*, Summer 1984). The researchers surveyed college students who watched "M*A*S*H" regularly for at least 1 year. Students were asked to evaluate 11 major "M*A*S*H" characters and to rank them in order of their preference as to whom they would like to have as a superior. Of the 411 students with GPA below 2.99, 222 selected Hawkeye Pierce as their first or second choice; of the 76 students with GPA above 3.75, 23 selected Hawkeye as their first or second choice. Is there sufficient evidence to indicate that college students with lower GPAs are more likely to choose Hawkeye as a desirable superior than college students with higher GPAs? Test using $\alpha = .01$. [*Note:* In the TV show, Hawkeye was a nonconformist in dress, speech, and action in relating to his superiors.]

11.97 *Personnel Psychology* (Winter 1983) examined the well-known Japanese concept of human resources management, called Theory Z. The Theory Z philosophy emphasizes trusting, intimate, and subtle relationships between managers and subordinates designed to maximize worker loyalty, commitment, and motivation. Two groups of managers—100 Japanese managers and 211 American managers—were administered the Sarnoff Survey of Attitudes Toward Life (SSATL), designed to measure motivation for upward mobility in three major areas: advancement, money, and forward striving. (Higher scores indicate a greater degree of motivation.) The accompanying table gives summary statistics for the three scales of measurement.

| | American | | Japanese | | | p-value for testing |
	$\bar{x}$	s	$\bar{x}$	s	z value	$H_0: \mu_1 = \mu_2$
Advancement	16.75	4.75	23.92	3.20	−15.66	<.001
Money	14.80	3.60	18.12	2.90	−8.72	<.001
Forward striving	34.24	5.55	37.79	3.50	−6.85	<.001

Source: Howard, A., Shudo, K., and Umeshima, M. "Motivation and values among Japanese and American managers." *Personnel Psychology*, Winter 1983, Vol. 36, No. 4, pp. 883–898.

a. For each measure of motivation, verify the *z* value for testing whether the SSATL score for American managers is less than the corresponding mean for Japanese managers.

b. Interpret the *p*-value for each test of part **a**.

c. In their discussion, the authors mention several "precautions [that] should be heeded before accepting the results at face value." These include:

1. Of the Japanese sample, 15% were nonmanagement, compared to none for the American sample.

2. The type of industry varies for the Japanese sample, whereas the American sample was drawn from one company.

3. The American sample represented different departments, whereas nearly all the Japanese were in personnel or training fields. Why might these facts bias the results of the study?

■ CASE STUDY 11.1

Comparing Low-Bid Prices to DOT Estimates in Highway Construction

Consider the data described in Appendix A.6. Recall (Case Study 3.2) that the data set contains information on the low-bid price, status (fixed or competitive), and Department of Transportation (DOT) engineer's estimate of the fair market price for a sample of 279 road construction contracts awarded in the state of Florida. In this case study, our goal is to compare the mean low-bid price to the mean DOT estimated price for each of the two groups of road contracts—fixed and competitive.

In theory, the mean low-bid price should be higher than the mean DOT estimate for fixed contracts. However, no significant difference should exist with competitive contracts. Consequently, we want to test each of the following two hypotheses:

Hypothesis 1: H_0: $\mu_{1,\text{FIXED}} = \mu_{2,\text{FIXED}}$

versus H_a: $\mu_{1,\text{FIXED}} > \mu_{2,\text{FIXED}}$

Hypothesis 2: H_0: $\mu_{1,\text{COMP}} = \mu_{2,\text{COMP}}$

versus H_a: $\mu_{1,\text{COMP}} \neq \mu_{2,\text{COMP}}$

where μ_1 = population mean low-bid price and μ_2 = population mean DOT estimated price.

a. Determine whether the data in Appendix A.6 should be analyzed using the independent samples test or the test for matched pairs. Explain your reasoning.

b. Summary statistics for low-bid price, DOT estimated price, and the difference between low-bid price and DOT estimate are provided in the SAS printouts, Figures 11.16 and 11.17. Figure 11.16 gives the descriptive statistics for the 85 fixed contracts and Figure 11.17 gives the descriptive statistics for the 194 competitive contracts. Use the relevant information to conduct the tests. Interpret the results.

FIGURE 11.16

Descriptive Statistics for Fixed Contracts

```
------------------------------------ STATUS=FIXED ------------------------------------
```

N Obs	Variable	N	Minimum	Maximum	Mean	Std Dev
85	LOWBID	85	46896.64	5654862.60	714474.02	970703.93
	DOTEST	85	43145.61	5447586.66	646845.93	887595.19
	DIFF	85	-94075.97	785525.72	67628.09	132551.16

FIGURE 11.17

Descriptive Statistics for Competitive Contracts

```
------------------------------------ STATUS=COMP ------------------------------------
```

N Obs	Variable	N	Minimum	Maximum	Mean	Std Dev
194	LOWBID	194	22853.20	10480320.24	1332340.41	2064752.78
	DOTEST	194	21960.00	10743600.26	1454153.64	2215461.67
	DIFF	194	-2740448.43	1279101.77	-121813.23	362772.39

■ CASE STUDY 11.2 ■

Analyzing the Commitment Data: Stayers Versus Leavers

In Case Study 5.1, we introduced the *Academy of Management* (Oct. 1993) study of employee commitment to an aerospace firm. Recall that the researchers measured continuance, affective, and moral commitment by administering a questionnaire to a sample of 270 of the firm's employees. One year after the questionnaire was administered, the researchers found that 48 of the 270 sampled employees had left the firm for another job. Thus, one objective of the study was to compare the overall level of commitment of these 48 "leavers" with the overall level of commitment of the 222 employees who remained with the firm ("stayers"). In theory, the stayers should have been more committed to the firm than the leavers.

This case study involves a computer analysis of the commitment data described in Appendix A.7. (The complete data set is available on a $3\frac{1}{2}''$ diskette from the publisher.)

a. An employee's overall level of commitment to the firm is determined by summing the continuance, affective, and moral commitment scales. The higher this sum, the greater the employee's commitment level. Use a computer to calculate the overall commitment level for each of the 270 sampled employees.

b. Calculate descriptive statistics on the overall commitment levels for each of the two groups of employees, stayers and leavers. Interpret the results. [*Note:* The variable Leave on the data set differentiates between the two groups: Leave = 1 for leavers and Leave = 0 for stayers.]

c. Test the researchers' hypothesis that the mean commitment level of stayers exceeds the corresponding mean for leavers. (Use $\alpha = .05$). Interpret the results.

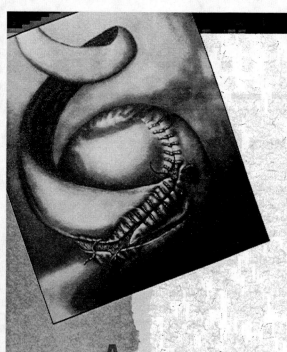

Chapter 12

SIMPLE LINEAR REGRESSION AND CORRELATION

At major colleges and universities, administrators (e.g., deans, chairpersons, provosts, presidents) are among the highest paid state employees. Is there a link between the raises administrators receive and their performance on the job? This and other questions concerning the relationship between two variables will be discussed in this chapter, and you will learn more about the raise–performance relationship of college administrators in Case Study 12.1.

■ CONTENTS

12.1 Bivariate Relationships

The procedures discussed in the previous four chapters are most useful in cases where we are interested in testing hypotheses about or estimating the values of population parameters based on random sampling. However, a more important concern may be the relationship between two different random variables, x and y, known as a **bivariate relationship**. For example, real estate appraisers, tax assessors, real estate investors, and home buyers may be interested in the relationship between the appraised value of a property, x, and its sale price, y; or an automobile dealer may be interested in the bivariate relationship between the size of his sales force, x, and his yearly sales revenue, y; or a concessions manager at a baseball park may be interested in the bivariate relationship between a game's total attendance, x, and the number of hot dogs purchased, y; and so on. In each case, the object of this interest is not merely academic. The real estate investor wants to know whether the appraised value of a property is a good indicator of the property's actual selling price (if it were to be put on the market for sale); the auto dealer would like to know whether the size of his sales force is a reliable predictor of his yearly sales revenue; and the concessions manager wishes to determine whether total game attendance is a good indicator of the number of hot dogs that will be purchased at that game.

How can we determine whether one variable, x, is a reliable predictor of another variable, y? To answer this question, we must be able to *model* the bivariate relationship—that is, describe how the two variables, x and y, are related using a mathematical equation. In this chapter, we present a method useful for modeling the (straight-line) relationship between two variables—a method called **simple linear regression analysis**.

12.2 Straight-Line Probabilistic Models

Consider the Federal Trade Commission's tar, nicotine, and carbon monoxide rankings of domestic cigarettes described in Appendix A.4. Suppose you want to model the relationship between the carbon monoxide (CO) ranking and the nicotine content of the cigarette brands. Do you believe that an *exact* mathematical relationship exists between the two variables? That is, would it be possible to state or calculate the exact CO ranking of a cigarette brand if you knew the nicotine content of the brand? In reality, the answer is a very definite no! The amount of carbon monoxide in the smoke of any given cigarette will depend not only on the nicotine content of the brand, but also on such variables as the tar content, length, filter-type, light type, and menthol flavor of the cigarette. You can probably think of additional variables that play an important role in determining the FTC's carbon monoxide ranking of a cigarette. How can we construct a model, then, for two variables for which no exact relationship exists? We illustrate with an example.

EXAMPLE 12.1
Plotting Data

The nicotine and CO measurements for a sample of 20 different cigarette brands extracted from the data described in Appendix A.4 are given in Table 12.1 on page 582. Hypothesize a reasonable model for the relationship between CO ranking and nicotine content.

Table 12.1 Carbon Monoxide and Nicotine Data for Example 12.1

Brand	CO	Nicotine	Brand	CO	Nicotine
1	15	.9	11	6	.5
2	6	.4	12	22	1.2
3	13	1.3	13	15	.8
4	12	.8	14	17	1.3
5	12	1.2	15	13	1.0
6	9	.7	16	11	.7
7	13	1.0	17	14	1.1
8	16	1.1	18	14	1.4
9	13	1.1	19	12	.9
10	12	.9	20	8	.4

SOLUTION Let y represent the carbon monoxide ranking of a cigarette brand, and let x represent the brand's nicotine content (both measured in milligrams). We can gain insight into the bivariate relationship by constructing a **scattergram** for the sample data. A scattergram is constructed by plotting the pairs of sample observations in Table 12.1 on a two-dimensional plot (x values on the horizontal axis and y values on the vertical axis).

Figure 12.1 shows a scattergram for the sample data in Table 12.1 From the scattergram, a pattern is detected: CO ranking (y) tends to increase as nicotine content (x) increases. Thus, we could select a model that proposes a straight-line relationship between y and x. Such a **deterministic model**—one that attempts to predict y exactly for a given x value—might be adequate if all the points in Figure 12.1 fell exactly on a straight line. However, you can see that this idealistic situation will not occur for the data in Table 12.1. No matter how you draw a straight line through the points of Figure 12.1, at least some (if not most) of the points will deviate from the line.

A more reasonable model is one that will allow for unexplained variation in CO ranking caused by important variables not included in the model (such as those discussed earlier) or simply by random phenomena that cannot be modeled or explained. Models that account for this **random error** are called **probabilistic models**, as shown in the box.

General Form of a Probabilistic Model

$y = $ Deterministic component $+$ Random error

where $y = $ variable to be predicted.

Assumption: The mean value of the random error equals 0. This is equivalent to assuming that the mean value of y, $E(y)$, equals the deterministic component of the model, i.e.,

$E(y) = $ Deterministic component

FIGURE 12.1

Scattergram of CO
Ranking Versus
Nicotine Content for
Example 12.1

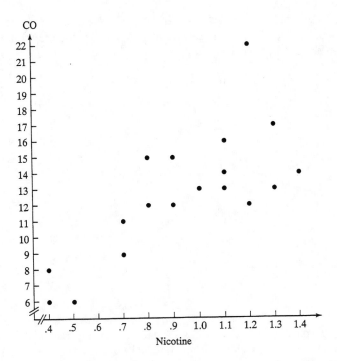

Note that probabilistic models include two components: a **deterministic component** and a **random error component.** In regression, we assume that the deterministic component represents the mean value of y, denoted $E(y)$. The deterministic
component will always be a function of the x variables in the model. The random error component, typically denoted by the Greek symbol ε, allows for random fluctuation of the y values about their mean, $E(y)$. Consequently, the probabilistic model
relating CO ranking (y) to nicotine content (x) will be of the form

$$y = E(y) + \varepsilon$$

where $E(y)$ will be a straight-line function of x. ■

EXAMPLE 12.2
Straight-Line Model

Refer to Example 12.1 and the probabilistic model $y = E(y) + \varepsilon$. Write the straight-
line equation relating $E(y)$ to nicotine content (x).

SOLUTION A straight-line equation involves two parameters, the y-intercept and slope
of the line. We will use the Greek symbols β_0 and β_1 to represent the y-intercept and
slope, respectively, since they are population parameters that will be known only if we
have access to the entire population of (x, y) measurements. Therefore, the equation of
the deterministic portion of the model is

$$E(y) = \beta_0 + \beta_1 x$$

A graph of this model is shown in Figure 12.2. Note that β_0 (the y-intercept) is the point at which the line cuts through the y-axis and β_1 (the slope) is the amount change in y for every 1-unit increase in x.

FIGURE 12.2

The Straight-Line Model

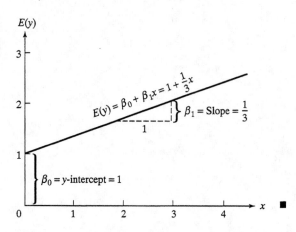

In this chapter, we consider only the simplest of probabilistic models—the **straight-line model**—which derives its name from the fact that the deterministic portion of the model graphs as a straight line. The elements of the straight-line model are summarized in the box.

The Straight-Line Probabilistic Model

$$y = \beta_0 + \beta_1 x + \varepsilon$$

where

$y =$ Variable to be predicted, called the **dependent** (or **response**) **variable**

$x =$ Variable to be used as a predictor of y, called the **independent variable**

$E(y) = \beta_0 + \beta_1 x$ is the deterministic portion of the model (the equation of a straight line)

β_0 (beta zero) $= y$-intercept of the line, i.e, the point at which the line intercepts or cuts through the y-axis (see Figure 12.2)

β_1 (beta one) $=$ Slope of the line, i.e., amount of increase (or decrease) in the deterministic component of y for every 1-unit increase in x (see Figure 12.2)

$\varepsilon =$ Random error

In the sections that follow, we will use the sample data to estimate the slope (β_1) and the y-intercept (β_0) of the deterministic portion of the straight-line model.

EXERCISES

■ *Learning the Mechanics*

12.1 Suppose y is exactly related to x by the equation $y = 1.5 + 2x$.
   a. Find the value of y that corresponds to $x = 1$.
   b. Find the value of y that corresponds to $x = 2$.
   c. Plot the two (x, y) points found in parts **a** and **b** on graph paper, and draw a line through the points. This line corresponds to the equation $y = 1.5 + 2x$.
   d. Find the value of y that corresponds to $x = 1.5$. Plot this point on the graph of part **c** and confirm that it falls on the line that passes through the points found in parts **a** and **b**.
   e. Part **d** illustrates an important relationship between graphs and equations: All the points that satisfy the equation $y = 1.5 + 2x$ have a common property. What is it?

12.2 Refer to Exercise 12.1.
   a. Find the y-intercept for the line and interpret its value.
   b. Find the slope of the line and interpret its value.
   c. If you increase x by 1 unit, how much will y increase or decrease?
   d. If you decrease x by 1 unit, how much will y increase or decrease?
   e. What is the value of y when $x = 0$?

12.3 Answer the questions posed in Exercise 12.1, using the line $y = 1.5 - 2x$.

12.4 Refer to Exercise 12.3.
   a. Find the y-intercept for the line and interpret its value.
   b. Find the slope of the line and interpret its value.
   c. If you increase x by 1 unit, how much will y increase or decrease?
   d. What is the value of y when $x = 0$?
   e. What do the two lines in Exercises 12.1 and 12.3 have in common? How do they differ?

12.5 Graph the lines corresponding to each of the following equations:
   a. $y = 1 + 3x$ **b.** $y = 1 - 3x$ **c.** $y = -1 + \frac{1}{2}x$
   d. $y = -1 - 3x$ **e.** $y = 2 - \frac{1}{2}x$ **f.** $y = -1.5 + x$
   g. $y = 3x$ **h** $y = -2x$

12.6 Give the values of β_0 and β_1 corresponding to each of the lines of Exercise 12.5.

12.3 Estimating the Model Parameters: The Method of Least Squares

The following example illustrates the technique we will use to **fit the straight-line model to the data**, i.e., to estimate the slope and y-intercept of the line using information provided by the sample data.

EXAMPLE 12.3

Estimating β_0 and β_1

Suppose we want to model the relationship between the sale price, y, and the total appraised value, x, of a residential property located in an upscale neighborhood. Based on our practical knowledge of real estate appraisal, we hypothesize the deterministic component of the probabilistic model as

$$E(y) = \beta_0 + \beta_1 x$$

If we were able to obtain the appraised value and sale price of *every* property in the neighborhood, i.e., the entire population of (x, y) measurements, then the values of the population parameters β_0 and β_1 could be determined exactly. Of course, we will never have access to the entire population of (x, y) measurements, since a great majority of the properties in the neighborhood will not be sold during the year. The problem, then, is to estimate the unknown population parameters based on the information contained in a sample of (x, y) measurements. Suppose we randomly sample five properties in the neighborhood that were sold during the past year. The sale prices and total appraised property values (measured in \$100,000) are given in Table 12.2.* How can we best use the sample information to estimate the unknown y-intercept β_0 and the slope β_1?

SOLUTION Estimates of the unknown parameters β_0 and β_1 are obtained by finding the best-fitting straight line through the sample data points of Table 12.2. (These points are plotted in Figure 12.3.) We will denote the estimates as $\hat{\beta}_0$ and $\hat{\beta}_1$, respectively. The procedure we will use to find the best fit is known as the **method of least squares**, and the best-fitting line, called the **least squares line**, is written

$$\hat{y} = \hat{\beta}_0 + \hat{\beta}_1 x$$

where $\hat{y}$ is the predicted value of sale price, y.

Table 12.2 Sale Price–Appraised Value Data for Example 12.3

Property	Total Appraised Property Value x, \$100,000	Sale Price y, \$100,000
1	2	2
2	3	5
3	4	7
4	5	10
5	6	11

*The sample size ($n = 5$) is unrealistically small to demonstrate the calculations involved in a simple linear regression.

FIGURE 12.3

Scattergram of Sale Price–Appraised Value Data of Table 12.2

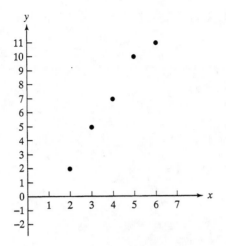

The first step in finding the least squares lines is to construct a sums of squares table to find the sums of the x values (Σx), y values (Σy), the squares of the x values (Σx^2), and the cross-products of the corresponding x and y values (Σxy). The sums of squares table for the sale price–appraised value data is given in Table 12.3. [*Note*: We have also included Σy^2 in Table 12.3. This value will be used later in the regression analysis.]

Table 12.3   Sums of Squares for Data of Table 12.2

	x	y	x^2	xy	y^2
	2	2	4	4	4
	3	5	9	15	25
	4	7	16	28	49
	5	10	25	50	100
	6	11	36	66	121
Totals	$\Sigma x = 20$	$\Sigma y = 35$	$\Sigma x^2 = 90$	$\Sigma xy = 163$	$\Sigma y^2 = 299$

The second step is to substitute the values of Σx, Σy, Σx^2, and Σxy into the formulas for SS_{xy} and SS_{xx} given in the box:

$$SS_{xy} = \Sigma xy - \frac{(\Sigma x)(\Sigma y)}{n} = 163 - \frac{(20)(35)}{5}$$

$$= 163 - 140 = 23$$

$$SS_{xx} = \Sigma x^2 - \frac{(\Sigma x)^2}{n} = 90 - \frac{(20)^2}{5}$$

$$= 90 - 80 = 10$$

Next, use these values of SS_{xy} and SS_{xx} to compute the estimate $\hat{\beta}_1$, as shown in the box.

Slope of the Least Squares Line

$$\hat{\beta}_1 = \frac{SS_{xy}}{SS_{xx}}$$

where

$$SS_{xx} = \Sigma x^2 - \frac{(\Sigma x)^2}{n}$$

$$SS_{xy} = \Sigma xy - \frac{(\Sigma x)(\Sigma y)}{n}$$

Substituting, we find $\hat{\beta}_1$, the slope of the least squares line, to be

$$\hat{\beta}_1 = \frac{SS_{xy}}{SS_{xx}} = \frac{23}{10} = 2.3$$

Finally, calculate $\hat{\beta}_0$, the y-intercept of the least squares line, as follows:

---

y-Intercept of the Least Squares Line

$$\hat{\beta}_0 = \bar{y} - \hat{\beta}_1 \bar{x}$$

For our example, we obtain

$$\hat{\beta}_0 = \bar{y} - \hat{\beta}_1 \bar{x} = \frac{\Sigma y}{5} - \hat{\beta}_1\left(\frac{\Sigma x}{5}\right)$$

$$= \frac{35}{5} - (2.3)\left(\frac{20}{5}\right)$$

$$= 7 - (2.3)(4) = 7 - 9.2 = -2.2$$

Therefore, $\hat{\beta}_0 = -2.2$, $\hat{\beta}_1 = 2.3$, and the least squares line is

$$\hat{y} = -2.2 + (2.3)x$$

A graph of this line is shown in Figure 12.4.

FIGURE 12.4

Least Squares Line
for Example 12.3

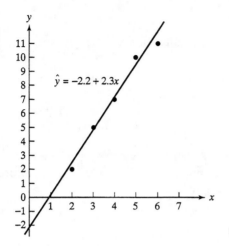

This five-step least squares procedure is summarized in the box.

Steps to Follow in Fitting a Least Squares Line to a Set of Data

1. Plot the data in a scattergram.
2. Construct a table (similar to Table 12.3) to find Σx, Σy, Σx^2, and Σxy.
3. Substitute the values into the formulas for SS_{xy} and SS_{xx}:

$$SS_{xy} = \Sigma xy - \frac{(\Sigma x)(\Sigma y)}{n}$$

$$SS_{xx} = \Sigma x^2 - \frac{(\Sigma x)^2}{n}$$

where n is the sample size (number of pairs of observations).
4. Substitute the values into the formula for $\hat{\beta}_1$. Then find $\hat{\beta}_0$.

$$\hat{\beta}_1 = \frac{SS_{xy}}{SS_{xx}} \qquad \hat{\beta}_0 = \bar{y} - \hat{\beta}_1 \bar{x}$$

(continued)

> **5.** Use the computed values of $\hat{\beta}_0$ and $\hat{\beta}_1$ to form the equation of the least squares line:
>
> $$\hat{y} = \hat{\beta}_0 + \hat{\beta}_1 x$$
>
> *Note*: A graph of the least squares line will always pass through the point $(\bar{x}, \bar{y})$.

EXAMPLE 12.4

Estimating β_0 and β_1

Refer to Example 12.3. Use a computer to find the least squares line.

SOLUTION Virtually all statistical computer software packages have routines for performing a simple linear regression analysis. The SAS regression printout for the data in Table 12.2 is displayed in Figure 12.5.

FIGURE 12.5

SAS Printout for Sale Price–Appraised Value Regression

Dependent Variable: Y

Analysis of Variance

Source	DF	Sum of Squares	Mean Square	F Value	Prob>F
Model	1	52.90000	52.90000	144.273	0.0012
Error	3	1.10000	0.36667		
C Total	4	54.00000			

Root MSE	0.60553	R-square	0.9796
Dep Mean	7.00000	Adj R-sq	0.9728
C.V.	8.65043		

Parameter Estimates

Variable	DF	Parameter Estimate	Standard Error	T for H0: Parameter=0	Prob > |T|
INTERCEP	1	-2.200000	0.81240384	-2.708	0.0733
X	1	2.300000	0.19148542	12.011	0.0012

The least squares estimates of the y-intercept and slope are shaded in Figure 12.5 under the column titled **Parameter Estimate**. Note that the estimate of the y-intercept ($\hat{\beta}_0 = -2.200000$) and the estimate of the slope ($\hat{\beta}_1 = 2.300000$) given on the printout agree with our previous hand-calculated values. Thus, the least squares line is

$$\hat{y} = -2.2 + 2.3x \quad ■$$

EXAMPLE 12.5

Why the Line Fits "Best"

Refer to Example 12.3. In what sense is the least squares line the "best-fitting" straight line to the data of Table 12.3?

SOLUTION In deciding whether a line provides a good fit to a set of data, we examine the vertical distances, or **deviations**, between the data points and the fitted line. (Since we are attempting to predict y, a measure of fit will involve the difference between the observed value y and the predicted value $\hat{y}$—a quantity that is represented by the *vertical* deviation between the data point and the fitted line.) The deviations for the least squares line

$$\hat{y} = -2.2 + 2.3x$$

are shown in Figure 12.6a.

Let us compare the deviations of the least squares line with the deviations of another fitted line (one fitted visually), given by the equation

$$\hat{y} = -1 + 2x$$

The deviations of the visually fitted line are shown in Figure 12.6b. Notice first that some of the deviations are positive, some are negative, and that even though three of the five data points fall exactly on the visually fitted line, the individual deviations tend to be smaller for the least squares line than for the visually fitted line. Second, note that the sum of squares of deviations, $SSE = \Sigma(y - \hat{y})^2$, is smaller for the least squares line. (The values of SSE for the least squares and visually fitted lines are given at the bottom of Figures 12.6a and 12.6b, respectively.) In fact, it can be shown that **there is one and only one line that will minimize the sum of squares of deviations of the points about the fitted line. It is the least squares line.**

FIGURE 12.6

Deviations about the Least Squares and Visually Fitted Lines of Example 12.5

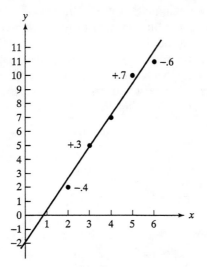

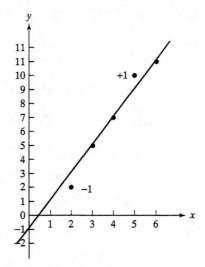

SSE = $\Sigma(y - \hat{y})^2$
   $= (-.4)^2 + (.3)^2 + (0)^2 + (.7)^2 + (-.6)^2$
   $= 1.10$

a. Least squares line: $\hat{y} = -2.2 + 2.3x$

SSE = $\Sigma(y - \hat{y})^2$
   $= (-1)^2 + (0)^2 + (0)^2 + (1)^2 + (0)^2$
   $= 2$

b. Visually fitted line: $\hat{y} = -1 + 2x$

> **Least Squares Criterion for Finding the "Best-Fitting" Line**
>
> Choose the line that minimizes the sum of squared deviations,
>
> $$SSE = \Sigma(y - \hat{y})^2$$
>
> This is called the **least squares line**, or the **least squares prediction equation**.

The fact that the least squares line is the one that minimizes the sum of squared deviations does not guarantee that it is the "best" line to fit the data. However, intuitively, it would seem that this is a desirable property for a good-fitting line.[*] A second advantage of the method of least squares is that we know the sampling distributions of the estimates of β_0 and β_1, something that would be unknown for lines fitted intuitively or visually. A third desirable property is that, under certain conditions, the sampling distributions of the least squares estimators of β_0 and β_1 will have smaller standard deviations than other types of estimators.

EXAMPLE 12.6
Practical Application

One aspect of the preliminary evaluation of a new food product is determining the nutritive quality of the product. This is often accomplished by feeding the food product to animals (e.g., rats) whose metabolic processes are very similar to our own. General Foods Corporation used this technique to evaluate the protein efficiency of two forms of a product (known by the pseudonym H)—one solid and the other liquid.[†] Thirty male rats, all newly weaned, were used in the experiment. Ten rats were randomly assigned a diet of solid H, 10 a diet of liquid H, and 10 a standard (control) diet. During the feeding period, each rat was permitted to eat as much as it wished. At the end of 28 days, the total protein intake x (in grams) and the weight gain y (in grams) were recorded for each of the 30 rats. General Foods fit a straight line to the 10 (x, y) data points for each diet by the method of least squares. The three least squares prediction equations are as follows:

Liquid H: $\hat{y} = 109.3 + 3.72x$

Solid H: $\hat{y} = 106.7 + 3.66x$

Control: $\hat{y} = 50.6 + 2.91x$

  a. Interpret the estimated y-intercept and slope for each diet.
  b. Predict the weight gain of a rat on liquid H if the rat's 28-day protein intake is 40 grams.

---

[*]*The sum of the deviations from the least squares line will also always equal 0. Since there are many other fitted lines that also have this property, we do not use this as the only criterion for choosing the "best-fitting" line.*

[†]*Source: Street, E. and Carroll, M.D. "Preliminary evaluation of a new food product." In Statistics: A Guide to the Unknown, Tanur et al., eds. San Francisco: Holden-Day, 1978, pp. 269–278.*

SOLUTION   **a.**   First, we will interpret the least squares slopes. Recall that the slope is the change in y for every 1-unit increase in x. Therefore, $\hat{\beta}_1$ represents the estimated change in weight gain (y) for every 1-gram increase in total protein intake (x) for rats on that particular diet. Since all the least squares slopes are *positive*, we are estimating a positive change (i.e., an *increase*) in y.

Liquid H: For every 1-gram increase in total protein intake (x), we estimate weight gain (y) to increase $\hat{\beta}_1 = 3.72$ grams.

Solid H: For every 1-gram increase in total protein intake (x), we estimate weight gain (y) to increase $\hat{\beta}_1 = 3.66$ grams.

Control: For every 1-gram increase in total protein intake (x), we estimate weight gain (y) to increase $\hat{\beta}_1 = 2.91$ grams.

You can see that liquid H yields the greatest estimated increase in weight gain for every 1-gram increase in protein intake. For this reason, General Foods concentrated on developing the liquid version of the new food product.

The y-intercept of the least squares line is the point at which the line crosses the y-axis. This point has an x value of 0. Consequently, the y-intercept can be interpreted as the predicted weight gain (y) for rats with a total protein intake of $x = 0$ grams. In this experiment, the estimated y-intercept is meaningless since it is impractical for rats on any diet to have a total protein intake of 0 grams after 28 days.

In simple linear regression, the estimated y-intercept will usually not have a practical interpretation. It will, however, be practical if the value $x = 0$ is meaningful and is within the range of sample x values.

b.   To predict the weight gain y of a rat with a protein intake of 40 grams, we substitute $x = 40$ into the least squares prediction equation for liquid H:

Liquid H: $\hat{y} = 109.3 + 3.72(40) = 258.1$ grams

Thus, we estimate that the rat will gain 258.1 grams in weight if it gets 40 grams of protein while on the 28-day liquid H diet. [*Note:* We will obtain a measure of reliability for a prediction such as this in Section 12.9]. ■

EXERCISES

■ *Learning the Mechanics*

12.7   Consider the data listed in the table.

x	−1	0	1	2	3
y	−1	1	2	4	5

   a. Calculate SS_{xy}.   **b.** Calculate SS_{xx}.   **c.** Calculate $\bar{y}$.
   d. Calculate $\bar{x}$.   **e.** Find $\hat{\beta}_1$.   **f.** Find $\hat{\beta}_0$.

12.8   Consider the five data points:

x	−1	0	1	2	3
y	−1	1	1	2.5	3.5

   a. Construct a scattergram for the data.
   b. Find the least squares prediction equation.
   c. Graph the least squares line on the scattergram and visually confirm that it provides a good fit to the data points.

12.9   Consider the four data points shown in the table.

x	1	1.5	1.9	2.5
y	3.1	2.2	1.0	.3

   a. Construct a scattergram for the data.
   b. Find the least squares prediction equation.
   c. Graph the least squares line on the scattergram and visually confirm that it provides a good fit to the data points.

12.10   Consider the following seven data points:

x	−5	−3	−1	0	1	3	5
y	.8	1.1	2.5	3.1	5.0	4.7	6.2

   a. Construct a scattergram for the data.
   b. Find the least squares prediction equation.
   c. Graph the least squares line on the scattergram and visually confirm that it provides a good fit to the data points.

12.11   Consider the four data points in the accompanying table.

x	−3.0	2.4	−1.1	2.0
y	2.7	.4	1.3	.5

a. Construct a scattergram for the data.

b. Find the least squares prediction equation.

c. Graph the least squares line on the scattergram and visually confirm that it provides a good fit to the data points.

■ Applying the Concepts

12.12 Public welfare expenditures by state governments have increased, on average, by $2 billion per year for the past 40 years. What determines the amount states spend each year on public welfare? This was the question studied in an article published in the *Journal of Socio-Economics* (Vol. 22, 1993). The dependent variable of interest was y, total annual public welfare expenditures for all 50 states from 1946 to 1987. To determine the best predictor of welfare expenditure, y was plotted against each of the following six independent variables for the 42 years: unemployment rate (x_1), total amount given to charity (x_2), Gross National Product (x_3), total amount allocated for grants-in-aid (x_4), percentage of states with Democratic governors (x_5), and percentage of states with Democratic legislatures (x_6). The six MINITAB scattergrams are shown here.* Examine the scattergrams and determine which of the six independent variables are likely to be linearly related to welfare expenditures y.

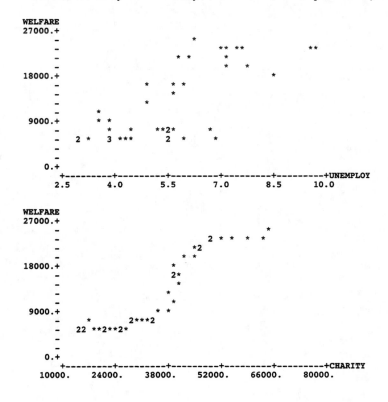

---

*Source: Mogull, R.G. "Determinants of states' welfare expenditures." The Journal of Socio-Economics, Vol. 22, No. 3, pp. 259–270 (Figures 2–5, 8–9).

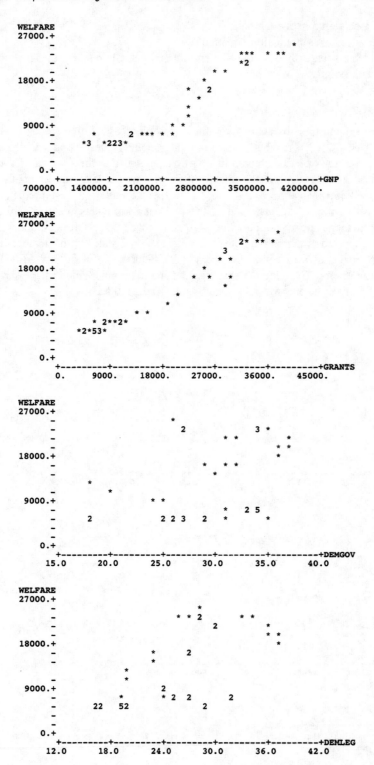

12.13 Modern warehouses use computerized and automated guided vehicles for materials handling. Consequently, the physical layout of the warehouse must be carefully designed to prevent vehicle congestion and optimize response time. Optimal design of an automated warehouse was studied in the *Journal of Engineering for Industry* (Aug. 1993). The layout assumes that vehicles do not block each other when they travel within the warehouse, i.e., that there is no congestion. The validity of this assumption was checked by simulating (on a computer) warehouse operations. In each simulation, the number of vehicles was varied and the congestion time (total time one vehicle blocked another) was recorded. The data are shown in the accompanying table. Of interest to the researchers is the relationship between congestion time (y) and number of vehicles (x).

Number of Vehicles	Congestion Time, minutes	Number of Vehicles	Congestion Time, minutes
1	0	9	.02
2	0	10	.04
3	.02	11	.04
4	.01	12	.04
5	.01	13	.03
6	.01	14	.04
7	.03	15	.05
8	.03		

Source: Pandit, R. and Palekar, U. S. "Response time considerations for optimal warehouse layout design." *Journal of Engineering for Industry*, Transactions of the ASME, Vol. 115, Aug. 1993, p. 326 (Table 2).

a. Construct a scattergram for the data.
b. Find the least squares line relating number of vehicles (x) to congestion time (y).
c. Plot the least squares line on the graph, part **a**.
d. Interpret the values of $\hat{\beta}_0$ and $\hat{\beta}_1$.

12.14 For a company to maintain a competitive edge in the marketplace, spending on research and development (R&D) is essential. To determine the optimum level for R&D spending and its effect on a company's value, a simple linear regression analysis was performed (*Research Management*, Sept./Oct. 1986). Data collected for the largest R&D spenders (based on 1981–1982 averages) were used to fit a straight-line model relating y to x, where

y = Price/earnings (P/E) ratio

x = R&D expenditures/sales (R/S) ratio

The data for 20 of the companies used in the study are provided in the table on page 598.
a. Construct a scattergram for the data.
b. Find the least squares prediction equation.
c. Graph the least squares line on the scattergram.
d. Use the least squares prediction equation to predict the P/E ratio y for a company with an R/S ratio of $x = \$.070$. [*Note:* We will find a measure of the reliability of this prediction in Section 12.9.]

Company	P/E Ratio y	R/S Ratio x	Company	P/E Ratio y	R/S Ratio x
1	5.6	.003	11	8.4	.058
2	7.2	.004	12	11.1	.058
3	8.1	.009	13	11.1	.067
4	9.9	.021	14	13.2	.080
5	6.0	.023	15	13.4	.080
6	8.2	.030	16	11.5	.083
7	6.3	.035	17	9.8	.091
8	10.0	.037	18	16.1	.092
9	8.5	.044	19	7.0	.064
10	13.2	.051	20	5.9	.028

Source: Wallin, C. C. and Gilman, J. J. "Determining the optimum level for R&D spending." *Research Management*, Vol. 14, No. 5, Sept./Oct. 1986, pp. 19–24 (adapted from Figure 1, p. 20).

12.15 Each year, *Fortune* ranks the top American cities according to their ability to provide high-quality, low-cost labor for companies that are relocating. One important measure used to form the rankings is the *labor market stress index* (y), which indicates the availability of workers in the city. (The higher the index, the tighter the labor market.) A second important variable is the *unemployment rate* (x). The values of these two variables for each of the top 10 cities in 1990 are listed in the table.

Rank	City	Labor Market Stress Index y	Unemployment Rate x
1	Salt Lake City	107	4.5%
2	Minneapolis–St. Paul	107	3.8%
3	Atlanta	100	5.1%
4	Sacramento	100	4.9%
5	Austin (Texas)	80	5.4%
6	Columbus (Ohio)	100	4.8%
7	Dallas/Fort Worth	100	5.5%
8	Phoenix	93	4.3%
9	Jacksonville (Florida)	87	5.7%
10	Oklahoma City	80	4.6%

Source: *Fortune*, Oct. 22, 1990, pp. 58–63.

a. Construct a scattergram for the data.
b. Find the least squares prediction equation.
c. Graph the least squares line on the scattergram.
d. Interpret the values of $\hat{\beta}_0$ and $\hat{\beta}_1$.

12.16 Refer to the *Journal of Information Systems* (Spring 1992) study of a computerized intrusion-detection system, Exercise 6.19. In addition to input-output (I/O) units, the central processing unit (CPU) time (in seconds) utilized by a sample of 44 system users was recorded. The data for both variables are listed here. A simple linear regression analysis relating CPU times (y) to I/O units (x) was conducted on the data. The results are shown in the accompanying SAS printout.

a. Locate the estimates of β_0 and β_1 on the printout.

b. Interpret the results, part **a**.

CPU Time	I/O Units	CPU Time	I/O Units	CPU Time	I/O Units
54	15	55	5	15	2
41	17	54	4	27	3
28	1	37	1	28	0
32	0	18	0	19	0
17	0	53	0	21	0
23	20	42	9	20	0
19	0	40	0	13	1
20	6	28	1	27	3
30	1	52	0	102	6
14	0	19	0	54	0
26	0	35	1	62	14
19	0	46	7	59	0
23	2	38	9	23	4
16	0	15	0	16	0
13	9	15	10		

Source: O'Leary, D. E. "Intrusion-detection systems." *Journal of Information Systems*, Spring 1992, p. 68 (Table 2).

Dependent Variable: CPU

Analysis of Variance

Source	DF	Sum of Squares	Mean Square	F Value	Prob>F
Model	1	937.54390	937.54390	2.975	0.0919
Error	42	13236.45610	315.15372		
C Total	43	14174.00000			

Root MSE	17.75257	R-square	0.0661	
Dep Mean	32.00000	Adj R-sq	0.0439	
C.V.	55.47678			

Parameter Estimates

Variable	DF	Parameter Estimate	Standard Error	T for H0: Parameter=0	Prob > |T|
INTERCEP	1	28.894324	3.22564861	8.958	0.0001
IO_UNITS	1	0.904965	0.52468333	1.725	0.0919

12.17 Two processes for hydraulic drilling of rock are dry drilling and wet drilling. In a dry hole, compressed air is forced down the drill rods to flush the cuttings and drive the hammer; in a wet hole, water is forced down. An experiment was conducted to determine whether the time y it takes to dry drill a distance of 5 feet in rock increases with depth x (*The American Statistician*, Feb. 1991). The results for one portion of the experiment are shown in the accompanying table followed by a MINITAB simple linear regression printout.

Depth at Which Drilling Begins *x, feet*	Time to Drill 5 Feet *y, minutes*	Depth at Which Drilling Begins *x, feet*	Time to Drill 5 Feet *y, minutes*
0	4.90	225	8.28
25	7.41	250	4.84
50	6.19	275	8.29
75	5.57	300	8.91
100	5.17	325	8.54
125	6.89	350	11.79
150	7.05	375	12.12
175	7.11	395	11.02
200	6.19		

Source: Penner, R. and Watts, D. G. "Mining information." *The American Statistician*, Vol. 45, No. 1, Feb. 1991, p. 6 (Table 1).

```
The regression equation is
DRILTIME = 4.79 + 0.0144 DEPTH

Predictor      Coef       Stdev      t-ratio        p
Constant       4.7896     0.6663       7.19      0.000
DEPTH          0.014388   0.002847     5.05      0.000

s = 1.432      R-sq = 63.0%      R-sq(adj) = 60.5%

Analysis of Variance

SOURCE         DF         SS           MS          F        p
Regression      1         52.378       52.378      25.54    0.000
Error          15         30.768        2.051
Total          16         83.146

Unusual Observations
Obs.   DEPTH   DRILTIME      Fit  Stdev.Fit   Residual   St.Resid
 11      250      4.840     8.387     0.376     -3.547     -2.57R

R denotes an obs. with a large st. resid.
```

a. Construct a scattergram for the data.

b. Find the least squares prediction equation on the MINITAB printout.

c. Graph the least squares line on the scattergram.

d. Interpret the values of $\hat{\beta}_0$ and $\hat{\beta}_1$.

12.18 A study was conducted to model the thermal performance of integral-fin tubes used in the refrigeration and process industries (*Journal of Heat Transfer*, Aug. 1990). Twenty-four specially manufactured integral-fin tubes with rectangular-shaped fins made of copper were used in the experiment. Vapor was released downward into each tube and the vapor-side heat transfer coefficient (based on the outside surface area of the tube) was measured. The dependent variable for the study is the heat transfer enhancement ratio, y, defined as the ratio of the vapor-side coefficient of the fin tube to the vapor-side coefficient of a smooth tube evaluated at the same temperature. Theoretically, heat transfer will be related to the area at the top of the tube that is "unflooded" by condensation of the vapor. The data in the table are the unflooded area ratio (x) and heat transfer enhancement (y) values recorded for the 24 integral-fin tubes.

Unflooded Area Ratio x	Heat Transfer Enhancement y	Unflooded Area Ratio x	Heat Transfer Enhancement y
1.93	4.4	2.00	5.2
1.95	5.3	1.77	4.7
1.78	4.5	1.62	4.2
1.64	4.5	2.77	6.0
1.54	3.7	2.47	5.8
1.32	2.8	2.24	5.2
2.12	6.1	1.32	3.5
1.88	4.9	1.26	3.2
1.70	4.9	1.21	2.9
1.58	4.1	2.26	5.3
2.47	7.0	2.04	5.1
2.37	6.7	1.88	4.6

Source: Marto, P. J. et al. "An experimental study of R-113 film condensation on horizontal integral-fin tubes." *Journal of Heat Transfer*, Vol. 112, Aug. 1990, p. 763 (Table 2).

a. Use the accompanying ASP printout to find the least squares line relating heat transfer enhancement y to unflooded area ratio x.

```
          SIMPLE LINEAR REGRESSION: HEAT(y) vrs. RATIO(x)

MODEL:  HEAT(y) = 2.42639RATIO(x) + 0.213389CNST

              COEF.   SD. ER.     t(22)     P-VALUE  PT. R SQ.
            --------  --------  ---------  ----------  --------
RATIO(x)  2.42639  0.228252  10.6303    3.92489E-10  0.837041
    CNST  0.213389  0.439      0.486081  0.631717     0.0106256

R SQ. = 0.837041,  ADJ. R SQ. = 0.829634,  D. W. = 1.49972
SQ. ROOT MSE = 0.453826,  F(1/22) = 113.003 (P-VALUE = 3.92489E-10)
```

b. Plot the data points, and graph the least squares line.
c. Interpret the values of $\hat{\beta}_0$ and $\hat{\beta}_1$.

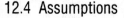
12.4 Assumptions

In the remainder of this chapter, we describe the statistical methods (e.g., tests of hypotheses and confidence intervals) appropriate for making inferences from a simple linear regression analysis. As with most statistical procedures, the validity of the inferences depends on certain assumptions being satisfied. These assumptions, made about the random error term in the straight-line probabilistic model, are summarized in the accompanying box.

Assumptions About the Random Error ε Required for a Simple Linear Regression Analysis

1. The mean of the probability distribution of ε is 0. That is, for each setting of the independent variable x, the average of the errors over an infinitely long series of experiments is 0.*

2. The variance of the probability distribution of ε is constant for all settings of the independent variable x and is equal to σ^2, i.e., the variance of ε is equal to σ^2 for all values of x.

3. The probability distribution of ε is normal.

4. The errors associated with any two observations are independent. That is, the error associated with one value of y has no effect on the errors associated with other y values.

Figure 12.7 shows a pictorial representation of the assumptions given in the box. For each value of x shown in the figure, the relative frequency distribution of the errors is normal with mean 0 and with a constant variance (all the distributions shown have the same amount of spread or variability) equal to σ^2.

Statistical techniques are available for detecting when one or more of the assumptions are grossly violated. These methods are based on an analysis of the least squares errors of prediction, or **residuals**. (We present an analysis of residuals in Chapter 13.) In practice, however, you will never know whether the data satisfy exactly the four assumptions. Fortunately, the estimators and test statistics used in a simple linear regression have sampling distributions that remain relatively stable for minor departures from the assumptions.

There is an additional assumption that is implied in a regression analysis, but often forgotten—namely, the assumption that the relationship between the mean value of y, $E(y)$, and the independent variable x is correctly modeled by a straight line. In a real application, the relationship between $E(y)$ and x probably possesses some curvature. Therefore, when we conduct a simple linear regression analysis, we are as-

---

*The assumption that $E(\varepsilon) = 0$ is not guaranteed by the method of least squares. The method of least squares yields a sample mean error of 0, i.e., $[\Sigma(y - \hat{y})]/n = 0$, for all models regardless of whether the model is the correct one. The assumption that $E(\varepsilon) = 0$ in simple linear regression is equivalent to assuming that the form of the correct model is a straight line.

FIGURE 12.7

The Probability
Distribution of the
Random Error
Component, ε

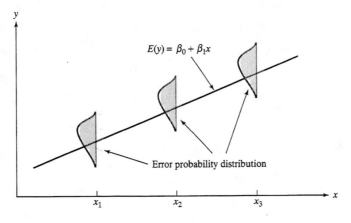

FIGURE 12.8

Hypothetical
Comparison of the
True Relationship
Between $E(y)$ and x
with the Simple
Linear Regression
Model

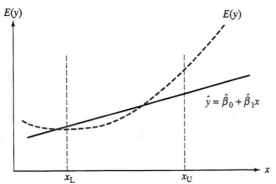

suming that this curvature is minimal over the set of values for which x is measured. The implications of this assumption can be seen in Figure 12.8. If x is measured over the interval between two points, say, x_L and x_U, a simple linear regression analysis may produce a very good prediction equation for estimating $E(y)$ or predicting y values of x between x_L and x_U, but very poor estimates and predictions for values of x outside this range. The rule, then, is never to attempt to predict values of y for values of x outside the range of values used in the regression analysis.

12.5 Measuring Variability Around the Least Squares Line

Is the sale price y of Example 12.3 really related to total appraised property value x, or is the linear relation that we seem to see a result of chance? That is, could it be the case that x and y are completely unrelated, and that the apparent linear configuration of the data points in the scattergram of Figure 12.4 is due to random variation? The statistical method that will answer this question requires that we know how much y will vary for a given value of x. That is, we must know the value of the quantity, called σ^2, that measures the variability of the y values about the least squares line. This value is the variance, σ^2, of the random error identified in Section 12.4.

Figure 12.9a on page 604 shows a hypothetical situation where the value of σ^2 is small. Note that there is very little variation in the y values about the least squares

FIGURE 12.9

Illustrations of Error
Variance, σ^2

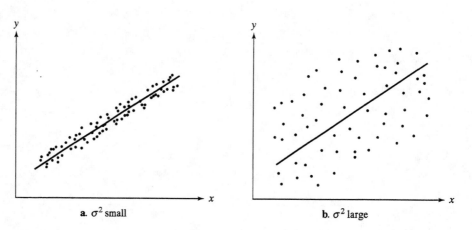

a. σ^2 small   **b.** σ^2 large

line. In contrast, Figure 12.9b illustrates a situation where σ^2 is large; the y values deviate greatly about the least squares line.

Since the variance σ^2 will rarely be known, we will estimate its value using the sum of the squared deviations (sum of the squared errors, SSE) and the procedure shown in the box.

Estimation of σ^2, a Measure of the Variability of the y Values About the Least Squares Line

An estimate of σ^2 is given by[*]

$$s^2 = \frac{\text{SSE}}{n-2}$$

where

$$\text{SSE} = \Sigma(y - \hat{y})^2 = \text{SS}_{yy} - \hat{\beta}_1 \text{SS}_{xy}$$

$$\text{SS}_{yy} = \Sigma(y - \bar{y})^2 = \Sigma y^2 - \frac{(\Sigma y)^2}{n}$$

Warning: When performing these calculations, you may be tempted to round the calculated values of SS_{yy}, $\hat{\beta}_1$, and SS_{xy}. We recommend carrying at least six significant figures for each of these quantities to avoid substantial rounding errors in the calculation of SSE.

[*Note:* The denominator of s^2 is termed the **number of degrees of freedom for error variance estimation.**]

---

[*]*The divisor of s^2, $n - 2$, represents the number of degrees of freedom available for estimating σ^2. The value results from the fact that we "lose" 2 degrees of freedom for estimating each of the model parameters, $\hat{\beta}_0$ and $\hat{\beta}_1$.*

EXAMPLE 12.7
Estimating σ^2

Refer to the simple linear regression relating sale price to total appraised value, Example 12.3. Estimate the value of the error variance σ^2 based on the data of Table 12.3.

SOLUTION According to the formulas given in the box, the first step is to compute SS_{yy}. We have

$$SS_{yy} = \Sigma y^2 - \frac{(\Sigma y)^2}{n}$$

$$= (2)^2 + (5)^2 + (7)^2 + (10)^2 + (11)^2 - \frac{(35)^2}{5}$$

$$= 299 - 245 = 54$$

Recall from Example 12.3 that $\hat{\beta}_1 = 2.3$ and $SS_{xy} = 23$. Thus, we compute

$$SSE = SS_{yy} - \hat{\beta}_1 SS_{xy}$$
$$= 54 - (2.3)(23) = 54 - 52.9 = 1.1$$

Notice that this value of SSE agrees with the value previously given in Figure 12.6a. Our estimate of σ^2 is therefore

$$s^2 = \frac{SSE}{n-2} = \frac{1.1}{5-2} = \frac{1.1}{3} = .36667$$

We could also compute the estimated standard deviation s by taking the square roots of s^2. In this example, we have

$$s = \sqrt{s^2} = \sqrt{.36667} = .6055$$

Since s measures the spread of the distribution of the y values about the least squares line, we should not be surprised to find that most of the observations lie within $2s = 2(.6055) = 1.211$ of the least squares line. From Figure 12.10 on page 606, we see that, for this example, all five data points have y values that lie within $2s$ of $\hat{y}$, the least squares predicted value.   ■

Practical Interpretation of s, the Estimated Standard Deviation of σ

Given the assumptions outlined in the box in Section 12.4, we expect most of the observed y values to lie within $2s$ of their respective least squares predicted values, $\hat{y}$.

FIGURE 12.10

Observations Within 2s of the Least Squares Line

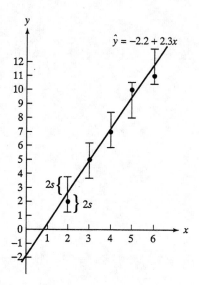

EXAMPLE 12.8
Estimating σ

Refer to Example 12.7. Use a computer to find SSE and estimates of σ^2 and σ for the simple linear regression.

SOLUTION The SAS regression printout for this example is reproduced in Figure 12.11. The value of SSE is found under the column headed **Sum of Squares** in the row labeled **Error** at the top of the printout. This quantity, shaded in the figure, is SSE = 1.1000.

The estimate of σ^2 is shaded in Figure 12.11 as **Mean Square** for **Error** and is located immediately to the right of SSE. Note that $s^2 = .36667$.

Finally, the estimate of σ is found (shaded) in the figure under the heading **Root MSE**. Thus, $s = .60553$. Note that except for rounding errors, these values of SSE, s^2, and s agree with our hand-calculated values in previous examples.

FIGURE 12.11

SAS Printout for Example 12.8

Dependent Variable: Y

Analysis of Variance

Source	DF	Sum of Squares	Mean Square	F Value	Prob>F
Model	1	52.90000	52.90000	144.273	0.0012
Error	3	1.10000	0.36667		
C Total	4	54.00000			

Root MSE	0.60553	R-square	0.9796		
Dep Mean	7.00000	Adj R-sq	0.9728		
C.V.	8.65043				

Parameter Estimates

Variable	DF	Parameter Estimate	Standard Error	T for H0: Parameter=0	Prob > |T|
INTERCEP	1	-2.200000	0.81240384	-2.708	0.0733
X	1	2.300000	0.19148542	12.011	0.0012

EXERCISES

■ *Learning the Mechanics*

12.19 Suppose you fit a least squares line to 10 data points and calculate SSE = .22.
  a. Find s^2, the estimate of σ^2.
  b. Find s, the estimate of σ.

12.20 The data for Exercise 12.8 are reproduced here.

x	−1	0	1	2	3
y	−1	1	1	2.5	3.5

  a. Calculate SSE for the data.
  b. Calculate s^2 and s.

12.21 The data for Exercise 12.10 are reproduced in the table.

x	−5	−3	−1	0	1	3	5
y	.8	1.1	2.5	3.1	5.0	4.7	6.2

  a. Calculate SSE for the data.
  b. Calculate s^2 and s.

■ *Applying the Concepts*

12.22 The data for the *Journal of Engineering for Industry* study, Exercise 12.13, are reproduced here:

Number of Vehicles	Congestion Time, minutes	Number of Vehicles	Congestion Time, minutes
1	0	9	.02
2	0	10	.04
3	.02	11	.04
4	.01	12	.04
5	.01	13	.03
6	.01	14	.04
7	.03	15	.05
8	.03		

Source: Pandit, R. and Palekar, U. S. "Response time considerations for optimal warehouse layout design." *Journal of Engineering for Industry,* Transactions of the ASME, Vol. 115, Aug. 1993, p. 326 (Table 2).

a. Find SSE and s^2 for the data.

b. Calculate s, the estimate of σ.

c. Interpret the value of s obtained in part **b**.

12.23 The data for the *Research Management* study discussed in Exercise 12.14 are reproduced in the table.

Company	P/E Ratio y	R/S Ratio x	Company	P/E Ratio y	R/S Ratio x
1	5.6	.003	11	8.4	.058
2	7.2	.004	12	11.1	.058
3	8.1	.009	13	11.1	.067
4	9.9	.021	14	13.2	.080
5	6.0	.023	15	13.4	.080
6	8.2	.030	16	11.5	.083
7	6.3	.035	17	9.8	.091
8	10.0	.037	18	16.1	.092
9	8.5	.044	19	7.0	.064
10	13.2	.051	20	5.9	.028

Source: Wallin, C. C. and Gilman, J. J. "Determining the optimum level for R&D spending." *Research Management*, Vol. 14, No. 5, Sept./Oct. 1986, pp. 19–24 (adapted from Figure 1, p. 20).

a. Find SSE and s^2 for the data.   **b.** Calculate s, the estimate of σ.

c. Interpret the value of s obtained in part **b**.

12.24 The data for Exercise 12.15 are reproduced in the accompanying table.

Rank	City	Labor Market Stress Index y	Unemployment Rate x
1	Salt Lake City	107	4.5%
2	Minneapolis–St. Paul	107	3.8%
3	Atlanta	100	5.1%
4	Sacramento	100	4.9%
5	Austin (Texas)	80	5.4%
6	Columbus (Ohio)	100	4.8%
7	Dallas/Fort Worth	100	5.5%
8	Phoenix	93	4.3%
9	Jacksonville (Florida)	87	5.7%
10	Oklahoma City	80	4.6%

Source: *Fortune*, Oct. 22, 1990, pp. 58–63.

    a. Find SSE and s^2 for the data.

    b. Calculate s, the estimate of σ.

    c. Interpret the value of s.

12.25 The data and MINITAB printout for Exercise 12.17 are reproduced here:

Depth at Which Drilling Begins x, feet	Time to Drill 5 Feet y, minutes	Depth at Which Drilling Begins x, feet	Time to Drill 5 Feet y, minutes
0	4.90	225	8.28
25	7.41	250	4.84
50	6.19	275	8.29
75	5.57	300	8.91
100	5.17	325	8.54
125	6.89	350	11.79
150	7.05	375	12.12
175	7.11	395	11.02
200	6.19		

Source: Penner, R. and Watts, D. G. "Mining information." *The American Statistician*, Vol. 45, No. 1, Feb. 1991, p. 6 (Table 1).

```
The regression equation is
DRILTIME = 4.79 + 0.0144 DEPTH

Predictor      Coef       Stdev     t-ratio        p
Constant     4.7896      0.6663        7.19    0.000
DEPTH       0.014388    0.002847        5.05    0.000

s = 1.432     R-sq = 63.0%     R-sq(adj) = 60.5%

Analysis of Variance

SOURCE       DF         SS           MS        F        p
Regression    1      52.378       52.378    25.54    0.000
Error        15      30.768        2.051
Total        16      83.146

Unusual Observations
Obs.   DEPTH   DRILTIME      Fit  Stdev.Fit  Residual  St.Resid
 11      250      4.840    8.387      0.376    -3.547    -2.57R

R denotes an obs. with a large st. resid.
```

    a. Find SSE and s on the printout.

    b. Interpret the value of s obtained in part **a**.

12.26 Refer to the *Journal of Information System* study, Exercise 12.16. The SAS printout for the simple linear regression of the data is reproduced on page 610. Locate an estimate of σ on the printout, and give a practical interpretation of its value.

```
           Dependent Variable: CPU

                         Analysis of Variance

                               Sum of          Mean
           Source        DF    Squares         Square      F Value    Prob>F

           Model          1    937.54390      937.54390     2.975     0.0919
           Error         42  13236.45610      315.15372
           C Total       43  14174.00000

               Root MSE        17.75257     R-square       0.0661
               Dep Mean        32.00000     Adj R-sq       0.0439
               C.V.            55.47678

                         Parameter Estimates

                       Parameter     Standard     T for H0:
           Variable  DF  Estimate       Error    Parameter=0   Prob > |T|

           INTERCEP   1   28.894324    3.22564861     8.958       0.0001
           IO_UNITS   1    0.904965    0.52468333     1.725       0.0919
```

▌12.6 Making Inferences About the Slope β_1

After fitting the model to the data and computing an estimate of σ^2, we can statistically check the usefulness of the model. That is, we can use a statistical procedure (a test of hypothesis or confidence interval) to determine whether the least squares straight-line (linear) model is a reliable tool for predicting y for a given value of x.

EXAMPLE 12.9
How to Test the Model

Consider the probabilistic model

$$y = \beta_0 + \beta_1 x + \varepsilon$$

How do we determine statistically whether this model is useful for prediction purposes? In other words, how could we test whether x provides useful information for the prediction of y?

SOLUTION Suppose x is **completely unrelated** to y. What could we say about the values of β_0 and β_1 in the probabilistic model, if in fact x contributes no information for the prediction of y? We think you will agree that for y to be independent of x, the true slope of the line, β_1, must be equal to 0. Therefore, to test the null hypothesis that x contributes no information for the prediction of y against the alternative that these variables are linearly related with a slope differing from 0, we test

H_0: $\beta_1 = 0$

H_a: $\beta_1 \neq 0$

If the data support the alternative hypothesis, we will conclude that x does contribute information for the prediction of y using the straight-line model, although the true relationship between $E(y)$ and x could be more complex than a straight line. ■

The test of hypothesis for β_1 is based on the sample estimator, $\hat{\beta}_1$ and the standard error of $\hat{\beta}_1$ (denoted $s_{\hat{\beta}_1}$). It can be shown (proof omitted) that $s_{\hat{\beta}_1} = s / \sqrt{SS_{xx}}$ in simple linear regression.

Using the hypothesis-testing techniques developed in Chapters 10 and 11, we set up the test for the predictive ability of the model as shown in the next box. Inferences based on this hypothesis test require the standard least squares assumptions about the random error term listed in the box in Section 12.4. However, the test statistic has a sampling distribution that remains relatively stable for minor departures from the assumptions. That is, our inferences remain valid for practical cases in which the assumptions are nearly, but not completely, satisfied.

Test of Hypothesis for Determining Whether the Straight-Line Model Is Useful for Predicting y from x

One-Tailed Test

H_0: $\beta_1 = 0$
H_a: $\beta_1 > 0$ (or H_a: $\beta_1 < 0$)

Two-Tailed Test

H_0: $\beta_1 = 0$
H_a: $\beta_1 \neq 0$

Test statistic: $\quad t = \dfrac{\hat{\beta}_1}{s_{\hat{\beta}_1}} = \dfrac{\hat{\beta}_1}{s / \sqrt{SS_{xx}}}$

Rejection region:
$t > t_\alpha$ (or $t < -t_\alpha$)

Rejection region:
$|t| > t_{\alpha/2}$

where the distribution of t is based on $(n - 2)$ degrees of freedom, t_α is the t value such that $P(t > t_\alpha) = \alpha$, and $t_{\alpha/2}$ is the t value such that $P(t > t_{\alpha/2}) = \alpha/2$.

Assumptions: See Section 12.4

[*Note:* The test statistic is derived from the sampling distribution of the least squares estimator of the slope, $\hat{\beta}_1$.]

EXAMPLE 12.10
Testing the Model

Refer to the appraised value–sale price problem of Example 12.3. At significance level $\alpha = .05$, test the hypothesis that total appraised property value x contributes useful information for the prediction of sale price y; i.e., test the predictive ability of the least squares straight-line model

$$\hat{y} = -2.2 + 2.3x$$

SOLUTION Testing the usefulness of the model requires testing the hypotheses

H_0: $\beta_1 = 0$

H_a: $\beta_1 \neq 0$

With $n = 5$ and $\alpha = .05$, the critical value based on $(5 - 2) = 3$ df is obtained from Table 6 of Appendix B:

$$t_{\alpha/2} = t_{.025} = 3.182$$

Thus, we will reject H_0 if $|t| > 3.182$.

To compute the test statistic, we need the values of $\hat{\beta}_1$, s, and SS_{xx}. In previous examples, we computed $\hat{\beta}_1 = 2.3$, $s = .6055$, and $SS_{xx} = 10$. Hence, our test statistic is

$$t = \frac{\hat{\beta}_1}{s/\sqrt{SS_{xx}}} = \frac{2.3}{.6055/\sqrt{10}} = 12.01$$

Since this calculated t value falls in the upper tail of the rejection region (see Figure 12.12), we reject the null hypothesis and conclude that the slope β_1 is not 0.

FIGURE 12.12

Rejection Region for Example 12.10

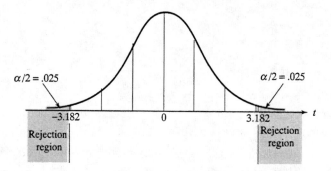

At the $\alpha = .05$ level of significance then, the sample data provide sufficient evidence to conclude that total appraised property value *does* contribute useful information for the prediction of sale price using the linear model. ▪

If the test statistic in Example 12.10 had not fallen in the rejection region, would we have concluded that $\beta_1 = 0$? The answer to this question is "no" (recall the discussion on Type II errors in Chapter 10). Rather, we acknowledge that additional data might indicate that β_1 differs from 0, or that a more complex relationship (other than a straight line) may exist between y and x.

EXAMPLE 12.11
Interpreting the *p*-Value

Refer to Example 12.10. Use a computer to obtain the test statistic and *p*-value for the hypothesis test H_0: $\beta_1 = 0$ versus H_a: $\beta_1 \neq 0$. Interpret the result.

SOLUTION The SAS printout of the simple linear regression for the sale price–appraised value problem is given in Figure 12.13. The value of the test statistic for testing β_1 is

FIGURE 12.13

SAS Printout for
Example 12.11

Dependent Variable: Y

Analysis of Variance

Source	DF	Sum of Squares	Mean Square	F Value	Prob>F
Model	1	52.90000	52.90000	144.273	0.0012
Error	3	1.10000	0.36667		
C Total	4	54.00000			

Root MSE	0.60553	R-square	0.9796
Dep Mean	7.00000	Adj R-sq	0.9728
C.V.	8.65043		

Parameter Estimates

Variable	DF	Parameter Estimate	Standard Error	T for H0: Parameter=0	Prob > |T|
INTERCEP	1	-2.200000	0.81240384	-2.708	0.0733
X	1	2.300000	0.19148542	12.011	0.0012

found under the column heading **T for HO: parameter = 0** in the lower portion of the printout. The value (shaded) is $t = 12.011$, which agrees with our hand-calculated test statistic in Example 12.10.

The observed significance level (or *p*-value) of the two-tailed test is given to the immediate right under the column **Prob > |T|**. The quantity (shaded) is $p = .0012$. Since the *p*-value is less than $\alpha = .05$, there is evidence to reject the null hypothesis in favor of the alternative that the slope differs from 0. Thus, our conclusion is the same as that in Example 12.10: There is sufficient evidence that total appraised property value (x) and sale price (y) are linearly related.

[*Note:* The *p*-value for a one-tailed test of a β parameter in regression is obtained by dividing the two-tailed *p*-value on the SAS printout in half when the sign of $\hat{\beta}_1$ agrees with the sign of β_1 in the alternative hypothesis. Consequently, since $\hat{\beta}_1$ is positive, the *p*-value for testing the alternative hypothesis $H_a: \beta_1 > 0$ is $p = .0012/2 = .0006$. The *p*-value for testing $H_a: \beta_1 < 0$ is actually $p = 1 - .0012/2 = .9994$.] ■

In addition to testing whether the slope β_1 is 0, we may also be interested in estimating its value with a confidence interval. The procedure is illustrated in the following example.

EXAMPLE 12.12
Confidence Interval for β_1

Using the information supplied in Example 12.10, construct a 95% confidence interval for the slope β_1 in the straight-line model relating sale price to total appraised property value.

SOLUTION The methods of Chapter 8 can be used to construct a confidence interval for β_1. The interval, derived from the sampling distribution of $\hat{\beta}_1$, is given in the box.

> **A $(1 - \alpha)100\%$ Confidence Interval for the Slope β_1**
>
> $$\hat{\beta}_1 \pm t_{\alpha/2}\left(\frac{s}{\sqrt{SS_{xx}}}\right)$$
>
> where the distribution of t is based on $(n - 2)$ degrees of freedom and $t_{\alpha/2}$ is the value of t such that $P(t > t_{\alpha/2}) = \alpha/2$.

For a 95% confidence interval, $\alpha = .05$. Therefore, we must find the value of $t_{.025}$ based on $(n - 2) = (5 - 2) = 3$ df. In Example 12.10, we found that $t_{.025} = 3.182$. Also we have $\hat{\beta}_1 = 2.3$, $s = .6055$, and $SS_{xx} = 10$. Thus, a 95% confidence interval for the slope in the model relating sale price to total appraised property value is

$$\hat{\beta}_1 \pm t_{.025}\left(\frac{s}{\sqrt{SS_{xx}}}\right) = 2.3 \pm 3.182\left(\frac{.6055}{\sqrt{10}}\right) = 2.3 \pm .61$$

Our interval estimate of the slope parameter β_1 is then 1.69 to 2.91. ■

EXAMPLE 12.13
Interpreting the Confidence Interval for β_1

Interpret the interval estimate β_1 derived in Example 12.12.

SOLUTION Since all the values in the interval $(1.69, 2.91)$ are positive, we say that we are 95% confident that the slope β_1 is positive. That is, we are 95% confident that the mean sale price, $E(y)$, increases as total appraised property value, x, increases. In addition we can say that for every 100,000-dollar increase in the appraised value x of the property, the increase in mean sale price $E(y)$ of the property could be as small as \$169,000 or as large as \$291,000. However, the rather large width of the interval reflects the small number of data points (and, consequently, a lack of information) in the experiment. We could expect a narrower interval if the sample size were increased. ■

EXERCISES

■ **Learning the Mechanics**

12.27 Suppose you want to test H_0: $\beta_1 = 0$ versus H_a: $\beta_1 \neq 0$ in a simple linear regression model. Give the degrees of freedom associated with the value of the test statistic for each of the following sample sizes.
    a. $n = 6$ **b.** $n = 10$ **c.** $n = 25$ **d.** $n = 50$

12.28 For each of the following combinations of H_a, $\hat{\beta}_1$, s^2, SS_{xx}, n, and α, specify the rejection region, test statistic value, and your conclusion for testing the null hypothesis H_0: $\beta_1 = 0$.

a. $H_a: \beta_1 \neq 0$, $\hat{\beta}_1 = .7$, $s^2 = .36$, $SS_{xx} = 10$, $n = 5$, $\alpha = .05$
b. $H_a: \beta_1 > 0$, $\hat{\beta}_1 = 1.5$, $s^2 = .10$, $SS_{xx} = 10$, $n = 5$, $\alpha = .10$
c. $H_a: \beta_1 < 0$, $\hat{\beta}_1 = -.011$, $s^2 = 3.880$, $SS_{xx} = 21,752$, $n = 7$, $\alpha = .01$

12.29 The data given in Exercises 12.8 and 12.20 are reproduced here.

x	−1	0	1	2	3
y	−1	1	1	2.5	3.5

a. Test the null hypothesis that the slope β_1 of the line equals 0 against the alternative hypothesis that β_1 is not equal to 0. Use $\alpha = .10$.
b. Compute the approximate observed significance level of the test.
c. Find a 90% confidence interval for the slope β_1.

12.30 The data given in Exercises 12.10 and 12.21 are reproduced here.

x	−5	−3	−1	0	1	3	5
y	.8	1.1	2.5	3.1	5.0	4.7	6.2

a. Test the null hypothesis that the slope β_1 of the line equals 0 against the alternative hypothesis that β_1 is not equal to 0. Use $\alpha = .10$.
b. Compute the approximate observed significance level of the test.
c. Find a 90% confidence interval for the slope of β_1.

■ *Applying the Concepts*

12.31 The data for the *Journal of Engineers for Industry* study, Exercises 12.13 and 12.22, are reproduced here. Test for a positive linear relationship between congestion time (*y*) and number of vehicles (*x*). Use $\alpha = .01$.

Number of Vehicles	Congestion Time, minutes	Number of Vehicles	Congestion Time, minutes
1	0	9	.02
2	0	10	.04
3	.02	11	.04
4	.01	12	.04
5	.01	13	.03
6	.01	14	.04
7	.03	15	.05
8	.03		

Source: Pandit, R. and Palekar, U. S. "Response time considerations for optimal warehouse layout design." *Journal of Engineering for Industry,* Transactions of the ASME, Vol. 115, Aug. 1993, p. 326 (Table 2).

12.32 Researchers conducted an analysis to compare return on equity for companies that aim at maximizing shareholder wealth to those with alternative corporate goals (*Quarterly Journal of Business & Economics*, Autumn 1986). Monthly holding period returns were averaged for the stocks of shareholder wealth maximizer companies and for companies holding alternative goals, and the difference between the averages (called monthly portfolio return differences) was calculated for each of $n = 72$ months. The return differences (y) were then regressed on monthly Standard & Poor's 500 Composite Stock Index (x), using the straight-line model

$$y = \beta_0 + \beta_1 x + \varepsilon$$

The regression results are summarized as follows:

$$\hat{y} = .00008 - .01748x \qquad SSE = .322 \qquad SS_{xx} = 2.914$$

a. Conduct a test to determine whether the monthly portfolio return differences are linearly related to the monthly S&P 500 Stock Index. Use $\alpha = .10$.
b. Construct a 90% confidence interval for the slope of the straight-line model.
c. Interpret the confidence interval obtained in part **b**, and explain what it tells you about the relationship between monthly portfolio return differences and the monthly S&P 500 Stock Index.

12.33 The *Research Management* study data, Exercises 12.14 and 12.23, are reproduced here. Do the data provide sufficient evidence to indicate that R/S ratio contributes information for the prediction of P/E ratio? Test using $\alpha = .05$.

Company	P/E Ratio y	R/S Ratio x	Company	P/E Ratio y	R/S Ratio x
1	5.6	.003	11	8.4	.058
2	7.2	.004	12	11.1	.058
3	8.1	.009	13	11.1	.067
4	9.9	.021	14	13.2	.080
5	6.0	.023	15	13.4	.080
6	8.2	.030	16	11.5	.083
7	6.3	.035	17	9.8	.091
8	10.0	.037	18	16.1	.092
9	8.5	.044	19	7.0	.064
10	13.2	.051	20	5.9	.028

Source: Wallin, C. C. and Gilman, J. J. "Determining the optimum level for R&D spending." *Research Management*, Vol. 14, No. 5, Sept./Oct. 1986, pp. 19–24 (adapted from Figure 1, p. 20).

12.34 In Exercise 2.16, we presented data on the foreign revenue of 20 multinational firms (i.e., firms with both domestic and foreign investments). Is there a positive linear relationship between the foreign revenue (measured as a percent of total revenue) and the foreign assets (measured as a percent of total assets) of multinational firms? Use the data in the table and the accompanying SPSS printout to conduct the analysis. Test using $\alpha = .10$.

Firm	Foreign Revenue, %	Foreign Assets, %	Firm	Foreign Revenue, %	Foreign Assets, %
Exxon	73.2	55.8	Procter & Gamble	39.9	32.2
IBM	58.9	48.6	Philip Morris	19.6	14.8
GM	26.6	25.2	Eastman Kodak	40.9	28.0
Mobil	64.7	51.1	Digital	54.1	44.2
Ford	33.2	26.9	GE	12.4	8.8
Citicorp	52.3	39.4	United Technologies	32.9	26.7
EI duPont	39.8	29.5	Amoco	26.1	32.7
Texaco	42.3	26.6	Hewlett-Packard	53.3	38.7
ITT	43.3	23.6	Xerox	34.6	25.4
Dow Chemical	54.1	44.6	Chevron	20.5	22.6

Source: *Forbes,* July 23, 1990, pp. 362–363

```
* * * *   M U L T I P L E   R E G R E S S I O N   * * * *

Equation Number 1    Dependent Variable..   FOREV

Multiple R           .92825
R Square             .86166
Adjusted R Square    .85397
Standard Error      6.10121

Analysis of Variance
                 DF      Sum of Squares      Mean Square
Regression        1         4173.32066       4173.32066
Residual         18          670.04484         37.22471

F =    112.11156      Signif F =  .0000

------------------ Variables in the Equation ------------------

Variable            B         SE B        Beta        T    Sig T

FORASS         1.218908    .115119     .928255     10.588  .0000
(Constant)     1.782570   3.959089                  .450   .6579
```

12.35 The data for the *Fortune* study of the top American cities for business, Exercises 12.15 and 12.24, are reproduced here. Do the data provide sufficient evidence of a linear relationship between labor market stress index (y) and unemployment rate (x)? Use $\alpha = .01$.

Rank	City	Labor Market Stress Index y	Unemployment Rate x
1	Salt Lake City	107	4.5%
2	Minneapolis–St. Paul	107	3.8%
3	Atlanta	100	5.1%
4	Sacramento	100	4.9%

(continued)

Rank	City	Labor Market Stress Index y	Unemployment Rate x
5	Austin (Texas)	80	5.4%
6	Columbus (Ohio)	100	4.8%
7	Dallas/Fort Worth	100	5.5%
8	Phoenix	93	4.3%
9	Jacksonville (Florida)	87	5.7%
10	Oklahoma City	80	4.6%

Source: Fortune, Oct. 22, 1990, pp. 58–63.

12.36 Refer to *The American Statistician* investigation of dry drilling in rock, Exercises 12.17 and 12.25. The MINITAB printout of the analysis is reproduced here. Is there evidence to indicate that dry drill time y increases with depth x? Test using $\alpha = .10$.

```
The regression equation is
DRILTIME = 4.79 + 0.0144 DEPTH

Predictor      Coef      Stdev    t-ratio        p
Constant     4.7896     0.6663       7.19    0.000
DEPTH       0.014388   0.002847       5.05    0.000

s = 1.432       R-sq = 63.0%     R-sq(adj) = 60.5%

Analysis of Variance

SOURCE       DF         SS          MS         F        p
Regression    1     52.378      52.378     25.54    0.000
Error        15     30.768       2.051
Total        16     83.146

Unusual Observations
Obs.   DEPTH   DRILTIME      Fit  Stdev.Fit   Residual   St.Resid
 11      250      4.840     8.387     0.376     -3.547      -2.57R

R denotes an obs. with a large st. resid.
```

12.37 The ASP printout for the *Journal of Heat Transfer* study of the straight-line relationship between heat transfer enhancement (y) and unflooded area ratio (x), Exercise 12.18, is reproduced here. Construct a 95% confidence interval for β_1, the slope of the line. Interpret the result.

```
        SIMPLE LINEAR REGRESSION: HEAT(y) vrs. RATIO(x)

MODEL:  HEAT(y) = 2.42639RATIO(x) + 0.213389CNST

            COEF.    SD. ER.     t(22)     P-VALUE  PT. R SQ.
          -------- --------- ---------- ----------- ---------
RATIO(x)  2.42639  0.228252   10.6303   3.92489E-10  0.837041
    CNST  0.213389 0.439       0.486081  0.631717    0.0106256

R SQ. = 0.837041,  ADJ. R SQ. = 0.829634,  D. W. = 1.49972
SQ. ROOT MSE = 0.453826,  F(1/22) = 113.003 (P-VALUE = 3.92489E-10)
```

12.7 The Coefficient of Correlation

In Section 12.6, we discovered that the least squares slope, $\hat{\beta}_1$, provides useful information on the linear relationship between two variables y and x. Another way to measure association is to compute the **Pearson product moment correlation coefficient r**. The correlation coefficient, defined in the box, provides a quantitative measure of the strength of the linear relationship between x and y in the sample, just as does the least squares slope $\hat{\beta}_1$. However, unlike the slope, the correlation coefficient r is *scaleless*. The value of r is always between -1 and $+1$, no matter what the units of x and y are.

Definition 12.1

The **Pearson product moment coefficient of correlation r** is a measure of the strength of the linear relationship between two variables x and y in the sample. It is computed (for a sample of n measurements on x and y) as follows:

$$r = \frac{SS_{xy}}{\sqrt{SS_{xx}SS_{yy}}}, \quad -1 \le r \le 1$$

Since both r and $\hat{\beta}_1$ provide information about the utility of the model, it is not surprising that there is a similarity in their computational formulas. In particular, note that SS_{xy} appears in the numerators of both expressions, and, since both denominators are always positive, r and $\hat{\beta}_1$ will always be of the same sign (either both positive or both negative). A value of r near or equal to 0 implies little or no linear relationship between y and x. And, if $r = 1$ or $r = -1$, all the points fall exactly on the least squares line. Positive values of r imply that y increases as x increases; negative values imply that y decreases as x increases. See Figure 12.14 and the box on page 620.

EXAMPLE 12.14
Calculating r

The data for Example 12.3 are reproduced in Table 12.4. Calculate the coefficient of correlation r between total appraised value x and sale price y. Interpret the result.

Table 12.4 Sale Price-Appraised Value Data for Example 12.14

Property	Total Appraised Property Value x, $100,000	Sale Price y, $100,000
1	2	2
2	3	5
3	4	7
4	5	10
5	6	11

FIGURE 12.14

Values of *r* and Their
Implications

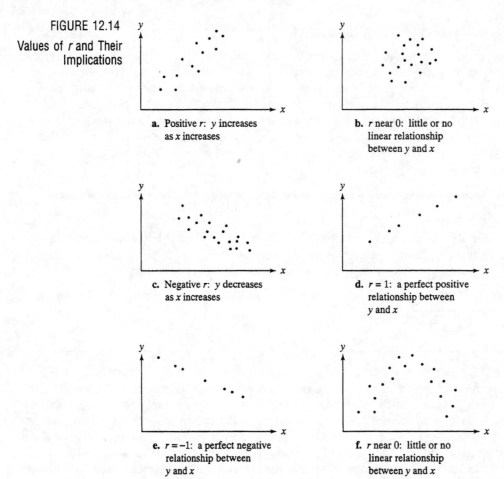

a. Positive *r*: *y* increases
as *x* increases

b. *r* near 0: little or no
linear relationship
between *y* and *x*

c. Negative *r*: *y* decreases
as *x* increases

d. *r* = 1: a perfect positive
relationship between
y and *x*

e. *r* = −1: a perfect negative
relationship between
y and *x*

f. *r* near 0: little or no
linear relationship
between *y* and *x*

Practical Interpretation of the Correlation Coefficient, r

$r > 0$:   *y* increases as *x* increases

$r = 1$:   A perfect positive linear relationship between *y* and *x*

$r < 0$:   *y* decreases as *x* increases

$r = -1$:   A perfect negative linear relationship between *y* and *x*

$r = 0$:   No linear relationship between *y* and *x*

SOLUTION From previous calculations (see Examples 12.3 and 12.7), we found $SS_{xy} = 23$, $SS_{xx} = 10$, and $SS_{yy} = 54$. Then, the coefficient of correlation is

$$r = \frac{SS_{xy}}{\sqrt{SS_{xx}SS_{yy}}} = \frac{23}{\sqrt{(10)(54)}}$$

$$= .9898$$

Thus, sale price and total appraised value are highly correlated—at least for this sample of five residential properties. The implication is that a strong positive linear relationship exists between these variables. We must be careful, however, not to jump to any unwarranted conclusions. For instance, the property appraiser may be tempted to conclude that a high total appraised value will *always* result in a higher sale price. The implication of such a conclusion is that there is a **causal** relationship between the two variables. However, **high correlation does not imply causality**. Many other factors, such as location, size of the property, and quality of the construction, may contribute to the increase in sale price. ■

> ### Warning
>
> High correlation does not imply causality. If a large positive or negative value of the sample correlation coefficient is observed, it is incorrect to conclude that a change in x causes a change in y. The only valid conclusion is that a linear trend *may* exist between x and y.

Keep in mind that the correlation coefficient r measures the correlation between x values and y values in the sample, and that a similar linear coefficient of correlation exists for the population from which the data points were selected. The **population correlation coefficient** is denoted by the symbol ρ (rho). As you might expect, ρ is estimated by the corresponding sample statistic, r. Or, rather than estimating ρ, we might want to test the hypothesis H_0: $\rho = 0$ against H_a: $\rho \neq 0$, i.e., test the hypothesis that x contributes no information for the prediction of y using the straight-line model against the alternative that the two variables are at least linearly related. However, we have already performed this identical test in Section 12.6 when we tested H_0: $\beta_1 = 0$ against H_a: $\beta_1 \neq 0$.

It is easy to show that $r = \hat{\beta}_1 \sqrt{SS_{xx}/SS_{yy}}$. Thus, $\hat{\beta}_1 = 0$ implies $r = 0$, and vice versa. Consequently, the null hypothesis H_0: $\rho = 0$ is equivalent to the hypothesis H_0: $\beta_1 = 0$. When we tested the null hypothesis H_0: $\beta_1 = 0$ in connection with the sale price–appraised value example, the data led to a rejection of the hypothesis for $\alpha = .05$. This implies that the null hypothesis of a zero linear correlation between the two variables (sale price and total appraised value) can also be rejected at $\alpha = .05$. The only real difference between the least squares slope $\hat{\beta}_1$ and the coefficient of correlation r is the measurement scale. Therefore, the information they provide about the utility of the least squares model is to some extent redundant. Furthermore, the slope β_1 gives us additional information on the amount increase (or decrease) in y for every

1-unit increase in x. For this reason, we recommend using the slope to make inferences about the existence of a positive or negative linear relationship between two variables. For those who prefer to test for a linear relationship between two variables using the coefficient of correlation r, we outline the procedure in the next box.

Test of Hypothesis for Linear Correlation

One-Tailed Test   *Two-Tailed Test*

H_0: $\rho = 0$ H_0: $\rho = 0$
H_a: $\rho > 0$ (or $\rho < 0$) H_a: $\rho \neq 0$

$$\text{Test statistic:}\quad t = \frac{r\sqrt{n-2}}{\sqrt{1-r^2}}$$

Rejection region: $t > t_\alpha$ *Rejection region:* $|t| > t_{\alpha/2}$
(or $t < -t_\alpha$)

where the distribution of t depends on $(n-2)$ df and t_α and $t_{\alpha/2}$ are the critical values obtained from Table 6 of Appendix B.

Assumptions: The sample of (x, y) values is randomly selected from a (bivariate) normal population.[*]

The next example illustrates how the correlation coefficient r may be a misleading measure of the strength of the association between x and y in situations where the true relationship is nonlinear.

EXAMPLE 12.15
Practical Application

Underinflated or overinflated tires can increase tire wear and decrease gas mileage. A manufacturer of a new tire tested the tire for wear at different pressures with the results shown in Table 12.5. Use the computer to calculate the coefficient of correlation r for the data. Interpret the result.

SOLUTION A SAS printout of the correlation analysis is shown in Figure 12.15. The value of r, shaded on the printout, is $r = -.114$. This relatively small value for r describes a weak linear relationship between pressure (x) and mileage (y). The manufacturer, however, would be remiss in concluding that tire pressure has little or no impact on wear of the tire. On the contrary, the relationship between pressure and wear is fairly strong, as the scattergram in Figure 12.16 illustrates. Note that the relationship is not linear, but curvilinear; the underinflated tires (low pressure values) and overinflated tires (high pressure values) both lead to low mileages.

---
[*]*A bivariate normal population will result if the probability distributions of both x and y are normal.*

Table 12.5   Data for Example 12.15

Pressure x, pounds per sq. inch	Mileage y, thousands	Pressure x, pounds per sq. inch	Mileage y, thousands
30	29.5	33	37.6
30	30.2	34	37.7
31	32.1	34	36.1
31	34.5	35	33.6
32	36.3	35	34.2
32	35.0	36	26.8
33	38.2	36	27.4

FIGURE 12.15

SAS Printout of
Correlation Analysis
of Data in Table 12.5

```
Pearson Correlation Coefficients / Prob > |R| under Ho: Rho=0 / N = 14

                                  X                     Y

              X             1.00000              -0.11371
                            0.0                   0.6987

              Y            -0.11371               1.00000
                            0.6987                0.0
```

FIGURE 12.16

Scattergram of Data
in Table 12.5

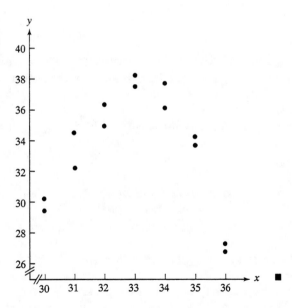

Example 12.15 points out the danger of using r to determine how well x predicts y: The correlation coefficient r describes only the *linear* relationship between x and y. For nonlinear relationships, the value of r may be misleading, and we need to resort to other methods for describing and testing such a relationship. Regression models for curvilinear relationships are presented in Chapter 13.

EXERCISES

■ *Learning the Mechanics*

12.38 What value does r assume if all the sample points fall on the same straight line and if the line has:
  a. A positive slope?   **b.** A negative slope?

12.39 The five data points for Exercise 12.8 are reproduced here. Find the correlation coefficient r and interpret its value.

x	−1	0	1	2	3
y	−1	1	1	2.5	3.5

12.40 The seven data points for Exercise 12.10 are reproduced here. Find the correlation coefficient r and interpret its value.

x	−5	−3	−1	0	1	3	5
y	.8	1.1	2.5	3.1	5.0	4.7	6.2

12.41 For each of the following situations, specify the test statistic and rejection region, and state your conclusion for testing the null hypothesis H_0: There is no linear correlation between x and y.
  a. H_a: The variables x and y are positively correlated; $r = .68, n = 10, \alpha = .01$
  b. H_a: The variables x and y are negatively correlated; $r = -.68, n = 52, \alpha = .01$
  c. H_a: The variables x and y are linearly correlated; $r = -.84, n = 10, \alpha = .10$

■ *Applying the Mechanics*

12.42 Give an example of two economic or business variables that are:
  a. Positively correlated   **b.** Negatively correlated

12.43 For each of the following pairs of variables, is the correlation expected to be positive or negative?
  a. $y =$ the number of buyers of new automobiles in a specific month (say, February), and $x =$ the prime interest rate
  b. $y =$ the demand for a product, and $x =$ price of the product

12.44 Investors in real estate investment trust (REIT) stock generally prefer REITs that are internally managed and that reward management both for share performance and for performance relative to industry competitors. To better understand management compensation patterns in the REIT industry, the *Real Estate Review* (Summer 1993) studied a sample of 16 internally managed REITs. The main purpose was to establish a relationship between CEO compensation and REIT performance. Data collected on the 16 REITs from the National Association of Real Estate Investment Trusts revealed a correlation coefficient of $r = .328$ between CEO cash compensation and the 1-year annualized total return for the REIT. Is there sufficient evidence to establish a positive linear relationship between CEO cash compensation and REIT performance? Test using $\alpha = .05$.

12.45 Refer to the *Journal of Organizational Behavior* (1992) study of workload and psychological strain in the dental profession, Exercise 11.38. Recall that one measure of psychological strain in dentists was job satisfaction, measured on a 20-point scale. Job satisfaction (y) was regressed against a quantitative independent variable that measured the congruence (x) between a dentist's preferred work hours and typical work hours. The simple linear regression analysis on data collected for $n = 318$ self-employed dentists resulted in a coefficient of correlation of $r = .01$. Make a statement about a possible linear relationship between job satisfaction and workload congruence for self-employed dentists.

12.46 Refer to the *Research Management* study of 20 large R&D spenders, Exercise 12.14. The data on price/earnings ratio (y) and R&D expenditures/sales ratio (x) for the 20 firms are reproduced here.

Company	P/E Ratio y	R/S Ratio x	Company	P/E Ratio y	R/S Ratio x
1	5.6	.003	11	8.4	.058
2	7.2	.004	12	11.1	.058
3	8.1	.009	13	11.1	.067
4	9.9	.021	14	13.2	.080
5	6.0	.023	15	13.4	.080
6	8.2	.030	16	11.5	.083
7	6.3	.035	17	9.8	.091
8	10.0	.037	18	16.1	.092
9	8.5	.044	19	7.0	.064
10	13.2	.051	20	5.9	.028

Source: Wallin, C. C. and Gilman, J. J. "Determining the optimum level for R&D spending." *Research Management*, Vol. 14, No. 5, Sept./Oct. 1986, pp. 19–24 (adapted from Figure 1, p. 20).

a. Find the correlation coefficient r and interpret its value.

b. Do the data provide sufficient evidence to indicate that x and y are linearly correlated? Test using $\alpha = .05$.

12.47 In the business world, the term *Machiavellian* is often used to describe one who employs aggressive, manipulative, exploiting, and devious moves to achieve personal and corporate objectives. Hunt and Chanko (*Journal of Marketing*, Summer 1984) investigated Machiavellian tactics in marketing. One question concerned the relationship between age and Machiavellianism. Do young marketers tend to be more Machiavellian than older marketers? A sample of 1,076 members of the American Marketing Association were administered a questionnaire that measured tendency toward Machiavellianism. (The higher the score, the greater the tendency toward Machiavellianism). The sample correlation coefficient between age and Machiavellianism score was found to be $r = -.20$. Is there evidence of a negative linear relationship between age of marketers and Machiavellianism score? Test using $\alpha = .05$.

12.48 Refer to the *Journal of Personal Selling & Sales Management* (Summer 1990) study of gender differences in the industrial sales force, Exercise 11.94. Two variables of interest to the researchers were level of organizational commitment (y) and total months experience in sales (x). For the 244 males in the study, the coefficient of correlation between x and y was $r_{males} = -.35$. For the 153 females in the study, the correlation coefficient was $r_{females} = -.06$.
  a. Interpret the value of r_{males}.
  b. Interpret the value of $r_{females}$.
  c. For each gender, test the hypothesis of no linear correlation between organizational commitment (y) and experience in years (x).

12.49 The relationships of five different work time dimensions with on-the-job performance were investigated in the *Journal of Business & Psychology* (Fall 1993). The researchers theorized that each work time dimension is positively related to performance. These five work time dimensions are (1) scheduling, (2) synchronization, (3) allocation of time, (4) autonomy of time use, and (5) future orientation. Based on data gathered from 122 managers at clothing manufacturing firms, the correlations shown in the accompanying table were obtained. Use this information to test the researchers' theories at a significance level of $\alpha = .05$.

Work Time Dimension	*Correlation (r) with Work Performance*
1. Scheduling	.22
2. Synchronization	.07
3. Allocation of time	−.25
4. Autonomy of time use	−.41
5. Future orientation	.44

Source: Lim, Y. M. and Seers, A. "Time dimensions of work: Relationships with perceived organizational performance". *Journal of Business & Psychology*, Vol. 8, No. 1, Fall 1993, p. 97 (Table 1).

12.50 An automated system for marking large numbers of student computer programs, called AUTOMARK, has been used successfully at McMaster University in Ontario, Canada. AUTOMARK takes into account both program correctness and program style when marking student assignments. To evaluate the effectiveness of the automated system, AUTOMARK was used to grade the FORTRAN 77 assignments of a class of 33 students. These grades were then compared to the grades assigned by the instructor. The results are shown in the table.

Automark Grade x	*Instructor Grade* y	*Automark Grade* x	*Instructor Grade* y	*Automark Grade* x	*Instructor Grade* y
12.2	10	18.2	15	19.0	17
10.6	11	15.1	16	19.3	17
15.1	12	17.2	16	19.5	17
16.2	12	17.5	16	19.7	17

(continued)

Automark Grade x	Instructor Grade y	Automark Grade x	Instructor Grade y	Automark Grade x	Instructor Grade y
16.6	12	18.6	16	18.6	18
16.6	13	18.8	16	19.0	18
17.2	14	17.8	17	19.2	18
17.6	14	18.0	17	19.4	18
18.2	14	18.2	17	19.6	18
16.5	15	18.4	17	20.1	18
17.2	15	18.6	17	19.2	19

Source: Redish, K. A. and Smyth, W. F. "Program style analysis: A natural by-product of program compilation." *Communications of the Association for Computing Machinery,* Vol. 29, No. 2, Feb. 1986, p. 132 (Figure 4).

a. Construct a scattergram for the data. After examining the scattergram, do you think that x and y are correlated? If correlation is present, is it positive or negative?

b. Find the correlation coefficient r and interpret its value.

c. Do the data provide sufficient evidence to indicate that x and y are linearly correlated? Test using $\alpha = .05$.

12.51 An investigation sought to determine whether there were certain collective behaviors, affective reactions, or performance outcomes associated with the maturity level of small groups (*Small Group Behavior*, May 1988). Fifty-eight undergraduate students enrolled in MIS or communications courses at a medium-size university participated in the experiment. A 10-item questionnaire (see Exercise 6.13) was used to measure the maturity level, y, of the students on a scale of 0–100, where more mature students received higher scores. One of several other variables measured was the number, x, of meetings held with their groups outside of regular class sessions. The correlation coefficient relating y to x was found to be $r = .46$. Is this sufficient evidence to indicate a positive correlation between group maturity and outside-of-class meetings? Test using $\alpha = .01$.

12.8 The Coefficient of Determination

So far, we have discussed a numerical descriptive measure of the correlation between two variables (Section 12.7) and a method of evaluating the usefulness of the straight-line model (Section 12.6). The correlation coefficient r measures the strength of the straight-line (linear) relationship between two variables x and y. An inference about the slope β_1 of a straight-line model (either a hypothesis test or confidence interval) leads to a determination of whether the independent variable x in the model contributes information for the prediction of the dependent variable y. In this section, we define an alternative numerical descriptive measure of how well the least squares line fits the sample data. This measure, called the **coefficient of determination**, is very useful for assessing how much the errors of prediction of y can be reduced by using the information provided by x.

EXAMPLE 12.16

Best Predictor of y without x

Refer to the sale price–total appraised value examples. Suppose you do not use x, the total appraised property value, to predict y, the sale price. If you have access to a sample of property sale prices only, what quantity would you use as the best predictor for any y value?

SOLUTION   If we have no information on the relative frequency distribution of the y values other than that provided by the sample, then $\bar{y}$, the sample average sale price, would be the best predictor for *any* y value. With $\bar{y}$ as our predictor, the sum of squared prediction errors would be

$$\Sigma(\text{Actual } y - \text{Predicted } y)^2 = \Sigma(y - \bar{y})^2$$

which is the familiar quantity SS_{yy}. The magnitude of SS_{yy} is thus an indicator of how well $\bar{y}$ behaves as a predictor of y.   ■

EXAMPLE 12.17

Best Predictor of y Using x

Refer to Example 12.16. Suppose now that you use the information on total appraised property value, x, to predict sale price, y. How do we measure the additional information provided by using the value of x in the least squares prediction equation, rather than $\bar{y}$, to predict y?

SOLUTION   If we use the information on x to predict y, then the sum of squares of the deviations of the y values about the predicted values obtained from the least squares equation $\hat{y} = \hat{\beta}_0 + \hat{\beta}_1 x$ is

$$SSE = \Sigma(y - \hat{y})^2$$

A convenient way of measuring how well the least squares equation performs as a predictor of y is to compute the reduction in the sum of squares of deviations that can be attributed to x, expressed as a proportion of SS_{yy}. This quantity, called the **coefficient of determination**, is

$$\frac{SS_{yy} - SSE}{SS_{yy}}$$

It can be shown that this proportion is equal to the square of the simple linear coefficient of correlation r.   ■

> **Definition 12.2**
>
> The **coefficient of determination** is
>
> $$r^2 = \frac{SS_{yy} - SSE}{SS_{yy}} = 1 - \frac{SSE}{SS_{yy}}, \quad \text{where } 0 \le r^2 \le 1$$
>
> It represents the proportion of the sum of squares of deviations of the y values about their mean that can be attributed to a linear relationship between y and x. (It may also be computed as the square of the coefficient of correlation.)

Note that r^2 is always between 0 and 1, since r is between -1 and $+1$. Thus, $r^2 = .75$ means that 75% of the sum of squares of deviations of the y values about their mean is attributable to the linear relationship between y and x. In other words, the error of prediction can be reduced by 75% when the least squares equation, rather than $\bar{y}$, is used to predict y.

EXAMPLE 12.18
Calculating r^2

Calculate the coefficient of determination for the appraised value–sale price data of Example 12.3 and interpret its value. The data are repeated in Table 12.6 for convenience.

Table 12.6

Property	Appraised Value x, $100,000	Sale Price y, $100,000
1	2	2
2	3	5
3	4	7
4	5	10
5	6	11

SOLUTION We will use the formula given in Definition 12.2 to compute r^2. From previous calculations, we have $SS_{yy} = 54$ and $SSE = 1.1$. Therefore

$$r^2 = \frac{SS_{yy} - SSE}{SS_{yy}} = \frac{54 - 1.1}{54} = \frac{52.9}{54} = .9796$$

Note that this value also appears (shaded) on the SAS printout for the simple linear regression analysis, Figure 12.17 on page 630. We interpret this value as follows: The use of total appraised property value, x, to predict sale price, y, with the least squares line

FIGURE 12.17
SAS Printout for
Example 12.18

```
Dependent Variable: Y

                        Analysis of Variance

                          Sum of           Mean
    Source        DF     Squares          Square      F Value      Prob>F

    Model          1    52.90000        52.90000      144.273      0.0012
    Error          3     1.10000         0.36667
    C Total        4    54.00000

            Root MSE     0.60553     R-square      0.9796
            Dep Mean     7.00000     Adj R-sq      0.9728
            C.V.         8.65043

                        Parameter Estimates

                      Parameter      Standard     T for H0:
    Variable   DF     Estimate          Error     Parameter=0     Prob > |T|

    INTERCEP    1    -2.200000      0.81240384       -2.708         0.0733
    X           1     2.300000      0.19148542       12.011         0.0012
```

$$\hat{y} = -2.2 + 2.3x$$

accounts for approximately 98% of the total sum of squares of deviations of the five sample sale prices about their mean. That is, we can reduce the total sum of squares of our prediction errors by nearly 98% by using the least squares equation $\hat{y} = -2.2 + 2.3x$, instead of $\bar{y}$, to predict y. Because this phrasing can sound awkward, most analysts prefer the more practical interpretation: "About 98% of the sample variation in sale price (y) can be explained by the linear relationship between y and appraised value (x)." ▪

Practical Interpretation of the Coefficient of Determination, r^2

About $100(r^2)\%$ of the sample variation in y can be explained by (or attributed to) using x to predict y in the straight-line model.

Since the two numerical descriptive measures r and r^2 are very closely related, there may be some confusion as to when each should be used. Our recommendations are as follows: If you are interested only in measuring the strength of the linear relationship between two variables x and y, use the coefficient of correlation r. However, if you want to determine how well the least squares straight-line model fits the data, use the coefficient of determination r^2.

EXERCISES

▪ **Learning the Mechanics**

12.52 For a set of $n = 30$ data points, $SS_{xx} = 39$, $SS_{yy} = 12$, and $SS_{xy} = 19$. Find r^2.

12.53 For a set of $n = 20$ data points, $SS_{yy} = 210$ and $SSE = 31$. Find r^2.

12.54 Refer to the data of Exercises 12.8, 12.20, and 12.29. Calculate the coefficient of determination r^2 and interpret its value.

12.55 Refer to the data of Exercises 12.10, 12.21, and 12.30. Calculate the coefficient of determination r^2 and interpret its value.

▪ **Applying the Concepts**

12.56 The Environmental Protection Agency (EPA) evaluates state pollution-control policies through the use of an emissions-to-job (E/J) ratio. The E/J ratio is obtained by dividing the amount (in pounds) of annual toxic emissions of an industry in a state by the number of jobs the state provides in that industry. *Environmental Technology* (Oct. 1993) investigated the relationship between E/J ratio and spending on pollution control in the chemical industry. Data collected for $n = 19$ large chemical-producing states were used to conduct a simple linear regression analysis, where $x =$ a state's pollution abatement capital expenditures (PACE), in millions of dollars (relative to other states), and $y =$ a state's chemical industry E/J ratio, in pounds per job. [*Note:* Positive x represents overspending on pollution control, whereas negative x represents underspending.] The analysis yielded a least squares line with a negative slope and $r^2 = .587$.
a. Interpret the value of r^2.
b. Calculate the correlation coefficient r and interpret the result.
c. In theory, underspending on pollution control will result in higher emissions and fewer jobs (i.e., a higher E/J ratio). Test the theory (at $\alpha = .01$) using the results of the straight-line regression.

12.57 The Mixed Arithmetic-Perceptual (MA-P) model is a componential model of graphic interaction that was developed based on analyses of humans interacting with graphical displays on the computer. The assumptions of the MA-P model were tested in a research article reported in the *SIGCHI Bulletin* (July 1993). Using simple linear regression, the researcher modeled response time y (in milliseconds) in a standard graph problem as a function of the number x of processing steps required to solve the problem. A summary of the regression results for $n = 8$ problems is given here:

$$\hat{y} = 1,346 + 450x \qquad r^2 = .91$$

a. Interpret the value of $\hat{\beta}_1$.
b. Interpret the value of r^2.
c. Conduct a test of model adequacy at $\alpha = .01$. *Hint:* Base the test on the value of r, the correlation coefficient.

12.58 Refer to the P/E ratio and R/S ratio data of Exercise 12.14. Calculate r^2 and interpret its value.

12.59 Refer to the data on labor market stress index and unemployment rate, Exercise 12.15. Calculate r^2 and interpret its value.

12.60 The SAS printout relating CPU time to I/O units, Exercise 12.16, is shown on page 632. Find r^2 and interpret its value.

Dependent Variable: CPU

Analysis of Variance

Source	DF	Sum of Squares	Mean Square	F Value	Prob>F
Model	1	937.54390	937.54390	2.975	0.0919
Error	42	13236.45610	315.15372		
C Total	43	14174.00000			

Root MSE	17.75257	R-square	0.0661	
Dep Mean	32.00000	Adj R-sq	0.0439	
C.V.	55.47678			

Parameter Estimates

Variable	DF	Parameter Estimate	Standard Error	T for H0: Parameter=0	Prob > |T|
INTERCEP	1	28.894324	3.22564861	8.958	0.0001
IO_UNITS	1	0.904965	0.52468333	1.725	0.0919

12.61 The MINITAB printout relating drill time and depth of penetration, Exercise 12.17, is shown here. Find r^2 and interpret its value.

The regression equation is
DRILTIME = 4.79 + 0.0144 DEPTH

Predictor	Coef	Stdev	t-ratio	p
Constant	4.7896	0.6663	7.19	0.000
DEPTH	0.014388	0.002847	5.05	0.000

s = 1.432   R-sq = 63.0%   R-sq(adj) = 60.5%

Analysis of Variance

SOURCE	DF	SS	MS	F	p
Regression	1	52.378	52.378	25.54	0.000
Error	15	30.768	2.051		
Total	16	83.146			

Unusual Observations

Obs.	DEPTH	DRILTIME	Fit	Stdev.Fit	Residual	St.Resid
11	250	4.840	8.387	0.376	-3.547	-2.57R

R denotes an obs. with a large st. resid.

12.62 The SPSS printout relating foreign revenue and foreign assets, Exercise 12.34, follows. Find r^2 and interpret its value.

* * * *   M U L T I P L E   R E G R E S S I O N   * * * *

Equation Number 1   Dependent Variable..   FOREV

Multiple R	.92825
R Square	.86166
Adjusted R Square	.85397
Standard Error	6.10121

Analysis of Variance

	DF	Sum of Squares	Mean Square
Regression	1	4173.32066	4173.32066
Residual	18	670.04484	37.22471

F =   112.11156   Signif F =   .0000

------------------ Variables in the Equation ------------------

Variable	B	SE B	Beta	T	Sig T
FORASS	1.218908	.115119	.928255	10.588	.0000
(Constant)	1.782570	3.959089		.450	.6579

12.63 Refer to the data on AUTOMARK grade and instructor grade provided in Exercise 12.50. Find r^2 and interpret its value.

12.9 Using the Model for Estimation and Prediction

After we have statistically checked the usefulness of our straight-line model and are satisfied that x contributes information for the prediction of y, we are ready to accomplish our original objective—using the model for prediction and estimation.

The most common uses of a probabilistic model for making inferences can be divided into two categories and are listed in the box.

Uses of the Probabilistic Model for Making Inferences

1. Use the model for estimating the mean value of y, $E(y)$, for a specific value of x.

2. Use the model for predicting a particular y value for a given value of x.

In the first case, we want to estimate the mean value of y for a very large number of experiments at a given x value. For example, we may want to estimate the mean sale price for all properties in the upscale neighborhood that are appraised at $300,000. In the second case, we wish to predict the outcome of a single experiment (predict an individual value of y) at the given x value. For example, we may want to predict the sale price of a particular property located in the neighborhood that has been appraised at $300,000.

We will use the least squares model

$$\hat{y} = \hat{\beta}_0 + \hat{\beta}_1 x$$

both to estimate the mean value of y, $E(y)$, and to predict a particular value of y for a given x.

EXAMPLE 12.19
Point Estimator of $E(y)$

Refer to Example 12.3. We found the least squares model relating sale price, y, to total appraised property value, x, to be

$$\hat{y} = -2.2 + 2.3x$$

Give a point estimate for the mean sale price of all properties in the neighborhood that have been appraised at $300,000. Recall that both x and y are measured in $100,000.

SOLUTION We need to find an estimate of $E(y)$. On the basis of the least squares model, our estimate is simply $\hat{y}$. Then, when $x = 3$, we have

$$\hat{y} = -2.2 + (2.3)(3) = -2.2 + 6.9 = 4.7$$

Thus, the estimated mean sale price for all properties with appraised values of $300,000 is $470,000. ▪

EXAMPLE 12.20
Point Estimator of y

Refer to Example 12.19. Use the least squares model to predict the sale price of a particular property whose total appraised value is $300,000.

SOLUTION Just as we use $\hat{y}$ from the least squares model to estimate $E(y)$, we also use $\hat{y}$ to predict a particular value of y for a given value of x. Again, when $x = 3$, we obtain $\hat{y} = 4.7$. Thus, we predict that a property in the neighborhood appraised at $300,000 would be sold for $470,000. ▪

Since the least squares model is used to obtain both the estimator of $E(y)$ and the predictor of y, how do the two model uses differ? The difference lies in the accuracies with which the estimate and the prediction are made. These accuracies are best measured by the repeated sampling errors of the least squares line when it is used as an estimator and predictor, respectively. These errors are given in the box.

Sampling Errors for the Estimator of the Mean of y
and the Predictor of an Individual y

1. The standard deviation of the sampling distribution of the estimator $\hat{y}$ of the mean value of y at a fixed x is

$$\sigma_{\hat{y}} = \sigma \sqrt{\frac{1}{n} + \frac{(x - \bar{x})^2}{SS_{xx}}}$$

where σ is the square root of σ^2, the measure of variability discussed in Section 12.4.

2. The standard deviation of the prediction error for the predictor $\hat{y}$ of an individual y value at a fixed x is

$$\sigma_{(y - \hat{y})} = \sigma \sqrt{1 + \frac{1}{n} + \frac{(x - \bar{x})^2}{SS_{xx}}}$$

where σ is the square root of σ^2, the measure of variability discussed in Section 12.4.

Since the true value of σ will rarely be known, we estimate σ by s. The sampling errors are then used in estimation and prediction intervals as shown in the boxes.

A $(1 - \alpha)100\%$ Confidence Interval for the Mean Value of y at a Fixed x

$$\hat{y} \pm (t_{\alpha/2}) s_{\hat{y}} = \hat{y} \pm (t_{\alpha/2}) s \sqrt{\frac{1}{n} + \frac{(x - \bar{x})^2}{SS_{xx}}}$$

A $(1 - \alpha)100\%$ Prediction Interval for an Individual y at a Fixed x

$$\hat{y} \pm (t_{\alpha/2}) s_{(y-\hat{y})} = \hat{y} \pm (t_{\alpha/2}) s \sqrt{1 + \frac{1}{n} + \frac{(x - \bar{x})^2}{SS_{xx}}}$$

EXAMPLE 12.21
Confidence Interval for $E(y)$

Find a 95% confidence interval for the mean sale price of all properties located in the neighborhood (referred to in previous examples) that have been appraised at $300,000.

SOLUTION   For a total appraised property value of $300,000, $x = 3$ and the confidence interval for the mean of y is

$$\hat{y} \pm (t_{\alpha/2}) s \sqrt{\frac{1}{n} + \frac{(x - \bar{x})^2}{SS_{xx}}} = \hat{y} \pm (t_{.025}) s \sqrt{\frac{1}{5} + \frac{(3 - \bar{x})^2}{SS_{xx}}}$$

where the distribution of t is based on $(n - 2) = 3$ degrees of freedom. Recall from previous examples that $\hat{y} = 4.7$, $s = .6055$, $\bar{x} = 4$, and $SS_{xx} = 10$. From Table 6 of Appendix B, $t_{.025} = 3.182$. Thus, we have

$$4.7 \pm (3.182)(.6055) \sqrt{\frac{1}{5} + \frac{(3 - 4)^2}{10}} = 4.7 \pm (3.182)(.6055)(.548)$$

$$= 4.7 \pm 1.055$$

or $(3.645, 5.755)$. Hence the 95% confidence interval for the mean sale price of all neighborhood properties appraised at $300,000 is $364,500 to $575,550. Note that the small sample ($n = 5$ properties) is reflected in the large width of the confidence interval. ■

EXAMPLE 12.22
Prediction Interval for y

Using a 95% prediction interval, predict the sale price of a particular property located in the neighborhood if its total appraised value is $300,000.

SOLUTION   For $x = 3$, the 95% prediction interval for y is computed as

$$\hat{y} \pm (t_{\alpha/2}) s \sqrt{1 + \frac{1}{n} + \frac{(x - \bar{x})^2}{SS_{xx}}} = 4.7 \pm (3.182)(.6055)\sqrt{1 + \frac{1}{5} + \frac{(3 - 4)^2}{10}}$$

$$= 4.7 \pm (3.182)(.6055)(1.140)$$

$$= 4.7 \pm 2.197$$

or (2.503, 6.897). Thus, we predict that the sale price for a particular property appraised at $300,000 will fall within the interval from $250,300 to $689,700. Again, the large width of this interval can be attributed to the unusually small number of data points (only five) used to fit the least squares line. The width of the prediction interval could be reduced by using a larger number of data points. ■

EXAMPLE 12.23
Using a Computer

Refer to Examples 12.21 and 12.22. Use a computer to find:

a. A 95% confidence interval for $E(y)$ when $x = 3$.
b. A 95% prediction interval for y when $x = 3$.

SOLUTION

a. A portion of the SAS printout not previously shown is given in Figure 12.18. For $x = 3$ (i.e., a total appraised property value of $300,000), the least squares predicted value of y, shaded in the **Predict Value** column, is $\hat{y} = 4.7000$. The endpoints of a 95% confidence interval for the mean, $E(y)$, for each value of x in the sample data are shaded in the columns labeled **Lower95% Mean** and **Upper95% Mean**. For $x = 3$, the 95% confidence interval ranges from 3.6445 to 5.7555. Thus, the mean sale price for properties appraised at $300,000 falls between $364,450 and $575,550, with 95% confidence. These results agree with those in Example 12.21.

FIGURE 12.18

Portion of the SAS Printout with 95% Confidence Limits for $E(y)$

Obs	X	Dep Var Y	Predict Value	Std Err Predict	Lower95% Mean	Upper95% Mean	Residual
1	2	2.0000	2.4000	0.469	0.9073	3.8927	-0.4000
2	3	5.0000	4.7000	0.332	3.6445	5.7555	0.3000
3	4	7.0000	7.0000	0.271	6.1382	7.8618	0
4	5	10.0000	9.3000	0.332	8.2445	10.3555	0.7000
5	6	11.0000	11.6000	0.469	10.1073	13.0927	-0.6000

```
Sum of Residuals                 -8.88178E-16
Sum of Squared Residuals             1.1000
Predicted Resid SS (Press)           4.4337
```

b. The endpoints of a 95% prediction interval for an individual value of y are given for each value of x in the sample in Figure 12.19, under the columns **Lower95% Predict** and **Upper95% Predict**. The 95% prediction interval for y with $x = 3$, shaded on the printout, is (2.5028, 6.8972). We predict that the sale price for a particular property appraised at $300,000 will fall between $250,280 and $689,720.

FIGURE 12.19

Portion of SAS
Printout with 95%
Prediction
Limits for *y*

Obs	X	Dep Var Y	Predict Value	Std Err Predict	Lower95% Predict	Upper95% Predict	Residual
1	2	2.0000	2.4000	0.469	-0.0376	4.8376	-0.4000
2	3	5.0000	4.7000	0.332	2.5028	6.8972	0.3000
3	4	7.0000	7.0000	0.271	4.8890	9.1110	0
4	5	10.0000	9.3000	0.332	7.1028	11.4972	0.7000
5	6	11.0000	11.6000	0.469	9.1624	14.0376	-0.6000

```
Sum of Residuals              -8.88178E-16
Sum of Squared Residuals       1.1000
Predicted Resid SS (Press)     4.4337
```

The difference between this result and the interval we computed in Example 12.22 ($250,300 to $689,700) is due to rounding error.   ■

In comparing the results of Examples 12.21–12.23, it is important to note that the prediction interval for an individual property sale price is wider than the corresponding confidence interval for the mean sale price (see Figure 12.20). By examining the formulas for the two intervals, you can see that this will always be true.

FIGURE 12.20

95% Confidence
Interval for $E(y)$ and
Prediction Interval for
y When $x = 3$

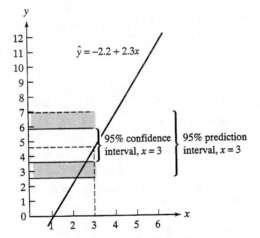

Additionally, over the range of the sample data, the widths of both intervals increase as the value of *x* gets further from $\bar{x}$ (see Figure 12.21 on page 638). Thus, the more the value of *x* deviates from the sample mean $\bar{x}$, the less useful the interval will be in practice. In fact, when *x* is selected far enough away from $\bar{x}$ so that it falls outside the range of the sample data, it is dangerous to make any inferences about $E(y)$ or *y*, as the following warning box explains.

Warning

Using the least squares prediction equation to estimate the mean value of *y* or to predict a particular value of *y* for values of *x* that fall *outside the range* of the values of *x* contained in your sample data may lead to errors of estimation or

(continued)

prediction that are much larger than expected. Although the least squares model may provide a very good fit to the data over the range of x values contained in the sample, **it could give a poor representation of the true model for values of x outside this region.**

FIGURE 12.21

Comparison of Widths of 95% Confidence Interval and Prediction Interval

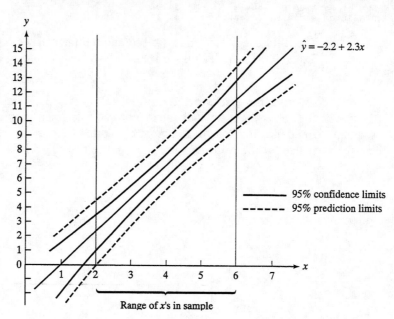

EXERCISES

■ **Learning the Mechanics**

12.64 In fitting a least squares line to $n = 22$ data points, suppose you computed the following quantities:

$$SS_{xx} = 25 \qquad \bar{x} = 2$$

$$SS_{yy} = 17 \qquad \bar{y} = 3$$

$$SS_{xy} = 20$$

a. Find the least squares line.
b. Calculate SSE.
c. Calculate s^2.
d. Find a 95% confidence interval for the mean value of y when $x = 1$.
e. Find a 95% prediction interval for y when $x = 1$.
f. Find a 95% confidence interval for the mean value of y when $x = 0$.

12.65 A simple linear regression analysis based on $n = 20$ data points produced the following results:

$\hat{y} = 2.1 + 3.4x$

$SS_{xx} = 4.77$ $\qquad\qquad \bar{x} = 2.5$

$SS_{yy} = 59.21$ $\qquad\qquad \bar{y} = 10.6$

$SS_{xy} = 16.22$

a. Calculate SSE and s^2.
b. Find a 95% confidence interval for $E(y)$ when $x = 2.5$. Interpret the interval.
c. Find a 95% confidence interval for $E(y)$ when $x = 2.0$. Interpret the interval.
d. Find a 95% confidence interval for $E(y)$ when $x = 3.0$. Interpret the interval.
e. Examine the widths of the confidence intervals obtained in parts **b**, **c**, and **d**. What happens to the width of the confidence interval for $E(y)$ as the value of x moves away from the value of $\bar{x}$?
f. Find a 95% prediction interval for a value of y to be observed in the future when $x = 3.0$. Interpret the interval.
g. Compare the width of the confidence interval from part **d** with the width of the prediction interval from part **f**. Explain why for a given value of x, a prediction interval for y is always wider than a confidence interval for $E(y)$.

12.66 The data of Exercises 12.8, 12.20, and 12.29 are reproduced here.

x	−1	0	1	2	3
y	−1	1	1	2.5	3.5

a. Estimate the mean value of y when $x = 1$, using a 90% confidence interval. Interpret the interval.
b. Suppose you plan to observe the value of y for a particular experimental unit with $x = 1$. Find a 90% prediction interval for the value of y that you will observe. Interpret the interval.
c. Which of the two intervals constructed in parts **a** and **b** is wider?

12.67 The data for Exercises 12.10, 12.21, and 12.30 are reproduced in the table.

x	−5	−3	−1	0	1	3	5
y	.8	1.1	2.5	3.1	5.0	4.7	6.2

a. Estimate the mean value of y when $x = -1$, using a 90% confidence interval. Interpret the interval.
b. Suppose you plan to observe the value of y for a particular experimental unit with $x = -1$. Find a 90% prediction interval for the value of y that you will observe. Interpret the interval.
c. Which of the two intervals is wider?

▪ *Applying the Concepts*

12.68 Refer to Exercise 12.13. Consider an automated warehouse that operates $x = 10$ vehicles.
  a. Find a 90% prediction interval for the congestion time (y) at this warehouse. Interpret the result.
  b. Find a 90% confidence interval for the mean congestion time, $E(y)$, at all warehouses with $x = 10$ vehicles. Interpret the result.

12.69 In Exercise 12.14, you found the least squares prediction equation relating P/E ratio y of a firm to R/S ratio x, and used it to predict P/E ratio when $x = .070$.
  a. Find a 99% prediction interval for this value of y and interpret it.
  b. Find a 99% confidence interval for $E(y)$ when $x = .070$. How does the interpretation of this interval differ from the interpretation of the interval of part **a**?

12.70 Refer to Exercise 12.17. A 95% prediction interval for drill time y when drilling begins at a depth of 300 feet is shown on the accompanying MINITAB printout. Interpret this result.

```
The regression equation is
DRILTIME = 4.79 + 0.0144 DEPTH

Predictor       Coef       Stdev     t-ratio        p
Constant      4.7896      0.6663        7.19    0.000
DEPTH       0.014388    0.002847        5.05    0.000

s = 1.432      R-sq = 63.0%      R-sq(adj) = 60.5%

Analysis of Variance

SOURCE          DF          SS          MS         F        p
Regression       1      52.378      52.378     25.54    0.000
Error           15      30.768       2.051
Total           16      83.146

Unusual Observations
Obs.    DEPTH   DRILTIME      Fit Stdev.Fit   Residual   St.Resid
  11      250      4.840     8.387     0.376     -3.547     -2.57R

R denotes an obs. with a large st. resid.

   Fit  Stdev.Fit          95% C.I.         95% P.I.
 9.106      0.450    ( 8.147, 10.065)   ( 5.906, 12.306)
```

12.71 In forestry, the diameter of a tree at breast height (which is fairly easy to measure) is used to predict the height of the tree (a difficult measurement to obtain). Silviculturists working in British Columbia's boreal forest conducted a series of spacing trials in an attempt to predict the heights of several species of trees. The data in the accompanying table are the breast height diameters (in centimeters) and heights (in meters) for a sample of 36 white spruce trees. A SAS printout of a simple linear regression analysis of the data follows.

Breast Height Diameter x, cm	Height y, m	Breast Height Diameter x, cm	Height y, m
18.9	20.0	16.6	18.8
15.5	16.8	15.5	16.9
19.4	20.2	13.7	16.3

(continued)

Breast Height Diameter x, cm	Height y, m	Breast Height Diameter x, cm	Height y, m
20.0	20.0	27.5	21.4
29.8	20.2	20.3	19.2
19.8	18.0	22.9	19.8
20.3	17.8	14.1	18.5
20.0	19.2	10.1	12.1
22.0	22.3	5.8	8.0
23.6	18.9	20.7	17.4
14.8	13.3	17.8	18.4
22.7	20.6	11.4	17.3
18.5	19.0	14.4	16.6
21.5	19.2	13.4	12.9
14.8	16.1	17.8	17.5
17.7	19.9	20.7	19.4
21.0	20.4	13.3	15.5
15.9	17.6	22.9	19.2

Source: Scholz, H., Northern Lights College, British Columbia.

Dependent Variable: HEIGHT

Analysis of Variance

Source	DF	Sum of Squares	Mean Square	F Value	Prob>F
Model	1	183.24469	183.24469	65.101	0.0001
Error	34	95.70281	2.81479		
C Total	35	278.94750			

Root MSE	1.67773	R-square	0.6569
Dep Mean	17.90833	Adj R-sq	0.6468
C.V.	9.36845		

Parameter Estimates

Variable	DF	Parameter Estimate	Standard Error	T for H0: Parameter=0	Prob > |T|
INTERCEP	1	9.146839	1.12131310	8.157	0.0001
DIAMETER	1	0.481474	0.05967333	8.069	0.0001

Obs	DIAMETER	Dep Var HEIGHT	Predict Value	Std Err Predict	Lower95% Mean	Upper95% Mean	Residual
37	20	.	18.7763	0.300	18.1675	19.3852	.

a. Construct a scattergram for the data.
b. Find the *y*-intercept and slope of the least squares line on the printout.
c. Plot the least squares line on your scattergram.

d. Do the data provide sufficient evidence to indicate that the breast height diameter x contributes information for the prediction of tree height y? Test using $\alpha = .05$.

e. Find a 95% confidence interval for the average height of white spruce trees with a breast height diameter of 20 cm on the printout. Interpret the interval.

12.72 Refer to Exercise 12.18. Use the information in the accompanying ASP printout to find a 95% confidence interval for the mean heat transfer coefficient of all tubes with an unflooded area ratio of 1.95. Interpret the results.

```
          SIMPLE LINEAR REGRESSION: HEAT(y) vrs. RATIO(x)

MODEL:  HEAT(y) = 2.42639RATIO(x) + 0.213389CNST

FORECAST OF HEAT(y) WHERE:

          RATIO(x) = 1.95
          CNST = 1

95% CONFIDENCE LIMITS FOR A SINGLE FORECAST:
             SD.ER.     t(22)  T*SD.ER.    LOWER FORECAST  UPPER
          ---------   -------  ---------   -------  --------  ------
  FORECAST 0.46346    2.07387  0.961157    3.98369  4.94485   5.906
E(FORECAST) 0.0940047  2.07387  0.194954    4.74989  4.94485   5.1398
```

12.73 Refer to Exercise 12.50. Find a 90% prediction interval for the instructor assigned grade of a FORTRAN77 assignment that received an AUTOMARK score of 18. Interpret the interval.

12.10 Simple Linear Regression: A Complete Example

In the previous sections, the basic elements of a simple linear regression analysis have been presented using a small (and unrealistic) data set. To solidify our thoughts, we present a complete simple linear regression analysis of a portion of the data described in Appendix A.1.

Recall that Appendix A.1 contains the sale prices and total appraised values of residential properties sold in 1993 in six Tampa, Florida, neighborhoods. For this analysis, consider only the 54 properties sold in the Tampa Palms neighborhood. These data are listed in Table 12.7. Our goal is to use these data in Table 12.7 and assess the straight-line model

$$y = \beta_0 + \beta_1 x + \varepsilon$$

where y = sale price of a property in Tampa Palms and x = total appraised value of a property in Tampa Palms. If the model is deemed adequate, we would like to use it to predict the sale price of a property appraised at $200,000 in Tampa Palms.

STEP 1 A scattergram of the data in Table 12.7 is shown on the SPSS printout, Figure 12.22. Note that sale price (y) tends to increase as total appraised value (x) increases. Thus, a straight-line model is a reasonable first choice for a model relating y to x.

STEP 2 The simple linear regression results are summarized in the MINITAB printout, Figure 12.23 on page 644. The least squares estimates of β_0 and β_1, shaded on the printout, are $\hat{\beta}_0 = 5,729$ and $\hat{\beta}_1 = 1.13$. Consequently, the best-fitting least squares line is

Table 12.7 Data on Sales and Appraisals of Tampa Palms Properties

Property	Sale Price	Appraisal	Property	Sale Price	Appraisal
1	$ 95,000	$ 79,760	28	$ 475,000	$ 341,306
2	116,500	98,480	29	138,000	106,773
3	156,900	110,655	30	110,000	95,339
4	111,000	96,859	31	172,000	142,258
5	100,100	100,861	32	196,000	166,178
6	100,000	105,230	33	195,000	151,310
7	130,000	94,798	34	190,000	170,154
8	170,400	139,850	35	206,000	179,231
9	211,500	170,341	36	170,000	125,353
10	185,000	155,137	37	174,700	153,656
11	179,700	170,662	38	137,000	116,389
12	208,000	185,939	39	154,000	124,438
13	208,900	187,457	40	147,500	119,211
14	210,000	206,264	41	164,300	128,671
15	255,000	223,853	42	180,000	139,803
16	150,000	142,815	43	162,000	120,173
17	149,900	129,292	44	805,000	669,129
18	360,000	280,250	45	155,900	127,981
19	425,000	368,903	46	136,000	121,030
20	130,000	111,000	47	175,000	144,690
21	170,000	154,568	48	267,000	195,355
22	152,500	141,368	49	203,000	171,300
23	144,500	124,636	50	159,900	123,626
24	310,000	335,873	51	121,000	102,760
25	293,000	299,460	52	120,000	104,425
26	300,000	329,575	53	124,900	98,871
27	345,000	324,252	54	108,000	94,485

FIGURE 12.22
SPSS Scattergram of
the Data in Table 12.7

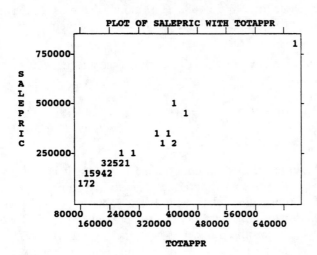

FIGURE 12.23

MINITAB Simple
Linear Regression
Printout

```
The regression equation is
SALEPRIC = 5729 + 1.13 TOTAPPR

Predictor        Coef       Stdev     t-ratio        p
Constant         5729        6899        0.83    0.410
TOTAPPR       1.13081     0.03501       32.30    0.000

s = 25448        R-sq = 95.3%      R-sq(adj) = 95.2%

Analysis of Variance

SOURCE        DF          SS          MS          F        p
Regression     1  6.75477E+11  6.75477E+11  1043.02    0.000
Error         52  33676208128    647619392
Total         53  7.09153E+11

     Fit  Stdev.Fit           95% C.I.           95% P.I.
  231891        3615   ( 224635, 239146)  ( 180300, 283481)
```

$$\hat{y} = 5{,}729 + 1.13x$$

Our practical interpretation of the slope $\hat{\beta}_1 = 1.13$ is as follows: For every \$1 increase in total appraised value (x), we estimate sale price (y) to increase by \$1.13. The value of the y-intercept $\hat{\beta}_0 = 5{,}729$ has no practical interpretation since an appraised value of \$0 ($x = 0$) is nonsensical and/or impractical.

STEP 3   For any inferences derived from the simple linear regression to be valid, the following assumptions about the random error ε in the model must be approximately satisfied:

1.   Mean of ε is 0
2.   Variance of ε is constant (σ^2) for all x values
3. ε has a normal distribution
4. ε's are independent

The estimate of σ, the model standard deviation, is shaded on the MINITAB printout, Figure 12.23. Note that $s = 25{,}448$. This implies that most of the actual Tampa Palms property sale prices will fall within $2s = \$50{,}896$ of their predicted prices using the least squares model.

STEP 4   **a.** *Test of model utility:* To determine the adequacy of the model, we want to test

$$H_0: \quad \beta_1 = 0$$

$$H_a: \quad \beta_1 > 0$$

We have selected an upper-tailed test since it is reasonable to expect sale price and appraised value to be positively linearly related if a straight-line relationship exists. The two-tailed p-value of the test, shaded on Figure 12.23, is approximately .000. Since the sign of $\hat{\beta}_1$ is positive (agreeing with the sign of β_1 in H_a), the one-tailed p-value is $p = .000/2 = .000$. Consequently, we have sufficient evidence to reject H_0; there is evidence of a positive linear relationship between sale price and appraised value of properties sold in Tampa Palms.

b. *Confidence interval for slope:* We gain additional information about the relationship by forming a confidence interval for the slope β_1. A 95% confidence interval is $\hat{\beta}_1 \pm (t_{.025}) s_{\hat{\beta}_1}$; where the value of $\hat{\beta}_1$ and its standard error, $s_{\hat{\beta}_1}$, are shown (shaded) on the printout. The value of $t_{.025}$, based on $n - 2 = 52$ df, is (from Table 6, Appendix B) approximately 2.0. Therefore, the 95% confidence interval is

$$\hat{\beta}_1 \pm (t_{.025}) s_{\hat{\beta}_1} = 1.13 \pm (2.0)\,(.035)$$

$$= 1.13 \pm .07 = (1.06, 1.20)$$

For every \$1 increase in total appraised value (x), we estimate that the mean increase in sale price (y) falls between \$1.06 and \$1.20.

c. *Coefficients of determination and correlation:* The coefficient of determination, shaded on Figure 12.23, is $r^2 = .953$. This implies that about 95% of the sample variation in sale price (y) is explained by the linear relationship with appraised value (x).

The coefficient of correlation r, which measures the strength of the linear relationship between y and x, is not shown on the MINITAB printout and must be calculated. Using the fact that $r = \sqrt{r^2}$ in simple linear regression and that r and $\hat{\beta}_1$ have the same sign, we find

$$r = +\sqrt{r^2} = \sqrt{.953} = .976$$

Thus, r shows further evidence of a strong positive linear relationship between y and x. The test of model adequacy, the confidence interval for β_1, r^2, and r all indicate that the straight-line model is useful for predicting sale price.

STEP 5   Recall that we want to use the model to predict the sale price of a Tampa Palm's residential property appraised at \$200,000. The bottom of the MINITAB printout, Figure 12.23, shows a 95% prediction interval for the sale price of this type of property. This interval (shaded) is (180,300, 283,481). Thus, we are 95% confident that the sale price for a property appraised at \$200,000 in Tampa Palms falls between \$180,300 and \$283,481.

Caution: We have made no attempt to verify the assumptions on ε made in step 3. If one or more of these assumptions are violated, the above inferences are suspect. In Chapter 13, we present a formal method for checking these assumptions, called a **residual analysis**.

SUMMARY

In this chapter, we introduced *bivariate relationships* and an extremely useful tool—the *method of least squares*—for fitting a straight-line model to a set of data. This procedure, along with associated statistical tests and estimations, is called a *regression analysis*.

After hypothesizing the *straight-line probabilistic model*

$$y = \beta_0 + \beta_1 x + \varepsilon$$

perform the steps outlined in the box.

Steps in a Simple Linear Regression Analysis

1. Collect the sample of (x, y) data points, and plot the data in a scattergram. Check the pattern to be sure that a linear relationship is reasonable.

2. Use the method of least squares to estimate the unknown parameters in the deterministic component, $\beta_0 + \beta_1 x$. Obtain the estimates by applying the computational formulas given in this chapter or by using a computer printout. The least squares estimates will yield a model $\hat{y} = \hat{\beta}_0 + \hat{\beta}_1 x$ with a sum of squared errors (SSE) that is smaller than that produced by any other straight-line model.

3. Check that the assumptions about the random error component (outlined in the box in Section 12.4) are satisfied. (We will explain how to do this in Chapter 13.) You should also determine s^2 (either by hand calculation or from a computer printout), an estimate of σ^2, the variance of the random error component.

4. Assess the usefulness of the hypothesized model—that is, determine how well x performs as a predictor of y. Included here are making inferences about the slope β_1 and computing the coefficient of determination, r^2.

5. Finally, if you are satisfied with the model, use it to estimate the mean y value, $E(y)$, for a given x value or to predict an individual y value for a specific x.

KEY TERMS

Bivariate relationships

Coefficient of correlation, r

Coefficient of determination, r^2

Deterministic component

Least squares line (prediction equation)

Linear regression analysis

Method of least squares

Probabilistic models

Random error component

Slope of line, β_1

y-intercept of line, β_0

KEY FORMULAS

Least squares estimates of β's:
$$\hat{\beta}_1 = \frac{SS_{xy}}{SS_{xx}} \qquad \hat{\beta}_0 = \bar{y} - \hat{\beta}_1 \bar{x}$$

where
$$SS_{xy} = \Sigma xy - \frac{(\Sigma x)(\Sigma y)}{n}$$

$$SS_{xx} = \Sigma x^2 - \frac{(\Sigma x)^2}{n}$$

$$SS_{yy} = \Sigma y^2 - \frac{(\Sigma y)^2}{n}$$

Sum of squared errors:
$$SSE = SS_{yy} - \hat{\beta}_1 SS_{xy}$$

Estimated variance of ε:
$$s^2 = \frac{SSE}{n-2}$$

Standard error of $\hat{\beta}_1$:
$$\sigma_{\hat{\beta}_1} = \sigma / \sqrt{SS_{xx}} \quad \text{where } \sigma \approx s$$

Coefficient of correlation:
$$r = \frac{SS_{xy}}{\sqrt{SS_{xx}SS_{yy}}}$$

Coefficient of determination:
$$r^2 = 1 - \frac{SSE}{SS_{yy}}$$

Standard error of estimating E(y):
$$\sigma_{\hat{y}} = \sigma \sqrt{\frac{1}{n} + \frac{(x - \bar{x})^2}{SS_{xx}}} \quad \text{where } \sigma \approx s$$

Standard error of predicting y:
$$\sigma_{(y - \hat{y})} = \sigma \sqrt{1 + \frac{1}{n} + \frac{(x - \bar{x})^2}{SS_{xx}}} \quad \text{where } \sigma \approx s$$

SUPPLEMENTARY EXERCISES

12.74 Civil engineers often use the straight-line equation $E(y) = \hat{\beta}_0 + \hat{\beta}_1 x$ to model the relationship between the mean shear strength $E(y)$ of masonry joints and precompression stress x. To test this theory, a series of stress tests was performed on solid bricks arranged in triplets and joined with mortar (*Proceedings of the Institute of Civil Engineers*, Mar. 1990). The precompression stress was varied for each triplet; the ultimate shear load just before failure (called the shear strength) was recorded. The stress results for seven triplets (measured in N/mm^2) are shown in the accompanying table.

Triplet Test	1	2	3	4	5	6	7
Shear Strength, y	1.00	2.18	2.24	2.41	2.59	2.82	3.06
Precompression Stress, x	0	.60	1.20	1.33	1.43	1.75	1.75

Source: Riddington, J. R. and Ghazali, M. Z. "Hypothesis for shear failure in masonry joints." *Proceedings of the Institute of Civil Engineerings, Part 2*, Mar. 1990, Vol. 89, p. 96 (Figure 7).

a. Construct a scattergram for the data. After examining the scattergram, do you think that x and y are correlated? If correlation is present, is it positive or negative?
b. Find the correlation coefficient r, and interpret its value.
c. Do the data provide sufficient evidence to indicate that x and y are linearly correlated? Test using $\alpha = .05$.
d. Find the least squares prediction equation relating shear strength and precompression strength x.
e. Test the hypothesis $H_0: \beta_1 = 0$ (at $\alpha = .05$), and show that the result agrees with your answer to part **c**.
f. Find a 95% prediction interval for the shear strength of a masonry joint with a precompression stress of $x = 2$.
g. Why might the prediction interval of part **f** be less reliable than expected? Explain.

12.75 The Consumer Attitude Survey, performed by the University of Florida Bureau of Economic and Business Research (BEBR), is conducted using random-digit telephone dialings of Florida households. The reliability of a telephone survey such as this depends on the *refusal rate*, i.e., the percentage of dialed households that refuse to take part in the study. One factor thought to be related to refusal rate is personal income. The accompanying table gives the refusal rate, y, and personal income per capita, x, for 12 randomly selected Florida counties from a recent BEBR survey. Conduct a complete simple linear regression analysis of the data.

County	Refusal Rate y	Per Capita Income x	County	Refusal Rate y	Per Capita Income x
1	.296	$ 7,737	7	.429	$11,466
2	.498	12,330	8	.422	10,000
3	.386	12,058	9	.441	10,052
4	.327	9,927	10	.191	8,636
5	.500	6,904	11	.526	7,445
6	.333	9,463	12	.405	9,059

Source: Bureau of Economic and Business Research, University of Florida.

12.76 A medical item used to administer to a hospital patient is called a *factor*. For example, factors can be intravenous (I.V.) tubing, I.V. fluid, needles, shave kits, bedpans, diapers, dressings, medications, and even code carts. The coronary care unit at Bayonet Point Hospital (St. Petersburg, Florida) investigated the relationship between the number of factors per patient, x, and the patient's length of stay (in days), y. The data for a random sample of 50 coronary care patients are given in the table, followed by a SAS printout of the simple linear regression analysis.

Number of Factors x	Length of Stay y, days	Number of Factors x	Length of Stay y, days
231	9	354	11
323	7	142	7
113	8	286	9
208	5	341	10
162	4	201	5
117	4	158	11
159	6	243	6
169	9	156	6
55	6	184	7
77	3	115	4
103	4	202	6
147	6	206	5
230	6	360	6
78	3	84	3
525	9	331	9
121	7	302	7
248	5	60	2
233	8	110	2
260	4	131	5
224	7	364	4
472	12	180	7
220	8	134	6
383	6	401	15
301	9	155	4
262	7	338	8

Source: Bayonet Point Hospital, Coronary Care Unit.

a. Construct a scattergram of the data.
b. Find the least squares line for the data, and plot it on your scattergram.
c. Define β_1 in the context of this problem.
d. Test the hypothesis that the number of factors per patient (x) contributes no information for the prediction of the patient's length of stay (y) when a linear model is used (use $\alpha = .05$). Draw the appropriate conclusions.
e. Find a 90% confidence interval for β_1. Interpret your result.

f. Find the coefficient of correlation for the data. Interpret your result.

g. Find the coefficient of determination for the linear model you constructed in part **b**. Interpret your result.

h. Find a 95% prediction interval for length of stay of a coronary care patient who is administered a total of $x = 200$ factors.

i. Explain why the prediction interval obtained in part **h** in so wide. How could you reduce the width of the interval?

```
Dependent Variable: Y

                          Analysis of Variance

                            Sum of          Mean
         Source      DF     Squares         Square      F Value      Prob>F

         Model        1    126.58393      126.58393      28.683      0.0001
         Error       48    211.83607        4.41325
         C Total     49    338.42000

            Root MSE        2.10077      R-square       0.3740
            Dep Mean        6.54000      Adj R-sq       0.3610
            C.V.           32.12193

                          Parameter Estimates

                      Parameter     Standard     T for H0:
         Variable  DF  Estimate        Error     Parameter=0    Prob > |T|

         INTERCEP   1   3.306032     0.67297426      4.913        0.0001
         X          1   0.014755     0.00275502      5.356        0.0001


                 Dep Var   Predict   Std Err  Lower95%  Upper95%
         Obs   X      Y      Value    Predict   Predict   Predict  Residual

          1   200      .     6.2570    0.302    1.9898   10.5242       .

         Sum of Residuals          9.769963E-15
         Sum of Squared Residuals     211.8361
         Predicted Resid SS (Press)   234.7934
```

12.77 Some economists fear that the current unemployment compensation system in the United States distorts the number of layoffs in a downturn of the business cycle. The hypothesis is that the unemployment compensation subsidy causes firms to lay off more people than they would if they knew the layoffs would receive no outside subsidy. The table shows the unemployment compensation subsidy rate x (as a percentage of total revenues) and the layoff rate y (number of workers per 1,000) for 11 industries. As SPSS printout of a simple linear regression analysis of the data follows.

Industry	Subsidy Rate x	Layoff Rate y
Apparel	57%	12.54
Chemicals	32	1.78
Construction	31	7.10
Electrical machinery	29	8.38

(continued)

Industry	Subsidy Rate x	Layoff Rate y
Fabricated metals	27%	11.72
Food	36	5.10
Machinery	32	4.44
Misc. manufacturing	61	9.82
Primary metals	23	7.34
Retail	27	1.98
Wholesale trade	33	1.86

Source: Tropel, R. H. "On layoffs and unemployment insurance." *American Economic Review*, 1983, Vol. 83, pp. 541–559.

* * * * MULTIPLE REGRESSION * * * *

Equation Number 1   Dependent Variable..   LAYOFF

Variable(s) Entered on Step Number
   1..   SUBSIDY

Multiple R   .45880
R Square   .21050
Adjusted R Square   .12278
Standard Error   3.62461

Analysis of Variance

	DF	Sum of Squares	Mean Square
Regression	1	31.52580	31.52580
Residual	9	118.24010	13.13779

F =   2.39963   Signif F =   .1558

------------------ Variables in the Equation ------------------

Variable	B	SE B	Beta	T	Sig T
SUBSIDY	.144675	.093395	.458803	1.549	.1558
(Constant)	1.447817	3.470832		.417	.6864

a. Find the least squares prediction equation.

b. Do the data provide sufficient evidence to indicate that the unemployment compensation subsidy rate x contributes information for the prediction of the layoff rate y? Test using $\alpha = .05$.

c. Find a 95% confidence interval for the mean increase in layoff rate, y, for each percentage point increase in subsidy rate, x. Interpret your result.

12.78 Paper-and-pencil honesty tests of employees are common among retail stores, financial institutions, and warehouse operations where employees have access to cash and merchandise. Such tests are less costly than polygraphs and can be used in states where pre-employment polygraph examinations are illegal. P. R. Sackett and M. M. Harris reviewed a number of studies that examined the validity of paper-and-pencil honesty tests (*Personnel Psychology*, Summer 1984). In one study, $n = 80$ applicants for retail management positions were given both an honesty test and a polygraph examination. The sample correlation coefficient between the scores of the two tests was $r = .48$. An independent study of $n = 17$ warehouse employees showed a sample correlation coefficient of $r = .41$ between honesty test score and dollar amount of money and merchandise stolen.

a. Is there sufficient evidence to indicate that paper-and-pencil honesty test scores and polygraph examination scores of retail management applicants are positively correlated? Test using $\alpha = .05$.

b. Is there sufficient evidence to indicate that paper-and-pencil test scores of warehouse employees are correlated with dollar amount of theft? Test using $\alpha = .05$.

12.79 Most investment firms provide estimates, called *betas*, of systematic risks of securities. A stock's beta measures the relationship between its rate of return and the average rate of return for the market as a whole. The term derives its name from the beta-coefficient for the slope in simple linear regression, where the dependent variable is the stock's rate of return (y) and the independent variable is the market rate of return (x). Stocks with beta values (i.e., slopes) greater than 1 are considered "aggressive" securities since their rates of return are expected to move (upward or downward) faster than the market as a whole. In contrast, stocks with beta values less than 1 are called "defensive" securities since their rates of return move slower than the market. A stock with a beta value near 1 is called a "neutral" security because its rate of return mirrors the markets. The data in the accompanying table are monthly rates of return (in percent) for a particular stock and the market as a whole for seven randomly selected months. Conduct a complete simple linear regression analysis of the data. Based on your analysis, how would you classify this stock—aggressive, defensive, or neutral?

Month	Stock Rate of Return y	Market Rate of Return x
1	12.0	7.2
2	−1.3	0.0
3	2.5	2.1
4	18.6	11.9
5	9.0	5.3
6	−3.8	−1.2
7	−10.0	−4.7

12.80 Refer to Exercise 12.79. Does a stock's beta value depend on the length of the horizon over which the rates of return are calculated? Since some brokerage firms base their beta values on monthly data and others on annual data, the question is an important one for investors. H. Levy investigated the relationship between length of horizon (in months) and average beta value for each of the three types of stocks (*Financial Analysts Journal*, Mar–Apr. 1984). Varying the length of horizon from 1 to 30 months, Levy calculated rates of return for 144 stocks over the years 1946–1975. The stocks were divided into 38 aggressive, 38 defensive, and 68 neutral stocks based on their beta values. The table gives the average beta value for different horizons for each of the stock types.

Length of Horizon x, months	Aggressive stocks	Beta Values, y Defensive Stocks	Neutral Stocks
1	1.37	.50	.98
3	1.42	.44	.95
6	1.53	.41	.94
9	1.69	.39	1.00
12	1.83	.40	.98
15	1.67	.38	1.00
18	1.78	.39	1.02
24	1.86	.35	1.14
30	1.83	.33	1.22

a. Find the least squares simple linear regression equation relating average beta value, y, to length of horizon, x, for (i) aggressive stocks, (ii) defensive stocks, and (iii) neutral stocks.

b. For each type of stock, test the hypothesis that length of horizon is a useful linear predictor of average beta value. Test using $\alpha = .05$.

c. For each type of stock, construct a 95% confidence interval for the slope of the line. Which stocks have beta values that increase linearly as length of horizon increases? Which stocks have beta values that decrease linearly as length of horizon increases?

12.81 A supermarket chain conducted an experiment to investigate the effect of price p (in dollars) on the weekly demand y (in pounds) for a house brand of coffee. Eight supermarkets that had nearly equal past records of demand for the product were used in the experiment. Eight prices were randomly assigned to the stores and were advertised using the same procedures. The number of pounds of coffee sold during the following week was recorded for each store, as shown in the table.

Demand y	Price p
1,120	3.00
999	3.10
932	3.20
884	3.30
807	3.40
760	3.50
701	3.60
688	3.70

a. Let $x = 1/p$. Find the least squares prediction equation for fitting the model

$$E(y) = \beta_0 + \beta_1 x$$

to the data. (Use the ASP simple linear regression printout, shown at the top of page 654.)

```
              SIMPLE LINEAR REGRESSION: DEMAND vrs. X=1/PRICE

MODEL:  DEMAND = 6808.11X + -1180.48CNST

          COEF.   SD. ER.     t(6)     P-VALUE  PT. R SQ.
        -------- --------  --------- ----------- ---------
      X  6808.11  358.353   18.9983  1.37472E-6   0.983648
   CNST -1180.48  107.729  -10.9578  3.4303E-5    0.952409

   R SQ. = 0.983648,  ADJ. R SQ. = 0.980923,  D. W. = 1.68056
   SQ. ROOT MSE = 20.9038,  F(1/6) = 360.936 (P-VALUE = 1.37472E-6)
```

    b. Do the data provide sufficient evidence to indicate that the model contributes information for the prediction of demand?

    c. Plot the data (y versus $x = 1/p$), and graph the least squares prediction equation.

    d. Find the value of the coefficient of determination of the ASP printout and interpret it.

12.82 "In the analysis of urban transportation systems it is important to be able to estimate expected travel time between locations." T. M. Cook and R. A. Russell collected data in the city of Tulsa on the urban travel times and distances between location for two types of vehicles—large hoist compactor trucks and passenger cars. A simple linear regression analysis was conducted for each set of data (y = urban travel time in minutes, x = distance between location in miles) with the results summarized in the accompanying table.

Passenger Cars	*Trucks*
$\hat{y} = 2.50 + 1.93x$	$\hat{y} = 1.85 + 3.86x$
$r^2 = .676$; p-value $< .05$	$r^2 = .758$; p-value $< .01$

Source: Cook, T. M. and Russell, R. A. "Estimating urban travel times: A comparative study." *Transportation Research*, 14A, June 1980, pp. 173–175. Copyright 1980, Pergamon Press, Ltd.

    a. Is there sufficient evidence to indicate that distance between locations is linearly related to urban travel time for passenger cars? Test at $\alpha = .05$.

    b. Is there sufficient evidence to indicate that distance between locations is linearly related to urban travel time for trucks? Test at $\alpha = .01$.

    c. Interpret the values of r^2 for the two prediction equations.

    d. Estimate the mean urban travel time for all passenger cars traveling a distance of 3 miles on Tulsa's highways.

    e. Predict the urban travel time for a particular truck traveling a distance of 5 miles on Tulsa's highways.

    f. Explain how we could attach a measure of reliability to the inferences derived in parts **d** and **e**.

12.83 Several factors thought to influence market share for capital equipment businesses were recently investigated (*Industrial Marketing Management*, Vol. 14, 1985). One variable considered was product quality, measured as the difference between the percentage of sales derived from products superior to competition and the percentage of sales inferior to competition. Based on data collected for 333 capital equipment businesses, the correlation between market share and product quality was found to be $r = .373$. Is there sufficient evidence to indicate that product quality and market share for capital equipment businesses are positively correlated? Test using $\alpha = .01$.

12.84 A major portion of the effort expended in developing commercial computer software is associated with program testing. A study was undertaken to assess the potential utility of various product- and process-related variables in identifying error-prone software (*IEEE Transactions on Software Engineering*, Apr. 1985). A straight-line model relating the number y of module defects to the number x of unique operands in the module was fit to the data collected for a sample of software modules. The coefficient of determination for this analysis was $r^2 = .74$.

a. Interpret the value of r^2.

b. Based on this value, would you infer that the straight-line model is a useful predictor of number y of module defects? Explain.

■ CASE STUDY 12.1

The SOB Effect Among College Administrators

At major colleges and universities, administrators (e.g., deans, chairpersons, provosts, vice presidents, and presidents) are among the highest-paid state employees. Is there a relationship between the raises administrators receive and their performance on the job? This was the question of interest to a group of faculty union members at the University of South Florida called the United Faculty of Florida (UFF).

The UFF compared the April 1990 ratings of 15 University of South Florida administrators (as determined by faculty in a survey) to their subsequent raises in August 1990. The data for the analysis are listed in Table 12.8 [*Note:* Ratings are measured on a 5-point scale, where 1 = very poor and 5 = very good.] According to the UFF, the "relationship is inverse, i.e., the lower the rating by the faculty, the greater the raise. Apparently, bad administrators are more valuable than good administrators."* (With tongue in cheek, the UFF refers to this phenomenon as "the SOB effect.") The UFF based its conclusions on a simple linear regression analysis of the data in Table 12.8, where y = administrator's raise and x = average rating of administrator.

a. Initially, the UFF conducted the analysis using all 15 data points in Table 12.8. Fit a straight-line model to the data of Table 12.8. Is there evidence to support the UFF's claim of an inverse relationship between raise and rating?

b. A second simple linear regression was performed with only 14 of the data points in Table 12.8. The data for administrator #3 were eliminated based on the fact that he was promoted to dean in the middle of the 1989–1990 academic year. (No other reason was given for removing this data point from the analysis.) Perform the simple linear regression analysis using the remaining 14 data points in Table

Table 12.8 Raises and Ratings of University of South Florida Administrators

Administrator	Raise[a]	Average Rating (5-pt scale)[b]
1	$18,000	2.76
2	16,700	1.52
3	15,787	4.40
4	10,608	3.10
5	10,268	3.83
6	9,795	2.84
7	9,513	2.10
8	8,459	2.38
9	6,099	3.59
10	4,557	4.11
11	3,751	3.14
12	3,718	3.64
13	3,652	3.36
14	3,227	2.92
15	2,808	3.00

[a]*Source:* Faculty and A&P Salary Report, University of South Florida, Resource Analysis and Planning 1990.
[b]*Source:* Administrative Compensation Survey, *Chronicle of Higher Education*, Jan. 1991

12.8. Is there evidence to support the UFF's claim of an inverse relationship between raise and rating?

c. Based on the results of the regression, part **b**, the UFF computed estimated raises for selected faculty ratings of administrators. These are shown in Table 12.9. What problems do you perceive with using this table to estimate administrators' raises at the University of South Florida?

---

* *UFF Faculty Forum, University of South Florida Chapter, Vol, 3, No. 5 May 1991.*

Table 12.9 Estimated Raises for Selected Ratings

Ratings		Raise
Very Poor	1.00	$15,939
	1.50	13,960
Poor	2.00	11,980
	2.50	10,001
Average	3.00	8,021
	3.50	6,042
Good	4.00	4,062
	4.50	2,083
Very Good	5.00	103

d. The ratings of administrators listed in Table 12.8 were determined by surveying the faculty at the University of South Florida. All faculty are mailed the survey each year, but the response rate is typically low (approximately 10%–20%). The danger with such a survey is that only disgruntled faculty, who are more apt to give a low rating to an administrator, will respond. Many of these faculty also think they are underpaid and that the administrators are overpaid. Comment on how such a survey could bias the results shown in Table 12.9.

e. Based on your answers to the previous questions, would you support the UFF's claim?

■ CASE STUDY 12.2

Top Corporate Executives and Their Pay—Another Look

Each year, *Business Week* compiles its Executive Compensation Scoreboard based on a survey of executives at the 1,000 highest-ranked U.S. companies. In Case Studies 1.1 and 3.1, we examined the 1994 survey. In addition to total cash compensation (salary plus bonus, plus long-term compensation), *Business Week* reports the total shareholder return of the executive's company, measured by the dollar value of a $100 investment in the company made 3 years earlier. (The complete data set is described in Appendix A.2.) *Business Week* uses the ratio of total shareholder return to total executive cash compensation (in $thousands) as a useful benchmark in determining which executives are worth their pay. Another approach is to compare the measures of total pay and shareholder return using the methods of this chapter.

Recall that the CEOs in the 1994 Scoreboard are categorized by industry group, of which there are nine. The objective of this case study, as in Case Study 3.1, is to make pay-for-performance comparisons of executives within industry groups. To accomplish this, consider the straight-line model $E(y) = \beta_0 + \beta_1 x$, where y = to-

tal cash compensation and x = total shareholder return.

a. A SAS printout of the simple linear regression for CEOs in the industrial–high tech industry group is shown in Figure 12.24. Does there appear to be a linear relationship between total executive pay (y) and total shareholder return (x)? Interpret the results.

b. Is it wise to use the least squares prediction equation to construct a 95% prediction interval for the total cash compensation of a CEO in the industrial–high tech industry whose company has a 3-year shareholder return of $300 on an initial $100 investment? Explain.

c. The linear relationship (or lack thereof) between total pay and shareholder return that exists among industrial–high tech CEOs may differ for other industries. For each of the remaining eight industry groups described in Appendix A.2, conduct a simple linear regression analysis similar to that of part a. (The data are available on a $3\frac{1}{2}$″ diskette from the publisher.) Interpret the results.

FIGURE 12.24

SAS Printout for Case Study 12.2

Dependent Variable: TOTCOMP

Analysis of Variance

Source	DF	Sum of Squares	Mean Square	F Value	Prob>F
Model	1	11054008.692	11054008.692	0.184	0.6704
Error	34	2039530214.2	59986182.770		
C Total	35	2050584222.9			

Root MSE	7745.07474	R-square	0.0054
Dep Mean	7690.55556	Adj R-sq	-0.0239
C.V.	100.70891		

Parameter Estimates

Variable	DF	Parameter Estimate	Standard Error	T for H0: Parameter=0	Prob > |T|
INTERCEP	1	7021.872655	2023.0510919	3.471	0.0014
RETURN	1	2.121680	4.94248832	0.429	0.6704

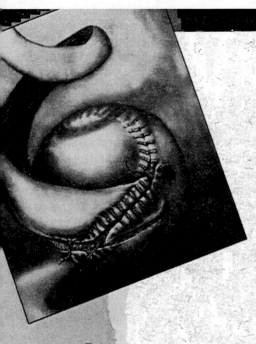

Chapter 13

MULTIPLE REGRESSION AND MODEL BUILDING

As a future college graduate, you expect the size of your paycheck to reflect your degree and on-the-job qualifications. But, will your salary depend on your gender? In this chapter, we extend the ideas of Chapter 12 and learn how to build a regression model relating a variable y to two or more independent variables. The problem of modeling the salary of a college graduate as a function of gender and other variables is addressed in Case Study 13.1.

■ CONTENTS

13.1 Introduction: The General Linear Model

Most practical applications of regression analysis require models that are more complex than the simple straight-line model. For example, a realistic probabilistic model for the carbon-monoxide ranking y of an American-made cigarette would include more variables than the nicotine content x of the cigarette (discussed in Chapter 12). Additional variables such as tar content, length, filter type, and menthol flavor might also be related to carbon-monoxide ranking. Thus, we would want to incorporate these and other potentially important independent variables into the model if we needed to make accurate predictions of the carbon-monoxide ranking y. A more complex probabilistic model relating y to various independent variables, say, $x_1, x_2, x_3, \ldots$, is called a **general linear statistical model**, or more simply, a **linear model**.

EXAMPLE 13.1
General Models

How does a general linear model differ from the following simple straight-line model?

$$y = \beta_0 + \beta_1 x + \varepsilon$$

SOLUTION General linear models are more flexible than straight-line models in the sense that they may include more than one independent variable. For example, a linear model for y, the carbon-monoxide ranking of a cigarette, could be written

$$y = \beta_0 + \beta_1 x_1 + \beta_2 x_2 + \beta_3 x_3 + \varepsilon$$

In addition to the independent variable x_1, the nicotine content of a cigarette, the model includes two other independent variables: the tar content, x_2, and the length of a cigarette, x_3. Note how the data for fitting general linear models would be collected: For each experimental unit—in our example, a cigarette—we would measure the dependent variable y and record the values of the independent variables x_1, x_2, and x_3. A general linear model might also include some independent variables that appear at higher orders, e.g., terms such as x_1^2, $x_1 x_2$, or x_3^3. For example,

$$y = \beta_0 + \beta_1 x_1 + \beta_2 x_2 + \beta_3 x_1 x_2 + \beta_4 x_1^2 + \beta_5 x_2^2 + \varepsilon$$

is a general linear model.* ∎

The formula for a general linear model is given in the box.

---

*The model is called linear *because it represents a linear function of the unknown parameters, β_0, β_1, β_2, ... That is, each term contains only one of the β parameters and each β is a coefficient of the remaining portion of the term. For example, the term $\beta_1 x_1 x_2^2$ satisfies this requirement, but the term $\beta_1 x_1^{\beta_2}$ does not because it contains two unknown parameters (β_1 and β_2) and, second, because β_2 appears as an exponent rather than as a multiplicative coefficient.*

The General Linear Model

$$y = \beta_0 + \beta_1 x_1 + \beta_2 x_2 + \cdots + \beta_k x_k + \varepsilon$$

where y is the dependent variable (the variable to be predicted) and $x_1, x_2, \ldots,$ x_k, are the independent variables.

$E(y) = \beta_0 + \beta_1 x_1 + \beta_2 x_2 + \cdots + \beta_k x_k$ is the deterministic portion of the model.

β_i determines the contribution of the independent variable x_i.

$\varepsilon = $ Random error component of the model.

[*Note:* Remember that the symbols $x_1, x_2, \ldots, x_k$ may represent higher-order terms. For example, x_1 might represent the nicotine content, x_2 might represent x_1^2, and so forth.]

In this chapter, we use the method of least squares to fit a general linear model to a set of data. This process, along with the estimation and test procedures associated with it, is called a **multiple regression analysis**. Because the computations involved in a multiple regression analysis are very complex, almost all regression analyses are performed on a computer.[*] In the following sections, we present several examples of a multiple regression analysis. In each case, we examine and interpret the printouts for one of the statistical computer software packages discussed in this text: SAS, SPSS, ASP, and MINITAB.

The steps to follow in a multiple regression analysis are similar to those in a simple linear regression, as illustrated in the box.

Steps to Follow in a Multiple Regression Analysis

1. Hypothesize the form of the linear model.
2. State assumptions about the random error, ε.
3. Estimate the unknown parameters $\beta_0, \beta_1, \beta_2, \ldots, \beta_k$.
4. Check whether the fitted model is useful for predicting y.
5. Check that the assumptions of step 2 are satisfied.
6. If we decide that the model is useful and the assumptions are satisfied, use it to estimate the mean value of y or to predict a particular value of y for given values of the independent variables.

---

[*] *Performing a multiple regression analysis without a computer requires knowledge of matrices and matrix theory.*

13.2 Model Assumptions

For the statistical tests, confidence intervals, and prediction intervals associated with a multiple regression analysis to be valid, certain assumptions must be satisfied. The second step in a multiple regression analysis is to make assumptions about the random error term in the general linear model hypothesized in step 1. These assumptions follow the same general pattern as for the straight-line model. The assumptions are given in the box.

Assumptions About the Random Error Term ε in the General Linear Model

1. The mean of the probability distribution of the random error is 0.
2. The variance σ^2 of the probability distribution of the random error is constant for all settings of the independent variables in the model.
3. The probability distribution of the random error is normal.
4. The errors associated with any two observations are independent.

Various statistical techniques exist for checking the validity of these assumptions, and there are remedies to be applied when they appear to be invalid. Some of these techniques are presented in Section 13.13. Fortunately, the assumptions need not hold exactly for the results of a multiple regression analysis to be valid. In fact, in many practical business applications they will be adequately satisfied.

13.3 Fitting the Model and Interpreting the β Estimates

Step 3 in a multiple regression analysis requires that we obtain sample data and calculate estimates of the unknown β parameters by fitting the model to the data. To fit a general linear model by the method of least squares, we choose the estimated model

$$\hat{y} = \hat{\beta}_0 + \hat{\beta}_1 x_1 + \hat{\beta}_2 x_2 + \cdots + \hat{\beta}_k x_k$$

that minimizes $\text{SSE} = \Sigma(y - \hat{y})^2$. In the following example, we use the computer to fit the model.

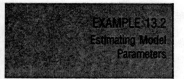

EXAMPLE 13.2
Estimating Model
Parameters

Suppose a property appraiser wants to model the relationship between the sale price of a residential property in a mid-size city and the following three independent variables: (1) appraised land value of the property, (2) appraised value of improvements (i.e., home value) on the property, and (3) area of living space on the property (i.e., home size). Consider the linear model

$$y = \beta_0 + \beta_1 x_1 + \beta_2 x_2 + \beta_3 x_3 + \varepsilon$$

where

y = Sale price (dollars)

x_1 = Appraised land value (dollars)

x_2 = Appraised improvements (dollars)

x_3 = Area (square feet)

To fit the model, the appraiser selected a random sample of $n = 20$ properties from the thousands of properties that were sold in a particular year. The resulting data are given in Table 13.1.

a. Use scattergrams to plot the sample data. Interpret the plots.

b. Use the method of least squares to estimate the unknown parameters β_0, β_1, β_2, and β_3 in the model.

Table 13.1 Real Estate Appraisal Data for 20 Properties

Property # (Obs.)	Sale Price y	Land Value x_1	Improvements Value x_2	Area x_3
1	68,900	5,960	44,967	1,873
2	48,500	9,000	27,860	928
3	55,500	9,500	31,439	1,126
4	62,000	10,000	39,592	1,265
5	116,500	18,000	72,827	2,214
6	45,000	8,500	27,317	912
7	38,000	8,000	29,856	899
8	83,000	23,000	47,752	1,803
9	59,000	8,100	39,117	1,204
10	47,500	9,000	29,349	1,725
11	40,500	7,300	40,166	1,080
12	40,000	8,000	31,679	1,529
13	97,000	20,000	58,510	2,455
14	45,500	8,000	23,454	1,151
15	40,900	8,000	20,897	1,173
16	80,000	10,500	56,248	1,960
17	56,000	4,000	20,859	1,344
18	37,000	4,500	22,610	988
19	50,000	3,400	35,948	1,076
20	22,400	1,500	5,779	962

Source: Alachua County (Florida) Property Appraisers Office.

SOLUTION
    a. SPSS scatterplots for examining the bivariate relationships between y and x_1, y and x_2, and y and x_3 are shown in Figure 13.1. Of the three variables, appraised improvements (x_2) appears to have the strongest linear relationship with sale price (y).

    b. The model hypothesized above is fit to the data of Table 13.1 using

FIGURE 13.1

SPSS Scatterplots for
the Data of Table 13.1

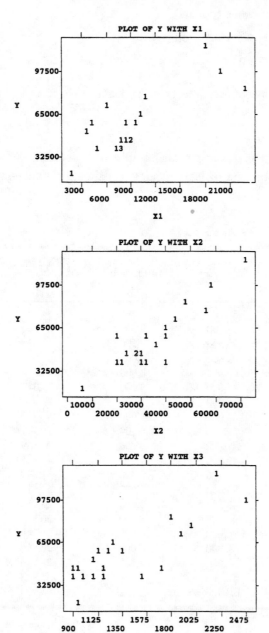

FIGURE 13.2

SAS Output for Sale
Price Model,
Example 13.2

Analysis of Variance

Source	DF	Sum of Squares	Mean Square	F Value	Prob>F
Model	3	8779676740.6	2926558913.5	46.662	0.0001
Error	16	1003491259.4	62718203.714		
C Total	19	9783168000.0			

Root MSE	7919.48254	R-Square	0.8974	
Dep Mean	56660.00000	Adj R-Sq	0.8782	
C.V.	13.97720			

Parameter Estimates

Variable	DF	Parameter Estimate	Standard Error	T for H0: Parameter=0	Prob > |T|
INTERCEP	1	1470.275919	5746.3245832	0.256	0.8013
X1	1	0.814490	0.51221871	1.590	0.1314
X2	1	0.820445	0.21118494	3.885	0.0013
X3	1	13.528650	6.58568006	2.054	0.0567

SAS. A portion of the SAS printout is reproduced in Figure 13.2. The least squares estimates of the β parameters appear (shaded) in the column labeled **Parameter Estimate**. You can see that $\hat{\beta}_0 = 1{,}470.275919$, $\hat{\beta}_1 = .814490$, $\hat{\beta}_2 = .820445$, and $\hat{\beta}_3 = 13.528650$. Therefore, the equation that minimizes SSE for this data set (i.e., the least squares prediction equation) is

$$\hat{y} = 1{,}470.28 + .8145x_1 + .8204x_2 + 13.53x_3 \quad ■$$

After obtaining the least squares prediction equation, the analyst will usually want to make meaningful interpretations of the β estimates. Recall that in the straight-line model (Chapter 12)

$$y = \beta_0 + \beta_1 x + \varepsilon$$

β_0 represents the y-intercept of the line and β_1 represents the slope of the line. From our discussion in Chapter 12, β_1 has a practical interpretation—it represents the mean change in y for every 1-unit increase in x. When the independent variables are quantitative (e.g., numeric variables), the β parameters in the multiple regression model of the form specified in Example 13.2 have similar interpretations. The difference is that when we interpret the β that multiplies one of the variables (e.g., x_1), we must be certain to hold the values of the remaining independent variables (e.g., x_2, x_3) fixed. The following example illustrates the point.

EXAMPLE 13.3
Graphing the Model

Suppose that the mean value $E(y)$ of a response y is related to two quantitative independent variables, x_1 and x_2, by the model

$$E(y) = \beta_0 + \beta_1 x_1 + \beta_2 x_2$$

where $\beta_0 = 1$, $\beta_1 = 2$, and $\beta_2 = 1$. In other words,

$$E(y) = 1 + 2x_1 + x_2$$

a. Graph the relationship between $E(y)$ and x_1 for $x_2 = 0$, 1, and 2. Interpret the graph.

b. Graph the relationship between $E(y)$, x_1, and x_2 in three dimensions. Interpret the graph.

SOLUTION   **a.** When $x_2 = 0$, the relationship between $E(y)$ and x_1 is given by

$$E(y) = 1 + 2x_1 + (0) = 1 + 2x_1$$

A graph of this relationship (a straight line) is shown in Figure 13.3. Similar graphs of the relationship between $E(y)$ and x_1 for $x_2 = 1$,

$$E(y) = 1 + 2x_1 + (1) = 2 + 2x_1$$

and for $x_2 = 2$,

$$E(y) = 1 + 2x_1 + (2) = 3 + 2x_1$$

also are shown in Figure 13.3. Note that the slopes of the three lines are all equal to $\beta_1 = 2$, the coefficient that multiplies x_1.

The model $E(y) = 1 + 2x_1 + x_2$ is an example of a **first-order linear model** in two quantitative independent variables, x_1 and x_2. Likewise, the model in Example 13.1 is an example of a first-order model in three quantitative independent variables. A first-order linear model in five quantitative independent variables is shown in the box.

A First-Order Linear Model Relating $E(y)$ to x_1, x_2, ..., x_5

$$E(y) = \beta_0 + \beta_1 x_1 + \beta_2 x_2 + \beta_3 x_3 + \beta_4 x_4 + \beta_5 x_5$$

where β_i represents the slope of the line relating y to x_i when all other x's are held fixed (i.e., β_i measures the change in y for every 1-unit increase in x_i, holding all other x's fixed).

Figure 13.3 exhibits a characteristic of all first-order models: If you graph $E(y)$ versus any one variable—say, x_1—for fixed values of the other variables, the response curve will always be a *straight line* with slope equal to β_1. If you repeat the process for other val-

FIGURE 13.3

Graphs of $E(y) = 1 + 2x_1 + x_2$ for $x_2 = 0, 1, 2.$

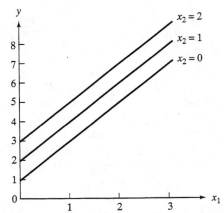

FIGURE 13.3

Graphs of $E(y) = 1 + 2x_1 + x_2$ for $x_2 = 0, 1, 2.$

FIGURE 13.4

The Plane
$E(y) = 1 + 2x_1 + x_2$

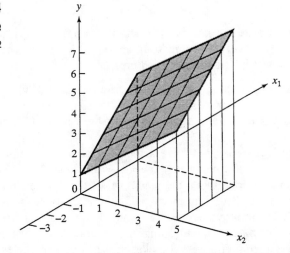

ues of the fixed independent variables, you will obtain a set of *parallel* straight lines. This indicates that the effect of the independent variable x_i on $E(y)$ is independent of all the other independent variables in the model, and this effect is measured by the slope β_i (see box).

b. A three-dimensional graph of the model $E(y) = 1 + 2x_1 + x_2$ is shown in Figure 13.4. Note that the model graphs as a plane. If you slice the plane at a particular value of x_2 (say, $x_2 = 0$), you obtain a straight line relating $E(y)$ to x_1 (e.g., $E(y) = 1 + 2x_1$). Similarly, if you slice the plane at a particular value of x_1, you obtain a straight line relating $E(y)$ to x_2. Since it is more difficult to visualize three-dimensional and, in general, k-dimensional surfaces, we will graph all the models presented in this chapter in two dimensions. The key to obtaining these graphs is to hold fixed all but one of the independent variables in the model. ■

EXAMPLE 13.4
Interpreting Model Parameters

Refer to the first-order model for sale price y considered in Example 13.2. Interpret the estimates of the β parameters in the model.

SOLUTION The least squares prediction equation, as given in Example 13.2, is $\hat{y} = 1{,}470.28 + .8145x_1 + .8204x_2 + 13.53x_3$. From Example 13.3, we know that with first-order models β_1 represents the slope of the y–x_1 line for fixed x_2 and x_3. That is, β_1 measures the change in $E(y)$ for every 1-unit increase in x_1 when all other independent variables in the model are held fixed. Similar statements can be made about β_2 and β_3; e.g., β_2 measures the change in $E(y)$ for every 1-unit increase in x_2 when all other x's in the model are held fixed. Consequently, we obtain the following interpretations:

$\hat{\beta}_1 = .8145$:   We estimate the mean sale price of a property, $E(y)$, to increase .8145 dollar for every \$1 increase in appraised land value (x_1) when both appraised improvements (x_2) and area (x_3) are held fixed.

$\hat{\beta}_2 = .8204$:   We estimate the mean sale price of a property, $E(y)$, to increase .8204 dollar for every \$1 increase in appraised improvements (x_2) when both appraised land value (x_1) and area (x_3) are held fixed.

$\hat{\beta}_3 = 13.53$:   We estimate the mean sale price of a property, $E(y)$, to increase \$13.53 for each additional square foot of living area (x_3) when both appraised land value (x_1) and appraised improvements (x_2) are held fixed.

The value $\hat{\beta}_0 = 1{,}470.28$ does not have a meaningful interpretation in this example. To see this, note that $\hat{y} = \hat{\beta}_0$ when $x_1 = x_2 = x_3 = 0$. Thus, $\hat{\beta}_0 = 1{,}470.28$ represents the estimated mean sale price when the values of all the independent variables are set equal to 0. Since a residential property with these characteristics—appraised land value of \$0, appraised improvements of \$0, and 0 square feet of living area—is not practical, the value of $\hat{\beta}_0$ has no meaningful interpretation. In general, $\hat{\beta}_0$ will not have a practical interpretation unless it makes sense to set the values of the x's simultaneously equal to 0. ■

> **Warning**
>
> The interpretation of the β parameters in the general linear model will depend on the terms specified in the model. The interpretations above are for a first-order linear model only. In practice, you should be sure that a first-order model is the correct model for $E(y)$ before making these β interpretations. [We discuss alternative models for $E(y)$ in Sections 13.9–13.11.]

13.4 Estimating and Interpreting σ^2

As in simple linear regression, the variance σ^2 of the random error term in a multiple regression model plays a key role in determining the utility of the model. In this section, we show how to obtain an estimate of σ^2 and give a practical interpretation of its value.

EXAMPLE 13.5
Finding σ^2 and σ

Refer to Example 13.2, where we fit the first-order linear model

$$E(y) = \beta_0 + \beta_1 x_1 + \beta_2 x_2 + \beta_3 x_3$$

Locate the minimum value of SSE on the SAS printout reproduced in Figure 13.5. Use this value to obtain estimates of σ^2 and σ, the variance and standard deviation, respectively, of the random error term in the probabilistic model.

FIGURE 13.5

SAS Printout for Sale
Price Model,
Example 13.5

Analysis of Variance

Source	DF	Sum of Squares	Mean Square	F Value	Prob>F
Model	3	8779676740.6	2926558913.5	46.662	0.0001
Error	16	1003491259.4	62718203.714		
C Total	19	9783168000.0			

Root MSE	7919.48254	R-Square	0.8974	
Dep Mean	56660.00000	Adj R-Sq	0.8782	
C.V.	13.97720			

Parameter Estimates

Variable	DF	Parameter Estimate	Standard Error	T for H0: Parameter=0	Prob > |T|
INTERCEP	1	1470.275919	5746.3245832	0.256	0.8013
X1	1	0.814490	0.51221871	1.590	0.1314
X2	1	0.820445	0.21118494	3.885	0.0013
X3	1	13.528650	6.58568006	2.054	0.0567

SOLUTION The minimum value of SSE, 1,003,491,259.4, is shaded in the row labeled **Error** under the column labeled **Sum of Squares** in the printout shown in Figure 13.5. Recall from Section 12.5 that we can use this quantity to estimate σ^2. The estimator for the straight-line model was $s^2 = \text{SSE}/(n - 2)$. Note that the denominator is

$n -$ (Number of estimated β parameters)

which, in the case of the straight-line model, is equal to $n - 2$. Since we must estimate two more parameters, β_2 and β_3, for the first-order model of Example 13.2, the estimator of σ^2 is

$$s^2 = \frac{\text{SSE}}{n - 4}$$

That is, the denominator becomes $(n - 4)$ because there are now four β parameters (including β_0) in the model.

The numerical estimate of σ^2 for this example is

$$s^2 = \frac{\text{SSE}}{20 - 4} = \frac{1,003,491,259.4}{16} = 62,718,203.7$$

Note that this estimate appears on the printout (shaded) as the **Mean Square** for **Error**. Similarly, the standard deviation $s = 7,919.48$ appears (shaded, to the right of the heading **Root MSE**) in Figure 13.5. ■

Estimator of σ^2: Multiple Regression

$$s^2 = \frac{\text{SSE}}{n - (\text{Number of estimated } \beta \text{ parameters})}$$

where n is the number of data points.

EXAMPLE 13.6
Interpreting s

Refer to Example 13.5. Interpret the value of s, the estimate of σ.

SOLUTION The interpretation of s in multiple regression is essentially the same as that for simple linear regression (see box in Section 12.6). Since s estimates the standard deviation of the errors of prediction, we expect most of the y values to lie within $2s$ of their least squares predicted value, $\hat{y}$. In Example 13.5, we found $s = 7,919.48$; hence, $2s = 2(7,919.48) = 15,838.96$. Consequently, we expect the first-order model with appraised land value (x_1), appraised improvements (x_2), and area (x_3) to predict the sale price (y) of a residential property to within about \$15,839 of its true value. ■

The importance of the estimator of σ is that we use its numerical value both to check the predictive ability of the model (Sections 13.5–13.7) and to provide a measure of the reliability of predictions and estimates when the model is used for those purposes (Section 13.8). Consequently, it is not surprising to find that when we are choosing between two different models, the model with the smaller value of s will likely be our preference.

13.5 Estimating and Testing Hypotheses About the β Parameters

Once you have fit a multiple regression model, you may want to determine the importance of one or more of the independent variables in the model (step 4). One way to do this is to conduct a test of hypothesis about the β parameter associated with the independent variable, as the following example illustrates.

EXAMPLE 13.7
Testing a β Parameter

Refer to the first-order model for sale price considered in Example 13.2. Test the hypothesis that appraised improvements, x_2, contributes significantly to the prediction of sale price, y. Use $\alpha = .05$.

SOLUTION If appraised improvements, x_2, is not useful for predicting sale price, y, then the true value of β_2 will be 0. Thus, we require a test of the hypotheses

H_0: $\beta_2 = 0$ (Appraised improvements not useful for predicting sale price)

H_a: $\beta_2 \neq 0$ (Appraised improvements is a useful predictor of sale price)

This test, a t test, is quite similar to the test about the slope of the simple straight-line model (refer to Section 12.6). The details for a test about any β parameter in the general linear model are given in the following box.

Test About an Individual Parameter Coefficient in the General Linear Model $y = \beta_0 + \beta_1 x_1 + \beta_2 x_2 + \cdots + \beta_k x_k + \varepsilon$

One-Tailed Test	Two-Tailed Test
H_0: $\beta_i = 0$	H_0: $\beta_i = 0$
H_a: $\beta_i > 0$	H_a: $\beta_i \neq 0$
(or H_a: $\beta_i < 0$)	

$$\text{Test statistic:} \quad t = \frac{\hat{\beta}_i}{s_{\hat{\beta}_i}}$$

Rejection region:	Rejection region:
$t > t_\alpha$ (or $t < -t_\alpha$)	$|t| > t_{\alpha/2}$

where

$n = $ Number of observations

$s_{\hat{\beta}_i} = $ Estimated standard deviation of the repeated sampling distribution of $\hat{\beta}_i$

and the distribution of t has degrees of freedom equal to ($n -$ Number of β parameters in the model).

Assumptions: See Section 13.2.

FIGURE 13.6

SAS Printout for the
Sale Price Model,
Example 13.7

                              Analysis of Variance

| | | Sum of | Mean | | |
Source	DF	Squares	Square	F Value	Prob>F
Model	3	8779676740.6	2926558913.5	46.662	0.0001
Error	16	1003491259.4	62718203.714		
C Total	19	9783168000.0			

Root MSE	7919.48254	R-Square	0.8974
Dep Mean	56660.00000	Adj R-Sq	0.8782
C.V.	13.97720		

                          Parameter Estimates

| | | Parameter | Standard | T for HO: | |
Variable	DF	Estimate	Error	Parameter=0	Prob > |T|
INTERCEP	1	1470.275919	5746.3245832	0.256	0.8013
X1	1	0.814490	0.51221871	1.590	0.1314
X2	1	0.820445	0.21118494	3.885	0.0013
X3	1	13.528650	6.58568006	2.054	0.0567

We use the symbol $s_{\hat{\beta}_2}$ to represent the estimated standard deviation of $\hat{\beta}_2$. Since the formula for $s_{\hat{\beta}_2}$ is very complex, we will not present it here. However, this will not cause difficulty because the printouts from most statistical software packages list the estimated standard deviation $s_{\hat{\beta}_i}$ for each of the estimated model coefficients $\hat{\beta}_i$ in the linear model as well as the corresponding calculated t values.

To test the null hypothesis that $\beta_2 = 0$, we again consult the SAS printout for the sale price model. From Figure 13.6, we see that the computed value of the test statistic corresponding to the test of H_0: $\beta_2 = 0$ (shaded under the column headed **T for HO: Parameter = 0**) is $t = 3.885$. The appropriate rejection region is obtained by consulting Table 6 of Appendix B. For $\alpha = .05$ and $(n - 4) = 16$ degrees of freedom, we have $t_{\alpha/2} = t_{.025} = 2.120$. Note that the critical t value used to specify the rejection region depends on $(n - 4)$ degrees of freedom because the first-order linear model contains four parameters $(\beta_0, \beta_1, \beta_2, \beta_3)$. Then the rejection region (shown in Figure 13.7) is

$$t > 2.120 \quad \text{or} \quad t < -2.120$$

Since $t = 3.885$ falls into the upper tail of the rejection region, we conclude that appraised improvements (x_2) makes an important contribution to the prediction model for the sale price of residential properties in the city.

This result could be obtained directly from the SAS printout, which lists the two-tailed observed significance level (p-value) for each t value under the column headed **Prob > |T|**. [*Reminder:* One-tailed observed significance levels are obtained by dividing the two-tailed p-values (shown on the SAS printout) in half when the sign of $\hat{\beta}_i$ agrees with the inequality sign of the alternative hypothesis.] The observed significance level .0013 corresponds to the x_2 term, and this implies that we would reject H_0: $\beta_2 = 0$ in favor of H_a: $\beta_2 \neq 0$ at any α level larger than .0013. Thus, there is very strong evidence of at least a linear relationship between sale price (y) and appraised improvements value (x_2) for these residential properties. ■

FIGURE 13.7

Rejection Region for
Test about β_2 in the
First-Order Linear
Model

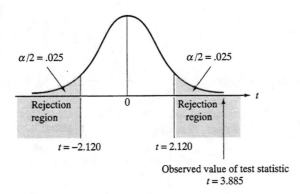

$\alpha/2 = .025$ $\alpha/2 = .025$

Rejection region   0   Rejection region

$t = -2.120$ $t = 2.120$

Observed value of test statistic
$t = 3.885$

EXAMPLE 13.8

Interpreting *p*-Values in the
First-Order Model

Refer to the SAS printout shown in Figure 13.6. Notice that the *p*-value for appraised land value (x_1) is .1314. Interpret this result.

SOLUTION Since the *p*-value is larger than $\alpha = .05$, we would fail to reject the null hypothesis H_0: $\beta_1 = 0$. Our first inclination might be to assume that $\beta_1 = 0$ and, therefore, that appraised land value is *not* useful for predicting sale price. However, such a decision is dangerous for two reasons. First, the fact that we are accepting H_0: $\beta_1 = 0$ leaves us vulnerable to making a Type II error with unknown probability of occurrence. Second, if $\beta_1 = 0$, the most we can say is that appraised land value (x_1) is not a useful *linear* predictor of sale price (y). There may, in fact, be a strong curvilinear (second-order) relationship between y and x_1. We explain in Section 13.10 how to determine whether such a relationship exists. ■

Warning

It is dangerous to conduct t tests on the individual β parameters in a *first-order linear model* for the purpose of determining which independent variables are useful for predicting y and which are not. If you fail to reject H_0: $\beta_i = 0$, several conclusion are possible:

1. There is no relationship between y and x_i.
2. A straight-line relationship between y and x_i exists (holding the other x's in the model fixed), but a Type II error occurred.
3. A relationship between y and x_i (holding the other x's in the model fixed) exists, but is more complex than a straight-line relationship (e.g., a curvilinear relationship may be appropriate).

The most you can say about a β parameter test is that there is either sufficient (if you reject H_0: $\beta_i = 0$) or insufficient (if you do not reject H_0: $\beta_i = 0$) evidence of a *linear* (*straight-line*) relationship between y and x_i.

EXAMPLE 13.9
Confidence Interval for a β Parameter

Refer to Example 13.2. Form a 95% confidence interval for the parameter β_2 in the first-order model. Interpret the result.

SOLUTION A confidence interval for any β parameter in a general linear model is given in the box. From Figure 13.5, (page 669), we see that $\hat{\beta}_2 = .820445$. The estimated standard deviations of the model coefficients appear in the SAS printout under the column labeled **Standard Error**. The value $s_{\hat{\beta}_2} = .21118494$ is shaded in Figure 13.6. Substituting the values of $\hat{\beta}_2$, $s_{\hat{\beta}_2}$, and $t_{.025} = 2.120$ (based on $n - 4 = 16$ degrees of freedom) into the formula for a confidence interval, we find the 95% confidence interval for β_2 to be

$$\hat{\beta}_2 \pm t_{\alpha/2}s_{\hat{\beta}_2} = .820445 \pm (2.120)(.21118494)$$

or (.372733, 1.268157). This interval can be used to estimate the change in mean sale price as appraised improvements value (x_2) is increased, holding the values of x_1 and x_3 fixed. It appears that for every \$1 increase in appraised improvements value, the mean sale price will increase by an amount between \$.37 and \$1.27. Note that all values in the interval are positive, reconfirming our test conclusion that β_2 is nonzero. ■

A $(1 - \alpha)100\%$ Confidence Interval for an Individual Parameter Coefficient in the General Linear Model

$$\hat{\beta}_i \pm t_{\alpha/2}\, s_{\hat{\beta}_i}$$

where

n = Number of observations

$s_{\hat{\beta}_i}$ = Estimated standard deviation of the repeated sampling distribution of $\hat{\beta}_i$

and the distribution of t has degrees of freedom equal to $(n -$ number of β parameters in the model), and $t_{\alpha/2}$ is the t value such that $P(t > t_{\alpha/2}) = \alpha/2$.

13.6 The Coefficient of Determination

Recall from Chapter 12 that the coefficient of determination, r^2, is a measure of how well a straight-line model fits a set of data. To measure how well a general linear model (for example, a first-order linear model) fits a set of data, we compute the multiple regression equivalent of r^2, called the **multiple coefficient of determination**, and denoted by the symbol R^2.

Definition 13.1

The **multiple coefficient of determination,** R^2, is defined as

$$R^2 = 1 - \frac{\text{SSE}}{\text{SS(Total)}} = \frac{\text{SSR}}{\text{SS(Total)}} \qquad 0 \leq R^2 \leq 1$$

where

SSE $= \text{Error sum of squares} = \Sigma(y - \hat{y})^2$

SS(Total)* $= \text{Total sum of squares} = \Sigma(y - \bar{y})^2$

SSR $= \text{Regression (or model) sum of squares} = \text{SS(Total)} - \text{SSE}$

Just as for the simple linear model, R^2 represents the proportion of the sum of squares of deviations [SS(Total)] of the y values about $\bar{y}$ that can be attributed to the regression model. Or, more practically, R^2 measures the percent of the sample variation in y that can be explained by the model. Thus, $R^2 = 0$ implies a complete lack of fit of the model to the data and $R^2 = 1$ implies a perfect fit, with the model passing through every data point. In general, the larger the value of R^2, the better the model fits the data.

EXAMPLE 13.10
Interpreting R^2

Refer to Example 13.2. Locate the value of R^2 on the SAS printout and interpret its value. Does the first-order linear model appear to provide a good fit to the sales data for the 20 randomly selected properties?

SOLUTION The SAS printout for the multiple regression is reproduced in Figure 13.8 on page 676. The value of R^2 (shaded) is shown to be $R^2 = .8974$. This high value implies that the first-order model with three independent variables (appraised land value, appraised improvements value, and home size) explains approximately 90% of the sample variation in sale prices. Thus, this large value of R^2 indicates that the model provides a good fit to the $n = 20$ sample data points. ≡

A large value of R^2 computed from the *sample* data does not necessarily mean that the model provides a good fit to all of the data points in the *population*. For example, a first-order linear model that contains three parameters will provide a perfect fit to a sample of three data points and R^2 will equal 1. Likewise, you will always obtain a perfect fit ($R^2 = 1$) to a set of n data points if the model contains exactly n parameters. Consequently, if you want to use the value of R^2 as a measure of how useful the model will be for predicting y, it should be based on a sample that contains substantially more data points than the number of parameters in the model.

---

*In Chapter 12, SS(Total) was denoted SS_{yy}.

FIGURE 13.8

SAS Printout for the
Sale Price Model,
Example 13.2

Analysis of Variance

Source	DF	Sum of Squares	Mean Square	F Value	Prob>F
Model	3	8779676740.6	2926558913.5	46.662	0.0001
Error	16	1003491259.4	62718203.714		
C Total	19	9783168000.0			

Root MSE	7919.48254	R-Square	0.8974	
Dep Mean	56660.00000	Adj R-Sq	0.8782	
C.V.	13.97720			

Parameter Estimates

Variable	DF	Parameter Estimate	Standard Error	T for H0: Parameter=0	Prob > |T|
INTERCEP	1	1470.275919	5746.3245832	0.256	0.8013
X1	1	0.814490	0.51221871	1.590	0.1314
X2	1	0.820445	0.21118494	3.885	0.0013
X3	1	13.528650	6.58568006	2.054	0.0567

Warning

In a multiple regression analysis, use the value of R^2 as a measure of how useful a linear model will be for predicting y only if the sample contains substantially more data points than the number of β parameters in the model.

As an alternative to using R^2 as a measure of model adequacy, the **adjusted multiple coefficient of determination**, denoted R_a^2, is often reported. The formula for R_a^2 is shown in the box.

The Adjusted Multiple Coefficient of Determination

The **adjusted multiple coefficient of determination** is given by

$$R_a^2 = 1 - \frac{(n-1)}{n-(k+1)}\left(\frac{\text{SSE}}{\text{SS(Total)}}\right)$$

$$= 1 - \frac{(n-1)}{n-(k+1)}(1-R^2)$$

Note: $R_a^2 \leq R^2$

R^2 and R_a^2 have similar interpretations. However, unlike R^2, R_a^2 takes into account ("adjusts" for) both the sample size n and the number of β parameters in the model. R_a^2 will always be smaller than R^2, and more importantly, cannot be "forced" to 1 by simply adding more and more independent variables to the model. Consequently, analysts prefer the more conservative R_a^2 when choosing a measure of model adequacy.

EXAMPLE 13.11
Interpreting R_a^2

Refer to Example 13.2. Locate the value of R_a^2 on the printout, Figure 13.8. Interpret its value.

SOLUTION The value of R_a^2 is shown on the SAS printout (Figure 13.8) directly beneath the value of R^2. Note that $R_a^2 = .8782$, a value only slightly smaller than R^2. Our interpretation is that after adjusting for sample size and the number of parameters in the model, approximately 88% of the sample variation in sale price can be "explained" by the first-order model. ▪

Despite their utility, R^2 and R_a^2 are only sample statistics. Consequently, it is dangerous to judge the usefulness of the model based solely on these values. In business, many models with relatively high R^2 values have ultimately been judged to be poor predictors of future y values. We discuss a more formal method of checking the predictive ability of a general linear model—a statistical test of hypothesis—in the following section.

13.7 Testing Whether the Model Is Useful for Predicting y

The object of step 4 in a multiple regression analysis is to conduct a test of the utility of a general linear model—that is, a test to determine whether the model is really useful for predicting y.

Conducting individual t tests on each β parameter in a model (Section 13.5) is generally *not* a good way to determine whether a model is contributing information for the prediction of y. For example, suppose you fit a first-order linear model in 10 quantitative independent variables and decide to conduct t tests on all 10 of the individual β's in the model, each at $\alpha = .05$. Even if all the β parameters (except β_0) in the model are in fact equal to 0, you will incorrectly reject the null hypothesis at least once and conclude that some β parameter is nonzero approximately 40% of the time.[*] In other words, the overall probability of a Type I error is about .40, not .05!

A better way to test the overall utility of a linear model in step 4 is to conduct a test involving *all* the β parameters (except β_0) simultaneously. The null and alternative hypotheses for this test of model utility are given in the box on page 678.

---

[*]*The proof of this result proceeds as follows:*

$P(Reject\ H_0\ at\ least\ once\ |\ \beta_1 = \beta_2 = \cdots = \beta_{10} = 0)$

$= 1 - P(Reject\ H_0\ no\ times\ |\ \beta_1 = \beta_2 = \cdots = \beta_{10} = 0)$

$\leq 1 - [P(Accept\ H_0:\ \beta_1 = 0\ |\ \beta_1 = 0) \cdot P(Accept\ H_0:\ \beta_2 = 0\ |\ \beta_2 = 0) \cdot \cdots \cdot P(Accept\ H_0:\ \beta_{10} = 0\ |\ \beta_{10} = 0)]$

$= 1 - [(1 - \alpha)^{10}] = 1 - (.95)^{10} = .401.$

> **Hypotheses for Testing Whether a General Linear Model Is Useful for Predicting y**
>
> H_0: $\beta_1 = \beta_2 = \cdots = \beta_k = 0$
>
> H_a: At least one of the β parameters in H_0 is nonzero.

Practically speaking, this test for model utility is a comparison of the predictive ability of the estimated general linear model (which uses the predictor $\hat{y} = \hat{\beta}_0 + \hat{\beta}_1 x_1 + \hat{\beta}_2 x_2 + \cdots + \hat{\beta}_k x_k$) with a model that contains no x's (which uses the best available predictor $\hat{y} = \bar{y}$). If the test shows that at least one of the β's is nonzero, then the value of $\hat{y}$ obtained from the estimated linear model will generally predict a future value of y more accurately than the sample mean $\bar{y}$. We illustrate a test of model utility in the following example.

EXAMPLE 13.12
Testing Model Utility

Refer to Example 13.2. Test (using $\alpha = .05$) whether the first-order linear model in the three quantitative independent variables is useful for predicting sale price, y, by testing the null hypothesis

H_0: $\beta_1 = \beta_2 = \beta_3 = 0$

against the alternative hypothesis,

H_a: At least one of the model parameters, β_1, β_2, and β_3, differs from 0

SOLUTION The test statistic used in the test for model utility is an F statistic. The formula for computing the F statistic is given in the next box. However, most statistical software packages with regression analysis routines give this F value. The F value for the sale price model (shaded in the SAS printout shown in Figure 13.8) is $F = 46.662$. To determine whether this F value is statistically significant, we read the value of the observed significance level given in the SAS printout. (For details on the test procedure, see Example 13.13.) The observed significance level for this test, .0001, is shaded in Figure 13.8 in the column headed **Prob > F**. This implies that we would reject the null hypothesis for any α level larger than .0001. Thus, we have strong evidence to reject H_0 and to conclude that at least one of the model coefficients, β_1, β_2, and β_3, is nonzero. Since the observed significance level is so small, there is ample evidence to indicate that the first-order model is useful for predicting the sale price of residential properties. ▪

Some software packages do not compute the value of the F statistic for testing the model and some do not compute its observed significance level. In such cases, you can calculate the F statistic directly using the formula shown in the box and reject

H_0: $\beta_1 = \beta_2 = \cdots = \beta_k$ for a given value of α if $F > F_\alpha$. The F test statistic is based on k numerator (where k is the number of β parameters in the model, excluding β_0) and $n - (k + 1)$ denominator degrees of freedom. The values of F_α for $\alpha = .10$, .05, .025, and .01 are given in Tables 8, 9, 10, and 11 of Appendix B. The test procedure is summarized in the box and illustrated in Example 13.13.

Procedure for Testing Whether the Overall Model Is Useful for Predicting y

H_0: $\beta_1 = \beta_2 = \cdots = \beta_k = 0$

H_a: At least one of the parameters, $\beta_1, \beta_2, \cdots, \beta_k$ differs from 0

Test statistic: $F = \dfrac{\text{Mean Square for Model}}{\text{Mean Square for Error}}$

$$= \left[\frac{\text{SS(Model)}}{\text{SSE}}\right]\left[\frac{n - (k + 1)}{k}\right]$$

$$= \left(\frac{R^2}{1 - R^2}\right)\left[\frac{n - (k + 1)}{k}\right]$$

Rejection region: $F > F_\alpha$

where

n = Number of observations

k = Number of parameters in the model (excluding β_0)

R^2 = Multiple coefficient of determination

and the distribution of F depends on k numerator degrees of freedom and $n - (k + 1)$ denominator degrees of freedom. Values of F_α for $\alpha = .10$, .05, .025, and .01 are given in Tables 8, 9, 10, and 11 of Appendix B.

EXAMPLE 13.13
Testing Model Utility

Refer to Example 13.12. Use the procedure outlined in the box to perform a test (with $\alpha = .05$) of the null hypothesis

H_0: $\beta_1 = \beta_2 = \beta_3 = 0$

against the alternative hypothesis

H_a: At least one of the parameters, β_1, β_2, and β_3, is nonzero

SOLUTION For this example, the number of data points is $n = 20$ and the number of parameters involved in H_0 is $k = 3$. Therefore, the rejection region for the test is

$$F > F_\alpha = 3.24$$

where $\alpha = .05$ and F is based on $k = 3$ numerator and $n - (k + 1) = 20 - (3 + 1) = 16$ denominator degrees of freedom, and $F_{.05}$ (given in Table 9 of Appendix B) is $F_{.05} = 3.24$.

To compute the value of the F statistic, we need to locate SS(Model) and SSE on the SAS printout shown in Figure 13.8. The value for SS(Model), shown in the **Model** row, is $SS(Model) = 8,779,676,740.6$. The corresponding value of SSE is $SSE = 1,003,491,259.4$. Then the computed value of the test statistic is

$$F = \frac{SS(Model)}{SSE} \left[\frac{n - (k + 1)}{k} \right]$$

$$= \frac{8,779,676,740.6}{1,003,491,259.4} \left(\frac{16}{3} \right)$$

$$= 46.662$$

[Note that this F value could also be calculated as MS(Model)/MS(Error), or by using the formula that involves R^2.]

Since the computed value of the test statistic, $F = 46.662$, exceeds the critical value, $F_{.05} = 3.24$, we reject H_0 and conclude that at least one of the parameters (β_1, β_2, and β_3) is nonzero. In other words, the model appears to be useful for predicting residential property sale prices. ■

After we have determined that the overall model is useful for predicting y using the F test, we may elect to conduct one or more t tests on the individual β parameters (see Section 13.5). However, the test (or tests) to be conducted should be decided a priori, i.e., prior to fitting the model. Also, we should limit the number of t tests conducted to avoid the potential problem of making too many Type I errors. Generally, the regression analyst will conduct t tests on only the "most important" β's. These are usually the β's associated with higher-order terms (x_1^2, $x_1 x_2$, etc.). We provide insight in identifying the most important β's in a linear model in Sections 13.9–13.10.

> ### Recommendation for Checking the Utility of a Multiple Regression Model
>
> 1. First, conduct a test of overall model adequacy using the F test, i.e., test
>
> $$H_0: \quad \beta_1 = \beta_2 = \cdots = \beta_k = 0$$
>
> *(continued)*

If the model is deemed adequate (i.e., if you reject H_0), then proceed to step 2. Otherwise, you should hypothesize and fit another model. The new model may include more independent variables or higher-order terms (see Sections 13.9–13.11).

2. Conduct t tests on those β parameters that you are particularly interested in (i.e., the "most important" β's). These usually involve only the β's associated with higher-order terms (x_1^2, $x_1 x_2$, etc.). However, it is a safe practice to limit the number of β's that are tested. Conducting a series of t tests leads to a high overall Type I error rate α.

Warning

Rejecting H_0: $\beta_1 = \beta_2 = \cdots = \beta_k = 0$ in a test of overall model adequacy does not necessarily imply that the model is "best" for predicting y. Another model may prove even more useful in terms of providing more reliable estimates and predictions.

13.8 Using the Model for Estimation and Prediction

After checking the utility of the linear model and finding it to be useful for prediction and estimation, we may decide to use it for those purposes (step 6). Our methods for prediction and estimation using any general linear model are identical to those discussed in Section 12.9 for the simple straight-line model. We will use the model to form a confidence interval for the mean $E(y)$ for a given value of x, or a prediction interval for a future value of y for a given x.

EXAMPLE 13.14
Estimating $E(y)$ for a Given x

Refer to Example 13.2. Using the first-order least squares model

$$\hat{y} = 1{,}470.28 + .8145x_1 + .8204x_2 + 13.53x_3$$

estimate the mean sale price, $E(y)$, for a property with an appraised land value of $x_1 = \$15{,}000$, an appraised improvements value of $x_2 = \$50{,}000$, and a home size of $x_3 = 1{,}800$ square feet. Use a 95% confidence interval.

SOLUTION Substituting $x_1 = 15{,}000$, $x_2 = 50{,}000$, and $x_3 = 1{,}800$ into the least squares prediction equation yields the following estimate of $E(y)$:

$$\hat{y} = 1{,}470.28 + .8145(15{,}000) + .8204(50{,}000) + 13.53(1{,}800)$$

$$= 79{,}061.98$$

FIGURE 13.9

(a) SAS Printout for Estimated Mean and Corresponding 95% Confidence Interval for $x_1 = 15,000$, $x_2 = 50,000$, and $x_3 = 1,800$.

Obs	X1	X2	X3	Y	Predict Value	Residual	Lower95% Mean	Upper95% Mean
21	15000	50000	1800	.	79061.4	.	73380.7	84742.1

(b) SAS Printout for Predicted Value and Corresponding 95% Prediction Interval for $x_1 = 15,000$, $x_2 = 50,000$, and $x_3 = 1,800$.

Obs	X1	X2	X3	Y	Predict Value	Residual	Lower95% Predict	Upper95% Predict
21	15000	50000	1800	.	79061.4	.	61337.9	96785

(Note that our value differs slightly from that shown on the printout in Figure 13.9a due to rounding.) To form a confidence interval for the mean, we need to know the standard deviation of the sampling distribution for the estimator $\hat{y}$. For general linear models, the form of this standard deviation is very complex. However, most regression packages (including SAS) allow us to obtain the confidence intervals for mean values of y at any given setting of the independent variables. The relevant portion of the SAS printout for the sale price example is shown in Figure 13.9a. The 95% confidence interval for $E(y)$, the mean sale price for all properties with an appraised land value of $x_1 = \$15,000$, an appraised improvements value of $x_2 = \$50,000$, and a home size of $x_3 = 1,800$ square feet, is shown (shaded) to be \$73,380.70 to \$84,742.10. ▪

EXAMPLE 13.15
Predicting y for a Given x

Refer to Example 13.2. Construct a 95% prediction interval for y, the sale price of a particular property with an appraised land value of $x_1 = \$15,000$, an appraised improvements value of $x_2 = \$50,000$, and a home size of $x_3 = 1,800$ square feet.

SOLUTION When $x_1 = 15,000$, $x_2 = 50,000$, and $x_3 = 1,800$, the predicted value for y is again $\hat{y} = 79,061.98$. However, the prediction interval for a particular value of y will be wider than the confidence interval for the mean value. This is reflected in the SAS printout shown in Figure 13.9b. The prediction interval (shaded) extends from \$61,337.90 to \$96,785.00. ▪

Just as in simple linear regression, it is dangerous to use any general linear model for extrapolation, i.e., making predictions outside the region in which the sample data fall. Checking the sample data given in Table 13.1, we see that appraised land value (x_1) ranges from \$1,500 to \$23,000, appraised improvements (x_2) ranges from \$5,779 to \$72,827, and home size (x_3) ranges from 899 to 2,455 square feet. Consequently, in Examples 13.14 and 13.15, we would not use the estimated model to make estimates or predictions for properties with values of the independent variables outside their respective ranges.* In general, the fitted model might not provide a good model for the relationship between the mean y and the value of x when stretched over a wider range of x values.

Warning

Do not use the least squares model to extrapolate y outside the region in which the sample data fall. In other words, do not predict y for values of the independent variables $x_1, x_2, \ldots, x_k$ that are not within the range of the sample data.

In the preceding sections, we have demonstrated the methods of multiple regression analysis by fitting a first-order linear model to a set of data. In the next three sections (Sections 13.9–13.11), we introduce other, more complex, models that are useful for relating a response variable y to a set of independent variables. Then, in Section 13.12, we show you how to compare models to determine which is "best" for predicting y.

EXERCISES

■ *Learning the Mechanics*

13.1 Write a first-order linear model relating the mean value of y, $E(y)$, to two quantitative independent variables.

13.2 Write a first-order linear model relating the mean value of y, $E(y)$, to four quantitative independent variables.

13.3 Consider the following first-order equation in two quantitative independent variables:

$$E(y) = 1 + 2x_1 + x_2$$

a. Graph the relationship between y and x_1 for $x_2 = 0$, 1, and 2.
b. How do the graphed lines in part **a** relate to each other? What is the slope of each line?
c. If a linear model is first-order in two independent variables, what type of geometric relationship will you obtain when $E(y)$ is graphed as a function of one of the independent variables for various values of the other independent variable?

13.4 Consider the first-order equation in three quantitative independent variables

$$E(y) = 1 + 2x_1 + x_2 - 3x_3$$

a. Graph the relationship between y and x_1 for $x_2 = 1$ and $x_3 = 3$.

---

*With two or more independent variables in the model, the values of x_1, x_2, etc., jointly *define the experimental region. An observation with values of the x's that fall within their respective sample ranges may still fall outside the experimental region.*

   b. Repeat part **a** for $x_2 = -1$ and $x_3 = 1$.

   c. How do the graphed lines in parts **a** and **b** relate to each other? What is the slope of each line?

   d. If a linear model is first-order in three independent variables, what type of geometric relationship will you obtain when $E(y)$ is graphed as a function of one of the independent variables for various combinations of values of the other independent variables?

13.5 Suppose $E(y)$ is related to four quantitative independent variables, x_1, x_2, x_3, and x_4, by the model

$$E(y) = \beta_0 + \beta_1 x_1 + \beta_2 x_2 + \beta_3 x_3 + \beta_4 x_4$$

Suppose you fit this model to a set of $n = 15$ data points and found $R^2 = .74$, SS(Total) $= 1.690$, and SSE $= .439$.

   a. Calculate s^2, the estimate of the variance of the random error.

   b. Calculate the F statistic for testing $H_0: \beta_1 = \beta_2 = \beta_3 = \beta_4 = 0$.

   c. Do the data provide sufficient evidence to indicate that the model contributes information for predicting y? Test using $\alpha = .05$.

13.6 Suppose you fit the first-order multiple regression model

$$y = \beta_0 + \beta_1 x_1 + \beta_2 x_2 + \varepsilon$$

to $n = 25$ data points and obtain the prediction equation

$$\hat{y} = 6.4 + 3.1 x_1 + .92 x_2$$

The estimated standard deviations of the sampling distributions of $\hat{\beta}_1$ and $\hat{\beta}_2$ are 2.3 and .27, respectively.

   a. Test $H_0: \beta_1 = 0$ against $H_a: \beta_1 > 0$. Use $\alpha = .05$.

   b. Test $H_0: \beta_2 = 0$ against $H_a: \beta_2 \neq 0$. Use $\alpha = .05$.

   c. Find a 90% confidence interval for β_1. Interpret the interval.

   d. Find a 99% confidence interval for β_2. Interpret the interval.

13.7 Suppose you fit the first-order multiple regression model

$$y = \beta_0 + \beta_1 x_1 + \beta_2 x_2 + \beta_3 x_3 + \varepsilon$$

to $n = 20$ data points and obtain $R^2 = .2623$. Test the null hypothesis $H_0: \beta_1 = \beta_2 = \beta_3 = 0$ against the alternative hypothesis that at least one of the β parameters is nonzero. Use $\alpha = .05$.

▪ *Applying the Concepts*

13.8 "Explaining variability in external audit fees" was the title of a research paper published in *Accounting and Business Research* (Vol. 23, 1992). The quantitative independent variables used to model audit fee (y) included total assets (x_1), number of audit locations (x_2), foreign assets (x_3), net income or loss (x_4), long-term debt assets (x_5), and number of security registration forms filed annually (x_6).

   a. Write a first-order model for audit fee (y) as a function of the six independent variables.

   b. Refer to part **a**. Give the null hypothesis appropriate for testing the overall adequacy of the model.

   c. The coefficient of determination for the model was $R^2 = .84$. Interpret this value.

13.9 According to the 1990 census, the number of homeless people in the U.S. is more than a quarter of a million. Yet, little is known about what causes homelessness. Economists at the City University of New York used multiple regression to assist in determining the factors that cause homelessness in American cities (*American Economic Review*, Mar. 1993). Data on the number y of homeless per 100,000 population in $n = 50$ metropolitan areas were obtained from the Department of Housing and Urban Development. In addition, the 16 independent variables listed in the accompanying table were measured for each city and a multiple regression analysis performed by fitting the first-order model

$$E(y) = \beta_0 + \beta_1 x_1 + \beta_2 x_2 + \cdots + \beta_{16} x_{16}$$

Independent Variable	β Estimate	t Value
Intercept	307.54	$(-)$
Rental price (10% percentile)	2.87	3.93
Vacancy rate (10% percentile)	-872.90	-1.58
Rent-control law (yes or no)	-15.50	$-.23$
Employment growth	-859.09	-2.71
Share of employment in service industries	-347.69	-1.33
Size of low-skill labor market	$-1,003.87$	$-.38$
Households (per 100,000) below poverty level	.013	1.22
Public welfare expenditures	.11	.59
AFDC benefits	$-.95$	-2.58
SSI benefits	1.07	2.14
Percent reduction in AFDC (non-poor percents)	146.62	1.49
AFDC accuracy rate	98.15	.13
Mental health in-patients (per 100,000)	$-.83$	-1.50
Fraction of births to teenage mothers	$-1,173.00$	-1.39
Blacks (per 100,000)	.004	1.78
1984 population (100,000's)	1.22	1.44

Source: Honig, M. and Filer, R. K. "Causes of intercity variation in homelessness." *American Economic Review*, Vol. 83, No. 1, Mar. 1993, p. 251 (Table 2).

a. Interpret the β estimate for the independent variable, rental price.
b. Test the hypothesis that the incidence of homelessness decreases as employment growth increases. Use $\alpha = .05$.
c. Test (at $\alpha = .05$) each of the 16 independent variables to determine which are significantly related to homelessness.
d. What is the danger in performing the t tests, part **c**?
e. For this model, $R_a^2 = .83$. Interpret this result.

13.10 Marketers are keenly interested in the factors that motivate coupon usage by consumers. Three dominant motivational factors are thought to be (1) price reduction, (2) time and effort required to collect coupons, and (3) self-satisfaction. Using questionnaire data collected for a sample of $n = 290$ shoppers, a trio of marketing researchers examined the relationship between coupon usage and these factors (*The Journal of Consumer Marketing*, Spring 1988). The multiple regression model took the form:

$$E(y) = \beta_0 + \beta_1 x_1 + \beta_2 x_2 + \beta_3 x_3$$

where

$y =$ Coupon redemption rate

$x_1 =$ Price-consciousness score

$x_2 =$ Time-value score

$x_3 =$ Satisfaction/pride score

The results are summarized as follows (t values for testing β's in parentheses):

$\hat{\beta}_1 = .09784\ (1.444)$ $R^2 = .11671$

$\hat{\beta}_2 = -.13134\ (-1.695)$ $F = 9.6893$

$\hat{\beta}_3 = .20019\ (2.571)$

a. Conduct an overall test of model accuracy. Use $\alpha = .10$.
b. In theory, coupon users are more price-conscious than nonusers. Test the theory using $\alpha = .10$.
c. Interpret the negative β estimate for time-value score (x_2).

13.11 Residential property appraisers make extensive use of multiple regression in their evaluation of property. Typically, the sale price (y) of a property modeled as a function of several home-related conditions (e.g., gross living area, location, number of bedrooms). However, appraisers are not interested in the predicted price, $\hat{y}$. Rather, they use the regression model as a tool for making value adjustments to the property. These adjustments are derived from the parameter estimates of the model. The *Real Estate Appraiser* (Apr. 1992) reported the results of a multiple regression on the price (y) of $n = 157$ residential properties recently sold in a northern Virginia subdivision. A table showing the results of the SAS analysis is reproduced here. Note that there are 27 independent variables in the model.

Dependent Variable: Sale Price

		Analysis of Variance			
Source	*DF*	*Sum of Squares*	*Mean Square*	*F Value*	*Prob > F*
Model	27	24,184,211,898	895,711,551.79	20.914	.0001
Error	129	5,524,834,283	42,828,172.73		
C Total	156	29,709,046,181			
Root MSE		6544.324	R-Square	.8140	
Dep Mean		173157.5	Adj R-Sq	.7751	
C.V.		3.779404			

(continued)

Parameter Estimates

Variable	Parameter Estimate	Std Error	95% Confidence Interval (@129df = 1.98)	T for H₀: Parameter = 0	Prob > |T|
Intercept	96,603	12,530	(71,794 to 121,412)	7.710	.0001
Time	150	123	(−94 to 394)	1.220	.2248
Lot Size	**.60**	**.30**	**(.01 to 1.19)**	**2.022**	**.0452***
Age	381	502	(−613 to 1,375)	.758	.4501
G.L.A.	**22.40**	**3.67**	**(15.13 to 29.67)**	**6.099**	**.0001***
Bedrooms	2,263	1,609	(−923 to 5,499)	1.407	.1619
Half Baths	**5,962**	**2,934**	**(153 to 11,771)**	**2.032**	**.0442***
Corner Lot	−1,481	1,692	(−4,831 to 1,869)	−.876	.3829
Cul-de-Sac	−56	2,557	(−5,119 to 5,007)	−.022	.9825
Back to Woods	**4,086**	**2,044**	**(39 to 8,133)**	**1.999**	**.0477***
Deck	2,408	2,167	(−1,883 to 6,699)	1.111	.2686
Fence	**2,896**	**1,271**	**(379 to 5,413)**	**2.279**	**.0243***
Shed	70	1,343	(−2,589 to 2,729)	.052	.9588
Patio	2,377	1,671	(−932 to 5,686)	1.423	.1572
Portico	−906	2,963	(−6,773 to 4,961)	−.306	.7603
Screen Porch	**5,021**	**2,038**	**(986 to 9,056)**	**2.463**	**.0151***
In-grnd Pool	**7,570**	**3,028**	**(1,575 to 13,565)**	**2.500**	**.0137***
Garage	**2,989**	**1,446**	**(126 to 5,852)**	**2.068**	**.0407***
Driveway	−1,844	3,222	(−8,224 to 4,536)	−.572	.5681
Fireplace	1,290	1,277	(−1,238 to 3,818)	1.010	.3144
Brick Facade	−2,140	2,369	(−6,381 to 2,551)	−.903	.3680
Updated Kit.	**4,171**	**1,470**	**(1,260 to 7,082)**	**2.837**	**.0053***
Remodel Kit.	**6,091**	**2,367**	**(1,404 to 10,778)**	**2.574**	**.0112***
Intercom	1,933	2,146	(−2,316 to 6,182)	.901	.3693
Cen. Vacuum	**−4,636**	**2,166**	**(−8,925 to −347)**	**−2.140**	**.0342***
Skylights	**7,744**	**2,622**	**(2,552 to 12,936)**	**−2.954**	**.0037***
Air Filter	874	2,506	(−4,088 to 5,836)	−.349	.7280
Bay Window	−3,174	2,086	(−7,304 to 956)	−1.522	.1305

*Indicates significance at the 5% significance level.

Source: Gilson, S. J. "A Case Study—Comparing the results: Multiple regression analysis vs. matched pairs in residential subdivision." *The Real Estate Appraiser*, Apr. 1992, p. 37 (Table 4).

a. Interpret the values of **F Value**, **Root MSE**, **R-Square**, and **Adj. R-Sq** shown on the print-out.

b. One the independent variables in the model is gross living area (GLA), measured in square feet. A 95% confidence interval for the β coefficient associated with GLA is shown on the printout. Interpret this interval.

c. Note that the independent variables with β coefficients significantly different from 0 (at

$\alpha = .05$) are highlighted in bold on the printout. The nonsignificant variables are not highlighted. Would you advise the property appraiser to ignore any value adjustments based on nonsignificant independent variables? Explain.

13.12 Is the suicide rate in the United States related to the health of the economy? This question was the topic of research reported in the *American Journal of Economics and Sociology* (Jan. 1992). The annual suicide rate y (measured as the number of suicides per 100,000 persons) was recorded over the period 1940–1984 ($n = 45$ years). In addition, the following independent variables were measured each year:

$x_1 =$ Gross National Product (GNP) in 1982 dollars

$x_2 =$ GNP for the previous year

$x_3 =$ Unemployment rate

$$x_4 = \begin{cases} 1 & \text{if World War II (1942–1945)} \\ 0 & \text{if not} \end{cases}$$

$x_5 =$ Female labor force participation rate

$x_6 =$ Divorce rate

$x_7 =$ Proportion of U. S. population that is Catholic

The regression results are summarized here. [*Note:* t values for β parameters are given in parentheses.]

$$\hat{y} = 1.57 + .48x_1 - .57x_2 + .01x_3 - .06x_4 - .01x_5 + .35x_6 + .01x_7$$
$$\quad (1.65) \quad (4.18) \quad (-6.34) \quad (4.14) \quad (-2.30) \, (-3.16) \quad (10.35) \quad (3.00)$$

$$R^2 = .92 \qquad R_a^2 = .90 \qquad F = 31.9$$

Interpret the regression results.

13.13 Personal computer (PC) technology is changing at a phenomenal rate. As such, the retail price of a PC may vary dramatically depending on when it is purchased and what features it includes. Retail price data were recently collected for IBM and IBM-compatible PCs. The data for $n = 60$ PCs, shown in the table, were used to fit the multiple regression model

$$E(y) = \beta_0 + \beta_1 x_1 + \beta_2 x_2$$

where

$y =$ Retail price ($)

$x_1 =$ Microprocessor speed (megahertz)

$$x_2 = \begin{cases} 1 & \text{if 386 CPU chip} \\ 0 & \text{if 286 CPU chip} \end{cases}$$

An SPSS printout of the analysis follows.

Retail Price y	Speed MHz	Chip	Retail Price y	Speed MHz	Chip
$5099	33	386	$3249	25	386
3995	25	386	2995	20	386
2230	20	386	3419	20	386
4395	33	386	1590	20	386
6299	25	386	3899	20	386
2549	16	386	2249	12	286
3499	16	386	5796	25	386
2995	16	386	4330	16	286
1649	10	286	2699	16	386
5499	20	386	5579	20	386
1695	12	286	2095	16	386
2595	20	386	2695	25	386
3695	33	386	2295	20	386
3499	33	386	3445	25	386
2845	20	386	2445	16	386
4195	33	386	3795	25	386
2895	20	386	2395	16	386
2195	12	286	1595	12	286
5625	25	386	2095	16	386
2495	20	386	2995	25	386
3795	33	386	2895	20	386
3295	25	386	3995	33	386
1995	16	386	2595	20	386
2795	25	386	4995	25	386
5795	33	386	2695	25	386
3995	33	386	3990	33	386
1850	12	286	2795	20	386
1895	16	386	1995	20	286
1795	16	286	1595	16	286
2645	16	386	2875	20	386

Source: Computer Monthly, Computer Shopper, and IBM Corporation flyers. Data compiled by Jerasimos N. Mantas, University of South Florida business student.

a. Write the least squares prediction equation.
b. Is the model adequate for predicting y? Test using $\alpha = .10$.
c. Construct a 90% confidence interval for β_1. Interpret the interval.
d. Is CPU chip (x_2) a useful predictor of price (y) in this model? Test using $\alpha = .10$.

```
* * * *   M U L T I P L E   R E G R E S S I O N   * * * *

Equation Number 1    Dependent Variable..   Y

Multiple R           .63263
R Square             .40022
Adjusted R Square    .37918
Standard Error    953.66516

Analysis of Variance
                    DF      Sum of Squares        Mean Square
Regression           2      34592103.00773      17296051.50386
Residual            57      51840202.92561        909477.24431

F =      19.01757      Signif F =   .0000

------------------ Variables in the Equation ------------------

Variable             B       SE B        Beta        T   Sig T

X2          357.184971  389.422935     .110908     .917   .3629
X1          104.838940   22.362982     .566873    4.688   .0000
(Constant)  648.022624  431.494302                1.502   .1387
```

13.14 A team of research physicians conducted a study to determine the effect of health education on the utilization of health services for hypertension patients (*Drug Topics*, Apr. 1993). Data collected for a sample of $n = 282$ new HMO enrollees with hypertension problems were used to fit the following regression model:

$$E(y) = \beta_0 + \beta_1 x_1 + \beta_2 x_2 + \beta_3 x_3 + \beta_4 x_4 + \beta_5 x_5$$

where

$y =$ Annual health care expenditures (dollars)

$x_1 =$ Age (years)

$$x_2 = \begin{cases} 1 & \text{if female} \\ 0 & \text{if male} \end{cases}$$

$$x_3 = \begin{cases} 1 & \text{if white} \\ 0 & \text{if nonwhite} \end{cases}$$

$x_4 =$ Number of concomitant maintenance medications (regimen)

$$x_5 = \begin{cases} 1 & \text{if enrolled in a health education program} \\ 0 & \text{if not} \end{cases}$$

The regression results are summarized in the following table.

Variable	β Estimate	p Value for Testing H_0: $\beta_i = 0$
Intercept	64.82	$< .05$
Age (x_1)	1.05	$< .05$
Gender (x_2)	−10.53	nonsignificant
Race (x_3)	.27	nonsignificant
Regimen (x_4)	9.46	$< .05$
Health education (x_5)	−92.97	$< .001$
$F = 37.84$, $R^2 = .4357$		

a. Write the least squares prediction equation for annual health care expenditures (y).
b. Interpret the estimates of β_1 and β_4.
c. Interpret the p-values shown in the table.
d. Interpret the F value.
e. Interpret the value of R^2.
f. Predict the annual health care expenditure of a 45-year old, male, white hypertension patient who maintains three medications, but who has not enrolled in a health-care education program.

13.15 In a special issue, *Management International Review* (Vol. 33, 1993) reported on a study of the effect of conformance quality on the performance of brand-name laundry detergents. Performance was measured as weekly market share (y) of the brand. The market share model took the form

$$E(y) = \beta_0 + \beta_1 x_1 + \beta_2 x_2 + \beta_3 x_3$$

where

$x_1 = $ Weekly price of brand (\$)

$x_2 = $ Number of times brand was displayed during the week

$$x_3 = \begin{cases} 1 & \text{if high-quality brand} \\ 0 & \text{low-quality brand} \end{cases}$$

Data for seven brands of laundry detergents were collected over a 100-week period and used to fit the model. The results are summarized here. (Observed significance levels for testing the β coefficients are given in parentheses.)

$$\hat{y} = .453 - .000407x_1 + .04x_2 + .108x_3$$
$$\quad\quad\quad (.000) \quad\quad (.002) \quad (.000)$$

a. Interpret $\hat{\beta}_1$.
b. Interpret $\hat{\beta}_2$.
c. Conduct a test to determine whether brand quality is a useful predictor of market share.
d. Predict the weekly market share of a high-quality brand of laundry detergent that sells for \$3.00 and is displayed twice during the week.

13.16 *Artificial Intelligence (AI) Applications* (Jan. 1993) discussed the use of computer-based technologies in building explanation systems for regression models. As an example, the authors presented a model for predicting the scenic beauty (y) of southeastern pine stands (measured on a numeric scale) as a function of age (x_1) of the dominant stand, stems per acre (x_2) in trees, and basal acre (x_3) per acre in hardwoods. A user of the AI system simply inputs the values of x_1, x_2, and x_3, and the system uses the least squares equation to predict the scenic beauty (y) value.

a. The AI system is designed to check the values of the input variables (x_1, x_2, and x_3) with the sample data ranges. If the input data are "out-of-range," a warning is issued about the potential inaccuracy of the predicted y value. Explain the reasoning behind this warning.
b. In addition to the predicted value, the AI system also generates information on how each independent variable can be manipulated to effect changes in the dependent variable. For

example, "if all else was held constant in the stand, allowing the age (x_1) of the dominant trees in the stand to mature by one year will *increase* scenic beauty (y)." From what portion of the regression analysis would the AI system extract this type of information?

13.17 In a production facility, an accurate estimate of man-hours needed to complete a task is crucial to management in making such decisions as the proper number of workers to hire, an accurate deadline to quote a client, or cost-analysis decisions regarding budgets. A manufacturer of boiler drums wants to use regression to predict the number of man-hours needed to erect the drums in future projects. To accomplish this, data for 35 boilers were collected. In addition to man-hours (y), the variables measured were boiler capacity ($x_1 = $ lb/hr), boiler design pressure ($x_2 = $ pounds per square inch or psi), boiler type ($x_3 = 1$ if industry field erected, 0 if utility field erected), and drum type ($x_4 = 1$ if steam, 0 if mud). The data are provided in the accompanying table. A MINITAB printout for the model $E(y) = \beta_0 + \beta_1x_1 + \beta_2x_2 + \beta_3x_3 + \beta_4x_4$ follows.

Man-Hours y	Boiler Capacity x_1	Design Pressure x_2	Boiler Type x_3	Drum Type x_4
3,137	120,000	375	1	1
3,590	65,000	750	1	1
4,526	150,000	500	1	1
10,825	1,073,877	2,170	0	1
4,023	150,000	325	1	1
7,606	610,000	1,500	0	1
3,748	88,200	399	1	1
2,972	88,200	399	1	1
3,163	88,200	399	1	1
4,065	90,000	1,140	1	1
2,048	30,000	325	1	1
6,500	441,000	410	1	1
5,651	441,000	410	1	1
6,565	441,000	410	1	1
6,387	441,000	410	1	1
6,454	627,000	1,525	0	1
6,928	610,000	1,500	0	1
4,268	150,000	500	1	1
14,791	1,089,490	2,170	0	1
2,680	125,000	750	1	1
2,974	120,000	375	1	0
1,965	65,000	750	1	0
2,566	150,000	500	1	0
1,515	150,000	250	1	0
2,000	150,000	500	1	0
2,735	150,000	325	1	0

(continued)

Man-Hours y	Boiler Capacity x_1	Design Pressure x_2	Boiler Type x_3	Drum Type x_4
3,698	610,000	1,500	0	0
2,635	90,000	1,140	1	0
1,206	30,000	325	1	0
3,775	441,000	410	1	0
3,120	441,000	410	1	0
4,206	441,000	410	1	0
4,006	441,000	410	1	0
3,728	627,000	1,525	0	0
3,211	610,000	1,500	0	0
1,200	30,000	325	1	0

Source: Kelly Uscategui, Former graduate student, University of South Florida.

```
The regression equation is
Y = - 3783 + 0.00875 X1 + 1.93 X2 + 3444 X3 + 2093 X4

Predictor        Coef        Stdev     t-ratio        p
Constant        -3783         1205       -3.14    0.004
X1          0.0087490    0.0009035        9.68    0.000
X2             1.9265       0.6489        2.97    0.006
X3             3444.3        911.7        3.78    0.001
X4             2093.4        305.6        6.85    0.000

s = 894.6       R-sq = 90.3%     R-sq(adj) = 89.0%

Analysis of Variance

SOURCE        DF           SS          MS        F        p
Regression     4    230854848    57713712    72.11    0.000
Error         31     24809760      800315
Total         35    255664608

SOURCE        DF       SEQ SS
X1             1    175007136
X2             1       490357
X3             1     17813090
X4             1     37544264

Unusual Observations
Obs.      X1          Y       Fit Stdev.Fit  Residual   St.Resid
 19  1089490      14791     12022      523      2769      3.81R

R denotes an obs. with a large st. resid.

    Fit  Stdev.Fit        95% C.I.         95% P.I.
   1936        239  (  1449,   2424) (    47,   3825)
```

a. Test the hypothesis that boiler capacity (x_1) is positively linearly related to man-hours (y). Use $\alpha = .05$.

b. Test the hypothesis that boiler pressure (x_2) is positively linearly related to man-hours (y). Use $\alpha = .05$.

c. Construct a 95% confidence interval for β_1 and interpret the result.

d. Construct a 95% confidence interval for β_3.

e. In Section 13.11, we will learn that β_3 represents the difference between the mean number of man-hours required for industrial and utility field erection boilers. Use this information to interpret the confidence interval of part **d**.

13.18 As a result of the U.S. surgeon general's warnings about the health hazards of smoking, Congress banned television and radio advertising of cigarettes in January 1971. The banning of prosmoking messages, however, also led to the virtual elimination of antismoking messages. In theory, if these antismoking commercials are more effective than prosmoking commercials, the net effect of the Congressional ban will be to increase the consumption of cigarettes and therefore benefit the tobacco industry. To test this hypothesis, researchers at the University of Houston built a cigarette-demand model based on data collected for 46 states over the 18-year period 1963–1980 (*The Review of Economics and Statistics*, Feb. 1986). For each state–year, the following independent variables were recorded:

x_1 = Natural logarithm of a price of a carton of cigarettes

x_2 = Natural log of minimum price of a carton of cigarettes in any neighboring state (This variable was included to measure the effect of "bootlegging" cigarettes in nearby states with lower tax rates.)

x_3 = Natural log of real disposable income per capita

x_4 = Per capita index of expenditures for cigarette advertising on television and radio (This value is 0 for the years 1971–1980, when the ban was in effect.)

The dependent variable of interest is y, the natural log of per capita consumption of cigarettes by persons of smoking age (14 years and older). The multiple regression model

$$E(y) = \beta_0 + \beta_1 x_1 + \beta_2 x_2 + \beta_3 x_3 + \beta_4 x_4$$

was fit to the $n = 828$ observations (46 states $\times$ 18 years) with the following results:

$$R^2 = .95 \qquad s = .047$$

a. Test the hypothesis that the model is useful for predicting y. (Use $\alpha = .05$.)
b. Interpret the value of s.
c. Give the null and alternative hypotheses appropriate for testing whether a decrease in per capita cigarette advertising expenditures is accompanied by an increase in per capita consumption of cigarettes over the period 1963–1980.
d. The value of $\hat{\beta}_4$ was determined to be .033. Interpret this value.
e. Does the value $\hat{\beta}_4 = .033$ support the alternative hypothesis of part **c**? Explain.

13.19 Because the coefficient of determination R^2 always increases when a new independent variable is added to the model, it may be tempting to include many variables in a model to force R^2 to be near 1. However, doing so reduces the degrees of freedom available for estimating σ^2, which adversely affects our ability to make reliable inferences. As an example, suppose you want to predict the selling price of a used car using 18 independent variables (such as make, model, year, and odometer reading). You fit the model

$$y = \beta_0 + \beta_1 x_1 + \beta_2 x_2 + \cdots + \beta_{17} x_{17} + \beta_{18} x_{18} + \varepsilon$$

where y = car price and $x_1, x_2, \ldots, x_{18}$ are the predictor variables. Using the relevant information on $n = 20$ used cars to fit the model, you obtain $R^2 = .95$.

a. Test to determine whether this value of R^2 is large enough for you to infer that this model is useful—i.e., that at least one term in the model is important for predicting selling price. Use $\alpha = .05$.

b. Calculate R_a^2. Interpret this result.

13.9 Model Building: Interaction Models

In Section 13.3, we demonstrated the relationship between $E(y)$ and the independent variables in a first-order linear model,

$$E(y) = \beta_0 + \beta_1 x_1 + \beta_2 x_2$$

When $E(y)$ is graphed against any one variable (say, x_1) for fixed values of the other variable (x_2), the result is a set of *parallel* straight lines (see Figure 13.10). When this situation occurs (as it always does for a first-order model), we say that the relationship between $E(y)$ and any one independent variable *does not depend* on the value of the other independent variable(s) in the model—that is, we say that the independent variables **do not interact**.

FIGURE 13.10

Graphs of $E(y)$ Versus x_1 for Fixed Values of x_2: First-Order Model

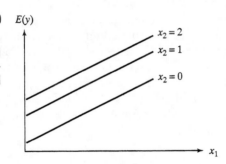

However, if the relationship between $E(y)$ and x_1 does, in fact, depend on the value of x_2 held fixed, then the first-order model is not appropriate for predicting y. In this case, we need another model that will take into account this dependence. Such a model is illustrated in the next example.

EXAMPLE 13.16

Graphing the Interaction Model

Refer to Example 13.3, where we graphed the first-order model, $E(y) = 1 + 2x_1 + x_2$. Now suppose that the mean value $E(y)$ of a response y is related to two quantitative independent variables, x_1 and x_2, by the model

$$E(y) = \beta_0 + \beta_1 x_1 + \beta_2 x_2 + \beta_3 x_1 x_2$$

where $\beta_0 = 1$, $\beta_1 = 2$, $\beta_2 = -1$, and $\beta_3 = 1$, i.e.,

$$E(y) = 1 + 2x_1 - x_2 + x_1x_2$$

Graph the relationship between $E(y)$ and x_1 for $x_2 = 0$, 1, and 2. Interpret the graph. [*Note:* Since this model contains the term x_1x_2, in addition to all of the terms of the model in Example 13.3, we will be able to see the effect of adding the second-order cross-product term (x_1x_2) to a first-order model.]

SOLUTION We obtain three response curves relating $E(y)$ to x_1—one for each of the values $x_2 = 0$, 1, and 2. For $x_2 = 0$:

$$E(y) = 1 + 2x_1 - (0) + x_1(0) = 1 + 2x_1 \qquad (\text{slope} = 2)$$

For $x_2 = 1$:

$$E(y) = 1 + 2x_1 - (1) + x_1(1) = 3x_1 \qquad (\text{slope} = 3)$$

For $x_2 = 2$:

$$E(y) = 1 + 2x_1 - (2) + x_1(2) = -1 + 4x_1 \qquad (\text{slope} = 4)$$

Note that the slope of each line is represented by $\beta_1 + \beta_3x_2 = 2 + x_2$. Graphs of these three straight lines are shown in Figure 13.11. The effect of adding a term involving the cross-product x_1x_2 can be seen in Figure 13.11. In contrast to Figure 13.10, the lines relating $E(y)$ to x_1 are no longer parallel. The effect on $E(y)$ of a change in x_1 (i.e., the slope) now *depends* on the value of x_2. When this situation occurs, we say that x_1 and x_2 **interact**. The cross-product term, $\beta_3x_1x_2$, is called an **interaction term**, and the model $E(y) = \beta_0 + \beta_1x_1 + \beta_2x_2 + \beta_3x_1x_2$ is called an **interaction model** with two quantitative variables (see the box on page 697).

FIGURE 13.11

Graphs of
$E(y) = 1 + 2x_1$
$- x_2 + x_1x_2$
for $x_2 = 0, 1, 2$

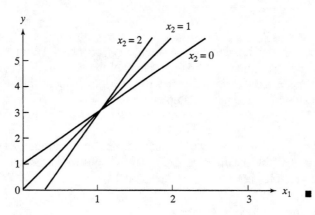

An Interaction Model Relating $E(y)$ to Two Quantitative
Independent Variables

$$E(y) = \beta_0 + \beta_1 x_1 + \beta_2 x_2 + \beta_3 x_1 x_2$$

where

$(\beta_1 + \beta_3 x_2)$ represents the change in $E(y)$ for every 1-unit increase in x_1, holding x_2 fixed

$(\beta_2 + \beta_3 x_1)$ represents the change in $E(y)$ for every 1-unit increase in x_2, holding x_1 fixed

A three-dimensional graph (generated by computer) of an interaction model in two quantitative x's is shown in Figure 13.12. Unlike the planar surface displayed in Figure 13.4, the interaction model traces a ruled surface (twisted plane) in three-dimensional space. If we slice the twisted plane at a fixed value of x_2, we obtain a straight line relating $E(y)$ to x_1; however, the slope of the line will change as we change the value of x_2.

FIGURE 13.12

Computer-Generated
Graph for an
Interaction Model
(Second-Order)

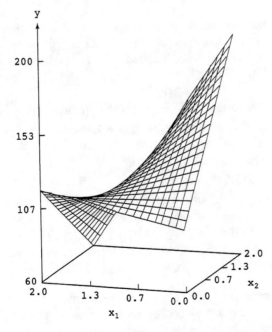

EXAMPLE 13.17

Analyzing an Interaction
Model

Although a regional express delivery service bases the charge for shipping a package on the package weight and distance shipped, its profit per package depends on the package size (volume of space that it occupies) and the size and nature of the load on the delivery truck. The company recently conducted a study to investigate the relationship between the cost y of shipment (in dollars) and the variables that control the shipping charge—package weight, x_1 (in pounds), and distance shipped, x_2 (in miles). Twenty packages were randomly selected from among the large number received for shipment, and a detailed analysis of the cost of shipment was made for each package, with the results shown in Table 13.2.

Table 13.2 Cost of Shipment Data for Example 13.17

Package	x_1	x_2	y	Package	x_1	x_2	y
1	5.9	47	2.60	11	5.1	240	11.00
2	3.2	145	3.90	12	2.4	209	5.00
3	4.4	202	8.00	13	.3	160	2.00
4	6.6	160	9.20	14	6.2	115	6.00
5	.75	280	4.40	15	2.7	45	1.10
6	.7	80	1.50	16	3.5	250	8.00
7	6.5	240	14.50	17	4.1	95	3.30
8	4.5	53	1.90	18	8.1	160	12.10
9	.60	100	1.00	19	7.0	260	15.50
10	7.5	190	14.00	20	1.1	90	1.70

a. Suppose the company believes that straight-line relationships exist between mean shipment cost, $E(y)$, and package weight (x_1), and between $E(y)$ and distance shipped (x_2), but that the rate of change of $E(y)$ with x_1 depends on x_2, and vice versa. Hypothesize an appropriate linear model for $E(y)$.

b. Fit the model to the data and graph the prediction equation.

c. Give the estimated slope of the line relating $E(y)$ to x_2 for a fixed package weight of $x_1 = 2$ pounds. Interpret this value.

d. Find the value of s and interpret it.

e. Find the value of R^2 and interpret it.

f. Is the model useful for the prediction of shipping cost y? Find the value of the F statistic on the printout, and give the observed significance level (p-value) for the test.

g. Is there evidence that the interaction term contributes to the prediction of shipping cost y?

SOLUTION a. Since the company expects the linear relationship between $E(y)$ and one x value (say, x_1) to depend on the other x value (x_2)—that is, since the company expects x_1 and x_2 to interact—the appropriate model is

$$E(y) = \beta_0 + \beta_1 x_1 + \beta_2 x_2 + \beta_3 x_1 x_2$$

b. An ASP printout for fitting the interaction model to $n = 20$ data

FIGURE 13.13

ASP Printout for
Interaction Model,
Example 13.17

INTERACTION MODEL

MODEL: Y = 0.019088X1 + 7.72085E-3X2 + 7.79574E-3X1*X2 + -0.140501CNST

	COEF.	SD. ER.	t(16)	P-VALUE	PT. R SQ.
X1	0.019088	0.158212	0.120649	0.905471	9.08931E-4
X2	7.72085E-3	3.90568E-3	1.97683	0.065558	0.196297
X1*X2	7.79574E-3	8.97664E-4	8.68448	1.88153E-7	0.824984
CNST	-0.140501	0.6481	-0.216789	0.831113	2.92873E-3

R SQ. = 0.985327, ADJ. R SQ. = 0.982576, D. W. = 2.24157
SQ. ROOT MSE = 0.64388, F(3/16) = 358.154 (P-VALUE = 7.12479E-15)

points is shown in Figure 13.13. You can see from the printout that the parameter estimates (shaded in Figure 13.13) are:

$$\hat{\beta}_0 = -.140501 \qquad \hat{\beta}_1 = .019088$$

$$\hat{\beta}_2 = .00772085 \qquad \hat{\beta}_3 = .00779574$$

Therefore, the prediction equation that relates shipping cost y to package weight, x_1, and distance shipped, x_2, is*

$$\hat{y} = -.140501 + .019088x_1 + .00772085x_2 + .00779574x_3$$

Graphs of the lines relating shipping cost (y) to distance shipped (x_2) for several package weight (x_1) values are portrayed in Figure 13.14. Notice that the lines are nonparallel, due to the interaction term.

FIGURE 13.14

Graph of the Least
Squares Prediction
Equation, Example
13.17

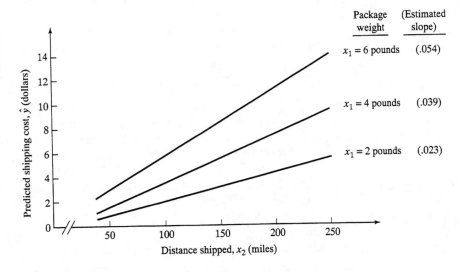

*ASP uses E notation to indicate that the decimal point for the number shown on the printout should be moved right or left. The notation E−3 for the value of $\hat{\beta}_2$ requires you to move the decimal 3 places to the left (−). In contrast, E+2 would require you to move the decimal 2 places to the right (+).

c. From the box, the slope of the $E(y)$–x_2 line is given by $\beta_2 + \beta_3 x_1$. Substituting the values of $\hat{\beta}_2$, $\hat{\beta}_3$, and x_1 into the equation, we obtain the estimated slope:

Estimated slope of the $E(y)$–x_2 line when $x_1 = 2$:

$$\hat{\beta}_2 + \hat{\beta}_3 x_1 = .00772085 + .00779574(2)$$

$$= .023$$

Thus, we estimate that mean shipping cost for a 2-pound package will increase $.023 for every additional mile shipped.

The estimated slopes for 2-, 4-, and 6-pound packages (computed in a similar fashion) are shown on Figure 13.14. You can see that the rate of increase of mean shipping cost with distance is faster for heavier packages.

d. The value of s, shaded on the printout, is $s = .64388$. Multiplying this value by 2, we obtain $2s = 2(.64388) = 1.28776$. Our interpretation is that we expect to predict shipping cost to within approximately $1.29 of its true value using the fitted interaction model.

e. The value of R^2, shaded in Figure 13.13, is .985327. This means that about 98.5% of the total sample variation in shipping cost (y) is explained by the model; the remainder of the variation is due to random error. [Note that the value of R_a^2, given next to R^2, is slightly smaller due to the adjustment for degrees of freedom.]

f. To determine whether the overall model is useful for predicting y, we test

$$H_0: \quad \beta_1 = \beta_2 = \beta_3 = 0$$

$$H_a: \quad \text{At least one } \beta_i \neq 0$$

The test statistic, shaded on the printout, is $F = 358.154$. Since $n = 20$ and $k = 3$, this F value depends on $k = 3$ numerator df and $n - (k + 1) = 20 - 4 = 16$ denominator df. The observed significance level (p-value) for the test, shown to the right of the F value on the printout (shaded), is $p = 7.12479\text{E}{-}15 \approx .000$. This means that if the model actually contributed no information for the prediction of y, the probability of observing a value of the F statistic as large as 358.154 would be extremely small. Thus, for any reasonable value of α, we will reject the null hypothesis and conclude that the model is adequate for predicting shipping cost.

g. Although we have decided that the overall model is useful for predicting y, we have not yet determined whether the interaction term contributes significantly to the model. That is, we do not know whether the relationship between $E(y)$ and x_2 depends on x_1. Consequently, we want to conduct a t test on β_3, the parameter in the interaction term. If $\beta_3 = 0$, then x_1 and x_2 do not interact and a first-order model is appropriate. Therefore, we want to test

$H_0:$ $\beta_3 = 0$ (no interaction between x_1 and x_2)

$H_a:$ $\beta_3 \neq 0$ (x_1 and x_2 interact)

The test statistic is given on the printout in the **X1∗X2** row (shaded) as $t = 8.68448$. The associated two-tailed p-value (also shaded) is $p = .000000188$. Thus, there is sufficient evidence at any reasonable value of α to indicate that package weight (x_1) and distance shipped (x_2) interact. This means that the slope of the straight-line relationship between mean shipping cost, $E(y)$, and one of the x's depends on the value of the other x (see Figure 13.14). ■

Example 13.17 illustrates an important point about conducting t tests on the β parameters in the interaction model. The "most important" β parameter in this model is the interaction β, β_3. [Note that this β is also the one associated with the highest-order term in the model, $x_1 x_2$.[*]] Consequently, we will want to test $H_0: \beta_3 = 0$ after we have determined that the overall model is useful for predicting y. Once interaction is detected (as in Example 13.17), however, tests on the first-order terms x_1 and x_2 should *not* be conducted since they are meaningless tests; the presence of interaction implies that both x's are important.

> **Warning**
>
> Once interaction has been deemed important in the model $E(y) = \beta_0 + \beta_1 x_1 + \beta_2 x_2 + \beta_3 x_1 x_2$, do not conduct t tests on the β coefficients of the first-order terms x_1 and x_2. These terms should be kept in the model regardless of the magnitude of their associated p-values shown on the printout.

EXERCISES

■ *Learning the Mechanics*

13.20 Write a first-order plus interaction model relating the mean value of y, $E(y)$, to two quantitative independent variables.

---

[*]When x_1 and x_2 are both quantitative variables, the cross-product, $x_1 x_2$, is considered a second-order term.

13.21 Write a first-order plus interaction model relating the mean value of y, $E(y)$, to three quantitative independent variables. [*Hint:* Include all possible two-way cross-product terms.]

13.22 In Exercise 13.3 you graphed the first-order model

$$E(y) = 1 + 2x_1 + x_2$$

Now consider the interaction model

$$E(y) = 1 + 2x_1 + x_2 - 3x_1x_2$$

a. Graph the relationship between y and x for $x_2 = 0$, 1, and 2 for the interaction model.
b. Compare the graph of part **a** to the graph of Exercise 13.3. How has the inclusion of the interaction term affected the graphs?
c. Give the slope of each line graphed in part **a**.

13.23 Suppose you fit the interaction model

$$y = \beta_0 + \beta_1x_1 + \beta_2x_2 + \beta_3x_1x_2 + \varepsilon$$

to $n = 32$ data points and obtain the following results:

$$\text{SS(Total)} = 479 \qquad \text{SSE} = 21 \qquad \hat{\beta}_3 = 10 \qquad s_{\hat{\beta}_3} = 4$$

a. Find R^2 and interpret its value.
b. Is the model adequate for predicting y? Test at $\alpha = .05$.
c. Use a graph to explain the contribution of the x_1x_2 term to the model.
d. Is there evidence that x_1 and x_2 interact? Test at $\alpha = .05$.

▪ *Applying the Concepts*

13.24 Refer to the *Management International Review* study of market shares of laundry detergents, Exercise 13.15. Recall that market share (y) was modeled as a first-order function of price (x_1), display (x_2), and quality (x_3), where $x_3 = 1$ if high-quality detergent or $x_3 = 0$ if low-quality detergent. The researchers also investigated whether the effect of a price change on brand share was dependent on brand quality.
a. Propose a model that will allow the researchers to test this hypothesis.
b. Propose a model that allows the effect of display on market share to depend on brand quality.

13.25 In theory, most academics advocate group decision making as a way to solve conflicts among a manager's subordinates. Many managers reject this proposition in practice, however, believing that conflict in groups is counterproductive. A study was conducted to examine this contradiction between accepted normative theory and current practice in Australia (*Organizational Behavior and Human Decision Processes*, Vol. 39, 1987). For one part of the study, multiple regression analysis was used to test "the proposition that the effective use of group discussion methods to resolve conflict depends on the manager's ability and willingness to encourage subordinates to confront conflict." A sample of 89 upper-level managers were asked to complete a questionnaire that measured (on a 7-point Likert scale) the following:

y = Average performance of manager's subordinates (i.e., subordinate performance)

x_1 = Manager's preferred level of subordinate participation in decision making when conflict is present (i.e., group decision method)

x_2 = Average of subordinates' perceptions of manager's inclination to legitimize conflict (i.e., conflict legitimization)

The interaction model $E(y) = \beta_0 + \beta_1 x_1 + \beta_2 x_2 + \beta_3 x_1 x_2$ was fit to the 89 data points, with the following results (t values in parentheses):

$$\hat{y} = 7.09 - .44x_1 - .01x_2 + .06x_1 x_2 \qquad R^2 = .22$$
$$\quad\;\; (-1.86) \;\; (-.01) \quad (1.85)$$

a. Conduct a test to determine whether the model is adequate for predicting subordinate performance y. Use $\alpha = .10$.

b. Use the least squares prediction equation to graph the estimated relationships between subordinate performance (y) and group decision method (x_1) for low-conflict legitimization $(x_2 = 1)$ and high-conflict legitimization $(x_2 = 7)$. Interpret the graphs.

c. Conduct a test to determine whether the relationship between subordinate performance (y) and manager's use of a group decision method (x_1) depends on a manager's legitimization of conflict (x_2). Use $\alpha = .10$.

d. Based on the result of part **c**, would you recommend that the researchers conduct t tests on β_1 and β_2? Explain.

13.26 Over the years, Graduate Record Examination (GRE) scores have been used to aid college administrators in the graduate school admission process. Some educators argue, however, that the GRE is biased against minority students, especially blacks, who are often unfairly denied admission to graduate study on the basis of test scores alone. Scott and Shaw (*Journal of Negro Education*, Jan. 1985) conducted a study to compare the relationship between GRE scores and performance of black and white graduate students at the University of Florida. The initial sample consisted of 75 black graduate students who were enrolled full time in the fall of 1982. Each of these black students was matched (by department, age, gender, and tenure) with a white graduate student, giving a combined sample of 150 students (75 white and 75 black). Data collected on GRE score and current grade point average (GPA) were used to fit the model

$$E(y) = \beta_0 + \beta_1 x_1 + \beta_2 x_2 + \beta_3 x_1 x_2$$

where

$$y = \text{GPA}$$

$$x_1 = \text{GRE score}$$

$$x_2 = \begin{cases} 1 & \text{if black} \\ 0 & \text{if white} \end{cases}$$

The least squares prediction equation and coefficient of determination follow:[*]

$$\hat{y} = 3.031 + .000498x_1 + .687x_2 - .000983x_1 x_2 \qquad R^2 = .05$$

$$s_{\hat{\beta}_3} = .0003738$$

[*] *Scott, R. R. and Shaw, M. E. "Black and white performance in graduate school and policy implications of the use of Graduate Record Examination scores in admissions." Journal of Negro Education, Vol. 54, No. 1, 1985, pp. 14–23. Some of the regression results shown here are approximated based on information provided in the article.*

a. Calculate the test statistic for checking model adequacy. Give the approximate p-value for the test.

b. Write the equation of the fitted line relating GPA to GRE score for white graduate students. [*Hint:* Substitute $x_2 = 0$ into the equation.]

c. Write the equation of the fitted line relating GPA to GRE score for black graduate students. [*Hint:* Substitute $x_2 = 1$ into the equation.]

d. Graph the lines from parts **b** and **c** on the same set of axes. What do you observe?

e. Test the hypothesis that the slopes of the lines relating GPA to GRE score differ for whites and blacks. [*Hint:* Test $H_0: \beta_3 = 0$.]

f. Predict the GPA of a black graduate student with a GRE score of 1200.

13.27 Stock market analysts are continually searching for reliable predictors of stock price. Consider the problem of modeling the price per share, y, of electric utility stocks. Two variables that are thought to influence stock price are return on average equity, x_1, and annual rate of dividend, x_2. The stock prices, returns on equity, and dividend rates for a sample of 16 nonnuclear electric utility stocks are shown in the accompanying table. The interaction model

$$E(y) = \beta_0 + \beta_1 x_1 + \beta_2 x_2 + \beta_3 x_1 x_2$$

was fit to the data. The resulting SAS printout follows.

Nonnuclear Stocks

y	x_1	x_2
25	15.2	2.60
20	13.9	2.14
15	15.8	1.52
34	12.8	3.12
20	6.9	2.48
33	14.6	3.08
28	15.4	2.92
30	17.3	2.76
23	13.7	2.36
24	12.7	2.36
25	15.3	2.56
26	15.2	2.80
26	12.0	2.72
20	15.3	1.92
20	13.7	1.92
13	13.3	1.60

Source: *United Business Investment Report.*

a. Write the least squares prediction equation for the electric utility stock.

b. Is the model useful for predicting the price of nonnuclear stocks? Test using $\alpha = .05$.

c. Is there evidence of interaction between return on equity and dividend rate in the model? Perform the test using $\alpha = .05$.

d. The SAS printout also includes 95% prediction intervals for price per share (y). Locate the lower and upper limits for a 95% prediction interval for y when $x_1 = 13.3$ and $x_2 = 1.60$ (observation #16).

e. Interpret the interval obtained in part **d**.

f. Would you recommend using the model to predict price per share of a nonnuclear stock with a dividend rate of 1.10? Explain.

Dependent Variable: Y

Analysis of Variance

Source	DF	Sum of Squares	Mean Square	F Value	Prob>F
Model	3	478.30855	159.43618	60.851	0.0001
Error	12	31.44145	2.62012		
C Total	15	509.75000			

Root MSE	1.61868	R-square	0.9383
Dep Mean	23.87500	Adj R-sq	0.9229
C.V.	6.77981		

Parameter Estimates

Variable	DF	Parameter Estimate	Standard Error	T for H0: Parameter=0	Prob > |T|
INTERCEP	1	-44.681773	25.23972659	-1.770	0.1021
X1	1	2.879579	1.74113100	1.654	0.1241
X2	1	25.062181	10.02876655	2.499	0.0280
X1X2	1	-0.959006	0.69103996	-1.388	0.1904

Obs	X1	X2	Dep Var Y	Predict Value	Std Err Predict	Lower95% Predict	Upper95% Predict	Residual
1	15.2	2.6	25.0000	26.3496	0.487	22.6663	30.0328	-1.3496
2	13.9	2.14	20.0000	20.4508	0.489	16.7667	24.1349	-0.4508
3	15.8	1.52	15.0000	15.8786	1.315	11.3344	20.4228	-0.8786
4	12.8	3.12	34.0000	32.0720	1.034	27.8869	36.2571	1.9280
5	6.9	2.48	20.0000	20.9310	1.336	16.3577	25.5043	-0.9310
6	14.6	3.08	33.0000	31.4270	0.697	27.5874	35.2665	1.5730
7	15.4	2.92	28.0000	29.7207	0.686	25.8900	33.5514	-1.7207
8	17.3	2.76	30.0000	28.5159	0.917	24.4620	32.5698	1.4841
9	13.7	2.36	23.0000	22.9086	0.415	19.2675	26.5497	0.0914
10	12.7	2.36	24.0000	22.2923	0.493	18.6056	25.9789	1.7077
11	15.3	2.56	25.0000	25.9726	0.486	22.2900	29.6552	-0.9726
12	15.2	2.8	26.0000	28.4466	0.577	24.7024	32.1908	-2.4466
13	12	2.72	26.0000	26.7403	0.701	22.8971	30.5836	-0.7403
14	15.3	1.92	20.0000	19.3234	0.732	15.4531	23.1937	0.6766
15	13.7	1.92	20.0000	17.6621	0.660	13.8533	21.4710	2.3379
16	13.3	1.6	13.0000	13.3085	1.083	9.0645	17.5524	-0.3085

13.28 One of the most promising methods for extracting crude oil employs a carbon dioxide (CO_2) flooding technique. CO_2, when flooded into oil pockets, enhances oil recovery by displacing the crude oil. In a microscopic investigation of the CO_2 flooding process, flow tubes were dipped into sample oil pockets containing a known amount of oil. The oil pockets were flooded with CO_2 and the percentage of oil displaced was recorded. The experiment was conducted at three different flow pressures and three different dipping angles. The displacement test data are recorded in the table on page 706.

Pressure x_1, pounds per square inch	Dipping Angle x_2, degrees	Oil Recovery y, percentage
1,000	0	60.58
1,000	15	72.72
1,000	30	79.99
1,500	0	66.83
1,500	15	80.78
1,500	30	89.78
2,000	0	69.18
2,000	15	80.31
2,000	30	91.99

Source: Wang, G. C. "Microscopic investigation of CO_2 flooding process." *Journal of Petroleum Technology.* Vol. 34, No. 8, Aug. 1982, pp. 1789–1797. Copyright © 1982, Society of Petroleum Engineers, American Institute of Mining Engineers. First published in the *JPT* August 1982.

a. Plot the sample data on a scattergram, with percentage oil recovery y on the vertical axis and pressure x_1 on the horizontal axis. Connect the points corresponding to the same value of dipping angle x_2. Based on the scattergram, do you believe that x_1 and x_2 interact?

b. An ASP printout for the interaction model

$$y = \beta_0 + \beta_1 x_1 + \beta_2 x_2 + \beta_3 x_1 x_2 + \varepsilon$$

is provided here. Give the prediction equation for this model.

INTERACTION MODEL

MODEL: Y = 7.69667E-3X1 + 0.554111X2 + 1.13333E-4X1*X2 + 54.5CNST

	COEF.	SD. ER.	t(5)	P-VALUE	PT. R SQ.
X1	7.69667E-3	3.23831E-3	2.37675	0.0634195	0.53047
X2	0.554111	0.259963	2.1315	0.08624	0.476072
X1*X2	1.13333E-4	1.67226E-4	0.677727	0.528032	0.084134
CNST	54.5	5.03416	10.826	1.16695E-4	0.959085

R SQ. = 0.964031, ADJ. R SQ. = 0.94245, D. W. = 1.33202
SQ. ROOT MSE = 2.50838, F(3/5) = 44.67 (P-VALUE = 4.93383E-4)

c. Construct a plot similar to the scattergram of part **a**, but use the predicted values from the interaction model on the vertical axis. Compare the two plots. Do you believe the interaction model will provide an adequate fit?

d. Check model adequacy using a statistical test with $\alpha = .05$.

e. Is there evidence of interaction between pressure x_1 and dipping angle x_2? Test using $\alpha = .05$.

f. Based on the result from part **e**, what model would you use to predict oil recovery y?

13.10 Model Building: Second-Order (Quadratic) Models

All of the linear models discussed in the previous sections proposed straight-line relationships between $E(y)$ and each of the independent variables in the model. In this section, we consider models that allow for curvature in the relationships. Each of these models is a **second-order model** because it will include an x^2 term.

First, we consider a special case of the general linear model—a case in which the model includes two terms, each including a single independent variable x. The form of this model, called the **quadratic model**, is

$$y = \beta_0 + \beta_1 x + \beta_2 x^2 + \varepsilon$$

Technically, the quadratic model includes only one independent variable, x, but we can think of the model as a general linear model in two independent variables with $x_1 = x$ and $x_2 = x^2$. The term involving x^2, called a **quadratic term** (or **second-order term**), enables us to hypothesize curvature in the graph of the response model relating y to x. Graphs of the quadratic model for two different values of β_2 are shown in Figure 13.15. When the curve opens upward, the sign of β_2 is positive (see Figure 13.15a); when the curve opens downward, the sign of β_2 is negative (see Figure 13.15b).

FIGURE 13.15

Graphs for Two
Quadratic Models

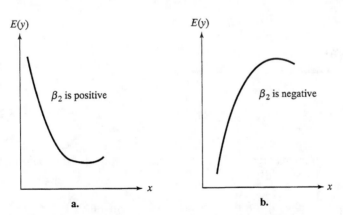

a.

b.

A Quadratic (Second-Order) Model in a Single Quantitative Independent Variable

$$E(y) = \beta_0 + \beta_1 x + \beta_2 x^2$$

where

β_0 is the y-intercept of the curve

β_1 is a shift parameter

β_2 is the rate of curvature

EXAMPLE 13.18
A Quadratic Model

Suppose the property appraiser of Example 13.2 wants to model the relationship between the sale price of a property located in a particular neighborhood and the corresponding appraised improvements value of the property. A random sample of 10 properties in the neighborhood that were sold last year was selected for the analysis. The resulting data are given in Table 13.3.

Table 13.3 Sale Price–Appraised
Improvements Value
for 10 Properties

Sale Price y, dollars	Appraised Improvements x, dollars
48,000	26,563
82,900	58,364
72,000	57,310
126,000	71,486
65,000	45,135
101,000	63,966
43,000	23,459
54,800	40,712
94,000	62,267
108,000	65,718

a. Construct a scattergram for the sale price–appraised improvements value data of Table 13.3.

b. Hypothesize a probabilistic model relating sale price to appraised improvements value for all properties in the neighborhood that were sold last year.

SOLUTION

a. A plot of the data of Table 13.3 is given in Figure 13.16. You can see that the sale price of the properties appears to increase in a curvilinear manner with appraised improvements value.

b. The apparent curvature in the graph relating appraised improvements value, x, to the sale price, y, provides some support for the inclusion of a quadratic term, x^2, in the response model. Thus, we think that the quadratic model

$$y = \beta_0 + \beta_1 x + \beta_2 x^2 + \varepsilon$$

might yield a better prediction equation than one based on the straight-line model of Chapter 12. ■

FIGURE 13.16

Scattergam of the
Sale Price–Appraised
Improvements Data
of Table 13.3

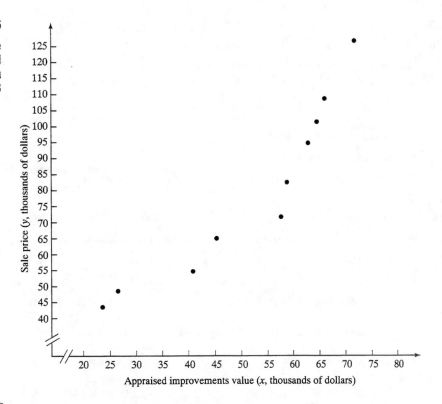

EXAMPLE 13.19
Analyzing the Quadratic
Model

Refer to Example 13.18.

a. Use the method of least squares to estimate the unknown parameters β_0, β_1, and β_2 in the quadratic model relating sale price, y, to appraised improvements value, x, for properties located in the neighborhood.

b. Graph the prediction equation.

c. Interpret the β estimates.

d. Is the overall model useful for predicting sale price y?

e. Is there sufficient evidence of upward curvature in the sale price–appraised improvements relationship?

SOLUTION

a. The quadratic model was fit to the data using SPSS. Part of the output of the SPSS multiple regression routine is reproduced in Figure 13.17. The least squares estimates of the β parameters appear (shaded) in the SPSS column labeled **B**. You can see that $\hat{\beta}_0 = 75{,}769.69820$, $\hat{\beta}_1 = -2.18924$, and $\hat{\beta}_2 = .00004009804$.*

---

*SPSS uses E notation to indicate that the decimal point for the number shown on the printout should be moved right or left. The notation **E − 05** for the value of $\hat{\beta}_2$ requires you to move the decimal 5 places to the left (−). In contrast, **E + 02** requires you to move the decimal 2 places to the right (+).

FIGURE 13.17

SPSS Printout for the
Quadratic Model,
Example 13.19

```
          * * * *   M U L T I P L E   R E G R E S S I O N   * * * *

Equation Number 1     Dependent Variable..    Y

Variable(s) Entered on Step Number
    1..    XX
    2..    X

Multiple R              .98703
R Square                .97422
Adjusted R Square       .96686
Standard Error     5025.82166

Analysis of Variance
                       DF      Sum of Squares       Mean Square
Regression              2     6682828816.80826    3341414408.40413
Residual                7      176812183.19175      25258883.31311

F =      132.28670      Signif F =  .0000


------------------ Variables in the Equation ------------------

Variable              B           SE B         Beta         T    Sig T

XX          4.009804E-05   8.06094E-06     2.286361     4.974   .0016
X              -2.189240       .758504    -1.326609    -2.886   .0234
(Constant)  75769.698201   16234.27331                  4.667   .0023


End Block Number   1    All requested variables entered.
```

Therefore, the equation that minimizes SSE for this data set is

$$\hat{y} = 75{,}769.69820 - 2.18924x + .00004009804x^2$$

b. From Figure 13.18, we see that the graph of the quadratic regression model provides a good fit to the data of Table 13.3.

c. According to the box, the β estimates (rounded) have the following interpretations:

$\hat{\beta}_0 = 75{,}770$ is the estimated y-intercept of the least squares curve shown in Figure 13.18. We also know that $\hat{\beta}_0$ represents the estimate of $E(y)$ when $x = 0$, which is meaningless in this example because a property with an appraised improvements value of $0 is not practical.

$\hat{\beta}_1 = -2.19$ is an estimate of the amount the curve in Figure 13.18 is shifted along the x-axis. This value rarely has a practical interpretation. Note that $\hat{\beta}_1$ is *not* a slope, and should not be interpreted as such.

$\hat{\beta}_2 = .00004$ is an estimate of the amount of curvature in the least squares curve in Figure 13.18. The sign of $\hat{\beta}_2$ is positive, which implies upward curvature in the sale price–appraised improvements relationship. We note here that the small value of $\hat{\beta}_2$ does *not* imply that the curvature is not significant, since the numerical scale of $\hat{\beta}_2$ depends on the scale of measurement. We will test the contribution of the quadratic coefficient in part **e**.

FIGURE 13.18

Graph of the Least
Squares Fit of the
Quadratic Model,
Example 13.19

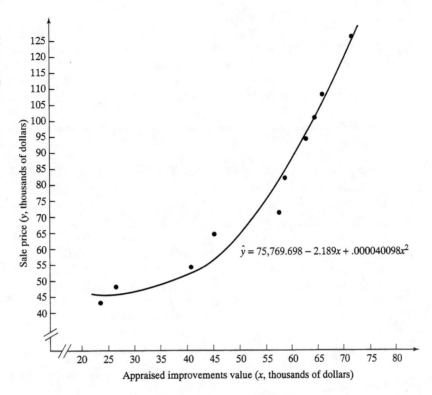

$$\hat{y} = 75,769.698 - 2.189x + .000040098x^2$$

d. To determine whether the overall model is useful for predicting y, we test

H_0: $\beta_1 = \beta_2 = 0$

H_a: At least one $\beta_i \neq 0$

The test statistic, shaded on the printout, is $F = 132.29$ and its associated p-value (also shaded) is approximately 0. Therefore, there is strong evidence of the utility of the model.

e. As noted earlier, β_2 measures the amount of curvature in the response curve. Thus, to determine whether curvature exists in the population, we test the null hypothesis H_0: $\beta_2 = 0$. Since we want to detect upward curvature, the alternative hypothesis is H_a: $\beta_2 > 0$. The t statistic is given on the SPSS printout (Figure 13.17) under the column labeled **T** in the **XX** row. This value (shaded) is $t = 4.974$. The two-tailed observed significance level, given under the **Sig T** column, is .0016. Recall that the p-value for a one-tailed test is half this value: $p = .0016/2 = .0008$. This implies that we will reject H_0 for any α value larger than .0008; thus, there is strong evidence of upward curvature in the population. ■

Note that we did not conduct a t test on β_1 in the quadratic model in Example 13.19. With the quadratic model, β_2 is the most important β (and also the β associated with the highest-order term in the model—namely, x^2) since it controls whether the relationship between y and x is linear or curvilinear. Once curvature has been detected (as in Example 13.19), there is no need to test a β parameter (e.g., β_1) that has no meaningful interpretation and risk making a Type II error unnecessarily.

Warning

Once curvature has been deemed important in the model $E(y) = \beta_0 + \beta_1 x + \beta_2 x^2$, do not conduct a t test on β_1. It is a safe practice to retain the $\beta_1 x$ term in the model regardless of the magnitude of the p-value shown on the printout.

The quadratic model in Example 13.19 is a second-order model in one quantitative independent variable. A second-order model in two quantitative independent variables is shown in the box. Note that the model contains all of the terms in a first-order model and, in addition, the second-order terms involving cross-products (interaction terms) and squares of the independent variables.

A Second-Order Model in Two Quantitative Independent Variables

$$E(y) = \beta_0 + \beta_1 x_1 + \beta_2 x_2 + \beta_3 x_1 x_2 + \beta_4 x_1^2 + \beta_5 x_2^2$$

A three-dimensional graph of the second-order model is shown in Figure 13.19. Note that the shape depends on the signs of the rate of the curvature parameters, β_4 and β_5.

A two-dimensional graph of a second-order model in two quantitative variables will look similar to the graph of a quadratic model, except that there will be one curve for each value of the second independent variable held constant.

FIGURE 13.19

Graphs of Three
Second-Order
Surfaces

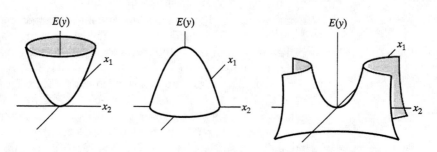

a. β_4 and β_5 positive   **b.** β_4 and β_5 negative   **c.** β_4 negative, β_5 positive

EXAMPLE 13.20
Graphing a Curvilinear
Model

Suppose the mean value $E(y)$ of a response y is related to two quantitative independent variables, x_1 and x_2, by the second-order model

$$E(y) = \beta_0 + \beta_1 x_1 + \beta_2 x_2 + \beta_3 x_1 x_2 + \beta_4 x_1^2 + \beta_5 x_2^2$$

where $\beta_0 = 1$, $\beta_1 = 2$, $\beta_2 = -1$, $\beta_3 = 1$, $\beta_4 = 1$, and $\beta_5 = 3$, i.e.,

$$E(y) = 1 + 2x_1 - x_2 + x_1 x_2 + x_1^2 + 3x_2^2$$

Graph the relationship between $E(y)$ and x_1 for $x_2 = 0$, 1, and 2. Interpret the graph. [*Note:* Since this model contains all of the terms in the interaction model of Example 13.16, we will be able to see the effect of adding terms involving x_1^2 and x_2^2 to the model.]

SOLUTION To reduce the tedium of graphing the three response curves relating $E(y)$ to x_1 for $x_2 = 0$, 1, and 2, we show a computer-generated (SAS) graph of the three curves in Figure 13.20.

The response curves in Figure 13.20 rise (or fall) in a manner similar to the lines shown in Figure 13.11. However, the graphs are curvilinear and the spacing between the curves has changed. These changes were produced by adding the second-order terms (those involving x_1^2 and x_2^2) to the model.   ■

FIGURE 13.20

SAS Graph of
$E(y) = 1 + 2x_1 - x_2$
$+ x_1 x_2 + x_1^2 + 3x_2^2$
for $x_2 = 0, 1, 2$

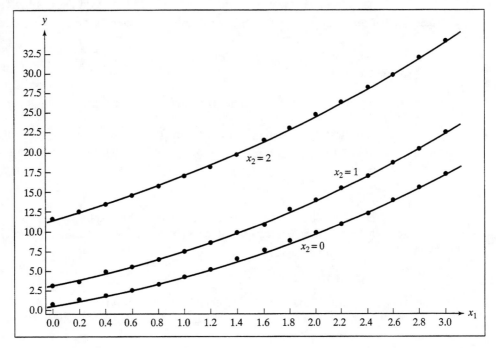

How can you choose an appropriate linear model with one or more quantitative independent variables to fit to a set of data? Since most relationships in the real world are curvilinear (at least to some extent), a good first choice would be a second-order linear model. If you are fairly certain that the relationships between $E(y)$ and the individual independent variables are approximately first-order and that the independent variables do not interact, you could select a first-order model for the data. If you have prior information that suggests there is moderate or very little curvature over the region in which the independent variables are measured, you could use the interaction model. However, keep in mind that for all multiple regression models, the number of data points must exceed the number of parameters in the model. Thus, you may be forced to use a first-order model rather than a second-order model simply because you do not have sufficient data to estimate all of the parameters in the second-order model.

Regression models can also be written to include qualitative independent variables. This topic is the subject of the next section.

EXERCISES

▪ *Learning the Mechanics*

13.29 Graph the following quadratic models side by side on the same sheet of graph paper.
   a. $y = 5 + x^2$
   b. $y = -5 + x^2$
   c. What effect does the change in the constant (β_0) have on the graph of a quadratic model?

13.30 Graph the following quadratic (second-order) models side by side on the same sheet of graph paper.
   a. $y = 1 - 2x + x^2$
   b. $y = 1 + 2x + x^2$
   c. $y = x^2$
   d. What effect does the inclusion of the first-order term $(2x)$ have on the graph of the response curve?
   e. What effect does the sign of the first-order term have on the graph of the response curve?

13.31 Graph the following quadratic models side by side on the same sheet of graph paper.
   a. $y = x^2$
   b. $y = 3x^2$
   c. $y = -x^2$
   d. What effect does the coefficient of x^2 have on the graph of a quadratic model?
   e. What effect does the sign of the coefficient of x^2 have on the graph of a quadratic model?

13.32 Suppose you fit the quadratic model

$$E(y) = \beta_0 + \beta_1 x + \beta_2 x^2$$

to a set of $n = 20$ data points and found $R^2 = .91$, SS(Total) $= 29.24$, and SSE $= 2.63$.
   a. Is there sufficient evidence to indicate that the model contributes information for predicting y? Test using $\alpha = .05$.

b. What null and alternative hypotheses would you test to determine whether upward curvature exists?

c. What null and alternative hypotheses would you test to determine whether downward curvature exists?

13.33 Write a second-order linear model relating the mean value of y, $E(y)$, to:
a. Two quantitative independent variables.
b. Three quantitative independent variables. [*Hint:* Include all possible two-way cross-product terms and squared terms.]

13.34 Consider the second-order model

$$E(y) = 1 + x_1 - x_2 + x_1 x_2 + 2x_1^2 + x_2^2$$

a. Graph the relationship between $E(y)$ and x_1 for $x_2 = 0$, 1, and 2.
b. Are the graphed curves in part **a** first-order or second-order?
c. How do the graphed curves in part **a** relate to each other?

13.35 Suppose you fit the second-order model

$$y = \beta_0 + \beta_1 x_1 + \beta_2 x_2 + \beta_3 x_1 x_2 + \beta_4 x_1^2 + \beta_5 x_2^2 + \varepsilon$$

to $n = 25$ data points and obtain the following values:

$\hat{\beta}_0 = 1.26$ $s_{\hat{\beta}_1} = 1.21$ $\text{SSE} = .41$

$\hat{\beta}_1 = -2.43$ $s_{\hat{\beta}_2} = .16$ $R^2 = .83$

$\hat{\beta}_2 = .05$ $s_{\hat{\beta}_3} = .26$

$\hat{\beta}_3 = .62$ $s_{\hat{\beta}_4} = 1.49$

$\hat{\beta}_4 = -1.81$ $s_{\hat{\beta}_5} = 3.65$

$\hat{\beta}_5 = -2.94$

a. Is there sufficient evidence to indicate that at least one of the parameters, β_1, β_2, β_3, β_4, and β_5, is nonzero? Test using $\alpha = .05$.
b. Test H_0: $\beta_4 = 0$ against H_a: $\beta_4 \neq 0$. Use $\alpha = .05$.
c. Test H_0: $\beta_5 = 0$ against H_a: $\beta_5 \neq 0$. Use $\alpha = .05$.
d. Use graphs to explain the consequences of the tests in parts **b** and **c**.

■ *Applying the Concepts*

13.36 Unions in the United States have officially opposed a free trade agreement with Mexico, fearing a decrease in wages. However, an article in the *Journal of Labor Research* (Spring 1993) used regression analysis to demonstrate that a Mexican free trade agreement will have little influence on union wages and should increase nonunion wages. The model for union wages (y) included the independent variable, years of completed education (x_1), among others.
a. The researcher hypothesized a curvilinear relationship between union wages (y) and education (x_1). Write a model for $E(y)$ as a function of x_1 that incorporates this hypothesis.
b. Refer to the model, part **a**. The researcher also hypothesized that education (x_1) will have

a positive net impact on union wages (y). Specifically, wages (y) will increase with education (x_1), but at a decreasing rate. Explain how to test this hypothesis.

13.37 In the pharmaceutical industry, a new chemical entity (NCE) is defined as a new chemical or biological compound tested in humans for therapeutic purposes for the first time. A study published in *Managerial & Decision Economics* (Sept. 3, 1988) reported that expenditures on research and development (R&D) of NCEs in the United Kingdom has increased dramatically over the 20 years 1964–1984. A plot of R&D expenditures (y) versus year (x) is shown here.

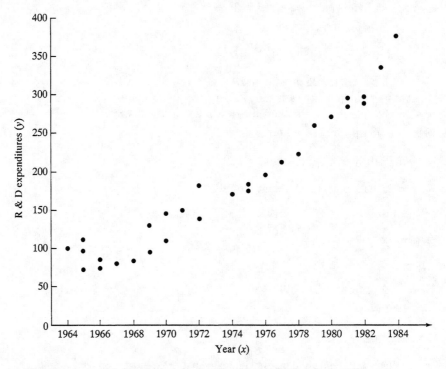

a. Propose a model for $E(y)$ that would seem to fit the data well.

b. What are the expected signs of the β's in the model, part **a**?

13.38 Research on the relationship between job performance and job turnover has yielded conflicting results. Some early studies found a negative relationship (i.e., the lower the performance, the greater the likelihood of turnover) among all types of workers, whereas others detected a positive relationship (i.e., the higher the performance, the greater the likelihood of turnover) among those employed in professional positions. These early studies, however, focused on the linear (first-order) relationship between these variables. The *Journal of Management* (Vol. 12, 1986) investigated the possibility of a curvilinear (second-order) relationship between job performance and turnover both for professional workers (accountants) and for nonprofessional workers (truck drivers). For each sample of workers the quadratic model $E(y) = \beta_0 + \beta_1 x + \beta_2 x^2$ was fit, where

x = Performance rating (1 = poor, ..., 4 = outstanding)

y = Probability of turnover (i.e., likelihood of worker leaving his or her job within 1 year)

The results are shown in the accompanying table.

Accountants (n = 169)	Truck Drivers (n = 107)
$\hat{\beta}_1 = -1.40$ $(t = -3.88)$	$\hat{\beta}_1 = -1.50$ $(t = -3.83)$
$\hat{\beta}_2 = 1.13$ $(t = 3.23)$	$\hat{\beta}_2 = 1.22$ $(t = 4.70)$
$R^2 = .114$	$R^2 = .298$

Source: Jackofsky, E. F., Ferris, K. R., and Breckenridge, B. G. "Evidence for a curvilinear relationship between job performance and turnover." *Journal of Management*, Vol. 12, No. 1, 1986, pp. 105–111.

a. Conduct a test of model adequacy for each of the two groups of workers. Use $\alpha = .05$.
b. Interpret the β estimates for each of the two groups of workers. Which of the $\hat{\beta}$'s have practical interpretations?
c. Is there evidence of upward curvature in the relationship between turnover and performance for accountants? Use $\alpha = .05$. What is the practical implication of this result?
d. Repeat part **c** for truck drivers.

13.39 Regression analysis was used to relate return on assets, y, to market share, x, for a sample of 5,400 businesses (*Business Economics*, Oct. 1984). The main objective of the analysis was to investigate the conventional wisdom in business strategy that "a better market share yields a higher profit." One of the models analyzed in the study was the quadratic model

$$E(y) = \beta_0 + \beta_1 x + \beta_2 x^2$$

The results of the multiple regression are as follows:

$$\hat{y} = .093 + .441x - .409x^2, \quad R^2 = .002, \quad t \text{ (for } \beta_2) = -2.39$$

a. Graph the least squares prediction equation. (Let market share x range from 0% to 60%.)
b. Interpret the value of R^2.
c. Is there sufficient evidence to indicate that market share, x, is a useful predictor of return on assets, y? Test using $\alpha = .05$.
d. As a result of the multiple regression analysis, the study concluded that "profits rise with size (of market share) up to some intermediate level and taper off thereafter." Do you agree with this statement?

13.40 A study reported in *Human Factors* (Apr. 1990) investigated the effects of recognizer accuracy and vocabulary size on the performance of a computerized speech recognition device. Accuracy (x_1) of the device, measured as the percentage of correctly recognized spoken utterances, was set at three levels: 90%, 95%, and 99%. Vocabulary size (x_2), measured as the percentage of words needed for the task, was also set at three levels: 75%, 87.5%, and 100%. The dependent variable of primary interest was task completion time (y, in minutes), measured from when a user of the recognition device spoke the first input until the recognizer displayed the last spoken word of the task. Data collected for $n = 162$ trials were used to fit a complete second-order model for task completion time (y), as a function of the quantitative independent variables accuracy (x_1) and vocabulary (x_2). The coefficient of determination for the model was $R^2 = .75$.

a. Write the complete second-order model for $E(y)$.

b. Interpret the value of R^2.

c. Conduct a test of overall model adequacy. Use $\alpha = .05$.

13.41 "Zoning" is defined as the distribution of vacant land to residential and nonresidential uses via policy set by local governments. Although the negative effects of zoning have been studied (e.g., distorting urban property markets, creating barriers to residential mobility, and impeding economic and social integration), little empirical evidence exists identifying the factors that encourage restrictive zoning practices. A recent study reported in the *Journal of Urban Economics* (Vol. 21, 1987) developed a series of multiple regression models that hypothesize several determinants of zoning. One of the models studied took the following form:

$$E(y) = \beta_0 + \beta_1 x_1 + \beta_2 x_1^2 + \beta_3 x_2$$

where

y = Percentage of vacant land zoned for residential use

x_1 = Proportion of existing land in nonresidential use

x_2 = Proportion of total tax base derived from nonresidential property

The model was fit to data collected for $n = 185$ municipal communities in northeastern New Jersey, with the following results:

Independent Variable	Parameter Estimate	Standard Error of Estimate	t Value	p Value
Intercept	92.26	3.07	30.05	$p < .01$
x_1	−96.35	46.59	−2.07	$p < .05$
x_1^2	166.80	120.88	1.38	$p > .10$
x_2	−75.51	13.35	−5.66	$p < .01$

Adjusted $R^2 = .25$ F = 21.86 (p < .01)

Source: Rolleston, B. S. "Determinants of restrictive suburban zoning: An empirical analysis." *Journal of Urban Economics*, Vol. 21, 1987, p. 15 (Table 4).

a. Construct a 95% confidence interval for β_3. Interpret the result.

b. Test the hypothesis that a curvilinear relationship exists between percentage (y) of land zoned for residential use and proportion (x_1) of existing land in nonresidential use.

c. Is the overall model statistically useful for predicting y?

d. Interpret the adjusted R^2 value.

13.42 Engineers at the University of Massachusetts studied the viability of using semiconductor lasers for solar lighting in spaceborne applications (*Journal of Applied Physics*, Sept. 1993). A series of $n = 8$ experiments with quantum-well lasers yielded the following observations on solar pumping threshold current (y) and waveguide Al mole fraction (x):

Threshold Current, y, A/cm^{-2}	Waveguide Al Mole Fraction, x
273	.15
175	.20
146	.25
166	.30
162	.35
165	.40
245	.50
314	.60

Source: Unnikrishnan, S. and Anderson, N. G. "Quantum-well lasers for direct solar photopumping." *Journal of Applied Physics*, Vol. 74, No. 6, Sept. 15, 1993, p. 4226 (data adapted from Figure 2).

a. The researchers theorize that the relationship between threshold current (y) and waveguide Al composition (x) will be represented by a U-shaped curve. Hypothesize a model that corresponds to this theory.

b. Plot the data points in a scattergram. Comment on the researchers' theory, part **a**.

c. Use the accompanying MINITAB printout to test the theory, part **a**.

```
The regression equation is
Y = 438 - 1684 X + 2502 X*X

Predictor      Coef      Stdev    t-ratio        p
Constant     438.31      60.54       7.24    0.001
X           -1684.3      357.3      -4.71    0.005
X*X          2502.3      470.6       5.32    0.003

s = 25.65      R-sq = 88.0%     R-sq(adj) = 83.2%

Analysis of Variance

SOURCE        DF          SS         MS        F        p
Regression     2       24163      12081    18.37    0.005
Error          5        3289        658
Total          7       27451
```

13.43 In the mid 1800s, the U.S. census inquired about the real property and personal wealth of individual households. Using census information from 1860 and 1870, J. R. Kearl and C. L. Pope examined the mobility of Utah households as measured by their wealth holdings (*The Review of Economics and Statistics*, May 1984). Holding occupation, time of entry into the economy, nativity, gender, place of residence, and internal migration constant, Kearl and Pope fit the quadratic model $E(y) = \beta_0 + \beta_1 x + \beta_2 x^2$, where y is the personal wealth (in dollars) of a Utah household and x is the age (in years) of the head of household. The results of the regression are summarized as follows:

$$\hat{y} = 52.39 + 74.21x - .71x^2$$

$$n > 20{,}000 \qquad t \text{ (for } \beta_1) = 13.79 \qquad t \text{ (for } \beta_2) = -.15$$

a. Graph the least squares prediction equation.

b. Is there evidence of a quadratic relationship in the wealth–age relationship for Utah households during 1860–1870? Test using $\alpha = .10$.

13.11 Model Building: Qualitative (Dummy) Variables

Multiple regression models can also be written to include **qualitative** (or **categorical**) independent variables. Qualitative variables, unlike quantitative variables, cannot be measured on a numerical scale. Therefore, we must code the values of the qualitative variable (called **levels**) as numbers before we can fit the model. These coded qualitative variables are called **dummy variables** since the numbers assigned to the various levels are arbitrarily selected.

EXAMPLE 13.21
Two-Level Dummy Variable Model

A female executive at a certain company claims that male executives earn higher salaries, on average, than female executives with the same education, experience, and responsibilities. To support her claim, she wants to model the salary y of an executive using a qualitative independent variable representing the gender of an executive (male or female).

    a. Write a model for mean executive salary, $E(y)$, using a dummy variable for the gender of an executive.

    b. Interpret the β parameters in the model.

SOLUTION

    a. A convenient method of coding the values of a qualitative variable at two levels involves assigning a value of 1 to one of the levels and a value of 0 to the other. For example, the dummy variable used to describe gender could be coded as follows:

$$x = \begin{cases} 1 & \text{if male} \\ 0 & \text{if female} \end{cases}$$

The choice of which level is assigned to 1 and which is assigned to 0 is arbitrary. The model then takes the following form:

$$E(y) = \beta_0 + \beta_1 x$$

    b. The advantage of using a 0–1 coding scheme is that the β coefficients are easily interpreted. The model in part **a** allows us to compare the mean executive salary $E(y)$ for males with the corresponding mean for females.

Males $(x = 1)$: $E(y) = \beta_0 + \beta_1(1) = \beta_0 + \beta_1$

Females $(x = 0)$: $E(y) = \beta_0 + \beta_1(0) = \beta_0$

First note that β_0 represents the mean salary for females (say, μ_F). When a 0–1 coding convention is used, β_0 will always represent the mean response associated with the level of the qualitative variable assigned the value 0 (called the **base level**). The difference between the mean salary for males and the mean salary for females, $\mu_M - \mu_F$, is represented by β_1—that is,

$$\mu_M - \mu_F = (\beta_0 + \beta_1) - (\beta_0) = \beta_1$$

Therefore, with the 0–1 coding convention, β_1 will always represent the difference between the mean response for the level assigned the value 1 and the mean for the base level. Thus, for the executive salary model, we have

$$\beta_0 = \mu_F$$
$$\beta_1 = \mu_M - \mu_F \quad ■$$

The model relating a mean response $E(y)$ to a qualitative independent variable at two levels is shown in the box.

A Model Relating $E(y)$ to a Qualitative Independent Variable with Two Levels

$$E(y) = \beta_0 + \beta_1 x$$

where

$$x = \begin{cases} 1 & \text{if level A} \\ 0 & \text{if level B} \end{cases}$$

Interpretation of β's:

$\beta_0 = \mu_B$ \quad (Mean for base level)

$\beta_1 = \mu_A - \mu_B$

For models that involve qualitative independent variables at more than two levels, additional dummy variables must be created. In general, the number of dummy variables used to describe a qualitative variable will be one less than the number of levels of the qualitative variable. The box on page 722 presents a model that includes a qualitative independent variable at three levels.

A Model Relating $E(y)$ to a Qualitative Independent Variable with Three Levels

$E(y) = \beta_0 + \beta_1 x_1 + \beta_2 x_2$

where

$$x_1 = \begin{cases} 1 & \text{if level A} \\ 0 & \text{if not} \end{cases} \qquad x_2 = \begin{cases} 1 & \text{if level B} \\ 0 & \text{if not} \end{cases} \qquad \text{Base level} = \text{Level C}$$

Interpretation of β's:

$\beta_0 = \mu_C$ (Mean for base level)

$\beta_1 = \mu_A - \mu_C$

$\beta_2 = \mu_B - \mu_C$

EXAMPLE 13.22
Three-Level Dummy
Variable Model

Refer to the problem of modeling the shipment cost, y, of a regional express delivery service, described in Example 13.17. Suppose we want to model $E(y)$ as a function of cargo type, where cargo type has three levels: fragile, semifragile, and durable. Costs for 15 packages of approximately the same weight and same distance shipped, but different cargo types, are listed in Table 13.4.

Table 13.4   Data for Example 13.22

Package	Cost y	Cargo Type	x_1	x_2
1	$17.20	Fragile	1	0
2	11.10	Fragile	1	0
3	12.00	Fragile	1	0
4	10.90	Fragile	1	0
5	13.80	Fragile	1	0
6	6.50	Semifragile	0	1
7	10.00	Semifragile	0	1
8	11.50	Semifragile	0	1
9	7.00	Semifragile	0	1
10	8.50	Semifragile	0	1
11	2.10	Durable	0	0
12	1.30	Durable	0	0
13	3.40	Durable	0	0
14	7.50	Durable	0	0
15	2.00	Durable	0	0

a. Write a linear model relating $E(y)$ to cargo type.

b. Interpret the β coefficients in the model.

c. A MINITAB printout of the model from part **a** is shown in Figure 13.21. Conduct the F test for overall model utility. Explain the practical significance of the result.

FIGURE 13.21

MINITAB Printout for Dummy Variable Regression, Example 13.22

```
The regression equation is
Y = 3.26 + 9.74 X1 + 5.44 X2

Predictor        Coef       Stdev    t-ratio        p
Constant        3.260       1.075       3.03    0.010
X1              9.740       1.521       6.41    0.000
X2              5.440       1.521       3.58    0.004

s = 2.404      R-sq = 77.4%      R-sq(adj) = 73.7%

Analysis of Variance

SOURCE          DF          SS          MS        F        p
Regression       2      238.25      119.13    20.61    0.000
Error           12       69.37        5.78
Total           14      307.62
```

SOLUTION

a. Since the qualitative variable of interest, cargo type, has three levels, we need to create $(3 - 1) = 2$ dummy variables. First, select (arbitrarily) one of the levels to be the base level—say, durable cargo. Then each of the remaining levels is assigned the value 1 in one of the two dummy variables as follows:

$$x_1 = \begin{cases} 1 & \text{if fragile} \\ 0 & \text{if not} \end{cases} \qquad x_2 = \begin{cases} 1 & \text{if semifragile} \\ 0 & \text{if not} \end{cases}$$

(Note that for the base level, durable cargo, $x_1 = x_2 = 0$.) Then the appropriate model is

$$E(y) = \beta_0 + \beta_1 x_1 + \beta_2 x_2$$

b. To interpret the β's, first write the mean shipment cost $E(y)$ for each of the three cargo types as a function of the β's:

Fragile $(x_1 = 1, x_2 = 0)$:

$$E(y) = \beta_0 + \beta_1(1) + \beta_2(0) = \beta_0 + \beta_1 = \mu_F$$

Semifragile $(x_1 = 0, x_2 = 1)$:

$$E(y) = \beta_0 + \beta_1(0) + \beta_2(1) = \beta_0 + \beta_2 = \mu_S$$

Durable $(x_1 = 0, x_2 = 0)$:

$$E(y) = \beta_0 + \beta_1(0) + \beta_2(0) = \beta_0 = \mu_D$$

Then we have

$$\beta_0 = \mu_D \quad \text{(Mean of the base level)}$$

$$\beta_1 = \mu_F - \mu_D$$

$$\beta_2 = \mu_S - \mu_D$$

Note that the β's associated with the nonbase levels of cargo type (fragile and semifragile) represent differences between a pair of means. As always, β_0 represents a single mean—the mean response for the base level (durable).

c. The F test for overall model utility tests the null hypothesis

$$H_0: \quad \beta_1 = \beta_2 = 0$$

Note that $\beta_1 = 0$ implies that $\mu_F = \mu_D$, and $\beta_2 = 0$ implies that $\mu_S = \mu_D$. Therefore, $\beta_1 = \beta_2 = 0$ implies that $\mu_F = \mu_S = \mu_D$. Thus, a test for model utility is equivalent to a test for equality of means, i.e.,

$$H_0: \quad \mu_F = \mu_S = \mu_D$$

From the MINITAB printout in Figure 13.21, $F = 20.61$. Since the p-value of the test (.000) is less than $\alpha = .05$, the null hypothesis is rejected. Thus, there is evidence of a difference between any two of the three mean shipment costs; that is, cargo type is a useful predictor of shipment cost y. ▪

The linear models described in Sections 13.9–13.11 form the basis for building models with quantitative independent variables and models with qualitative independent variables. More complex models, such as those with interactions between qualitative variables and those with both quantitative and qualitative variables (including interactions), may be required in practice, however.

EXERCISES

▪ Learning the Mechanics

13.44 Write a model relating $E(y)$ to a qualitative independent variable with two levels, A and B. Interpret the β parameters.

13.45 Write a model relating $E(y)$ to a qualitative independent variable with four levels, A, B, C, and D. Interpret the β parameters.

13.46 Consider the model relating $E(y)$ to a qualitative variable with three levels:

$$E(y) = \beta_0 + \beta_1 x_1 + \beta_2 x_2$$

where

$$x_1 = \begin{cases} 1 & \text{if level 1} \\ 0 & \text{if not} \end{cases} \qquad x_2 = \begin{cases} 1 & \text{if level 2} \\ 0 & \text{if not} \end{cases} \qquad \text{Base level} = \text{level 3}$$

The model was fit to $n = 100$ data points with the following result:

$$\hat{y} = 42.7 + 18.3x_1 - 7.7x_2$$

a. Estimate $E(y)$ when the qualitative variable is set at level 1.
b. Estimate $E(y)$ when the qualitative variable is set at level 2.
c. Estimate $E(y)$ when the qualitative variable is set at level 3.
d. Interpret $\hat{\beta}_0$, $\hat{\beta}_1$ and $\hat{\beta}_2$.
e. How would you test the hypothesis that $E(y)$ is the same for all three levels of the qualitative variable?

13.47 Consider the model relating $E(y)$ to a qualitative variable with five levels:

$$E(y) = \beta_0 + \beta_1 x_1 + \beta_2 x_2 + \beta_3 x_3 + \beta_4 x_4$$

where

$$x_1 = \begin{cases} 1 & \text{if level 1} \\ 0 & \text{if not} \end{cases} \qquad x_2 = \begin{cases} 1 & \text{if level 2} \\ 0 & \text{if not} \end{cases} \qquad x_3 = \begin{cases} 1 & \text{if level 3} \\ 0 & \text{if not} \end{cases}$$

$$x_4 = \begin{cases} 1 & \text{if level 4} \\ 0 & \text{if not} \end{cases} \qquad \text{Base level} = \text{level 5}$$

The model was fit to $n = 20$ data points with the following results:

$$\hat{y} = 20 - 5.6x_1 + 11.2x_2 - 1.7x_3 - 9.0x_4$$

$$\text{SSE} = 662 \qquad \text{SS(Total)} = 1{,}043$$

a. Interpret the estimates of the β parameters.
b. Interpret the following hypotheses in terms of the means of the five levels:

$$H_0: \quad \beta_1 = \beta_2 = \beta_3 = \beta_4 = 0$$

$$H_a: \quad \text{At least one } \beta \neq 0$$

c. Conduct the test specified in part **b**. Use $\alpha = .05$.

▪ *Applying the Concepts*

13.48 Refer to the *Accounting and Business Research* study of external audit fees, Exercise 13.8. In addition to the six quantitative independent variables, the following three qualitative predictors (with levels in parentheses) were used in a model of audit fee (y): opinion ("subject to" or not), industry (regulated or nonregulated), and firm type (Big 8 or non–Big-8 auditor).

a. Set up dummy variables for these three qualitative predictors.

b. Write. a model for audit fee (y) as a function of the three qualitative variables.

c. Interpret the β coefficients in the model, part **b**.

13.49 Refer to the *Real Estate Appraiser* study, Exercise 13.11. Interpret the 95% confidence intervals associated with the independent variables: back to woods, fence, screen porch, in-ground pool, garage, updated kitchen, remodeled kitchen, and skylights. [*Note:* Each of these variables is a dummy variable coded as 1 if yes and 0 if no.]

13.50 Refer to the *Academy of Management* (Mar. 1989) study of the relationship between wives' employment and husbands' well-being, Exercise 11.39. The researchers also used regression to analyze the data. The model $E(y) = \beta_0 + \beta_1 x$ was fit to data collected for $n = 413$ professional accountants, where y = husband's job satisfaction (measured on a 5-point scale) and x is a dummy variable for employment status of wife (1 = employed, 0 = unemployed).

a. The estimate of β_1 was negative and statistically significant at $\alpha = .01$. Interpret these results.

b. The value of the coefficient of determination was $R^2 = .02$. Interpret this result.

13.51 Refer to the *Journal of Labor Research* study of union wages, Exercise 13.36. The model for union wages (y) also included several qualitative independent variables. For example, the researcher wanted to account for differences in union wages across seven geographic regions: Great Lakes, Southeast, Southwest, Plains States, Rocky Mountains, Pacific, and Northeast.

a. Using Northeast as the base level, set up the dummy variables for regions.

b. Incorporate the dummy variables of part **a** into a model for union wages (y).

c. Interpret the β coefficients of the model, part **b**.

13.52 Because of the hot, humid weather conditions in Florida, the growth rates of beef cattle and the milk production of dairy cows typically decline during the summer. However, agricultural and environmental engineers have found that a well-designed shade structure can significantly increase the milk production of dairy cows. In one experiment, 30 cows were selected and divided into three groups of 10 cows each. Group 1 cows were provided with a man-made structure, group 2 cows with tree shade, and group 3 cows with no shade. Of interest was the mean milk production (in gallons) of the cows in each group.

a. Identify the independent variables in the experiment.

b. Write a model relating the mean milk production, $E(y)$, to the independent variables. Identify and code all dummy variables.

c. Interpret the β parameters of the model.

13.53 An article in *Financial Management* (Winter 1992) focused on an analysis of wealth gains and losses between buying-firm shareholders and selling-firm shareholders. In one portion of the study, the cumulative abnormal returns (y) of matched pairs of sellers and buyers of $n = 278$ firms was regressed against two independent variables:

$$x_1 = \begin{cases} 1 & \text{if price disclosed at sell-off announcement} \\ 0 & \text{if not} \end{cases}$$

$$x_2 = \begin{cases} 1 & \text{if divesting firm downgraded prior to sell-off announcement} \\ 0 & \text{if not} \end{cases}$$

Initially, the model $E(y) = \beta_0 + \beta_1 x_1 + \beta_2 x_2$ was fit to the data.

a. Give a practical interpretation of β_1 in the model.

b. Give a practical interpretation of β_2 in the model.

c. Now consider the interaction model, $E(y) = \beta_0 + \beta_1 x_1 + \beta_2 x_2 + \beta_3 x_1 x_2$. Repeat parts **a** and **b** for this model. [*Hint:* Interpret β_1 at the $x_2 = 0$ level; interpret β_2 at the $x_1 = 0$ level.]

13.54 The liquefaction of coal is a major contributor of synthetic fuels. An experiment was conducted to evaluate the performance of a diesel engine run on synthetic (coal-derived) and petroleum-derived fuel oil (*Journal of Energy Resources Technology*, Mar. 1990). The petroleum-derived fuel used was a number 2 diesel fuel (DF-2) obtained from Phillips Chemical Company. Two synthetic fuels were used: a blended fuel (50% coal-derived and 50% DF-2) and a blended fuel with advanced timing. The brake power (kW) and fuel type were varied in test runs, and engine performance was measured. The accompanying table gives the experimental results for the performance measure, mass burning rate per degree of crank angle. Initially, the researchers fit the first-order, main effects model

$$E(y) = \beta_0 + \beta_1 x_1 + \beta_2 x_2 + \beta_3 x_3$$

where

$y = $ Mass burning rate

$x_1 = $ Brake power

$$x_2 = \begin{cases} 1 & \text{if DF-2 fuel} \\ 0 & \text{if not} \end{cases}$$

$$x_3 = \begin{cases} 1 & \text{if blended fuel} \\ 0 & \text{if not} \end{cases}$$

Interpret the results shown in the MINITAB printout on page 728.

Brake Power x_1	Fuel Type	Mass Burning Rate y
4	DF-2	13.2
4	Blended	17.5
4	Advanced Timing	17.5
6	DF-2	26.1
6	Blended	32.7
6	Advanced Timing	43.5
8	DF-2	25.9
8	Blended	46.3
8	Advanced Timing	45.6
10	DF-2	30.7
10	Blended	50.8

(*continued*)

Brake Power x_1	Fuel Type	Mass Burning Rate y
10	Advanced Timing	68.9
12	DF-2	32.3
12	Blended	57.1

Source: Litzinger, T. A. and Buzza, T. G. "Performance and emissions of a diesel engine using a coal-derived fuel." *Journal of Energy Resources Technology*, Vol. 112, Mar. 1990, p. 32 (Table 3).

```
The regression equation is
Y = 13.3 + 4.36 X1 - 22.6 X2 - 7.36 X3

Predictor      Coef       Stdev     t-ratio         p
Constant      13.320      6.931        1.92     0.084
X1             4.3650     0.8057       5.42     0.000
X2           -22.600      5.464       -4.14     0.002
X3            -7.360      5.464       -1.35     0.208

s = 8.057       R-sq = 81.2%      R-sq(adj) = 75.6%

Analysis of Variance

SOURCE       DF         SS          MS        F        p
Regression    3     2807.90      935.97    14.42    0.001
Error        10      649.09       64.91
Total        13     3456.99

SOURCE       DF     SEQ SS
X1            1     1603.93
X2            1     1086.22
X3            1      117.76

Unusual Observations
Obs.      X1         Y      Fit Stdev.Fit  Residual   St.Resid
  3      4.0     17.50    30.78     4.70    -13.28      -2.03R

R denotes an obs. with a large st. resid.
```

13.12 Model Building: Comparing Nested Models

To be successful model builders, we require a statistical method that will allow us to determine (with a high degree of confidence) which one among a set of candidate models best fits the data. In this section, we present such a technique for **nested models**.

Definition 13.2

Two models are **nested** if one model contains all the terms of the second model and at least one additional term. The more complex of the two models is called the **complete** model, and the simpler of the two is called the **reduced** model.

EXAMPLE 13.23
Nested Models

In Example 13.17, we fit the straight-line interaction model for the mean shipment cost $E(y)$ of an express delivery package as a function of two quantitative variables: package weight, x_1, and distance shipped, x_2. The interaction model was

$$E(y) = \beta_0 + \beta_1 x_1 + \beta_2 x_2 + \beta_3 x_1 x_2$$

If we assume that the relationship between shipment cost (y), package weight (x_1), and distance shipped (x_2) is curvilinear, then the quadratic model is more appropriate:

$$E(y) = \beta_0 + \beta_1 x_1 + \beta_2 x_2 + \beta_3 x_1 x_2 + \beta_4 x_1^2 + \beta_5 x_2^2$$

Determine whether these two models are nested models.

SOLUTION Note that the curvilinear model contains quadratic terms for x_1 and x_2, as well as the terms in the interaction model. Therefore, the models are nested models. In this case, the interaction model is nested within the more complex curvilinear model. Thus, the curvilinear model is the **complete** model and the interaction model is the **reduced** model. ■

EXAMPLE 13.24
H_0 for Comparing Nested Models

Refer to Example 13.23. Suppose we want to determine whether the more complex curvilinear model contributes more information for the prediction of y than the interaction model. Propose the null and alternative hypotheses that will allow us to compare these two models.

SOLUTION If the curvilinear model *does not* contribute additional information for the prediction of y, then the two quadratic terms in the model are not necessary. Consequently, we carry out the test of the hypothesis that the parameters for the quadratic terms, x_1^2 and x_2^2, equal 0:

H_0: $\beta_4 = \beta_5 = 0$

H_a: At least one of the two parameters, β_4 and β_5, is nonzero

The terms being tested are those additional terms in the complete (curvilinear) model that are not in the reduced (interaction) model. ■

In Section 13.5, we presented both the t test for a single coefficient and the F test for *all* the β parameters (except β_0) in the model. We now need a test for a *subset* of the β parameters in the complete model. The test procedure is intuitive. First, we use the method of least squares to fit the reduced model, and calculate the corresponding sum of squares for error, SSE_R (the sum of squares of the deviations between observed and predicted y-values). Next, we fit the complete model, and calculate its sum of squares for error, SSE_C. Then, we compare SSE_R to SSE_C by calculating the difference, $SSE_R - SSE_C$. If the additional terms in the complete model are significant, then SSE_C should be much smaller than SSE_R, and the difference $SSE_R - SSE_C$ will be large.

Since SSE will always decrease when new terms are added to the model, the question is whether the difference $SSE_R - SSE_C$ is large enough to conclude that it is due to more than just an increase in the number of model terms and to chance. The formal statistical test utilizes an F statistic, as shown in the box.

F Test for Comparing Nested Models

    Reduced model: $E(y) = \beta_0 + \beta_1 x_1 + \cdots + \beta_g x_g$

    Complete model: $E(y) = \beta_0 + \beta_1 x_1 + \cdots + \beta_g x_g + \beta_{g+1} x_{g+1}$
                                  $+ \cdots + \beta_k x_k$

H_0: $\beta_{g+1} = \beta_{g+2} = \cdots = \beta_k = 0$

H_a: At least one of the β parameters under test is nonzero.

    Test statistic: $$F = \frac{(SSE_R - SSE_C)/(k - g)}{SSE_C/[n - (k + 1)]}$$

$$= \frac{(SSE_R - SSE_C)/\#\beta\text{'s tested in } H_0}{MSE_C}$$

where

  SSE_R = Sum of squared errors for the reduced model

  SSE_C = Sum of squared errors for the complete model

  MSE_C = Mean square error (s^2) for the complete model

  $k - g$ = Number of β parameters specified in H_0 (i.e., number of β parameters tested)

  $k + 1$ = Number of β parameters in the complete model (including β_0)

      n = Total sample size

  Rejection region: $F > F_\alpha$

where F in based on $v_1 = k - g$ numerator degrees of freedom and $v_2 = n - (k + 1)$ denominator degrees of freedom.

When the assumptions listed in Section 13.2 about the random error term are satisfied, this F statistic has an F distribution with v_1 and v_2 df. Note that v_1 is the number of β parameters being tested and v_2 is the number of degrees of freedom associated with s^2 in the complete model.

<table>
<tr><td>**EXAMPLE 13.25**
Applying the Nested F Test</td><td>In Example 13.17, we fit the interaction model for a set of $n = 20$ data points relating shipment cost to package weight and distance shipped. The SAS printout for this model is shown in Figure 13.22. Figure 13.23 shows the SAS printout for the curvilinear model fit to the same $n = 20$ data points. Referring to the printouts, we find the following:</td></tr>
</table>

Straight-line interaction model (reduced model):

   $SSE_R = 6.63331$ (see Figure 13.22)

Curvilinear model (complete model):

   $SSE_C = 2.74474$ (see Figure 13.23)

FIGURE 13.22

SAS Printout for the
Interaction Model of
Example 13.25

Analysis of Variance

Source	DF	Sum of Squares	Mean Square	F Value	Prob>F
Model	3	445.45219	148.48406	358.154	0.0001
Error	16	6.63331	0.41458		
C Total	19	452.08550			

Root MSE	0.64388	R-Square	0.9853	
Dep Mean	6.33500	Adj R-Sq	0.9826	
C.V.	10.16385			

Parameter Estimates

Variable	DF	Parameter Estimate	Standard Error	T for H0: Parameter=0	Prob > |T|
INTERCEP	1	-0.140501	0.64810001	-0.217	0.8311
X1	1	0.019088	0.15821160	0.121	0.9055
X2	1	0.007721	0.00390568	1.977	0.0656
X1X2	1	0.007796	0.00089766	8.684	0.0001

FIGURE 13.23

SAS Printout for the
Curvilinear Model of
Example 13.25

Analysis of Variance

Source	DF	Sum of Squares	Mean Square	F Value	Prob>F
Model	5	449.34076	89.86815	458.388	0.0001
Error	14	2.74474	0.19605		
C Total	19	452.08550			

Root MSE	0.44278	R-square	0.9939	
Dep Mean	6.33500	Adj R-sq	0.9918	
C.V.	6.98940			

Parameter Estimates

Variable	DF	Parameter Estimate	Standard Error	T for H0: Parameter=0	Prob > |T|
INTERCEP	1	0.827016	0.70228935	1.178	0.2586
X1	1	-0.609137	0.17990408	-3.386	0.0044
X2	1	0.004021	0.00799842	0.503	0.6230
X1X2	1	0.007327	0.00063743	11.495	0.0001
X1SQ	1	0.089751	0.02020542	4.442	0.0006
X2SQ	1	0.000015070	0.00002243	0.672	0.5127

Test the null hypothesis that the quadratic terms in the curvilinear model do not contribute information for the prediction of y.

SOLUTION The test statistic (from the box) is

$$F = \frac{(\text{SSE}_R - \text{SSE}_C)/2}{\text{SSE}_C/(20 - 6)} = \frac{(6.63331 - 2.74474)/2}{2.74474/14} = \frac{1.94428}{.19605} = 9.92$$

In this case, the F distribution depends on $v_1 = 2$ numerator df (since we are testing two β's in H_0) and $v_2 = 14$ denominator df (the df for error in the complete model). The critical value of F for $\alpha = .05$, $v_1 = 2$, and $v_2 = 14$ is found in Table 9 (Appendix B) to be

$$F_{.05} = 3.74$$

Thus, we will reject H_0 if $F > 3.74$ (see Figure 13.24). Since the test statistic, $F = 9.92$, exceeds 3.74, we are confident in concluding that the quadratic terms contribute to the prediction of y, shipment cost per package. The curvature terms should be retained in the model. ■

FIGURE 13.24

Rejection Region for the F Test of H_0: $\beta_4 = \beta_5 = 0$

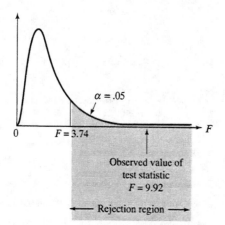

The nested model F test described previously can be used to determine whether *any* subset of terms should be included in a complete model by testing the null hypothesis that a particular set of β parameters simultaneously equals 0. For example, we may want to test to determine whether a set of interaction terms for quantitative variables or a set of main effect terms for a qualitative variable should be included in a model. If we reject H_0, the complete model is the better of the two nested models.

Suppose the F test in Example 13.25 yielded a test statistic that did not fall in the rejection region. Although we must be cautious about accepting H_0, most practitioners of regression analysis adopt the principle of **parsimony**. That is, in situations where two competing models are found to have essentially the same predictive power (as in this case), the model with the fewer number of β's (i.e., the more parsimonious model) is selected. Based on this principle, we would drop the two quadratic terms and select the straight-line interaction (reduced) model over the curvilinear (complete) model.

Definition 13.3

A **parsimonious model** is a general linear model with a small number of β parameters. In situations where two competing models have essentially the same predictive power (as determined by an F test), choose the more parsimonious of the two.

When the candidate models in model building are nested models, the F test developed in this section is the appropriate procedure to apply to compare the models. However, if the models are not nested, this F test is not applicable. In this situation, the analyst must base the choice of the best model on statistics such as R_a^2 and s. It is important to remember that decisions based on these and other numerical descriptive measures of model adequacy cannot be supported with a measure of reliability and are often very subjective in nature.

EXERCISES

■ Learning the Mechanics

13.55 Determine which pairs of the following models are "nested" models. For each pair of nested models, identify the complete and reduced model.

a. $E(y) = \beta_0 + \beta_1 x_1 + \beta_2 x_2$

b. $E(y) = \beta_0 + \beta_1 x_1$

c. $E(y) = \beta_0 + \beta_1 x_1 + \beta_2 x_1^2$

d. $E(y) = \beta_0 + \beta_1 x_1 + \beta_2 x_2 + \beta_3 x_1 x_2$

e. $E(y) = \beta_0 + \beta_1 x_1 + \beta_2 x_2 + \beta_3 x_1 x_2 + \beta_4 x_1^2 + \beta_5 x_2^2$

13.56 Suppose you fit the interaction model

$$E(y) = \beta_0 + \beta_1 x_1 + \beta_2 x_2 + \beta_3 x_3 + \beta_4 x_1 x_2 + \beta_5 x_1 x_3 + \beta_6 x_2 x_3$$

to $n = 25$ data points and obtain SSE $= 6,000$.

a. Give the reduced model appropriate for testing the null hypothesis

$$H_0: \quad \beta_4 = \beta_5 = \beta_6 = 0$$

b. Suppose the reduced model of part **a** resulted in SSE $= 8,500$. Calculate the value of the test statistic.

c. Find the rejection region for the test of part **a**. Use $\alpha = .05$.

d. Use the results of parts **b** and **c** to make the appropriate conclusion.

13.57 Consider the second-order model relating $E(y)$ to three quantitative independent variables, x_1, x_2, and x_3:

$$E(y) = \beta_0 + \beta_1 x_1 + \beta_2 x_2 + \beta_3 x_3 + \beta_4 x_1 x_2 + \beta_5 x_1 x_3 + \beta_6 x_2 x_3 + \beta_7 x_1^2 + \beta_8 x_2^2 + \beta_9 x_3^2$$

a. Specify the parameters involved in a test of the hypothesis that no curvature exists in the response surface.

b. State the hypothesis of part **a** in terms of the model parameters.

c. What hypothesis would you test to determine whether x_3 is useful for the prediction of $E(y)$?

■ *Applying the Concepts*

13.58 Refer to the *Journal of Personal Selling & Sales Management* (Summer 1990) study of gender differences in the industrial sales force, Exercise 12.48. Recall that a sample of 244 male sales managers and a sample of 155 female sales managers participated in the survey. One objective of the research was to assess how supervisory behavior affects intrinsic job satisfaction. Initially, the researchers fit the following reduced model to the data on each gender group:

$$E(y) = \beta_0 + \beta_1 x_1 + \beta_2 x_2 + \beta_3 x_3 + \beta_4 x_4$$

where

$y =$ Intrinsic job satisfaction (measured on a scale of 0 to 40)

$x_1 =$ Age (years)

$x_2 =$ Education level (years)

$x_3 =$ Firm experience (months)

$x_4 =$ Sales experience (months)

To determine the effects of supervisory behavior, four variables (all measured on a scale of 0 to 50) were added to the model: $x_5 =$ contingent reward behavior, $x_6 =$ noncontingent reward behavior, $x_7 =$ contingent punishment behavior, and $x_8 =$ noncontingent punishment behavior. Thus, the complete model is

$$E(y) = \beta_0 + \beta_1 x_1 + \beta_2 x_2 + \beta_3 x_3 + \beta_4 x_4 + \beta_5 x_5 + \beta_6 x_6 + \beta_7 x_7 + \beta_8 x_8$$

a. For each gender, specify the null hypothesis and rejection region ($\alpha = .05$) for testing whether any of the four supervisory behavior variables affect intrinsic job satisfaction.

b. The R^2 values for the four models (reduced and complete model for both samples) are given in the accompanying table. Interpret the results. For each gender, does it appear that the supervisory behavior variables have an impact on intrinsic job satisfaction? Explain.

| | R^2 | |
Model	Males	Females
Reduced	.218	.268
Complete	.408	.496

Source: Schul, P. L. et al. "Assessing gender differences in relationships between supervisory behaviors and job-related outcomes in the industrial sales force." *Journal of Personal Selling & Sales Management*, Vol. X, Summer 1990, p. 9 (Table 4).

c. The F statistics for comparing the two models are: $F_{\text{males}} = 13.00$ and $F_{\text{females}} = 9.05$. Conduct the tests, part **a**, and interpret the results.

13.59 Refer to the *Journal of Energy and Resources Technology* study of diesel engines, Exercise 13.54. Recall that the researchers fit the model

$$E(y) = \beta_0 + \beta_1 x_1 + \beta_2 x_2 + \beta_3 x_3$$

where

$y = $ Mass burning rate

$x_1 = $ Brake power

$$x_2 = \begin{cases} 1 & \text{if DF-2 fuel} \\ 0 & \text{if not} \end{cases}$$

$$x_3 = \begin{cases} 1 & \text{if blended fuel} \\ 0 & \text{if not} \end{cases}$$

```
The regression equation is
Y = - 10.8 + 7.82 X1 + 19.4 X2 + 12.8 X3 - 5.68 X1X2 - 2.95 X1X3

Predictor      Coef       Stdev     t-ratio       p
Constant    -10.830       8.277      -1.31     0.227
X1            7.815       1.126       6.94     0.000
X2           19.35       10.69        1.81     0.108
X3           12.79       10.69        1.20     0.266
X1X2         -5.675       1.380      -4.11     0.003
X1X3         -2.950       1.380      -2.14     0.065

s = 5.037      R-sq = 94.1%     R-sq(adj) = 90.5%

Analysis of Variance

SOURCE       DF         SS          MS         F         P
Regression    5     3253.98      650.80     25.65     0.000
Error         8      203.01       25.38
Total        13     3456.99

SOURCE       DF      SEQ SS
X1            1     1603.93
X2            1     1086.22
X3            1      117.76
X1X2          1      330.04
X1X3          1      116.03
```

The interaction model

$$E(y) = \beta_0 + \beta_1 x_1 + \beta_2 x_2 + \beta_3 x_3 + \beta_4 x_1 x_2 + \beta_5 x_1 x_3$$

was also fit using MINITAB, with the results shown in the accompanying printout. Conduct a test to determine whether brake power and fuel type interact. Test using $\alpha = .01$.

13.60 Research was recently undertaken to examine the effect of the several factors on managerial performance (*Journal of Vocational Behavior*, Oct. 1986). A sample of 100 management personnel from several divisions within a government agency took part in the study. Each manager completed a questionnaire designed to measure the following variables:

y = Performance rating (1 = unacceptable, ..., 5 = outstanding)

$$x_1 = \begin{cases} 1 & \text{if male} \\ 0 & \text{if female} \end{cases}$$

x_2 = Job tenure (years)

x_3 = Manager–subordinate work relationship rating (1 = unsatisfactory, ..., 5 = excellent)

x_4 = Effort level (average number of hours per week invested in job)

$$x_5 = \begin{cases} 1 & \text{if middle/upper-level manager} \\ 0 & \text{if lower-level manager} \end{cases}$$

x_6 = Subordinate-related managerial behavior score (low scores indicate little or no effort spent on counseling, evaluating, and training subordinates)

The data collected on the 100 managers were used to fit several regression models of managerial performance.

a. Initially, the model

$$E(y) = \beta_0 + \beta_1 x_1 + \beta_2 x_2 + \beta_3 x_3 + \beta_4 x_4$$

was considered to account for the influence of gender, job tenure, manager–subordinate work relationship, and effort level on performance rating. For this model, SSE = 352 and $R^2 = .11$. Calculate the F statistic for testing model adequacy. Is the model useful for predicting performance rating y? (Use $\alpha = .05$)

b. Terms for managerial level and subordinate-related behavior (i.e., $\beta_5 x_5 + \beta_6 x_6$) were added to the model of part **a**, resulting in SSE = 341 and $R^2 = .14$. Do these terms contribute additional information for the prediction of performance rating y? (Test using $\alpha = .05$.)

c. A third model was also considered:

$$E(y) = \beta_0 + \beta_1 x_1 + \beta_2 x_2 + \beta_3 x_3 + \beta_4 x_4 + \beta_5 x_5 + \beta_6 x_6 + \beta_7 x_5 x_6$$

The model resulted in SSE = 321 and $R^2 = .19$. Test the hypothesis that the interaction between managerial level (x_5) and subordinate-related behavior (x_6) is not important, i.e., test $H_0: \beta_7 = 0$. Use $\alpha = .05$.

d. Interpret the result of part **c** in terms of the problem.

13.61 Since 1978, when the U.S. airline industry was deregulated, researchers have questioned whether the deregulation has ensured a truly competitive environment. If so, the profitability of any major airline would be related only the overall industry conditions (e.g., disposable income and market share) but not to any unchanging feature of that airline. This "profitability" hypothesis was tested in *Transportation Journal* (Winter 1990) using multiple regression. Data for $n = 234$ carrier-years were used to fit the model

$$E(y) = \beta_0 + \beta_1 x_1 + \beta_2 x_2 + \beta_3 x_3 + \cdots + \beta_{30} x_{30}$$

where

y = Profit rate

x_1 = Real personal disposable income

x_2 = Industry market share

x_3–x_{30}: Dummy variables (coded 0–1) for the 29 air carriers investigated in the study

The results of the regression analysis are summarized in the table. Interpret the results. Is the "profitability" hypothesis supported?

Variable	β Estimate	t Value	p-Value
Intercept	1.2642	.09	.9266
x_1	−.0022	−.99	.8392
x_2	4.8405	3.57	.0003
x_3–x_{30}	(not given)	—	—

$R^2 = .3402$ $F(\text{Model}) = 3.49$, p-value $= .0001$
$F(\text{Carrier dummies}) = 3.59$, p-value $= .0001$

Source: Leigh, L. E. "Contestability in deregulated airline markets: Some empirical tests." *Transportation Journal,* Winter 1990, p. 55, (Table 4).

13.62 Consider the problem of modeling the price charged for motor transport service (such as trucking) in a particular state. In the early 1980s, several states removed regulatory constraints on the rate charged for intrastate trucking services. (Florida was the first state to embark on a deregulation policy on July 1, 1980). One of the goals of the regression analysis is to assess the impact of state deregulation on the supply price y charged per ton-mile. The following independent variables were selected:

x_1 = Distance shipped

x_2 = Weight of product

$$x_3 = \begin{cases} 1 & \text{if deregulation in effect} \\ 0 & \text{if not} \end{cases} \qquad x_4 = \begin{cases} 1 & \text{if large market} \\ 0 & \text{if small market} \end{cases}$$

Data collected for $n = 132$ shipments were used to fit the three models shown here. The results are summarized in the table.

MODEL 1. $E(y) = \beta_0 + \beta_1 x_1 + \beta_2 x_2 + \beta_3 x_1 x_2 + \beta_4 x_1^2 + \beta_5 x_2^2 + \beta_6 x_3 + \beta_7 x_4 + \beta_8 x_3 x_4$
$\qquad + \beta_9 x_1 x_3 + \beta_{10} x_1 x_4 + \beta_{11} x_1 x_3 x_4 + \beta_{12} x_2 x_3 + \beta_{13} x_2 x_4 + \beta_{14} x_2 x_3 x_4$
$\qquad + \beta_{15} x_1 x_2 x_3 + \beta_{16} x_1 x_2 x_4 + \beta_{17} x_1 x_2 x_3 x_4 + \beta_{18} x_1^2 x_3 + \beta_{19} x_1^2 x_4$
$\qquad + \beta_{20} x_1^2 x_3 x_4 + \beta_{21} x_2^2 x_3 + \beta_{22} x_2^2 x_4 + \beta_{23} x_2^2 x_3 x_4$

MODEL 2. $E(y) = \beta_0 + \beta_1 x_1 + \beta_2 x_2 + \beta_3 x_1 x_2 + \beta_4 x_3 + \beta_5 x_4 + \beta_6 x_3 x_4 + \beta_7 x_1 x_3$
$\qquad + \beta_8 x_1 x_4 + \beta_9 x_1 x_3 x_4 + \beta_{10} x_2 x_3 + \beta_{11} x_2 x_4 + \beta_{12} x_2 x_3 x_4 + \beta_{13} x_1 x_2 x_3$
$\qquad + \beta_{14} x_1 x_2 x_4 + \beta_{15} x_1 x_2 x_3 x_4$

MODEL 3. $E(y) = \beta_0 + \beta_1 x_1 + \beta_2 x_2 + \beta_3 x_1 x_2 + \beta_4 x_3 + \beta_5 x_4 + \beta_6 x_3 x_4$

Model	SSE	R^2	df(Error)
1	203,570	.83	108
2	227,520	.81	116
3	395,165	.67	125

a. What null hypothesis would you test to compare models 1 and 2?
b. Conduct the test specified in part **a**. Use $\alpha = .05$.
c. Note that the terms tested in part **a** are all quadratic terms. Given the result of the test, would you recommend keeping these terms in the model?
d. What null hypothesis would you test to compare models 2 and 3?
e. Conduct the test specified in part **d**. Use $\alpha = .05$
f. Based on the results of these tests, which of the three models would you recommend for predicting supply price y?
g. Based on the model you selected in part **f**, propose an alternative (simpler) model that will allow you test for the impact of deregulation. How would you conduct this test?

13.13 Residual Analysis

An analysis of **residuals**, the differences $(y - \hat{y})$ between the y values and their corresponding predicted values, often provides information that can lead to modifications and improvements in a regression model. These modifications may result from any one of three reasons: (1) the model itself has been misspecified, (2) one or more of the assumptions listed in Section 13.2 is violated, and (3) the data used to fit the model contain one or more unusual values.

Definition 13.4

A regression **residual** is defined as the difference between an observed y value and its corresponding predicted value:

$$\text{Residual} = (y - \hat{y})$$

Detecting Model Misspecification

One method for analyzing the residuals in a regression analysis is to plot the value of each residual versus the corresponding value of the independent variable, x. (If the model contains more than one independent variable, a plot would be constructed for each of the independent variables.) This plot will aid in detecting whether you have misspecified the model, as the following example illustrates.

EXAMPLE 13.26
Calculating and Plotting Residuals

Fit the first-order linear model, $E(y) = \beta_0 + \beta_1 x$, to the data shown in Table 13.5. Then calculate the residuals, plot them versus x, and analyze the plot.

Table 13.5 Data for Example 13.26

x	y	x	y
0	1	4	9
1	4	5	10
2	6	6	10
3	8	7	8

SOLUTION The least squares equation for the data can be obtained by using the formulas of Chapter 12 or by performing a standard regression analysis on a computer. The MINITAB printout for the simple linear regression is shown in Figure 13.25. You can see that the resulting prediction equation is

$$\hat{y} = 3.167 + 1.0952x$$

Substituting each value of x into this prediction equation, we can calculate $\hat{y}$ and the corresponding residual, $y - \hat{y}$. The value of x, the predicted value $\hat{y}$, and the residual $(y - \hat{y})$ are shown in Table 13.6 for each of the data points (see page 740).

FIGURE 13.25

MINITAB Printout for the Simple Linear Model, Example 13.26

```
The regression equation is
Y = 3.17 + 1.10 X

Predictor      Coef      Stdev     t-ratio      p
Constant      3.167      1.167      2.71      0.035
X            1.0952     0.2790      3.93      0.008

s = 1.808      R-sq = 72.0%      R-sq(adj) = 67.3%

Analysis of Variance

SOURCE       DF       SS         MS        F        p
Regression    1     50.381     50.381    15.41    0.008
Error         6     19.619      3.270
Total         7     70.000

Unusual Observations
Obs.    X        Y      Fit Stdev.Fit  Residual  St.Resid
  8   7.00    8.000   10.833    1.167    -2.833    -2.05R

R denotes an obs. with a large st. resid.
```

Table 13.6 Calculation of the Residuals for the Simple Linear Regression Analysis of the Example 13.26

x	y	$\hat{y}$	$(y - \hat{y})$
0	1	3.167	−2.167
1	4	4.262	−.262
2	6	5.357	.643
3	8	6.452	1.548
4	9	7.548	1.452
5	10	8.643	1.357
6	10	9.738	.262
7	8	10.833	−2.833

FIGURE 13.26

Analysis of Residuals for Example 13.26

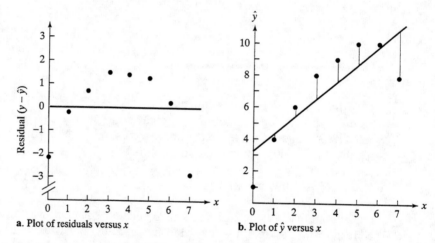

a. Plot of residuals versus x

b. Plot of $\hat{y}$ versus x

One way to analyze the residuals from Table 13.6 is to plot them versus the independent variable x. This plot is shown in Figure 13.26a. Instead of varying in a random pattern as x increases, the values of the residuals cycle from negative to positive to negative. This cyclical behavior is because we have fit a first-order (straight-line) linear model to data which a second-order model is appropriate—that is, we have misspecified the model. A plot of the data points on a graph of $\hat{y}$ versus x is shown in Figure 13.26b. The residuals, the vertical bars between the data points and the fitted line, are shown in color. Those below the $\hat{y}$ line are negative; those above it are positive. Figure 13.26 shows why fitting the wrong model to a set of data can produce patterns in the residuals when they are plotted versus an independent variable. For this simple example, the nonrandom (in this case, cyclical) behavior of the residuals can be eliminated by fitting the second-order model $E(y) = \beta_0 + \beta_1 x + \beta_2 x^2$ to the data. In general, certain patterns in the values of the residuals may suggest a need to modify the deterministic portion of the regression model, but the exact change that is needed may not always be obvious. ∎

Detecting Unequal Variances

A plot of the residuals may sometimes reveal the fact that the variance of y is not stable (as required by the assumptions stated in Section 13.2). For example, a plot of the residuals versus the predicted value $\hat{y}$ may display a pattern as shown in Figure 12.27. In the figure, the range in values of the residuals increases as $\hat{y}$ increases, thus indicating that the variance of the response variable y (and the random error, ε) becomes larger as the estimate of $E(y)$ increases in value.*

FIGURE 13.27

Residual Plot
Showing Changes in
the Variance of y

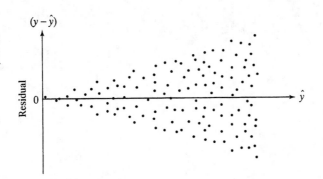

Residual plots of the type shown in Figure 13.27 are not uncommon because the variance of y often depends on the mean value of y. Variables that represent counts per unit of area, volume, time, etc. (i.e., Poisson random variables) are cases in point. Recall from Section 5.5 that for a Poisson random variable, the variance of y is equal to $E(y) = \mu$, i.e., $\sigma_y^2 = \mu$.

Since $\hat{y}$ is an estimator of $E(y)$, a plot of the residuals versus $\hat{y}$ may indicate how the range of the residuals (and hence, σ_y) varies as $E(y)$ increases. If the plot assumes the pattern shown in Figure 13.28a on page 742 and if you think it is possible that y is approximately a Poisson random variable, you may be able to stabilize the variance of the response by fitting $\sqrt{y}$ (instead of y) to the independent variables. Similarly, if y is a sample percentage or proportion, x/n, we would expect $\sigma_y = \sqrt{\pi(1-\pi)/n}$ to be small when π is near 0 or 1 and to reach a maximum when π is equal to .5 (see Section 5.4). A plot of the residuals versus $\hat{y}$ for this type of data (i.e., binomial data) would appear as shown in Figure 13.28b. To stabilize the variance for this type of data, fit $y^* = \sin^{-1}\sqrt{y}$, where y is expressed in radians.

A third situation that requires a variance-stabilizing transformation occurs with business and economic data where the response variable y follows a *multiplicative model*. Unlike the *additive* models discussed so far, in this model the dependent variable is written as the *product* of its mean and the random error component:

Multiplicative model: $y = [E(y)] \cdot \varepsilon$

The variance of this response will grow proportionally to the square of the mean, i.e., $\sigma_y^2 = [E(y)]^2 \sigma^2$, where σ^2 is the variance of the random error, ε. Data subject to

It can be shown (proof omitted) that for any regression model, Var(y) = Var(ε) = σ².

FIGURE 13.28

Plots of the Residuals
Versus $\hat{y}$ for
Poisson, Binomial,
and Multiplicative
Response Variables

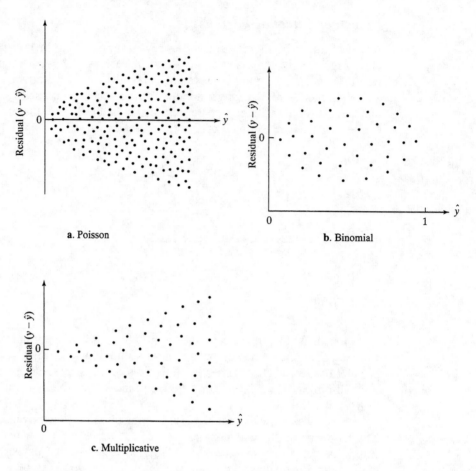

a. Poisson

b. Binomial

c. Multiplicative

multiplicative errors produce a pattern of residuals about $\hat{y}$ like that shown in Figure 13.28c. The appropriate transformation for this type of data is $y^* = \log(y)$.

The three variance-stabilizing transformations we have discussed are summarized in Table 13.7.

Table 13.7 Transformations to Stabilize the Variance of a Response

Residual Plot	*Type of Data*	*Characteristics*	*Transformation*
As shown in Figure 13.28a	Poisson	Counts per unit of time, distance, volume, etc.	$y^* = \sqrt{y}$
As shown in Figure 13.28b	Binomial	Proportions, percentages, or numbers of successes for a fixed number n of trials	$y^* = \sin^{-1}\sqrt{y}$ where y is proportion
As shown in Figure 13.28c.	Multiplicative	Business and economic data (e.g., salaries, prices)	$y^* = \log(y)$

EXAMPLE 13.27
Detecting Unequal
Variances

The data in Table 13.8 are the salaries, y, and years of experience, x, for a sample of 50 auditors. The first-order model $E(y) = \beta_0 + \beta_1 x$ was fit to the data using MINITAB. The MINITAB printout is shown in Figure 13.29, followed by a plot of the residuals versus $\hat{y}$ in Figure 13.30 on page 744. Interpret the results. Should the model be modified? If so, how?

Table 13.8   Salary Data for Example 13.27

Years of Experience x	Salary y	Years of Experience x	Salary y	Years of Experience x	Salary y
7	$26,075	21	$43,628	28	$99,139
28	79,370	4	16,105	23	52,624
23	65,726	24	65,644	17	50,594
18	41,983	20	63,022	25	53,272
19	62,308	20	47,780	26	65,343
15	41,154	15	38,853	19	46,216
24	53,610	25	66,537	16	54,288
13	33,697	25	67,447	3	20,844
2	22,444	28	64,785	12	32,586
8	32,562	26	61,581	23	71,235
20	43,076	27	70,678	20	36,530
21	56,000	20	51,301	19	52,745
18	58,667	18	39,346	27	67,282
7	22,210	1	24,833	25	80,931
2	20,521	26	65,929	12	32,303
18	49,727	20	41,721	11	38,371
11	33,233	26	82,641		

FIGURE 13.29

MINITAB Analysis for Example 13.27

```
The regression equation is
Y = 11369 + 2141 X

Predictor      Coef       Stdev      t-ratio        p
Constant      11369        3160         3.60     0.001
X             2141.3       160.8        13.31     0.000

s = 8642       R-sq = 78.7%      R-sq(adj) = 78.2%

Analysis of Variance

SOURCE       DF          SS              MS           F         p
Regression    1    13238774784    13238774784     177.25     0.000
Error        48     3585073152       74689024
Total        49    16823847936

Unusual Observations
Obs.      X        Y       Fit  Stdev.Fit   Residual    St.Resid
  31    1.0    24833     13511       3013      11322       1.40 X
  35   28.0    99139     71326       2005      27813       3.31R
  45   20.0    36530     54196       1259     -17666      -2.07R
R denotes an obs. with a large st. resid.
X denotes an obs. whose X value gives it large influence.
```

FIGURE 13.30

MINITAB Residual
Plot for the Data of
Example 13.27

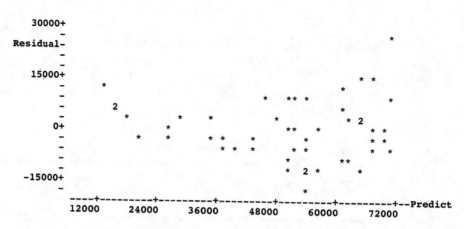

SOLUTION The MINITAB printout, Figure 13.29, suggests that the first-order model provides an adequate fit to the data. The R^2 value indicates that the model explains 78.7% of the sample variation in salaries. The t value for testing β_1, 13.31, is highly significant (p-value ≈ 0) and indicates that the model contributes information for the prediction of y. However, an examination of the residuals plotted against $\hat{y}$ (Figure 13.30) reveals a potential problem. Note the "cone" shape of the residual variability; the size of the residuals increases as the estimated mean salary increases.

This residual plot indicates the possibility of a multiplicative model and suggests that we employ the variance-stabilizing transformation $y^* = \log(y)$. We explore this possibility further in the next example. ■

EXAMPLE 13.28
Analyzing the Log Model

Consider the salary and experience data in Table 13.8. Use the logarithmic transformation on the dependent variable and relate $\log(y)$ to years of experience x with the linear model

$$\log(y) = \beta_0 + \beta_1 x + \varepsilon$$

    a.   Evaluate the adequacy of the model.

    b.   Interpret the value of $\hat{\beta}_1$.

SOLUTION   **a.**   The MINITAB printout in Figure 13.31 gives the regression analysis for the $n = 50$ measurements. The prediction equation is

$$\widehat{\log y} = 9.84 + .05x$$

with $R^2 = .863$ and $t = 17.43$ for testing $H_0: \beta_1 = 0$ (highly significant p-value ≈ 0). Both imply that the model contributes significantly to the prediction of $\log(y)$.

The residual plot, shown in Figure 13.32, indicates that the logarithmic transformation has stabilized the error variances. Note that the cone shape is gone; there is no apparent tendency of the residual variance to increase as mean salary increases. We therefore

FIGURE 13.31

MINITAB Printout for
the Data in Example
13.28

```
The regression equation is
LOGY = 9.84 + 0.0500 X

Predictor        Coef        Stdev      t-ratio        P
Constant      9.84133      0.05636      174.63      0.000
X            0.049978     0.002868       17.43      0.000

s = 0.1541     R-sq = 86.3%     R-sq(adj) = 86.1%

Analysis of Variance

SOURCE        DF          SS          MS        F         P
Regression     1      7.2118      7.2118    303.65    0.000
Error         48      1.1400      0.0238
Total         49      8.3519

Unusual Observations
Obs.     X       LOGY      Fit   Stdev.Fit   Residual   St.Resid
 19     4.0    9.6869   10.0412    0.0460     -0.3544     -2.41R
 31     1.0   10.1199    9.8913    0.0537      0.2286      1.58 X
 45    20.0   10.5059   10.8409    0.0225     -0.3350     -2.20R
R denotes an obs. with a large st. resid.
X denotes an obs. whose X value gives it large influence.
```

FIGURE 13.32

MINITAB Residual
Plot for the Data in
Example 13.28

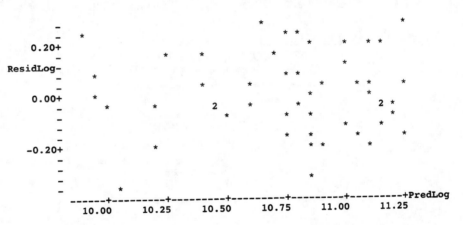

are confident that inferences using the logarithmic model are more reliable than those using the untransformed model.

b. Because we are using the logarithm of salary as the dependent variable, the β estimates have slightly different interpretations than previously discussed. In general, a parameter β in a log-transformed model represents the percentage increase (or decrease) in the dependent variable for a 1-unit increase in the corresponding independent variable. The percentage change is calculated by taking the antilogarithm of the β estimate and subtracting 1, i.e., $e^{\hat{\beta}_1} - 1$ (proof omitted). For example, the percentage change in auditor's salary associated with a 1-unit (i.e., 1-year) increase in years of experience x is $(e^{\hat{\beta}_1} - 1) = (e^{.05} - 1) = .051$. Thus, when all other independent variables are held constant, we estimate an auditor's salary to increase 5.1% for each additional year of experience. ■

Detecting Nonnormality

Of the four assumptions listed in Section 13.2, the assumption that the random error is normally distributed is the least restrictive when we apply regression analysis in practice. That is, moderate departures from the assumption of normality have very little effect on the validity of the statistical tests, confidence intervals, and prediction intervals. In this case, we say that regression is **robust** with respect to nonnormality. However, great departures from normality cast doubt on any inferences derived from the regression analysis.

The simplest way to determine whether the data grossly violate the assumption of normality is to construct either a relative frequency distribution (Section 2.4) or a stem-and-leaf display (Section 2.3) of the residuals, as illustrated in Example 13.29.

EXAMPLE 13.29
Residual Plot for Checking Normality

Refer to the complete second-order model for shipping cost (y), fit in Example 13.25. The residuals for the model (obtained by computer) are provided in Table 13.9. Construct a stem-and-leaf display for the residuals. Interpret the plot.

Table 13.9 Residuals for Complete Second-Order Fit to $n = 20$ Data Points, Example 13.25

Residuals			
−.011	.230	.144	−.153
−.196	.577	−.056	.090
.176	−.006	−.033	−.207
−.283	−.486	−.386	−.860
.133	.943	.162	.225

SOLUTION A computer-generated (MINITAB) stem-and-leaf display for the residuals is shown in Figure 13.33. Recall from Section 2.3 that if you turn the stem-and-leaf display on its side, it will look very much like a frequency distribution (or histogram). You can see from Figure 13.33 that the distribution of the residuals is mound-shaped and reasonably symmetric about 0. Consequently, it is unlikely that the normality assumption would be violated using these data.

FIGURE 13.33

MINITAB Stem-and-Leaf Display of the Residuals, Table 13.9

```
Stem-and-leaf of RESID      N  = 20
Leaf Unit = 0.10

     1    -0 8
     1    -0
     2    -0 4
     5    -0 322
    (6)   -0 110000
     9     0 01111
     4     0 22
     2     0 5
     1     0
     1     0 9   ■
```

When nonnormality of the random error term is detected, it can often be rectified by applying one of the transformations listed in Table 13.7. For example, if the relative frequency distribution (or stem-and-leaf display) of the residuals is highly skewed to the right (as it is for Poisson data), the square-root transformation on y will stabilize (approximately) the variance and, at the same time, will reduce skewness in the distribution of residuals. Nonnormality may also be due outliers, discussed next.

Detecting Outliers

Residual plots can also be used to detect **outliers**, values of y that appear to be in disagreement with the model. Since almost all values of y should lie within 3σ of $E(y)$, the mean value of y, we would expect most of them to lie within $3s$ of $\hat{y}$. If a residual is larger than $3s$ (in absolute value), we consider it an outlier and seek background information that might explain the reason for its large value.

Definition 13.5

A residual that is larger than $3s$ (in absolute value) is considered to be an **outlier**.

To detect outliers, we can construct horizontal lines located a distance of $3s$ above and below 0 (see Figure 13.34 on page 748) on a residual plot. Any residual falling outside the band formed by these lines would be considered an outlier. We would then initiate an investigation to seek the cause of the departure of such observations from expected behavior.

Although some analysts advocate elimination of outliers, regardless of whether cause can be assigned, others encourage the correction of only those outliers that can be traced to specific causes. The best philosophy is probably a compromise between these extremes. For example, before deciding the fate of an outlier, you may want to determine how much influence it has on the regression analysis. When an accurate outlier (i.e., an outlier that is not due to recording or measurement error) is found to have a dramatic effect on the regression analysis, it may be the model and not the outlier that is suspect. Omission of important independent variables or higher-order terms could be the reason why the model is not predicting well for the outlying observation. Several sophisticated numerical techniques (beyond the scope of this course) are available for identifying influential observations.

Detecting Correlated Errors

The assumption that the random errors are independent (uncorrelated) is most often violated when the data employed in a regression analysis are a **time series**. With time series data, the experimental units in the sample are time periods (e.g., years, months, or days) in consecutive time order.

For most business and economic time series, there is a tendency for the regression residuals to have positive and negative runs over time. For example, consider

FIGURE 13.34

3*s* Lines Used to
Locate Outliers

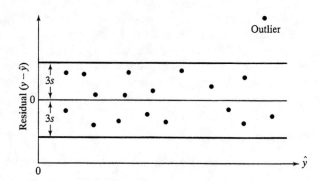

fitting a straight-line regression model to yearly time series data. The model takes the form

$$E(y) = \beta_0 + \beta_1 t$$

where *y* is the value of the time series in year *t*. A plot of the yearly residuals may appear as shown in Figure 13.35. Note that if the residual for year *t* is positive (or negative), there is a tendency for the residual for year $(t + 1)$ to be positive (or negative). That is, neighboring residuals tend to have the same sign and appear to be correlated. Thus, the assumption of independent errors is likely to be violated, and any inferences derived from the model are suspect.[*]

Remedial measures for this problem involve proposing complex time series models that include a model for both the deterministic and random error components. Time series models are the subject of Chapter 16.

FIGURE 13.35

Residual Plot for
Yearly Time Series
Model

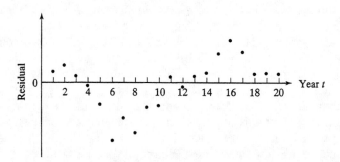

A Summary of Steps to Follow in a Residual Analysis

   1. Check for a **misspecified model** by plotting residuals $(y - \hat{y})$ against each independent variable in the model. A curvilinear trend

(continued)

---

[*]*A test of residual correlation is presented in Chapter 16.*

detected in a plot implies that a quadratic term for that particular x variable will probably improve model adequacy.

2. Check for **unequal variances** by plotting the residuals against the predicted values ($\hat{y}$). If you detect a pattern similar to one of those shown in Figure 13.28, refit the model using the appropriate variance-stabilizing transformation on y (see Table 13.7).

3. Check for **nonnormal errors** by constructing a stem-and-leaf display (or histogram) for the residuals. If you detect extreme skewness in the data, then either apply one of the transformations listed in Table 13.7 or look for one or more outliers (see step 4).

4. Check **outliers** by locating residuals that lie a distance of $3s$ or more above or below 0 on a residual plot versus $\hat{y}$. Before eliminating an outlier from the analysis, you should conduct an investigation to determine its cause. If the outlier is found to be the result of a coding or recording error, fix it or remove it. Otherwise, you may want to determine how influential the outlier is before deciding its fate.

5. Check for **correlated errors** by plotting the residuals in time order. If you detect runs of positive and negative residuals, propose a time series model to account for the residual correlation (see Chapter 16).

EXERCISES

■ *Learning the Mechanics*

13.63 Identify the problem(s) in each of the following residual plots:

a.

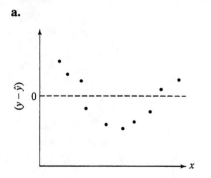

b.

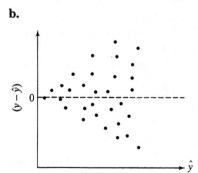

c.

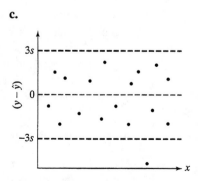

d.

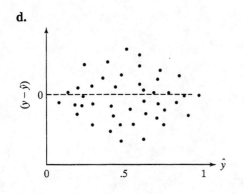

e.

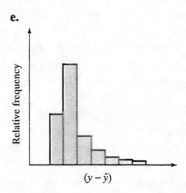

13.64 A first-order model is fit to the data shown in the table, with the following results:

$$\hat{y} = 2.588 + .541x \qquad s = .356$$

x	−2	−2	−1	−1	0	0	1	1	2	2	3	3
y	1.1	1.3	2.0	2.1	2.7	2.8	3.4	3.6	4.0	3.9	3.8	3.6

a. Calculate the residuals for the model.
b. Plot the residuals versus x. Do you detect any trends? If so, what does the pattern suggest about the model?
c. Plot the residuals versus $\hat{y}$. Identify any outliers on the plot.
d. Refer to the residual plot constructed in part **c**. Do you detect any trends? If so, what does the pattern suggest about the model?

13.65 A first-order model is fit to the data shown in the table, with the following results:

$$\hat{y} = -3.179 + 2.491x \qquad s = 4.154$$

x	2	4	7	10	12	15	18	20	21	25
y	5	10	12	22	25	27	39	50	47	65

a. Calculate the residuals for the model.
b. Plot the residuals versus x. Do you detect any trends? If so, what does the pattern suggest about the model?
c. Plot the residuals versus $\hat{y}$. Identify any outliers on the plot.
d. Refer to the residual plot constructed in part **c**. Do you detect any trends? If so, what does the pattern suggest about the model?

▪ *Applying the Concepts*

13.66 PCBs make up a family of hazardous chemicals that are often dumped, illegally, by industrial plants into the surrounding streams, rivers, or bays. The accompanying table reports the 1984 and 1985 concentrations of PCBs (measured in parts per billion) in water samples collected from 37 U.S. bays and estuaries. An official from the Environmental Protection Agency wants to model the 1985 PCB concentration (y) of a bay as a function of the 1984 PCB concentration (x). Consider the first-order model $E(y) = \beta_0 + \beta_1 x$. A SAS printout of the analysis, with residuals, is shown on page 752.

| | | PCB Concentration | |
Bay	State	1984	1985
Casco Bay	ME	95.28	77.55
Merrimack River	MA	52.97	29.23
Salem Harbor	MA	533.58	403.1
Boston Harbor	MA	17104.86	736
Buzzards Bay	MA	308.46	192.15
Narragansett Bay	RI	159.96	220.6
East Long Island Sound	NY	10	8.62
West Long Island Sound	NY	234.43	174.31
Raritan Bay	NJ	443.89	529.28
Delaware Bay	DE	2.5	130.67
Lower Chesapeake Bay	VA	51	39.74
Pamlico Sound	NC	0	0
Charleston Harbor	SC	9.1	8.43
Sapelo Sound	GA	0	0
St. Johns River	FL	140	120.04
Tampa Bay	FL	0	0
Apalachicola Bay	FL	12	11.93
Mobile Bay	AL	0	0
Round Island	MS	0	0
Mississippi River Delta	LA	34	30.14
Barataria Bay	LA	0	0
San Antonio Bay	TX	0	0
Corpus Christi Bay	TX	0	0
San Diego Harbor	CA	422.1	531.67
San Diego Bay	CA	6.74	9.3
Dana Point	CA	7.06	5.74
Seal Beach	CA	46.71	46.47
San Pedro Canyon	CA	159.56	176.9
Santa Monica Bay	CA	14	13.69
Bodega Bay	CA	4.18	4.89
Coos Bay	OR	3.19	6.6
Columbia River Mouth	OR	8.77	6.73
Nisqually Beach	WA	4.23	4.28
Commencement Bay	WA	20.6	20.5
Elliott Bay	WA	329.97	414.5
Lutak Inlet	AK	5.5	5.8
Nahku Bay	AK	6.6	5.08

Source: Environmental Quality, 1987–1988.

Dependent Variable: LNPCB85

Analysis of Variance

Source	DF	Sum of Squares	Mean Square	F Value	Prob>F
Model	1	145.58169	145.58169	251.172	0.0001
Error	35	20.28631	0.57961		
C Total	36	165.86800			

Root MSE	0.76132	R-square	0.8777
Dep Mean	2.94451	Adj R-sq	0.8742
C.V.	25.85556		

Parameter Estimates

Variable	DF	Parameter Estimate	Standard Error	T for H0: Parameter=0	Prob > |T|
INTERCEP	1	0.425110	0.20232699	2.101	0.0429
LNPCB84	1	0.850826	0.05368523	15.848	0.0001

Obs	BAY	LNPCB84	Dep Var LNPCB85	Predict Value	Residual
1	Casco	4.567261	4.3637	4.3111	0.0527
2	Merrmack	3.988428	3.4088	3.8186	-0.4097
3	Salem	6.281481	6.0017	5.7696	0.2321
4	Boston	9.747176	6.6026	8.7183	-2.1157
5	Buzzards	5.734829	5.2635	5.3045	-0.0410
6	Narragan	5.081156	5.4009	4.7483	0.6526
7	ELongIsl	2.397895	2.2638	2.4653	-0.2015
8	WLongIsl	5.461414	5.1666	5.0718	0.0947
9	Raritan	6.097827	6.2734	5.6133	0.6601
10	Delaware	1.252763	4.8803	1.4910	3.3893
11	LChesapk	3.951244	3.7072	3.7869	-0.0797
12	Pamilico	0	0	0.4251	-0.4251
13	Charlest	2.312535	2.2439	2.3927	-0.1488
14	Sapelo	0	0	0.4251	-0.4251
15	StJohns	4.94876	4.7961	4.6356	0.1605
16	Tampa	0	0	0.4251	-0.4251
17	Apalach	2.564949	2.5596	2.6074	-0.0479
18	Mobile	0	0	0.4251	-0.4251
19	RoundIsl	0	0	0.4251	-0.4251
20	MissRiv	3.555348	3.4385	3.4501	-0.0116
21	Baratara	0	0	0.4251	-0.4251
22	SanAnton	0	0	0.4251	-0.4251
23	CorpusCh	0	0	0.4251	-0.4251
24	SDiegoHa	6.047609	6.2779	5.5706	0.7073
25	SDiegoBa	2.046402	2.3321	2.1662	0.1659
26	DanaPt	2.086914	1.9081	2.2007	-0.2926
27	SealBch	3.865141	3.8601	3.7137	0.1464
28	SanPedro	5.078668	5.1812	4.7462	0.4351
29	SantaMon	2.70805	2.6872	2.7292	-0.0420
30	Bodega	1.644805	1.7733	1.8246	-0.0513
31	Coos	1.432701	2.0281	1.6441	0.3841
32	Columbia	2.279316	2.0451	2.3644	-0.3193
33	Nisquall	1.654411	1.6639	1.8327	-0.1688
34	Commence	3.072693	3.0681	3.0394	0.0286
35	Elliot	5.802028	6.0295	5.3616	0.6679
36	Lutak	1.871802	1.9169	2.0177	-0.1008
37	Nahku	2.028148	1.8050	2.1507	-0.3457

a. Is the model adequate for predicting y? Explain.

b. Construct a residual plot for the data. Do you detect any outliers? If so, identify them.

c. Refer to part **b**. Although the residual for Boston Harbor is not, by definition, an outlier, the EPA believes that it has strong influence on the regression due to its large y value. Remove the observation for Boston Harbor from the data and refit the model. Has model adequacy improved?

d. An alternative approach is to use the log transformations $y^* = $ natural $\log(y + 1)$ and $x^* = $ natural $\log(x + 1)$, and the fit model $E(y^*) = \beta_0 + \beta_1 x^*$. The SAS printout for this model follows. Conduct a test for model adequacy and perform a residual analysis. Interpret the results. In particular, comment on the residual value for Boston Harbor.

13.67 The data in the table, extracted from the *Real Estate Appraiser and Analyst*, were collected from $n = 10$ home sales. Property appraisers used the data to fit the model $E(y) = \beta_0 + \beta_1 x_1 + \beta_2 x_2$, where

$y = $ Sale price (in thousands of dollars)

$x_1 = $ Home size (square feet)

$x_2 = $ Condition rating (1 to 10)

Sale Price y, $ thousands	Home Size x_1, hundreds of sq. ft.	Condition Rating x_2, 1 to 10
60.0	23	5
32.7	11	2
57.7	20	9
45.5	17	3
47.0	15	8
55.3	21	4
64.5	24	7
42.6	13	6
54.5	19	7
57.5	25	2

Source: Andrews, R. L. and Ferguson, J. T. "Integrating judgment with a regression appraisal." *The Real Appraiser and Analyst*, Vol. 52, No. 2, Spring 1986 (Table I).

The resulting least squares prediction equation is

$$\hat{y} = 9.782 + 1.871x_1 + 1.278x_2$$

a. Calculate the residuals for the model.
b. Plot the residuals versus x_1. Do you detect any trends? If so, what does the pattern suggest about the model?
c. Plot the residuals versus x_2. Do you detect any trends? If so, what does the pattern suggest about the model?

13.68 The EPA gas mileage guide gives the engine size and estimated city miles per gallon ratings for the 11 gasoline-fueled subcompact and compact cars shown in the table. (The engine sizes are in total cubic inches of cylinder volume.) In an attempt to predict gas mileage from the engine size of subcompact and compact cars, the first-order model

$$y = \beta_0 + \beta_1 x + \varepsilon$$

is fit to the data. The resulting least squares model is $\hat{y} = 37.677 - .0724x$.

Car	Cylinder Volume x	Miles per Gallon y
VW Golf	97	37
Chevy Cavalier	173	19
Plymouth Horizon	97	31
Pontiac Firebird	151	23
Corvette	350	17
Honda Accord	119	27
Dodge Omni	97	31
Renault Alliance	85	35
Olds Firenza	173	19
Nissan Sentra	97	31
Ford Escort	114	32

Sources: *1986 Gas Mileage Guide, EPA Fuel Economy Estimates*, U.S. Dept. of Energy. *Words Automotive Yearbook*, 1986.

a. Calculate the regression residuals for this model.
b. Verify that the sum of the residuals is 0.
c. Plot these residuals against cylinder volume, x.
d. Do you detect any distinctive patterns or trends in this plot?
e. What does your answer to part c suggest about model adequacy or the usual assumptions made about the error term?

13.69 A certain type of rare germ serves as a status symbol for many of its owners. In theory, as the price of the germ increases, the demand will decrease at low prices, level off at moderate prices, and increase at high prices due to the status the owners believe than gain by obtaining the gem. Although a quadratic model would seem to match the theory, the model proposed to explain the demand for the gem by its price is the first-order model

$$y = \beta_0 + \beta_1 x + \varepsilon$$

where y is the demand (in thousands) and x is the retail price per carat (dollars). This model was fit to the 12 data points given in the table. The SPSS printout of the analysis is shown here.

x	100	700	450	150	500	800	70	50	300	350	750	700
y	130	150	60	120	50	200	150	160	50	40	180	130

a. Use the least squares prediction equation to calculate the regression residuals.
b. Plot the residuals against retail price per carat, x.
c. Can you detect any trends in the residual plot? What does this imply?

```
Multiple R              .23064
R Square                .05319
Adjusted R Square      -.04149
Standard Error         56.20658

Analysis of Variance
                    DF      Sum of Squares       Mean Square
Regression           1          1774.86785       1774.86785
Residual            10         31591.79882       3159.17988

F =        .56181       Signif F =   .4708


------------------ Variables in the Equation ------------------

Variable           B          SE B        Beta         T    Sig T

X                .04516      .06025      .23064      .750   .4708
(Constant)     99.81690    29.55565                 3.377   .0070
```

13.70 Breakdowns of machines that produce steel cans are very costly. The more breakdowns, the fewer cans produced, and the smaller the company's profits. To help anticipate profit loss, the owners of a can company would like to find a model that will predict the number of breakdowns on the assembly line. The model proposed by the company's statisticians is the following:

$$y = \beta_0 + \beta_1 x_1 + \beta_2 x_2 + \beta_3 x_3 + \beta_4 x_4 + \varepsilon$$

where y is the number of breakdowns per 8-hour shift,

$$x_1 = \begin{cases} 1 & \text{if afternoon shift} \\ 0 & \text{if otherwise} \end{cases} \qquad x_2 = \begin{cases} 1 & \text{if midnight shift} \\ 0 & \text{otherwise} \end{cases}$$

x_3 is the temperature of the plant (°F), and x_4 is the number of inexperienced personnel working on the assembly line. After the model is fit using the least squares procedure, the residuals are plotted against y, as shown in the accompanying figure.

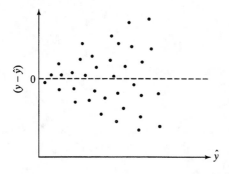

a. Do you detect a pattern in the residual plot? What does this suggest about the least squares assumptions?

b. Given the nature of the response variable y and the pattern detected in part **a**, what model adjustments would you recommend?

13.71 A recent study investigated the geopolitical and socioeconomic processes that shape the urban size distributions of the world's nations (*Economic Development and Cultural Change*, Oct. 1984). One of the goals of the study was to determine the factors that influence population size in each nation's largest city. Based on data collected for a sample of 126 countries, the following model was fit:

$$E(y) = \beta_0 + \beta_1 x_1 + \beta_2 x_2 + \beta_3 x_3 + \beta_4 x_4 + \beta_5 x_5 + \beta_6 x_6 + \beta_7 x_7 + \beta_8 x_8 + \beta_9 x_9 + \beta_{10} x_{10}$$

where

y = Logarithm of population (in thousands) of largest city in country

x_1 = Log of area (in thousands of square kilometers) of country

x_2 = Log of radius (in hundred kilometers) of city limits

x_3 = Log of national population (in thousands)

x_4 = Percentage annual change in national population (1960–1970)

x_5 = Log of energy consumption per capita (in kilograms of coal equivalent)

x_6 = Percentage of nation's population in urban areas

x_7 = Log of population (in thousands) of second largest city in country

$$x_8 = \begin{cases} 1 & \text{if seaport city} \\ 0 & \text{if not} \end{cases}$$

$$x_9 = \begin{cases} 1 & \text{if capital city} \\ 0 & \text{if not} \end{cases}$$

$$x_{10} = \begin{cases} 1 & \text{if city data are for metropolitan area} \\ 0 & \text{if not} \end{cases}$$

```
STEM LEAF                           #
   5  1                             1
   4  5                             1
   4
   3  79                            2
   3  1224                          4
   2  5899                          4
   2  000012233344                 12
   1  5789                          4
   1  00001113444                  11
   0  5566888                       7
   0  11111122223334               14
  -0  4433333322111000             16
  -0  9999988665                   10
  -1  44433332221110               14
  -1  88865                         5
  -2  444443100                     9
  -2  77665                         5
  -3  3000                          4
  -3  97                            2
  -4
  -4  6                             1
      ----+----+----+----+
MULTIPLY STEM.LEAF BY 10**-01
```

SAS Residual Plot for
Exercise 13.71

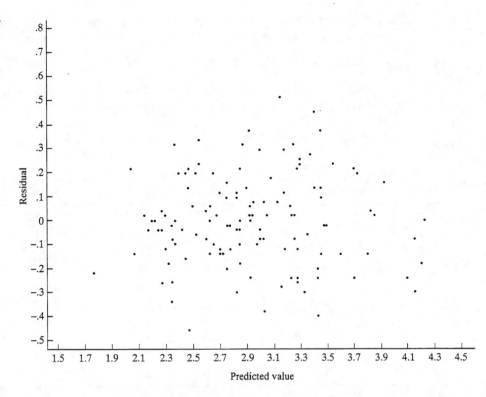

[*Note:*   All logarithims are log(base 10).]

The regression resulted in $R^2 = .879$ and MSE $= .036$.

a. Conduct a test for model adequacy. (Use $\alpha = .05$.)

b. A computer-generated (SAS) stem-and-leaf plot of all the residuals is shown here. Does it appear that the assumption of normal errors is satisfied?

c. A computer-generated (SAS) plot of the regression residuals versus $\hat{y}$ is also shown. Identify any outliers on the plot.

13.72 In Hawaii, condemnation proceedings are under way to enable private citizens to own the property that their homes are built on. Prior to 1980, only estates were permitted to own land, and homeowners leased the land from the estate (a law that dates back to the feudal period in Hawaii). To comply with the new law, a large Hawaiian estate wants to use regression analysis to estimate the fair market value of its land. A first proposal is the quadratic model

$$E(y) = \beta_0 + \beta_1 x + \beta_2 x^2$$

where

$y = $ Leased fee value (i.e., sale price of property)

$x = $ Size of property in square feet

Data collected for 20 property sales in a particular neighborhood, given in the accompanying table, were used to fit the model. The least squares prediction equation is

$$\hat{y} = -44.0947 + 11.5339x - .06378x^2$$

a. Calculate the predicted values and corresponding residuals for the model.
b. Plot the residuals versus $\hat{y}$. Do you detect any trends? If so, what does the pattern suggest about the model?
c. Based on your results, how should the estate proceed?

Property	Leased Fee Value y, thousands of dollars	Size x, thousands	Property	Leased Fee Value y, thousands of dollars	Size x, thousands
1	70.7	13.5	11	148.0	14.5
2	52.7	9.6	12	85.0	10.2
3	87.6	17.6	13	171.2	18.7
4	43.2	7.9	14	97.5	13.2
5	103.8	11.5	15	158.1	16.3
6	45.1	8.2	16	74.2	12.3
7	86.8	15.2	17	47.0	7.7
8	73.3	12.0	18	54.7	9.9
9	144.3	13.8	19	68.0	11.2
10	61.3	10.0	20	75.2	12.4

13.73 A large manufacturing firm wants to determine whether a relationship exists between the number of work-hours an employee misses per year, y, and the employee's annual wages, x (in thousands of dollars). A sample of 15 employees produced the data in the accompanying table. A first-order model was fit to the data with the following results:

$$\hat{y} = 222.64 - 9.60x \qquad r^2 = .073$$

Employee	y	x	Employee	y	x
1	49	12.8	9	191	7.8
2	36	14.5	10	6	15.8
3	127	8.3	11	63	10.8
4	91	10.2	12	79	9.7
5	72	10.0	13	543	12.1
6	34	11.5	14	57	21.2
7	155	8.8	15	82	10.9
8	11	17.2			

a. Interpret the value of r^2.

b. Calculate and plot the regression residuals. What do you notice?

c. After searching through its employees' files, the firm has found that employee 13 had been fired but that his name had not been removed from the active employee payroll. This explains the large accumulation of work-hours missed (543) by that employee. In view of this fact, what is your recommendation concerning this outlier?

d. Refit the model to the data, excluding the outlier, and find the least squares line. Calculate r^2 and comment on model adequacy.

13.74 The data for the *Communications of the Association for Computing Machinery* study, Exercise 12.50, are reproduced here. Recall that a straight-line model was used to predict instructor grade (y) from AUTOMARK grade (x). Use a graphical technique to check the normality assumption.

Automark Grade x	Instructor Grade y	Automark Grade x	Instructor Grade y	Automark Grade x	Instructor Grade y
12.2	10	18.2	15	19.0	17
10.6	11	15.1	16	19.3	17
15.1	12	17.2	16	19.5	17
16.2	12	17.5	16	19.7	17
16.6	12	18.6	16	18.6	18
16.6	13	18.8	16	19.0	18
17.2	14	17.8	17	19.2	18
17.6	14	18.0	17	19.4	18
18.2	14	18.2	17	19.6	18
16.5	15	18.4	17	20.1	18
17.2	15	18.6	17	19.2	19

Source: Redish, K. A. and Smyth, W. F. "Program style analysis: A natural by-product of program compilation." *Communications of the Association for Computing Machinery*, Vol. 29, No. 2, Feb. 1986, p. 132 (Figure 4).

13.14 Multicollinearity

Often, two or more of the independent variables used in the model for $E(y)$ will contribute redundant information. That is, the independent variables will be correlated with each other. For example, suppose we want to construct a model to predict the gasoline mileage rating, y, of a truck as a function of its load, x_1, and the horsepower, x_2, of its engine. In general, you would expect heavier loads to require greater horsepower and to result in lower mileage ratings. Thus, although both x_1 and x_2 contribute information for the prediction of mileage rating, some of the information is overlapping, because x_1 and x_2 are correlated. When the independent variables are correlated, we say that *multicollinearity* exists. In practice, it is not uncommon to observe correlations among the independent variables. However, a few problems arise when serious multicollinearity is present in the regression analysis.

Definition 13.6

Multicollinearity exists when two or more of the independent variables used in regression are correlated.

First, high correlations among the independent variables increase the likelihood of rounding errors in the calculations of the β estimates, standard errors, and so forth. Second, and more important, the regression results may be confusing and misleading.

EXAMPLE 13.30
Detecting Multicollinearity

Consider the model for gasoline mileage rating (y) of a truck:

$$E(y) = \beta_0 + \beta_1 x_1 + \beta_2 x_2$$

where $x_1 =$ load and $x_2 =$ horsepower. The model, fit to a sample data set, produced the following results:

$$\hat{y} = 12 + .2x_1 - .7x_2$$

$p = .76$ for testing $H_0: \beta_1 = 0$

$p = .45$ for testing $H_0: \beta_2 = 0$

$p = .001$ for testing $H_0: \beta_1 = \beta_2 = 0$

Detect and discuss any confusing or misleading results.

SOLUTION First, notice that the t tests for testing β_1 and β_2 are both nonsignificant at the $\alpha = .05$ level. However, the F test for $H_0: \beta_1 = \beta_2 = 0$ is highly significant ($p = .001$). The tests may seem to be contradictory, but really they are not. The t tests indicate that the contribution of one variable, say, $x_1 =$ load, is not significant after the effect of $x_2 =$ horsepower has been accounted for (because x_2 is also in the model). The significant F test, on the other hand, tells us that at least one of the two variables is making a contribution to the prediction of y (i.e., β_1, β_2, or both differ from 0). In fact, both are probably contributing, but the contribution of one overlaps with that of the other.

Multicollinearity can also have an effect on the signs of the parameter estimates. More specifically, a value of $\hat{\beta}_i$ may have the opposite sign from what is expected. From our discussion above, we expect the signs of both of the parameter estimates for the gasoline mileage rating model to be negative, yet the regression analysis for the model yields the estimates $\hat{\beta}_1 = .2$ and $\hat{\beta}_2 = -.7$. The positive value of $\hat{\beta}_1$ seems to contradict our expectation that heavy loads will result in lower mileage ratings. This is the danger of interpreting a β coefficient when the independent variables are correlated. Because the variables contribute redundant information, the effect of load x_1 on mileage rating is measured only partially by β_1.   ■

How can you avoid the problems of multicollinearity in regression analysis? One way is to conduct a designed experiment so that the levels of the x variables are uncorrelated.[*] Unfortunately, time and cost constraints may prevent you from collecting data in this manner. For these and other reasons, most data collected in business studies are observational. That is, the sample is selected and the values of the independent variables are observed with no attempt to control their values. Since observational data frequently consist of correlated independent variables, you will need to recognize when multicollinearity is present and, if necessary, make modifications in the analysis.

Several methods are available for detecting multicollinearity in regression. A simple technique is to calculate the coefficient of correlation, r, between each pair of independent variables in the model and use the procedure outlined in Section 12.7 to test for evidence of positive or negative correlation. If one or more of the r values is statistically different from 0, the variables in question are correlated, and a severe multicollinearity problem may exist.[†] Other indications of the presence of multicollinearity include those mentioned in the beginning of this section—namely, nonsignificant t tests for the individual β parameters when the F test for overall model adequacy is significant, and estimates with opposite signs from what is expected.[‡]

Detecting Multicollinearity in the Regression Model

$$E(y) = \beta_0 + \beta_1 x_1 + \beta_2 x_2 + \cdots + \beta_k x_k$$

The following are indicators of multicollinearity:

1. Significant correlations between pairs of independent variables in the model
2. Nonsignificant t tests for all (or nearly all) of the individual β parameters when the F test for overall model adequacy $H_0: \beta_1 = \beta_2 = \cdots = \beta_k = 0$ is significant
3. Signs opposite from what is expected in the estimated parameters

---

EXAMPLE 13.31
Detecting Multicollinearity

The Federal Trade Commission (FTC) annually ranks varieties of domestic cigarettes according to their tar, nicotine, and carbon monoxide contents (see Case Study 2.1). The U.S. surgeon general considers each of these three substances hazardous to a smoker's health. Past studies have shown that increases in the tar and nicotine

---

[*]*Designed experiments are the topic of Chapter 14.*

[†]*Remember that r measures only the pairwise correlation between x values. Three variables, x_1, x_2, and x_3, may be highly correlated as a group but may not exhibit large pairwise correlations. Thus, multicollinearity may be present even when all pairwise correlations are not significantly different from 0.*

[‡]*More formal methods for detecting multicollinearity, such as variance-inflation factors, are beyond the scope of this text. Consult the references for a discussion of these methods.*

contents of a cigarette are accompanied by an increase in the carbon monoxide emitted from the cigarette smoke. Table 13.10 presents data on tar, nicotine, and carbon monoxide contents (in milligrams), as well as weight (in grams), for a sample of 25 (filter) brands tested in a recent year. Suppose we want to model carbon monoxide content, y, as a function of tar content, x_1, nicotine content, x_2, and weight, x_3, using the model

$$E(y) = \beta_0 + \beta_1 x_1 + \beta_2 x_2 + \beta_3 x_3$$

The model is fit to the 25 data points in Table 13.10, and a portion of the SAS printout is shown in Figure 13.36. Examine the printout. Do you detect any signs of multicollinearity?

Table 13.10   FTC Cigarette Data for Example 13.31

Brand	Tar x_1, milligrams	Nicotine x_2, milligrams	Weight x_3, grams	Carbon Monoxide y, milligrams
Alpine	14.1	.86	.9853	13.6
Benson & Hedges	16.0	1.06	1.0938	16.6
Bull Durham	29.8	2.03	1.1650	23.5
Camel Lights	8.0	.67	.9280	10.2
Carlton	4.1	.40	.9462	5.4
Chesterfield	15.0	1.04	.8885	15.0
Golden Lights	8.8	.76	1.0267	9.0
Kent	12.4	.95	.9225	12.3
Kool	16.6	1.12	.9372	16.3
L&M	14.9	1.02	.8858	15.4
Lark Lights	13.7	1.01	.9643	13.0
Marlboro	15.1	.90	.9316	14.4
Merit	7.8	.57	.9705	10.0
Multifilter	11.4	.78	1.1240	10.2
Newport Lights	9.0	.74	.8517	9.5
Now	1.0	.13	.7851	1.5
Old Gold	17.0	1.26	.9186	18.5
Pall Mall Light	12.8	1.08	1.0395	12.6
Raleigh	15.8	.96	.9573	17.5
Salem Ultra	4.5	.42	.9106	4.9
Tareyton	14.5	1.01	1.0070	15.9
True	7.3	.61	.9806	8.5
Viceroy Rich Lights	8.6	.69	.9693	10.6
Virginia Slims	15.2	1.02	.9496	13.9
Winston Lights	12.0	.82	1.1184	14.9

Source: Federal Trade Commission.

SOLUTION   First, notice that a test of

$$H_0: \quad \beta_1 = \beta_2 = \beta_3 = 0$$

FIGURE 13.36

SAS Printout for FTC
Model of CO Content,
Example 13.31

Dependent Variable: CO

Analysis of Variance

Source	DF	Sum of Squares	Mean Square	F Value	Prob>F
Model	3	495.25781	165.08594	78.984	0.0001
Error	21	43.89259	2.09012		
C Total	24	539.15040			

Root MSE	1.44573	R-square	0.9186	
Dep Mean	12.52800	Adj R-sq	0.9070	
C.V.	11.53996			

Parameter Estimates

Variable	DF	Parameter Estimate	Standard Error	T for H0: Parameter=0	Prob > |T|
INTERCEP	1	3.202190	3.46175473	0.925	0.3655
TAR	1	0.962574	0.24224436	3.974	0.0007
NICOTINE	1	-2.631661	3.90055745	-0.675	0.5072
WEIGHT	1	-0.130482	3.88534182	-0.034	0.9735

is highly significant. The F value (shaded on the printout) is very large ($F = 78.984$) and the observed significance level of the test (also shaded) is small ($p = .0001$). Therefore, we can reject H_0 for any α greater than .0001 and conclude that at least one of the parameters β_1, β_2, and β_3 is nonzero. The t tests for two of the three individual β's, however, are nonsignificant. (The p-values for these tests are shaded on the printout.) Unless tar is the only one of the three variables useful for predicting carbon monoxide content, these results are the first indication of a potential multicollinearity problem.

The negative values for $\hat{\beta}_2$ and $\hat{\beta}_3$ (shaded on the printout) are a second clue to the presence of multicollinearity:

$$\hat{\beta}_2 = -2.63 \qquad \hat{\beta}_3 = -.130$$

From past studies, the FTC expects carbon monoxide content, y, to increase when either nicotine content, x_2, or weight, x_3, increases—that is, the FTC expects *positive* relationships between y and x_2 and between y and x_3, not negative ones.

All signs indicate that a serious multicollinearity problem exists. To confirm our suspicions, we calculate the coefficient of correlation, r, for each of the three pairs of independent variables in the model. These values are given in Table 13.11 on page 764. You can see that tar content, x_1, and nicotine content, x_2, appear to be highly correlated ($r = .977$), whereas weight, x_3, appears to be moderately correlated with both tar content ($r = .491$) and nicotine content ($r = .500$). In fact, all three sample correlations exceed the critical t value for a two-tailed test of $H_0: \rho = 0$ conducted at $\alpha = .05$ with $n - 2 = 23$ df. (See Section 12.7.) ■

Once you have detected that a multicollinearity problem exists, there are several alternative measures available for solving the problem. The appropriate measure to take depends on the severity of the multicollinearity and the ultimate goal of the regression analysis.

Table 13.11 Correlation Coefficients for the Three Pairs of Independent Variables in Example 13.31

Pair	Correlation Coefficient
x_1, x_2	.977
x_1, x_3	.491
x_2, x_3	.500

Solutions to Some Problems Created by Multicollinearity

1. Drop one or more of the correlated independent variables from the final model.
2. If you decide to keep all the independent variables in the model:
   a. Avoid making inferences about the individual β parameters based on the t statistics.
   b. Restrict inferences about $E(y)$ and future y values to values of the independent variables that fall within the range of the sample data.
3. To reduce rounding errors in higher-order regression models, code the independent variables so that first-, second-, and higher-order terms for a particular x variable are not highly correlated.

Some researchers, when confronted with highly correlated independent variables, choose to include only one of the correlated variables in the final model. If you are interested only in using the model for estimation and prediction (step 6), you may decide not to drop any of the independent variables from the model. In the presence of multicollinearity, we have seen that it is dangerous to interpret the individual β's. However, confidence intervals for $E(y)$ and prediction intervals for y generally remain unaffected *as long as the values of the independent variables used to predict y follow the same pattern of multicollinearity exhibited in the sample data.* That is, you must take strict care to ensure that the values of the x variables fall within the range of the sample data.

When fitting higher-order regression models [e.g., the second-order model $E(y) = \beta_0 + \beta_1 x + \beta_2 x^2$], the independent variables $x_1 = x$ and $x_2 = x^2$ will often be correlated. If the correlation is high, the computer solution may result in extreme rounding errors. For this model, the solution is not to drop one of the independent variables but to transform the x variable in such a way that the correlation between the coded x and x^2 values is substantially reduced. One transformation that works reasonably well is the z transform. That is, replace the variable x with its (approximate) z score

$$z_x \approx \frac{x - \bar{x}}{s}$$

More sophisticated procedures (e.g., ridge regression) for dealing with the multicollinearity problem are available, but they are beyond the scope of this text.

EXERCISES

■ *Applying the Concepts*

13.75 Consider the regression model $E(y) = \beta_0 + \beta_1 x_1 + \beta_2 x_2 + \beta_3 x_1 x_2$, where x_1 and x_2 are both quantitative variables. Suppose also that x_1 and x_2 are highly correlated. Assume the correlation between x_1 and x_2 is $r = .99$.
   a. Interpret the value of r.
   b. Based on your answer to part **a**, is it possible to change the value of x_1 while holding the value of x_2 fixed?
   c. Use your answer to part **b** to help explain why it is difficult to test for interaction between x_1 and x_2 in the presence of severe multicollinearity.

13.76 Refer to the study of electric utility stocks, Exercise 13.27. Recall that the average equity (x_1) and annual rate of dividend (x_2) were used to model the stock price (y) of nonnuclear stocks. Data were also collected for nuclear electric utility stocks, as shown in the table. The data were used to fit the interaction model $E(y) = \beta_0 + \beta_1 x_1 + \beta_2 x_2 + \beta_3 x_1 x_2$. The SAS printout of the analysis follows. Examine the printout for signs of multicollinearity.

Nuclear Stocks

y	x_1	x_2
21	15.1	2.36
31	15.0	3.00
26	11.2	3.00
11	12.1	1.96
24	16.3	3.00
8	11.9	1.40
18	14.9	1.80
23	11.8	2.56
13	13.4	2.06
14	16.2	1.94
35	17.1	2.96
13	13.3	2.20

Source: United Business Investment Report, Apr. 23, 1984.

```
                          Analysis of Variance

                          Sum of          Mean
        Source      DF    Squares        Square     F Value    Prob>F

        Model        3   640.93485     213.64495    13.217     0.0018
        Error        8   129.31515      16.16439
        C Total     11   770.25000

               Root MSE      4.02050    R-square    0.8321
               Dep Mean     19.75000    Adj R-sq    0.7692
               C.V.         20.35695

                          Parameter Estimates

                       Parameter     Standard    T for H0:
        Variable   DF   Estimate      Error     Parameter=0   Prob > |T|

        INTERCEP    1  -17.556340   40.05327713    -0.438      0.6727
        X1          1    0.518988    2.93598713     0.177      0.8641
        X2          1   10.889423   15.57141358     0.699      0.5042
        X1X2        1    0.132215    1.12491646     0.118      0.9093
```

13.77 A bioengineer wants to model the amount (y) of carbohydrate solubilized during steam processing of peat as a function of temperature (x_1), exposure time (x_2), and pH value (x_3). Data collected for each of 15 peat samples were used to fit the model

$$E(y) = \beta_0 + \beta_1 x_1 + \beta_2 x_2 + \beta_3 x_3$$

A summary of the regression results follows:

$$\hat{y} = -3{,}000 + 3.2x_1 - .4x_2 - 1.1x_3 \qquad R^2 = .93$$

$$s_{\hat{\beta}_1} = 2.4 \qquad s_{\hat{\beta}_2} = .6 \qquad s_{\hat{\beta}_3} = .8$$

$$r_{12} = .92 \qquad r_{13} = .87 \qquad r_{23} = .81$$

Based on these results, the bioengineer concludes that none of the three independent variables, x_1, x_2, and x_3, is a useful predictor of carbohydrate amount, y. Do you agree with this statement? Explain.

13.78 Refer to the FTC cigarette data of Example 13.31. The data are reproduced here for convenience.

Brand	Tar x_1, milligrams	Nicotine x_2, milligrams	Weight x_3, grams	Carbon Monoxide y, milligrams
Alpine	14.1	.86	.9853	13.6
Benson & Hedges	16.0	1.06	1.0938	16.6
Bull Durham	29.8	2.03	1.1650	23.5
Camel Lights	8.0	.67	.9280	10.2
Carlton	4.1	.40	.9462	5.4
Chesterfield	15.0	1.04	.8885	15.0
Golden Lights	8.8	.76	1.0267	9.0
Kent	12.4	.95	.9225	12.3
Kool	16.6	1.12	.9372	16.3
L&M	14.9	1.02	.8858	15.4

(continued)

Brand	Tar x_1, milligrams	Nicotine x_2, milligrams	Weight x_3, grams	Carbon Monoxide y, milligrams
Lark Lights	13.7	1.01	.9643	13.0
Marlboro	15.1	.90	.9316	14.4
Merit	7.8	.57	.9705	10.0
Multifilter	11.4	.78	1.1240	10.2
Newport Lights	9.0	.74	.8517	9.5
Now	1.0	.13	.7851	1.5
Old Gold	17.0	1.26	.9186	18.5
Pall Mall Light	12.8	1.08	1.0395	12.6
Raleigh	15.8	.96	.9573	17.5
Salem Ultra	4.5	.42	.9106	4.9
Tareyton	14.5	1.01	1.0070	15.9
True	7.3	.61	.9806	8.5
Viceroy Rich Lights	8.6	.69	.9693	10.6
Virginia Slims	15.2	1.02	.9496	13.9
Winston Lights	12.0	.82	1.1184	14.9

Source: Federal Trade Commission.

a. Fit the model $E(y) = \beta_0 + \beta_1 x_1$ to the data. Is there evidence that tar content (x_1) is useful for predicting carbon monoxide content (y)?

b. Fit the model $E(y) = \beta_0 + \beta_2 x_2$ to the data. Is there evidence that nicotine context (x_2) is useful for predicting carbon monoxide content (y)?

c. Fit the model $E(y) = \beta_0 + \beta_3 x_3$ to the data. Is there evidence that weight (x_3) is useful for predicting carbon monoxide content (y)?

d. Compare the signs of $\hat{\beta}_1$, $\hat{\beta}_2$, and $\hat{\beta}_3$ in the models of part **a**, **b**, and **c**, respectively, to the signs of the $\hat{\beta}$'s in the multiple regression model fit in Example 13.31. The fact that the $\hat{\beta}$'s change dramatically when the independent variables are removed from the model is another indication of a serious multicollinearity problem.

13.79 Hamilton (1987) illustrated the multicollinearity problem with an example using the data shown in the accompanying table. The values of x_1, x_2, and y in the table represent appraised land value, appraised improvements value, and sale price, respectively, of a randomly selected residential property. (All measurements are in thousands of dollars.)

x_1	x_2	y	x_1	x_2	y
22.3	96.6	123.7	30.4	77.1	128.6
25.7	89.4	126.6	32.6	51.1	108.4
38.7	44.0	120.0	33.9	50.5	112.0
31.0	66.4	119.3	23.5	85.1	115.6
33.9	49.1	110.6	27.6	65.9	108.3
28.3	85.2	130.3	39.0	49.0	126.3
30.2	80.4	131.3	31.6	69.6	124.6
21.4	90.5	114.4			

Source: Hamilton, D. "Sometimes $R^2 > r_{yx_2}^2$: Correlated variables are not always redundant." *The American Statistician*, Vol. 41, No. 2, May 1987, pp. 129–132.

a. Calculate the coefficient of correlation between y and x_1. Is there evidence of a linear relationship between sale price and appraised land value?

b. Calculate the coefficient of correlation between y and x_2. Is there evidence of a linear relationship between sale price and appraised improvements?

c. Based on the results in parts **a** and **b**, do you think the model $E(y) = \beta_0 + \beta_1 x_1 + \beta_2 x_2$ will be useful for predicting sale price?

d. Use a statistical computer software package to fit the model in part **c**, and conduct a test of model adequacy. In particular, note the value of R^2. Does the result agree with your answer to part **c**?

e. Calculate the coefficient of correlation between x_1 and x_2. What does the result imply?

f. Many researchers avoid the problems of multicollinearity by always omitting all but one of the "redundant" variables from the model. Would you recommend this strategy for this example? Explain. (Hamilton notes that in this case, such a strategy "can amount to throwing out the baby with the bathwater.")

SUMMARY

In this chapter, we have discussed some of the methodology of *multiple regression analysis*. Throughout, we presented several different types of *general linear models* of the form

$$y = \beta_0 + \beta_1 x_1 + \beta_2 x_2 + \cdots + \beta_k x_k + \varepsilon$$

The steps employed in a multiple regression analysis are much the same as those employed in a simple linear regression analysis (Chapter 12):

1. The form of the probabilistic model is hypothesized.
2. The appropriate model assumptions are made.
3. The model coefficients are estimated using the method of least squares.
4. The utility of the model is checked using the overall F test, t tests on individual β parameters, the F test for a partial set of β's, R^2, and the adjusted R^2.
5. A residual analysis is conducted to determine whether the data comply with the assumptions of step 2. Modifications to the model are made, if necessary.
6. If the model is deemed useful and the assumptions are satisfied, it may be used to make estimates and to predict values of y to be observed in the future.

We stress that this is not intended to be a complete coverage of multiple regression analysis. Whole texts have been devoted to this topic. However, we have presented the core necessary for a basic understanding of multiple regression and general linear models.

KEY TERMS

Adjusted R^2

Complete model

Dummy variable

F test for comparing nested models

F test for determining whether the overall model is useful for predicting y

First-order model

General linear model

Interaction

Interaction model

Multicollinearity

Multiple coefficient of determination: R^2

Multiple regression analysis

Nested models

Outlier

Parsimonious model

Quadratic model

Qualitative independent variable

Quantitative independent variable

Reduced model

Residual

Residual analysis

Second-order model

t test for testing an individual β parameter of a model

Variance-stabilizing transformation

KEY FORMULAS

Multiple coefficient of determination

$$R^2 = 1 - \frac{\text{SSE}}{\text{SS(Total)}} = \frac{\text{SSR}}{\text{SS(Total)}} \qquad R_a^2 = 1 - \left[\frac{(n-1)}{n-(k+1)}\right](1 - R^2)$$

Estimated variance of random error term

$$s^2 = \frac{\text{SSE}}{n-(k+1)} = \text{MSE}$$

Test of overall model utility

$H_0: \quad \beta_1 = \beta_2 = \cdots = \beta_k = 0$

Test statistic: $\quad F = \dfrac{\text{MS(Model)}}{\text{MSE}} = \dfrac{\text{SS(Model)}}{\text{SSE}}\left[\dfrac{n-(k+1)}{k}\right]$

$$= \left[\frac{R^2}{1-R^2}\right]\left[\frac{n-(k+1)}{k}\right]$$

where F depends on $v_1 = k$ and $v_2 = n-(k+1)\,\text{df}$

Test for comparing nested models

$H_0: \quad \beta_{g+1} = \beta_{g+2} = \cdots = \beta_k = 0$

Test statistic: $\quad F = \dfrac{(\text{SSE}_R - \text{SSE}_C)\,/(\#\,\beta\text{'s tested in } H_0)}{\text{MSE}_C}$

where

$\text{SSE}_R = $ SSE for reduced model (with g parameters)

$\text{SSE}_C = $ SSE for complete model (with k parameters)

$\text{MSE}_C = $ MSE for complete model

F depends on $v_1 = (k - g)$ and $v_2 = [n - (k + 1)]$ df

Regression residual

$(y - \hat{y})$

13.80 Multiple regression is the most commonly used statistical tool for settling employment discrimination cases. A recent issue of the *American Business Law Journal* (Vol. 27, 1993) presented a typical model for the monthly wage level y (in dollars) of an employee in a gender discrimination case:

$$E(y) = \beta_0 + \beta_1 x_1 + \beta_2 x_2 + \beta_3 x_3$$

where $x_1 = $ years of experience; $x_2 = $ years of formal training or education; and $x_3 = 1$ if female employee, 0 if male employee. The model was fit to sample data collected for 500 employees; the regression results are summarized here. (t-values for testing the β coefficients are in parentheses.)

$$\hat{y} = 404.6 + 289 x_1 + 442 x_2 - 397 x_3 \qquad R^2 = .90$$
$$\qquad\qquad\quad (2.66) \quad\; (1.02) \quad (-3.01)$$

Comment on the accuracy of the following statements about the regression analysis extracted from the article.

a. "The wage earnings for this sample can be expected to increase by \$289 on average for each year of experience, holding the other independent variables constant."

b. "We cannot say, with 95% [confidence], that the observed relationship between years of training and earnings is [statistically significant]."

c. "A female employee in this sample can expect to earn \$397 less on average than a male employee, after accounting for differences in experience, training or education."

d. "The independent variables, taken together, explain a very high proportion of the variation in [wage levels]."

e. "A complication may arise if two or more of the independent variables interact in affecting wage level. For example, an employer might conceivably discriminate in wage-setting against experienced female workers but not against new female employees. ... Fortunately, this can be tested for by [incorporating an interaction term between experience and sex]."

13.81 The impact of the Airline Deregulation Act of 1978 on the security returns in the airline industry was investigated in the *Quarterly Journal of Business and Economics* (Autumn 1984). The researchers examined the daily rates of returns of airline common stocks. For each airline, daily stock returns were recorded for each of 120 days prior to deregulation and 120 days after deregulation. Data for the total $n = 240$ observations (days) were then used to fit the model

$$E(y) = \beta_0 + \beta_1 x_1 + \beta_2 x_2 + \beta_3 x_1 x_2$$

where

y = Daily rate of return on the airline stock

x_1 = Average daily rate of return on the market

$$x_2 = \begin{cases} 1 & \text{if after deregulation} \\ 0 & \text{if prior to deregulation} \end{cases}$$

a. Write the equation of the line relating daily stock return y to average daily market return x_1 prior to deregulation (i.e., when $x_2 = 0$). Identify the y-intercept and slope of the line. [The slope is used to measure the stock's systematic risk and is often called the **β risk index** or **β value** for the stock. When the β value is greater than 1, the stock is classified as an *aggressive* or *risky* security since its daily rate of return is expected to move (upward or downward) faster than the market rate of return. In contrast, when the β value is less than 1, the stock is classified as a *defensive* or *stable* security since its daily rate of return moves slower than the market. A stock with a β value near 1 is called a *neutral* security because its daily rate of return mirrors the market.]

b. Write the equation of the line relating daily stock return y to average daily market return x_1 after deregulation (i.e., when $x_2 = 1$). Identify the y-intercept and slope of the line.

c. What hypothesis would you test to determine whether the model is adequate for predicting y?

d. What hypothesis would you test to determine whether deregulation had an effect on the measure of systematic risk (i.e., β value) associated with the airline stock? [*Hint:* Use your answers to parts **a** and **b**.]

e. The least squares prediction equations for three airline stocks are given in the accompanying table. Identify those stocks that have significant (at $\alpha = .10$) interaction between average market rate of return x_1 and deregulation x_2. For each of these stocks, how has deregulation affected the stock's β value?

Stock	$\hat{\beta}_0$	$\hat{\beta}_1$	$\hat{\beta}_2$	$\hat{\beta}_3$
Delta Airlines	−.0002	1.8557*	−.0005	−.6667*
United Airlines	.0023	1.8137*	−.0039	.1444
W.A.F., Inc.	.0024	1.9271*	.0035	1.7067*

*Asterisk identifies β coefficients significant at $\alpha = .10$.

Source: Davidson, W. N., Chandy, P. R., and Walker, M. "The stock market effects of airline deregulation." *Quarterly Journal of Business and Economics*, Autumn 1984, Vol. 23, No. 4, pp. 31–45.

13.82 Researchers at the Upjohn Company utilized multiple regression analysis in the development of a sustained release tablet.* One of the objectives of the research was to develop a model relating the dissolution y of a tablet (i.e., the percentage of the tablet dissolved over a specified period of time) to the following independent variables:

x_1 = Excipient level (i.e., amount of nondrug ingredient in the tablet)

x_2 = Process variable (e.g., machine setting under which tablet is processed)

a. Write the complete second-order model for $E(y)$.
b. Write a model that hypothesizes straight-line relationships between $E(y)$, x_1, and x_2. Assume that x_1 and x_2 do not interact.
c. Repeat part **b**, but add interaction to the model.
d. For the model in part **c**, what is the slope of the $E(y)$–x_1 line for fixed x_2?
e. For the model in part **c**, what is the slope of the $E(y)$–x_2 line for fixed x_1?

13.83 *IEEE Transactions on Software Engineering* (Apr. 1985) published a study on identifying error-prone software. A multiple regression analysis was conducted to identify the computer-module-related variables (called *metrics*) useful for predicting the number y of discovered module defects. For a certain product written in PL/S language, the following model was fit to data collected for $n = 253$ modules:

$$E(y) = \beta_0 + \beta_1 x_1 + \beta_2 x_2$$

where

x_1 = Number of unique operands in the module

x_2 = Number of conditional statements, loops, and Boolean operators in the module

The multiple coefficient of determination for the model was $R^2 = .78$. Is there sufficient evidence to indicate that the model is useful for predicting the number y of defects in modules of the software product? Test using $\alpha = .05$.

13.84 Refer to Exercise 12.82. In an attempt to improve the ability of the model to predict urban travel times, Cook and Russell added a second independent variable—weighted average speed limit between the two urban locations. The proposed model takes the form

$$y = \beta_0 + \beta_1 x_1 + \beta_2 x_2 + \varepsilon$$

where

y = Urban travel time (minutes)

x_1 = Distance between locations (miles)

x_2 = Weighted speed limit between locations (miles per hour)

This model was fit to the car and truck data sets, with the results shown in the accompanying table.

---
*Source: Klassen, R. A. *"The application of response surface methods to a tablet formulation problem."* Paper presented at Joint Statistical Meetings, American Statistical Association and Biometric Society, Aug. 1986, Chicago, Ill.

Passenger Cars	*Trucks*
$\hat{y} = 5.46 + 2.15x_1 - .09x_2$	$\hat{y} = 4.84 + 3.92x_1 - .09x_2$
$R^2 = .687;\ n \doteq 567$	$R^2 = .771;\ n = 918$

Source: Cook, T. M. and Russell, R. A. "Estimating urban travel times: A comparative study." *Transportation Research,* 14A, June 1980, pp. 173–175. Reprinted with permission. Copyright 1980, Pergamon Press, Ltd.

a. Is the model useful for predicting the urban travel times of passenger cars? Use $\alpha = .05$.
b. Interpret the β estimates of the model for passenger cars.
c. Is the model useful for predicting urban travel times of trucks? Use $\alpha = .05$.
d. Interpret the β estimates of the model for trucks.

13.85 Most homes in the United States are sold through a real estate broker, who receives a commission on each sale. As a future home buyer, you may want to know the extent to which brokerage commissions are incorporated into the selling price of the home. Stated more simply, is the price paid by a home buyer higher when property is sold through a real-estate broker than when sold directly by an owner? Evidence collected by researchers at Louisiana State University suggests that home buyers may, in fact, save in costs by purchasing owner-offered properties (*The Real Estate Appraiser and Analyst,* Winter 1985). Data on a sample of 111 transactions were used to fit the model

$$E(y) = \beta_0 + \beta_1 x_1 + \beta_2 x_2 + \beta_3 x_3 + \beta_4 x_4 + \beta_5 x_5 + \beta_6 x_6$$

where

y = Sale price (dollars)

x_1 = Age of home (years)

x_2 = Living area (square feet)

x_3 = Area (sq. ft.) of other improvements (e.g., garage, porch, etc.)

x_4 = Selling date

$$x_5 = \begin{cases} 1 & \text{if home was conventionally financed} \\ 0 & \text{if not} \end{cases}$$

$$x_6 = \begin{cases} 1 & \text{Brokerage commission (in dollars)} \quad \text{if home listed with real estate broker} \\ 0 & \hspace{5.3cm} \text{if not} \end{cases}$$

The regression results are summarized here. (The standard errors of the β estimates are given in parentheses.)

$$\hat{y} = 10.67 - 725x_1 + 27.50x_2 + 10.15x_3 + 470.12x_4 - 1{,}450x_5 + .43x_6 \qquad R^2 = .86$$
$$\hspace{1.1cm} (120.8) \hspace{0.6cm} (1.73) \hspace{0.7cm} (2.67) \hspace{0.9cm} (940.24) \hspace{0.7cm} (1{,}208.3) \hspace{0.4cm} (.25)$$

a. Is the model adequate for predicting the sale price of a home? Test using $\alpha = .10$.

b. Calculate a 90% confidence interval for β_1. Interpret your result.

c. Interpret the estimate of β_5.

d. Test the hypothesis that a brokerage commission increases the mean selling price of a home. Test using $\alpha = .10$.

13.86 The performance of an industry is often measured by the level of excess (or unutilized) capacity within the firm. A study examined the relationship between excess capacity (y) and several market variables in 273 U.S. manufacturing industries (*Quarterly Journal of Business & Economics*, Summer 1986). One of the qualitative variables used in the study was market concentration (low, moderate, or high).

a. Write a model for $E(y)$ as a function of market concentration.

b. Interpret the β coefficients in the model.

c. How would you test the hypothesis of no differences among the mean excess capacity levels of the three markets?

13.87 A study was conducted to determine whether entrepreneurs, newly hired (transferred) managers, and newly promoted managers differ in their risk-taking propensities (*Academy of Management Journal*, Sept. 1980). For the purposes of this study, entrepreneurs were defined as individuals who, within 3 months prior to the study, had ceased working for their employers to own and manage business ventures. Thirty-one individuals from each of the three groups were randomly selected to participate in the study. Each was administered a questionnaire that required the respondent to choose between a safe alternative and a more attractive but risky one. Test scores were designed to measure risk-taking propensity. (Lower scores are associated with greater conservatism in risk-taking situations.) The test scores for the three groups are summarized in the table.

Group	Sample Size	Sample Mean
Entrepreneurs	31	71.00
Transferred managers	31	72.52
Promoted managers	31	66.97
	93	

Suppose you were to fit the following model to the $n = 93$ data points:

$$E(y) = \beta_0 + \beta_1 x_1 + \beta_2 x_2$$

where

$y =$ Test score

$$x_1 = \begin{cases} 1 & \text{if entrepreneur} \\ 0 & \text{if not} \end{cases} \qquad x_2 = \begin{cases} 1 & \text{if transferred manager} \\ 0 & \text{if not} \end{cases} \qquad \text{Base level} = \text{Promoted manager}$$

a. Use the information in the table to find the least squares prediction equation.

b. How would you test the hypothesis that there are no differences among the mean risk-taking propensities of the three groups of managers?

13.88 *Multinational* is the term given to an industry with foreign investors. A study of 216 manufacturing industries in Mexico found that multinational presence in a firm has a positive influence on market concentration (*World Development,* Vol. 14, 1986). The result was revealed in a multiple regression analysis on the dependent variable *y*, market concentration index, using the following quantitative independent variables:

x_1 = Market size

x_2 = Market rate of growth

x_3 = Gross production in largest plants (expressed as a percentage of total gross production)

x_4 = Capital intensity (ratio of total assets to total number of employees)

x_5 = Advertising intensity (ratio of advertising to value added)

x_6 = Foreign share (i.e., gross output produced by foreign subsidiaries)

a. Write a first-order model for $E(y)$ as a function of the variables x_1–x_6.
b. Interpret β_6 in the model of part **a**.
c. Based on the results of the study, is β_6 positive or negative?
d. Write a second-order model for $E(y)$ that proposes interaction between the independent variables, but no curvature.
e. Using the model in part **d**, how would you test the hypothesis that effect of a multinational presence on market concentration is independent of the other independent variables in the model?

13.89 A naval base is considering modifying or adding to its fleet of 48 standard aircraft. The final decision regarding the type and number of aircraft to be added depends on a comparison of cost versus effectiveness of the modified fleet. Consequently, the naval base would like to model the projected percentage increase *y* in fleet effectiveness by the end of the decade as a function of the cost *x* of modifying the fleet. A first proposal is the quadratic model

$$E(y) = \beta_0 + \beta_1 x + \beta_2 x^2$$

The data provided in the table were collected on 10 naval bases of similar size that recently expanded their fleets. The data were used to fit the model. A SAS printout of the multiple regression analysis is presented here.

Percentage Improvement at End of Decade, y	Cost of Modifying Fleet x, million of dollars
18	125
32	160
9	80
37	162
6	110
3	90
30	140
10	85
25	150
2	50

```
Dependent Variable: Y

                          Analysis of Variance

                            Sum of         Mean
         Source      DF     Squares        Square      F Value    Prob>F

         Model        2    1368.77501    684.38750     33.079     0.0003
         Error        7     144.82499     20.68928
         C Total      9    1513.60000

              Root MSE        4.54855    R-square      0.9043
              Dep Mean       17.20000    Adj R-sq      0.8770
              C.V.           26.44504

                          Parameter Estimates

                      Parameter      Standard     T for H0:
         Variable  DF   Estimate       Error     Parameter=0   Prob > |T|

         INTERCEP   1   10.659036    14.55009061     0.733       0.4876
         X          1   -0.281606     0.28087588    -1.003       0.3494
         XX         1    0.002672     0.00125383     2.131       0.0706
```

a. Interpret the value R^2 on the printout.

b. Find the value s and interpret it.

c. Perform a test of overall model adequacy. Use $\alpha = .05$.

d. Is there sufficient evidence to conclude that the percentage improvement y increases more quickly for more costly fleet modifications than for less costly fleet modifications? Test with $\alpha = .05$.

e. Calculate the regression residuals and construct a plot of residuals versus x.

f. Examine the residual plot constructed in part **e.** Do you detect any outliers? Are there any trends?

g. Now consider the model

$$E(y) = \beta_0 + \beta_1 x_1 + \beta_2 x_1^2 + \beta_3 x_2 + \beta_4 x_1 x_2$$

where

$x_1 =$ Cost of modifying the fleet

$$x_2 = \begin{cases} 1 & \text{if American base} \\ 0 & \text{if foreign base} \end{cases}$$

The model is fit to the $n = 10$ data points and resulted in SSE $= 97.645$. Is there sufficient evidence to indicate that type of base (American or foreign) is a useful predictor of percentage improvement y? Test using $\alpha = .05$.

13.90 The following questions pertain to multicollinearity.

a. What problems result when multicollinearity is present in a regression analysis?

b. How can you detect multicollinearity?

c. What remedial measures are available when multicollinearity is detected?

13.91 The manager of a retail appliance store wants to model the proportion of appliance owners who decide to purchase a service contract for a specific major appliance. Since the manager believes that the proportion y decreases as the age x of the appliance (in years) increases, he will fit the first-order model

$$E(y) = \beta_0 + \beta_1 x$$

A sample of 50 purchasers of new appliances are contacted about the possibility of purchasing a service contract. Fifty owners of 1-year-old machines and 50 owners each of 2-, 3-, and 4-year-old machines are also contacted. One year later, another survey is conducted in a similar manner. The proportions y of owners deciding to purchase the service policy are shown in the table.

x	0	0	1	1	2	2	3	3	4	4
y	.94	.96	.70	.76	.60	.40	.24	.30	.12	.10

a. Fit the first-order model to the data.
b. Calculate the residuals and construct a residual plot versus $\hat{y}$.
c. What does the plot constructed in part **b** suggest about the variance of y?
d. Explain how you could stabilize the variances.

13.92 Power companies have to be able to predict the peak power load at their various stations to operate effectively. The peak power load is the maximum amount of power that must be generated each day to meet demand.

Suppose a power company located in the southern part of the United States decides to model daily peak power load, y, as a function of the daily high temperature, x, and the model is to be constructed for the summer months when demand is greatest. Although we would expect the peak power load to increase as the high temperature increases, the *rate* of increase in $E(y)$ might also increase as x increases. That is, a 1-unit increase in high temperature from 100°F to 101°F might result in a larger increase in power demand than would a 1-unit increase from 80°F to 81°F. Therefore, we postulate the second-order model

$$E(y) = \beta_0 + \beta_1 x + \beta_2 x^2$$

and we expect β_2 to be positive.

A random sample of 25 summer days is selected. The data are shown in the accompanying table. The SAS printout for the second-order model is also given on page 778.

Temperature x, °F	Peak Load y, megawatts	Temperature x, °F	Peak Load y, megawatts	Temperature x, °F	Peak Load y, megawatts
94	136.0	106	178.2	76	100.9
96	131.7	67	101.6	68	96.3
95	140.7	71	92.5	92	135.1
108	189.3	100	151.9	100	143.6
67	96.5	79	106.2	85	111.4
88	116.4	97	153.2	89	116.5
89	118.5	98	150.1	74	103.9
84	113.4	87	114.7	86	105.1
90	132.0				

a. Give the least squares prediction equation.
b. Find R^2 and s on the printout and interpret their values.
c. Is there evidence that the model is useful for predicting peak power load y? Test using $\alpha = .05$.

Analysis of Variance

Source	DF	Sum of Squares	Mean Square	F Value	Prob>F
Model	2	15011.7720	7505.89	259.69	0.0001
Error	22	635.8784	28.90		
C Total	24	15647.6504			

Root MSE	5.3762	R-square	.9594
Dep Mean	125.43	Adj R-sq	.9524
C.V.	4.2863		

Parameter Estimates

Variable	Parameter Estimate	Standard Error	T for H0: Parameter=0	Prob > |T|
INTERCEP	385.0481	55.1724	6.98	0.0001
X	-8.2925	1.2990	-6.38	0.0001
XX	0.0598	0.0075	7.93	0.0001

d. Test the hypothesis that the power load increases at an increasing rate with temperature. Use $\alpha = .05$.

e. Use the least squares prediction equation to calculate the residual for each of the peak loads given in the table.

f. Calculate the mean and the variance of the residuals. The mean should equal 0 and the variance should be close to the value of MSE given in the SAS printout.

g. Determine the proportion of the residuals that fall outside 3 estimated standard deviations ($3s$) of 0.

h. Plot the residuals against daily high temperature, x, and examine the graph for trends. What can you conclude about the assumptions concerning the random error term?

i. Construct a stem-and-leaf display for the residuals. Interpret the graph.

13.93 A chain of drug stores wants to model mean profit per week, $E(y)$, as a function of three advertising factors: type of design, choice of newspaper, and percentage discount offered on sale items. A first proposal is the model

$$E(y) = \beta_0 + \beta_1 x_1 + \beta_2 x_1^2 + \beta_3 x_2 + \beta_4 x_3 + \beta_5 x_2 x_3 + \beta_6 x_1 x_2 + \beta_7 x_1 x_3 + \beta_8 x_1 x_2 x_3$$
$$+ \beta_9 x_1^2 x_2 + \beta_{10} x_1^2 x_3 + \beta_{11} x_1^2 x_2 x_3$$

where

x_1 = Percentage discount

$$x_2 = \begin{cases} 1 & \text{if design } D_1 \\ 0 & \text{if design } D_2 \end{cases} \qquad x_3 = \begin{cases} 1 & \text{if newspaper } N_1 \\ 0 & \text{if newspaper } N_2 \end{cases}$$

a. Specify the parameters that would be involved in a test of the hypothesis, "The design of the advertising and the choice of newspaper have no effect on the mean value of the weekly profits."

b. Refer to part **a**. State the hypothesis that you would make regarding the parameter values.

c. Give the parameters that would be involved in a test of the hypothesis, "The relationship between mean weekly profit and percentage discount for each of the combinations of newspaper and design is first-order (i.e., a straight line)."

■ *CASE STUDY 13.1* ■

The Salary Race: Males Versus Females

Upon graduation from college, you will embark on a career in your chosen field of study. Once you accept a job, you'll join the ranks of workers who are preoccupied with the size of their paychecks. Are you being fairly compensated? Why does your friend in another city receive a larger salary for a less demanding job? What can you do to get a raise?

Certainly, we expect our compensation to be tied to our qualifications. Graduates with engineering degrees expect to be paid more than nursing graduates. Graduates with Ph.D. degrees expect higher starting salaries than graduates with bachelor degrees. But, will your starting salary depend on your gender?

We can obtain a partial answer to this question by examining a data set extracted from a recent Career Resource Center (CRC), University of Florida, questionnaire. The data set contains the staring salaries of approximately 900 graduates (bachelor degree) of the University of Florida in five different colleges: Business Administration, Engineering, Journalism, Liberal Arts and Sciences, and Nursing. In addition to starting salary and college, the gender (male or female) of the graduate was recorded.

Consider a multiple regression model relating starting salary y to the two qualitative independent variables, college (at 5 levels) and gender (at 2 levels). From Section 13.11, we require four dummy variables for college and one for gender. These are defined as follows:

$$\text{College: } x_1 = \begin{cases} 1 & \text{if Business Administration} \\ 0 & \text{if not} \end{cases}$$

$$x_2 = \begin{cases} 1 & \text{if Engineering} \\ 0 & \text{if not} \end{cases}$$

$$x_3 = \begin{cases} 1 & \text{if Liberal Arts and Sciences} \\ 0 & \text{if not} \end{cases}$$

$$x_4 = \begin{cases} 1 & \text{if Journalism} \\ 0 & \text{if not} \end{cases}$$

$$\text{Gender: } x_5 = \begin{cases} 1 & \text{if female} \\ 0 & \text{if male} \end{cases}$$

Note that we have arbitrarily selected nursing and male as the base levels for college and gender, respectively. A model relating mean starting salary, $E(y)$, to these two independent variables takes the form

$$E(y) = \beta_0 + \underbrace{\beta_1 x_1 + \beta_2 x_2 + \beta_3 x_3 + \beta_4 x_4}_{\substack{\text{College} \\ \text{terms}}} + \underbrace{\beta_5 x_5}_{\substack{\text{Gender} \\ \text{term}}}$$

a. Write the equation relating mean starting salary, $E(y)$, to college, for male graduates only.

b. Interpret β_1 in the model from part **a**.

c. Interpret β_2 in the model from part **a**.

d. Interpret β_3 in the model from part **a**.

e. Interpret β_4 in the model from part **a**.

f. Write the equation relating mean starting salary, $E(y)$, to college, for female graduates only.

g. Interpret β_1 in the model from part **f**. Compare to your answer to part **b**.

h. Interpret β_2 in the model from part **f**. Compare to your answer to part **c**.

i. Interpret β_3 in the model from part **f**. Compare to your answer to part **d**.

j. Interpret β_4 in the model from part **f**. Compare to your answer to part **e**.

k. For a given college, interpret the value of β_5 in the model.

l. The SAS printout of the multiple regression analysis is displayed in Figure 12.37 on page 780. Interpret the results. Part of your answer should include a statement about whether gender has an effect on average starting salary.

FIGURE 13.37

SAS Printout for the Model Relating Salary to College and Gender

Dependent Variable: SALARY

Analysis of Variance

Source	DF	Sum of Squares	Mean Square	F Value	Prob>F
Model	5	13609836905	2721967380.9	90.022	0.0001
Error	896	27092165483	30236791.833		
C Total	901	40702002387			

Root MSE	5498.79913	R-square	0.3344	
Dep Mean	26020.20510	Adj R-sq	0.3307	
C.V.	21.13280			

Parameter Estimates

Variable	DF	Parameter Estimate	Standard Error	T for H0: Parameter=0	Prob > |T|
INTERCEP	1	29215	739.33031785	39.515	0.0001
X1	1	-3928.938467	731.13739384	-5.374	0.0001
X2	1	1845.020611	778.46344679	2.370	0.0180
X3	1	-8375.343226	902.00089218	-9.285	0.0001
X4	1	-7349.696165	795.38316872	-9.240	0.0001
X5	1	-1142.171471	419.57634068	-2.722	0.0066

■ CASE STUDY 13.2

Building a Model for the Sale Price of a Residential Property

This case study concerns a problem of interest to real estate appraisers, tax assessors, real estate investors, and home buyers—namely, the relationship between the appraised value of a property and its sale price. The sale price for any given property will vary depending on the price set by the seller, the strength of appeal of the property to a specific buyer, and the state of the money and real estate markets. Therefore, we can think of the sale price of a specific property as possessing a relative frequency distribution. The mean of this distribution might be regarded as a measure of the fair value of the property. Presumably, this is the value that a property appraiser or a tax assessor would like to attach to a given property.

Recall that Appendix A.1 describes the appraised land and improvements values and the sale prices for residential properties sold in six neighborhoods in Tampa, Florida, during 1993. Therefore, the data of Appendix A.1 provide us with an opportunity to build a model for the mean sale price $E(y)$ of a property using the following independent variables:

1. Appraised land value of the property
2. Appraised value of the improvements on the property
3. Neighborhood in which the property is listed

The objectives of the study are twofold:

1. To determine whether the data indicate that appraised values of land and improvements are related to sale prices. That is, do the data supply sufficient evidence to indicate that these variables contribute information for the prediction of sale price?
2. To acquire the prediction equation relating appraised value of land and improvements to sale price and to determine whether this relationship is the same for a variety of neighborhoods. In other words, do the appraisers use the same appraisal criteria for various types of neighborhoods?

If the mean sale price $E(y)$ of a property were, in fact, equal to its appraised value x, the relationship between $E(y)$ and x would be a straight line with slope equal to 1,

as shown in Figure 13.38 on page 782. But it is unlikely that this ideal situation will exist. The property appraiser's data could be several years old and consequently may represent (because of inflation) only a percentage of the actual mean sale price. Also, it is not a foregone conclusion that the relationship between $E(y)$ and x is linear (a straight-line relationship). The appraiser might have a tendency to overappraise or underappraise properties in specific price ranges, say, very low-priced or very high-priced properties. If this were true, a second-order curve would provide a better model. Consequently, we will consider both first-order and second-order models for sale price y to determine whether the second-order terms improve the prediction equation.

Recall that we want to relate three independent variables to the sale price y: the qualitative factor, neighborhood (six levels), and the two quantitative factors, appraised land value and appraised improvements value. Consider the following three models as candidates for this relationship:

Model 1 is a first-order model for mean sale price $E(y)$ as a function of the two quantitative independent variables $x_1 =$ appraised land value and $x_2 =$ appraised improvements value. This model will assume that the straight-line relationships are identical for all six neighborhoods, i.e., that a first-order model is appropriate for relating sale price to x_1 and x_2 and that the relationship between the sale price and the appraised value of a property is the same for all neighborhoods. This model is

$$E(y) = \beta_0 + \underbrace{\beta_1 x_1}_{\substack{\text{Appraised land} \\ \text{value}}} + \underbrace{\beta_2 x_2}_{\substack{\text{Appraised} \\ \text{improvements value}}}$$

a. Sketch the relationships between mean sale price and appraised improvements (x_2) hypothesized by model 1 for different values of appraised land value (x_1). Show the relationships for $x_1 = \$10,000$, $x_1 = \$15,000$, and $x_1 = \$20,000$ on the same graph.

Model 2 will assume that the relationship between mean sale price $E(y)$ and x_1 and x_2 is first-order but that

FIGURE 13.38

The Theoretical Relationship Between Mean Sale Price and Appraised Value x

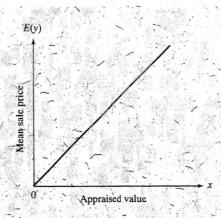

the straight-line relationships differ depending on the neighborhood. That is, model 2 assumes that neighborhood interacts with both x_1 and x_2. This model would be appropriate if the appraiser's procedure for establishing appraised values produced a linear relationship between mean sale price $E(y)$ and x_1 and x_2 that differed in at least two neighborhoods. Model 2 is

$$E(y) = \beta_0 + \overbrace{\beta_1 x_1}^{\substack{\text{Appraised land} \\ \text{value}}} + \overbrace{\beta_2 x_2}^{\substack{\text{Appraised} \\ \text{improvements value}}}$$

$$+ \overbrace{\beta_3 x_3 + \beta_4 x_4 + \beta_5 x_5 + \beta_6 x_6 + \beta_7 x_7}^{\text{Main effect terms for neighborhoods}} +$$

$$+ \overbrace{\beta_8 x_1 x_3 + \beta_9 x_1 x_4 + \cdots + \beta_{12} x_1 x_7}^{\text{Interaction, appraised land by neighborhood}}$$

$$+ \overbrace{\beta_{13} x_2 x_3 + \beta_{14} x_2 x_4 + \cdots + \beta_{17} x_2 x_7}^{\text{Interaction, appraised improvements by neighborhood}}$$

where

$x_1 =$ Appraised land value

$x_2 =$ Appraised improvements value

$$x_3 = \begin{cases} 1 & \text{if Avila} \\ 0 & \text{if not} \end{cases}$$

$$x_4 = \begin{cases} 1 & \text{if Carrollwood Village} \\ 0 & \text{if not} \end{cases}$$

$$\vdots$$

$$x_7 = \begin{cases} 1 & \text{if Town \& Country} \\ 0 & \text{if not} \end{cases}$$

The sixth neighborhood, Ybor City, was chosen as the base level for the qualitative variable. Consequently, the model will predict $E(y)$ for the Ybor City neighborhood when $x_3 = x_4 = \cdots = x_7 = 0$.

b. Using model 2, write the equation of the line relating $E(y)$ to appraised improvements (x_2) for properties with appraised land values of $x_1 = \$10,000$ in Ybor City.

c. Repeat part **b** for each of the following three sets of properties:

(i) $x_1 = \$50,000$, Northdale

(ii) $x_1 = \$80,000$, Northdale

(iii) $x_1 = \$20,000$, Ybor City

d. Use the equations of parts **b** and **c** to sketch the hypothesized relationships between $E(y)$ and x_2 for the four different combinations of x_1 and neighborhood. Show the lines on the same graph.

Model 3 is a second-order model that is similar to first-order model 2 except that we will add second-order terms corresponding to x_1^2, x_2^2, $x_1 x_2$, and all the interactions between these terms and the six dummy variables that define the neighborhoods. Consequently, the second-order model hypothesizes curvature in the relationship between $E(y)$ and x_1 and x_2, with different curves for each neighborhood. The second-order model is given as follows:

Second-order model in x_1 and x_2

$$E(y) = \beta_0 + \overbrace{\beta_1 x_1 + \beta_2 x_2 + \beta_3 x_1 x_2 + \beta_4 x_1^2 + \beta_5 x_2^2}$$

Main effect terms for neighborhoods
$$+ \overbrace{\beta_6 x_3 + \beta_7 x_4 + \beta_8 x_5 + \beta_9 x_6 + \beta_{10} x_7}$$

$$+ \beta_{11} x_3 x_1 + \beta_{12} x_3 x_2 + \beta_{13} x_3 x_1 x_2 + \beta_{14} x_3 x_1^2$$

$$+ \beta_{15} x_3 x_2^2 + \beta_{16} x_4 x_1 + \beta_{17} x_4 x_2 + \beta_{18} x_4 x_1 x_2$$

$$+ \beta_{19} x_4 x_1^2 + \beta_{20} x_4 x_2^2 + \cdots + \beta_{31} x_7 x_1 + \beta_{32} x_7 x_2$$

$$+ \beta_{33} x_7 x_1 x_2 + \beta_{34} x_7 x_1^2 + \beta_{35} x_7 x_2^2$$

e. Repeat parts **b**, **c**, and **d** for model 3.

f. Using an available statistical software package, fit the three models to the data described in Appendix A.1. (The data set of Appendix A.1 can be obtained on a $3\frac{1}{2}$" diskette from the publisher.)

g. Compare models 1 and 2 using the procedure outlined in this chapter. Test using $\alpha = .01$.

h. Compare models 2 and 3 using the procedure outlined in this chapter. Test using $\alpha = .01$.

i. Based on the results from parts **f** and **g**, which of these three models would you recommend for predicting sale price y?

The test in part g should reveal that the first-order prediction equations vary among neighborhoods, and we would expect the same result for the second-order model, i.e., we also expect the second-order model that predicts sale price as a function of the appraised values x_1 and x_2 to vary in shape from neighborhood to neighborhood. To test this theory, we would need to fit a second-order model that would imply the same quadratic relationship for all neighborhoods. This reduced model, **model 4**, is identical to model 3 except that all terms involving the neighborhood dummy variables, x_3, x_4, ..., x_7, have been omitted:

$$E(y) = \beta_0 + \beta_1 x_1 + \beta_2 x_2 + \beta_3 x_1 x_2 + \beta_4 x_1^2 + \beta_5 x_2^2$$

j. Fit model 4 to the data of Appendix A.1 using a statistical software package.

k. Determine whether the second-order relationships differ from neighborhood to neighborhood by comparing model 4 to model 3. Use $\alpha = .01$.

l. Interpret the values of R^2 and R_a^2 for the best of the four models.

m. Is the best model a useful predictor of sale price? Conduct a test for overall model adequacy using $\alpha = .01$.

n. Interpret the value of s for the best model. Do you believe the errors of prediction are small enough to indicate that the model could be of *practical* value in predicting sale prices?

o. List some other real-estate-related variables that might improve the predictive ability of the model.

p. Conduct a residual analysis for the best model. Interpret the results.

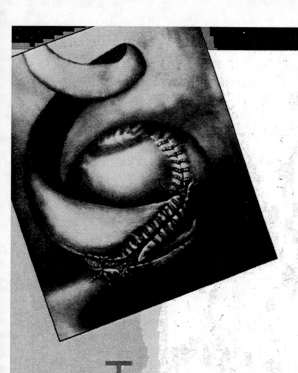

Chapter 16

TIME SERIES ANALYSIS AND FORECASTING

To operate effectively, power companies must be able to accurately predict daily peak demand for electricity. Consequently, they are continually developing and refining statistical models of daily peak demand. In this chapter, we present some statistical methods for analyzing data collected sequentially over time—time series data. Ultimately, we want to forecast a response at some future point in time. The problem of forecasting daily peak demand at Florida Power Corporation is addressed in Case Study 16.2.

■ CONTENTS

16.1 Introduction

You often hear from a television newscaster or read in your daily newspaper statements such as the following: "The Consumer Price Index rose to 489.8 in May, an increase of 2.3 over the previous month"; "The Dow Jones Industrial Average closed at 3,950 today in heavy trading"; "Inflation rate expected to fall below 7% by this time next year"; or "Corporation reports annual net loss of $1 million." Each of these numerical variables—Consumer Price Index (CPI), Dow Jones Industrial Average (DJA), inflation rate, and annual profit (or loss) of a firm—characterizes a particular business or economic phenomenon. However, they are all similar in that each is observed sequentially on a regular chronological basis, daily, monthly, or yearly. Business data that are collected sequentially over time are called **time series**.

Definition 16.1

A **time series** is a collection of data obtained by observing a response variable at periodic points in time.

Definition 16.2

If repeated observations on a variable produce a time series, the variable is called a **time series variable**. We use y_t to denote the value of the variable at time t.

The values of a time series may be plotted on the y-axis, with time on the x-axis, to provide an easily understood summary of the past and present values of the series. We illustrate this graphical descriptive technique with an example.

EXAMPLE 16.1
Plotting a Time Series

The data of Table 16.1 (see page 926) represent the annual average prime interest rates charged by U.S. banks for the years 1975–1994. Identify the time series variable, and plot its values.

SOLUTION The time series variable, i.e., the variable that is measured or observed yearly over the 20-year time period 1975–1994, is the average prime interest rate charged by U.S. banks. A graph of the time series, with prime rate on the y-axis and time (years) on the x-axis, is shown in Figure 16.1 on page 926.

16.2 Time Series Components

Researchers often approach the problem of describing the nature of a time series by first identifying four kinds of change, or variation, in the time series values. These

FIGURE 16.1

Graph of Prime
Interest Rate,
1975–1994

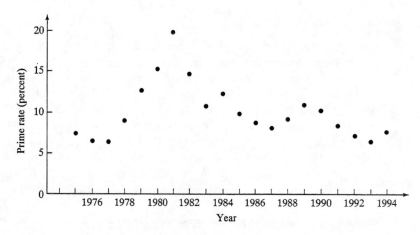

Table 16.1 Prime Interest Rates, Example 16.1

Year	Prime Rate %	Year	Prime Rate %
1975	7.86	1985	9.93
1976	6.84	1986	8.83
1977	6.82	1987	8.21
1978	9.06	1988	9.32
1979	12.67	1989	10.87
1980	15.27	1990	10.01
1981	18.87	1991	8.46
1982	14.86	1992	6.25
1983	10.79	1993	6.00
1984	12.04	1994	6.99

Source: *Survey of Current Business*, U.S. Department of Commerce, Bureau of Economic Analysis.

four components are commonly known as (1) **secular trend**, (2) **cyclical fluctuation**, (3) **seasonal variation**, and (4) **residual effect**.

EXAMPLE 16.2
Time Series Components

What does each of the four time series components attempt to explain?

SOLUTION The four components of a time series are most easily identified and explained pictorially. Figure 16.2 shows three typical time series plots, each of which identifies one of the four kinds of changes.

Figure 16.2a shows a **secular trend** in the time series values. The secular component describes the tendency of the value of the variable to increase or decrease over a long period of time. Thus, this type of change or variation is also known as the **long-term trend**. In Figure 16.2a, the long-term trend is of an increasing nature.

FIGURE 16.2

Illustrating the
Components of a
Time Series, Example
16.2

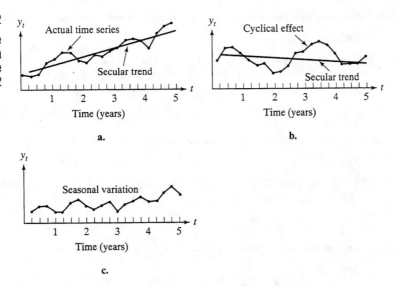

a.

b.

c.

However, this does not imply that the time series has always moved upward from month to month and from year to year. You can see that the series fluctuates, but that the trend has been an increasing one over that period of time.

The **cyclical fluctuation** in a time series, as shown in Figure 16.2b, is the wavelike or oscillating pattern (up and down fluctuations) about the secular trend that is attributable to business and economic conditions at the time. These wavelike fluctuations are sometimes called **business cycles**. During a period of general economic expansion, the business cycle lies above the secular trend, whereas during a recession, when business activity is likely to slump, the cycle lies below the secular trend. You can see that the cyclical fluctuation does not follow any definite trend, but moves rather unpredictably.

The **seasonal variation** in a time series describes the fluctuations that recur during specific portions of each year (e.g., monthly or seasonally). In Figure 16.2c, you can see that the pattern of change in the time series within a year tends to be repeated from year to year.

The final component, the **residual effect**, is what remains after the secular, cyclical, and seasonal components have been removed. This component is not systematic and may be attributable to unpredictable influences such as wars, hurricanes, presidential assassination, and randomness of human actions. Thus, the residual effect represents the random error component of a time series. ■

Definition 16.3

The **secular trend** (T_t) of a time series is the tendency of the series to increase or decrease over a long period of time. It is also known as the **long-term trend**.

Definition 16.4

The **cyclical fluctuation** (C_t) of a time series is the wavelike or oscillating pattern about the secular trend that is attributable to business and economic conditions at the time. It is also known as a **business cycle**.

Definition 16.5

The **seasonal variation** (S_t) of a time series describes the fluctuations that recur during specific portions of the year (e.g., monthly or seasonally).

Definition 16.6

The **residual effect** (R_t) of a time series is what remains after the secular, cyclical, and seasonal components have be removed.

In many practical applications of time series, one of the objectives is to **forecast** (predict) some future value of the series. To obtain forecasts, some type of model that can be projected into the future must be used to describe the time series. One of the most widely used models is the **additive model**[*]

$$y_t = T_t + C_t + S_t + R_t$$

where T_t, C_t, S_t, and R_t represent the secular trend, cyclical fluctuation, seasonal variation, and residual effect, respectively, of the time series variable, y_t. Various methods exist for estimating the components of the model and forecasting the time series. These range from simple **descriptive techniques**, which rely on smoothing the pattern of the time series, to complex **inferential models**, which combine regression analysis with specialized time series models.

Several descriptive techniques are presented in Sections 16.3–16.5, and forecasting using the general linear regression model of Chapter 13 is discussed in Section 16.6. The remainder of the chapter is devoted to the more complex and more powerful time series models.

---

[*]*Another useful model is the **multiplicative model**, $y_t = T_t C_t S_t R_t$. Note that this model can be written in the form of an additive model by taking natural logarithms:*

$log\ y_t = log\ T_t + log\ C_t + log\ S_t + log\ R_t$

16.3 Index Numbers

Various descriptive methods are available for identifying and characterizing a time series. A popular descriptive technique employs **index numbers**. Index numbers are used to measure how much a variable changes over time, relative to a **base period**. For example, we may be interested in comparing the prime rate in 1981 (a year in which a major recession occurred) with the prime rate in 1995. An index number will allow us to make this comparison.

Definition 16.7

An **index number** is a number that measures the relative change in a variable over time. Index numbers are often used to characterize time series phenomena.

Index numbers may be computed from a single time series variable (e.g., world share of oil production), or they may be a composite of several time series variables. For example, an index familiar to everyone is the Consumer Price Index (CPI). The CPI, compiled monthly by the U.S. Bureau of Labor, measures overall price changes of a variety of consumer goods (including food, clothing, television equipment, housing, and transportation) relative to the base year of 1972. The CPI combines the prices of approximately 400 items into a single index that is often used to gauge the increase in the cost of living. Two other important business indexes that combine or aggregate several variables are the Dow Jones Industrial Average (DJA) and the Wholesale Price Index.

In this section, we present three different types of index numbers found to be useful in describing time series.

Simple Index Numbers

Index numbers based on a single time series variable, such as the price of gold, are called **simple index numbers**. In Example 16.3, we illustrate the steps necessary for calculating a simple index number.

Definition 16.8

A **simple index number** is based on the relative changes over time in the value of a single time series variable.

EXAMPLE 16.3
Computing a Simple Index

The price of gold (dollars per troy ounce) is shown in Table 16.2 for the years 1971–1993 (see page 930).

Table 16.2 Gold Prices (Dollars per Troy Ounce),
Example 16.3

Year	Price	Year	Price	Year	Price
1971	$ 41.25	1979	$307.80	1987	$408.91
1972	58.61	1980	606.01	1988	436.93
1973	97.81	1981	450.63	1989	381.28
1974	159.70	1982	374.18	1990	384.07
1975	161.40	1983	449.03	1991	362.04
1976	124.80	1984	360.29	1992	344.50
1977	148.30	1985	317.30	1993	383.69
1978	193.50	1986	367.87		

Source: Survey of Current Business, U.S. Department of Commerce.

a. Calculate the simple index number for the price of gold for this period.

b. Interpret the results.

SOLUTION

a. The first step in calculating an index number is to select the *base period*—that is, the time period (month, year, etc.), upon which the index is to be based. In this example, since the price of gold is measured each year, we will choose a particular year as a base period. The base period is selected with some purpose in mind since all comparisons of the price of gold will be made relative to the price in the base year. Usually, an economist will choose a year during which price levels are "normal," i.e., undisturbed by unusual or extenuating factors (defining price normality is a complex, if not impossible, problem). Many current business and economic indexes, including the CPI, use 1972 as a base period, and for this example, we will also.

After the base period is selected, the next step is to compare the value of the time series variable at two different times—the time being indexed, say, t, and the base period, say, t_0. In our example, $t_0 = 1972$; thus, we will compare the price of gold in year t with the price of gold in 1972. In general, index numbers are expressed as percentages. We shall use the percentage

$$\left(\frac{\text{Price of gold in year } t}{\text{Price of gold in base year 1972}} \right) 100$$

as a *simple index* of the price of gold at a year t. This percentage will then be computed for all years from 1971 through 1993.

Let us start with the year $t = 1971$. To compute the gold price index for 1971, say, I_{1971}, first form the ratio

$$\frac{\text{Price of gold in 1971}}{\text{Price of gold in 1972}} = \frac{41.25}{58.61} = .704$$

Expressing this ratio as a percentage, we have

$$I_{1971} = \left(\frac{41.25}{58.61}\right) 100 = (.704)100 = 70.4$$

Thus, the gold price index for the year 1971 is 70.4%. Notice that the gold price index for the base year $t_0 = 1972$ is

$$I_{1972} = \left(\frac{\text{Price of gold in 1972}}{\text{Price of gold in 1972}}\right) 100$$

$$= \left(\frac{58.61}{58.61}\right) 100 = 100.0$$

It is always true that **the index number for the base period is 100%**. The complete gold price index for 1971–1993 is shown in Table 16.3.

Table 16.3   Simple Index for Gold Prices
of Example 16.3

Year	Index	Year	Index	Year	Index
1971	70.4	1979	525.2	1987	697.7
1972	100.0	1980	1,034.0	1988	745.5
1973	166.9	1981	768.9	1989	650.5
1974	272.5	1982	638.4	1990	593.9
1975	275.4	1983	766.1	1991	617.7
1976	212.9	1984	614.7	1992	587.8
1977	253.0	1985	541.4	1993	654.6
1978	330.1	1986	627.7		

b. The index numbers of Table 16.3 reflect relative price changes in gold from the base year of 1972. Since the indexes are percentages, they represent the percentage change in gold price relative to the base year of 1972. For example, the index for 1971 is 70.4. Thus, we say that the price of gold in 1971 was 70.4% of the price in the base year 1972. Or, equivalently, the 1971 price was 29.6% less than the 1972 price. Now consider the 1987 gold price index of 697.7. This value implies that the price of gold in 1987 was 697.7% of the price in 1972; i.e., the price of gold increased 597% relative to the base year of 1972. The remaining index values are interpreted similarly.

The graph of the gold price index for 1971–1993 is shown in Figure 16.3. Notice that the plot makes it easy to identify the highly inflationary period beginning in 1974 and the extreme jump in gold prices in 1980. This is one of the primary values of simple indexes—they make price fluctuations and trends easier to identify and compare. ▪

FIGURE 16.3

Graph of Gold Price Index for Example 16.3

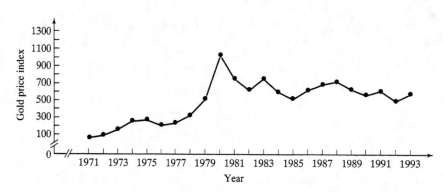

Calculating a Simple Index Number for a Time Series

1. Select the base period, i.e., the time t_0 upon which the index is to be based.

2. Letting y_t represent the value of the time series variable at time t, compute the ratio

$$\frac{y_t}{y_{t_0}}$$

3. The simple index I_t for the time series variable at time t is the ratio in step 2 expressed as a percentage, i.e.,

$$I_t = \left(\frac{y_t}{y_{t_0}}\right)100$$

4. Repeat steps 2 and 3 for each value y_t of the time series.

As previously stated, simple index numbers will always be based on a single time series variable. However, business and economic time series analysts are frequently more interested in examining index numbers for a composite of several variables, such as a combination of wholesale prices of manufactured goods.

Simple Composite Index Numbers

Index numbers computed from a combination of several time series variables or commodities are called **composite index numbers**. The construction of a composite index requires choosing a method of combining the commodities that compose the index. The simplest method of combining these time series variables is to sum them. A composite index based on this sum is called a **simple composite index**.

Definition 16.9

A **simple composite index** is based on the relative change over time in the sum of the values of two more time series variables.

EXAMPLE 16.4
Computing a Simple
Composite Index

The annual personal consumption expenditures (in billions of dollars) of U.S. citizens for food, transportation, and medical care from 1986–1991 are given in Table 16.4.

    a.   Calculate the simple composite index for total annual expenditures for these three products using the base period $t_0 = 1980$.

    b.   Interpret the index.

Table 16.4   Annual Personal Consumption
Expenditures for Example 16.4

Year	Food	Transportation	Medical	Total
1980	394.9	77.4	200.6	672.9
1986	447.1	86.2	251.5	784.8
1987	452.7	89.6	266.8	809.1
1988	460.0	94.5	278.2	832.7
1989	497.1	98.2	309.0	904.3
1990	523.8	102.6	329.8	956.2
1991	543.7	109.3	351.6	1,004.6

Source: Statistical Abstract of the United States, U.S. Bureau of the Census, 1994.

SOLUTION   **a.**   To compute a simple composite index, we first must sum the values of the respective time series variables—in this example, the sum of the annual personal consumption expenditures for food, transportation, and medical care. The sum of these annual expenditures is shown in the column labeled TOTAL in Table 16.4. This column of numbers is used to compute the simple composite index.

    If we let y_t represent the total annual expenditures during year t, the simple composite index (using 1980 as a base) is

$$I_{1986} = \left(\frac{y_{1986}}{y_{1980}}\right)100 = \left(\frac{784.8}{672.9}\right)100 = 116.6$$

$$I_{1987} = \left(\frac{y_{1987}}{y_{1980}}\right)100 = \left(\frac{809.1}{672.9}\right)100 = 120.2$$

and so forth. The complete simple composite index for total annual expenditures for personal consumption expenditures from 1986 to 1991 is given in Table 16.5.

Table 16.5 Simple Composite Index for Total Annual Personal Consumption Expenditures for Example 16.4

Year	Index	Year	Index
1986	116.6	1989	134.4
1987	120.2	1990	142.1
1988	123.7	1991	149.3

b. Our interpretation of the simple composite index is identical to that of the simple index. For example, the 1991 index value of 149.3 represents a 49.3% increase (relative to the base year of 1980) in total annual personal consumption expenditures for food, transportation, and medical care in the United States. ■

Calculating a Simple Composite Index Number for a Time Series

1. Select the base period, i.e., the time t_0 upon which the index is to be based.

2. If the index consists of k time series variables with respective values $Q_{1t}, Q_{2t}, \ldots, Q_{kt}$ at time t, calculate

y_t = Sum of the time series variables at time t

$\quad = \Sigma Q_{it} = Q_{1t} + Q_{2t} + \cdots + Q_{kt}$

y_{t_0} = Sum of the time series variables at time t_0

$\quad = \Sigma Q_{it_0} = Q_{1t_0} + Q_{2t_0} + \cdots + Q_{kt_0}$

3. Calculate the index,

$$I_t = \left(\frac{y_t}{y_{t_0}}\right)100$$

4. Repeat steps 2 and 3 for each value y_t of the composite time series.

Weighted Composite Index Numbers

Although it is easy to compute, a simple composite index has a major drawback. Time series variables with large values exert a greater influence on the index than those with smaller values. For example, with a simple composite price index, commodities with high prices tend to dominate the index more than those with low prices. The index therefore depends on the quantity of each commodity that is included. A more meaningful measure of composite time series is the **weighted composite index**. The time series values are weighted before being summed, where the weights are multipliers chosen to reflect the relative importance of each value. Typically, the weight assigned to a commodity in a composite price index is the quantity of the item consumed.

Definition 16.10

A **weighted composite index** is based on the relative change over time in the weighted sum of two or more time series variables. Usually, the time series variables are prices and the weights are quantities purchased.

EXAMPLE 16.5
Computing a Weighted Composite Index

Consider the information on the prices of milk products for the years 1989–1993, as provided in Table 16.6. Using 1984 as a base period, calculate a weighted composite price index for the milk products if the weights are the total quantities of the products consumed in 1984. Interpret the results.

Table 16.6 Milk Prices (Dollars) for Example 16.5

| Year | Average Price Per Pound | |
	Dry Milk	Fluid Milk
1984	$ .912	$ .135
1989	.993	.133
1990	.948	.137
1991	.893	.123
1992	1.030	.131
1993	1.074	.128
Total quantity consumed (million pounds)		
1984	119.6	1,355

Source: Survey of Current Business, U.S. Dept. of Commerce, Bureau of Economic Analysis.

SOLUTION The first step in calculating a weighted composite price index is to multiply the commodity prices at time t by the corresponding weights. In this example, we need to multiply the average price per unit of dry milk and fluid milk for each year by the corresponding quantity of the commodity consumed during 1984. The two products are then summed to give the value of the composite time series that is to be indexed. These preliminary calculations are shown in Table 16.7.

Table 16.7 Preliminary Calculations for Weighted Composite Index of Example 16.5

| Year | Weighted Price = (Price) × (Quantity) | | Sum of Weighted Prices |
	Dry Milk	Fluid Milk	
1984	(.912) (119.6) = 109.1	(.135) (1,355) = 182.9	292.0
1989	(.993) (119.6) = 118.8	(.133) (1,355) = 180.2	299.0
1990	(.948) (119.6) = 113.4	(.137) (1,355) = 185.6	299.0
1991	(.893) (119.6) = 106.8	(.123) (1,355) = 166.7	273.5
1992	(1.030) (119.6) = 123.2	(.131) (1,355) = 177.5	300.7
1993	(1.074) (119.6) = 128.4	(.128) (1,355) = 173.4	301.8

After computing the weighted sums (the rightmost column of Table 16.7), we calculate the index in the usual manner. Letting y_t represent the weighted sum in year t, we have (using 1984 as the base):

$$I_{1989} = \left(\frac{y_{1989}}{y_{1984}}\right)100 = \left(\frac{299.0}{292.0}\right)100 = 102.4$$

$$I_{1990} = \left(\frac{y_{1990}}{y_{1984}}\right)100 = \left(\frac{299.0}{292.0}\right)100 = 102.4$$

and so forth. The complete weighted composite milk products price index is given in Table 16.8.

Table 16.8 Weighted Composite Index for Milk Prices in Example 16.5

Year	Index
1989	102.4
1990	102.4
1991	93.7
1992	103.0
1993	103.4

Notice from Table 16.6 that the quantity of fluid milk consumed in 1984 is much greater than the quantity of dry milk consumed. By using consumption as a weighting factor, we attach greater importance to fluid milk price changes in our composite index of dairy prices. In effect, we are saying that the price of fluid milk affects the consumer more heavily than dry milk (based on total consumption), and we want the composite price index to reflect this.

Again, our interpretation of the index numbers in Table 16.8 is analogous to those of the previous sections. For example, the 1991 index of 93.7 indicates that, using 1984 consumption as a weighting factor, the composite price of the two milk products (dry milk and fluid milk) is 6.3% lower than the composite price in the base year of 1984. ■

Calculating a Weighted Composite Index Number for a Time Series

1. Select the base period, i.e., the time t_0 upon which the index is to be based.
2. Choose the weights to be attached to each of the time series variables in the composite.* (The weights should reflect the relative importance of each variable. For a price index, the weights are usually the quantities consumed of the respective variables.)
3. If the index consists of k time series variables with respective values $Q_{1t}, Q_{2t}, \ldots, Q_{kt}$ at time t, and the respective weights are denoted by $W_1, W_2, \ldots, W_k$, then calculate

   y_t = Weighted sum of the time series variables at time t

   $$= \Sigma W_i Q_{it} = W_1 Q_{1t} + W_2 Q_{2t} + \cdots + W_k Q_{kt}$$

   y_{t_0} = Weighted sum of the time series variables at time t_0

   $$= \Sigma W_i Q_{it_0} = W_1 Q_{1t_0} + W_2 Q_{2t_0} + \cdots + W_k Q_{kt_0}$$

4. Calculate the index,

   $$I_t = \left(\frac{y_t}{y_{t_0}}\right) 100$$

5. Repeat steps 3 and 4 for each value y_t in the composite time series.

We conclude this section with a warning. There is little doubt that index numbers provide useful descriptive summaries of the degree of relative change in business

*A composite index that uses the original base period weights for the calculations, as in Example 16.5, is called a **Laspeyres index**. A second method of computing a weighted composite index, called a **Paasche index**, uses weights computed for the period at which the index is being calculated.

and economic activity. However, there is a danger of using index numbers for more than they are intended. For example, the Consumer Price Index (CPI) measures how prices of a market basket of goods, *purchased by moderate-income, urban Americans,* have changed. But the CPI is frequently used to gauge the cost of living for *all* Americans. While the CPI does reflect the cost of living to some degree, *all* Americans certainly do not purchase the same goods in the same quantities as urban Americans with moderate incomes. Thus, using the CPI to measure the cost of living of, say, low-income, inner-city families would be improper.

Warning

Do not use index numbers for more than they are intended. In particular, it is inappropriate to generalize the results of an index or to use a single index to predict future business or economic events.

EXERCISES

■ Learning the Mechanics

16.1   Consider the time series y_t, $t = 1, 2, \ldots, 5$, shown in the table.

t	y_t
1	5
2	8
3	10
4	20
5	22

a. Calculate a simple index number for y_5 using $t = 1$ as a base period.
b. Calculate a simple index number for y_4 using $t = 2$ as a base period.
c. Calculate a simple index number for y_5 using $t = 2$ as a base period.

16.2   Consider the two time series, y_t and x_t, shown in the table.

t	y_t	x_t
1	5	83
2	8	82
3	10	70
4	20	55
5	22	48

a. For each value of t, sum the values y_t and x_t.

b. Use the sums, part **a**, to calculate the simple composite index number for $t = 3$ using $t = 1$ as a base period.

c. Use the sums, part **a**, to calculate the simple composite index number for $t = 5$ using $t = 2$ as a base period.

16.3 Refer to the two time series, y_t and x_t, Exercise 16.2. Consider a weighted composite index using $t = 1$ as a base period and the weights $w_1 = 10$ for y_t and $w_2 = .5$ for x_t.

a. Multiply the weights by the values of the time series at time $t = 1$, and sum these products.

b. Multiply the weights by the values of the time series at time $t = 5$, and sum these products.

c. Use the results, parts **a** and **b**, to compute a weighted composite index number for $t = 5$.

▪ *Applying the Concepts*

16.4 Since the energy shortage, the price of foreign crude oil has skyrocketed. Consequently, crude oil imports into the United States have declined. The data in the table are the amounts of crude oil (millions of barrels) imported into the United States from the Organization of Petroleum Exporting Countries (OPEC) for the years 1974–1993.

Year	t	Imports, y_t	Year	t	Imports, y_t
1974	1	926	1984	11	553
1975	2	1,171	1985	12	479
1976	3	1,663	1986	13	771
1977	4	2,058	1987	14	876
1978	5	1,892	1988	15	987
1979	6	1,866	1989	16	1,232
1980	7	1,414	1990	17	1,282
1981	8	1,067	1991	18	1,233
1982	9	633	1992	19	1,247
1983	10	540	1993	20	1,339

Source: Statistical Abstract of the United States, U.S. Bureau of the Census, 1994.

a. Using 1977 as the base period (a year when oil prices skyrocketed), calculate the simple index for OPEC imports from 1974 to 1993.

b. Interpret the index number for 1993.

16.5 The accompanying table records the monthly number of mortgage applications (in thousands) for new home construction processed by the Federal Housing Administration (FHA) for the period 1991–1993.

Mortgage Applications, thousands		
	1991	1992	1993
January	8.0	7.2	5.7
February	6.7	7.5	7.0

(continued)

Mortgage Applications, thousands

	1991	1992	1993
March	8.2	10.1	7.7
April	9.4	9.4	8.2
May	10.5	7.9	7.7
June	8.8	7.7	8.4
July	10.1	8.8	8.3
August	7.4	7.5	8.6
September	7.1	7.1	7.4
October	8.7	7.3	8.8
November	6.6	7.1	9.2
December	6.5	6.5	7.1

Source: Survey of Current Business, U.S. Department of Commerce,
Bureau of Economic Analysis.

a. Using January 1991 as the base period, calculate and plot the simple index for monthly number of mortgage applications between January 1991 and December 1994.

b. Interpret the value of the index you obtained for July 1992.

16.6   The Gross Domestic Product (GDP) is a measure of total U.S. output and is, therefore, an important indicator of the U.S. economy. The GDP is the sum of several components. One of these is personal consumption expenditures, which is itself the sum of durable goods, nondurable goods, and services. The amounts (in billions of dollars) spent on durable goods, nondurable goods, and services in the United States for the period 1984–1993 are given in the accompanying table.

GDP Component

Year	Durable Goods	Nondurable Goods	Services
1984	335.5	867.3	1,128.7
1985	368.7	913.1	1,347.5
1986	402.4	939.4	1,458.0
1987	413.6	974.4	1,568.3
1988	455.2	1,052.3	1,727.6
1989	474.6	1,130.0	1,845.5
1990	480.3	1,193.7	1,983.3
1991	446.1	1,251.5	2,190.1
1992	480.3	1,290.5	2,324.0
1993	538.0	1,139.2	2,501.0

Source: Survey of Current Business, U.S. Department of Commerce, Bureau of Economic Analysis.

a. Using 1984 as a base period, construct a simple composite index for personal consumption for the years 1984–1993.

b. Graph the entire simple composite index of part **a.**

c. Interpret the value of the index for 1993.

16.7 The *Consumer Confidence Index* is designed to measure consumers' appraisal of current economic conditions and their expectations for the future. Each month, the Confidence Board conducts a nationwide survey of 5,000 households and determines the number of people who expect to find employment or increase their personal income 6 months from the time of the interview. This number is compared to the average number during the base period of 1970 to form the monthly Consumer Confidence Index. Suppose the February 1995 Consumer Confidence Index was 95.4. Interpret the index.

16.8 The following table contains the average wholesale prices (in dollars per 100 pounds) of beef steers and hogs for the period 1986–1990. Using 1986 as the base, construct a yearly weighted composite price index for the two products if the weights are total production of the items in 1986. Interpret the index.

	Price, $ per 100 pounds	
Year	*Beef*	*Pork*
1986	57.74	50.73
1987	64.60	47.11
1988	69.58	43.25
1989	74.44	43.91
1990	78.89	54.72
Total production (thousands of animals)		
1986	35,913	77,290

Source: Survey of Current Business, U.S. Department of Commerce, Bureau of Economic Analysis.

16.9 A tradition pulse rate of the economic health of the accommodations (hotel–motel) industry is the trend in room occupancy. Average monthly occupancies for two recent years are given in the table for hotels and motels in the cities of Atlanta, Georgia, and Phoenix, Arizona.

Year 1 Month	*Percentage of Rooms Occupied* Atlanta	Phoenix	Year 2 Month	*Percentage of Rooms Occupied* Atlanta	Phoenix
January	59	67	January	64	72
February	63	85	February	69	91
March	68	83	March	73	87
April	70	69	April	67	75
May	63	63	May	68	70
June	59	52	June	71	61
July	68	49	July	67	46

(continued)

Year 1 Month	Percentage of Rooms Occupied		Year 2 Month	Percentage of Rooms Occupied	
	Atlanta	Phoenix		Atlanta	Phoenix
August	64	49	August	71	44
September	62	56	September	65	63
October	73	69	October	72	73
November	62	63	November	63	71
December	47	48	December	47	51

Source: Trends in the Hotel Industry.

a. Calculate a simple index for the Atlanta monthly occupancy series using January, year 1, as the base period.

b. Calculate a simple index for the Phoenix monthly occupancy series using January, year 1, as the base period.

c. Plot the simple index for both cities on the same graph and interpret the results. (Use two different colors so you will be able to distinguish between the two series.)

16.10 The accompanying table shows the number of transactions per quarter at a New York City bank for the years 1993 and 1994. Using quarter I of 1993 as the base period, construct a simple composite index for the quarterly number of transactions at the New York City bank from 1993 to 1994. Graph the quarterly index and interpret your results.

Year	Quarter	Withdrawals		Deposits	
		Savings	Checking	Savings	Checking
1990	I	41.2	561.8	86.7	392.1
	II	50.8	490.0	71.1	424.0
	III	33.9	733.7	75.3	630.5
	IV	27.5	811.9	66.5	557.6
1991	I	20.8	852.5	70.9	610.4
	II	32.0	814.0	89.2	731.1
	III	39.4	966.1	107.5	500.3
	IV	18.5	1,045.5	93.4	872.2

16.11 A major portion of total consumer credit is extended in the categories of automobile loans and revolving credit. Amounts outstanding (in billions of dollars) in each category for the period 1986–1993 are given in the table.

| | Loan Amount Outstanding, $ billions | |
Year	Automobile	Revolving Credit
1980	112.3	54.9
1986	247.3	137.0
1987	266.0	153.9
1988	281.2	174.8
1989	292.5	198.5
1990	284.7	222.6
1991	260.9	243.6
1992	259.6	254.3
1993	278.3	281.5
	Number of Outstanding Loans	
1980	40,000	100,000

Source: *Statistical Abstract of the United States,* U.S. Bureau of the Census, 1994.

a. Compute a weighted composite index for the series using 1980 as the base period. Use as weights the number of outstanding loans in 1980 in each category.

b. Graph and interpret the index.

16.4 Smoothing Methods

Other descriptive methods, in addition to index numbers, are available for characterizing a time series. Unlike index numbers, however, some of these methods attempt to remove the rapid fluctuations that sometimes occur in a time series so that the tendency of the variable to increase or decrease over a long period of time (i.e., the long-term trend) can be more easily seen. For this reason, they are sometimes called **smoothing techniques**. In this section, we present two popular smoothing methods.

Moving Average Method

A widely used smoothing technique is called the **moving average method**. A moving average, M_t, at time t is formed by averaging the time series values over adjacent time periods. Moving averages aid in identifying the long-term trend of a time series because the averaging tends to modify the effect of rapid fluctuations. That is, a plot of the moving averages yields a "smooth" time series curve that clearly depicts the long-term trend.

Definition 16.11

An *N*-point moving average is the average of the time series values over *N* adjacent time periods.

EXAMPLE 16.6
Computing Moving
Averages

Consider the 1991–1994 quarterly power loads for a utility company located in a southern part of the United States, given in Table 16.9.

Table 16.9   Quarterly Power Loads, 1991–1994

Year	Quarter	Time t	Power Load y_t, megawatts
1991	I	1	103.5
	II	2	94.7
	III	3	118.6
	IV	4	109.3
1992	I	5	126.1
	II	6	116.0
	III	7	141.2
	IV	8	131.6
1993	I	9	144.5
	II	10	137.1
	III	11	159.0
	IV	12	149.5
1994	I	13	166.1
	II	14	152.5
	III	15	178.2
	IV	16	169.0

A graph of the quarterly time series, Figure 16.4, shows the pronounced seasonal variation, i.e., the fluctuation that recurs from year to year. The quarterly power loads tend to be highest in the summer months (quarter III) with another smaller peak in the winter months (quarter I), and lowest during the spring and fall (quarters II and IV). To clearly identify the long-term trend of the series, we need to average, or "smooth out," these seasonal fluctuations.

FIGURE 16.4

Graph of Quarterly
Power Loads, Table
16.9

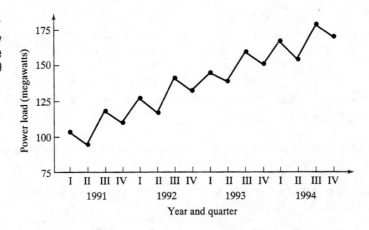

a. Calculate a 4-point moving average for the quarterly time series.

b. Graph the 4-point moving average and interpret the results.

SOLUTION

a. The first step in calculating a moving average for quarterly data is to sum the observed time values y_t—in this example, quarterly power loads—for the four quarters during the initial year 1991. Summing the values from Table 16.9, we have

$$y_1 + y_2 + y_3 + y_4 = 103.5 + 94.7 + 118.6 + 109.3$$

$$= 426.1$$

This sum is called a **4-point moving total**, which we denote by the symbol S_t. It is customary to use a subscript t to represent the time period at the midpoint of the four quarters in the total. Since for this sum, midpoint is between $t = 2$ and $t = 3$, we will use the conventional procedure of "dropping it down one line" to $t = 3$. Thus, our first 4-point moving total is $S_3 = 426.1$.

We find the next moving total by eliminating the first quantity in the sum, $y_1 = 103.5$, and adding the next value in the time series sequence, $y_5 = 126.1$. This enables us to keep four quarters in the total of adjacent time periods. Thus, we have

$$S_4 = y_2 + y_3 + y_4 + y_5 = 94.7 + 118.6 + 109.3 + 126.1$$

$$= 448.7$$

Continuing this process of "moving" the 4-point total over the time series until we have included the last value, we find

$$S_5 = y_3 + y_4 + y_5 + y_6 \quad = 118.6 + 109.3 + 126.1 + 116.0 \ = 470.0$$

$$S_6 = y_4 + y_5 + y_6 + y_7 \quad = 109.3 + 126.1 + 116.0 + 141.2 \ = 492.6$$

$$\vdots \qquad\qquad \vdots \qquad\qquad\qquad\qquad\qquad \vdots \qquad\qquad\qquad \vdots$$

$$S_{15} = y_{13} + y_{14} + y_{15} + y_{16} = 166.1 + 152.5 + 178.2 + 169.0 \ = 665.8$$

The complete set of 4-point moving totals is given in the appropriate column of Table 16.10 on page 946. Notice that three data points will be "lost" in forming the moving totals.

After the 4-point moving totals are calculated, the second step is to determine the **4-point moving average**, denoted by M_t, by dividing each of the moving totals by 4. For example, the first three values of the 4-point moving average for the quarterly power load data are:

$$M_3 = \frac{y_1 + y_2 + y_3 + y_4}{4} = \frac{S_3}{4} = \frac{426.1}{4} = 106.5$$

$$M_4 = \frac{y_2 + y_3 + y_4 + y_5}{4} = \frac{S_4}{4} = \frac{448.7}{4} = 112.2$$

$$M_5 = \frac{y_3 + y_4 + y_5 + y_6}{4} = \frac{S_5}{4} = \frac{470.0}{4} = 117.5$$

All of the 4-point moving averages are given in the appropriate column of Table 16.10.

Table 16.10 4-Point Moving Average for the Quarterly Power Load Data

Year	Quarter	Time t	Power Load y_t	4-Point Moving Total S_t	4-Point Moving Average M_t	Ratio y_t/M_t
1991	I	1	103.5	—	—	—
	II	2	94.7	—	—	—
	III	3	118.6	426.1	106.5	1.113
	IV	4	109.3	448.7	112.2	.974
1992	I	5	126.1	470.0	117.5	1.073
	II	6	116.0	492.6	123.2	.942
	III	7	141.2	514.9	128.7	1.097
	IV	8	131.6	533.3	133.3	.987
1993	I	9	144.5	554.4	138.6	1.043
	II	10	137.1	572.2	143.1	.958
	III	11	159.0	590.1	147.5	1.078
	IV	12	149.5	611.7	152.9	.978
1994	I	13	166.1	627.1	156.8	1.059
	II	14	152.5	646.3	161.6	.944
	III	15	178.2	665.8	166.5	1.071
	IV	16	169.0	—	—	—

b. Both the original power load time series and the 4-point moving average are graphed in Figure 16.5. Notice that the moving average has smoothed the time series, i.e., the averaging has modified the effects of the short-term or seasonal variation. The plot of the 4-point moving average clearly depicts the secular (long-term) trend component of the time series. ■

Moving averages are not restricted to 4 points. For example, you may wish to calculate a 7-point moving average for daily data, a 12-point moving average for

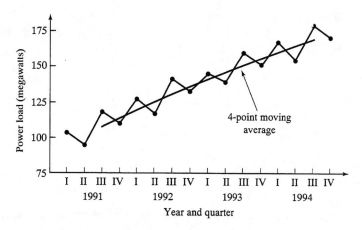

FIGURE 16.5

Quarterly Power Loads and 4-Point Moving Average

monthly data, or a 5-point moving average for yearly data. Although the choice of the number of points is arbitrary, you should search for the number N that yields a smooth series, but is not so large that many points at the end of the series are "lost." The method of constructing an N-point moving average is outlined in the box.

Calculating an N-Point Moving Average

1. Select N, the number of consecutive time series values $y_1, y_2, \ldots, y_n$ that will be averaged. (The time series values must be equally spaced.)

2. Calculate the N-point moving total, S_t, by summing the time series values over N adjacent time periods, where

$$S_t = \begin{cases} y_{t-(N-1)/2} + \cdots + y_t + \cdots + y_{t+(N-1)/2} & \text{if } N \text{ is odd} \\ y_{t-N/2} + \cdots + y_t + \cdots + y_{t+N/2-1} & \text{if } N \text{ is even} \end{cases}$$

3. Compute the N-point moving average, M_t, by dividing the corresponding moving total by N:

$$M_t = \frac{S_t}{N}$$

Exponential Smoothing

Another popular smoothing method is called **exponential smoothing**. Like the moving average method, exponential smoothing tends to deemphasize (or "smooth") most of the random effects. However, exponential smoothing averages only past and current values of the time series.

To obtain an exponentially smoothed time series, we first need to choose a weight w, between 0 and 1, called the **exponential smoothing constant**. The exponentially smoothed series, denoted E_t, is then calculated as follows:

$$E_1 = y_1$$
$$E_2 = wy_2 + (1 - w)E_1$$
$$E_3 = wy_3 + (1 - w)E_2$$
$$\vdots \qquad \vdots$$
$$E_t = wy_t + (1 - w)E_{t-1}$$

You can see that the exponentially smoothed value at time t is simply a weighted average of the current time series value, y_t, and the exponentially smoothed value at the previous time period, E_{t-1}. Smaller values of w give less weight to the current value, y_t, whereas larger values give more weight to y_t.

Definition 16.12

The **exponentially smoothed value** at time t is the weighted average of the time series values at time t and time $(t - 1)$.

Calculating an Exponentially Smoothed Series

1. The data consist of n equally spaced time series values, y_1, y_2, $\ldots, y_n$.
2. Select a smoothing constant, w, between 0 and 1. (Smaller values of w give less weight to the current value of the series and yield a smoother series. Larger values of w give more weight to the current value of the series and yield a more variable series.)
3. Calculate the exponentially smoothed series, E_t, as follows:

$$E_1 = y_1$$
$$E_2 = wy_2 + (1 - w)E_1$$
$$E_3 = wy_3 + (1 - w)E_2$$
$$\vdots$$
$$E_n = wy_n + (1 - w)E_{n-1}$$

EXAMPLE 16.7
Computing an
Exponentially Smoothed
Series

Refer to Example 16.6 and the quarterly power load data given in Table 16.9. Calculate and graph the exponentially smoothed series using a smoothing constant of $w = .7$.

SOLUTION Substituting $w = .7$ and $1 - w = .3$ into the formulas given in the preceding box, we have

$$E_1 = y_1 = 103.5$$

$$E_2 = .7y_2 + (1 - .7)E_1$$

$$= .7(94.7) + .3(103.5) = 97.3$$

$$E_3 = .7y_3 + (1 - .7)E_2$$

$$= .7(118.6) + .3(97.3) = 112.2$$

$$\vdots$$

The exponentially smoothed values (using $w = .7$) for all the quarterly power loads are given in Table 16.11. Both the actual and the smoothed time series values are graphed in Figure 16.6. You can see that the exponentially smoothed series is less variable than the actual series, making it easier to identify the long-term trend.

Table 16.11   Quarterly Power Load with Exponential Smoothing

Year	Quarter	Time t	Power Load y_t	Exponentially Smoothed Power Load E_t
1991	I	1	103.5	103.5
	II	2	94.7	97.3
	III	3	118.6	112.2
	IV	4	109.3	110.2
1992	I	5	126.1	121.3
	II	6	116.0	117.6
	III	7	141.2	134.1
	IV	8	131.6	132.4
1993	I	9	144.5	140.9
	II	10	137.1	138.2
	III	11	159.0	152.8
	IV	12	149.5	150.5
1994	I	13	166.1	161.4
	II	14	152.5	155.2
	III	15	178.2	171.3
	IV	16	169.0	169.7

FIGURE 16.6

Plot of Exponentially
Smoothed Power
Loads

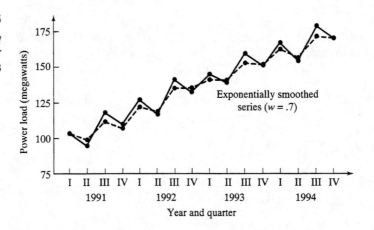

In the next section, we show how to obtain forecasts of the time series using both moving averages and exponential smoothing.

EXERCISES

■ *Learning the Mechanics*

16.12 Consider the time series y_t, $t = 1, 2, 3, 4, 5$, shown in the table.

t	y_t
1	2
2	10
3	12
4	8
5	15

  a. Calculate the sums $(y_1 + y_2)$, $(y_2 + y_3)$, $(y_3 + y_4)$, and $(y_4 + y_5)$. These are 2-point moving totals.
  b. Calculate the 2-point moving averages corresponding to each of the sums, part **a**.
  c. Plot the moving averages, part **b**.

16.13 Refer to the time series, Exercise 16.12.
  a. Calculate the sums $(y_1 + y_2 + y_3)$, $(y_2 + y_3 + y_4)$, and $(y_3 + y_4 + y_5)$. These are the 3-point moving totals.
  b. Calculate the 3-point moving averages corresponding to each of the sums, part **a**.
  c. Plot the moving averages, part **b**.

16.14 Refer to the time series, Exercise 16.12. Calculate the exponentially smoothed value of y_3 for each of the following smoothing constants.
  a. $w = .2$ **b.** $w = .5$ **c.** $w = .75$

■ *Applying the Concepts*

16.15 The quarterly numbers of new privately owned housing starts (in thousands of dwellings) in the United States from winter 1989 through spring 1994 are recorded in the accompanying table.

Year	Quarter	Housing Starts	Year	Quarter	Housing Starts
1989	I	290.6	1992	I	262.0
	II	390.9		II	340.6
	III	346.2		III	322.1
	IV	303.6		IV	276.7
1990	I	300.8	1993	I	240.6
	II	320.8		II	367.2
	III	307.1		III	355.6
	IV	233.0		IV	322.0
1991	I	185.4	1994	I	293.9
	II	300.8		II	421.6
	III	284.8			
	IV	152.0			

Source: Standard & Poor's Statistical Service: Current Statistics, Jan. 1995, New York, Standard & Poor's Corporation.

a. Plot the quarterly time series. Can you detect a long-term trend?

b. Calculate the 4-point moving average for the quarterly housing starts.

c. Graph the 4-point moving average on the same set of axes you used for the graph in part **a.** Is the long-term trend more evident? What effects has the moving average method removed or smoothed?

16.16 Refer to the quarterly housing starts data given in Exercise 16.15.

a. Calculate the exponentially smoothed series for housing starts using a smoothing constant of $w = .2$.

b. Plot the exponentially smoothed series. Can you detect the long-term trend?

16.17 The Consumer Price Index (CPI) for the years 1980–1993 (using 1967 as a base period) is shown in the table.

Year	CPI	Year	CPI
1980	246.8	1987	340.1
1981	272.4	1988	354.2
1982	289.1	1989	371.3
1983	298.4	1990	391.3
1984	311.1	1991	401.6
1985	322.2	1992	413.2
1986	328.4	1993	425.6

Source: Survey of Current Business, U.S. Department of Commerce, Bureau of Economic Analysis.

a. Graph the time series. Can you detect a long-term trend?

b. Calculate and plot a 3-point moving average for the CPI. Compare the plot with that obtained in part **a**.

16.18 Refer to the CPI data given in Exercise 16.17.

a. Calculate and plot the exponentially smoothed series for the CPI using a smoothing constant of $w = .4$.

b. Calculate and plot the exponentially smoothed series for the CPI using a smoothing constant of $w = .8$.

c. Compare the two plots obtained in parts **a** and **b**. Which plot yields a smoother series?

16.19 Standard & Poor's 500 Composite Stock Index (S&P 500) is a stock market index that financial experts use to monitor stock market activity. The accompanying table contains end-of-quarter values of the S&P 500 for the years 1985–1992.

Year	Quarter	S&P 500	Year	Quarter	S&P 500
1985	I	180.6	1989	I	294.8
	II	191.8		II	317.9
	III	182.0		III	349.1
	IV	211.2		IV	353.4
1986	I	232.3	1990	I	339.9
	II	245.3		II	358.0
	III	238.2		III	306.0
	IV	248.6		IV	330.2
1987	I	291.7	1991	I	372.2
	II	304.0		II	378.3
	III	321.8		III	387.2
	IV	247.0		IV	388.5
1988	I	258.8	1992	I	407.4
	II	273.5		II	408.3
	III	271.9		III	418.5
	IV	277.7		IV	435.6

Source: Standard & Poor's Statistical Service: Current Statistics, Jan. 1993, New York, Standard & Poor's Corporation.

a. Calculate a 4-point moving average for the quarterly stock market index.

b. Plot the quarterly index and the 4-point moving average on the same graph. Can you identify the long-term trend of the time series?

16.20 Refer to the S&P 500 data given in Exercise 16.19.

a. Calculate and plot the exponentially smoothed series for the quarterly S&P 500 using a smoothing constant of $w = .3$.

b. Explain how you could obtain a series smoother than the series calculated in part **a**.

16.21 Refer to Exercise 16.5. The monthly mortgage applications data for 1991–1993 are reproduced in the table.

Mortgage Applications, Thousands

	1991	1992	1993
January	8.0	7.2	5.7
February	6.7	7.5	7.0
March	8.2	10.1	7.7
April	9.4	9.4	8.2
May	10.5	7.9	7.7
June	8.8	7.7	8.4
July	10.1	8.8	8.3
August	7.4	7.5	8.6
September	7.1	7.1	7.4
October	8.7	7.3	8.8
November	6.6	7.1	9.2
December	6.5	6.5	7.1

Source: Survey of Current Business, U.S. Department of Commerce, Bureau of Economic Analysis.

a. Examine the graph of the time series you constructed in part **a** of Exercise 16.5. Can you detect a long-term trend?

b. Calculate and plot a 6-point moving average for the monthly number of mortgage applications. Compare the two plots.

16.5 Forecasting Using Smoothing Techniques

In Section 16.4, we described two methods for smoothing a time series: moving averages and exponential smoothing. These smoothing techniques attempt to remove the rapid fluctuations in a time series so that the secular (long-term) trend can be more easily seen. Once the secular trend is identified, forecasts for future values of the time series are easily obtained. We illustrate the two methods with examples.

EXAMPLE 16.8
Forecasting with Moving Averages

Refer to Example 16.6, where we constructed a 4-point moving average for the 1991–1994 quarterly power loads of a utility company. The actual time series values and the moving averages are reproduced in Table 16.12 and plotted in Figure 16.7 on page 954. Use the moving average method to forecast the power load for quarter I of 1995.

SOLUTION To forecast a future value of the time series using the moving average method, simply extend the moving average M_t on the graph (Figure 16.7) to the future time period. You can see from Figure 16.7 that a graphical extension of the 4-point moving average for the quarterly power loads to quarter I of 1995 ($t = 17$) yields a moving average of approximately $M_{17} = 172$. This value, 172 megawatts, represents the *unadjusted* forecast for quarter I of 1995.

Table 16.12 4-Point Moving Averages for the Quarterly Power Load Data

Year	Quarter	Time t	Power Load y_t	4-point Moving Total S_t	4-point Moving Average M_t	Ratio y_t/M_t
1991	I	1	103.5	—	—	—
	II	2	94.7	—	—	—
	III	3	118.6	426.1	106.5	1.113
	IV	4	109.3	448.7	112.2	.974
1992	I	5	126.1	470.0	117.5	1.073
	II	6	116.0	492.6	123.2	.942
	III	7	141.2	514.9	128.7	1.097
	IV	8	131.6	533.3	133.3	.987
1993	I	9	144.5	554.4	138.6	1.043
	II	10	137.1	572.2	143.1	.958
	III	11	159.0	590.1	147.5	1.078
	IV	12	149.5	611.7	152.9	.978
1994	I	13	166.1	627.1	156.8	1.059
	II	14	152.5	646.3	161.6	.944
	III	15	178.2	665.8	166.5	1.071
	IV	16	169.0	—	—	—

FIGURE 16.7

Quarterly Power Loads and 4-Point Moving Average

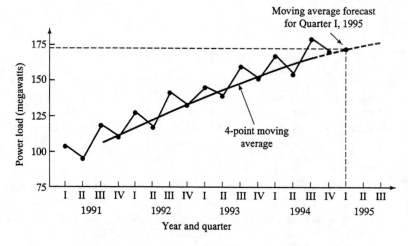

EXAMPLE 16.9
Seasonal Adjustment to Moving Average Forecast

Refer to Example 16.8. The graph in Figure 16.7 clearly shows the seasonal variation in the quarterly power loads. Each year, the power loads peak in quarter III (summer) and quarter I (winter) and fall in quarter II (spring) and quarter IV (fall.) Calculate an adjusted forecast for quarter I of 1995 to account for the pronounced seasonal variation in the series.

SOLUTION The ratio between the observed power load, y_t, and the 4-point moving average, M_t, for each quarter measures the seasonal effect (primarily attributable to temperature differences) for that quarter. The ratios y_t/M_t are calculated and shown in the last column of Table 16.12. The average of the ratios for a particular quarter, multiplied by 100, can be used to form a **seasonal index** for that quarter. For example, the seasonal index for quarter I is

$$\frac{1.073 + 1.043 + 1.059}{3}(100) = 105.8$$

implying that the time series values in quarter I is, on the average, 105.8% of the moving average value for that time period.

To adjust the forecast for quarter I, 1995, for seasonal variation, multiply the future moving average value $M_{17} = 172$ (obtained in Example 16.8) by the seasonal index for quarter I, then divide by 100:

$$F_{17} \approx M_{17}\left(\frac{\text{Seasonal index for quarter I}}{100}\right)$$

$$= 172\left(\frac{105.8}{100}\right) = 182$$

where F_{17} is the forecast of y_{17}. Therefore, the seasonally adjusted moving average forecast for the power load in quarter I of 1995 is approximately 182 megawatts. ■

The method of forecasting with a general N-point moving average is outlined in the box on page 956.

One problem with using a moving average to forecast values of a time series is that values at the ends of the series are "lost," thereby requiring that we subjectively extend the graph of the moving average into the future. No exact calculation of a forecast is available because the moving average at a future time period t requires that we know one or more future values of the series. Alternatively, the exponential smoothing technique will lead to forecasts that can be explicitly calculated, as Example 16.10 illustrates.

Forecasting Using an N-Point Moving Average Method

1. Obtain the N-point moving average (refer to the box in Section 16.4).
2. Graph the moving average M_t on the vertical axis with time t on the horizontal axis. (This plot should reveal a "smooth" curve that identifies the long-term trend of the time series.[*]) Extend the graph to a future time period to obtain the forecasted value of M_t.
3. For a future time period t, the forecast of y_t is

$$F_t = \begin{cases} M_t & \text{if little or no seasonal variation exists in the time series} \\ M_t \left(\dfrac{\text{Seasonal index}}{100} \right) & \text{otherwise} \end{cases}$$

where the seasonal index for a particular quarter (or month) is the average of past values of the ratios

$$\frac{y_t}{M_t} (100)$$

for that quarter (or month).

EXAMPLE 16.10
Forecasting with Exponential Smoothing

Refer to Example 16.7, where we calculated the exponentially smoothed quarterly power load series using a smoothing constant of $w = .7$. The exponentially smoothed values are reproduced in Table 16.13. Calculate the exponentially smoothed forecast of the power load in quarter I of 1995.

SOLUTION Exponentially smoothed forecasts are obtained by taking a weighted average of the most recent value of the time series, y_t, and the most recent exponentially smoothed value, E_t. If n is the last time period in which y_t is observed, then the forecast for a future time period t is given by

$$F_t = wy_n + (1 - w)E_n$$

Therefore, the forecast for the power load in quarter I of 1995 ($t = 17$) is calculated as follows:

$$F_{17} = wy_{16} + (1 - w)E_{16} = .7(169.0) + .3(169.7) = 169.2$$

---

[*]When the number N of points is small, the plot may not yield a very smooth curve. However, the moving average will be smoother (or less variable) than the plot of the original time series values.

Table 16.13   Quarterly Power Load with Exponential Smoothing

Year	Quarter	Time t	Power Load y_t	Exponentially Smoothed Power Load E_t
1991	I	1	103.5	103.5
	II	2	94.7	97.3
	III	3	118.6	112.2
	IV	4	109.3	110.2
1992	I	5	126.1	121.3
	II	6	116.0	117.6
	III	7	141.2	134.1
	IV	8	131.6	132.4
1993	I	9	144.5	140.9
	II	10	137.1	138.2
	III	11	159.0	152.8
	IV	12	149.5	150.5
1994	I	13	166.1	161.4
	II	14	152.5	155.2
	III	15	178.2	171.3
	IV	16	169.0	169.7

The steps for calculating exponentially smoothed forecasts are given in the next box. Note that the right-hand side of the forecast equation does not depend on the future time period t; hence, forecasts for all future time periods are the same. For example, the forecasts of the quarterly power loads of all future quarters will be 169.2 megawatts, the same as the value for quarter I of 1995. This points out one disadvantage of the exponential smoothing forecasting technique. Since the exponentially smoothed forecast is constant for all future values, any changes in trend and/or seasonality are not taken into account. Therefore, exponentially smoothed forecasts are appropriate only when the trend and seasonal components of the time series are relatively insignificant.

Forecasting Using Exponential Smoothing

1. Calculate the exponentially smoothed series E_t with smoothing constant w ($0 < w < 1$) as shown in the box in Section 16.4.

2. Calculate the forecast for any future time period t as follows:

$$F_t = wy_n + (1 - w)E_n, \quad t = n + 1, n + 2, \ldots$$

where E_n is the exponentially smoothed value for the last time period in which y_t is observed.

We conclude this section with a comment. A major disadvantage of forecasting with smoothing techniques (the moving average method or exponential smoothing) is that no measure of the forecast error (or reliability) is known. Although forecast errors can be calculated *after* the future values of the time series have been observed, we prefer to have some measure of the accuracy of the forecast *before* the actual values are observed. For this reason, smoothing techniques are generally regarded as descriptive rather than as inferential procedures. On the other hand, forecasts with inferential models (such as regression models) are accompanied by measures of the *standard error of the forecast*, which allow us to construct prediction intervals for the future time series value. We discuss inferential time series forecasting models in the remaining sections of this chapter.

> **Warning**
>
> Many forecasting methods based on smoothing techniques have been proposed. There are usually no measures of reliability for these forecasts, and thus the risk associated with making decisions based on them cannot be assessed. These forecasting techniques should be used with care.

EXERCISES

■ *Learning the Mechanics*

16.22 Refer to the 2-point moving average you calculated and plotted in Exercise 16.12. Extend the graph to obtain a forecast for y_6.

16.23 Refer to the exponentially smoothed series you calculated in Exercise 16.14a.
a. Use the smoothed values to forecast y_6.
b. Use the smoothed values to forecast y_7.

16.24 Consider a 3-point moving average for the monthly time series shown here.

| | Year 1 | | | Year 2 | |
Month	y_t	M_t	Month	y_t	M_t
January	4	—	January	8	4
February	2	5	February	2	6
March	9	4	March	8	5
April	1	4	April	5	5
May	2	2	May	2	5
June	3	5	June	8	7
July	10	6	July	11	10

(continued)

	Year 1			*Year 2*		
Month	y_t	M_t	Month	y_t	M_t
August	6	8	August	11	12
September	8	11	September	14	15
October	17	10	October	20	15
November	5	8	November	11	11
December	2	5	December	2	—

a. Calculate a seasonal index for the month of February.

b. Calculate a seasonal index for the month of October.

c. Calculate a seasonal index for the month of June.

■ *Applying the Concepts*

16.25 What are the drawbacks to using the moving average method to forecast a time series?

16.26 What are the drawbacks to using the exponential smoothing technique to forecast a time series?

16.27 Can you measure the reliability of the forecasts obtained using a smoothing technique? Why is this a problem?

16.28 Refer to Exercise 16.4. The amounts of crude oil (millions of barrels) imported into the United States from the Organization of Petroleum Exporting Countries (OPEC) for the years 1974–1993 are reproduced here.

Year	t	Imports, y_t	Year	t	Imports, y_t
1974	1	926	1984	11	553
1975	2	1,171	1985	12	479
1976	3	1,663	1986	13	771
1977	4	2,058	1987	14	876
1978	5	1,892	1988	15	987
1979	6	1,866	1989	16	1,232
1980	7	1,414	1990	17	1,282
1981	8	1,067	1991	18	1,233
1982	9	633	1992	19	1,247
1983	10	540	1993	20	1,339

Source: Statistical Abstract of the United States, U.S. Bureau of the Census, 1994.

a. Calculate and plot a 3-point moving average for annual OPEC oil imports.

b. Calculate and plot the exponentially smoothed series for annual OPEC oil imports using a smoothing constant of $w = .3$.

c. Forecast OPEC oil imports in 1995 using the moving average method.

d. Forecast OPEC oil imports in 1995 using exponential smoothing with $w = .3$.

16.29 Refer to Exercise 16.15. The quarterly number of new privately owned housing starts (in thousands of dwellings) in the United States from winter 1989 through spring 1994 are reproduced here.

Year	Quarter	Housing Starts	Year	Quarter	Housing Starts
1989	I	290.6	1992	I	262.0
	II	390.9		II	340.6
	III	346.2		III	322.1
	IV	303.6		IV	276.7
1990	I	300.8	1993	I	240.6
	II	320.8		II	367.2
	III	307.1		III	355.6
	IV	233.0		IV	322.0
1991	I	185.4	1994	I	293.9
	II	300.8		II	421.6
	III	284.8			
	IV	152.0			

Source: Standard & Poor's Statistic Service: Current Statistics, Jan. 1995, New York, Standard & Poor's Corporation.

a. In Exercise 16.15, you calculated the 4-point moving average for the quarterly series. Use this information to calculate the seasonal index for the number of housing starts in quarter III.

b. Use the moving average method to forecast the number of housing starts in quarter III of 1994.

16.30 Refer to the quarterly housing starts data, Exercise 16.29. In Exercise 16.16, you calculated the exponentially smoothed series using $w = .2$. Use the exponentially smoothed series to forecast the number of new housing starts in quarter III of 1994.

16.31 Refer to Exercise 16.17. The Consumer Price Index (CPI) for the period 1980–1993 (using 1967 as a base period) is reproduced here.

Year	CPI	Year	CPI
1980	246.8	1987	340.1
1981	272.4	1988	354.2
1982	289.1	1989	371.3
1983	298.4	1990	391.3
1984	311.1	1991	401.6
1985	322.2	1992	413.2
1986	328.4	1993	425.6

Source: Survey of Current Business, U.S. Department of Commerce, Bureau of Economic Analysis.

a. In Exercise 16.17, you calculated a 3-point moving average for the CPI. Use the moving average method to forecast the CPI in 1994.

b. In Exercise 16.18, you calculated the exponentially smoothed CPI series using $w = .4$. Use the exponentially smoothed values to forecast the CPI in 1994.

16.32 Refer to Exercise 16.19. The end-of-quarter values of the Standard & Poor's 500 Stock Average (S&P 500) for the years 1985–1992 are reproduced here.

Year	Quarter	S&P 500	Year	Quarter	S&P 500
1985	I	180.6	1989	I	294.8
	II	191.8		II	317.9
	III	182.0		III	349.1
	IV	211.2		IV	353.4
1986	I	232.3	1990	I	339.9
	II	245.3		II	358.0
	III	238.2		III	306.0
	IV	248.6		IV	330.2
1987	I	291.7	1991	I	372.2
	II	304.0		II	378.3
	III	321.8		III	387.2
	IV	247.0		IV	388.5
1988	I	258.8	1992	I	407.4
	II	273.5		II	408.3
	III	271.9		III	418.5
	IV	277.7		IV	435.6

Source: Standard & Poor's Statistical Service: Current Statistics, Jan. 1993, New York, Standard & Poor's Corporation.

a. In Exercise 16.19, you calculated the 4-point moving average for the S&P 500 series. Use the moving average method to forecast the quarterly S&P 500 for quarter I, 1994.

b. In Exercise 16.20, you calculated the exponentially smoothed series for the S&P 500 using $w = .3$. Calculate the exponentially smoothed forecast of the quarterly S&P 500 in 1994.

16.33 An article in the *Journal of Accountancy* (Oct. 1988) demonstrated the use of microcomputer spreadsheet software for trend analysis. Three exponentially smoothed forecasts of year-end balance were developed.

a. The first exponentially smoothed forecast was obtained by placing "emphasis on the early years" in the annual time series. Give a value of the weighting constant w that would satisfy this requirement.

b. The second forecast was obtained by placing "equal emphasis on all years" in the time series. Give the value of w for this forecast.

c. The third forecast was obtained by placing "emphasis on recent years" in the time series. Give a value of w that satisfies this requirement.

16.6 Forecasting Using Regression

One way of describing the long-term trend of a time series is to fit a line to the sample data, using the method of least squares discussed in Chapter 12. That is, if a plot of the sample data reveals a linear trend, we way hypothesize that the secular component of the time series can be explained by the simple linear regression (straight-line) model

$$E(y_t) = \beta_0 + \beta_1 t$$

where y_t is the time series value at time t. The least squares prediction equation can then be used to forecast future values of the time series. Unlike the smoothing forecasting methods of Section 16.5, the regression model allows us to calculate prediction intervals for the forecasts to assess their reliability.

EXAMPLE 16.11
Modeling Secular Trend

Refer to the data on the quarterly power loads, given in Table 16.9 (page 944). Since the graph of the data shown in Figure 16.7 (page 954) reveals a linearly increasing long-term trend, the straight-line model

$$E(y_t) = \beta_0 + \beta_1 t$$

seems plausible for the secular trend.

a. Use the data of Table 16.9 to fit the model by the method of least squares.

b. Plot the least squares line. Is the straight-line model appropriate for describing the long-term trend?

SOLUTION

a. The ASP printout of the simple linear regression for the data of Table 16.9 is given in Figure 16.8. The printout identifies the least squares estimates of the y-intercept β_0 and slope β_1 as

$$\hat{\beta}_0 = 95.6625$$

$$\hat{\beta}_1 = 4.89926$$

Thus, the least squares line that explains the secular trend for the quarterly power load is

$$\hat{y}_t = \hat{\beta}_0 + \hat{\beta}_1 t = 95.6625 + 4.89926t$$

b. A graph of the power load data and the least squares line is shown in Figure 16.9. You can see that the power loads fluctuate about the line (seasonal variation), but the overall long-term trend is clearly depicted.

FIGURE 16.8

ASP Printout for
Least Squares Fit
(Straight Line) to
y_t = Power Load,
Example 16.11

STRAIGHT-LINE REGRESSION MODEL FOR QUARTERLY POWER LOADS

```
MODEL:  LOAD = 4.89926T + 95.6625CNST

           COEF. SD. ER.    t(14)      P-VALUE  PT. R SQ.
        --------- ------- ------- ----------- ---------
      T  4.89926 0.45062 10.8723 3.28399E-8   0.894105
   CNST 95.6625  4.35729 21.9546 3.02734E-12  0.971774

   R SQ. = 0.894105,  ADJ. R SQ. = 0.886541,  D. W. = 3.68473
   SD. ER. EST. = 8.30903,  F(1/14) = 118.206 (P-VALUE = 3.28399E-8)
```

FIGURE 16.9

Plot of Quarterly
Power Loads and
Least Squares Line
for Example 16.11

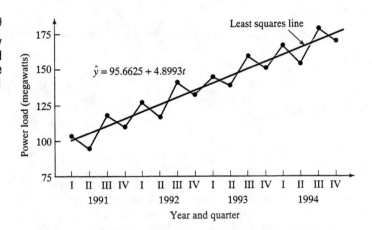

The fact that the least squares line provides a good description of the secular trend is supported by the information given in the ASP printout shown in Figure 16.8. A test of H_0: $\beta_1 = 0$ is highly significant (p-value ≈ 0) and $r^2 = .894$.   ■

In addition to the secular (long-term) trend of a time series, you may want to include terms for cyclical or seasonal (short-term) variation in the model before using it for forecasting. For example, it is clear that seasonal variation exists in the quarterly power load series (see Example 16.9.) Consequently, our forecasts should be improved by the addition of seasonal variation terms in the regression model. This requires that we propose a multiple regression model (Chapter 13).

EXAMPLE 16.12
Modeling Trend and
Seasonal Variation

Refer to the 1991–1994 quarterly power loads listed in Table 16.9 (page 944).

a. Propose a model for quarterly power load, y_t, that will account for both the secular trend and seasonal variation present in the series.

b. Fit the model to the data, and use the least squares prediction equation to forecast the utility company's quarterly power loads in 1995. Construct 95% prediction intervals for the forecasts.

SOLUTION **a.** A common way to describe seasonal differences in a time series is with dummy variables. For quarterly data, a model that includes both trend and seasonal components is

$$E(y_t) = \beta_0 + \underbrace{\beta_1 t}_{\substack{\text{Secular} \\ \text{trend}}} + \underbrace{\beta_2 Q_1 + \beta_3 Q_2 + \beta_4 Q_3}_{\text{Seasonal component}}$$

where

$t = $ Time period, ranging from $t = 1$ for quarter I of 1991 to $t = 16$ for quarter IV of 1994

$y_t = $ Power load (megawatts) in time t

$$Q_1 = \begin{cases} 1 & \text{if quarter I} \\ 0 & \text{if not} \end{cases} \qquad Q_2 = \begin{cases} 1 & \text{if quarter II} \\ 0 & \text{if not} \end{cases}$$

$$Q_3 = \begin{cases} 1 & \text{if quarter III} \\ 0 & \text{if not} \end{cases} \qquad \text{Base level} = \text{quarter IV}$$

The β coefficients associated with the seasonal dummy variables determine the mean increase (or decrease) in power load for each quarter, relative to the base level quarter, quarter IV.

b. The model is fit to the data from Table 16.9 using SAS. The resulting SAS printout is shown in Figure 16.10. Note that the model appears to fit the data quite well: $R^2 = .997$, indicating that the model accounts for 99.7% of the sample variation in power loads over the 4-year period; $F = 968.96$ strongly supports the hypothesis that the model has predictive utility (p-value $= .0001$); and the standard deviation, **Root MSE** $= 1.53$, implies that the model predictions will usually be accurate to within approximately $\pm 2(1.53)$, or about ± 3.06 megawatts.

Forecasts and corresponding 95% prediction intervals for the 1995 power loads are reported in the bottom portion of the printout in Figure 16.10. For example, the forecast for power load in quarter I of 1995 is 184.7 megawatts with the 95% prediction interval (180.5, 188.9.) Therefore, using a 95% prediction interval, we expect the power load in quarter I of 1995 to fall between 180.5 and 188.9 megawatts. ■

Note that the prediction intervals for $t = 17$, 18, 19, and 20 of Example 16.12 widen as we attempt to forecast farther into the future. Intuitively, we know that the farther into the future we forecast, the less certain we are of the accuracy of the forecast because some unexpected change in business and economic conditions may make the model inappropriate. Since we have less confidence in the forecast for, say, $t = 20$

FIGURE 16.10

SAS Printout of Least
Squares Fit to
Quarterly Power
Loads

Dependent Variable: Y

Analysis of Variance

Source	DF	Sum of Squares	Mean Square	F Value	Prob>F
Model	4	9101.67800	2275.41950	968.962	0.0001
Error	11	25.83138	2.34831		
C Total	15	9127.50938			

Root MSE	1.53242	R-square	0.9972	
Dep Mean	137.30625	Adj R-sq	0.9961	
C.V.	1.11606			

Parameter Estimates

Variable	DF	Parameter Estimate	Standard Error	T for H0: Parameter=0	Prob > |T|
INTERCEP	1	90.206250	1.14931396	78.487	0.0001
T	1	4.964375	0.08566480	57.951	0.0001
Q1	1	10.093125	1.11364246	9.063	0.0001
Q2	1	-4.846250	1.09704478	-4.418	0.0010
Q3	1	14.364375	1.08696452	13.215	0.0001

Obs	ID	Dep Var Y	Predict Value	Std Err Predict	Lower95% Predict	Upper95% Predict	Residual
1	1991_1	103.5	105.3	0.923	101.3	109.2	-1.7637
2	1991_2	94.7	95.3	0.923	91.3518	99.2	-0.5887
3	1991_3	118.6	119.5	0.923	115.5	123.4	-0.8637
4	1991_4	109.3	110.1	0.923	106.1	114.0	-0.7637
5	1992_1	126.1	125.1	0.785	121.3	128.9	0.9788
6	1992_2	116.0	115.1	0.785	111.4	118.9	0.8538
7	1992_3	141.2	139.3	0.785	135.5	143.1	1.8788
8	1992_4	131.6	129.9	0.785	126.1	133.7	1.6788
9	1993_1	144.5	145.0	0.785	141.2	148.8	-0.4787
10	1993_2	137.1	135.0	0.785	131.2	138.8	2.0963
11	1993_3	159.0	159.2	0.785	155.4	163.0	-0.1787
12	1993_4	149.5	149.8	0.785	146.0	153.6	-0.2787
13	1994_1	166.1	164.8	0.923	160.9	168.8	1.2637
14	1994_2	152.5	154.9	0.923	150.9	158.8	-2.3612
15	1994_3	178.2	179.0	0.923	175.1	183.0	-0.8363
16	1994_4	169.0	169.6	0.923	165.7	173.6	-0.6362
17	1995_1	.	184.7	1.149	180.5	188.9	.
18	1995_2	.	174.7	1.149	170.5	178.9	.
19	1995_3	.	198.9	1.149	194.7	203.1	.
20	1995_4	.	189.5	1.149	185.3	193.7	.

Sum of Residuals	6.252776E-13
Sum of Squared Residuals	25.8314
Predicted Resid SS (Press)	55.6184

than for $t = 17$, it follows that the prediction interval for $t = 20$ must be wider to attain a 95% level of confidence. For this reason, time series forecasting (regardless of the forecasting method) is generally confined to the short term.

Many descriptive forecasting techniques have proved their merit by providing good forecasts for particular applications. Nevertheless, the advantage of forecasting using the regression approach is clear: Regression analysis provides us with a measure of reliability for each forecast through prediction intervals.

Forecasting Using Regression

STEP 1 Hypothesize a model for the deterministic component:

$$E(y_t) = \beta_0 + \beta_1 x_{1t} + \beta_2 x_{2t} + \cdots + \beta_k x_{kt}$$

(You may consider time t as one of the independent variables in the model.)

STEP 2 Collect the time series data (in equally spaced data points).

STEP 3 Obtain the least squares prediction equation,

$$\hat{y} = \hat{\beta}_0 + \hat{\beta}_1 x_{1t} + \hat{\beta}_2 x_{2t} + \cdots + \hat{\beta}_k x_{kt}$$

STEP 4 Assess the adequacy of the model.

STEP 5 If the model is deemed adequate, the forecast for a future time period t $(t = n + 1, n + 2, \ldots)$ is

$$F_t = \hat{y}_t$$

Corresponding prediction intervals for the forecast also should be obtained.

EXERCISES

■ *Applying the Concepts*

16.34 The accompanying table records the volume of wheat (in thousands of bushels) harvested by members of a farmers' marketing cooperative for the period 1981–1994. The cooperative is interested in detecting the long-term trend of the wheat harvest.

Year	Time	Wheat Harvested	Year	Time	Wheat Harvested
1981	1	75	1988	8	91
1982	2	78	1989	9	92
1983	3	82	1990	10	92
1984	4	82	1991	11	93
1985	5	84	1992	12	96
1986	6	85	1993	13	101
1987	7	87	1994	14	102

a. Graph the wheat harvest time series.

b. Propose a model for the long-term linear trend of the time series.

c. Fit the model, using the method of least squares. Plot the least squares line on the graph of part **a**. Can you identify the long-term trend?

d. How well does the linear model describe the long-term trend? [*Hint:* Check the value of r^2.]

e. Use the least squares model to forecast the volume of wheat harvested in 1995. Construct a 95% prediction interval for the forecast.

16.35 A realtor working in a large city wants to identify the secular trend in the weekly number of one-family houses sold by her firm. For the past 15 weeks she has collected data on the firm's home sales, as shown in the table.

Week t	Homes Sold y_t	Week t	Homes Sold y_t	Week t	Homes Sold y_t
1	59	6	137	11	88
2	73	7	106	12	75
3	70	8	122	13	62
4	82	9	93	14	44
5	115	10	86	15	45

a. Plot the time series. Is there visual evidence of a quadratic trend?

b. The realtor hypothesizes the model $E(y_t) = \beta_0 + \beta_1 t + \beta_2 t^2$ for the secular trend of the weekly time series. Fit the model to the data, using the method of least squares. (You will need access to a statistical computer software package.)

c. Plot the least squares model on the graph of part **a**. How well does the quadratic model describe the secular trend?

d. Use the model to forecast home sales in week 16 with a 95% prediction interval.

16.36 Refer to the quarterly S&P 500 values given in Exercise 16.32.

a. Hypothesize a time series model to account for trend and seasonal variation.

b. Fit the model in part **a** to the data.

c. Use the least squares model from part **b** to forecast the S&P 500 for quarters III and IV of 1994. Obtain 95% prediction intervals for the forecasts.

16.37 The total annual revenue (in $ millions) produced from passengers using intercity motor carriers in the United States is listed in the table for the years 1982–1991.

Year	Revenue $ millions	Year	Revenue $ millions
1982	969	1987	751
1983	876	1988	825
1984	861	1989	890
1985	836	1990	738
1986	765	1991	793

Source: Statistical Abstract of the United States, 1994.

a. Propose a regression model for total annual revenue that accounts for long-term trend.

b. Plot the data in a scattergram. Can you detect trend in the time series?

c. Fit the model, part **a**, to the data. Is the model adequate for predicting annual revenue?

d. Forecast the total revenue of intercity motor carriers in 1993. Include 95% prediction limits around the forecast.

16.38 The annual price (in cents per pound) of galvanized steel from 1971 to 1989 is shown in the table.

Year	t	y_t	Year	t	y_t	Year	t	y_t
1971	1	9.61	1978	8	20.47	1985	15	30.30
1972	2	10.88	1979	9	22.32	1986	16	30.30
1973	3	10.59	1980	10	23.88	1987	17	30.49
1974	4	12.39	1981	11	26.88	1988	18	31.05
1975	5	14.80	1982	12	26.75	1989	19	31.05
1976	6	16.07	1983	13	28.43			
1977	7	18.10	1984	14	30.30			

Source: Standard & Poor's *Trade Securities Statistics* (Annual), New York, Standard & Poor's Corporation.

a. Plot the time series. Is there visual evidence of a linear trend? A quadratic trend? Propose a regression model that is likely to fit the data well.

b. Use a statistical software package to fit the model, part **a**, to the data.

c. Plot the least squares line on the graph of part **a**. How well does the model describe the time series?

d. Use the fitted least squares model to forecast the price of galvanized steel for the years 1990–1995. Obtain 95% prediction intervals for the forecasts, and verify that the width of the interval increases the farther you forecast into the future.

16.39 An analysis of seasonality in returns of stock traded on the London Stock Exchange was published in the *Journal of Business* (Vol. 60, 1987.) One of the objectives was to determine whether the introduction of a capital gains tax in 1965 affected rates of return. The following model was fit to data collected over the years 1956–1980:

$$y_t = \beta_0 + \beta_1 D_t + \varepsilon_t$$

where y_t is the difference between the April rates of return of the two stocks on the exchange with the largest and smallest returns in year t, and D_t is a dummy variable that takes on the value 1 in the post-tax period (1966–1980) and a value of 0 in the pre-tax period (1956–1965).

a. Interpret the value of β_1.

b. Interpret the value of β_0.

c. The least squares prediction equation was found to be $\hat{y}_t = -.55 + 3.08 D_t$. Use the equation to estimate the mean difference in April rates of returns of the two stocks during the pretax period.

d. Repeat part **c** for the posttax period.

e. Obtain a forecast of the difference in April rates of return of the two stocks in 1995.

16.40 The data on monthly occupancy rate at hotels/motels in two cities, Exercise 16.9, is reproduced here. Let y_t = occupancy rate for Phoenix in month t.

Year 1 Month	Percentage of Rooms Occupied Atlanta	Phoenix	Year 2 Month	Percentage of Rooms Occupied Atlanta	Phoenix
January	59	67	January	64	72
February	63	85	February	69	91
March	68	83	March	73	87
April	70	69	April	67	75
May	63	63	May	68	70
June	59	52	June	71	61
July	68	49	July	67	46
August	64	49	August	71	44
September	62	56	September	65	63
October	73	69	October	72	73
November	62	63	November	63	71.
December	47	48	December	47	51

Source: Trends in the Hotel Industry.

a. Propose a model for $E(y_t)$ that accounts for possible seasonal variation in the monthly series. [*Hint:* Consider a model with dummy variables for the 12 months, January, February, etc.]

b. Fit the model of part **a** to the data.

c. Test the hypothesis that the monthly dummy variables are useful predictors of occupancy rate. [*Hint:* Conduct a partial F test.]

d. Use the fitted least squares model from part **b** to forecast the Phoenix occupancy rate in January of year 3 with a 95% prediction interval.

e. Repeat parts **a–d** for the Atlanta monthly occupancy rates.

16.41 The Employee Retirement Income Security Act (ERISA) of 1974 was originally established to enhance retirement security income. J. Ledolter and M. L. Power investigated the effects of ERISA on the growth in the number of private retirement plans (*Journal of Risk and Insurance*, Dec. 1983). Using quarterly data from 1956 through the third quarter of 1982 ($n = 107$ quarters), Ledolter and Power fit quarterly time series models for the number of pension qualifications and the number of profit-sharing plan qualifications. One of the various models investigated was the quadratic model $E(y_t) = \beta_0 + \beta_1 t + \beta_2 t^2$, where y_t is the logarithm of the dependent variable (number of pension or number of profit-sharing qualifications) in quarter t. The results are summarized here:

Pension plan qualifications: $\hat{y}_t = 6.19 + .039t - .87t^2$

$$t \text{ (for } H_0: \beta_2 = 0) = -1.39$$

Profit-sharing plan qualifications: $\hat{y}_t = 6.22 + .035t - .73t^2$

$$t \text{ (for } H_0\text{: } \beta_2 = 0) = -1.61$$

a. Is there evidence that the quarterly number of pension plan qualifications increases at a decreasing rate over time? Test using $\alpha = .05$. [*Hint:* Test H_0: $\beta_2 = 0$ against H_a: $\beta_2 < 0$.]

b. Forecast the number of pension plan qualifications for the fourth quarter of 1982 (i.e., $t = 108$). [*Hint:* Since y_t is the logarithm of the number of pension plan qualifications, to obtain the forecast, you must take the antilogarithm of $\hat{y}_{108}$, i.e., $e^{\hat{y}_{108}}$.]

c. Is there evidence that the quarterly number of profit-sharing plan qualifications increases at a decreasing rate over time? Test using $\alpha = .05$. [*Hint:* Test H_0: $\beta_2 = 0$ against H_a: $\beta_2 < 0$.]

d. Forecast the number of profit-sharing plan qualifications for the fourth quarter of 1982 (i.e., $t = 108$). [*Hint:* Since y_t is the logarithm of the number of profit-sharing plan qualifications, to obtain the forecast, you must take the antilogarithm of $\hat{y}_{108}$, i.e., $e^{\hat{y}_{108}}$.]

16.7 Time Series Forecasting Models

The examples in the previous two sections illustrate an important point. Smoothing techniques lack a measure of reliability for time series forecasts and, consequently, should be used with care. To assess the reliability of forecasts, we must first construct a *regression model*. However, there are two problems associated with forecasting time series using the regression approach.

PROBLEM 1　We are using the least squares prediction equation to forecast values outside the region of observation of the independent variables. For example, in Example 16.12, we are forecasting for values of t between 17 and 20 (the four quarters of 1995), even though the observed power loads are for t values between 1 and 16. We noted with warning boxes in both Chapters 12 and 13 that it is risky to use a least squares regression model for prediction outside the range of the observed data because some unusual change, economic or political, may make the model inappropriate for predicting future events. Because forecasting always involves predictions about future values of a time series, this problem obviously cannot be avoided; however, we must keep the risk in mind and recognize the dangers of this type of prediction.

PROBLEM 2　Recall the standard assumptions made about the random error component of the multiple regression model (Section 13.2). We assume that the errors have mean 0, constant variance, normal probability distributions, and are *independent*. The latter assumption is often violated in time series that exhibit short-term trends. As an illustration, refer to the plot of the power load data given in Figure 16.9. Notice that the power loads for the winter and summer months (quarters I and III) lie above the least squares trend line, whereas the power loads for the spring and fall months (quarters II and IV) fall below the line for each year shown. Since the variation in the power loads is systematic, the implication is that the errors are correlated. (We outline a formal statistical test for correlated errors in the next section.) Violation of this standard regression assumption could lead to unreliable forecasts.

Time series models have been developed specifically for the purpose of making forecasts when the errors are known to be correlated. These models include terms for secular, cyclical, and seasonal variation, and an **autoregressive term** for correlated errors that result from short-term effects. This autoregressive term is often incorporated into the residual component of the time series model, i.e.,

R_t = Autoregressive (correlated) errors

whereas the secular, cyclical, and seasonal variations are usually incorporated into the deterministic portion of the model, as shown in the box.

Time Series Model

$$y_t = \underbrace{T_t + C_t + S_t}_{\substack{\text{Deterministic} \\ \text{component}}} + \underbrace{R_t}_{\substack{\text{Random} \\ \text{error}}}$$

where

T_t = Secular trend   (usually, $T_t = \beta_0 + \beta_1 t$ for a straight-line trend or
   $T_t = \beta_0 + \beta_1 t + \beta_2 t^2$ for a curvilinear trend)

C_t = Cyclical variation

S_t = Seasonal variation   (usually, dummy variables representing seasons, e.g.,
   $S_t = \beta_2 Q_1 + \beta_3 Q_2 + \beta_4 Q_3$ for quarterly data)

R_t = Residual variation   (usually, R_t = autoregressive error)

If properly constructed, time series models can be powerful business forecasting tools. Because of their complexity, the successful construction of time series models requires much experience, and as with regression modeling, entire texts are devoted to the subject. In the remaining sections of this chapter, we discuss autocorrelated errors and autoregressive models

16.8 Testing for Autocorrelation: The Durbin–Watson Test

As pointed out in the previous section (problem 2 in Section 16.7), the standard regression assumption of independent errors is often violated with time series data. The reason is that *time series residuals* tend to be correlated with one another.

Recall that a time series residual is computed as the difference between the observed value of the time series, y_t, and the corresponding predicted value obtained from using the fitted time series model, $\hat{y}_t$, i.e., $(y_t - \hat{y}_t)$. For most business economic time series, there is a tendency for the residuals to have positive and negative runs over time. For example, consider fitting a straight-line regression model to yearly time series data. A plot of the yearly time series residuals may appear as in Figure 16.11. Note that if the residual for year t is positive (or negative), there is a tendency for the residual for year $(t + 1)$ to be positive (or negative). That is, neighboring residuals tend to have the same sign, and appear to be correlated. We call the correlation among the time series residuals at different points in time **autocorrelation**.

Definition 16.13

Autocorrelation is the correlation between time series residuals at different points in time. The special case in which neighboring residuals one time period apart (at times t and $t + 1$) are correlated is called **first-order autocorrelation**.

FIGURE 16.11

Residual Plot for Yearly Time Series Model

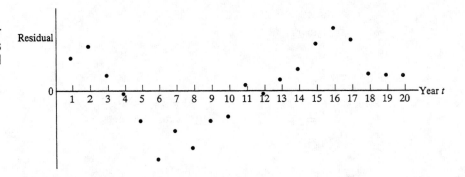

A special case of autocorrelation that has many applications to business and economic phenomena is the case in which neighboring residuals one time period apart (say, time t and $t + 1$) are correlated. This type of correlation is called **first-order autocorrelation**.* The more general type of autocorrelation (non–first-order autocorrelation) is beyond the scope of this text. Therefore, whenever we use the term *autocorrelation*, we are referring to the first-order case. In the following examples, we outline a test of hypothesis appropriate for detecting the presence of first-order autocorrelation among residuals.

EXAMPLE 16.13
Testing for Residual Autocorrelation

Due to seasonality and economic trends, most time series models exhibit positively autocorrelated errors. Therefore, consider testing the hypothesis

H_0: No residual autocorrelation

against the alternative hypothesis

H_a: Positive residual autocorrelation

---

*In general, correlation between time series residuals m time periods apart is **mth-order autocorrelation**.

The appropriate test statistic is the **Durbin–Watson d statistic**. Since most statistical software packages include a regression routine that calculates d, we are concerned more with the interpretation of d than with its computation.[*] Thus, what is the range of the values of d, and what values of d lead us to conclude that autocorrelation is present?

SOLUTION The value of d always falls in the interval from 0 to 4, i.e., $0 \leq d \leq 4$. If the residuals are *uncorrelated*, then d is approximately equal to 2; if the residuals are *positively autocorrelated*, d is less than 2; and, if residuals are *negatively correlated*, d is greater than 2. The closer d gets to 0 or 4, the stronger the autocorrelation (positive or negative, respectively). The interpretation of the d statistic is summarized in the box.

Interpretation of the Durbin–Watson d Statistic

> *Range of d:* $\quad 0 \leq d \leq 4$
> *Uncorrelated residuals:* $\quad d \approx 2$
> *Positive autocorrelation:* $\quad d < 2$
> $\quad$ (Strong positive autocorrelation: $\quad d \approx 0$)
> *Negative autocorrelation:* $\quad d > 2$
> $\quad$ (Strong negative autocorrelation: $\quad d \approx 4$)

For a test for positive autocorrelation, then, we will reject the null hypothesis in favor of the alternative if the d statistic is "too small," i.e., significantly less than 2. Durbin and Watson (1951)[†] provide tables for the lower-tail values of the d statistic. We illustrate the use of these tables in the following examples. ■

EXAMPLE 16.14
Critical Values of d

A reproduction of part of Table 15 of Appendix B is shown in Table 16.14 on page 974. The table gives critical values of the Durbin–Watson d Statistic for $\alpha = .05$. (Critical values based on $\alpha = .01$ are given in Table 16 of Appendix B.) You can see that the values in the table depend on two parameters: n, the sample size, and k, the number of independent variables in the time series model. Use the table to specify the appropriate rejection region for a test for positive autocorrelation at $\alpha = .05$, when $n = 35$ and $k = 1$.

---

[*]*The computing formula for d is $d = \sum_{t=2}^{n} (\hat{R}_t - \hat{R}_{t-1})^2 / \sum_{t=1}^{n} \hat{R}_t^2$, where n is the number of observations (time periods) and $\hat{R}_t$ is the residual at time t, i.e., $\hat{R}_t = (y_t - \hat{y}_t)$.*

[†]*Source: Durbin, J. and Watson, G. S. "Testing for serial correlation in least squares regression. II." Biometrika, 1951, Vol. 38, pp. 159–178.*

Table 16.14 Reproduction of Part of Table 15 of Appendix B ($\alpha = .05$)

n	$k=1$ d_L	d_U	$k=2$ d_L	d_U	$k=3$ d_L	d_U	$k=4$ d_L	d_U	$k=5$ d_L	d_U
31	1.36	1.50	1.30	1.57	1.23	.1.65	1.16	1.74	1.09	1.83
32	1.37	1.50	1.31	1.57	1.24	.1.65	1.18	1.73	1.11	1.82
33	1.38	1.51	1.32	1.58	1.26	.1.65	1.19	1.73	1.13	1.81
34	1.39	1.51	1.33	1.58	1.27	.1.65	1.21	1.73	1.15	1.81
35	1.40	1.52	1.34	1.58	1.28	.1.65	1.22	1.73	1.16	1.80
36	1.41	1.52	1.35	1.59	1.29	.1.65	1.24	1.73	1.18	1.80
37	1.42	1.53	1.36	1.59	1.31	.1.66	1.25	1.72	1.19	1.80
38	1.43	1.54	1.37	1.59	1.32	.1.66	1.26	1.72	1.21	1.79
39	1.43	1.54	1.38	1.60	1.33	.1.66	1.27	1.72	1.22	1.79
40	1.44	1.54	1.39	1.60	1.34	.1.66	1.29	1.72	1.23	1.79

SOLUTION Unlike the z, t, F, and other test statistics, the complexity of the sampling distribution of d prevents us from specifying a single point, d_α, that acts as a boundary between the rejection and nonrejection regions. Instead, upper and lower bounds on the critical value of d are specified.

For $\alpha = .05$, $n = 35$, and $k = 1$, the upper bound is given by $d_U = 1.52$ and the lower bound is $d_L = 1.40$. Since small values of d provide sufficient evidence of positive autocorrelation, we can *definitely* reject H_0 if d is *smaller than the lower bound* d_L, i.e., if $d < 1.40$. Similarly, there is insufficient evidence to reject H_0 if d is *greater than the upper bound* d_U, i.e., if $d > 1.52$. If d falls between the bounds, i.e., if $1.40 < d < 1.52$, then more information is needed before we can reach any conclusion about the presence of autocorrelation. For this reason, the interval (d_L, d_U) is sometimes called the **inconclusive region**. A graphical depiction of the rejection region for the Durbin–Watson d test is shown in Figure 16.12.

FIGURE 16.12

Rejection Region for the Durbin–Watson d Test

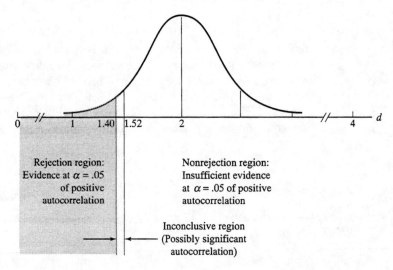

EXAMPLE 16.15	A leading pharmaceutical company that produces a hypertension pill would like to model annual revenue generated by this product. Company researchers utilized data collected over the years 1980–1994 to fit the model

Application of the *d* Test

$$E(y_t) = \beta_0 + \beta_1 x_t + \beta_2 t$$

where

$y_t =$ Revenue in year t (in millions of dollars)

$x_t =$ Cost per pill in year t

$t =$ Year (1, 2, ..., 15)

The SAS printout for the regression analysis appears in Figure 16.13. A company statistician suspects that the assumption of independent errors may be violated and that, in fact, the regression residuals are positively autocorrelated. Test this claim using $\alpha = .05$.

SOLUTION The null and alternative hypotheses for the test are given by

H_0:   No residual autocorrelation

H_a: Positive (first-order) autocorrelation

and the appropriate test statistic is the Durbin–Watson d statistic from the bottom of the SAS printout: $d = .776$.

FIGURE 16.13

SAS Printout for Example 16.15

Dependent Variable: Y

Analysis of Variance

Source	DF	Sum of Squares	Mean Square	F Value	Prob>F
Model	2	48.82325	24.41163	206.187	0.0001
Error	12	1.42075	0.11840		
C Total	14	50.24400			

Root MSE	0.34409	R-square	0.9717	
Dep Mean	7.32000	Adj R-sq	0.9670	
C.V.	4.70064			

Parameter Estimates

Variable	DF	Parameter Estimate	Standard Error	T for H0: Parameter=0	Prob > |T|
INTERCEP	1	3.261191	1.87880228	1.736	0.1082
T	1	0.391588	0.07045937	5.558	0.0001
X	1	1.587609	4.12905034	0.384	0.7073

Durbin-Watson D	0.776
(For Number of Obs.)	15
1st Order Autocorrelation	0.485

For $n = 15$ observations (years), $k = 2$ independent variables (x_t and t), and $\alpha = .05$, the upper and lower bounds obtained from Table 15 of Appendix B are $d_L = .95$ and $d_U = 1.54$. Since the computed value ($d = .776$) is less than the lower bound ($d_L = .95$), there is sufficient evidence at $\alpha = .05$ to conclude that the residuals are positively correlated. ■

Two-tailed tests and tests for negative autocorrelation (although rare in practice) are similar to the test for positive autocorrelation. These tests, which are based on the symmetry of the sampling distribution of d, are outlined in the box.

Durbin–Watson d Test

One-Tailed Test	*Two-Tailed Test*
H_0: No autocorrelation H_a: Positive autocorrelation [or H_a: Negative autocorrelation]	H_0: No autocorrelation H_a: Positive or negative autocorrelation
Test statistic: d (obtained from a regression printout)	*Test statistic:* d (obtained from a regression printout)
Rejection region: $d < d_{L,\alpha}$ [or $(4 - d) < d_{L,\alpha}$ if H_a: Negative autocorrelation]	*Rejection region:* $d < d_{L,\alpha/2}$ or $(4 - d) < d_{L,\alpha/2}$
where $d_{L,\alpha}$ is the lower tabled value corresponding to k independent variables and n observations	where $d_{L,\alpha/2}$ is the lower tabulated value corresponding to k independent variables and n observations
Caution: If $d_{L,\alpha} < d < d_{U,\alpha}$, the test is inconclusive (i.e., "possibly significant").	*Caution:* If $d_{L,\alpha/2} < d < d_{U,\alpha/2}$ or $d_{L,\alpha/2} < (4 - d) < d_{L,\alpha/2}$, the test is inconclusive (i.e., "possibly significant").

If strong evidence of autocorrelation is detected, as in Example 16.15, then the least square results and any inferences drawn from them are suspect. In the following section, we present a time series model that accounts for (first-order) autocorrelation in the random errors.

EXERCISES

■ *Learning the Mechanics*

16.42 Define autocorrelation. Explain why autocorrelation is important in time series modeling and forecasting.

16.43 Find the values of d_L and d_U from Tables 15 and 16 of Appendix B for each of the following situations:
 a. $n = 30$, $k = 3$, $\alpha = .05$ **b.** $n = 40$, $k = 1$, $\alpha = .01$ **c.** $n = 35$, $k = 5$, $\alpha = .05$

16.44 Suppose you fit the time series model

$$E(y_t) = \beta_0 + \beta_1 t + \beta_2 t^2$$

to quarterly time series data collected over a 10-year period ($n = 40$ quarters).
 a. Set up the test of hypothesis for positively autocorrelated residuals. Specify H_0, H_a, the test statistic, and the rejection region. Use $\alpha = .05$.
 b. Suppose the Durbin–Watson d statistic is calculated to be 1.14. What is the appropriate conclusion?

■ *Applying the Concepts*

16.45 Exploratory research published in the *Journal of Professional Services Marketing* (Vol. 5, 1990) examined the relationship between deposit share of a retail bank and several marketing variables. Quarterly deposit share data were collected for the years 1981–1985 for each of nine retail banking institutions. The model analyzed took the form:

$$y_t = \beta_0 + \beta_1 P_{t-1} + \beta_2 S_{t-1} + \beta_3 D_{t-1} + \varepsilon_t$$

where

$\quad y_t = $ Deposit share of bank in quarter t, $t = 1, 2, \ldots, 20$

$\quad P_{t-1} = $ Expenditures on promotion-related activities in quarter $t - 1$

$\quad S_{t-1} = $ Expenditures on service-related activities in quarter $t - 1$

$\quad D_{t-1} = $ Expenditures on distribution-related activities in quarter $t - 1$

A separate model was fit for each bank with the results shown in the table.

Bank	R^2	p-Value for Global F	Durbin–Watson d[a]
1	.914	.000	1.3
2	.721	.004	3.4
3	.926	.000	2.7
4	.827	.000	1.9
5	.270	.155	.85

(continued)

Bank	R^2	p-Value for Global F	Durbin–Watson d[a]
6	.616	.012	1.8
7	.962	.000	2.5
8	.495	.014	2.3
9	.500	.011	1.1

[a]*Note*: The values of *d* shown are approximated based on other information provided in the article.

a. Interpret the value of R^2 for each bank.

b. Test the overall adequacy of the model for each bank.

c. Conduct the Durbin–Watson *d* test for each bank. Interpret the practical significance of the tests.

16.46 The consumer purchasing value of the dollar from 1970 to 1993 is illustrated by the data in the accompanying table, where the purchasing power of the dollar (compared to 1982) is listed for each year. The first-order model $E(y_t) = \beta_0 + \beta_1 t$ was fit to the data using SAS. The SAS printout is displayed here.

Year, t	Value, y	Year, t	Value, y
1970	$2.55	1982	$1.00
1971	2.47	1983	.98
1972	2.39	1984	.96
1973	2.19	1985	.95
1974	1.90	1986	.97
1975	1.72	1987	.95
1976	1.65	1988	.93
1977	1.55	1989	.88
1978	1.43	1990	.84
1979	1.29	1991	.82
1980	1.14	1992	.81
1981	1.04	1993	.79

Source: Statistical Abstract of the United States, 1994.

a. Plot the regression residuals (shown on the printout) against *t*. Is there a tendency for the residuals to have long positive and negative runs? How do you account for this?

b. Locate the Durbin–Watson *d* statistic for this model on the printout. Test the hypothesis that the time series residuals are positively correlated. Test at $\alpha = .05$.

Dependent Variable: Y

Analysis of Variance

Source	DF	Sum of Squares	Mean Square	F Value	Prob>F
Model	1	6.44178	6.44178	120.391	0.0001
Error	22	1.17716	0.05351		
C Total	23	7.61893			

Root MSE	0.23132	R-square	0.8455	
Dep Mean	1.34167	Adj R-sq	0.8385	
C.V.	17.24094			

Parameter Estimates

Variable	DF	Parameter Estimate	Standard Error	T for H0: Parameter=0	Prob > |T|
INTERCEP	1	149.644019	13.51615991	11.071	0.0001
T	1	-0.074843	0.00682113	-10.972	0.0001

Durbin-Watson D	0.106
(For Number of Obs.)	24
1st Order Autocorrelation	0.855

Obs	T	Dep Var Y	Predict Value	Residual
1	1970	2.5500	2.2024	0.3476
2	1971	2.4700	2.1275	0.3425
3	1972	2.3900	2.0527	0.3373
4	1973	2.1900	1.9778	0.2122
5	1974	1.9000	1.9030	-0.00299
6	1975	1.7200	1.8281	-0.1081
7	1976	1.6500	1.7533	-0.1033
8	1977	1.5500	1.6785	-0.1285
9	1978	1.4300	1.6036	-0.1736
10	1979	1.2900	1.5288	-0.2388
11	1980	1.1400	1.4539	-0.3139
12	1981	1.0400	1.3791	-0.3391
13	1982	1.0000	1.3042	-0.3042
14	1983	0.9800	1.2294	-0.2494
15	1984	0.9600	1.1546	-0.1946
16	1985	0.9500	1.0797	-0.1297
17	1986	0.9700	1.0049	-0.0349
18	1987	0.9500	0.9300	0.0200
19	1988	0.9300	0.8552	0.0748
20	1989	0.8800	0.7803	0.0997
21	1990	0.8400	0.7055	0.1345
22	1991	0.8200	0.6307	0.1893
23	1992	0.8100	0.5558	0.2542
24	1993	0.7900	0.4810	0.3090

16.47 Forecasts of automotive vehicle sales in the United States provide the basis for financial and strategic planning of large automotive corporations. Olson and Janakiraman (1985) developed the following forecasting model for y, total monthly passenger car and light truck sales (in thousands):

$$E(y) = \beta_0 + \beta_1 x_1 + \beta_2 x_2 + \beta_3 x_3 + \beta_4 x_4 + \beta_5 x_5$$

where

x_1 = Average monthly retail price of regular gasoline

$x_2 = $ Annual percentage change in GNP per quarter

$x_3 = $ Monthly Consumer Confidence Index

$x_4 = $ Total number of vehicles scrapped (millions) per month

$x_5 = $ Vehicle seasonality

The model was fit to monthly data collected over a 12-year period ($n = 144$ months) with the following results.[*]

$$\hat{y} = -676.42 - 1.93x_1 + 6.54x_2 + 2.02x_3 + .08x_4 + 9.82x_5$$

$$R^2 = .856 \qquad \text{Durbin–Watson } d = 1.01$$

a. Is there sufficient evidence to indicate that the model contributes information for the prediction of y? Test using $\alpha = .05$.

b. Is there sufficient evidence to indicate that the regression errors are positively correlated? Test using $\alpha = .05$.

c. Comment on the validity of the inference concerning model adequacy in light of the result of part **b**.

16.48 The accompanying table gives the factory sales (in thousands) of passenger cars in the United States for the years 1992 and 1993. The straight-line model $E(y_t) = \beta_0 + \beta_1 t$ is fit to the data using the method of least squares, with the following results:

$$\hat{y}_t = 467.78 - 1.31t \qquad \text{Durbin-Watson } d = 1.58$$

Month	Time, t	1992 Sales, y	Time, t	1993 Sales, y
January	1	404	13	440
February	2	444	14	479
March	3	506	15	596
April	4	506	16	539
May	5	548	17	545
June	6	572	18	562
July	7	362	19	305
August	8	418	20	426
September	9	474	21	459
October	10	529	22	547
November	11	458	23	543
December	12	464	24	495

Source: *Survey of Current Business*, U.S. Dept. of Commerce.

[*]*Source:* Olson, S. J. and Janakiraman, J. "Proposed U.S. passenger car and light truck sales forecast model." *Paper presented at SAS Users Group International Conference, Reno, Nevada, 1985.*

    a. Calculate and plot the regression residuals against t. Is there a tendency for the residuals to have long positive and negative runs?

    b. Is there evidence at $\alpha = .05$ level of significance that the residuals are autocorrelated?

16.49 Refer to Exercise 16.34.

    a. Use the least squares straight-line model to compute the regression residuals.

    b. Construct a residual plot over time (years). Is there visual evidence of residual autocorrelation?

    c. Use a computer to obtain the value of the Durbin–Watson d statistic. Is there evidence to indicate that the residuals are autocorrelated? Test using $\alpha = .05$.

16.50 B. N. Song compared the annual consumption for two lower-developed countries (LDCs)—Korea, a poor LDC, and Italy, a rich LDC (*Economic Development and Cultural Change*, Apr. 1981). Using data form the post–Korean War period, Song modeled annual consumption y_t as a function of total labor income x_{1t} and total property income x_{2t}, with the following results (assume that data for $n = 40$ years were used in the analysis):

Korea: $\hat{y}_t = 7.81 + .91x_{1t} + .57x_{2t}$

          $s = 1.29$

          $d = 2.09$

Italy: $\hat{y}_t = 1{,}043.4 + .85x_{1t} + .40x_{2t}$

          $s = 290.5$

          $d = 1.07$

    a. Is there evidence of positively autocorrelated residuals in the consumption model for Korea? Test using $\alpha = .05$.

    b. Is there evidence of positively autocorrelated residuals in the consumption model for Italy? Test using $\alpha = .05$.

16.51 T. C. Chiang considered several time series forecasting models of future foreign exchange rates for U.S. currency (*The Journal of Financial Research*, Summer 1986). One popular theory among financial analysts is that the forward (90-day) exchange rate is a useful predictor of the future spot exchange rate. Using monthly data on exchange rates for the British pound for $n = 81$ months, Chiang fit the model

$$E(y_t) = \beta_0 + \beta_1 x_{t-1}$$

where

     $y_t = \log(\text{spot rate})$ in month t

     $x_t = \log(\text{forward rate})$ in month t

The method of least squares yielded the following results:

$$\hat{y}_t = -.009 + .986x_{t-1} \quad (t = 47.9)$$

     $s = .0249$ $R^2 = .957$ Durbin–Watson $d = .962$

a. Is the model useful for predicting future spot exchange rates for the British pound? Test using $\alpha = .05$.

b. Interpret the values of s and R^2.

c. Is there evidence of positive autocorrelation among the residuals? Test using $\alpha = .05$.

d. Based on the results of parts **a–c**, would you recommend using the least squares model to forecast spot exchange rates?

16.9 Forecasting Using Autoregressive Error Models

Once you have determined that the time series residuals are autocorrelated, you should avoid using the fitted least squares model for forecasting. When the standard regression assumption of independent errors is violated, the forecasts will have larger errors than expected. However, if the autocorrelated residuals can be accounted for in the time series model, then better forecasts can be obtained.

Recall that a time series model can be written as

$$y_t = E(y_t) + R_t$$

where $E(y_t)$ is the deterministic component and R_t is the residual component of the model. In time series analysis, it is assumed that the R_t's are autocorrelated and a pair of models is proposed—one model for the deterministic component, $E(y_t)$, and one model for the autocorrelated residuals, R_t.

A useful model for autocorrelated residuals is the **first-order autoregressive model**

$$R_t = \phi R_{t-1} + \varepsilon_t$$

where ϕ ("phi") is a constant coefficient that lies between -1 and 1, and the random error ε has mean 0, constant variance, is normally distributed and *independent*. This model implies that the values of R_t are autocorrelated with the constant ϕ as the correlation coefficient. When ϕ is positive, the residuals are positively autocorrelated; when ϕ is negative, the residuals are negatively autocorrelated; and, when ϕ is 0, the residuals are uncorrelated. The closer ϕ is to 1 or -1, the stronger the autocorrelation (either positive or negative, respectively).

First-Order Autoregressive Model

$$R_t = \phi R_{t-1} + \varepsilon_t$$

where R_t is the time series residual at time t, $-1 \leq \phi \leq 1$, and ε_t represents uncorrelated random error at time t.

Since positive autocorrelations generate cyclic behavior in the time series residuals, first-order autoregressive models used for business and economic time series generally have positive values for ϕ.

<table>
<tr><td>**EXAMPLE 16.16**</td><td rowspan="4">The Dow Jones Industrial Average (DJA) is a widely followed stock market indicator. The values of the DJA from 1971 to 1990 are given in Table 16.15. Suppose we want to model the yearly DJA, y_t, as a function of t, where t is the number of years since 1970 (i.e., $t = 1$ for 1971, $t = 2$ for 1972, ..., $t = 20$ for 1990). Propose and fit a time series model that includes a long-term trend and autocorrelated residuals.</td></tr>
<tr><td>Modeling Autocorrelated</td></tr>
<tr><td>Errors</td></tr>
</table>

Table 16.15 Dow Jones Industrial Average (DJA)

Year	DJA	Year	DJA
1971	885	1981	899
1972	951	1982	1,047
1973	924	1983	1,259
1974	759	1984	1,212
1975	802	1985	1,547
1976	975	1986	1,896
1977	835	1987	2,276
1978	805	1988	2,061
1979	839	1989	2,508
1980	964	1990	2,679

Source: Wall Street Journal.

SOLUTION The appropriate time series model can be written as

$$y_t = E(y_t) + R_t$$

where the long-term trend, $E(y_t)$, is given by

$$E(y_t) = \beta_0 + \beta_1 t$$

and the autocorrelated residuals, R_t, are represented by the autoregressive model

$$R_t = \phi R_{t-1} + \varepsilon_t$$

Combining the two components into one model, we have

$$y_t = \beta_0 + \beta_1 t + \phi R_{t-1} + \varepsilon_t$$

Note that the model contains three unknown parameters: β_0, β_1, and ϕ. To estimate these parameters, a modification of the least squares method is used. The mathematical details of this technique are beyond the scope of this text. However, several statistical software packages are available that compute the estimates using the modified least squares method (e.g., the AUTOREG procedure in SAS). The SAS AUTOREG printout for the data of Table 16.15 is shown in Figure 16.14 on page 984.

FIGURE 16.14

Straight-Line Autoregressive Model for Dow Jones Industrial Average

Autoreg Procedure

Dependent Variable = DJA

Ordinary Least Squares Estimates

SSE	1998865	DFE	18
MSE	111048	Root MSE	333.2387
SBC	292.9962	AIC	291.0047
Reg Rsq	0.7303	Total Rsq	0.7303
Durbin-Watson	0.3298		

Variable	DF	B Value	Std Error	t Ratio	Approx Prob
Intercept	1	358.931579	154.80	2.319	0.0324
T	1	90.211278	12.92	6.981	0.0001

Estimates of Autocorrelations

Lag	Covariance	Correlation	-1 9 8 7 6 5 4 3 2 1 0 1 2 3 4 5 6 7 8 9 1
0	99943.24	1.000000	| |******************** |
1	72059.18	0.721001	| |************** |

Preliminary MSE = 47988.51

Estimates of the Autoregressive Parameters

Lag	Coefficient	Std Error	t Ratio
1	-0.72100099	0.16806119	-4.290110

Yule-Walker Estimates

SSE	703545.1	DFE	17
MSE	41385	Root MSE	203.433
SBC	275.8415	AIC	272.8543
Reg Rsq	0.5519	Total Rsq	0.9051

Variable	DF	B Value	Std Error	t Ratio	Approx Prob
Intercept	1	434.929919	256.82	1.694	0.1086
T	1	92.279852	20.17	4.576	0.0003

The format of the SAS printout for the time series model is different from that of the standard SAS regression printout. The estimates of the β's in the deterministic component, $E(y_t)$, appear at the bottom of the printout under the column heading **B Value**. These values (rounded) are $\hat{\beta}_0 = 434.93$ and $\hat{\beta}_1 = 92.28$.

The estimate of the first-order autoregressive parameter ϕ is given in the middle portion of the printout titled **ESTIMATES OF THE AUTOREGRESSIVE PARAMETERS** beneath the column heading **COEFFICIENT**. The value shown (rounded) is $-.721$. However, the SAS autoregressive model is defined so that ϕ has the *opposite sign* from the value contained in our model. As a result, we must multiply the estimate of ϕ shown in the SAS printout by -1 to obtain the estimate for our model. Therefore, we have $\hat{\phi} = (-.721)(-1) = .721$.

The fitted time series models are

$$\hat{y}_t = 434.93 + 92.28t + \hat{R}_t \quad \text{and} \quad \hat{R}_t = .721\hat{R}_{t-1}$$

or

$$\hat{y}_t = 434.93 + 92.28t + .721\hat{R}_{t-1}$$

The value $\hat{\beta}_1 = 92.28$ is positive and significant at $\alpha = .10$ (p-value $\approx .0003/2 =$ .00015 for a one-tailed test), indicating that the DJA is increasing over time. The value $\hat{\phi} = .721$ is also positive, implying that the time series residuals are possibly positively autocorrelated. The fact that we have included an autoregressive component in our model to account for possible residual autocorrelation will lead us to more reliable forecasts. Note the value of MSE shown in the printout, **MSE** = 41,385. The estimate of σ is then **ROOT MSE** = 203. Thus, we expect to predict the yearly DJA to within 2(203), or about 406 points of the actual value. ■

In the presence of residual autocorrelation, we expect to obtain more reliable forecasts using a time series model with autoregressive errors than with the ordinary least squares model. The forecasting procedure for the first-order autoregressive model is illustrated in the following examples.

EXAMPLE 16.17
Forecasting with
Autoregressive Models

Refer to the DJA model discussed in Example 16.16. Use the fitted model to forecast the DJA for the years 1991, 1992, and 1993 (i.e., $t = 21$, 22, and 23, respectively).

SOLUTION The fitted model of Example 16.16 is given by

$$\hat{y}_t = 434.93 + 92.28t + .721\hat{R}_{t-1}$$

Consider first the forecast for 1991 ($t = 21$). Substituting $t = 21$ into the estimated model, we have

$$\hat{y}_{21} = 434.93 + 92.28(21) + .721\hat{R}_{20}$$

To complete the calculation of the forecast, however, we require an estimate of the residual for 1990, $\hat{R}_{20}$. By definition, the residual in year t is equal to the difference between the observed DJA in year t and its corresponding predicted value, i.e., $\hat{R}_t = y_t - \hat{y}_t$, or

$$\hat{R}_t = y_t - (434.93 + 92.28t)$$

Substituting $t = 20$, we obtain

$$\hat{R}_{20} = y_{20} - [434.93 + 92.28(20)]$$
$$= 2,679 - 2,280.5 = 398.5$$

Thus, our forecast for 1991 is

$$\hat{y}_{21} = 434.93 + 92.28(21) + .721\hat{R}_{20}$$
$$= 434.93 + 92.28(21) + .721(398.5) = 2{,}660.1$$

The forecasts for the remaining years are obtained by using the recursive relation

$$\hat{y}_t = 434.93 + 92.28t + .721\hat{R}_{t-1}$$

For 1992, $t = 22$ and

$$\hat{y}_{22} = 434.93 + 92.28(22) + .721\hat{R}_{21}$$

where

$$\hat{R}_{21} = .721\hat{R}_{20}$$
$$= .721(398.5) = 287.3$$

Then the forecast for 1992 is

$$\hat{y}_{22} = 434.93 + 92.28(22) + .721(287.3) = 2{,}672.2$$

Similarly, for 1993, $t = 23$ and

$$\hat{y}_{23} = 434.93 + 92.28(23) + .721\hat{R}_{22}$$

where

$$\hat{R}_{22} = .721\hat{R}_{21} = .721(287.3) = 207.1$$

Then the forecast for 1993 is

$$\hat{y}_{23} = 434.93 + 92.28(23) + .721(207.1) = 2{,}706.7 \quad ■$$

The general procedure for forecasting with time series models with first-order autoregressive residuals is outlined in the accompanying box.

**Forecasting Using Time Series Models
with First-Order Autoregressive Residuals**

$$y_t = \beta_0 + \beta_1 x_{1t} + \beta_2 x_{2t} + \cdots + \beta_k x_{kt} + R_t$$

$$R_t = \phi R_{t-1} + \varepsilon_t$$

STEP 1 Use a statistical software package to obtain the estimated model:

(continued)

$$\hat{y}_t = \hat{\beta}_0 + \hat{\beta}_1 x_{1t} + \hat{\beta}_2 x_{2t} + \cdots + \hat{\beta}_k x_{kt} + \hat{R}_t \quad t = 1, 2, \ldots, n$$

$$\hat{R}_t = \hat{\phi} \hat{R}_{t-1}$$

STEP 2 Compute the estimated residual for the last time period in the data $(t = n)$ as follows:

$$\hat{R}_n = y_n - \hat{y}_n$$

$$= y_n - (\hat{\beta}_0 + \hat{\beta}_1 x_{1n} + \hat{\beta}_2 x_{2n} + \cdots + \hat{\beta}_k x_{kn})$$

STEP 3 Forecasts of future values are obtained as follows:

$$F_{n+1} = \hat{\beta}_0 + \hat{\beta}_1 x_{1,n+1} + \hat{\beta}_2 x_{2,n+1} + \cdots + \hat{\beta}_k x_{k,n+1} + \hat{\phi} \hat{R}_n$$

$$F_{n+2} = \hat{\beta}_0 + \hat{\beta}_1 x_{1,n+2} + \hat{\beta}_2 x_{2,n+2} + \cdots + \hat{\beta}_k x_{k,n+2} + \hat{\phi}^2 \hat{R}_n$$

$$F_{n+3} = \hat{\beta}_0 + \hat{\beta}_1 x_{1,n+3} + \hat{\beta}_2 x_{2,n+3} + \cdots + \hat{\beta}_k x_{k,n+3} + \hat{\phi}^3 \hat{R}_n$$

$$\vdots$$

$$F_{n+m} = \hat{\beta}_0 + \hat{\beta}_1 x_{1,n+m} + \hat{\beta}_2 x_{2,n+m} + \cdots + \hat{\beta}_k x_{k,n+m} + \hat{\phi}^m \hat{R}_n$$

(where $\hat{R}_n$ is obtained from step 2).

How reliable are the DJA forecasts obtained in Example 16.17? To assess this, we need to place prediction limits on their values. The formulas for computing approximate prediction limits are given in the box.

Approximate 95% Forecasting Limits Using Time Series Models with First-Order Autoregressive Residuals

Forecast	Forecasting Limits
F_{n+1}	$\pm 2\sqrt{\mathrm{MSE}}$
F_{n+2}	$\pm 2\sqrt{\mathrm{MSE}(1 + \hat{\phi}^2)}$
F_{n+3}	$\pm 2\sqrt{\mathrm{MSE}(1 + \hat{\phi}^2 + \hat{\phi}^4)}$
$\vdots$	$\vdots$
F_{n+m}	$\pm 2\sqrt{\mathrm{MSE}(1 + \hat{\phi}^2 + \hat{\phi}^4 + \cdots + \hat{\phi}^{2(m-1)})}$

EXAMPLE 16.18
Constructing 95% Forecast Limits

Refer to Example 16.17. Construct approximate 95% prediction limits for the DJA forecasts for 1991–1993. Comparisons with the actual DJA for these years are shown in Table 16.16.

Table 16.16 Comparisons of Forecast and Actual DJAs: 1991–1993

	Forecast DJA (Example 16.17)	Actual DJA
1991	$\hat{y}_{21} = 2{,}660.1$	$y_{21} = 3{,}015$
1992	$\hat{y}_{22} = 2{,}672.2$	$y_{22} = 3{,}160$
1993	$\hat{y}_{23} = 2{,}706.7$	$y_{23} = 3{,}520$

SOLUTION For the forecast F_{n+1} (i.e., the DJA forecast for 1991), the 95% prediction interval is given by

$$F_{n+1} \pm 2\sqrt{\text{MSE}}$$

where MSE is the mean square error obtained from the printout shown in Figure 16.14: MSE = 41,385. The approximate 95% prediction interval for the 1991 DJA is then obtained by substitution into the formula:

$$F_{21} \pm 2\sqrt{\text{MSE}} = 2{,}660.1 \pm 2\sqrt{41{,}385}$$

$$= 2{,}660.1 \pm 406.9$$

or (2,253.2, 3,067.0).

For the forecast F_{n+2} (i.e., the DJA forecast for 1992), the 95% prediction interval is given by

$$F_{n+2} \pm 2\sqrt{\text{MSE}\,(1 + \hat{\phi}^2)}$$

where $\hat{\phi}$ is the estimated first-order autocorrelation coefficient obtained from the printout. Since $\hat{\phi} = .721$, the approximate 95% prediction interval for the DJA forecast for 1992 is

$$F_{22} \pm 2\sqrt{\text{MSE}\,(1 + \hat{\phi}^2)} = 2{,}672.2 \pm 2\sqrt{41{,}385 + (1 + .721)^2}$$

$$= 2{,}672.2 \pm 501.6$$

or (2,170.6, 3,173.8).

The approximate 95% prediction interval for the forecast F_{n+3}, is

$$F_{n+3} \pm 2\sqrt{\text{MSE}\,(1 + \hat{\phi}^2 + \hat{\phi}^4)} = F_{23} \pm 2\sqrt{\text{MSE}\,(1 + \hat{\phi}^2 + \hat{\phi}^4)}$$

$$= 2{,}706.7 \pm 2\sqrt{41{,}385 + (1 + .721^2 + .721^4)}$$

$$= 2{,}706.7 \pm 544.4$$

or $(2{,}162.3, 3{,}251.1)$.

Notice that the actual DJA falls within its 95% prediction interval for both 1991 and 1992. However, the actual DJA for 1993 falls above its corresponding prediction interval. Probably the best measure of the usefulness of a forecasting technique is a comparison of the forecasts against the future values of the time series. The fact that the 1991 and 1992 forecast intervals capture the actual DJA strongly supports the usefulness of the model for *short-term* forecasting. In fact, the coefficient of determination for the model (shown on the printout in Figure 16.14 as **TOTAL RSQ**) is $R^2 = .9051$. This implies that over 90% of the variation in the observed DJAs is explained by the model. The usefulness of the model for longer-term forecasts is suspect, however, since the 1993 interval missed the actual DJA.

Note, also, that the prediction intervals get wider as we forecast farther into the future. This is because we are extrapolating outside the range of the time period containing the data. The farther ahead we forecast, the less confidence we have that the structure of the fitted model will not change during the forecasting period; consequently, the forecasts are less reliable. This is another reason why forecasts should be confined to the short term whenever possible. ■

The forecasting techniques outlined in this section apply to time series models with first-order autoregressive residuals. The more complex the autoregressive model, the more complex the forecasting process becomes.

EXERCISES

■ *Learning the Mechanics*

16.52 Write the regression–autoregression pair of models that would be fit to annual time series data if a straight-line secular trend were being postulated in the regression model. Explain the role of each of the parameters in the models.

16.53 Repeat Exercise 16.52 assuming that a quadratic secular trend is postulated.

16.54 The annual time series model $y_t = \beta_0 + \beta_1 t + \phi R_{t-1} + \varepsilon_t$ was fit to data collected for $n = 30$ years with the following results:

$$\hat{y}_t = 10 + 2.5t + .64\hat{R}_{t-1}$$

$$y_{30} = 82$$

$$\text{MSE} = 4.3$$

    a. Calculate forecasts for y_t for $t = 31$, $t = 32$, and $t = 33$.

    b. Construct approximate 95% prediction intervals for the forecasts obtained in part **a**.

16.55 The quarterly time series model $y_t = \beta_0 + \beta_1 t + \beta_2 t^2 + \phi R_{t-1} + \varepsilon_t$ was fit to data collected for $n = 48$ quarters, with the following results:

$$\hat{y}_t = 220 + 17t + .3t^2 + .81\hat{R}_{t-1}$$

$$y_{48} = 350$$

$$\text{MSE} = 10.5$$

    a. Calculate forecasts for y_t for $t = 49$, $t = 50$, and $t = 51$.

    b. Construct approximate 95% prediction intervals for the forecasts obtained in part **a**.

▪ **Applying the Concepts**

16.56 Suppose you are interested in buying gold on the commodities market. Your broker has advised you that your best strategy is to sell back the gold at the first substantial jump in price. Hence, you are interested in a short-term investment. Before buying, you would like to model the closing price of gold, y_t, over time (in days), t.

    a. Write a first-order model for the deterministic portion of the model, $E(y_t)$.

    b. If a plot of the daily closing prices for the past month reveals a quadratic trend, write a plausible model for $E(y_t)$.

    c. Since the closing price of gold on day $(t + 1)$ is very highly correlated with the closing price on day t, your broker suggests that the random error components of the model are correlated. Given this information, postulate a model for the error term, R_t.

16.57 Numerous studies have been conducted to examine the relationship between seniority and productivity in business. A problem encountered in such studies is that individual output is often difficult to measure. G. A. Krohn developed a technique for estimating the experience–productivity relationship when such a measure is available (*Journal of Business & Economic Statistics*, Oct. 1983). Krohn modeled the batting average of a Major League baseball player in year $t(y_t)$ as a function of the player's age in year $t(x_t)$ and an autoregressive error term (R_t).

    a. Write a model for $E(y_t)$ that hypothesizes, as did Krohn, a curvilinear relationship with x_t.

    b. Write a first-order autoregressive model for R_t.

    c. Use the models from parts **a** and **b** to write the full time series autoregressive model for y_t.

16.58 Suppose a CPA firm wants to model its monthly income, y_t. The firm is growing at an increasing rate, so that the mean income will be modeled as a second-order function of t.

    a. Write a model for $E(y_t)$ to reflect the second-order function of time t.

    b. Write a model for the error term R_t that accounts for the residual correlation.

16.59 The Gross Domestic Product (GDP) is a measure of total U.S. output, and is, therefore, an important indicator of the U.S. economy. The quarterly GDP values (in billions of dollars) from 1990 to 1993 are given in the table. Let y_t be the GDP in quarter t, $t = 1, 2, 3, \ldots, 16$.

| | Quarter | | | |
Year	I	II	III	IV
1990	4,881	4,900	4,903	4,855
1991	4,824	4,841	4,832	4,838
1992	4,874	4,892	4,998	5,068
1993	5,078	5,102	5,139	5,218

Source: Survey of Current Business.

a. Hypothesize a time series model for quarterly GDP that includes a straight-line long-term trend and autocorrelated residuals.
b. The SAS printout for the time series model $y_t = \beta_0 + \beta_1 t + \phi R_{t-1} + \varepsilon_t$ follows (see page 992). Write the least squares prediction equation.
c. Interpret the estimates of the model parameters, β_0, β_1, and ϕ.
d. Interpret the value of R^2 and **Root MSE**.
e. Forecast GDP for the first three quarters of 1994, and calculate approximate 95% forecast limits. Do these bounds contain the actual 1994 GDP values shown in the accompanying table?

Quarter	1994 GDP
I	5,261
II	5,314
III	5,359

Source: Survey of Current Business.

16.60 Refer to Exercises 16.34 and 16.49.
  a. Hypothesize a time series model for annual volume of wheat harvested, y_t, that takes into account the residual autocorrelation.
  b. Fit the autoregressive time series model, part **a**. Interpret the estimates of the model parameters.
  c. Forecast annual volume of wheat harvest for 1995. Place approximate 95% confidence bounds on the forecast.

16.61 Refer to Exercise 16.41 and the study on the long-term effects of the Employment Retirement Income Security Act (ERISA). Ledolter and Power also fit quarterly time series models for the number of pension plan terminations and the number of profit-sharing plan terminations from the first quarter of 1956 through the third quarter of 1982 ($n = 107$ quarters). To account for residual correlation, they fit straight-line autoregressive models of the form

$$y_t = \beta_0 + \beta_1 t + \phi R_{t-1} + \varepsilon_t$$

The results were as follows:

Pension plan terminations: $\quad \hat{y}_t = 3.54 + .039t + .40\hat{R}_{t-1}$

Profit-sharing plan terminations: $\quad \hat{y}_t = 3.54 + .039t + .22\hat{R}_{t-1}$

SAS printout for Exercise 16.59

Autoreg Procedure

Dependent Variable = GDP

Ordinary Least Squares Estimates

SSE	78083.02	DFE	14
MSE	5577.359	Root MSE	74.68171
SBC	186.8382	AIC	185.2931
Reg Rsq	0.6813	Total Rsq	0.6813
Durbin-Watson	0.2883		

Variable	DF	B Value	Std Error	t Ratio	Approx Prob
Intercept	1	4764.35000	39.163	121.653	0.0001
T	1	22.15735	4.050	5.471	0.0001

Estimates of Autocorrelations

Lag	Covariance	Correlation	-1 9 8 7 6 5 4 3 2 1 0 1 2 3 4 5 6 7 8 9 1
0	4880.189	1.000000	| |********************|
1	3590.525	0.735735	| |************** |

Preliminary MSE = 2238.515

Estimates of the Autoregressive Parameters

Lag	Coefficient	Std Error	t Ratio
1	-0.73573478	0.18784084	-3.916799

Yule-Walker Estimates

SSE	24720.72	DFE	13
MSE	1901.593	Root MSE	43.60726
SBC	171.9881	AIC	169.6703
Reg Rsq	0.5335	Total Rsq	0.8991

Variable	DF	B Value	Std Error	t Ratio	Approx Prob
Intercept	1	4787.81640	60.725	78.844	0.0001
T	1	22.33703	5.794	3.855	0.0020

a. Interpret the estimates of the model parameters for pension plan terminations.
b. Interpret the estimates of the model parameters for profit-sharing plan terminations.
c. The values of MSE for the quarterly time series models of retirement plan terminations are as follows:

Pension plan terminations: MSE = .0440

Profit-sharing plan terminations: MSE = .0402

Forecast the number of pension plan terminations for the fourth quarter of 1982 (i.e., $t = 108$). Assume that $y_{107} = 7.5$. [*Hint:* Recall that y_t is the logarithm of the number of pension plan terminations. Therefore, to obtain the forecast value, you must take the anti-logarithm of $\hat{y}_{108}$, i.e., the forecasted number of pension plan terminations is $e^{\hat{y}_{108}}$.]

d. Place approximate 95% confidence bounds on the forecast obtained in part **c**. [*Hint:* First, calculate upper and lower confidence limits for y_{108}, then take antilogarithms.]

e. Repeat parts **c** and **d** for the number of profit-sharing plan terminations in the fourth quarter of 1982. Assume that $y_{107} = 7.6$.

16.10 Forecasting Using Lagged Values of the Dependent Variable

In previous examples, we discussed a variety of choices for the deterministic component $E(y_t)$ of the time series models. All these models were functions of independent variables, such as t, x_t, x_{t-1}, and seasonal dummy variables. Often, the forecast of y_t can be improved by adding **lagged values of the dependent variable** to the model. For example, since the price y_t of a stock on day t is highly correlated with the price on the previous day (i.e., on day $t-1$), a useful model for $E(y_t)$ is

$$E(y_t) = \beta_0 + \beta_1 y_{t-1}$$

Models with lagged values of y_t tend to violate the standard regression assumptions outlined in Section 13.3; thus, they must be fit using specialized methods.

Box and Jenkins[*] developed a method of analyzing time series models based on past values of y_t and past values of the random error ε_t. The general model, called an **autoregressive moving average model** and denoted **ARMA** $(\boldsymbol{p}, \boldsymbol{q})$, takes the form

$$y_t + \phi_1 y_{t-1} + \phi_2 y_{t-2} + \cdots + \phi_p y_{t-p} = \varepsilon_t + \theta_1 \varepsilon_{t-1} + \theta_2 \varepsilon_{t-2} + \cdots + \theta_q \varepsilon_{t-q}$$

The left side of the equation is called a **pth-order autoregressive model** for y_t, whereas the right side of the equation is called a **qth-order moving average model** for the random error ε_t.

The analysis of an ARMA (p, q) model is divided into three stages: (1) identification, (2) estimation, and (3) forecasting. In the identification stage, the values of p and q are determined from the sample data. That is, the order of both the autoregressive portion and the moving average portion of the model are identified.[†] For example, the analyst may find the best fit to be an ARMA model with $p = 2$ and $q = 0$. Substituting $p = 2$ and $q = 0$ into the previous equation, we obtain the ARMA$(2, 0)$ model

$$y_t + \phi_1 y_{t-1} + \phi_2 y_{t-2} = \varepsilon_t$$

Note that since $q = 0$, there is no moving average component to the model.

---

[*]*Source:* Box, G. E. P. and Jenkins, G. M. Time Series Analysis: Forecasting and Control, *2nd ed. San Francisco: Holden-Day, 1977.*

[†] *This step involves a careful examination of a plot of the sample autocorrelations. Certain patterns in the plot allow the analyst to identify p and q.*

Once the model is identified, the second stage involves obtaining estimates of the model's parameters. In the case of the ARMA(2, 0) model, we require estimates of the autoregressive parameters ϕ_1 and ϕ_2. Tests for model adequacy are conducted, and, if the model is deemed adequate, the estimated model is used to forecast future values of y_t in the third stage.

Analysis of ARMA (p, q) models for y_t requires a level of expertise that is beyond the scope of this text. Even with this level of expertise, the analyst cannot hope to proceed without the aid of a sophisticated computer program. Procedures for identifying, estimating, and forecasting with ARMA (p, q) models are available in SAS, SPSS, and MINITAB.

SUMMARY

Many practical business problems require analysis of *time series data*, i.e., data that are collected sequentially over time. Various methods are available for describing time series. These methods usually require the calculation of index numbers—*simple, simple composite*, or *weighted composite index numbers*—that characterize a time series phenomenon by measuring how much the time series variable changes over time. Other descriptive techniques attempt to smooth the time series to make it easier to identify the *long-term trend*. These smoothing techniques include *moving averages* and *exponential smoothing*.

Time series are often modeled as a combination of four components: *secular, seasonal, cyclical*, and *residual*. Both descriptive and inferential techniques are available for *estimating* the time series components and *forecasting* future values of the time series. The *moving average method* uses estimates of the secular and seasonal components to forecast future values of a time series. However, the method requires you to extrapolate the moving average into the future to obtain the forecasts. *Exponential smoothing* is an adaptive forecasting method for time series with little or no secular or seasonal trends that leads to explicit forecasts.

A *regression model* is an inferential time series model that allows you to construct prediction intervals for the forecasts. The deterministic portion of the model accounts for the trend and seasonal components. However, the regression approach assumes that the random error term is uncorrelated. Since many business and economic time series exhibit autocorrelated errors, the *Durbin–Watson d statistic* is important for testing *residual autocorrelation*. When autocorrelation is present, time series models that include an *autoregressive model* as the residual component are very useful forecasting tools. The reliability of the forecasts can be assessed by constructing prediction intervals about the forecast value.

The business forecaster should be careful to distinguish between descriptive and inferential time series models. If a descriptive model (e.g., smoothing technique) is used to project future values of the series, no assessment of forecast reliability is possible.

KEY TERMS

ARMA models
Autocorrelation
Autoregressive models
Cyclical fluctuation
Durbin–Watson test
Exponential smoothing
Forecasting

Index numbers
Lagged values
Long-term trend
Moving average
Residual variation
Seasonal variation
Secular (long-term) trend

Simple composite index
Simple index
Time series
Time series models
Weighted composite index

KEY FORMULAS

Simple index: $\quad I_t = \left(\dfrac{y_t}{y_{t_0}} \right) 100$

where t_0 is the base period

Simple composite index: $\quad I_t = \left(\dfrac{y_t}{y_{t_0}} \right) 100$

$$y_t = Q_{1t} + Q_{2t} + \cdots + Q_{kt}$$
$$y_{t_0} = Q_{1t_0} + Q_{2t_0} + \cdots + Q_{kt_0}$$

Weighted composite index: $\quad I_t = \left(\dfrac{y_t}{y_{t_0}} \right) 100$

where

$$y_t = W_1 Q_{1t} + W_2 Q_{2t} + \cdots + W_k Q_{kt}$$
$$y_{t_0} = W_1 Q_{1t_0} + W_2 Q_{2t_0} + \cdots + W_k Q_{kt_0}$$

N-point moving average: $\quad M_t = S_t/N$

where

$$S_t = \begin{cases} y_{t-(N-1)/2} + \cdots + y_t + \cdots + y_{t+(N-1)/2} & \text{if } N \text{ is odd} \\ y_{t-N/2} + \cdots + y_t + \cdots + y_{t+N/2-1} & \text{if } N \text{ is even} \end{cases}$$

Exponential smoothing: $\quad E_t = wy_t + (1-w)E_{t-1}$

where $0 < w < 1$

Moving average forecast:

$$F_t = \begin{cases} M_t & \text{if little or no seasonal variation exists} \\ M_t \cdot \left(\dfrac{\text{Seasonal index}}{100} \right) & \text{otherwise} \end{cases}$$

where M_t is the moving average value graphically extended to future time t

Exponential smoothing forecast:

$$F_t = wy_n + (1 - w)E_n, \quad t = n + 1, n + 2, \ldots$$

where y_n is the last observed value of the time series and E_n is the last exponentially smoothed value

Forecasting Using a Time Series Model with First-Order Autoregressive Residuals

m-step-ahead forecast:

$$F_{n+m} = \hat{\beta}_0 + \hat{\beta}_1 x_{1,n+m} + \hat{\beta}_2 x_{2,n+m} + \cdots + \hat{\beta}_k x_{k,n+m} + \hat{R}_{n+m}$$

where

$$\hat{R}_{n+m} = \hat{\phi}^m \hat{R}_n \qquad \hat{R}_n = y_n - \hat{y}_n$$

Approximate 95% forecasting limits:

$$F_{n+m} \pm 2\sqrt{\text{MSE}\,(1 + \hat{\phi}^2 + \hat{\phi}^4 + \cdots + \hat{\phi}^{2(m-1)})}$$

SUPPLEMENTARY
EXERCISES

16.62 The level at which commercial lending institutions set consumer credit interest rates has a significant effect on the volume of buying and selling of new automobiles. The data in the table
are the annual average interest rates on 48-month, fixed-rate loans on new automobiles for the
period 1980–1993.

Year	Interest Rate, %	Year	Interest Rate, %
1980	14.30	1987	10.46
1981	16.54	1988	10.86
1982	16.83	1989	12.07
1983	13.92	1990	11.78
1984	13.71	1991	11.14
1985	12.91	1992	9.29
1986	11.33	1993	8.09

Source: Statistical Abstract of the United States, U.S. Bureau of the Census, 1994.

a. Calculate a simple index for the annual average interest rates using 1980 as the base period. Interpret the index for 1993.

b. Calculate and plot a 3-point moving average for the interest rates. Do you detect a long-term trend?

c. Calculate and plot the exponentially smoothed interest rate series using a smoothing constant of $w = 2$. Do you detect a long-term trend?

16.63 The level of production of metals in the United States is one measure of the strength of the industrial economy. The table lists the 1994 January–August production (in thousand tons) for three metals important to U.S. industry.

Month	Pig Iron	Production Aluminum	Lead
January	4,413	292.5	43.17
February	4,425	260.9	40.21
March	4,436	286.4	48.45
April	4,419	269.5	48.26
May	4,438	277.5	47.92
June	4,445	267.6	47.10
July	4,518	275.5	52.53
August	4,440	274.4	47.08

Source: Standard & Poor's Statistical Service: Current Statistics, Jan. 1995.

a. Compute the simple composite index of production for the 8-month period, using January 1994 as the base period.

b. Interpret the value of the production index for August 1994.

16.64 The accompanying table lists the space shuttle system expenditures (in millions of dollars) by NASA for 1973 through 1995.

Year	Outlay	Year	Outlay
1973	58	1985	2,636
1974	325	1986	2,606
1975	1,543	1987	4,165
1976	2,619	1988	2,378
1977	2,258	1989	2,522
1978	2,062	1990	2,471
1979	2,251	1991	2,630
1980	2,751	1992	2,775
1981	2,724	1993	2,857
1982	2,932	1994	2,571
1983	3,014	1995	2,420
1984	3,127		

Source: Statistical Abstract of the United States, U.S. Bureau of the Census, 1995.

a. Plot the time series.

b. Calculate and plot the simple index for the series using 1982 as the base period. Interpret the index.

c. Calculate 3-point, 5-point, and 7-point moving averages. Plot each moving average series on the same graph. Which moving average best characterizes the long-term trend of space shuttle expenditures?

d. Calculate the exponentially smoothed series for the time series using smoothing constants $w = .1$, $w = .5$, and $w = .8$. Plot each smoothed series on the same graph. Which series best characterizes the long-term trend of space shuttle expenditures?

e. Graphically extend the moving average you chose in part **c** to forecast the outlay for the space program in 1996. Comment on the reliability of this forecast.

f. Use exponential smoothing (with smoothing constant $w = .8$) to forecast the outlay for the space program in 1996. Comment on the reliability of this forecast.

16.65 In 1974, Congress adopted the Federal-Aid Highway Amendments, which reduced the highway speed limit to 55 miles per hour (mph). Since that time, controversy over the social efficiency of the decision has grown. T. H. Ferrester, R. F. McNown, and L. D. Singell conducted an analysis to estimate the effect of 55 mph speed limit on traffic fatalities (*Southern Economic Journal*, Jan. 1984). Time series data for the United States from 1952 to 1979 ($n = 28$ years) were used to fit a regression model relating traffic fatalities y_t to $k = 7$ independent variables.

x_{1t} = Real earned income

x_{2t} = Vehicle miles

x_{3t} = Ratio of number of youths to number of adults

x_{4t} = Percentage of all car purchases that are imported cars

x_{5t} = Average highway speed

x_{6t} = Percentage of cars traveling between 45 and 60 mph

$$x_{7t} = \begin{cases} 0 & \text{if 55 mph speed limit imposed} \\ 1 & \text{otherwise} \end{cases}$$

The results of the multiple regression are summarized as follows:

$$\hat{y}_t = -20,016.4 + 7,544.85x_{1t} - .01046x_{2t} - 36,758.0x_{3t} - 117.609x_{4t} + 1,325.22x_{5t}$$
$$- 415.742x_{6t} + 9,678.08x_{7t}$$

$$R^2 = .987 \qquad F = 217.23 \qquad d = 1.97$$

a. Is there evidence that the model is useful for predicting annual traffic fatalities? Test using $\alpha = .05$.

b. Is there evidence that the regression residuals are autocorrelated? Test using $\alpha = .05$. (Since Table 15 of Appendix B does not show critical values for $k = 7$ independent variables, use those based on $k = 5$.)

16.66 The number of industrial and commercial failures in the United States is given in the table by type of firm for the years 1986–1993. Using 1980 as the base period, construct a simple composite industrial and commercial failures index. Interpret the index.

			Number of Failures		
Year	*Commercial Service*	*Construction*	*Manufacturing and Mining*	*Retail Trade*	*Wholesale Trade*
1980	1,594	2,355	1,599	4,910	1,284
1986	20,911	7,035	5,641	13,509	4,808
1987	23,802	6,735	4,900	12,240	4,336
1988	22,686	6,791	4,698	11,488	4,455
1989	12,779	7,120	4,284	11,120	3,687
1990	16,063	8,072	5,090	12,826	4,376
1991	22,852	11,963	7,006	17,242	6,170
1992	26,871	12,452	7,550	19,084	6,744
1993	24,287	10,411	6,396	15,482	5,930

Source: *Survey of Current Business*, U.S. Department of Commerce, Bureau of Economic Analysis.

16.67 The average monthly retail prices (in cents per pound) of cotton and wool were recorded for the period beginning January 1993 and ending December 1993. This monthly time series appears in the table.

	Retail Prices, ¢ Per Pound	
	Cotton	*Wool*
January	53.7	145
February	55.4	135
March	56.4	120
April	56.2	114
May	56.4	119
June	54.4	124
July	54.4	118
August	53.0	125
September	54.0	117
October	54.6	115
November	55.6	120
December	60.3	120

Source: *Survey of Current Business*, U.S. Department of Commerce, Bureau of Economic Analysis.

a. In January 1990, cotton sold for 60.2¢ per pound and wool sold for 294¢ per pound. Calculate a simple composite price index for the textile products using January 1990 as the base period. Plot the index values.

b. Consumption figures for the two products in the base period of January 1990 are as follows: cotton, 605 million pounds; wool, 10.9 million pounds. Using consumption as a weighting factor and January 1990 as the base period, compute a weighted composite price index for the products.

c. Plot the weighted composite index on the same graph as the simple composite index. Compare the two indexes. Which index do you think better characterizes the increase in price of the textile products? Explain.

16.68 The accompanying table shows U.S. beer production for the years 1973–1993. Suppose you are interested in forecasting U.S. beer production in 1994. Since a plot of the time series y_t reveals a linearly increasing trend, you hypothesize the model

$$E(y_t) = \beta_0 + \beta_1 t$$

for the secular trend.

Year	t	U.S. Beer Production y_t, Millions of Barrels	Year	t	U.S. Beer Production y_t, Millions of Barrels
1973	1	149	1984	12	193
1974	2	156	1985	13	194
1975	3	161	1986	14	197
1976	4	164	1987	15	195
1977	5	171	1988	16	197
1978	6	179	1989	17	199
1979	7	184	1990	18	204
1980	8	194	1991	19	202
1981	9	194	1992	20	202
1982	10	196	1993	21	207
1983	11	196			

Source: Standard & Poor's Statistical Service: Current Statistics, New York, Standard & Poor's Corporation, Jan. 1995.

a. Fit the model to the data using the method of least squares.

b. Plot the least squares model from part **a** and extend the line to forecast y_{22}, the U.S. beer production (in millions of barrels) in 1994. How reliable do you think this forecast is?

c. Calculate and plot the residuals for the model obtained in part **a**. Is there visual evidence of residual autocorrelation?

d. How could you test to determine whether residual autocorrelation exists? If you have access to a computer package, carry out the test. Test using $\alpha = .05$.

e. Hypothesize a time series model that will account for the residual autocorrelation. If you have access to a computer package with a modified least squares routine, fit the model.

f. Compute a 95% prediction interval for y_{22}, the U.S. beer production in 1994. Why is this forecast preferred to that of part **b**?

16.69 Civilian employment is broadly classified by the federal government into two categories—agricultural and nonagricultural. The nonagricultural employment category is further subclassified into wage and salary workers, self-employed workers, and unpaid family members. The average numbers of hours worked per year (in thousands) for the three classes of nonagricultural workers are given in the table for the 1986–1993 period.

Year	Wage & Salary	Self-employed	Unpaid Family Members
1980	88,525	7,000	413
1986	98,299	7,881	255
1987	100,771	8,201	260
1988	103,021	8,519	260
1989	105,259	8,605	279
1990	105,715	8,760	252
1991	104,520	8,899	225
1992	105,540	8,619	232
1993	107,011	9,003	218

Source: Statistical Abstract of the United States, U.S. Bureau of the Census, 1994.

a. Compute simple indexes for each of the three time series using 1980 as the base period.

b. Which class of workers has shown the highest growth in hours worked in 1993 compared to 1980? Which class has shown the least growth?

c. Calculate and plot a simple composite index for the total number of hours worked per year by workers in the three groups, using 1980 as the base period.

16.70 In May 1978, the first casino (Resorts International Hotel and Casino) opened in Atlantic City, New Jersey. In the first few years following casino openings, employment in hotels and other lodging places accelerated along Atlantic City's Boardwalk, as shown in the table.

Year	Quarter	Employment in Atlantic City Hotels
1978	I	1,711
	II	4,065
	III	5,787
	IV	5,019
1979	I	5,459
	II	9,184
	III	12,168
	IV	11,842
1980	I	13,730
	II	14,964
	III	18,058
	IV	21,393

Source: Business Review, Jan./Feb. 1982.

a. Use a smoothing technique to forecast employment in Atlantic City hotels in quarter I of 1981. Comment on the reliability of this forecast.

b. Propose a time series model for the quarterly series that will account for secular trend, seasonal variation, and residual autocorrelation. If you have access to a computer package with a modified least squares routine, fit the model.

c. Use the fitted time series model of part **b** to forecast employment in quarter I of 1981. Place an approximate 95% prediction interval about the forecast.

   d. Actual employment in quarter I of 1981 was 22,772. Check to determine whether the forecasting technique of part **c** has captured this value.

   e. Would you recommend using the fitted model from part **b** for forecasting quarterly employment in 1991? Explain.

16.71 Suppose a firm is interested in forecasting its sales revenue for each of the next 5 years. The yearly sales data (revenue in $ thousands) for the firm's 35 years of operation are given in the table. A plot of the data reveals a linearly increasing trend, so the model

$$E(y_t) = \beta_0 + \beta_1 t$$

seems plausible for the secular trend. The SAS printout for the least squares fit is reproduced here.

t	y_t	t	y_t	t	y_t
1	4.8	13	48.4	25	100.3
2	4.0	14	61.6	26	111.7
3	5.5	15	65.6	27	108.2
4	15.6	16	71.4	28	115.5
5	23.1	17	83.4	29	119.2
6	23.3	18	93.6	30	125.2
7	31.4	19	94.2	31	136.3
8	46.0	20	85.4	32	146.8
9	46.1	21	86.2	33	146.1
10	41.9	22	89.9	34	151.4
11	45.5	23	89.2	35	150.9
12	53.5	24	99.1		

Dependent Variable: Y

Analysis of Variance

Source	DF	Sum of Squares	Mean Square	F Value	Prob>F
Model	1	65875.20817	65875.20817	1615.724	0.0001
Error	33	1345.45355	40.77132		
C Total	34	67220.66171			

Root MSE	6.38524	R-square	0.9800
Dep Mean	77.72286	Adj R-sq	0.9794
C.V.	8.21540		

Parameter Estimates

Variable	DF	Parameter Estimate	Standard Error	T for H0: Parameter=0	Prob > |T|
INTERCEP	1	0.401513	2.20570829	0.182	0.8567
T	1	4.295630	0.10686692	40.196	0.0001

Durbin-Watson D	0.821
(For Number of Obs.)	35
1st Order Autocorrelation	0.590

a. Write the least squares prediction equation.
b. Is there sufficient evidence to indicate that the model is useful for predicting yearly sales? Test using $\alpha = .05$.
c. Examine the residual plot shown here. Do the residuals appear to be correlated? Explain.

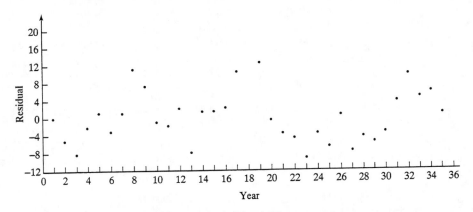

d. Conduct a test to determine whether positive residual correlation exists. Test using $\alpha = .05$.
e. Propose a model that will account for first-order autocorrelation among the residuals.
f. The SAS printout for the straight-line autoregressive model of part e is reproduced below. Identify the key elements on the printout and interpret their values.

Autoreg Procedure

Dependent Variable = Y

Ordinary Least Squares Estimates

SSE	1345.454	DFE	33
MSE	40.77132	Root MSE	6.385242
SBC	234.1562	AIC	231.0455
Reg Rsq	0.9800	Total Rsq	0.9800
Durbin-Watson	0.8207		

Variable	DF	B Value	Std Error	t Ratio	Approx Prob
Intercept	1	0.40151261	2.2057	0.182	0.8567
T	1	4.29563025	0.1069	40.196	0.0001

Estimates of Autocorrelations

Lag	Covariance	Correlation	-1 9 8 7 6 5 4 3 2 1 0 1 2 3 4 5 6 7 8 9 1
0	38.44153	1.000000	|********************|
1	22.66605	0.589624	|***********|

Preliminary MSE = 25.07708

Estimates of the Autoregressive Parameters

Lag	Coefficient	Std Error	t Ratio
1	-0.58962415	0.14277861	-4.129639

(continued)

SAS Printout (Autoregressive Model) for Exercise 16.71 *(continued)*

Yule-Walker Estimates

SSE	877.6854	DFE	32	
MSE	27.42767	Root MSE	5.237143	
SBC	223.1868	AIC	218.5208	
Reg Rsq	0.9412	Total Rsq	0.9869	

Variable	DF	B Value	Std Error	t Ratio	Approx Prob
Intercept	1	0.40575699	3.9970	0.102	0.9198
T	1	4.29593038	0.1898	22.630	0.0001

g. Use the autoregressive model to forecast sales revenues for the firm for each of the next 5 years. Place approximate 95% confidence bounds around the forecasts.

16.72 The data on annual OPEC oil imports, Exercises 16.4 and 16.28, are reproduced here.

Year	t	Imports, y_t	Year	t	Imports, y_t
1974	1	926	1984	11	553
1975	2	1,171	1985	12	479
1976	3	1,663	1986	13	771
1977	4	2,058	1987	14	876
1978	5	1,892	1988	15	987
1979	6	1,866	1989	16	1,232
1980	7	1,414	1990	17	1,282
1981	8	1,067	1991	18	1,233
1982	9	633	1992	19	1,247
1983	10	540	1993	20	1,339

Source: Statistical Abstracts of the United States, U.S. Bureau of the Census, 1994.

a. Plot the time series.
b. Hypothesize a straight-line autoregressive time series model for annual amount of imported crude oil, y_t.
c. If you have access to a computer package, fit the proposed model to the data.
d. From the output, write the modified least squares prediction equation for y_t.
e. Forecast the amount of foreign crude oil imported into the United States from OPEC in 1994. Place approximate 95% prediction bounds on the forecast value.

■ CASE STUDY 16.1

Analyzing the Price of Your Favorite Stock

Consider the daily closing prices of your favorite stock during the past 5 years. Suppose you want to analyze the time series consisting of the closing stock price on the last day of each month using the smoothing methods outlined in this chapter.

a. Record and plot the closing prices on the last day of each month for the 5-year period. [*Note:* You can obtain these monthly closing prices from the monthly periodical, *Security Owner's Stock Guide*, published by Standard & Poor's Corporation and available at your university library.] Can you identify the long-term trend of this monthly time series?

b. Use the moving average method to clearly identify the long-term trend of the month-ending closing prices. [*Hint:* You will need to try several different numbers of points to obtain a smooth series.]

c. The moving average of part **b** will also help you to identify any seasonal or cyclical fluctuations. Compare the actual time series value, y_t, to the moving average M_t, by forming the ratio

$$\left(\frac{y_t}{M_t}\right) 100$$

for each value of t in the monthly series. The larger this ratio, the greater the seasonal or cyclical variation.

d. Use exponential smoothing to clearly identify the long-term trend of the monthly time series. Use a value of w that will yield a smoother series.

e. Obtain the moving average forecast by extrapolating a graph of the moving average of part **b** to the future month.

f. Adjust the moving average forecast to account for any seasonal variation in the series.

g. Obtain the exponentially smoothed forecast of the stock price for the future month.

h. One drawback to the exponential smoothing forecast method is that the secular (long-term) trend component of the time series is not taken into account. The **Holt–Winters forecasting model** is an extension of the exponential smoothing method that explicitly recognizes the long-term trend in a time series.* The Holt–Winters model for y_t is

$$E_t = \begin{cases} y_2, & \text{if } t = 2 \\ wy_t + (1 - w)(E_{t-1} + T_{t-1}), & \text{if } t > 2 \end{cases}$$

$$T_t = \begin{cases} y_2 - y_1, & \text{if } t = 2 \\ v(E_t - E_{t-1}) + (1 - v)T_{t-1}, & \text{if } t > 2 \end{cases}$$

where $0 < w < 1$ and $0 < v < 1$. Note that the model consists of both an exponentially smoothed component, E_t (with smoothing constant w), and a trend component, T_t (with smoothing constant v). After we calculate E_t and T_t for $t = 2, 3, 4, \ldots, n$ (E_1 and T_1 are not defined), the Holt–Winters forecast for a future time period, say $t = n + k$, is

$$F_{n+k} = E_n + kT_n$$

Obtain the Holt–Winters forecast of the stock price for the future month. (Use the value of w selected in part **g** and $v = .5$.)

i. Suppose you also want forecast stock closing prices 2 and 3 months into the future. Which of the three forecasting methods—moving average, exponential smoothing, or Holt–Winters—would you recommend? Why?

j. Obtain the 2-month-ahead and 3-month-ahead forecasts using the technique you selected in part **i**.

k. What is the major disadvantage of forecasting with any of the three smoothing techniques?

---

*The Holt–Winters model can also be adapted to allow for seasonal variation in the time series.

■ CASE STUDY 16.2

Modeling Peak Electricity Demands at Florida Power Corporation

To operate effectively, power companies must be able to predict daily peak demand for electricity. *Demand* (or *load*) is defined as the rate (measured in megawatts) at which electric energy is delivered to customers. Since demand is normally recorded on an hourly basis, daily peak demand refers to the maximum hourly demand in a 24-hour period. Power companies are continually developing and refining statistical models of daily peak demand.

Time series models of daily peak-demand serve a twofold purpose. First, the models provide short-term *forecasts* that will assist in the economic planning and dispatching of electric energy. Second, models that relate peak demand to one or more weather variables provide estimates of historical peak demands under a set of alternative weather conditions. That is, since changing weather conditions represent the primary source of variation in peak demand, the model can be used to answer the often asked question, "What would the peak daily demand have been had normal weather prevailed?" This second application, commonly referred to as *weather normalization*, is mainly an exercise in *backcasting* (i.e., adjusting historical data) rather than forecasting.

In this case study, we consider a study designed to compare several alternative methods of modeling 1983 daily peak demands for the Florida Power Corporation (FPC).* The data for the study consist of daily observations on peak demand recorded by the FPC for the period beginning November 1, 1982, and ending October 31, 1983, and several factors that are known to influence demand. It is typically assumed that demand consists of two components, a non–weather-sensitive "base" demand that is not influenced by temperature changes, and a weather-sensitive demand component that is highly responsive to changes in temperature.

The principal factor that affects the usage of non-weather-sensitive appliances (such as refrigerators, generators, lights, and computers) is the *day of the week*. Typically, Saturdays have lower peak demands than weekdays due to decreased commercial and industrial activity, whereas Sundays and holidays exhibit even lower peak demand levels as commercial and industrial activity declines even further.

The single most important factor effecting the usage of weather-sensitive appliances (such as heaters and air conditioners) is *temperature*. During the winter months, as temperatures drop below comfortable levels, customers begin to operate their electric heating units, thereby increasing the level of demand placed on the system. Similarly, during the summer months, as temperatures climb above comfortable levels, the use of air conditioning drives demand upward. Since the FPC serves 32 counties along west-central and northern Florida, it was necessary to get information on temperature conditions from multiple weather stations. This was accomplished by identifying three primary weather stations within the FPC service area and recording the temperature value at the hour of peak demand each day at each station. A weighted average of these three daily temperatures was used to represent coincident temperature (i.e., temperature at the hour of peak demand) for the entire FPC service area, where the weights were proportional to the percentage of total electricity sales attributable to the zones surrounding each of the three weather stations.

To summarize, the dependent variable (y_t) and the independent variables recorded for each of the 365 days of the November 1982–October 1983 year were

Dependent variable:

y_t = Peak demand (in megawatts) observed on day t

Source: Jacob. M. F. "A time series approach to modeling daily peak electricity demands." Paper presented at the SAS Users Group International Annual Conference, Reno, Nevada, 1985.

Independent variables:

Day of the week: Weekday, Saturday, or Sunday/holiday

Temperature: Coincident temperature (in degrees), i.e., the temperature recorded at the hour of the peak demand on day t, calculated as a weighted average of three daily temperatures.

In any modeling procedure, it is often helpful to plot the data in a scattergram. Figure 16.15 shows a graph of the daily peak demand (y_t) from November 1982 through October 1983. The effects of seasonal weather on peak demand are readily apparent from the figure. One way to account for this seasonal variation is to include dummy variables for months in the model. However, since temperature is such a strong indicator of the weather, the FPC opted for a simpler model with temperature as the sole seasonal weather variable.

Figure 16.16 on page 1008 presents a scatterplot of daily peak demands versus coincident temperature. Note the nonlinear relationship that exists between the two variables.

During the cool winter months, peak demand is inversely related to temperature; lower temperatures cause increased usage of heating equipment, which, in turn, cause higher peak demands. In contrast, the summer months reveal a positive relationship between peak demand and temperature; higher temperatures yield higher

peak demands due to greater usage of air conditioners. You might think that a second-order (quadratic) model would be a good choice to account for the U-shaped distribution of peak demands shown in Figure 16.16. The FPC, however, rejected such a model for two reasons:

1. A quadratic model yields a symmetrical shape (i.e., a parabola) and would, therefore, not allow independent estimates of the winter and summer peak demand–temperature relationship.

2. In theory, there exists a mild temperature range where peak demand is assumed to consist solely of the non–weather-sensitive base demand component. For this range, a temperature change will not spur any additional heating or cooling and, consequently, has no impact on demand. The lack of linearity in the bottom portion of the U-shaped parabola fit by the quadratic model would tend to yield overestimates of peak demand at the extremes of the mild temperature range and underestimates for temperatures in the middle of this range (see Figure 16.17).

The solution was to model daily peak demand with a **piecewise linear regression model**. This approach has the advantage of allowing the peak demand–temperature relationship to vary between some prespecified temperature ranges, as well as providing a mechanism for joining the separate pieces.

FIGURE 16.15

Daily Peak Megawatt Demands, November 1982–October 1983

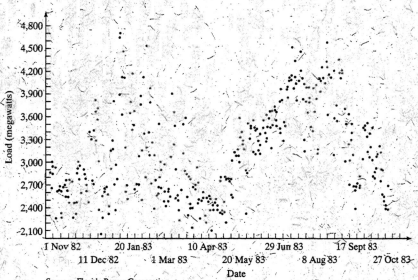

Source: Florida Power Corporation.

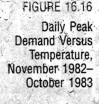

FIGURE 16.16

Daily Peak Demand Versus Temperature, November 1982– October 1983

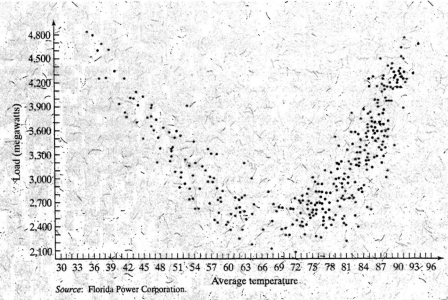

Source: Florida Power Corporation.

FIGURE 16.17

Theoretical Relationship Between Daily Peak Demand and Temperature

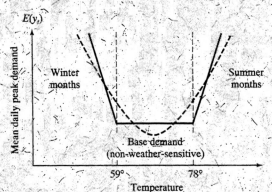

With the piecewise linear specification as the basic model structure, the following multiple regression model (**model 1**) of daily peak demand was proposed:

$$y_t = \beta_0 + \underbrace{\beta_1(x_{1t} - 59)x_{2t} + \beta_2(x_{1t} - 78)x_{3t}}_{\text{Temperature}}$$

$$+ \underbrace{\beta_3 x_{4t} + \beta_4 x_{5t}}_{\text{Day of the week}} + \varepsilon_t$$

where

$x_{1t} = $ Coincident temperature on day t

$$x_{2t} = \begin{cases} 1 & x_{1t} < 59 \\ 0 & \text{if not} \end{cases}$$

$$x_{3t} = \begin{cases} 1 & \text{if } x_{1t} > 78 \\ 0 & \text{if not} \end{cases}$$

$$x_{4t} = \begin{cases} 1 & \text{if Saturday} \\ 0 & \text{if not} \end{cases}$$

$$x_{5t} = \begin{cases} 1 & \text{if Sunday or holiday} \\ 0 & \text{if not} \end{cases} \quad \text{(Base Level = Weekday)}$$

a. -Show that model 1 proposes three different straight-line relationships between peak demand (y_t) and coincident temperature x_{1t}, one for each of the three temperature ranges corresponding to winter months (less than 59°), non–weather-sensitive months (between 59° and 78°), and summer months (greater than 78°). [*Hint:* For winter months ($x_{1t} < 59$), we have $x_{2t} = 1$ and $x_{3t} = 0$, whereas for weekdays, $x_{4t} = x_{5t} = 0$. Substituting $x_{2t} = 1$, $x_{3t} = 0$, $x_{4t} = 0$, and $x_{5t} = 0$ into the model, we obtain the equation of the demand–temperature line for weekdays during winter months:

$$E(y_t) = \beta_0 + \beta_1(x_{1t} - 59)(1) + \beta_2(x_{1t} - 78)(0)$$
$$+ \beta_3(0) + \beta_4(0)$$
$$= \beta_0 + \beta_1(x_{1t} - 59)$$
$$= (\beta_0 - 59\beta_1) + \beta_1 x_{1t}$$

Perform similar calculations for weekdays during summer months and non–weather-sensitive months.]

b. Model 1 also allows for variations in demand due to day of the week (Saturday, Sunday/holiday, or weekday). Since interaction between temperature and day of the week is omitted, what is the model assuming about the differences between mean peak demand for weekdays or weekends/holidays for the three temperature ranges?

c. Refer to part a. Show that the slope of the demand–temperature line for winter months (when $x_{1t} < 59$) is β_1. Do you expect β_1 to be positive or negative? [*Hint:* Use Figure 16.17.]

d. Refer to part a. Show that the slope for summer months (when $x_{1t} > 78$) is β_2. Do you expect β_2 to be positive or negative?

Model 1 is a multiple regression model that relies on the standard regression assumptions of independent errors (i.e., errors uncorrelated). This may be a serious shortcoming in view of the fact that the data are in the form of a time series. To account for possible autocorrelated residuals, the following time series model (**model 2**) was proposed:

$$y_t = \beta_0 + \beta_1(x_{1t} - 59)x_{2t} + \beta_2(x_{1t} - 78)x_{3t}$$
$$+ \beta_3 x_{4t} + \beta_4 x_{5t} + R_t$$
$$R_t = \phi R_{t-1} + \varepsilon_t$$

Model 2 proposes a regression–autoregression pair of models for daily peak demand (y_t). The deterministic component, $E(y_t)$, is identical to the deterministic component of model 1; however, a first-order autoregressive model is chosen for the random error component.

e. What type of autocorrelation (positive or negative) occurs when ϕ in model 2 is positive? Negative?

f. The SAS multiple regression computer printout for model 1 is shown in Figure 16.18, and a plot of the least squares fit is shown in Figure 16.19 on page 1010. Interpret the values of R^2, F, and ROOT MSE on the printout.

g. Refer to the model 1 printout shown in Figure 16.18. Test the hypotheses

$$H_0: \quad \phi = 0$$
$$H_a: \quad \phi > 0$$

using the Durbin–Watson test. (Use $\alpha = .05$.) Interpret the results.

h. The SAS printout for model 2 is shown in Figure 16.20 on page 1011. Find and interpret the values of R^2 (TOTAL RSQ) and ROOT MSE on the printout. Compare these values to the values obtained in part f. Do these results support the conclusion reached by the Durbin–Watson test in part g?

i. Use model 2 and the information provided in Table 16.17 to forecast daily peak demand for the first 7 days in November 1983. The estimated model,* obtained from Figure 16.20, is given by

$$\hat{y}_t = 2{,}812.967 - 65.337(x_{1t} - 59)x_{2t}$$
$$+ 83.455(x_{1t} - 78)x_{3t} - 130.828 x_{4t}$$
$$- 275.551 x_{5t} + \hat{R}_t$$
$$\hat{R}_t = .6475 \hat{R}_{t-1}$$

j. Construct approximate 95% prediction intervals for the forecasts of part i. Determine whether actual

---

*Remember that the estimate of ϕ is obtained by multiplying the value reported on the SAS printout by (-1).

FIGURE 16.18

SAS Printout for Multiple Regression Model of Daily Peak Demand, Model 1

Dependent Variable: LOAD

Analysis of Variance

Source	DF	Sum of Squares	Mean Square	F Value	Prob>F
Model	4	106565982	26641495.5	441.729	0.0001
Error	360	21712247	60311.8		
C Total	364	128278229			

Root MSE	245.585	R-square	0.8307	
Dep Mean	3191.863	Adj R-sq	0.8289	
C.V.	7.694			

Parameter Estimates

Variable	DF	Parameter Estimate	Standard Error	T for H0: Parameter=0	Prob > |T|
INTERCEP	1	2670.171	21.251829	126.644	0.0001
AVTW	1	-82.038953	2.941928	-27.886	0.0001
AVTS	1	114.443	3.050468	37.516	0.0001
SAT	1	-164.932	37.990216	-4.341	0.0001
SUN	1	-285.114	35.328293	-8.070	0.0001

Durbin-Watson D	0.705
(For Number of Obs.)	365
1st Order Autocorrelation	0.648

FIGURE 16.19

Daily Peak Demand Versus Temperature: Actual Versus Fitted Piecewise Linear Model

Source: Florida Power Corporation.

demand (see Table 16.17) falls within the corresponding prediction interval for each of the 7 days.

k. Consider the problem of using model 2 for weather normalization. Suppose the temperature on Saturday, March 5, 1983 (i.e., $t = 125$), was $x_{1,121} = 25°$, unusually cold for that day. Normally, temperatures range from 40° to 50° on March 5 in the FPC service area. Substitute $x_{1,121} = 45°$ into the prediction equation to obtain an estimate of the peak demand expected if normal weather conditions had prevailed on March 5, 1983. Calculate an approximate 95% prediction interval for the estimate. [*Hint:* Use $\hat{y}_{121} \pm 2\sqrt{MSE}$.]

Table 16.17 Actual Peak Demands for the First 7 Days of November 1983

Date	t	Actual Demand y_t	Actual Temperature x_{1t}
Tues., Nov. 1	366	2,799	76
Wed., Nov. 2	367	2,784	77
Thurs., Nov. 3	368	2,845	77
Fri., Nov. 4	369	2,701	76
Sat., Nov. 5	370	2,512	72
Sun., Nov. 6	371	2,419	71
Mon., Nov. 7	372	2,749	68

FIGURE 16.20

SAS Printout for First-Order Autoregressive Time Series Model of Daily Peak Demand, Model 2

```
                           Autoreg Procedure

Dependent Variable = LOAD

                    Ordinary Least Squares Estimates

              SSE         21712247      DFE              360
              MSE         60311.8       Root MSE         245.585
              Reg Rsq     0.8307        Total Rsq        0.8307
              Durbin-Watson  0.7052


       Variable     DF      B Value      Std Error    t Ratio  Approx Prob

       INTERCEP      1      2670.171     21.251829    126.644     0.0001
       AVTW          1       -82.038953   2.941928    -27.886     0.0001
       AVTS          1       114.443      3.050468     37.516     0.0001
       SAT           1      -164.932     37.990216     -4.341     0.0001
       SUN           1      -285.114     35.328293     -8.070     0.0001


                      Estimates of Autocorrelations

  Lag  Covariance  Correlation  -1 9 8 7 6 5 4 3 2 1 0 1 2 3 4 5 6 7 8 9 1

   0    59485.6    1.000000   |                    |********************|
   1    38519.4    0.647541   |                    |*************        |


                    Preliminary MSE = 35542.75

              Estimates of the Autoregressive Parameters

           Lag    Coefficient     Std Error        t Ratio
            1      -0.64754083     0.039887        -16.23458


                       Yule-Walker Estimates

              SSE         9939789       DFE              359
              MSE         26787.44      Root MSE         166.3943
              Reg Rsq     0.7626        Total Rsq        0.9225


       Variable     DF      B Value      Std Error    t Ratio  Approx Prob

       INTERCEP      1      2812.967     29.879088     94.145     0.0001
       AVTW          1       -65.337453   2.663925    -24.527     0.0001
       AVTS          1        83.455      3.853199     21.659     0.0001
       SAT           1      -130.828     22.413602     -5.837     0.0001
       SUN           1      -275.551     21.373678    -12.892     0.0001
```

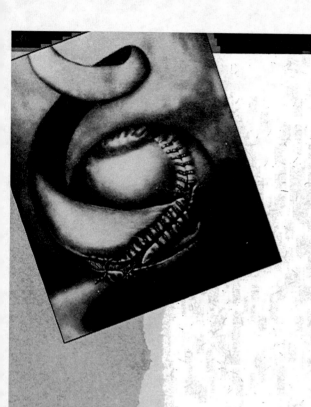

Appendix A

DATA SETS

■ CONTENTS

A.1 Sales and Appraisals of Residential Properties in Tampa, Florida

ASCII file name: A1SALES.DAT
Number of observations: 707

Variable	Column(s)	Type	Description
PROPERTY	1–3	QN	Property identification number
NBRHOOD	7–14	QL	Neighborhood (AVILA, CWDVILL, NORTDALE, TAMPALMS, TOWNCTRY, or YBORCITY)
LOCATION	21–22	QL	Location (NE, NW, SE, SW)
LANDVAL	28–34	QN	Appraised land value (dollars)
IMPROVAL	39–45	QN	Appraised value of improvements (dollars)
TOTALVAL	49–55	QN	Total appraised value (LANDVAL + IMPROVAL)
SALEPRIC	60–66	QN	Sale price (dollars)
SALTOAPR	70–77	QN	Ratio of sale price to total appraisal

Data for the First 25 Observations Are Listed Here.

PROPERTY	NBRHOOD	LOCATION	LANDVAL	IMPROVAL	TOTALVAL	SALEPRIC	SALTOAPR
1	AVILA	NE	40600	129632	170232	231200	1.35815
2	AVILA	NE	43384	106541	149925	210600	1.40470
3	AVILA	NE	39400	93495	132895	155000	1.16633
4	AVILA	NE	34000	118532	152532	166000	1.08830
5	AVILA	NE	38189	99429	137618	158500	1.15174
6	AVILA	NE	39180	117058	156238	180000	1.15209
7	AVILA	NE	34850	79745	114595	132000	1.15188
8	AVILA	NE	34000	94535	128535	155800	1.21212
9	AVILA	NE	38300	102962	141262	159000	1.12557
10	AVILA	NE	34000	92204	126204	148000	1.17270
11	AVILA	NE	33033	118744	151777	204000	1.34408
12	AVILA	NE	36125	90045	126170	165500	1.31172
13	AVILA	NE	21473	96439	117912	151500	1.28486
14	AVILA	NE	121665	348561	470226	300000	0.63799
15	AVILA	NE	124526	280947	405473	315000	0.77687
16	AVILA	NE	89529	114102	203631	245000	1.20316
17	AVILA	NE	95528	362992	458520	430000	0.93780
18	AVILA	NE	196459	303073	499532	605000	1.21113
19	AVILA	NE	129439	355958	485397	452500	0.93223
20	AVILA	NE	113998	535227	649225	775000	1.19373
21	AVILA	NE	439317	1037067	1476384	1146000	0.77622
22	AVILA	NE	45806	124545	170351	317500	1.86380
23	AVILA	NE	28608	119518	148126	166000	1.12067
24	AVILA	NE	26392	89872	116264	159000	1.36758
25	CWDVILL	NW	14000	41633	55633	77500	1.39306

A.2 *Business Week*'s 1994 Executive Compensation Scoreboard

ASCII file name: A2CEO.DAT

Number of observations: 360

Variable	Column(s)	Type	Description
COMPANY	1–28	QL	Company or corporation
INDUSTRY	30–32	QL	Industry type (CP, FS, IHT, ILT, R, S, TR, TEL, or U)
CEO	34–46	QL	Last name of chief executive officer
SALARY	48–52	QN	1993 salary ($ thousands)
CHANGE	55–58	QN	Change in salary from 1992 ($ thousands)
LONGTERM	61–65	QN	Long-term compensation ($ thousands)
TOTCOMP	67–72	QN	Total compensation ($ thousands)
RETURN	74–76	QN	Rate of return ($) on a $100 investment made 3 years earlier
RATING	79	QN	Pay-for-performance ratio (1 = excellent, 2 = above average, 3 = average, 4 = below average, 5 = poor)

Data for the First 25 Observations Are Listed Here.

COMPANY	INDUSTRY	CEO	SALARY	CHANGE	LONGTERM	TOTCOMP	RETURN	RATING
Boeing	IHT	Shrontz	1421	3	170	4961	102	4
General Dynamics	IHT	Mellor	2777	-28	4510	26852	580	3
Lockheed	IHT	Tellep	1413	5	203	4550	221	3
Martin Marietta	IHT	Augustine	1651	18	1946	9956	213	4
McDonnell Douglas	IHT	McDonnell	1055	54	0	2591	286	2
United Technologies	IHT	Daniell	1901	88	885	7198	41	4
AMR	TR	Crandall	630	1	300	2822	139	2
Delta Air Lines	TR	Allen	495	-4	276	2127	103	2
Maytag	CP	Hadley	878	34	307	2605	184	1
Whirlpool	CP	Whitwam	2100	6	9737	16531	297	3
Chrysler	CP	Eaton	2950	146	6287	14187	436	3
Dana	CP	Morcott	1254	16	348	3654	216	2
Eaton	CP	Butler	1269	32	160	3397	216	1
General Motors	CP	Smith	1375	84	45	2743	171	1
Paccar	CP	Pigott	752	-42	413	4263	204	2
Banc One	FS	McCoy	2063	6	708	7434	209	3
Bank of Boston	FS	Stepanian	1569	21	153	6068	370	2
Bank of New York	FS	Bacot	2876	63	0	5486	349	2
BankAmerica	FS	Rosenberg	2200	9	342	9794	190	4
Bankers Trust New York	FS	Sanford	8866	142	2945	24308	203	5
Barnett Banks	FS	Rice	2210	43	972	6284	241	3
Boatmen's Bancshares	FS	Craig	961	3	409	3701	209	2
Chase Manhattan	FS	Labrecque	2257	63	2080	7692	357	2
Chemical Banking	FS	McGillic	3350	49	3398	11048	407	3
Citicorp	FS	Reed	4150	90	2240	9787	298	3

A.3 Characteristics of HMO Physicians in a Managed-Care System

ASCII file name: A3HMO.DAT

Number of observations: 186

Variable	Column(s)	Type	Description
PRIMSPEC	1–10	QL	Primary Specialty (FAMILY, GENERAL, INTERNAL, OBSTETRICS, PEDIATRICS, or OTHER)
SECSPEC	22	QL	Secondary Specialty (Y = yes, N = no)
CERTIF	24	QL	Certification level (0 = uncertified/board ineligible, 1 = certified, 2 = uncertified/eligible)
GENDER	26	QL	Gender (M = male, F = female)
MEDSCHL	28–30	QL	Country of medical school (USA or FOReign)
MEDRESID	32–34	QL	Country of medical residence (USA or FOReign)
EXP	37–38	QN	Years of experience
COST	41–46	QN	Total costs accrued per patient per month ($)
MBMNTH	50–54	QN	Total patient-months

Data for the First 25 Observations Are Listed Here.

PRIMSPEC	SECSPEC	CERTIF	GENDER	MEDSCHL	MEDRESID	EXP	COST	MBMNTH
PEDIATRICS	N	1	M	USA	USA	37	47.6	2108
PEDIATRICS	Y	1	M	FOR	USA	35	25.9	18
PEDIATRICS	N	2	M	FOR	USA	0	53.7	430
PEDIATRICS	N	1	F	FOR	USA	21	74.1	255
INTERNAL	N	1	M	FOR	USA	8	18.2	12
OTHER	N	0	M	FOR	FOR	0	141.4	707
INTERNAL	N	0	M	FOR	FOR	38	8.0	71
FAMILY	N	1	M	USA	FOR	22	20.5	88
PEDIATRICS	N	1	M	USA	FOR	23	21.6	1001
PEDIATRICS	N	1	F	FOR	USA	0	32.0	577
INTERNAL	N	1	M	FOR	USA	20	45.1	650
OBSTETRICS	N	1	M	USA	USA	14	8.9	18
INTERNAL	N	1	M	USA	FOR	41	56.3	344
FAMILY	N	1	M	USA	USA	24	1.8	38
PEDIATRICS	N	1	M	FOR	USA	13	137.2	80
PEDIATRICS	N	1	F	FOR	FOR	26	12.1	427
GENERAL	N	0	M	FOR	FOR	32	20.0	69
FAMILY	N	1	M	USA	FOR	30	71.3	507
FAMILY	N	1	F	FOR	FOR	0	69.7	123
FAMILY	N	1	M	USA	USA	8	67.0	563
FAMILY	N	2	M	FOR	USA	45	45.1	958
PEDIATRICS	N	0	M	FOR	USA	0	7.7	82
INTERNAL	N	1	M	FOR	USA	12	79.9	397
PEDIATRICS	N	1	F	USA	USA	14	14.3	243
INTERNAL	N	1	M	USA	USA	16	103.7	1779

A.4 Federal Trade Commission Rankings of Domestic Cigarette Brands

ASCII file name: A4FTC.DAT

Number of observations: 500

Variable	*Column(s)*	*Type*	*Description*
BRAND	1–23	QL	Cigarette brand name
LENGTH	25–27	QN	Length (millimeters)
MENTHOL	29–30	QL	Menthol type (M = menthol, NM = nonmenthol)
FILTER	32–33	QL	Filter type (F = filter, NF = nonfilter)
LIGHT	35	QL	Light type (R = regular, L = light, E = extra-light)
PACK	37–38	QL	Pack type (SP = soft pack, HP = hard pack)
TAR	40–41	QN	Tar content (milligrams)
NICOTINE	43–45	QN	Nicotine content (milligrams)
CO	47–48	QN	Carbon monoxide content (milligrams)

Data for the First 25 Observations Are Listed Here.

BRAND	LENGTH	MENTHOL	FILTER	LIGHT	PACK	TAR	NICOTINE	CO
Alpine	85	M	F	R	SP	15	1.0	15
Alpine	100	M	F	R	SP	15	1.1	14
Alpine	85	M	F	L	SP	9	.7	10
Alpine	100	M	F	L	SP	9	.7	11
Alpine	80	M	F	R	HP	15	1.0	14
Alpine	80	M	F	L	HP	9	.7	10
American Filter	100	NM	F	R	SP	16	1.3	16
American Filter	85	NM	F	R	SP	16	1.3	14
American Lights	100	NM	F	L	SP	12	1.0	12
American Lights	85	NM	F	L	SP	11	.9	12
American Lights	100	M	F	L	SP	11	.9	11
B&H De-Nic	85	M	F	L	HP	9	.1	8
B&H De-Nic	100	NM	F	L	HP	8	.1	8
B&H De-Nic	100	M	F	L	HP	8	.1	8
B&H De-Nic	85	NM	F	L	HP	8	.1	8
Barclay	85	NM	F	R	HP	4	.3	3
Barclay	85	NM	F	R	SP	4	.3	3
Barclay	100	NM	F	R	SP	5	.4	4
Belair	85	M	F	R	SP	10	.8	10
Belair	100	M	F	R	SP	10	.8	9
Belair Lo Price	85	M	F	R	SP	14	1.2	13
Belair Lo Price	100	M	F	R	SP	14	1.2	13
Belair Lo Price	85	M	F	L	SP	9	.8	10
Belair Lo Price	100	M	F	L	SP	10	.9	10
Benson and Hedges	85	NM	F	R	HP	14	1.2	11

A.5 Diameters of Manufactured Steel Rods

ASCII file name: A5RODS.DAT
Number of observations: 500

Variable	Columns	Type	Description
DIAMETER	1–7	QN	Diameter (centimeters)

Data for the First 25
Observations Are
Listed Here.

DIAMETER

```
1.000
1.005
1.002
1.003
1.001
1.002
1.000
1.005
1.001
1.001
1.003
1.000
1.000
1.001
1.004
1.000
1.002
1.005
1.004
1.000
1.003
1.001
1.001
1.002
1.004
```

A.6 Sealed-Bid Data for Fixed and Competitive Highway Construction Contracts

ASCII file name: A6BIDS.DAT
Number of observations: 279

Variable	Column(s)	Type	Description
LOWBID	1–6	QN	Price bid by lowest bidder ($ thousands)
DOTEST	8–12	QN	DOT engineer's estimate of fair price ($ thousands)
LBERAT	14–17	QN	Ratio of low bid price to DOT estimate
STATUS	20	QL	Collusion status (1 = fixed, 0 = competitive)
DIST	22	QL	Florida district (1, 2, 3, 4, or 5)
BIDS	25–26	QN	Number of bidders
DAYS	28–31	QN	Estimated number of days to complete work
ROAD	33–36	QN	Length of road (miles)
PCTASPH	38–41	QN	Percentage of costs allocated to liquid asphalt
PCTBASE	43–46	QN	Percentage of costs allocated to base material
PCTEXCAV	48–51	QN	Percentage of costs allocated to excavation
PCTMOBIL	53–56	QN	Percentage of costs allocated to mobilization
PCTSTRUC	60–63	QN	Percentage of costs allocated to structures
PCTTRAFF	65–68	QN	Percentage of costs allocated to traffic control
SUB	71	QL	Use of subcontractor (1 = yes, 0 = no)

Data for the First 25 Observations Are Listed Here.

LOWBID	DOTEST	LBERAT	STATUS	DIST	BIDS	DAYS	ROAD	PCTASPH	PCTBASE	PCTEXCAV	PCTMOBIL	PCTSTRUC	PCTTRAFF	SUB
363	386	0.94	0	1	3	100	7.2	62.6	0.0	9.1	2.0	11.7	9.2	0
152	175	0.87	1	1	3	75	0.0	15.3	1.2	14.2	4.7	1.8	14.8	0
240	195	1.23	1	1	3	65	0.2	8.3	0.0	10.5	4.9	22.3	6.0	0
1559	1925	0.81	0	1	10	250	3.6	19.0	29.9	23.8	1.2	16.6	4.1	0
144	253	0.57	0	1	8	90	23.7	31.6	24.5	16.0	0.3	8.3	0.9	0
1187	1573	0.75	0	1	5	230	2.6	28.2	21.4	24.2	0.8	14.8	2.3	0
24	33	0.73	0	5	7	60	0.3	10.5	22.9	22.0	2.1	8.5	3.1	0
170	176	0.96	1	5	4	125	2.4	49.6	11.1	17.1	3.5	5.8	5.0	0
1082	1086	1.00	0	1	6	400	0.0	17.3	21.8	7.4	1.0	34.8	3.5	0
433	545	0.79	0	5	5	230	0.0	15.7	24.0	32.2	2.2	16.3	2.3	0
669	597	1.12	1	1	3	120	0.0	0.0	0.0	81.4	6.9	0.0	4.9	0
1884	1550	1.22	1	1	3	350	0.0	12.0	21.1	11.5	6.5	29.5	4.9	0
82	93	0.88	0	1	2	70	0.0	31.5	13.4	15.4	5.7	17.3	6.7	0
272	224	1.21	1	1	4	110	0.0	11.2	21.0	15.5	3.7	17.6	13.8	1
3300	2806	1.18	1	1	4	525	4.4	17.9	32.3	13.3	4.5	14.4	6.1	0
582	785	0.74	0	2	4	200	0.0	9.7	24.7	33.1	0.3	8.2	16.5	0
240	429	0.56	0	2	10	120	4.7	18.9	29.1	37.9	1.5	4.6	0.4	0
333	376	0.88	0	2	8	140	3.9	18.0	28.4	28.9	0.6	13.2	0.4	0
801	1031	0.78	0	2	8	425	0.0	17.6	21.8	32.6	0.4	8.3	0.3	0
1748	1493	1.17	0	2	6	445	0.0	15.7	14.8	28.2	0.3	27.4	2.1	0
6584	5949	1.11	0	1	7	675	.	1.7	24.1	23.3	3.9	14.4	0.0	0
7098	8297	0.86	0	1	9	510	0.0	21.0	20.6	27.6	2.6	21.5	1.8	0
158	187	0.85	0	1	2	60	6.1	92.4	0.0	0.0	0.0	0.0	7.6	0
1354	1618	0.84	0	1	7	200	4.3	33.0	15.5	33.0	1.8	7.5	3.2	0
372	327	1.14	1	5	2	120	.	52.2	3.7	10.4	10.5	3.8	7.8	0

A.7 Commitment and Turnover of Employees of an Aerospace Firm

ASCII file name: A7COMM.DAT

Number of observations: 270

Variable	Column(s)	Type	Description
ID	4–6	QL	Employee identification number
AGE	9–10	QN	Age (years)
GENDER	13	QL	Gender (1 = male, 0 = female)
ORGTEN	18–20	QN	Organizational tenure (months with firm)
JOBTEN	25–27	QN	Job tenure (months in current job)
THINKQ	33	QN	Thinking of quitting (1–5-point scale)
SEARCH	40	QN	Searching for a new job (1–5-point scale)
INTLV	46–47	QN	Intentions to leave (2–11-point scale)
CONCOM	52–53	QN	Continuance commitment (3–21-point scale)
AFFCOM	59–60	QN	Affective commitment (14–98-point scale)
MORCOM	66–67	QN	Moral commitment (4–28-point scale)
LEAVE	73	QL	Leave status (0 = stay, 1 = quit)

Data for the First 25 Observations Are Listed Here.

ID	AGE	GENDER	ORGTEN	JOBTEN	THINKQ	SEARCH	INTLV	CONCOM	AFFCOM	MORCOM	LEAVE
1	49	1	51	51	2	3	4	9	64	24	0
2	23	0	6	7	2	5	5	8	63	21	1
3	45	1	28	48	2	2	3	13	66	23	0
4	49	0	45	123	1	2	3	6	65	22	0
5	36	0	2	45	1	1	3	13	70	26	0
6	35	0	21	21	1	1	4	9	69	28	0
7	60	0	239	239	2	2	3	14	55	26	0
8	34	1	11	11	2	2	4	9	65	14	0
9	29	1	43	43	5	5	11	9	56	20	0
10	29	1	19	22	1	3	8	10	58	14	0
11	25	0	4	4	1	1	3	15	68	20	0
12	40	0	64	117	2	2	4	18	64	22	0
13	39	1	1	178	2	2	3	13	61	25	0
14	38	1	38	54	2	2	5	9	54	12	0
15	47	1	92	107	2	3	3	13	65	27	0
16	35	1	41	41	2	3	4	13	61	17	0
17	32	0	3	4	2	3	4	9	66	25	0
18	64	1	152	166	1	1	2	13	56	20	0
19	27	1	61	75	2	3	4	13	65	23	1
20	29	1	50	50	1	2	3	12	61	20	1
21	24	1	21	21	4	4	8	10	63	20	0
22	50	0	87	152	2	3	5	21	56	24	0
23	29	0	5	15	2	3	5	6	57	18	0
24	61	0	57	110	3	2	2	14	51	21	0
25	55	0	164	164	2	1	2	15	62	28	0

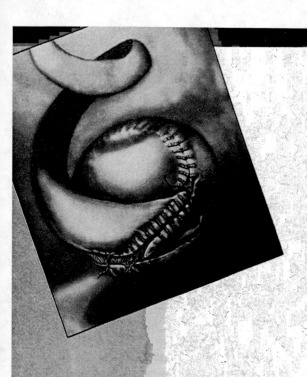

Appendix B

STATISTICAL TABLES

■ CONTENTS

Table 1 Random Numbers

Row	1	2	3	4	5	6	7	8	9	10	11	12	13	14
1	10480	15011	01536	02011	81647	91646	69179	14194	62590	36207	20969	99570	91291	90700
2	22368	46573	25595	85393	30995	89198	27982	53402	93965	34095	52666	19174	39615	99505
3	24130	48360	22527	97265	76393	64809	15179	24830	49340	32081	30680	19655	63348	58629
4	42167	93093	06243	61680	07856	16376	39440	53537	71341	57004	00849	74917	97758	16379
5	37570	39975	81837	16656	06121	91782	60468	81305	49684	60672	14110	06927	01263	54613
6	77921	06907	11008	42751	27756	53498	18602	70659	90655	15053	21916	81825	44394	42880
7	99562	72905	56420	69994	98872	31016	71194	18738	44013	48840	63213	21069	10634	12952
8	96301	91977	05463	07972	18876	20922	94595	56869	69014	60045	18425	84903	42508	32307
9	89579	14342	63661	10281	17453	18103	57740	84378	25331	12566	58678	44947	05585	56941
10	85475	36857	53342	53988	53060	59533	38867	62300	08158	17983	16439	11458	18593	64952
11	28918	69578	88231	33276	70997	79936	56865	05859	90106	31595	01547	85590	91610	78188
12	63553	40961	48235	03427	49626	69445	18663	72695	52180	20847	12234	90511	33703	90322
13	09429	93969	52636	92737	88974	33488	36320	17617	30015	08272	84115	27156	30613	74952
14	10365	61129	87529	85689	48237	52267	67689	93394	01511	26358	85104	20285	29975	89868
15	07119	97336	71048	08178	77233	13916	47564	81056	97735	85977	29372	74461	28551	90707
16	51085	12765	51821	51259	71452	16308	60756	92144	49442	53900	70960	63990	75601	40719
17	02368	21382	52404	60268	89368	19885	55322	44819	01188	65255	64835	44919	05944	55157
18	01011	54092	33362	94904	31273	04146	18594	29852	71585	85030	51132	01915	92747	64951
19	52162	53916	46369	58586	23216	14513	83149	98736	23495	64350	94738	17752	35156	35749
20	07056	97628	33787	09998	42698	06691	76988	13602	51851	46104	88916	19509	25625	58104
21	48663	91245	85828	14346	09172	30168	90229	04734	59193	22178	30421	61666	99904	32812
22	54164	58492	22421	74103	47070	25306	76468	26384	58151	06646	21524	15227	96909	44592
23	32639	32363	05597	24200	13363	38005	94342	28728	35806	06912	17012	64161	18296	22851
24	29334	27001	87637	87308	58731	00256	45834	15398	46557	41135	10367	07684	36188	18510
25	02488	33062	28834	07351	19731	92420	60952	61280	50001	67658	32586	86679	50720	94953
26	81525	72295	04839	96423	24878	82651	66566	14778	76797	14780	13300	87074	79666	95725
27	29676	20591	68086	26432	46901	20849	89768	81536	86645	12659	92259	57102	80428	25280
28	00742	57392	39064	66432	84673	40027	32832	61362	98947	96067	64760	64584	96096	98253
29	05366	04213	25669	26422	44407	44048	37937	63904	45766	66134	75470	66520	34693	90449
30	91921	26418	64117	94305	26766	25940	39972	22209	71500	64568	91402	42416	07844	69618
31	00582	04711	87917	77341	42206	35126	74087	99547	81817	42607	43808	76655	62028	76630
32	00725	69884	62797	56170	86324	88072	76222	36086	84637	93161	76038	65855	77919	88006
33	69011	65795	95876	55293	18988	27354	26575	08625	40801	59920	29841	80150	12777	48501
34	25976	57948	29888	88604	67917	48708	18912	82271	65424	69774	33661	54262	85963	03547
35	09763	83473	73577	12908	30883	18317	28290	35797	05998	41688	34952	37888	38917	88050

(continued)

Table 1 (continued) Random Numbers

Row	1	2	3	4	5	6	7	8	9	10	11	12	13	14
36	91576	42595	27958	30134	04024	86385	29880	99730	55536	84855	29080	09250	79656	73211
37	17955	56349	90999	49127	20044	59931	06115	20542	18059	02008	73708	83517	36103	42791
38	46503	18584	18845	49618	02304	51038	20655	58727	28168	15475	56942	53389	20562	87338
39	92157	89634	94824	78171	84610	82834	09922	25417	44137	48413	25555	21246	35509	20468
40	14577	62765	35605	81263	39667	47358	56873	56307	61607	49518	89656	20103	77490	18062
41	98427	07523	33362	64270	01638	92477	66969	98420	04880	45585	46565	04102	46880	45709
42	34914	63976	88720	82765	34476	17032	87589	40836	32427	70002	70663	88863	77775	69348
43	70060	28277	39475	46473	23219	53416	94970	25832	69975	94884	19661	72828	00102	66794
44	53976	54914	06990	67245	68350	82948	11398	42878	80287	88267	47363	46634	06541	97809
45	76072	29515	40980	07391	58745	25774	22987	80059	39911	96189	41151	14222	60697	59583
46	90725	52210	83914	29992	65831	38857	50490	83765	55657	14361	31720	57375	56228	41546
47	64364	67412	33339	31926	14883	24413	59744	92351	97473	89286	35931	04110	23726	51900
48	08962	00358	31662	25388	61642	34072	81249	35648	56891	69352	48373	45578	78547	81788
49	95012	68379	93526	70765	10592	04542	76463	54328	02349	17247	28865	14777	62730	92277
50	15664	10493	20492	38391	91132	21999	59516	81652	27195	48223	46751	22923	32261	85653
51	16408	81899	04153	53381	79401	21438	83035	92350	36693	31238	59649	91754	72772	02338
52	18629	81953	05520	91962	04739	13092	97662	24822	94730	06496	35090	04822	86774	98289
53	73115	35101	47498	87637	99016	71060	88824	71013	18735	20286	23153	72924	35165	43040
54	57491	16703	23167	49323	45021	33132	12544	41035	80780	45393	44812	12515	98931	91202
55	30405	83946	23792	14422	15059	45799	22716	19792	09983	74353	68668	30429	70735	25499
56	16631	35006	85900	98275	32388	52390	16815	69298	82732	38480	73817	32523	41961	44437
57	96773	20206	42559	78985	05300	22164	24369	54224	35083	19687	11052	91491	60383	19746
58	38935	64202	14349	82674	66523	44133	00697	35552	35970	19124	63318	29686	03387	59846
59	31624	76384	17403	53363	44167	64486	64758	75366	76554	31601	12614	33072	60332	92325
60	78919	19474	23632	27889	47914	02584	37680	20801	72152	39339	34806	08930	85001	87820
61	03931	33309	57047	74211	63445	17361	62825	39908	05607	91284	68833	25570	38818	46920
62	74426	33278	43972	10119	89917	15665	52872	73823	73144	88662	88970	74492	51805	99378
63	09066	00903	20795	95452	92648	45454	09552	88815	16553	51125	79375	97596	16296	66092
64	42238	12426	87025	14267	20979	04508	64535	31355	86064	29472	47689	05974	52468	16834
65	16153	08002	26504	41744	81959	65642	74240	56302	00033	67107	77510	70625	28725	34191
66	21457	40742	29820	96783	29400	21840	15035	34537	33310	06116	95240	15957	16572	06004
67	21581	57802	02050	89728	17937	37621	47075	42080	97403	48626	68995	43805	33386	21597
68	55612	78095	83197	33732	05810	24813	86902	60397	16489	03264	88525	42786	05269	92532
69	44657	66999	99324	51281	84463	60563	79312	93454	68876	25471	93911	25650	12682	73572
70	91340	84979	46949	81973	37949	61023	43997	15263	80644	43942	89203	71795	99533	50501
71	91227	21199	31935	27022	84067	05462	35216	14486	29891	68607	41867	14951	91696	85065
72	50001	38140	66321	19924	72163	09538	12151	06878	91903	18749	34405	56087	82790	70925
73	65390	05224	72958	28609	81406	39147	25549	48542	42627	45233	57202	94617	23772	07896
74	27504	96131	83944	41575	10573	08619	64482	73923	36152	05184	94142	25299	84387	34925
75	37169	94851	39117	89632	00959	16487	65536	49071	39782	17095	02330	74301	00275	48280

(continued)

Table 1   *(continued)* Random Numbers

Column Row	1	2	3	4	5	6	7	8	9	10	11	12	13	14
76	11508	70225	51111	38351	19444	66499	71945	05422	13442	78675	84081	66938	93654	59894
77	37449	30362	06694	54690	04052	53115	62757	95348	78662	11163	81651	50245	34971	52924
78	46515	70331	85922	38329	57015	15765	97161	17869	45349	61796	66345	81073	49106	79860
79	30986	81223	42416	58353	21532	30502	32305	86482	05174	07901	54339	58861	74818	46942
80	63798	64995	46583	09785	44160	78128	83991	42865	92520	83531	80377	35909	81250	54238
81	82486	84846	99254	67632	43218	50076	21361	64816	51202	88124	41870	52689	51275	83556
82	21885	32906	92431	09060	64297	51674	64126	62570	26123	05155	59194	52799	28225	85762
83	60336	98782	07408	53458	13564	59089	26445	29789	85205	41001	12535	12133	14645	23541
84	43937	46891	24010	25560	86355	33941	25786	54990	71899	15475	95434	98227	21824	19585
85	97656	63175	89303	16275	07100	92063	21942	18611	47348	20203	18534	03862	78095	50136
86	03299	01221	05418	38982	55758	92237	26759	86367	21216	98442	08303	56613	91511	75982
87	79626	06486	03574	17668	07785	76020	79924	25651	83325	88428	85076	72811	22717	50585
88	85636	68335	47539	03129	65651	11977	02510	26113	99447	68645	34327	15152	55230	93448
89	18039	14367	61337	06177	12143	46609	32989	74014	64708	00533	35398	58408	13261	47908
90	08362	15656	60627	36478	65648	16764	53412	09013	07832	41574	17639	82163	60859	75567
91	79556	29068	04142	16268	15387	12856	66227	38358	22478	73373	88732	09443	82558	05250
92	92608	82674	27072	32534	17075	27698	98204	63863	11951	34648	88022	56148	34925	57031
93	23982	25835	40055	67006	12293	02753	14827	23235	35071	99704	37543	11601	35503	85171
94	09915	96306	05908	97901	28395	14186	00821	80703	70426	75647	76310	88717	37890	40129
95	59037	33300	26695	62247	69927	76123	50842	43834	86654	70959	79725	93872	28117	19233
96	42488	78077	69882	61657	34136	79180	97526	43092	04098	73571	80799	76536	71255	64239
97	46764	86273	63003	93017	31204	36692	40202	35275	57306	55543	53203	18098	47625	88684
98	03237	45430	55417	63282	90816	17349	88298	90183	36600	78406	06216	95787	42579	90730
99	86591	81482	52667	61582	14972	90053	89534	76036	49199	43716	97548	04379	46370	28672
100	38534	01715	94964	87288	65680	43772	39560	12918	86537	62738	19636	51132	25739	56947

Source: Abridged from W. H. Beyer (ed.), *CRC Standard Mathematical Tables*, 24th edition. (Cleveland: The Chemical Rubber Company), 1976.

Table 2 Cumulative Binomial Probabilities

a. $n = 5$

							π						
k	.01	.05	.1	.2	.3	.4	.5	.6	.7	.8	.9	.95	.99
0	.9510	.7738	.5905	.3277	.1681	.0778	.0313	.0102	.0024	.0003	.0000	.0000	.0000
1	.9990	.9774	.9185	.7373	.5282	.3370	.1875	.0870	.0308	.0067	.0005	.0000	.0000
2	1.0000	.9988	.9914	.9421	.8369	.6826	.5000	.3174	.1631	.0579	.0086	.0012	.0000
3	1.0000	1.0000	.9995	.9933	.9692	.9130	.8125	.6630	.4718	.2627	.0815	.0226	.0010
4	1.0000	1.0000	1.0000	.9997	.9976	.9898	.9687	.9222	.8319	.6723	.4095	.2262	.0490

b. $n = 6$

							π						
k	.01	.05	.1	.2	.3	.4	.5	.6	.7	.8	.9	.95	.99
0	.9415	.7351	.5314	.2621	.1176	.0467	.0156	.0041	.0007	.0001	.0000	.0000	.0000
1	.9985	.9672	.8857	.6554	.4202	.2333	.1094	.0410	.0109	.0016	.0001	.0000	.0000
2	1.0000	.9978	.9841	.9011	.7443	.5443	.3437	.1792	.0705	.0170	.0013	.0001	.0000
3	1.0000	.9999	.9987	.9830	.9295	.8208	.6562	.4557	.2557	.0989	.0158	.0022	.0000
4	1.0000	1.0000	.9999	.9984	.9891	.9590	.8906	.7667	.5798	.3446	.1143	.0328	.0015
5	1.0000	1.0000	1.0000	.9999	.9993	.9959	.9844	.9533	.8824	.7379	.4686	.2649	.0585

c. $n = 7$

							π						
k	.01	.05	.1	.2	.3	.4	.5	.6	.7	.8	.9	.95	.99
0	.9321	.6983	.4783	.2097	.0824	.0280	.0078	.0016	.0002	.0000	.0000	.0000	.0000
1	.9980	.9556	.8503	.5767	.3294	.1586	.0625	.0188	.0038	.0004	.0000	.0000	.0000
2	1.0000	.9962	.9743	.8520	.6471	.4199	.2266	.0963	.0288	.0047	.0002	.0000	.0000
3	1.0000	.9998	.9973	.9667	.8740	.7102	.5000	.2898	.1260	.0333	.0027	.0002	.0000
4	1.0000	1.0000	.9998	.9953	.9712	.9037	.7734	.5801	.3529	.1480	.0257	.0038	.0000
5	1.0000	1.0000	1.0000	.9996	.9962	.9812	.9375	.8414	.6706	.4233	.1497	.0444	.0020
6	1.0000	1.0000	1.0000	1.0000	.9998	.9984	.9922	.9720	.9176	.7903	.5217	.3017	.0679

(continued)

Table 2 *(continued)* Cumulative Binomial Probabilities

d. n = 8

						π							
k	.01	.05	.1	.2	.3	.4	.5	.6	.7	.8	.9	.95	.99
0	.9227	.6634	.4305	.1678	.0576	.0168	.0039	.0007	.0001	.0000	.0000	.0000	.0000
1	.9973	.9423	.8131	.5033	.2553	.1064	.0352	.0085	.0013	.0001	.0000	.0000	.0000
2	.9999	.9942	.9619	.7969	.5518	.3154	.1445	.0498	.0113	.0012	.0000	.0000	.0000
3	1.0000	.9996	.9950	.9437	.8059	.5941	.3633	.1737	.0580	.0104	.0004	.0000	.0000
4	1.0000	1.0000	.9996	.9896	.9420	.8263	.6367	.4059	.1941	.0563	.0050	.0004	.0000
5	1.0000	1.0000	1.0000	.9988	.9887	.9502	.8555	.6346	.4482	.2031	.0381	.0058	.0001
6	1.0000	1.0000	1.0000	.9999	.9987	.9915	.9648	.8936	.7447	.4967	.1869	.0572	.0027
7	1.0000	1.0000	1.0000	1.0000	.9999	.9993	.9961	.9832	.9424	.8322	.5695	.3366	.0773

e. n = 9

						π							
k	.01	.05	.1	.2	.3	.4	.5	.6	.7	.8	.9	.95	.99
0	.9135	.6302	.3874	.1342	.0404	.0101	.0020	.0003	.0000	.0000	.0000	.0000	.0000
1	.9966	.9288	.7748	.4362	.1960	.0705	.0195	.0038	.0004	.0000	.0000	.0000	.0000
2	.9999	.9916	.9470	.7382	.4623	.2318	.0898	.0250	.0043	.0003	.0000	.0000	.0000
3	1.0000	.9994	.9917	.9144	.7297	.4826	.2539	.0994	.0253	.0031	.0001	.0000	.0000
4	1.0000	1.0000	.9991	.9804	.9012	.7334	.5000	.2666	.0988	.0196	.0009	.0000	.0000
5	1.0000	1.0000	.9999	.9969	.9747	.9006	.7461	.5174	.2703	.0856	.0083	.0006	.0000
6	1.0000	1.0000	1.0000	.9997	.9957	.9750	.9102	.7682	.5372	.2618	.0530	.0084	.0001
7	1.0000	1.0000	1.0000	1.0000	.9996	.9962	.9805	.9295	.8040	.5638	.2252	.0712	.0034
8	1.0000	1.0000	1.0000	1.0000	1.0000	.9997	.9980	.9899	.9596	.8658	.6126	.3698	.0865

f. n = 10

						π							
k	.01	.05	.1	.2	.3	.4	.5	.6	.7	.8	.9	.95	.99
0	9044	.5987	.3487	.1074	.0282	.0060	.0010	.0001	.0000	.0000	.0000	.0000	.0000
1	.9957	.9139	.7361	.3758	.1493	.0464	.0107	.0017	.0001	.0000	.0000	.0000	.0000
2	.9999	.9885	.9298	.6778	.3828	.1673	.0547	.0123	.0016	.0001	.0000	.0000	.0000
3	1.0000	.9990	.9872	.8791	.6496	.3823	.1719	.0548	.0106	.0009	.0000	.0000	.0000
4	1.0000	.9999	.9984	.9672	.8497	.6331	.3770	.1662	.0473	.0064	.0001	.0000	.0000
5	1.0000	1.0000	.9999	.9936	.9527	.8338	.6230	.3669	.1503	.0328	.0016	.0001	.0000
6	1.0000	1.0000	1.0000	.9991	.9894	.9452	.8281	.6177	.3504	.1209	.0128	.0010	.0000
7	1.0000	1.0000	1.0000	.9999	.9984	.9877	.9453	.8327	.6172	.3222	.0702	.0115	.0001
8	1.0000	1.0000	1.0000	1.0000	.9999	.9983	.9893	.9536	.8507	.6242	.2639	.0861	.0043
9	10000	1.0000	1.0000	1.0000	1.0000	.9999	.9990	.9940	.9718	.8926	.6513	.4013	.0956

(continued)

Table 2 *(continued)* Cumulative Binomial Probabilities

g. *n* = 15

						π							
k	.01	.05	.1	.2	.3	.4	.5	.6	.7	.8	.9	.95	.99
0	.8601	.4633	.2059	.0352	.0047	.0005	.0000	.0000	.0000	.0000	.0000	.0000	.0000
1	.9904	.8290	.5490	.1671	.0353	.0052	.0005	.0000	.0000	.0000	.0000	.0000	.0000
2	.9996	.9638	.8159	.3980	.1268	.0271	.0037	.0003	.0000	.0000	.0000	.0000	.0000
3	1.0000	.9945	.9444	.6482	.2969	.0905	.0176	.0019	.0001	.0000	.0000	.0000	.0000
4	1.0000	.9994	.9873	.8358	.5155	.2173	.0592	.0093	.0007	.0000	.0000	.0000	.0000
5	1.0000	.9999	.9978	.9389	.7216	.4032	.1509	.0338	.0037	.0001	.0000	.0000	.0000
6	1.0000	1.0000	.9997	.9819	.8689	.6098	.3036	.0950	.0152	.0008	.0000	.0000	.0000
7	1.0000	1.0000	1.0000	.9958	.9500	.7869	.5000	.2131	.0500	.0042	.0000	.0000	.0000
8	1.0000	1.0000	1.0000	.9992	.9848	.9050	.6964	.3902	.1311	.0181	.0003	.0000	.0000
9	1.0000	1.0000	1.0000	.9999	.9963	.9662	.8491	.5968	.2784	.0611	.0022	.0001	.0000
10	1.0000	1.0000	1.0000	1.0000	.9993	.9907	.9408	.7827	.4845	.1642	.0127	.0006	.0000
11	1.0000	1.0000	1.0000	1.0000	.9999	.9981	.9824	.9095	.7031	.3518	.0556	.0055	.0000
12	1.0000	1.0000	1.0000	1.0000	1.0000	.9997	.9963	.9729	.8732	.6020	.1841	.0362	.0004
13	1.0000	1.0000	1.0000	1.0000	1.0000	1.0000	.9995	.9948	.9647	.8329	.4510	.1710	.0096
14	1.0000	1.0000	1.0000	1.0000	1.0000	1.0000	1.0000	.9995	.9953	.9648	.7941	.5367	.1399

h. *n* = 20

						π							
k	.01	.05	.1	.2	.3	.4	.5	.6	.7	.8	.9	.95	.99
0	.8179	.3585	.1216	.0115	.0008	.0000	.0000	.0000	.0000	.0000	.0000	.0000	.0000
1	.9831	.7358	.3917	.0692	.0076	.0005	.0000	.0000	.0000	.0000	.0000	.0000	.0000
2	.9990	.9245	.6769	.2061	.0355	.0036	.0002	.0000	.0000	.0000	.0000	.0000	.0000
3	1.0000	.9841	.8670	.4114	.1071	.0160	.0013	.0000	.0000	.0000	.0000	.0000	.0000
4	1.0000	.9974	.9568	.6296	.2375	.0510	.0059	.0003	.0000	.0000	.0000	.0000	.0000
5	1.0000	.9997	.9887	.8042	.4164	.1256	.0207	.0016	.0000	.0000	.0000	.0000	.0000
6	1.0000	1.0000	.9976	.9133	.6080	.2500	.0577	.0065	.0003	.0000	.0000	.0000	.0000
7	1.0000	1.0000	.9996	.9679	.7723	.4159	.1316	.0210	.0013	.0000	.0000	.0000	.0000
8	1.0000	1.0000	.9999	.9900	.8867	.5956	.2517	.0565	.0051	.0001	.0000	.0000	.0000
9	1.0000	1.0000	1.0000	.9974	.9520	.7553	.4119	.1275	.0171	.0006	.0000	.0000	.0000
10	1.0000	1.0000	1.0000	.9994	.9829	.8725	.5881	.2447	.0480	.0026	.0000	.0000	.0000
11	1.0000	1.0000	1.0000	.9999	.9949	.9435	.7483	.4044	.1133	.0100	.0001	.0000	.0000
12	1.0000	1.0000	1.0000	1.0000	.9987	.9790	.8684	.5841	.2277	.0321	.0004	.0000	.0000
13	1.0000	1.0000	1.0000	1.0000	.9997	.9935	.9423	.7500	.3920	.0867	.0024	.0000	.0000
14	1.0000	1.0000	1.0000	1.0000	1.0000	.9984	.9793	.8744	.5836	.1958	.0113	.0003	.0000
15	1.0000	1.0000	1.0000	1.0000	1.0000	.9997	.9941	.9490	.7625	.3704	.0432	.0026	.0000
16	1.0000	1.0000	1.0000	1.0000	1.0000	1.0000	.9987	.9840	.8929	.5886	.1330	.0159	.0000
17	1.0000	1.0000	1.0000	1.0000	1.0000	1.0000	.9998	.9964	.9645	.7939	.3231	.0755	.0010
18	1.0000	1.0000	1.0000	1.0000	1.0000	1.0000	1.0000	.9995	.9924	.9308	.6083	.2642	.0169
19	1.0000	1.0000	1.0000	1.0000	1.0000	1.0000	1.0000	1.0000	.9992	.9885	.8784	.6415	.1821

(continued)

Table 2 (*continued*) Cumulative Binomial Probabilities

i. $n = 25$

							π						
k	.01	.05	.1	.2	.3	.4	.5	.6	.7	.8	.9	.95	.99
0	.7778	.2774	.0718	.0038	.0001	.0000	.0000	.0000	.0000	.0000	.0000	.0000	.0000
1	.9742	.6424	.2712	.0274	.0016	.0001	.0000	.0000	.0000	.0000	.0000	.0000	.0000
2	.9980	.8729	.5371	.0982	.0090	.0004	.0000	.0000	.0000	.0000	.0000	.0000	.0000
3	.9999	.9659	.7636	.2340	.0332	.0024	.0001	.0000	.0000	.0000	.0000	.0000	.0000
4	1.0000	.9928	.9020	.4207	.0905	.0095	.0005	.0000	.0000	.0000	.0000	.0000	.0000
5	1.0000	.9988	.9666	.6167	.1935	.0294	.0020	.0001	.0000	.0000	.0000	.0000	.0000
6	1.0000	.9998	.9905	.7800	.3407	.0736	.0073	.0003	.0000	.0000	.0000	.0000	.0000
7	1.0000	1.0000	.9977	.8909	.5118	.1536	.0216	.0012	.0000	.0000	.0000	.0000	.0000
8	1.0000	1.0000	.9995	.9532	.6769	.2735	.0539	.0043	.0001	.0000	.0000	.0000	.0000
9	1.0000	1.0000	.9999	.9827	.8106	.4246	.1148	.0132	.0005	.0000	.0000	.0000	.0000
10	1.0000	1.0000	1.0000	.9944	.9022	.5858	.2122	.0344	.0018	.0000	.0000	.0000	.0000
11	1.0000	1.0000	1.0000	.9985	.9558	.7323	.3450	.0778	.0060	.0001	.0000	.0000	.0000
12	1.0000	1.0000	1.0000	.9996	.9825	.8462	.5000	.1538	.0175	.0004	.0000	.0000	.0000
13	1.0000	1.0000	1.0000	.9999	.9940	.9222	.6550	.2677	.0442	.0015	.0000	.0000	.0000
14	1.0000	1.0000	1.0000	1.0000	.9982	.9656	.7878	.4142	.0978	.0056	.0000	.0000	.0000
15	1.0000	1.0000	1.0000	1.0000	.9995	.9868	.8852	.5754	.1894	.0173	.0001	.0000	.0000
16	1.0000	1.0000	1.0000	1.0000	.9999	.9957	.9461	.7265	.3231	.0468	.0005	.0000	.0000
17	1.0000	1.0000	1.0000	1.0000	1.0000	.9988	.9784	.8464	.4882	.1091	.0023	.0000	.0000
18	1.0000	1.0000	1.0000	1.0000	1.0000	.9997	.9927	.9264	.6593	.2200	.0095	.0002	.0000
19	1.0000	1.0000	1.0000	1.0000	1.0000	.9999	.9980	.9706	.8065	.3833	.0334	.0012	.0000
20	1.0000	1.0000	1.0000	1.0000	1.0000	1.0000	.9995	.9905	.9095	.5793	.0980	.0072	.0000
21	1.0000	1.0000	1.0000	1.0000	1.0000	1.0000	.9999	.9976	.9668	.7660	.2364	.0341	.0001
22	1.0000	1.0000	1.0000	1.0000	1.0000	1.0000	1.0000	.9996	.9910	.9018	.4629	.1271	.0020
23	1.0000	1.0000	1.0000	1.0000	1.0000	1.0000	1.0000	.9999	.9984	.9726	.7288	.3576	.0258
24	1.0000	1.0000	1.0000	1.0000	1.0000	1.0000	1.0000	1.0000	.9999	.9962	.9282	.7226	.2222

Table 3 Exponentials

c	e^{-c}	c	e^{-c}	c	e^{-c}	c	e^{-c}
.00	1.000000	2.50	.082085	5.00	.006738	7.50	.000553
.05	.951229	2.55	.078082	5.05	.006409	7.55	.000526
.10	.904837	2.60	.074274	5.10	.006097	7.60	.000501
.15	.860708	2.65	.070651	5.15	.005799	7.65	.000476
.20	.818731	2.70	.067206	5.20	.005517	7.70	.000453
.25	.778801	2.75	.063928	5.25	.005248	7.75	.000431
.30	.740818	2.80	.060810	5.30	.004992	7.80	.000410
.35	.704688	2.85	.057844	5.35	.004748	7.85	.000390
.40	.670320	2.90	.055023	5.40	.004517	7.90	.000371
.45	.637628	2.95	.052340	5.45	.004296	7.95	.000353
.50	.606531	3.00	.049787	5.50	.004087	8.00	.000336
.55	.576950	3.05	.047359	5.55	.003887	8.05	.000319
.60	.548812	3.10	.045049	5.60	.003698	8.10	.000304
.65	.522046	3.15	.042852	5.65	.003518	8.15	.000289
.70	.496585	3.20	.040762	5.70	.003346	8.20	.000275
.75	.472367	3.25	.038774	5.75	.003183	8.25	.000261
.80	.449329	3.30	.036883	5.80	.003028	8.30	.000249
.85	.427415	3.35	.035084	5.85	.002880	8.35	.000236
.90	.406570	3.40	.033373	5.90	.002739	8.40	.000225
.95	.386741	3.45	.031746	5.95	.002606	8.45	.000214
1.00	.367879	3.50	.030197	6.00	.002479	8.50	.000204
1.05	.349938	3.55	.028725	6.05	.002358	8.55	.000194
1.10	.332871	3.60	.027324	6.10	.002243	8.60	.000184
1.15	.316637	3.65	.025991	6.15	.002133	8.65	.000175
1.20	.301194	3.70	.024724	6.20	.002029	8.70	.000167
1.25	.286505	3.75	.023518	6.25	.001930	8.75	.000158
1.30	.272532	3.80	.022371	6.30	.001836	8.80	.000151
1.35	.259240	3.85	.021280	6.35	.001747	8.85	.000143
1.40	.246597	3.90	.020242	6.40	.001661	8.90	.000136
1.45	.234570	3.95	.019255	6.45	.001581	8.95	.000130
1.50	.223130	4.00	.018316	6.50	.001503	9.00	.000123
1.55	.212248	4.05	.017422	6.55	.001430	9.05	.000117
1.60	.201897	4.10	.016573	6.60	.001360	9.10	.000112
1.65	.192050	4.15	.015764	6.65	.001294	9.15	.000106
1.70	.182684	4.20	.014996	6.70	.001231	9.20	.000101
1.75	.173774	4.25	.014264	6.75	.001171	9.25	.000096
1.80	.165299	4.30	.013569	6.80	.001114	9.30	.000091
1.85	.157237	4.35	.012907	6.85	.001059	9.35	.000087
1.90	.149569	4.40	.012277	6.90	.001008	9.40	.000083
1.95	.142274	4.45	.011679	6.95	.000959	9.45	.000079
2.00	.135335	4.50	.011109	7.00	.000912	9.50	.000075
2.05	.128735	4.55	.010567	7.05	.000867	9.55	.000071
2.10	.122456	4.60	.010052	7.10	.000825	9.60	.000068
2.15	.116484	4.65	.009562	7.15	.000785	9.65	.000064
2.20	.110803	4.70	.009095	7.20	.000747	9.70	.000061
2.25	.105399	4.75	.008652	7.25	.000710	9.75	.000058
2.30	.100259	4.80	.008230	7.30	.000676	9.80	.000056
2.35	.095369	4.85	.007828	7.35	.000643	9.85	.000053
2.40	.090718	4.90	.007447	7.40	.000611	9.90	.000050
2.45	.086294	4.95	.007083	7.45	.000581	9.95	.000048
						10.00	.000045

Table 4   Cumulative Poisson Probabilities

Tabulated values are $\sum_{x=0}^{k} p(x)$

Poisson Mean μ

k	.5	1.0	1.5	2.0	2.5	3.0	3.5	4.0	4.5	5.0
0	.6065	.3679	.2231	.1353	.0821	.0498	.0302	.0183	.0111	.0067
1	.9098	.7358	.5578	.4060	.2873	.1991	.1359	.0916	.0611	.0404
2	.9856	.9197	.8088	.6767	.5438	.4232	.3208	.2381	.1736	.1247
3	.9982	.9810	.9344	.8571	.7576	.6472	.5366	.4335	.3423	.2650
4	.9998	.9963	.9814	.9473	.8912	.8153	.7254	.6288	.5321	.4405
5	1.0000	.9994	.9955	.9834	.9580	.9161	.8576	.7851	.7029	.6160
6	1.0000	.9999	.9991	.9955	.9858	.9665	.9347	.8893	.8311	.7622
7	1.0000	1.0000	.9998	.9989	.9958	.9881	.9733	.9489	.9134	.8666
8	1.0000	1.0000	1.0000	.9998	.9989	.9962	.9901	.9786	.9597	.9319
9	1.0000	1.0000	1.0000	1.0000	.9997	.9989	.9967	.9919	.9829	.9682
10	1.0000	1.0000	1.0000	1.0000	.9999	.9997	.9990	.9972	.9933	.9863
11	1.0000	1.0000	1.0000	1.0000	1.0000	.9999	.9997	.9991	.9976	.9945
12	1.0000	1.0000	1.0000	1.0000	1.0000	1.0000	.9999	.9997	.9992	.9980
13	1.0000	1.0000	1.0000	1.0000	1.0000	1.0000	1.0000	.9999	.9997	.9993
14	1.0000	1.0000	1.0000	1.0000	1.0000	1.0000	1.0000	1.0000	.9999	.9998
15	1.0000	1.0000	1.0000	1.0000	1.0000	1.0000	1.0000	1.0000	1.0000	.9999
16	1.0000	1.0000	1.0000	1.0000	1.0000	1.0000	1.0000	1.0000	1.0000	1.0000
17	1.0000	1.0000	1.0000	1.0000	1.0000	1.0000	1.0000	1.0000	1.0000	1.0000
18	1.0000	1.0000	1.0000	1.0000	1.0000	1.0000	1.0000	1.0000	1.0000	1.0000
19	1.0000	1.0000	1.0000	1.0000	1.0000	1.0000	1.0000	1.0000	1.0000	1.0000
20	1.0000	1.0000	1.0000	1.0000	1.0000	1.0000	1.0000	1.0000	1.0000	1.0000

Poisson Mean μ

k	5.5	6.0	6.5	7.0	7.5	8.0	8.5	9.0	9.5	10.0
0	.0041	.0025	.0015	.0009	.0006	.0003	.0002	.0001	.0001	.0000
1	.0266	.0174	.0113	.0073	.0047	.0030	.0019	.0012	.0008	.0005
2	.0884	.0620	.0430	.0296	.0203	.0138	.0093	.0062	.0042	.0028
3	.2017	.1512	.1118	.0818	.0591	.0424	.0301	.0212	.0149	.0103
4	.3575	.2851	.2237	.1730	.1321	.0996	.0744	.0550	.0403	.0293
5	.5289	.4457	.3690	.3007	.2414	.1912	.1496	.1157	.0885	.0671
6	.6860	.6063	.5265	.4497	.3782	.3134	.2562	.2068	.1649	.1301
7	.8095	.7440	.6728	.5987	.5246	.4530	.3856	.3239	.2687	.2202
8	.8944	.8472	.7916	.7291	.6620	.5925	.5231	.4557	.3918	.3328
9	.9462	.9161	.8774	.8305	.7764	.7166	.6530	.5874	.5218	.4579
10	.9747	.9574	.9332	.9015	.8622	.8159	.7634	.7060	.6453	.5830
11	.9890	.9799	.9661	.9467	.9208	.8881	.8487	.8030	.7520	.6968
12	.9955	.9912	.9840	.9730	.9573	.9362	.9091	.8758	.8364	.7916
13	.9983	.9964	.9929	.9872	.9784	.9658	.9486	.9261	.8981	.8645
14	.9994	.9986	.9970	.9943	.9897	.9827	.9726	.9585	.9400	.9165
15	.9998	.9995	.9988	.9976	.9954	.9918	.9862	.9780	.9665	.9513
16	.9999	.9998	.9996	.9990	.9980	.9963	.9934	.9889	.9823	.9730
17	1.0000	.9999	.9998	.9996	.9992	.9984	.9970	.9947	.9911	.9857
18	1.0000	1.0000	.9999	.9996	.9992	.9993	.9987	.9976	.9957	.9928
19	1.0000	1.0000	1.0000	1.0000	.9999	.9997	.9995	.9989	.9980	.9965
20	1.0000	1.0000	1.0000	1.0000	1.0000	.9999	.9998	.9996	.9991	.9984

Table 5   Normal Curve Areas

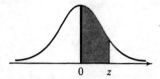

z	.00	.01	.02	.03	.04	.05	.06	.07	.08	.09
.0	.0000	.0040	.0080	.0120	.0160	.0199	.0239	.0279	.0319	.0359
.1	.0398	.0438	.0478	.0517	.0557	.0596	.0636	.0675	.0714	.0753
.2	.0793	.0832	.0871	.0910	.0948	.0987	.1026	.1064	.1103	.1141
.3	.1179	.1217	.1255	.1293	.1331	.1368	.1406	.1443	.1480	.1517
.4	.1554	.1591	.1628	.1664	.1700	.1736	.1772	.1808	.1844	.1879
.5	.1915	.1950	.1985	.2019	.2054	.2088	.2123	.2157	.2190	.2224
.6	.2257	.2291	.2324	.2357	.2389	.2422	.2454	.2486	.2517	.2549
.7	.2580	.2611	.2642	.2673	.2704	.2734	.2764	.2794	.2823	.2852
.8	.2881	.2910	.2939	.2967	.2995	.3023	.3051	.3078	.3106	.3133
.9	.3159	.3186	.3212	.3238	.3264	.3289	.3315	.3340	.3365	.3389
1.0	.3413	.3438	.3461	.3485	.3508	.3531	.3554	.3577	.3599	.3621
1.1	.3643	.3665	.3686	.3708	.3729	.3749	.3770	.3790	.3810	.3830
1.2	.3849	.3869	.3888	.3907	.3925	.3944	.3962	.3980	.3997	.4015
1.3	.4032	.4049	.4066	.4082	.4099	.4115	.4131	.4147	.4162	.4177
1.4	.4192	.4207	.4222	.4236	.4251	.4265	.4279	.4292	.4306	.4319
1.5	.4332	.4345	.4357	.4370	.4382	.4394	.4406	.4418	.4429	.4441
1.6	.4452	.4463	.4474	.4484	.4495	.4505	.4515	.4525	.4535	.4545
1.7	.4554	.4564	.4573	.4582	.4591	.4599	.4608	.4616	.4625	.4633
1.8	.4641	.4649	.4656	.4664	.4671	.4678	.4686	.4693	.4699	.4706
1.9	.4713	.4719	.4726	.4732	.4738	.4744	.4750	.4756	.4761	.4767
2.0	.4772	.4778	.4783	.4788	.4793	.4798	.4803	.4808	.4812	.4817
2.1	.4821	.4826	.4830	.4834	.4838	.4842	.4846	.4850	.4854	.4857
2.2	.4861	.4864	.4868	.4871	.4875	.4878	.4881	.4884	.4887	.4890
2.3	.4893	.4896	.4898	.4901	.4904	.4906	.4909	.4911	.4913	.4916
2.4	.4918	.4920	.4922	.4925	.4927	.4929	.4931	.4932	.4934	.4936
2.5	.4938	.4940	.4941	.4943	.4945	.4946	.4948	.4949	.4951	.4952
2.6	.4953	.4955	.4956	.4957	.4959	.4960	.4961	.4962	.4963	.4964
2.7	.4965	.4966	.4967	.4968	.4969	.4970	.4971	.4972	.4973	.4974
2.8	.4974	.4975	.4976	.4977	.4977	.4978	.4979	.4979	.4980	.4981
2.9	.4981	.4982	.4982	.4983	.4984	.4984	.4985	.4985	.4986	.4986
3.0	.4987	.4987	.4987	.4988	.4988	.4989	.4989	.4989	.4990	.4990

Source: Abridged from Table I of A. Hald, *Statistical Tables and Formulas* (New York: John Wiley & Sons, Inc.), 1952. Reproduced by permission of A. Hald and the publisher.

Table 6   Critical Values for Student's *t*

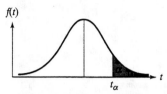

ν	$t_{.100}$	$t_{.050}$	$t_{.025}$	$t_{.010}$	$t_{.005}$	$t_{.001}$	$t_{.0005}$
1	3.078	6.314	12.706	31.821	63.657	318.31	636.62
2	1.886	2.920	4.303	6.965	9.925	22.326	31.598
3	1.638	2.353	3.182	4.541	5.841	10.213	12.924
4	1.533	2.132	2.776	3.747	4.604	7.173	8.610
5	1.476	2.015	2.571	3.365	4.032	5.893	6.869
6	1.440	1.943	2.447	3.143	3.707	5.208	5.959
7	1.415	1.895	2.365	2.998	3.499	4.785	5.408
8	1.397	1.860	2.306	2.896	3.355	4.501	5.041
9	1.383	1.833	2.262	2.821	3.250	4.297	4.781
10	1.372	1.812	2.228	2.764	3.169	4.144	4.587
11	1.363	1.796	2.201	2.718	3.106	4.025	4.437
12	1.356	1.782	2.179	2.681	3.055	3.930	4.318
13	1.350	1.771	2.160	2.650	3.012	3.852	4.221
14	1.345	1.761	2.145	2.624	2.977	3.787	4.140
15	1.341	1.753	2.131	2.602	2.947	3.733	4.073
16	1.337	1.746	2.120	2.583	2.921	3.686	4.015
17	1.333	1.740	2.110	2.567	2.898	3.646	3.965
18	1.330	1.734	2.101	2.552	2.878	3.610	3.922
19	1.328	1.729	2.093	2.539	2.861	3.579	3.883
20	1.325	1.725	2.086	2.528	2.845	3.552	3.850
21	1.323	1.721	2.080	2.518	2.831	3.527	3.819
22	1.321	1.717	2.074	2.508	2.819	3.505	3.792
23	1.319	1.714	2.069	2.500	2.807	3.485	3.767
24	1.318	1.711	2.064	2.492	2.797	3.467	3.745
25	1.316	1.708	2.060	2.485	2.787	3.450	3.725
26	1.315	1.706	2.056	2.479	2.779	3.435	3.707
27	1.314	1.703	2.052	2.473	2.771	3.421	3.690
28	1.313	1.701	2.048	2.467	2.763	3.408	3.674
29	1.311	1.699	2.045	2.462	2.756	3.396	3.659
30	1.310	1.697	2.042	2.457	2.750	3.385	3.646
40	1.303	1.684	2.021	2.423	2.704	3.307	3.551
60	1.296	1.671	2.000	2.390	2.660	3.232	3.460
120	1.289	1.658	1.980	2.358	2.617	3.160	3.373
∞	1.282	1.645	1.960	2.326	2.576	3.090	3.291

Source: This table is reproduced with the kind permission of the Trustees of Biometrika from E. S. Pearson and H. O. Hartley (eds.), *The Biometrika Tables for Statisticians*, Vol. 1, 3rd ed., *Biometrika*, 1966.

Table 7 Critical Values for the χ^2 Statistic

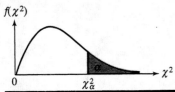

Degrees of Freedom	$\chi^2_{.995}$	$\chi^2_{.990}$	$\chi^2_{.975}$	$\chi^2_{.950}$	$\chi^2_{.900}$
1	.0000393	.0001571	.0009821	.0039321	.0157908
2	.0100251	.0201007	.0506356	.102587	.210720
3	.0717212	.114832	.215795	.351846	.584375
4	.206990	.297110	.484419	.710721	1.063623
5	.411740	.554300	.831211	1.145476	1.61031
6	.675727	.872085	1.237347	1.63539	2.20413
7	.989265	1.239043	1.68987	2.16735	2.83311
8	1.344419	1.646482	2.17973	2.73264	3.48954
9	1.734926	2.087912	2.70039	3.32511	4.16816
10	2.15585	2.55821	3.24697	3.94030	4.86518
11	2.60321	3.05347	3.81575	4.57481	5.57779
12	3.07382	3.57056	4.40379	5.22603	6.30380
13	3.56503	4.10691	5.00874	5.89186	7.04150
14	4.07468	4.66043	5.62872	6.57063	7.78953
15	4.60094	5.22935	6.26214	7.26094	8.54675
16	5.14224	5.81221	6.90766	7.96164	9.31223
17	5.69724	6.40776	7.56418	8.67176	10.0852
18	6.26481	7.01491	8.23075	9.39046	10.8649
19	6.84398	7.63273	8.90655	10.1170	11.6509
20	7.43386	8.26040	9.59083	10.8508	12.4426
21	8.03366	8.89720	10.28293	11.5913	13.2396
22	8.64272	9.54249	10.9823	12.3380	14.0415
23	9.26042	10.19567	11.6885	13.0905	14.8479
24	9.88623	10.8564	12.4011	13.8484	15.6587
25	10.5197	11.5240	13.1197	14.6114	16.4734
26	11.1603	12.1981	13.8439	15.3791	17.2919
27	11.8076	12.8786	14.5733	16.1513	18.1138
28	12.4613	13.5648	15.3079	16.9279	18.9392
29	13.1211	14.2565	16.0471	17.7083	19.7677
30	13.7867	14.9535	16.7908	18.4926	20.5992
40	20.7065	22.1643	24.4331	26.5093	29.0505
50	27.9907	29.7067	32.3574	34.7642	37.6886
60	35.5346	37.4848	40.4817	43.1879	46.4589
70	43.2752	45.4418	48.7576	51.7393	55.3290
80	51.1720	53.5400	57.1532	60.3915	64.2778
90	59.1963	61.7541	65.6466	69.1260	73.2912
100	67.3276	70.0648	74.2219	77.9295	82.3581
150	109.142	112.668	117.985	122.692	128.275
200	152.241	156.432	162.728	168.279	174.835
300	240.663	245.972	253.912	260.878	269.068
400	330.903	337.155	346.482	354.641	364.207
500	422.303	429.388	439.936	449.147	459.926

(continued)

Table 7   *(continued)*

Degrees of Freedom	$\chi^2_{.100}$	$\chi^2_{.050}$	$\chi^2_{.025}$	$\chi^2_{.010}$	$\chi^2_{.005}$
1	2.70554	3.84146	5.02389	6.63490	7.87944
2	4.60517	5.99147	7.37776	9.21034	10.5966
3	6.25139	7.81473	9.34840	11.3449	12.8381
4	7.77944	9.48773	11.1433	13.2767	14.8602
5	9.23635	11.0705	12.8325	15.0863	16.7496
6	10.6446	12.5916	14.4494	16.8119	18.5476
7	12.0170	14.0671	16.0128	18.4753	20.2777
8	13.3616	15.5073	17.5346	20.0902	21.9550
9	14.6837	16.9190	19.0228	21.6660	23.5893
10	15.9871	18.3070	20.4831	23.2093	25.1882
11	17.2750	19.6751	21.9200	24.7250	26.7569
12	18.5494	21.0261	23.3367	26.2170	28.2995
13	19.8119	22.3621	24.7356	27.6883	29.8194
14	21.0642	23.6848	26.1190	29.1413	31.3193
15	22.3072	24.9958	27.4884	30.5779	32.8013
16	23.5418	26.2962	28.8454	31.9999	34.2672
17	24.7690	27.5871	30.1910	33.4087	35.7185
18	25.9894	28.8693	31.5264	34.8053	37.1564
19	27.2036	30.1435	32.8523	36.1908	38.5822
20	28.4120	31.4104	34.1696	37.5662	39.9968
21	29.6151	32.6705	35.4789	38.9321	41.4010
22	30.8133	33.9244	36.7807	40.2894	42.7956
23	32.0069	35.1725	38.0757	41.6384	44.1813
24	33.1963	36.4151	39.3641	42.9798	45.5585
25	34.3816	37.6525	40.6465	44.3141	46.9278
26	36.5631	38.8852	41.9232	45.6417	48.2899
27	36.7412	40.1133	43.1944	46.9630	49.6449
28	37.9159	41.3372	44.4607	48.2782	50.9933
29	39.0875	42.5569	45.7222	49.5879	52.3356
30	40.2560	43.7729	46.9792	50.8922	53.6720
40	51.8050	55.7585	59.3417	63.6907	66.7659
50	63.1671	67.5048	71.4202	76.1539	79.4900
60	74.3970	79.0819	83.2976	88.3794	91.9517
70	85.5271	90.5312	95.0231	100.425	104.215
80	96.5782	101.879	106.629	112.329	116.321
90	107.565	113.145	118.136	124.116	128.299
100	118.498	124.342	129.561	135.807	140.169
150	172.581	179.581	185.800	193.208	198.360
200	226.021	233.994	241.058	249.445	255.264
300	331.789	341.395	349.874	359.906	366.844
400	436.649	447.632	457.305	468.724	476.606
500	540.930	553.127	563.852	576.493	585.207

Table 8   Critical Values for the F Statistic: $F_{.10}$

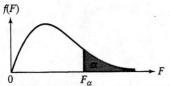

v_1	Numerator Degrees of Freedom								
v_2	1	2	3	4	5	6	7	8	9
1	39.86	49.50	53.59	55.83	57.24	58.20	58.91	59.44	59.86
2	8.53	9.00	9.16	9.24	9.29	9.33	9.35	9.37	9.38
3	5.54	5.46	5.39	5.34	5.31	5.28	5.27	5.25	5.24
4	4.54	4.32	4.19	4.11	4.05	4.01	3.98	3.95	3.94
5	4.06	3.78	3.62	3.52	3.45	3.40	3.37	3.34	3.32
6	3.78	3.46	3.29	3.18	3.11	3.05	3.01	2.98	2.96
7	3.59	3.26	3.07	2.96	2.88	2.83	2.78	2.75	2.72
8	3.46	3.11	2.92	2.81	2.73	2.67	2.62	2.59	2.56
9	3.36	3.01	2.81	2.69	2.61	2.55	2.51	2.47	2.44
10	3.29	2.92	2.73	2.61	2.52	2.46	2.41	2.38	2.35
11	3.23	2.86	2.66	2.54	2.45	2.39	2.34	2.30	2.27
12	3.18	2.81	2.61	2.48	2.39	2.33	2.28	2.24	2.21
13	3.14	2.76	2.56	2.43	2.35	2.28	2.23	2.20	2.16
14	3.10	2.73	2.52	2.39	2.31	2.24	2.19	2.15	2.12
15	3.07	2.70	2.49	2.36	2.27	2.21	2.16	2.12	2.09
16	3.05	2.67	2.46	2.33	2.24	2.18	2.13	2.09	2.06
17	3.03	2.64	2.44	2.31	2.22	2.15	2.10	2.06	2.03
18	3.01	2.62	2.42	2.29	2.20	2.13	2.08	2.04	2.00
19	2.99	2.61	2.40	2.27	2.18	2.11	2.06	2.02	1.98
20	2.97	2.59	2.38	2.25	2.16	2.09	2.04	2.00	1.96
21	2.96	2.57	2.36	2.23	2.14	2.08	2.02	1.98	1.95
22	2.95	2.56	2.35	2.22	2.13	2.06	2.01	1.97	1.93
23	2.94	2.55	2.34	2.21	2.11	2.05	1.99	1.95	1.92
24	2.93	2.54	2.33	2.19	2.10	2.04	1.98	1.94	1.91
25	2.92	2.53	2.32	2.18	2.09	2.02	1.97	1.93	1.89
26	2.91	2.52	2.31	2.17	2.08	2.01	1.96	1.92	1.88
27	2.90	2.51	2.30	2.17	2.07	2.00	1.95	1.91	1.87
28	2.89	2.50	2.29	2.16	2.06	2.00	1.94	1.90	1.87
29	2.89	2.50	2.28	2.15	2.06	1.99	1.93	1.89	1.86
30	2.88	2.49	2.28	2.14	2.05	1.98	1.93	1.88	1.85
40	2.84	2.44	2.23	2.09	2.00	1.93	1.87	1.83	1.79
60	2.79	2.39	2.18	2.04	1.95	1.87	1.82	1.77	1.74
120	2.75	2.35	2.13	1.99	1.90	1.82	1.77	1.72	1.68
∞	2.71	2.30	2.08	1.94	1.85	1.77	1.72	1.67	1.63

Denominator Degrees of Freedom (vertical axis label)

Source: From M. Merrington and C. M. Thompson, "Tables of Percentage Points of the inverted Beta (*F*)-Distribution." *Biometrika*, 1943, 33, pp. 73–88. Reproduced by permission of the *Biometrika* trustees.

(continued)

Table 8   (*continued*)

v_2 \ v_1	Numerator Degrees of Freedom									
	10	12	15	20	24	30	40	60	120	∞
1	60.19	60.71	61.22	61.74	62.00	62.26	62.53	62.79	63.06	63.33
2	9.39	9.41	9.42	9.44	9.45	9.46	9.47	9.47	9.48	9.49
3	5.23	5.22	5.20	5.18	5.18	5.17	5.16	5.15	5.14	5.13
4	3.92	3.90	3.87	3.84	3.83	3.82	3.80	3.79	3.78	3.76
5	3.30	3.27	3.24	3.21	3.19	3.17	3.16	3.14	3.12	3.10
6	2.94	2.90	2.87	2.84	2.82	2.80	2.78	2.76	2.74	2.72
7	2.70	2.67	2.63	2.59	2.58	2.56	2.54	2.51	2.49	2.47
8	2.54	2.50	2.46	2.42	2.40	2.38	2.36	2.34	2.32	2.29
9	2.42	2.38	2.34	2.30	2.28	2.25	2.23	2.21	2.18	2.16
10	2.32	2.28	2.24	2.20	2.18	2.16	2.13	2.11	2.08	2.06
11	2.25	2.21	2.17	2.12	2.10	2.08	2.05	2.03	2.00	1.97
12	2.19	2.15	2.10	2.06	2.04	2.01	1.99	1.96	1.93	1.90
13	2.14	2.10	2.05	2.01	1.98	1.96	1.93	1.90	1.88	1.85
14	2.10	2.05	2.01	1.96	1.94	1.91	1.89	1.86	1.83	1.80
15	2.06	2.02	1.97	1.92	1.90	1.87	1.85	1.82	1.79	1.76
16	2.03	1.99	1.94	1.89	1.87	1.84	1.81	1.78	1.75	1.72
17	2.00	1.96	1.91	1.86	1.84	1.81	1.78	1.75	1.72	1.69
18	1.98	1.93	1.89	1.84	1.81	1.78	1.75	1.72	1.69	1.66
19	1.96	1.91	1.86	1.81	1.79	1.76	1.73	1.70	1.67	1.63
20	1.94	1.89	1.84	1.79	1.77	1.74	1.71	1.68	1.64	1.61
21	1.92	1.87	1.83	1.78	1.75	1.72	1.69	1.66	1.62	1.59
22	1.90	1.86	1.81	1.76	1.73	1.70	1.67	1.64	1.60	1.57
23	1.89	1.84	1.80	1.74	1.72	1.69	1.66	1.62	1.59	1.55
24	1.88	1.83	1.78	1.73	1.70	1.67	1.64	1.61	1.57	1.53
25	1.87	1.82	1.77	1.72	1.69	1.66	1.63	1.59	1.56	1.52
26	1.86	1.81	1.76	1.71	1.68	1.65	1.61	1.58	1.54	1.50
27	1.85	1.80	1.75	1.70	1.67	1.64	1.60	1.57	1.53	1.49
28	1.84	1.79	1.74	1.69	1.66	1.63	1.59	1.56	1.52	1.48
29	1.83	1.78	1.73	1.68	1.65	1.62	1.58	1.55	1.51	1.47
30	1.82	1.77	1.72	1.67	1.64	1.61	1.57	1.54	1.50	1.46
40	1.76	1.71	1.66	1.61	1.57	1.54	1.51	1.47	1.42	1.38
60	1.71	1.66	1.60	1.54	1.51	1.48	1.44	1.40	1.35	1.29
120	1.65	1.60	1.55	1.48	1.45	1.41	1.37	1.32	1.26	1.19
∞	1.60	1.55	1.49	1.42	1.38	1.34	1.30	1.24	1.17	1.00

Denominator Degrees of Freedom

Table 9   Critical Values for the F Statistic: $F_{.05}$

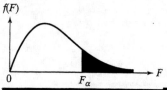

v_2 \ v_1	Numerator Degrees of Freedom								
	1	2	3	4	5	6	7	8	9
1	161.4	199.5	215.7	224.6	230.2	234.0	236.8	238.9	240.5
2	18.51	19.00	19.16	19.25	19.30	19.33	19.35	19.37	19.38
3	10.13	9.55	9.28	9.12	9.01	8.94	8.89	8.85	8.81
4	7.71	6.94	6.59	6.39	6.26	6.16	6.09	6.04	6.00
5	6.61	5.79	5.41	5.19	5.05	4.95	4.88	4.82	4.77
6	5.99	5.14	4.76	4.53	4.39	4.28	4.21	4.15	4.10
7	5.59	4.74	4.35	4.12	3.97	3.87	3.79	3.73	3.68
8	5.32	4.46	4.07	3.84	3.69	3.58	3.50	3.44	3.39
9	5.12	4.26	3.86	3.63	3.48	3.37	3.29	3.23	3.18
10	4.96	4.10	3.71	3.48	3.33	3.22	3.14	3.07	3.02
11	4.84	3.98	3.59	3.36	3.20	3.09	3.01	2.95	2.90
12	4.75	3.89	3.49	3.26	3.11	3.00	2.91	2.85	2.80
13	4.67	3.81	3.41	3.18	3.03	2.92	2.83	2.77	2.71
14	4.60	3.74	3.34	3.11	2.96	2.85	2.76	2.70	2.65
15	4.54	3.68	3.29	3.06	2.90	2.79	2.71	2.64	2.59
16	4.49	3.63	3.24	3.01	2.85	2.74	2.66	2.59	2.54
17	4.45	3.59	3.20	2.96	2.81	2.70	2.61	2.55	2.49
18	4.41	3.55	3.16	2.93	2.77	2.66	2.58	2.51	2.46
19	4.38	3.52	3.13	2.90	2.74	2.63	2.54	2.48	2.42
20	4.35	3.49	3.10	2.87	2.71	2.60	2.51	2.45	2.39
21	4.32	3.47	3.07	2.84	2.68	2.57	2.49	2.42	2.37
22	4.30	3.44	3.05	2.82	2.66	2.55	2.46	2.40	2.34
23	4.28	3.42	3.03	2.80	2.64	2.53	2.44	2.37	2.32
24	4.26	3.40	3.01	2.78	2.62	2.51	2.42	2.36	2.30
25	4.24	3.39	2.99	2.76	2.60	2.49	2.40	2.34	2.28
26	4.23	3.37	2.98	2.74	2.59	2.47	2.39	2.32	2.27
27	4.21	3.35	2.96	2.73	2.57	2.46	2.37	2.31	2.25
28	4.20	3.34	2.95	2.71	2.56	2.45	2.36	2.29	2.24
29	4.18	3.33	2.93	2.70	2.55	2.43	2.35	2.28	2.22
30	4.17	3.32	2.92	2.69	2.53	2.42	2.33	2.27	2.21
40	4.08	3.23	2.84	2.61	2.45	2.34	2.25	2.18	2.12
60	4.00	3.15	2.76	2.53	2.37	2.25	2.17	2.10	2.04
120	3.92	3.07	2.68	2.45	2.29	2.17	2.09	2.02	1.96
∞	3.84	3.00	2.60	2.37	2.21	2.10	2.01	1.94	1.88

Source: From M. Merrington and C. M. Thompson, "Tables of Percentage Points of the inverted Beta (*F*)-Distribution." *Biometrika*, 1943, 33, pp. 73–88. Reproduced by permission of the *Biometrika* trustees.

(continued)

Table 9 *(continued)*

v_2 \ v_1	Numerator Degrees of Freedom									
	10	12	15	20	24	30	40	60	120	∞
1	241.9	243.9	245.9	248.0	249.1	250.1	251.1	252.2	253.3	254.3
2	19.40	19.41	19.43	19.45	19.45	19.46	19.47	19.48	19.49	19.50
3	8.79	8.74	8.70	8.66	8.64	8.62	8.59	8.57	8.55	8.53
4	5.96	5.91	5.86	5.80	5.77	5.75	5.72	5.69	5.66	5.63
5	4.74	4.68	4.62	4.56	4.53	4.50	4.46	4.43	4.40	4.36
6	4.06	4.00	3.94	3.87	3.84	3.81	3.77	3.74	3.70	3.67
7	3.64	3.57	3.51	3.44	3.41	3.38	3.34	3.30	3.27	3.23
8	3.35	3.28	3.22	3.15	3.12	3.08	3.04	3.01	2.97	2.93
9	3.14	3.07	3.01	2.94	2.90	2.86	2.83	2.79	2.75	2.71
10	2.98	2.91	2.85	2.77	2.74	2.70	2.66	2.62	2.58	2.54
11	2.85	2.79	2.72	2.65	2.61	2.57	2.53	2.49	2.45	2.40
12	2.75	2.69	2.62	2.54	2.51	2.47	2.43	2.38	2.34	2.30
13	2.67	2.60	2.53	2.46	2.42	2.38	2.34	2.30	2.25	2.21
14	2.60	2.53	2.46	2.39	2.35	2.31	2.27	2.22	2.18	2.13
15	2.54	2.48	2.40	2.33	2.29	2.25	2.20	2.16	2.11	2.07
16	2.49	2.42	2.35	2.28	2.24	2.19	2.15	2.11	2.06	2.01
17	2.45	2.38	2.31	2.23	2.19	2.15	2.10	2.06	2.01	1.96
18	2.41	2.34	2.27	2.19	2.15	2.11	2.06	2.02	1.97	1.92
19	2.38	2.31	2.23	2.16	2.11	2.07	2.03	1.98	1.93	1.88
20	2.35	2.28	2.20	2.12	2.08	2.04	1.99	1.95	1.90	1.84
21	2.32	2.25	2.18	2.10	2.05	2.01	1.96	1.92	1.87	1.81
22	2.30	2.23	2.15	2.07	2.03	1.98	1.94	1.89	1.84	1.78
23	2.27	2.20	2.13	2.05	2.01	1.96	1.91	1.86	1.81	1.76
24	2.25	2.18	2.11	2.03	1.98	1.94	1.89	1.84	1.79	1.73
25	2.24	2.16	2.09	2.01	1.96	1.92	1.87	1.82	1.77	1.71
26	2.22	2.15	2.07	1.99	1.95	1.90	1.85	1.80	1.75	1.69
27	2.20	2.13	2.06	1.97	1.93	1.88	1.84	1.79	1.73	1.67
28	2.19	2.12	2.04	1.96	1.91	1.87	1.82	1.77	1.71	1.65
29	2.18	2.10	2.03	1.94	1.90	1.85	1.81	1.75	1.70	1.64
30	2.16	2.09	2.01	1.93	1.89	1.84	1.79	1.74	1.68	1.62
40	2.08	2.00	1.92	1.84	1.79	1.74	1.69	1.64	1.58	1.51
60	1.99	1.92	1.84	1.75	1.70	1.65	1.59	1.53	1.47	1.39
120	1.91	1.83	1.75	1.66	1.61	1.55	1.50	1.43	1.35	1.25
∞	1.83	1.75	1.67	1.57	1.52	1.46	1.39	1.32	1.22	1.00

Denominator Degrees of Freedom

Table 10 Critical Values for the F Statistic: $F_{.025}$

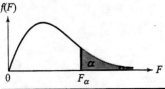

v_1 / v_2	Numerator Degrees of Freedom								
	1	2	3	4	5	6	7	8	9
1	647.8	799.5	864.2	899.6	921.8	937.1	948.2	956.7	963.3
2	38.51	39.00	39.17	39.25	39.30	39.33	39.36	39.37	39.39
3	17.44	16.04	15.44	15.10	14.88	14.73	14.62	14.54	14.47
4	12.22	10.65	9.98	9.60	9.36	9.20	9.07	8.98	8.90
5	10.01	8.43	7.76	7.39	7.15	6.98	6.85	6.76	6.68
6	8.81	7.26	6.60	6.23	5.99	5.82	5.70	5.60	5.52
7	8.07	6.54	5.89	5.52	5.29	5.12	4.99	4.90	4.82
8	7.57	6.06	5.42	5.05	4.82	4.65	4.53	4.43	4.36
9	7.21	5.71	5.08	4.72	4.48	4.32	4.20	4.10	4.03
10	6.94	5.46	4.83	4.47	4.24	4.07	3.95	3.85	3.78
11	6.72	5.26	4.63	4.28	4.04	3.88	3.76	3.66	3.59
12	6.55	5.10	4.47	4.12	3.89	3.73	3.61	3.51	3.44
13	6.41	4.97	4.35	4.00	3.77	3.60	3.48	3.39	3.31
14	6.30	4.86	4.24	3.89	3.66	3.50	3.38	3.29	3.21
15	6.20	4.77	4.15	3.80	3.58	3.41	3.29	3.20	3.12
16	6.12	4.69	4.08	3.73	3.50	3.34	3.22	3.12	3.05
17	6.04	4.62	4.01	3.66	3.44	3.28	3.16	3.06	2.98
18	5.98	4.56	3.95	3.61	3.38	3.22	3.10	3.01	2.93
19	5.92	4.51	3.90	3.56	3.33	3.17	3.05	2.96	2.88
20	5.87	4.46	3.86	3.51	3.29	3.13	3.01	2.91	2.84
21	5.83	4.42	3.82	3.48	3.25	3.09	2.97	2.87	2.80
22	5.79	4.38	3.78	3.44	3.22	3.05	2.93	2.84	2.76
23	5.75	4.35	3.75	3.41	3.18	3.02	2.90	2.81	2.73
24	5.72	4.32	3.72	3.38	3.15	2.99	2.87	2.78	2.70
25	5.69	4.29	3.69	3.35	3.13	2.97	2.85	2.75	2.68
26	5.66	4.27	3.67	3.33	3.10	2.94	2.82	2.73	2.65
27	5.63	4.24	3.65	3.31	3.08	2.92	2.80	2.71	2.63
26	5.61	4.22	3.63	3.29	3.06	2.90	2.76	2.69	2.61
29	5.59	4.20	3.61	3.27	3.04	2.88	2.76	2.67	2.59
30	5.57	4.18	3.59	3.25	3.03	2.87	2.75	2.65	2.57
40	5.42	4.05	3.46	3.13	2.90	2.74	2.62	2.53	2.45
60	5.29	3.93	3.34	3.01	2.79	2.63	2.51	2.41	2.33
120	5.15	3.80	3.23	2.89	2.67	2.52	2.39	2.30	2.22
∞	5.02	3.69	3.12	2.79	2.57	2.41	2.29	2.19	2.11

Denominator Degrees of Freedom

(continued)

Table 10   *(continued)*

v_1 v_2	Numerator Degrees of Freedom									
	10	12	15	20	24	30	40	60	120	∞
1	968.6	976.7	984.9	993.1	997.2	1001	1006	1010	1014	1018
2	39.40	39.41	39.43	39.45	39.46	39.46	39.47	39.48	39.49	39.50
3	14.42	14.34	14.25	14.17	14.12	14.08	14.04	13.99	13.95	13.90
4	8.84	8.75	8.66	8.56	8.51	8.46	8.41	8.36	8.31	8.26
5	6.62	6.52	6.43	6.33	6.28	6.23	6.18	6.12	6.07	6.02
6	5.46	5.37	5.27	5.17	5.12	5.07	5.01	4.96	4.90	4.85
7	4.76	4.67	4.57	4.47	4.42	4.36	4.31	4.25	4.20	4.14
8	4.30	4.20	4.10	4.00	3.95	3.89	3.84	3.78	3.73	3.67
9	3.96	3.87	3.77	3.67	3.61	3.56	3.51	3.45	3.39	3.33
10	3.72	3.62	3.52	3.42	3.37	3.31	3.26	3.20	3.14	3.08
11	3.53	3.43	3.33	3.23	3.17	3.12	3.06	3.00	2.94	2.88
12	3.37	3.28	3.18	3.07	3.02	2.96	2.91	2.85	2.79	2.72
13	3.25	3.15	3.05	2.95	2.89	2.84	2.78	2.72	2.66	2.60
14	3.15	3.05	2.95	2.84	2.79	2.73	2.67	2.61	2.55	2.49
15	3.06	2.96	2.86	2.76	2.70	2.64	2.59	2.52	2.46	2.40
16	2.99	2.89	2.79	2.68	2.63	2.57	2.51	2.45	2.38	2.32
17	2.92	2.82	2.72	2.62	2.56	2.50	2.44	2.38	2.32	2.25
18	2.87	2.77	2.67	2.56	2.50	2.44	2.38	2.32	2.26	2.19
19	2.82	2.72	2.62	2.51	2.45	2.39	2.33	2.27	2.20	2.13
20	2.77	2.68	2.57	2.46	2.41	2.35	2.29	2.22	2.16	2.09
21	2.73	2.64	2.53	2.42	2.37	2.31	2.25	2.18	2.11	2.04
22	2.70	2.60	2.50	2.39	2.33	2.27	2.21	2.14	2.08	2.00
23	2.67	2.57	2.47	2.36	2.30	2.24	2.18	2.11	2.04	1.97
24	2.64	2.54	2.44	2.33	2.27	2.21	2.15	2.08	2.01	1.94
25	2.61	2.51	2.41	2.30	2.24	2.18	2.12	2.05	1.98	1.91
26	2.59	2.49	2.39	2.28	2.22	2.16	2.09	2.03	1.95	1.88
27	2.57	2.47	2.36	2.25	2.19	2.13	2.07	2.00	1.93	1.85
28	2.55	2.45	2.34	2.23	2.17	2.11	2.05	1.98	1.91	1.83
29	2.53	2.43	2.32	2.21	2.15	2.09	2.03	1.96	1.89	1.81
30	2.51	2.41	2.31	2.20	2.14	2.07	2.01	1.94	1.87	1.79
40	2.39	2.29	2.18	2.07	2.01	1.94	1.88	1.80	1.72	1.64
50	2.27	2.17	2.06	1.94	1.88	1.82	1.74	1.67	1.58	1.48
120	2.16	2.05	1.94	1.82	1.76	1.69	1.61	1.53	1.43	1.31
∞	2.05	1.94	1.83	1.71	1.64	1.57	1.48	1.39	1.27	1.00

Denominator Degrees of Freedom

Table 11 Critical Values for the F Statistic: $F_{.01}$

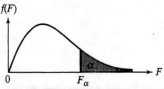

v_2 \ v_1	Numerator Degrees of Freedom								
	1	2	3	4	5	6	7	8	9
1	4,052	4,999.5	5,403	5,625	5,764	5,859	5,928	5,982	6,022
2	98.50	99.00	99.17	99.25	99.30	99.33	99.36	99.37	99.39
3	34.12	30.82	29.46	28.71	28.24	27.91	27.67	27.49	27.35
4	21.20	18.00	16.69	15.98	15.52	15.21	14.98	14.80	14.66
5	16.26	13.27	12.06	11.39	10.97	10.67	10.46	10.29	10.16
6	13.75	10.92	9.78	9.15	8.75	8.47	8.26	8.10	7.98
7	12.25	9.55	8.45	7.85	7.46	7.19	6.99	6.84	6.72
8	11.26	8.65	7.59	7.01	6.63	6.37	6.18	6.03	5.91
9	10.56	8.02	6.99	6.42	6.06	5.80	5.61	5.47	5.35
10	10.04	7.56	6.55	5.99	5.64	5.39	5.20	5.06	4.94
11	9.65	7.21	6.22	5.67	5.32	5.07	4.89	4.74	4.63
12	9.33	6.93	5.95	5.41	5.06	4.82	4.64	4.50	4.39
13	9.07	6.70	5.74	5.21	4.86	4.62	4.44	4.30	4.19
14	8.86	6.51	5.56	5.04	4.69	4.46	4.28	4.14	4.03
15	8.68	6.36	5.42	4.89	4.56	4.32	4.14	4.00	3.89
16	8.53	6.23	5.29	4.77	4.44	4.20	4.03	3.89	3.78
17	8.40	6.11	5.18	4.67	4.34	4.10	3.93	3.79	3.68
18	8.29	6.01	5.09	4.58	4.25	4.01	3.84	3.71	3.60
19	8.18	5.93	5.01	4.50	4.17	3.94	3.77	3.63	3.52
20	8.10	5.85	4.94	4.43	4.10	3.87	3.70	3.56	3.46
21	8.02	5.78	4.87	4.37	4.04	3.81	3.64	3.51	3.40
22	7.95	5.72	4.82	4.31	3.99	3.76	3.59	3.45	3.35
23	7.88	5.66	4.76	4.26	3.94	3.71	3.54	3.41	3.30
24	7.82	5.61	4.72	4.22	3.90	3.67	3.50	3.36	3.26
25	7.77	5.57	4.68	4.18	3.85	3.63	3.46	3.32	3.22
26	7.72	5.53	4.64	4.14	3.82	3.59	3.42	3.29	3.18
27	7.68	5.49	4.60	4.11	3.78	3.56	3.39	3.26	3.15
28	7.64	5.45	4.57	4.07	3.75	3.53	3.36	3.23	3.12
29	7.60	5.42	4.54	4.04	3.73	3.50	3.33	3.20	3.09
30	7.56	5.39	4.51	4.02	3.70	3.47	3.30	3.17	3.07
40	7.31	5.18	4.31	3.83	3.51	3.29	3.12	2.99	2.89
60	7.08	4.98	4.13	3.65	3.34	3.12	2.95	2.82	2.72
120	6.85	4.79	3.95	3.48	3.17	2.96	2.79	2.66	2.56
∞	6.63	4.61	3.78	3.32	3.02	2.80	2.64	2.51	2.41

Denominator Degrees of Freedom (left axis label)

Source: From M. Merrington and C. M. Thompson, "Tables of Percentage Points of the inverted Beta (F)-Distribution." *Biometrika*, 1943, 33, pp. 73–88. Reproduced by permission of the *Biometrika* trustees.

Table 11   (continued)

v_2 \ v_1	Numerator Degrees of Freedom									
	10	12	15	20	24	30	40	60	120	∞
1	6,056	6,106	6,157	6,209	6,235	6,261	6,287	6,313	6,339	6,366
2	99.40	99.42	99.43	99.45	99.46	99.47	99.47	99.48	99.49	99.50
3	27.23	27.05	26.87	26.69	26.60	26.50	26.41	26.32	26.22	26.13
4	14.55	14.37	14.20	14.02	13.93	13.84	13.75	13.65	13.56	13.46
5	10.05	9.89	9.72	9.55	9.47	9.38	9.29	9.20	9.11	9.02
6	7.87	7.72	7.56	7.40	7.31	7.23	7.14	7.06	6.97	6.88
7	6.62	6.47	6.31	6.16	6.07	5.99	5.91	5.82	5.74	5.65
8	5.81	5.67	5.52	5.36	5.28	5.20	5.12	5.03	4.95	4.86
9	5.26	5.11	4.96	4.81	4.73	4.65	4.57	4.48	4.40	4.31
10	4.85	4.71	4.56	4.41	4.33	4.25	4.17	4.08	4.00	3.91
11	4.54	4.40	4.25	4.10	4.02	3.94	3.86	3.78	3.69	3.60
12	4.30	4.16	4.01	3.86	3.78	3.70	3.62	3.54	3.45	3.36
13	4.10	3.96	3.82	3.66	3.59	3.51	3.43	3.34	3.25	3.17
14	3.94	3.80	3.66	3.51	3.43	3.35	3.27	3.18	3.09	3.00
15	3.80	3.67	3.52	3.37	3.29	3.21	3.13	3.05	2.96	2.87
16	3.69	3.55	3.41	3.26	3.18	3.10	3.02	2.93	2.84	2.75
17	3.59	3.46	3.31	3.16	3.08	3.00	2.92	2.83	2.75	2.65
18	3.51	3.37	3.23	3.08	3.00	2.92	2.84	2.75	2.66	2.57
19	3.43	3.30	3.15	3.00	2.92	2.84	2.76	2.67	2.58	2.49
20	3.37	3.23	3.09	2.94	2.86	2.78	2.69	2.61	2.52	2.42
21	3.31	3.17	3.03	2.88	2.80	2.72	2.64	2.55	2.46	2.36
22	3.26	3.12	2.98	2.83	2.75	2.67	2.58	2.50	2.40	2.31
23	3.21	3.07	2.93	2.78	2.70	2.62	2.54	2.45	2.35	2.26
24	3.17	3.03	2.89	2.74	2.66	2.58	2.49	2.40	2.31	2.21
25	3.13	2.99	2.85	2.70	2.62	2.54	2.45	2.36	2.27	2.17
26	3.09	2.96	2.81	2.66	2.58	2.50	2.42	2.33	2.23	2.13
27	3.06	2.93	2.78	2.63	2.55	2.47	2.38	2.29	2.20	2.10
28	3.03	2.90	2.75	2.60	2.52	2.44	2.35	2.26	2.17	2.06
29	3.00	2.87	2.73	2.57	2.49	2.41	2.33	2.23	2.14	2.03
30	2.98	2.84	2.70	2.55	2.47	2.39	2.30	2.21	2.11	2.01
40	2.80	2.66	2.52	2.37	2.29	2.20	2.11	2.02	1.92	1.80
60	2.63	2.50	2.35	2.20	2.12	2.03	1.94	1.84	1.73	1.60
120	2.47	2.34	2.19	2.03	1.95	1.86	1.76	1.66	1.53	1.38
∞	2.32	2.18	2.04	1.88	1.79	1.70	1.59	1.47	1.32	1.00

Denominator Degrees of Freedom

Table 12   Factors Used When Constructing Control Charts

Number of Observations in Sample	Chart for Averages		Chart for Ranges		
n	A_2	d_2	d_3	D_3	D_4
2	1.880	1.128	.853	0	3.276
3	1.023	1.693	.888	0	2.575
4	.729	2.059	.880	0	2.282
5	.577	2.326	.864	0	2.115
6	.483	2.534	.848	0	2.004
7	.419	2.704	.833	.076	1.924
8	.373	2.847	.820	.136	1.864
9	.337	2.970	.808	.184	1.816
10	.308	3.078	.797	.223	1.777
11	.285	3.173	.787	.256	1.744
12	.266	3.258	.778	.284	1.719
13	.249	3.336	.770	.308	1.692
14	.235	3.407	.762	.329	1.671
15	.223	3.472	.755	.348	1.652
16	.212	3.532	.749	.364	1.636
17	.203	3.588	.743	.379	1.621
18	.194	3.640	.738	.392	1.608
19	.187	3.689	.733	.404	1.596
20	.180	3.735	.729	.414	1.586
21	.173	3.778	.724	.425	1.575
22	.167	3.819	.720	.434	1.566
23	.162	3.858	.716	.443	1.557
24	.157	3.895	.712	.452	1.548
25	.153	3.931	.709	.459	1.541

Source: *ASTM Manual on Quality Control of Materials,* American Society for Testing Materials, Philadelphia, Pa., 1951. Copyright ASTM. Reprinted with permission.

Table 13   Values of K for Tolerance Limits for Normal Distributions

	$1 - \alpha = .95$			$1 - \alpha = .99$		
n \ γ	.90	.95	.99	.90	.95	.99
2	32.019	37.674	48.430	160.193	188.491	242.300
3	8.380	9.916	12.861	18.930	22.401	29.055
4	5.369	6.370	8.299	9.398	11.150	14.527
5	4.275	5.079	6.634	6.612	7.855	10.260
6	3.712	4.414	5.775	5.337	6.345	8.301
7	3.369	4.007	5.248	4.613	5.488	7.187
8	3.136	3.732	4.891	4.147	4.936	6.468
9	2.967	3.532	4.631	3.822	4.550	5.966
10	2.839	3.379	4.433	3.582	4.265	5.594
11	2.737	3.259	4.277	3.397	4.045	5.308
12	2.655	3.162	4.150	3.250	3.870	5.079
13	2.587	3.081	4.044	3.130	3.727	4.893
14	2.529	3.012	3.955	3.029	3.608	4.737
15	2.480	2.954	3.878	2.945	3.507	4.605
16	2.437	2.903	3.812	2.872	3.421	4.492
17	2.400	2.858	3.754	2.808	3.345	4.393
18	2.366	2.819	3.702	2.753	3.279	4.307
19	2.337	2.784	3.656	2.703	3.221	4.230
20	2.310	2.752	3.615	2.659	3.168	4.161
25	2.208	2.631	3.457	2.494	2.972	3.904
30	2.140	2.549	3.350	2.385	2.841	3.733
35	2.090	2.490	3.272	2.306	2.748	3.611
40	2.052	2.445	3.213	2.247	2.677	3.518
45	2.021	2.408	3.165	2.200	2.621	3.444
50	1.996	2.379	3.126	2.162	2.576	3.385
55	1.976	2.354	3.094	2.130	2.538	3.335
60	1.958	2.333	3.066	2.103	2.506	3.293
65	1.943	2.315	3.042	2.080	2.478	3.257
70	1.929	2.299	3.021	2.060	2.454	3.225
75	1.917	2.285	3.002	2.042	2.433	3.197
80	1.907	2.272	2.986	2.026	2.414	3.173
85	1.897	2.261	2.971	2.012	2.397	3.150
90	1.889	2.251	2.958	1.999	2.382	3.130
95	1.881	2.241	2.945	1.987	2.368	3.112
100	1.874	2.233	2.934	1.977	2.355	3.096
150	1.825	2.175	2.859	1.905	2.270	2.983
200	1.798	2.143	2.816	1.865	2.222	2.921
250	1.780	2.121	2.788	1.839	2.191	2.880
300	1.767	2.106	2.767	1.820	2.169	2.850
400	1.749	2.084	2.739	1.794	2.138	2.809

(continued)

Table 13 (*continued*) Values of K for Tolerance Limits for Normal Distributions

	$1 - \alpha = .95$			$1 - \alpha = .99$		
n \ γ	.90	.95	.99	.90	.95	.99
500	1.737	2.070	2.721	1.777	2.117	2.783
600	1.729	2.060	2.707	1.764	2.102	2.763
700	1.722	2.052	2.697	1.755	2.091	2.748
800	1.717	2.046	2.688	1.747	2.082	2.736
900	1.712	2.040	2.682	1.741	2.075	2.726
1000	1.709	2.036	2.676	1.736	2.068	2.718
∞	1.645	1.960	2.576	1.645	1.960	2.576

Source: From *Techniques of Statistical Analysis* by C. Eisenhart. M. W. Hastay, and W. A. Wallis. Copyright 1947, McGraw-Hill Book Company, Inc. Reproduced with permission of McGraw-Hill.

Table 14 Sample Size n for Nonparametric Tolerance Limits

	$1 - \alpha$					
γ	.50	.70	.90	.95	.99	.995
.995	336	488	777	947	1,325	1,483
.99	168	244	388	473	662	740
.95	34	49	77	93	130	146
.90	17	24	38	46	64	72
.85	11	16	25	30	42	47
.80	9	12	18	22	31	34
.75	7	10	15	18	24	27
.70	6	8	12	14	20	22
.60	4	6	9	10	14	16
.50	3	5	7	8	11	12

Source: Tables A-25d of Wilfrid J. Dixon and Frank J. Massey, Jr., *Introduction to Statistical Analysis*, 3rd. ed., McGraw-Hill Book Company, New York, 1969. Used with permission of McGraw-Hill Book Company.

Table 15 Critical Values for the Durbin–Watson d Statistic ($\alpha = .05$)

n	$k = 1$		$k = 2$		$k = 3$		$k = 4$		$k = 5$	
	d_L	d_U	d_L	d_U	d_L	d_U	d_L	d_U	d_L	d_U
15	1.08	1.36	.95	1.54	.82	1.75	.69	1.97	.56	2.21
16	1.10	1.37	.98	1.54	.86	1.73	.74	1.93	.62	2.15
17	1.13	1.38	1.02	1.54	.90	1.71	.78	1.90	.67	2.10
18	1.16	1.39	1.05	1.53	.93	1.69	.82	1.87	.71	2.06
19	1.18	1.40	1.08	1.53	.97	1.68	.86	1.85	.75	2.02
20	1.20	1.41	1.10	1.54	1.00	1.68	.90	1.83	.79	1.99
21	1.22	1.42	1.13	1.54	1.03	1.67	.93	1.81	.83	1.96
22	1.24	1.43	1.15	1.54	1.05	1.66	.96	1.80	.86	1.94
23	1.26	1.44	1.17	1.54	1.08	1.66	.99	1.79	.90	1.92
24	1.27	1.45	1.19	1.55	1.10	1.66	1.01	1.78	.93	1.90
25	1.29	1.45	1.21	1.55	1.12	1.66	1.04	1.77	.95	1.89
26	1.30	1.46	1.22	1.55	1.14	1.65	1.06	1.76	.98	1.88
27	1.32	1.47	1.24	1.56	1.16	1.65	1.08	1.76	1.01	1.86
28	1.33	1.48	1.26	1.56	1.18	1.65	1.10	1.75	1.03	1.85
29	1.34	1.48	1.27	1.56	1.20	1.65	1.12	1.74	1.05	1.84
30	1.35	1.49	1.28	1.57	1.21	1.65	1.14	1.74	1.07	1.83
31	1.36	1.50	1.30	1.57	1.23	1.65	1.16	1.74	1.09	1.83
32	1.37	1.50	1.31	1.57	1.24	1.65	1.18	1.73	1.11	1.82
33	1.38	1.51	1.32	1.58	1.26	1.65	1.19	1.73	1.13	1.81
34	1.39	1.51	1.33	1.58	1.27	1.65	1.21	1.73	1.15	1.81
35	1.40	1.52	1.34	1.58	1.22	1.65	1.22	1.73	1.16	1.80
36	1.41	1.52	1.35	1.59	1.29	1.65	1.24	1.73	1.18	1.80
37	1.42	1.53	1.36	1.59	1.31	1.66	1.25	1.72	1.19	1.80
38	1.43	1.54	1.37	1.59	1.32	1.66	1.26	1.72	1.21	1.79
39	1.43	1.54	1.38	1.60	1.33	1.66	1.27	1.72	1.22	1.79
40	1.44	1.54	1.39	1.60	1.34	1.66	1.29	1.72	1.23	1.79
45	1.48	1.57	1.43	1.62	1.38	1.67	1.34	1.72	1.29	1.78
50	1.50	1.59	1.46	1.63	1.42	1.67	1.38	1.72	1.34	1.77
55	1.53	1.60	1.49	1.64	1.45	1.68	1.41	1.72	1.38	1.77
60	1.55	1.62	1.51	1.65	1.48	1.69	1.44	1.73	1.41	1.77
65	1.57	1.63	1.54	1.66	1.50	1.70	1.47	1.73	1.44	1.77
70	1.58	1.64	1.55	1.67	1.52	1.70	1.49	1.74	1.46	1.77
75	1.60	1.65	1.57	1.68	1.54	1.71	1.51	1.74	1.49	1.77
80	1.61	1.66	1.59	1.69	1.56	1.72	1.53	1.74	1.51	1.77
85	1.62	1.67	1.60	1.70	1.57	1.72	1.55	1.75	1.52	1.77
90	1.63	1.68	1.61	1.70	1.59	1.73	1.57	1.75	1.54	1.78
95	1.64	1.69	1.62	1.71	1.60	1.73	1.58	1.75	1.56	1.78
100	1.65	1.69	1.63	1.72	1.61	1.74	1.59	1.76	1.57	1.78

Source: From J. Durbin and G. S. Watson, "Testing for serial correlation in least squares regression, II." *Biometrika*, 1951, 30 pp. 159–178. Reproduced by permission of the *Biometrika* Trustees.

Table 16   Critical Values for the Durbin–Watson d Statistic ($\alpha = .01$)

	$k = 1$		$k = 2$		$k = 3$		$k = 4$		$k = 5$	
n	d_L	d_U	d_L	d_U	d_L	d_U	d_L	d_U	d_L	d_U
15	.81	1.07	.70	1.25	.59	1.46	.49	1.70	.39	1.96
16	.84	1.09	.74	1.25	.63	1.44	.53	1.66	.44	1.90
17	.87	1.10	.77	1.25	.67	1.43	.57	1.63	.48	1.85
18	.90	1.12	.80	1.26	.71	1.42	.61	1.60	.52	1.80
19	.93	1.13	.83	1.26	.74	1.41	.65	1.58	.56	1.77
20	.95	1.15	.86	1.27	.77	1.41	.68	1.57	.60	1.74
21	.97	1.16	.89	1.27	.80	1.41	.72	1.55	.63	1.71
22	1.00	1.17	.91	1.28	.83	1.40	.75	1.54	.66	1.69
23	1.02	1.19	.94	1.29	.86	1.40	.77	1.53	.70	1.67
24	1.04	1.20	.96	1.30	.88	1.41	.80	1.53	.72	1.66
25	1.05	1.21	.98	1.30	.90	1.41	.83	1.52	.75	1.65
26	1.07	1.22	1.00	1.31	.93	1.41	.85	1.52	.78	1.64
27	1.09	1.23	1.02	1.32	.95	1.41	.88	1.51	.81	1.63
28	1.10	1.24	1.04	1.32	.97	1.41	.90	1.51	.83	1.62
29	1.12	1.25	1.05	1.33	.99	1.42	.92	1.51	.85	1.61
30	1.13	1.26	1.07	1.34	1.01	1.42	.94	1.51	.88	1.61
31	1.15	1.27	1.08	1.34	1.02	1.42	.96	1.51	.90	1.60
32	1.16	1.28	1.10	1.35	1.04	1.43	.98	1.51	.92	1.60
33	1.17	1.29	1.11	1.36	1.05	1.43	1.00	1.51	.94	1.59
34	1.18	1.30	1.13	1.36	1.07	1.43	1.01	1.51	.95	1.59
35	1.19	1.31	1.14	1.37	1.08	1.44	1.03	1.51	.97	1.59
36	1.21	1.32	1.15	1.38	1.10	1.44	1.04	1.51	.99	1.59
37	1.22	1.32	1.16	1.38	1.11	1.45	1.06	1.51	1.00	1.59
38	1.23	1.33	1.18	1.39	1.12	1.45	1.07	1.52	1.02	1.58
39	1.24	1.34	1.19	1.39	1.14	1.45	1.09	1.52	1.03	1.58
40	1.25	1.34	1.20	1.40	1.15	1.46	1.10	1.52	1.05	1.58
45	1.29	1.38	1.24	1.42	1.20	1.48	1.16	1.53	1.11	1.58
50	1.32	1.40	1.28	1.45	1.24	1.49	1.20	1.54	1.16	1.59
55	1.36	1.43	1.32	1.47	1.28	1.51	1.25	1.55	1.21	1.59
60	1.38	1.45	1.35	1.48	1.32	1.52	1.28	1.56	1.25	1.60
65	1.41	1.47	1.38	1.50	1.35	1.53	1.31	1.57	1.28	1.61
70	1.43	1.49	1.40	1.52	1.37	1.55	1.34	1.58	1.31	1.61
75	1.45	1.50	1.42	1.53	1.39	1.56	1.37	1.59	1.34	1.62
80	1.47	1.52	1.44	1.54	1.42	1.57	1.39	1.60	1.36	1.62
85	1.48	1.53	1.46	1.55	1.43	1.58	1.41	1.60	1.39	1.63
90	1.50	1.54	1.47	1.56	1.45	1.59	1.43	1.61	1.41	1.64
95	1.51	1.55	1.49	1.57	1.47	1.60	1.45	1.62	1.42	1.64
100	1.52	1.56	1.50	1.58	1.48	1.60	1.46	1.63	1.44	1.65

Source: From J. Durbin and G. S. Watson, "Testing for serial correlation in least squares regression, II." *Biometrika*, 1951, 30, pp. 159–178. Reproduced by permission of the *Biometrika* Trustees.

Table 17   Critical Values for the Wilcoxon Rank Sum Test: Independent Samples

a. $\alpha = .025$ one-tailed; $\alpha = .05$ two-tailed

n_2 \ n_1	3		4		5		6		7		8		9		10	
	T_L	T_U	T_L	T_U	T_L	T_U	T_L	T_U	T_L	T_U	T_L	T_U	T_L	T_U	T_L	T_U
3	5	16	6	18	6	21	7	23	7	26	8	28	8	31	9	33
4	6	18	11	25	12	28	12	32	13	35	14	38	15	41	16	44
5	6	21	12	28	18	37	19	41	20	45	21	49	22	53	24	56
6	7	23	12	32	19	41	26	52	28	56	29	61	31	65	32	70
7	7	26	13	35	20	45	28	56	37	68	39	73	41	78	43	83
8	8	28	14	38	21	49	29	61	39	73	49	87	51	93	54	98
9	8	31	15	41	22	53	31	65	41	78	51	93	63	108	66	114
10	9	33	16	44	24	56	32	70	43	83	54	98	66	114	79	131

b. $\alpha = .05$ one-tailed; $\alpha = .10$ two-tailed

n_2 \ n_1	3		4		5		6		7		8		9		10	
	T_L	T_U	T_L	T_U	T_L	T_U	T_L	T_U	T_L	T_U	T_L	T_U	T_L	T_U	T_L	T_U
3	6	15	7	17	7	20	8	22	9	24	9	27	10	29	11	31
4	7	17	12	24	13	27	14	30	15	33	16	36	17	39	18	42
5	7	20	13	27	19	36	20	40	22	43	24	46	25	50	26	54
6	8	22	14	30	20	40	28	50	30	54	32	58	33	63	35	67
7	9	24	15	33	22	43	30	54	39	66	41	71	43	76	46	80
8	9	27	16	36	24	46	32	58	41	71	52	84	54	90	57	95
9	10	29	17	39	25	50	33	63	43	76	54	90	66	105	69	111
10	11	31	18	42	26	54	35	67	46	80	57	95	69	111	83	127

Source: From F. Wilcoxon and R. A. Wilcox, "Some Rapid Approximate Statistical Procedures," 1964, pp. 20–23. Reproduced with the permission of American Cynamid Company.

Table 18   Critical Values for the Wilcoxon Paired-Difference Signed Ranks Test

One-tailed	Two-tailed	n = 5	n = 6	n = 7	n = 8	n = 9	n = 10
$\alpha = .05$	$\alpha = .10$	1	2	4	6	8	11
$\alpha = .025$	$\alpha = .05$		1	2	4	6	8
$\alpha = .01$	$\alpha = .02$			0	2	3	5
$\alpha = .005$	$\alpha = .01$				0	2	3
		n = 11	n = 12	n = 13	n = 14	n = 15	n = 16
$\alpha = .05$	$\alpha = .10$	14	17	21	26	30	36
$\alpha = .025$	$\alpha = .05$	11	14	17	21	25	30
$\alpha = .01$	$\alpha = .02$	7	10	13	16	20	24
$\alpha = .005$	$\alpha = .01$	5	7	10	13	16	19
		n = 17	n = 18	n = 19	n = 20	n = 21	n = 22
$\alpha = .05$	$\alpha = .10$	41	47	54	60	68	75
$\alpha = .025$	$\alpha = .05$	35	40	46	52	59	66
$\alpha = .01$	$\alpha = .02$	28	33	38	43	49	56
$\alpha = .005$	$\alpha = .01$	23	28	32	37	43	49
		n = 23	n = 24	n = 25	n = 26	n = 27	n = 28
$\alpha = .05$	$\alpha = .10$	83	92	101	110	120	130
$\alpha = .025$	$\alpha = .05$	73	81	90	98	107	117
$\alpha = .01$	$\alpha = .02$	62	69	77	85	93	102
$\alpha = .005$	$\alpha = .01$	55	61	68	76	84	92
		n = 29	n = 30	n = 31	n = 32	n = 33	n = 34
$\alpha = .05$	$\alpha = .10$	141	152	163	175	188	201
$\alpha = .025$	$\alpha = .05$	127	137	148	159	171	183
$\alpha = .01$	$\alpha = .02$	111	120	130	141	151	162
$\alpha = .005$	$\alpha = .01$	100	109	118	128	138	149
		n = 35	n = 36	n = 37	n = 38	n = 39	
$\alpha = .05$	$\alpha = .10$	214	228	242	256	271	
$\alpha = .025$	$\alpha = .05$	195	208	222	235	250	
$\alpha = .01$	$\alpha = .02$	174	186	198	211	224	
$\alpha = .005$	$\alpha = .01$	160	171	183	195	208	
		n = 40	n = 41	n = 42	n = 43	n = 44	n = 45
$\alpha = .05$	$\alpha = .10$	287	303	319	336	353	371
$\alpha = .025$	$\alpha = .05$	264	279	295	311	327	344
$\alpha = .01$	$\alpha = .02$	238	252	267	281	297	313
$\alpha = .005$	$\alpha = .01$	221	234	248	262	277	292
		n = 46	n = 47	n = 48	n = 49	n = 50	
$\alpha = .05$	$\alpha = .10$	389	408	427	446	466	
$\alpha = .025$	$\alpha = .05$	361	379	397	415	434	
$\alpha = .01$	$\alpha = .02$	329	345	362	380	398	
$\alpha = .005$	$\alpha = .01$	307	323	339	356	373	

Source: From F. Wilcoxon and R. A. Wilcox, "Some Rapid Approximate Statistical Procedures," 1964, p. 28. Reproduced with the permission of American Cynamid Company.

Table 19 Critical Values of Spearman's Rank
Correlation Coefficient

The α-values correspond to a one-tailed test of
$H_0: \rho = 0$. The value should be doubled for
two-tailed tests.

n	$\alpha = .05$	$\alpha = .025$	$\alpha = .01$	$\alpha = .005$
5	.900	—	—	—
6	.829	.886	.943	—
7	.714	.786	.893	—
8	.643	.738	.833	.881
9	.600	.683	.783	.833
10	.564	.648	.745	.794
11	.523	.623	.736	.818
12	.497	.591	.703	.780
13	.475	.566	.673	.745
14	.457	.545	.646	.716
15	.441	.525	.623	.689
16	.425	.507	.601	.666
17	.412	.490	.582	.645
18	.399	.476	.564	.625
19	.388	.462	.549	.608
20	.377	.450	.534	.591
21	.368	.438	.521	.576
22	.359	.428	.508	.562
23	.351	.418	.496	.549
24	.343	.409	.485	.537
25	.336	.400	.475	.526
26	.329	.392	.465	.515
27	.323	.385	.456	.505
28	.317	.377	.448	.496
29	.311	.370	.440	.487
30	.305	.364	.432	.478

Source: From E. G. Olds, "Distribution of Sums of Squares of Rank
Differences for Small Samples." *Annals of Mathematical Statistic*, 1938, 9.
Reproduced with the permission of the Editor, *Annals of Mathematical
Statistics.*

Table 20   Critical Values for the Theil Zero-Slope Test

x	4	5	8	9	12	13	16	17	20	21	24	25	28	29	32	33	36	37	40
0	.625	.592	.548	.540	.527	.524	.518	.516	.513	.112	.510	.509	.508	.507	.506	.506	.505	.505	.505
2	.375	.408	.452	.460	.473	.476	.482	.484	.487	.488	.490	.491	.492	.493	.494	.494	.495	.495	.495
4	.167	.242	.360	.381	.420	.429	.447	.452	.462	.464	.471	.472	.477	.478	.481	.482	.484	.484	.486
6	.042	.117	.274	.306	.369	.383	.412	.420	.436	.441	.451	.454	.461	.463	.468	.469	.473	.474	.477
8		.042	.199	.238	.319	.338	.378	.388	.411	.417	.432	.436	.446	.448	.455	.457	.462	.464	.468
10		.008	.138	.179	.273	.295	.345	.358	.387	.394	.413	.418	.430	.434	.442	.445	.452	.453	.459
12			.089	.130	.230	.255	.313	.328	.362	.371	.394	.400	.415	.419	.430	.433	.441	.443	.449
14			.054	.090	.190	.218	.282	.299	.339	.349	.375	.382	.400	.405	.417	.421	.430	.433	.440
16			.031	.060	.155	.184	.253	.271	.315	.327	.356	.364	.385	.390	.405	.409	.420	.423	.431
18			.016	.038	.125	.153	.225	.245	.293	.306	.338	.347	.370	.376	.392	.397	.409	.413	.422
20			.007	.022	.098	.126	.199	.220	.271	.285	.320	.330	.355	.362	.380	.385	.399	.403	.413
22			.002	.012	.076	.102	.175	.196	.250	.265	.303	.314	.341	.348	.368	.373	.388	.393	.404
24			.001	.006	.058	.082	.153	.174	.230	.246	.286	.297	.326	.334	.356	.362	.378	.383	.395
26			.000	.003	.043	.064	.133	.154	.211	.228	.270	.282	.312	.321	.344	.350	.368	.373	.386
28				.001	.031	.050	.114	.135	.193	.210	.254	.266	.298	.308	.332	.339	.358	.363	.377
30				.000	.022	.038	.097	.118	.176	.193	.238	.251	.285	.295	.320	.328	.347	.353	.369
32					.016	.029	.083	.102	.159	.177	.223	.237	.272	.282	.309	.317	.338	.344	.360
34					.010	.021	.070	.088	.144	.162	.209	.222	.259	.270	.298	.306	.328	.334	.351
36					.007	.015	.058	.076	.130	.147	.195	.209	.246	.257	.287	.295	.318	.325	.343
38					.004	.011	.048	.064	.117	.134	.181	.196	.234	.246	.276	.285	.308	.315	.334
40					.003	.007	.039	.054	.104	.121	.169	.183	.222	.234	.265	.274	.299	.306	.326
42					.002	.005	.032	.046	.093	.109	.156	.171	.211	.223	.255	.264	.290	.297	.318
44					.001	.003	.026	.038	.082	.098	.145	.159	.200	.212	.244	.254	.280	.288	.309
46					.000	.002	.021	.032	.073	.088	.134	.148	.189	.201	.234	.244	.271	.279	.301
48						.001	.016	.026	.064	.079	.123	.138	.178	.191	.224	.235	.262	.271	.293
50						.001	.013	.021	.056	.070	.113	.128	.168	.181	.215	.225	.254	.262	.285
52						.000	.010	.017	.049	.062	.104	.118	.158	.171	.206	.216	.245	.254	.277
54							.008	.014	.043	.055	.095	.109	.149	.162	.197	.207	.237	.245	.270
56							.006	.011	.037	.049	.087	.101	.140	.153	.188	.199	.228	.237	.262
58							.004	.009	.032	.043	.079	.093	.131	.144	.179	.190	.220	.229	.255
60							.003	.007	.027	.037	.072	.085	.123	.136	.171	.182	.212	.222	.247
62							.002	.005	.023	.032	.066	.078	.115	.128	.163	.174	.204	.214	.240
64							.002	.004	.020	.028	.059	.071	.108	.120	.155	.166	.197	.206	.233
66							.001	.003	.017	.024	.054	.065	.101	.112	.147	.158	.189	.199	.226
68							.001	.002	.014	.021	.048	.059	.094	.105	.140	.151	.182	.192	.219
70							.001	.002	.012	.018	.044	.054	.087	.099	.133	.144	.175	.185	.212
72							.000	.001	.010	.015	.039	.049	.081	.092	.126	.137	.168	.178	.205
74								.001	.008	.013	.035	.044	.075	.086	.119	.130	.161	.171	.199
76								.001	.007	.011	.031	.040	.070	.080	.113	.124	.155	.165	.192
78								.000	.006	.009	.028	.036	.065	.075	.107	.117	.148	.158	.186
80									.005	.008	.025	.032	.060	.070	.101	.111	.142	.152	.180
82									.004	.007	.022	.029	.055	.065	.095	.106	.136	.146	.174
84									.003	.005	.019	.026	.051	.060	.090	.100	.130	.140	.168
86									.002	.005	.017	.023	.047	.056	.085	.095	.124	.134	.162
88									.002	.004	.015	.021	.043	.052	.080	.090	.119	.129	.156
90									.002	.003	.013	.018	.039	.048	.075	.085	.114	.123	.151
92									.001	.002	.011	.016	.036	.044	.070	.080	.108	.118	.146
94									.001	.002	.010	.014	.033	.041	.066	.075	.103	.113	.140
96									.001	.002	.009	.013	.030	.037	.062	.071	.099	.108	.135
98									.001	.001	.007	.011	.027	.034	.058	.067	.094	.103	.130
100									.000	.001	.006	.010	.025	.031	.054	.063	.089	.098	.125

Table 20   (continued)

| | n | | | | | | | | | | | | | | | | | n |
x	6	7	10	11	14	15	18	19	22	23	26	27	30	31	34	35	38	39
1	.500	.500	.500	.500	.500	.500	.500	.500	.500	.500	.500	.500	.500	.500	.500	.500	.500	.500
3	.360	.386	.431	.440	.457	.461	.470	.473	.478	.479	.483	.484	.486	.487	.488	.489	.490	.490
5	.235	.281	.364	.381	.415	.423	.441	.445	.456	.458	.465	.467	.472	.473	.477	.478	.480	.481
7	.136	.191	.300	.324	.374	.385	.411	.418	.434	.438	.448	.451	.458	.460	.465	.466	.470	.472
9	.068	.119	.242	.271	.334	.349	.383	.391	.412	.417	.431	.434	.444	.446	.453	.455	.460	.462
11	.028	.068	.190	.223	.295	.313	.354	.365	.390	.397	.414	.418	.430	.433	.442	.444	.450	.452
13	.008	.035	.146	.179	.259	.279	.327	.339	.369	.377	.397	.402	.416	.420	.430	.433	.440	.443
15	.001	.015	.108	.141	.225	.248	.300	.314	.348	.357	.380	.386	.402	.407	.418	.422	.431	.433
17		.005	.078	.109	.194	.218	.275	.290	.328	.338	.363	.371	.389	.394	.407	.411	.421	.424
19		.001	.054	.082	.165	.190	.250	.267	.308	.319	.347	.355	.375	.381	.396	.400	.411	.414
21		.000	.036	.060	.140	.164	.227	.245	.289	.301	.331	.340	.362	.368	.384	.389	.401	.405
23			.023	.043	.117	.141	.205	.223	.270	.283	.316	.325	.349	.355	.373	.378	.392	.396
25			.014	.030	.096	.120	.184	.203	.252	.265	.300	.310	.336	.343	.362	.368	.382	.387
27			.008	.020	.079	.101	.165	.184	.234	.248	.285	.296	.323	.331	.351	.357	.373	.377
29			.005	.013	.063	.084	.147	.166	.217	.232	.270	.281	.310	.318	.340	.347	.363	.368
31			.002	.008	.050	.070	.130	.149	.201	.216	.256	.268	.298	.306	.329	.336	.354	.359
33			.001	.005	.040	.057	.115	.133	.186	.201	.242	.254	.286	.295	.319	.326	.345	.350
35			.000	.003	.031	.046	.100	.119	.171	.187	.229	.241	.274	.283	.308	.316	.336	.341
37				.002	.024	.037	.088	.105	.157	.173	.216	.228	.262	.272	.298	.306	.327	.333
39				.001	.018	.029	.076	.093	.144	.160	.203	.216	.251	.261	.288	.296	.318	.324
41				.000	.013	.023	.066	.082	.131	.147	.191	.204	.239	.250	.278	.286	.309	.315
43					.010	.018	.056	.072	.120	.135	.179	.192	.228	.239	.268	.277	.300	.307
45					.007	.014	.048	.062	.109	.124	.168	.181	.218	.229	.259	.267	.291	.298
47					.005	.010	.041	.054	.099	.114	.157	.170	.208	.219	.249	.258	.283	.290
49					.003	.008	.034	.047	.089	.104	.147	.160	.198	.209	.240	.249	.274	.282
51					.002	.006	.029	.040	.080	.094	.137	.150	.188	.199	.231	.240	.266	.274
53					.002	.004	.024	.034	.072	.086	.127	.141	.178	.190	.222	.232	.258	.266
55					.001	.003	.020	.029	.064	.078	.118	.132	.169	.181	.213	.223	.250	.258
57					.001	.002	.016	.025	.058	.070	.110	.123	.160	.172	.205	.215	.242	.250
59					.000	.001	.013	.021	.051	.063	.102	.115	.152	.164	.196	.206	.234	.243
61						.001	.011	.017	.045	.057	.094	.107	.144	.155	.188	.198	.227	.235
63						.001	.009	.014	.040	.051	.087	.099	.136	.147	.180	.191	.219	.228
65						.000	.007	.012	.035	.046	.080	.092	.128	.140	.173	.183	.212	.221
67							.005	.010	.031	.041	.073	.085	.121	.132	.165	.176	.205	.214
69							.004	.008	.027	.036	.067	.079	.114	.125	.158	.168	.198	.207
71							.003	.006	.024	.032	.062	.073	.107	.118	.151	.161	.191	.200
73							.003	.005	.021	.028	.057	.067	.100	.112	.144	.154	.184	.193
75							.002	.004	.018	.025	.052	.062	.094	.105	.137	.148	.177	.187
77							.001	.003	.015	.022	.047	.057	.088	.099	.131	.141	.171	.180
79							.001	.003	.013	.019	.043	.052	.083	.093	.125	.135	.165	.174
81							.001	.002	.011	.017	.039	.048	.077	.088	.119	.129	.158	.168
83							.001	.002	.010	.015	.035	.044	.072	.082	.113	.123	.152	.162
85							.000	.001	.008	.013	.032	.040	.067	.077	.107	.117	.147	.156
87								.001	.007	.011	.029	.036	.063	.072	.102	.112	.141	.150
89								.001	.006	.009	.026	.033	.059	.068	.097	.107	.135	.145
91								.001	.005	.008	.023	.030	.054	.063	.092	.101	.130	.139
93								.000	.004	.007	.021	.027	.051	.059	.087	.096	.125	.134
95									.003	.006	.019	.025	.047	.055	.082	.092	.120	.129
97									.003	.005	.017	.022	.043	.052	.078	.087	.115	.124
99									.002	.004	.015	.020	.040	.048	.074	.083	.110	.119
101									.002	.004	.013	.018	.037	.045	.070	.078	.105	.114

Appendices C–F

COMPUTER SOFTWARE TUTORIALS

The following appendices provide keystroke commands for selected statistical software packages:

Appendix C: SAS

Appendix D: SPSS

Appendix E: MINITAB

Appendix F: ASP

These appendices are in the free *Computer Software Tutorials: SAS, SPSS, MINITAB, ASP* manual that accompanies this text.

ANSWERS
TO ODD-NUMBERED
EXERCISES

■ *Chapter 1*

1.1   **a.** Qualitative   **b.** Quantitative   **c.** Qualitative   **d.** Quantitative
       e. Quantitative   **f.** Qualitative

1.3   **a.** Canadian manufacturing workers
       b. Behavior type: qualitative; age: quantitative; managerial level: qualitative; number of employees supervised: quantitative; performance rating: quantitative

1.5   **a.** Qualitative   **b.** Qualitative   **c.** Qualitative   **d.** Quantitative
       e. Quantitative

1.7   **a.** Quality of all gear shifts produced
       b. Status (defective or not) of each of the 50 gear shifts tested per hour

1.9   **a.** Analytic   **b.** Annual prime interest rates from 1987 to 1993
       c. Prime interest rates for all years, past, present, and future

1.11   **a.** Merit increase: quantitative   **b.** Sample

1.15   Not every person will return the questionnaire

1.17   Sample probably not selected at random; may not be representative of population

1.21   **a.** Quantitative   **b.** Qualitative   **c.** Qualitative   **d.** Quantitative

1.23   **a.** Enumerative   **b.** All consumers   **c.** 1,000 consumers polled
       d. Qualitative   **e.** Infiniti ads are best-recalled commercial

1.25   **a.** Performance ratings for all type A workers; performance ratings for all type B workers
       b. Job performance; quantitative
       c. Yes
       d. Calculate the difference between the average performance rating of the sample of type A workers and the average performance rating of the sample of type B workers
       e. No

1.27   **a.** Analytic   **b.** Annual sales for all years, past and future

■ *Chapter 2*

2.1   **a.** Pipe material; location; stability of soil; corrosiveness of soil
       b. Bar graph, pie chart

2.3   **a.** Qualitative   **b.** (5, 40); (3, 40); (6, 48); (4, 40)   **c.** 10; 4; 3; 8
       d. .40; .16; .12; .32

2.5   Average rating is least likely to occur

2.9   **c.** Population

2.11   Employed in service industry, bachelor's degree, married

2.13   **a.** 21, 22, 23, 24, 25, 26, 27, 28, 29, 30, 31

b.

21	3, 5
22	4, 6, 7, 8
23	4, 7
24	1
25	4
26	5, 6, 7, 8
27	0, 4
28	5, 8
29	1
30	3, 3
31	6, 9
32	0

2.15 **a.**

1	1, 2, 1, 6, 6
2	1
3	5, 3
4	5, 3, 0
5	9, 3, 0
6	3, 7, 5, 4
7	3, 6, 4
8	6, 4, 4, 9, 2
9	4, 7

2.19 **a.** Stem is leftmost digit (6, 7, 8, or 9) **b.** .923

2.21 Brand name

2.23 **a.** 8.6   **b.** 1.8   **c.** 1.05–2.85, 2.85–4.65, 4.65–6.45, 6.45–8.25, 8.25–10.05

2.25 **a.** .02, .02, .06, .08, .20, .14, .10, .08, .06, .04, .06, .04, .06, .04
 b. No

2.27 **a.** Quantitative   **b.** Histogram; 64%

2.29 **a.** .16   **b.** .27

2.33 Yes

2.39 **a.** Bar chart   **b.** 16%   **c.** 200   **d.** Sample

2.41 **b.** Yes; yes

2.43 **a.** Bar graph   **c.** $\dfrac{1}{50} = .02$

2.47 **a.** Qualitative
 c. The majority of the business graduates receiving job offers (60%) were accounting majors

2.49 **a.** Qualitative   **b.** Bar graph or pie chart
 d. Approx. 13.2%   **e.** Approx. 44.9%

■ *Chapter 3*

3.1 **a.** 12   **b.** 40   **c.** 7   **d.** 21   **e.** 144

3.3 **a.** 11.2   **b.** 12   **c.** 30

3.5 **a.** 6   **b.** 50   **c.** 42.8

3.7 Mean = 4.6; median = 4

3.9 **a.** Mean = 5; median = 5; mode = 5 **b.** Mean = 12; median = 5; mode = 5
c. Mean = 0; median = 0; mode = 0 **d.** Mean = 0; median = 4.5; mode = 9

3.11 **a.** Mean = 630.32, median = 633, modes = 608, 616, 635, 651
c. Mean = 29.488, median = 30.1, mode = 12

3.13 Mean = 91.044, median = 92

3.15 **b.** Mean = 9.33; median = 7; mode = 5; yes

3.17 **a.** Mean = .188, median = .11, modes = .25, .11, .03, and .05; mean or median
b. Mean = .085, median = .03, mode = 0; median
c. Mean = .133, median = .07, mode = .03; mean or median

3.19 **a.** Variance = 9; standard deviation = 3
b. Variance = 144; standard deviation = 12
c. Variance = .0025; standard deviation = .05

3.21 Range = 8; variance = 3.66; standard deviation = 1.91

3.23 **a.** Approx. 70% **b.** Approx. 95% **c.** Approx. 100%

3.25 **a.** 74.31 **b.** 20.94 **c.** (32.43, 116.19)

3.27 **a.** $\bar{x} = 33.68$, $s^2 = 1{,}104.48$, $s = 33.23$
b. At least 75% (if not mound-shaped); approx. 95% (if mound-shaped)
c. 88%

3.29 **a.** Mound-shaped, nearly symmetric **b.** Empirical rule
  c. .967

3.31 **b.** Mean = 159.38, median = 77.4, std. dev. = 262.5
d. Mean = 114.26, median = 76.0, std. dev. = 90.0

3.33 **a.** 80%; 20% **b.** 50%; 50% **c.** 24%; 76%
d. 75%; 25% **e.** 25%; 75%

3.35 **a.** −1.6 **b.** .6 **c.** 1.6

3.37 **a.** $Q_L = 3.5$; $M = 6.1$; $Q_U = 8.2$ **b.** 1.2

3.39 $M = 1.2013$, $Q_L = 1.1136$, $Q_U = 1.3095$

3.41 **a.** $Q_L = 17$, $Q_U = 29$ **b.** 20 **c.** 1.37

3.43 **b.** $Q_L = 13$, $M = 15$, $Q_U = 18$ **c.** 19

3.45 **a.** $Q_L = 2$, $M = 7.1$, $Q_U = 19.2$ **b.** $z = 3.54$

3.49 **a.** 12.60; yes **b.** Measurement from a different population

3.51 **a.** Yes; 10.55 is a suspect outlier; 8.05, 8.72, 8.72, and 8.80 are highly suspect outliers
b. 8.05 is an outlier **c.** No **d.** No outliers

3.53 **b.** Suspect outliers: 49.7 and 58.5; highly suspect outliers: 76.5

3.55 **a.** 41.135 **b.** 40.4 **c.** Mean or median **d.** 15.97

3.57 **b.** Mean = 8.36, median = 6, mode = 5; median
c. range = 36, variance = 79.94, std. dev. = 8.94 **d.** Yes, $z = 3.09$

3.59 **b.** .95 **c.** Between 7.06 and 27.70 **d.** Between .80 and 28.32

3.61 **b.** Not likely ($z = 2.30$) **c.** Decrease; decrease
d. $\bar{x} = 3.72$, $s = 2.59$

3.63 **b.** −1.56 **c.** −2.23

3.65   **a.** Mean $= 117.82$, median $= 117.5$, mode $= 97$
b. Range $= 62$, variance $= 225.33$, standard deviation $= 15.01$

c.

Interval	Number in Interval	Number Expected by Empirical Rule
$\bar{x} \pm s$ (102.81, 132.83)	31	34
$\bar{x} \pm 2s$ (87.80, 147.84)	49	48
$\bar{x} \pm 3s$ (72.79, 162.85)	50	Almost all

d. No outliers
e. 137

3.67   **a.** Common stock price: $(-10.46, 44.10)$; cash dividends per share: $(-25.35, 57.69)$; earnings per share: $(-18.63, 75.21)$
b. Approx. .95   **c.** No; yes

■ *Chapter 4*

4.1   **a.** $\frac{1}{6}$
4.3 $\frac{2}{365} = .0054795$
4.5   .076
4.9   **a.** $\frac{1}{2}, \frac{1}{2}, \frac{1}{2}$ **b.** $\bar{A} = \{4, 5, 6\}$; $\bar{B} = \{2, 4, 6\}$; $\bar{C} = \{1, 3, 5\}$
         c. $\frac{1}{2}, \frac{1}{2}, \frac{1}{2}$ **d.** B and C are complementary events
4.11   **a.** $\frac{1}{4}$ **b.** $\frac{1}{4}$ **c.** $\frac{3}{4}$ **d.** At least 1 tail; $\frac{3}{4}$
4.15   **a.** Basic browns, true-blue greens, greenback greens, sprouts, grousers
         b. .28, .11, .11, .26, .24   **c.** .52   **d.** .48
4.17   **a.** .18   **b.** .28   **c.** .99   **d.** .58
4.19   **a.** (40, 300), (40, 350), (40, 400), (45, 300), (45, 350), (45,400), (50, 300), (50, 350), (50, 400)
         b. No
4.21   **a.** $\frac{8}{168}$ **b.** $\frac{2}{7}$
4.23   **a.** .97   **b.** .04   **c.** No
4.25   **b.** .28   **c.** .56
4.27   **a.** No   **b.** $\frac{1}{17,000,000,000,000}$ **c.** Greater than .5
4.29   **a.** (AA, AB, AC); $\frac{3}{9}$ **b.** (AB, BB, CB); $\frac{3}{9}$ **c.** (AB); $\frac{1}{3}$
         d. Yes   **e.** $\frac{1}{9}$
4.31 $P(A) = .55, P(B|A) > \frac{1}{3}$
4.33   **a.** $\frac{50}{188} = .266$ **b.** $\frac{47}{50} = .94$ **c.** No
4.35   **a.** $\frac{228}{234} = .974$ **b.** $\frac{3}{25} = .12$
4.37 $\frac{1}{8,000} = .000125$
4.39   **a.** 3.27×10^{-25} **b.** .9999999776   **c.** .000000024
4.41   **a.** .00000001   **b.** Claim is probably false

4.43   **a.** $\frac{8}{36}$ **b.** $\frac{4}{36}$ **c.** $\frac{8}{36}$ **d.** $\frac{4}{36}$

4.45   .6

4.47   **a.** .468   **b.** .204   **c.** .021   **d.** .563
           e. .585   **f.** .256

4.49   .24

4.51   **a.** .63   **b.** .57   **c.** .21   **d.** .41
           e. 0   **f.** .79   **g.** $\frac{41}{63}$

4.53   .2088

4.55   **a.** $\frac{47}{52}$ **b.** $P(\text{Lose savings} \mid \text{Video player}) = \frac{35}{47}$ **c.** $\frac{35}{52}$

4.57   **a.** .80   **b.** .20

4.59 $(P_1, P_2), (P_1, P_3), (P_1, P_4), (P_1, P_5), (P_1, P_6), (P_1, P_7), (P_1, P_8), (P_2, P_3), (P_2, P_4), (P_2, P_5),$
           $(P_2, P_6), (P_2, P_7), (P_2, P_8), (P_3, P_4), (P_3, P_5), (P_3, P_6), (P_3, P_7), (P_3, P_8), (P_4, P_5), (P_4, P_6),$
           $(P_4, P_7), (P_4, P_8), (P_5, P_6), (P_5, P_7), (P_5, P_8), (P_6, P_7), (P_6, P_8), (P_7, P_8)$

4.61   No

4.63   **a.** .57   **b.** .098   **c.** .143

4.65   **a.** .0344   **b.** .1250   **c.** .1384

4.67   **a.** $\frac{6}{16}$ **b.** $\frac{15}{16}$ **c.** No

4.69   **a.** .06   **b.** .94

4.71   **a.** .25   **d.** .75

4.73   **a.** $\frac{24}{36}$ **b.** $\frac{5}{36}$ **c.** $\frac{1}{6}$

4.75   **a.** .493   **b.** .507   **c.** .476

■ *Chapter 5*

5.1   **a.** −5, 0, 2, 5   **b.** 2   **c.** .5   **d.** .2

5.3   **a.** .8, .16, .032, .0064, .00128   **b.** .99968; no   **c.** .96

5.5   **a.** Yes   **c.** .15   **d.** .75

5.7 $\mu = .3$, $\sigma = 3.0$

5.9   **a.** Between \$5 and \$30   **b.** \$15   **c.** (.1, 2.7)

5.11   **a.** $\mu = 1.4$, $\sigma = .65$

5.13   **a.** 24   **b.** 4   **c.** 10   **d.** .064   **e.** .2304

5.15   **a.** .0625, .25, .375, .25, .0625   **b.** .3125   **c.** .6875

5.17   **a.** .8369   **b.** .9976   **c.** .0308   **d.** .3087

5.19   **a.** $\mu = 1$, $\sigma = .95$ **b.** $\mu = 1.5$, $\sigma = 1.16$ **c.** $\mu = 2$, $\sigma = 1.34$
           d. $\mu = 2.5$, $\sigma = 1.5$

5.21   **b.** .0574   **c.** .9984   **d.** $\mu = 9$, $\sigma^2 = .9$

5.23   No

5.25   **a.** 2   **b.** 1.34

5.27   **a.** .1719

5.29   **a.** .838   **b.** .002

5.31 **a.** .402   **b.** .161

5.33 **a.** .011109   **b.** .135335   **c.** .002479   **d.** .272532
          e. .025   **f.** .047   **g.** .224

5.35 **b.** $\mu = 2.5$; $\sigma = 1.58$ **c.** 2.5 ± 3.16; .958

5.37 **a.** .3233   **b.** .0361   **c.** .1353   **d.** .4060

5.39 **a.** .10   **b.** .074

5.41 **a.** .2510   **b.** .5578   **c.** $(.2231)^3 = .0111$

5.43 90 ± 18.97

5.45 .0679

5.47 **a.** $\frac{1}{15}, \frac{8}{15}, \frac{6}{15}$ **c.** $\mu = 1.33$; $\sigma = .596$ **d.** 1.33 ± 1.192; $\frac{14}{15} = .933$

5.49 **a.** $\frac{350}{792}$ **b.** $\frac{246}{792}$ **c.** $\frac{21}{792}$ **d.** $\frac{196}{792}$
          e. 2.92   **f.** .88   **g.** $\frac{735}{792} = .928$

5.51 **a.** $\frac{4}{7}$ **b.** $\frac{4}{35}$

5.53 **a.** $\frac{1}{455}$ **b.** $\frac{235}{455}$

5.55 .467

5.57 **a.** $\frac{91}{228}$ **b.** $\frac{1}{114}$ **c.** $\frac{137}{228}$

5.59 **b.** $\mu = 3.33$; $\sigma = 2.79$ **c.** 3.33 ± 5.58; .942

5.61 **a.** .24   **b.** .216   **c.** .64   **d.** .052
          e. .6   **f.** 2.5   **g.** 1.94

5.63 **a** Geometric distribution with $\pi = .001$ **b.** .995
          c. Claim is probably false since $P(x \leq 5) = .005$

5.65 **a.** 2.5   **b.** .130

5.67 **a.** .226   **b.** $\mu = 20$; $\sigma^2 = 380$; $\sigma = 19.49$ **c.** 20 ± 38.98

5.69 .049; .0956; .1399; .1821

5.71 **a.** 0   **b.** .3980   **c.** .0352
          d. Either the percentage of troubled employees is less than 20% or one or more of the sampled
          employees are not being entirely honest

5.73 **a.** .9975   **b.** .9502   **c.** .9478

5.75 **a.** .7763   **b.** .1118

5.77 **a.** $\frac{1}{19}$ **b.** $\frac{17}{38}$ **c.** $\frac{1}{2}$

5.79 **a.** .1393   **b.** .5858

5.81 **a.** .7617   **b.** $\mu = 2.63$; $\sigma^2 = 4.29$; $\sigma = 2.07$

5.83 **a.** .1125   **b.** .4679   **c.** .0111

5.85 **a.** 25,256.57   **b.** 152.27   **c.** 36.41
          d. True percentage is higher than 8.2%

■ *Chapter 6*

6.1 **a.** .3849   **b.** .4319   **c.** .1844   **d.** .4147   **e.** .0918

6.3 **a.** .25   **b.** .92   **c.** 1.28   **d.** 1.65   **e.** 1.96

6.5 **a.** .75   **b.** -1.00 **c.** -1.625 **d.** 2.00   **e.** -2.00

6.7   **a.** -1.28 **b.** -1.04 **c.** $-.52$ **d.** .00

6.9   **a.** .0351   **b.** .2578   **c.** .2119

6.11 **a.** .9406   **b.** .0068

6.13 **a.** .0869   **b.** .2743

6.15 **a.** 0   **b.** 1   **c.** 0   **d.** $-.675$ **e.** .675

6.17 **a.** .9671   **b.** .2611   **c.** No

6.19 No; skewed right

6.21 IQR/$s \approx 1.17$; approx. normal

6.25 Old: IQR/$s = .46$, no; new: IQR/$s = 1.27$, yes

6.27 **a.** Yes   **b.** No   **c.** No   **d.** Yes

6.29 **a.** .2500   **b.** .2483

6.31 **a.** .0139   **b.** .4052   **c.** .017, .416; yes

6.33 .8186

6.35 **a.** $\mu = 6$, $\sigma = 2.31$ **b.** $\mu = 0$, $\sigma = 2.89$
         c. $\mu = .5$, $\sigma = .29$ **d.** $\mu = 67.5$, $\sigma = 4.33$

6.37 **a.** $\mu = 150$, $\sigma = 28.87$ **b.** (92.26, 207.74)   **c.** 1.0

6.39 **a.** $\mu = 7$, $\sigma = .29$ **b.** .3

6.41 **a.** $\mu = 1.375$, $\sigma^2 = .2552$ **b.** 1.0   **c.** .286

6.43 **a.** .0183   **b.** .7769   **c.** .5

6.45 **a.** 1,000,000   **b.** .135   **c.** .777

6.47 Yes; $P(x \geq 15) = .0235$

6.49 **a.** .3679   **b.** .6065   **c.** .1353   **d.** .0041

6.51 **a.** .0122   **b.** \$256.4 million

6.53 **a.** Yes   **b.** .1335   **c.** .26

6.55 **a.** $\sigma = 10$ **b.** .753   **c.** .135

6.57 **a.** $\mu = 5$, $\sigma^2 = 8.33$ **b.** .3

6.59 **a.** .7642   **b.** .2037   **c.** 54,175 miles

6.61 **a.** Approx. 0
         b. Percentage of adults who believe tax is unfair is greater than 60%

6.63 **a.** .0228   **b.** ≈ 0 **c.** 30.08   **d.** EPA estimate is too high

■ *Chapter 7*

7.1   **c.** Mean $= 4.74$; standard deviation $= 1.28$

7.3   **a.** μ; 1

7.9   **a.** $\mu_{\bar{x}} = 10$; $\sigma_{\bar{x}} = 2$ **b.** $\mu_{\bar{x}} = 20$; $\sigma_{\bar{x}} = 1$
         c. $\mu_{\bar{x}} = 50$; $\sigma_{\bar{x}} = 30$ **d.** $\mu_{\bar{x}} = 100$; $\sigma_{\bar{x}} = 20$

7.11 **a.** .9932   **b.** .2061   **c.** .0159

7.13 **a.** Approx. normal with $\mu_{\bar{x}} = 28.5$ and $\sigma_{\bar{x}} = 5.98$ **b.** .6203   **c.** .5987

7.15 **a.** .0166   **b.** Strong evidence that $\mu > 3.00$

7.17 **a.** .1314

7.19 **a.** Approx. normal with $\mu_{\bar{x}_{25}} = 17$ and $\sigma_{\bar{x}_{25}} = 2$
  b. Approx. normal with $\mu_{\bar{x}_{100}} = 17$ and $\sigma_{\bar{x}_{100}} = 1$
  c. $P(15 < \bar{x}_{100} < 19)$
  d. .6826; .9544

7.21 **a.** .4325 **b.** Approx. 0 **c.** No **d.** Yes
  e. Most likely $\mu < 35$

7.23 **a.** 1.452; 2.548 **b.** .0026

7.25 **a.** .3023 **b.** .0668

7.27 **a.** .0139 **b.** Yes

7.29 **a.** Approx. normal with $\mu_{\bar{x}} = 8,000$ and $\sigma_{\bar{x}} = 237.17$ **b.** .0174 **c.** .9652

7.31 **a.** .8757 **b.** .5636

■ *Chapter 8*

8.3 **a.** 81 ± 1.97 **b.** 81 ± 2.35 **c.** 81 ± 3.10

8.5 **a.** $5.7 \pm .66$ **b.** 5.7 ± 1.03

8.9 **a.** $1.94 \pm .13$ **b.** Increase n or decrease confidence coefficient

8.11 **a.** .95 **d.** Sampling rates are normal

8.13 **c.** .97

8.15 **a.** 2.898 **b.** 2.262 **c.** 1.761

8.17 **a.** 33 ± 4.97 **b.** 33 ± 2.22 **c.** 33 ± 1.65

8.21 **a.** $\bar{x} = 25,964.7$, $s = 42,807.8$ **b.** $25,964.7 \pm 20,034.4$
  c. Distribution of salaries is approx. normal **d.** Not random sample of CEOs

8.23 **a.** $.604 \pm .117$ **b.** Narrower

8.25 **a.** 74.31 ± 15.57 **b.** Yes

8.27 **a.** .031 **b.** .016 **c.** .043

8.29 **a.** $.2 \pm .078$ **b.** $.2 \pm .035$

8.31 **a.** .075 **b.** $.075 \pm .028$

8.33 **a.** $.64 \pm .028$ **c.** Narrower

8.35 **a.** $.75 \pm .1225$ **b.** Yes

8.37 $.18 \pm .035$

8.39 **a.** $\mu_{(\bar{x}_1-\bar{x}_2)} \approx 10$, $\sigma_{(\bar{x}_1-\bar{x}_2)} \approx 1.31$ **b.** $\mu_{(\bar{x}_1-\bar{x}_2)} \approx 13$, $\sigma_{(\bar{x}_1-\bar{x}_2)} \approx 2$

8.43 **a.** 9.8 ± 7.94 **b.** 9.8 ± 9.61 **c.** 9.8 ± 13.14

8.45 **a.** -5 ± 1.36

8.47 **a.** .1 **b.** $.1 \pm .27$ **d.** Increase n's

8.51 $.103 \pm .116$

8.53 **a.** $\bar{d} = 1.75$, $s_d = 2.63$ **c.** 1.75 ± 4.18

8.55 19.3 ± 1.44

8.57 **a.** $-4.83 \pm .997$ **b.** $\mu_{\text{DCF}} < \mu_{\text{F}}$

8.59 $0 \pm .09$

8.61 **a.** Same items selected at both supermarkets
b. 95% confident that $\mu_{\text{Winn}} < \mu_{\text{Publix}}$

8.63 **a.** $\mu_{(p_1-p_2)} \approx -.1$, $\sigma_{(p_1-p_2)} \approx .057$ **b.** $\mu_{(p_1-p_2)} \approx .05$, $\sigma_{(p_1-p_2)} \approx .037$
c. $\mu_{(p_1-p_2)} \approx -.2$, $\sigma_{(p_1-p_2)} \approx .033$

8.65 **a.** $.1 \pm .070$ **b.** $.1 \pm .109$

8.67 **a.** $.41 \pm .105$

8.69 **a.** $.195 \pm .137$

8.71 $.078 \pm .035$

8.73 **a.** 683   **b.** 246   **c.** 427

8.75 **a.** 57   **b.** 99   **c.** 596

8.77 245

8.79 4,802

8.81 752

8.83 **a.** 16.0128, 1.68987   **b.** 26.2962, 7.96164   **c.** 25.1882, 2.15585
d. 34.1696, 9.59083

8.85 **a.** (2.13, 2.97)   **b.** (.015, .029)   **c.** (25.3, 42.5)   **d.** (.97, 3.56)

8.87 (.0028, .0105)

8.89 **a.** (4.73, 9.44)   **b.** No

8.91 **a.** (147.5, 544.1)
b. Population of foreign revenue percentages is approx. normal; yes

8.93 $.21 \pm .024$

8.95 **a.** .420   **b.** .279   **c.** $.141 \pm .049$ **d.** Males

8.97 28,160

8.99 **a.** $-.071 \pm .048$

8.101 **a.** -14.08 ± 1.95 **b.** Yes   **c.** 629

8.103 (37.81, 358.3)

8.105 **a.** .692   **b.** $.692 \pm .298$ **c.** Small sample
d. Increase n or reduce confidence coefficient; increase n **e.** 568

8.107 (.101, .371)

■ *Chapter 9*

9.1 680 ± 7.47

9.3 $.81 \pm .025$

9.5 $779,030 \pm 305,620.84$

9.7 **a.** 371 ± 18.89 **b.** $100,912 \pm 5,138.05$

9.9 $353,698.8 \pm 17,975.0$

9.11 43

9.13 2,252

9.15   327

9.17 $477,100 \pm 10,624$

9.19   **a.** $9.93 \pm .336$ **b.** $9.93 \pm .309$

9.21 $.0214 \pm .0076$

9.23 $n_1 = 50; n_2 = 20; n_3 = 131$

9.25 $n_1 = 92; n_2 = 37; n_3 = 239$

9.27   Panhandle: 128; central: 385; south: 769

9.29   **a.** Test markets; all test markets   **b.** Cost savings
        c. L.A.: 45; Chic.: 23; N.Y.: 45

9.31 $4,889.6 \pm 1,412.65$

9.35 171.8 ± 87.7

9.37   7

9.39   10

9.41   8

9.43   **a.** 461.7 ± 27.21 **b.** $1,846,800 \pm 108,857.05$ **c.** $.44 \pm .137$ **d.** $n = 167$

9.45   **a.** 44.82 ± 8.80 **b.** $242,035.71 \pm 47,511.21$ **c.** $.357 \pm .048$ **d.** 14

9.47 $.079 \pm .016$

9.49 $25,964.7 \pm 16,780.6$

9.51 $2,217.39 \pm 555.13$

■ *Chapter 10*

10.3 $H_0: \mu = 60, H_a: \mu > 60$

10.5 $H_0: \pi = .04, H_a: \pi < .04$

10.7   One-tailed: 3, 4, 5; two-tailed: 2, 6

10.9   Type I: claim $\mu > 60$ when $\mu = 60$, Type II: claim $\mu = 60$ when $\mu > 60$

10.11   Type I: claim $\pi < .04$ when $\pi = .04$, Type II: claim $\pi = .4$ when $\pi < .04$

10.13   **a.** $\alpha = P(\text{Reject } H_0 | H_0 \text{ true})$ **b.** Chance of error is α
        c. $\alpha + \beta = 1$ implies an error will always occur

10.15 β is unknown

10.17   **a.** -3.33 **b.** -2.36 **c.** 2.36 **d.** 1.18

10.19   **a.** $\alpha = .025$ **b.** $\alpha = .05$ **c.** $\alpha = .01$

10.21   **a.** $z = -2.65$ **b.** $z < -2.33$ **c.** Reject H_0 at $\alpha = .01$

10.23   **a.** $.0250$ **b.** $.05$ **c.** $.0038$ **d.** $.1056$

10.25   **a.** $.0022$ **b.** $.0571$ **c** $.0139$ **d.** $.003$

10.27   Evidence to conclude $\mu > 60$

10.29   Insufficient evidence to conclude $\pi < .04$

10.31 $.004$; reject H_0

10.33   Power $= 1 - \beta$

10.35   **a.** $1,016.31$ **b.** 74.91 **c.** 13.63

10.37 **a.** .5080   **b.** .3859   **c.** .1814

10.39 .0756

10.41 Reject H_0; do not reject H_0

10.45 Decreases

10.47 **a.** $z < -2.58$ or $z > 2.58$ **b.** $z < -2.33$ or $z > 2.33$
          c. $z < -2.05$ or $z > 2.05$

10.49 **a.** $H_0: \mu = 22, H_a: \mu < 22$ **b.** $H_0: (\pi_1 - \pi_2) = 0, H_a: (\pi_1 - \pi_2) \neq 0$
          c. $H_0: (\mu_1 - \mu_2) = 0, H_a: (\mu_1 - \mu_2) > 0$ **d.** $H_0: (\mu_1 - \mu_2) = 0, H_a: (\mu_1 - \mu_2) > 0$
          e. $H_0: \pi = \frac{1}{6}, H_a: \pi \neq \frac{1}{6}$

10.51 **a.** $z > 2.33$ **b.** $z = 1.57$ **c.** Do not reject H_0 **f.** .0582
          g. .2420   **h.** Approx. 1

10.53 **a.** Type I: claim $\mu_1 > \mu_2$ when $\mu_1 = \mu_2$; Type II: claim $\mu_1 = \mu_2$ when $\mu_1 > \mu_2$

■ *Chapter 11*

11.1 **a.** .33   **b.** -10.64 **c.** -1.67

11.3 **a.** $t < -2.145$ or $t > 2.145$ **b.** $t < -2.977$ or $t > 2.977$
          c. $t < -1.761$ **d.** $t > 1.533$ **e.** $t > 1.318$

11.5 **a.** $z = -1.84$; do not reject H_0 **b.** $z = -1.84$; reject H_0
          c. .0329   **d.** .0329

11.7 **a.** $H_0: \mu = 88,000, H_a: \mu \neq 88,000$

11.9 $z = .87$; do not reject H_0

11.11 **a.** Yes; $z = 2.27$ **b.** $t = 1.07$; do not reject H_0 **c.** .0116; $p > .10$

11.15 Reject H_0

11.17 **a.** $z > 1.28$; $z = 1.41$; reject H_0 **b.** $z < -1.645$; $z = -1.53$; do not reject H_0
          c. $|z| > 2.58$; $z = -6.33$; reject H_0

11.19 **a.** $H_0: \pi = .52, H_a \; \pi \neq .52$

11.21 $z = 1.33$; reject H_0

11.23 Do not reject H_0; $z = 2.30$

11.25 Reject H_0; $z = 9.82$

11.27 **a.** $|z| > 2.58$ **b.** $|z| > 1.645$ **c.** $z > 1.645$ **d.** $z < -1.645$

11.29 **a.** $z = 2.03$; reject H_0 **b.** $z = 1.02$; do not reject H_0

11.31 $t = 1.53$; do not reject H_0

11.33 **a.** $H_0: \mu_1 - \mu_2 = 0, H_a: \mu_1 - \mu_2 > 0$ **b.** $z > 1.645$ **c.** Reject H_0

11.35 Statement valid

11.37 **a.** $t = -.0187$; do not reject H_0 **b.** $t = -.019$; do not reject H_0

11.39 **a.** $H_0: \mu_1 - \mu_2 = 0, H_a: \mu_1 - \mu_2 < 0$ **c.** Reject H_0
          b. $t > 2.132$; $t = 13.42$; reject H_0

11.41 **a.** $|z| > 2.58$; $z = 9.20$; reject H_0
          c. $t < -1.476$; $t = -3.27$; reject H_0

11.43 **a.** $t = 1.34$; do not reject H_0

11.45 $t = -2.63$; reject H_0

11.47 Yes; $t = 2.48$

11.49 No; $t = -.45$

11.51 **a.** $t = 3.08$; reject H_0 **b.** $t = 1.54$; do not reject H_0

11.53 **a.** $z = 1.04$; do not reject H_0 **b.** $z = 3.29$; reject H_0

11.55 Yes; $z = 5.89$

11.57 $z = 2.51$; reject H_0

11.59 No; $z = -2.28$

11.61 Yes, $z = -4.05$

11.63 **a.** $\chi^2 = 19.2$ **b.** $\chi^2 = 18.7$ **c.** $\chi^2 = 30.38$ **d.** $\chi^2 = 396$

11.65 **a.** $\chi^2 = 6.975$; do not reject H_0

11.67 $\chi^2 = 21.95$; reject H_0

11.69 Yes, $\chi^2 = 688$

11.71 **a.** $\chi^2 = 2.97$; do not reject H_0 **b.** One-tailed

11.73 **a.** 2.40 **b.** 3.35 **c.** 1.65 **d.** 5.86

11.75 **a.** 1.42 **b.** 3.88 **c.** 1.77

11.77 $F = 5.87$; reject H_0

11.79 $F = 2.47$; do not reject H_0

11.81 $F = 3.41$; reject H_0

11.83 $z = -1.69$; do not reject H_0

11.85 $z = -2.09$; reject H_0

11.87 **a.** $H_0: \mu_d = 0; H_a: \mu_d \neq 0$ **c.** $t = 1.58$; do not reject H_0

11.89 Yes, $\chi^2 = 54$

11.91 $z = 4.74$; reject H_0

11.93 Yes; $\chi^2 = 133.9$

11.95 $t = 3.01$; reject H_0

11.97 **b.** Reject H_0 at $\alpha = .05$ for all three areas

■ *Chapter 12*

12.1 **a.** 3.5 **b.** 5.5 **d.** 4.5 **e.** Points fall exactly on the line

12.3 **a.** $-.5$ **b.** -2.5 **d.** -1.5 **e.** Points fall exactly on the line

12.7 **a.** 15 **b.** 10 **c.** 2.2 **d.** 1
  e. 1.5 **f.** .7

12.9 **b.** $\hat{y} = 4.986 - 1.934x$

12.11 **b.** $\hat{y} = 1.255 - .398x$

12.13 **b.** $\hat{y} = -.00105 + .00321x$

12.15 **b.** $\hat{y} = 130.69 - 7.26x$

12.17 **b.** $\hat{y} = 4.79 + .014x$

12.19 **a.** .0275 **b.** .16583

12.21 **a.** 1.8157 **b.** $s^2 = .363, s = .603$

12.23 **a.** SSE $= 77.414$, $s^2 = 4.301$ **b.** 2.074

12.25 **a.** SSE $= 30.768$, $s = 1.432$

12.27 **a.** 4   **b.** 8   **c.** 23   **d.** 48

12.29 **a.** $t = 7.00$; reject H_0 **b.** $p < .01$ **c.** $1.05 \pm .353$

12.31 $t = 7.44$, reject H_0

12.33 Yes; $t = 4.48$

12.35 No; $t = -1.33$

12.37 $2.43 \pm .473$

12.39 .971

12.41 **a.** $t = 2.623$; $t > 2.896$; do not reject H_0
       b. $t = -6.558$; $|t| > 2.70$; reject H_0 **c.** $t = -4.379$; $|t| > 1.86$; reject H_0

12.43 **a.** Negative   **b.** Negative

12.45 $t = .178$, do not reject H_0

12.47 Yes; $t = -6.69$

12.49 Scheduling: $t = 2.47$, reject H_0; Synchron: $t = .77$, do not reject H_0;
       Alloc.: $t = -2.83$, do not reject H_0; Autonomy: $t = -4.92$, do not reject H_0;
       Future: $t = 5.37$, reject H_0

12.51 Yes; $t = 3.88$

12.53 .852

12.55 .927

12.57 **c.** $t = 7.79$, reject H_0

12.59 .181

12.61 .630

12.63 .687

12.65 **a.** SSE $= 4.055$; $s^2 = .225$ **b.** $10.6 \pm .22$ **c.** $8.90 \pm .32$
       d. $12.3 \pm .32$ **e.** Wider   **f.** 12.3 ± 1.05

12.67 **a.** $2.767 \pm .482$ **b.** 2.767 ± 1.307 **c.** Prediction interval is wider

12.69 **a.** (4.955, 17.368)   **b.** (9.463, 12.861)

12.71 **b.** $\hat{\beta}_0 = 9.174$, $\hat{\beta}_1 = .481$ **d.** Yes, $t = 8.069$ **e.** (18.17, 19.39)

12.73 (13.72, 18.235)

12.75 $\hat{y} = .3537 + .000004426x$, SSE $= .1022$, $s = .1011$, $t = .256$ (do not reject H_0), $r^2 = .0065$

12.77 **a.** $\hat{y} = 1.4478 + .144675x$ **b.** No; $t = 1.549$ (p-value $= .1558$)
       c. $.144675 \pm .21125$

12.79 $\hat{y} = -1.329 + 1.762\,x$; $r^2 = .995$; $s = .744$; $t = 32.54$ (reject H_0); aggressive

12.81 **a.** $\hat{y} = -1{,}180.48 + 6{,}808.11x$ **b.** Yes, reject H_0; $t = 19.00$ **d.** .9836

12.83 Yes; $t = 7.31$

■ *Chapter 13*

13.1 $E(y) = \beta_0 + \beta_1 x_1 + \beta_2 x_2$

13.3 **b.** Parallel lines (same slope); slope $= 2$ **c.** Parallel lines

13.5   **a.** .0439   **b.** 7.12   **c.** Yes; reject H_0

13.7   Do not reject H_0; $F = 1.90$

13.9   **b.** $t = -2.71$, reject H_0

c. Rental price, empl. growth, AFDC benefits, SSI benefits   **d.** Inflated α error

13.11 **a.** $F = 20.914$, reject H_0: $\beta_1 = \beta_2 = \cdots = \beta_{27} = 0$; $s = 6{,}544$; $R^2 = .814$; $R_a^2 = .7751$

b. $(15.13, 29.67)$ **c.** No; inflated α-error; no higher-order terms in model

13.13 **a.** $\hat{y} = 648.023 + 104.839x_1 + 357.185x_2$ **b.** Yes, $F = 19.017$

c. 104.839 ± 37.368 **d.** No, $t = .917$

13.15 **c.** Reject H_0: $\beta_3 = 0$ $(p = .000)$ **d.** .64

13.17 **a.** $t = 9.68$ $(p = .000)$, reject H_0 **b.** $t = 2.97$ $(p = .006/2 = .003)$, reject H_0

c. $.00875 \pm .0018$ **d.** $3{,}444.3 \pm 1{,}861.7$

e. Infer that $\mu_{\text{Industrial}} > \mu_{\text{Utility}}$

13.19 **a.** Do not reject H_0; $F = 1.06$ **b.** .05

13.21 $E(y) = \beta_0 + \beta_1 x_1 + \beta_2 x_2 + \beta_3 x_3 + \beta_4 x_1 x_2 + \beta_5 x_1 x_3 + \beta_6 x_2 x_3$

13.23 **a.** .956   **b.** Yes, $F = 202.79$ **d.** Yes, $t = 2.5$

13.25 **a.** $F = 7.99$; reject H_0 **c.** $t = 1.85$; reject H_0; $\beta_3 = 0$ **d.** No

13.27 **a.** $\hat{y} = -44.682 + 2.880x_1 + 25.062x_2 - .959x_1 x_2$

b. Yes, reject H_0 $(F = 60.85, p\text{-value} = .0001)$

c. No, do not reject H_0: $\beta_3 = 0$ $(t = -1.39, p\text{-value} = .1904)$

d. $(9.06, 17.55)$

f. No; $x_2 = 1.10$ is outside the range of the sample data

13.29 **c.** Changes y-intercept

13.31 **d.** Changes rate of curvature

e. Controls nature of curvature (upward or downward)

13.33 **a.** $E(y) = \beta_0 + \beta_1 x_1 + \beta_2 x_2 + \beta_3 x_1 x_2 + \beta_4 x_1^2 + \beta_5 x_2^2$

b. $E(y) = \beta_0 + \beta_1 x_1 + \beta_2 x_2 + \beta_3 x_3 + \beta_4 x_1 x_2 + \beta_5 x_1 x_3 + \beta_6 x_2 x_3 + \beta_7 x_1^2 + \beta_8 x_2^2 + \beta_9 x_3^2$

13.35 **a.** Yes, $F = 18.55$ **b.** Do not reject H_0; $t = -1.215$

c. Do not reject H_0; $t = -.8055$

13.37 **a.** $E(y) = \beta_0 + \beta_1 x + \beta_2 x^2$ **b.** $\beta_2 > 0$

13.39 **c.** Yes; $F = 5.41$ **d.** Yes; reject H_0: $\beta_2 = 0$; $t = -2.39$

13.41 **a.** -75.71 ± 26.17 **b.** Do not reject H_0; $t = 1.38$ **c.** Yes; $F = 21.86$

13.43 **b.** No; $t = -.15$

13.45 $E(y) = \beta_0 + \beta_1 x_1 + \beta_2 x_2 + \beta_3 x_3$, where

$$x_1 = \begin{cases} 1 & \text{if A} \\ 0 & \text{if not} \end{cases}, \quad x_2 = \begin{cases} 1 & \text{if B} \\ 0 & \text{if not} \end{cases}, \quad x_3 = \begin{cases} 1 & \text{if C} \\ 0 & \text{if not} \end{cases};$$

$\beta_0 = \mu_D, \beta_1 = \mu_A - \mu_D, \beta_2 = \mu_B - \mu_D, \beta_3 = \mu_C - \mu_D$

13.47 **a.** $\hat{\beta}_0 = \bar{x}_5 = 20$, $\hat{\beta}_1 = \bar{x}_1 - \bar{x}_5 = -5.6$, $\hat{\beta}_2 = \bar{x}_2 - \bar{x}_5 = 11.2$, $\hat{\beta}_3 = \bar{x}_3 - \bar{x}_5 = -1.7$, $\hat{\beta}_4 = \bar{x}_4 - \bar{x}_5 = -9.0$

b. H_0: $\mu_1 = \mu_2 = \mu_3 = \mu_4 = \mu_5$ **c.** $F = 2.16$; do not reject H_0

13.49 For each qualitative variable, the mean price differs for the two levels

13.51 a. $x_1 = \begin{cases} 1 & \text{if GL} \\ 0 & \text{if not} \end{cases}$, $x_2 = \begin{cases} 1 & \text{if SE} \\ 0 & \text{if not} \end{cases}$, $x_3 = \begin{cases} 1 & \text{if SW} \\ 0 & \text{if not} \end{cases}$

$x_4 = \begin{cases} 1 & \text{if PS} \\ 0 & \text{if not} \end{cases}$, $x_5 = \begin{cases} 1 & \text{if RM} \\ 0 & \text{if not} \end{cases}$, $x_6 = \begin{cases} 1 & \text{if P} \\ 0 & \text{if not} \end{cases}$

b. $E(y) = \beta_0 + \beta_1 x_1 + \beta_2 x_2 + \beta_3 x_3 + \beta_4 x_4 + \beta_5 x_5 + \beta_6 x_6$

c. $\beta_0 = \mu_{\text{NE}}$, $\beta_1 = \mu_{\text{GL}} - \mu_{\text{NE}}$, $\beta_2 = \mu_{\text{SE}} - \mu_{\text{NE}}$, $\beta_3 = \mu_{\text{SW}} - \mu_{\text{NE}}$, $\beta_4 = \mu_{\text{PS}} - \mu_{\text{NE}}$, $\beta_5 = \mu_{\text{RM}} - \mu_{\text{NE}}$, $\beta_6 = \mu_{\text{P}} - \mu_{\text{NE}}$

13.53 a. $\beta_1 = \mu_{\text{Disclosed}} - \mu_{\text{Undisclosed}}$ for any level of x_2

b. $\beta_2 = \mu_{\text{Downgraded}} - \mu_{\text{Not downgraded}}$ for any level of x_1

c. $\beta_1 = \mu_{\text{Disclosed}} - \mu_{\text{Undisclosed}}$ when $x_2 = 0$; $\beta_2 = \mu_{\text{Downgraded}} - \mu_{\text{Not downgraded}}$ when $x_1 = 0$

13.55 e (complete) and any other model; d (complete) and b; d (complete) and a; c (complete) and b; a (complete) and b

13.57 a. $\beta_7, \beta_8, \beta_9$ **b.** $H_0: \beta_7 = \beta_8 = \beta_9 = 0$ **c.** $H_0: \beta_3 = \beta_5 = \beta_6 = \beta_9 = 0$

13.59 a. $F = 8.79$; reject H_0

13.61 No; reject $H_0: \beta_3 = \beta_4 = \cdots = \beta_{30} = 0$, $F = 3.59$

13.63 a. Misspecified model: quadratic term missing   **b.** Unequal variances

c. Outlier   **d.** Unequal variances   **e.** Nonnormal errors

13.65 a. 3.197, 3.215, -2.258, .269, -1.713, -7.186, -2.659, 3.359, -2.132, 5.904

b. Yes; needs curvature   **c.** No outliers   **d.** Yes; needs curvature

13.67 a. .796, $-.219$, -1.004, .077, -1.071, 1.116, .868, .827, .223, -1.612

b. No   **c.** Possibly; needs curvature term $\beta_3 x_2^2$

13.69 a. 25.67, 18.57, -60.14, 13.41, -72.40, 64.06, 47.02, 57.93, -63.36, -75.62, 46.31, -1.43

c. Yes; model needs curvature term

13.71 a. $F = 83.54$; reject H_0 **b.** Yes   **c.** No outliers

13.73 b. -50.76, -47.44, -15.96, -33.72, -54.64, -78.24, 16.84, -46.52, 43.24, -64.96, -55.96, -50.52, 436.5, 37.88, -36.00; one outlier

c. Delete

d. $\hat{y} = 191.26 - 9.58x$; $r^2 = .483$

13.75 b. No

13.77 No; appears that multicollinearity exists

13.79 a. .0025; no   **b.** .4341; no   **c.** No

d. $\hat{y} = -45.154 + 3.097x_1 + 1.032x_2$; $F = 39,222$; $R^2 = .9998$

e. $-.8998$; x_1 and x_2 are highly correlated   **f.** No

13.81 a. $E(y) = \beta_0 + \beta_1 x_1$; y-int. $= \beta_0$, slope $= \beta_1$

b. $E(y) = (\beta_0 + \beta_2) + (\beta_1 + \beta_3)x_1$; y-int. $= \beta_0 + \beta_2$, slope $= \beta_1 + \beta_3$

c. $H_0: \beta_1 = \beta_2 = \beta_3 = 0$ **d.** $H_0: \beta_3 = 0$ **e.** Delta; WAF

13.83 Yes; $F = 443.18$

13.85 a. $F = 106.48$; yes   **b.** -725 ± 198.7 **d.** $t = 1.72$; reject $H_0: \beta_6 = 0$

13.87 a. $\hat{y} = 66.97 + 4.03x_1 + 5.55x_2$ **b.** $H_0: \beta_1 = \beta_2 = 0$

13.89 a. .904318   **b.** 4.54854755   **c.** $F = 33.08$; reject H_0, p-value $= .0003$

d. Yes; reject $H_0: \beta_2 = 0$, p-value $= .0706/2 = .0353$

e. .791, −2.0062, 3.7682, 1.8362, −6.0142, −3.9582, 6.3938, 3.9718, −3.539, −1.259
f. No; no   **g.** No, do not reject H_0: $\beta_3 = \beta_4 = 0$; $F = 1.21$

13.91 **a.** $\hat{y} = .94 - .214x$ **b.** 0, .02, −.026, .034, .088, −.112, −.058, .002, .036, .016
c. Football shape; unequal variances
d. Use the transformation $y^* = \sin^{-1}\sqrt{y}$ and fit the model $y^* = \beta_0 + \beta_1 x + \varepsilon$

13.93 **a.** $\beta_3, \beta_4, \ldots, \beta_{11}$ **b.** H_0: $\beta_3 = \beta_4 = \cdots = \beta_{11} = 0$
c. H_0: $\beta_2 = \beta_9 = \beta_{10} = \beta_{11} = 0$

■ *Chapter 14*

14.1 **b.** 7.502   **c.** 2.381   **d.** 1   **e.** 11   **f.** 3.15

g.

Source	df	SS	MS	F
Treatments	1	7.502	7.502	3.15
Error	11	26.190	2.381	
Total	12	33.692		

h. Reject H_0 if $F > 4.84$ **i.** Do not reject H_0

14.3 **a.** df(Error) = 30; SSE = 37.7; MST = 6.175; MSE = 1.257; $F = 4.91$
b. 5   **c.** Yes; reject H_0

14.5 **a.** Completely randomized   **b.** A/R, A/P, and Control groups
c. df(groups) = 2, df(error) = 42, SSE = 321.47, MS(groups) = 35.755, $F = 4.67$
d. Group means differ at $\alpha = .05$

14.7 Yes, reject H_0; $F = 9.50$

14.9 **a.** No, do not reject H_0 **b.** Reject H_0, p-value = .065

14.11 **a.** H_0: $\mu_1 = \mu_2 = \mu_3$
b. df(size) = 2, df(error) = 121, SS(size) = 15.48, SS(Total) = 205.48, MS(size) = 7.74, MSE = 1.57

14.13 **a.** df(Error) = 15, df(Total) = 23, SSB = 74.5, SS(Total) = 135, MST = 9.033, MSE = 2.227, F(Treatments) = 4.06, F(Blocks) = 6.69
b. No, do not reject H_0
c. Yes, reject H_0 at $\alpha = .05$

14.15 Do not reject H_0; $F = 1.45$ ($p = .149$)

14.17 **b.**

Source	df	SS	MS	F
Periods	2	9,726	4,863	1.04
Months	3	68,258	22,753	4.48
Error	6	27,947	4,658	
Total	11	105,932		

    c. No; $F = 1.04$ **d.** 68.25 (compared to 85.30)   **e.** $F = 4.88$; reject H_0

14.19 **a.** STAAD-III (1), STAAD-III (2), DRIFT

    c. Reject H_0 at $\alpha = .05$; $F = 4.79$ ($p \approx .043$)

14.21 **a.** df$(A) = 2$, df(Error) $= 18$, df(Total) $= 23$, SS$(B) = 559$, SS$(AB) = 5$, SSE $= 36$, MS$(A) = 50$, MS$(B) = 559$, $F(A) = 25$, $F(B) = 279.5$, $F(AB) = 1.25$

    b. Do not reject H_0; $F = 1.25$ **c.** Reject H_0; $F = 25.0$ **d.** Reject H_0; $F = 279.5$

14.23 **a.** Factors (levels): accounts receivable (completed, not completed); verification (completed, not completed); treatments: CC, CN, NC, NN

    c. Yes

14.25 No evidence of interaction; no evidence of room order main effect; evidence of aid type main effect

14.27 **a.** Evidence of $N \times I$ interaction; ignore tests for main effects

    b. Agree; interaction implies differences among N means depend on level of I

14.29 **a.** SS$(P) = 1.55$, SS$(D) = 22.26$, SS$(PD) = .61$, SSE $= 114.40$, SS(Total) $= 138.82$, $F(P) = 1.08$, $F(D) = 15.57$, $F(PD) = .43$

    b. No evidence of $P \times D$ interaction, $F = .43$; no evidence of P main effect, $F = 1.08$; evidence of D main effect, $F = 15.57$

14.31 **a.** 3.930   **b.** 3.355   **c.** Approx. 3.00   **d.** 2.845

14.33 $(\mu_1 - \mu_2)$: 2.53; $(\mu_1 - \mu_3)$: 2.70; $(\mu_2 - \mu_3)$: 2.53 (using $t \approx 2.79$)

14.35 5.26 (using $t = 3.930$) for all pairwise comparisons

14.37 **a.** Policy 1 differs from each of policies 3–18; 2 and 3 differ from 4–18; 4 differs from 8–18; 5, 6, and 7 differ from 9–18; 8 differs from 12–18; 9, 10, and 11 differ from 16–18

    b. Yes

14.39 **b.** Yes

    c. 75% vocab: means for all 3 accuracy levels are significantly different; 87.5% vocab: means for all 3 accuracy levels are significantly different; 100% vocab: 99% and 95% accuracy levels are not significantly different, whereas 90% accuracy mean is significantly larger than the other two means

14.41 **a.** .03   **b.** $\mu_E > (\mu_M, \mu_L)$

14.43 Complete: $E(y) = \beta_0 + \beta_1 x_1 + \beta_2 x_2$, where $x_1 = \begin{cases} 1 & \text{if A/R} \\ 0 & \text{if not} \end{cases}$, $x_2 = \begin{cases} 1 & \text{if A/P} \\ 0 & \text{if not} \end{cases}$;

Reduced: $E(y) = \beta_0$

14.45 **a.** Complete: $E(y) = \beta_0 + \beta_1 x_1 + \beta_2 x_2 + \beta_3 x_3 + \beta_4 x_4 + \cdots + \beta_{34} x_{34}$, where

$$x_1 = \begin{cases} 1 & \text{if excellent} \\ 0 & \text{if not} \end{cases}, \quad x_2 = \begin{cases} 1 & \text{if average} \\ 0 & \text{if not} \end{cases},$$

and $x_3 - x_{34}$ are dummy variables for manager;

Reduced: $E(y) = \beta_0 + \beta_3 x_3 + \beta_4 x_4 + \cdots + \beta_{34} x_{34}$

14.47 **a.** Complete: $E(y) = \beta_0 + \beta_1 x_1 + \beta_2 x_2 + \beta_3 x_3 + \cdots + \beta_{10} x_{10} + \beta_{11} x_1 x_3 + \beta_{12} x_1 x_4 + \cdots + \beta_{26} x_2 x_{10}$, where

$$x_1 = \begin{cases} 1 & \text{if A} \\ 0 & \text{if not} \end{cases}, \quad x_2 = \begin{cases} 1 & \text{if B} \\ 0 & \text{if not} \end{cases}, \quad x_3 = \begin{cases} 1 & \text{if 1 hour} \\ 0 & \text{if not} \end{cases}, \dots, x_{10} = \begin{cases} 1 & \text{if 8 hours} \\ 0 & \text{if not} \end{cases};$$

Reduced: $E(y) = \beta_0 + \beta_1 x_1 + \beta_2 x_2 + \beta_3 x_3 + \cdots + \beta_{10} x_{10}$

14.57 **a.** Reject H_0; $F_{.05} \approx 2.21$ **b.** $\mu_T < (\mu_V, \mu_R, \mu_L, \mu_S)$

14.59 **b.** Yes, $F = 13.00$ **c.** $B = .62$; $\mu_Y > (\mu_X, \mu_Z)$

14.61 $\mu_R < (\mu_{KD}, \mu_{LW}, \mu_{KW}) < \mu_{LD}$

14.63 **a.**

Source	df	SS	MS	F
Plan	3	154.11	51.37	10.21
Error	13	65.42	5.03	
Total	16	219.53		

c. Yes, reject H_0: $F_{.05} = 3.41$

d. The following treatment pairs are significantly different: (3, 2) and (3, 4)

e. $E(y) = \beta_0 + \beta_1 x_1 + \beta_2 x_2 + \beta_3 x_3$, where

$$x_1 = \begin{cases} 1 & \text{if plan 1} \\ 0 & \text{if not} \end{cases}, \quad x_2 = \begin{cases} 1 & \text{if plan 2} \\ 0 & \text{if not} \end{cases}, \quad x_3 = \begin{cases} 1 & \text{if plan 3} \\ 0 & \text{if not} \end{cases}$$

14.65 **a.** Yes; $F = 52.81$ **b.** $(\mu_{YO}, \mu_{OW}) <$ all other means; $\mu_{BW} < \mu_{YA}$

14.67 **a.**

Source	df	SS	MS	F
Ratio, R	2	32.00	16.00	2.68
Length, L	2	10.67	5.33	.89
RL	4	95.33	23.83	4.00
Error	27	161.00	5.96	
Total	35	299.00		

b.

		Ratio		
		2:1	4:1	8:1
	6	26.5	28.25	25.75
Length	9	28.0	26.25	28.25
	12	22.0	28.0	28.5

d. Yes; reject H_0 **e.** No; do not reject H_0 **f.** When no interaction is present

14.69 **a.** SS(Groups) = 14.6, SSE = 112.585, SS(Total) = 127.185, $F = 5.77$
b. Yes; $F = 5.77$

14.71 a.

Source	df	SS	MS	F
Method	2	.19	.10	.08
Brand	5	605.70	121.14	93.18
Error	10	13.05	1.30	
Total	17	618.94		

b. No; do not reject H_0 **c.** No

■ Chapter 15

15.1   **a.** 167.2   **b.** 180.7   **c.** 153.7   **d.** Process out of control

15.3 $\bar{x} = 1.4985$, $s = .0085$, UCL $= 1.5239$, LCL $= 1.4731$

15.5   **a.** $\bar{x} = 5.895$, $s = .35314$, LCL $= 4.836$, UCL $= 6.954$ **b.** Yes

15.7   **a.** $A_2 = .577$, $d_2 = 2.326$ **b.** $A_2 = .266$, $d_2 = 3.258$ **c.** $A_2 = .223$, $d_2 = 3.472$
     d. $A_2 = .162$, $d_2 = 3.858$

15.9   **c.** 5.93   **d.** 4.75   **e.** LCL $= 1.071$, UCL $= 10.789$
     f. No; mean for sample 12 is outside control limits

15.11   **a.** 4.99114   **b.** LCL $= 4.93923$, UCL $= 5.04305$ **c.** Yes

15.13   **b.** $\bar{\bar{x}} = .40336$, LCL $= .40300$, UCL $= .40371$
     c. No; sample means for hours 10, 12, and 18 fall outside the control limits
     d. $\bar{\bar{x}} = .40333$, LCL $= .40296$, UCL $= .40371$; yes

15.15   **a.** $D_3 = 0$, $D_4 = 3.276$ **b.** $D_3 = .223$, $D_4 = 1.777$ **c.** $D_3 = .348$, $D_4 = 1.652$
     d. $D_3 = .434$, $D_4 = 1.566$

15.17   LCL $= 0$, UCL $= 12.231$

15.19 $\bar{R} = .13917$, LCL $= .01893$, UCL $= .25941$; yes

15.21 $\bar{R} = .00062$, LCL $= 0$, UCL $= .00131$; no, ranges for hours 9 and 13 fall outside control limits

15.23   Yes

15.25   Evidence of trend in sequences d and f

15.27   No trends

15.29   Sample means for seven consecutive hours (9–15) fall above the center line; evidence of trend

15.31   **a.** .0364   **b.** LCL $= 0$, UCL $= .0926$
     c. No; fraction for sample 21 is outside limits

15.33   **b.** .075   **c.** LCL $= 0$, UCL $= .25169$; yes

15.35   Yes, $p = .11$ for this sample lies outside the control limits

15.37   **a.** 2.5   **b.** LCL $= 0$, UCL $= 7.24$ **c.** No

15.39   **b.** 4.8   **c.** LCL $= 0$, UCL $= 11.37$; yes   **d.** No evidence of trend

15.41   **b.** $\bar{c} = 8.00$, LCL $= 0$, UCL $= 16.49$ **c.** Yes; yes

15.43   **a.** 4.433   **b.** 2.934   **c.** 2.677   **d.** 3.518
     e. 5.079   **f.** 7.855

15.45 **a.** 68.2 ± 27.08 (using $K = 2.355$) **b.** (25, 107)

15.47 **a.** $.40336 \pm .00104$ **b.** Yes **c.** $n = 93$; (.4023, .4043)

15.49 **a.** 26 ± 29.11; $1 - \alpha = 1.00$
b. Specific cause, because 93.12 falls outside the tolerance interval

15.51 **b.** LCL = 12.3452, UCL = 13.5298 **c.** LCL = 12.2811, UCL = 13.5939
d. Yes for both sets of limits **e.** 12.9375 ± 1.6334

15.53 **b.** $\bar{c} = 9.92$, LCL = .47, UCL = 19.37 **c.** Yes

15.55 **a.** $1{,}312 \pm 1{,}238.15$

■ *Chapter 16*

16.1 **a.** 440 **b.** 250 **c.** 275

16.3 **a.** 91.5 **b.** 244 **c.** 266.67

16.5 **a.**

Year	Jan.	Feb.	Mar.	Apr.	May	June
1991	100.0	83.7	102.5	117.5	131.2	110.0
1992	90.0	93.7	126.2	117.5	98.7	96.2
1993	71.2	87.5	96.2	102.5	96.2	105.0

Year	July	Aug.	Sept.	Oct.	Nov.	Dec.
1991	126.2	92.5	88.7	108.7	82.5	81.2
1992	110.0	93.7	88.7	91.2	88.7	81.2
1993	103.7	107.5	92.5	110.0	115.0	88.7

16.9 **a.**

Year	Jan.	Feb.	Mar.	Apr.	May	June
1	100.00	106.78	115.25	118.64	106.78	100.00
2	108.47	116.95	123.73	113.56	115.25	120.34

Year	July	Aug.	Sept.	Oct.	Nov.	Dec.
1	115.25	108.47	105.48	123.73	105.08	79.66
2	113.56	120.34	110.17	122.03	106.78	79.66

b.

Year	Jan.	Feb.	Mar.	Apr.	May	June
1	100.00	126.86	123.88	102.99	94.03	77.61
2	107.46	135.82	129.85	111.94	104.48	91.04

Year	July	Aug.	Sept.	Oct.	Nov.	Dec.
1	73.13	73.13	83.58	102.99	94.03	71.64
2	68.66	65.67	94.03	108.96	105.97	76.12

16.11 a.

1986	*1987*	*1988*	*1989*	*1990*	*1991*	*1992*	*1993*
236.3	260.8	287.8	316.1	337.1	348.6	358.8	393.5

16.13 a. 24, 30, 35   **b.** 8.0, 10.0, 11.67

16.15 b.

	I	*II*	*III*	*IV*
1989	—	—	332.8	335.4
1990	317.8	308.1	290.4	261.6
1991	256.6	251.0	230.7	249.9
1992	259.8	269.2	300.3	295.0
1993	301.6	310.0	321.3	334.7
1994	348.3	—	—	—

c. Yes; secular variation

16.17 b.

1980	*1981*	*1982*	*1983*	*1984*	*1985*	*1986*	*1987*
—	269.4	286.6	299.5	310.6	320.6	330.2	340.9

1988	*1989*	*1990*	*1991*	*1992*	*1993*
355.2	372.3	388.1	402.0	413.5	—

16.19

	I	*II*	*III*	*IV*
1985	—	—	191.5	204.4
1986	217.8	231.8	241.1	256.0
1987	270.6	291.5	291.2	283.0
1988	275.3	262.8	270.5	279.5
1989	290.6	309.9	328.9	340.1
1990	350.1	339.4	341.6	346.7
1991	367.0	381.6	390.3	397.8
1992	405.7	417.4	—	—

16.21 b.

Year	*Jan.*	*Feb.*	*Mar.*	*Apr.*	*May*	*June*
1991	—	—	—	8.60	8.95	9.07
1992	7.77	7.88	8.10	8.30	8.57	8.57
1993	6.88	7.03	7.13	7.45	7.88	8.15

Year	*July*	*Aug.*	*Sept.*	*Oct.*	*Nov.*	*Dec.*
1991	8.88	8.77	8.12	7.73	7.25	7.27
1992	8.07	7.72	7.58	7.38	6.87	6.78
1993	8.10	8.20	8.45	8.23	—	—

16.23 a. 9.13   **b.** 9.13

16.25 Must subjectively extend graph of moving averages into the future

16.27 No

16.29 a. 110.23   **b.** ≈ 415

16.31 a. ≈ 433 **b.** 414.1

16.33 a. $w < .5$ **b.** $w = .5$ **c.** $w > .5$

16.35 b. $\hat{y}_t = 39.4879 + 19.13032t - 1.31529t^2$ **d.** $(-31.2506, 48.9693)$

16.37 a. $E(y_t) = \beta_0 + \beta_1 t$ **c.** $\hat{y}_t = 912.13 - 14.86t$; yes (at $\alpha = .10$), $t = -2.27$
     d. 748.67 ± 165.62

16.39 a. $\beta_1 = \mu_{post} - \mu_{pre}$ **b.** μ_{pre} **c.** $-.55$ **d.** 2.53   **e.** 2.53

16.41 a. No; $t = -1.39$ $(-t_{.05} = -1.645)$ **b.** 2,003.48   **c.** No; $t = -1.61$ $(-t_{.05} = -1.645)$
     d. 1,901.81

16.43 a. $d_L = 1.21$; $d_U = 1.65$ **b.** $d_L = 1.25$; $d_U = 1.34$ **c.** $d_L = 1.16$; $d_U = 1.80$

16.45 b. Model adequate at $\alpha = .05$ for all banks except bank 5
     c. Reject H_0 (two-tailed test at $\alpha = .05$) for banks 2 and 5; fail to reject H_0 for banks 4, 6, and
     8; test inconclusive for banks 1, 3, 7, and 9

16.47 a. $F = 164.07$; yes   **b.** $d = 1.01$; yes   **c.** Result may be overly optimistic

16.49 a. -1.11, $-.03$, 2.05, .14, .22, $-.70$, $-.61$, 1.47, .55, -1.36, -2.28, -1.20, 1.89, .97
     b. Possibly   **c.** No, do not reject H_0; $d = 1.43$

16.51 a. Yes; reject H_0: $\beta_1 = 0$; $t = 47.9$ **c.** Yes; $d = .962$
     d. No; evidence of autocorrelated errors

16.53 $y_t = \beta_0 + \beta_1 t + \beta_2 t^2 + R_t$; $R_t = \phi R_{t-1} + \varepsilon_t$

16.55 a. $F_{49} = 336.91$, $F_{50} = 323.41$, $F_{51} = 309.46$
     b. F_{49}: 336.91 ± 6.48; F_{50}: 323.41 ± 8.34; F_{51}: 309.46 ± 9.36

16.57 a. $E(y_t) = \beta_0 + \beta_1 x_t + \beta_2 x_t^2$ **b.** $R_t = \phi R_{t-1} + \varepsilon_t$
     c. $y_t = \beta_0 + \beta_1 x_t + \beta_2 x_t^2 + \phi R_{t-1} + \varepsilon_t$

16.59 a. $y_t = \beta_0 + \beta_1 t + \phi R_{t-1} + \varepsilon_t$ **b.** $\hat{y}_t = 4{,}787.82 + 22.34t + .736\,\hat{R}_{t-1}$
     d. $R^2 = .8991$, $s = 43.61$
     e. Quarter I: $5{,}221.14 \pm 87.21$; Quarter II: $5{,}229.34 \pm 108.29$; Quarter III: $5{,}241.28 \pm 118.15$;
     yes

16.61 c. 2,136.2   **d.** $(1{,}404.3, 3{,}249.7)$ **e.** 1,944.0; $(1{,}301.8, 2{,}902.9)$

16.63 a.

Jan.	Feb.	Mar.	Apr.	May	June	July	Aug.
100.0	99.5	100.5	99.7	100.3	100.2	102.0	100.3

16.65 a. Yes, $F = 217.23$ **b.** No, $d = 1.97$

16.67 a.

Jan.	Feb.	Mar.	Apr.	May	June	July
56.1	53.7	49.8	48.1	49.5	50.4	48.7

Aug.	Sept.	Oct.	Nov.	Dec.
50.3	48.3	47.9	49.6	50.9

b.

Jan.	Feb.	Mar.	Apr.	May	June	July
86.0	88.3	86.7	88.9	89.4	86.5	86.3

Aug.	Sept.	Oct.	Nov.	Dec.
84.4	85.7	86.5	88.2	95.4

16.69 a. Wage & salary:

1986	1987	1988	1989	1990	1991	1992	1993
111.0	113.8	116.4	118.9	119.4	118.1	119.2	120.9

Self-employed:

1986	1987	1988	1989	1990	1991	1992	1993
112.6	117.2	121.7	122.9	125.1	127.1	123.1	128.6

Unpaid family:

1986	1987	1988	1989	1990	1991	1992	1993
61.7	62.9	62.9	67.6	61.0	54.4	56.2	52.8

b. Self-employed; unpaid family

c.

1986	1987	1988	1989	1990	1991	1992	1993
110.9	113.9	116.5	119.0	119.6	118.5	119.2	121.2

16.71 a. $\hat{y}_t = .40151261 + 4.29563025t$ **b.** Yes; p-value = .0001
  c. Yes, long positive and long negative runs
  d. Reject H_0; $d = .821$ **e.** $y_t = \beta_0 + \beta_1 t + \phi R_{t-1} + \varepsilon_t$
  f. $\hat{y}_t = .405757 + 4.295930t + .58962\hat{R}_{t-1}$; R^2(adjusted) = .987
  g. F_{36}: 155.14 ± 10.47; F_{37}: 159.40 ± 12.16; F_{38}: 163.68 ± 12.69; F_{39}: 167.96 ± 12.87; F_{40}: 172.25 ± 12.94

■ *Chapter 17*

17.1 a.

Category	1	2	3	4
Expected Number	10	30	30	30

b. 6.25139

c. H_a: At least two of the cell probabilities differ from .1, .3, .3, .3, respectively

d. No; $\chi^2 = 3.933$, do not reject H_0

17.3 a.

Brown	Yellow	Red	Orange	Green	Tan
111	74	74	37	37	37

b. 13.54   **c.** Reject H_0

17.5 a. .25, .25, .25, .25   **b.** 9, 9, 9, 9   **c.** 14.667   **d.** Yes, reject H_0

17.7 Yes; $\chi^2 = 40.7$

17.9 Yes; $\chi^2 = 14.77$

17.11 a.

	1	2	3
1	15.697	30.945	27.358
2	19.303	38.055	33.642

b. 3.74

17.13 $\chi^2 = 1.12$, do not reject H_0

17.15 a. $\chi^2 = 4.97$, reject H_0 **b.** Reject H_0 for $\alpha > .026$

17.17 a. Reject H_0; $\chi^2 = 16.06$ **b.** $-.28 \pm .11$

17.19 a. $\chi^2 = 1.56$; do not reject H_0

17.21 $\chi^2 = 31.87$, reject H_0

17.23 b. Reject H_0

17.25 Reject H_0: $\chi^2 = 18.91$

17.27 a. 1.0070   **b.** .3606   **c.** .9851   **d.** 1.2840

17.29 a. $\chi^2 = 2.929$ ($p = .0870$), reject H_0 at $\alpha = .10$

b. Odds of owning PC increase by 5.6% for every $1,000 increase in annual income

17.31 a. Reject H_0; $\chi^2 = 20.43$ **c.** Yes; $\chi^2 = 4.63$ **d.** (.00048, .40027)

17.33 a. Reject H_0; $\chi^2 = 5.61$ **c.** $.087 \pm .062$

17.35 a. Yes; $\chi^2 = 12.57$, reject H_0 **b.** Yes; $z = 3.14$, reject H_0

17.37 Yes; $\chi^2 = 35.66$

17.39 Yes; $\chi^2 = 16.19$, reject H_0

17.41 a. Yes; $\chi^2 = 313.15$, reject H_0 **b.** $.181 \pm .069$

17.43 a.

	Native	Naturalized	Other
FM	648.01	17.43	29.56
OCC	137.99	3.71	6.29
IL	69.00	1.86	3.15

b. $\chi^2 = 2.11$; do not reject H_0

■ *Chapter 18*

18.1   **a.** .8125   **b.** .0118   **c.** .0547

18.3   **a.** 80   **b.** H_0: $\eta = 80$, H_a: $\eta < 80$
    c. One-tailed p-value $= .046$; reject H_0 at $\alpha = .05$

18.5   **a.** No   **b.** No; assumption of normality is violated
    c. $S = 14$, p-value $= .0577$; reject H_0

18.7   **a.** Reject H_0; p-value $= .0023$

18.9   **a.** $T_1 \le 24$ or $T_1 \ge 56$ **b.** $T_1 \ge 84$ **c.** $T_1 \le 22$

18.11   **a.** $z = -3.16$; reject H_0 if $z < -1.645$ **b.** $z = 2.18$; reject H_0 if $z > 1.28$
    c. $z = 2.33$; reject H_0 if $|z| > 1.96$

18.13   **b.** H_0: Distributions of change in swollen joints for collagen and placebo populations are identical
    c. Reject H_0 at $\alpha = .05$

18.15 $T_C = 35$; do not reject H_0

18.17   No; $T_1 = 66$

18.19   Do not reject H_0; p-value $= .3036/2 = .1518$

18.21   No, do not reject H_0; $T_1 = 88.5$

18.23   **a.** Reject H_0 if $T^- \le 2$ **b.** Reject H_0 if T (smaller of T^+ and T^-) ≤ 4

18.25   Reject H_0; $T^+ = 1$

18.27   Reject H_0; p-value ≈ 0; yes

18.29   **a.** Do not reject H_0 **b.** Reject H_0

18.31   Reject H_0; $T^+ = 2$

18.33   **a.** Completely randomized
    b. H_0: All three population relative frequency distributions are identical
    c. $H > 5.99147$ **d.** $T_1 = 46$, $T_2 = 21.5$, $T_3 = 68.5$ **e.** $H = 12.47$
    f. Reject H_0

18.35   No, do not reject H_0; $H = .98$

18.37   **a.** H_0: The distributions of changes in bond prices for the four underwriters are identical; H_a: At least two of the four distributions differ in location
    b. 1.21
    c. No, do not reject H_0; $\chi^2_{.01} = 11.3449$

18.39   **a.** Reject H_0; $H = 11.42$

18.41   Yes, reject H_0; $H = 9.1$

18.43   Reject H_0; $F_r = 6.78$

18.45   Do not reject H_0; $F_r = 1.18$

18.47   **a.** Invalid   **b.** Do not reject H_0; $F_r = 3.5$

18.49   **b.** $r_s = .893$ **c.** Yes, reject H_0; $r_{.025} = .786$

18.51 $C = 15$, reject H_0

18.53   Reject H_0

18.55   Yes, reject H_0, $r_s = .745$

18.57   **a.** $C = -13$ **b.** No, do not reject H_0

18.59 Yes; $F_r = 12.80$

18.61 Do not reject H_0; $T_2 = 126$

18.63 No, $S = 5$; *p*-value $= 1.00$

18.65 **a.** Aggressive: .870; defensive: $-.946$; neutral: .874
b. Reject H_0 for each stock
c. Aggressive: $C = 27$; defensive: $C = -31$; neutral: $C = 26$; reject H_0 for all three stocks

18.67 Yes, reject H_0; $F_r = 10.67$

18.69 Yes, reject H_0; $H = 11.44$

■ *Chapter 19*

19.1 Actions, states of nature, outcomes, objective variable

19.3 *Actions:* a_1, Settle out of court; a_2, Go to court. *States:* S_1, Win court case; S_2, Lose court case. *Outcomes:* Settle out/Win, $-\$800{,}000$; Settle out/Lose, $-\$800{,}000$, Go to court/Win, $-\$50{,}000$; Go to court/Lose, $-\$2{,}000{,}000$. *Objective variable:* Net loss.

19.5 *Actions:* a_1, Buy restaurant; a_2, Do not buy restaurant. *States:* S_1, Low demand; S_2, Medium demand; S_3, High demand. *Outcomes:* Buy/Low, $-\$125{,}000$; Buy/Medium, $+\$50{,}000$, Buy/High, $+\$200{,}000$; Do not buy/Low, $\$0$, Do not buy/Medium, $\$0$, Do not buy/High, $\$0$. *Objective variable:* Net profit.

19.9 **a.**

| | | State of Nature | |
		Repay	Default
Action	Grant loan	3,000	−13,000
	Do not grant loan	0	0

b.

| | | State of Nature | |
		Repay	Default
Action	Grant loan	0	13,000
	Do not grant loan	3,000	0

19.11 **a.**

| | | State of Nature | | | | |
		Sell 1	2	3	4	5
	Buy 1	10	10	10	10	10
	2	5	20	20	20	20
Action	3	0	15	30	30	30
	4	−5	10	25	40	40
	5	−10	5	20	35	50

b.

		State of Nature				
		Sell 1	2	3	4	5
Action	Buy 1	0	10	20	30	40
	2	5	0	10	20	30
	3	10	5	0	10	20
	4	15	10	5	0	10
	5	20	15	10	5	0

19.13 a.

		State of Nature	
		Success	Failure
Action	Increase budget	1,600,000	400,000
	Do not increase budget	200,000	200,000

b.

		State of Nature	
		Success	Failure
Action	Increase budget	0	0
	Do not increase budget	1,400,000	200,000

19.15 a.

		State of Nature				
		.5	10	15	20	25
Action	Market wine	−2.85	0	1.5	3	4.5
	Do not market wine	0	0	0	0	0

b.

		State of Nature				
		.5	10	15	20	25
Action	Market wine	2.85	0	0	0	0
	Do not market wine	0	0	1.5	3	4.5

19.27 a. $EP(a_1) = 21$, $EP(a_2) = -8$, $EP(a_3) = -7.5$; choose a_1

b.

		State of Nature			
		S_1	S_2	S_3	S_4
Action	a_1	10	0	0	15
	a_2	40	30	50	0
	a_3	0	15	40	60

$EOL(a_1) = 4$, $EOL(a_2) = 33$, $EOL(a_3) = 32.5$; choose a_1

    c. Yes

19.29 a_2

19.31 **a.** $EP(a_1) = 34{,}000$, $EP(a_2) = 22{,}000$, $EP(a_3) = 22{,}000$; choose a_1
    b. Choose a_1

		State of Nature			
		S_1	S_2	S_3	$EOL(a_i)$
	a_1	0	110,000	60,000	56,000
Action	a_2	150,000	0	40,000	68,000
	a_3	150,000	20,000	0	68,000

19.33 **a.** $EP(a_1) = 10$, $EP(a_2) = 17.75$, $EP(a_3) = 22.5$, $EP(a_4) = 22$, $EP(a_5) = 17.75$; choose a_3
    (buy 3 boxes)

19.35 **a.** a_4 **b.** a_1

    c.

		State of Nature		
		S_1	S_2	S_3
	a_1	0	0	105
Action	a_2	50	20	105
	a_3	125	70	85
	a_4	25	15	0

    d. a_4

19.37 **a.** a_3 **b.** a_1

19.39 **a.** Limited tickets   **b.** Unlimited tickets   **c.** Limited tickets

19.41 **a.** .006   **b.** .005   **c.** .006   **d.** .017   **e.** $\frac{6}{17}$ **f.** $\frac{5}{17}$ **g.** $\frac{6}{17}$

19.43 .818

19.45 .7294

19.47 $P(S_1|I) = .3158$, $P(S_2|I) = .2368$, $P(S_3|I) = .2368$, $P(S_4|I) = .2105$

19.49 **a.** $P(S_1|I) = .3191$, $P(S_2|I) = .1702$, $P(S_3|I) = .5106$
    b. $EP(a_1) = 540.38$, $EP(a_2) = 455.26$; choose a_1

19.51 **a.**

		State of Nature	
		Pass (.6)	Doesn't pass (.4)
Action	Stay	2,500,000	−1,500,000
	Lease	500,000	500,000

b. $P(\text{Pass}|I) = .9231, P(\text{No pass}|I) = .0769$
d. $EP(\text{Stay}) = 2,192,400; EP(\text{Leave}) = 500,000;$ choose stay

19.53 a.

		State of Nature	
		5% defective (.8)	10% defective (.2)
Action	Reject	−1,000	0
	Accept	0	−4,100

b. Rejected   **c.** $P(5\%|I) = .6667, P(10\%|I) = .3333$ **d.** Choose reject
e. $P(5\%|I) = .5, P(10\%|I) = .5$ **f.** Choose reject

19.55 a. *Actions:* Go to court; Settle out of court. *States of nature:* Win; Lose. *Outcomes:* Go to court/Win, 0; Go to court/Lose, −1,000,000; Settle out of court/Win, −250,000; Settle out of court/Lose, −250,000. *Objective variable:* Loss

b.

		State of Nature	
		Win	Lose
Action	Go to court	0	−1,000,0000
	Settle out of court	−250,000	−250,000

d. Settle   **e.** Go to court   **f.** Settle   **g.** Settle

19.57 b.

		State of Nature					
		Sell 3	4	5	6	7	8
Action	Buy 3	60	60	60	60	60	60
	4	55	80	80	80	80	80
	5	50	75	100	100	100	100
	6	45	70	95	120	120	120
	7	40	65	90	115	140	140
	8	35	60	85	110	135	160

c.

		State of Nature					
		Sell 3	4	5	6	7	8
Action	Buy 3	0	20	40	60	80	100
	4	5	0	20	40	60	80
	5	10	5	0	20	40	60
	6	15	10	5	0	20	40
	7	20	15	10	5	0	20
	8	25	20	15	10	5	0

d. Buy 6 dozen   **f.** Buy 8 dozen   **g.** Buy 3 dozen   **h.** Buy 7 dozen

19.59 **a.** *Actions:* Issue; Do not issue. *States of nature:* Favorable, No reaction; Unfavorable. *Outcomes:* Issue/Favorable, 5; Issue/No reaction, 0; Issue/Unfavorable, −7; Do not issue/Favorable, 0; Do not issue/No reaction, 0; Do not issue/Unfavorable, 0. *Objective variable:* Point increase in poll.

b.

		State of Nature		
		Favorable	*No reaction*	*Unfavorable*
Action	*Issue*	5	0	−7
	Do not issue	0	0	0

c. Maximax: Issue; maximin: Do not issue

d.

		State of Nature		
		Favorable	*No reaction*	*Unfavorable*
Action	*Issue*	0	0	7
	Do not issue	5	0	0

Minimax decision: Do not issue

19.61 **a.**

		States of Nature				
		.00	*.05*	*.10*	*.15*	*.20*
Action	a_1	−46,000	−46,000	−46,000	−46,000	−46,000
	a_2	−40,000	−42,000	−44,000	−46,000	−48,000

b. $EP(a_1) = -46,000$, $EP(a_2) = -42,400$; choose a_2
c. Defective: choose a_2; nondefective: choose a_2

INDEX